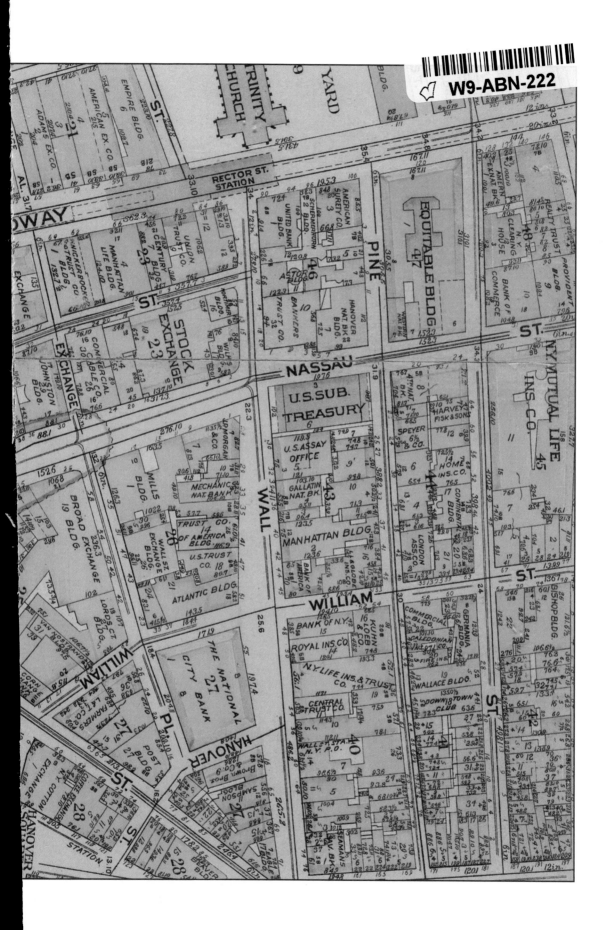

Greater Gotham

VOLUME TWO OF THE *GOTHAM* SERIES

Greater
Gotham

A History of
New York City
from 1898 to 1919

Mike Wallace

OXFORD
UNIVERSITY PRESS

OXFORD
UNIVERSITY PRESS

Oxford University Press is a department of the University of Oxford.
It furthers the University's objective of excellence in research, scholarship,
and education by publishing worldwide. Oxford is a registered trade mark of
Oxford University Press in the UK and certain other countries.

Published in the United States of America by Oxford University Press
198 Madison Avenue, New York, NY 10016, United States of America.

Library of Congress Cataloging-in-Publication Data

Names: Wallace, Mike, 1942– author. | Burrows, Edwin G., 1943– Gotham.
Title: Greater Gotham : a history of New York City from 1898 to 1919 /
    Mike Wallace.
Description: New York, NY : Oxford University Press, 2018.
Identifiers: LCCN 2017005224 | ISBN 9780195116359 (hardback :
acid-free paper)
Subjects: LCSH: New York (N.Y.) — History — 1898–1951.
Classification: LCC F128.5 .W227 2018 | DDC 974.7/104 — dc23 LC
record available at https://lccn.loc.gov/2017005224

Cover: C. S. Hammond & Company, "Bird's Eye View of New York and
    Vicinity," 1912. (New York Public Library, Lionel Pincus and Princess
    Firyal Map Division)
Front endpaper (Wall Street 1911): G. W. Bromley and Walter S. Bromley,
    "Plate 1: Bounded by Liberty Street, Maiden Lane, East River (Piers 1–14),
    South Street, Battery Park, and Hudson River (Piers 2–37), West Street," 1911.
    (New York Public Library, Lionel Pincus and Princess Firyal Map Division)
Back endpaper (Lower East Side, 1911): G. W. Bromley and Walter S. Bromley,
    "Plate 5: Bounded by Broome Street, Attorney Street, Division Street,
    Chatham Square, Park Row, Pearl Street, and Centre Street," 1911. (New
    York Public Library, Lionel Pincus and Princess Firyal Map Division)

9 8 7 6 5 4 3 2 1
Printed by Edwards Brothers Malloy, United States of America

A mi querida esposa, Carmen Boullosa

Contents

INTRODUCTION

Vantage Points

O NEW YEAR'S EVE 1897, thousands of people turned out in Union Square, braving a cold and driving rain, to march in a celebratory parade. By 10:00 p.m. the dignitary-filled carriages, regimental bands, singing societies, civic organizations, trade associations, and ethnic groups (among them Cuban, German, Hungarian, Irish, and Italian) had taken their places on cross streets to the east and west of the square, waiting to feed into the line of march. The illuminated floats were also ready to roll, some commercial (sponsored by Broadway theaters, the fruit trade, the Siegel-Cooper department store), others political, like the Democratic Party's, which bore a giant mock-up of its Tammany Tiger mascot, equipped with electric eyes.

At 10:15, umbrellas aloft, the procession set off from Everett House—a famous old hostelry at Fourth Avenue and 17th Street—and began wending its way down Broadway, heading for Manhattan's City Hall Park. There the walkers would link up with thousands more celebrants, already assembled, and together take part in one of the greatest Festivals of Connection in the city's history.

It had long been a civic tradition for Gothamites to take to the streets—in disciplined hierarchical ranks or milling free-form crowds—to hail the establishment of some new link that promised to enhance the flow of people or commerce into their rapidly burgeoning city.

New Yorkers had gathered in 1788 to acclaim the new federal constitution. Five thousand men and boys, representing sixty-odd trades and professions, marched with floats and banners forecasting the prosperity that would accrue to Gotham from membership in a stronger national union. "This Federal Ship Will Our Commerce Revive," read a ship joiners' banner, "And Merchants and Shipwrights and Joiners Will Thrive."

Gothamites had gathered again in 1825 for the official opening of the Erie Canal—hailing a link between the granary of the Midwest and their Hudson River gateway to the sea, which its promoters forecast would make New York "one of the greatest commercial cities in the world." An aquatic assemblage of vessels greeted the *Seneca Chief*, a canal boat just arrived from Lake Erie bearing casks of lake water that were ceremoniously poured into the harbor (a "wedding of the waters") while the Battery's guns boomed and citizens cheered from wharves and rooftops. A land parade followed immediately, with professionals and artisans "bearing their respective standards and the implements of their arts" trooping from the Battery up to City Hall through streets packed with more than 100,000 people, nearly two-thirds of the population. Finally a huge nighttime throng elbowed into the park to gawk at a City Hall lit up with 1,542 wax candles and 764 oil lamps, to gaze at glowing transparencies depicting the canal, and to gasp at a dazzling display of fireworks.

In 1838 there was a spontaneous and exuberant rejoicing at the landfall of the *Sirius*, a paddle-wheeled steam packet nineteen days out of Cork, and the arrival a scant four hours later of a second steamer, the *Great Western*, fourteen days out of Bristol, making it doubly clear that New York would extend its domination of the transatlantic sea lanes from the age of sail into the era of steam.

In 1842 vast numbers assembled to cheer the opening of the Croton Aqueduct, bringing water to a parched and flammable Manhattan (at that point still coterminous with New York). A parade five miles long, pronounced "the largest procession ever known in the city," made its way down Broadway into Park Row with noisy jubilation, as church bells pealed and a 100-gun salute attended the eruption of a 50-foot plume of water from a fountain in City Hall Park.

In 1858 the inauguration of the Atlantic Cable—initiating instantaneous communication with Europe and solidifying Gotham's status as media portal of America—triggered multiple and immense popular demonstrations; at one, the fireworks were so enthusiastic they set the City Hall cupola on fire.

In 1883 the opening of the Brooklyn Bridge—the first grappling hook thrown across the East River—was accompanied by a vociferous welcome (particularly in Brooklyn) of this physical linkage of two great and ofttimes rivalrous island cities.

The 1897 New Year's Eve festivities were hailing the city's own municipal consolidation. At midnight, New York and Brooklyn (the nation's first- and fourth-largest metropoli), together with Queens, the Bronx, and Staten Island, would merge into a super-city—"Greater New York," as many were calling it—thus establishing definitive demographic primacy over contenders like Chicago and Philadelphia, numbers two and three.

Around 11:00 p.m. the marchers, soaked but still celebratory, some having fortified themselves at saloons along the way, began cascading into the streets adjacent to City Hall Park. The crowds filled Broadway from Chambers down to Park Place, on the park's western flank, and flowed across Mail Street, just above the Post Office, to Park Row, on its eastern side, and thence up to Printing House Square and the Brooklyn Bridge. The park itself—kept clear for dignitaries and performers by long lines of shoulder-to-shoulder police—was brilliantly illuminated by 500 magnesium lights. City Hall was bedecked with thousands of "incandescent lamps." And the windows of the tall buildings overlooking this stage set were filled with spectators, giving the appearance (enthused one reporter) of "tiers and tiers of boxes in a greater theatre than the world has ever seen." In the park, bands and choral societies regaled the swelling audience while competing for a silver punch bowl, with vaudevillian entrepreneur Tony Pastor and his fellow judges straining, as was the crowd, to hear over the wind and din.

As midnight approached, the rain turned to damp snow. When Trinity's bells chimed the hour, the assemblage (led by the 800 massed voices of a congeries of German singing societies) joined in a rousing "Auld Lang Syne," while Greater New York's new blue and white flag was hoisted slowly up the City Hall flagstaff, illuminated by the million-candle-power glare of thirty-seven focused searchlights. Then a coordinated cacophony rolled over the assembled merry-makers: a battery of field guns near the Post Office boomed out a 100-gun salute; 500 35-inch aerial bombs were rapid-fired from 1-ton mortars; red and green rockets soared aloft; the city's tugs and steamers shrieked their whistles in the harbor; and all together the crash of cannon, roar of exploding bombs, braying horns, shouting men, and the throbbing from a huge brass band created a saturation of sound that, it was said, "rent the very clouds."

It was a fittingly mass witnessing of the birth of an urban Goliath. Greater New York was now twice as large as any other US city. Manhattan had already ranked number one in the 1890 census, when its populace of 1,515,301 had easily overmatched Chicago's 1,099,850, Philly's 1,046,964, and Brooklyn's 806,343. But the 1900 census revealed a drastically transformed demoscape: Chicago had surged during the '90s to 1,698,575, and Philadelphia had posted a respectable increase to 1,293,697. Gotham, with 3,437,202 people, had moved into another league altogether, one of planetary scale, in which it was outranked only by London (6,506,954 in 1901). New York could now safely march into the twentieth century hoisting the title—as an 1898 commemorative Consolidation volume dubbed it—"Second City of the World."

ONE OF *GREATER GOTHAM*'S SEVERAL TASKS will be to explore the roots and ramifications of Consolidation.

The people principally responsible for promoting the grand merger were a coterie of businessmen—financiers, industrialists, merchants, landowners, lawyers, and corporate managers—at the helm of the city's and the nation's economy. Their goal was to overcome what they believed to be a lunatic competition between the municipalities gathered around the great harbor, rivalries that were getting in the way of solving common problems. Among the items on their action agenda were upgrading the ailing port, cleaning up the worsening pollution of the waterways, building an infrastructure that would tie the former competitors together and improve their connections to the continent and wider world, dealing with phenomena like crime and epidemics that did not respect political borders, providing homes in which to house an expected influx of immigrants, finding locations in which to place the city's growing number of industries, improving the area's life support systems (water, power, food supply, waste removal) upon which millions now depended, overpowering parochial and corrupt politicians who couldn't or wouldn't think in citywide terms, and warding off challenges to New York's economic primacy from other fast-growing cities, notably Chicago.

The model for accomplishing all this, they believed, was the corporate reconstruction of American capitalism over which they themselves were presiding. They believed they had made a great discovery: that free-market capitalism was bad for business and society and polity; that ruinous competition was inefficient, irrational, immoral, destabilizing and outmoded, a relic of olden days, primitive, even savage. They believed, too, that they had a better alternative—replacing competition with consolidation—which they did by engineering a colossal merger movement. In a scant few years (1898–1904) bankers of the stature of J. P. Morgan conglomerated thousands of competing companies into hundreds of mega-corporations, some on the order of United States Steel. As they were convinced the same methodology could be applied in a variety of spheres, civic as well as commercial, the corporate elite, together with like-minded professional allies, would make prodigious efforts to remold their headquarters city in the image of their new enterprises.

One of the chief products of this transformative time, in addition to the giant corporations housed in huge skyscrapers and the beginnings of an overseas American empire, was the corporate class itself, which might be styled as *trinitarian*. As befit the primary architects and principal beneficiaries of the era's international, national, and metropolitan projects, the city's top 1 percent—an expression that had some currency in the era—was simultaneously an imperial, corporate, and municipal entity. Most of the people who'd pushed for municipal consolidation were charter members of the cohort that promoted corporate mergers and overseas expansion. This elite's multiple and overlapping character was particularly evident in individual biographies. Elihu Root, now virtually unknown but a titan of the period, was simultaneously imperial proconsul, corporate lawyer, and municipal politician. Similar multi-tasking was characteristic of many of the heads of Gotham's great banks, trust companies, insurance firms, industrial corporations, mercantile and commercial establishments, and real estate concerns, as well as many of the trinitarians' adjuncts among the city's upper echelon of attorneys, academics, managers, and professionals.

The city's corporate class was by no means monolithic. Members had differing styles and clashing interests. But most shared what might be called a class *mentalité*, a conception of how the world worked (or should work). This turn-of-the-century zeitgeist—which stressed the superiority of consolidation over competition—provided those who shared it with a tremendous and empowering sense of legitimacy, a conviction that they had the wind of history at their back, billowing their sails and thrusting them into the future. They were *progressive*, agents of a new and higher form of civilization, one that required rising above the competitive scramble of the marketplace and attaining the lofty altitude from which the future could be actively planned, not passively endured. Being capitalists, they were pursuing *private* profit, not the *common* wealth, but many were convinced of their program's social utility and believed the greater good would come wagging along behind it.

The corporate elite was cohesive as well as powerful and principled. Its members were overwhelmingly of Anglo-Protestant descent, and they assumed that having been first on the scene made Gotham *their* city, by right of cultural primogeniture. They had received it from their predecessor class, New York's great nineteenth-century merchants and landowners, who had displayed a similar proprietorial sensibility, particularly when it came to keeping up with European capitals in producing urban embellishments like parks, museums, and Crystal Palaces. Now the twentieth-century patricians believed they had the right and responsibility to improve and pass on what they had inherited.

They would, accordingly, seek to promote New York's physical, economic, cultural, and social development, to make it a metropolis that was beautiful, efficient, and a profitable field for investment. Applying the methods and ideology of consolidation, they would work to reshape its borders, rationalize its transport and life support systems, and remodel its cultural and political institutions. As they were then also presiding over an expansion of overseas investment, they would seek to make Gotham, the de facto seat of America's budding empire, into a truly imperial metropolis, whose monumental buildings and elegant boulevards would proclaim the grandeur and glory of the coming new age.

Several of these goals were achieved in the century's first two decades. The era's gargantuan infrastructure projects helped bind the boroughs together (via subways, bridges, and roadways) and better linked the harbor and its hinterland to the country and the planet (via trains, ships, and assorted tubes and tunnels). Improved transit facilitated a housing boom on the urban periphery, which allowed some dispersion of the citizenry out of the over-crammed core and provided shelter for many of the overseas and continental immigrants. The new arrivals also generated an enormous demand for food, drink, clothing, heat, light, entertainment, and commodities of many kinds. This in turn helped swell the city's industrial plant, boom its commercial sector (both wholesale and retail), and underwrite mass entertainment innovations such as movies and amusement parks. The accelerated velocity of the movement of people and things into and out of the city helped work a qualitative transformation in the city's scale, dynamics, composition, and appearance. By the end of World War I, Greater Gotham had gone from being a project on paper to being a fact on the ground.

A *colossal* fact. After twenty years of frenetic building, New York had morphed into a City Gigantic. Everywhere one looked, some component part had bulked up to extraordinary size. In these years the city accumulated a sheaf of world records. It had the planet's *tallest* skyscraper, its *biggest* office building, and its *largest* department store, hotel, corporate employer, bankers club, steamship fleet, electrical-generating plant, bakery, ballroom, library stacks, steel-arch bridge, integrated transit system, armory, apartment house, terra-cotta manufactory, paper box factory, telephone equipment factory, factory made of concrete, garment-manufacturing center, hospital social service department, and program of organized athletics. Also the *longest* bar, the *richest* man, and the *first* auto highway.

Then there was the basket of blue ribbons accumulated at the national level. New York—the biggest city, in the most populous state—had the country's biggest port, bank, insurance company, and dry-goods wholesaler; it contained the largest enclaves of Jews, Italians, Irish, Germans, and African Americans; it was the nation's largest urban consumer market. It boasted the USA's largest corporation, museum, theater, racetrack, baseball stadium, sugar refinery, building contractor, railroad bridge, Catholic orphanage, high school, university, restaurant, subway system, police force, prison population, system of charities, public workforce, and municipal debt.

This *Guinness Book of Records* approach to describing Gotham's early-twentieth-century development was an appealing one. A flood of boosterish accounts (in print and film) of its king-sized wonders attracted tourists—the basis of yet another growth industry—who came from near and far to marvel. This way of celebrating the newest New York was particularly attractive for those who had promoted Consolidation and those who had participated in the mega construction spree that made it real. It was a popular perspective at the Chamber of Commerce on Liberty Street, the organization that had been one of political amalgamation's leading proponents. It was popular, too, at the Bankers Club of New York on the top three floors of the Equitable Building, at the 44th Street quarters of the City Club, and at the Engineers Club, the American Society of Civil Engineers, the Building Trades Club, the United States Realty and Construction Company (and its subsidiary the Fuller Company), the Building Trades Employers Association, and the United Board of Building Trades (its union counterpart), as well as in the drafting room of architects McKim, Mead & White and at Alfred Stieglitz's 291 Gallery, where the photographer displayed images of the city's skyscrapers and construction sites.

This prideful self-congratulatory viewpoint was both merited and misleading—accurate in its touting of the parts (biggest this, largest that) but less convincing in its characterization of the whole. With its wide-angle lens focused on Gotham's arterial efficiency and productive energy, it encouraged the assumption that a successful metropolitan order had been wrought out of multi-municipal chaos. Now the city *worked*.

But did it? That depended on which New York you looked at, which New Yorkers you asked, and what criteria for success were applied. In these years an immense other city emerged, fed by a phenomenal burst of immigration, and the newcomers, being overwhelmingly working-class or poor, tended to have different concerns than did the corporate elite.

AS NEW YORK EXPANDED OUT INTO THE WORLD, the world arrived at its doorstep. In 1900 the newly consolidated city contained 3,437,202 souls. In 1920 it numbered 5,620,048, and of this total, well over 40 percent were either first- or second-generation immigrants.

The immigration story dates back to the Dutch, of course, and the peopling of the city continued throughout the seventeenth, eighteenth, and nineteenth centuries, most crucially by northern Europeans and sub-Saharan Africans. In the early twentieth century, the metropolis embraced massive migration from southern and eastern Europe, along with smaller inflows from northern Europe, the Middle and Far East, the Caribbean, and Central/South America—and the US countryside, as southern blacks and rural whites headed for the big city. These newcomers would have a tremendous impact on the city's labor force and political order.

As before, but on a whole new scale, newcomers didn't trickle in individually; they arrived en masse, swelling existing enclaves or launching new ones, some pocket-sized but many vast enough to allow them to bear the mark of a particular ethnic culture. By 1920 there were significant encampments of African Americans, Armenians, Australians, Belgians, Bengalis, Bohemians, Bosnians, Canadians, Central Americans, Chinese, Cubans, Croats, Czechs, Dutch, English, Finns, French, Germans, Greeks, Hungarians, Irish, Italians, Jamaicans, Jews, Mexicans, Norwegians, Poles, Puerto Ricans, Russians, Scots, Serbians, Slovaks, South Americans, Spaniards, Swedes, Swiss, Syrians, Turks, Welsh, and West Indians—in addition to those created or expanded by domestic migrants from the American North, West, and South.

On the whole the corporate elite was happy with immigration. It was the newcomers, after all, who built the city—the sandhogs tunneling under the Hudson, the high-steel workers throwing up skyscrapers—labored in its factories and offices, and consumed its innumerable products. The problem was that the ethnic bastions sustained alien languages, religions, and cultures, creating a polyglot and decentralized cityscape, irritatingly at odds with their notion of a smoothly consolidated terrain. Even the economy was carved up into occupational niches, and politically the newcomers tended to vote as blocs (and seldom for the Republican candidates the 1 percent tended to favor). To a degree the city's mandarins took comfort from assuming that these foreigners and their children would accept Anglo-Protestant primacy in the present and remodel themselves in the future according to elite precepts and tenets. But the process of assimilation, while making some headway, seemed vexingly slow. Worse, many ethnics didn't accept cultural primogeniture; they denied that the Anglos' earlier arrival fixed forever their preeminence. Some even argued that New York should be considered not an offshoot fragment of northwestern Europe but a world city, a multi-cultural rather than a homogeneous metropolis. If true, this would morally entitle newcomers (at least the white ones) to a say in the city's development and direction. The immigrants would not be clay on the trinitarians' potter's wheel.

Worse still, they carried in their historical kit bags a set of radically different notions of how to arrange the city's economy and polity, perspectives that focused less on material progress than on social relations, less on economic efficiency and profitability than on the attainment of social and economic justice.

To some degree they had been attracted to New York precisely *because* it had a lengthy tradition of concern with such issues. In the colonial era, the city had hosted proponents of religious toleration and freedom of the press, slave insurrectionists, Protestant dissenters, republican anti-monarchists, American revolutionaries, Paine-ite deists, antifederalists, and manumissionists. The nineteenth century brought political democratizers and advocates of public education, public health, public schools, public welfare, and public works in times of depression. The city had been home to union organizers, financial reformers, land reformers, housing reformers, women's rights activists, civil rights activists, tenant activists, abolitionists, sexual radicals, English co-operators, Irish nationalists, German socialists, Parisian Communards, Henry George–ite single-taxers, radical Catholics, radical Methodists, bohemians, revolutionary poets, settlement workers, historic preservationists, and anti-imperialists.

In the twentieth century, as *Greater Gotham* will demonstrate, many of these activists remained on the scene. They were joined by muckrakers, progressives, Jewish socialists, Italian anarchists, Wobblies, women's suffragists and suffragettes, feminists, birth controllers, opponents of child labor, proponents of industrial unionism, rent strikers, free speech advocates, pacifists, multi-culturalists, Ash Can and modernist artists, radical writers, consumer activists, housing activists, welfare and labor reformers plugged into the latest European initiatives, Harlem-based opponents of racism, and Greenwich Village–based cultural and sexual radicals.

Therefore, whether or not Greater New York in the 1900s and '10s was to be considered a success story, whether or not it *worked*, depended on the observer and where she or he was standing. Thus the post-Consolidation developments looked quite different when viewed from the editorial office of *McClure's Magazine*, a hive of muckraking investigative journalists; or from headquarters of the Municipal Ownership League, where Samuel Seabury and William Randolph Hearst denounced local corporations; or the Scarlet Room in the uptown Delmonico's, where Tammany chief Charles Francis Murphy held sway.

The state of the city was read differently, too, at Lillian Wald's Henry Street Settlement house; Big Tim Sullivan's Comanche Club House; the *World* office of Joseph Pulitzer; the East Broadway tower housing Abe Cahan's *Jewish Daily Forward*; the headquarters of the Socialist Party; Cardinal Farley's archiepiscopal residence on Madison Avenue; Rabbi Stephen Wise's Free Synagogue; the Reverend Dr. Storrs's Church of the Pilgrims in Brooklyn; the Great Hall of the Ellis Island Immigration Station; the Brunswick Saloon that served as headquarters for striking Irish, Italian, and black longshoremen in 1907; the shirtwaist makers' local of the International Ladies' Garment Workers Union; the Hester Street Chazar Market, where pushcart peddlers and day laborers assembled; the Forsyth Street meeting hall of the Ladies' Anti-Beef Trust Association; the McKinley Hall meeting place of the New York Rent Protective Association; the New Brighton Athletic Club headquarters of Paolo Vacarelli's Five Points gang; Margaret Sanger's birth control clinic in Brownsville; Mabel Dodge's salon; Polly's café in Greenwich Village; the Lower East Side cafés where Russian refugee radicals congregated; Carlo Tresca's *L'Avvenire* office in East Harlem; the *Messenger* office of A. Philip Randolph and Chandler Owen; Hubert Harrison's Harlem soapbox; the Circolo Avanti in Brooklyn; Emma Goldman's East 13th Street apartment; the Ferrer Center; the Woman Suffrage Party; the Rand School of Social Science; the Blackwell Island's Workhouse; the Municipal Lodging House; or any of the many Bowery flophouses.

THIS BOOK, TOO, HAS MULTIPLE VANTAGE POINTS—varying altitudes from which it surveys the historical cityscape. These were laid out in the general introduction to *Gotham*, published in 1999. While I will not assume that readers of this volume have read the former one— *Greater Gotham* can stand on its own two covers—I think it's useful to recall those points of perspective, to indicate how the story of Greater New York in the first two decades of the twentieth century was woven into the tapestry of the city's earlier history.

At the highest level of analysis—akin to a satellite's-eye view—the *Gotham* project examines New York's changing role in the global scheme of things. In the period covered by the first volume, the territory we now call New York City transitioned from Lenape country to backwater trading post on the periphery of the Dutch empire, to significant provincial seaport in the English empire, to antebellum intermediary between industrializing Europe and the agricultural North American continent, to post–Civil War underwriter of American industrialization by facilitating the flow of capital and workers from Europe.

In the years examined in this volume, Gotham took a giant stride forward on its journey from the edge to the center of the world. The city's financial sector engineered a reconstruction of American capitalism, creating giant corporations that were primarily headquartered in New York. These Gotham-based businesses rushed to expand overseas, particularly in the Western Hemisphere, where they established a fledgling commercial empire and, with the assistance of military forces dispatched by Washington, butted heads with European rivals. As the Wall Street financial complex grew in strength and reach, it began to rival that of London's Lombard Street. During World War I, the European combatants, seeking the wherewithal with which to destroy one another, sold off their accumulated holdings of stock in American railroads, mines, fields, and factories. When those billions proved insufficient, they borrowed billions more, transforming the United States virtually overnight from a debtor to a creditor nation and leaving New York poised to wrest financial leadership of the global capitalist system from London.

THE SECOND VANTAGE POINT—with New York viewed, metaphorically, from the window of a jet airliner—explores the relations between city and country. Over the course of its first three centuries, Gotham segued from tiny Dutch hamlet on the edge of a vast and verdant continent to English seaboard port that supported an expanding commercial agricultural hinterland, to momentary political centrality as capital of the new United States, to antebellum sparkplug of westward agricultural expansion, to key transmitter to the nation of European industrial and cultural goods, to post–Civil War facilitator of American industrialization, funneling European capital and labor to the continent.

In the early twentieth century, New York emerged as the unofficial capital of the country. As the biggest city in the most electoral-rich state, and home to the deepest-pocketed campaign contributors, it had outsized impact on national politics. (For most of the period, New Yorker Theodore Roosevelt was either president or a strenuous player on the national scene.) The Wall Street financial-industrial corporate complex largely directed (or disrupted) the workings of the nation's economic order. The city's industrial sector churned out products for the national as well as the local market. Its media and entertainment sectors disseminated information and cultural commodities to the interior.

Gothamic neighborhood names became nationally, even internationally, recognized as synecdoches—stand-ins for national-level functions indelibly associated with the metropolis— Wall Street (finance), Madison Avenue (advertising), Times Square (entertainment), Fifth Avenue (both high society and great department stores), Greenwich Village (cultural radicalism), Union Square (economic and political radicalism), Broadway (theater, movies), Coney Island (amusement parks), Ellis Island (immigration), and the Bowery (poverty).

What one made of this metropolitan preeminence varied with one's viewpoint. Gotham's towers and theaters and department stores, its Fifth Avenue society and Times Square entertainments and Tin Pan Alley tunes, had ardent admirers across the country. The city had bitter detractors, too, like the heartland's farmers and small businessmen dragged down in the 1907–8 recession triggered by Wall Street speculators, or the many who feared the metropolis's overweening economic and cultural power, or those who objected to its ability to influence national politics through its munificent campaign contributions.

A THIRD VANTAGE POINT—with the analytic lens now hovering at helicopter level—affords a perspective on the repeated rearrangements of New York's macro-economy in response to changing international and national contexts. *Gotham* recounted how the city grew by taking on new functions, growing ever more complex. The Dutch village was reliant on the trade in beavers and slaves. The English town flourished by shipping food and other essentials to the West Indian sugar islands, with profits from trade supplemented by those from privateering, slaving, fencing pirate loot, and provisioning British forays against the French. The Caribbean connection also helped spawn a subsidiary artisanal sector, which manufactured the tools of commerce (ships, barrels, rope) and processed incoming raw materials (sugar into rum, hides into shoes). After the Revolution, antebellum New York remained preeminently a seaport, whose wharves and warehouses expanded dramatically; so did Brooklyn's, though Kings County retained a healthy agricultural base. Manhattan, however, added an adjunct financial sector (banks, insurance companies, stock market), fostered new forms of wholesale and retail marketing (auction houses, department stores), developed new means of communication (newspapers, telegraph, intercontinental cable), augmented its capacity for hosting and entertaining (hotels, restaurants, theaters), and churned out manufactured goods for the new markets opened up by the Erie Canal, becoming the nation's largest manufacturing center. After the Civil War, New York's financial sector expanded to underwrite continental industrialization and western expansion, and a business services sector emerged to manage the new corporate economy and merchandise its products.

Greater Gotham records how the financial sector attained preeminence, and how the collateral boom in office construction (skyscrapers) elevated the real estate development sector to major player. The Cheopsian construction projects that made Consolidation a reality (subways, bridges, gas mains, electrical plants, and waterworks) strengthened the building and engineering trades. New immigrant-driven demand for shelter did the same for the housing industry, and demand for food and drink spurred industrial-scale provisioning (notably of bread, beef, and beer). Giantism produced some enormous industrial complexes, notably in the refining of oil and sugar, but most manufacturing was not consolidated, remaining a highly competitive terrain with vast numbers of small factories (notably in garments). The port expanded, and its lengthened piers, acres of warehouses, and enhanced rail networks helped New York sustain its supremacy in wholesaling and retailing. The entertainment industry emerged as an independent powerhouse, with New Yorkers hawking plays, vaudeville acts, books, magazines, newspapers, sheet music, records, and movies to the nation—and to visiting tourists, whose care and feeding became itself a highly profitable sector.

THE FOURTH VANTAGE POINT DROPS DOWN to bird's-eye level, from which perspective we'll examine the alternation of peaks of prosperity with troughs of hard times that gave everyday life in the city its undulating quality. In the colonial era, ups and downs were shaped primarily by the imperial dynamics of war and trade. In the nineteenth century, with its imbrication in the world capitalist economy, New York commenced its characteristic roller coaster ride in earnest, now surging to heights of prosperity, now plunging into sloughs of depression. The canal-era boom of the 1820s–'30s raced to culmination and crisis in 1837, then tumbled into a seven-year depression. The rail-spurred prosperity of 1844–57 was interrupted by the

Panic of 1857, reignited by the Civil War, then snuffed out by the Panic of 1873, which inaugurated a stretch of hard times. Industrialization-based resurgence in the 1880s gave way to the terrible depression of the 1890s.

Greater Gotham begins with the return of prosperity in 1898. Ushered in by corporate consolidation and war with Spain, a great boom got under way, the economy surging upward with the skyscrapers. The high times lasted a decade, until the Panic of 1907 ushered in the nasty and brutish but short recession of 1907–8. Partly because of vigorous private and public interventions, the post-panic period of 1908–15 was not one of sustained depression but rather one of constant flux, with brief recoveries cut short by fresh downturns. The people of New York suffered through a particularly fierce drop-off in 1913–15, from which they were rescued (as so often) by the approach of, and then entry into, war (1915–18). During that seven-year stretch (1908–1915), when as much time was spent in gloom as in boom, the jaunty boosterism of the early 1900s didn't vanish—the economic upticks provided sufficient purchase points for continuing optimism—but hard times did fertilize a resurgence of labor upheavals, socialist and syndicalist challenges, and a variety of cultural, gender, and racial radicalisms, some of which would be harshly suppressed during World War I.

THE FINAL VANTAGE POINT IS THAT FROM GROUND LEVEL, when, having completed our analytic descent from the stratosphere, we get to walk around on terra firma. Indeed, much of *Greater Gotham* will take place on the streets, poking into various domains—the canyons of Wall Street, the docks and industrial sites, the entertainment zones and shopping districts, and many of the neighborhoods that sprawled throughout the boroughs.

At this street level we'll be meeting hundreds of individuals and innumerable varieties of Gothamites—actors, ad men, anarchists, anthropologists, architects, automobilists, bohemians, boxers, Bull Moosers, butchers, chorus girls, coal yard operators, Coney Island barkers, consumer activists, corporate lawyers, dance maniacs, department store shoppers, detectives, developers, district leaders, dockworkers, electrical engineers, Ellis Island officials, fight fans, film directors, firemen, fiscal reformers, gangsters, garbage workers, generals, health care providers, historians, home builders, Labor Day paraders, librarians, ministers, muckrakers, novelists, opera stars, pacifists, painters, philanthropists, planners, political scientists, politicians, priests, printers, rabbis, rent strikers, restaurateurs, sanitary engineers, settlement workers, slaughterhouse workers, social workers, socialists, speculators, subway workers, suffragists, symphony conductors, taxi drivers, union organizers, vaudevillians, and zookeepers. Among others.

WE BEGIN AT THE TOP—via a reprise of *Gotham*'s last chapters—with the city's foremost bankers and industrialists, whose ranks included the likes of John D. Rockefeller and J. P. Morgan. We do so not only because these men of enormous wealth wielded tremendous power in the city (albeit always contested, not least by one another) but because at this moment, gripped by their vision of an ideal moral economy, they were launching a transformation of American business that would have multiple and profound impacts on New York City. So now it's back to January 1, 1898—Day One for Greater Gotham—when, as thousands cheered, the door to the twentieth century swung open.

PART ONE

CONSOLIDATIONS AND CONTRADICTIONS

"The New York Stock Exchange, Trinity Church and Wall Street," 1903. (New York Public Library, Miriam and Ira D. Wallach Division of Art, Prints and Photographs)

1

Mergers

Since at least the 1870s American businessmen had been trying to solve a vexing problem—the problem of "competition," a word that in their lexicon was almost invariably yoked with "ruinous." As practical entrepreneurs, rather than academics and ideologues, they *loathed* competition—as well they might have. "Cut-throat" competition led to price wars, declining profits, wage cuts, unionization, strikes, repression, political upheaval, economic crisis, and, all too often, their company's bankruptcy. Nowhere had the pattern been more painfully evident than in the railroad business. Companies repeatedly indulged in rampant overbuilding and competitive rate slashing, resulting in battered bottom lines, and in heightened vulnerability to the bursting of financial bubbles that speculators were forever blowing.

No fools, railroad directors—*pace* Fourth of July pieties about the free market—had done their damnedest to transcend the competitive regime of which they were so often victims. They tried establishing "pools"—voluntary agreements to fix prices and allocate market share—but someone always cheated, out of greed or mistrust; and pools, having no legal standing, were unenforceable. Railroads tried buying out competitors, but ran up against state-level incorporation laws that forbade companies they chartered from acquiring or even collaborating with one another, lest they collude in boosting prices. States also barred their corporate creations from owning businesses in other states, lest jobs and tax revenues be diverted beyond their borders. Efforts to loosen these legal strictures were dashed by massive opposition from consumers, notably farmers—populists who feared "the deadly fangs of monopoly," as the Colored Alliance of Virginia put it in 1891.

Investment banks like Drexel, Morgan, and Kuhn, Loeb—overwhelmingly based in New York City (though with contingents in Boston and Philadelphia)—were also alarmed that the railroads, whose bonds they had marketed to local and European capitalists, were imperiled by ruinous competition and rampant speculation. To protect investors, and their own reputations, bankers had tried to halt the competitive donnybrooks but failed to make headway.

A seeming breakthrough had come in the 1880s, not in railroading or manufacturing but in processing—the refining of crude oil or raw sugar—which a few businessmen proved able to dominate, and thus acquire the leverage to impose order on a wider industry. In both oil and sugar, the consortiums that attained this degree of control either originated in or were swiftly drawn to Gotham, then establishing itself as the country's commercial and financial command post.

In oil, John D. Rockefeller astutely sized up the wild new industry that had trapped hundreds of small producers in what he too called "ruinous competition." Each pumped as much oil as possible; increased supply drove down prices; staying afloat demanded upping output, which drove prices down further. "Every man assumed to struggle hard to get all of the business," Rockefeller recalled later in life, "even though in so doing he brought to himself and the competitors in the business nothing but disaster." If the oil sector was to be made profitable, escaping from the competition trap was the first prerequisite. Free-market capitalism had to be tamed, disciplined, civilized, centralized.

Rockefeller's alternative to competition he called "cooperation." Not the kind of cooperation envisioned by the Knights of Labor—a cooperative commonwealth based on the solidarity of working people—but rather the imposition from above of a giant cartel that would reduce overcapacity, stabilize prices, rationalize the industry, and make lots of money for its progenitors. Cooperation had an ethical dimension, too. A devout Baptist, Rockefeller believed rapacious business practices morally abhorrent because they dissolved the bonds of Christian fellowship. Cooperation-via-cartelization would suppress antisocial egotism. This gave his vision a moral edge, lifting it above being a mere moneymaking scheme and enhancing its ability to challenge the status quo.

But victory in "the battle of the new idea of cooperation against competition," Rockefeller knew, could only be won in the economic trenches. So John D. and his younger brother William, with their Cleveland associates in the Standard Oil Company (Ohio), spent the 1870s and 1880s buying up rival refineries, arranging rebates from railroads for shipping oil to market, establishing their own pipelines to bypass railroads and send crude directly from thousands of western wells to eastern seaboard cities, and setting up or buying out eastern refineries to produce kerosene for metropolitan markets, and the more distant consumers accessible by sea. Gotham being the nation's biggest urban market and biggest port, the Standard's economic center of gravity slowly shifted eastward. The Rockefellers established major refinery complexes on either side of Manhattan—in Bayonne, New Jersey, and along Newtown Creek on the Brooklyn-Queens border—while also building up an elaborate export business, overseen by brother William, who had been dispatched to Gotham back in 1866.

Growth brought new problems. It was hard, given legal limitations on multi-state operations, for the Standard to coordinate bases in New York, Cleveland, Pittsburgh, Philadelphia, and Baltimore. So a new organizational structure was established. Separate companies were set up in key states: Standard Oil of New York was created on August 1, 1882, with William as president; Standard Oil of New Jersey followed four days later, with John at the helm. Then the various companies were sutured together. The owners of each Standard firm placed their common stock in a "trust"—a legal device for people who wanted to put control of property in trustworthy hands while retaining its economic benefits—and received in exchange trust certificates (negotiable securities). The Standard Oil Trust was thus a union not of corporations—still frowned upon by courts—but of stockholders, whose board of nine New York–based trustees controlled 90 percent of American refineries.

John himself now moved to Gotham. He had long felt the city's pull. With his family, he had routinely spent part of each winter there, usually staying (from 1877 on) at the

Buckingham, a residential hotel on Fifth Avenue and 50th. In 1883, with the trust now centered in the city that was home as well to Standard's enormous refining and export operations, he relocated, purchasing in 1884 a (relatively) modest four-story town house a few blocks north of the Buckingham, at 4 West 54th Street. The Rockefellers also set about building a new and permanent headquarters for Standard Oil, William having been operating out of unsuitably small offices on Pearl Street or lower Broadway. They purchased the site across from Bowling Green on which Alexander Hamilton's home had once stood, and spent nearly a million dollars constructing a granite, nine-story building, of which they took occupancy in 1885 (on May 1, still Moving Day in New York). It had no name or corporate logo outside, just a number, but 26 Broadway would soon win global name recognition as shorthand for the Oil Trust itself.

Control of the processing, transport, and marketing of oil had given the Rockefellers the chokehold they needed to discipline producers. Now they took the final step and began moving into production themselves. Swallowing up other firms, crushing competitors and holdouts by fair means and foul, the Standard by 1891 controlled a quarter of American oil production; by 1898, a third. They had brought every aspect of the industry, from "well to wick," under the umbrella of One Big Company, its dominion justified as providing a bulwark against competition. It had also made the Rockefellers immensely rich.

The other major general in the war on competition, Henry Osborne Havemeyer, had his base of operations on Williamsburg's East River waterfront, not far from the Rockefellers' refineries at Newtown Creek. The Havemeyers were not recent transplants. They were deeply rooted in New York and its sugar industry. Henry's grandfather and great-uncle had opened their first refinery in Greenwich Village (on what is today Vandam Street) back in 1802. Henry's uncle William F. had been diverted from sugar into politics, serving three terms as mayor of New York, but his father, Frederick C., had in 1856 moved the operation to Brooklyn, where, employing the latest European technology, he launched the Williamsburg works on South 3rd Street and Kent Avenue; it would become the world's largest. Nevertheless, when Henry and his brother Theodore took the helm in the 1870s, they still faced market instability and declining profit rates. So in 1887, following in the Rockefellers' footsteps, the Havemeyers and seventeen other companies—possessing between them about three-quarters of the nation's refining capacity—folded their firms into the Sugar Refineries Company, popularly known as the Sugar Trust.

Or unpopularly known. For many consumers and competitors, the word "trust" was evolving into its opposite, evoking monopolistic and exploitative practices. Opponents sued the Sugar Trust, claiming violations of New York State's corporation law, and in June 1890, the Court of Appeals declared the trust illegal and ordered it dissolved. The Ohio Supreme Court meted out the same treatment to Standard Oil, finding it had violated its state charter by transferring control to out-of-state trustees in New York; it was forced, though only on paper, to wind up its affairs in 1892.

The sugar men found a haven in New Jersey, which, in 1889, had just passed the most accommodating corporation law in the country. James B. Dill, a New York lawyer, had pointed out to legislators that the state could make lots of money allowing companies to hold shares in other companies, even those chartered in other states. If competitors could gather under a single corporate umbrella, they might exempt themselves from antitrust prosecution. New Jersey loved the idea, and jumped into the business of fostering mergers. The state created a Corporation Trust Company (CTC), which advertised New Jersey's legal wares, and offered to do all the work of incorporation. The CTC even provided a fictive legal home for new-hatched firms, in the form of a plaque affixed to its building, obviating the need to have an office in Jersey, much less do business there.

At first companies shied away from taking the state up on its offer, concerned they might fall afoul of the new (1890) Sherman Act, the federal law that had just outlawed trusts, in response to growing unease about these proliferating *fleurs du mal*. The Jersey law seemed such an obvious subterfuge. Its "holding companies" looked, walked, and quacked like trusts. But Havemeyer, his operation having been shut down in New York, had little alternative. And so, with the blessing of attorney Elihu Root—pillar of the New York bar and Havemeyer adviser since 1880—Henry plunged across the Hudson River. The Sugar Trust, formally laid to rest in June 1890, was reincarnated in January 1891 as the American Sugar Refining Company. In the next few years, through absorption (or demolition) of most remaining competitors, the Sugar Trust (as it remained stubbornly known to press and populace) came to control well over 90 percent of the national output, virtually extinguishing price competition as a problem.

Now other firms journeyed to Jersey, and plaques began to cover the Corporation Trust Company's walls.

Among them was a consortium of metropolitan area rope makers. In 1887, plagued by competition, four cordage manufacturers had joined forces in a Twine Trust, to bring the "advantages of combination" to the business. Several of the firms had been part of New York and Brooklyn's maritime-manufacturing complex since the eighteenth century. These included the Tucker and Carter Cordage Company, which traced its ancestry to Tucker's Rope Walk, founded in 1728; L. Waterbury and Company, which Noah Waterbury had opened in Brooklyn in 1816 on Ten Eyck Street; the smaller but well-respected William Wall's Sons; and the Elizabethport Cordage Company, a post–Civil War upstart in New Jersey. Between them they operated 2,800 spindles, 30 percent of the national total.

They wanted more. So in 1890 they set up a New Jersey–style corporation—the National Cordage Company—and went public, that is, issued stocks to raise money with which to buy up competitors. This was a bold and novel proposition. Industrial securities were not popular with investment bankers or deep-pocketed lenders like insurance companies and savings banks, which stuck to government bonds and railroad securities. Manufacturing seemed too risky a sphere, riven as it was by uncontrollable warfare among a myriad of small firms. Competition kept their profit margins low, and their vulnerability to market fluctuations high; indeed, manufacturers were frequently swept away in the storms that routinely ravaged the economic landscape. The few investors willing to take a chance on industrials were mainly up in Boston, where they had grown accustomed to dealing with Massachusetts textile firms.

Then, in 1890, August Belmont & Co., since 1837 the New York agency of the House of Rothschild, stepped up to underwrite the $15 million stock offering for National Cordage. By 1892, using these funds, the company had established control over 90 percent of the production and sale of rope and twine in the United States. In 1893 New York's *Commercial and Financial Chronicle* dubbed it "the great industrial corporation."

The year 1890 also saw nicotine magnate James Buchanan Duke head to Jersey. The North Carolina chewing-tobacco manufacturer had switched to cigarette production in the mid-1880s and moved his operations to Manhattan—the largest urban tobacco market in the nation and an industry center since Pierre Lorillard had opened his snuff factory on Chatham Street back in 1760. Duke had constructed a massive factory at Second Avenue and 38th Street, using cheap female labor and the new Bonsack cigarette-rolling machines that could turn out 200 cigarettes a minute. By 1889 he was producing over 800 million annually. Industry competition was ferocious, however, so the following year Duke merged with his four leading rivals in the giant new American Tobacco Corporation, a New Jersey company (though its real headquarters were in New York, at 111 Fifth Avenue, at 18th Street). In 1890 the combined ex-competitors, now leagued in the Tobacco Trust (as it was popularly if technically incorrectly known), produced 90 percent of the nation's cigarette supply.

Even the House of Morgan now tested the industrial waters. In 1892 Morgan merged Thompson-Houston with Edison General Electric to form General Electric. The incorporation was a cautious, sober affair—a simple confluence of existing shares, with no public offering—certainly nothing as audacious as National Cordage's gambit.

Which was just as well, as the economy and market were soon shaken by the first tremors of the 1893 financial earthquake, which quickly toppled the Twine Trust, and its bankruptcy helped topple the larger economy. The ensuing 1893–97 depression flattened far taller trees. The nation's railroads—grossly over-built and over-indebted—were blown down one after another until firms controlling over one-third the country's trackage had gone belly up.

The mid-'90s crisis was far more than simply an economic catastrophe; it was accompanied by a political crisis, rooted in a revolt of the unemployed. With roughly 20 percent of the non-agricultural workforce out of work, class warfare broke out, especially where corporations cut wages or seized the opportunity to crush unions. Federal troops and state militias battled hundreds of thousands of miners and railroad workers in uprisings spanning a score of states.

In New York, layoffs had commenced during the summer of 1893 and reached fearsome levels during the freezing winter months. In January 1894 a house-to-house canvass discovered about 70,000 unemployed, of whom roughly 25 percent were female. An additional 25,000 were reported to be down and out in Brooklyn, with destitution among African Americans particularly terrible. As early as August 1893, angry socialists and unionists began collecting food, establishing soup kitchens, and organizing "hunger demonstrations" on the East Side and in Union Square. In addition, the Socialist Labor Party, the Central Labor Union, and the American Federation of Labor petitioned the state and city to provide direct emergency relief and set up public works projects.

Anarchists favored more direct action. During one August demonstration, Emma Goldman told an assemblage that rather than tamely petitioning the authorities, they should march by the homes of the wealthy and demand relief. On another occasion she addressed (in German) a jobless audience at the Golden Rule Hall (125 Rivington Street). According to one witness she told them: "If you are hungry and need bread, go and get it. The shops are plentiful and the doors are open." Such militancy provoked hysteria among the respectable. Goldman was tried and found guilty of inciting a riot—though a riot hadn't happened. After ten months in the Blackwell's Island penitentiary, the new-minted martyr was welcomed back to the Lower East Side by a crowd of thousands.

Protests by the unemployed and homeless, and calls for government intervention to provide public work, were nothing new in New York. There had been riots in 1837, marches on Wall Street in 1857, mass demonstrations in 1874, and political revolt in 1886. But what was worrying some elites was the steady escalation of these protests—in the growing breadth of those affected and the deepening force of their anger. The 1890s depression seemed to be provoking new levels of militancy on all sides—a march on Washington, huge strikes met with federal troops, and a surge of socialist and anarchist challenges to the capitalist order itself. "We are on the eve of a very dark night," said Morgan's chief lawyer, Francis Lynde Stetson, in 1894, "unless a return of commercial prosperity relieves popular discontent."

This discontent flowed into the political arena during the 1896 presidential campaign. Populists and silverite Democrats backed William Jennings Bryan's call for inflating the currency on behalf of debtors. This was anathema to New York elite creditors. Even those (like Morgan) who had favored Democrats (like Grover Cleveland)—because Republicans were pro-tariff, while Gotham's bankers and merchants favored free trade—now jumped ship. They rallied behind former Ohio governor William McKinley, once they'd been assured that the Republican candidate would support the gold standard and refuse to abort the fledgling merger movement. Gotham's businessmen poured record amounts into the McKinley campaign. J. P. Morgan and the Rockefellers' Standard Oil each gave $250,000, their two donations alone equaling Bryan's entire war chest.

All this depression-era disorder underscored again the importance of addressing root causes of the economic crisis, foremost among them, many believed, being excessive competition. And for some, notably Rockefeller, it also pointed toward the solution—cartelized cooperation—attested to by Standard Oil's relative immunity from hard times. The firm, said JDR, had "held things together so steady that our fortunate laboring men got their pay, though in other concerns many of them were compelled to go, and without bread."

J. P. Morgan & Co. (which succeeded Drexel, Morgan in 1895) now set out to wring competition from the hard-hit railroad business. Bankrupt companies were "Morganized" by transferring a majority of their stock to "voting trusts" run by Morgan and other investment bankers (notably Jacob Schiff of Kuhn, Loeb), who now moved from dispensing advice to making decisions. By 1900 much of the country's trackage had been consolidated into six huge systems controlled by Wall Street bankers, who had picked up millions of dollars in fees, and tied the corporations to their purse strings for future financing. The bankers also physically resituated the firms' headquarters, putting them in lower Manhattan, where they could keep an eye on them. Before being Morganized more than two-thirds of the railroad offices were outside New York; afterward most had moved to the city.

At the same time, hard times began evaporating. Recent crop disasters in Europe, Asia, and South America had driven up the price of American wheat to $1 a bushel. Ecstatic farmers paid off burdensome mortgages, and started a round of heavy purchases. Agricultural traffic boosted railroad earnings, which spurred the iron and steel industry. The year 1898 brought government spending on the war in Cuba, and discoveries of gold in South Africa and the Yukon. The combination of stimuli jolted the economy into action. Factories started up, the unemployed began trooping back to work, and the country clambered its way toward prosperity.

By 1898, therefore, all the prerequisites for a perfect storm of mergers were in place: the desire for systemic change to overcome competition; the return of prosperity; great quantities of capital seeking investment; a White House that would soft-pedal enforcement of antitrust laws; the development of the holding company; and a newfound possibility for profit in assembling giant corporations. The result was an explosion of consolidation that began in earnest in late 1898, when Pierpont Morgan entered the iron and steel business.

FROM MORGAN'S PERSPECTIVE, THE INDUSTRY, though booming again (it had just surpassed Britain's to become the world's largest), was also facing an overproduction crisis that demanded preemptive consolidation. Elbert Gary agreed. Gary was general counsel for Illinois Steel, itself a merger of several Chicago-area mills. Gary proposed amalgamating Illinois Steel (a basic producer) with Minnesota Mining (a provider of iron ore) to create a self-contained, centrally managed firm. Morgan agreed, and in September 1898 he forged Federal Steel as a New Jersey holding company, with Gary as president. Next, in 1899, Morgan and Gary began amalgamating competing manufacturers of finished steel products (tubes, hoops, wire, nails) into two huge conglomerates—the National Tube Company (comprising fourteen former foes) and American Bridge (embracing twenty-five ex-competitors). Then, in 1900, Morgan had his new manufacturing goliaths start buying their basic metal from Federal Steel, moving the ensemble of firms toward becoming an autonomous entity.

COMMERCIAL MIGHT *VERSUS* DIVINE RIGHT.
THE MODERN TRUST KING BRINGS DISMAY TO THE OLD KINGS OF EUROPE.

"Commercial Might versus Divine Right: The Morgan Trust King Brings Dismay to the Old Kings of Europe." *Puck*, May 21, 1902. (Everett Collection Historical/Alamy Stock Photo)

This roused a not-so-sleepy giant, Andrew Carnegie, king of the industry, the largest steelmaker on earth. His Carnegie Steel had prospered by ruthlessly slashing costs, particularly wages, achieved by crushing the Amalgamated Association of Iron and Steel Workers in the ferocious Homestead strike of 1892; de-unionization had allowed him to jam wages down and hike hours up. He also made a point of keeping dividend payouts low and plowing profits back into technological upgrades of the production process. Exploitation and efficiency allowed him to make money throughout the depression, and to begin doubling his profits each year in the recovery period ($11 million in 1898, $21 million in 1899, $40 million in 1900). In April 1900 he consolidated Carnegie Steel with his chief fuel supplier, H. C. Frick Coke, and made Charles Schwab president of the resulting Carnegie Company—the largest corporation in the United States, three times the size of Standard Oil.

Carnegie was a warrior; he loved to fight. Morgan, by threatening his customer base, was clearly a danger. Carnegie's visceral response was to assume battle stations. "A struggle is inevitable," he told Schwab with some relish; "it is a question of survival of the fittest." He announced a counterassault. As Morgan had entered primary steel production, Carnegie would start making finished products, beginning with tubes. As he could almost certainly do so more efficiently, he would almost certainly win the ensuing price war.

On the other hand, he knew that Morgan's Federal Steel was a powerful and deep-pocketed foe, and while he might win the war, the campaign would be long and expensive. Also, Carnegie, who turned 65 in 1900, wanted to turn his energies to philanthropy, to give money away, not make more of it. The only way to transmute his illiquid assets into dispensable cash was to sell the company, and the only purchaser who could conceivably come up with the necessary funds was Pierpont Morgan. Still, Carnegie had his dander up.

It was precisely this that Morgan despised in Carnegie—the Scotsman's Darwinian business ethics. The banker considered the entrepreneur a dangerous adventurer who embodied the competitive ethos Morgan was out to overcome. Carnegie, Morgan believed, had "demoralized steel by undermining coordination, order, and ultimately stability"; the industry would be far better off without him. But all-out war between Federal Steel and the Carnegie Company would be tremendously disruptive, and best avoided.

So the two men began an elaborate dance, with overtures and withdrawals carried out through intermediaries, in various venues around town. Carnegie himself was on the scene, having left Pittsburgh back in 1870, drawn as much by Gotham's intellectual and cultural life as its centrality to business affairs. He had lived (with his mother) in various apartment hotels before buying a town house at 5 West 51st Street, three blocks south of John D. Rockefeller, on the occasion of his marriage in 1886.

Finally, on December 12, 1900, a fruitful link was established at the University Club, a luxurious structure at 1 West 54th completed the year before by architects McKim, Mead & White (all of whom were members). A dinner had been arranged to introduce Charles Schwab, the Carnegie Company's relatively unknown president, to Manhattan's moguls. Schwab gave a speech on his vision of the steel industry's future. It dovetailed perfectly with Morgan's. The two had a brief private chat afterward. More talks followed in January, and a deal was hammered out. Schwab gave Morgan a list of all the competing companies that should be included. Morgan then set up United States Steel (USS) as a New Jersey holding company in 1901. Capitalized at $1.4 billion—the world's first billion-dollar corporation—it had the wherewithal to buy out all those on Schwab's list, and plenty left over to reward the promoters handsomely. Carnegie got his asking price of $480 million (in USS securities) at a time when the entire federal budget was $350 million. This made the now former steelmaker—as Morgan informed him—"the richest man in the world."

United States Steel Corporation, Gold Bond issued to Andrew Carnegie, 1901. (Museum of American Finance)

The merger also made John D. Rockefeller the second richest. Schwab insisted that Rockefeller be brought into the giant steel consolidation because he controlled the nation's biggest deposits of iron ore, and a transportation system to move the product. Back in the 1890s depression, Rockefeller had picked up some iron mines in northern Minnesota cheaply, because the ore was powdery and considered to be of doubtful commercial utility. Carnegie had snorted at this amateur, blundering into his domain, referring to him derisively as "Rockafellow." But Rockefeller's scientists figured out how to use the ore, and he bought up more of the Mesabi Range. He also created a fleet of ships to carry the ore across the Great Lakes, and sank rival shippers by ruthlessly undercutting them. By the time Carnegie awoke to his need for more ore, Rockefeller had locked up the richest deposits and was in a position to charge Carnegie exorbitantly for ore and transport. Worse, Rockefeller was capable of creating a giant Steel Trust on the Standard Oil model and going head-to-head with Carnegie (who now began calling him "Wreckafellow").

In 1896, rather than clash, they had come to terms. Carnegie Steel agreed to take the full output of Rockefeller's mines, at way below market price; Rockefeller agreed to ship it all, plus 600,000 tons from Carnegie's own mines, on his railroads and steamers. In addition, they entered into a non-competition pact: Carnegie would not lease or buy new mines; Rockefeller would stay out of steel. So it was that six years later, Schwab reminded Morgan that leaving Rockefeller out of the new combine would leave it vulnerable to extortionate pricing for indispensable ore. In the end JPM paid JDR $80 million for the mines (in USS stock) and another $8.5 million for the fifty-six steamers of his Great Lakes fleet.

Morgan was less than thrilled about this aspect of the deal. He was not keen on Rockefeller, in part because Standard Oil had cash reserves greater than those of many banks, so Rockefeller could not be intimidated by Wall Streeters, even the mighty Morgan.

Culturally the two men were as chalk and cheese; they lived in different Gothams.

Morgan moved in a world of ultra-rich grandees; he was fond of cigars, port, steam yachts, and Manhattan club life. He was also a High Church Episcopalian—St. George's at 16th Street and Rutherford Place was generally known as "Morgan's Church"—and he enjoyed hobnobbing with bishops.

Rockefeller was Low Church, the family having joined the Fifth Avenue Baptist Church (at 46th Street), which became generally known as "Rockefeller's Church." A temperate man, he eschewed the club scene and indulged few urban pleasures besides carriage riding in Central Park.

To Rockefeller, Morgan seemed haughty, sybaritic, and arrogant. For Morgan's taste, Rockefeller was dry, prudish, and ascetic. On first meeting they instantly repelled one another. Rockefeller: "For my part, I have never been able to see why any man should have such a high and mighty feeling about himself." Morgan, more elementally: "I don't like him." (Lord Revelstoke, of London's House of Barings, recorded a more caustic commentary, telling a partner that in private conversation Morgan had "inveighed bitterly against the growing power of the Jews and of the Rockefeller crowd, and said more than once that our firm and his were the only two composed of white men in New York.")

Nevertheless, both detested competition, and both knew a good deal when they saw one. Thus was born United States Steel, composed of 228 formerly separate and locally owned companies in 127 cities and 18 states, now rolled into one gigantic enterprise. It produced roughly two-thirds of the country's steel output, more than Germany and Great Britain put together, nearly one-fourth the world's total. Its $1.4 billion capitalization was four times the federal budget. It had over 160,000 employees—making it the world's largest employer—who labored in 149 steel mills, 213 manufacturing plants, and 41 mines. It owned over a thousand miles of track, and as much land as Massachusetts, Vermont, and Rhode Island combined.

Schwab was president, and Gary chair of the executive committee, but there were more money men than steel executives on the board, including Morgan and three of his partners, and Rockefeller and his son. And the headquarters were not in Pittsburgh but in New York City. In 1901 the new mega-corporation moved into the fittingly named Empire Building, a twenty-story 1898 structure at 71 Broadway (corner of Rector), just across from the Trinity Church cemetery—a block and a half from Morgan's 23 Wall Street and two blocks up from Rockefeller's 26 Broadway.

EVEN BEFORE THE DEAL WAS DONE, the financial markets had registered the coming of changing times. In November 1898 Wall Street had begun to "boil"—in the vernacular of brokers on the New York Stock Exchange. Boom days followed one another in rapid succession. The rate of escalation, it was widely agreed, had seldom if ever been seen in Wall Street's history. On December 27 volume nearly hit 1 million shares, the most sensational day in memory. Too sensational to last, said some graybeards. But the market's eloquent rebuttal, as one observer noted, was "the continual click, click, click, of the Stock Exchange ticker quoting figures mounting higher not only every day, but virtually every minute." Taking stock at year's end, analysts found that "during 1898 hundreds of millions on hundreds of millions of dollars were added to the current market values of securities dealt on the New York Stock Exchange."

It didn't stop. The market kept rocketing upward during the first weeks of 1899, with million-share days becoming commonplace. "Money is in abundance all over the country," the *New York Times* rejoiced, "and from all over the country it has seemed recently bound toward Wall Street." Some said the market was surging simply because the economy had revived, and that was certainly true in part. Gotham was accustomed to the booms and busts hardwired into its capitalist economy. These had alternated with the almost biblical regularity of Pharaoh's dreams (seven years of fat cows and golden grain, seven years of lean cattle and withered wheat). As the nation's financial center, New York had experienced these disruptions acutely, beginning with the first market crash of 1792, before there even *was* a stock exchange. Financial crises had erupted in 1819, 1837, 1857, 1873, and 1893, in each case followed by periods of depression, with each trough deeper than the preceding one. Yet each had eventually given way to a period of abundance, with each new surge reaching ever giddier heights, as now seemed the case again.

But the frenzy on Wall Street reflected something more than the passing of the 1893–97 depression, something more than the latest upswing in the "business cycle." In 1898 financial analysts were beginning to spot things that smacked more of secular transformation than cyclical variation. "There have been developments in the affairs of corporations of the most favorable sort," it was said. "Wonderful strides" were being made that were "directly affecting values."

Big Steel was "forging buoyantly forward" and pulling the whole economy with it, but it wasn't just about heavy metals. A plethora of funds seeking investment was driving "rumors of deals, mergers, and absorptions" throughout the economy, the *New York Times* noted, especially in manufacturing. A "Bull fever" was a-hoof, as "many new industrial combinations were being brought out, and their shares presented an attractive field for speculation." In January of 1899 the *Times* noted that "American railways are in an era of consolidation and concentration. Lesser and competing roads are being merged into greater systems." It seemed that consolidations of "the greatest properties" were in the works.

They were indeed. In 1899 a maelstrom of mergers struck the Exchange. In sector after sector—rubber and paper, chemicals and explosives, machinery and metal products, sugar refining and tobacco products, oil and mining, railroads and shipping—an urge to merge, a desire to acquire, swept through hundreds of competing companies. Bitter rivals trooped to the table to integrate their interests—subsuming assets and identities in gigantic corporations.

Back in 1897, only 69 firms had disappeared into consolidated entities; in 1898—when the phenomenon began registering on Wall Street seismographs—the number had jumped to 303. But in 1899 the total surged to 1,208, a simply unheard-of number.

And they kept on coming. By 1904, when the great merger wave crested and tapered off, roughly 4,200 firms had winked out, their place in the economic firmament taken by 250 or so bright and shining supernovae. Among these were United States Steel, American Sugar Refining, International Harvester, American Smelting and Refining, Amalgamated Copper, United Fruit, and combinations in whiskey, tobacco, beer, coal, wool, bicycles, matches, even chewing gum (American Chicle).[1]

The old competitive order was being dismantled with incredible speed. A new corporate economy was emerging. And Gotham was at the vortex of events, for the giant new entities that had been assembled and financed in New York City were now being housed and head-quartered there.

---

1. It's a reasonable bet (though hardly a guarantee) that if an American corporation has the word "United," "Consolidated," "Amalgamated," "National," or "General" in its title, it dates to this first merger wave.

The process fed on itself. The concentration of capital and management—the super-dense accumulation of money and power—gave New York terrific financial gravitational force; it sucked in millionaires and corporations as fast as they were created, and yanked some already existing ones out of other cities' orbits.

Consider AT&T. In 1885 Bell Telephone, a Boston-based company, had established a subsidiary, American Telephone and Telegraph (AT&T), incorporated in New York State, to build and operate the system's long distance lines. In 1899, with the merger movement now in full swing, Bell decided to expand its national operations, but proved unable to obtain sufficient financing in Massachusetts, where the state's corporation law restricted capitalization to $10 million. So Bell transferred its assets to its AT&T subsidiary. AT&T became the parent and Bell the child, and many of its functions were shifted south to the old (1888) Telephone Building at 18 Cortlandt Street, newly expanded (in 1897) with an adjoining add-on at 15 Dey. As the century expired, the *New York Times* predicted this move would "make New York instead of Boston the centre of the vast Bell telephone system." This vision notched closer to realization in 1902 when Boston capitalists, forced to turn for financing to a Morgan-headed New York syndicate, were also forced to grant the Manhattanites increased representation in management. And in 1907, Wall Streeters having recently underwritten the $100 million bond offering that allowed AT&T to buy out competitors and virtually monopolize the industry nationwide, Morgan became the company's principal banker, and effective power shifted from Boston to New York.

The bottom-line reality was neatly summarized a few years later by New Haven Railroad president (and Bostonian) Charles Mellen, who when asked why he had gone to Wall Street rather than State Street to raise money replied: "Because I can get the money in New York when it is needed and I can't get it in Boston." The depth of the city's capital pool was another reason that so many of the largest industrial combinations had their main offices in New York City.

And yet, at the very moment that Gotham was exerting this tremendous centripetal pull, drawing the nation's financial and managerial resources to the Hudson, the mass of accumulated capital was generating a powerful centrifugal force, as it sought new and distant outlets abroad. It was not merely coincidental that the height of the great merger movement (1898–1904) overlapped precisely with the emergence of an American overseas empire.

2

Acquisitions

The United States had been an imperial power from its inception. It hadn't projected force overseas, but hadn't needed to: the North American continent had itself been the target of opportunity. Between the Revolution and the Civil War, the Republic had steadily extended its domain westward, often at gunpoint, and over the bodies of Indians and Mexicans. But advocates of expansion had insisted that theirs was not an imperial project, because conquered territories were eventually incorporated into the Union as states, and because conquered peoples became citizens, not colonial subjects (setting aside the Indians driven onto "reservations").

This republican expansionism continued after the Civil War into the era when European nations began carving up Africa and Asia to guarantee access to resources needed for industrialization. The United States did the same with its "Winning of the West," from the Sand Creek Massacre (1864) to the Battle of Wounded Knee (1890). Expansionists could still plausibly deny they were engaged in Euro-style imperialism, because the expropriations remained within continental boundaries, and the Constitution still followed the flag. Nevertheless, the end result was similar to that achieved by the Europeans. The United States secured mountains of iron, coal, and copper for mills and factories, fields and grazing lands for feeding the workforce, and forest products for housing it. Imperialism (a.k.a. Western expansion) went hand in hand with industrialization.

Gotham had been integral to this thrust into North America, even though geographically it had grown ever more distant from the center of action, as the western front advanced toward the Pacific. New York had been the prime funnel for Euro-capital—with bankers like J. P. Morgan and Jacob Schiff vetting railroad, ranching, and mining projects, on behalf of British, German, Dutch, and French investors. New York also funneled Euro-labor to fields and factories, with Irish, German, Italian, Polish, Welsh, and Jewish workers among the many nationalities who passed through Gotham on their way west, or who stayed to labor in the city's own industrial sector and bolster its consumer market.

As the premier national seaport, moreover, Gotham was the principal export point for industrial products railed in from the West, or manufactured in Gotham itself. The oil the Rockefellers pumped east to New York–area refineries was processed into kerosene, then dispatched to foreign shores, with Standard Oil of New York capturing over 70 percent of the world market. James Buchanan Duke's American Tobacco Company rolled cigarettes for the global millions. The Singer Manufacturing Company, headquartered at 34 Union Square, had been churning out sewing machines since the 1860s at its works in Elizabethport, New

"All Nations Use Singer Sewing Machines," ca. 1892. (Library of Congress Prints and Photographs Division)

Jersey, just across the Arthur Kill from northwest Staten Island. These were shipped abroad and sold via a network of company-owned or franchised retail outlets in Canada, Mexico, Russia, Scotland, England, Spain, Cuba, Venezuela, Uruguay, and Peru. By 1886 more than half of Singer's total earnings were harvested abroad, and its sales agencies virtually blanketed the planet. In the 1890s, to handle this business, Singer moved its central office to larger quarters, an eleven-story structure at 149 Broadway (on the northwest corner of Liberty Street).

New York exported capital as well as commodities. As metropolitan wealth accumulated—won chiefly in mercantile pursuits—affluent New Yorkers had begun investing in ventures abroad, notably in Latin America. Usually they were welcomed by cash-strapped regimes, nowhere more so than in Mexico during Porfirio Díaz's dictatorship (1876–1911). Díaz opened his country to New York capital in order to develop Mexico's infrastructure and resources. Gotham businessmen were attracted by the dictatorial stability. They also liked the fact that many Porfirian projects involved building transport and communication lines that connected to New York itself, thus extending the city's commercial hinterland.

One of the earliest entrepreneurs to ford the Rio Grande was James Scrymser, who in 1865, on returning to Gotham from Civil War service, decided to enter the submarine cable business by connecting the United States to Cuba. The 26-year-old Captain Scrymser won backing from Moses Taylor, long the leading merchant in the New York–Havana sugar trade. Taylor had segued into finance, rolling over his immense mercantile profits into shares in the City Bank of New York, of which he'd become president in 1856. Having helped underwrite the Atlantic Cable connecting New York to London, Taylor now did the same for Scrymser's linking of Florida with Cuba; it became operational in 1867. Moving on to grander projects, Scrymser set up a Mexican Telegraph Company, with J. P. Morgan a backer. In 1878 he got a concession from Díaz to lay cable under the Gulf of Mexico from Vera Cruz to Galveston, Texas, where it spliced into Western Union lines running on to New York City and its transatlantic link to Europe. That accomplished, he set up a Central and South American Telegraph Company. After getting Morgan's funding commitment (over dinner at the Union League Club), Scrymser, again with Díaz's support, ran cable from Mexico to Panama, and then down the west coast of the continent to Lima, Peru, 4,000 miles in all; it opened for business in 1882.

Díaz also welcomed railroad investments from the likes of Russell Sage, Jay Gould, J. P. Morgan, and Moses Taylor—the Mexican National Railroad was known as a New York project— and outfits like the Mexican-American Construction Company (32 Nassau Street) were called in to lay tracks. Cattle became big business, too, paced by the Hearst family ranch, with over a million acres in Chihuahua. (The Hearst papers were highly laudatory of dictator Díaz.)

Mining also drew New York firms to Mexico. Phelps Dodge was an old and established metals firm, founded in 1834 by Gotham merchant William Earl Dodge and his father-in-law, Anson Greene Phelps. The company had initially imported tin and copper into Brooklyn, then branched out into mining investments in Arizona, then (in 1895) bought the Moctezuma Copper Company in northeastern Sonora; in time it would account for well over half of Mexico's copper output.

Meyer Guggenheim, on the other hand, was a newcomer to mining. A Swiss Jewish immigrant to Philadelphia, Guggenheim had become a successful importer and manufacturer of embroidery when, in 1881, he purchased a one-third interest in two Colorado lead and silver mines, a business of which he knew nothing. But when they proved to be bonanzas he undertook their development himself. By 1887 the 130 miners he'd hired (and whose strikes

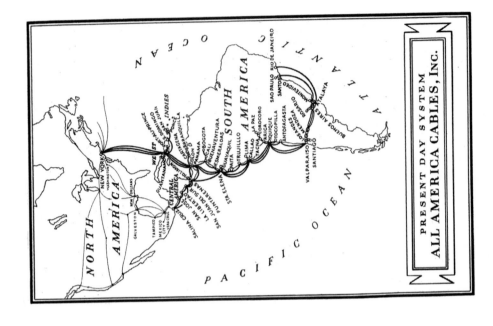

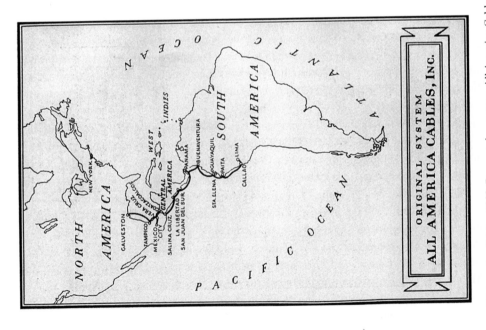

Original system, All America Cables, 1882. Present-day system, All America Cables, 1928. (Courtesy of Bill Glover, Atlantic-Cable.com)

he'd repeatedly crushed), had extracted 9 million ounces of silver, and the Guggenheim family was reaping three-quarters of a million dollars each year. In 1888, seeing that the cost of smelting (separating metal from ore) was eating up much of his profit, Meyer built his own smelter in Pueblo, Colorado, the largest in the world. Nevertheless, competition, labor costs, and more strikes (against brutal twelve-hour days) presented ongoing problems.

At this point Guggenheim moved in two directions—east to New York and south to Mexico. He and his family headed to Gotham, partly because that's where the business action was, and partly because Philadelphia "society" would never open its ranks to Jews no matter how wealthy they were. By 1889 he and his wife were resettled in a large brownstone at 36 West 77th Street, opposite the Museum of Natural History; three of his sons, Daniel, Solomon, and Isaac, were ensconced in the west 50s, just off Fifth, amid a covey of Rockefellers, Vanderbilts, and Astors; and the firm—M. Guggenheim's Sons—had been housed at 2 Wall Street. Then, in 1890, Daniel was dispatched to negotiate with Díaz. The development-minded dictator was delighted to approve a smelter in the sleepy northern town of Monterrey; it opened in 1892, with armed troops stationed there to prevent unrest, and another smelter, near Aguascalientes, became operational in 1894. Díaz also allowed the Guggenheims to buy or lease mines, and search for new ones, anywhere in Mexico. Daniel returned to Gotham to oversee all mining and smelting operations, and Solomon went to Mexico, where mines and railroads were soon added to the family holdings.

GIVEN THESE AND OTHER SUCCESS STORIES, New York's merchants, bankers, and manufacturers saw no pressing need to seek imperial control over foreign territory. They were content to construct a *commercial* empire, using their superior financial and technological resources to develop economic rather than political hegemony, and relying on affiliated local elites to supply political muscle as needed. The internationally minded businessmen did insist on some basic ground rules: there should be free flow of capital (no barriers to American investment) and open doors (unrestricted access to foreign markets and materials). But it seemed perfectly possible to attain these desired arrangements without an expensive military apparatus.

This began to change in the century's last decades. The problem, once again, was competition, this time between rivalrous national economies, on a global playing field. Spurred by the international depression of the 1870s, Europeans began securing colonies whose markets and resources were placed off-limits to other powers, including the now-industrializing Americans. Europeans also began contesting established American footholds in Europe itself: the discovery of oil at the Russian port of Baku on the Caspian Sea touched off fierce struggles between Standard Oil and European competitors, battles that spread into the Middle East.

Tensions grew in the Western Hemisphere as well. Great Britain had long dominated Latin America's markets and supplied the bulk of its credit needs. Increasingly New Yorkers found themselves bumping up against entrenched British positions in the course of expanding their own, as when James Scrymser tried to extend his cable operations to Brazil, only to discover the British had been granted a monopoly. The Germans, alarmingly, had started a massive naval buildup and clearly had designs on Latin America, even the Caribbean. Theodore Roosevelt argued that as Europe had inaugurated a new age of imperialism, the United States must get into the Great Game and compete vigorously, or risk being cut off from markets and raw materials in a world increasingly carved up into colonies and protectionist blocs.

In this context the anemic condition of America's military seemed increasingly troubling. In the late 1880s two New Yorkers helped oversee creation of a more substantial American fleet. The initiatives of financier William Whitney, secretary of the navy in Grover Cleveland's first administration (1885–89), included construction of the USS *Maine*, launched from the Brooklyn Navy Yard in 1889. Whitney's buildup had been continued by Benjamin Franklin Tracy, his counterpart in Benjamin Harrison's Republican regime (1889–93). A leading Brooklyn lawyer, Tracy believed the Gulf of Mexico and the Pacific were the coming theaters of naval action, and he promoted the building of steel-hulled battleships, as American interests abroad were "too important to be left longer unprotected."

The depression of the mid-1890s added greater urgency to this reconsideration of American foreign policy. It was widely believed that a major cause of the economic crisis was "overproduction." It seemed that US capitalism's ability to produce goods had outraced the US market's ability to consume them. Foreign markets, though far smaller than the domestic one, were now deemed essential to diminishing the dangerous glut. Not surprisingly, this became gospel in New York, the country's preeminent entrepôt; its Chamber of Commerce and its Board of Trade and Transport both warned Congress in 1896 that "the necessity of finding new markets is an imperative one." But farmers too called for expanding exports, as did the new National Association of Manufacturers, founded in Cincinnati in 1895.

The idea also took hold—argued most forcefully by Charles Arthur Conant—that America suffered from a surplus of capital as well as commodities. Conant was a highly respected scholar and financial journalist—Washington correspondent (1889–1901) of the *New York Journal of Commerce* and international financial editor of the New York *Bankers Magazine*. In 1902 he segued into banking himself, becoming treasurer of the Morton Trust Company, a leading underwriter of corporate consolidations. In articles like "Can New Openings Be Found for Capital?" (1899) Conant argued that the recurrent crises of industrial capitalism were rooted in an excess of savings over outlets for investment. This was evidenced by diminishing returns on domestic capital and rising levels of unemployment.

Much of this "surplus capital" had coursed into the New York Stock Exchange to fuel the merger movement. But this had actually exacerbated the systemic dilemma, as the new industrial giants generated more surplus commodities and surplus capital to be sopped up. The solution, Conant believed, lay in finding abroad "new outlets for American capital and new opportunities for American enterprise," particularly through developing the infrastructure of capital-scarce countries in Asia, Africa, and Latin America. Here the merger movement was advantageous, for the huge corporations could compete more effectively in world markets. The state should assist this process by forestalling or removing foreign constraints on US capital, whether imposed by rival empires or revolutionary regimes, and by promoting a vigorous internationalization of the investment system itself. Conant was optimistic that if equal access was guaranteed, the US would win global economic preeminence. So too would New York. As Conant told the American Bankers Association in 1900, the growing role of New York City in "the circle of international money markets" had "raised the question whether the star of financial supremacy was not to move westward from the precincts of [London's] Lombard Street to our own chief city."

This new consensus spurred calls to forcefully invoke the Monroe Doctrine, America's 1823 warning to Europeans against recolonizing the Latin American republics that had just broken away from Spain. Realistically the US hadn't had the military capacity to prevent such incursions, but this hadn't been a problem so long as it and England (with its powerful navy) were not direct competitors. But during the '90s depression, with England now a rival and Germany on the move, fantasies were floated of making Latin America a European-free zone. If "we could wrest the South American markets from Germany and England and permanently hold them," wrote the *Bankers Magazine* in 1894, "this would be indeed a conquest worth perhaps a heavy sacrifice." Some actual jousting took place in the mid-1890s, as the second Cleveland administration (1893–97) deployed its enhanced naval strength against British interests in Brazil in 1893, in Nicaragua in 1894, and in Venezuela in 1895–96, in the latter case nearly precipitating a war with England.

THE 1898 INTERVENTION IN CUBA came in this context, though ironically, the survival of Spain's centuries-long rule had not hitherto been a major source of concern. Cuba under the Spanish seemed not terribly dissimilar from Mexico under Díaz. Perhaps Spain wasn't as enthusiastic about the growing American investment on the island, but it had neither the will nor the wherewithal to block it. Cuban cane producers—driven out of a major market when Europe switched to sugar beets for sweets—had turned to US capital to modernize their mills. They had also become almost totally reliant on US buyers—in truth, on one buyer, Havemeyer's American Sugar Refining Company (ASRC) up in New York. Nor had Spain interfered when US refinery interests began moving into production in Cuba itself, seeking to control their source of supply. With its purchase of the Trinidad Sugar Company in 1892, the Sugar Trust began a vertical integration of the industry that transcended national borders. Other New York companies were equally comfortable operating under the Spanish umbrella, and Gotham-based firms provided Cuba with lighting, waterworks, telephones, omnibuses, and hotels. By the mid-1890s, American investment in the island surpassed $50 million.

This cozy state of affairs evaporated after the Cubans, in 1895, launched their latest struggle to throw off Spanish rule. The order to commence hostilities had come from Gotham itself, issued by José Martí, the Cuban writer-revolutionary who had been living in the city since 1880; his Partido Revolucionario Cubano (PRC) was headquartered on Front Street (between Wall and Pine), near the pier of the Ward Line, a major Caribbean carrier.

Martí himself died in battle in 1895, but the war he'd ignited caught fire. Cuban guerrillas laid waste to sugar plantations in an effort to render the island economically useless to its imperial overlords. Spain countered with its monstrous *reconcentrado* initiative, which herded hundreds of thousands into barbed-wired encampments, wherein tens of thousands perished of starvation and disease.

Sympathy for the rebels had grown in Gotham, fanned by the PRC and the Cuban Junta (the PRC's fund-raising and propaganda wing), both controlled by Martí's successor, Tomás Estrada Palma. The Junta channeled arms, food, and medical supplies to the island, lobbied Congress to support the Cuban cause, won backing from the influential Americans (among them Theodore Roosevelt) in the Cuban League of the United States (at 115 Broadway), and promoted sympathetic reporting by Gotham's sensationalist press, paced by William Randolph Hearst's *Journal* and Joseph Pulitzer's *World*.

Then, on February 15, 1898, the USS *Maine* exploded in Havana's harbor. On March 28, a US Naval Court of Inquiry declared the sinking had been caused by a mine. Spain, near-universally, was presumed the culprit. Sentiment for armed intervention surged. On April 4 a special issue of Hearst's *Journal* loudly beat the drum for war; it sold over a million copies. The new rallying cry became "Remember the *Maine* / To Hell with Spain."

New Yorkers were particularly receptive to the anti-Iberian message. The city's Dutch and English founders had been profound opponents of the Spanish Empire, and of the Catholic Church to which Spain gave crucial support. Schoolbook accounts of conquistadors and inquisitors perpetuated this inherited antipathy, and indeed convinced many of the

Grand Cuban-American Fair, Madison Square Garden, May 25–30, 1896. (Library of Congress Prints and Photographs Division)

singular and seemingly inherent depravity of Spaniards. One New York publisher recharged this link between past and present by bringing out a new English edition of Bartolomé de Las Casas's sixteenth-century *Short Account of the Destruction of the Indies*, with the souped-up title *An Historical and True Account of the Cruel Massacre and Slaughter of 20,000,000 People in the West Indies by the Spaniards* (1898), adding, lest the point be lost, the subtitle: *Horrible Atrocities of Spaniards in Cuba*. Other black marks against the Spanish included a belief that they were less than "white" given their historic intermingling with Moors and Africans, a dismay at Spain's harsh centuries-long effort to "purify" its national bloodstream of those colored components, and outrage at their supposed sexual appetites. (Hearst's *Journal* ran made-up stories about lustful Spanish brutes ravishing pure Cuban women.) Added to their Catholicism, their presumed destruction of the *Maine*, and the all-too-real atrocities they were committing in Cuba, the result was a bill of indictment deemed by many to warrant war.

Protestant ministers joined the yellow press in pushing for intervention. R. Heber Newton, pastor of the Episcopal All Souls' Church (at Madison Avenue and 66th Street), believed that "the long story of Spain's rapacity and extortion, of her oppression and cruelty, of her treachery and perfidy" had reached a culmination in Cuba that required retribution. "It is no pleasant thing to be appointed by Providence the executioner upon a great nation," said Newton, but it was patently America's duty to "unsheath its sword from its scabbard and proceed to the work of the Lord."

Felix Adler, longtime leader of the Society for Ethical Culture, rejected vengeance as a legitimate ground for war. But he did argue, in an April 10 talk at Carnegie Hall, that physical force could be justly deployed if done "out of respect for human rights," notably the "inalienable right of a people to be self-governing." Indeed, *failure* to act could be considered immoral, Adler added, noting that the refusal of European powers to stop the massacre of Armenians by Turks in 1894–96 was considered by many to be an "everlasting stain" on their escutcheon. The US, moreover, could intervene to win independence for Cuba with a clear conscience because it would come to the fight with "clean hands." "We are not moved," Adler argued, "by the desire for aggrandizement."

Not all were swept away by anti-Spanish fervor. In an April debate at the Central Labor Union (CLU), a delegate from the Longshoremen's Union declared that the "cruelty exhibited in Cuba is no peculiarity of the Spanish race," citing the recent wave of lynchings in the United States. He urged continued diplomatic pressure rather than military intervention. But war proponents carried the day in the CLU, if by a narrow majority, citing destruction of the *Maine* as the principal casus belli.

Most of the city's business community, though distressed by Spain's inability to provide stability, resisted bellicosity. Even New York's sugar interests at first urged only that President McKinley pressure Spain into granting Cuba greater autonomy, in order to defuse the crisis. But as the costs of conflict became apparent, they sought more vigorous intervention: a January 1898 petition from seventy leading Gotham businessmen and firms active in Cuba asked the president to help end their "tremendous losses" and restore "a most valuable commercial field."

But most of Wall Street continued to favor a hands-off policy, fearing war might abort what looked like a fledgling recovery from the long depression. Some were concerned that an independent Cuba might be less amenable to US interests than it had been as Spain's colony, might even become a black republic on the model of Haiti. Their reluctance generated nationwide opprobrium. New York's money men, it was charged, by blocking a humanitarian crusade, were putting profits over people. Wall Street (buzzed the *Sacramento Evening Bee*) was the "Benedict Arnold of the Union," the "Judas Iscariot of humanity."

The clamor finally convinced many New York businessmen that peace was proving as debilitating as war, and that Spain's empire had outlived its usefulness. There was also the political fallout to consider, a case argued by attorney Elihu Root, a power in the Republican Party and in Gotham's corporate circles. On April 2, 1898, Root advised McKinley not to "retard the enormous momentum of the people bent upon war" lest he bring the Democrats to power in the upcoming 1900 presidential election. War with the Spanish—whom Root considered an inferior race and dismissed as "dagos"—was a small price to pay for maintaining conservative Republican control. Besides, though he didn't spell this out to McKinley, Spain was patently the easiest European power to beat.

On April 19 Congress authorized the president to use force to evict Spain and liberate Cuba, while disavowing "any disposition or intention to exercise sovereignty, jurisdiction, or control over said island" (though it pointedly did not extend recognition to the Cuban government-in-exile in New York). Within days the country was at war, and a blockade of Cuba was set in motion. Gotham immediately donned patriotic dress: Broadway was bunted and beflagged from the Battery to 42nd Street; rush orders went out to manufacturers for more of the red, white, and blue. Here and there, in areas where Cubans concentrated (like the Pearl Street cigar-making district), the lone-star Cuban flag (designed and debuted in Gotham back in 1850) was lavishly displayed.

Crowds congregated in front of the newspaper offices to read war bulletins; the enormous gatherings at the *Times* building rendered Nassau and Spruce Streets unpassable. Harbor defenses were bolstered to ward off a feared invasion by the Spanish fleet. In Brooklyn, a hastily organized 1st Marine Battalion left for Cuba from the Navy Yard dock while the Yard's band played "The Girl I Left Behind Me."

On April 23 McKinley called for 125,000 volunteers to aid the undermanned professional army, which had been mainly engaged in suppressing the last flickers of Indian resistance out west. National Guardsmen flocked to their armories to sign up for a two-year hitch. (Some Brooklynites made enlistment contingent on their unit's maintaining its "Brooklyn" designation.) Newly formed volunteer outfits set up recruiting tents in Union Square, Madison Square, Bowling Green, the Bowery, and City Hall—drawing in thousands of clerks, messengers, mechanics. On Wall Street a Bankers and Brokers Regiment was planned. Theodore Roosevelt decided to resign as assistant secretary of the navy and raise a regiment of western cowboys and New York clubmen—the Rough Riders—to be coloneled by Leonard Wood, a military surgeon who was also the president's doctor.

On the distaff side, professional nurses and society women rushed to the Red Cross Hospital at 233 West 100th Street. The only training school for Red Cross nurses in the country, it had been founded in 1895 by the New York branch, with the approval of National Red Cross president Clara Barton; its student nurses had hitherto worked in the New York Lying-In Hospital or the Willard Parker (for contagious diseases). Now, with financial aid from the likes of real estate baron John Jacob Astor IV and Jacob Schiff, and involvement by a contingent of prominent society women, the New York operation expanded with tremendous speed. It recruited nurses to care for the army, sent outfitted ambulances to the front

"Colonel Theodore Roosevelt, of the 'Rough Riders.'" *Harper's Pictorial History of the War with Spain,* vol. 2, 1899.

lines, and oversaw a network of hospitals, warehouses, and auxiliaries—all quite independently of Barton—down in Cuba. Alarmed that her national organization might be supplanted by the Gothamites' creation, Barton would move her headquarters from Washington to Manhattan.

Then, in a relative twinkling, the war was won. On May 1, a scant week after it started, Commodore George Dewey's Asiatic Squadron destroyed the decrepit Spanish fleet in Manila Bay. (Washington got the news from Pulitzer's *World*, whose communication system outclassed the military's.) By May 27 the US Navy had bottled up Spain's fleet in Santiago de Cuba's bay. In June the main invasion force arrived on the scene. In early July it captured the San Juan Heights overlooking Santiago, making the city indefensible. The Spanish fleet tried to escape and was destroyed. On July 17 the Spanish surrendered. A week later US troops invaded Puerto Rico, where in short order they took Ponce and Mayaguez. On August 12 they were advancing on Arecibo when word arrived that an armistice had been signed. In the Philippines, on August 13, US forces (not having gotten the news) attacked Manila, and the Spanish surrendered there as well.

The war begun in spring was thus effectively over by summer. Negotiation and ratification of a peace treaty took a little longer. On December 10, in Paris, Spain renounced its rights to Cuba, ceded Puerto Rico and Guam to the United States, and sold it the Philippines for $20,000,000, a deal ratified by the US Senate on February 6, 1899, with the treaty formally proclaimed on April 11, 1899.

New York, having been in the center of the action at the war's beginning, now laid plans to occupy center stage at its conclusion. In the spring of 1899 the city's political, economic, and cultural elites came together to propose an imperial Festival of Connection, hailing the links that had been established, this time at gunpoint, with far-flung islands. Gotham requested and received Navy Department permission for (now) Admiral Dewey to make Gotham (not Washington) his first port of call. The metropolis promised to throw a colossal homecoming party for the conquering hero when he returned from the Pacific in September. A reception committee appointed by Mayor Robert A. Van Wyck got to work preparing two immense parades, one by land, the other by sea, as per the Erie Canal celebration of 1825.

In May the city's National Sculpture Society offered to contribute a temporary triumphal arch, erected out of staff, the plaster-and-wood-shavings confection used to build Chicago's White City exposition in 1893. Eighty-three feet high, it would be a cross between Rome's Arch of Titus (commemorating the taking of Jerusalem by imperial legions) and Paris's Arc de Triomphe (commissioned by Napoleon after his victory at Austerlitz). It would rise at Madison Square, astride Fifth Avenue at 24th Street, where Broadway made its way downtown.

The arch was in place on Friday, September 29, 1899, when boats participating in the day's aquatic procession lined up in the harbor above the Narrows. At the head of the nautical parade was the admiral's flagship, the *Olympia*, with Dewey aboard. It was followed by vessels bearing the mayor and governor and assorted civic officials, warships of the North Atlantic Squadron paced by the cruiser USS *New York* (Rear Admiral Sampson's flagship at the Battle of Santiago) and the USS *Brooklyn* (flagship of Commodore Schley's Flying Squadron at the same encounter), a squadron of 94 private yachts (headed by the *Corsair*, under the command of its owner, John Pierpont Morgan, in his capacity as commodore of the New York Yacht Club), 92 merchant vessels, and finally 135 tugboats and barges. The assemblage then steamed impressively up the Hudson to Grant's Tomb, where the *Olympia*'s guns thundered a salute from one hero to another, and the other vessels U-turned and dropped anchor at their designated places along the length of Manhattan. The watery pageant continued at night when illuminated lighters passed down the East and North (as the Hudson was still often called) Rivers, on either side of Manhattan, shooting off fireworks and then meeting up at the Battery for an even more spectacular display.

The next day the celebration came ashore. Dewey, who had spent the night at the Waldorf-Astoria, stopped first at City Hall, then traveled by barouche up to Claremont Heights, where about 30,000 were assembled. They then marched down Riverside Drive to 72nd Street, to Central Park West, to 59th, to Fifth Avenue, and then down Fifth (the avenue's businessmen having beaten off an effort by rival merchants to shunt the flow to Broadway) to the reviewing stand at 24th, where Dewey watched the parade, and on down to Washington Square, passing an estimated 2 million people on the way.

"Surely no Roman general, surely no Roman Emperor ever received such a tribute from the populace of the Eternal City," boasted the *Times*, positioning Gotham as the symbolic capital of a new American Empire. A souvenir booklet agreed that "New York has achieved a triumph as complete and remarkable in its way as the brilliant victory it is meant to commemorate." But after the cheering died down, and New Yorkers began poring over the burst of new books devoted to familiarizing Americans with their acquisitions—titles like *Our New Possessions*, and *Our Island Empire: A Hand-book of Cuba, Porto Rico, Hawaii, and the Philippine Islands*—it remained unclear exactly what this empire might mean for the country and its chief metropolis. Nor—given that in December 1898 the Philippines had declared themselves independent of America as well as Spain, and fighting had broken out between Filipino forces and the US occupation army—was it even clear that the possessions obtained during the previous spring and summer were truly "ours."

WITH THE UNITED STATES NOW IN POSSESSION OF CUBA, Puerto Rico, the Philippines, and Guam, the necessity of deciding what to do with them put the issue of overseas empire squarely on the table. In the ensuing debates and decisions New Yorkers played a central role, none more so than Elihu Root, who became McKinley's (and later Roosevelt's) secretary of war (1899–1904), and still later (1905–9) served as Roosevelt's secretary of state.

When McKinley asked Root to accept the War portfolio, he demurred, pleading his complete ignorance of things military. Undeterred, McKinley replied: "I don't need anyone who knows anything about war or the army. I need a lawyer to administer these Spanish islands we've captured and you are the lawyer I want."

Elihu Root was not just any lawyer; he was Gotham's preeminent corporate attorney, whose clients included the biggest companies (Standard Oil, the Sugar Trust) and the wealthiest titans (Morgan, Belmont, Whitney, James J. Hill,). He was also a heavyweight in the Republican Party, a pillar of the New York bar, and—though not born into it—a fixture in Gotham society.

Root had grown up in Clinton (near Utica, in upstate New York), where his father was a professor at Hamilton College, from which Elihu graduated in 1864. Hamilton alumni eased Root's move down to Gotham. One facilitated his entry to NYU Law School (Class of '67). Another introduced him to the minister at the West Presbyterian Church on 42nd Street (across from Bryant Park), where he taught Sunday school and became active in the Young Men's Christian Association (headed by the likes of J. P. Morgan). Another linked him to a bank president for whom he undertook a complicated reorganization in 1869, which led to further such commissions. And a fourth put Root up for membership in the Union League Club (ULC), where New York's worlds of business, Republican politics, and male camaraderie intersected. At the club he met Salem H. Wales, a director of the Bank of North America,

Elihu Root, ca. 1908. (Library of Congress Prints and Photographs Division)

who was prominent in Republican Party politics and Fifth Avenue society. In 1878 Root married Wales's daughter Clara, and the couple moved to a town house at 30 East 55th Street purchased and furnished by the bride's parents.

Root rose rapidly in his profession, focusing after 1885 on corporation work, devising ways for big businesses to operate without falling afoul of existing law. He also rose in New York City Republican and reform politics, and in the Union League Club, of which he was elected president in 1898. The following year McKinley, who had treated the ULC as a talent pool, drawing its members into high administration positions and ambassadorial posts, tapped Root for secretary of war and overseer of empire. With his Roman bangs he even looked the part of an American proconsul.

Root became one of McKinley's key advisers, a position he would fill for Theodore Roosevelt after McKinley was assassinated. McKinley, who had been reelected in 1900 with Roosevelt as his running mate, was murdered in September 1901, and TR ascended to the presidency. The new state of affairs strengthened Root's already considerable influence, as he and Roosevelt went way back in Gotham. Seventeen years earlier Root had been one of a group of eminent New Yorkers that supported Roosevelt's entry into local politics, and he'd become the younger man's mentor as well as friend. Root was one of the few who could chide or josh the testy TR, who professed even to enjoy Root's acerbic wit, calling him "the brutal friend to whom I pay the most attention." In February 1904, convinced he'd accomplished what he'd set out to do, and eager to get back to New York, Root resigned as secretary of war. Back in Gotham his law practice flourished immediately, becoming the most lucrative in the country, involving him in nearly every major corporate litigation. He joined numerous bank and insurance company boards. He was elected president of the Association of the Bar of the

City of New York. He and his wife (who had hated Washington) reestablished themselves in Manhattan society. Architect Thomas Hastings was designing them a splendid town house on Park Avenue at 71st. But when Secretary of State John Hay died on July 1, 1905, and Roosevelt asked Root to come back as secretary of state, he acquiesced. (Many thought this put him in line for the presidency.) He would serve until the end of Roosevelt's second term. During the decade-long debates over imperialism, therefore, Root was the key point person, bringing to the discussion his personal and legal skills as a consummate problem solver and all around "wise man." But Root also transmitted the perspectives that circulated in the circles wherein he traveled, the commanding heights of New York's business, legal, and political sectors.

BACK IN THE FALL OF 1899, as if preparing for a court case, Root boned up on his subject by working his way through what he called "a short list of books which would do for a beginning in the colonial business." Then he assessed the specific situation of each of the new possessions.

In the Philippines, the key decision had been made before Root arrived. At war's end McKinley had hoped to keep just Manila, as a strategic gateway to Asian markets, though the reality of imperial competition—German warships were already on the scene—led him to claim the whole archipelago. But ordering its occupation (in December 1898) had touched off an insurrection (in February 1899) by the new Philippine Republic (Emilio Aguinaldo, president). So when Root assumed command, war had been raging for half a year.

Root was in complete agreement with the policy, and when quick victory proved elusive, he threw in more troops, swelling the total to 70,000 in 1900. He promulgated the official line that the rebels were "half-civilized" bandits under a "half-breed" leader, whereas most Filipinos were ready "to accept American sovereignty" and learn "the rudiments of government under the tuition of the American soldier." As this tutelage included brutal counterinsurgency tactics, exacerbated by racism, the war spurred on the protest movement that had emerged the minute it became clear that the United States intended to annex the islands.

It had started and remained strongest in Boston, where in November 1898 an Anti-Imperialist League had been constituted. Heavy on lawyers and university professors, especially from Harvard, the group warned that opting for empire would doom the American Republic as it had Rome's. The same argument was advanced by the smaller but more diverse movement that sprang up in New York City.

Reformers and journalists like E. L. Godkin and Carl Schurz inverted the imperialists' race-based justification for conquest (that Filipinos were incapable of self-government), by noting that if the United States annexed the Philippines it would allow "alien, inferior, and mongrel races" (Godkin) or "barbarous Asiatics...far less good-natured, tractable and orderly than the negro" (Schurz) to migrate to the mainland, where they would govern not only themselves, but white Americans as well.

Union leaders—notably Samuel Gompers of the American Federation of Labor, who had gotten his start as a cigar-makers organizer in New York—were angry that a war for Cuban liberation had turned into a war for imperial acquisition. Gompers, who signed on as a League vice president, feared annexation would lead to Asian immigration, and floods of cheap or contract laborers would undercut American wages. Or perhaps, Gompers worried, American employers would simply move their factories to Manila and exploit cheap labor over there. Either way he saw the New Empire as serving the interests of trusts and corporations, not working people. Many in the labor movement agreed—in early 1899, the Central Labor Union of New York City opposed annexation—though some trade unions accepted the businessmen's brief that territorial expansion, by creating a market for surplus goods, would forestall another depression.

Another Anti-Imperialist League recruit was Andrew Carnegie—a bit oddly, as at that point he was still the nation's leading manufacturer of steel plating for battleships. Nevertheless, Carnegie opposed annexing the Philippines. He denied that colonization was a prerequisite for trade; indeed, he thought it would weaken the economy by triggering an arms race with the Europeans, costing the nation millions that should be spent on building up commercial infrastructure. Carl Schurz agreed it was "a barbarous notion that in order to have a profitable trade with a country we must own it."

Mark Twain, another League enlistee, had caustic things to say about the effort of the "Blessings-of-Civilization Trust" to uplift "our Brother who Sits in Darkness." He warned that in addition to losing its moral compass, the US was entering "a quagmire from which each fresh step renders the difficulty of extrication immensely greater."

The Anti-Imperialist League's efforts gained traction when word of American atrocities leaked out (despite Root's best efforts). Well-sourced reports arrived of Filipinos being massacred wholesale; of deliberate American military efforts to turn their territory into "a howling wilderness'" of US troops waterboarding and otherwise torturing Philippine prisoners and herding civilians into *reconcentrados*, the very tactic reviled when employed by the Spanish in Cuba. Calls for Root's resignation multiplied, but he hung tough. Claiming that the Filipinos, who were "but little advanced from pure savagery," had committed their own atrocities, he vigorously defended the army against criticism, admitting to only a few bad apples, which had been plucked out. But the enterprise had been irrevocably stained.

In the end the Americans triumphed—a denouement that Roosevelt hailed as "glorious"—but the price had been chillingly high. After more than three years of intense fighting—the war ended in July 1902—over 4,200 US soldiers were dead, 20,000 Philippine soldiers had been killed, and at least 200,000 civilians had perished. This soured many, even TR for all his boasting, on the idea of further military adventures in pursuit of territory.

Whatever second thoughts Secretary Root may have had, the Philippines were now an American acquisition, and he set about pondering how best to incorporate them into America's economic orbit. To aid him in this, he dispatched economist Arthur Conant to Manila in 1901 to consider how to modernize the islands to make them attractive to US investors. Conant focused on currency reform and on establishing a Philippine monetary and banking system to facilitate transfers of capital and repatriation of profits. This was but an early step in what would become a broader effort to transform US colonies or protectorates—creating a sociopolitical environment friendly to capitalist development by instituting fiscal, budgetary, and tax "modernizations."

Nor, despite the bloodshed and uproar, did Root have any intention of abandoning the military arm. Quite the opposite. In tandem with reformers in the officer corps who were tired of low budgets and frontier duties, and who wanted to play in the same league as their counterparts in Europe, Root proceeded to reshape the military establishment in ways that made it a more useful (and disciplined) tool for projecting American power abroad. The lawyer saw the army as an ailing business concern, plagued by unclear lines of authority, and bedeviled by internal competition between virtually autonomous bureaus. Root proposed the kind of central direction and control that was customary in well-run corporations, with power concentrated at the top, in the hands of a general staff of professionally educated officers (Root pushed for a War College), and above them the civilian appointee elite. The Army Bill of 1903 enacted much of his program into law.

Root also worked at strengthening links between Wall Street and the officer corps. The city's top businessmen had long lionized military leaders—Sherman and Grant were among those who not only moved to New York but worked on Wall Street—but Root burnished the connection for a new century. The battlefield death of General Henry W. Lawton in the Philippines was an occasion for demonstrating that Root and his colleagues honored military traditions. Lawton had died poor, leaving his wife and four young children practically penniless. So Root wrote personal notes to the metropolitan elite, among them John D. Rockefeller, J. P. Morgan, and August Belmont, noting of the Lawton family that there was "nothing but our sense of obligation between them and want," and a comfortable sum was soon settled on the widow.

PUERTO RICO OFFERED A DIFFERENT PATHWAY to direct colonization. The US invasion had been quick, virtually bloodless, and welcomed by most Puerto Ricans, with many favoring annexation (and eventual statehood) as being in the island's best interest. But Root—whose War Department had jurisdiction over the occupied territory—had a different view. He drew up a frame of governance that precluded citizenship and excluded statehood (because Americans shouldn't "dilute our electorate"). Instead he called for giving Puerto Rico the "greatest possible measure of self-government which she is competent to exercise"—which turned out to be virtually none. He proposed a highly centralized structure consisting of a governor and legislative council, both appointed by the US president. Some council seats (though not a majority) would be reserved for local elites, but Root rejected an elective assembly, as he believed the vast majority of Puerto Ricans couldn't be trusted to vote wisely. Congress embodied most of his suggestions in the 1900 Foraker Act, though it did insist on an elected lower house. The legislators justified the denial of statehood and citizenship by designing a new tailor-made category of possession—"unincorporated territories" (i.e., not incorporated into the Union). Puerto Rico would be part of the US vis-à-vis other foreign states but would remain a foreign state for purposes of domestic law. The Supreme Court approved this arrangement in 1901 in one of the Insular Cases, a decision Root drolly summarized as finding that "the Constitution follows the flag—but doesn't quite catch up with it."

Root also fought to eliminate tariff barriers between Puerto Rico and the mainland, arguing that free trade was essential to revive the moribund sugar industry and make the island economically viable. He was rousingly seconded in this call by his clients the Havemeyers, whose American Sugar Refining Company would not have to pay taxes on its imported and indispensable raw material. Others in McKinley's pro-tariff Republican administration balked, but Root carried the day, partly by mobilizing the Merchants' Association of New York, a bastion of free-trade forces, to lobby vigorously for the exception.

The 1901 decision to end taxing the export of sugar to the mainland had an immediate and startlingly powerful effect on Puerto Rico's economy. New York capital poured into the sugar sector, huge modern mills were constructed, and before the decade was out, sugar production had shot up 331 percent. Puerto Rican, Spanish, and French mill owners also prospered in the boom, but almost half of the island's ground cane would soon be produced by New York–based sugar corporations, each vertically integrated with the Sugar Trust's refineries. At the same time that sugar boomed, coffee crashed. It had been the island's principal export crop, grown by a multitude of small farmers. But after 1898 it lost its protected markets in Cuba and Spain, while gaining nothing from its integration into the US orbit, because there were no American tariffs on coffee. This left Puerto Rico free to compete in the US market with Brazil, which had long ago established an impregnable position. Disaster soon ensued.

BOTH PUERTO RICO AND THE PHILIPPINES were exceptional cases, and for Root neither pointed the way toward a replicable neo-imperial strategy. Cuba did.

Cuba was a far richer prize than Puerto Rico or the Philippines. It already boasted substantial US investments, and at war's end it was securely occupied by the American military. But in this case possession was not nine-tenths of the law, given that before the war Congress had passed the Teller Amendment, which had renounced annexation. Gotham's sugar interests pushed to undo this promise: a package of articles entitled "The Future of Cuba: New York Business Men Advocate Annexation" was dispatched to newspapers all across the country. And in 1900 the *New York Sun* argued that "the wealth and intelligence of the island are generally in favor of [annexation], and the agitators and their tools, the ignorant Negroes, are opposed to it"; clearly, the US was backing the wrong side. But Leonard Wood—Teddy Roosevelt's Rough Riders compatriot and now the island's military commander—quickly discovered there was little or no sympathy for annexation anywhere in Cuba.

Root, Wood's superior, had his own reservations about simply up and leaving, based not on short-term profitability but on long-term strategic calculations. He was concerned that Europeans might move in to fill the vacuum, a matter of increasing salience as the United States moved closer to building an isthmian canal. "The American people will within a few years have to either abandon the Monroe Doctrine or fight for it," said Root pugnaciously in April 1900, "and we are not going to abandon it." He was also reluctant to leave existing or future US investments to the possibly untender mercies of an independent country, possessed of an army consisting of battle-hardened insurrectionaries, and with no home-grown Díaz in sight. Cuba was too strong and too weak to let go of, yet full-scale Euro-style colonization was politically impossible, militarily difficult, and to Root's way of thinking ultimately unwise.

His solution was to agree to withdraw troops but to require, as the price for leave-taking, a guaranteed right to return. In a draft of his terms the secretary said the United States must retain the option of intervening "for the preservation of Cuban independence and the maintenance of a stable government, adequately protecting life, property, and individual liberty." Root thus rejected a full-time occupation in favor of just-in-time military actions, on a need-to-intervene basis. Root also demanded the right to approve Cuba's external affairs and to require it to "keep healthy finances and acquire no public debt." He also mandated the transfer of land for a naval base (which would rise at Guantánamo Bay). Senator Orville Platt attached these conditions, virtually word for word, in a rider to a military appropriations bill that became law in February 1901, superseding the Teller Amendment. With immense reluctance, Cubans wrote them into their constitution in 1902. Cuba had become an American protectorate, neither independent nor a colony.

To sweeten this bitter pill, Root sought to eliminate duties on sugar and tobacco, as he had in Puerto Rico, but the Cuban case proved a much harder sell. Squawks went up from the US beet sugar industry out west, claiming with some justice that the initiative was a ploy by New York's cane sugar "refining trust" to reap windfall profits. The Havemeyers' ASRC neatly overcame this obstacle by buying up a controlling interest in the major beet companies, whose caviling abruptly ceased. Even then, the 1903 reciprocity treaty granted Cuban cane only a 20 percent discount, while requiring that American products get a break of 25 percent to 40 percent, with the goal of transforming Cuba into a marketplace for American goods.

To prepare the ground for this new relationship, the Americans brought in experts to reshape the island's social infrastructure. Many were reformers from New York City, who had established new best practices in a variety of social domains, which they now sought to transfer to Cuba. To improve sanitary conditions, McKinley appointed George E. Waring Jr.—hero of Gotham's reformers for his impressive street-cleaning achievements in the Strong administration—but Waring contracted yellow fever in Havana and died shortly after returning to New York. John McCullagh, chief of New York's police department, was called in to reorganize the Havana force. And Root convinced Charlton Lewis, president of the Prison Association of New York, to examine Cuban courts and prisons. But the principal agents of transformation would be American—overwhelmingly New York—businessmen.

An article in the *New York World* on July 20, 1898, had predicted that a new invasion of Cuba would follow the war. "Whatever may be decided as to the political future of Cuba," it stated, "its industrial and commercial future will be directed by American enterprise with American capital." The prognostication was overstated—Cubans, Spaniards, Britons, and Germans would be important players—but basically correct. Capital raced south, in a fiscal version of the Oklahoma land rush. And because the surge coincided with the corporate merger movement, the new arrivals were flush with immense quantities of cash freshly raised on Wall Street.

On April 25, 1900, the Cuba Company was incorporated in New Jersey in "order to develop Cuba," and in particular to build a 350-mile-long cross-island railroad to connect Havana with Santiago, the island's eastern port. Proposed and promoted by William Cornelius Van Horne, former head of the Canadian Pacific Railroad, the Cuba Company drew in a bevy of New Yorkers as incorporators, directors, and shareholders, among them such giants as railroad magnates Hill and Harriman; financier William C. Whitney and transportation magnate Thomas F. Ryan; bankers Schiff, Belmont, Levi Morton, and George Baker; the Rockefellers' Standard Oil partner Henry Flagler; John W. Mackay, president of the Commercial Cable Company; and corporate lawyer Paul Cravath. The Cuba Company, instantly the largest foreign investment in the country, completed the Cuba Central Rail Road within two years.

The new line, in turn, helped open up the eastern end of the island for modern sugar production. Several New York syndicates jumped in, accumulating enormous tracts of land on which they erected mammoth mills. Several of these were then consolidated into the Cuban-American Sugar Company. (First chartered in New Jersey in 1899, it was reorganized and expanded in 1906, with financial backing from Henry Havemeyer and the National City Bank.) All these threads led back to the American Sugar Refining Company (at 117 Wall) and the putatively independent but actually interlocked National Sugar Refining Company (at 129 Front Street, a block away).

James Duke's American Tobacco Company (ATC) was also Caribbean-bound. The ATC had garnered all but total control of cigarette production in the United States but had been stymied in mastering the domestic cigar industry. Now, in 1901, Duke organized the American Cigar Company (ACC), consolidated twenty or so domestic manufacturers within it, and bought up a network of retail outlets. Then—the ground prepared—he entered Cuba in 1902. Using the proceeds of massive stock offerings on Wall Street, the ACC bought up the major local producers, built the largest cigar factory in Havana, and soon controlled over 85 percent of the island's tobacco manufacturing, and 90 percent of its tobacco exports. (In Puerto Rico, too, Duke's organization became the main buyer and processor of tobacco leaves from the island's small farmers, and by decade's end controlled 75–90 percent of the cigar output.)

New York capital swarmed into other key sectors, too. One Wall Street syndicate beat out British interests to win the franchise for electrifying Havana's street railways. Another organized the Havana Central Railroad to transport cane and tobacco from the hinterlands to Havana Bay. These rail projects, in turn, generated multiplier effects: Cuba became the best customer for USA-made railroad freight cars, and its second-largest buyer of steel rails; Havana Central alone bought ten 40-ton locomotives from General Electric. The Spanish American Light and Power Company of New York (113 Wall) provided gas; the Cuban American Govin family of New York owned four major Havana dailies; and in 1899 two Gotham promoters founded the North American Trust Company of New York, got the contract as fiscal agent for the occupation government, and after reorganization in 1901, with additional capital infusions from J. P. Morgan, emerged as the Banco Nacional de Cuba, soon the island's leading bank.

To the $50 million Americans had invested in Cuba by 1898 were added another $30 million by 1902, when the US occupation ended. And by 1906, investment totaled almost $160 million, though at that point the "independent" regime ran into trouble.

Tomás Estrada Palma, who had spent most of the previous twenty-five years in New York running the government-in-exile, had been elected Cuba's president in 1902. He'd been unopposed because his Liberal opponents, who favored continued opposition to the Platt Amendment (on which Estrada Palma had signed off), withdrew from the race, charging the United States with rigging the electoral system to ensure Estrada Palma's victory. In 1906, though deeply unpopular, he won again, thanks to rampant fraud. The defeated Liberals, who included most of the leaders of the disbanded revolutionary army, reassembled a formidable force and threatened insurrection. Estrada Palma resigned, stating he could no longer "protect North American lives and property." Roosevelt now intervened, though he professed to "loathe the thought of assuming any control over the island such as we have over Puerto Rico and the Philippines." The reoccupation would last until 1909 and be reestablished again in 1912.

Back in 1900 Charles Conant had argued, in an article entitled "The United States as a World Power—Their Advantages in the Competition for Commercial Empire," that in order to dispose of its surplus capital abroad, the country had three options. It could follow Europe in seizing, administering, and investing in the modernizing of colonies; it could develop markets and investment outlets in nominally independent countries but maintain control of them by applications of naval power; or it could try to win international agreement for an open-door policy that mandated an equal right to trade and invest in any nation or colony, without special privileges for any nation, including itself. Conant favored the third option, convinced the United States could count on its superior productivity to win any open competition. That would be the option of choice in China, where the US presence was weak. But in Latin America, where it was strong, recurrent intervention became de facto policy.

ROOSEVELT AND ROOT MADE THIS OFFICIAL in the course of an intervention in the Dominican Republic. From 1893 to 1899, the Santo Domingo Improvement Company (SDIC), a collection of Wall Street crony capitalists, had worked closely with Dominican dictator Ulises Heureaux, hoping to foster a Díaz-like modernization program, but succeeded mainly in running up huge debts to Europeans and plunging the country into economic chaos. Heureaux was assassinated in 1899, and the reviled Improvement Company expelled and its debts repudiated in 1901. After several years of turmoil, European creditors began threatening to exact repayment at cannon point, as they had in Venezuela in 1903, when Britain, Germany, and Italy bombarded the country for that reason. In early 1904, to forestall this, TR sent a warship, but also decided to issue a full-fledged enunciation of future policy.

At a Waldorf-Astoria dinner of the Cuba Society of New York, Root read aloud a May 20, 1904, letter the president had written him (and which he had almost certainly had a hand in drafting). In it, Roosevelt denied that the US "has any land hunger or entertains any projects as regards other nations save such as are for their welfare." If, continued Roosevelt/Root, "a nation shows that it knows how to act with decency in industrial and political matters, if it keeps order and pays its obligations, then it need fear no interference from the United States." However, if "brutal wrongdoing, or an impotence which results in a general loosening of the ties of a civilized society may finally require intervention by some civilized nation," then "in the Western Hemisphere the United States cannot ignore this duty." This last gloved threat was restated more bare-knuckledly when Roosevelt—reiterating his May corollary to the Monroe Doctrine in a December message to Congress—noted the United States was prepared to unilaterally undertake "the exercise of an international police power."

In January 1905 TR came to an informal understanding with Dominican leaders. The island's customs revenue would now be collected by a fiscal agent appointed by the United States and deposited in the National City Bank in New York. The bank would then disburse 45 percent to the Dominicans for ordinary government functions, while the other 55 percent would go to pay down debt to the SDIC and European creditors. The US also imposed financial controls—barring tax increases or government spending without an American okay. This arrangement, which had all the earmarks of a Root-directed reorganization of a bankrupt railroad, was formally embedded in a treaty between the countries in 1906 by Root, now secretary of state, and accepted by the Senate the following year. At that point the entire Dominican debt was refinanced via a $20 million bond issue by Kuhn, Loeb, the first time the State Department and private bankers acted in official concert.

When Kuhn, Loeb was considering a loan to the Dominican Republic, Jacob Schiff asked a London associate, the banker Sir Ernest Cassel, "If they do not pay, who will collect these customs duties?" To which Cassel replied, "Your marines and ours." American marines would indeed splash ashore repeatedly in the coming years, to collect debts or "restore order," invading—sometimes repeatedly—Haiti, Nicaragua, Honduras, Cuba, post-Díaz Mexico, and Panama. Thus in 1909 troops were sent to Nicaragua to back a Conservative uprising against an unamenable Liberal president, who among other sins had been seeking loans in London and talking canal deals with Germany. The United States also re-funded Nicaragua's national debt via a loan from Brown Brothers and J. & W. Seligman. By way of security, the New York bankers were granted a lien on the national railroad and control of the National Bank of Nicaragua. (The country's currency would henceforth be countersigned by a Brown Brothers representative.) When fighting flared again in 1912, US Marines reoccupied the country to ensure Conservative control.

Some of the marines grew grumpy at being asked to undertake such chores. Major Smedley Butler, a battalion commander of US forces in Nicaragua during 1909–12, wrote his wife in the latter year: "It is terrible that we should be losing so many men fighting the battles of these d——d spigs—all because Brown Bros. have some money down here." But now it was official. When diplomacy failed to produce the desired stability, the fallback position was force. Washington would ride shotgun on Wall Street's stagecoach. The new commercial empire would have one base in NY, the other in DC.

NOT ALL OVERSEAS INVESTMENTS required military escort; sometimes the simple command of spectacular amounts of capital, made possible by the new order on Wall Street, was sufficient. Economist Conant had argued that giant companies spawned by the merger movement should concentrate on extending the railroad grid and extractive industries to underdeveloped countries. This was a prescription New York capitalists were delighted to follow.

Mexico under Díaz continued to welcome entrepreneurs, especially in railroads, mining, and oil. In 1897 the United States had $200 million in direct investment, which mounted to $650 million by 1911, much of it from Gotham's grandest clans; and in 1899, the House of Morgan participated in a sovereign bond issue for the Mexican government, the first time an American firm had acted as a syndicate manager, a milestone in US finance. These investments were not viewed as an unmixed blessing by Mexicans. Members of the Mexican elite with mining and smelting interests, for example, saw themselves being crushed beneath the Díaz-favored Guggenheim juggernaut. Among the powerful families who saw their interests being sacrificed to foreign entrepreneurs was that of Francisco Madero, who challenged Díaz's rule in 1910, setting off a revolutionary upheaval that would damage the Guggenheims' mining and smelting interests.

In 1910, partly in an effort to spread their international risk, the Guggenheims ventured down to Chile, which had been the world's leading copper producer in the 1870s, although the industry had stagnated in subsequent decades. Given its moribund state, the Chilean government was willing to allow foreign investors to operate in this sector virtually tax-free. The Guggenheims purchased a site known as Chuquicamata, a mountain with hundreds of millions of tons of low-grade copper ore. Raising money through a bond issue floated in New York, they set up a mining company, a power plant, a railroad, and a port, and soon their huge mechanical shovels had made of Chuquicamata the largest open pit mine in the world. Combining state-of-the-art mining technology with cheap Chilean labor allowed them to undersell domestic producers on the New York metals market; in less than a decade American interests accounted for 87 percent of Chile's copper output.

J. P. Morgan was drawn into copper, too, especially in Peru, where he partnered with James Ben Ali Haggin—who owned mines out west and lived in Fifth Avenue splendor—to form the Cerro de Pasco Corporation, headquartered on Broad Street. Morgan also linked up with the Guggenheims in Alaska, after Daniel Guggenheim came to him in 1906 for help in financing a $20 million railroad, to run from the coast to inland copper deposits. Morgan was already in Alaska, building a line from the ice-free port at Valdez to coal fields on the Bering River. Now he merged the two enterprises, forming the Morgan-Guggenheim syndicate, and the partners (or "Morganheims" as they were informally known) proceeded to buy or control most of the region's fisheries, canneries, steamship lines, copper mines, coal fields, and land, turning Alaska into a virtual colony of corporate New York by 1910.

THE GRANDEST DEVELOPMENT PROJECT OF ALL—the making of the Panama Canal—also stemmed from a collaboration between the nation's commercial and military centers. New York merchants had been seeking alternatives to the route around the Horn since 1851, when Commodore Vanderbilt had set up a lake-steamer-and-carriage-road transport system across Nicaragua, to speed the shipment of gold to Gotham from San Francisco. Now more than ever a canal seemed critical, both commercially (for selling surplus commodities in Asian markets) and militarily (for shifting battleships from one ocean to another).

By 1901 Congress was on the verge of authorizing a canal across Nicaragua when a rival route issued a credible challenge. After a French company had tried but failed in 1889 to dig

American Bank Note Co., Nicaraguan Five *Centavo* Stamp, 1900

its way across Panama—a province of Colombia—its right-of-way had been inherited by a Paris-based successor, the New Panama Canal Company, which hoped to sell its concession to the United States. To coax Congress into switching from Nicaragua to Panama, it hired William Nelson Cromwell, co-founder of the Wall Street corporate law firm of Sullivan & Cromwell and lobbyist extraordinaire. In 1902 Cromwell managed to bring Congress around, but in 1903 Colombia balked at closing the deal.[1] So Cromwell (and his private-sector allies, who, by some accounts, included J. P. Morgan) instigated and aided an independence bid by Panamanian nationalists, who had long chafed under Colombian rule. It was a public/private insurrection: the New Yorkers arranged financing for the uprising, and Roosevelt sent warships and marines to prevent Colombia from suppressing it. The November 3 rebellion went smoothly. US recognition was virtually instantaneous. The newly independent state of Panama received $10 million for granting the United States virtual sovereignty over a 10-mile-wide Canal Zone strip. Panama promptly named J. P. Morgan its fiscal agent. He helped them invest their new wealth by putting $6 million into first mortgages on New York real estate and $2.8 million into various New York banks. From the city's perspective, however, much greater wealth would flow from the canal than was provided by such short-term infusions: when finished in 1914, it would usher in an enormous expansion of transoceanic trade, much of which would steam into Gotham's harbor.

THOUGH THE SPANISH WAR and the great merger wave both erupted in 1898, each had been part of a larger process—overseas expansion, corporate reconstruction—that had been long in the making and would stretch on into the twentieth century. So too the creation of Greater New York had an extensive backstory, and its ramifications would ripple on through subsequent decades. The movement for municipal consolidation, moreover, was deeply intertwined with the movements for incorporation and expansion, as it was the same people who were reconstituting US relations with the world, and refashioning the national economy, who were chiefly responsible for creating the second-largest city on earth.

---

1. The change of mind was lubricated by a clever maneuver involving a postage stamp printed in 1900 by New York's American Bank Note Company (then at 78–86 Trinity Place) on behalf of the Nicaraguan government. It proudly (but inadvisedly) displayed a smoking volcano, known as Momotombo. After a devastating eruption in April 1902 killed 30,000 in Martinique, Cromwell and his fellow lobbyist Bunau Varilla planted an article in the *New York Sun* noting that Momotombo had also recently erupted. Nicaraguan authorities panicked and, rather than pointing out the volcano was over a hundred miles from the proposed canal route, simply lied and denied it had erupted at all. The lobbyists promptly sent one of the Nicaraguan stamps to each senator, labeling them evidence of geological instability provided by the would-be host country itself. Three days later the Senate opted for Panama.

3

Consolidation

The notion of consolidating the harbor's two principal cities had popped up from time to time since at least the 1830s but only began to gain traction after the Civil War, thanks in good measure to its compelling presentation by attorney Andrew Haswell Green. In the 1850s Green was the junior partner of Samuel J. Tilden, one of New York's first corporate lawyers, whose practice, run out of 43 Wall Street, focused on reorganizing and merging railroads that fell victim to that boom era's hyper-competitiveness. It may have been in Tilden's office that Green developed his fervor for consolidation as the antidote to ruinous competition in another arena.

In 1868 Green first suggested that an orderly development of the larger metropolitan region required a centralized authority that could end parochial bickering between the multiple political entities grouped around the harbor. Specifically, he suggested bringing "the City of New York and the County of Kings, a part of Westchester County and a part of Queens and Richmond, including the various suburbs of the City, under one common municipal government, to be arranged in departments under a single executive head." Green admitted this was not practicable at that moment. But he felt confident that the arguments for territorial consolidation would "increase in cogency as population augments," while the resistance offered by "small jealousies and petty interests" would become less effectual.

It was not until 1887, however, that Gotham's most powerful players signed on to Green's campaign, and his project began to rumble toward realization. In that year the New York State Chamber of Commerce officially urged that Brooklyn be added to New York. The assembled merchants and businessmen expressed concern that the port was losing ground to the more efficient facilities of New Orleans, Baltimore, Boston, and Philadelphia. More generally, the slovenly state of metropolitan infrastructure—decaying docks, clogged streets, and turtle-paced transit systems—was costing the city its competitive edge, but efforts to coordinate port administration, build new bridges, and improve city services were being thwarted by divided political jurisdictions. The Chamber considered political competition between the area's municipalities annoyingly irrational, just as many of its members were then decrying ruinous economic competition. As a step toward proper planning of piers, wharves, warehouses, and transportation, the Chamber urged putting "New York and its environs under one general scheme of municipal rule." As the Chamber was a very old (1768) and very powerful institution—members in this era included Morgan, Rockefeller, Carnegie, Schiff, Belmont, Baker, William Waldorf Astor, and Daniel and Isaac Guggenheim—its wishes carried weight.

Another reason such magnates sought political amalgamation was that erecting a larger frame of governance would hopefully facilitate rule by men like themselves. Civil service reform veteran Dorman B. Eaton and municipal efficiency advocate Albert Shaw pointed to the newly authorized (1888) London County Council as a form of metropolitan-scale government whose at-large elections would allow the "best elements of business life" to edge out politicians who excelled at ward-level combat. "There were no saloon-keepers or ward bosses in this London council," Shaw advised.

In 1888, the *Real Estate Record and Builders Guide*—organ of New York's propertied and development interests—also came out for consolidation. Only a centralized authority, it argued, could push through the improvements that would boost land values, and provide insurance companies, savings banks, and estate trustees with profitable investment opportunities.

In 1888 Mayor Abram Hewitt—iron manufacturer and Chamber of Commerce stalwart—proposed a vast and coordinated program of public improvements, and hitched it to a grand vision of New York's future. "With its noble harbor protected from injury, and the channels of its approach straightened and deepened"; with its wharves and docks improved and its streets paved and cleansed; with "cheap and rapid transit throughout its length and breadth" and "salubrious and attractive parks" sprinkled throughout the area; and with a system of taxation "so modified that the capital of the world may be as free to come and go as the air of heaven"—then, Hewitt said, "the imagination can place no bounds to the future growth of this city in business, wealth, and the blessings of civilization." Indeed, New York's "imperial destiny as the greatest city in the world is assured by natural causes, which cannot be thwarted except by the folly and neglect of its inhabitants."

For all its upbeat energy, this "imperial" urban vision—like those of nationalist jingoes, railroad magnates, and corporate financiers—was also fueled by fear. Inaction might leave the field to rival empire builders, which in New York's case meant Chicago. In 1889 the midwestern metropolis swallowed up 133 square miles of suburban terrain, and when the 1890 Census was tallied, the results showed it gaining fast on Gotham. The *Real Estate Record* assessed the threat bluntly: "New York would undoubtedly lose a great deal in prestige the world over—and in actual dollars and cents, too—should Chicago or any other city on the continent count a larger population." European banking and export firms might shift their American branches to the heartland; corporate headquarters would soon follow, taking professional firms along; the market prices of stocks and commodities would be set in the interior; manufacturing would slip away; New York's property values would scud downward; it would get ever harder to market Gotham's bonds on international capital markets. Doomsayers recalled how the power and prestige of Philadelphia, once America's chief city, had slowly bled away once it was surpassed numerically by its Hudson River rival.

With the Chamber and real estate industry now backing Green's proposal, the state legislature in 1890 established a Municipal Consolidation Commission to flesh it out (with Green as chair), and in several addresses that year Green produced a more detailed schema and a more thoroughgoing set of justifications.

The heart of his objection to the status quo was ruinous competition. "There is probably nowhere another three and a half millions of people so thoroughly assimilated as the populations grouped about this port," Green wrote, "yet there is not, in the world over, another like area so disturbed by multiplicity of conflicting authorities." He found it astonishing that the "many-headed municipalities, shievalities, baliwicks, and townships which mottle the varied space" had managed to survive "for a century without precipitating the anarchy inherent in them." No one was minding the store. Caring for the great harbor at the core of the region's commercial life was "the concern of all" but "the duty of none." As a result the vast shoreline had fallen prey to those who—devoted to "niggard scheme[s] of individual profit"—were depleting the general system "by encroachment, appropriation and misuse."

Consolidation would enable the intelligent and foresighted planning required to deal with the manifold problems that transcended borders. The harbor was drowning in pollution. Shipping was chaotic and inefficient. So were the city's markets. Manufacturing needed attention. Rapid transit wasn't rapid. New connections to the interior were essential, most crucially a bridge across the Hudson. Only a Greater New York, Green believed, could muster the resources to act without waiting for state or national governments. The port was also vulnerable to the new steel-clad navies of potential enemies; only a combined effort by harbor-mates could induce Washington to strengthen its defenses.

The city needed to plan for a vast expansion of population. Immigrants had been flooding in from overseas, and that would surely continue. So would migration from the countryside, as the mechanization of agriculture sent displaced farm workers beelining toward urban factories. People now living, Green prophesied, would someday see more than half the US population living in cities! Incorporating this massive influx could not be left to helter-skelter development. Planning the region as a single unit could balance population between center and suburbs. If a Greater City controlled its outlying territories, it could reserve them for, say, healthful parks, rather than letting them be gobbled up piecemeal. And only a Greater City could solve the "difficult question of taxation of non-residents that now exists," with people on the periphery drawing sustenance from New York's commerce but contributing little to its governance.

If the region at the Hudson's mouth didn't present "a consolidated front to all rivalries" rather than sticking with the "loose municipal formations in which we permit ourselves to be divided," then the center of economic gravity would shift inland and Gotham would find itself reduced to second-fiddle status—the mere seaport appendage of some interior metropolis (read: Chicago). New York would then be compared with Southampton, not London; Le Havre, not Paris; Hamburg, not Berlin; Veracruz, not Mexico City; Osaka, not Tokyo.

But there were even greater dangers out there than rival cities. Green believed New York was in mortal peril from "lawless enterprise," by which he meant the great modern combinations of capital—"monopolies, pools and trusts." For a man who'd spent much of his legal career helping Samuel Tilden arrange mergers—or perhaps precisely because of that experience—Green was extremely wary about the growth of corporations. They had, he said, "invaded every field of work and every sphere of business." Their impact was nowhere more evident than in cities, where "people live, move, and have their being by sufferance of the corporate power." A citizen buys food from one corporation, water from another, light from a third, heat from a fourth, works on the road of a fifth, is paid in bills from a sixth, has his life insured by a seventh, and is buried on the grounds of an eighth. "There is not a moment of his life in which he is not admonished of the all-pervading presence of the corporate power."

This phenomenon was "substantially a new creation," he correctly observed. (Early manifestations like American Tobacco and the Twine Trust were then much in the news.) Green denied he was hostile to these "modern forms of corporate contrivances"—they were, indeed, "improvements upon cruder conditions"—but he insisted they "must be regulated and controlled by governmental intervention." But which government? For Green the populace massed in cities represented a potentially effective countervailing power. Alas, at a time when all private interests, "actuated by selfish motives," were tending to consolidation, the only interests *not* combining were "our unselfish, thoughtless peoples, and their fatuous municipalities, which in broken form, carry on desultory and futile war against the organized forces of relentless and absentee capitalism."

Green was hopeful about the outcome of this war "between the corporate power and the power of the people" because he discerned evolutionary trends at work in the history of great cities—and of New York especially—that were the counterpart of those spawning the great corporations. Both developments were part of mankind's great progression from barbarism to civilization. But if Green was hopeful, he wasn't smug. There were no guarantees that "the scheme of civilization, even in the hands of the Caucasian race, is beyond the hazards of deterioration." New York unfortunately still had those who clung to barbaric traditions and sought "to preserve their clans and clanships." Only through a struggle between retrograde and progressive forces could evolutionary destiny be attained: "The encounter," exhorted Green in 1890, sounding quite like John D. Rockefeller, is one "between the retreating forces of the tribal system and the coming forces of the cooperative system, between barbaric tradition and educated aspiration, to which there can be but one result, when the frontier lines of the Manhattan, the Montauks and the Raritans shall be obliterated, and New York, Brooklyn, Long Island City and Staten Island shall be one politically as they are already in every other relation."

The method for achieving this was annexation. The successful 1874 absorption of lower Westchester by New York, and the earlier annexation of Williamsburg by Brooklyn, pointed the way forward. Those communities "have already merged early rivalries and jealousies in union of forces for cooperative work, thus covering divided areas by one harmonious administration." Annexation was the only way to bulk up fast, gaining the numbers to retain the front rank. Immigration was inconstant and slow. Chicago, like London and Paris, and Brooklyn for that matter, had "become great and prosperous, not alone by accumulation of number, within their first restricted bounds, but by expansion, annexation, and consolidation."

Green urged New York to recognize and grasp its imperial destiny. New York had become in fact the second city of the world but was refusing to claim its title. It should do so, joyously. "Cities are the crowns, the signs, the factors of empire," Green proclaimed, and "the imperial city has won an honorable renown throughout the world which all her colonies may proudly inherit and which they cannot avoid accepting." (An impolitic reference to Brooklyn that was soon to haunt him.)

Green's Consolidation Commission now laid out the scope of the proposed Greater New York—Manhattan, Kings and Richmond Counties, and in Queens, Long Island City plus the Towns of Newtown, Flushing, Jamaica, and specified parts of Hempstead—and rested its case. The issue now moved to the political arena.

It seemed at first that an unstoppable array of forces was mobilized behind Consolidation, chiefly in "imperial" Manhattan. These included merchants and industrialists who wanted a unified shipping and rail network; real estate owners who sought higher land values; insurance companies, savings banks, and estates trustees who envisioned new investment opportunities in the suburbs; businessmen and professionals who thought a larger city would transfer power from Tammany to the "best men"; and reformers who believed it would provide cheap land for working-class housing, which, they were convinced, would put an end to poverty, crime, and socialism. The leading business groups, clubs, and commercial associations were on board, as were the city's major papers including the *World, Herald, Sun, Tribune,* and *Times.* It's true that some Northern Manhattan and Bronx developers feared a siphoning off of population and tax dollars to Brooklyn and Queens; responding to these fears, the *Real Estate Record and Builders Guide* reversed itself in 1894. Others fretted that Greater New York might lead to a "Greater Tammany," or create endless quarrels between New York and Brooklyn, "like two cats tied together by their tails and thrown over a clothesline."

But the toughest resistance came from across the East River, more precisely from the old Anglo-Protestant bastion of Brooklyn Heights. These worthies had a peculiar relationship with Manhattan. They were well aware that Brooklyn was fundamentally dependent on New York: part bedroom suburb, part industrial hinterland, part agricultural supplier, part commercial backup. Yet they had also fashioned a separate identity, organized in large part around their presumed superiority to Manhattan.

Protestant middle-class Brooklynites liked to think theirs was a "city of homes and churches": free from millionaires and the snobbish ways of Fifth Avenue; free from the huddled immigrant masses and the squalor of Five Points or Hell's Kitchen; free from the sin-drenched Tenderloin and Bowery, the corruptions of Tammany ward heelers, the fast-paced life of the scurrying big city. Their Brooklyn was genteel . . . but not provincial. They boasted of their modern cultural apparatus (Prospect Park, the *Brooklyn Eagle,* the Montauk Club, the Long Island Historical Society, the Brooklyn Academy of Music, and on the drawing boards a Brooklyn Museum that would surpass the Metropolitan). Consolidation with Manhattan, said the Rev. Dr. Storrs of the Church of the Pilgrims (at Remsen and Henry), could endanger all this by opening a door to the "political sewage of Europe," with its coterie of riots, corruption, and the "brutal and criminal domination" of Tammany Hall.

This was a badly overstated case. It's true that the big rich stayed mainly in Manhattan, though the Pratts, Lows, and Pierreponts were no pikers. But the percentage of non-Protestants in each city, while different (52.7 percent in New York, 40 percent in Brooklyn), hardly justified such sweeping characterizations. The working-class Irish, Germans, Italians, Jews, and African Americans may have been out of sight (from the perspectives of the Montauk Club or Church of the Pilgrims), but they were hardly out of power, as repeated failures to impose a Dry Sunday attested. And while Brooklyn boss Hugh McLaughlin was subtler than Manhattan boss Richard Croker, his Willoughby Street Democratic machine was in some ways more powerful than Tammany's. The barbarians, so to speak, were already inside the gates.

But three insuperable problems stood between Brooklyn and continued municipal independence. First, the city was running out of cash and credit. Like Manhattan, it was subject to the state constitution's requirement that municipal debt not exceed 10 percent of assessed valuation of taxable real estate, and all those homes and churches couldn't support the level of borrowing power afforded by New York's office buildings. Second, the city was running out of water and desperately needed to tap into Manhattan's gushing supply. Third, there was a potent fifth column of affluent Manhattanites—also inside the gates—who recognized the profound interconnectedness of the two conurbations, and in 1892, at a Montauk Club meeting, they formed a Brooklyn Consolidation League (BCL) to back Green's proposal.

These pro-merger merchants, bankers, real estate developers, large retailers, and streetcar-company presidents stressed the benefits of Consolidation for Brooklyn: new East River bridges, access to Croton water, lower taxes for property owners, greater borrowing power, and establishment of an integrated transport system and real estate market. To those concerned about threats to moral order and good government, the BCL men argued that if the virtuous of Brooklyn linked arms with the best men of Manhattan, the united forces of good government would overwhelm the politicos. In the face of such advantages, demands for continued suburban autonomy amounted to "senile sentimentalism."

Notwithstanding this array of forces, when Green got the legislature to put a nonbinding referendum on the 1894 ballot, Brooklyn, like the other municipalities and towns, voted in favor of Consolidation, but the majority was about 0.2 percent—politically a wash. Indeed, the near-rejection galvanized opponents to organize their own lobby—the League of Loyal Citizens of Brooklyn—which bombarded Albany with demands for a recount they were sure would bury Consolidation forever.

Ironically, the same 1894 election brought a cooling of Consolidation ardor in Manhattan, when the hitherto-stymied coalition of political and moral reformers captured the mayoralty. In September 1894 a constellation of Chamber of Commerce luminaries—including Elihu Root, J. P. Morgan, Cornelius Vanderbilt, William E. Dodge, Abram Hewitt, Jacob Schiff, and James Speyer—had engineered formation of a Committee of Seventy (so named to evoke the group that had toppled Tweed). Under its banner the committee established a formidable campaign operation, run out of the Chamber of Commerce building, on behalf of their mayoral candidate, William L. Strong. A millionaire dry-goods merchant turned banker, Strong was a longtime member of the Union League Club, former president of the Business Men's Republican Club, and prominent figure in the Chamber itself. His inner core of supporters were similarly wealthy Yankee Protestant or German Republicans, most of whom were active in the City Club, Good Government Clubs, Civil Service Reform Association, and various moral reform agencies; Root was one of Strong's leading champions, and his lawyer as well.

In November, Democrats paid the traditional penalty of incumbency during hard times and police scandals, and Republicans, in fusion with dissident Democrats, swept Strong into office. This victory, together with the triumph of Republican Frederick Wurster in Brooklyn the following year, diminished the sense of urgency about revamping government to get rid of Tammany. As the League of Loyal Citizens argued: "The gang is out. Decency and ability reign." Why chance reviving Tammany by voting for Consolidation? Given Brooklyn's opposition (as evidenced by the sliver-thin referendum mandate) and Manhattan's dampened enthusiasm, the legislature wavered, though in 1895 it did authorize the annexation to New York of another 14,000 acres of southern Westchester lying east of the Bronx River. Brooklyn, in the meantime, absorbed Kings County's last remaining independent towns.

By 1895 the Consolidation movement seemed dead. Then Boss Thomas Platt resurrected it. The state's Republican leader decided he could enhance his party's chances in Manhattan—heretofore impregnable Tammany territory—by combining it with the more Republican-friendly Brooklyn. And given the Republicans' strong 1894 showing throughout the region, Platt had hopes of capturing the first mayoralty of a consolidated metropolis. By stepping forward as the would-be Father of Greater New York, Platt would demonstrate to his big business backers how capable he was of energetic leadership on their behalf.

In 1896, accordingly, Platt rammed a bill through the legislature calling for consolidation of precisely the territories Green's commission had proposed—to take effect as of January 1, 1898. The new law empowered Republican Governor Levi Morton (the Gotham banker and former US vice president had also been elected in the 1894 anti-Tammany sweep) to appoint a panel to draft a new charter. As required by the state constitution, the bill was submitted to mayors of the affected cities.

Brooklyn's Wurster vetoed it. So did Mayor Strong. Poised on the brink of victory, the Chamber of Commerce crowd allied to the Strong administration had gotten cold feet. Maybe the deal was *too* favorable to Brooklyn. Maybe Manhattan taxpayers would get stuck with the tab for improvements in the Bronx, or be forced to shoulder debts racked up by profligate villages in Queens. Maybe Tammany would capture the mayoralty. The Union League Club, the City Club, the Reform Club, the Association of the Bar of the City of New York, the Real Estate Exchange, the Board of Trade and Transportation—all counseled delay.

Platt shut his ears and pressed ahead relentlessly. The recalcitrant mayors were overridden on April 22. Governor Morton signed on May 11, 1896, and then appointed a Charter Commission that included both notable consolidationists like Green (though he would fall sick and be unable to participate in the drafting process) and a strong contingent from Brooklyn (which Platt was anxious to placate). The members were virtually all corporate lawyers, real estate developers, bankers, merchants, or politicians; no representatives of labor were included.

These gentlemen prepared an immense and rambling document that represented a series of compromises. It strengthened the mayor and the Board of Estimate and maintained the position of independently elective comptroller—features applauded by taxpayers and bond holders. It retired the Common Council, after more than 200 years of service, and replaced it with a two-chambered Municipal Assembly. This body, together with the five newly instituted borough governments (complete with elected borough presidents) was intended to satisfy the desire of Brooklyn's Loyal Leaguers for decentralized, local self-government. It also gave the Republicans four potential footholds should Tammany keep control of Manhattan. Platt got the 900-page document safely through the legislature by March 23, without, he boasted, "the crossing of a 't' or the dotting of an 'i.' " After one last stubborn mayoral veto from William Strong had been overcome, the Charter of Greater New York was presented to the new governor, Frank Black, for his signature, which he affixed on May 5, 1897.

WITH CONSOLIDATION LOOMING just six months ahead, attention now shifted to the November 1897 municipal elections, the winner of which would preside over the new-minted metropolis. For the Good Government reformers who had put Strong in office in 1894, planning had begun in December 1896, when the core of the coalition gathered in the office of Elihu Root to create a permanent political party, one devoted to the full time pursuit of municipal power. Root suggested the title of Citizens' Union (CU) and drafted its declaration of principles. Foremost among these was the importance of disconnecting local from state and national politics—a move facilitated by the charter's shifting of municipal balloting to odd-numbered years. Cities (said the Citizens) should be run like businesses, with efficiency and competency the watchwords, not party loyalty. Businessmen—chiefly Republicans, with a sprinkling of anti-Tammany Democrats—occupied central positions in the nonpartisan party, with Root, Morgan, Hewitt, Schiff, Speyer, and Dodge particularly prominent. Around this nucleus clustered crucial auxiliaries: corporate lawyers and other professionals; Protestant clergymen and reform-minded women; settlement house workers and organized charities. The Good Government Clubs were converted into Citizens' Union district headquarters. For a standard bearer the CU chose Seth Low, the stout and stolid burgher who had been a two-term mayor of Brooklyn and was currently president of Columbia University; Low had also served on the Charter Commission and so was up to speed on the prerogatives and powers of his intended office.

Low's troops were met on the field of electoral battle by a Tammany army generaled by Boss Richard Croker, the Citizens' Union's arch-nemesis, who had come out of semiretirement to direct the campaign. The Democrats selected for their candidate Robert A. Van Wyck [pronounced *Whyk*, not Wick], an obscure municipal court judge. With no independent base, no money, no personal pizzazz, indeed nothing much more going for him than a venerable city name, Van Wyck was a perfect Croker creature. Democratic district leaders rallied their forces behind him at a rollicking ratification meeting, featuring fireworks and a band booming out "There'll Be a Hot Time in the Old Town To-Night."

But the decision that determined the outcome would be made by Boss Platt. He was prepared to fuse his regular Republican machine with the Citizens' Union forces—as he had done in 1894, successfully electing Mayor Strong—but he was mightily displeased with his potential ally's nonpartisan professions. There was much at stake. The new mayor would get to hire an army of 35,000 municipal employees and control a city budget of $100 million a year, a patronage treasure chest second only to that commanded by the president of the United States. Platt approached Root, a CU leader but a staunch Republican on state and national issues, sounding him out about being cut in for some negotiated percentage of the jobs. Root was amenable. More to the point, so was candidate Low, who knew full well he couldn't win without the Republicans. The bulk of the Citizens' Union, however, was dead set against a deal. They saw the 1897 election as the most fundamental contest since the Civil War, one that might well determine the future of American democracy, possibly the fate of Western Civilization. Compromise was out of the question. So Platt gave up. Between such unseemly rigidity and the undoubted pliability of Boss Croker, his ostensible rival but brother-under-the-skin politico, the choice was easy. "I would rather see the Tammany ticket elected," Platt announced, "than to have Seth Low chosen as Mayor." True to his word, he ran his own Republican candidate, former secretary of the navy Benjamin F. Tracy, who came in a poor third but threw the election to Tammany.

In November, therefore, scant weeks before Consolidation would take effect, they rolled into power, and jeering Democrats marched through the streets chanting, "Well, well, well, Reform has gone to hell!" It would be Croker and Van Wyck who would control the new urban colossus—and, worse, for a charter-mandated four year term. No surprise that reformers saw little to celebrate: outgoing Mayor Strong declined to back the planned jamboree on New Year's Eve, and it had been William Randolph Hearst, publisher of the *New York Journal*, who stepped forward to underwrite and organize the floats and fireworks.

And so it came to pass that on that rainy final night of 1897, as celebrants set off from Union Square toward City Hall, spirits over at Citizens' Union headquarters and the Chamber of Commerce were as damp as the weather.

They were pretty soggy, too, just across the East River, a short stroll over the bridge from the boisterous Manhattan revels, where glum Brooklynites gathered at their former city hall, now demoted, like their city itself, to mere borough status. Many in Kings County felt like victims of an imperial expansion they had tried but failed to halt. Accordingly, rather than a "celebration," local officials were holding what they billed as an "observance."

A stream of guests came to call on shortly-to-be-former Mayor Wurster and a clutch of other ex-mayors. When Wurster, in making some remarks, recalled he had seen "no way clear

TAMMANY TIMES

A NATIONAL DEMOCRATIC NEWSPAPER.

VOLUME TEN.　　　NEW YORK, DECEMBER 27TH, 1897.　　NUMBER THIRTY-THREE.

EXIT REFORMERS.

FATHER KNICKERBOCKER'S NEW YEAR'S HOUSE-CLEANING.

"Exit Reformers." *Tammany Times*, December 27, 1897.

but to veto the Consolidation bill"—a reference to the failed effort to halt what had become unstoppable—he was greeted with lengthy and tumultuous applause. Similar approbation greeted his denial that Brooklyn had come to the marriage "a penniless bride."

St. Clair McKelway, editor of the *Brooklyn Eagle*, was a bit more candid about the relative poverty that had led cash-strapped Brooklyn to the altar, thus winning access to Manhattan's amply filled coffers. He emphasized that the merger would create a common treasury from which Brooklyn could make withdrawals, perhaps even take out more than it

"The City of Greater New York," 1905. (Library of Congress Prints and Photographs Division)

Manhattan Bridge.   Manhattan Beach.

Navy Yard.   N. Y. & Brooklyn Bridge.   Prospect Park.   Coney Island.   Sandy Hook.   Highlands of Navesink.

Park Row Building.   Greenwood Cemetery.   Fort Hamilton.   Narrows.   Quarantine.   Staten Island.

Bay Ridge.   Governors Island.   Fort Wadsworth.

South Brooklyn.   Battery.

Ellis Island.   Statue of Liberty

YORK

BOROUGH OF BROOKLYN.   BOROUGH OF RICHMOND.

put in. Still, McKelway urged Brooklynites to hold fast to their separate identity and to sustain their separate schools, libraries, institutes, and churches: "Let us be no branch office," he told the gathering.

The observance concluded with the reading of a poem, "The Passing of Brooklyn," by Will Carleton. "We are grieved [ran one stanza] that a maiden of sweetness / Full of life's vigor and joy and completeness, / We are aggrieved that this fair, comely maiden / At midnight must die." In an effort to finesse this melancholy fact, the poet wheeled in "Father Time," who consoled the doomed maiden by insisting: "You are no corse [sic], fit for tears or pity / You are the soul of the great coming city!"

The next day—Consolidation Day, January 1, 1898—was even more galling for the businessmen reformers. They had to watch from the sidelines as power was transferred to Tammany from not one but three mayors (Strong of Manhattan, Wurster of Brooklyn, and Patrick Gleason of Long Island City). Around midday, thousands crowded into City Hall, while a regimental band played popular airs, and Mayor Van Wyck, duly sworn in, met with well-wishers. Among them was George Washington Plunkitt, a West Side Tammany district leader, who with his usual blunt candor told Van Wyck that the party faithful from his district were "on hand in a body, Mr Mayor, and every man wants a job." At 12:55, the social proprieties observed, the mayor withdrew, accompanied by Boss Croker's chief lieutenant, to "make some appointments."

THE MOMENTARILY BALKED BUSINESSMEN would not retire from the municipal field. In the years to come they would devote considerable time, money, and energy to seeking metropolitan political dominance, with maddeningly mixed results. Matters were profoundly different on the national level. At the very moment of their city-level setback, the city's trinitarian class, with spectacular success, set out to reconstruct US capitalism. Over the next ten years, 1898–1907, they would preside over the greatest boom in American history, one that would have an immense impact on the city's social and spatial fabric, and enhance its national and global standing. These epic transformations would be directed from a minuscule patch of Manhattan real estate over which they exercised near-total mastery, the tiny territory where, back in the seventeenth century, Dutch New Amsterdam had huddled below its protective wall.

4

Wall Street

Back in 1886, during the celebration of the Statue of Liberty's unveiling, a festive parade had threaded its way through lower Manhattan. As it passed along Wall Street—so a reporter for the *New York Times* noted—"many imps of office boys" began unreeling spools of ticker tape and hurling them out the windows. "In a moment the air was white with curling streamer." Some were "caught in the meshes of electric wires and made a snowy canopy, and others floated downward and were caught by the crowd." Finding this "altogether too much fun," the brokers shouldered their clerks aside and sent more and more ribbons skimming through the air, until "every window appeared to be a paper mill spouting out squirming lines of tape." Such, the story concluded, "was Wall-street's novel celebration."

Fifteen years farther on, Wall Street was again being inundated by a blizzard of paper, but now on a daily basis, as vast quantities of stocks and bonds—tangible by-products of the massive merger movement—descended on the financial center. At the center of this typhoon of paper sat the New York Stock Exchange (NYSE), on the southwest corner of Broad and Wall. Between 1896 and 1901 the volume of stocks being traded there increased sixfold. New issues were scooped up and resold in frantic bursts of speculation, producing a cyclonic churning of the market. On one day in January 1901 an astonishing 2 million shares were traded. Jacob Schiff wrote a friend that "it is almost terrifying to contemplate the way in which the market has risen, by leaps and bounds."

Commission houses were snowed under; brokers and clerks toiled till midnight, trying to dig out; the Exchange had to declare a special holiday to catch up with the paperwork. The cramped old building—dating to 1865—was clearly overtaxed. In 1899 the board of governors decided to rebuild and expand. Eight New York architects were invited to participate in a design competition. The Exchange selected the neoclassical entry of George B. Post. On April 29, 1901, the brokers moved out so the building could be demolished and took up temporary quarters in the colossal Produce Exchange (also by George Post) at the foot of Broadway, where normally only commodities such as wheat, pork, and beans were bought

By 1888, only two years after the dedication of the Statue of Liberty, the ticker tape parade had become a New York ritual. "The Humors of the Presidential Campaign in New York City: A Political Procession Passing down Wall Street—An Avalanche of Telegraphic Tape." *Frank Leslie's Illustrated Newspaper*, October 27, 1888.

and sold. Two days later, a staggering 3,250,000 shares changed hands, dispatching all prior records to the dustbin of NYSE history.

In 1903 the gleaming new Exchange building opened at 18 Broad Street. Post had fashioned an elegant temple of mammon. Its portico—featuring six 52-foot-high Corinthian columns and a pediment containing a marble sculptural group by John Quincy Adams Ward—gave the structure an air of magisterial repose, belying the frantic activity of brokers within. The cavernous trading floor, one of the largest interior spaces in the city, had originally been designed to rise from the second floor, thus allowing the street level to be leased out to a revenue-producing bank. But the governors thoughtfully rejected Post's plan, fearing it "would hamper the brokers' freedom of movement in times of panic or failure," and reserved the ground floor for their own use, allowing hasty exits in times of crisis. In 1903, however, there were no panics or failures on the horizon. The mighty financial machinery in the engine room of American capitalism was thrumming away reassuringly, powering the great boom that had gotten under way in 1898.

THE STOCK EXCHANGE WAS NOT THE ONLY PART of the Wall Street complex to undergo upgrading and reconstruction in the first flush of the new century. The tributaries feeding the Exchange and enabling the great merger movement—investment banks, commercial banks, trust companies, and insurance firms—were expanding their physical plant, wrestling with succession issues, and tussling over their place in the new financial order of things, while at the same time they were collectively fashioning business practices and social arrangements that kept a lid on the ruinous competition they all decried.

Nearly all of these institutions—which supplied NYSE brokers with stocks to sell, and the capital with which to buy them—were conveniently situated within a few blocks of the sanctum sanctorum.

Investment banks were both the most essential and the nearest to hand. The House of Morgan, unquestioned leader of that fraternity, was directly across the street from the Exchange, in a mansarded building on the southeast corner of Wall and Broad (hence its nickname "the Corner"). Investment bankers like Pierpont Morgan helped corporations arrange their initial public offerings of stock, and facilitated later trips to the NYSE well to raise capital for new mergers, for plant expansion, or for operating expenses. Investment bankers "underwrote" these stocks—purchasing them from the issuing corporation, then reselling them (hopefully at a higher price) directly to investors, or to intermediary bankers in various European capitals; or they turned them over to NYSE brokers to flog on the trading floor, as Morgan had recently done so successfully with shares of United States Steel.

Morgan himself was at the peak of his game in 1903, a globe-girdling colossus, imperious, autocratic, forceful, even frightening, all of which he looked in the famous photo snapped by Edward Steichen in 1903, his eyes glaring out at viewers as if he were a train bearing down on them. In truth he'd been in a particularly bad mood at that moment, Steichen having asked him to turn his head sideways, which would have highlighted his horribly acned nose, puffy and inflamed, about which he was deeply sensitive. In less fraught moments he could be more accepting, as when he told a Russian minister of finance, who had suggested surgery, that "everybody knows my nose. It would be impossible for me to appear on the streets of New York without it."

Still, Morgan was getting on—in 1903 he turned 66—and was facing dynastic difficulties. It's an ironic fact that the investment banks then engineering gigantic and bureaucratic corporations were themselves small partnerships, often family affairs, and vulnerable to the kind of succession crises commonly considered the peculiar bane of monarchies. In Morgan's case, he wasn't convinced that John Pierpont Junior ("Jack") was up to snuff. In 1898 Jack had been more or less exiled to the London office, where for the next seven years, though having a grand time hobnobbing with British aristocrats, he nevertheless sulked at being excluded from the financial action—he'd had to read about US Steel in the newspapers. Even after he was brought back to New York in 1905, the heavy lifting was done by others.

Much of the Morganization of the American economy was the achievement of half a dozen partners, with a support staff of fewer than 150. The pressure on them was ferocious; many burned out, died young, or proved unready for the big leagues. Robert Bacon, left in charge of the Northern Pacific fracas, bobbled it, and retired soon after (his nerves shot) to a less taxing position as Elihu Root's assistant secretary of state. A likelier candidate for succession was George Walbridge Perkins, a live-wire executive at the New York Life Insurance Company, which in the 1890s he'd transformed into the biggest outfit in the business. A flamboyant and outgoing glad-hander, Perkins was PR-savvy, something Morgan was definitely not, and he ably served as the firm's public face and liaison to the world of politics. He was also ideologically articulate: an ardent believer in Morgan's anti-competition gospel, he vigorously touted the virtues of giant corporations. Taken on board in 1901, Perkins quickly made his bones by organizing International Harvester in 1902, another mega-merger, and it appeared as if the House's leadership had been lined up for the new century. Morgan moved more slowly in upgrading the House itself, sticking with the 1873 Second Empire Drexel Building until 1912, when he purchased the property from the widow of his former partner, paying the highest price per square foot in the annals of Gotham real estate, and authorized construction thereupon of an Italian Renaissance marble palace, *smaller* than its predecessor, completed in 1914.

Morgan's only near-peer in the investment banking world—Jacob Schiff—was right nearby. Kuhn, Loeb's offices had been one block north of the Exchange, at the corner of Nassau and Pine, until 1903, when they were relocated a few steps eastward, to larger quarters at Pine and William. Schiff, the blue-eyed, white-bearded, impeccably dressed patrician, was having succession issues of his own. He himself had married Therese Loeb, the daughter of founder Solomon Loeb, and he was now grooming his own son, Mortimer, for a leadership role. But there were in-house competitors, notably the Warburg brothers, Paul and Felix. Not only had they too married into the firm—Felix had wedded Schiff's daughter Frieda, and Paul tied the knot with Nina Loeb, another of the founder's daughters—but they were also scions of M. M. Warburg & Co., Hamburg's most distinguished banking family. This marital/financial connection was critical for Kuhn, Loeb.[1] Like other German Jewish bankers in Gotham, the firm had been able to breach Wall Street's anti-Semitic barriers, winning grudging acceptance from Morgan and his Anglo-Protestant ilk, because they could tap into pools of German capital. And while Schiff had developed contacts in London as well—notably Sir Ernest Cassel, a transplanted German Jewish financier who was an adviser to the Prince of Wales—the ability to sell securities to German compatriots remained an important source of their power on the street; that made the Warburgs contenders in the Kuhn, Loeb succession sweepstakes.

---

1. And had been since Kuhn, Loeb's beginnings, Solomon Loeb having married Fanny Kuhn, sister of Abraham Kuhn. The same dynastic dimension was evidenced at many other Wall Street firms, corporations as well as partnerships. The accumulation and transfer of capital was often transacted by way of weddings arranged on the "marriage market," the social infrastructure maintained by upper-class women. Thus did Fifth Avenue contribute to Wall Street consolidations.

There was still another aspirant, Otto Herman Kahn, though he seemed less likely to rise in the Kuhn, Loeb hierarchy. Kahn, born and raised in Mannheim, Germany, had gone to London in 1888 to work in a Deutsche Bank subsidiary. He had wanted to move up, to the London office of Speyer & Co., an ancient (1644) and distinguished banking house in Frankfurt, but was only able to land a spot in its New York office, established in 1837 and run since 1899 by James Speyer, who in 1902 built a Florentine palace just across Pine Street from Kuhn, Loeb, their longtime competitor in Frankfurt finance. The Speyers blossomed in the new imperial arena—underwriting the Philippine Railway and the Republic of Cuba—and were running neck and neck with J. & W. Seligman (1846), where currently Isaac Newton Seligman presided over the family firm. But both had slipped below Kuhn, Loeb, and it was on that firm that Kahn now fixed his eye. He segued there in the approved manner by marrying Addie Wolff, the daughter of the other senior principal, Abraham Wolff, who pressured Schiff into accepting his new son-in-law as partner. Schiff acquiesced, though he wasn't crazy about Kahn, whose service with the rival Speyers made him suspect. But Kahn would shine at Kuhn, Loeb, first for his banking prowess, amply demonstrated when he struck up a close working relationship with the firm's most important client, railroad magnate Edward H. Harriman, and for his unparalleled ability to promote the firm's public image in the wider public sphere (rather as Perkins was doing for the House of Morgan), particularly in the city's glittery cultural community.

Perhaps the smoothest investment bank transition into the new century was that of Belmont & Co., still at 23 Nassau. When August Belmont Sr. died, back in 1890, August Belmont Jr. inherited the presidency of the firm his father had founded back in 1837, as an agency of England's House of Rothschild. (Junior also inherited Senior's passion for race-horses, becoming chairman of the Jockey Club, which often met in his office at the bank, and in 1902, in conjunction with his colleagues in the Westchester Racing Association, bought 650 acres on the Queens-Nassau county line where he built Belmont Park [1905], the fanciest racetrack in the nation.)

In addition to these venerable firms, there were some scrappy newcomers. If one could measure status by proximity to the Exchange, the ascent of Goldman, Sachs in the Wall Street pecking order might have been gleaned from its move to 43 Exchange Place, just around the corner. The firm had indeed come a long way since Marcus Goldman, son of a Bavarian cattle drover, had arrived in Gotham in 1869 and carved out a spot as a merchant peddler. In the morning Goldman would buy commercial paper (promissory notes or bills of exchange) from wholesale jewelers on Maiden Lane and leather merchants on John Street, at a discount; in the afternoon he'd resell them to commercial banks, making a small profit on the spread. By the late 1890s Goldman, Sachs & Co. (Marcus having been joined by his son-in-law) was the country's largest dealer in such instruments.

Goldman had decided to join the major leagues by becoming an investment banker and getting in on the great merger wave shortly before he died in 1904. His son Henry pursued the project, only to have Morgan, Speyer & Co., and Kuhn, Loeb tell him he wasn't welcome at the head table. Barred from railroad and industrial finance, Henry turned to opportunities the majors wouldn't touch. He started with several rival Jewish cigar manufacturers with whom he had had financial dealings, proposing they merge into one mega-company to make and retail their products. There were two impediments. One, the firms had few tangible assets that could serve as collateral, and two, Goldman didn't have enough capital to underwrite the deal. He solved the first by deciding that the cigar makers' customer base, which generated substantial earnings, itself constituted sufficient collateral, a break with conventional banking wisdom. And he sorted out the second by bringing to the table a cash-rich firm, run by his friend Philip Lehman, with whom he dined daily at Delmonico's. Philip was one of five Lehman brothers (their office was just around the corner at 22 William) who were commodity traders (chiefly cotton and coffee) but who also aspired to get into underwriting securities. Henry and Philip linked Goldman Sachs clients with Lehman Brothers capital and successfully (and profitably) launched United Cigar (later General Cigar) in 1906. The team now applied the same financial calculus—underwriting mergers based more on earnings than assets—to full-time retailers, another category with which the Morgans and Schiffs wouldn't deal. Goldman had worked previously with Julius Rosenwald of the Chicago-based Sears, Roebuck, selling its commercial paper so the distributor could raise capital to buy merchandise in New York City. Now, with Lehman's money, Goldman pulled off a $10 million public stock offering, then promptly did the same for Frank Woolworth, the five-and-ten-cent-store magnate, whose request for financing Morgan had turned down.

TO SOME DEGREE MORGAN'S DISINTEREST might be put down to his having bigger fish to finance. Increasingly, Wall Street's investment banks were arranging the underwriting of overseas issues, principally for railroads and mines and communications ventures in the Western Hemisphere. More dramatically, investment bankers were beginning to float stocks and bonds of European origin. After a good half century of New York's serving as point of *entry* for English, German, French, and Dutch capital—the wherewithal for industrializating the continent—there were signs and portents of a reversal of flow. Most startling was the decision in 1900 of the British exchequer, faced with the tremendous costs of fighting the Boer War, to float securities worth £10 million in the New York market, chiefly through J. P. Morgan. The issue was a resounding success, as were four subsequent war loans between 1900 and 1902.

Wall Street watchers sat up and took notice, starting with English stockbrokers, who feared that "permanent injury has been done to the London market" and wondered gloomily if one day New York might not "cut out" the City. In 1902 Secretary of State John Hay boisterously anticipated just that, proclaiming that "the financial center of the world, which required thousands of years to journey from the Euphrates to the Thames and Seine, seems passing to the Hudson between daybreak and dark." The Gotham-based *Bankers Magazine* was more cautious. While "the financial centre of the world still remains fixed at London despite enthusiastic American assertions to the contrary," weren't there signs that this "superiority" was "beginning to wane?" Wasn't it the case that "New York, the great commercial centre of the United States, is rapidly gaining as a market where capital may be obtained for cosmopolitan enterprise"? Additional evidence supporting this perspective was soon forthcoming, when during the 1904–5 Russo-Japanese War a Schiff-led syndicate funded millions of dollars' worth of Japanese government bonds, which contributed greatly, as Schiff had intended, to the defeat of the anti-Semitic czarist regime. More broadly, between 1900 and 1913, nearly 250 foreign loans were issued in the United States. Still, the country remained a minor financial power on the international scene, and as late as 1914, the United States remained a debtor nation. British investors were owed $20 billion; French financiers held $10 billion in foreign loans, and the Germans another $5 billion; whereas all outstanding American foreign loans totaled less than $1 billion.

THE SECOND CATEGORY OF INSTITUTIONS essential to Stock Exchange workings were commercial banks—what most people thought of when they thought of banks: entities that accepted deposits and loaned them out. *National* commercial banks, meaning those that had "national" in their name, were chartered by the US Treasury Department's comptroller of the currency. They were authorized, under the Civil War–era National Bank Acts, to issue bank notes—currency—if they first purchased US government bonds and deposited them with the treasury as backing for the notes they were issuing. New York's national banks were also legally designated as central reserve banks, institutions in which thousands of "correspondent" banks across the country were allowed to park a percentage of *their* required reserves in interest-bearing accounts. This boon to New York City, which reflected its financial preeminence and helped sustain it, was diminished somewhat when Chicago and St. Louis demanded and got "reserve" status in 1887. And the correspondent system was not without its drawbacks. The funds flowed in and out, depending on the agricultural cycle and the state of business in the interior. If it was planting time, or business was slack, rural sectors sent idle capital to New York banks; at harvest time, or when business was hopping, capital was withdrawn from Gotham to be employed in more profitable pursuits. It was as if the continent were tilted from side to side each season, sending money sloshing this way and that.

This volatility in turn impacted stock trading. Legally speaking, commercial banks were not allowed to invest directly in the stock market—to shield depositors' accounts from risky speculation—though this restriction was often ignored or evaded by one means or another, such as setting up supposedly arm's-length subsidiaries. There were other ways, however, that commercial banks lubricated the New York Stock Exchange machinery. Increasingly they accepted stocks as collateral for loans—to corporations, to individuals, and to brokers on the Exchange floor. Loans to the latter, known as call loans (because they could be recalled at any time), were made to brokers, who then reloaned the funds to would-be stock purchasers, enabling them to buy stocks on credit; buyers paid only a small percentage (a "margin") in cash, and the broker-lender retained the stock itself as collateral. This leveraging made for enhanced profits if the stock went up. But if the stock went down—thus eroding the value of the loan's collateral—brokers would require debtors to cough up more money. If they didn't, the brokers could sell off the stock immediately, before it fell further. This introduced a potential source of serious instability, for both brokers and their commercial-banker backers, which both happily ignored as the boom roared on.

Two of the city's leading commercial banks were each one block away from the NYSE, both on Wall Street itself. Walking west toward Trinity Church brought one to the First National Bank at the northeast corner of Wall and Broadway. As the name suggests, it had been the city's first national bank, co-founded in 1863 and presided over since 1877 by the taciturn George Baker, a proper Victorian gentleman replete with muttonchop whiskers and an ample paunch, garlanded with a gold watch chain. In 1881 Baker had replaced First National's original low-rise headquarters with the nine-story United Bank Building (jointly owned with the Bank of the Republic). Baker's forte was buying and rehabbing railroads, and establishing new corporations on which he then served as a director. First National was itself a corporation, as national banks were required to be, and its directors included financiers of the first rank, among them Morgan (a friend and ally since the 1870s), J. D. Rockefeller, J. H. Hill, and H. C. Frick. Its depositors were a similarly stellar body of corporate and individual investors (including Baker himself), who kept large amounts in the bank, which collectively constituted a select market for new securities.

First National being a corporation, not a partnership, Baker was less trammeled by family considerations in hiring executives, and his choice of first lieutenant was the vigorous and genial Henry Pomeroy Davison, who had risen by merit, not pedigree. Davison, son of a farm tools dealer in a small Pennsylvania town, had skipped college, worked for a bank in

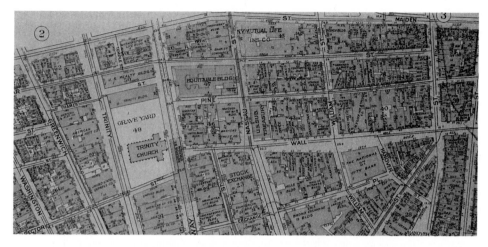

G. W. Bromley and Walter S. Bromley, "Plate 1: Bounded by Liberty Street, Maiden Lane, East River (Piers 1–14), South Street, Battery Park, and Hudson River (Piers 2–37), West Street," 1911. (New York Public Library; Astor, Lenox, and Tilden Foundations; Lionel Pincus and Princess Firyal Map Division)

Bridgeport, and moved to New York in 1893, where he worked in two of First National's farm team banks—the Astor and the Liberty—before being made vice president in the big leagues.

Baker's was one of the first national banks to wriggle free of legislative restrictions on speculating in stocks, by setting up First Security Company in 1908, onto which he could offload risky underwriting and margin loans (though the firewall between them would prove all too permeable).

Walking back to the Exchange and continuing on Wall Street a block farther led to the dramatic new-but-old headquarters of the National City Bank at 55 Wall, which occupied the entire south side of the block between William and Hanover. For almost a century, beginning back when it was founded in 1812 as the City Bank of New York, it had been housed across the street at 52 Wall. There it had grown steadily under Moses Taylor and his successor (and son-in-law), Percy R. Pyne, and then astronomically under James Stillman, who took over as president in 1891.

Stillman attracted deposits from many of New York's super-rich—including himself, having (in 1902) a personal fortune of $50 million—but no one else was as crucial to the bank's success as William Rockefeller. A decidedly different flavor of Rockefeller than John, William had none of his older brother's disdain for financiers. Indeed, as president of the phenomenally cash-rich Standard Oil of New York he had parlayed his position into one of exceptional prominence on Wall Street. He'd also adopted a lifestyle far closer to Morgan's than that of John, who disapproved of speculative wheeling and dealing as much as he did Lucullan wining and dining. Access to William's millions helped National City Bank—soon known as the Oil Bank—win a leading position among Gotham's financial establishments.[2] Its immense treasure chest served as a prime source of the funds used to purchase the stocks being marketed by the likes of Morgan and Kuhn, Loeb.

2. The millions decidedly did not come from John D.'s pockets, as he had serious reservations about Stillman's character and regretted his association with William. When asked privately about his own stake in National City he responded: "It is called, I am told, the Rockefeller institution. But I don't control it . . . . Why, I declare I don't even know where it is located" (this latter protestation being presumably an example of dry midwestern humor).

Given such explosive growth, National City Bank, like the NYSE, was clearly in need of a new space, but Stillman preferred to acquire a vintage one. Just across Wall Street sat the second Merchants' Exchange, built between 1836 and 1842 to replace the first exchange, which had burned in the Great Fire of 1835. Since 1862, 55 Wall had been used as the US Custom House, but by the end of the 1890s the federal agency had outgrown the building and moved out. Stillman bought it and had Stanford White design an expansion plan that double-decked it, setting four Corinthian-columned stories atop Isaiah Rogers's original four Ionic ones, and keeping the old dome to crown the colossal banking chamber that occupied the lower structure. On moving day, December 19, 1908, $70 million in cash and $500 million in securities were hauled in tin boxes across the street from 52 Wall and into 55's 300-ton armor-plated safe that sat smack in the middle of the banking floor, the light from the glass dome above illuminating the steam coils surrounding the strongbox, which were "designed to parboil in an instant any person bent on burglary."

Though a corporation, National City was nevertheless enmeshed in family networks, principally at the ownership level, Stillman's two daughters having married William Rockefeller's two sons; a banking dynasty was busy being born. But though the president brought his son, James A. Stillman, into the firm, he turned to a professional for a potential successor. Stillman had worked closely with Frank Vanderlip, assistant secretary of the treasury, on funding the war with Spain, and in 1901 enticed him into leaving Washington to become a vice president of the bank. Like others of his generation, Vanderlip would prove a politically savvy spokesperson—both for National City and for the New York financial community in general.

TRUST COMPANIES, THE THIRD CATEGORY OF NYSE-related institutions, were not subject to the constraints governing commercial banks. Technically they weren't banks at all but rather fiscal institutions set up to hold and manage properties entrusted to their care. Originally

Vault, National City Bank, ca. 1910. (Image No. x2010.7.1.1053, Wurts Brothers/Museum of the City of New York)

they oversaw family trust funds, acted as executors of wills, or administrated estates. With the growth of corporations, trusts extended their fiduciary services to include acting as fiscal agents for companies.

Not being part of the national banking system, they were not allowed to issue bank notes. But neither were they required (as were national banks) to keep a minimum of 25 percent of their deposits on hand. Indeed, before 1906 trusts were not required to hold any reserves, an advantage they used to muscle their way into banking, luring depositors away from commercial bank rivals by offering higher interest rates. They grew rapidly. In 1900 there were thirty-one trust companies in New York City; by 1913 the number had more than tripled. Assets soared, too: between 1897 and 1907, New York State trust holdings jumped from $400 million to $1.3 billion.

Much of this money was then poured into the stock market. Legally unencumbered, trusts in effect became investment banks—underwriting new issues, trading securities—but with resources approaching those of commercial banks.

Banks were not happy about the rise of trusts. It was bad enough when they competed for interest-bearing deposits, worse when they stole clients who'd been referred to them for trust work. In 1903 a group of New York banks fought back by forming their own trust company, the appropriately named Bankers Trust. This outfit could be trusted not to compete with its owners: J. P. Morgan held a controlling interest, John D. Rockefeller bought a substantial stake, and George Baker dispatched Henry Davison to get it up and running—along with a newcomer, Thomas Lamont, who worked at Baker's Liberty Bank. Three months after opening its doors at 143 Liberty Street, it had nearly $6 million in deposits. In another month it had outgrown its original premises and moved to 10 Wall Street, virtually next door to Morgan and the NYSE.

The trusts nevertheless continued to grow and multiply, spreading out through lower Manhattan, and following the monied who were migrating uptown. The reassuringly named Knickerbocker Trust—the city's third-largest—had a downtown branch at 60 Broadway. But it also commissioned Stanford White (a good friend of Knickerbocker's president, Charles T. Barney) to build a magnificent uptown branch at the northwest corner of Fifth Avenue and 34th Street, just across from the Waldorf-Astoria, where until recently A. T. Stewart's mansion had stood. Its new (1904) Corinthian-columned, marble Roman temple radiated trustworthiness.

FINALLY, TOWERING OVER ALL OTHERS as a source of capital for the merger wave and its accompanying boom were the life insurance companies—headed by the Big Three: the Mutual Life Insurance Company of New York (at 34 Nassau, between Liberty and Cedar), the Equitable Assurance Company (at 120 Broadway, between Cedar and Pine), and the New York Life Insurance Company (an outlier, in 346 Broadway at Leonard, several blocks above City Hall). These were huge entities—gigantic reservoirs of money. Their combined income from premiums in 1905 was greater than the sum harvested annually by the federal government. Their combined assets—a billion dollars that year—were greater than the amount of currency in circulation in the United States, and twice Great Britain's gold supply.

They were also major players on the international scene, with three-quarters of a billion dollars' worth of insurance in force abroad, overwhelmingly in Europe, where they catered to the German, English, and French equivalents of the business, professional, and white-collar groups who made up the bulk of the US life insurance market. New York Life also had a big presence in Latin America and Russia; Equitable had policyholders in almost a hundred nations.

Officially, their raison d'être was not profit but public service. Two of them were "mutuals"—owned entirely by their policyholders, to whom were rebated any profits—and even New York Life, a corporation owned by its shareholders, was limited to dividends of 7 percent. All were allowed to invest their accumulated premiums, but only in the name of enhancing their ability to meet claims by policyholders. Traditionally they had been barred from buying stocks and restricted to government securities, municipal bonds, farm mortgages, and the like. But once the feverish boom got under way, company executives couldn't pass up participation, and they figured out ways of plunging in.

One route was to deposit huge sums with banks and trust companies, which used the cash to buy securities, as the firms themselves could not. The Big Three were spurred on in this endeavor by bankers and trust company executives who, desperate to get access to these immense moneypots, piled onto their boards of directors (especially their finance committees), thus winning a say from the inside as to where the funds would be invested. More proactively, they bought up huge chunks of trust companies and then directed the flow of their capital. Things got so intertwined it was hard at times to tell who was calling the shots: Guaranty Trust Company was half owned by Mutual Life; Jacob Schiff of Kuhn, Loeb sold $22 million worth of bonds in 1904 to Equitable, on whose finance committee he sat (reaping $500,000 on the deal); and J. P. Morgan vice president George Perkins sold $39 million worth of securities to...New York Life vice president George Perkins, the dual-hatted Perkins serving on both institutions simultaneously from 1901 to 1906.

All in all, by one means or another, in 1904 the Big Three had come to own around $2.25 billion of stocks and bonds. And this did not count the nearly $45 million of European securities they had purchased, roughly three-fourths the total of US overseas investment.

THE WORLD OF WALL STREET was not without its internal rivalries—banks vs. trusts, Jews vs. Protestants, bulls vs. bears, the Morgan/First National Bank/US Steel cluster vs. the Rockefeller/National City Bank/Standard Oil cluster. But these were offset by powerful centripetal factors—notably a latticework of business associations generated inside the industry itself, and a matrix of personal relationships nurtured in lower Manhattan's social institutions.

Three business practices fostered cooperation among even the most competitively-minded Wall Streeters: the necessity of syndicates, the establishment of interlocking directorates, and membership in the New York Clearing House.

During the great merger wave there was no way the House of Morgan or any other financial firm could, by itself, raise the stupendous sums needed to float giant new corporations. Syndicates were the solution. These were pickup teams—of commercial banks, trusts, brokerages, life insurance companies, and super-rich individuals—invited by an originating house, usually one of the city's leading investment banks, to underwrite a percentage of the amount to be underwritten. Invitees never declined, lest they not be asked again, or lest others not come when they themselves called. The ethos of cooperation was strengthened by the fact that syndicate participation was often extremely lucrative. The one J. P. Morgan put together for US Steel—its roster read like an all-star team of Gotham's banks and millionaires—did very well indeed. For underwriting $200 million worth of stock, members divided up a profit of $62.5 million—though they supplied only $25 million in actual cash, and undertook only minimal risk in guaranteeing the rest.

Wall Street's denizens' awareness that they had collective interests that transcended those of their individual firms was also reinforced by their participation in a network of interlinked directorships. Bankers and trust company executives swapped seats on one another's boards, and on those of their client corporations and affiliated insurance companies. Interlocking directorates were ultimately a way of assuring one's business a reliable supply of capital, and also a method of accumulating inside market information, of being in the know. Directorships paid handsomely, too, no small inducement. While such overlapping did not guarantee peace and harmony, it did help forge a code of conduct. It became, as Jacob Schiff explained, not "good form to create unreasonable interference or competition."

The Clearing House—an ornate five-story domed Italian Renaissance structure (1896) at 83 Cedar Street—was a more workaday but nevertheless vital force for cooperation. Since 1853 it had provided a practical way to settle up interbank transactions at the end of each business day. It also served as lender of last resort for member banks, who could borrow from others to tide themselves over any temporary flurry of withdrawals, thus forestalling the "runs" to which any bank was vulnerable, and which, once begun, might well spread to others and create a general "panic." Trusts were not members but were allowed to clear through banks that were; this task was undertaken primarily by the National Bank of Commerce (at Nassau and Cedar), the city's (and perforce the country's) second-largest commercial bank, with Morgan the dominant director.

Another species of constraint on rampant pursuit of self-interest was the cultivation of amiable social relations in lower-Manhattan enclaves. Of particular importance were the downtown dining clubs—workplace counterparts of the men's clubs that dotted their uptown residential neighborhoods. Here Wall Street players of all stripes could congregate at lunchtime to schmooze in luxurious and restful settings with others, with whom they had perhaps been locked in combat all morning. The oldest of these, the Down-Town Association, dated to 1860; it had its own building at 60 Pine and catered primarily to brokers and financiers. Others were also occupationally focused, like the Merchants' Club (1871) in the New York Life Building, or the Lawyers Club (1887) in the Equitable Building. A new generation of associations had ridden in on the merger wave and its booming aftermath: the City Midday Club (1901) at 25 Broad; the Whitehall Lunch Club (1910) in the Whitehall Building (17 Battery Place), for shipping-industry executives; and the Recess Club (1911) in the Knickerbocker Trust building, at 60 Broadway, where members included J. P. Morgan, Jacob Schiff, Otto Kahn, Cornelius Vanderbilt, and Charles M. Schwab. "Every one of the big cliques is represented," it was reported, with the club's internal pecking order based strictly on wealth. Members were ranked in collegiate order, with "seniors" worth $30 million and up, "juniors" in the $15–$30 million category, and so forth. Less exclusive than the Recess (which had only 200 members) was the new Bankers Club of New York (1915) in the Equitable Building, whose 1,500 members could choose from among several themed dining rooms (Italian Renaissance, Grecian Classic, Georgian, etc.).

Another dining club—the Pilgrims of the United States (1903)—was part of a matched set with the Pilgrims of Great Britain (1902), both dedicated to "fostering good fellowship" between their respective English-speaking nations. Anglophilia was a powerful component of Wall Street's culture. The Pilgrims met several times a year for banquets—in London at the Carlton Hotel, in New York at Delmonico's or the Waldorf—usually when distinguished visitors were visiting from across the pond, notably new ambassadors or generals. Membership was drawn principally from the equivalent financial and social establishments, including in London the likes of Lord Kitchener, Cecil Rhodes, and members of the royal family, and in New York the Astors, Baker, Belmont, Butler, Carnegie, Choate, Depew, Duke, Morgan, Root, the Rockefellers, and Schwab; Episcopal Bishop Henry C. Potter presided over the US association.

The ultimate club—a thousand members strong—was Wall Street's oldest, and arguably still the most powerful institution in the city: the New York Chamber of Commerce. Since its founding at Fraunces Tavern in 1768, the Chamber had never had a permanent home. In the new century this no longer seemed tolerable to its members or its leadership—notably President Morris Jesup, now retired from banking but vigorously active in a host of metropolitan cultural institutions, and the Chamber's three vice presidents, J. P. Morgan, John D. Rockefeller, and Andrew Carnegie. A building fund was put together. It quickly gathered pledges of well over a million dollars, secured a site (from member and real estate speculator Henry Morgenthau) at 65 Liberty Street (between Broadway and Nassau), and set architect member James B. Baker to designing a pantheon for the masters of the metropolis. When it was opened in 1902 by President Roosevelt and ex-president Cleveland, the Beaux-Arts extravaganza—New York's closest approach to the opulence of the Paris Opera— featured a 60′ × 90′ Great Hall on the second floor. From its gilded, paneled, and skylighted ceiling above to the 2,750-pound hand-tufted rug below (designed and furnished by member William Sloane of W. & J. Sloane), it was a resplendent setting for the Chamber's regular meetings. It was also festooned with a collection of portraits of members past, by the likes of artists Asher Durand and Charles Willson Peale, with additional tribute paid to the institution's history in four sculptural groups by Daniel Chester French, one of which depicted De Witt Clinton flanked by a crouched worker with a shovel, reminding all of the Chamber's far-sighted support of the Erie Canal.

CURIOUSLY, LAWYERS WERE BARRED from Chamber membership (and had been since colonial days). This obscured the degree to which the burden of binding together Wall Street's disparate interest groups was borne by an adjutant caste of corporate attorneys. The upper echelons of the legal profession had by now completed the transition, begun in the 1870s, from courtroom to boardroom. Corporate clients had less need of litigation than of continuous legal advice on the construction, maintenance, and reorganization of their companies. Most "office lawyers" (as opposed to "trial lawyers") were concerned with day-to-day tactical issues. But the giants of the profession worked closely with top owners and managers on grand strategic planning. And because they dealt with an array of firms, and sat on numerous corporate boards, leading lawyers focused on the systemic issues confronting all their clients, helping competitors understand what they had in common.

For their own firms, corporate lawyers tended to opt for one of two structures, one mimicking the corporations themselves, the other more akin to small investment banks which, like J. P. Morgan & Co., were really the lengthened shadow of one man. By 1915 fifty-one firms in Gotham had five or more attorneys; fourteen boasted more than ten. In 1908 Cravath, Swaine & Seward had three partners and sixteen salaried associates hired straight from law school as possible future partners. Some of these "law factories" not only undertook domestic corporate work but labored abroad assisting US business expansion overseas. The head of the sizable Sullivan & Cromwell firm—William Nelson Cromwell, of Panama Canal fame— not only helped J. P. Morgan organize US Steel but aided client banks (European as well as American) in buying securities in other countries.[3]

---

3. Facilitating the international flow of capital appealed to young John Foster Dulles, who was initially turned down by Cromwell, as his law degree was only from George Washington, not Harvard or Yale. But in 1911 Cromwell relented immediately on receipt of a letter supporting young Dulles from his grandfather John Watson Foster—international lawyer, diplomat, and former secretary of state.

At the opposite extreme were small firms built largely around one legal titan—like Joseph H. Choate, counsel for Rockefeller's Standard Oil, or Francis Lynde Stetson, organizer and general counsel of Morgan's United States Steel. The preeminent example was Elihu Root, whose firm of Root & Clark had consisted, in 1891, of Root, Clark, and a clerical staff of four. When he went off in 1899 to serve as McKinley's and then Roosevelt's secretary of war, Root passed his firm on to other hands, principally those of Henry Lewis Stimson.[4] When he returned to Wall Street in 1904 and re-shouldered his practice, he was working virtually on his own but still managed to become the highest-paid attorney in Gotham's history, join many corporate and bank boards, and serve as president of the Association of the Bar of the City of New York.

What both kinds of firms had in common was the background of their principals— Anglo-Protestant Republicans trained in a tiny handful of acceptable law schools—though, in the same way that finance and industry made room for a German Jewish wing, exceptions were made in the legal profession as well, precisely because they had a powerful client base among Jewish bankers and industrialists. Thus the firm that handled much of the Guggenheim family's legal work was Guggenheimer, Untermyer & Marshall (37 Wall Street). Samuel Untermyer, son of Bavarian Jewish immigrants, had been brought to New York as a child, graduated from City College and Columbia Law (1878), and started a practice with his half brother Randolph Guggenheimer, which was joined in 1895 by Louis Marshall, who would become a significant figure in Gotham's Jewish community.

SO THIS WAS THE CLUBBY WORLD OF WALL STREET, where financiers spent most of their time dealing with one another, or with industrial chieftains and legal consiglieri. But they were also well aware that their tiny domain was at the center of the reconstruction of American capitalism, an enterprise in which, for reasons both practical and ideological, they sought to involve other social actors. Some brokers and promoters began appealing to small investors, hoping to coax new kinds of capital into the Exchange, by tapping into the savings of mid-level corporate managers, well-paid professionals, and small businessmen. It was also part of an effort to bolster their legitimacy by shedding the disreputable legacy of the freebooting era of Daniel Drew, Jim Fisk, and Jay Gould, when investor lambs were routinely shorn and slaughtered. Thus the reassuring mission statement the New York Stock Exchange inscribed on its new pediment: "Business Integrity Protecting the Industries of Man."

Yet the market remained a rough-and-tumble operation, whose far-from-level playing field was still dominated by highly skilled professionals who thought nothing of trampling on small fry. Brokers were not mere technicians, after all; the best of them could shove the market in desired directions. Morgan didn't just dump his newly minted US Steel shares on

---

4. Root hired Stimson in 1891 at the recommendation of his biggest client, William C. Whitney, then building his streetcar empire. Stimson's grandfather Henry Clark Stimson had been senior partner of a Wall Street stock brokerage firm after the Civil War, whose clients had included Leonard Jerome, Jay Gould, and Commodore Vanderbilt. He lost much of his fortune in the Panic of 1873, but enough remained to support a comfortable retirement in an East 34th Street brownstone. His son—young Stimson's father—opted for medicine, becoming a surgeon at Presbyterian Hospital. But Henry chose the law. Educated at Phillips Academy (in Andover, Massachusetts), Yale (Skull and Bones), and then Harvard Law (Class of 1890), he started out in the office of his Yale friend Sherman Evarts, son of one of the great lawyers of the previous generation, and in 1893 became a partner in Root and Clark, where he did corporate work while absorbing Root's attention to bigger structural issues. When his mentor went down to DC in 1899, Stimson and another young partner, Bronson Winthrop, changed the firm's name (in 1901) to Winthrop & Stimson; many clients left, but others were drawn to Stimson's reputation for solid reliable counsel, and he became a well-known corporate lawyer. In 1906, at the behest of Secretary of State Root, President Theodore Roosevelt appointed Stimson US attorney for the Southern District of New York, where he made a distinguished record prosecuting corporate wrongdoing.

the Exchange; he turned to ace stockbroker James R. Keene, known as "the Silver Fox of Wall Street," who by adroit buying and selling created an illusion of tremendous demand, which in turn produced the desired result, a steadily rising price. Some were sharkier still, like Bernard Baruch, son of Simon Baruch, the celebrated physician who had campaigned successfully for the establishment of public baths. Young Baruch had worked in a brokerage after graduating from City College. Then, with his earnings and commissions, he bought a seat on the Exchange and embarked on a campaign of daring speculations, with a penchant for short selling, bear raids, and trading on inside information. Baruch then crossed over into investment banking by assembling speculative syndicates of wealthy investors, notably the Guggenheims. By 1903 he was a millionaire; by 1910, one of the Street's best known, and most feared, financiers. These were not waters for amateurs to paddle about in.

Small investors (and some substantial ones) also balked at buying the common stock issued in oceanic quantities by merger promoters, given a widespread wariness about how much water they contained. Critics calculated that Morgan's $1.4 billion capitalization of US Steel had added nearly 50 percent to the already inflated value of its constituent firms.

Merger defenders argued that the extra shares represented the profits to be won through increased efficiency, economies of scale, administrative rationalization, and an imposing percentage of market share.

Investors countered that overcapitalization seemed mainly about lining promoters' pockets—a grander way for New York gamblers to skin the country—while it also increased market volatility and led companies to overprice their goods, gouging consumers to benefit shareholders.

Exchange defenders denied overcapitalization could long exist, as the stock market itself would arrive at a fair valuation, wringing out water in the course of buying and selling.

Critics riposted that it wasn't exactly easy to evaluate true corporate worth because most companies withheld even basic information about sales, costs, and profits, resisting any efforts to penetrate their veil of secrecy. When sugar mogul Henry Havemeyer was asked in 1899 what stockholders were entitled to know about companies in which they invested, he harrumphed: "Let the buyer beware; that covers the whole business. You cannot wet-nurse people....They have got to wade in and get stuck and that is the way men are educated and cultivated."

Financial journalism had emerged partly as a way to extract and publicize such information, but it wasn't much help to small investors, as it was really aimed at insiders. The *Wall Street Journal*—which since 1896 had been publishing its Dow Jones Industrial Average on a daily basis—was written explicitly for "operators, bankers and capitalists." The paper's "Investment and Speculation" column pointedly discouraged market participation by any other than securities professionals. Even John D. Rockefeller claimed to be leery, saying, "If I were to give advice it would be to keep out of Wall Street."[5]

---

5. Not that he took his own advice. It's true that when JDR retired from day-to-day involvement with Standard Oil (he stopped going to 26 Broadway altogether in 1897, though his 30 percent ownership allowed him as much control as he cared to exercise), he shifted from earning money to giving it away. But it's at least as accurate to say he shifted from earning money through producing oil products to earning money from avidly playing the market (with expert advice, to be sure). Rockefeller redirected much of the $3 million or so he received yearly in Standard Oil dividends into a vast portfolio, with sizable stakes in sixteen railroad companies, nine banks and financial houses, nine real estate firms, six steel corporations, and six steamship companies, and he took large shares in loans floated by foreign governments. Kuhn, Loeb was his favored investment banker, as Rockefeller was convinced, not without reason, that the House of Morgan treated him badly.

The industry came up with two ways to allay small investors' fears. One was to work through savings banks, whose probity was widely accepted, by encouraging them to invest—cautiously—on their depositors' behalf. New York State helped out by restricting such institutions to rock-solid instruments, like first-class mortgage bonds of railroads that had paid dividends for at least ten years. By 1904 savings banks had accumulated over $2 billion of such securities. The other approach was to offer those seeking steady income a separate instrument, *preferred* stock, which offered regular dividends but no ownership share, hence no shot at big-time capital gains; such shares, moreover, were reassuringly backed by the hard actual value of company assets like mines, refineries, or factories.

Some at the leading edge of the corporate revolution had even grander visions, verging on the utopian. In a speech he gave in 1904, Frank Vanderlip, vice president of the National City Bank, foresaw a future in which "the people own the stocks and bonds of the corporations, and they become true owners of the country's wealth." In this fantasy, capitalism would merge with democracy, and the United States would become a nation of citizen-stockholders.

AS SUCH NOTIONS SUGGESTED, the financial-industrial class securely nested in lower Manhattan was supremely self-confident about the value and virtue of its historical mission, and convinced of its right and responsibility to steer the national economy from the New York corporate cockpit. What was good for Wall Street was good for the USA.

Many in the country—and city—disagreed.

Even before the great merger movement of 1898–1904 wound down, hard questions were being raised about it. Many middle-class Americans—long accustomed to a system that dispersed economic power among a myriad of competing small-scale entrepreneurs—worried that their interests, and perhaps the fate of the Republic itself, were imperiled by the growing power of great companies. Such concerns were given form and focus by a sudden explosion of investigative journalism. Like the corporate revolution, the movement that probed it was centered in New York City.

5

Critics and Crisis

MUCKRAKERS

In November 1902, the new issue of *McClure's Magazine*, selling at newsstands around town for ten cents, began running a series on the history of Standard Oil. Author Ida Tarbell acknowledged the company's "real greatness," applauding in particular its elimination of wasteful competition. But Tarbell also spelled out—in calm and analytical prose—the methods Rockefeller had employed to achieve such ends: bribery, treachery, fraud, coercion, and intimidation. Coming from an independent oil-producer family, she knew whereof she wrote.

Tarbell's exposé was not the first of the genre. Henry Demarest Lloyd's book *Wealth against Commonwealth* had excoriated Rockefeller's company back in the depression year of 1894. Populists and socialists had long preached an anti-corporate gospel. But many middle-class urbanites hadn't found radical literature palatable. They did, however, read with growing gusto the new mass-market magazines, like *McClure's*, that were casting a critical eye on the great merger wave and its ramifications.

McClure's had been launched back in 1893 by Samuel S. McClure, whose widowed mother had brought him as a child from Ireland to Indiana, where he grew up on a farm, dirt poor. McClure got into student journalism while working his way through college, then apprenticed (in Boston) at the *Wheelman*, a biking magazine, then moved in 1884 to New York, where he worked briefly at the *Century Magazine* (the successor to *Scribner's*). Like other

Cover, *McClure's Magazine*, December 1903.

prestigious monthlies, such as the stately *Harper's*, the *Century* was aimed at a genteel audience, the kind of families who could afford the relatively steep cover price of thirty-five cents. Editors offered their readers uplifting and refined works of fiction and poetry by English and American authors, and articles on politics and current events, written by moderate reformers, that were free from any taint of working-class radicalism or rural populism.

McClure soon went out on his own. Launching the pioneering McClure Newspaper Syndicate, he bought articles and short stories from popular American and English writers, then sold reprint rights to newspapers and magazines across the country. In June 1893 McClure used his syndicate earnings to launch his own national periodical, priced at fifteen cents—just as the economy tanked. Worse, in October, *Munsey's Magazine*—a rival monthly that Frank Munsey had been struggling to keep afloat since 1891 at a twenty-five-cent price point—responded to the depression (and the growth of newspaper Sunday supplements) by dropping it down to a dime. *Munsey's* promptly took off, its circulation shooting from 40,000 that month to 500,000 the following April. McClure quickly followed suit, shaving a nickel off his price, and sales leapt from 60,000 copies per month in 1894 to 250,000 in 1896 to over 350,000 by the turn of the century.

Both men were now selling magazines below the cost of production. They were able to do so because the big money came from selling advertising. Ads, in turn, were an artifact of the boom in mass-produced consumer goods, especially those items—like cereal, crackers, and soap—that were rapidly leaving the domain of household production. These goods were manufactured instead by nationwide corporations, then branded and hawked through ads increasingly placed—at the advice of agencies like J. Walter Thompson—in nation-spanning magazines. *Century* and *Harper's* had been doing advertising since the 1880s—the ad revolution was already under way—but their promotions had been segregated in discrete sections at the back. Munsey and McClure sprinkled ads throughout their pages, and with increasing prodigality: a typical *Munsey's* issue had nineteen pages' worth in 1894, ninety-two by 1900.

To some extent, the explosion in circulation was a function of returning good times, as professional and middle-class readers had more money to spend on entertainment and edification, as well as on the new household commodities to which magazine ads were guides and enticements. But what really drew affluent eyes to this particular kind of vehicle was a shift in style and content.

The monthlies adopted new design strategies, made possible by new technologies. The switch from wood engraving to halftone engraving drastically reduced the cost of reproducing illustrations and photos, and at the same time gave the periodicals a contemporary and journalistic "look." The editors also adopted a new "voice"—the editorial "we" was abandoned, as was the custom of addressing a presumed "gentle reader"; bluntly colloquial language vanquished leisurely prose.

Subjects changed in tandem with style. Readers were urged to abandon idle fantasizing for a vigorous embrace of "real" life. Coverage of metropolitan doings became more prominent. Articles sought to reveal the concealed, to offer an "inside" look at politics and current affairs, to provide fact-laden analyses of how things *worked*. (*McClure's* also carried a lot of popular-science stories.) And they were often accompanied not by gauzy illustrations but by the kind of photographic "evidence" that technology made newly possible.

Sam McClure had an even more vaulting ambition. He wanted to lay out a comprehensive critique of American society, and by 1901 he'd decided that the two great issues confronting the country were the growth of giant corporations, and the concomitant surge in political corruption. To get stories on these subjects, McClure couldn't sit back in the editor's easy chair and see what came in over the transom. He had to find crackerjack writer-reporters, set them to investigating some piece of the larger puzzle, and pay them a handsome monthly salary for doing so, freeing them up to spend weeks or months, even years, researching and writing articles. McClure estimated that the Tarbell stories cost $4,000 apiece.

They were well worth it. The first *McClure's* issue running Tarbell's takedown of Standard Oil was snapped up. So were the succeeding eighteen installments, which ran from 1902 to 1904. As the magazine's circulation boomed, McClure (and some of his competitors) quickly realized that exposés of big corporations were hot and saleable properties. More first-rate journalists joined the *McClure's* stable because—as one of them (Ray Stannard Baker) reminisced about his first office visit—*McClure's* offered "the most stimulating, yes intoxicating editorial atmosphere then existent in America—or anywhere else."

Not all the monthlies adopted McClure's critical stance. Frank Munsey, who himself did a fair amount of speculating on Wall Street, hailed mergers as progressive. He defended the giant new corporations (and advertising agencies) for bringing producers and consumers closer together, eliminating middlemen, and expanding sales to more than cover the increase in costs of production (a business model with which he was profoundly familiar). But in the century's first decade, most of his peers opted for excoriation.

In short order, a dozen or so popular journals—almost all of them New York City concerns—were competing to bring ever more vivid disclosures to a national audience. They tended to cluster considerably to the north of Wall Street, mostly between 14th and 34th Streets, especially along Fourth and Fifth Avenues. Thus *Collier's* was at 416–24 West

13th Street, *Everybody's* at Union Square, and in ascending order one could find *Leslie's Monthly* (141 Fifth, at 21st), *Munsey's* (in location, at least, huddling with peers, at 175 Fifth and 23rd), *McClure's* (44 East 23rd, at Fourth), *Cosmopolitan* (381 Fourth, at 27th), and *American Magazine* (341 Fifth, at 33rd).

Editors took aim at a vast range of targets but were particularly drawn to Wall Street, especially after the door to its inner sanctum got kicked wide open in a piece written not by a journalist digging up facts but by an insider revealing them. In 1904 *Everybody's* began running a series called "Frenzied Finance," by Thomas W. Lawson, a rich Bostonian speculator and stock promoter. According to Lawson's revelations, rendered in appropriately frenzied prose, he had conceived the notion (in 1899) of consolidating competing copper mining interests out west—doing for copper what Rockefeller had for oil, and Morgan had for steel.

This required big-monied backers. Lawson took the idea to Standard Oil capo Henry Huttleson Rogers—known as "Hell-Hound Rogers" for his ruthless rapacity, though widely acknowledged a charming man after business hours—as well as William Rockefeller and James Stillman. They decided to back Lawson's scheme. Rogers and Rockefeller would start by acquiring Anaconda Copper, a giant mining venture in Butte, Montana, then the most prolific copper-producing district in the world. First the duo took title to the mine properties, borrowing the entire purchase price of $39 million from Stillman's National City Bank. Next they created a New Jersey holding company—Amalgamated Copper—and announced it would issue $75 million worth of stock (an extravagant overcapitalization). Then the partners hyped the stock, stoking a speculative fever. Lawson announced Amalgamated would be "one of the great monopolies of the world"; that its stock, issued at 100, would quickly go to 150 or 175; that an investment of $5,000 would net $75,000 in a matter of days; and that John D. Rockefeller was behind the offering. (JDR was furious but never publicly dissociated himself from the deal.) On May 4, 1899, in two hours flat, the public plunked down $75 million and offered tens of millions more; the police had to drive away crowds of disappointed investors besieging National City Bank, which floated the stock.

Now the quartet used the proceeds to retire the $39 million loan from Stillman and pocketed the remaining $36 million. Then they began dumping stock to drive down the price; terrified small holders sold at a loss; then the insiders resumed buying and jerked the price back up again. Two years later they doubled down. In 1901, after another blaze of publicity, Rogers & Co. raised Amalgamated's capitalization from $75 million to $155 million. Again the stock was taken up in a flash; again the gang of four unloaded vast quantities of paper, driving the price down from 100 to 33; again thousands of small fry sold out and lost their shirts; again the insiders bought it back at bargain rates, then yanked up the price and harvested another round of profits. The confederates took the public for as much as $100 million—an amount that dwarfed the pickings of Drew, Fisk, and Gould, back in the days that had supposedly been transcended by the new order of "Business Integrity" (the words engraved on the new Stock Exchange). As one irate citizen wrote the US Bureau of Corporations: "Rogers has taken more millions from the Amalgamated minority stock holders than all the thieves in the 46 state prisons."

Lawson, who claimed he'd been double-crossed by his partners, wrote a tell-all account and took it to Erman Ridgway, ambitious editor of the struggling *Everybody's*. Claiming that "I have unwittingly been made the instrument by which thousands upon thousands of investors in America and Europe have been plundered," Lawson launched into an exposé of "the System" (the name he gave his former partners). Copies of the July 1904 issue were snatched from the stands; within months, *Everybody's* circulation vaulted past 500,000 to top *McClure's* and *Munsey's*. "Frenzied Finance" ran for over three years, until February 1908, when monthly sales reached 750,000. Circulation dropped back down to 500,000 at series' end, but with the magazine now selling 150 pages of advertising each month, it still cleared a hefty profit.

IN THE DECEMBER 1904 INSTALLMENT of "Frenzied Finance" Lawson had announced, "I am now going to cause a life insurance blaze," and, with the assistance of Joseph Pulitzer's *World*, he proceeded to fan a conflagration. The clamor in the press drove hitherto somnolent legislators and industry-dominated regulators into launching an investigation, of which Charles Evans Hughes was appointed chief counsel. The youthful, red-bearded Hughes had been a respected but low-profile attorney, best known for tracking down concealed corporate assets in bankruptcy cases, until he'd been picked, early in 1905, to lead a public investigation of gas company rates. Having performed brilliantly in the spring, he was asked for a repeat performance in the fall. He delivered. From September to December 1905, in the mahogany-paneled Aldermanic Chamber of City Hall, Hughes conducted a remorseless, devastating dissection of the life insurance industry's three giants. He laid bare the conflict of interest inherent in the interlocks with banks and trusts (with J. P. Morgan–cum–New York Life executive George Perkins coming in for special grilling). He exposed the use of policyholder premiums for campaign contributions. He revealed the juggling of books.

These and other of Hughes's wholesale findings (submitted in February 1906) were retailed to readers of *McClure's* in "The Story of Life Insurance," a series that ran from May to November 1906, authored by journalist Burton Jesse Hendrick, who supplemented Hughes's work with his own research.

Hendrick argued that the Big Three's executives had become more interested in sexy high finance than in boring life insurance, and had diverted policyholder funds into complicated and risky stocks, rather than into sound and often more profitable real estate mortgages. Their goal was profit, power, and life in the fast lane. Directors and top management were thrilled by their extravagant salaries, their access to directorships, their participation in syndicates, their receipt of stock market tips or other insider perks (as when James Stillman allowed New York Life president John A. McCall to buy National City Bank stock at 200, at a time its market value was 300). The odor of corruption was so pervasive that even the strongly pro-corporate *Commercial and Financial Chronicle* found in the disclosures "so much that is unsavory, so much that offends the moral sense."

Equally disturbing was the corruption of the political process made possible by such concentrated financial power. The companies made unsecured loans to influential public figures, underwrote political campaigns, or simply bribed reporters, editors, and legislators to obtain favorable coverage or special treatment. These revelations alarmed *McClure's* readers—small businessmen, professionals, shopkeepers, better-off workers—many of whom were also holders of insurance policies whose premiums rose along with executive salaries.

In the ensuing storm of outrage, Hughes submitted a series of proposals to the legislature, which by now had slipped from the companies' control. In 1906 all were passed virtually as Hughes had written them. The new laws required the insurance industry to stick to its core business. Companies were prohibited from underwriting securities, required to divest themselves of stock they held in banks or trust companies, barred from buying common stock, limited to "conservative and durable investments," and forced to set a maximum limit on their surplus and distribute any excess to policyholders. Lobbying was regulated; campaign contributions, forbidden. Within a year twenty-nine states had followed New York in adopting regulatory reforms.

The laws had a significant impact. The insurance industry was effectively removed from the mix of institutions funneling capital to the New York Stock Exchange. George Perkins resigned from New York Life. And in November 1906 Charles Evans Hughes was elected governor of New York.

IN THE MEANTIME NEWSPAPER MOGUL William Randolph Hearst had been campaigning to do for national politics what Hughes and Hendrick were doing in New York State—mobilize a public protest that set some limits on the ability of money to influence politics. Hearst had been an antitrust and anticorruption crusader since his *San Francisco Examiner* days, and he transferred that battle to his New York newspapers. In 1905 he carried his campaign into a new medium. That May, having long been eager to enter the magazine field, Hearst purchased *Cosmopolitan*, which since its founding in 1886 had been a family, then a literary, magazine. Bringing in investigative reporters like Charles Edward Russell, he set out to boost the magazine's visibility—and his own, Hearst having entered politics.

For a series on "The Treason of the Senate," he turned to David Graham Phillips, a successful novelist who had just published *The Deluge*, featuring a hero, based on Thomas W. Lawson, who "tears away the mask from our American Monte Carlo, the gambling hell of Wall Street."[1] In a February 1906 teaser for the forthcoming series, Hearst promised a "terrible arraignment" of US senators, for whom the merest "nod of a Havemeyer, an Armour or a Morgan" would outweigh "a petition signed by a million of the common people." Citing the 1904 book *Poverty* by Robert Hunter, head of the University Settlement House, Hearst suggested that as "one per cent. of the families living in the United States hold more property than the remaining ninety-nine per cent.," then it followed, given the policies and attitude of the United States Senate, "that it is not the ninety-nine, but merely the one per cent that is really represented by that sedate and decorous body, so often referred to as the 'Rich Man's Club.'"

Phillips's first installment, which appeared in *Cosmopolitan* in March 1906, charged the Senate with being the agent of "treasonous" corporate interests, which were "as hostile to the American people as any invading army could be, and vastly more dangerous," because they "manipulate the prosperity produced by all, so that it heaps up riches for the few." His first case study was of New York's "Misrepresentatives"—Thomas Collier Platt (who, as Republican boss of the state legislature, which in those days selected United States senators, had selected himself), and Chauncey M. Depew, whom Phillips lit into as an obsequious "servant of the plutocracy," notably of the Vanderbilts and their railroad interests. Eschewing Tarbell's moderate tone, Phillips went for the jugular, claiming that the wife of one of the younger Vanderbilts once refused to have Depew at her table, saying to her husband: "I do not let my butler sit down with me....Why should I let yours?" But Phillips and Hearst justified heated rhetoric because they believed—not without justification (as evidenced most recently by Hughes's insurance investigation)—that corporate oligarchs wielded an unhealthy influence in the corridors of power.

NEW YORK MAGAZINES CONTINUED TO CHURN OUT indignant, fact-packed articles, rummaging for skeletons in the closets of every major industry—and political machines, universities, and churches as well. Between 1903 and 1912, almost 2,000 of these pieces were published,

---

1. Phillips's usage drew on gambling "hells"—the businesses devoted to games of chance that were then blooming throughout Manhattan, particularly in the Wall Street area.

in journals whose readership, once numbering in the hundreds of thousands, now comprised 25 million people.[2] Finley Peter Dunne's fictional (and dialect-ical) saloonkeeper Mr. Dooley summed up the change: "Time was," he told his straight man, Mr. Hennessy, when magazine reading "was very ca'ming to the mind," a matter of "Prom'nent lady authoresses makin' pomes at the moon....Th' idee ye got fr'm these here publications was that life was wan glad sweet song....But now whin I pick me fav-rite magazine off th' flure, what do I find? Ivrything has gone wrong....I used to be nervous about burglars, but now I'm afraid iv a night call fr'm the prisidint iv th' First National Bank."

The exposés did puncture the professions of financial and industrial leaders, and suggest that the new corporations were not as moral, rational, or progressive as they claimed to be, that indeed they might yet overwhelm state and society. Ray Stannard Baker, writing for *Collier's*, worried about the power Morgan and his Wall Street colleagues had assumed over the American economy. "Is it possible," Baker asked, "that the time will come when an imperial 'M' will repose within the wreath of power?"

But if the investigative articles were long on description, they were short on prescription.

Their authors and editors were not Populists, whose opposition to the new corporate order—and its citadel city of New York—was far more profound. Those largely rural critics had protested metropolitan domination of the national financial system by "the money kings of Wall Street," whom they charged with exploiting the debtor classes by constricting the money supply (tethering it to gold), thus rationing credit and depressing prices. They had proposed wresting control of the monetary system from Gotham's private banks and vesting it in the hands of the US Treasury, which they believed would meet the credit needs of the "producing classes." They also wanted the government to run the railroads, and the telegraph, too. And they sought a graduated income tax to remedy the inequities fostered by the "money power." But the Populists had been beaten as a political force in 1896, largely by "gold bugs" headquartered in New York, and though William Jennings Bryan recaptured the Democratic nomination in 1900 and 1908, and continued to thunder against the money power, few Gotham-based magazines championed his cause.

Nor were most authors or publishers socialists (though some were). Most hadn't given up on capitalism. They did not call for the expropriation or extirpation of giant corporations. Like many of their urban middle-class readers, the investigative journalists believed that Wall Street—though not New York City (their hometown, after all)—was becoming a threat to the Republic. On the other hand, most believed that their personal future (and that of their city) was now willy-nilly linked to corporate industry and finance, which were themselves (as Morgan and Rockefeller argued) the product of an evolutionary development that was

---

2. This didn't count book readers. Charles Edward Russell's series in *Everybody's* on "The Greatest Trust in the World"—the Chicago meatpackers—spurred along a cognate project by Upton Sinclair. A Baltimorean brought to the Bronx in 1888 at the age of 10, Sinclair had supported his education at City College and Columbia by writing dime novels for the downtown publishers Street and Smith. He set out to become a great writer. His first serious fiction made no great impression. But in 1904 the *Appeal to Reason*, a midwestern socialist magazine, staked Sinclair to a seven-week stay among Chicago workers and published, in installments, the raging novel that resulted. New York City publishers refused to bring *The Jungle* out as a book—exposés could be *too* hot—and with the help of his friend Jack London, Sinclair had decided to self-publish. Then Walter Hines Page of Doubleday, Page & Co. decided to gamble on it. *The Jungle*'s instant and spectacular success triggered a new wave of additional exposés—in *Collier's* as well as other journals—and helped win regulatory reforms. This had not been Sinclair's intent, exactly; he was into exposing abysmal working conditions, not the condition of meat. He was also well aware that the big packers had actually pushed for government regulation in the 1890s after Europeans barred American beef from their markets as a menace. The consumer-oriented reforms had won reentry but hadn't done much for labor. As Sinclair lamented: "I aimed at the public's heart and by accident hit its stomach."

superior to the competitive order they were replacing. Many socialists believed this, too; they just thought evolution had one last replacement up its sleeve.

Most writers were "progressives," a fuzzy term for an ambivalent politics. They wanted to defend the common weal against private power but not abort the prosperity the corporate economy seemed capable of generating. They wanted to balance economic growth with social justice but avoid class struggle. They wanted democratic government to curb oligarchic capital but were unclear about who should do the regulating and how much regulation was required.

For much of the first decade of the new century, the man they most trusted to sort out this situation was New Yorker Theodore Roosevelt. As Mr. Dooley drily noted, TR was himself of mixed mind about the giant new corporations: "On th' wan hand I wud stamp them undher fut; on th' other hand, not so fast." Roosevelt accepted the argument that consolidation was apparently inevitable and probably progressive, but he worried about the overweening power wielded by the new conglomerates. Given his limited confidence in their willingness to set public good above private profit, he argued it was the right and duty of government to ensure that they did. Given that the Morgans and Rockefellers believed, to the contrary, that the economy would best be left in their trustworthy hands, the stage was set for a confrontation over national policy that would dominate much of TR's presidency (1901–9). As so many of the leading protagonists were New Yorkers, their shared prior history in the metropolis would shape the contours of the struggle, and color the nature of its resolution.

TEDDY

"I do not," Theodore Roosevelt sniffed in 1900, "see very much of the big-moneyed men in New York simply because very few of them possess the traits which would make them companionable to me or would make me feel that it was worth while dealing with them." The notion of dining with them, he added, "fills me with frank horror." Roosevelt professed himself impervious to the charms of mere money. "I am simply unable to make myself take the attitude of respect toward the very wealthy men which such an enormous multitude of people evidently feel. I am delighted to show any courtesy to Pierpont Morgan or Andrew Carnegie or James J. Hill, but as for regarding any of them as, for instance, I regard . . . Peary, the Arctic explorer, or [James Ford] Rhodes, the historian—why, I could not force myself to do it even if I wanted to, which I don't."

This attitude of aristocratic condescension was bred in the bone. Roosevelt was a seventh-generation New Yorker—Claes Martenszen van Rosenvelt having arrived circa 1649—and very conscious of his pedigreed position. "I stand 19th in the class," he reported from Harvard as an undergraduate. "Only one gentleman stands ahead of me." This gave him the cultural self-confidence and assured social status that allowed him to adopt a dismissive attitude toward Morgan.[3]

Yet while the Roosevelts' money was thoroughly patinaed, the family was very much a part of the Morganesque elite. True, its roots were in commerce—the importation of hardware and then plate glass—but that business had gone under in the depression of the 1870s. By then Grandpa Cornelius had shuttled the family fortune into banking (he had in the 1840s become a founding director of Chemical Bank) and Manhattan real estate (he'd set up

---

3. Roosevelt was also a voracious reader and prodigious writer, having by 1900 penned essays, travel diaries, biographies, and a history of New York City; he was as much a cultivated intellectual as a politician.

a Broadway Improvement Association to manage his extensive and lucrative holdings). By 1868 Cornelius was one of New York's ten bona fide millionaires.

The family business passed to James Alfred Roosevelt and his younger brother Theodore Sr. The former ran the firm; the latter helped out but really threw himself into philanthropy, becoming widely admired for his work with hospitals, museums, and poor children. He transmitted to his son the conviction that inherited wealth brought with it the responsibility of public service. Teddy thus belonged to a small stratum of pedigreed Knickerbockers who felt superior to the merely monied but who had themselves transitioned successfully to contemporary forms of wealth creation. His response to the giant corporations was as complicated as his relationship with their owners and upper-echelon managers, the newer and richer city elite.

TR entered politics as a representative of Gotham's upper class. In 1882 he launched the City Reform Club, a collation of Socially Registered Anglo-Dutch Protestants, devoted to ensuring that "the respectable, educated, refined young men of this city should have more weight in public matters." That same year he entered the state assembly, having run and won from a wealthy neighborhood, with strong backing from such club men and business leaders as Elihu Root, Morris K. Jessup... and Pierpont Morgan. A friend of TR's father, Morgan had worked with Roosevelt Sr. in founding the Museum of Natural History and the Metropolitan Museum of Art.

Roosevelt performed as expected until union organizer Samuel Gompers, pushing a bill to outlaw cigar manufacture in workers' homes, walked him through some tenement sweatshops, which shocked him into supporting the proposed law, despite its being (as Roosevelt said) "in a certain sense a socialistic one." Roosevelt also came to despise the unsavory practices of financiers like Jay Gould, whom he denounced as a member "of that most dangerous of all dangerous classes, the wealthy criminal class." Roosevelt would carry this self-branding—as an upper-class patrician willing to criticize elite wrongdoing and address working-class grievances—from local to national politics.

In the crucial mayoral election of 1886, however, he set aside working-class concerns to run again as monied New York's white knight, vigorously opposed to labor-backed Henry George and Tammany-backed Abram Hewitt. Nominated by Chauncey Depew at a Republican convention presided over by Elihu Root (who became his campaign manager), TR was endorsed by the *New York Times*, which predicted that the "uptown vote" would rally behind him "to effectually squelch communism and socialism." That held true at first. Wall Street businessmen organized a Roosevelt Club. The Stock Exchange, Produce Exchange, and Real Estate Exchange promised their support. The Union League Club backed him. Dry-goods men held Roosevelt rallies. In the end, however, many of his troops, terrified at the possibility of a George victory, defected to the Democratic camp, helping give Hewitt the victory.

Roosevelt became a national figure in the run-up to the Spanish-Cuban-American War, in part by railing at Wall Street resistance to military intervention, which he denounced as the "craven fear and brutal selfishness of the mere money-makers." When Morgan and others came around on the war, however, he quickly repaired frayed links with his classmates. In 1898, now a war hero, he accepted the Republican gubernatorial nomination for New York State and ran a successful campaign, to which Morgan reportedly gave $10,000.

Roosevelt became governor just as the merger movement emerged as an unavoidable political issue. (Bryan had injected it into the presidential campaign.) He spoke about it for the first time in his January 1900 message to the legislature, staking out a position (much of it cribbed from letters sent him by Elihu Root) from which, for all his rhetorical bobbing and weaving, he never fundamentally departed: merged corporations were not in themselves injurious to the public; abuses by corporate managers might well be.

As governor, Roosevelt was no lapdog. He supported a corporate franchise tax that Wall Street opposed, blocked tax loopholes it favored. At the same time, he strengthened his relations with the "responsible" corporate elite, notably by aiding George W. Perkins of New York Life in beating back unwanted insurance legislation. The two men hit it off and strengthened their association, which was easy to do in lower Manhattan. Roosevelt asked Perkins to serve on a civic commission to preserve the Palisades (the cliffs along the Hudson's west bank). Perkins agreed, then solicited a contribution from J. P. Morgan, who gave Perkins not only a donation but a job as the bank's vice president. Perkins, now close to both Roosevelt and Morgan, became an important intermediary between the country's political and economic leadership.

Overall, however, TR made enough enemies as governor—so he wrote Henry Cabot Lodge in April 1900—that some "big corporation men, are especially anxious to have me gotten out of New York somehow." Boss Platt, who had his own problems with the obstreperous Roosevelt, decided to kick him upstairs by making him McKinley's running mate. TR resisted, seeing the vice presidency as a dead end. But Perkins, a power in the Republican Party, both helped win the nomination for Roosevelt and convinced him to accept it. After victory in November the new vice president threw a dinner in Morgan's honor at the Union League Club (he'd been a big campaign contributor), telling Root (with tongue only partly in cheek) that the affair "represents an effort on my part to become a conservative man, in touch with the influential classes, and I think I deserve encouragement."

After McKinley's assassination made him president, TR ran a draft of his first Annual Message to Congress by Perkins, now Morgan's right-hand man, and by Morgan partner Robert Bacon, TR's friend and Harvard classmate, among others. They heartily approved of his defense of "great industrial combinations" as being the result of "natural causes in the business world," and likewise his insistence that the great antagonism aroused by "the creation of great corporate fortunes" was unwarranted, as the captains of industry had "on the whole done great good to our people." Roosevelt did admit in this December 1901 speech that "real and grave evils have arisen, one of the chief of them being overcapitalization," which had "many baleful consequences." Nevertheless, "combination and concentration in business should be, not prohibited, but supervised and within reasonable limits controlled," ideally by the federal government. Before such controls could be established, however, greater "knowledge of the facts" was required, something "to be obtained only through publicity, which is the one sure remedy we can now invoke." Roosevelt was thinking of an official government inquiry, but McClure and his colleagues took his call for publicity as license for their wave of investigative exposés of those "baleful consequences."

If Morgan and others on Wall Street were more or less pleased with Roosevelt's debut speech, they were shocked and appalled two months later when, without consulting Wall Street—neither Morgan nor Root nor Perkins—he ordered the Justice Department to prosecute a Morgan creation, the Northern Securities Company, under the Sherman Antitrust Act. Morgan, furious, met with Roosevelt and Attorney General Philander Knox, complained about the lack of advance warning, and suggested (a tad imperiously), "If we have done anything wrong, send your man to my man and they can fix it up." TR demurred. Morgan asked: "Are you going to attack my other interests, the Steel Trust and others?" Roosevelt replied: "Certainly not— unless we find out that . . . they have done something that we regard as wrong." Afterward, TR marveled at Morgan's "regarding me as a big rival operator"—a "most illuminating illustration of the Wall Street point of view"—and it strengthened his determination to establish the supremacy of a civic-minded president over a money-minded banker.

A détente was hammered out that in effect institutionalized the "your man, my man" approach Morgan had proposed. Roosevelt prevailed on Congress to create a Department of Commerce and Labor, which would house a Bureau of Corporations, an agency to which corporations would send the data the government needed to distinguish between "bad" and "good" companies. Any disputes would be resolved in a gentlemanly way, behind closed doors. Morgan accepted this discreet administrative oversight of the new corporate order in exchange for exemption from antitrust prosecution.

And there were positive benefits. New York City businessmen had understood since Alexander Hamilton's day, and the era of the Erie Canal, that government—"good" government—could be useful to them. Gotham's political and economic leaders had a history of recognizing when their interests overlapped, and this facility was extended from conversations in New York to the dialogue between the nation's political and economic capitals, in this critical first decade of the new corporate order, allowing the patrician Roosevelt and the plutocrat Morgan to fashion a modus operandi. It didn't hurt that, despite their differences in age and style, their positions in Gotham's class firmament were so proximate, or that their paths had crossed so often.

Morgan cooperated with Roosevelt on the capital/labor front, too, most dramatically in 1902 when a mammoth coal strike got under way in the Pennsylvania anthracite fields. With nearly a quarter-million workers out, management stubbornly refusing to bargain, and winter approaching, the price of coal in Frost Belt cities shot up; in Gotham it went from $5–$6 a ton to $20. Elihu Root convinced Roosevelt that Morgan—who indirectly controlled the recalcitrant mine owners—might be helpful. The secretary of war took a midnight sleeper to New York, where he and Morgan conferred aboard the *Corsair*, the latter's yacht, anchored off Manhattan. The banker agreed to apply pressure, the owners agreed to arbitration, and the miners returned to work. "If it had not been for your going into the matter," Roosevelt said in thanking Morgan, "I do not see how the strike could have been settled at this time."

Where Morgan opted to show respect, even bend the knee, the more myopic Rockefeller and his minions treated the federal government as a meddlesome and secondary power. It wasn't that JDR was opposed to all regulation. He and other Standard Oil leaders urged a national incorporation law as preferable to dealing with dozens of pesky states; in this they were as one with Morgan and Perkins. But prying by the Bureau of Corporations, which Morgan was prepared to accept, Rockefeller deemed intolerable. So JDR hadn't intervened when Standard Oil's de facto head, the aggressive John D. Archbold, set out to block the bureau's enabling legislation by prodding Rockefeller Jr. into sending telegrams to six senators urging its defeat ("It must be stopped"). Roosevelt found out and in February 1903 trumpeted (inaccurately) to reporters that JDR *Sr.* had personally intervened to ward off government oversight. Coupled with the devastating impact of Tarbell's Standard Oil series, then running in *McClure's*, the public relations blunder allowed Roosevelt to brand Rockefeller's company as the archetypal "bad" corporation.

As the 1904 election approached, many Wall Street Republicans grumbled about Roosevelt and sought to deny him the nomination. Elihu Root derailed their efforts with a passionate address in February to the Union League Club. "I am told," he told the assembled worthies, "that he is not popular in the City of New York; that he, who was born and grew to manhood among us, old member of this club . . . that he is not safe. . . . But I say to you that he has been, during these years since President McKinley's death, the greatest conservative force for the protection of property and our institutions in the city of Washington." By the time Root finished recounting how TR had "dared to say, I will veto an unfair measure against capital," hosannas rose from the floor, along with shouts of "Three cheers for President Roosevelt." ("It has become almost flat for me to express to you my realization of all you have done for me," the President wrote Root.)

And indeed, when TR dispatched his campaign's avuncular finance chair, Cornelius Bliss, up to Gotham, the old New York merchant and money man was welcomed with open wallets, especially as it had become clear the president would be reelected by a massive majority. Roosevelt's opponent—another New Yorker, Alton B. Parker, a Democrat in the mold of Grover Cleveland—had his backers on Wall Street, notably August Belmont Jr. and Thomas Fortune Ryan, but they were outnumbered by the Republican rich. Morgan, Frick, Gould, Harriman, Stillman, Depew, Perkins (who in addition to issuing a personal check gave one from New York Life, which would get him in trouble the following year), and John D. Archbold of Standard Oil (whose check for over $100,000 TR later ordered returned to sender, though only after it had already been spent)—this roster, together with other millionaires and corporations, provided Roosevelt over $2 million.

After his electoral triumph TR eased off on comments critical of capital, even tried to stanch the flood of investigative reporting he'd helped unleash. In October 1905 he wrote Sam McClure urging him to throttle back his attacks on business. Then (in March 1906) came the first piece in David Graham Phillips's "Treason of the Senate" series for Hearst's *Cosmopolitan*. (Roosevelt loathed Hearst—"the most potent single influence for evil we have in our life"—and Hearst loathed him back.) And while TR knew full well that senators, as creatures of state legislatures, were beholden to party machines or corporate contributors— the burden of Phillips's argument—he also knew that freedom from electoral challenge made them relatively invulnerable, and he needed their votes to pass his programs. So days after Phillips's attack on New York senators Platt and Depew (the latter one of Roosevelt's earliest supporters), the president gave a speech at Washington's Gridiron Club in which he spoke of the "man with the muck-rake" (borrowing the phrase from Bunyan's *Pilgrim's Progress*) who "in newspapers and magazines makes slanderous and mendacious attacks upon men in public life." He followed this in April with a public speech in which, while admitting that some who exposed wicked politicians or businessmen performed an "indispensable" public service, he nevertheless railed against unnamed "wild preachers of unrest and discontent, the wild agitators against the existing order," whom he called "the most dangerous opponents of real reform." The journalists thus attacked as "muck-rakers" adopted the term of opprobrium as a badge of honor, as colonial American rebels had done with "Yankee Doodle," but the assault had a chilling effect.

Nevertheless, later that year Roosevelt resumed his assault on Rockefeller and Standard Oil. The Bureau of Corporations had reported that the corporation had continued to collude with the railroads in illegal rebating practices. In private, Roosevelt denounced Standard Oil directors as "the biggest criminals in the country." In public, in November 1906, his Justice Department filed suit under the Sherman Antitrust Act charging the company with having illegally monopolized the oil industry and calling for its dissolution. Archbold moaned, "Darkest Abyssinia never saw anything like the course of treatment we received at the hands of the administration following Mr. Roosevelt's election in 1904." An enraged Henry C. Frick told *New York Evening Post* publisher Oswald Garrison Villard (though not for publication) that TR had promised to lay off big business in exchange for campaign contributions ("He got down on his knees before us"), only to renege after winning ("We bought the son of a bitch and then he did not stay bought"). *Pace* the furious Frick, it's highly unlikely that Roosevelt offered specific quids for their cash quo. Certainly not where Rockefeller's Standard Oil was concerned, as proving it was "bad" was essential if other (virtually *all* other) companies, like Morgan's US Steel, were to be adjudged "good"—the simple but effective rhetorical ground on which TR pitched his argumentative tent. Only if firms that "sinned against the light" received condign punishment could virtuous corporations receive a government seal of approval. Hence Roosevelt's reported response—"That's bully!"— when in August 1907 Judge Kenesaw Mountain Landis not only fined Standard Oil a staggering $29 million but said the company was no better than a common thief.

But in the summer of 1907 Roosevelt, Rockefeller, and Morgan—and the whole cast of characters in New York and Washington—had a much bigger problem on their collective plate, for the entire economy of the United States seemed to be coming unhinged.

PANIC OF 1907

The great boom had been roaring along for nearly a decade, interrupted only occasionally by brief market dips. Yet there had been signs and portents, on a global scale, that the financial engine was sputtering—in part for lack of fuel. The international capitalist economy, by design, had been tethered to gold, and the supply of precious metal had not been keeping up with demand. So much capital had been devoured by the merger movement, and by military adventures (the Boer and Russo-Japanese Wars), and rescue missions (the San Francisco earthquake), that by 1906 a worldwide capital shortage had developed, reflected in rising interest rates and confidence rattling financial tremors: the Egyptian stock exchange crashed, Japanese banks failed, and the Bank of England, feeling squeezed, repatriated gold, further depleting US reserves.

In March 1907 a sudden squall hit the New York Stock Exchange. Panicky selling drove prices down, wiping out $2 billion in value. Frick, Schiff, Harriman, and William Rockefeller huddled in secret and debated pooling a $25 million emergency fund. Morgan, in London, thought this premature, and indeed the market soon rallied, thanks to swift action by Treasury Secretary George B. Cortelyou. The scion of another ancient Gotham clan—its founding ancestor arrived in New Netherland in 1652, shortly after the ur-Roosevelt stepped ashore— Cortelyou had served TR as the first secretary of commerce and labor (1903–4) and as postmaster general (1905–7), then been handed the Treasury portfolio, a scant ten days before the market tanked. Cortelyou's deposit of $12 million of US gold in New York banks helped arrest the slide and won him instant respect on Wall Street.

Nevertheless, matters resumed their downward trend over the summer. Gold reserves dropped 10 percent between May and August. The stock market slid another 8.1 percent— making a decline of 24.4 percent for the year's first three quarters. And August brought the Judge Landis decision, after which Standard Oil shares slumped from 500 to 421, tugging the market down with them. Many on the Street shared Rockefeller Sr.'s fear (as expressed to his son) that such "persecutions against business interests" presaged "very disastrous results to our commercial fabric." But in response to calls on TR to lighten up on big capital, the president suggested darkly (in an August 20 speech) that perhaps the crisis was being confected to achieve precisely that end, that perhaps "certain malefactors of great wealth" had combined "to bring about as much financial stress as possible, in order to discredit the policy of the Government and thereby secure a reversal of that policy, so that they may enjoy unmolested the fruits of their own evil-doing."

Apart from anxiety about illiquidity and antitrust action, the Street was haunted by an uneasy sense that the speculative binge of the previous two years had weakened the foundation of the New York capital markets. An unhealthy feedback loop seemed to be at work. The merger promoters' lavish stock handouts manufactured instant millionaires, who rushed to deploy their winnings in the Wall Street casino. They were abetted by Gotham's financial institutions, notably the trust companies, whose call loans allowed wheeler-dealers to buy, on margin, the bloated securities promoters were flogging, loans increasingly secured only by the waterlogged stocks themselves. For nearly a decade, the rising tide of easy money and low interest rates had lifted even these leaky boats. Now money was harder to come by, and cost more to borrow.

Also, autumn was arriving. Fall was always a tight time, as rural banks drew down from New York central reserve banks to meet the demands of harvesting and marketing crops; this diminution of funds led the New York banks to curtail loans to brokers, driving up the cost of call money and damping down the stock market. Jacob Schiff had warned about the rigidities of this antiquated system just the previous year when he'd told the New York Chamber of Commerce in January 1906 that if "the currency conditions of this country are not changed materially . . . you will have such a panic in this country as will make all previous panics look like child's play."

Still, stock prices held until mid-October, when a particularly audacious speculator, the grandly named Frederick Augustus Heinze, administered a mega-voltage shock to the financial system. The Brooklyn-born Heinze, after graduating from Columbia's School of Mines, raised a capital stake in Manhattan, moved west to Butte in 1889, and made a fortune smelting ore dug up by Montana's small producers, then became a mine owner himself. In 1899, when these independents were targeted for takeover by the Amalgamated Copper Company (the would-be monopoly promoted by "Hell Hound" Rogers and William Rockefeller), Heinze led a resistance movement, tying the Standard Oil crowd up in court for years and finally forcing a furious Rogers to buy him out.

In the spring of 1906 he returned to New York from the Montana copper fields, 12 million Amalgamated dollars in his pocket, determined to make a huge splash by cornering the copper market—in stocks, not metal. Heinze teamed up with his broker brother Otto, and the notorious speculator Charles W. Morse. (A few years back he'd cornered New York City's ice supply, winning the sobriquet of "Ice King.") Together they won control of a string of banks and trust companies whose depositors' money they would use for the maneuver. Finally, on October 16, 1907, they sprang their trap, only to discover to their horror they had either miscalculated the amount of copper securities in circulation, or been blindsided by someone dumping a big block of stock on the market (perhaps, it was whispered on the Street, the vengeful Hell Hound Rogers).

This left their patched-together network of institutional backers short on cash and vulnerable to runs. Word spread that the Mercantile National Bank was in trouble. Depositors rushed to withdraw their savings. The firm quickly closed its doors and turned for help to its fellow banks in the Clearing House. That body agreed to a rescue, on condition that Heinze and Morse be dumped—indeed, they were forced out of the stock business altogether—after which support was announced and the run halted.

A very different fate awaited the Knickerbocker Trust Company, the city's third-largest. Rumors spread that its president, Charles T. Barney, a leading figure in Gotham's financial

Advertisement, Knickerbocker Trust Company. *Trow's General Directory of the Boroughs of Manhattan and Bronx, City of New York*, vol. 120 (July 1, 1907).

and social circles, had secretly supported the copper corner scheme. (Barney had underwritten prior Morse speculations.) Its depositors panicked and rushed to the great bronze doors on Fifth Avenue. Barney rushed to the Clearing House. But the Knickerbocker, being a trust, not a bank, was not a member; it cleared only by courtesy of the National Bank of Commerce, effectively controlled by J. P. Morgan.

Morgan too had been busy. All too aware that if the panic got out of hand, it could bring down the trusts, the banks, the Stock Exchange, and the US economy, he had set up a war room in his library at 36th and Madison and organized two committees of financiers. One, the high command, consisted of himself, James Stillman of National City Bank, and George Baker of First National. The other, drawn from the junior officer corps, included Perkins (from Morgan's shop), Davison (from Baker's), and Benjamin Strong (the secretary of Bankers Trust); this group would survey the condition of all threatened trusts and decide which merited saving. In truth few of these bankers thought *any* trusts were worth saving, having run risky businesses (to say nothing of having lured away the banks' customers). "We hadn't any use for their management," Perkins recalled, "and knew that they ought to be closed, but we fought to keep them open in order not to have runs on other concerns." When Barney presented his appeal, the junior team crash-surveyed the Knickerbocker's books. The trust was, they said, gutted of ready cash but not insolvent, hence salvageable. Nevertheless,

"Opening Knickerbocker Trust," 1908. (Library of Congress Prints and Photographs Division, George Grantham Bain Collection)

on Monday, October 21, the National Bank of Commerce announced it would no longer clear for the Knickerbocker. Morgan had excommunicated the trust, and now it was turned over to the secular arm—the company's 17,000 depositors, who the next day stormed the building to get their money out. After doling out cash to shopkeepers, mechanics, clerks, frock-coated men, silk-dressed ladies, and messengers from other banks bearing large checks—$8 million was disbursed in two hours—the Knickerbocker suspended payments. For all the Corinthian solidity of Stanford White's creation, it turned out that you couldn't tell a bank by its columns.[4]

The decision to pull the plug on the Knickerbocker may have slaked Morgan's anti-trust-company ire, but it didn't stabilize the situation; quite the opposite. Now the Trust Company of America (TCA), at Broadway and Liberty, took its place on the hot seat. Morgan dispatched Benjamin Strong to appraise TCA's situation, the young banker reported it was savable, and this time the high command began dispatching cash to the stricken trust. Most of the money came from National City Bank vaults, which received an infusion of $10 million from John D. Rockefeller Sr., who announced to the press that, if necessary, he would give half of all the securities he possessed ("and I have cords of them, gentlemen, cords of them") to maintain America's credit. "They always come to Uncle John when there is trouble," Rockefeller purred.

"They" also turned to the federal government, which had even deeper pockets. On the day the Knickerbocker went down, Secretary Cortelyou caught a train to Manhattan and met that evening at a Madison Avenue hotel with Morgan, Stillman, Baker, Perkins, and A. Barton Hepburn, president of the Chase National Bank. Cortelyou pledged to deposit $25 million of Treasury funds in national banks (not a penny would go directly to trusts), leaving it, in effect, up to Morgan as to how to deploy the money.

Nevertheless, by Thursday, October 24, the fourth straight day of the panic, the trouble washed over the Exchange. As banks around the United States began to withdraw their reserves from Gotham, and as trust companies called in outstanding loans to get cash back into their vaults, the interest rates on call money, already at 70 percent, spurted to 125 percent, more or less choking off the supply of funds to NYSE brokers, making it impossible to conduct business. Stock prices plummeted. Hysteria gripped the Exchange. (The street-level exits came in handy.) Its president told Morgan he would have to shut it down. Morgan told him to sit tight, then summoned the city's bankers and told them that unless they raised $25 million in the next ten minutes, at least fifty brokerages would fail. The money was promptly forthcoming ($8 million from Stillman, $4 million from Baker, $2.5 million from the National Bank of Commerce, the rest from eleven other commercial banks), and loaned out across the street (at rates ranging to 60 percent). The Exchange got through the day. But the next day was just as bad: Friday brought waves of selling, margin calls, collapsing prices, call loans at 150 percent, depositors besieging trusts (whose tellers stalled on payouts), and another (less successful) round of hat-passing.

Over the weekend another potential domino turned up: the city of New York itself. On Sunday, Mayor George McClellan told the high command that New York needed $30 million to meet payroll and maturing obligations (chiefly contracts for municipal improvements). Ordinarily this wouldn't have been a problem, but with money scarce and rates astronomical

---

4. On being turned away from the Clearing House, Barney had resigned as president, symbolically falling on his sword in hopes of removing the stigma of his association with Morse. It made no difference. Three weeks later he killed himself for real, committing suicide in his town house at Park Avenue and 38th Street, a few blocks from his neighbor Pierpont Morgan.

"Wall Street during the Money Panic," 1907. (Fotosearch/Getty Images)

it had become impossible to borrow. Without help, Gotham would be bankrupt within a week. Quickly, as if dashing off a sidebar to the main story, Morgan worked out a solution. The Clearing House would issue certificates—honored by member banks—that would be swapped for $30 million worth of 6 percent municipal revenue bonds. It was done the next day. The mayor offered thanks "for the great public spirit you have shown."

Now the Big Three set out to flood the system with money. First, as in the case of New York, they arranged for the Clearing House to issue $100 million of certificates, in effect ersatz currency. They also arranged to import gold from Europe, particularly from banks that saw an opportunity to buy US securities on the cheap. On November 8 the first shipment ($12.4 million) arrived from Liverpool aboard the *Lusitania*, after a record-breaking five-day dash across the Atlantic. All told, more than $50 million arrived in November, and another $40 million debarked in December. The biggest contributor was the federal government. Secretary Cortelyou increased his commitment of Treasury funds to $69 million, virtually exhausting the government's own supply of gold, then got presidential permission to issue $150 million of government and Panama gold bonds (for financing canal construction), and to authorize banks that bought the bonds to use them as reserves on which to issue currency notes. The injection of all this cash ended the panic in November 1907, arresting the fall in the value of all listed US stocks at the point when they had declined 37 percent.[5]

---

5. Friday, November 1, brought a last coda, the threatened failure of one of the city's largest brokerage houses, Moore and Schley, which owed roughly $35 million to various banks and trusts, borrowings secured by shares of Tennessee Coal, Iron & Railroad Company (TCI), an independent steel producer headquartered in Birmingham, Alabama. But the value of those shares had fallen sharply, and cashing them in would leave the brokerage short. Morgan feared the firm's failure would ricochet through Wall Street and likely wreck the still-fragile recovery. In a last-minute maneuver, Morgan got US Steel to exchange its strong bonds for the weak TCI stock, which solved the problem. Roosevelt had signed off on the deal (the alternative having been presented to him as immediate catastrophe). Nevertheless, critics denounced what they saw as a profitable gambit by the giant steel company to strengthen its monopoly position in the market.

THE BANKS HAD BEEN SAVED. But not the people.

The panic brought a severe nationwide contraction in its wake, the kind of downturn that wasn't supposed to happen anymore. Orders were canceled, crop movements retarded; industrial production dropped; workers got laid off. Nationally, unemployment bounded from 2.8 percent to 8 percent. News about joblessness traveled overseas fast, and immigration dropped from 1,200,000 in 1907 to roughly 750,000 in 1909. The sober *Commercial and Financial Chronicle* declared that "the industrial paralysis and prostration was the very worst ever experienced in the country's history."[6]

It was certainly grim in Gotham during the bitter winter of 1907–8. The city was awash in unemployed men and women. In January 1908 the *New York Times* estimated that a quarter-million were vainly seeking work. The garment and building trades were battered. The ranks of piano makers, machinists, iron molders, jewelers, lithographers, cigar makers, artificial-flower and paper-box makers—were diminished, it was thought, by a third to a half. Unskilled workers probably fared worse. And there was an influx of unemployed from out of state, notably New England mill and factory towns.

People survived. They shoehorned into tenement spaces (fifteen to eighteen occupied an apartment of three small rooms) or lodging houses, the back rooms of saloons, river barges, parked carts, and the streets. Pawnbrokers did a brisk business. So did army and navy recruiting stations, the main one at 25 Third Avenue (at Astor Place) and the many others scattered around town. But the suffering could be overwhelming. Beckie Blass, 28, was the wife of a Williamsburg tailor who'd been unemployed for over six months. The family with its two children often went for days without food. Mrs. Blass, driven mad by watching her children starve, tried to throw herself in front of a car, was dragged back by a crowd, then tried to kill her 9-month-old baby by dashing its head against the sidewalk. Police intervened, and, once subdued, she was taken off to Kings County Hospital.

Organized working people called for remedial measures. In March 1908 a socialist-led Unemployed Conference of New York, composed of 130 labor organizations, called for a massive demonstration in Union Square to urge city, state, and federal officials to respond to "the industrial depression now existing, which is causing want and suffering to hundreds of thousands of working people in this city and to millions throughout the country." As during previous breakdowns of the private economy—in 1819, 1837, 1857, 1873, 1893—the organized unemployed sought a program of "useful public works upon a large scale," a cyclically recurring demand in Gotham. They also wanted an eight-hour day, which would allow a wider distribution of available employment, and an "exhaustive legislative investigation" into the causes of the crisis. Many thousands showed up on March 28 and were peaceably awaiting the first speakers when mounted police charged the crowd, clubbing participants out of the square—echoing previous depression-time crackdowns, notably the 1874 police assault in Tompkins Square Park. When one demonstrator demanded that Inspector Max Schmittberger respect their right to free speech, the veteran officer waved his baton and replied, "The club is mightier than the Constitution."

---

6. The New York–generated panic had repercussions abroad. For the first time since 1857 Gotham had birthed a global crisis, which spread quickly to, among others, Chile, Denmark, France, Italy, Japan, Mexico, and Sweden. The impact in Mexico had severe political repercussions. US investment—so central to the Díaz regime—all but ceased at the end of 1907. Mexico's own markets collapsed, the credit system seized up, and food prices rose beyond the reach of the poor—whose ranks swelled as penniless Mexican laborers returned home after losing their jobs in the States. The intensified dissatisfaction with the Díaz dictatorship that resulted played a part in helping turn the minor Madero insurrection of 1910 into a full-fledged revolution.

"A New Plan: Scouting for Recruits in City Hall Park, New York." *Harper's Weekly*, March 21, 1908.

Some elite voices joined the public works chorus. Jacob Schiff urged Mayor McClellan to back such projects—"The parks, the streets, the speedways, and various other communal properties need work to be done upon them"—and argued that putting several hundred thousand dollars into circulation "would prevent a great amount of suffering and tend to maintain the self-respect of thousands of our people." But the predominant stance was the one outlined by the *New York Times*, which insisted that public works would *undermine* the self-respect of workingmen and should be used only as a device for "sifting the lazy from the others among the professed unemployed. Actual hard work is an excellent test of character, and . . . should be applied wherever charity is sought by able-bodied persons."

The charity societies agreed. Private agencies like the New York Association for Improving the Condition of the Poor and the Charity Organization Society increased their caseload but continued to stress that aiding able-bodied men would encourage dependency. They opposed any who established breadlines. More charitably inclined organizations found it hard to raise sufficient funds. At one point the United Hebrew Charities had to close its doors for lack of money. An emergency appeal brought in only enough to reopen on a bare-boned basis.[7]

In the end no significant public works program was set up, partly due to opposition from elites, and partly because not long after the Union Square affair, the crisis eased.

THE RECESSION OF 1907–8, THOUGH SHARP, WAS SHORT. Thanks largely to vigorous private and public interventions, the 1907 financial panic did not become a curtain raiser on the

---

7. Schiff gave $20,000 to establish a Self Respect Fund that gave loans only to families that had never before sought assistance. He also got behind a United Hebrew Charities plan to establish a privately financed National Employment Exchange "conducted on strictly business principles." Its first office opened in 1909 at Battery Park, the start-up costs underwritten by Schiff, Morgan, J. D. Rockefeller, Paul Warburg, Baker, Harriman, and Gary, among others, but barely dented the problem.

"Parade of Unemployed Men, Carrying Signs, New York," 1909. (Library of Congress Prints and Photographs Division, George Grantham Bain Collection)

order of those of 1837, 1873, and 1893, each of which ushered in a lengthy period of unrelieved depression. The post-panic period of 1908–14 was rather one of constant flux. After the hard winter of 1907–8, a recovery began in June 1908. The city (and country) enjoyed steady growth over the next eighteen months, though the stock market and industrial production didn't reach pre-panic levels until late 1909, and they didn't stay that high for long. The recovery peaked in January 1910, and the economy roller-coastered down again through 1910 and 1911, bottoming out in January 1912. The next round of prosperity was shorter, topping out a year later in January 1913, after which the economy sagged through 1913 and 1914, touching bottom in December of the latter year. During that seven-year stretch, twice as much time was spent in recession than in prosperity.

The 1907 panic proved a pivot point on another score. The near-meltdown galvanized the city's financial elite into seeking the best way to avoid another one, being all too aware that a recurrence might prove fatal to their economic order. Their initiatives advanced two different strategies: one called for *tightening* the grip of Wall Street on the national economy; the other proposed bringing the federal government into the picture by establishing a national bank (albeit one under Wall Street's control).

THE SENIOR COMMANDERS WHO HAD DIRECTED the rescue effort emerged from the crisis convinced that the remedy lay in further consolidating the financial industry itself, and keeping it in their hands. Morgan, Stillman, and Baker believed it was their right and responsibility to oversee the banking system and regulate the nation's money supply. Calling themselves "the Trio," they informally set up shop as, in effect, a privately run central bank. At one point they considered a formal integration—a super-merger—but decided against it, concerned (correctly) about the likely negative public reaction. Former rivalries, notably that between the Morgan and Rockefeller blocs, diminished significantly, partly thanks to their leaders having worked together on combating the panic. (JDR, commenting on the way he and JPM had shored up scores of financial institutions, asked drily, "Now, wasn't that a pretty nice thing for two such very, very bad men to do?") In the next few years, the Trio arranged a series of mergers that strengthened their control over the trust sector by making Guaranty Trust and Bankers Trust—which they effectively dominated—the first and second largest in the nation. Morgan and his associates also gained sway over all three of the big insurance companies, and they continued their program of corporatizing the industrial economy: between 1908 and 1912 the Trio underwrote, on their own or with others, $1.3 billion worth of mergers.

This gambit proved unsustainable, not least because the three old men were running out of steam. James Stillman, tuckered out from combating the panic, moved to Paris in 1908, leaving Frank Vanderlip (vice president since 1901) in de facto control, then making him president the following year. Stillman retained overriding authority, partly by continuing as chairman of the board, more surely through his stock ownership. But Vanderlip now became a major spokesman for National City Bank, for the Rockefeller interests, and for the banking community as a whole.

George Baker similarly ceded the presidency to longtime First National executive Francis L. Hine but kept a hand on the tiller through his position as board chair.

Baker also obliged his old friend Pierpont Morgan by agreeing to the latter's request that Harry Davison be released from First National service to work at J. P. Morgan & Co. Morgan had been impressed by Davison's work during the panic, and he knew the younger man was a true believer in his gospel of industrial consolidation. So at the end of 1908 Davison moved two blocks east from Broadway to Broad, and Morgan (now 71) set about grooming him to be chief operating executive. (JPM Junior was still deemed not to measure up, but Senior was enough of a dynast to want his son to serve as constitutional monarch, with a regent to run the bank.)

Two years later George Perkins left the firm, seeing that the mantle of Morgan would not be settling on his shoulders. Perkins had been too independent, had made too many decisions without consulting Senior, been contemptuous of Junior, and the Hughes insurance investigation had tarnished his image and that of the bank. Perkins was replaced by another Baker boy, Thomas W. Lamont, a Harvard graduate who had worked as a reporter for the *New York Tribune* and was as aware of the importance of public relations as Perkins had been. Lamont had been discovered by Davison, who recruited him to help build up Bankers Trust, then brought him to First National as vice president. Having done yeoman work during the panic, Lamont was gathered into the House of Morgan in 1910. Benjamin Strong, another Davison discovery, had also been given a position at Bankers Trust (in 1904). Strong would rise to its presidency, an ascension boosted by marrying 18-year-old Katherine Converse, the daughter of Edmund C. Converse, Bankers Trust's founding president and a close Morgan associate.

This new generation of bankers, and others of their cohort like Paul Warburg of Kuhn, Loeb, did not believe that the Trio's answer to the problems of the financial system—total consolidation in the Gotham elite's hands—was viable, not least given the age of its principals. As junior officers and circumspect heirs-apparent they didn't point this out publicly, but the conventional wisdom was voiced by Nelson Aldrich, the powerful US senator, chairman of the Senate Finance Committee, and father-in-law of John D. Rockefeller Jr.: "Something has got to be done. We may not always have Pierpont Morgan with us to meet a banking crisis."

Also, it was clear to Vanderlip, Davison, Warburg, and Strong et al. that for all Morgan's heroic role, it had taken the resources of the United States Treasury to stave off collapse.

They believed it was time to bring in the national government, by creating a bank that could centralize the nation's reserves at the federal level, and serve as a reliable lender of last resort, expanding the money supply as needed. They preferred that such an institution be formally (or at least actually) run by the New York banking community, even if politics and public relations might dictate basing it in Washington. And they began having quiet conversations about what such an alternative federal reserve system might look like.

THE PANIC OF 1907 PROVED PIVOTAL AS WELL for Teddy Roosevelt. He had long insisted that the new corporate order was acceptable, even progressive, if the barrel could be rid of a few bad apples and a federal regulatory regime established. This conviction grew harder to sustain in the panic's sour aftermath. True, his administration had worked closely with Morgan, and he'd been nudged into expressing kind words about "those influential and splendid businessmen . . . who have acted with such wisdom and public spirit." But it soon became apparent that the current of opinion on Wall Street, which blamed the president for the crisis, was broader than he'd supposed.

On the evening of November 21, 1907, with the embers of the initial panic still aglow, the New York Chamber of Commerce held its annual banquet at the Waldorf-Astoria. As customary, the master of ceremonies proposed a toast to the president's health. All stood. All remained silent. Finally, one man in a far corner shouted "Hip Hip," but not one of the thousand-plus guests followed through with "Hurrah"—a snub that contrasted sharply with the cheers and lusty applause that greeted a speaker who blamed the crisis on "irresponsible government" and hailed the "strong, patriotic, resourceful bankers and financiers of this great city, led by the uncrowned king of them all, J. P. Morgan," for having spared the country a catastrophe. All this was page-one headline news the next day.

The day after that, TR penned a private response in a letter to writer Hamlin Garland. "As for the New York financiers, their hangers-on, the innocent men whom they have deceived, or who follow them and the newspapers that they own or inspire," wrote Roosevelt, "why, I have to expect that these people will attack me." The ill will was mutual, he made clear, reiterating an old theme: "I neither respect nor admire the huge monied men to whom money is the be-all and end-all of existence; to whom the acquisition of untold millions is the supreme goal of life, and who are too often utterly indifferent as to how these millions are obtained." Several days later, in another letter, he employed language reminiscent of the Populists: "The business community of New York (by which I mean the New York plutocracy and those who are in the pay of or are led by the plutocracy) is a rather preposterous body," he argued, as they "will themselves tell you how much they suffer from the scoundrelism [of the Harrimans and the Rockefellers] . . . but the minute that any action is taken to get rid of the rascality, they fall into a perfect panic and say that business conditions must not be jeopardized."

Publicly, the president was almost as pugnacious. In his Annual Message to Congress (December 3, 1907), he lobbed the blame back to his critics, and pointed out that when wealthy men "indulge in reckless speculation—especially if it is accompanied by dishonesty—they jeopardize not only their own future but the future of all their innocent fellow-citizens, for they expose the whole business community to panic and distress." It was essential to find a way "to prevent the spasms of high money and speculation which now obtain in the New York market."

Over the next year, pot and kettle engaged in mutual recrimination. In particular TR's critics kept up a drumfire of opposition to his proposed regulations—he had suggested federal oversight of the Stock Exchange and endorsed a ban on corporate funding of campaigns. Roosevelt fixed more attention on the link between the bad apples and the others in the barrel. In his last Annual Message (December 8, 1908) he told Congress: "Too often we see the business community in a spirit of unhealthy class consciousness deplore the effort to hold to account under the law the wealthy men who in their management of great corporations, whether railroads, street railways, or other industrial enterprises, have behaved in a way that revolts the conscience of the plain, decent people."

On January 31, 1909—his presidency at the point of expiration—Roosevelt dashed off a Special Message to Congress complaining of "attacks by these great corporations" and "certain wealthy men" who "have banded together to work for a reaction." They had placed in newspapers across the country "huge advertisements attacking with envenomed bitterness the Administration's policy of warring against successful dishonesty," and had underwritten a flood of books, pamphlets, and speeches on the same theme. TR denounced these writers and speakers, in prose that the most incendiary of muckrakers might have envied, as "the representatives of predatory wealth—of the wealth accumulated on a giant scale by all forms of iniquity, ranging from the oppression of wageworkers to unfair and unwholesome methods of crushing out competition, and to defrauding the public by stock jobbing and the manipulation of securities." These predators were "the most dangerous members of the criminal class—the criminals of great wealth." It was essential that the federal government control such "law-defying wealth; in the first place to prevent its doing dire evil to the Republic, and in the next place to avoid the vindictive and dreadful radicalism which, if left uncontrolled, it is certain in the end to arouse."

Wall Street's response to the Special Message included the surmise that Roosevelt had simply lost his mind. The *New York Times* and *New York Evening Mail* both spoke of the president's tendency toward "delusion," and the *New York Sun* said that his "portentous diatribe" should be studied by psychologists. One New York banker bundled this theory with two others, claiming that "the President is crazy, and furthermore…[was] indulging immoderately in drink and is an opium fiend." As Henry Adams wrote a friend, "The reaction against Roosevelt, socially, is violent."

On this note TR left office. He'd refused to run again, and instead thrown William Howard Taft's hat in the ring to be his anointed successor. (Earlier, believing Elihu Root the most qualified, he had urged him to consider running. But Root had not been interested, and by now it was not certain they would continue to see eye to eye, Root being firmly fixed in the Republican mainstream, and Roosevelt eddying toward its left bank.) Taft won, and TR decamped to Africa on a yearlong safari. Pierpont Morgan was reputed, perhaps apocryphally, to have offered a toast on his departure, saying: "America expects that every lion will do its duty."

ROOSEVELT WASN'T THE ONLY WALL STREET CRITIC IN TOWN. In the aftermath of the panic there had been a swelling chorus of criticism—not only about Wall Street's role in creating the crisis, but about Morgan's success in quelling it. Yes, it appeared that he and his confederates had rescued the economy and the country from near certain collapse. But if true, was it appropriate, in a republic, for one man or one class to have such power? Increasingly, political leaders stepped forward to say no.

Some of these critics were moderate in tone. In 1908 New York's Governor Charles Evans Hughes appointed a Committee on Speculation in Securities and Commodities, and charged it with addressing one of the chief presumed causes of the breakdown. But in the end, while admitting that what some speculators engaged in was "virtually gambling," the group suggested that speculators also provided useful services, like helping stabilize prices, and that it was hard (as it had been since Hamilton's day) to separate the good kind of speculation from the bad. The New York committee, moreover, was hobbled by fears that imposing stricter regulations might cause the Exchange to flee to more accommodating states—libertine New Jersey lay just across the river. In the end, Hughes's committee's report (1909) called on the NYSE to regulate its own house, which it notoriously hadn't, and likely wouldn't: the only violation that could really get a member expelled was cutting his commission, thus undercutting his colleagues.

Stronger and louder voices were blowing in from the western prairies. Some belonged to Democrats. Bryan's wing had once again wrested control of the party from the Gotham-based Grover Cleveland crowd, and Bryan himself was once again its presidential candidate in 1908. Some of the most ferocious criticisms came from an insurgent wing of the Republican Party. They called themselves Progressive Republicans, and their standard-bearer was Wisconsonite Robert La Follette. In the depressed 1890s the state's dissidents had decried the sway of big business and called for the direct election of senators, for primaries that could end-run party machines, for progressive taxation, and for the enlistment of University of Wisconsin experts to help in drafting well-researched and progressive legislation. La Follette was elected governor in 1901, then sent to the Senate in 1905, where he quickly became the leader of a small group of senatorial progressives.

In March 1908 La Follette had a major dustup with Nelson Aldrich, leader of the conservative Republican senators (and close ally of Wall Street), when Aldrich proposed legislation that would, in any future crisis, authorize issuance of emergency currency. La Follette, in a stinging critique, denounced this as an attempt to routinize big-bank bailouts. During the recent panic "the last resort of the frenzied speculator" had been the national treasury, and if Aldrich had his way, the future would no doubt witness "periodic raids on the public funds." La Follette launched a futile filibuster, in which he charged (borrowing the phraseology of a correspondent) that "the men who are urging this new bill might as well urge a currency issued by Standard Oil, redeemed by the steel trust, secured by the New York Stock Exchange and to bear on its face the picture of John D. Rockefeller." Congress brushed him aside and passed the Aldrich-Vreeland Act (1908), which allowed national banks to issue emergency notes secured by negotiable corporate securities and state and municipal bonds.

La Follette expanded his critique, arguing that the source of the nation's economic woes wasn't a matter of "bad" trusts or banks, or this or that plutocrat, but rather the entire edifice of the nation's financial arrangements, and the entire class of those who commanded it, people who overwhelmingly lived in New York City. Shifting to the kind of argument Gotham's elite had thought safely interred after the Populist Party's 1896 defeat, La Follette focused not only on industrial corporations but on financial ones as well.

In 1908, on the Senate floor, La Follette denounced "a comparatively small clique which has succeeded in dominating the finances of the country." He came prepared with a list of a hundred men who "control[led] the industrial, financial and commercial life of the American people," those who controlled the New York banks that had centralized economic power in Gotham. "In the grasp of these 100 men is the destiny of the Republic." The roster included Astor, Baker, Belmont, Brady, Cravath, Depew, Dodge, Duke, Frick, Gary, Gould, Guggenheim, Harriman, Havemeyer, Mackay, Morgan, Morton, Perkins, Rockefeller, Rogers, Ryan, Schiff, Schwab, Speyer, Stillman, Vanderbilt, and Whitney. He called them the "Money Trust," a term plucked from the Populist and Bryanite lexicon. And he suggested that while the Hundred had once had their internal divisions—chiefly between the Morgan and Rockefeller blocs—their interests had now become so intertwined that soon they would "be knit together and a great financial monopoly become a reality."

This Money Trust, moreover, had *engineered* the recent economic crisis. "The panic was the result of a plot," La Follette thundered, which had been intended to torpedo the movement for regulating Wall Street, by seemingly proving that government tampering led inevitably to crisis. Congressman Charles A. Lindbergh Sr. of Minnesota also favored the "Money Trust" formulation but believed in a plot of a different color, one aimed at whipping up support for a Wall Street–controlled national bank.

The plot theories didn't gain wide traction. What did resonate with many in the middle classes, and even some segments of the business community, was La Follette's challenge to the Morganizers' self-presentation as a progressive force. His counter-narrative suggested that the Money Trust, headquartered in New York, was a parasitic presence, a malignant force that issued watered stock, indulged in speculative swindles, and had nearly brought the country to its knees.

OTHER PEOPLE'S MONEY

In Gotham, investigative reporters followed up on La Follette's lead. Until 1910 Lincoln Steffens, one of the most prominent muckrakers, had focused primarily on exposing corrupt political bosses. Now he launched an in-depth analysis of Wall Street, hiring as legman Walter Lippmann, a recent Harvard grad of socialist leanings. Steffens's series—which beginning in September 1910 ran for eight months in *Everybody's Magazine*—probed deeper than had Tom Lawson's insider account, because it considered Wall Street as a system. Ferreting out the connections that laced together New York's financial and corporate institutions, Steffens depicted Wall Street as a web of power at whose center crouched Morgan, whom Steffens dubbed "the boss of the United States."

Steffens's revelations fueled mounting calls for an official investigation. In April 1912 Congress authorized hearings (chaired by Louisianan Arsène Pujo) to determine, once and for all, if a Money Trust existed. The Pujo Committee chose as counsel Samuel Untermyer, a suave and savvy corporation lawyer in New York, whose experiences in organizing industrial consolidations had led him to reverse his earlier Morganesque views about the virtues of combination. Untermyer's inquiry revealed that the partners and directors of five New York City financial firms—J. P. Morgan & Co., the First National Bank, the National City Bank, Bankers Trust, and Guaranty Trust (the latter two dominated by Morgan)—between them held 341 directorships on the boards of America's 112 biggest corporations, railroads, insurance firms, trading companies, and public utilities. These top financial firms constituted, if not a trust, then a "community of interest"—a "business and financial system" which "if not corrected is likely to lead to a moneyed oligarchy more despotic and more dangerous to industrial freedom than anything civilization has ever known." Its physical location was not in doubt. "The financial resources of the country," one congressman summed up, "have been concentrated in the city of New York, until they now dominate more than 75 percent of the moneyed interests of America, more than 75 percent of the industrial corporations which are combined in the trusts, and practically all of the great trunk railways running from ocean to ocean."

Untermyer summoned Wall Street's leadership to Washington for questioning. Morgan, the star witness, arrived clad in striped pants, velvet-collared coat, and silk top hat, accompanied by a sixteen-person entourage. Jacob Schiff, George Perkins, William Rockefeller, and George Baker testified, too. The New York financiers vigorously denied the existence of a Money Trust. There was, to be sure, an extensive degree of financial centralization: that was an inevitable concomitant of industrial concentration. Yes, their metropolis did play a preeminent role, but that too was only natural: economic laws dictated that "every country create some city as the great financial centre." But concentration didn't mean control. Gotham's bankers did not rule the corporate boards on which they sat. Nor did they command the flow of currency and credit. "All the banks in Christendom," Morgan thundered, "could not control money."

The Pujo Committee didn't buy this assessment. In a report submitted in February 1913, it proposed congressional action to prevent further financial consolidation in New York, and to place Wall Street itself under federal supervision. Among the twenty-plus recommendations were calls to regulate the New York Stock Exchange, scrutinize the issuance of new securities, outlaw stock manipulation, and control margin trading.

The Pujo/Untermyer assessment was widely publicized in 1913 by Louis D. Brandeis, a close adviser of Woodrow Wilson, who had just been elected president. In a *Harper's Weekly* series of nine articles, later collected in *Other People's Money and How the Bankers Use It* (1914), Brandeis charged that Wall Street bankers exercised a virtually complete control over the flow of credit and capital, that they used their power to favor the corporations on whose boards they sat, and that they discouraged competition, blocked new inventions, reaped unjustifiable underwriting fees, profited from insider trading, and, in general, levied tribute on stockholders, bank depositors, investors, workers, and consumers. In Brandeis's view the whole system needed to be dismantled. "We must break the Money Trust," *Other People's Money* concluded, "or the Money Trust will break us."

Some critics who accepted this wholesale repudiation of Wall Street urged using antitrust laws to break up New York's "money monopoly." Others wanted the federal government to assume direct control of the money and credit supply, supplanting the banker oligarchy altogether. In the end, neither of these came to pass. Instead, the financial system was reorganized along lines suggested by the rising generation of the Wall Street banking elite. They believed that deflecting popular outrage, and arranging for federal support to prevent panics, dictated creation of a central bank, the likes of which had not been seen in the United States since the presidency of Andrew Jackson.

IN 1908 THE ALDRICH-VREELAND ACT, which had authorized the issuance of emergency money, also established a National Monetary Commission, headed by Senator Aldrich, to study the banking and currency system. The commission spent four years pondering, producing detailed studies of US methods, traveling in Europe examining practices, and compiling volumes of statistics and analysis. The essential work of planning an alternative, however, was not left to congressmen and economists but was undertaken by Aldrich himself, in close (and clandestine) association with Wall Street. Given the growing uproar about the Money Trust, had bankers' participation been known, it would have been the kiss of death. (Aldrich's name alone might well have sunk any proposal, given that in 1901 his daughter Abigail Aldrich had married John D. Rockefeller Jr., in the society wedding of the decade.)

On the evening of November 22, 1910, a small group of men, dressed as duck hunters, arrived, separately, at the Hoboken train station, where they boarded a sealed-off, blinds-drawn railroad car owned by Nelson Aldrich that had been hooked up to the end of a southbound train. Their destination was Jekyll Island, a secluded retreat off the coast of Georgia. (The entire island had been bought by a consortium of millionaires.) Their ranks included Aldrich; Henry P. Davison of the Morgan bank; Frank A. Vanderlip of the National City Bank; Charles D. Norton, vice president of George Baker's First National Bank; and Paul Warburg of Kuhn, Loeb. For over a week, having successfully dropped from sight, the men (who addressed one another by first names only, lest staff alert the press) labored on designing a new banking system. What they came up with—thanks in particular to Paul Warburg's deep familiarity with the workings of Germany's Reichsbank—was a National Reserve Association, to be established in Washington, with fifteen branches throughout the country (politically savvy concessions to those who opposed further concentration of financial power in New York City). Each branch would be governed by boards of directors elected by the member banks in its district, and each would be responsible for holding the reserves of member banks, funds that would be made available to any bank that was basically sound but under temporary pressure. Eliminating the need to constrict credit in a crisis would head off bank runs and avert financial panics.

The Jekyll Island draft, its real authors incognito, was guised as the Aldrich bill and submitted to Congress in 1912, where it ran into roadblocks. Woodrow Wilson won the Democratic nomination that summer of 1912, on a platform, reflecting Bryanite suspicions, strongly opposed to the Aldrich bill, and any "domination by what is known as the Money Trust." Wilson, much influenced by Brandeis, and by the Untermyer hearings running concurrently with his campaign, warned against Wall Street, saying that "concentration of the control of credit" might "at any time become infinitely dangerous to free enterprise." When Wilson won that November, and the Democrats took both houses, it looked like the Aldrich bill was dead on arrival.

The new president, however, believed the Aldrich plan was "60–70 percent correct," and it became the basis for the Federal Reserve Act (1913), with the principal addition being a DC-based seven-member Federal Reserve Board set atop the system, to be selected by the president, not the bankers.

To the public, it seemed that Wall Street had been bridled, that democratic command of the nation's finances had been regained. This perception had its advantages. The great New York financiers could better shrug off charges of being an all-powerful Money Trust, passing responsibility for economic affairs to the publicly controlled Fed. ("If all such prejudices, political and sectional, against New York and its bankers can be overcome by such measures as have been adopted in the Federal Reserve Act," wrote one of its designers, "I should feel that the work now being done has been well repaid.") In fact the opposite was true. Though the bankers lost their battle for full private control—the smarter ones had never even pushed for it—they would still decide who got credit and what they paid for it. And while it appeared that governing authority had shifted south to Washington, appearances were misleading. For one thing, the refusal of Congress to accept even one of the Pujo Committee's recommendations for regulating Wall Street left the Federal Reserve Board without power to oversee the Stock Exchange. For another, it swiftly took New York players on board. In 1914 Paul Warburg, perhaps the most influential designer of the final system, resigned from Kuhn, Loeb and was appointed to the Fed. (Bryanites were notable by their absence.) Moreover, William Gibbs McAdoo, who Wilson chose as secretary of the treasury—a position that gave him an ex-officio seat on the board—also relocated from New York, where he had been a close business and financial associate of J. P. Morgan.

Most telling, the New York Fed, which became the system's focal point, was firmly in the Morgan orbit. The money-center bankers chose as their governor Benjamin Strong Jr., by then president of the Morgan-dominated Bankers Trust. (Strong had not been at Jekyll

Island but was almost immediately inducted into the First Name Club, as Jekyll veterans called their inner circle.) The New York Fed soon seized or was handed prerogatives that flowed from its members' disproportionate financial power and undisputed preeminence in dealings with European central banks and foreign exchange markets. It was named sole agent for open market operations of all Fed banks. An extralegal council of governors was formed, with Strong as chair, that rivaled the authority of the central board.

Wall Street's position had been strengthened, moreover, by having a lender of last resort at its back. It both offered insulation against instability and encouraged riskier speculative gambits. And the Fed's wielding of the national banking community into a unified force, with New York its de facto head, insulated Gotham financiers from challenges to their preeminence by rival cities.

Wall Street had thus buttressed its economic and social power with quasi-formal political authority—the House of Morgan became known as the Fed House—and this goal had been in the minds of the Fed's creators. Representative Carter Glass, a key figure in passage of the legislation, made clear that "the proponents of the Federal Reserve Act had no idea of impairing the rightful prestige of New York as the financial metropolis of this hemisphere. They rather expected to confirm its distinction, and even hoped to assist powerfully in wresting this scepter from London and eventually making New York the financial center of the world."

6

Who Rules New York?

BOSSES AND BUSINESSMEN

Gotham's financiers and corporate officials, though paladins of the private sector, were imbued with a sense of entitlement to rule the public sphere—indeed, of their responsibility to do so. In many cases, particularly at the presidential level, they were able to exercise this imperative directly, aided by the fact that New York was the biggest city in the biggest and most electoral-vote-laden state in the Union. Between 1868 and 1916, in every presidential and vice-presidential contest except that of 1896, there was a New Yorker in the field of major party contenders—on four occasions *more* than one—and in seven of those eleven races a New York candidate wound up in the winners' circle.[1] They could also obtain a desired result more obliquely, by providing (or withholding) funding for political candidates, be they Democratic, Republican, or independent. Would-be presidents and governors trooped to Wall Street because that's where the money was, and this gave the city's elite tremendous influence in the political arena. During the 1898–1907 boom years, in particular, the Morgans and Rockefellers et al. had been able to translate their economic power into political muscle, channeling huge resources into the electoral arena to help the Republican Party, their chosen

---

1. 1868 (Seymour), 1872 (Greeley), 1876 (Tilden), 1880 (Arthur*), 1884 (Cleveland*), 1888 (Morton,* Cleveland), 1892 (Cleveland,* Reid), 1900 (Roosevelt*), 1904 (Roosevelt,* Parker), 1908 (Sherman*), 1912 (Sherman/Butler, Roosevelt), 1916 (Hughes). Names in parentheses are New York major-party candidates; those with asterisks won their race.

pestle, grind away obstacles to the new corporate order they were building. In the process they had emerged as the closest approximation to a ruling class the United States had ever had.

The corporate elite had had every expectation of exercising a similar degree of control over their own municipality. The charter their consolidationist movement fashioned had established a powerful municipal governance structure. It granted Greater New York's mayor far more authority than was held by any other city executive in the United States, power barely checked by any legislative balance. Municipal consolidation created a more centralized framework, one that would, they hoped, facilitate elite rule, as had London's establishment of a metropolitan-scale government.

Some had even dreamed of creating a proper seat of governance for a new political order, believing the old City Hall, built in 1802–12, lacking in grandeur, to say nothing of sufficient office space in which to manage burgeoning municipal affairs. In 1893, with Andrew Haswell Green's merger drive proceeding full tilt, an architectural competition sought proposals for scrapping City Hall and rearing in its place one gargantuan structure to house all of city government. The contest elicited a bevy of knock-offs of the Paris Hôtel de Ville. But then a rumpus was raised—one of the earliest historic preservation campaigns—and the jewel-like building was saved; Green himself participated in the rescue mission, believing the legitimacy conferred by continuity to be more valuable than any benefits that might accrue from a grand architectural statement. Others advanced the alternative of ditching not City Hall but its surrounding buildings; one 1903 proposal reimagined it as the splendidly isolated centerpiece of a vast Civic Center, twice the size of the Place de la Concorde or Trafalgar Square. Either solution would have given New York an imperial hub from which laws and directives, harmony and order would radiate outward like grand axial boulevards.

Whatever structure was devised for the Greater City's center of government, the elite had every intention and expectation of occupying it—and thus reversing their historic marginalization at the hands of Tammany Hall. From the colonial era to the mid-nineteenth century their antecedents—the old merchant class—had ruled the political roost more or less automatically. Then professional politicians had entered Eden and engineered their expulsion, by capitalizing on the possibilities of a democratized franchise to incorporate arriving immigrants into the political process, and muster them en masse into the Democratic Party. Since then, though the elite continued to run the economy, the politicians pretty much ran the polity. Which meant they could turn this control to their personal advantage, by, for instance, forcing businessmen to pay tribute whenever they needed something from the municipality, such as streetcar franchises. The politicos were also able to impede the largely Anglo-Protestant elite's efforts at imposing their cultural authority on alien masses.

Being sidelined by, and having to cut deals with, petty grafters who were kept in place by working-class voters was not simply costly; it was infuriating, a perceived inversion of the natural order of things. Developments in the mid-1890s, concurrent with the drive to Consolidation, had given grounds for optimism that the upper crust might arrange a Restoration. In 1894 the powerful Chamber of Commerce and its associated "good government" organizations had burst into local politics, determined to wrest power from Tammany and hand it back to the city's "best men." The "goo-goos'" ad hoc effort had succeeded in putting their man in the mayoral chair, winning a two-year term for merchant and banker William Strong. But then, just on the verge of triumph, with charter in hand, came the disastrous 1897 election in which the Citizens' Union reform party had been crushed by Boss Richard Croker and his candidate Robert Van Wyck.

Just as feared, the Democrats then embarked on four merry years of trough feeding. Taking advantage of the opportunities Consolidation presented, Tammany men padded payrolls, rigged contracts, accepted kickbacks, shook down municipal employees, sold judgeships and franchises, and parlayed inside public information into lucrative private sector deals. They did well for themselves and were proud of it. When Croker was hauled before a state legislative hearing in 1899 and asked, "Then you are working for your own pocket, are you not?" he replied: "All the time; the same as you."

This kind of effrontery enraged the now-sidetracked reformers who had tasted power during the Strong regime. The "city should be governed by the commercial classes and the property owners," hissed William F. King, president of the Merchants' Association, in 1901, "not by the vicious, not by the corrupt, not by the politicians and those who follow them blindly." Businessmen despised the saloonkeepers and tradesmen who staffed the Board of Aldermen. The Citizens' Union's executive director, James B. Reynolds, semi-facetiously proposed inviting them to dinner at the elite City Club, but only if "we could lock up the valuables and could place one member next to each alderman whose duty it would be to watch the silver."

In truth the Croker-Van Wyck regime, though bad, was not quite as terrible as upper-class reformers made out. Tammany contractors did most of the work they were overpaid for. Experts were retained in key departments. Administrators adhered (more or less) to civil service regulations. The comptroller kept honest books and unified the financial records of the formerly separate municipalities to the satisfaction of bondholders. Property taxes were kept low. The treasury wasn't looted.

But Tammany did use its control of the municipality to extract revenue from legitimate and illegitimate businessmen alike, swelling income streams that afforded the machine a fiscal base and considerable autonomy. These dealings were revealed by the Mazet Investigating Committee launched in 1899 by the upstate Republicans who held power in Albany. From the five volumes of testimony generated by the yearlong probe, two instances of major league corruption leapt out.

One was the so-called Ice Trust. Croker and Van Wyck gave the American Ice Company, owned by Charles W. Morse (of later copper-corner infamy), the exclusive right to land ice at the municipal docks, giving Morse a de facto monopoly. In return he handed his enablers large quantities of "Ice Trust" stock—the mayor alone got a half-million dollars' worth—without the inconvenience of having to pay for it. Worse, Morse dispensed with the traditional practice of selling small chunks for a nickel and offered only hundred-pound blocks, which was hard on the poor, who needed ice to keep milk for their children from spoiling; a rise in infant deaths duly followed.

Making an even bigger splash than revelations about the Ice Trust were those concerning a purported Vice Trust. With the formation of Greater New York, the various borough police forces had been folded into a single New York Police Department (NYPD). Croker-Van Wyck then turned control of the new department over to "Big Bill" (260 pounds) Devery, the crooked cop who had been cashiered in 1894 after the Lexow hearings but clawed his way back to power. Chief Devery, it was charged, had not only expanded the business of accepting payoffs from gambling establishments, in return for the police turning a blind eye, but had centralized it, forming a syndicate with Frank Farrell, a professional gambler, and State Senator Timothy D. "Big Tim" Sullivan, a Tammany power broker, which channeled the income stream upward. While the degree of triumviral control was probably overstated, it was patently clear that New York was once again a wide-open town.

Confronted with such brazenness, upstate Republicans set out to clip Tammany's wings. In this initiative they were joined by the Democratic Party machine in Brooklyn—where Boss Hugh McLaughlin, having held power since the Civil War, had refused to follow the bosses of the Bronx, Queens, and Staten Island in bending the knee to the Manhattan machine. Together they set up a Charter Revision Commission in 1900 that throttled back mayoral power. The commission cut the mayor's term in half, so that if Tammany—God forbid—captured the office again in 1901, it would only be able to do two years' worth of damage. More fundamentally it parceled out a considerable piece of the mayor's power to the borough presidents, whose role in the original structure had been mostly ceremonial. Now they were added to the Board of Estimate and Apportionment, the powerful administrative-and-legislative body that managed the public purse and a good deal else. After 1901 the board would be composed of three citywide elected officials—the mayor, the president of the Board of Aldermen (the city's new unicameral legislature), and the comptroller (who oversaw finances)—each of whom had three votes; and the five elected borough presidents, their voting strength weighted according to population, with Manhattan and Brooklyn having two votes each, while Queens, Richmond, and the Bronx each got one. The mayor's power was further diluted by abolition of the mayoral-dominated Board of Public Improvements, a body that had had considerable discretion over land use. Local projects paid for out of general city funds (roads, sewers, public buildings) now required approval from the Board of Estimate and the Board of Aldermen, but would be implemented by the borough presidents, providing each with a warehouse of patronage plums.

Andrew Green was not alone in being dismayed at this partial re-decentralization of power, which undercut one of the major purposes of Consolidation—facilitating a citywide approach to municipal improvements. Even those who accepted this devolution of authority to the boroughs as a necessary constraint on Tammany Hall were more determined than ever to eject ward heelers from power and replace them with "men of the highest character and intelligence."

In 1901, accordingly, the Citizens' Union struck up an alliance with the Republican Party, a "fusion" as it was known, and once again ran Seth Low, who promised to give the city "a business administration."

Croker came up with a crafty counterthrust, nominating Edward Morse Shepard, a civil service reformer, distinguished corporate lawyer (he represented railroad and mining interests), and independent Brooklyn Democrat who opposed the McLaughlin machine. Shepard had actually supported Low's campaign in 1897 and had called Tammany Hall "the most burning and disgraceful blot upon the municipal history of this country," but time, and the prospect of power, had healed all wounds. Shepard's selection discombobulated reformers, though it shouldn't have, as tactically-savvy Tammany had long since demonstrated a willingness to nominate respectable (if accommodating) figures in a crisis, as it had picked steelmaster Abram Hewitt to battle Henry George back in 1886.

In the end, however, Fusion had a winning card in its hand—the Mazet exposé of Tammany's Vice Trust, particularly its prostitution division—which it proceeded to play brilliantly. Frank Moss, Mazet's chief counsel, had charged that brothel owners were being protected by well-rewarded Tammany policemen—the same accusations that had been leveled by the Lexow investigation back in the mid-1890s, when Moss had been its associate counsel. This led Henry Codman Potter, bishop of the Episcopal Diocese of New York, to publish (on November 15, 1900) an indignant open letter of protest to Van Wyck, which was sloughed off by the mayor. Potter's intervention sparked formation two weeks later of a

Committee of Fifteen, an extremely high-powered group of bankers, corporate execs, Wall Street lawyers, academics, and civic leaders. Chaired by William Baldwin Jr., president of the Long Island Rail Road, it included financier Jacob Schiff, banker Levi P. Morton, former Chamber of Commerce president Charles Stewart Smith, Columbia economist Edwin R. A. Seligman, and Ethical Culture Society founder Felix Adler. (Two labor representatives were tardily added in response to complaints about its plutocratic profile.)

The Committee of Fifteen now hired detectives to ferret out locations of brothels and gambling "hells," concentrating on Chinatown, Mulberry Street's Little Italy, and the Lower East Side. Using this information, they obtained warrants and, in late February 1901, launched a series of raids on targeted addresses, each led by a member of the committee dressed in full formal evening wear and silk topper. (Some suggested the lofty gentlemen were "trying to purify the Bowery with eau de cologne.")

To provide cover of law for these initiatives, the Fifteen enlisted the aid of William Travers Jerome. Like them, Jerome—a nephew of financier and art patron Leonard Jerome—was a member in good standing of New York Society. An attorney and maverick Democrat, he had served as associate counsel to the Lexow investigation, managed Mayor Strong's campaign in 1894, and been rewarded in 1895 with a judgeship on the Court of Special Sessions. Now, in March 1901, Judge Jerome, axe in hand, began smashing his way into gambling dens and brothels. Close behind him came a retinue of reporters, photographers, and assistant vigilantes from the Committee of Fifteen—as well as some "stalwart young men" provided by two vigilante outfits, the Society for the Prevention of Crime and the City Vigilance League, both associated with the Reverend Charles Parkhurst, pastor of the Madison Square Presbyterian Church and a prominent social reformer. Once inside, Jerome would pull a Bible out of his hip pocket, set up court behind a craps table, arrest those found on the premises, and sledgehammer the gambling equipment. In a matter of months, the axe-wielding jurist had physically invaded and closed forty-five brothels and sixty-nine gambling dens. "This is the law," Jerome declared. "The police won't enforce it. It is for the citizen to act."

The rampaging judge made great copy. The press called him the "St. George of Manhattan." But by June some of the Committee of Fifteen, notably Jacob Schiff, had grown uncomfortable with the campaign—there had been mounting complaints about its disturbing similarity "to the prying and snuffling of Carrie Nationism" (in the *World*'s words)—and it was phased out.[2] Jerome went on to bigger things. In early October 1901, the Fusionists gave him their nomination to become district attorney. For the next fifty-five days he barnstormed Manhattan, paying particular attention to Tammany's Lower East Side stronghold, where he hammered away at the issue of prostitution, seeking to build a bridge to traditionally Democratic voters. At an October 21 rally in the Odd Fellows Hall (106 Forsyth Street),

---

2. Nation, a militant midwestern temperance reformer, was already notorious even before she visited the city in August 1901, which only increased the antipathy. She arrived in her poke bonnet and black alpaca dress, with a hatchet as large as a small broadaxe strapped to her waist, ready to take on the sin-filled metropolis. Trailed by an army of reporters and policemen, Nation stormed into the lobby of the Hotel Victoria on Fifth Avenue and demanded a naked statue of Diana be covered up, threatening "a little hatchetation" in the event of noncompliance. She then proceeded down Fifth Avenue in an open barouche, hatchet slung over her shoulder like a rifle, shouting "Rummies! Murderers! Hell-holes!" at passing saloons. She traveled by steamer to Coney Island, chasing the boat's waiters who were carrying tray-loads of beer. Once at the resort, she sold miniature hatchets, snatched cigars from passersby, and tried to smash up a bar. When arrested, she resisted the officer—denouncing him as "purple and bloated from beer drinking"—until he whacked her on the knuckles with a nightstick, breaking a small bone, and dragged her off in a Black Maria. Carrie Nationism was too tacky for New York. When she spoke at Carnegie Hall, the audience roared with laughter. The *Times* admitted her "unsexed" performances had "a somewhat revolting interest" but declared there was "no reason why anybody, except a policeman, should take Mrs. Nation seriously." She soon abandoned the metropolis to its wicked ways, but her activities colored responses to Jerome's similar enterprise.

"Carry Nation at the Dewey Theater, New York, N.Y.," 1901. (Kansas State Historical Society)

packed with mostly Jewish working-class men, he waved around a leather belt studded with the brass checks Allen Street madams gave their customers to prove they had paid, and demanded to know: "Is the honor of Jewish women sold for brass checks nothing to you?" Challenging their "manhood," he called on them to "stop the police growing rich off the shame of fallen women," adding that "if these conditions existed in other communities there would be a Vigilance Committee organized and somebody would get lynched." At the same time, Jerome, in fact no prig, insisted he had no interest in enforcing the puritanical Sunday drinking laws (as had Mayor Strong, to his great political cost).

THE TUMULTUOUS RECEPTION GIVEN JEROME by working-class men on the Lower East Side in 1901 was due in part to the ground having been prepared by upper-middle-class women. New York polling places were still off-limits to females, but lack of the franchise hadn't stopped some from intervening in the political process. In the 1890s the Reverend Parkhurst had called on the women of Gotham to battle Tammany corruption by enlisting in the Strong campaign for good government. At his urging, Josephine Shaw Lowell, the grand dame of

New York social reformers, had agreed to head up a new entity, the Woman's Municipal League (WML), which would arrange parlor talks, hold mass meetings, and distribute literature to "instruct the ignorant people of the slums what right and purity of politics are." Concerns about women venturing out of their proper domestic sphere and intruding on male territory were countered by arguments that their superior virtue made them ideal social/moral housekeepers, and that while traditional "dirty" politics were admittedly no place for a lady, the new "clean" nonpartisan reform movements were perfectly acceptable. It did mean, however, said Parkhurst—a strong opponent of female suffrage ("manhoodmania," he called it)—that the ladies had to check their votes-for-women politics at the WML door, lest they call into question the organization's "disinterested" status; Lowell, though herself pro-suffrage, acquiesced.

Avowedly partisan political female organizations also emerged in the 1890s. Republican Party auxiliaries like the West End Women's Republican Association (1894) appealed to educated middle-class women, especially wives and daughters of Republican politicians, whose menfolk told them that working to clean up the city by electing good men was not only acceptable, but their duty. Republican ladies engaged in all the campaign activities WML women did, and daringly added door-to-door canvassing. In the 1896 presidential campaign they established their own headquarters, prepared literature in various languages, and walked the tenement districts, braving derision and the occasional potato (as organizer Helen Boswell recalled) "thrown by the irate Irish ladies." The Republican women were back in the 1900 campaign, going apartment to apartment in Russian and Polish Jewish quarters, as well as those of Little Italy, Little Syria, and the like, gaining access to Tammany households where Republican men would have been decidedly unwelcome. Once invited in, they presented party positions and collected data (how many men were old enough to vote, how many

Dr. C. H. Parkhurst, ca. 1910. (Library of Congress Prints and Photographs Division, George Grantham Bain Collection)

were unnaturalized), obtaining it "from their foreign sisters rather than from the men themselves who are less approachable." Taking a leaf from Tammany's playbook, if they found the housewife in need of food or medical attention for her children, the visitor might provide temporary relief or arrange for a doctor to stop by. As the president of the West End Women's Republican Association observed, a woman in need "will use all her influence for the first person who alleviates her sufferings, and can usually be counted upon to control her husband's vote."

In 1901, the Woman's Municipal League threw itself into the Fusion campaign, pitting (as did Jerome) Democratic voters' moral sensibilities against their loyalty to Tammany Hall. Particularly effective on the Lower East Side were members like Lillian Wald, well known there from her work with the Henry Street Settlement, and Consumers' League co-founder Maud Nathan, scion of a distinguished New York Sephardic family (her great-grandfather, a rabbi, attended President Washington's inaugural ceremony); Nathan found that Russian Jewish women came to her talks (translated simultaneously into Yiddish) because they had "confidence in me as a co-religionist."

Like Jerome, the WML women focused on the prostitution issue, notably by producing a sixteen-page pamphlet, *Facts for Fathers and Mothers*. Drawing on the writings of Bishop Potter, Judge Jerome, Manhattan District Attorney Eugene Philbin, the University Settlement Society, and the Society for the Prevention of Cruelty to Children, *Facts* presented graphic stories about young New York girls being lured by "cadets" (procurers) into brothels where they were forcibly inducted into prostitution, with the purchased acquiescence of the police and Tammany Hall. Published with assistance from the City Club, hundreds of thousands of copies were printed, which were mailed to registered voters and given to clergymen, settlement houses, working girls' clubs, and women's Republican clubs to distribute.[3]

The onslaught began to tell on Tammany. Croker promised his own investigation, but was balked by powerful subordinates like Big Tim Sullivan, boss of the Lower East Side, who was furious about Jerome's raids on gambling operations under his protection. Similarly, when Republican state legislators axed his ally, Bill Devery, by abolishing his office of chief of police, Sullivan pressured Mayor Van Wyck into appointing Devery as deputy police commissioner, with even greater powers than before.

Sullivan was relatively up-front about defending gambling against puritans. He publicly took the lead in contesting those who wanted to outlaw boxing and horse racing, and argued restrictions were bad for the tourist industry. "The best way to ruin a large cosmopolitan city like ours," he would say in 1907, "which virtually lives off our visiting strangers, is to enforce or keep on the statute books such blue laws which don't belong to our age." He loudly denied

---

3. Though there was considerable overlap with the approach of the all-male Committee of Fifteen, some WML members did press for a more complex understanding of the causes of prostitution. Shortly after the committee set up shop, Maud Nathan wrote (in a letter to the *Times*) that while she was "heartened" that such prominent gentlemen had taken the field against vice and corruption, none seemed to touch on the "outrageous conditions under which many of our young girls are forced to work in our factories and workshops." Indeed, she noted some of the very businessmen "who are at present eager to stem the tide of vice ... are men who have earned the unenviable reputation of paying notoriously low wages ... while they have been heaping up profits and have been making annual 'charitable bequests.'" These shafts reached their target, at least to the degree that the final report of the Committee of Fifteen—*The Social Evil: With Special Reference to Conditions Existing in the City of New York* (1902)—noted that "it is undoubtedly true that a chronic state of poverty has a powerful influence in impelling women to accept a vicious life." The report even acknowledged the impact of the capitalist business cycle, noting that there were many women "whose normal income is sufficient to permit them to lead honorable lives, but who are left at times of temporary depression with no means of escaping starvation except prostitution."

having any link to prostitution. This may have been true, but his associates certainly did: Martin Engel, boss of the next-door Eighth District, looked out for the interests of his brother, Max Engel, who ran a string of brothels along Allen Street, the Jewish red-light district. And Sullivan himself was vice president of the Max Hochstim Association, putatively a Jewish fraternal group that provided death benefits and burial plots, but was also a front for the Independent Benevolent Association, an alliance of real estate agents, concert saloon owners, and brothel managers that dominated prostitution on the Lower East Side; if not directly under Big Tim's protection, the likes of Hochstim (an Engel lieutenant) could count on his passive consent.

As the campaign drove toward the finish line, getting more incandescent by the day, Sullivan felt behooved to act. He handed over the district leadership to his trusted lieutenant and cousin "Little Tim" Sullivan, who then, together with Florrie Sullivan, another Big Tim cousin, set about publicly assaulting local brothels—smashing up the premises and beating up pimps. To no avail.

Seth Low won with 52 percent of the vote, the margin of victory widely believed to have been provided by dissident Democrats; the *New York Times* estimated 43,000 had crossed party lines. Jerome in his DA race did even better, running 14,000 votes ahead of Low, and triumphing in seven of ten heavily Jewish East Side districts, usually solid for Tammany, that were precisely the territory women's organizations had been canvassing in every election since 1896. Suffragist Harriot Stanton Blatch hailed the results as demonstrating how strong "woman's power" could be when aroused.

DURING HIS TWO-YEAR TERM (1902–3), Mayor Low enacted a series of administrative improvements; cut taxes and spending; facilitated the work of reformers in housing, education, and public health; fired Tammany hacks (including Devery); and staffed his administration with gentlemen from the City Club and *Social Register* (whose memberships overlapped considerably). A "true business-like energy" prevailed, rejoiced the *Review of Reviews*. It seemed the political millennium had arrived.

Big Tim Sullivan (right) and his half-brother, Larry Mulligan-Hicks, 1913. (Library of Congress Prints and Photographs Division, George Grantham Bain Collection)

But Low, like Strong before him, dissipated his support. He gave fellow Republicans the lion's share of appointments, alienating his Democratic and Citizens' Union backers. Prosecuting utilities drove some big businessmen back toward the corrupt but pliable Tammany. Enforcing Sunday drinking laws (a concession to the Parkhurst wing) alienated Germans. And his patrician goo-goo-ism alienated many plebeians. As one critic remarked, Low and company "believed in government by the good, they being the good."

Worse still, by the time his term was up, Low was facing a revitalized Tammany Hall. Croker had stepped down after the 1901 debacle—the old Fourth Avenue Tunnel brawler, born penniless, retiring to his baronial Irish estate to raise Thoroughbred racehorses—and by 1902 power had passed to the more formidable Charles Francis Murphy.

Murphy was born in 1858 to poor Irish immigrants in the Gas House District—the tenement territory between 14th and 27th Streets that lay to the east of the posh precincts of Stuyvesant, Gramercy, and Madison Squares, running to the East River. He and his eight siblings were raised as devout Catholics; the family attended the Church of the Epiphany on Second Avenue. After quitting school at 14 Murphy worked in a wire factory, then in Roach's Shipyard as a caulker, and then as a horsecar driver on the crosstown Blue Line plodding back and forth between the East River and the Hoboken ferry.

In 1880 Murphy opened a saloon on Second Avenue. For five cents, men from the nearby gas plants and lumberyards could get a schooner of beer and a bowl of soup. Prospering, Murphy opened three more drinking establishments. One of them, at 20th Street, became headquarters of the Anawanda Club, the local Tammany organization.

Murphy became a model district leader. Shrewd and methodical, he kept records on each voter. If someone hadn't voted by three o'clock on Election Day, a party functionary was dispatched to corral him. Murphy, no glad-hander, was dignified and taciturn; his colleagues called him "Silent Charlie" (though not to his face). He was, however, readily available. Stationed beneath an old gas lamp on Second Avenue for several hours each night, he dispensed favors to constituents and was personally (often anonymously) generous to those in need. He piled up the largest majorities in the city for the Tammany ticket.

Like Croker, Murphy also worked for his own pocket. Appointed a dock commissioner by Mayor Van Wyck in 1897 (the only official salaried job he ever held), Murphy set up a dock-leasing system that channeled business to the New York Contracting and Trucking Company his brother founded; the firm would eventually be awarded $15 million worth of contracts.

Murphy set his face firmly against "vice." Personally upright and abstemious, he also needed to diminish Tammany's vulnerability to Jerome-style attacks. When he became boss of bosses in 1902, to clean up the machine's image he off-loaded all responsibility for past venality onto Bill Devery's ample shoulders, and very publicly barred the former police chief from any position of standing in the Democratic Party. Sullivan was far too powerful to treat in such a manner, and besides, he'd been instrumental in Murphy's elevation, but Big Tim helped out by kicking himself upstairs to Congress, thus removing from the local scene, at least for the moment, a prime irritant to reformer sensibilities. (The *Times* considered this a mixed blessing, finding it appalling that "a person who is simply not fit to be at large in a civilized community" would represent the district that "includes the financial center of the United States of America.")

Murphy now cultivated improved relations with the city's upper class. The aristocratic J. Sergeant Cram, with whom he'd worked on the Van Wyck Dock Commission, showed Murphy around Fifth Avenue, took him riding in Central Park, taught him how to eat peas with a fork. He moved his family to a house at 305 East 17th Street, overlooking toney Stuyvesant Square, and bought a fifty-acre estate (Good Ground) out on Long Island, where he installed a nine-hole golf course. Murphy also shifted his informal court to a private room at the ultra-fashionable Delmonico's restaurant, the latest (1897) incarnation of which was uptown at Fifth Avenue and 44th Street; it was well situated for meetings with respectable businessmen, who wouldn't be caught dead at "the Wigwam," Tammany headquarters down at 141 East 14th Street. From the sidelines Devery jeered that Murphy "has got into a habit of tucking up his trousers at the bottom and wearing glasses, and instead of being a respectable gas house gentleman he goes on Fifth Avenue."

Murphy demonstrated the value of respectability and uptown connections when he engineered Tammany's comeback in 1903. For his mayoral candidate against Low, he chose not a hack but young George McClellan Jr., son of the Civil War general. A cultured, scholarly, well-tailored Princeton graduate, McClellan had the class credentials to win uptown credibility yet was also an experienced politician who had been president of the Board of Aldermen and served four terms in the US House of Representatives.

In November Tammany and McClellan swept Low and the reformers out of office. The *Times* and *Tribune*, shocked, pronounced the cause of self-government hopeless. Teddy Roosevelt declared: "The dog has returned to its vomit." But the 1903 election results engendered more penetrating analyses about why reform had been rejected, the most notable of which were penned by two of the era's sharpest political commentators, men who shared presidential first names—George Washington Plunkitt and Lincoln Steffens—though little else, coming as they did from opposite classes and opposite coasts of the continent.

PLUNKITT WAS BORN IN 1842, IN SENECA VILLAGE, a West Side site later swallowed up by Central Park. He began his working life as driver of a cart, then became a butcher's boy in the Washington Market, and later went into the butcher business for himself. He entered politics by rounding up sixty friends, neighbors, and relations who agreed to be his followers, bundling them into a George Washington Plunkitt Association, and going to the local district leader, who welcomed him with lit cigars for having delivered three score votes—a "marketable commodity." He rose in the ranks, becoming district leader of the Fifteenth Assembly District (43rd/50th/ Eighth/Hudson River), in the heart of Hell's Kitchen. In 1869 he was elected to the state assembly, and went on to serve intermittently in the state senate between 1884 and 1904.

Plunkitt had no office. He received his constituents, transacted business, and dispensed political philosophy from his rostrum at a bootblack stand in the marble lobby of the New York County Courthouse (the one built by Boss Tweed). Journalist William L. Riordan transcribed several interviews with him, published them as mini-essays in various local papers, then in 1905 collected them in a small book, prefaced with Murphy's imprimatur, that became an instant classic: *Plunkitt of Tammany Hall.*

Addressing the question "Why Reform Administrations Never Succeed Themselves!," Plunkitt explained that reformers just didn't understand that "politics is as much a regular business as the grocery or the dry-goods or the drug business. You've got to be trained up to it or you're sure to fail." The key to success was providing unremitting assistance to constituents. "What tells in holdin' your grip on your district," Plunkitt explained, "is to go right down among the poor families and help them in the different ways they need help. I've got a regular system for this. If there's a fire in Ninth, Tenth, or Eleventh Avenue, for example, any hour of the day or night, I'm usually there with some of my election district captains as soon

"The Most Striking Cartoon of the Campaign: 'The Tiger Now Has a Bridge Pass'—A Daily Paper Several Days after the Election, by Courtesy of the New York *Herald*.'" "Glimpses of a Great Campaign," *World's Work*, December 1, 1903.

as the fire engines. [His home was on the scene, at 323 West 51st.] If a family is burned out I don't ask whether they are Republicans or Democrats, and I don't refer them to the Charity Organization Society, which would investigate their case in a month or two and decide they were worthy of help about the time they are dead from starvation. I just get quarters for them, buy clothes for them if their clothes were burned up, and fix them up till they get things runnin' again. . . . The consequence is that the poor look up to George W. Plunkitt as a father, come to him in trouble—and don't forget him on election day." Plunkitt was also an avenue to employment. "I can always get a job for a deservin' man," he explained, adding, "I know every big employer in the district and in the whole city, for that matter, and they ain't in the habit of sayin' no to me when I ask them for a job."

Plunkitt provided circuses as well as bread—all the district leaders did—but it was his colleague Big Tim Sullivan who chiefly developed the art of political entertainment, another reason for Low's loss.

Like Plunkitt, Sullivan provided social services. He went bail for constituents in trouble with the law (or put in a word with Tammany judges), sent flowers to sickbeds and funerals, helped out with getting a pushcart license or citizenship papers. Since the depression year of 1894 he'd been feeding thousands of local residents free Christmas dinners at the Sullivan Association (207 Bowery, just below Rivington); every February he gave away thousands of vouchers for free shoes and wool socks, redeemable at local stores; and he provided coal to the poorest—during the 1902 miners strike, he organized distribution of half a ton to every needy family in the district. Like Plunkitt, Sullivan contrasted Tammany's warmheartedness with the reformers' chilly charity: "I never ask a hungry man about his past. I feed him, not because he is good, but because he needs food. Help your neighbor," his motto might have been, "but keep your nose out of his affairs."

But where Sullivan was truly pace-setting was in his melding of electoral organizing with commercial entertainment. Partly this flowed from his immersion in the city's communication industry. Born on Greenwich Street in 1863, he'd gone to work at age 7 on Newspaper

"Ex-Senator George Washington Plunkitt, on His Rostrum, the New York County Court-House Bootblack Stand." William L. Riordon, *Plunkitt of Tammany Hall*, 1905.

Row bundling papers for delivery, but then became a wholesale news dealer and manager for a large circulation agency—an unusual résumé for a Tammany boss. Sullivan was also drawn to commercial culture because his district was bisected by the Bowery, still the locus of working-class theaters, concert saloons, lager beer gardens, dime museums, restaurants, and oyster bars. It was a magnet for locals out for a cheap night on the town, for tourists, for uptown slummers—and for Sullivan, who early on became an entertainment entrepreneur. After cutting his teeth in the business, managing Bowery burlesque and music halls, in 1898 he and a partner remodeled the Volks Garden—farther north, on East 14th Street near the Wigwam—as the Dewey Theater (after the admiral), which scantily clad chorus girls helped make the most popular theater in the Union Square rialto district. Still farther uptown, he bought a piece of the Metropole Hotel at 142 West 43rd Street, just off Times Square, whose café, popular with boxers, gamblers, and actresses, became his midtown headquarters (in sharp contrast to Murphy's choice of nearby Delmonico's).

From the beginning Sullivan admixed his commercial and political projects, arranging for local vaudeville performers to entertain the men at his Christmas dinners. But he really hit his stride when he turned the fairly traditional practice of Sunday steamboat outings into a spectacular entertainment extravaganza. With help from his theatrical producer friends, Sullivan began hosting annual Labor Day "chowders" for his constituents, as many as 15,000 of them. They'd begin with Big Tim leading a street parade to an East River dock where steamboats waited to ferry his followers to Harlem River Park or College Point. There they feasted on a clam fritter breakfast, a fish and chicken dinner, and oceans of beer for the men and enjoyed track and field competitions, baseball games, prizefights (with gambling on the side), and dancing. A late-night return was capped by a torchlight parade and fireworks. Tickets cost five dollars, although the great majority didn't pay but rather received them gratis from saloonkeepers and other businessmen who bought bunches of them to stay in Big Tim's good graces. This Tammany style was profoundly popular and contrasted markedly and favorably with the Low regime's earnest sobriety, another reason Democrats made a comeback in 1903.

But if Tammany's system was all that effective, why was a comeback necessary in the first place? Why had neither bread nor circus prevented the 1901 reformer victory? Plunkitt tackled the question head-on. "Tammany was beat in 1901," he argued, because the people "saw that some Tammany men grew rich, and supposed they had been robbin' the city treasury or levyin' blackmail on disorderly houses [read: brothels], or workin' in with the gamblers and lawbreakers." But they—and he—hadn't, Plunkitt insisted: "I've made a big fortune out of the game, and I'm gettin' richer every day, but I've not gone in for dishonest graft—blackmailin' gamblers, saloonkeepers, disorderly people, etc.—and neither has any of the men who have made big fortunes in politics." The money came from "honest graft," not "dishonest graft," and between the two there was "all the difference in the world."

Honest graft? He elucidated: "My party's in power in the city, and it's goin' to undertake a lot of public improvements. Well, I'm tipped off, say, that they're going to lay out a new park at a certain place. I see my opportunity and I take it. I go to that place and I buy up all the land I can in the neighborhood. Then the board of this or that makes its plan public, and there is a rush to get my land, which nobody cared particular for before. Ain't it perfectly honest to charge a good price and make a profit on my investment and foresight? Of course, it is. Well, that's honest graft." It was, he claimed, "just like lookin' ahead in Wall Street or in the coffee or cotton market," probably referring to the speculation and insider trading that were both rampant and legal. But the key point for Plunkitt was that politicians hadn't gotten rich by looting the treasury or protecting "evildoers" because they didn't have to: "Why should the Tammany leaders go into such dirty business, when there is so much honest graft lyin' around?" In effect, he deflected accusations of major malfeasance by owning up to (what he hoped would be considered) minor peccadilloes.

LINCOLN STEFFENS, ONE OF THE PREEMINENT MUCKRAKERS of the day, saw eye to eye with Plunkitt on some matters, but his gaze was more penetrating, in part because he was the product of a very different culture. Born in 1866 into a wealthy Sacramento family, Steffens graduated in 1889 from the University of California at Berkeley and moved on to postgraduate studies in Berlin, in Heidelberg, and at the Sorbonne, for which his father footed the bill. He'd been planning on more "observing and studying" in London, but his father pulled the financial plug, so in 1892 he sailed to Gotham, loaded down with a trunk's worth of the latest English fashions. (He'd become something of a dandy, affecting a goatee and bangs.) Awaiting him was a note from his father suggesting it was time for him to study the "practical side" of life, and the best way to do so was to "stay in New York and hustle." He enclosed a check for a hundred dollars, "which should keep you till you can find a job and support yourself."

Steffens père actually provided something better than cash—a letter of introduction that led to a reporter's position at the *New York Evening Post*. There he covered the Wall Street beat (interviewing Morgan and tracking the Panic of 1893), added a police beat (aided by Jacob Riis, then police reporter for the *New York Sun*), and dealt with politics (interviewing Croker, covering Parkhurst's crusade and the Lexow hearings). All this afforded him a crash immersion in the inner workings of New York's polity, economy, and social structure. In late 1897 he became city editor of the *Commercial Advertiser*, New York's longest-surviving newspaper (1794), which had been on its last legs, and turned it around in two years by bringing on college grads as investigative reporters. In 1901 Sam McClure enticed him away with a $5,000 salary to become managing editor of *McClure's Magazine*.

McClure had concluded that the two great issues confronting the country were the growth of industrial trusts (he had set Ida Tarbell to work on that story), and the expansion of political corruption, which he turned over to Steffens. Deciding to study the matter in a comparative and scientific manner, Steffens plotted out a multi-locational series about municipal misgovernance, beginning with "Tweed Days in St. Louis," which ran in the October 1902 *McClure*'s, one issue before Tarbell's first installment on the Rockefellers. Then it was on to similarly corrupt Minneapolis, Pittsburgh, and Philadelphia, before finally attending to Seth Low's New York, which Steffens considered a heartening exception to the general misrule. In Gotham, "the honest men are in," and the upcoming election (the piece was written in September 1903) "was to decide whether they are to be kept in, which is a very different matter." Any people is capable "of rising in wrath to overthrow bad rulers," Steffens suggested, but "revolt is not reform, and one revolutionary administration is not good government." The question was whether—with "nothing but mild approval and dull duty to impel" it—the city would "vote intelligently to sustain a fairly good municipal government." At that moment it seemed extremely doubtful. Why? Because, it seemed, Low was "not a loveable character"; the city did not like the way he smiled.

This was less absurd than it appeared to be. Low, Steffens argued, was the "ideal product of the New York theory that municipal government is business, not politics, and that a business man who would manage the city as he would a business corporation, would solve for us all our troubles." This meant Low hadn't been out developing the "political strength" needed to win elections—unlike Tammany Hall, whose leaders dispensed "kindness and petty privileges," smiled "friendly smiles," gave picnics, and provided jobs. They were corrupt, but they shared some of the spoils, thus creating a "corruption with consent." The handouts, after all, cost them little in relation to the vast amounts they raked in through control of the city government. Worse, the smiling bosses betrayed their constituents by scrimping on services like education and health care and by allowing vice to blossom in the neighborhoods.[4] Worse still, it seemed to Steffens that the up-and-coming Murphy, who "acts with force, decision, and skill," had learned from Croker's and Sullivan's missteps, and would curtail the machine's worst excesses, thus reconciling the people to its rule. And indeed, when the New York piece was reprinted in his 1904 book, *The Shame of the Cities*, Steffens had to append a postscript reporting that Tammany was back in the saddle.

Steffens raised a more fundamental objection to the reformers' notion that corruption could be curtailed by deep-sixing depraved politicians and installing honest businessmen. In his opinion, it was precisely "the better classes—the business men—[who] are the sources of corruption." It took two to do the corruption tango, after all, and businessmen were the paymasters, though they were "rarely pursued and caught."[5] The alliance between bosses and economic elites (with corporations making campaign contributions in exchange for franchises, favorable legislation, or being left alone) was not all that different from the much-decried alliance between bosses and underworld entrepreneurs (with saloonkeepers and

4. If Tammany could be incorporated and its earnings paid out in dividends, Steffens mused hyperbolically, its stock would be worth more than Standard Oil's, its power greater than US Steel's.

5. Steffens made an interesting exception to this rule in the case of Gotham. Noting that "most of the big businesses represented in New York have no plants there," just "head offices," and observing also that Wall Street dealt with the whole United States, apart from a small group that specialized in local corporations and thus "g[a]ve Tammany a Wall Street connection," the city's major corporate officials and financiers needed little from the municipality per se, hence weren't dependent on Tammany. These men—"bribers though they may be" in Albany and Washington—could afford to be honest citizens at home, and it was precisely from this class that the reformers were drawn.

gambling impresarios making payoffs to be left alone). Yet upper-crust corruption seemed merely normal. What reformers were therefore up against, though they didn't realize it, was "a regularly established custom of the country, by which our political leaders are hired, by bribery, by the license to loot, and by quiet moral support, to conduct the government of city, State and Nation, not for the common good, but for the special interests of private business." Not until the citizenry realized that corruption was systemic and endemic, and that it was engaged in by "good" people as well as "bad," would they develop the inclination and ability to attack it.[6]

Steffens dulled the edge of this critique somewhat by arguing that reformers were further deluded in believing that if corruption was exposed people would rise against it. The truth was that most people knew perfectly well that corruption flourished all around them but tolerated it, either because they hoped to gain from it, or were too lazy to take responsibility for self-governance: the boss, he argued, was "the product of a freed people that have not the spirit to be free." If true, what hope was there of challenging the system? Steffens advanced instead the anemic argument that because the bosses were themselves businessmen, entrepreneurs in the political marketplace, they would ultimately obey the law of supply and demand. Hence "all we have to do is establish a steady demand for good government." This demand could be fanned by publicity, by the dissemination of facts. But this nostrum was not all that different (or more effective) than the solution proposed by the reformers he derided.[7]

There were, however, other ways to approach the issue. Yes, in 1903, Tammany's triumph seemed to presage a long and comfortable rule. But the machine had two formidable weaknesses.

The first was a shrinking electoral base. Tammany had long been sustained chiefly by Irish and German votes. But the older immigrants were being rapidly displaced by newer ones. In 1880 first- and second-generation Irish had constituted 27 percent of the populace of what would become Greater New York; by 1910 they had slipped to 14 percent. Germans

---

6. Steffens argued that corruption was not the result of misbehavior by bad men but was inherent in the system. "One business man's bribe was nothing but a crime, but a succession of business briberies over the years was a corruption of government to make it represent business." This was ultimately the result of the separation of political from economic leadership. "In a country where business is dominant, business men must and will corrupt a government which can pass laws to hinder or help business." He tried to explain this to his friend Roosevelt. Writing in 1905 after the Hughes insurance investigation showed big money had swamped the president with campaign contributions, Steffins suggested TR consider returning contributions from corporations seeking national legislation and encourage small individual contributions instead. Doing so "would make the millions feel that it was their government," and that "you and your administration were beholden to the many, not to the few." Roosevelt responded in high dudgeon: "I do not know of a single corporation which contributed last year which now desires legislation." Morgan, Rockefeller, et al. had given because they believed Teddy "stood for the good of the country."

7. Steffens really liked bosses better than reformers. They were crooks, but they were honest crooks, and the candor of Plunkitt types was refreshing. Steffens doesn't appear to have read Plunkitt, though he was given to Plunkitt-like assertions such as "Society is made up of legitimate grafters." Plunkitt, on the other hand, did read Steffens, and though he believed the reporter "gets things all mixed up" because he "can't see no difference between honest graft and dishonest graft," found him nevertheless on target in dismissing the common reformer notion that corruption flourished because ignorant immigrants sustained the machines in power. "Steffens made one good point in his book," Plunkitt allowed, when he said "that Philadelphia, ruled almost entirely by Americans, was more corrupt than New York, where the Irish do almost all the governin.'" Quite right, said the boss of Hell's Kitchen: "The Irish was born to rule, and they're the honestest people in the world." Recalling that once "a Republican superintendent of the Philadelphia almshouse stole the zinc roof off the buildin' and sold it for junk," he declared with mock indignation, "Show me the Irishman who would steal a roof off an almhouse! He don't exist."

Plunkitt also offered a rebuttal to the notion that the government of cities was any worse than it had been in the old days, at least in relation to opportunities. "A half a century ago," he explained, "our cities were small and poor. There wasn't many temptations lyin' around for politicians. There was hardly anything to steal, and hardly any opportunities for even honest graft." So "what credit was there in bein' honest under them circumstances? It makes me tired to hear of old codgers back in the thirties or forties boastin' that they retired from politics without a dollar except what they earned in their profession or business. If they lived today, with all the existin' opportunities, they would be just the same as twentieth-century politicians."

dropped from 23 percent to 15 percent over the same period. By 1910, by contrast, Jews—the vast majority of whom were Russian, Polish, and Austro-Hungarian—were just over 25 percent of the population, and the Italians had climbed to about 11 percent.

To be sure, many newcomers were not registered voters, or even citizens—thanks in no small measure to Tammany pols' reluctance to aid in naturalizing them at anywhere near the rate they had incorporated the Irish.[8] Clearly, however, this was not a winning long-term strategy. The bosses realized they must widen their electoral base. But for an organization based on patronage, not principle, this was not so simple. The number of available positions was limited. While some Jews and Italians were made ethnic lieutenants and given minor party posts, Irish chieftains reserved the great mass of city jobs for their core constituency.

In partial compensation, they included the newcomers in their social service networks and made symbolic bows to their cultures. Tammany leaders donned yarmulkes, attended brises, gave out Passover as well as Christmas baskets. For the Italians, Big Tim Sullivan got Columbus Day declared a state holiday. And when a gang of Irish toughs harassed a group of orthodox Jews, Sullivan—in a pointed message to his compatriots—got them evicted from their clubhouse and had it turned into a synagogue.

In the short run Murphy and his men maintained control. But exclusivity left the machine vulnerable to opponents able to mobilize the new ethnics.

Tammany's second vulnerability was that the party was not ideological. The bosses had no vision of what to do with their power. They had no agenda to advance. They had no fundamental objection to the status quo's class structure or political economy. They didn't see politics as an instrument of social or municipal transformation. Indeed, they maintained their laissez-faire suspicion of strong municipal authority, a wariness born of fighting off repeated Protestant efforts to use state power to impose cultural values. This vision vacuum made little difference in day-to-day affairs. But it left them vulnerable to those capable of advancing a popular program for social change.

It was these two chinks in Tammany's armor that made the flowering of Jewish socialism, smack in the middle of Tim Sullivan's bailiwick, a potentially lethal challenge.

RADICALS AND REGULATORS

The first substantial cohort of socialist organizers, many of them former students in or on the fringe of the anti-czarist movement, arrived on the Lower East Side in the mid-1880s, fleeing, like other Jews, from the pogroms that followed the 1881 assassination of Alexander II. They clustered in a distinct sub-community—"the Russian Colony"—eventually numbering about a thousand. Initially they viewed themselves as constituting an American outpost of the Russian revolutionary movement, but they soon refocused their attention on their situation in Gotham. Unable to support themselves as teachers, as they would have in Russia, they entered the garment factories and there encountered a rapidly expanding and highly exploited Jewish proletariat, which they began to consider organizing.

In this they were inspired by the German Americans who had preceded them to New York. Not, however, the uptown German Jewish bourgeoisie, focused as it was on compassionate

---

8. Republicans at the federal and state levels also slowed Southern and Eastern European entry into politics. The Naturalization Law of 1906 demanded the ability to speak English. (In practice, reading or reciting from memory passages from the US Constitution satisfied the requirement.) It also asked for stringent proof of lawful entry, required five years continuous residency, and barred radicals. Rejection rates soared; in the case of Italians, one out of five was turned down.

philanthropy or on teaching the Eastern Europeans how to mind their P's and Q's. Rather they turned to the German socialists, their near neighbors, just above Grand Street in Kleindeutschland (Little Germany).

The German quarter was at its peak in the 1880s, chockablock with labor lyceums, assembly halls, clubs, and saloons, all of which German-speaking Russian intellectuals loved to frequent. Many of Kleindeutschland's residents had been members of Germany's Socialist Workers Party, the largest socialist party in Europe. In Gotham they had organized the Socialist Labor Party (SLP)—since 1877 the principal vehicle of American socialism, though as of 1887 fewer than 10 percent were native-born Americans. German socialists, being internationalists and secularists, welcomed the Russian Jews and helped them organize a Jewish radical movement.

One of the new recruits was Morris Hillquit, born Moishe Hillkowitz in Riga in 1869. When his father's business failed in the mid-1880s, the family straggled over from Latvia to New York and in 1885 squeezed into a two-room apartment on Clinton Street. Morris worked as a shirtmaker and joined the SLP in 1887. He got an NYU law degree in 1893 (by working nights teaching English to immigrants) and commenced a successful Nassau Street practice, rising all the while in SLP ranks—until 1899, when, unhappy with the SLPs shift to a spiky sectarianism, he and fifty or so comrades jumped ship. Teaming up with a Chicago-based socialist organization recently formed by railroad union leader Eugene Debs, the New Yorkers and midwesterners became in 1901 the dual core of the Socialist Party of America (SP), and Hillquit became of its leading theoreticians.

New York's SP members rejected "revolution," if that meant a violent worker insurrection. Violence, Hillquit argued, was impractical and self-defeating. It was, moreover, unnecessary. History, thanks to capitalism, was evolving in a socialist direction. Corporate leaders had socialized labor, centralized industry, and replaced primitive entrepreneurs with modern monopolies. J. P. Morgan and his ilk believed they were the vanguard of progress. Hillquit thought so, too: for all their evils, the giant trusts were a progressive development. But corporate capitalism wasn't the end of history. It fostered injustice and kept breaking down. It needed to be replaced by a superior system. Given the Laws of History, such a development was virtually inevitable.

The party's task—here Hillquit drew inspiration from Germany's Social Democratic Party—was mobilizing the people to win power through the ballot. By "the people," Hillquit meant well-organized proletarians—the skilled union workers then flocking to the American Federation of Labor (AFL). This dictated a strategy of wooing and winning AFL members to a course of political action. With a strong trade union base, the party could elect Socialist candidates. Once in public office—again following a Euro-parliamentary model—radical representatives would enact immediate reforms. While initially leaving the capitalist structure intact, these improvements in daily life would build support for socialism.

The cockpit for these political initiatives would be the city. In Hillquit's scheme of things, the central government would be limited to making general laws and managing national industries. To forestall formation of monolithic state bureaucracies, real power would be retained at the grassroots level, in autonomous cities. The local party, accordingly, entered the political arena to sell New Yorkers on the idea of municipal socialism.

On June 22, 1901, the Socialists met at the Labor Lyceum (64 East 4th Street)—for decades a center for socialist activities such as classes, lectures, rallies, social gatherings, and the publishing of the *New Yorker Volkszeitung*. The 137 delegates from around the city had come to hammer out a platform and select a mayoral candidate. Morris Hillquit presided.

Many of the planks they settled on dealt with long-standing labor issues. Gotham, the delegates decided, should guarantee city employees an eight-hour day and a minimum wage, "women to be paid equally with men"; establish municipal pensions for aged and disabled workmen; set up a free employment bureau; and "undertake public works in times of depression, to give men employment."

The platform also addressed broader quality-of-life concerns. New York "should provide for the education of all children, establishing day nurseries, kindergartens, ample schools, free meals and clothing, when needed," and "improve the free library system." Neighborhood differentials should be evened out: though the "residential portion of New York is beautiful"—no surprise given that "vast sums of money are spent on beautifying the surroundings of the rich"—"the workingman's portion is filthy and hideous," and serious attempts should be made "to introduce public parks, baths, playgrounds, &c., for the workingman." In addition, "tenement laws should be improved," and the city itself should "erect fire-proof tenement houses, with all needed provisions."

On the macroeconomic front, the city should "acquire and operate all industries which require a franchise for their operation" and "supply the people at cost with pure food, medicines, fuel, and ice."

As for politics, the Democratic Party was flagrantly corrupt and had "frequently proved its hostility to labor." The Republican Party was as one with the Democrats "in its servility to the capitalistic class." Nor—taking a swipe at Jerome and the Committee of Fifteen—would existing evils be remedied by "so-called reformers," who in their "well fed morality amuse themselves by hounding" poor working women who had been forced into prostitution.

For its mayoral candidate the Socialist Party chose Benjamin Hanford. Born in Cleveland in 1861, he had learned the printer's trade in Iowa, moved to Chicago, where he became a militant unionist, then headed east to New York, where he became an activist member of Typographical Union No. 6 and signed up with the Socialists.

The new party didn't entice many Democratic voters away from their allegiance to Tammany. In 1901 Hanford received but 1.7 percent of the popular tally. The party did slightly better in the 1903 mayoral contest. And in 1904 the Socialist candidate for Congress running in the Ninth District in the heart of the Lower East Side racked up 21 percent, while in their debut performance on the US presidential scene the Midwest/New York ticket of Debs and Hanford garnered more than 400,000 votes, placing third (behind Roosevelt and Parker) in a field of six presidential candidates. But in 1905 their progress faltered when, in Gotham's most hotly contested mayoral race since 1886, they were unexpectedly blindsided by a maverick member of the capitalist class, the multi-millionaire publishing mogul William Randolph Hearst.

AFTER PLAYING A HIGH-PROFILE PART in the 1898 war with Spain, Hearst had been depressed at how little he'd gotten out of it, compared to Roosevelt, whom he loathed and envied. TR had returned from Cuba a war hero and ridden into the governor's mansion. Perhaps, Hearst mused, he should have raised his own cowboy regiment instead of slugging it out with Pulitzer, selling newspapers. Even if belatedly, he was determined to plunge into politics, and in 1899 he announced his signature issue: the "DESTRUCTION OF CRIMINAL TRUSTS."

Hearst had been an anti-trust and anti-corruption crusader since his *San Francisco Examiner* days, when he'd excoriated the Southern Pacific, and he now launched a similar campaign in his New York newspapers. From 1899 on, the *New York Morning Journal* (in 1902 renamed the *New York American*), and the *New York Evening Journal,* paid close attention to the expanding merger movement—issuing weekly, sometimes daily, reports on consolidations in various industries, and denouncing the growth of these "Trust Frankensteins," which had become "more powerful than the people's government."

During the Croker-Van Wyck years Hearst took up arms against several New York Frankensteins, notably the wannabe or actual monopolies in water and energy.

In the mid-1890s New York had been looking at a future water shortfall of 500 million gallons a day. Given that the Croton watershed was at its limits, and the Hudson basically unusable, the obvious next place to tap was up in the Catskill Mountains, long fabled for the purity of their water. Banking on this, a group of New York City speculators had formed a corporation, the Ramapo Company, and set out to get a hammerlock on the Catskills' liquid assets. In 1895, with assistance from Republican boss Platt, they got legislative authority to buy options on critical properties. In 1899, with assistance from Democratic boss Croker, they pushed the Van Wyck regime to commit the city to buying water from their company for the next forty years— at twice the price of Croton water. Hearst screamed "corrupt bargain" and supported Comptroller Bird Coler, an independent Brooklyn Democrat, in holding up the deal long enough to generate an engineers' report that argued the city could undertake the project on its own for approximately one-fifth what Ramapo was demanding. Soon the deal was dead.

In the arena of gas and electric generation and distribution, the field was already highly centralized, with the Rockefellers' Consolidated Gas a leading player. Critics complained the energy companies overcharged for their services, paid little or nothing to the city for their franchises, wriggled out of agreements to provide free lighting to public buildings, ripped up streets but seldom restored them, and arrogantly secured immunity from public control by contributing heavily to politicians. In the spring of 1899 Hearst unleashed an attack on Consolidated Gas, galvanizing a protest movement that led the state legislature to temporarily drive rates down 20 percent, and in 1901, partly at Hearst's urging, the Low administration began demanding that Consolidated Gas negotiate the rates it charged for street lighting rather than dictating them.

Hearst did more than critique existing arrangements; he proposed alternative ones. In 1899 he called for "public ownership of public franchises," suggesting in particular creation of a municipal gas plant. Taking a stand for municipal ownership was a shrewd tactic. It appealed to many working people yet was acceptable to many conservatives. The powerful Merchants' Association had played a key role in sinking the Ramapo's bid to privatize the water supply, believing it would give monopoly profits to a small group of crony capitalists, at the expense of the broader business community. The prestigious New York City Club also favored continued municipal ownership of the water supply.

Since Erie Canal days, New York businessmen had often been willing to socialize the cost of constructing key utilities, using public funds to facilitate private development. They were confirmed in this inclination at the turn of the century by their awareness that many European cities had embarked on just such initiatives, with businessmen taking the lead in expanding public enterprise. Glasgow had municipalized its gas supply in 1869, Birmingham followed suit five years later, and by 1889 half the gasworks in the German Empire were municipally owned, with Frankfurt having an electric plant as well. The London County Council voted to municipalize water, gas, electricity, the docks, and streetcars, at the behest of a so-called Progressive coalition of business and professional men with socialists and workingmen, though Parliament, controlled by anti-tax conservatives, stymied most of these initiatives.

New Yorkers were well aware of these European initiatives. Albert Shaw, editor of the *American Review of Reviews*, provided regular reports on the municipalization movement and in 1895 brought out two volumes on the subject—*Municipal Government in Great Britain* and *Municipal Government in Continental Europe*—while from the left, John Burns, a leading English advocate of "municipal socialism," lectured in Gotham on the progress of London's Progressives.

The notion had been taken up by respectable members of Gotham's reform community, though they tended to distance themselves from any socialistic implications. In 1897 the Reform Club's organ, *Municipal Affairs*, published an article entitled "New York City Should Own the Gas Supply." This was, said its author, Edward M. Grout, "purely a business proposition." The city was already running businesses—docks, bridges, sanitation, markets—why not power supply? Given that gas production had become a monopoly, and competition could not be counted on to restrain price gouging, it should be run by public authorities. Grout ticked off all the European cities—and American ones as well—who had followed this path: 700 in all. Public power was "neither socialistic, communistic, nor populistic," Grout insisted, but rather a sign of "progress." Similarly, in 1900 a committee of the august Chamber of Commerce declared "that the city should own its own water supply, and that it should acquire, if it can be done on fair terms, the gas and electrical supplies of the city," adding that "the experience of municipal governments in Great Britain abundantly proves that such ownership has tended to the public welfare."

His platform now firmly established, Hearst dove into electoral politics, starting at the top. William Jennings Bryan was running for president again in 1900. Hearst wanted to join him on the ticket, but Bryan went with the more conservative Adlai Stevenson. When the Democrats lost to McKinley—a victorious war president presiding over a boom—Hearst continued his labors on behalf of the party, preparing to run for the top spot in 1904. He hit a speed bump in 1901 when McKinley was assassinated and Hearst's vitriolic campaign editorials came back to haunt him.

Hearst recovered in 1902, courtesy of Tammany, which gave him the Democratic nomination to Congress—a reward for past services and expected future funding. With Murphy's imprimatur Hearst didn't need to campaign at all, but he did so, vigorously, all the while mastering the tactics of the professional politician's trade. He appealed for the immigrant vote by having his papers support Irish independence and report on events in Russia of concern to Jews. He spent lavishly on helping the needy: feeding the hungry, importing and selling coal below cost, handing out Christmas toys to 40,000 children. He demonstrated a Sullivanian flair in organizing crowd-pleasing extravaganzas. And—far more than Tammany—he championed workers and was endorsed by many unions.

Hearst won, but he rarely showed up in Congress during his term, preferring to spend his time pursuing the 1904 Democratic nomination. He spent a million and a half dollars organizing "Hearst for President" clubs, and hailed unions while hammering trusts. As his pledged delegate count mounted steadily, so did the anxiety level of the party's conservative wing. *Times* publisher Adolph Ochs warned that Hearst was "appealing with equal fervor and greater recklessness to the very prejudices and passions aroused by the utterances of Bryan." Tammany boss Murphy agreed that Hearst was too radical, and that his candidacy would be disastrous. So did big Democratic backers like August Belmont and Thomas Fortune Ryan. To "expel the Hearst poison," as the *Times* put it, the right wing rallied behind the conservative Wall Street lawyer and Court of Appeals Chief Justice Alton B. Parker.

Parker carried the St. Louis convention. In the ensuing contest between two New Yorkers—a reflection of Gotham's overweening influence as the biggest city in the most electoral-rich state in the Union—Tammany carried Manhattan, the Bronx, Queens, and Richmond for Parker, but Roosevelt won Brooklyn and every other county in the state, giving him a commanding majority.

BALKED AT THE TOP IN 1904, Hearst lowered his sites in 1905 and took aim at the mayoralty. Murphy renominated George McClellan for another term—now to be four years in length, thanks to another charter revision. As Tammany's man, McClellan seemed assured of victory, but then Hearst entered the lists on a third-party ticket, and the race became a donnybrook.

In December 1904, weeks after the national election was over, Hearst and others formed the Municipal Ownership League (MOL). The organization's goal was to replace private monopolies with publicly owned utilities, which would have the collateral benefit of diminishing the corporate payoffs that Tammany used to maintain its grip on power. Hearst printed an MOL application form in the *American* and the *Journal*; a thousand readers enrolled in the first week.

The most impressive recruit was Judge Samuel Seabury, scion of an impeccably conservative New York family. The first Samuel Seabury had been a leading Tory opponent of Alexander Hamilton and the first bishop of the Episcopal Church. Subsequent Seaburys—Samuel's grandfather and father—had each in turn been rector of the Church of the Annunciation on West 14th Street and professor of canon law at the General Theological Seminary. Samuel switched from the pulpit to the bar (which he passed in 1894) and entered reform politics by joining a Good Government Club and working in the Strong campaign.

Then he read *Progress and Poverty* and became a staunch anti-monopolist. He went to visit Henry George, worked for the old man in his climactic last campaign, joined the Manhattan Single Tax Club, and became its president in 1897. In this capacity he made his first attack on the utility companies. Noting that Parisian gas companies paid substantial taxes to their city, he charged that New York's firms were using "their privileges as a means of plundering all the people."

Seabury's attacks helped win him election to a City Court judgeship during the Citizens' Union sweep of 1901, but he continued from the bench to publish articles and give speeches urging the state to give the city the right to own and operate public utilities and to confiscate existing companies (with just compensation). In 1905 he collected these pieces in a 200-page booklet, *Municipal Ownership and Operation of Public Utilities in New York City*. (In writing it Seabury drew heavily on two works by the eminent muckraker Gustavus Myers: *History of Public Franchises in New York City* (1900) and *The History of Tammany Hall* (1901), both of which recounted assorted swindles.)

Seabury and Hearst continued to stress that many European cities had opted for public ownership. To underscore this, and thus bolster its own legitimacy, the MOL dispatched to Europe a committee including Hearst and James Graham Phelps Stokes, another millionaire reformer, for a summer-long inspection tour of cities where municipalization had worked, and Hearst ran stories illustrating those successes in his papers.[9]

9. Stokes was a scion of one of New York's wealthiest families. His great-grandfather had founded Phelps, Dodge. His father, Anson Phelps Stokes, was a banker and real estate developer. He himself had extensive mining and railroad interests out west. But he had also inherited the family's liberal strain—best evidenced in his unmarried aunts, who had founded the Phelps-Stokes Fund to give money to American Indians, African Americans, and slum residents of New York City. Young Stokes worked for the YMCA, then joined Hartley House, then the University Settlement, where in 1903 he met Rose Pastor, a Jewish former factory girl, now journalist and settlement worker. The 1905 marriage between a Protestant millionaire and a Yiddish Cinderella generated enormous press coverage, which drew additional attention to the MOL.

Seabury and Hearst also called on the Republican state legislature to investigate possible collusion between the Democratic city government and Consolidated Gas. The legislature agreed, partly to bash Tammany, partly to placate the many businessmen and citizens riled by high-priced energy. The position of counsel was offered to Charles Evans Hughes, an attorney as yet unknown beyond legal circles.

Like Seabury, Hughes had come from a ministerial background, but after undergraduate studies at Brown he'd opted for studying law at Columbia and moved down to the city from upstate New York. After passing the bar in 1884 he practiced commercial law, rather than entering a large Wall Street firm and dealing with corporate clients. Though respectable and prosperous, Hughes was thus an outsider, well positioned for his duties. Few expected much from his investigation, however, given that many state legislators were deeply beholden to utility corporations. (Consolidated Gas was a major campaign contributor.) Hearst slammed Hughes as a "FRIEND OF ROCKEFELLER" because Hughes attended the same church as JDR and taught young Rockefeller Jr. in its Sunday school.

But Hughes surprised almost everybody with his spring 1905 grilling of a series of arrogant and uncooperative energy officials. His probing revealed that their companies, wildly overcapitalized, had pegged gas rates high enough to pay dividends on watered as well as asset-backed stock, giving shareholders a return of 20–30 percent on actually invested capital. He also compared rates with those of other cities and confirmed that Consolidated Gas and New York Edison were overcharging. He suggested they could cut gas prices by a quarter, and electric bills by a third, and still make a reasonable profit, more than the minimum of 6 percent to which they were entitled by law. Hughes also confirmed muckraker charges of fraudulent bookkeeping, tax evasion, and bribing of legislators.

Hughes then drafted corrective measures for the legislators to consider. He rejected Hearst and Seabury's call for municipal ownership, chiefly from fears it would redound to Tammany's benefit, not an unreasonable concern. ("I'm all for municipal ownership," Boss Plunkitt enthused. "It's a grand idea, the city owning the railroads, the gas works and all that. Just see how many thousands of new places there would be for Tammany workers!") He also refused to endorse a breakup of the Gas Trust to restore competition, deeming it no longer practical. Instead Hughes advocated and won passage of a 1905 law mandating public regulation by an appointed body—a State Commission of Gas and Electricity—that would have the authority to inspect power companies' books, regulate their issue of stocks and bonds, specify standards for their products, and set rates.

Hughes's regulatory approach was very much in the vein of what President Roosevelt was advocating on the national level. And just as the nationwide corporations preferred federal regulation to dealing with scores of states, so the New York State energy companies considered dealing with three commissioners—unelected and hence less responsive to popular pressure—to be a better bet than remaining accountable to multiple municipal legislatures. Especially as some cities, notably Gotham, had been agitating for public power, a potentially mortal threat, and Hughes's law specifically precluded New York City from operating a power plant without state-commission approval. Not surprisingly, the Municipal Ownership League and the Citizens' Union protested the ceding of all regulatory power to an appointed state body as undemocratic and a violation of home rule.

In October Hearst was officially nominated for mayor by the MOL. Republicans tried to get Hughes to run against him, but the lawyer was in the midst of the insurance investigation, which he'd been appointed to run after his gas triumph. The GOP nominated instead William Ivins, a moderate reformer.

Hearst now put together a multi-class coalition. He appealed to the well-to-do and middle-class reform crowd with his plan to starve Tammany by municipalizing utilities. He personalized the issue by charging Murphy with having taken corporate payoffs—the probable source of his luxurious Long Island villa—and threatening reprisals: "Look Out, Murphy!" read a Hearst cartoon caption under an image of the Tammany boss in convict stripes. "It's a Short Lockstep from Delmonico's to Sing Sing." And the publisher promised that he, Hearst, would be beholden only to the people; he didn't quite say that as a millionaire he would be unbribable, but he didn't have to.

He also aimed at the Irish and German skilled workers who had been in the forefront of the Henry George insurgency back in the 1880s. He defended unions, strikes, and pro-labor legislation; established a Workingmen's Municipal Ownership Association; and demanded cheaper gas, better schools, and lower transportation rates. Hearst also pushed ethnic and gender buttons: appealing to Irish nationalism by attacking McClellan as a "hireling of Great Britain"; supporting Jewish causes by helping raise funds for pogrom victims; and working with Harriot Stanton Blatch, daughter of Elizabeth Cady Stanton, in setting up a Women's League for Hearst.

The Democrats denounced Hearst as a socialist. Tammany campaign headquarters on Park Row, across from City Hall, was decorated with two large pictures, one of Mayor McClellan paired with an American flag, one of Hearst matched with a red flag. Bourke Cockran, Tammany's star orator, told a huge Democratic rally in Union Square that Hearst— "an apostle of riot, an advocate of disorder, a promoter of Socialism"—would encourage class conflict. If he was elected, the "foundations of society would be shattered and the whole fabric of social order reduced to ruin."

The Socialists, however, denounced Hearst as a humbug. His "pseudo-socialistic daily press" was just "feigning an ultra radical attitude." His anti-Tammany credentials were of extremely recent vintage: he had accepted its 1902 nomination for Congress and done his damndest to get its presidential nod in 1904. He was no friend of labor—being just another capitalist—and his implicit claims of descent from George were ludicrous: "Hearst is a pygmy as compared to Henry George." True, his municipal ownership issue seemed to mirror the Socialists' own advocacy of city-owned streetcars, gas plants, and waterworks. But until the municipal government was controlled by working people, whatever it owned would not be safely in the public domain. Still, Hillquit had to admit that Hearst had helped rouse "the spirit of revolt against existing conditions"; he only hoped this would redound to the benefit of Socialist journalist Algernon Lee, the SP's candidate for mayor.

On Election Day, new-Tammany Murphy slipped on old-Tammany brass knuckles. Hearst poll watchers were beaten up and chased away by hired muscle; Hearst ballots were dumped in the East River; repeaters from Philadelphia were trooped to the polls; votes were cast in the name of dead people. McClellan won, but even with rampant fraud, Hearst came within an eyelash of victory, losing by roughly 3,500 votes out of 600,000 cast for the three candidates. The publisher demanded a recount, backed by the likes of Bishop Potter and Andrew Carnegie; privately even Roosevelt, who detested Hearst, thought "if he was entitled to the seat he should have it." But neither the courts nor the state legislature was willing to intervene and overturn.

Post-election analysis suggested Hearst's support was broadly based. Particularly alarming to Murphy was a *New York Herald* report that 72 percent of workingmen had gone for the publisher. He had done particularly well with second-generation Irish workers, those less in need of the machine's jobs and services, and had appealed strongly to Jewish voters. Clearly, the idea of an activist municipal government devoted to working-class interests had tremendous potential appeal.

IN 1906 HEARST, ON A ROLL, took aim at the governorship—renaming the Municipal Ownership League as the Independence League, the better to attract upstate voters. His bid immediately commanded national attention. Lincoln Steffens profiled "Hearst, the Man of Mystery" in the *American Magazine*, noting that if he "did literally the things he says he will do, it means that this child of the privileged class will really try to abolish privilege." On the other hand, Steffens reported, many reformers, who agreed with Hearst on curbing the trusts, nevertheless thought he too much resembled the corporate capos he was attacking. His power, after all, was based on money and ownership of a press. His party was a one-man show; he seemed more autocrat than democrat.

Certainly the Socialists thought so. They denounced Hearst as an unprincipled demagogue, found his seeming socialism a matter of "political clothes stealing," and nominated their own gubernatorial candidate; they also chose Hillquit to run for Congress, making his electoral debut against an incumbent backed by Hearst.

Then, in August, Charlie Murphy upended the race by announcing his preferred gubernatorial candidate was...William Randolph Hearst. Murphy even lurched leftward (at least rhetorically) by endorsing Hearst's calls for municipal ownership of public utilities and a war against "criminal combinations of capital." Accusations of a corrupt bargain began to fly—Hearst was rumored to have promised Murphy a half million if he won—but there were simpler, less conspiratorial explanations. Murphy understood that if Hearst ran as a third-party candidate, the likeliest winner of the ensuing Hearst/Tammany tussle would be the Republicans. Hearst loudly insisted he was still opposed to Murphy, but quietly went along with the arrangement, as it was evident that this unnatural alliance had immeasurably increased Hearst's chances of winning.

"Hearst in War, Hearst in Peace, Hearst in the Hearts of His Countrymen," 1906. (Library of Congress Prints and Photographs Division)

To no one was this more evident than Theodore Roosevelt. The president viewed Hearst rather as Alexander Hamilton had Aaron Burr, as an unprincipled Cataline, a dangerous demagogue. TR's private correspondence was filled with fulminations. Hearst "preaches the gospel of envy, hatred and unrest"; if he got the chance he might "play the part of some of the least worthy creatures of the French Revolution"; he was "the most potent single influence for evil we have in our life."

For all TR's venom against the person of the publisher, he saw something even more menacing in Hearst's rising star, and that was the working-class support he had mobilized. Roosevelt confided to Henry Cabot Lodge that "I am horrified at the information I receive on every hand as to Hearst's strength on the East Side among laborers," itself a reflection of the "great growth of socialistic and radical spirit among the workingmen." "The labor men are very ugly," he wrote in another letter, "and no one can tell how far such discontent will spread." Writing to the chair of the Republican National Committee, Roosevelt called for a "savage and aggressive fight against Hearstism."

First he needed a strong Republican nominee, and as he wrote his consigliere Elihu Root, Charles Evans Hughes was clearly the strongest possible candidate. When TR raised this with the Republican leaders in Albany, however, they protested vehemently—Hughes was far more liberal than they. But Roosevelt rode roughly over them, something he'd been eager to do for some time, and which was now feasible given the specter of Hearstism and the fact that Hughes's insurance investigation had laid bare flagrant corruption by those self-same Republican bosses. When they dug in their heels anyway, Roosevelt went public with a full presidential endorsement, and the bosses caved. They even accepted a TR-style platform that called for "the regulation of all public utility corporations."

Roosevelt now plotted out every step of Hughes's campaign, taking the low road as well as the high. He advised one editor that Hearst's private life was "disreputable," his wife being a former vaudevillian, and hence he was not someone anyone who believed that "sound home relations form the basis of national citizenship" would want in the executive mansion. When TR was sent some damaging information on the publisher by a friend in California, he immediately wrote Hughes that "I believe your manager should act on them at once"; rumors of louche living soon began appearing in opposition papers and magazines.

Finally, Roosevelt rolled out his top gun. On November 1, he dispatched Secretary of State Root to New York to deliver the following message: "I say to you, with [the president's] authority, that he regards Mr. Hearst to be wholly unfit to be Governor, as an insincere, self-seeking demagogue, who is trying to deceive the workingmen of New York by false statements and false promises." Hearst's election, said Root, would do serious injury to Roosevelt's work against "corporate wrongdoing." And then he dropped his biggest bombshell, declaring, again on presidential authority, that when TR, in his first message to Congress, had denounced unspecified anarchists and agitators for having inflamed the assassin who murdered McKinley, "HE HAD MR. HEARST SPECIFICALLY IN HIS MIND."

Thrown on the defensive days before the election, Hearst was able to do little more than denounce Root as a tool of the corporations. It wasn't enough. Hearst polled a substantial majority in Greater New York, but Hughes carried upstate by an even bigger margin, winning the governorship by less than 60,000 votes out of nearly 1.5 million cast.

One result of the 1906 outcome was that regulation triumphed over municipalization as the primary device for dealing with local corporations. In 1907, fulfilling now-Governor Hughes's promise, New York State established a Public Service Commission—an expanded version of the Gas and Electric Commission—and gave it authority over nearly all public utilities.

A second result was that upper- and middle-class reformers finally abandoned the idea of winning power via an independent municipal third party. The 1903 defeat of the Citizens' Union had been the initial blow, and the Hearst campaigns of 1905 and 1906, apart from having failed to dislodge Tammany, had demonstrated that third parties could be put to discomfiting uses. They did not, however, withdraw from politics. Many retreated into the Republican Party. Though it was clearly doomed to minority status in a Democratic town, the organization dominated state and national politics. And keeping the local Republican machine in good working order preserved a vehicle that could be used to recapture the city, if sufficient numbers of independents and disaffected Democrats could again be enticed into a fusion campaign. Until such a propitious moment, reformers would forgo direct political challenges to Tammany. Instead of seeking to control the governmental apparatus, they settled instead for shaping the way it operated.

EXPERTS

The theoretical underpinnings for this new strategy had been laid out by Frank J. Goodnow, a professor of the new science of public administration. The Brooklyn-born academician had gotten a law degree from Columbia but switched fields in 1882, joining Columbia's just-established School of Political Science (1881). Goodnow rose to become a full professor in 1891, and in 1903 was appointed the Eaton Professor of Administrative Law and Municipal Science and also chosen as the first president of the American Political Science Association. "Science" was a highly prestigious noun at the turn of the century, promising dispassionate solutions for political conundrums.

In one of his major works—*Politics and Administration* (1900)—Goodnow wrestled with the boss-ridden state of municipal government and suggested that reformers were approaching the problem in the wrong way. The first step toward achieving a structure that was both representative and efficient was to recognize there were two distinct components of government—politics and administration—which should be separated as much as possible. Politics—the "determination of public policy"—should be left to politicians and legislators, while "the execution of that policy" should be given over to professional managers, trained in the science of administration. Render unto politicians the things that are political, was Goodnow's advice, but leave administration to the experts.

One corollary of this dictum was that administrators and political leaders should be selected by different procedures: "Where you want skill, you must appoint; where you want responsibility elect." Another was that administrators once appointed should be freed from interference by politicians. Just as judges were independent, so should administrators be. And to ensure their autonomy, they should be granted tenure, rather than being made subject to dismissal each time a new party won. Civil service examinations were OK as devices to keep incompetent amateurs *out*, but Goodnow wanted to keep competent professionals *in*. Making public service a permanent career would also liberate administrators from parochial (ward or ethnic) concerns, and allow them to concentrate on the wider city's needs.

Elite Good Government reformers who had been banging their heads against electoral walls were drawn to this diagnosis and prescription. If they couldn't win politically, perhaps they could conquer administratively, ceding City Hall to Tammany (if reluctantly) and instead infiltrating the departments, which ran the metropolis on a daily basis. This approach was particularly appealing to the generation of patricians and professionals then rising to prominence in organizations that had been spearheading the Good Government approach but were now prepared to rethink it.

This shift in personnel and principles was particularly apparent at the City Club, long a backbone (and pocketbook) of the reform movement. When founded in 1892 it had unquestionably been the instrument of Gotham's wealthiest businessmen and most socially prominent citizens, with 90 percent of its members listed in the *Social Register*. Members had seen their organization as simultaneously a civic association and a social club on par with the Union League, the Metropolitan, and the Century, to which many of them also belonged.

Its social cachet continued on in the new century, boosted by the elegant new clubhouse that went up in 1904 at 55 West 44th Street—New York's equivalent of London's Pall Mall, the seat of gentlemen's clubs. But as membership grew from roughly 500 in 1892 to 1,250 in 1912, the percentage of the socially registered fell to 75 percent in 1902, 60 percent in 1904, and 44 percent in 1912. The center of gravity shifted to professionals and a broader array of businessmen, many of whom were active in the city's civic, charitable, and social organizations. A sampling of 667 members in 1905 included 195 lawyers, 51 bankers, 52 manufacturers, 50 merchants, 31 physicians and surgeons, 23 engineers, 23 educators, 18 architects, 16 publishers, 14 social and civic workers, and 13 clergymen.[10] The club claimed it was nonpartisan, and it was, more or less, so far as major parties were concerned—of 344 who expressed a political preference, 200 were independents, 111 Republicans, and 31 Democrats—but union members and Socialists were conspicuously absent.

As the club's composition shifted, so too did its focus. From 1892 to 1903 it concentrated on defeating Tammany and electing Good Men. After 1903 it largely withdrew from the hurly-burly of politics. Adopting the Goodnow line (the professor himself served on the board of trustees from 1902 to 1905), it replaced calls for political rectitude with demands for administrative efficiency. Deploying their powerful assets—money, economic muscle, social status, and professional credentials—the City Clubbers would conquer territory inside the government they'd been unable to win on the electoral battlefield.

The reversal was effected under two sequential club presidents, Lawrence Veiller (1903–6) and George McAneny (1907–9). Veiller, a social worker, settlement house volunteer, and housing activist, began the reorientation. It was expanded under McAneny, who had a more varied vita. Born poor in Jersey City in 1869, McAneny had worked as a newsboy, and then as a reporter for Pulitzer's *New York World*, before being drawn into civil service reform by Carl Schurz and becoming in 1894 secretary of the National Civil Service Reform League. McAneny remained an active lobbyist on that issue until 1903, when he began studying law in the office of Edward M. Shepard, special counsel to the Pennsylvania Railroad, a giant corporation for which McAneny would undertake lobbying work. Under Veiller and McAneny's direction, City Club committees (often headed by former commissioners) surveyed city problems, monitored government activities, deluged officials with suggestions, and filed taxpayer suits to compel action.

The City Club was not alone in shifting attention from politics to administration. The Reform Club maintained a staff of statisticians and economists to track the city and its

---

10. The abundance of attorneys was a reflection of the profession's overcrowded condition. Of the roughly 16,000 lawyers working in New York City in 1911, only about 30 percent found it a paying profession. Many corporate law firms assigned some young partners to almost full-time *pro bono publico* service. This was not unwelcome, as reform work was seen as a way of advancing one's legal career.

problems and published *Municipal Affairs*, the first journal of its kind in the United States. The Citizens' Union subsided into watchdog status after its 1903 shellacking at the polls, and so did the Woman's Municipal League.

These and other traditional civic associations were now joined by more novel institutions called "foundations." In 1901 John D. Rockefeller decided to organize the "business of benevolence." First he established a series of foundations, each supporting a distinct project. Then, in 1909, he created the all-purpose Rockefeller Foundation, popularly known as the Benevolence Trust. Andrew Carnegie followed suit with several targeted foundations capped, in 1911, by the Carnegie Corporation of New York, which he endowed with $135 million. The premier Gotham-related version was born after the miserly railroad magnate Russell Sage died in 1906, leaving $65 million to his wife, the 78-year-old Margaret Olivia Sage. After consulting with Robert De Forest, her husband's lawyer, on how best to spend it, Mrs. Sage set up the Russell Sage Foundation (1907) with a $10 million endowment. Dedicated to improving "social and living conditions" in the United States, it focused particularly on urban problems. Though it was national in scope, she did require that no less than one-quarter of the endowment's income be applied to "the needs of my own city and its vicinity." (Mrs. Sage now delighted in lavishing her notoriously stingy husband's fortune on, and affixing his name to, various benevolent enterprises. "I am nearly eighty years old," she smiled, "and I feel as if I were just beginning to live.")

In the long run, these multi-million-dollar enterprises would have substantial impact on public policy in New York City.[11] But the most immediate and hands-on exemplar of the new approach was the Bureau of Municipal Research (BMR), the brainchild of William H. Allen, a bright young man with a PhD in political science who had been working for the Association for Improving the Condition of the Poor. In 1903 Allen suggested establishing a nonpartisan agency of experts to apply modern "techniques of business management" to "public affairs and civic problems." He took the concept to R. Fulton Cutting, president of the Citizens' Union (whose candidate, Seth Low, had just been battered by Murphy's George McClellan). Intrigued, Cutting set up a Bureau of City Betterment within the Citizens' Union, in January 1906, as a one-year demonstration project. To direct its affairs, Allen chose Henry Bruère, a University of Chicago graduate who was involved with the settlement house movement.

A team of eager young men in high collars and bowler hats now set out to assess the work done by Manhattan Borough President John F. Ahearn's office, which was responsible for streets, sewers, and public baths, among other things. Ahearn, a Tammany man, stonewalled them by denying access to records to which they were entitled, by law, to review. Rather than commence lengthy legal proceedings to obtain a court order, Bruère and his crew took to the streets. Cross-checking supposedly fulfilled contracts to repair potholes with the actual condition of Eighth Avenue between 42nd and 59th Streets, they found the streets as pockmarked as ever. When they presented Ahearn with evidence of this and other instances of either corruption or incompetence, he ignored them. So they went public—publishing a pamphlet, complete with damning photographs, entitled *How Manhattan Is Governed* (1906), which created a stir in the press.

---

11. The foundations generated considerable distrust. Many suspected the wealthy were out to promote their influence in ways unaccountable to the public. Congressional hearings were held in New York in 1915 on "Centralization of Industrial Control and Operation of Philanthropic Foundations." Despite critical testimony, the government declined to ban them, opting instead for congressional regulation.

Ahearn now demanded an official (i.e., Tammany-controlled) investigation—the time-honored way of sweeping such challenges under the Democratic Party's capacious rug. But McClellan, after his 1905 reelection, had begun to distance himself from Tammany. The mayor had hoped to be nominated for the governorship in 1906 and had been furious when Murphy backed Hearst instead. With his eyes still fixed on higher office, McClellan decided to put some daylight between himself and the bosses. Which is why he turned over the Ahearn investigation not to a Murphy-picked tribunal but to an independent-minded young lawyer, John Purroy Mitchel. When the 28-year-old Columbia College and NYU Law graduate confirmed the Bureau of City Betterment's findings, Republican governor Hughes (in December 1907) removed Ahearn from office, not for corruption but for incompetence and mismanagement, the first time an American official had been discharged for such reasons. The bureau and its Citizens' Union backers were thrilled. As one member exulted, "The hoo-rah reformer is not the only one who can get results."[12]

The bureau also proved it could wield carrots as well as sticks. When invited by the Health Department to investigate its workings, the bureau's men pored over records the department threw open for them and then issued accolades, particularly of the department's innovations in child health care, which helped *increase* its budget. The Board of Estimate was so impressed by the bureau's work that it commissioned a similar assessment of the Finance Department. Back in 1904 McClellan had appointed a commission to do this—it had included Columbia's Goodnow and NYU professor Frederick A. Cleveland, a specialist in municipal accounting—but they had found the records a total and impenetrable mess. The bureau now proceeded to straighten things out and install an up-to-date accounting system. In this way it signaled its willingness to work with city officials—providing them with services and personnel, publicizing their achievements, strengthening their hand vis-à-vis the politicians.

With the bureau's promise so amply demonstrated, Citizens' Union chief Cutting prevailed on John D. Rockefeller, Andrew Carnegie, E. H. Harriman, Kuhn, Loeb, and J. P. Morgan & Co. to establish Allen and Bruère's operation as a separate institution, renamed the Bureau of Municipal Research (BMR). In May 1907 the BMR began operations on the ninth floor of 261 Broadway, from which (appropriately) it could oversee City Hall below. Its trustees included Cutting, McAneny of the City Club, Frank Vanderlip of National City Bank, and the presidents of the Carnegie Foundation and Rockefeller's General Education Board. The chair was Columbia economics professor Edwin R. A. Seligman, scion of the German Jewish banking family, a leading authority on public finance, a prominent member of the City Club, and a supporter of Greenwich House, tenement reform, and Felix Adler's Society for Ethical Culture (of which he'd assumed the presidency in 1906). Allen became secretary, Bruère became director, and the two were soon joined by Professor Cleveland as technical director. The trio quickly became known as "the ABC."

The ABC's goals differed from the muckrakers'. They were interested not in digging up dirt but in providing "constructive publicity"—demystifying the budget in order "to keep the public informed of what public officials are doing." In effect they sought to serve as the public's CPA. (The status of certified public accountant had been established by law in 1896.) But while they would watch every penny, they promised not to pinch them. Their new

---

12. Ahearn's removal was immediately reversed when Tammany aldermen, led by Little Tim Sullivan, instantly reelected the deposed B. P. to the same office. The City Club and Citizens' Union then sued, and the case dragged on through the courts for two years before Ahearn was finally ousted. But in the meantime, additional investigations of Tammany chieftains had successfully toppled the borough presidents of Queens and the Bronx.

budgetary systems would, to be sure, reveal where savings could be made, but the ABC denied they were simply flacking for the wealthy taxpayers who groused endlessly about the waste, corruption, and extravagance of city government for which they had to foot the bill.[13] Rather, cutting waste would free up resources that could be better spent on municipal betterment. This was stressed in their 1908 Budget Exhibit, an elaborate array of lectures and displays that attracted 50,000 citizens to the new City Investing Building (165 Broadway), including Governor Hughes and the sympathetic Comptroller Herman Metz. In 1911 the municipality itself took over the Budget Exhibit and made it an annual event.

Also in 1911, the Bureau of Municipal Research leaders took steps to ensure they wouldn't become "mornin' glories" that "withered up in a short time"—Boss Plunkitt's taunt about the fate of amateur reformers. The BMR established a Training School for Public Service, intended precisely to produce a cadre of expert administrators that could give the reform movement staying power. Founded with a handsome gift from Mary Averell Harriman, widow of railroad magnate Edward H. Harriman (an early BMR supporter who had died in 1909, leaving her roughly $70 million), it was inspired by the example of German cities such as Dresden, Leipzig, and Munich, which offered instruction in municipal administration.

A key figure in the Training School's development was a junior colleague of Goodnow's at Columbia, Charles Austin Beard, then an adjunct professor of politics. Beard believed with Goodnow that expert administrative leadership was crucial for improved municipal governance. As he also believed in mixing scholarship with public service, from 1909 on he had devoted three afternoons a week to BMR work downtown at 261 Broadway. In 1912 he took on substantial responsibilities at the new Training School, and in 1915 he became its director.

For all his enthusiasm and participation, Beard began worrying early on that the BMR was focusing too narrowly on budgetary and financial issues, and restricting its purview to the purely municipal. In his 1912 book, *American City Government*, Beard offered a caveat to Goodnow's now-regnant perspective, suggesting that "strictly speaking, there can be no such thing as 'municipal science,' because the most fundamental concerns of cities, the underlying economic foundations, are primarily a matter of state and national, not local, control." The problems city dwellers faced—congestion, low wages, crime, unemployment, the stark division between classes—might be partially alleviated through municipal action, but all such local solutions, even municipal ownership, which he favored, would be subject to "the limitations inherent in the dependence of the city upon the larger social and economic tissue of which it is a part." That was why "mere business efficiency in administration," while helpful, could have only marginal impact.[14]

---

13. Many of the propertied grousers managed to evade their obligations, partly by failing to declare their less tangible forms of wealth, such as corporate securities, which formed an increasing percentage of their assets. Some also simply lied about their holdings: for all their cattiness about crooked aldermen, twenty members of the Chamber of Commerce were found to have perjured themselves on such matters. Even much real estate escaped taxation. As Henry George had noted long before, unimproved land held for speculation in suburban areas was grossly under-assessed. William Vanderbilt's taxable personal property was valued at $40 million, but he paid taxes on only a half million. This upper-class tax evasion shifted the burden to the middle classes, whose holdings were primarily in real estate. They would provide a major source of support for the municipal reform movement. (The propertyless poor escaped direct taxation.)

14. In his own scholarly work, Beard would go beyond assessing battles within the bosses/businessmen/socialists triad, or examining formal governmental structures, and instead analyze the economic underpinnings of municipal politics. He would focus on contention between key city interest groups—landowners, manufacturers, shippers, possessors of franchises, recipients of tax favors, bondholders, municipal bankers, private utilities, favored contractors, liquor, gambling, and vice rings, as well as the politics-for-profit city machines. This kind of interest group analysis would also characterize his 1913 book *An Economic Interpretation of the Constitution.*

THE BMR'S STOCK CONTINUED TO RISE in the next administration. In 1909 Boss Murphy denied the renegade McClellan the nomination for a third term, effectively ending his career, and turned for a Tammany candidate to State Supreme Court Justice William Jay Gaynor. It seemed a clever choice. A Montague Street lawyer and erudite gentleman (he read Homer in the original), Gaynor had won a solid reputation as a civic reformer by ferreting out fraud and corruption in Brooklyn. Elected to the bench, he became an advocate of individual liberties. Gaynor had also developed a popular following. Himself the son of Irish immigrants, he appealed to his compatriots as a man who liked his whiskey straight and who opposed zealots out to purify the public's morals. (Of the Reverend Parkhurst Gaynor said: "He thinks he is pious, when he is only bilious.")

Gaynor had also long been backed by the Hearst press as a crusader for municipal ownership of rapid transit, and he himself had campaigned for Hearst in 1905 and 1906. Yet Gaynor, a political realist, was prepared to cut a deal with Murphy (as Hearst himself had done).

The nonpartisan reformers, disaffected Democrats, and Republicans decided this might be a propitious moment for taking another shot at winning control of the municipal government, rather than settling for merely influencing it. They joined in backing a fusion slate that included attorney Otto Bannard for mayor; John Purroy Mitchel (the hero of the Ahearn fight) for the presidency of the Board of Aldermen; George McAneny, who had resigned as president of the City Club in order to run for the borough presidency of Manhattan; and William A. Prendergast (a BMR supporter) seeking the comptrollership.

Now Hearst again strode to center stage. Enraged at Gaynor's acceptance of the Democratic nomination, Hearst demanded he refuse it. The strong-willed Gaynor turned him down cold. So Hearst entered the race himself on a third-party ticket—basically what remained of the Independence League—and launched a vituperative campaign. But the peppery judge proved a match for the journalist. Gaynor denounced not only Hearst's "ragbag newspapers" but his personal behavior. (One pamphlet, *Orgies in a Yacht*, depicted Hearst as a debauchee.) "Morally speaking," Gaynor snapped, "his mind must be a howling wilderness."

Hearst proved unable to outflank Gaynor on the corruption front, and former supporters dropped away, notably Samuel Seabury. Prepared to see Gaynor elected even with Murphy's support, Seabury had grown impatient with Hearst's dictatorial style, and his hypocrisy, noting, "It is not so long ago that Mr. Hearst saw no impropriety in accepting for himself a Democratic endorsement." Labor too did not turn out in force, having been seriously disaffected by Hearst's betrayal in the previous race, and many Irish supporters opted to stay in the Wigwam. Murphy successfully mobilized the Democratic masses for Gaynor, who carried 42 percent of the Greater New York vote. But while Fusion's mayoral candidate lost, the rest of the slate won a resounding victory, leaving reformers in overwhelming control of the Board of Estimate, and McAneny, Prendergast, and Mitchel installed in power.

To add injury to injury, Gaynor, Tammany's supposed man in City Hall, when asked after his election what he intended to do for Murphy, announced he would "give him a few kind words." As Murphy's influence in the Gaynor administration waned, that of the Bureau of Municipal Research waxed. Prendergast and McAneny introduced proposals as fast as the BMR could draft and type them. Departments were reorganized. Tammany men were ousted. Yet Gaynor never fulfilled his promise as a reform mayor. On August 9, 1910, months after taking office, he was shot in the throat by a would-be assassin—a disgruntled laborer who had been dismissed from the Docks Department. Though he survived, Gaynor's already sulphurous temper worsened. He alienated reformers, Republicans, and Democrats alike and died in 1913, shortly after launching a quixotic campaign for reelection as an independent.

NOW THE REENERGIZED REFORMERS SET OUT TO COMPLETE their return to power by putting one of their own in the mayor's seat. They were convinced that in the youthful John Purroy Mitchel they had found a man who combined impeccable reform credentials with widespread political appeal.

Mitchel came from radical Irish stock. The British had banished his grandfather, a famous rebel patriot, to Australia, from whence he had escaped to New York City, where he was greeted with a grand reception at City Hall. His son, John Purroy's father, rose in city politics to become fire marshal. Marrying Mary Purroy, a public school teacher whose father had been president of the Board of Aldermen, he settled down to a comfortable existence in suburban Fordham. There, in a stone-walled house replete with fruit trees and gardens, Mitchel was born in 1879. In 1894 he entered St. John's College, whose campus adjoined the family's property. In 1896 he transferred to Columbia. In 1902 he completed New York Law School. In 1907 he'd been working as a city investigator when he was tapped by McClellan for a starring role in the removal of Borough President Ahearn, and that in turn led to his election in 1909 as president of the Board of Aldermen.

"Attempted Assassination of Mayor William J. Gaynor," 1910. (Image No. 43.119, Brown Brothers/Museum of the City of New York)

In 1913 Mitchel was nominated by an ad hoc Citizens' Municipal Committee of lawyers, bankers, and business executives (including Andrew Carnegie, William K. Vanderbilt, and the John D. Rockefellers, Senior and Junior both). He was endorsed by the Republicans, the Citizen's Union, and the City Club. The BMR's Henry Bruère—with whom Mitchel had worked closely during the Gaynor years—designed his campaign platform. George McAneny became his running mate as candidate for the aldermanic presidency.

For all his upper-class Anglo-Saxon backing, the Irish Catholic Mitchel knew how to appeal to his countrymen. At one Cooper Union rally of 2,500 Irish Americans, he personally led the throng in singing "The Wearin' of the Green." Mitchel also reached out to social workers and municipal populists by promising better schools, more parks and playgrounds, purer food and water, improved public health, cleaner streets, and freedom from vice. Finally he gained Hearst's support by calling for city-run rapid transit, and municipal ownership of utilities, while reassuring the upper classes he was no closet socialist.

Mitchel buried Murphy's candidate by the largest margin since Consolidation, winning 57.1 percent of the citywide vote to Edward McCall's 37.3 percent; muckraker Charles Edward Russell, running on the Socialist ticket, garnered 5.1 percent, more than doubling that party's previous total. Mitchel had succeeded in bringing together the Irish, Jewish, and German municipal populists who'd backed Hearst with the native-stock traditional reformers who'd backed Low. His running mates did equally well: Fusion candidates swept fifteen of the sixteen seats on the Board of Estimate. It was a total disaster for Tammany Hall—Mitchel even captured Murphy's own district—and the machine now entered into painful exile.

Mitchel hoped to keep them there "for all time." The key to doing so, he believed, was to prove "what a city government in New York can be, if administered solely with a view of achieving continuous efficiency." To accomplish this, he virtually turned the city over to the Bureau of Municipal Research for his four-year term (1914–17).[15]

First he appointed the Bureau's Bruère as city chamberlain. Despite its archaic title, it was not a musty ceremonial seat but rather the city's treasurer, a post whose holder shared power over Gotham's financial affairs with the comptroller. More, Mitchel made Bruère his chief adviser; some began calling him "the Warwick of New York." BMR staff now bustled about, reorganizing departments, revising the budget system, and centralizing control over expenditures. Adopting other BMR proposals, Mitchel created a host of new city agencies, installed professionals and social workers in power, standardized municipal salaries and titles, and clamped down on spending.

The ABC also hoped to transform the municipal work force—a hive, they were sure, of patronage hacks. The BMR was enamored of industrial efficiency experts like Frederick Taylor, who advocated that managers appropriate workers' craft knowledge in order to gain control over the production process; Taylor's *Shop Management* (1903) was required reading at the bureau's Training School for Public Service. The ABC longed to do the same for municipal governance, using time sheets, efficiency tests, and time-and-motion studies to develop precise records of employee performance, weed out superfluous officials, and increase the productivity of those that remained. They got their chance when Mitchel appointed Henry Moskowitz, head of the Madison Street Settlement, to be president of the Civil

15. Some on Rockefeller's staff believed that with a progressive mayor in office, the bureau had become redundant. But others— including Junior—thought a reform regime backed by Rockefeller resources might permanently transform the way the city did business. "Our effort should be not merely to get an honest and economic administration," his advisers concluded, "but to raise the standard so high as to make the Mitchel Mayoralty a memorable object lesson of Good Government and thereby a substantial asset of the reformer in future Municipal campaigns."

Service Commission, and Moskowitz, in turn, unleashed a youthful BMR zealot named Robert Moses on the city bureaucracy.

Moses had been born in New Haven in 1888 to affluent German Jewish parents. (His father owned a department store.) The family moved down to New York City in 1897, where Robert enjoyed a luxurious upbringing in a town house just off Fifth Avenue, at 20 East 46th Street. After graduating from Yale in 1909, he studied public administration at Oxford, where he became a devout Anglophile (affecting a British accent), and in particular a devotee of the British civil service.

Moses deeply admired England's two-tier system of administration, which reserved the upper division for highly educated members of the upper class and employed clerks who passed exams to do the "lower and more mechanical work." He had a similarly profound regard for Britain's colonial administration, having visited and approved of Kitchener's Egypt, and dismissed those who would give "subject peoples" a greater role in self-governance, believing they already occupied as many places "as they are reasonably capable of filling." Moses urged the United States to follow suit, attracting the "best men" to the upper ranks of public service not with knighthoods but with salaries substantial enough to "compete with the large corporations for administrative talent," while making sure that lower-tier workers didn't organize "unions of public employees" to agitate for "higher salaries," by relying "in the last analysis" on "the remorseless exercise of the executive power of suppression and dismissal to solve this question."

After graduating from Oxford in 1911, and studying political science for a term at the University of Berlin, Moses returned to New York in the summer of 1912, enrolled in Columbia's School of Political Science, and over the next year worked on his PhD thesis *The Civil Service of Great Britain* (with advice from Professor Goodnow); it was accepted and published in 1914. In the summer of 1913 he had also joined the BMR's Training School, which seemed to be following in Oxford's excellent footsteps, preparing university men (most BMR students were Ivy Leaguers) for "upper division" service. He quickly grew impatient with the nature and pace of the instruction, and offered to serve on the regular BMR staff, for no salary, an offer the ABC didn't refuse. But there too he soon chafed at not being where the real action was, in the government itself. Then came Mitchel's election and his appointment of Moskowitz, who dispatched Moses to take on the civil service.

Setting a team of assistants to watch city workers perform their jobs, Moses instructed them to break down the bureaucrats' tasks into components that could be graded with mathematical precision. (Examiners were forbidden to take "human factors" into consideration.) Those who scored poorly would be demoted or suffer a pay cut—unless Moses deemed their jobs unnecessary, in which case they would be fired. This prospect created hysteria in the ranks. Tammany mounted an adroit counteroffensive. And Mitchel backed away from Moses, partly as many of his own reformer appointees might not have made the grade.

Many years later, Moses would faint-praise the Mitchel administration, saying it was "an honest outfit, committed to saving rubber bands, using both ends of the pencil and similar efficiency devices," and in truth the ABC did relish the minutiae of cost cutting. On one occasion Allen went to J. P. Morgan and asked him to aid the BMR by handing the banker a dozen erasers, which he had bought in a local shop for 32¢ each, but for which the police department had paid $1.50, from the same store; Allen walked out with a $10,000 donation. The Mitchel administration did begin to get a (not undeserved) reputation for penny pinching, and in particular for not delivering on its promises to working-class constituents. But in the bigger picture, it facilitated an ongoing loosening of the public purse strings that had been going on since Consolidation, one that reversed a policy of fiscal conservatism that had been set in place back in Tweed's day.

The ur-boss had borrowed liberally for funding public works (and padding construction contracts), driving up city debt from $43 million in 1867 to $87 million in 1871, at which point propertied taxpayers had risen up and imposed an austerity regime. In 1884 it was enshrined in the state constitution, when an amendment limited municipal indebtedness to 10 percent of the assessed value of the city's real estate. The penitent Tammany machine got with the program too, and city borrowing slowed in relation to the growth of wealth and population. The tax rate dropped as well, from 2.94 percent in 75 to 1.72 percent in 1895. The city's credit was restored, but public projects lagged. The Consolidation movement—though led by fiscal retrencher Andrew Haswell Green—was seen as the prelude to a massive expansion of needed public works, and so it proved to be.

During the early-twentieth-century administrations—Van Wyck (1898–1901), Low (1902–3), McClellan (1904–9), Gaynor (1910–13), and Mitchel (1914–17)—late-nineteenth-century fiscal conservatism gave way to an era of rising expenditures, higher taxes, and increasing debt. The new dispensation claimed that the municipality, by borrowing to develop infrastructure, would promote metropolitan growth, raise the value of real estate, and reap increased tax levies, which would allow it to pay off the bondholders who had loaned the money to build the public works. The key to making this happen was the city's ability to maintain access to the capital markets—getting the great investment banking houses like J. P. Morgan and Kuhn, Loeb, and bond specialists like William A. Read, to market municipal paper. And instrumental to winning that support was the city's installation of the accounting and management reforms for which the Bureau of Municipal Research had been the most ardent champion. When Bruère declared that New York's financial reporting system was now equal to that of the Pennsylvania Railroad, it was music to bankers' ears.

Which is why, throughout all the electoral gyrations of the turbulent post-Consolidation decades, with their manifold political, social, and cultural consequences, Gotham was able to go on a sustained city-building bender—a three-dimensional expansion spree, embracing both the private and public sector, that sent New York soaring upward, spreading outward, and burrowing underground, creating a metropolis the likes of which the world had never seen.

PART TWO

CONSTRUCTION AND CONNECTION

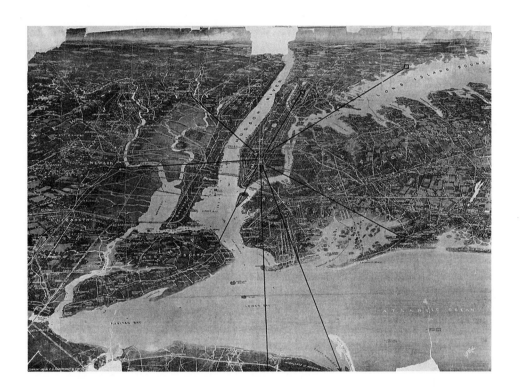

"Found in the Heart of Greater New York and the Metropolitan District...The John Wanamaker Store is easily reached from all residence centers and by its Free Delivery automobile service, reaches all home centers. The store is directly on the great main avenue of travel, and the subway station within the store connects it with the great railroad stations and every part of the community." The lines radiating from Wanamaker's in Manhattan point to the department store's delivery stations throughout Greater New York and areas beyond the city's limits. 1913. (New York Public Library, Lionel Pincus and Princess Firyal Map Division)

7

Sky Boom

SKYLINE

At the turn of the century Harry Black, head of the Chicago-based Fuller Construction Company, set out to make his mark on New York City. Actually Black, though a whiz at promotion and finance, knew little about building. But in 1894 he had met George Fuller, a pioneer skyscraper man, joined his company, and married his daughter. When Fuller died in 1900, Black took over the firm.

Despite Chicago's ongoing demand for tall buildings, Black was convinced that booming Manhattan was the place to be. Already it had reclaimed the world's height record, lost momentarily to Chicago—the current title holder was the thirty-story Park Row Building (1899) at City Hall Park—and calls for twenty-plus-story structures were now routine.

Black moved Fuller Company headquarters to New York and set out to make a splashy debut. He purchased a wedge of property at 23rd Street, where Broadway sheared its way across Fifth Avenue, and prepared to raise a skyscraper. It was a gambler's choice. The odd triangular site posed tricky technical problems. It lay far to the north of Wall Street. And given its proximity to Madison Square, any tall building would be markedly conspicuous, for good or ill.

For a design Black turned to Chicago's preeminent architect, Daniel Burnham, the acclaimed master planner of the 1893 World's Columbian Exposition (Chicago's quadricentennial celebration of Columbus's first voyage). Burnham's firm proposed an elegant and dramatic solution, a structure that would fit neatly into the V-shaped plot and soar straight upward for 300 feet (twenty-one stories) to command the neighborhood. Then Black brought in Paul Starrett, a Fuller construction chief, to translate plan into limestone and terra-cotta reality. Starrett was one of five brothers, all of whom would become prodigious builders. This would be his first New York project.

Even before the scaffolding came down from the shimmering Flatiron Building—so dubbed for its resemblance to the ubiquitous wrinkle remover—it was clear Black had a triumph on his hands. The *Architectural Record* called it "quite the most notorious thing in New York"—a tower that was attracting "more attention than all the other buildings now going up put together." After its official opening in 1902, its fame rippled across continents and oceans.

"Flat-Iron Corner after Snow Storm, New York," 1905. (New York Public Library, Art and Picture Collection)

The Flatiron's popularity was remarkable, especially as it had not captured the "world's tallest" title. In part, its sexy cachet was a matter of ankles. Something in the aerodynamics of its acutely angled edge sent wind gusts whipping along 23rd Street, tossing up skirts of passing shoppers as effectively as did the Blow Hole at Coney Island. This titillating fact was transmitted to the country via vaudeville routines and humor weeklies. (Less amusingly, when winds blew in from the northeast they were—as a lawsuit brought by a neighboring merchant deposed—"deflected with great force and violence down and into the street," throwing pedestrians "with great violence to the pavement," and smashing the plaintiff's plate-glass windows.)

The Flatiron's commercial success spurred further skyscraper construction. The Fuller Company followed up with another wedge-shaped edifice—the twenty-four-story Times Tower (1904) at Broadway and 42nd Street. Here again Black was a pioneer, planting a striking structure in an underdeveloped uptown locale. But most builders stuck to downtown venues, sending dense clusters of tall towers shouldering upward throughout the Wall Street area, around City Hall Park, along Broadway to Union Square, and up Fifth Avenue to the Flatiron. By 1908 there were 366 tall buildings (nine stories or more) in lower Manhattan, nearly four times the number a decade before.

That year one downtown newcomer shot up startlingly out of the skyscraper pack, seized the world's height record, and usurped the Flatiron's place as New York's most sensational tall structure. The Singer Sewing Machine Company had Paris-trained architect Ernest Flagg design a tower to set atop their recently reconstructed fourteen-story French Renaissance headquarters at 149 Broadway (northwest corner of Liberty). The slender Beaux-Arts spire rose 47 stories, its bulbous, mansarded, lantern-topped pinnacle peaking exuberantly at 612 feet, *twice* the height of the Flatiron.

"The Singerhorn," as some called it, became New York's new darling. A 30-foot-long white pennant (with SINGER emblazoned in red letters) flapped from its summit; it could be seen from virtually anywhere in the city. At night, thirty projector searchlights bathed the shaft, and 1,600 incandescent lamps outlined the dome, making the luminous column visible 40 miles away. Thousands paid fifty cents for a ride to the "observation balcony" on the fortieth floor. Some took a shortcut down: the viewpoint attracted death trippers rather than ankle fetishists and soon became known as Suicide Pinnacle.

The Singer Company's triumph inspired the Metropolitan Life Insurance Company to reach for new heights. The firm, which had lagged behind the Big Three insurers (Mutual, Equitable, New York Life), had undertaken an aggressive series of mergers, and by the time of Hughes's 1905 insurance company revelations (which left it unscathed) it had absorbed ten former rivals. In the next few years Met Life leapt ahead of the industry heavyweights to become the world's largest insurance firm, and embarked on a collateral building program to underscore its new preeminence.

Already miffed that its twelve-story headquarters on 23rd Street had been upstaged by the Flatiron, Met Life had been quietly buying up buildings and lots in the remainder of the block bounded by Madison, Fourth, 23rd, and 24th. By 1905 only one holdout remained, the Reverend Parkhurst's Madison Square Presbyterian Church (1854), on the southeast corner of Madison and 24th, from whose pulpit the militant minister had long inveighed against "rum-soaked libidinous" Tammany Hall. Met Life acquired and demolished the building, then helped cover the cost of raising a new church for Parkhurst just across the street—a Stanford White Italian Renaissance masterpiece whose 30-foot-tall granite columns bespoke a determined permanence. The block secured, Met Life commissioned Napoleon Le Brun & Sons to

"Metropolitan Life Insurance Building, Madison Square," ca. 1910. (Library of Congress Prints and Photographs Division)

"Woolworth Building Illuminated at Night, with Singer Tower and World Building," 1915. (Museum of Science and Industry, Chicago/Getty Images)

fashion a tower that would outshine Singer's. The firm designed an outsized (almost cartoonish) blowup of the Campanile of St. Mark's Square in Venice, topped for good measure with a searchlight. At 700 feet the Met Life tower (1909) had captured the "world's tallest" prize.

Only to lose it four years later after Frank Woolworth, the retailing king, hired architect Cass Gilbert to devise, and builder Theodore Starrett to erect, a gleaming white terra-cotta headquarters. (Theodore, Paul's brother, was head of the Thompson-Starrett construction concern, the Fuller Company's chief rival.) Woolworth, having merged his original company with five rival mass retailers, wanted a structure commensurate with his worldwide empire of over 600 five-and-ten-cent stores.

Completed in 1913, the Woolworth Building stole the city's heart. People loved its soaring verticality: from atop the twenty-nine-story base, just across from City Hall, a twenty-story tower streamed upward 792 feet (making it the highest structure on earth apart from the 1,024-foot Eiffel Tower). They adored its grand public lobby, a golden marble cavern with vaulted ceilings of mosaic glass. And they thrilled to its spectacular nighttime presence. When its 80,000 incandescents and high-intensity beams were first switched on, the flash was visible a hundred miles away.

EACH NEW TALL TOWER FASCINATED CITIZENS and tourists alike. During a postcard craze that reached epidemic levels by 1905, people snapped up the new "skyscraper cards," taller and narrower than normal. Increasingly, however, attention focused less on individual buildings than on their collective impact.

In 1896 William Randolph Hearst's *Journal* had published a panoramic drawing of the lower part of Manhattan and captioned it "The Skyline of New York." The word caught on almost immediately. The following year, architectural critic Montgomery Schuyler wrote an article for *Harper's Weekly* entitled "The Sky-line of New York." (Schuyler, the conservative muttonchopped scion of an ancient New York clan, had worked as a newspaper reporter and editor at the *World* and the *Times*, developed an interest in architecture, and in 1891 with others had launched the *Architectural Record*.) No fan of skyscrapers (he would write a scathing assessment of the Flatiron), Schuyler asserted that few tall towers were distinguished in themselves. But "in the aggregation," he was forced to admit, an "immense impressiveness lies."

Over the next decade, the skyline replaced the harbor as New York's emblem, just as financiers supplanted merchants in the city's economy. Brooklyn-based profiles of Manhattan (emphasizing boats, wharves, and bridges) gave way to Jersey-based perspectives in which the waterfront merely foregrounded the pride of skyscrapers basking along the island's spine.

Skyline views grasped the city in a glance, an apt way of seeing in an era of consolidation. They also helped reshape notions of urbanity. The word "city" had long connoted a dense horizontal agglomeration of human-scaled buildings. In the early twentieth-century, it would conjure up a Gotham-rooted image of a constellation of megaliths that accentuated towering verticality and superhuman scale.

Tall towers quickly became so quintessential a New York phenomenon that they took on an air of inevitability. The explanation for their existence seemed obvious, almost trivial. Manhattan land was limited, hence expensive, so building tall made sense; new technologies—steel cage construction and elevators—made it possible to do so.

Such conventional wisdom raises more questions than it answers. If skyscrapers were an epiphenomenon of costly land, why did they arise in Chicago, a city surrounded by vast tracts of level terrain, while being blocked in London and Paris, where real estate was expensive?

Similarly, if skyscraper feasibility was a simple artifact of widely available technology, why was tower construction so concentrated in one city?

And why lower Manhattan? There was plenty of land elsewhere on the island, which since 1898 was only part of a much vaster city. Why the huddling within colonial-era boundaries, along former Dutch cow paths and English country lanes? Geology doesn't bear the explanatory weight sometimes attached to it. For while it's true that the depth of bedrock—the Manhattan schist so admirably suited for supporting skyscrapers—dove farther below street level between downtown and midtown, elsewhere, in Cleveland for instance, tall buildings had been planted on far more subterranean underpinnings. Understanding why New Yorkers demanded skyscrapers, who supplied them and how, and why they rose where and when they did, reveals a good deal about the city's central dynamics in the early twentieth century.

WHY SKIES?

First and foremost, tall towers were the physical manifestation of America's consolidating and internationalizing corporate economy. When great enterprises crystallized, expanded, or merged, they usually set up new (or enlarged existing) headquarters in lower Manhattan—US capitalism's financial and managerial hub—virtually next door to the banks that were financing and overseeing them.

Giant corporations needed enormous central staffs. The top brass—managers, accountants, lawyers, and engineers—assessed market possibilities, arranged financing, oversaw far-flung factories, monitored the flow of commodities, drew up contracts, audited books, tracked profits, and allocated dividends. They in turn depended on a rank-and-file army of typists, stenographers, bookkeepers, receptionists, copyists, file clerks, and messengers to process letters and telegrams, packing slips and invoices, bills and receipts, paychecks and contracts. These immense convocations of white-collar employees required massive amounts of office space, with ample natural light. Skyscrapers delivered. Met Life's clerical staff expanded from 530 in 1893 to 1,080 in 1897 and to over 2,800 by 1908; its headquarters boasted more typewriters than any other office building in the world.

Skyscrapers also enhanced brand recognition; they served, in effect, as outsize variants of an electric pickle sign the Heinz Company had flashed over Broadway. High visibility seemed especially appealing to corporations with high-volume sales to the public. Singer parlayed its tower's notoriety into increased sewing machine sales to Lower East Side seamstresses and Russian housewives; Met Life used its headquarters logo to promote nickel-and-dime-premium "industrial" policies; Frank Woolworth bluntly described his building as "a giant signboard to advertise around the world a spreading chain of five and ten cent stores."

Skyscrapers provided symbols of corporate identity. A tall building was like an architectural trademark, registered on Manhattan's skyline. These giant totems exalted their company's enterprise, expressed its optimism, demonstrated its potency, carved out its space in the capitalist universe.

This in turn generated a competitive "mine's bigger than yours" dynamic. Firms felt impelled to keep up with or surpass rivals lest a height deficiency suggest a larger infirmity. The ensuing race for space reminded some observers of contemporary imperialism. For others it recalled urban feudalism. A visiting German historian argued in 1904 that "New York is the San Gimignano of today, its bankers and wholesalers playing Montecchi and Capuleti with each other." This helps explain huddling. Downtown Manhattan was the crucial stage set, *the*

H. J. Heinz Co. electric advertising sign, ca. 1901–2. (The Henry Ford)

place for companies to strut their stuff. A skyscraper in Queens or the Bronx would not serve the same publicizing function.

Individual as well as corporate egos got involved. Frank Woolworth, who had given Cass Gilbert the marching order to overtop the Met Life tower, furnished his fortieth-floor office (later the "Empire Room") as if it were Napoleon's own, filled with Empire furniture, a full-length portrait and life-size bust of Napoleon, etc.

For a time, investment, commercial, and savings banks, along with trust companies, remained relatively free from the imperative to scramble upward, preferring a conspicuous nonconsumption of space. Firms ranging from the Bowery Savings Bank to J. P. Morgan & Co. opted for squat solidity. Partly this was because low-rise (and many-columned) structures were thought to suggest trustworthiness. The Knickerbocker Trust Company's one-story McKim, Mead & White building positively radiated prudence. But the notion that one could tell a financial book by its architectural cover was badly bruised when Knickerbocker's follies helped precipitate the Panic of 1907, after which tall banks became more common. Thus Bankers Trust reared a thirty-one-story campanile in 1912 whose seven-story pyramidal roof became its symbol. And the twelve-story Jarmulowsky Bank at Canal and Orchard (also 1912) was topped by a two-story, domed-and-columned *tempietto*, festooned with eagles, which loomed over its Lower East Side depositors.

Skyscrapers helped with broader image problems. Confronted with muckrakers branding their new concentrations of capital as menaces to the Republic, newly defensive and public-relations-minded corporations adopted architectural self-presentations that associated them with esteemed civic traditions. Humanist Renaissance rhetoric—exemplified by Metropolitan Life's Venetian bell tower—was deemed particularly serviceable. Lest anyone not grasp its iconographical intentions, Met Life put out a pamphlet—*The Metropolitan Tower: A Symbol of Refuge, Warning, Love, Inspiration, Beauty, Strength* (1915)—whose text aligned the company's "high tower" with "righteousness and purity in business corporations" (and, for good measure, with "protest against the exploitation of the poor.")

The company could have added *Profit* to the list of its tower's virtues, for corporate executives well knew that unused space in their dramatic headquarters could be leased out at premium prices. Met Life told prospective tenants that having an office in their tower was a form of "natural advertising," as "there is hardly a man who does not know of this building, who has not a picture of it stored in his brain." So successful was this pitch that Met Life's president boasted the tower had cost the company nothing, since "the tenants footed the bill."

The Singer Company barely occupied its tower at all; after reserving the thirty-fourth floor for executive offices, it rented out the rest to professional and commercial tenants. Bankers Trust, similarly, used only the lower three floors, renting all those above to legal firms and brokers willing to pay high rates for its prime location and iconic building; the bank housed its own staff in less expensive space elsewhere.

Indeed, some of the tall towers springing up were purpose-built to be rented out, financed not by corporations but by syndicates of investors. As speculative developers came to discern the truth enunciated by architect Cass Gilbert in 1900—that a skyscraper was a "machine that makes the land pay"—the process of constructing, financing, and renting out of office space in mega-buildings emerged as one of Gotham's central industries.

Tenants seeking less than 1,000 square feet, the equivalent of four or five office units, swarmed to these white-collar hives, drawn by proximity to the big corporate and financial players, and to key institutions like the Stock Exchange. They also liked the proximity to their building mates—rather as jewelers or flower merchants or butter-and-egg wholesalers clustered in distinctive districts. More broadly, the dense matrix of giant office structures created a nurturant business ecology similar to the weave of variegated small manufacturing concerns that had made New York, despite its sparsity of giant factories, the nation's premier industrial city.

CORPORATE DESIRES—FOR RENTAL PROFITS, OFFICE SPACE, advertising spin-offs, distinctive logos, marketplace status, and a beneficent public image—thus powered the skyscraper boom. But in addition to their self-interested motives, there was a wind of metropolitan opinion blowing early in the new century, one that billowed businessmen's inclinations to build tall.

Many New Yorkers, gripped by a Promethean frenzy, cheered the construction on. For these Gothamites, soaring buildings signaled prosperity, power, and movement into the front rank of world-class cities. Some went further, arguing the skyscraper boom marked a turning point in the history of civilization itself. All previous world wonders lay across the Atlantic— the Tower of Babel, the Pyramid of Cheops, the great Gothic cathedrals. But the tall towers, which many considered their modern successors, were uniquely an American and preeminently a New York phenomenon. The torch had been passed: mankind's new frontier lay in the sky over Manhattan. It was manifestly the city's destiny to probe its limits.[1]

Imaginative projects outraced actual construction. In 1906 builder Theodore Starrett called for a hundred-story super-tower that would incorporate all "the cultural, commercial

---

1. Such assessments were ratified by travelers from abroad. European visitors, like kings from the East, came to witness the new birth. A poetic Dutch architect in 1910 declared Manhattan's skyscrapers "seem a consummation of that dream / Of Babel's towers, these buildings that arise / And towering seem almost to touch the skies." European languages seemed to falter before Gotham's triumphant towers: the best translation Germans and Dutch could manage for "skyscraper" was "cloudscraper," a distinctly lower level of imagination.

Moses King, *King's Dream of New York*, 1908. (Image from the collection of The Skyscraper Museum)

and industrial activities of a great city." Factories would inhabit the bottom; next would come offices, then residences and a hotel. The segments would be separated by public plazas and by a general market on the twentieth floor, a cluster of theaters on the fortieth, a "shopping district" at the sixtieth, and on the top a roof garden, amusement park, and swimming pool.

In 1908 Moses King published in his popular guidebook a sketch (by Harry M. Pettit) of the city such thrusting might produce. "King's Dream of New York" portrayed the future metropolis as a fantastic City of Towers, with the new Singer Building dwarfed by dozens of taller rivals. Citizens negotiated their way through the sky-opolis along aerial footbridges and rail bridges strung between the towers at awesome heights. Higher still, giant dirigibles floated at flagpole moorings, awaiting scheduled departure times for Europe, Japan, the North Pole, and the Panama Canal.

The passion for tall buildings was further fanned in some breasts by aesthetic rapture. Writers groping for a vocabulary to describe the new urban vista redeployed metaphors depicting the natural landscape. In an early effort, an 1899 *Scribner's* commentator depicted the skyline as "a cluster of mountains, with their bright peaks glistening in the sun far above the dark shadows of the valleys in which the streams of business flow, down to the wharves and so out over the world."

"Comparison of Victoria Falls (400 Feet High) with Niagara Falls (168 Feet High) and with the Sky Line of New York. Only the Singer Building's Tower Rises above the Crest." *Scientific American*, June 29, 1907.

The "Imperator" 900 feet. Woolworth Building 750 feet.
THE LONGEST SHIP AND THE TALLEST BUILDING

"The Longest Ship and the Tallest Building. The 'Imperator' 900 Feet. Woolworth Building 750 Feet."
Scientific American, September 14, 1912. (Image from the collection of The Skyscraper Museum)

A decade later, when writer and aesthete John Charles Van Dyke authored *The New New York* (1909), such imagery was better developed. Arguing that the sun "works as busily and as potently on the face wall of a sky-scraper as on the canyon walls of the Colorado or the snow caps of Monte Rosa," Van Dyke offered a paean to Manhattan's "sublime" sierras, celebrating their appearance at different times of day and season. In a spring rain: "How very beautiful the high ridge of sky-scrapers looks shrouded in that silver-gray mist, their tops half-disappearing in the upper blend of rain and clouds." In the full noonday light: "with dark shadows flung down the great walls and high lights leaping from cornice to gilded dome." In late afternoon: "when the sun is setting over New Jersey and its yellow light flushes the tops of the high buildings and turns the window-panes to flaming fire." On summer evenings: when a tall tower might run from "a red glow at sunset through pink, mauve, and lilac, until, with twilight gone, it settles into a blue."

If the skyscrapers were magnificent by day, by night they were mesmerizing. "It is then," wrote Ezra Pound on a 1910 visit, "that the great buildings lose reality and take on their magical powers. They are immaterial; that is to say one sees but the lighted windows. Squares after squares of flame, set and cut into the aether. Here is our poetry, for we have pulled down the stars to our will." At such times, Pound said, New York was "the most beautiful city in the world."

"The Singer Tower Compared to Other Tall Structures in the World." *A History of the Singer Building Construction: Its Progress from Foundation to Flag Pole*, 1908.

The poetry of the skyline and the prospects for the city often reinforced one another, as they did for young Lewis Mumford in the course of a twilight stroll across the Brooklyn Bridge. "Three-quarters of the way across the Bridge," he later recalled, "I saw the skyscrapers in the deepening darkness become slowly honeycombed with lights until, before I reached the Manhattan end, these buildings piled up in a dazzling mass against the indigo sky. Here," Mumford exulted, "was my city, immense, overpowering, flooded with energy and light.... At that moment," he recalled, the world "opened before me, challenging me, beckoning me, demanding something of me that it would take more than a lifetime to give, but raising all my energies by its own vivid promise to a higher pitch."

With utilitarian calculations reinforced by such transcendent emotions, little wonder that many hailed skyscraper builders as heroes.

BUILDERS, ENGINEERS, FINANCIERS

Who were the builders? And how did they accomplish such astonishing feats, and in such short periods of time? (As Singer's managers bragged, while Cologne's Cathedral took 641 years to complete, and the Pyramid of Cheops required the labor of 100,000 men, their tower was thrown up by 1,200 laborers in a scant twenty months.)

New York's great leap upward relied on three developments: a consolidation of the construction business, the emergence of new technologies, and the establishment of novel methods of financing.

Skyscrapers got built by general contracting firms—large-scale enterprises akin to their corporate clients. Previously most contractors were small-scale and single-purpose, focusing on a particular type of construction, like stonework. New style concerns—of which the

Fuller Company was the preeminent example—consolidated all aspects of building under a single management and signed a single contract assuming total responsibility for all aspects of raising a building. Then they administered—in-house or via subcontractors—the thousands of operations involved in raising a skyscraper.

To an amazing degree the men who perfected this approach in Gotham were all named Starrett—one or another of five Kansas-born brothers, sons of a Presbyterian preacher father and a Quaker teacher mother. The Starrett family relocated to Chicago, where in 1887 the eldest brothers, Theodore and Paul, both began their careers in the office of Burnham & Root. Paul became a draftsman and was made superintendent of two Columbian Exposition buildings in 1893. In 1897 he joined the Fuller Company, worked in Baltimore and Washington, then in 1900 came to New York, where company head Harry Black put him in charge of construction. After his Flatiron triumph, Paul oversaw the raising of (among others) the Times Building, Pennsylvania Station, the General Post Office, Macy's, several hotels (including the Pennsylvania, Commodore, and Plaza), the Hippodrome, and the Met Life Tower. With subsidiary offices in Chicago, St. Louis, Boston, and Baltimore, Fuller was the largest building concern in the United States. Paul's brother Theodore also worked first for Burnham & Root in Chicago (as a structural engineer), then switched to the Fuller Company in New York, where he in 1899 he supervised construction of the eighteen-story Beaux-Arts Broadway-Chambers Building, architect Cass Gilbert's first in New York. In 1900 Theodore went out on his own and cofounded the Thompson-Starrett Company, using Fuller methodology to rival the Fuller Company, of which his brother Paul assumed command; Theodore would eventually employ the other three members of the clan at Thompson-Starrett. In some years, competing Starretts would together dominate most skywork in the city.

The secret of their tremendous efficiency, Theodore argued in 1907, was their consolidation of contractors under centralized control, echoing the approach of the financial and corporate leaders then directing the great merger movement. "Larger armies are more effective than the aggregate of the smaller ones under disunited leadership," he explained: "The builder who has a complete army under his command can do things which the commander of a single company cannot do." Not that such generalship was easy: Theodore claimed that "if John D. Rockefeller had tackled the building business instead of the oil business he would have quit early or died of exhaustion long before he reached his goal." William Starrett, another of the master-builder family, echoed the martial lingo. "Building skyscrapers," he said, "epitomizes the warfare and the accomplishment of our progressive civilization."

The foot soldiers of this construction army—bricklayers, masons, plasterers, painters, iron setters, electricians, and plumbers—gathered themselves into disciplined American Federation of Labor platoons. Sam Parks, a militant ironworker organizer, led the United Board of Building Trades, an umbrella labor organization. A series of strikes and organizing drives made union membership virtually mandatory for access to a skyscraper site. Labor peace settled over the booming industry, disrupted sporadically by jurisdictional squabbles between building-trades unions, but sustained overall by good wages and under-the-table payoffs to corrupt union leaders (Parks notoriously among them). And after a skyscraper was completed, keeping a tower running properly required a secondary army of mostly unionized engineers, firemen, locksmiths, glaziers, painters, plumbers, and janitors, and mostly ununionized scrubwomen and elevator operators.

STRUCTURAL, MECHANICAL, AND ELECTRICAL ENGINEERS furnished the second skyboom prerequisite, a host of technological breakthroughs. Chief among these were pneumatic caissons.

Close cousins to the devices used to raise the Brooklyn Bridge, they were airtight bottomless boxes, inside which workers dug down through sand and ooze while piped-in compressed air kept sub-surface water at bay. When the caisson hit bedrock, the sandhogs exited through airlocks and filled the boxes with concrete, forming a solid foundation pier. (It took sixty-nine of them to support the Woolworth Building's 223,000 tons.) In addition, power driven trip-hammers replaced the old pile drivers, giant double-drummed engines operated the derricks that hoisted steel beams and millions of bricks to the rising floors, and pneumatic hammers used compressed air to fasten beams and girders together. (One of these, operated by two men, could drive almost twice as many rivets in a day as had an entire gang using the old manual method.) Electric lights allowed crews to work both night and day, one reason erecting a skyscraper took, on average, just a year.

Technology solved a host of non-construction problems, too. When skyscrapers shot past the range of hydraulic elevators, the Otis Elevator Company, just in time, developed high-speed, electric, gearless traction elevators; by 1907 they were standard equipment for tall towers. The skyscrapers also outran the capacity of fire companies to deliver water. When firemen dragged hoses above the seventh or eighth story, gravity forced the water back down the tubes, and when it encountered the water being forced upward by pumping engines, it promptly burst the hoses. The solution was the metal standpipe, which, after a series of sky-scraper fires in 1899, was made mandatory in all new buildings over 100 feet tall. These were six-inch-wide wrought-iron pipes, capable of withstanding a thousand pounds of pressure to the square inch. They ran from cellar to roof, with connectors at each floor for attaching fire hoses, and a Y-shaped "Siamese" connector outside at sidewalk level, for linking to hydrants and pumpers. In a November 1902 test of the Flatiron's system, fire engines connected to the mains on one hand and the standpipe on the other successfully sent thousands of gallons of pressurized water shooting straight up 300 feet to and out of the top.

THE SKYBOOM'S THIRD PREREQUISITE WAS MONEY—lots of it. Sometimes the corporations themselves footed the bill, though Frank Woolworth was unique in plunking down his building's entire $13.5 million cost in cash. Increasingly, however, skyscrapers were built as speculative ventures by specialized development companies that, in effect, brokered the buildings into being. They borrowed money from savings banks or insurance companies, bought land, employed an architect and engineer, hired a building contractor, and engaged an agent to rent or sell space to a substantial corporation or masses of small tenants.

The most successful of these new concerns would be a mega-firm, established by Harry Black, that handled all these tasks in-house. For all his triumphs at the Fuller Company helm, Black had been envious of great consolidators like Morgan who were then transforming banking, industry, and commerce. So he set out to do the same for real estate by expanding his construction company laterally into financing, sales, and management. His path was eased by the fact that another real estate pioneer—Henry Morgenthau—had been putting together just the sort of financial operation with which Black had been hoping to hook up.

Henry Morgenthau had been born in Mannheim, a city in the Grand Duchy of Baden, in 1856. His father, a successful Jewish cigar manufacturer, had suffered a severe setback in 1862 when a new US tariff effectively barred German tobacco products. The family emigrated to New York in 1866, but his father was never able to reestablish himself. Henry attended City College and later Columbia Law School (teaching in a public school to pay his way). After admission to the bar he worked in a small law office, then in 1879 opened a partnership specializing in real estate law—handling mortgages and foreclosures, particularly in

Harlem, a largely Jewish middle-class domain. With capital provided by his brother-in-law (a wealthy dry-goods merchant), Morgenthau began buying groups of three to five houses, then reselling them quickly for a small profit. In 1889 he went out on his own.

In 1891 he scored his first big deal. Aware of rumors that a rapid transit line for upper Manhattan was in the offing, he deduced that Washington Heights would blossom, and 181st Street would become a particularly valuable location. Morgenthau bought an option (for $50,000) to buy a tract of sixteen city blocks (for $1,000,000) from Levi P. Morton (then vice president of the United States) and his associate, banker George Bliss. He then put together a syndicate of prominent investors, which consummated the purchase. Next he arranged an auction at the Real Estate Exchange (65 Liberty Street) to resell pieces of the tract to smaller speculators. With help from newspaper publisher James Gordon Bennett, who gave the sale "generous attention" in the *New York Herald* (Bennett having large possessions in the neighborhood), Morgenthau successfully sold off everything and cleared a hefty profit.

Morgenthau became known as one of the best judges of real estate in the city, and began operating in ever higher business and social circles, for ever higher stakes. After Consolidation, the churning of New York real estate became sexy, exciting, and potentially very lucrative. Speculative syndicates bloomed—outfits like the Knickerbocker Real Estate Company, whose stockholders included Solomon Loeb (of Kuhn, Loeb), and sugar magnate Henry O. Havemeyer (who had extensive real estate interests). Morgenthau dealt with the newly rich, with ancient landlord clans like the Astors, and with the giant insurance companies now playing the real estate field. Metropolitan Life had gotten into the game in 1893, when it created a Real Estate Division to take advantage of the numerous foreclosures that depression year and acquire hundreds of properties. In 1898 the company added a Bond and Mortgage Division, which by 1905 had issued $38 million in mortgage loans and owned $17.5 million in real estate assets.

Surveying the booming field in 1899, as the merger movement was going into hyperdrive, Morgenthau asked himself: "Why not induce some leading financiers to join me in the formation of a real estate trust company which would do for real estate what banking institutions have done for the railroads and industries?" In August 1899 he and some associates set up the Central Realty Bond & Trust, with $3 million in capital, then set out to enlist participation of the colossi of New York, among them James Stillman of National City Bank and Frederick P. Olcott, president of Central Trust. Such men were curious but cautious. "To most of them," Morgenthau recalled, "real estate was a closed book." They considered land a frozen asset and preferred to deal only in liquid ones. Morgenthau explained that the financiers could "capitalize real estate equities" by buying land through a corporation whose shares could be bought and sold with ease. He laid out the likely certainty that, given the city's growth in commerce and population, there were fabulous profits to be made in New York real estate. He reminded the magnates that many substantial capitalists had entered the field but that their relatively modestly scaled corporations lacked the resources to handle really big deals.

Given Morgenthau's track record, representatives of Gotham's three biggest capital pools (banks, trusts, and insurance companies) signed on to get a piece of the real estate action. Stillman joined the board and served on the executive committee. Olcott came on, too. So did Augustus D. Juilliard, a director of Mutual Life (also a merchant, philanthropist, and patron of musicians), Equitable's James Hazen Hyde, Henry Havemeyer, and the amiable former mayor Hugh J. Grant, who knew the political lay of the land.

By December 1899 the press was abuzz with stories about the new "skyscraper trust." Its stock price doubled in its first three months; profit on capital was 100 percent its first year. Morgenthau was "suddenly catapulted from my comparatively unknown law office"—from which he now resigned—"into the very midst of high finance." Only one thing was lacking: the ability to control the construction side of the business. And at that moment Harry Black materialized with a proposal to join forces.

In March 1901 Black reorganized the Fuller Company as a New Jersey holding company and welcomed onto its board Central Realty's Morgenthau, Grant, Stillman, and other worthies. He welcomed, too, the $20 million in capital they brought along. (No shares were sold to the public.) "Great Building Concern Organized," bannered the *New York Times* at month's end, the story noting that while both Central and Fuller would retain their separate corporate identities, it was assumed they "will in the future be closely allied."

This wasn't enough for Harry Black. "My motto," he bragged, "is 'bigger and bigger.'" And indeed, just fifteen months later—July 1902—Black upped the ante considerably, incorporating a huge new entity, the United States Realty and Construction Company (USR). Not only was USR a formal alliance between Fuller and Central (which became subsidiaries of the parent corporation) and with a leading real estate company (New York Realty), but it brought to its table some of the greatest principals of the emerging corporate order, notably Charles M. Schwab, president of US Steel; Charles Steele, a J. P. Morgan partner; and banker James Speyer. The new firm, whose stock was listed on the NYSE, would command $66 million of capital.

Black told the press that "U.S. Realty's operations will be confined very largely to New York, with the exception of the construction business of the Fuller Company, which will be carried on as usual throughout the important cities of the country." He emphasized that his USR and Schwab's USS would have very close relations. ("Naturally, as we will be the largest consumers of structural steel in the world, our terms as to price and delivery will be most favorable"—enabling Black to undercut competitors.)

US Realty would work all sides of the skyscraper business—buying a site, making a building loan, erecting structures, managing properties. In its first large endeavor it bought and combined two sites adjacent to Trinity's graveyard and raised thereon two tall and narrow limestone structures. The first replaced the five-story Trinity Building (1852) with a twenty-story tower of the same name (1905), and the second, right next door, was the eponymous United States Realty Building (1907); the two were connected by a futuristic rooftop skywalk in 1912. Both were speculative ventures; both were swiftly rented out to bankers, attorneys, brokers, engineers, and trust companies. A mighty development engine, US Realty now began to churn out skyscrapers and apartment houses, train stations and hotels, lofts and department stores.

Thompson-Starrett was hard-pressed to keep up, valued as it was at only $1 million, a scant one-sixty-sixth of Black's giant operation. Yet it remained US Realty's main rival, in part by winning new financial backers, among them the Title Guarantee and Trust Company and some Standard Oil interests, thus gaining its own pipeline to New York's capital pools. The money men did insist on some changes. They thought Theodore Starrett a genius as a builder but profligate as a manager, and also lacking in polish. So they turned to a money man to ride herd on him and handle sales, Louis Jay Horowitz. The Polish-born Horowitz had come to New York in 1892 and worked as a stock clerk and shoe salesman. In 1898 Horowitz sank his savings and some borrowed funds into building a Brooklyn apartment house, which he sold for a profit, rolling over his returns into a new project. He set up the Brooklyn Heights Improvement Company and became a fixture on the Joralemon and Court Street law-and-real-estate circuit. When he took on a project beyond his little firm's capacity, he turned to Thompson-Starrett, which in 1903 took him on board as Ted Starrett's finance man.

"Organization Chart, Thompson-Starrett Company Building Construction." *The Modern Building Organization*, 1911. (New York Public Library)

Horowitz cultivated the ways of the wealthy (morning horseback rides in Central Park), and the new investors approvingly made him president in 1910, in which capacity he beat out the Fuller Company to win the contract for Frank Woolworth's tower.

The bottom line of all this activity was that (as *Moody's Magazine* claimed in March 1907) New York City's real estate market was "becoming more and more the favorite investment field of the largest capitalists and shrewdest financiers throughout the United States and even in Europe." A "constantly increasing volume of money is being attracted to it," *Moody's* noted, as well it might have been, given that assessed land values had climbed to $6 billion dollars, up nearly a billion in two years. The value of metropolitan real estate, *Moody's* crowed, was now "greater than the entire wealth of many states and even many foreign countries."[2]

TOO SMALL?

While this cascade of capital accelerated Gotham's skyward surge, other forces were also promoting the escalation in height, ones that muckraker Lincoln Steffens had spotted at the very beginning of the boom years. In a shrewd 1897 article for *Scribner's Magazine* entitled "The Modern Business Building," Steffens focused not on corruption—his usual frame of analysis—but rather on a contradiction he discerned at the heart of the emerging skyscraper industry.

Building tall increased rental income: each new floor added more tenants to the rent rolls; that was the incentive for aiming high. The increase in rents, in turn, boosted the value of the underlying property (that value being essentially capitalized rent). Skyscrapers not only "made the land pay" in the sense of extracting profits via building rents; they made the land itself more valuable.

There were, however, some downsides to all this.

As building heights and land values went up, so did assessed taxes. So did the cost of insurance and maintenance and mortgage-carrying charges. All these increased expenses had to be deducted from increased profits.

---

2. "It is 25 per cent more than the entire wealth of Holland, Spain, Sweden and Norway...one-fifth that of Russia...one-tenth that of Great Britain and Ireland. It is indeed an imperial city in an empire state."

Tall office buildings were also subject to rapid depreciation. The velocity of technological change had significant consequences. Updating outmoded elevators, for instance—which owners more or less had to do if they wanted to hold on to fickle tenants—was costly.

Height competition between developers also cut into profits. It wasn't just that higher buildings were intrinsically more appealing—had better views—and so drew off tenants from now shorter ones. Much more troubling was that if your neighbor built a tower taller than yours, his building could (and often did) literally overshadow yours, blocking not only views but sunlight.

This was not merely an aesthetic complaint. Natural light was still the most important source of illumination. Incandescent bulbs were weak and inefficient. Offices were more appealing if they had large windows and high ceilings that allowed daylight to penetrate more deeply into the interior—along with fresh air, particularly important given New York's sultry summers. Skyscraper interiors, accordingly, were laid out as a ring of rentable space surrounding a central core of circulatory and mechanical services. The shallower the ring, the better. A 15-foot-deep office maximized light and air and fetched a high rent; 25- or 50-footers had gloomy interiors and brought lower returns. But even the best-arranged layout availed naught if a competitor's building went up across the street, blocking the light. Tenants—no loyalty there!—were all too likely to leap to a higher peak.

Thanks to the surge of investment, competition heated up. Because speculative office building was no longer related to demonstrated present need but rather keyed to presumed future demand, it soon generated more space than was currently required, as railroad competition had led to an oversupply of trackage. Landlords were forced into bidding wars for tenants (as the railroads had struggled to win passengers and freight), which drove down rental prices, and depressed the rate of profit. The average return on skyscrapers was around 5 percent, but it could drop to less than half that when supply outraced demand.

An overtopped owner had three choices. 1) Accept declining rents, even though mortgage payments, insurance premiums, taxes, and maintenance costs would remain fixed, or increase. 2) Retire from the combat zone by moving to a new location, though thanks to Harry Black and others, skyscrapers were now sprouting uptown, too; besides, relocation removed one from the center of the action. 3) Stay downtown but escalate. The only viable way to offset depreciation, Steffens deduced early on, was to invest in "newer and higher structures."

Here, however, another contradiction came into play. The taller the desired building, the more elevators were needed to handle the increase in vertical traffic. But elevators ate into rentable floor space. At some point they hogged so much of it that it wasn't worth going higher. The only solution lay in assembling bigger base plots—ideally entire square blocks—so the point of diminishing returns would arrive at a more elevated altitude.

Large sites, however, were hard to come by downtown, broken up as it was into small parcels, all of them occupied. Big plots were difficult to assemble in the absence of catastrophic fires, like those that had leveled much of Chicago in 1871 and had destroyed much of lower Manhattan itself back in 1835. Not surprisingly, land assembly was one of the services Harry Black offered. "If a bank or an industrial company had outgrown its quarters and required a larger space," Black explained in 1902, "the U.S. Realty would show the directors how they might trade their present property in on a more desirable plot and finance a new and larger building with rentable space that would carry the investment."

In practice, assembling a "more desirable plot" often meant tearing down what you had, plus whatever was sitting upon such adjacent pieces of land as you could (often surreptitiously) buy up. Demolishing existing stock had the additional virtue of generating a fresh supply of tenants. When overbuilding outstripped demand, Steffens observed, "the only sure source of tenants is in the continuance of the process, as the tearing down of more old buildings for the next year's crop of new buildings supplies the tenants for this May's openings." This process Steffens called a "perpetual motion quest."

The result was that Gotham's torrent of building was accompanied by a hurricane of demolition: 21,000 buildings were torn down in Manhattan between 1898 and 1908. "One might almost fancy that the town had been bombarded by a hostile fleet, such rents and gashes appear everywhere in the solid masonry," wrote cultural critic Randall Blackshaw in the *Century Magazine* in 1902, "ranging from the width of a single building to that of a whole block front." As Hugh Thompson put it in a perceptive 1912 essay, "The Remaking of New York": "Nowhere in the country is space so precious, and nowhere are such miracles of construction and destruction practised upon it." And nowhere in New York was the "perpetual motion" more frenzied than along lower Broadway. "The spirit of change is making the familiar street unrecognizable," wrote a reporter for the *Brooklyn Eagle* during the summer of 1901. Block after block of buildings was coming down—"probably not more than a hundred old buildings can now feel safe"—creating a cityscape that alternated skeletons of rising structures with rubble from just dismantled ones.[3]

At first it was mostly small and old buildings that came down. But as demand soared and land values leapt, casualties began appearing in the ranks of recently erected skyscrapers themselves. The twenty-story Gillender Building at Wall and Nassau had been built in 1897, the year in which Steffens published his analysis. But by 1909 the land on which it stood had appreciated so spectacularly (to $822 a square foot) that its owner couldn't resist selling. And as Bankers Trust had the wherewithal to buy, down it came, in 1910, after a life span of only thirteen years. Four years later Gotham's ur-skyscraper bit the dust. Bradford Gilbert's eleven-story Tower Building (50 Broadway, 1889)—the first in New York to employ steel cage construction—had been so badly overtowered that it no longer generated enough revenue to pay its own taxes.[4]

Some jokesters expected the 1909 tower itself to be a merely provisional structure, soon to be replaced by something newer and larger. In one contemporary cartoon a character announces, "They're going to pull down the Metropolitan Tower and make room for a sky-scraper."

Skyscrapers began to attract murderous fantasies about New York's destruction—which had long been current in the culture—the way they did lightning bolts. In critic Ambrose Bierce's "Ashes of the Beacon" (1905), a future historian recalls the violent demolition of insurance company towers this way: "The smoldering resentment of years [about the insurance abuses revealed in that year's investigation] burst into flames, and within a week all that was left of insurance in [Ancient] America was the record of a monstrous and cruel delusion written in the blood of its promoters." In 1911 George Allan England, a socialist activist and former insurance clerk, produced "The Last New Yorkers: A Weird Story of Love and

---

3. As a 1910 *Scientific American* article put it: "So soon as the march of improvement or development renders it certain that there is more profit in 'scrapping' an existing machine, plant, or building, and replacing it by another more efficient or of greater capacity, it is a matter of sound business policy to send that machine to the 'junk heap' or turn the 'wrecking gang' loose upon that building."

4. Office buildings were not the only structures vulnerable to obsolescence; hotels quickly became outmoded in an era of rapid technological change. Black's roving eye fell on McKim, Mead, & White's deluxe 400-room Plaza Hotel at the Grand Army Plaza (58th/59th and Fifth). Though *King's Handbook of New York City* declared it one of the grandest in the world, and though it had been only completed in 1890, fifteen years later it was antiquated and runty: constructed without a steel frame, it was only eight stories high. So in 1905 Black, along with other investors, bought it up, tore it down, and hired architect Henry Janeway Hardenbergh (famous for his Waldorf-Astoria and Dakota apartment house) to build a new, massive Plaza, nineteen stories tall. Opened in 1907, it occupied an entire city block, and had 753 rooms, with some suites having as many as 17 rooms. It was not only ultra-luxurious but featured all the latest gadgetry: push-button maid service, electric dumbwaiters, individual room thermostats, a built-in vacuum-cleaning system.

"In Newest New York," ca. 1910–20. (Metropolitan Life Insurance Company Archives)

Adventure in the Ruins of a Fallen Metropolis." The 103-episode epic, serialized in *Munsey's Cavalier and Scrap Book*, opened with the hero and heroine, a consultant engineer and his stenographer, awakening from centuries of suspended animation on the forty-eighth floor of the Metropolitan Life Tower, amid the ruins of New York.

The net result of all this creation and destruction was the rapid ascension of Manhattan's skyline. By the end of 1912, the borough had 1,510 buildings in the nine-to-seventeen-story range and 891 still loftier ones (from eighteen to fifty-five)—far more than any other city, anywhere. How far into the empyrean this "perpetual quest" would take New York was anyone's guess. One of the droller predictions was depicted in a 1902 cartoon on the cover of *Life* (a humor magazine), in which ballooning sightseers—in 1920—were informed by their guide, as they floated over a sinkhole of Manhattan-like dimensions, that the "depression down there is where New York City stood. But with all its sky-scrapers and underground tunnels it suddenly sunk one day and they haven't been able to find it since."[5]

---

5. Another of this Manhattan-gets-its-comedownance-genre was "The Tilting Island," published in *Everybody's* in 1909. In this telling, there had been a gradual sinking of the downtown portion of Manhattan into the harbor, until one day "the tallest tower [disappeared] below the sea." A Columbia geology professor attributed the disaster to "the recent construction boom in the downtown district," which had massed the weight of "twenty stories of steel, thirty stories, forty stories" on one end of the island, atop a "hitherto undiscovered fault line," making the "whole island tilt" like "the hand of man on the edge of the plate."

"Sightseeing in 1920. The Conductor: That depression down there is where New York City stood. But with all its sky-scrapers and underground tunnels it suddenly sunk one day, and they haven't been able to find it since." *Life*, February 6, 1902.

CITY BEAUTICIANS

Many New Yorkers applauded the development tornado roaring up Broadway. But there were others in Gotham who found the proliferation of skyscrapers appalling. Their distaste and dismay were rooted in the strikingly different vision they had in their heads of what New York ought to look like in the coming century, a vision in which skyscrapers were about as welcome as the Snake in the Garden. These New Yorkers dreamed of a horizontal, not a vertical, city, a metropolis of monumental (but low-rise) buildings of classic design, a cityscape of spacious open plazas linked together by grand and leafy boulevards. They wanted *not* a scattershot, profit-driven, chaotic, and ugly city but one that was orderly, civic-minded, planned, and beautiful.

They knew it was possible to fashion such a city because they'd seen one, in Chicago, in 1893, at the World's Columbian Exposition that had been erected on swamplands reclaimed from Lake Michigan. The evanescent White City had been a dazzling affair of grand Roman buildings, Venetian lagoons, and Baroque avenues, that had attracted millions of astonished Americans to goggle at it, then promptly vanished.

One group of New Yorkers had done more than goggle; they'd largely designed and built it. Daniel Burnham, the Chicago architect in overall charge of shaping the fair, had turned immediately to Gotham professionals for assistance. First Central Park's Frederick Law Olmsted (then approaching 70) helped choose the site and lay out the grounds. Then a crew of distinguished eastern architects—Charles McKim and Richard Morris Hunt chief among them—helped hammer out the critical decisions: the adoption of a uniform color (white), a uniform cornice height (60 feet), and a uniform vocabulary (neoclassical). Finally, New Yorkers were asked to erect the most prestigious structures (vast but temporary edifices of wood and plaster wrapped around steel sheds). Hunt did the centerpiece Administration Building, McKim handled the Agriculture Building, and George B. Post put up the gargantuan Manufactures Building (three times as large as St. Peter's, four times the size of the Colosseum).

What its designers loved about the exposition, even more than the Roman grandeur of its individual parts, was the way the parts fitted together into a planned whole. In its very structure, the fair transcended competition and embodied the virtues of cooperation. Architectural critic Montgomery Schuyler had declared the White City "first of all a success of unity, a triumph of 'ensemble.'"

Genteel New Yorkers were deeply affected by the contrast between the fair's orderly and uplifting environment and their own city's degrading squalor, as recently depicted by Jacob Riis in *How the Other Half Lives* (1890). Though the comparison was depressing, it was also energizing. One distinguished visitor, the Reverend William Rainsford, rector of St. George's Episcopal Church (better known as "Morgan's minister"), saw it as an inspiration: "If things looked dark in New York," Rainsford said, "there was another city whose white, classic loveliness stood, for one summer." Urban reformer Frederic C. Howe recalled that "people left it with the inquiry: 'Why cannot cities be built like a world's fair; why should we not employ architects and artists in their designing; why should we not live in cities as beautiful as this fugitive play city, that will disappear at the end of the summer?'" The *Social Economist*, a Gotham journal, summarized the new spirit: "The World's Fair at Chicago puts New York City on its mettle to do some great thing."

Several New Yorkers returned from Chicago imbued with a desire to remake their messy metropolis in its gleaming image, notably Richard Morris Hunt. In 1893 the grand old man of New York architecture, together with leading artists and men of affairs, formed the Municipal Arts Society (MAS); Hunt became its first president. The members' ambition was to "crystalize together" architects, sculptors and painters in a campaign to beautify the city's streets and public places.[6] Their massed talents and energies, they believed, could transform the metropolis so thoroughly that the results would "outlast that great exhibition at Chicago for hundreds of years to come." Their handiwork might also inspire civic loyalty among New Yorkers. "To make us love our city," the MAS argued, "we must make our city lovely."[7]

This phalanx of artists and businessmen set out to make New York a "City Beautiful," a term coined in England in 1896 and popularized in Gotham around 1899. Their initial goal was extremely modest—they would donate one artwork to the city each year—but they quickly grew more ambitious and aimed at rearranging New York's infrastructure as well as embellishing its public spaces. For many this meant declaring war on the 1811 Grid, which they loathed. Ernest Flagg, himself a Beaux-Arts-trained architect, spoke for many when he raged at the primitive utilitarians of 1811 for having condemned succeeding generations "to hopeless monotony and humdrum commercialism." New Yorkers had been cheated out of the "grand metropolitan air which distinguishes most of the great capitals of Europe." For Flagg and his colleagues, a beautiful city was a Baroque city. Their heroes were the seventeenth- and early-eighteenth-century monarchs (or latter-day avatars like Baron Haussmann) who had demolished cramped medieval spaces and erected magnificent open

---

6. The willingness of these eminent architects and sculptors to work together had been spurred by their delight in working together in Chicago on producing a coordinated ensemble, along with the accompanying after-hours socializing. St. Gaudens, moved by the collaborative spirit, remarked to Burnham: "Look here, old fellow, do you realize that this is the greatest meeting of artists since the fifteenth century?"

7. By 1898 the MAS had incorporated, and its 350 members included such business and professional luminaries as Post, Carnegie, Deforest, Gilder, La Farge, Lamb, Low, McKim, and Schiff.

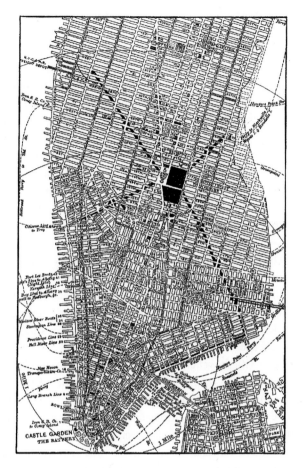

J. F. Harder, "Areas Proposed to Be Condemned for Avenues, Extension of Union Square." "The City's Plan," *Municipal Affairs* 2 (1898).

stage sets. Now, with the opportunity afforded by Consolidation, they hoped to burst New York's historic fetters.

In 1899 architect Julius F. Harder proposed a multi-step "logical plan" for transforming New York into a radial city. First, transplant City Hall to Union Square. Then expand this new Civic Center to appropriately grand dimensions by muscling its borders several blocks deeper into surrounding neighborhoods. Next send great arterial boulevards rolling out majestically in all directions: northward, up Fourth Avenue, to Grand Central; southwest along Christopher Street to the ferry terminal; and northwest, northeast, and southeast to majestic new bridges or transport stations. Not only would these highways afford magnificent vistas, but by scything their way through dangerous tenement quarters, they would offer quick and easy access for police and firemen.[8]

8. Many of the plans that followed Harder's advocated similar tactics, exuberantly performing imaginary surgery on the old order. The Municipal Art Society's 1904 contribution urged cutting a boulevard from near Cooper Union straight through the Lower East Side to Delancey Street, from whence it would carom back to the Bowery, whacking out another great chunk of working-class housing. Extending Sixth and Seventh Avenues southward would take out the less respectable swatches of Greenwich Village, and thrusting Franklin Street eastward would have similarly appealing consequences: as the *Times* noted, "Chinatown would be opened to the public gaze and perhaps destroyed."

In January 1903 the MAS escalated again. Arguing that a beautification scheme "must have as its basis the fundamental plan upon which the city is to improve and develop," the society urged establishment of a commission to draft just such a master blueprint for Gotham. It was absurd, the members argued, that a city destined to become "a greater centre than the world has ever seen" was being developed with no governing guidelines other than those embedded in the grid. For possible models, they reached back to Mayor Abram Hewitt's ambitious proposal of 1888, and in March 1903 they organized at the National Arts Club an exhibition on planning, one that assembled and displayed various illustrative initiatives. They also said attention had to be paid to the economic as well as aesthetic dimensions of planning. With support from the Merchants' Association and the Manufacturers' Association—attracted by this broader perspective—they won establishment of a New York City Improvement Commission.

Up and running by March 1904, the commission issued an initial report by December and a full-scale proposal in 1907, which took its cues mainly from extant proposals like Harder's proposed radial city centered on Union Square. The commissioners called for a grand Civic Center. They advocated fostering interborough unity with a network of interconnecting parks and parkways. (One such ran from the Bronx parks down to Riverside Park, across to Central Park, and then east, along 59th Street—widened into a 160-foot boulevard—across a new bridge, and on to an étoile in Queens.) They proposed breaking up the grid with assorted circles, curves, and diagonals. Above all, they insisted, "if New York is to take its place as one of the great Metropolitan Cities of the World" then all its parts must be made "consistent, the one with the other, and form a homogeneous whole."

Reaction to the commission's report was underwhelming, with critics more in evidence than cheerleaders. The *Times* was disheartened by the proposed price tag—the regal parkway across 59th Street alone would involve acquiring and demolishing properties worth $15 million—and it feared that the wretched grid could never be "corrected by any Haussmannizing process that would be worth its cost." Others noted and rejected the *political* price of "Haussmannizing." One commentator suggested that perhaps "the kind of beauty that makes Paris charming can only exist where private rights and personal liberty are or have been trampled on."

The Improvement Commission's work fell flat in large part because the city's movers and shakers were not prepared to cede any planning powers to the state, much less the extravagant and wrenching kinds of interventions the commissioners sought. Daniel Burnham would encounter similar objections in Chicago when in 1909 he proposed an even more grandiose plan. Only in special circumstances—as in Washington, DC, or Manila (a colonial possession)—would government have the authority to restructure an already built environment.

But the tepid response to the 1907 Plan stemmed also from the fact that events had patently passed it by. For nearly ten years, New York City had been in the grip of a mighty building boom. Its most striking feature—apart from individual structures (libraries, train stations, universities) done in the monumental style Beauticians favored—was the jagged eruptions, as if from Manhattan's schist, of colossal towers shaped by no plan, part of no soothing ensemble.

From their point of view, skyscrapers were the enemies of a well-ordered city. Products of a commercial, not a civic, culture, each was a private venture that paid no heed to the larger cityscape. Worse, each builder sought to advance at the expense of the others, as had the railroads and manufacturers whose ruinous competition was so deplored by Morganizers. Each tower had clawed its way up, the better to steal another's tenants, setting off a scramble that had led to rampant overbuilding, and attendant deleterious effects ranging from darkly canyoned streets to overcrowded transport.

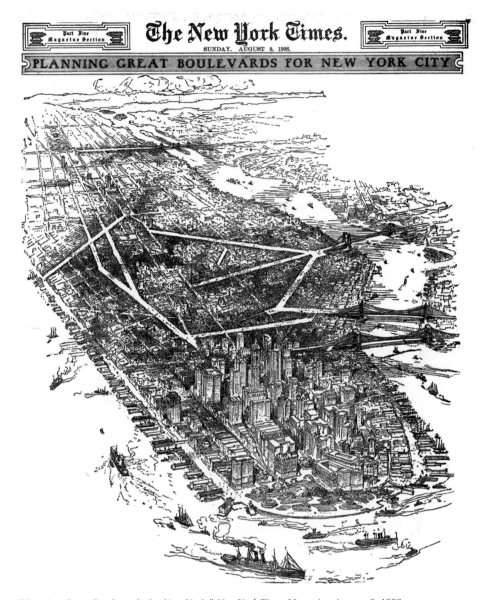

"Planning Great Boulevards for New York." *New York Times Magazine*, August 9, 1908.

The Beautifiers hewed to a different social calculus—one that privileged the larger municipal good (as they understood it)—and sought to create a harmonious cityscape. From their vantage point, the downtown extrusion of towers was a cancerous growth—now metastasizing uptown—that exalted the commercial over the civic, the private over the public, the part over the whole, the selfish over the common weal.

This was the burden of many of Montgomery Schuyler's critical essays. He decried the building craze as "wild work"—the product of "savage and unregulated energy"—and deplored the skyscrapers themselves as "new commercial Babels." The landscape they produced was "bewildering and stupefying in the mass, with no ensemble but that of universal strife and struggle." Like Frankenstein, he concluded, "we stand appalled before the monsters of our own creation."

The contrast with Europe was particularly depressing. After touring new garden cities in England, Walter Weyl, an economist and University Settlement resident, found US cities "overgrown, anarchic" Babylons, products of a "clash of egotistical interests." Frederick Howe agreed that American cities were commercial "accidents," bereft of any "sense of unity, of permanence, of the rights of the whole community." This perspective was ratified by visitors from Europe itself. One English journalist, G. W. Steevens (in his *Land of the Dollar*), found that in Manhattan's business quarter, "the very buildings cry aloud of struggling, almost savage, unregulated strength. . . . It is the outward expression of the freest, fiercest individualism. The very houses are alive with the instinct of competition, and strain each one to overtop its neighbors."

This competitive privatism was another reason Beautifiers hated the grid, which they believed enabled it. Intended from the beginning to facilitate the purchase and sale of individual parcels—the landscape broken up into bite-sized, prepackaged commodities—the street plan had fostered a way of seeing the city as "real estate," a matrix of opportunities rather than an urban commonwealth. Each plot traveled its unique trajectory, and every transaction aimed at some private end, hampered by no larger consideration. The grid made for a city of flux and flexibility. Particular parcels could transform their identity overnight, shape-shifting from residential to commercial to industrial and back again, without reference to any coordinated plan of action. The result, according to one's values, was dire chaos or admirable adaptability.

Other grounds for tower antipathy were advanced by novelist Henry James, who in 1904–5 revisited his native city after two decades abroad. James penned a brooding elegy that recalled his "old New York" as a picture "now so violently overpainted." The most disheartening new brushstrokes were the skyscrapers, "invidious presences" that "cruelly overtopped" a once serenely scaled town. His patrician gaze discerned little of beauty in them. Brutally piling story upon story, they pursued not grace but profit. While James admitted that on rare occasion a "vast money-making structure quite horribly, quite romantically justified itself, looming through the weather with an insolent cliff-like sublimity," on the whole he condemned them as "mercenary monsters." Echoing Schuyler, he protested the mess they made of the cityscape: from the rivers they appeared "like extravagant pins in a cushion already overplanted, and stuck in as in the dark, anywhere and anyhow."

James zeroed in on the ephemerality of the buildings. "They never begin to speak to you, in the manner of the builded majesties of the world as we have heretofore known such—towers or temples or fortresses or palaces—with the authority of things of permanence or even of things of long duration," James suggested. "One story is good only till another is told, and sky-scrapers are the last word of economic ingenuity only till another word be written." That was why a "consciousness of the finite, the menaced, the essentially invented state, twinkles ever, to my perception, in the thousand glassy eyes of these giants of the mere market."

This aura of temporariness suffused the larger city's culture: "Crowned not only with no history, but with no credible possibility of time for history, and consecrated by no uses save the commercial at any cost, they are simply the most piercing notes in that concert of the expensively provisional into which your supreme sense of New York resolves itself." This provisionality and ahistoricity fostered a "poverty of public life," reflected in the fact that the "city has no public squares which, either because of the sacredness of their associations or the excellence of their encircling buildings, have aroused in the minds of its inhabitants any feelings of pride and affection." Deprived of temporal moorings, Gotham's citizens were stranded in the present, adrift on the surface of things.[9]

FOR ALL ITS BITE, JAMES'S INDICTMENT—like those of many Beautifiers—was a bit abstract. The city's past seemed the prey of inexorable forces, rather than particular historical agents. But there were other critics, closer to the muckraker temperament, who had no qualms about identifying more precise targets.

Journalist Herbert Croly had been born in New York City in 1869 to the famed female journalist Jane Cunningham Croly—better known by her pseudonym, Jenny June—and David Goodman Croly, a reporter for the *Post* and the *Herald*, and then managing editor at the *New York World*, and later still the *Daily Graphic*; David also cofounded, edited, and wrote a column in the *Real Estate Record and Builders Guide (RERBG)*, the industry's bible. Herbert attended the City College of New York for one year, then entered Harvard in 1886, dropping out and in again repeatedly, until departing definitively, without a degree, in 1899. In 1900 Croly became an editor of the *Architectural Record* (a spinoff of the *RERBG*, for which he had also written). He stayed until 1906, during which time he wrote several essays touching on the relation between the consolidating city and its skyscrapers.

The Greater New York merger, in opening up possibilities for bold intervention in the cityscape, magnified reformer frustration when these opportunities were not seized upon. In 1899 a local paper fretted that "we are laying out the new districts of the Greater New York, not as the ideal city or the city beautiful, or even as the city of common sense. We are merely permitting it to grow under the stimulus of private greed and real estate speculation." Croly concurred but noted that this was a much older story than imagined. "Private, special and business interests have been dominant in New York ever since the Revolution," he wrote in 1903, "and have left an indelible mark upon the public life and appearance of the city." In truth, Croly argued, "there has never been any attempt commensurate with its resources to plan it adequately and conveniently, or to adorn it appropriately. On the contrary, the streets have been made a gift to real estate speculators and builders to deform as suited their interests: and they have done and are still doing their worst." The failure of the 1904–7 Improvement Commission came as no surprise to Croly. Not that he was crazy about City Beautiful plans: "The vision of a local pseudo-classic Beaux-Artist New Jerusalem, which is the only kind of an ideal city the civic art reformer ever imagines, seems to the writer a very insipid ideal," he wrote in 1904. The stifling symmetry and monotony of the proposed urban utopia would, he argued, sacrifice New York's "proper character and vitality." "For me the skyscraper and the furnace-stack," he added in a moment of enthusiasm.

But if skyscrapers were a welcome sign of energy, it was of a "blind and uninformed" variety. The basic fact was that "the interest of the whole people in a beautiful and convenient

---

9. Churches—major memory markers of an era when noncommercial buildings were central to the public landscape—were particularly menaced. With "the new landmarks crushing the old quite as violent children stamp on snails and caterpillars," James wrote, ecclesiastical structures were "hideously threatened." Even if they survived, they were overwhelmed by surrounding towers. James advanced an "inexorable law of the growing invisibility of churches," lamenting in particular the fate of "poor old Trinity," next door to which Harry Black's United States Realty had just erected the New Trinity Building—replete with "a south face as high and wide as the mountain-wall that drops the Alpine avalanche, from time to time, upon the village, and the village spire, at its foot." This sentiment was widely shared by clerics and allies who resented their lost dominance of the sky. Ralph Adams Cram, an eminent architect of churches, decried the "mercantile buildings that lift absurdly above them, crushing them into ignominy." "Hideously threatened": This proved true even for Stanford White's replacement church at Madison Square. For all the seeming durability of its green granite columns, when Met Life expanded northward once again, in 1919, it too fell prey to the wrecker's ball, with pieces of it carted off to the Metropolitan Museum for preservation (only to be later still demolished).

city demands the distribution of population and business in the most liberal manner and according to an organic plan," whereas "the interest of the real estate speculator demands congestion and concentration of business and population, which enormously increases real estate values." That was why "the local owners of real estate are always the most stubborn opponents of improvements in the public interest which in any way impair their chances of reaping their unearned reward from the growth of the city." Croly advised the authors of the 1907 Plan that "it will be found in the long run that the radical and comprehensive improvement of our large cities in convenience and good looks will be effected only, as it were, over the dead body of the great American real estate speculator."

Given the unlikelihood of being able to stop the development tornado in its tracks, City Beautifiers lowered their sights, and settled on the more modest goal of setting limits on how high a building could go. In the aftermath of the 1907 panic, they were joined by a most unlikely set of allies—the real estate speculators themselves—in their campaign to draw a line in the sky.

TOO TALL!

As an example of how Gotham was dominated by profit maximizers, Herbert Croly pointed to the relatively progressive state of affairs in Boston and Chicago: "Whereas in those cities, a restriction, although a small one, is or has been placed upon the height of fireproof buildings, in New York such structures are restricted only by the amount of elevator service, which it pays to provide."

Back in 1891 Boston had imposed a height limit of 125 feet (about ten stories), and later established an 80-foot cap outside the business district, to keep even modest towers from invading residential districts. Boston's success in maintaining a low profile was traceable in part to the fact that roughly three-quarters of downtown was owned by old family trusts—conservative investors who sought reliable income and eschewed risk.

Chicago had no such constraining force, but it too, in 1893, had passed an ordinance imposing a ceiling of 130 feet. There, however, waivers were dispensed liberally by a pliant municipal government, and the ceiling itself was lifted on occasion—doubling to 260 feet at some points—but was then forced down again by Chicago Beautifiers. As a result, the city had nearly as many tall buildings as New York, but none as high.

It was a different story in Europe. Rigorous height limitations had been imposed on Paris in the eighteenth century, and by the early twentieth these had spread throughout the continent. Paris then had a 75-foot maximum in effect; Berlin's was set at 78, Zurich's 43, Vienna's 82. And these were non-negotiable. Harry Black tried repeatedly to hawk skyscrapers in London and Paris, and perhaps ignite a space race there, but got nowhere.

In New York, conversely, it was the culture and law of limitlessness—the absolute right of property owners to do as they pleased with their property (barring noxious or dangerous uses)—that proved unbroachable.

Early efforts, like those of Charles Lamb, went nowhere. Lamb, who with his brother ran a commercial decorating firm specializing in the interior design of churches, was a City Beautiful evangelist who in 1898 wrote an article for *Municipal Affairs* in which he urged mandating a stepped-back pyramid envelope as a way to allow light to reach the street. The idea, which he said he borrowed from Paris, proved a non-starter.

In 1903 Lamb denounced the Flatiron as "an example of the greed of the corporation controlling it and owning it," adding that "architecturally, it is unfit to be in the center of the city." The controlling corporation, of course, was Harry Black's. Lamb didn't much care for Black, given his ties to corrupt union boss Sam Parks and his reputation for dodgy stock manipulations, and above all because his "skyscraper trust" had figured out how to funnel Wall Street capital into real estate speculation, opening the door to rampant overdevelopment. His critique went unheeded.

In 1906, when Lamb was elected president of the Municipal Art Society, he pledged the organization would present a heights limitation bill "following somewhat the law of Paris." Development forces howled him down. The *Times* dismissed the notion as "oppressive and absurd." Vigorous lobbying by the real estate industry squelched legislative initiatives. A dispirited Montgomery Schuyler wrote what seemed the movement's epitaph: "It were a fond imagination that the individualistic New Yorker, whose rampant individualism is, in fact, in this matter, the source of all our woes, would submit to such limitation of his right to do what he will with his own."

But throughout the years of Lamb's campaign, the skyboom had been at full throttle. "There can be no doubt that the present is a period of unparalleled speculation in New York real estate," the *Nation* had said in 1902. "The Prices now being paid in Manhattan are wholly unexampled." The speculative frenzy had mounted steadily, hitting a new peak in 1905 when conveyances were up 40 percent over the previous year, and rents for new towers pinnacled at $3.50 a square foot (while older buildings fetched only $1.75), helping push construction starts to new highs in 1906. In the mad rush skyward, talk of limits was brushed aside.

Then came the 1907 panic on the New York Stock Exchange. Almost immediately the effects reverberated through the real estate market. Values tanked. Rentals in first-class buildings dropped to $2.00 a square foot, or even $1.75. Construction slid sharply. Many builders went bankrupt. US Realty—which had been acting on the assumption that demand for office space (and attendant land values) could only go in one direction, now found their stock plummeting, and the firm proved unable to declare dividends. Paul Starrett, whom Harry Black had advised to invest heavily in the company, lost his shirt.

Suddenly, the climate of opinion on height limitation shifted, and a conversation broke out, kicked off by Ernest Flagg, a man whose pro-height credentials were, literally, second to none. On December 29, 1907, amid the rubble of the collapsed real estate industry, Flagg wrote an article that began "High buildings are becoming a nuisance and a peril." Streets were becoming congested and dark ("little better than deep cañons"). And those "dismal ravines" were lined with "huge masses, devoid of any good qualities but revenue production, [which] rear their heads like monuments to greed, and make our city a by-word to the cultivated foreigner accustomed to the orderly appearance of the cities of the old world."

Flagg could say this without being called a hypocrite because he believed his Singerhorn was part of the solution, not part of the problem. He proposed legislation that would allow towers to rise to any height, but to occupy only one-quarter of their plot (the needle-like Singer covered only one-sixth). This would greatly lessen the shadowcasting of neighbors into darkness. He also (being a Beaux-Arts man himself) urged uniform cornice heights (*à la française*) set in a fixed ratio to the width of the street, but no more than 100 or 150 feet (eight to twelve stories). With other restrictions, this would replace Gotham's "wild-Western appearance" with "a metropolitan air" that better befit "a city which claims rank with the other great capitals of the world." A reinvigorated Montgomery Schuyler championed Flagg's initiative in a 1908 article, "To Curb the Skyscraper," applauding the architect's desire "to 'citify,' to regularize, in a word, to Parisianize the city."

For a while, skyscraper regulation was the talk of the town. There were discussions at the City Club, testimonies at City Hall, special stories in the Sunday supplements. The normally boosterish *Real Estate Record and Builders Guide* worried about an "Invasion of New York City by Darkness." The New York Board of Trade recommended setbacks. And in 1908, heeding the tumult, the city government set up a Committee on the Limitation of Height and Area as a subset of the Building Code Revision Commission of New York City, to which Flagg presented his proposals. Developers were so concerned that limits were just around the corner that they raced to file building plans before the law was changed.

The Building Code Revision Commission, however, had other fish to fry, namely the preservation of archaic but, for Tammany Hall, lucrative rules. The existing code still required that walls grow thicker at the bottom as buildings grew taller—a ludicrous provision now that steel girders carried the weight. But Lincoln Steffens estimated Tammany collected a "commission" of 1 percent of the construction cost of any plans that were granted a variance by the Department of Buildings—which brought in millions each year. Rather than endanger the golden goose, Tammany simply derailed the whole revision, taking height restriction down with it.

Then, suddenly, with the 1907–8 panic over, speculative building roared back into business, and 1909 proved the biggest building year in the city's history, with nearly a thousand buildings set in upward motion. The regulatory movement immediately lost steam.

After two wild years, the real estate market collapsed again—battered by a generally shaky economy and the newly bloated oversupply of office space—and this time it stayed on the mat. From 1911 on, property values at best remained flat, though in some areas buildings lost half to two-thirds their value. Vacancies spread, bankruptcies ensued, and many Wall Street towers fell back into the unwilling hands of their lenders. Banks and insurance companies grew concerned. (Met Life alone had over $200 million tied up in New York real estate.) The mighty US Realty Company nearly went under. In 1911 Harry Black himself declared: "New York is overbuilt." Speculation remained becalmed year after year. In 1914 the industry was still mired in "depression," according to the *Real Estate Record*; the following year it reported "unprecedented stagnation."

The height conversation recommenced, this time in the larger context of what one prominent real estate man called "ruinous competition." Jockeying for skyline preeminence, it now seemed clear, had produced some winners but many more losers. "Wholesale theft of daylight is the cause of over-supply of rentable space," said the *RERBG* in 1911, and oversupply drove down rents and scared off investors. At a 1913 convention of building owners and managers, one speaker said, "Many of the skyscrapers in New York are monuments of uselessness."

Gotham's developers began thinking the unthinkable. Perhaps the glorious drive skyward *had* been overdone. Perhaps rampant individualism and competition were as harmful in real estate as in railroading, steel, and oil. Perhaps there *were* advantages to bringing in the state or city to regulate skyscraper construction.

ZONING

The man who brokered a response to the crisis with which both City Beautifiers and the real estate industry could live was George McAneny, who in 1910 had become borough president of Manhattan. In that capacity he would tackle a variety of big projects, but one of his principal concerns became the regulation of skyscrapers and, more broadly, of land use throughout the city.

McAneny forged a coalition among four constituencies.

First was the real estate industry and associated financiers who were eager to preserve property values but hesitant about accepting any infringement on their power to build what and where they willed. Second was a constellation of Fifth Avenue merchants, dismayed at the arrival of a particular type of tower—manufacturing lofts—into their hitherto exclusively commercial domain (from 23rd Street to 50th); they had organized a vigorous lobbying group, the Fifth Avenue Association, to repel the intruders. Third were the civic-minded business-men and lawyers in groups like the City Club and Municipal Art Society—City Beautifier strongholds. Fourth was the Committee on Congestion of Population in New York City (CCP), rooted in social reform circles and focused principally on alleviating terrible condi-tions in the tenement quarters; though skyscrapers were not of great concern to the CCP, it did have a Committee on Streets and Highways, which backed height restrictions; and it did have an interest in expanding suburban housing, which won it support from those who, like Henry Morgenthau, had large holdings in the outer boroughs.

Arguably, McAneny's land-use reform coalition included a fifth constituency: the net-work of city planners, engineers, architects, and public health experts who sought to create and empower a municipal bureaucracy that could strengthen the public's ability to control its own destiny, rather than leaving its fate in private hands. This group counted McAneny him-self among its ranks: he had chaired the City Club's Committee on City Planning and in 1910 had told the Saint Nicholas Society, "We have got to build a city fifty years or one hundred years ahead."

IN 1911 A DELEGATION FROM THE FIFTH AVENUE ASSOCIATION (FAA) visited McAneny and urged municipal intervention to keep manufacturers at bay. In response, the borough presi-dent created a Fifth Avenue Commission (six of whose seven members were also in the FAA), which recommended that height and bulk limitations be imposed on loft buildings. But the proposed remedy was so nakedly self-interested that it failed to gain political traction. McAneny, accordingly, set out to mobilize a broader base.

In February 1913 McAneny got the Board of Estimate and Apportionment (on which he sat ex officio) to establish a Committee on the Height, Size, and Arrangement of Buildings (of which he became chair). It would work to "limit the heights of buildings, to reduce fire hazards, to avoid the shutting off of light and air from other buildings and public streets, and to prevent unwholesome and dangerous congestion both in living conditions and in street and traffic conditions."

It, in turn, appointed a Heights of Buildings Commission (HBC), an advisory body that represented most of the interested private parties—real estate agents, retailers, builders, bro-kers, architects, planners, lawyers, and representatives from the Fifth Avenue Association, City Club, and Chamber of Commerce. The HBC was chaired by Edward M. Bassett, a Brooklyn-born lawyer (Columbia Law, Class of 1886), a planner, and an opponent of sky-scraper proliferation.

The HBC pretty quickly agreed on a height-limitation plan that married Charles Lamb's setbacks and Ernest Flagg's towers, but they worried about its passing judicial muster. To bolster the case for its being a legitimate exercise of the constitutional "police power," they adopted two tactics. First, they narrowed its rationale, claiming (dubiously) it was essentially a fire safety and public health measure (even bringing in a neurologist to testify about motion sickness in tall-tower elevators). Second, they broadened the mission—spectacularly—by making height regulation but a small part of a much vaster project aimed at promoting the *general* welfare by zoning the *entire* city, and by imposing restrictions not only on height but also on use.

The idea for zoning had come from several of the constituencies, notably the City Club, the Committee on Congestion, and Chairman Bassett himself. But in all cases the New York advocates were importing approaches to urban development pioneered in Europe, chiefly in Germany, and particularly in Frankfurt and Düsseldorf. The HBC itself followed up by dispatching agents to investigate how zoning worked abroad, and they returned laden with maps, specifications, and assessments that were overwhelmingly positive about its ability to promote orderly urban growth. What the German municipalities had done was district their entire cities into specific use areas—residential, industrial, commercial, and mixed. This protected each quarter from invasion by the other, and undermined the ability of speculators to exploit the uncertainty and fear of one or another set of users. The Germans also carved out a second set of districts, regulating the height of buildings by gearing them to specific multiples of street widths. A third set of area-based regulations governed the percentage of each lot that could be covered.

To bring the zoning idea before a larger public, McAneny got the Board of Estimate to co-underwrite (with the Merchants' Association) another City Planning Exhibition (in November 1913, at the New York Public Library) with contributions from over 200 cities.

In December the HBC released its zoning proposal, a variant of the German model. It suggested three use districts (residential, commercial, or unrestricted), five height districts, and five kinds of area districts (regulating the size of yards and courts). Two-thirds of the greater city (and two-fifths of Manhattan) was tentatively set aside for strictly residential use. In commercial districts, manufacturing would be effectively barred. Building heights were a multiple of street width, the formula varying with location, but no building could climb higher than fourteen stories without being progressively set back from the street (Lamb's approach), though (following Flagg's suggestion) unlimited development was permitted on 25 percent of the site.

With an eye toward cultivating popular support and judicial approbation, the commission stressed that zoning would provide for the citizenry's "health, safety, morals, and convenience." To the business community it emphasized that zoning would stabilize property values, avoid loss of light and air, diminish insurance rates, and reduce the burden on transportation. Their plan, the commissioners stressed, was not the product of idealistic reformers out to benefit the poor; as one member insisted: "This was not class legislation of any sort."

The proposal elicited a mixed response. Most powerful interests lined up behind it. The City Club, the Fifth Avenue Association, the New York Chamber of Commerce, and the New York Real Estate Board (representing the largest realty firms) favored it. Smaller firms hurt in the slump, owners of unimproved property, and unreconstructed laissez-faire types opposed any limits at all. (One outfit—the United Real Estate Owners' Associations—denounced it as a probably unconstitutional "blow at the fundamental right to private ownership.") So did the building trade unions, who feared a reduction in construction. Politically, the ayes had it, and the state legislature amenably amended New York's charter in February 1914, giving the Board of Estimate and Apportionment authority to zone the city.

In June 1914 the board set up one last committee, even more top-heavy with representatives of real estate men and financiers, and charged it with preparing a detailed plan. The Commission on Building Districts and Restrictions (CBDR) labored two years more. Again chaired by Edward Bassett, it mapped out the metropolis, district by district, showing the height and use of every building in the city—over $8 billion worth of real property—while other maps traced the historical transformation of particular neighborhoods. Height limitations were laid down—with the highest permitted ratio from ground level to first setback

(2.5 times the street width) awarded to the Wall Street area, and the lowest, which in effect precluded tall towers, assigned to the outer boroughs, virtually ensuring they would remain bedroom or factory communities. In general, buildings along avenues could rise straight up for fourteen to eighteen floors before a setback, and those on side streets from nine to twelve floors. The limitations were capacious enough to accommodate virtually every existing large building in Manhattan.

WHILE THE CBDR PORED OVER GOTHAM'S TOPOGRAPHY (1914–16), political support swelled for a grand compromise between the real estate industry and skyscraper critics, thanks in part to the public response to two drastically different towers.

Beautifiers had decried not only skyscrapers' altitude but their aesthetics. Given their White City and urban European models, skyscrapers weren't really architecture at all, but merely engineering artifacts and moneymaking machines. This animus softened somewhat as the boom wore on and towers of real architectural merit went up. The Singer and Met Life towers were widely praised. But it was Cass Gilbert's Woolworth Building that proved the game changer.

It had been an article of faith that skyscrapers lived only on the dollar side of the commercial/civic divide. Woolworth set out to challenge this. He asked Gilbert to wrap his corporate totem in a secular Gothic envelope—specifically suggesting the Victoria Tower of the Houses of Parliament as a model—in order to stake a claim to civic merit. When the tower was done, Woolworth sought out critical approbation, and got it. In 1913 he commissioned a commemorative art book for distribution to a small elite audience. He asked Montgomery Schuyler, the ur-skyscraper-critic, to write the text. Schuyler agreed and offered effusive praise for the tower as "the culminating triumph of commercial architecture" and the "noblest offspring" of steel cage construction. Most critics accepted that at last a suitable architectural expression had been found for the skyscraper. *American Architect*, longtime opponent of towers, said that

Test of fire protection system, Woolworth Building. *Fire and Water Engineering*, June 11, 1913. (Cass Gilbert Architectural Collection, Image No. 78899d, New-York Historical Society)

there could be "no further doubt" that "a satisfactory solution to the architectural difficulties of the tall building" had been found.

In 1916 Woolworth added a patina of piety, commissioning a gilded, prayer-book-like booklet called *The Cathedral of Commerce,* and inviting Dr. S. Parkes Cadman to write the foreword. Minister since 1901 of the Central Congregational Church in Brooklyn (on Hancock, then Spencer Street, between Bedford and Franklin Avenues), Cadman, a popular orator, waxed grandiloquent. "When seen at nightfall bathed in electric light as with a garment, or in the lucid air of a summer morning, piercing space like a battlement of the paradise of God which St. John beheld, it inspires feelings too deep even for tears," he declaimed. "The writer," Cadman added, "looked upon it and at once cried out 'the Cathedral of Commerce' "—thus reconciling Christianity and commerce, as had an earlier pulpit master, Henry Ward Beecher. Architect Gilbert dissented from this characterization, insisting he'd had no intention of evoking a cathedral, but did admit he'd aimed at showing that a building dedicated to commerce could "inspire thoughts of a higher and more spiritual life." And he allowed as how he believed a Gothic skyscraper gained "in spirituality the higher it mounts."

IF THE WOOLWORTH BUILDING HELPED RECONCILE City Beautifiers to skyscrapers, the Equitable Building helped convert any remaining holdouts in the real estate fraternity to accepting public restraints on their right to build tall.

In the late nineties, at the beginning of the real estate boom, the Equitable Life Assurance Society had been unhappily ensconced in its headquarters at 120 Broadway. When the building first opened in 1870, it had been a trailblazer with its 130-foot height (twice that of the typical commercial structure) and its status as the first office building to feature passenger elevators. Now it was considered a dinosaur. Equitable, looking to expand, had bought up the block on which the building sat (Broadway/Cedar/Nassau/Pine) and conferred with Daniel Burnham about building a super-tall replacement. The 1905 insurance scandal had put things on hold. Then, on January 9, 1912, the building burned in a spectacular blaze; the sixteen-degree temperature froze the water firemen played on it, creating a Second Empire palace of ice.

The day after the fire, plans were set in motion for a replacement. The one hitch was a post-scandal law that barred insurance companies from investing in buildings not solely for their own use. Equitable sold the property to a syndicate of developers, including T. Coleman du Pont, possessor of a chemical-company fortune, while agreeing to take three floors for its own use, and to come up with an arm's-length way to help finance the project.

Du Pont, another would-be Napoleon of New York real estate, now announced plans to build the biggest office building in the world, biggest by volume, not height. A thirty-nine-story no-frills office block that would maximize return on investment, it would shoot straight up from the property line, encompassing 1.2 million square feet of rentable space, capable of housing 20,000 employees. It would also cast deep shadows, generate intolerable congestion, suck up tenants from other skyscrapers, and drastically exacerbate the existing glut—all this just as the depression-spurred debate on regulation was getting under way.

To build it, du Pont turned to Louis Horowitz of Thompson-Starrett. When the construction company tore down the ruins of Equitable's old building that summer of 1912, nearby towers were suddenly flooded with sunshine; some, like Chase National and Fourth National Banks, luxuriated in light for the first time in their existence. Then they learned of du Pont's plan, which would hurl them back into darkness, along with many others. The new monster, said one broker, would tower over its immediate surroundings, casting "a chilling, killing blight upon them, and sapping their vitality."

Du Pont's soon-to-be neighbors, horrified, rallied to halt the project. Harry Black's United States Realty—whose Trinity and USR buildings were right across Broadway—took the lead in assembling a consortium, including several leading banks; the effort was spearheaded by Black's vice president George T. Mortimer, who would soon join the 1913 Heights of Building Commission. At first the group suggested du Pont donate the $13.5 million site to the city for a park—a proposal, Horowitz huffed, which "outranks, for nerve, anything of which I ever heard." He countered that du Pont might consider selling the property to them, at full price, after which they could plant all the flowers they wished, for all he cared. (Horowitz was, of course, Harry Black's chief rival, and hardly inclined to do him any favors.) Next the consortium appealed to the city to condemn the site for a park, another nonstarter, as the city would not only have to pay the multi-million-dollar sale price but also forgo a million or so in annual taxes. Then they offered du Pont $2.5 million to limit his building to eight stories. He laughed them out the door. With their helplessness in the face of "architectural aggression" thus brought starkly home to them, these leading real estate, financial, and corporate moguls grew ever more determined to seek municipal intervention.

In June 1914 du Pont began construction, which was finished the following May, just as the Commission on Building Districts and Restrictions was seeking public commentary on its zoning work in progress. The Equitable Building became exhibit A in favor of its proposal. The building's noontime shadow, critics noted, stretched almost a fifth of a mile, cutting off direct sunlight from the Broadway fronts of buildings as tall as twenty-one stories. Tenants had fled the darkened buildings, and their property owners had claimed a loss of rental income, forcing the city to reduced their assessed valuations by roughly $1 million. As 80 percent of Gotham's budget came from taxes on property or buildings, the city itself now had a demonstrable interest in reining in such rogue operators.

By now the critics were pushing on an open door. When the CBDR's final report came out in March 1916, there was all but universal support for the zoning ordinance, and for the commission's conclusion that "New York City has reached a point beyond which continued unplanned growth cannot take place without inviting social and economic disaster. It is too big a city, the social and economic interests involved are too great to permit the continuance of the *laissez faire* methods of earlier days." Even the Equitable Life Assurance Society signed on.

In July the Board of Estimate and Apportionment enacted it into law. The *New York Times* cheered: "The do-as-you-please policy of running up a building to any height, irrespective of the size of the plot or the rights of adjoining owners to light and air, has ceased. It is to be hoped, for the good of the city, forever." Other municipalities scrambled to follow New York's lead. By 1918 zoning commissions were at work in at least nine other cities; within twenty years, over 1,200 municipalities would adopt similar zoning ordinances.

George McAneny hailed the zoning law of 1916 as "the greatest single achievement in city planning in America," but some veteran reformers argued that it was in truth a substitute for planning, even a setback to it. It didn't involve the city in directing and shaping its future growth—as had been the case in Frankfurt; rather, it essentially froze the status quo, protecting owners from land uses that threatened property values. Zoning aimed less at promoting the general welfare than at providing a safer environment for speculation. As one disappointed reformer noted, "In the greatest city in the New World nothing was done to direct growth, in the interest of beauty, health, and safety, until Mammon cried out in distress."

The new law did, however, have one immediate effect on the cityscape. It didn't halt construction of tall towers, but it did force architects to squeeze their structures into spatial envelopes resembling Babylonian ziggurats. There would be no more Equitable Buildings. The 1918 arrival of a setback tower at 27 West 43rd Street hinted at the shape of things to come.

AT THE SAME TIME THAT NEW YORK WAS SHOOTING SKYWARD, it was stretching out laterally, refurbishing or adding conduits, by land and sea, that connected it to the continent and the wider world.

8

Arteries

TRAINS AND TUNNELS

As the century began, trains seeking to enter the metropolis faced great obstacles. Of the twelve major rail lines converging on New York City, nine dead-ended in New Jersey—their iron horses impotently pawing the Hudson riverbank. Manhattan-bound passengers (140 million arrived during 1906) had to detrain and board ferries at Jersey City or Hoboken, a cumbersome and, depending on the weather, frustrating business.

Alexander J. Cassatt, from 1899 president of the Pennsylvania Railroad (PRR), was determined to correct this situation. The Pennsy had long stuck to its Philadelphia last, but in 1871, when it had become clear that New York would dominate the country's export-import traffic, the line had established service across the Jersey flatlands to the Hudson. After 1892 PRR passengers arrived at an immense vaulted train shed in the Paulus Hook section of Jersey City, where they could transfer to ferries headed for Courtlandt Street, directly across the river. Such a state of affairs was acceptable for regional lines like the Erie or Jersey Central, but the Pennsylvania was the nation's biggest and richest system. It was therefore extremely vexing that its only serious rival, the Vanderbilt's New York Central, was able to shepherd *its* patrons directly onto Gotham terra firma—via a bridge at Albany and tracks down the Hudson's east bank—depositing them at Grand Central Depot (42nd and Fourth Avenue). Cassatt wanted his own Manhattan beachhead.

Given the difficulties of spanning the mile-wide Hudson with a bridge, the obvious solution was a tunnel. But the river had defeated all efforts to burrow beneath it. Back in the 1870s an adventurous entrepreneur named De Witt Clinton Haskin (he'd been born in New York in 1824 just as Clinton was finishing the Erie Canal) had attempted to link Manhattan with Hoboken via two single-track tubes. Sandhogs had used compressed air to keep waters at bay while they dug, but after a disastrous blowout in 1880 killed twenty men, the firm went belly up. Some bondholders tried again. By bringing in British capital and deploying shield technology, the company managed to bore its way under 4,000 feet of riverbed before running out of money and subsiding into bankruptcy in 1892.

In that same year William Steinway, the piano manufacturer and Queens booster, opened a second front. In an effort to establish trolley service between Long Island City and Manhattan, the New York and Long Island Railroad, in which Steinway was the principal investor, began construction of a tunnel under the East River; but a dynamite disaster that killed five people brought on lawsuits that ruined the company.

In 1894 an English engineer, Charles M. Jacobs, successfully completed New York's first tunnel: a modest 10-foot-wide tube under the East River that carried gas mains (and an adjacent service track) from the Ravenswood section of Long Island City to Manhattan's East 71st Street for the East River Gas Company.

In 1901 William Gibbs McAdoo took up the quest for a subaquatic Hudson connection. A 30-year-old Georgia-born and Chattanooga-based lawyer who'd moved to New York in 1897, McAdoo learned about Haskins's tunnel interruptus from John Randolph Dos Passos, a corporate attorney and former tunnel investor, and promptly caught the connectivitis bug. Dos Passos introduced McAdoo to tunnel engineer Jacobs, and in October the two men, clad in hip boots and yellow oilskins, visited the abandoned diggings. When Jacobs declared that completing the project was perfectly feasible technically, McAdoo incorporated a New York and New Jersey Railroad Company, issued $8.5 million of stock, bought up rights to the old company, wound up his law practice, and in fall 1902 threw himself full-time into completing the conduit. His goal was to run electrified inter-urban light-rail cars for commuters from the Jersey Shore to Manhattan's West Side, where connections could be made to elevated and trolley lines.

In early 1903, with the renewed digging going well, McAdoo escalated by launching a second set of tubes, a mile farther south, that would link Jersey City and its big rail terminals directly to the Wall Street area. The north tunnel holed-through in March 1904. The southern one followed suit in September 1905. In 1906 McAdoo set up the Hudson and Manhattan (H&M) Railroad, which floated a $100 million bond issue to finish the business; it attracted some of the city's wealthiest, including J. P. Morgan, Cornelius Vanderbilt II, and Elbert Gary of US Steel. Fiscally fortified, the system was rapidly finished. By 1908 passengers could travel from Hoboken's Lachine terminal to Christopher Street; by 1910 they could ride all the way to a new H&M terminal at Sixth Avenue and 33rd. In 1909 the second tunnel began carrying passengers from Exchange Place in Jersey City (after 1910 they could board the train at Newark) to a subterranean station at Courtlandt Street. Atop it sat two twenty-two-story skyscrapers—the Hudson Terminal Buildings—which McAdoo had ordered up in 1906 from Harry Black and Paul Starrett's Fuller Company. Together, the twin towers at 30 and 50 Church Street (divided by Dey) constituted the largest office-building complex in the world, and its 900 leaseholders generated additional income for McAdoo's line.

No sooner had McAdoo's project gotten off/under the ground than Alexander Cassatt decided to tunnel, too. The Pennsylvania tubes would not only be far larger—geared to handling

"Interior View of the Hudson River Tunnel between New York and New Jersey," ca. 1908. (Mary Evans Picture Library/Alamy Stock Photo)

big trains coming in from the continent—but they'd be part of a vast reorganization of the entire rail route into and out of Gotham, a financial/engineering project of unprecedented magnitude and complexity.

In 1901 Cassatt, himself a civil engineer, convinced himself that electric engines could replace steam locomotives—an indispensable precondition for going with tunnels—by visiting Paris to see the electrified Orléans railway wend its way under city streets to the new Gare d'Orsay. In 1902 he hired McAdoo's tunnel expert, Charles Jacobs, to run his engineering design team. This was an amicable arrangement (Jacobs would work on both projects at once) because Cassatt never considered McAdoo a competitor but rather a junior partner in a systemic metropolitan realignment. Over the next two years Cassatt, Jacobs, and a corps of engineers hammered out a plan with several parts.

First, trains approaching Gotham from the interior would be shunted off from the main line just east of Newark, and then run on a 5-mile causeway across the Hackensack Meadows, pausing midway at a new station—to be called Manhattan Transfer—where they would swap their steam locomotives for electric engines, and also offload passengers desiring to ride McAdoo's Hudson and Manhattan directly to Wall Street. From there trains would travel through a tunnel to be bored through Bergen Hill (the lower end of the Palisades) and then, at Weehawken, continue on under the Hudson to a point beneath Manhattan's Eighth Avenue and 33rd Street.

From there (ran part two of the engineers' plan) the company would dig a crosstown tunnel to carry trains across Manhattan and beneath the East River, emerging in Long Island City, Queens, where they would link up with the Long Island Rail Road, a line in which the Pennsy had bought a controlling interest in 1900. A little farther east, the PRR would construct the largest passenger-car yard in the world, a mammoth 192-acre storage, repair, and turnaround facility called Sunnyside Yards.

"Hudson and Manhattan Tube," ca. 1910. (Hoboken Historical Museum)

In the final phase of the master plan, Sunnyside Yards would in turn be connected to the Bronx mainland by an aptly named New York Connecting Railroad. This short but crucial line would curve north through Queens and west across Hell Gate over a to-be-built railroad bridge, arriving at the Oak Point Yard of the New York, New Haven & Hartford line, in the Port Morris area. This road, which in 1903 came under the control of New York investors led by J. P. Morgan, was the main trunk line leading on to southern New England and points north.

At the center of this seamless river of rails, where the Hudson and East River tunnels confluesced, Cassatt intended to build a great train depot, Pennsylvania Station.

BEFORE THESE PLANS COULD BE BROUGHT TO FRUITION, certain obstacles had to be overcome. The Pennsylvania needed a franchise from the city and wanted it granted in perpetuity. This raised Hearst's hackles, and in 1902 his papers denounced it as a "Colossal Robbery." It was, he declared, "infamous that the rights of the people in these franchises, worth hundreds of millions to the Pennsylvania Company, should be given away forever." The Tammany-controlled Board of Aldermen—whose acquiescence was essential—also objected, and the aldermen supported as well a demand from the Central Federated Union, Gotham's largest labor organization, that the franchise include a clause guaranteeing an eight-hour day. The railroad refused on both counts, and Tammany eventually yielded, but only after its acquiescence was lubricated by the Pennsylvania's awarding a $2 million excavation contract (the nation's biggest ever) to the New York Contracting and Trucking Company, which was, not coincidentally, run by Boss Charlie Murphy's brother. Equally amicable relations with Boss Platt's Albany Republicans were facilitated by Cassatt's retaining the legal services of Platt's son (at $10,000 a year).

Next, the PRR had to acquire the four square blocks of real estate bounded by West 31st and 33rd Streets and Seventh and Ninth Avenues, an area described by one chronicler as "given up to the French and negro colonies." The company quietly retained the real estate agent who managed the Astor family's vast holdings, and he dispatched buyers carrying wads of cash and contracts to acquire titles—as surreptitiously as possible—to brownstones, tenements, and the cafés and saloons owned by black prizefighters that marked the heart of the old Tenderloin district. "Dives disappear before derrick and stone masons," exulted the *Herald*, which considered this a species of urban renewal. But squeezing black tenants northward would have momentous consequences for the area's social ecology.

Most crucially, the Pennsy's New York Extension required staggering amounts of capital. Given the enormity of the sums, assembling it was not easy, even with the aid of Gotham's leading investment bankers. Floating a $100 million convertible bond sale in May 1905—the largest of its kind in railroad annals—took the combined syndicate-creation efforts of both Kuhn, Loeb and the House of Morgan. In May 1906, Cassatt went back to the market well for another $50 million, then obtained yet another $50 million one month after that (this time from French investors). At this point Schiff cautioned Cassatt: "Do no more financing in this market for some time to come," he said, as "your company's immense requirements are beginning somewhat to frighten its shareholders." Still, over time, all the pieces of the plan found funding.

WORK ON THE HUDSON RIVER AND EAST RIVER TUNNELS by a multi-national crew of sandhogs (some had worked on tunnels in Egypt and South America) commenced in 1904, and ran concurrently with construction of the Sunnyside Yards. By 1910 all pieces were in readiness, and the centerpiece, Pennsylvania Station, was itself approaching completion.

Back in April 1902 Cassatt had handed Charles McKim, of McKim, Mead & White, a difficult design problem. As all the trackage would be submerged 45 feet below ground, the conventional approach to terminals—a great vaulted shed—was unnecessary. Cassatt toyed with putting up a skyscraper to generate rental income, as McAdoo would do. But McKim—not a great skyscraper fan—convinced Cassatt that a commercial structure wouldn't satisfy the railroad's wish to be seen as a civic benefactor. He urged the PRR to provide Gotham with a magnificent gateway worthy of an imperial city.

For McKim—a leading City Beautifularian—only a low-rise neoclassical structure would do. Believing the emerging American Empire more "nearly akin to the life of the Roman Empire than that of any other known civilization," he turned to the Eternal City for an

"New York's first Under-River Tunnel," 1902. (New York Public Library, Art and Picture Collection)

architectural model. (McKim had helped establish the American Academy in Rome in 1897, with financial backing from J. P. Morgan, precisely so American students could learn first hand "the splendid standards of Classic and Renaissance art" and escape the undue influence of Parisians.) The public buildings of ancient Rome, in addition to their aesthetic excellence, offered functional lessons as well, as they had been intended to accommodate great moving crowds. McKim not only patterned Penn Station's general waiting room on the *frigidarium* (cold-water room) of the Baths of Caracalla; he went to Rome and hired workmen to stroll around the ruins so he could ponder scale and flow. McKim turned to Rome for some of his building materials, too, obtaining cream-colored travertine stone from the same quarries that once had supplied the emperors.

Then construction began. Tammany chief Murphy's company hired 2,000 men (doubtless loyal Democrats) to clear the entire site, then excavated an 8-acre hole to a depth of 50 feet. Crowds gaped and painters set up easels as 3 million cubic yards of earth and mica schist were blasted, dug, and hauled away by small steam locomotives to the scows waiting at West Side piers to ferry them to fills. (The process reminded many of the contemporary excavation of the Panama Canal.) Then Paul Starrett and his George A. Fuller Company were brought in to erect the steel frame and affix to it a half-million cubic feet of pink Milford Massachusetts granite.

By 1910 the massive construction crews had Pennsylvania Station ready for dedication. The colossal colonnaded structure, hailed as an architectural triumph, was praised for its efficiency, too. The Roman waiting room and the adjacent steel-and-glass Concourse facilitated the smooth circulation of huge crowds, with long-distance passengers and daily commuters channeled in orderly flows, up and down and in and out of bridges, ramps, tunnels, staircases, elevators, arcades, and finally exits.

"Concourse, Penn. [Pennsylvania] Station," ca. 1910–15. (Library of Congress Prints and Photographs Division)

The railroad hoped the surrounding neighborhood, shorn of its low-lifes, would become a great commercial complex. To further this goal, Cassatt set out to improve the neighborhood tone (and recoup some of the mounting land costs) by selling at cost the large parcel between Eighth and Ninth Avenues to the U.S. Postal Service, then seeking a new main post office in Manhattan. McKim, Mead & White and the Fuller Company would again collaborate on another colonnaded structure, directly atop the PRR train tracks, so that an ingenious chute system could drop mailbags to postal cars below. (The architects inadvertently provided the mail service with an unofficial motto when they emblazoned on the façade's frieze a passage from Herodotus describing the messenger service of the Persian Empire: "Neither snow, nor rain, nor heat, nor gloom of night stays these couriers from the swift completion of their appointed rounds.") On the Seventh Avenue side, the firm erected the Hotel Pennsylvania (1919), yet another McKim, Mead & White–Fuller Company collaboration-cum-columns; the largest hostelry in the world, it was leased and operated by the Statler Company.

Despite their efforts, the territory around the station resisted further upgrading. This contrasted sharply with the transformation wrought in the vicinity of its great rival on 42nd Street.

AT THE TURN OF THE CENTURY, the managers of the New York Central were alarmed. They had just finished wrapping a new façade around the old (1871) Grand Central Depot and tacking on extra stories. Now this makeover would be wildly outclassed by a brand-new station that, in addition, would give Manhattan access to their biggest rival. What to do?

In 1903—one year after the line premiered its future-oriented Twentieth Century Limited service to Chicago—the Central decided to build its station anew, following a bold proposal laid out by William John Wilgus, the Central's chief engineer. Wilgus had grown up in a Central family. His father, a modestly paid freight agent in the railroad's Buffalo terminal, had been unable to provide his son professional schooling. So Wilgus was apprenticed to a civil engineer, then went west and worked on railroads, specializing in electrification. In

"Pennsylvania Railroad Station, New York City: Seventh Avenue and Thirty-Second Street, Looking towards Long Island," 1910. (Library of Congress Geography and Map Division)

1897 the Central offered him the post of engineer of the Eastern Division. He took it, moved to Gotham, rose rapidly, and by 1899 was in charge of the entire line.

In March 1903 Wilgus presented a fully fleshed-out proposal to senior management. He suggested the company blast away all 48 acres of the land it owned, down to 60 feet below grade, and insert therein two immense underground platforms, one above the other, the lower for local commuter service, the upper for long-distance trains. Atop this vast subterranean complex—stretching from west of Lexington to east of Madison, from 56th to 42nd—would rise a brand-new Grand Central Terminal.

Like Cassatt, Wilgus called for electrifying incoming trains, for only thus could an underground station be made viable. Besides, given a recent catastrophe, steam engines were on the way out. In January 1902 a commuter train murking its way through the steam-and-smoke-filled Park Avenue tunnel, had plowed into the rear of a stationary New Haven train, killing seventeen passengers. An enraged state legislature decreed in May 1903 that after 1908 steam trains running on predominantly passenger tracks would be forbidden to enter Manhattan at all. Electricity would soon be mandatory as well as modern.

Wilgus admitted the price tag for the whole package would be a steep $40 million, roughly half the annual revenue of the entire Central system. (In the end it would be closer to $70 million.) But he pointed out that once the old yards and tracks were covered over, the company would be in possession of a whopping chunk of new-made prime real estate. On it the Central could construct commercial buildings—supported by steel piers placed between the tracks—and collect a fortune in rentals, offsetting if not exceeding its costs. As the practical engineer put it in a poetic moment: "Thus from the air would be taken wealth."

In 1903 architects entered a competition to choose the new Grand Central's designer. McKim, Mead & White, already at work on Penn Station, submitted an uncharacteristically spectacular conception. Stanford White's plan called for a fourteen-story terminal, topped by a sixty-story tower, capped by a 300-foot plume of steam spray illuminated at night by crimson lights. But the job was given to the little-known Minnesota firm of Reed and Stem (Charles Reed being Wilgus's brother-in-law), which also proposed topping the terminal with rental space, though a more modest twelve stories. Their decision did not stand, however, as the Minnesotans were forced to share design authority with the local firm of Warren and Wetmore (Whitney Warren being William K. Vanderbilt's cousin). Warren, another Beaux-Arts graduate, opted for City Beautifulesque low-lying monumentality, and, with Vanderbilt's strong support, Reed was overruled, the tower left on the drafting room floor.

Design, demolition, and construction proceeded for a decade, while service continued unabated. When the great doors officially swung open to the public in February 1913, thousands rushed in to marvel at the results. The exterior was applauded for its three imperial Roman arches, its multiple columns, and its south façade's sculptural triad of Mercury flanked by Hercules and Minerva. But the innards brought the greatest gasps.

The new mega-station's forty-eight platforms (dwarfing Pennsylvania's eleven) and its 70 acres of underground tracks and yards (to Pennsy's mere 25) could accommodate 1,100 cars. Twenty million passengers had passed through in 1910; the figure would almost double in the next decade. In the new statistical sweepstakes of "passenger miles"—a mobile measurement of traveler-as-commodity—neither the Pennsylvania nor any other station in the world even came close. Grand Central was another of the age's circulatory marvels. An interconnecting system of sloping ramps smoothly guided incoming and outgoing, or suburban and continental, passengers to their respective destinations. Train platforms and baggage rooms were handily adjacent to cab stands on 42nd Street or on Park Avenue, which had been wrapped around the station on elevated ramps.

But why leave? Warren envisioned the terminal as a bustling "bazaar"—a destination in its own right—and the place certainly had everything: art gallery, theater, Oyster Bar, emergency hospital, and post office; private dressing rooms where suburbanites could slip into evening wear; clubrooms, hairdressing parlors, barbers, bathtubs, and a profusion of small shops. Above all, it had the great soaring Concourse, another barrel-vaulted Roman bath, featuring a staircase as grand as the Paris Opera's, and a ceiling that was a mockup of the starry heavens. Vaster than St. Peter's nave, it was, some thought, equally "sublime."

If one *did* manage to tear oneself away from watching or participating in the endless spectacle, one stepped outside (or passed through underground corridors) into Terminal City, the complex of buildings rising above the Central's territory. Though it would never become quite the mini–City Beautiful the road envisioned, with uniform cornice lines restricted to the height of the terminal, travelers could walk to an impressive array of structures, most done in neoclassical limestone, including hotels (the Belmont, Barclay, Biltmore, Chatham, Commodore, Park Lane, and Ritz-Carlton), shops (Brooks Brothers, Abercrombie & Fitch),

THE "TERMINAL CITY," SHOWING WORK WHEN COMPLETED.   DRAWN BY VERNON HOWE BAILEY.

"The 'Terminal City,' Showing Work When Completed," 1913. (New York Public Library, Art and Picture Collection)

Warren & Wetmore, "Plan, Grand Central Terminal: Track Lay-Out to the North of the Concourse & Park Avenue," ca. 1907. (Columbia University, Avery Architectural and Fine Arts Library)

office buildings, the Yale Club, and the YMCA. Still more remarkable were the transformations being wrought along Park Avenue itself, under which the tracks ran. The Central had long refused to cover over the old steam vents, but when it became clear that property values on the terminal's periphery were rising at the rate of 25 percent a year, it soon constructed an unbroken promenade. In short order the avenue would shed its identity as host to industrial buildings and working-class homes and begin to rival Fifth Avenue as an abode of millionaires.

More portentous still, as prescient observers noticed, the combination of the two giant train stations, which together funneled millions of commuters and commercial travelers into the West 30s and East 40s, was fostering a burst of office and hotel construction and a bevy of restaurants and theaters that bade fair to boost the status of midtown Manhattan from second-string business district to full-fledged rival of hitherto unassailable Wall Street.

Most critical of all, these rail-based reorganizations inserted the newly consolidated city more securely into the national land transport grid—the counterpart of a contemporaneous drive to improve Gotham's aquatic links to the planet.

BOATS AND DOCKS

Turn-of-the-century visitors sailing or steaming up the Narrows into the Upper Bay encountered a magnificent profusion of traffic swarming the sea lanes: huge full-rigged ships, barks, and brigs; sloops and coasting schooners laden with country produce; white-and-gold excursion steamboats with bands playing and flags flying; great funneled transatlantic liners belching smoke; tugs hauling long lines of canal boats or garbage scows; Standard Oil tankers loaded with kerosene; magenta-and-olive ferryboats, yachts, oil lighters, dredgers, elevator boats, oyster sloops, catboats, barges topped with railroad cars; and all this accompanied by clanging bells, shrieking whistles, snorting steam, and shouting men. It was exciting, bracing, intensely alive, richly romantic.

To New York's merchants, it looked more like a disaster zone.

The Port was slipping. To be sure it still did a vast and, in absolute terms, a growing business. Over 6,000 steamers and sailing vessels arrived each year from foreign ports; perhaps another 15,000 entered from domestic waters. The city still handled nearly two-thirds of the nation's imports (quantities of coffee, sugar, molasses, wool, and manufactures were going up) and over one-third of the country's exports. But its *relative* share of both had been and was continuing to drop. Baltimore and Philadelphia, though smaller, were closer to the interior and as good or better at handling bulk cargoes. Chicago, St. Louis, New Orleans, and San Francisco—cheaper and closer to producers—were steadily eroding eastern port predominance. For all its surface vigor, the port's vital signs were down, and its commercial leaders were worried.

They were also alarmed by how few of the thousands of vessels clearing Sandy Hook were American owned or American made. The United States had lost control of the carrying trade of its own commerce. In 1900 a mere 14 percent of the tonnage in and out of the port sailed in US-flag shipping. In strictly foreign commerce it was worse: 90 percent of the country's imports and 94 percent of its exports traveled in foreign bottoms. Worse still, apart from two respectable-sized firms (neither in New York), surviving US shippers were small fry and hypercompetitive. There were no consolidated giants in the marine economy, none that could even dream of competing with the great European firms. Aided by government subsidies and lower shipbuilding costs, the English (Cunard, White Star), the Germans (Hamburg-American, North German Lloyd), and the French (French Line) commanded the transatlantic trade.

These huge enterprises carried enormous weight around the harbor. Literally. One of the greatest problems confronting the port was the growing size and draft of foreign-flag passenger vessels. Beginning with Inman's *City of New York* (1888), a twin-screw express grossing over 10,000 tons, the Europeans had been building ever bigger, faster, more luxurious ships. In the early 1890s Cunard moved to the front with its *Campania* and *Lucania*, only to lose out to North German Lloyd's *Kaiser Wilhelm der Grosse*, which was trumped in 1899 by the White Star Line's *Oceanic*—at 685 feet and 17,000 tons, the first transatlantic steamer to surpass in size the old *Great Eastern* that had arrived in New York harbor to such acclaim back in 1860. The *Oceanic* stayed the last word in sumptuous travel only until 1907, when Cunard launched its 790-foot, 31,000-ton superliners the *Mauretania* and *Lusitania*.

By this point, however, an American contender had entered the lists, the ubiquitous J. P. Morgan. The Great Consolidator had long stuck to land-based transport, but after the Spanish-American and Boer Wars touched off an export surge, boosting industry profits, he set out to forge a Shipping Trust. First he merged America's two leading transatlantic firms (Philadelphia's International Navigation Company and Baltimore's Atlantic Transport Line). Then, aware that given US weakness, any marine combine worth its salt would have to include or neutralize the dominant European firms, he organized the International Mercantile Marine (IMM), and brought Britain's White Star and Leyland lines into the combination by the simple but very expensive expedient of paying shareholders ten times current earnings. Though the resulting Anglo-American fleet of over 120 steamships was the world's largest, Morgan pressed ahead, struck a deal with Germany's leading lines (after a tête-à-tête with Kaiser Wilhelm) to divide up the North Atlantic, and turned to swallow the one remaining holdout whose incorporation was critical—Britain's Cunard Steamship Company.

This proved impossible. Cunard's shares were too widely held to buy up control on the open market. Worse, Cunard appealed successfully to the British government for help in warding off the American threat. When the British Admiralty argued that Morgan-owned liners might not be available in a wartime emergency, Parliament agreed to grant Cunard lavish subsidies (to build the *Mauretania* and the *Lusitania*) and maintain British supremacy at sea. A debilitating rate war ensued between Cunard and Morgan's heavily watered and wobbling trust. In an all-out bid to gain supremacy, the IMM's White Star Line decided (in 1907) to build three mammoth and super-luxurious ships, the *Olympic*, *Titanic*, and *Britannic*, to capture the carriage trade from Cunard. Morgan, enthusiastic, arranged for a personal Tudor-style suite on the *Titanic*'s B deck (with special cigar holders in the bathroom) and attended its Belfast christening in May 1911. In April 1912 the 852-foot, 46,000-ton *Titanic* set out on its maiden voyage to New York. When the sumptuous floating city collided with an iceberg, and over 1,500 of the passengers and crew perished (in part because the magnificent accoutrements didn't include enough lifeboats), it took Morgan's debt-laden International Mercantile Marine with it. The company entered receivership in 1915, ending New York's bid to regain commercial supremacy. "The ocean," said the *Wall Street Journal*, had proven "too big for the old man."

Despite the catastrophe, the race for size continued, with Germans now taking the lead. The Hamburg-American unleashed its *Imperator* in 1912. At 906 feet, 52,000 tons, four screws, and six decks, it was the maritime wonder of the day, until the same line's *Vaterland* came down the ways in 1913, 42 feet longer and 2,000 tons bigger than its predecessor. Cunard responded with the *Aquitania*, a smaller ship, in effect throwing in the size towel, emphasizing safety and luxury instead. The *Aquitania* arrived in New York on her maiden voyage in June 1914, accompanied by shrieking whistles and dipping colors as she steamed up the harbor.

But while New York continued to fête each new arrival, and its wealthy flocked to book passage on these floating palaces, the giant vessels were also giant headaches; they outstretched the port's largest piers and sorely tested the capacity of its river channels. One of the first items on the consolidated city's transportation agenda was attending to these issues.

"New Chelsea Piers on the Hudson," 1912. (Library of Congress Prints and Photographs Division)

Problem number one was access to the harbor. Vessels arrived from the open sea by way of the Gedney and Main Channels, which swept in a horseshoe course around the 6-mile-long sandbar stretching between Sandy Hook and Coney Island. Though dredged to a depth of 30 feet back in the 1880s, these channels were too shallow for the new steel behemoths.

In 1899 a federal Rivers and Harbors Act appropriated funds to sluice out the old–foot-deep East Channel, which cut directly through the bar, to a depth of 40 and a width of 2,000 feet and mark its pathway with eighteen gas buoys. The work began in 1901 and was not completed until 1914, though the channel was in use by 1907. The new route—renamed the Ambrose Channel, honoring John Wolf Ambrose, longtime advocate of harbor improvement—diverged from the old Gedney Channel at a spot marked by the Ambrose lightship and sliced 5 miles off the approach route.[1]

Revamping Manhattan's antiquated docks was also on the agenda. The hodgepodge of ramshackle wooden pier-sheds offered an embarrassing contrast to the sleek new steamers (to say nothing of the massive stone quays of Hamburg and Liverpool). Mayor William Strong's administration's Dock Department had commenced construction of five new Hudson River piers, between Gaansevoort and West 11th Street. Completed in 1902, they were leased to the Cunard, White Star, and Leyland companies. But as ever grander liners kept steaming into port, the 259-foot-long Gansevoort piers were rapidly outdated. Cunard and other companies began warning that without longer docks they might have to consider moving to New Jersey.

---

1. After 1895 vessels entering the port would have an easier time, no matter which route they chose, thanks to yet another consolidation. Until then, piloting had been a highly competitive business. The first to reach an incoming ship got the job of escorting it into the harbor; hence thirty boats cruised constantly outside the harbor and raced one another with a vigor (and inefficiency) equal to the old volunteer fire companies' scrambles to reach conflagrations. In 1895 the New York Pilots' Association and a New Jersey equivalent were created, and the two combined to work out a regular and more practical arrangement.

In 1902 the city hired the architectural firm of Warren and Wetmore (shortly to start work on Grand Central) to construct a set of nine 800-foot docks running for three-quarters of a mile along the Chelsea waterfront between Little West 12th and 22nd Streets. The Chelsea Docks, completed in 1907, were hailed by the City Improvement Commission as a masterpiece of "harmony and symmetry." The piers presented a continuous Beaux-Arts façade, two stories high, of reinforced concrete and pink granite, replete with heroic cement sculptures recounting the history of trade, and huge cast-iron globes proclaiming the city's international preeminence. In a triumph of City Beautiful planning, passengers could now arrive (through streets swept free of hay barges and "street arabs") at pier-shed entryways embellished with vast arched windows, ascend in bronze elevators to superb waiting rooms, and board the *Olympic* or the *Mauretania* in style.

IMMIGRATION ISLAND

At the same time First and Second Class passengers were debarking at the Chelsea Piers, so were the immigrants in Third Class or Steerage, who had experienced a very different crossing. H. G. Wells, while sailing westward in 1906 on Cunard's *Carmania*, wrote of its 4,000-plus souls that they formed "a city rather than a ship," one that embraced a full social spectrum. "We've the plutocracy up here, there's a middle-class on the second-class deck, and forward a proletariat," Wells observed, noting that "it's possible to go slumming aboard." Daring mid-voyage explorers who did venture down to the hold, wherein hundreds were cattled, would have encountered an unbearable stench—a "pestilential air," as investigator Edward A. Steiner put it in his *On the Trail of the Immigrant* (1906)—along with miserable food and gloomy darkness. When these travelers stumbled up to the light and down the gangplanks they found that their journey, unlike that of their upper-class shipmates, still had one lap to go, a ferry ride to Ellis Island. And it was that last lap—experienced by millions of arriving immigrants, drawn across the Atlantic by the opportunity to find work in the continent's booming factories, mines, fields, and sweatshops—that presented yet another challenge to the port's ability to function.

Beginning in 1899, the already substantial Jewish migration from Eastern Europe of the 1880s and 1890s surged to new heights with the flight of Romanians from famine and repression. After 1903 Russian Jews poured into the port, as the czarist regime countered strikes and revolutionary activities throughout the Pale with ruthless massacres. German Jews aided their co-religionists' westward exodus, negotiating special rates with railroad and steamship lines. Still, steerage prices from Bremen to New York averaged over thirty dollars—a small fortune for many—and conditions below decks on steamers like the *Kaiser Wilhelm*, while much improved, remained harrowing. Nevertheless, between 1901 and 1914 over a million and a half managed the journey, with Gotham the overwhelming destination of choice.

Still vaster human cargoes arrived from Naples. One disaster after another befell southern Italy: harvest failures, slumped agricultural prices, and soaring village populations that put intolerable pressure on thin resources. As landless farm laborers organized unions and co-ops, the Italian government decided mass emigration was worth encouraging—one senator proclaimed it "a safety valve, or security against envy and class odium"—and a 1901 act smoothed the way to the exit. Urged along by the authorities, and encouraged by *padrone* labor recruiters and cheap steerage rates, Italians took to the seas. Some still aimed for the wheatfields of Argentina, but increasingly they made for North America, and of these over 95 percent headed to the Hudson River. In the early 1890s, 60,000–70,000 had arrived each year.

Guadeloupean immigrants at Ellis Island, ca. 1911. (Manuscripts and Archives Division, The New York Public Library)

The depression had halved that figure. The boom restored and surpassed it. In 1900, 100,000 arrived (making Italians the most numerous single nationality group entering the U.S.) and the numbers climbed steadily, peaking, in 1907, at over 285,000. The figures were halved again in the ensuing recession and then lurched up and down until peaking again in 1914 with just under 284,000. The largest single off-loading occurred in 1909, when the liner

Ultonia docked and a record 2,111 Italians walked down the gangplank. Between 1901 and 1914, just over 3 million arrived in the United States.[2]

While Eastern and Southern Europeans predominated, other nationalities continued to stream into the country and its leading port. In the 1901–14 period, over half a million Irish came, driven west by continuing crop failures and industrial recessions. Added to these arrivees were substantial contingents (according to census data) of Armenians, Australians, Belgians, Canadians, Central Americans, Cubans, Czechs, Dutch, English, Finns, French, Germans, Greeks, Hungarians, Mexicans, Moroccans, Norwegians, Poles, Scots, South Americans, Spaniards, Swedes, Swiss, Syrians, Turks, Welsh, and West Indians—leaving aside non-aliens like Puerto Ricans, southern blacks, and rural whites—a torrent of immigrants that would press hard on the city's capacity to receive them.

This challenge was met by a bravura demonstration of what might be called *civic* engineering. In 1897 the United States Immigration Station, which had moved to Ellis Island from Castle Garden in 1892, burned down. Processing continued in makeshift tents and buildings while construction of a mammoth new station proceeded—one, according to the terms of the competition, that would be in keeping with "the magnitude of the nation to which these structures were to be the entrance." When completed, the 385-foot-long Beaux-Arts structure (spiced with four Byzantine-looking copper-covered towers at each corner) proved to be a masterpiece of internal circulation. With relative ease, 5,000 arrivals a day (8,000 if pressed) could be shuttled from one department to the next. In one twenty-four-hour period in the spring of 1907, Ellis managed to sort and sift more than 15,000 people.

"Immigrants after Their Arrival in Ellis Island by Ship," 1902. (Ullstein Bild/Getty Images)

---

2. Many went back. Between 1897 and 1907, 41 percent of the total number of Italians landing at Italian ports were returnees from the USA.

"12 New Americans a Minute." *Sunday World Magazine*, April 29, 1906.

Within twenty-four hours, if all went well, they could be showered, fed, tagged, chalked, their possessions inspected, their persons and politics probed, and—if not rejected—passed on to the ferries that ran twenty-four hours a day to the railheads in Jersey, or to the Battery and its awaiting crush of porters, hackmen, runners, and sharpers. (The latter practiced a vast range of frauds—starting with charging five dollars to help new arrivals purchase an elevated pass available for five cents at the station a few yards away, and working up to more ingenious methods of extraction.)

The sortees and siftees were ambivalent about their handling. It was somewhat better than Castle Garden had been, especially after President Roosevelt set Commissioner William Williams, heretofore a Wall Street lawyer, to reforming the complex. Williams was honest and efficient; he even posted signs reminding officials to be courteous to the aliens. Nevertheless, bureaucratic arrogance and cultural condescension abounded, and arrivees resented being processed like objects.

There were certainly exceptions to the general officiousness and outright inhumanity. Fiorello La Guardia, a young Ellis interpreter, later recalled that "I never managed during the years I worked there to become callous to the mental anguish, the disappointment and the despair I witnessed almost daily. . . . At best the work was an ordeal." For the most part, however, immigrants relied on landsmen for support. The Hebrew Immigrant Aid Society (HIAS, 1892), one of the first major institutions set up and administered by New York's Eastern European Jews, was particularly helpful. The HIAS stationed a representative on the island, protested steerage conditions to German and British shipping lines, pressured the Hamburg-American line into posting Yiddish notices explaining ship regulations, steered greenhorns past sharpers (some of whom were posing as pious Jews), handed out Yiddish bulletins offering hardheaded advice, and ran an employment bureau. In 1912 over 150,000 sought help at its offices at 229 East Broadway.

What worried immigrants and their helpers most was the fear that Ellis aimed more to screen arrivals out than to welcome them in. They were not wrong to worry. As one journalist noted: "The day of the emigrants' arrival in New York was the nearest earthly likeness to the final Day of Judgment, when we have to prove our fitness to enter Heaven." And Williams set ever higher standards. In 1900 he decreed that immigrants would henceforth need twenty-five dollars to be admitted, an immense sum for most. His aim, as he wrote Roosevelt, was to exclude "all below a certain physical and economic standard." The New York immigrant community, led by the *Jewish Daily Forward*, hammered at this restriction and got it relaxed. But more were in the offing. In 1903 congressional legislation fulfilled President Roosevelt's wish that "we should aim to exclude absolutely not only all persons who are known to be believers in anarchistic principles . . . but also all persons who are of a low moral tendency or of unsavory reputation." Some would have gone further and imposed literacy requirements, but they were beaten back. In these years, Ellis would filter the flood but not dam it.

MOVING FREIGHT

If people entering and leaving the port were now handled with greater efficiency, it was thanks in large measure to federal and municipal initiatives and funding. In contrast, freight had a tougher time accessing and exiting the city, in part because responsibility for transporting agricultural goods and industrial products was fragmented among a variety of contending public and private players.

The port's freight problems were structural and geographical. Nearly all the goods coming into the port from the continent arrived by train to New Jersey and had to be transferred by barge to New York, where they were either consumed or shipped out on oceangoing vessels. And vice versa: most of the goods arriving in New York from overseas that were not consumed in the metropolis had to be gotten across the river to New Jersey where the freight lines awaited them. A vast marine fleet of tugboats, lighters, and car floats, most owned by the railroad companies, did the ferrying—taking food, fuel, or manufactured goods to docks they owned or leased along the Manhattan waterfront. As demand for dock space far exceeded supply, massive tie-ups were routine. The surrounding streets bulged with long lines of trucks and wagons waiting hours to reach the docksheds to offload outward-bound items from thousands of small Manhattan manufacturers, or to pick up commodities ranging from coal to cabbages.

Adding to this aquatic confusion was the terrestrial congestion generated by the New York Central's freight line. Branching off at Spuyten Duyvil from the main route into the

"Car Floats, Harlem River Landing, New Haven Railroad." *New York, the Metropolis: The Book of Its Merchants' Association and of Co-Operating Public Bodies*, 1902.

city, its steam engines dragged cars filled with milk, hay, grain, produce, and coal straight down the West Side at street level. Having run along the Hudson to the freight yards at 60th Street, trains could carry on down Eleventh Avenue to the yards at 30th Street, then continue south along Tenth Avenue to West Street, where the tracks ran on, right alongside the piers, to Canal Street, where they jagged inland to Hudson Street and the now-ancient (1868) block-long St. John's Terminal. Not only did New York Central rail cars hinder access to and from the docks, but they often maimed or killed pedestrians—usually the poor women and children who darted about scooping up coal spilled from cars. A coalition of civic groups (the Municipal Art Society, the City Club, the Citizens' Union, and the Women's League for the Protection of Riverside Park) sought to ban the tracks—Eleventh Avenue acquired the nickname "Death Avenue"—but with large numbers of jobs dependent on the line, nothing was done apart from the city's requiring a horseman to ride ahead of the locomotive, waving a red flag. As traffic on those tracks slowed from a walk to a crawl, even the Central began to resort to barges, running car floats from its Jersey subsidiary to its own float docks at the 60th and 30th Street yards, dumping yet more goods into the maelstrom.

The chaos, it was widely believed, would get considerably worse when the Panama Canal opened in 1914. Still another inundation was expected in 1918, when the Erie Canal's facelift was finished. By the turn of the twentieth century, the old waterway had become so badly outmoded that much of the midwestern grain trade, formerly barged to Gotham, was now railed to Montreal, Boston, Philadelphia, and Baltimore. In response, New York State (in 1903) had authorized a massive modernization that would allow diesel barges to replace mule-drawn vessels.

The problem, it seemed, was that no one was minding the store. The Department of Docks had broad authority to oversee the waterfront, but when under Tammany control its officials and inspectors awarded contracts, handed out leases, and enforced ordinances in a highly selective (and well-requited) manner. Charlie Murphy, before replacing Richard Croker as boss of Tammany Hall, served a profitable apprenticeship as a dock commissioner (1897–1901), and his colleague George Washington Plunkitt boasted with disarming frankness that control of Dock Department patronage was a license "to make hay while the sun shines." The politicos benefitted from congestion, so why try to overcome it?

In 1907 railroad magnate James J. Hill sent tremors through Gotham's business and civic circles when he declared that New York, having become "the dearest place in the world to do business," had now "reached the climax of her commercial supremacy." Unless angioplasty was performed on the arteries of commerce, "traffic will be forced to seek other outlets; business other locations."

Thus spurred, a host of city, state, and federal officials, along with private experts, came up with proposals to reform freight handling in the Port of New York.

One of the quickest off the mark was William Wilgus, who in 1907 resigned from the Pennsylvania Railroad—having realized he would never rise to its presidency—and became a consulting engineer. Wilgus now advanced a comprehensive and innovative plan on an even grander scale than his remake of Grand Central. Massive freight yards should be built in New Jersey, Wilgus argued, where all the railroads could send their goods to be repackaged into closed containers (a Wilgus invention), and then put on flatcars that would be whisked, through a new cross-Hudson freight tunnel, to a Manhattan terminal at 60th street. From there they would be rolled on into a 60-mile-long electrified network of small-bore tunnels, running just 11 feet beneath the city streets, to strategically placed freight terminals for storage and distribution, or directly to warehouses and factories equipped with special freight elevators. (As a bonus, the freight cars could haul away not only manufactured goods but also mail, garbage, and rubble excavated from building sites.) Once this underground freight matrix was in place, the New York Central's death-dealing trains could be replaced by an elevated belt freight line that encircled Manhattan and was open to all the roads. To further diminish the quantity of goods coming in by boat, Wilgus advocated a regional belt line as well, which would run through a new tunnel under the Narrows linking Staten Island with Brooklyn. Once street and harbor congestion was reduced, shipping capacity could be expanded and rail routes rationalized.

The engineering, said Wilgus, was perfectly feasible—and who knew better than he? While expensive, it would be cost-effective—if all the lines split the cost. The plan would also require interstate cooperation, and Wilgus urged New York and New Jersey to jointly follow the lead of London and Liverpool, which had established "Port Authorities" to manage harbor operations. He even drafted bills authorizing such an authority and submitted them to the two legislatures. New Jersey actually passed theirs, almost exactly as Wilgus had written it, and Woodrow Wilson, Jersey's new governor, signed it in 1911.

But that was as far as it got. The New York Central and the many Manhattan interests integrated with it balked. The New Jersey competitors refused to pursue a joint solution. And there was no political support in Albany for working with Trenton. The idea of a port authority was back-burnered. The freight delivery subway went nowhere.

Wilgus's initiative did, however, inspire Calvin Tomkins, whom reform Mayor William Gaynor appointed commissioner of docks in 1910. Tomkins was a cultivated businessman, a close associate of artists, and a leader in civic reform efforts. But he was most toasted in commercial circles for his expertise about transporting freight into and out of New York, gained from experience moving his company's building materials around the harbor. When Tomkins took office, he did launch an assault on Tammany profit-skimming, but he was convinced that the waterfront's snarl-up was due less to corruption by politicians than to competition among corporations. Tomkins was a municipal ownership man. The "port must be developed as a unit," he believed, and "administered by the City for the benefit of all," if New York was ever to break free of "the makeshift policy of separate subports constructed by great private corporations," which had led to "the chaos of jarring private rivalry and mutual obstruction."

In 1909 Tomkins had had a hand in winning exclusion of borrowing for dock improvements from the city's debt limit, on the grounds that enhancing the piers would generate a revenue stream that would offset the costs. In 1910 the city floated $73 million in bonds, backed by the income from leases on municipal docks. Tomkins aimed to invest this money in a grand restructuring. His plan borrowed much from Wilgus, and from various European cities whose approach to harbor development he studied closely. The vision began with a huge assembly yard, to be built in Newark Meadows for all the New Jersey railroads; next, a connecting freight tunnel, to be built jointly by New York and New Jersey, would funnel goods under the Hudson to a city-built elevated line along the West Side waterfront that would replace Death Avenue's tracks; finally, Gotham would build new municipal piers and warehouses below the Chelsea docks. The newly rationalized system would be overseen by the municipality and by a Port Authority, which Tomkins joined Wilgus in advocating. But again—despite much agreement that his proposal was intelligently designed and technologically feasible—its execution was blocked by obdurate existing interests.

Given this failure to act, some influential voices (including Tomkins's) suggested finessing the Manhattan mess by creating a new port elsewhere. The alternative that gained the most political traction in New York—New Jerseyites plumped for Newark—was the development, from scratch, of a deep-water harbor–cum–industrial center in Jamaica Bay.

One of the earliest progenitors of this notion had been Andrew Haswell Green himself. It was in large measure because he believed the bay could become "the greatest shipping center in the world" that he had drawn Greater New York's boundaries to encompass it. In 1905 Comptroller Edward M. Grout made the first public case for it, in a short pamphlet that urged improving "the Water Front of the City of New York other than that of Manhattan Island." Jamaica Bay, as Grout and a growing body of advocates noted, could provide space within its 32 square miles for more ships than could Manhattan's entire perimeter, and it was just twenty minutes from blue water. In 1906 the city appointed a Jamaica Bay Improvement Commission, which began discussions with the federal Corps of Engineers and New York State about dredging and bulkhead construction. In 1910 the city (with Tomkins's support) appropriated a million dollars to launch the enterprise. Also in 1910 the federal government dredged Rockaway Inlet and dug a main channel into the bay, which linked to a city-created channel, that produced Mill Basin. Dredged material was used to fill in marshes and create new upland in that area. Industrial plants were established there, worker housing went up, and plans were laid to extend Flatbush Avenue and other city services, linking the new proto-port to Brooklyn.

Another proposed connectivity scheme, also following Green's lead, urged digging a canal across Long Island from Flushing to Jamaica Bay. This would allow the revived New York State Barge Canal's traffic coming down the Hudson to head directly for the new port. (The cross-island canal was actually surveyed and priced out by state engineers.) Others suggested the proposed rail tunnel from Staten Island to Bay Ridge should be extended on to Jamaica Bay. Some argued the bay should be made a free port, as had Hamburg, enabling raw material to be brought in duty-free, manufactured at plants along the new-made shoreline, and shipped out, untaxed, to other countries.

WHAT SEEMED A PROMISING POSSIBILITY in Jamaica Bay—thanks to joint federal, state, and municipal government initiatives—was already a reality along the lengthy stretch of Brooklyn's shoreline that ran from Bay Ridge to Newtown Creek. And here it was private developers who were the principal pioneers, as had long been the case in Brooklyn: viz., the Atlantic and Erie Basins, the Empire and Red Hook Stores.

SCIENTIFIC AMERICAN

[Entered at the Post Office of New York, N. Y., as Second Class Matter. Copyright, 1910, by Munn & Co., Inc.]

A POPULAR ILLUSTRATED WEEKLY OF THE WORLD'S PROGRESS

Vol. CIII.—No. 1.
Established 1845.

NEW YORK, JULY 2, 1910.

[10 CENTS A COPY.
[$3.00 A YEAR.

"The Jamaica Bay Improvement: The City of New York in Co-Operation with the Federal Government is About to Begin at Jamaica Bay a Scheme of Construction of Channels, Bulkheads, and the Reclamation of Land Which, When Ultimately Completed, Will Provide this Port with 150 Additional Miles of Water Front." *Scientific American*, July 2, 1910.

In 1895 the Brooklyn Wharf and Warehouse Company (BWWC) was incorporated. A would-be Warehouse Trust, it proceeded to consolidate thirty-one hitherto-competing companies, from Main Street (in what is now Dumbo) to the Erie Basin (at Gowanus Bay). All members of the new combine now offered uniform rates for docking and storage, and shared a connecting railroad. But the company was short-lived. It had saddled itself with a heavy debt load, having paid extravagant sums to its constituent warehouse owners, just as the port's grain trade weakened. Jacking up rates to cover losses drove shippers to other facilities, toppling it into bankruptcy.

Soon reorganized as the New York Dock Company, the firm adopted a new strategy of replacing antiquated warehouses with modern facilities, only to stumble into another problem. Manufacturers were increasingly interested in shipping their goods straight out of the factory, bypassing warehouses altogether, if they had direct access to transportation. The New York Dock Company had the transport connections, but not enough upland space to build accommodation for manufacturers, so the locus of innovation shifted south to Sunset Park.

In 1895, at the foot of 40th Street, Irving T. Bush had launched a modest shipping business, consisting of one pier, one warehouse, an old railroad engine, and two boats. But Bush's vision of his project's future was considerably more capacious. As he surveyed the "endless lost motion and constant waste expense in moving the merchandise that made up the commerce of New York," Bush diagnosed the problem as a structural disjuncture: ships on one shore, railroads on the other, and factories scattered helter-skelter with no regard to transport. "Why not bring them to one place," he thought, "and tie the ship, the railroad, the warehouse, and the factory together with ties of railroad tracks?" Using the substantial bequest left him by his father, Rufus T. Bush, from the sale of his South Brooklyn oil refinery business to Standard Oil, he began to do just that.

In 1902 he incorporated Bush Terminal, Inc., sold shares on Wall Street, and bought adjacent property (far more was available in Sunset Park than had been in Red Hook). Over the next decade he erected long, wide, roomy, covered piers. He also built massive eight-story buildings, first wood and brick, later white-painted fireproof reinforced concrete, each floor of which spanned 3 acres. Some space he rented out for storage, some for manufacturing. He added an internal circulatory rail system linking pierheads to warehouses to manufactories and connected the entire complex to the rest of South Brooklyn. He also convinced the federal government to dredge a channel that allowed oceangoing vessels to dock at his facilities and arranged with the New Jersey railroads to accept and provide cargos via car floats, which he connected to his piers using state-of-the-art transfer bridges. The whole enterprise was directed from Bush Tower (1918), a thirty-story skyscraper and merchandise mart on 42nd Street in Manhattan.

Bush Terminal was not an amalgamation of competitors in the classic merger-era mode. Rather it hosted scores (later hundreds) of independent manufacturers, some big, many small, and provided them with centrally run services, manned by terminal staff: rail transport to and from their door, packaging and storing, building maintenance and banking, medical and eating facilities—amenities few small businesses would have been able to provide for themselves. *Bush Magazine*, the terminal's in-house publication, had as its logo a honeycomb surrounded by the words "Efficiency and economy through cooperation."

Bush had had difficulty at first in convincing Jersey-based rail companies to deliver to his relatively isolated South Brooklyn address, and had resorted to stratagems like placing orders himself with midwest firms and demanding the goods be shipped directly to his docks.

But thanks in large part to his own activities, Brooklyn's commercial center of gravity shifted slowly southward, a process dramatically accelerated by the Pennsylvania Railroad's decision to establish a direct freight connection even farther down the shore, at 65th Street.

In 1899 the Pennsy bought 900 acres in the Greenville area of Jersey City for an enlarged freight yard and marine car-float terminal, which conveyed railroad cars directly across the harbor to Bay Ridge, Brooklyn, where its subsidiary, the Long Island Rail Road, received them at its 65th Street terminal. In 1905 the Long Island line embarked on the Bay Ridge Improvement, which, when finished in 1918, linked the Bay Ridge terminal to a junction with the New York Connecting Railroad and thence, via the Hell Gate Bridge, on to New England. Freight rail cars could now be run smoothly, without breaking bulk, from Florida to Maine via Jersey City to South Brooklyn, skipping the Manhattan quagmire altogether.

ONE LAST COLOSSAL PROJECT EMBODIED AND CELEBRATED the tremendous efforts made, if with varying degrees of success, to improve the Port of New York in this period. It was initiated by Washington. The federal government was thrilled by the vast flood of commodities entering the harbor, as import taxes collected in Gotham constituted a significant portion of the US Treasury's total income. But the collector of the port was having trouble monitoring the influx, even with more than 2,000 officials to help him, and his huge staff had overflowed the old Mercantile Exchange at 55 Wall Street where the Customs establishment had been housed since 1863.

In 1899 an architectural competition was announced for a new Custom House, to be situated at Bowling Green, site of the original Fort Amsterdam. Entrants had to design a mammoth office building, but also a structure that would, in City Beautiful fashion, serve as gateway to the city and nation. The winning design by Cass Gilbert called for a neo–French Renaissance structure, a Beaux-Arts approach the architect believed would best celebrate the "wealth and luxury of the great port."

When completed in 1907, the massive building attracted attention as much for its exterior statuary as its monumental scale. A bevy of sculptors had provided twelve emblematic personifications of those seafaring powers (Genoa, Venice, Holland, and the like) whose commercial glory had presaged America's. And sculptor Daniel Chester French had produced four great groups similarly intent on situating the United States (and New York) in the global (and racial) scheme of things. His *Four Continents*, as glossed by Gilbert, included *Asia*, seated on a throne of skulls, its people "borne down by superstition, tyranny and oppression"; *Africa*, "somnolent" though prepared perhaps "to awake with all the power of brute force"; *Europe*, an enthroned "Imperial figure of the highest intelligence" who currently ruled the roost; and *America*, a "beautiful, alert, young female figure" holding in her hand the "torch of Progress," who was clearly rising "to meet the future."

REFURBISHING THE TRANSPORT SYSTEM HAD ITS DOWNSIDE. Ships and trains now efficiently disgorged people into a city already swollen by Consolidation to 5 million souls. How could the old life-support systems sustain such a mega-population? Where would the metropolis get sufficient supplies of water, or food, or power? How could it eliminate its wastes? In the century's first two decades, New York would solve each of these problems—in some cases just barely, in others brilliantly enough to set new standards for the world.

In refashioning its infrastructure, the metropolis engaged in yet another battle over the proper role of the public sector in municipal development. Out of the debate came a de facto division of labor, similar to that worked out in transport. Where providing a service seemed profitable, private businesses—themselves consolidated into huge enterprises—retained control (as they had in rails). Where costs or risks gave capitalists pause, the city or state stepped in (as they had at sea). As the lines of division were seldom neat and tidy, debates on provision of city services—such as the water supply—were often explosive.

WATER

Greater New York was a thirsty super-city. It was drinking, washing, flushing, firefighting, and manufacturing at a rate of 370 million gallons a day—and wasting at least half of it, given leaky pipes and the citizenry's rejection of metering or other conservation efforts. The metropolis had survived the nineteenth century by constantly extending its Croton system. Since 1892 another round had been in the works. When finished in 1906, the New Croton Dam—the highest masonry dam in the world—would channel additional millions into the city's reservoir system (newly enhanced by a holding bin in the Bronx on the site of the old Jerome Park racetrack), which fed the city's 1,706 miles of water mains.

It wouldn't be enough, said the engineers. The expanded Croton system might handle Manhattan and the Bronx for a while, though water pressure was dropping, but what about the other boroughs? Brooklyn still relied on its patchwork system of wells and water from Nassau County's streams and surface runoff, but booming demand and faltering supply were engendering periodic water famines, and hopes of siphoning off water from Suffolk County had been foreclosed by preemptive legislative action. Queens and Staten Island still depended on local wells run by private water companies; many had been polluted by growing commercial development. All three boroughs demanded more water; it was why many of their residents had supported Consolidation in the first place.

Once the effort to privatize water delivery was shot down, with the defeat of the Ramapo Company's initiative, plans got under way to entrust the project to the public sector. To ensure adequate financing, New York State voters passed a constitutional amendment in 1905 that exempted water-supply projects from the municipal debt limit formula: the city was authorized to float $200 million worth of bonds for the Catskill system, which would be backed by the flow of revenue from water rates. At the same time, the city created a quasi-independent Board of Water Supply (BWS) to oversee the project. To keep Tammany's hands out of the till, BWS members were to be appointed by the mayor only from candidate lists provided by the city's business and financial interests. The BWS quickly revamped the city's ossified technical staff, appointing J. Waldo Smith, a reservoir expert, as chief engineer. By 1911 he would be overseeing an engineering corps of 1,348 and directing an army of 25,000 contractors and laborers.

In 1905 the board laid out the grand design. As the Ramapo men had guessed, New York's choice for a watershed fell upon the Esopus Valley, 90 miles to its northwest. It had probably been a lake in preglacial times; Smith proposed to dam it, drown it, and make it a lake again. Using eminent domain granted by the legislature, the imperial city condemned and acquired 8,000 acres. This required removing residents, some of them descended from the 1740s settlers, from nine villages, exhuming 2,800 bodies from thirty-two cemeteries, and rerouting 11 miles of railroad track and 69 miles of highways.

With the valley's bodies (live and dead) dislodged, work began on the Ashokan Reservoir. Labor power came from the vast reservoir of newly arrived Southern Italians, and from blacks fresh from the American South who chiefly served as mule drivers. Workers were housed in reasonably well appointed (and segregated) barrack camps, complete with schools, chapels, and YMCAs and patrolled by Board of Water Supply Police.[3] The workmen erected 12 miles of dam and dikes, which, when completed, impounded 130 billion gallons of water, enough to cover all of Manhattan to a depth of 30 feet.

Closer to New York, two additional holding basins were dug. The Kensico Reservoir, formed by a dam across the Bronx River 3 miles north of White Plains, was designed to receive and store 29 billion gallons' worth of Catskill water (a fifty-day emergency reserve) while passing the main flow along to the Hill River Reservoir, an equalizing station 16 miles farther south in Yonkers. Kensico was so close to the city that—in a City Beautifulizing touch—its granite dam was embedded with architectural flourishes fashioned by expert stonemasons, on the (correct) assumption that visitors would drive up to picnic there.

Between the Ashokan and Kensico Reservoirs, engineers and workmen designed and laid a heroic aqueduct, twice as long as anything the Romans ever attempted. Boring through hills and mountains, dipping beneath creeks and rivers, the Catskill Aqueduct dove deep below Storm King Mountain, drove on under the Hudson River a thousand feet beneath the surface, and carried on to the waiting Kensico and Hill River vessels.

One last link remained, the 18-mile run down to the city itself. To handle the water—by this point under enough pressure to blow apart the strongest tubing—engineers designed the

"Celebration Ceremonies Attending the Holing Through of the Last Heading of the City Tunnel." Catskill Aqueduct, Contract No. 65, January 12, 1914. (New York Public Library, Science, Industry and Business Library)

---

3. These conditions, though problematic, were much improved from those experienced by Italians working on the New Croton Dam, who'd been exploited by *padroni*. Stuck in shanties, forced to pay monopoly prices for shovels, pickaxes, and food, and to labor more than the legal eight hours, the Italian quarry workers had gone on strike in 1900. Then-Governor Roosevelt had denounced the "riotous Italians," though admitting they were "decidedly oppressed," and sent up the elite 7th Regiment, which broke the strike.

world's longest pipeline, City Tunnel No. 1, to be run through bedrock at depths ranging from 200 to 800 feet below the street. Italian crews sank twenty-five shafts along the tunnel's route, mainly in parks and public places. (Shaft 21 at Clinton and South Street is deeper than the Woolworth Building is high.) Then, lowered to the bottom by elevator, they bored laterally to connect with the other work gangs. By 1914 they had created a tube, lined with concrete, that ran from the Bronx under the East River to its terminus beneath Flatbush. Next, riser pipes and valves were installed to pump water up to the street-main level. Finally, a cast-iron pipe-siphon was laid in a trench dredged along the floor of the Narrows to a newly constructed Silver Lake Reservoir on Staten Island, while a last pipeline shuttled water north to Queens.

When the entire $177 million system went into operation in 1917, it sent a billion and a half gallons a day cascading down from the mountains, 126 miles into New York City, with enough momentum to shoot unaided to the top of a twenty-eight-story building. A minifestival of connection in October hailed the epic achievement, though with less spectacle than the occasion warranted, in part as the system was virtually invisible.[4] Still, though crowds of onlookers had compared the Penn Station excavation with the Panama Canal, engineers and workmen knew that the magnificent Catskill system was its real rival.

POWER

Greater New York ate energy as voraciously as it drank water. In the first decades of the twentieth century, the city's homes, offices, streets, commercial buildings, and industrial plants consumed vast amounts of gas and electricity for their lights, stoves, furnaces, motors, and appliances. To meet this demand, energy producers engineered a dramatic transformation in the way power was generated and distributed—a development marked by corporate consolidations, technological revolutions, and battles over private versus municipal ownership.

Amid all the changes one thing remained the same: New York City was still powered by coal. The coal was burned directly, or used to generate electricity, or turned into manufactured gas (though some gasification processes began employing oil as well). The coal was principally hard (anthracite)—preferred as less polluting—but when hard was in short supply, power companies turned to soft (bituminous), a smoky second best.

Anthracite still came overwhelmingly from Pennsylvania, though it no longer arrived by canal. The old Delaware and Hudson Canal that since 1828 had barged hard coal from northeastern Pennsylvania to Kingston on the Hudson River carried its last load in 1898, after which it was closed and drained. Instead, coal came in from the anthracite fields via railroad—on lines like the Delaware, the Jersey Central, and the Susquehanna (a.k.a. the Susie-Q). Significant amounts of bituminous also arrived—from Pennsylvania, and from fields in the Pocahontas region of West Virginia, shipped up in coastal colliers from Hampton Roads.

On reaching the Hudson's harbor, coal was stored in Jersey towns like Bayonne, Weehawken, Hoboken, and Elizabethport, and from there barged as needed to the metropolis. Some of these storage sites were enormous, notably Shadyside, near Edgewater, opposite Grant's Tomb. Built in 1903, in the aftermath of the 1902 anthracite coal strike that had nearly exhausted the city's supply, it could hold 300,000 tons—about six days' worth at a time when roughly 50,000 tons were consumed every twenty-four hours.

---

4. So were some of the celebrations: sandhogs and dignitaries had formal "holing-through" dinners 800 feet below ground, when two sections of tunnel were joined.

Once the coal reached the metropolis proper, it entered two very different distribution streams.

The first (ancient) structure involved the sale by coal companies—often subsidiaries of the conveying railroads (e.g., the Delaware & Lachine Coal Company)—to New York wholesalers—concerns like Williams & Peters, which like many of its ilk had offices at 1 Broadway, as did the Wholesale Coal Trade Association of New York. They in turn contracted with retailers, the owners of coal yards. Scattered around the city, they tended to locate on the waterfront, for easy receipt of the fuel; the largest could store 15,000 tons, most far less. These merchants—grouped in the New York Retail Coal Dealers' Association, and doing collective business at the Retail Coal Dealers' Exchange (58th and Lexington)—would make deliveries to end users, usually at night or on Sunday, using four-to-six-horse teams to haul their loads through city streets. Yards (and basement or grocery sub-retailers) also sold by the pail to the poor—at a higher profit margin than they reaped on larger orders. In cold snaps or strikes, discounts might be offered. Then crowds of tenement dwellers, mainly women and children, would gather in long lines at yards like H. Barbers' Sons, at 377 Water Street, or Robert Gordon & Son, at 46th and the North River, where coal (while it lasted) might be had for ten or fifteen cents a pail, enough to keep a stove hot for an hour. The private charity establishment continued to oppose free wintertime governmental provision of coal to the poor, as had once been common practice in Gotham. Whenever the state legislature tried to reauthorize the practice, usually during crises, leaders like Edward T. Devine, head of the Charity Organization Society, and Homer Folks of the New York State Charities Aid Association rushed to Albany to oppose the idea, declaring that public aid would be demoralizing and that charity should be left to the private sector (i.e., them.)

There was, however, a completely separate distribution system, one that sold huge quantities of coal to giant businesses, which turned it into gas or electricity or steam. That system underwent a major restructuring in the new century. Competing producers coalesced into giant corporations. The new behemoths refashioned the inefficient system of having a myriad of small-scale producers supply only their immediate environs. Instead they constructed giant centralized energy factories, whose product was distributed to substations, and from there on to business, municipal, and residential users.

Gas producers led the way. Back in the 1880s, Manhattan's many manufactured-gas companies, panic-stricken by the arrival of electricity, had conglomerated in self-defense. Primacy of place had been seized by the straightforwardly named Consolidated Gas Company (1884) backed by William Rockefeller and Henry Huttleston Rogers of Standard Oil, though powerful companies—dominated by such titans as Russell Sage and J. P. Morgan—continued to contest

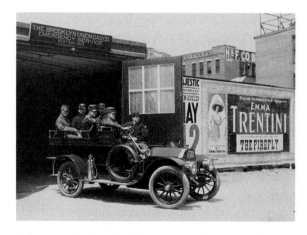

Emergency Service, Brooklyn Union Gas Company, ca. 1915. (Image No. x2010.11.13663, Museum of the City of New York)

its rule. Over the next decades Consolidated completely absorbed (or gained effective control over) major competitors, winning a virtual lock on gas production in Manhattan and the West Bronx. In Brooklyn, it was much the same story: in 1895 seven local utilities, facing low profits because of price wars and stiff competition from electricity, amalgamated into the Brooklyn Union Gas Company, which in turn came under the sway of the Standard Oil crowd.

The availability of capital and new tunnel technology now allowed gas to be produced in enormous plants, distant from dense population centers, and pumped to consumers from afar. The first was the Ravenswood works of the East River Gas Company, which sent its output through the tunnel under Blackwell's Island that Charles Jacobs had engineered back in 1894. By 1906, with demand now far ahead of what Ravenswood could supply, the Astoria Light, Heat & Power Company, a wholly owned subsidiary of Consolidated Gas, put its enormous Astoria plant into operation. Perched on the waterfront at the northwestern tip of Queens (north of 20th Avenue and west of 37th Street), the world's largest cooking-gas-generating plant sent its product to Manhattan and Bronx via the world's largest mains—6 feet in diameter. Gas thus delivered could be stored in huge tanks erected around the city, like those (the world's largest) on East 20th just west of Avenue A (in the "Gas House District"), or in more open country, like one in Elmhurst built in 1910 to serve western Queens (being 230 feet high, it became an instant landmark).

Electricity production underwent a similar development, featuring many of the same players. The old Edison Electric Illuminating Company of New York—the lengthened shadow of Edison himself—had built the original Pearl Street Station, thus setting the pattern of relying on direct current. As DC had a limited range, many such stations were needed. In this climate, rivals flourished, and the electrical industry became a welter of competing companies. Then Anthony N. Brady, an Albany utilities financier, moved down to Gotham, where—with backing from streetcar magnates William Whitney and Thomas Fortune Ryan—he merged several rival firms into the New York Gas and Electric Light, Heat, and Power Company (1898). In 1899 Consolidated Gas, fearful of competition from such electric companies, purchased a controlling interest in Brady's firm, in Edison Electric Illuminating, and in the United Electric Light and Power Company (the third-largest electric company, which had been founded by H. H. Westinghouse). In 1901 it merged all three into the New York Edison Company—Brady was made its president—which thus became a Consolidated Gas subsidiary.

A single group of financiers and executives now controlled Manhattan's gas and electric power production—a centralization that would be ratified architecturally when they tore down their 1856 headquarters building at 15th Street and Irving Place, which they had inherited from a Consolidated Gas ancestor company, and hired Henry Hardenbergh to design (and the Fuller Company to build) an imposing eighteen-story structure, raised in stages between 1910 and 1914.

Brady also gathered Brooklyn electric power companies into the fold, acquiring control of Edison Electric Illuminating Company of Brooklyn, which became a subsidiary of New York Edison. And Henry Rogers managed to become the czar of Staten Island utilities—the principal owner of its electric and gas companies, and its trolleys, railroads, and ferries as well.

The New York Steam Company was able to retain its independence and still expand its operations. Its downtown plant on Greenwich Street (between Courtlandt and Dey), near the Hudson River, was joined by an uptown counterpart on 59th Street, at the East River.

THE WATERSIDE STATIONS OF THE NEW YORK EDISON COMPANY WHICH EXTEND FROM
FIRST AVENUE TO EAST RIVER AND FROM THIRTY-EIGHTH TO FORTIETH STREETS

Waterside, ca. 1915. *Forty Years of Edison Service, 1882–1922: Outlining the Growth and Development of the Edison System in New York City*, 1922.

Together these supplied steam for heat and power to office buildings, lofts, theaters, and private residences.

CORPORATE CONSOLIDATION FACILITATED TECHNOLOGICAL UPGRADING. Pioneering engineer/executive Thomas E. Murray, who came down from Albany with Brady, helped develop the enormous Waterside generating station (yet another "world's largest"), at 38th Street and the East River; it opened in 1901. In 1906 it was joined by and linked to Waterside No. 2, one block to the north. Together these immense energy factories, manned by 700 workers, and burning 1,500 tons of coal a day in summer, 2,000 in winter, produced high-voltage (6,600 volts) alternating current. In 1912 it was fed into 384 miles of subterranean high-tension transmission cables, which carried current to thirty-odd substations throughout Manhattan and the Bronx. There it was converted to 240-volt DC current and sent off into an underground network of 646 miles of mains and 319 miles of feeders. (Manholes at each street intersection and handholds on streetlight utility poles allowed for testing and repairs.)

Different New York Edison substations became associated with particular subsets of the company's 59,000-strong customer base. The one at 30–32 Horatio Street supplied shipping and wholesale firms on the riverfront. That at 115 East 12th fed large East Side manufactories, East River dry docks, and 14th Street theaters and cafés. The West 16th station served department stores. That on 26th Street furnished power to offices along Broadway and Fifth Avenue. New York Edison also supplied power to a rapidly growing network of customers in the Bronx (28,582 in 1912). And its Brooklyn counterpart sent power, via 3,350 miles of conductors, to many large manufacturing and commercial concerns, notably Bush Terminal, New York Dock Company, and the Erie Basin dry docks.

"New York Edison—What 'At Your Service' Means." *Sun*, May 12, 1914.

Perhaps the most visible sign of ongoing electrification was the changeover in street illumination. In 1903 gas still ruled the streets—42,777 gas lamps to 16,668 electric lights, with the latter predominantly in the commercial and wealthy residential districts. The development (in 1907) of tungsten filaments and (in 1913) of nitrogen-filled incandescent lamps revolutionized street lighting. By 1916 improved illumination had spread to the most crowded tenement districts, and New York had become the first major city to convert fully to electricity. The City Beautiful movement left its mark on this development, taking advantage of tungsten-lamp flexibility to promote ornamental designs. The Bishop's Crook lamppost,

"Trimming a Lamp." *Thirty Years of New York, 1882–1912: Being a History of Electrical Development in Manhattan and the Bronx*, 1913.

with its scroll of acanthus leaves curving toward a center rosette, became a signature feature of Gotham street furniture.

WHILE NEW YORKERS WERE PLEASED with their enhanced energy supply, they were angry at the corporate conglomerates that provided it. Just as muckrakers protested the concentration of power at the national level, so too a wide range of metropolitan voices—from radical socialists to conservative businessmen—were raised against the control of public utilities by private interests. Hearst, Seabury, and their Municipal Ownership League were among those who called for municipal gas and electric-lighting plants, emphasizing that many European cities had long since opted for public power. Their calls for a probe of Consolidated Gas profiteering and collusion with Tammany Hall led to their charges being confirmed by Charles Evans Hughes's investigation. Hughes, however, rejected municipal ownership and instead advocated and won passage of a 1905 law mandating public regulation by an independent body.

In 1906 the new State Commission of Gas and Electricity, after another study of the company books, determined that while Consolidated Gas had issued $80 million of stock and bonds, the actual value of the property employed in manufacture and distribution of gas was only $30 million. The commission accordingly mandated a lowering of price from $1 to 80¢ per 1,000 cubic feet. As the true cost of production was 60.75¢, that would generate a more modest but fair return of 8 percent. To ensure that requiring reduction would withstand judicial scrutiny—independent commissions being relatively new phenomena—the legislature (in 1906) passed a law imposing the same terms by direct fiat. Consolidated Gas fought the

Banana docks, South Street, 1906. (Image No. x2011.34.4388, Detroit Publishing Co./Museum of the City of New York)

so-called Eighty Cents Law all the way to the US Supreme Court, arguing the 20 percent reduction was confiscatory, but the justices ruled against them in 1909. This put on a firm footing the power of the Public Service Commission—an expanded version of the Gas and Electric Commission—which New York State had created in 1907 and given authority over nearly all public utilities. A new hybrid relationship between public oversight and private ownership had been set in place.

FOOD IN

The distribution of food into the city was also a private/public affair. The centerpiece of the system was the great Washington Market, locus of retail and wholesale produce marketing since the late eighteenth century. At its heart was the 1884 city-built structure that occupied the entire block bounded by Washington, West, Fulton, and Vesey. In 1915 the municipality modernized its interior, dividing it up into stalls that were leased to retail food merchants of every kind.

But what most people understood by the term "Washington Market" was the 58-acre territory that spilled westward from the retail building to the Hudson piers, and northward—along West, Washington, and Hudson Streets—up a dozen blocks to Laight. These choked and narrow streets were crammed with wholesale jobbers and commission men doing business out of old Federal and Greek Revival brownstones. Wooden shed roofs jutting out from the second floor formed the sidewalk stalls wherein these private merchants dealt in items such as grapes, apples, plums, pears, lettuce, peppers, radishes, and string beans.

Into this dense ganglion ran bundles of transport nerves. New York Central's West Side freight line terminated there. Steamers, schooners, ferries, and lighters from upstate New York, South Jersey, Pennsylvania, and points west disgorged fruits and vegetables at the Hudson docks. And cargo ships off-loaded products—bananas, fruits, onions, figs—from more distant shores.

"Horse Drawn Wagons," lower west side docks, ca. 1900–1910. (Mariners' Museum and Park)

All these goods had to compete with the daily deluge of other commodities swamping the West Side shoreline. Boats and barges had to scrabble for access to and from the chaotic and congested docks, with the result that a great deal of perishable food rotted before it could be off-loaded. More and more voices were raised, deploring the disorder, waste, inefficiency, and consequent high costs of doing business at the unregulated central market. Critics charged that because it was a private affair, there was, so to speak, no one minding the store.

About a mile north lay the West Washington Market, product of an earlier attempt to ease downtown congestion. Back in 1879 the city had moved the farmers' market—consisting of wagons ferried in from Long Island, New Jersey, and Staten Island—up to the site of old Fort Gansevoort. In a 30-acre area framed by Little West Twelfth, Washington, Gansevoort, and West, restaurateurs, grocers, and consumers could buy produce directly from local growers.

The municipality had also relocated the meat and live poultry stalls from the old West Washington Market, then in front of the Erie Railroad's piers at Chambers Street. They were resettled in ten city-built, two-story, red-brick and terra-cotta buildings between West Street and the river, just below 14th Street, directly across from the Gansevoort Farmers' Market. This new West Washington Market, which had opened in 1889, now flourished mightily, thanks to the new and nearby municipal Gansevoort and Chelsea Piers, and the New York Central freight line. They were serviced, too, by the Manhattan Refrigerating Company, a private company that constructed (beginning in 1897) an ensemble of nine cold-storage warehouses that eventually filled the Gansevoort/Horatio/Washington/West block. From 1906, the company also boasted a power plant that pumped brine-cooled water to the market in underground iron pipes beneath West Street. Here refrigerator cars brought dressed meat from the West Side abattoir district (between 34th and 60th Streets).

The newest of those uptown slaughterhouses grew out of a battle between wholesalers, retailers, and consumers—the last a new entrant into the mix of food industry players. In 1902 meat prices rose sharply, the result, it was widely believed, of the establishment of a price-fixing consortium by big midwestern meatpackers—wholesalers like Swift and Armour—unpopularly known as the Beef Trust. In response, thousands of immigrant Jewish East Side women, most of them wives of garment workers, broke into butcher shops and burned meat or flung it into the street. Quickly becoming more organized, they formed a Ladies' Anti–Beef Trust Association and established a formal boycott of kosher meat retailers. Posters went up featuring a skull and crossbones, and a text in Hebrew: "Boycott! Boycott! Eat no meat while the Trust is taking meat from the bones of your children and women." This they enforced by physically barring entry to any potential purchasers. With support from Socialist, Zionist, and Orthodox organizations—despite some dismay at such unfeminine tactics—the boycott spread rapidly to Harlem, Brooklyn, and the Bronx. Dozens of women were beaten by police, arrested, fined. When a judge told the boycotters they were not allowed to riot in the street, one retorted: "If all we did was to weep at home, nobody would notice it; so we have to do something to help ourselves." Three weeks into the protest, the Retail Butchers Association itself affiliated with the boycott, and the resulting drop-off in demand forced wholesalers to roll back prices.

All too soon, however, prices crept up again, so the city's 35,000 butchers decided to bypass the wholesalers altogether by setting up their own co-op abattoir. Forming the New York Butchers Dressed Meat Company, they sold shares of stock, purchased land between 39th and 40th Streets from Eleventh Avenue down to the river, and set out to build a state-of-the-art facility. When the old Manhattan Abattoir at 34th Street had been doing business back in the 1870s, cattle had been landed on the Hudson River shore and held there in pens before being channeled to the shambles through a "cow tunnel" under 12th Avenue, thus eliminating the potential goring of passing pedestrians by runaway steers. East Side firms (like United States Beef, and Schwarzschild and Sulzberger), clustered in the mid-40s between First Avenue and the East River, similarly sprawled out their pens horizontally. But the new company took a leaf from the vertical city thrusting up downtown and in August 1906 opened a six-story abattoir—a mini-skyscraper by slaughterhouse standards. Cattle arrived at the company's own pier, hoofed up a ramp to the roof, and spent their last hours there in repose, eating, drinking, and contemplating the Hudson, before being dropped by electric elevators to the fifth-floor killing beds, where they were dispatched in accordance with kosher practice, processed as they descended or shuttled to adjacent specialized plants, and reached street level as sides of beef, ready to be sent down to wholesalers in the meatpacking district below 14th Street. The new abattoir was widely praised for its efficiency and cleanliness, qualities in marked contrast to the horrible conditions that prevailed in Beef Trust plants in Chicago—a state of affairs that had just been revealed (in February) by Upton Sinclair's *Jungle*, and outlawed (in June) by the Pure Food and Drug Act.

DIRECTLY ACROSS MANHATTAN FROM THE WASHINGTON MARKET lay the Fulton Market, a city-run general emporium on the East River opened in 1822. Its fortunes had waned over the nineteenth century as butchers and other retailers decamped, following their moneyed clientele northward. The market's fishmongers stayed and flourished, however, because South Street was the principal port of call for the fishing fleet; hence it was there that fish were freshest. By 1831 they had separated from other retailers and moved to a wooden shed across South Street on the bulkhead running from dock to dock (between Fulton and Beekman). By around 1910, when a new steel building was added to the complex, most of the fishmongers had shifted into wholesale operations, receiving aquatic produce not only from local schooners but also by rail from waters as distant as Alaska and Oregon, Nova Scotia and Maine. A "fish train" came down from Boston to the Bronx each morning and off-loaded cod, etc., from points farther north that were then boated to South Street. In turn wholesalers supplied hotels, boardinghouses, restaurants, and retailers around the metropolitan region. The Fulton Market had developed its own distinct identity as a congeries of private entrepreneurs, who rented public space but experienced little public regulation.

In addition to these primary facilities, there was a series of secondary, largely retail public markets (some relatively ancient). These included Catharine, Clinton, Centre, Jefferson, Tompkins, Union, Essex, Grand, and Harlem, in Manhattan; the Westchester and Bronx Produce House to the north; and Wallabout Market, a square of Dutch gabled buildings adjoining the Brooklyn Navy Yard, that had opened in 1884.

Finally, there was the immense tertiary sector of grocers, hucksters, pushcart vendors, and standmen who congregated at the wholesale markets at four in the morning in winter, earlier in summer, to purchase goods for resale throughout Greater New York.

This sector, too, had its problems. By 1900 thousands of immigrants were peddling pushcarts, far too many to be able to negotiate trips to the jam-packed Washington Market. Many had instead settled into fixed locations, creating de facto open-air markets, to which carting agencies delivered the goods they would sell. Essentially unregulated, these peddlers were also unprotected, and at the mercy of cops who extorted payoffs for overlooking the archaic law barring pushcarts from stopping in one place for more than thirty minutes. The

"Push Cart Market—New York," ca. 1910–15. (Library of Congress Prints and Photographs Division, George Grantham Bain Collection)

unsupervised markets grew dirty, indeed stank; the one at Hester Street, a principal Lower East Side allée (and open-air hiring location for day-laborers), became known colloquially as the Chazar Market (*chazar* meaning "pig" in Yiddish and Hebrew), a doubly disparaging term in a widely kosher community.

These conditions provoked concern and study. In 1906 Mayor McClellan organized a Pushcart Commission, which included Lawrence Veiller, secretary of the City Club, and settlement worker Lillian Wald, among others. It urged establishing an East Side district where peddlers could stand, as of right, if they bought a license, and from which horse-and-cart peddlers would be banned. On a larger scale, in 1913 a Mayor's Market Commission worried not only about costly inefficiencies and lack of regulation and quality control at the wholesale markets but about the city's food supply—in dramatic contrast to its water supply—falling out of public control. Commissioners and advisers compared Gotham's private entities unfavorably with Europe's magnificent public markets, such as London's Covent Garden and Paris's Les Halles. Berlin's municipalized market, it was noted, was more sanitary and cheaper to run than New York's and actually generated a profit for the city. Critics proposed replacing Washington Market with a municipally owned and city-run wholesale terminal (rail-connected) market. They also urged terminal markets be established in each borough; it seemed absurd that items which arrived in the Bronx were sent down to lower Manhattan and then brought back again. The commissioners also called for an official Department of Markets. This was finally established in 1917, and authorized to begin building wholesale terminal markets, beginning with one in the Bronx.

GARBAGE OUT

For all the complaints about the manner in which food reached the city, there was considerably greater dismay at the way food—once eaten—left it.

George Waring had left the Department of Street Cleaning (DSC) in remarkably good shape at the end of 1897 (after which he went to Cuba as a sanitation expert, contracted yellow fever, and died in 1898). The impact of his reforms on the city's streetscape had been so striking that even the new Tammany regime, fearful of voter wrath should muck and mire return, retained the recycling regime he had instituted in 1896. Waring had mandated that households divide their refuse into three categories, each to be collected (and disposed of) separately: ashes (the residue of burned coal or wood); rubbish (dry refuse, like paper, cardboard, tin cans, bottles, shoes, carpets, furniture); and garbage (animal and vegetable refuse). In addition to carrying away these residential wastes, sanitation workers collected street sweepings, chiefly dirt and assorted carcasses. (Commercial establishments were not under municipal purview and dealt with private cartmen.)

Ashes were hauled off to landfills on Rikers Island, the Corona lowlands, Jamaica Bay, and Newark Meadows. In Brooklyn, city workers took ashes to local collection stations scattered about the borough, often in train-yard sidings, where employees of the Brooklyn Ash Removal Company transferred them into iron tanks, which were lifted by cranes onto trolley- or locomotive-drawn cars, and then taken to and dumped in "waste lands" like those around Barren Island. After 1909 Brooklyn Ash shifted attention to filling in the tidal salt marshes known as Flushing Meadows, beginning formation of the Corona Ash Dump (soon to be known as Mount Corona).

Rubbish was incinerated—following European practice—using a process that produced energy as a by-product. The incinerator on Delancey Street, under the Williamsburg Bridge, burned 1,050 cubic yards of rubbish daily—one-fifth of all collected in Manhattan and the Bronx—converting it into enough electrical current to light the surrounding buildings and keep the bridge aglow all night.

Garbage—of which in 1903 Manhattan alone produced 220 tons on its lightest winter day and 1,100 on the heaviest day of summer—was recycled through "reduction." In 1896 Waring had contracted with the New York Sanitary Utilization Company to transform garbage into marketable commodities at a plant on Barren Island. Every day, seven or eight garbage scows, carrying between them 500 to 1,000 tons, came alongside the disposal plant, where the refuse was carried by endless chain elevators into "digestors," which cooked and stewed the material until it dislodged oil and grease, from which could be derived, among many other things, glycerin, an essential element in the chemical, textile, leather, ink, and (as nitroglycerine) construction industries. The 500-man workforce of blacks, Irish, Italians, and Poles produced tens of thousands of tons of oils, grease, and fertilizers, worth over $10 million a year.

Street leavings were accumulated by an army of DSC workers—expanded after Consolidation to encompass Brooklyn's thoroughfares—who swept up at least once every day. Their gatherings consisted chiefly of dirt—which was then often admixed with ashes and sent to landfills—but included as well an assortment of bodies. Each weekday morning the horseboat would arrive at Barren Island, carrying as many as fifty dead horses, not to mention expired cows, cats, dogs, and enormous rats.

For twenty years this regimen had replaced the traditional practice of barging everything out to sea and dumping it. But after 1917, when a fire destroyed the Barren Island works, the city's resolution faltered. At first a new base of operations was opened at Lake's Island, near Fresh Kills in Staten Island, by the Metropolitan By-Products Company, but the horrible odors fomented a near rebellion on Staten Island, and in 1918 it was shut down, and ocean dumping resumed.

THE POLLUTION PRODUCED BY GARBAGE was only a dirty drop in the bucket compared to the effluvia flowing from New York's (in 1902) 1,467 miles of sewers. With the gradual phasing out of backyard privies, and the rapid increase in population and per-capita water use, the volume of sewage pouring into the rivers and harbors surrounding New York soared after the turn of the century. At Consolidation, the city was dumping roughly 300 million gallons of raw sewage each day; by 1910, 600 million gallons per day gushed from massive pipes, often situated under piers, and left to the presumedly cleansing tides.

In the harbor these essentially household products mingled with industrial wastes disgorged into the Passaic, Rahway, Bronx, and Harlem Rivers, Newtown Creek, and the Gowanus Canal, as private companies relieved themselves of often toxic externalities.

The Gowanus had become the busiest commercial canal in the United States, as much of the timber, sand, and brownstone being used to build booming Brooklyn passed along it. But its banks were laden as well with foundries, slaughterhouses, cement makers, flour mills, gas houses, and other fouling enterprises—like the dye works that gave the Gowanus its nickname of "Lavender Lake." The resulting stench, exacerbated by its being a dead-end ditch, was mitigated somewhat after the installation in 1911 of a flushing tunnel—a 12-foot-wide brick conduit under Degraw Street that used a ship's propeller to expel the fetid water into Buttermilk Channel.

Newtown Creek was worse. The 4-mile-long tidal arm of the East River—which bore more tons of freight annually than did the 1,000-mile-long Mississippi River—was lined with hundreds of refineries and factories. Spill-offs from the oil and kerosene works, varnish and paint manufacturers, sulfuric-acid makers, fertilizer factories, vinegar distillers, and ink producers produced a truly obnoxious brew. There was some very modest relief when Standard Oil, having outgrown the creek's capacity, shifted much of its refining to New Jersey. By 1900 Rockefeller's firm boasted that its Bayonne refinery was the largest in the world, producing roughly 20,000 barrels of kerosene daily, and by 1904 the oil works had drawn 235 collateral manufacturing establishments to Bayonne. In 1908 Standard expanded again, opening the massive Bayway plant several miles farther south along the Arthur Kill in Linden, New Jersey. By 1919 the 17-mile corridor between the two giant plants had been largely filled in with chemical works, fertilizer plants, varnish factories, metalworks, and more refineries, the latter turning out over 100,000 barrels of finished product daily. A goodly percentage of this wound up, courtesy of massive oil spills, in the Upper Bay, by way of the Kill Van Kull. In the harbor it met up with yet another torrent of commercial waste and residential sewage pouring in via the Passaic River, the acid fumes from which blistered the paint on houses along the banks. (It was not reassuring when New Jersey announced, in 1902, that given high death rates in Newark and Jersey City, a Passaic Valley Sewage Commission was being established, whose notion of a solution proved to be building a joint sewer line that

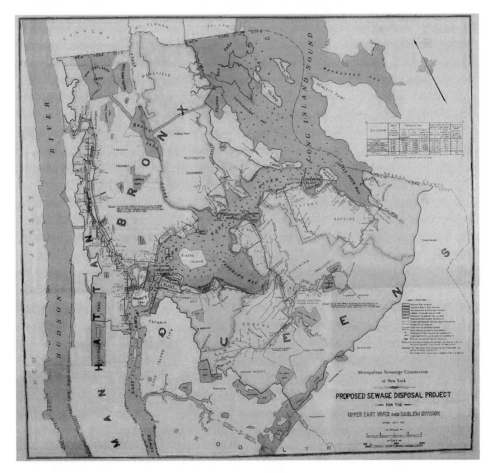

"Proposed Sewage Disposal Project for the Upper East River and Harlem Division." *Report of the Metropolitan Sewerage Commission of New York: Main Drainage and Sewage Disposal Works for New York City, Reports of Experts and Data Relating to the Harbor*, 1914.

would bypass the stricken cities and dump detritus directly in the middle of the bay, where it could be shared by all.)

As a result of this battering from east and west, the once-sparkling bay water turned black, mucky, and effervescent. Those who collected driftwood at the Battery for home fuel found it coated with an inch-thick layer of grease. The free-floating river baths the city had established for the poor, and the beaches along the Jersey and Long Island shores, stank revoltingly. The value of shore properties slithered downward. The oyster industry faced extinction.

A chorus of complaints galvanized the legislature into establishing, in 1903, the New York Bay Pollution Commission. After two years of study it affirmed what residents' noses already knew—unrestricted harbor dumping was generating an environmental disaster. Then it called, ringingly, for more study. That, at least, was forthcoming. In 1906 the state established the Metropolitan Sewerage Commission (MSW). It hired chemists, bacteriologists, microscopists. Directed by George A. Soper, a young sanitary engineer, they dropped dyes in sewers, tracked the colored effluvia, mapped the harbor's currents from floating labs. Their reports (issued in 1910, 1912, and 1914) proved with scientific precision that the hundreds of millions of gallons of untreated sewage dumped in the bay each day did not get flushed out to sea. Much of it sank to the harbor bottom, which was now covered with black sludge, in places 10 feet deep, a fermenting and putrefying mass that gave off carbonic acid, ammonia waste, and bubbles of methane gas. Much of it rose to the surface, forming great floating cesspools of sludge dotted with "jet-black masses of erupting gases." In 1907 a Merchants' Association investigation noted that children bathing and swimming in the East River at 96th Street would wait until a patch of sewage floated by before diving in, but would sometimes surface in the middle of the next one, emerging with their head and shoulders a "mass of filth." In 1914 New York City began closing public beaches in Manhattan, Brooklyn (except for Coney), the Bronx (as far as Clason Point), Queens, and Staten Island (from Fort Wadsworth to Kill Van Kull, and all of Arthur Kill).

Also in 1914, in an 800-page report, the Metropolitan Sewage Commission laid out a plan for a comprehensive counteroffensive. It proposed building intercept sewers parallel to the waterfront to capture the effluvia and direct it to screening plants where enough impurities could be filtered out to permit discharge of the remainder. To oversee construction of such a wastewater treatment system it recommended creation of a commission, modeled on the Board of Water Supply then building the Catskill system. That said, it disbanded.

Though Soper continued to press for reform, virtually nothing was done. Powerful industrial players resisted change. Competing jurisdictions couldn't come together on a unified strategy. Neighborhoods didn't want treatment plants in their backyard. And there was no overriding public health menace to mobilize the citizenry, a consequence in no small part of the sewer system's success. Its channeling dangerous wastes away from communities, in tandem with crystal-clear water sluicing in from the mountains, had produced a sharp drop in deaths from waterborne disease. There had been no major cholera or typhoid epidemics since the 1860s. And while diarrheal diseases still came in third as a cause of death, behind tuberculosis and pneumonia, they'd been cut in half between 1870 and 1900 and were continuing to drop. So though some New Yorkers now described Manhattan as "a body of land entirely surrounded by sewage," the mortality rate during the 1910s slid to a record low of just under fifteen deaths per thousand, making Gotham one of healthiest of the great cities.

BEFORE THE TWENTIETH CENTURY WAS TWO DECADES OLD, therefore, Greater New York had applied itself to unclogging and enhancing its circulatory systems. Ships, trains, commodities, power, water, food, and garbage now moved in and out of its borders in greater quantity and with greater velocity than ever before. This was chiefly thanks to a profusion of conduits: new aqueducts, improved canals, rail bridges, high-voltage conductors, conveyor belts, sewage pipes, electric elevators, station ramps, ship channels, revamped docks, immigrant-processing stations, and tunnels in profusion—railroad tunnels, trolley tunnels, gas tunnels, cooling tunnels, heating tunnels, flushing tunnels, cow tunnels—as if Gotham had become Gopher City.

But there remained one last flow to facilitate: the movement of people within and throughout the expanded city. New York's transit lines were limited and clogged. Serving a mushrooming population and making Consolidation a reality required the unsnarling of old pathways and the creation of brand-new ones, beginning with the basics: bridges, to improve inter-borough, inter-island connections.

9

Ligaments

BRIDGES

The Brooklyn Bridge—as of Consolidation Day still the sole link between Manhattan Island and Long Island—was terribly overburdened.[1] Each year, tens of millions jostled and fought their way across on foot while millions more crammed their way into cable cars, wagons, and carriages. Then, between 1903 and 1917, four major bridges were thrown across the East River, like grappling hooks, binding the new boroughs together and relieving pressure on the Roeblings' creation.

First came the Williamsburg Bridge. Because it was intended to carry elevated trains and trolleys as well as pedestrians and horse-drawn vehicles, its designers opted for a utilitarian approach. When it opened in 1903, it received engineering plaudits for being the longest suspension bridge in the world, and won social kudos for relieving the pressure of population. Within a year it was dubbed the "Jews' Highway" (by the *New York Tribune*) for facilitating an exodus of Jews from the Lower East Side to the old German community of

---

1. And overbought. True to their founding myth of the Dutch having picked up Manhattan Island for $24 in trinkets, New Yorkers reveled in stories of putting one over on visiting rubes by selling them the Brooklyn Bridge. One turn-of-the-century confidence man named George C. Parker would forge impressive-looking documents proving he was the bridge's owner, then convince his marks they could make a fortune by controlling access to the roadway. Several of his victims actually tried to erect toll barriers and had to be summarily ejected by the police. Two notorious goniffs—the Gondorf brothers, Charles and Fred—also sold it repeatedly, sometimes for hundreds of dollars; in one instance they demanded $500, but because the mark didn't have enough cash on him to pay full freight, they sold him *half* the bridge for $250.

Williamsburg. The bridge did more than just facilitate; its construction itself displaced nearly 20,000 people.

The Williamsburg Bridge, however, got low marks for beauty, notably from Gustav Lindenthal, the Austrian-born engineer who had been hired by Seth Low's reform administration in 1902 as commissioner of the Department of Bridges. In tune with City Beautiful sensibilities, Lindenthal wanted bridges to be aesthetic as well as efficient. (He himself leaned toward a romantic Habsburgian style.) But, as he complained to the Municipal Art Society, though his predecessors had opted for "the ugliest possible" solution, the project was too far along for any but modest alterations.

"Blackwell's Island Bridge," 1903. (Art and Picture Collection, The New York Public Library)

Queensboro Bridge, Manhattan side, 3:50 p.m., April 11, 1909. (Courtesy New York City Municipal Archives)

He and his associates had more impact on the cantilevered Blackwell's Island Bridge, linking Manhattan (at 59th Street) with Queens (at Queens Boulevard). They humanized its heavy industrial appearance with whimsical steel finials and dome-topped masonry towers. But significant changes were made in their design after Mayor McClellan and Tammany Hall took office in 1904 and ousted Lindenthal from the commissionership.

The structure, when completed in March 1909, took its name, at first, from the institution-filled Blackwell's Island over which it soared. Queens real estate brokers and property owners petitioned for a change to Queensboro, more indicative of its final destination. Besides, they found the name Blackwell's "unpleasantly suggestive of a penal institution and a poorhouse"; indeed, soon after it opened, friends or relatives of prisoners in the jail below began dropping food and clothes to them from the bridge's pedestrian way. Irish American societies opposed the change, thinking it sounded too British, but to no avail.

Nine months later, on the last day of 1909, the Manhattan Bridge opened, and here too the end result was not what Lindenthal had called for. He had proposed replacing traditional steel-wire cables with nickel-steel chains, a plan scrapped by Tammany's new commissioner, on both aesthetic and engineering grounds (and perhaps political, too, given the Roebling Wire Works' close ties to the Democratic Party). The new team didn't stint on embellishments, however, and architects Carrère & Hastings were brought in to fashion a grand stone archway (based on the Porte St. Denis in Paris) at the Canal Street entrance in Manhattan, while Daniel Chester French sculpted appropriately monumental figures for the somewhat less imposing gateway on the Brooklyn side at Flatbush Avenue.

After his ouster, Lindenthal returned to the private sector. He had long tried to interest the Pennsylvania Railroad (PRR) in a cross-Hudson bridge, only to see the corporation reject his plan in favor of the tunnel solution. But now, in 1904, he was taken on by the PRR to work on the New York Connecting Railroad, and its indispensable link to the mainland, the magnificent Hell Gate Bridge, the longest, heaviest, strongest steel arch bridge in the world at that time. This project was designed for inter-city rail traffic: when it opened in 1917 the first PRR train across it was the Washington/Boston Federal Express. Hell Gate also inspired talk of building a *tri*-borough bridge, running nearly parallel to the New York Connecting Railroad but adding a lateral extension to upper Manhattan at East 125th Street; a bill to that effect was introduced in the state legislature in 1920. For the time being, travelers relied on a new series of swing bridges over the Harlem River that stitched Manhattan directly to the Bronx: Third Avenue (1898), Willis Avenue (1901), 145th Street (1905), University Heights (1908), and Madison Avenue (1910). In addition to these arteries, a host of capillaries were created, like the Borden Avenue Bridge (1908) spanning the narrow waters of Dutch Kills, a tributary of Newtown Creek, in the industrial neighborhood of Sunnyside, Queens; and the Pelham Bay Bridge (1908) over where the Hutchinson River and Eastchester Bay meet.

Only the gap between Staten Island and the other boroughs remained unbridgeable. New York did, however, municipalize ferry service to Richmond, and construct new City Beautiful ferry terminals to service it. Carrère & Hastings's St. George and Stapleton Terminals (both 1908) established grand water gateways between Staten Island and Manhattan's Whitehall Street Ferry Terminal (1907). Next to Whitehall the city erected a Municipal Ferry Building (1909), a Beaux-Arts palace featuring three monumental steel archways and a lobby lined with cast-iron columns and stained-glass windows (now the Battery Maritime Building). It was built to house the South Brooklyn Ferry, a line that had been taken over in 1906 from the patrician banker brothers W. Bayard and R. Fulton Cutting

"View Showing Five Bridges Spanning the East River. The New York Connecting Railroad Bridge at Hell Gate Is Shown in Foreground. The Proposed Tri-Borough Bridge Would Parallel This Route a Short Distance to the South." Chamber of Commerce, Borough of Queens, *Queens Borough, New York City, 1910–1920: The Borough of Homes and Industry*, 1920.

"The Completion of Hell Gate Railroad Bridge: Engineers and Workers, October 11, 1916." (Library of Congress Prints and Photographs Division)

(and for which, some argued, they had been all too handsomely reimbursed); it provided service to 39th Street, virtually next door to the burgeoning Bush Terminal.

ELS, CABLES, TROLLEYS

For all the impressive achievements in bridging inter-borough gaps, it proved tremendously difficult to get elevateds and trolleys—the intended beneficiaries—to traverse them. You could lead an iron horse to water, it turned out, but you couldn't make it cross. This was but one of the many grievances twentieth-century New Yorkers had against their two rapid transit systems.

Citizens were particularly dissatisfied with the elevateds. Service was badly congested and notoriously slow—it took at least forty-five minutes to get to Harlem from the Battery—and the els were limited in range. For these and other problems people blamed the monopoly that operated the lines. Control of the Manhattan Elevated Company—put together by the unsavory Jay Gould—had passed with Gould's death in 1892 to his equally unpopular son George, and to Russell Sage and J. P. Morgan. Competition-free and paying handsome dividends on heavily watered stock, the complacent company showed little interest in improvements. The Manhattan Elevated delayed electrification until 1903, nearly a decade after Chicago had junked its heavy and dirty steam engines.

The problems with the second transit system—street-level trolleys—were also attributed to the grip of a monopoly, though one that had, admittedly, transcended problems of the former competitive regime. During the 1890s, entrepreneurs backed by big capital had engineered another consolidationist roundup. William Collins Whitney, the master strategist, was a dapper and well-connected attorney, who had married Flora Payne, the sister of Standard Oil partner Oliver Hazard Payne. Whitney's associate was Thomas Fortune Ryan,

Elevated railroad at 110th Street, ca. 1910. (Image No. x2010.11.8933, Museum of the City of New York)

a Virginia-born stockbroker and a genius at the mechanics of financing. Together, these two remade New York's surface-transit system—with the aid of vast sums from Standard Oil backers and Philadelphia financiers, the high-powered legal advice of Elihu Root, and Democrat-backer Whitney's cozy connections with Tammany boss Richard Croker. Borrowing the techniques of national merger makers, Whitney and Ryan had bought up the old independent horsecar companies using vast quantities of highly watered stock, and by century's end their Metropolitan Street Railway Company had absorbed its last rival.

Whitney and Ryan (with help from Root) then knitted their acquisitions into an integrated system. They instituted a highly popular system of free transfers that finally made it possible to travel long distances for a nickel. They replaced many of the remaining horses—6,000 were still hauling streetcars in 1900, more than in all other US cities combined—with electric trolleys. By 1902 the Metropolitan Street Railway had converted 114 miles of line to electricity, drawing power from underground conduits.

The new system proved hugely attractive to the burgeoning populace. Together with the elevateds, New York's transit lines carried over a billion passengers in 1903, more than all the steam railroads in North and South America combined. But in transportation, sometimes nothing fails like success. The flood of new users swamped the system. Trolley cars were mobbed, especially at rush hour. Overhead, life on the els was equally miserable: "Travelers must stand," one complainant reported, "swaying precariously and squeezed and jostled by similar unfortunates, often rude and ill tempered." Streetcar traffic backed up in an almost unbroken procession for miles, gridlocking at intersections despite the introduction of cops at corners.

More strikingly, there were no through connections from Manhattan to Brooklyn. The boroughs had consolidated politically, but their transit companies had not followed suit. Brooklyn was ruled by an independent outfit, the Brooklyn Rapid Transit Company (BRT). Another conglomerating enterprise, it was controlled by gas-and-electric magnate Anthony Brady, who had amalgamated and electrified almost all the borough's els, rails, and trolleys. The Manhattan and Brooklyn firms had then reached a gentlemen's agreement not to intrude on one another's territory. The BRT trunk lines along Myrtle Avenue and Fulton Street, accordingly, fed into downtown Brooklyn and over the Brooklyn Bridge but not an inch farther than Park Row, right next to City Hall. There they dumped their passengers and returned home. Conversely, in the evening, Brooklyn-bound commuters converged on the Park Row terminal by foot, trolley, or elevated, creating the mother of all maelstroms.

The 1903 opening of the Williamsburg Bridge didn't help. Though a BRT elevated ran along Brooklyn's Broadway from rural Canarsie and East New York through Bushwick and Williamsburg, the BRT (in cahoots with the Metropolitan) refused for five years to run its lines across to Delancey Street on the Lower East Side (and vice versa). Mayor McClellan was only able to get trolley service rolling in 1904 by threatening to refuse the BRT access to the Brooklyn Bridge.

Apart from its poor service, Whitney and Ryan's Metropolitan Street Railway (like the Gould/Sage/Morgan Manhattan Elevated Railway) drew muckraker attacks for its minuscule remuneration to the city for franchises, its connections to Tammany Hall, its interlinks with the Gas Trust and Wall Street financiers, its overcharging, and its refusal to expand into new territories in a planned and comprehensive way. Despite these complaints, the Metropolitan made few improvements. The company's funds were earmarked for other uses. Ryan and Whitney shelled out vast sums for leases of subsidiary lines, disbursed huge dividends on watered stock, and paid massive carrying charges on debts incurred for acquisitions and electrification. Revenues, on the other hand, were limited by a law that imposed a nickel fare. And attempts to cut costs by working employees more than ten hours and crimping on wages generated a series of strikes, some bloody. In 1899 both the Metropolitan and the BRT called in police to break union protests.

At the turn of the century, therefore, both the Metropolitan Street Railway Company and the Manhattan Elevated Company were chugging along profitably, their revenues guaranteed by their riderships' absence of alternatives. This monopoly status was about to be challenged.

PLANNING THE SUBWAY

Prescient New Yorkers—back as far as Alfred E. Beach's Pneumatic Railway (1870)—had argued that rapid transit had to go underground. By the 1880s and 1890s many citizens— uptown and outer-borough real estate interests, downtown businessmen, tenement residents, and would-be suburbanites—were clamoring for a subway.

The problem, given the immense costs involved, was how to pay for it. Three possibilities emerged.

Back in the 1886 mayoral election, Henry George had proposed that the city itself finance, construct, and operate its own rapid transit system. Taxes on speculative real estate profits would cover the costs. People would ride free. In 1893 social worker Charles B. Stover reactivated the idea, which gained substantial political support from New York's unionized tradesmen.

The city's real estate and mercantile elites shuddered at the prospect. Some stressed that municipalization would turn the project over to Tammany. Others—the principled laissez-faire types—denounced a public system as inherently "paternal, communistic, [and] socialistic" and insisted instead that private businessmen do it. But no capitalist would undertake such a risky project, certainly not without heavy subsidies and a perpetual franchise. As the prestigious Citizens' Union observed, "Private enterprise has failed utterly to supply the city's need."

The solution finally adopted had been laid out by Mayor Abram Hewitt back in 1888: public financing and ownership; private construction and operation. Hewitt suggested the city raise funds by issuing municipal bonds; it could borrow money more cheaply than private entrepreneurs. This would require public ownership, as the state constitution banned loaning public credit to private firms. Tammany corruption could be avoided by contracting out construction and operation to a private company. This, Hewitt argued, was not socialism but enlightened use of the state (as per the Erie Canal, Croton waterworks, and Brooklyn Bridge), and squarely in the republican tradition of Alexander Hamilton and De Witt Clinton. In 1891 Jacob Schiff seconded this position, making clear that banks would not fund subways—they were too costly—and the only way to get rapid transit was "at the expense of the city."

Leading commercial groups got behind this approach. In 1894 the powerful Chamber of Commerce—persuaded by members Hewitt and Schiff—worked out the winning formula and pushed it through the Republican-controlled state legislature. The law established a self-perpetuating Rapid Transit Commission (RTC) that was, in effect, an arm of the Chamber. In addition to the mayor and comptroller, the RTC would include the Chamber's president (ex officio) and five citizens, named in the measure, four of whom were millionaires. If any resigned, the RTC had sole power to replace them. The commissioners were given authority to issue bonds, design the system, choose the route, let the contracts, and supervise the work. They chose William Barclay Parsons, scion of an elite colonial New York family, and an 1882 graduate of Columbia's School of Mines, to be their engineering eyes and ears. Parsons built docks in Cuba, worked as chief surveyor of China's Canton–Hankow Railway for the American China Development Company, and in 1904 was made a consultant on the Panama Canal; engineers, too, roamed the rim of empire.

The city's unions accepted this scenario as the best they could get. The price of their support was a five-cent fare and a municipal referendum on the question of public ownership. Despite some grumbling in upper-class circles at such "anarchism," a referendum was scheduled for 1894. A broad coalition set out to drum up support, including seventy labor unions (who hoped subway construction would generate employment in the midst of the national depression), Henry George and his supporters, immigrant associations, black organizations, Christian social reformers, the Chamber of Commerce, the Real Estate Exchange, retailers, manufacturers, and bankers. In the largest turnout in New York City's history, public development and municipal ownership of a subway system was approved by three-fourths of the voters.

It took another five years to make the key engineering decisions, sort out the routing, find a private partner, and negotiate the terms.

When Parsons became the RTC's chief engineer, electric traction was a tested but not a proven technology. Parsons went to Europe in 1894 to visit those cities (notably London) that were in the forefront of its development, and he found it promising. In the next few years Glasgow, Budapest, and Boston demonstrated conclusively that electric engines could replace steam ones, and Parsons pressed ahead, following the same calculus that led the Pennsylvania Railroad to opt for tunneling under the Hudson (using electricity) rather than bridging it (using steam).

Property owners along lower Broadway (backed by a balky judiciary) also slowed progress. An 1872 amendment to the state constitution—sponsored by Tilden and other Tweed-era reformers to block corrupt deals between city officials and railroad promoters—had required that rapid transit commissions secure consent from at least half the property owners (by value) along a proposed right-of-way before construction. By the 1890s much of the property along lower Broadway was in the hands of estate guardians, trustees of charitable institutions, and large corporations that feared a subway would depress values. Many other north-south thoroughfares were also off-limits. An act of 1891 forbade any route on Fifth Avenue, and it was tacitly understood that Central Park West, West End Avenue, and Riverside Drive were reserved for affluent housing. So a way to route the subway up Manhattan had to be plotted out.

The commissioners also had to come to terms with Tammany, which, determined to get access to this patronage-rich enterprise, erected various roadblocks over the next few years.

Finally, in 1900, the last pieces came together with a smoothness suggesting behind-the-scenes concessions.

In January the RTC awarded the construction job to John B. McDonald. McDonald had experience: he had been general superintendent of the Croton Dam and done extensive railroad work, notably an 1894 B&O tunnel under Baltimore. Perhaps more important, the Irish-American contractor was on excellent terms with Tammany.

So was Democrat August Belmont Jr., the man to whom McDonald turned for financial assistance. The contract required McDonald to pay the city's huge interest charges on the money it borrowed for the project, and to post an enormous bond as well. McDonald had no such resources. But Belmont, like his late father, was one of the city's most powerful bankers, with access to Rothschild funds. Belmont, moreover, had been locked out of the lucrative New York transport scene (and associated real estate possibilities) by the Manhattan Elevated (Gould/Sage/Morgan) and Metropolitan Street Railway (Whitney/Ryan/Standard Oil) combines. He was eager and ready to enter the great game.

Belmont now took charge. He chartered two companies: a construction outfit to build the line under McDonald's direction (and Parsons's supervision), and the Interborough Rapid Transit Company (IRT) to operate it. Belmont also organized a syndicate that brought in the House of Morgan to arrange financing.

Finally, on March 24, 1900, all was ready. Twenty-five thousand citizens assembled in City Hall Park to watch the groundbreaking ceremonies. As John Philip Sousa's band played and fireworks exploded from atop the Pulitzer Building, the crowd chanted, "To Harlem in fifteen minutes!" while Mayor Van Wyck turned the first clods of earth.

BUILDING THE SYSTEM

THE TASK CONFRONTING THE ENGINEERS and the 7,700 workers was complicated. Parsons and the RTC had decided against London's deep-tunnel system in favor of a cut-and-cover approach. This meant digging trenches—and removing over 3 million cubic yards of earth—from city streets already home to an intricate undergrowth of steam pipes, sewers, gas mains, water tunnels, electric cables, trolley conduits, phone lines, and telegraph wires. There were also depressions to bridge and rises to be blasted through.

"Subway Construction: Park Row and City Hall Park, from Street Level. Building with Columns at Right is the Original Hall of Records." November 13, 1902. (Courtesy New York City Municipal Archives)

The work was not only demanding; it was dangerous and poorly paid. Dynamite explosions and cave-ins cost fifty-four men their lives; hundreds more were injured or maimed. The laborers, a multi-national crew (though chiefly just-arrived Italians), were paid $2.00 to $2.25 for a ten-hour day if unskilled and about $2.50 if skilled. They soon formed AFL locals and struck for higher wages and shorter hours, with vociferous support from the Italian colonies. McDonald countered by hiring more blacks, Greeks, Germans, and Irishmen, and calling in the police, touching off riotous street battles. In the end, the workers gained few concessions.

For the historically minded among them, there were some compensations. As they dug and threaded their way along, the IRT men found their path recapitulating the city's past and anticipating its future.

From the Post Office just below City Hall, the line plowed north on Park Row, alongside the old Commons where Whitfield once preached and Stamp Act protestors once rallied. (Excavation turned up colonial coins, weapons, and tools.) Then—barred from Broadway— it ran north under Centre Street, where Aaron Burr's hollowed-out pine-log waterpipes were unearthed, and cut through the filled-in Collect Pond (the malarial bog on which the Five Points was built) and the old canal that had drained it. Heading up Elm Street and Lafayette Place, it tacked under Fourth Avenue (beneath the site of the 1849 Astor Place riots), plunged (at Murray Hill) beneath the old Park Avenue tunnel, and cruised straight on to Grand Central. Here, at 42nd and Park, Belmont (in 1906) would order up the lavish twenty-three-story Hotel Belmont, complete with a passageway that would let him swing his special subway car, the *Mineola*, with its mahogany inlay and plate glass, directly onto the underground system for joyrides. (As Mrs. Belmont observed: "A private railroad car is not an acquired taste. One takes to it immediately.")

At 42nd Street the route zigged left across town to Broadway and zagged right into the former Longacre Square (the newly rechristened Times Square), maneuvering through the new *Times* building then under construction (above the pressroom, below the first floor). Here it headed straight up Broadway, through the emerging theater district, past the old carriage quarter, under a shored-up Columbus statue, up the soon-to-boom West Side, and beneath a new acropolis emerging on Morningside Heights. Then, breaking into the open, it traversed a viaduct that soared over the old village of Manhattanville at 125th Street, until it resubmerged at 133rd and rolled to its initial terminus at 145th Street. Over the next four years it would press on under Broadway to and under Eleventh Avenue, to Fort George, surfacing again at Dyckman Street (where huge mastodon bones were uncovered), crossing over the new Harlem River Ship Canal Bridge to Marble Hill (225th Street), and rolling on through the Bronx to Broadway and 242nd Street, a stone's throw from the 1748 Van Courtland House.

A spin-off line, which would in short order have epochal consequences for both Harlem and the Bronx, shunted off at 96th Street, cut under Central Park at 104th, and sliced diagonally northeastward to emerge under and continue up Lenox Avenue. Proceeding north to 140th Street, it veered to the right, passed beneath the Harlem River at 145th Street, and slid under the Bronx's East 149th Street until it emerged and continued on Westchester Avenue, on along Southern Boulevard, and up Boston Road to West Farms Square and 180th Street at Bronx Park.

One last piece of trackage remained. A 1902 contract authorized McDonald to open up a second (southern) front. From City Hall this line ran under Park Row and down Broadway (former objections having dissipated) to Bowling Green at the Battery, with stops at Fulton and Wall finally integrating the financial district to the underground network. At South Ferry yet another tunnel was dug under the East River, allowing trains to carry on, below Joralemon Street and the old Brooklyn City (now Borough) Hall, to the junction of Flatbush and Atlantic Avenues, giving IRT riders access (by 1908) to the Long Island Rail Road terminal there. The colossal logjam at the Brooklyn Bridge was, at last, a thing of the past.

WHILE MOST DUG, OTHERS BUILT the "World's Greatest Powerhouse." IRT engineers designed an immense ultra-modern generating plant at 59th Street and Eleventh Avenue to feed electricity to its system. When completed, coal—which arrived by barge to a special Hudson River pier—was carried on belt conveyors through a tunnel to the powerhouse. Hoisted to giant hoppers, coal then dropped down into six independent generating stations (encompassing fifty-two boilers), each of which had its own enormous chimney, rising 162 feet into the West Side air. The engines and alternators could collectively produce 100,000 horsepower, more than any other electric plant ever built, and deliver it to transformers and converters housed around the city in substations. These in turn passed on 625 volts of direct current to third rails in the subway tunnels.

Not only was the powerhouse a technological triumph; it was also a striking piece of architecture. The IRT's contract—drawn as the City Beautiful movement was hitting its stride—had insisted all visible parts of the subway be designed "with a view to the beauty of their appearance, as well as to their efficiency." Stanford White created the powerhouse facework. The various substations were designed to blend in with their neighborhoods.

The passenger stations also looked to Europe for aesthetic inspiration. For entryways, the IRT men turned not to Paris (and its Art Nouveau Métro) but to Budapest. The Hungarians had modeled their stations on the *kushk*—a summerhouse with mosque-like roof that had graced gardens in ancient Persia and Turkey—and New York's subway engineers transmuted them into cast-iron-and-glass "kiosks." Below ground, the stations were finished with tiles, marble, pottery, faience, and ceramic mosaics. In some stops, special panels denoted a historic building or event associated (sometimes obliquely) with the location. (Fulton Street featured the *Clermont*; Grand Central displayed the New York Central's logo;

Powerhouse, Interborough Rapid Transit Company, ca. 1904. (Pierre P. Pullis. Art and Picture Collection, The New York Public Library)

Columbus Circle boasted the *Santa Maria*; Astor Place presented a beaver, rather than the riot.) Finally, oak ticket booths with bronze window grilles were installed, ready to serve paying customers.

But the first customers rode free—Henry George's vision realized—though, alas, only for a day. On Thursday, October 27, 1904, New York set out to celebrate the opening of the IRT with a Festival of Connection rarely equaled in the city's history. Flags and bunting were up everywhere that afternoon, and factories gave workers a half holiday. Crowds congregated at City Hall and kiosks along the line; church bells rang, whistles screeched, sirens screamed, and ocean liners boomed their foghorns. At first, however, this traditional approach seemed oddly misplaced, as all the celebratory action was out of sight.

Just after 2:30 p.m., with Mayor McClellan at the controls, an olive-green train loaded with bewhiskered and silk-hatted dignitaries pulled out of the City Hall station. McClellan, his hand glued to a silver throttle, ran it flat-out until nervous aides persuaded him to relinquish command to a professional at 103rd Street. Soon the train burst sedately into the sunlight at the viaduct over Manhattan Valley as people who packed the hillsides cheered this first tangible display. When it pulled into 145th Street, having completed a 9.1-mile journey of twenty-eight stations, it had taken just twenty-six minutes. Additional VIP trains chugged up and down the route until 6:00 p.m. At that point, seventy of the most powerful and prominent joyriders trooped off to a testimonial dinner for Belmont at Sherry's, a repast that featured a perfect facsimile—40 feet long—of the 72nd Street station, complete with an operating set of IRT toy trains.

Now it was the people's turn. At 7:00 p.m. the crowds poured into the stations, free of charge. They were handed a little booklet Columbia professor Charles Chandler had written, assuring them the subway air was as pure as that in their own homes. An estimated 150,000 people rode up and down the line, in a carnivalesque mood, thrilling, said the *Tribune*, to "the

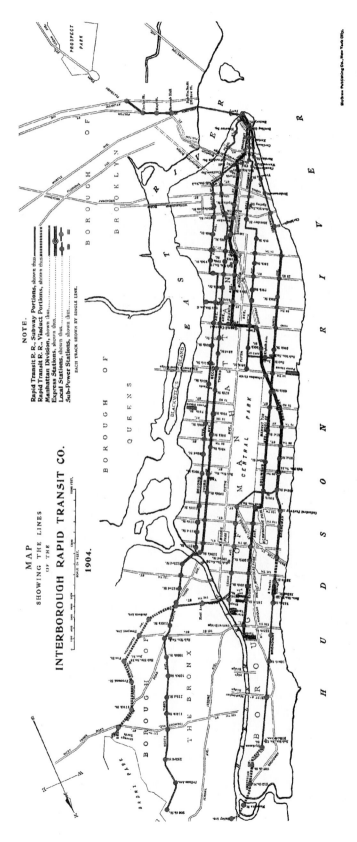

"Map Showing the Lines of the Interborough Rapid Transit Co." *The New York Subway: Its Construction and Equipment*, 1904. (Image No. 80001d, New-York Historical Society)

novelty of the whirlwind rush through the long tunnel, the thunder of grinding wheels and the mad dance of flying shadows past the car windows."

One Henry Barret took a more jaundiced view. He discovered, shortly after entering the 28th Street station, that he had been deftly parted from his $500 diamond horseshoe pin— thus becoming the city's first victim of underground crime.

A rather different association between subways and crime was made by the chief of police that day. During the festivities he told Mrs. McDonald: "This subway is going to ab- solutely preclude the possibility of riots in New York. If a riot should break out at any time

Mayor George B. McClellan Jr. (center) and executives of the Interborough Rapid Transit Company, cab of the first IRT train, October 27, 1904, at City Hall Station. (New-York Historical Society)

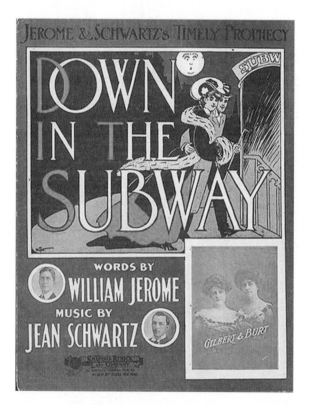

"Down in the Subway: Jerome & Schwarz' Timely Prophecy," 1904. (Kirk Collection, Special Collections Department, Cunningham Memorial Library, Indiana State University)

now we could clear the road and send out a trainload of a thousand men, dropping as many of them off at every station as necessary, and have an armed force in Harlem in fifteen minutes."

What most astonished one sharp-eyed *Times* reporter, however, was just how speedily the novelty wore off over the course of the day. Even as crowds of the yet-uninitiated surrounded station exits, gawking in amazement as people emerged from a hole in the ground, the emergees themselves—now seasoned veterans—headed matter-of-factly homeward, "having finished what will be to them the daily routine of the rest of their lives."

EXPANDING THE SYSTEM

OVER THE NEXT FEW YEARS, JUBILATION GAVE WAY TO EXASPERATION.

Crowds jammed the subways from day one. Designed to carry 400,000 passengers daily, the IRT was soon averaging 800,000. Everyone expected matters would be quickly alleviated by expansion, but years went by and things got worse.

Crushed riders were not alone in their eagerness for development. Once it became apparent that where the IRT ran, land values soared, outer-borough real estate promoters deluged the Rapid Transit Commission with appeals to send tracks their way.[2] Brooklyn developers extracted a promise that the next subway would be in Kings County, but construction of a route down Fourth Avenue to Bay Ridge, adopted in 1905, remained stuck on the drawing boards. Bronx developers pleaded for the IRT to push north from West Farms along White Plains Road; other Bronxites, particularly Chancellor MacCracken of NYU, sought a Jerome Avenue line. But nothing happened.

The IRT was in no hurry. Crowding annoyed passengers but profited the company enormously. Ridership doubled between 1905 and 1908, topping the planned maximum capacity by one-third. The company earned a 17–18 percent annual profit operating the city-built line, paid high dividends (soaring from 2 percent in 1904 to 9 percent in 1907), and accumulated a whopping surplus. It was under no pressure to add new lines on its own account, especially as competition from surface transit had vanished.

Even before the first subway opened, Belmont had taken over the elevated system. Gould and his associates had signed a lease in 1902 giving the IRT control of the Manhattan Railway Company for 999 years, in exchange for a 7 percent annual rental.

That left only the trolleys. The Metropolitan Street Railway, already weakened by Ryan and Whitney's profligate ways, faced disaster when the subway opened. Ryan (his partner having died in 1904) decided to brazen his way past catastrophe: he would force Belmont to take over his tottering firm and its load of liabilities.

Ryan announced to the city that *he* would undertake the subway expansion Belmont refused to, and on excellent terms for New York. (He made this threat credible by acquiring control of the Equitable Life Assurance Company, a bottomless source of investment funds.)

2. Some of these operators—*pace* businessmen's denunciations of Tammany corruption—engaged in precisely the kind of "honest graft" touted by Boss Plunkitt. Charles T. Barney, president of Knickerbocker Trust and an active land speculator, became a director of the IRT in 1900. He didn't stay long, but departed laden with insider information about routes, station locations, and construction timetables. Organizing a syndicate of bankers, which commanded nearly $7 million in capital, Barney and friends began snapping up vacant properties in Harlem, Washington Heights, and Fort George (in 1901), then moved on to Inwood and the Bronx (in 1902). As early as February 1904, he and his associates began selling off lots, and by 1907 they had harvested all their profits. Other IRT insiders followed suit, including August Belmont himself, who together with the Rothschilds and J. P. Morgan bought property on City Island in the Bronx. Henry Morgenthau waited until 1904, when the subway was nearing completion, then enlisted the aid of real estate broker/operator J. Clarence Davies, in buying up 2,500 plots abutting the new lines.

"The Public Be Jammed!" ca. 1905. (Library of Congress Prints and Photographs Division, Cabinet of American Illustration)

Belmont resisted but eventually capitulated, unwilling to risk the erosion of his monopoly position. In December 1905 Belmont and Ryan set up a holding company embracing the IRT and the Metropolitan Street Railway. The merger sent the Metropolitan's stock soaring. Ryan waited until it hit the top and then sold out for a handsome profit, leaving the shell of the old streetcar company to collapse into receivership, taking numerous small investors down with it. An irked Belmont, left to pick up the pieces, complained that the forced take-over had cost the IRT $40 million. On the other hand, he had eliminated his last serious rival. As a New York *Tribune* headline summed up the new situation: "Belmont Is Traction King; Belmont Now in Position to Sandbag City."

The deal had created the largest integrated transport system on the face of the earth. The IRT now controlled all surface, elevated, and subway lines in Manhattan and the Bronx. When statisticians added in riders on the BRT, which had an equally firm stranglehold on Brooklyn, they discovered that Greater New York's transit system moved (in 1906) almost 1.2 billion people annually.

The IRT and its banker backers were thus dealing from great strength in negotiating with the city. Belmont was amenable to expansion, but only where it was immediately profitable. He was prepared to turn the Z-shaped first system into an H by running a new line up Lexington Avenue from Grand Central, and another down the West Side from Times Square to the new Pennsylvania Station and points south. But he was not interested in pushing ahead of the existing market into sparsely settled areas; he sought the fat, not the lean. Nor did he want to commit any of the IRT's own money to new construction. He (and the House of Morgan) told the city it must pay for any new lines; once completed, the IRT would operate them—if it was guaranteed a hefty rate of profit.[3]

BELMONT'S HARDBALLING GENERATED ENEMIES.

The muckraking community, then battling the Gas Trust, charged that the Rapid Transit Commission was giving away the municipal store. Ray Stannard Baker noted in a 1905

---

3. This situation was not unique to New York; in Toronto, Glasgow, Munich, and Cologne, city councils battled with commercial companies unwilling to extend lines and service beyond the dense inner core where returns on invested capital were highest.

McClure's article that Belmont was getting access to the streets, money for building, exemption from taxation, and control of the line for fifty, perhaps seventy-five years. Yes, he had to reimburse the city for the interest it paid on the money it borrowed on his behalf—but it was much cheaper for Belmont to pay the 3.25 percent the city could get as a public entity than if he'd gone to the capital markets himself. Yes, he had to pay for the equipment—but the city was obligated to buy it back at the end of the contract period. As one commissioner wrote Andrew Haswell Green: "I know it is the fashion to speak of this subway as an instance of municipal ownership. It may be such three generations hence. To-day it is merely a lending of municipal credit with exemption from taxation." Boston, Baker noted, not only built its subway but kept control of it.

The IRT's own workforce was alienated. Belmont did settle one strike in 1904 through arbitration, but in 1905 he broke a strike of the Amalgamated Association, and thereafter refused any dealings with the union.

IRT intransigence also dismayed reform organizations intent on comprehensive citywide development. The City Club (especially its president, George McAneny), the Municipal Art Society, and various philanthropists and civic leaders urged subway-led development of the outer boroughs as a solution to Manhattan's slum congestion.

William Randolph Hearst and Judge Samuel Seabury called for real municipalization. They wanted a giant network of new lines to be built and operated by the city, not by the rapacious IRT.

Slowly a disparate coalition, ranging from the Citizens' Union and the Merchants' Association to the unions and the radicals, began to call on the city to build its own municipal subway to compete with the giant monopolies.

The first victim of this rising clamor was the Rapid Transit Commission. Once hailed, now jeered, the Chamber-dominated group seemed undemocratic, powerless, unable or unwilling to confront the monopolies. When Charles Evans Hughes was elected governor in 1906, defeating Hearst, he had the legislature sweep the RTC away and give control of transit to the same Public Service Commission (PSC) that had been given oversight of gas and electric utilities.

The PSC quickly churned out ideas for citywide route expansion but soon discovered that despite its new supervisory powers, it had no power to force the private companies to extend their systems, nor sufficient funds to build a comprehensive public one. The state constitution's limitation of the city's debt to 10 percent of the assessed value of its real estate was one obstacle; the Panic of 1907 and ensuing hard times was another. Pro-municipal-development forces urged the city to construct at least a few new lines and let the IRT add on to its own system. But the IRT refused to build if the city became a competitor. Its fiscal representative, J. P. Morgan Jr., bluntly told New York it must choose. If it wanted IRT participation, it must scrap plans for an independent system and provide substantial inducements to the company.

The PSC was left with one card to play against the IRT syndicate: the possibility of enticing competitors to enter its bailiwick. In 1910 William Gibbs McAdoo—fresh from his under-river engineering triumphs—offered to equip and operate a city-built line and turn it over to municipal control in ten years if service proved unsatisfactory. McAneny (elected Manhattan borough president in 1909) applauded this, noting McAdoo was in a position to link his Hudson tubes to an expanded line, thus giving the city a regional transit system. This alarmed Belmont, and prodded him into sweetening the IRT's offer. That weakened McAdoo's ability to deliver, as his finances were stretched, and the IRT's move frightened away other investors who didn't want to compete with Belmont's monopoly, backed by the House of Morgan. McAdoo was forced to withdraw his proposal.

But what finally scared the IRT into action was a 1911 proposal from the powerful Brooklyn Rapid Transit company that *it* be allowed to invade the IRT's lucrative territory by running a line from Brooklyn up Broadway to the burgeoning mid-Manhattan market. This precipitated two years of tough bargaining between the PSC, the IRT, and the BRT. In 1913, brokered by McAneny, a deal was finally cut.

The participants agreed to split the cost of a massive expansion of Greater New York's transit system. Most money would come from the city (roughly $200 million), though the two firms anted up substantial contributions (the IRT $77 million; the BRT $61 million). The new lines would be owned by the city. The companies would operate them (on a forty-nine-year lease). For this they would be paid a sum equal to the profit they were getting from existing lines (14–15 percent) plus 6 percent on their investment. They would take this "preferential" payment, intended to reduce the risk of expanding into thinly populated areas, out of operating revenues before the city got a dime. The new lines would be so comprehensive—expanding trackage from 181 to 614 miles—that real estate interests all over the metropolis would profit, and hence put their political muscle behind the wheels. Working people would get the five-cent fare guaranteed.

Critics screamed sellout. Why guarantee the IRT its current profit rate, based as it was on inadequate service and indecent congestion? Why subsidize the companies and the Wall Street interests behind them? "Tammany would not dare give any corporation what these eminently respectable gentlemen are giving to Morgan and Belmont and this traction monopoly," howled the *Evening World*. But proponents argued that a) there was no choice and b) construction would redound to the city's long-term benefit. In fact, however, by guaranteeing profits for the private company, the city was creating potential problems down the road: if revenues roared in, it could handle the payouts, if not, there would be pressure to raise the fare, pitting labor against watered capital. Nevertheless, in March 1913 the Board of Estimate ratified the "Dual Contracts"—226 parchment pages of fine print bound up in red leather—and the gigantic building project got under way.

By 1920 nearly 323 miles of new lines had been added, more than doubling the trackage extant in 1913. Some serviced densely populated areas; others speared into undeveloped parts of the city.

In Manhattan, the IRT got to complete its H. One line (the upper-right leg of the H) ran from Grand Central up Lexington Avenue to the Bronx, where it connected with the Jerome Avenue Line (today's #4) to Woodlawn, and the Pelham Line to Pelham Bay Park (#6). The other IRT line (today's #1) ran down the lower-left leg, south from Times Square to the hitherto marooned Penn Station on Seventh Avenue, then carrying on down the West Side to South Ferry. (In 1916, while working through landfill at Greenwich and Dey, crews turned up the charred hull of Adriaen Block's *Tyger*, the ship that had caught fire and sunk in 1613, three centuries earlier.) At Chambers Street, a line to Brooklyn curled east, through the purpose-dug Clark Street Tunnel, on to the LIRR terminal at Flatbush and Atlantic. From there it traveled under Eastern Parkway to Brownsville and East New York (#3), with a spur under Nostrand Avenue to Flatbush (#2).

For its part, the BRT completed the trunk line down Fourth Avenue—through Sunset Park and on to Bay Ridge (traversing the area through which Washington's forces had retreated, back in the 1776 Battle of Long Island). Along the Fourth Avenue line, connections branched off through Borough Park, Bensonhurst, and Park Slope to Coney Island via the

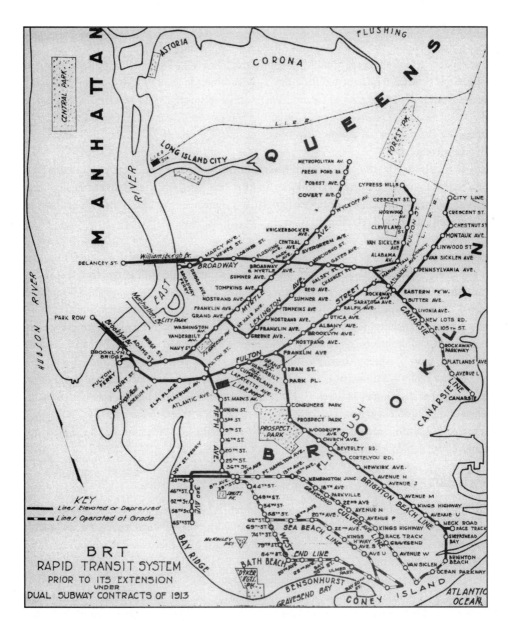

"Brooklyn Rapid Transit System Prior to Its Extension under Dual Subway Contracts of 1913," 1912. (Courtesy of David Pirmann)

old steam railroads—the Sea Beach (today's N), West End (D), Culver (F), and Brighton (B)—now converted to rapid transit feeder lines. In the opposite direction, the BRT's Fourth Avenue road and its tributaries triumphally funneled Brooklynites into Manhattan, via two routes. One (today's N) took the high road, over the Manhattan Bridge straight to Canal Street; the other (today's R) took the low road, under the East River, via South Ferry and City Hall up to the same Canal Street station. (It was while digging their way up Broadway, in 1912, that workmen broke into the 1870 Alfred Ely Beach tunnel, wherein they found the tunneling shield used in building it, and some remains of Gotham's ur-subway-car). From Canal Street the line ran up under Broadway and Seventh Avenue, then swerved east under 59th Street and undercrossed the river to the Queensborough Bridge Plaza. The BRT got yet another Brooklyn-Manhattan connection: a line running from Canarsie through Bushwick that tunneled under the East River and across Manhattan along 14th Street (L).

Queens also got a direct Manhattan connection. Today's #7 line ran from Broadway and 42nd Street eastward into the old Steinway Tunnel—built in the 1890s to provide trolley-car access from Long Island City to Grand Central and now upgraded. From Hunters Point, the road carried on to Queensborough Bridge Plaza and then east (via Queens Boulevard and Roosevelt Avenue) as an elevated to Woodside and Corona (#7), or north to Astoria at Ditmars Avenue (N).

In the Bronx, the IRT's Lexington Avenue line fed into a Jerome Avenue elevated, which proceeded up to Woodlawn (#4), and into another line (#6), which traveled to Pelham Bay Park. Finally, its original line to Bronx Park (#2) was pushed up along White Plains Road to near the city limits at 241st Street.

MORE THAN ANYTHING ELSE, the subway system made Greater New York a reality. In a way, it also brought the City Beautiful into being. Above ground, the pining of artists and architects since Olmsted's day for a system of interconnecting verdant boulevards had been frustrated—apart from scattered pieces of parkway. But below the metropolitan surface, there now lay a magnificent integrated network of roadbeds. Sweeping majestically from borough to borough, conjoining in great underground étoiles, they created a colossal, Haussmanesque, radial city, most of which, ironically, was utterly invisible.

Above ground, a different kind of irony was at work. Greater New York had now bound itself together with hoops of steel. But at the very moment of its effective consolidation, an agent of dissolution began putt-putting about on the city's streets. Misread at first as a harmless toy, this little nemesis would prove to be a vehicle for undermining the unification achieved at such enormous cost.

THE AUTOMOBILING CLASS

On a summer day in 1901, an automobile ran down two-year-old Louis Camille, son of Italian immigrants, on a Lower East Side street. The chauffeur, who had been driving two businessmen to their Wall Street offices, was assaulted by a crowd of enraged neighborhood residents until rescued by the police.

Over the next dozen years, motorists killed about a thousand children as they played in the streets.[4] Communities fought back. One wealthy woman being chauffeured through Italian East Harlem was stoned and knocked unconscious. Another driver was slain by his victim's irate father. Suburbanites too resented the invasion of arrogant "scorchers." Sheriffs routinely set up Sunday afternoon speed traps to snare the mobile rich. Tarrytown police stretched ropes across the road that yanked drivers out of their seats. Some vigilante groups shot at speeders.

New York's *Horseless Age*, the country's first specialized auto periodical, berated "many of the newspapers circulating chiefly among the working class [which] try to make capital out of class hatred and lose no opportunity to hold up the automobile as a means of oppression

---

4. Adults, too, were mown down. The city's first traffic fatality came on September 13, 1899, when Henry Hale Bliss, a wealthy real estate salesman, stepped off a trolley heading south on Central Park West, into the path of an electric cab carrying a doctor back from a house call in Harlem. In 1901 the state legislature passed the first auto law. It required registration of all vehicles and the display of the owner's initials "in a conspicuous place" on the back of the automobile (a proto-license-plate). It also allowed municipalities to set speed limits, with the *minimum* velocity being 8 miles per hour.

of the poor by the wealthy." But the president of Princeton University blamed the motorists themselves—they embodied the "arrogance of wealth, with all its independence and carelessness"—and suggested that "nothing has spread socialistic feelings in this country more than the use of the automobile."

Woodrow Wilson's association of autos with rich people was nowhere more accurate than in New York City, capital of the emerging car culture. By 1900 a near-majority of the 8,000 automobiles in the United States were owned by financiers, industrialists, merchants, or wealthy professionals in the New York metropolitan area. There were several reasons for this dense concentration.

First, car ownership was an expensive proposition. Apart from the steep purchase price, there were the high costs of maintenance. A chauffeur was essential, as much to repair as to pilot the frail and temperamental vehicles. As late as 1914 one-third of the drivers in New York City were chauffeurs. An indoor garage was also essential, as most early models were open-air, fair-weather machines.

An automobile was thus a rich man's plaything. Not only did New York have more millionaires than anyplace else, but many were horse fanciers who now transferred their affections to machines. Diamond Jim Brady was the first to flirt, startling the town (and scaring its horses) when he test-drove (in 1895) an electric brougham. ("Brady Drives First Horseless Carriage Seen in New York," ran the headline; "Appearance Ties Up Traffic for Two Hours.") The new fad flamed through the precincts of the wealthy. William Rockefeller traded in his steeds and carriages for cars; William Randolph Hearst zipped around in a speedy French auto; William Gibbs McAdoo commuted to Yonkers in a big red Mercedes, blasting its bugle horn to scatter pedestrians; Thomas Lamont's French import had ebony woodwork, a writing desk, and a washstand table; his boss J. P. Morgan's claret-colored, 50-horsepower Rolls-Royce had silver flower vases, velvet carpets, silk curtains, and "JPM" on the door. *Harper's Weekly* noted that over 200 New Yorkers had between five and ten vehicles apiece. As John Jacob Astor told the papers in 1905, "A stable of cars is coming to be recognized as the proper thing for a man of wealth." Astor should have known; he had thirty-two of them.

The car enthusiasts soon formed a club, as had horsemen and yachtsmen before them. The Automobile Club of America (ACA, 1899)—headquartered in the Waldorf-Astoria—drew on the cream of the city's elite, including Vincent Astor, George Baker, August Belmont, Chauncey Depew, J. B. Duke, Stuyvesant Fish, Henry Clay Frick, George Gould, E. H. Harriman, John T. Havemeyer, John D. and William Rockefeller, James Stillman, Cornelius and William Vanderbilt, and William C. Whitney, among others.

The ACA held banquets, sponsored parades down Fifth Avenue, and hired crack lawyers to ward off legal constraints on motorists. Their efforts deflected state or city driving tests until 1917 (long after London and Paris required them), overturned speed limits they deemed too low, and voided legislation aimed at hit-and-run drivers. (Forcing motorists to stay at the scene of an accident was held to violate their constitutional rights against self-incrimination.) The ACA also proclaimed itself the national voice of all American motorists. It soon dominated the fledgling American Automobile Association (AAA), a Chicago-based national federation of local clubs.

Another reason for New York's auto-primacy was that it offered better roads to drive on than most other cities (to say nothing of the American countryside, whose rutted lanes were often impassable). Vaux and Olmsted's parkways were ideal for the fragile vehicles: they barred heavy teaming and public transport, had good pavements and shallow grades, and lacked sharp corners. Car drivers battled their way into Central Park (in 1899), over the

"N.Y.C. Auto Wrecked in Central Park," ca. 1910–15. (Library of Congress Prints and Photographs Division, George Grantham Bain Collection)

opposition of horse owners and livery stable keepers, and promenaded in machines where they'd once paraded in carriages. (By 1912 the Park Department had asphalted the drives to make them even more hospitable for autos.) Racier drivers headed for the Harlem River Speedway, much to the annoyance of the trotting fraternity for whom it had been built; in 1919, after a long fight, it was formally opened to cars. The fast crowd also zoomed up and down Riverside Drive—where Hearst, during his stint in the House of Representatives, became the first congressman arrested for speeding.[5]

New York, as the nation's emporium, became the center of automotive marketing efforts, some of them quite spectacular. From the first, the metropolis was the focus for long-distance races promoted by publishers and manufacturers to sell magazines and cars. In 1895 New York became home to the first two specialized auto periodicals, *Motocycle* and *Horseless Age*; *Cosmopolitan*, *Harper's Weekly*, and *Outing* also regularly covered the car culture. In 1896 *Cosmopolitan* sponsored a dash from Manhattan's City Hall to a country club in Ardsley, New York, with four Duryeas and a lone Benz the only entrants. In 1901 Ransom E. Olds sold 750 of his Curved Dash Oldsmobiles in the metropolis, after a record-breaking run from Detroit that averaged 14 miles per hour. And on February 12, 1908, 250,000 jammed Times Square to watch six cars start off on a race to Paris via Seattle, Japan, and Siberia.

A more genteel species of marketing took place at the annual New York Auto Show. This weeklong affair—launched in 1900 under the auspices of the ACA and the National Association of Automobile Manufacturers—was held, like the Horse Show, at Madison Square Garden. By 1905 it had become a "sort of festival for society and the automobiling

---

5. Pennsylvania Railroad engineers lowered an automobile into their tunnel and became the first group to motor under the Hudson.

"New York–Paris Race: Lelouvier Starting," February 11, 1908. (Library of Congress Prints and Photographs Division, George Grantham Bain Collection)

"New York–Paris Race: Cars Lined Up for Race (1908)," February 11, 1908. (Library of Congress Prints and Photographs Division, George Grantham Bain Collection)

class" and, simultaneously, the nation's leading industrial exposition. The J. Walter Thompson agency, a specialist in marketing to targeted income groups, assured car manufacturers (in 1901) that their advertising dollars would not be wasted by the firm: "We can ensure that automobiles shall not be extensively advertised to the working classes nor bargain jack-knives to the well-to-do."

From marketing device to sport of tycoons proved a short step, as auto enthusiasts quickly made New York into the national hub of car racing. William K. Vanderbilt, through from an old railroading family (the 26-year-old was the Commodore's great-grandson), created the Vanderbilt Challenge Cup competition in 1904. An enthusiastic participant in European contests—in 1902 he'd raced from Monte Carlo to Paris in his "Red Devil" Mercedes in seventeen hours—he also wanted to encourage US manufacturers to improve American machines, still overmatched by European superior craftsmanship. Vanderbilt donated the 10-gallon, 30-pound, Tiffany silver "cup"; a $2,000 prize added to the allure. By 1906 the third Vanderbilt Race drew 200,000 fans from around the country to the tourney over nearly 300 miles of Long Island's turnpikes and country roads, probably the largest crowds ever at any sporting event in the New York metropolitan area. The races also attracted considerable protest. With drivers hitting speeds over 70 miles per hour, and spectators pressing recklessly onto the roadway, accidents were plentiful. The *Times* denounced the spectacle as "a terror and a juggernaut, like that which led the nobility and privileged classes into the excesses which precipitated the French Revolution." The competition's reputation was not helped by an ugly international incident in 1906 when Vanderbilt ran over a peasant child in Italy and was barely rescued from an enraged crowd.

Vanderbilt's response to criticism was to build, with some wealthy friends, a forty-five-mile-long, sixteen-foot-wide, concrete, auto-only road that ran through private estates on the North Shore; a private road, it was intended to be made self-sustaining from auto tolls. Only the first nine-mile stretch of Vanderbilt's Long Island Motor Parkway was ready by 1908, so much of the course still ran on narrow public highways, flanked by ever larger crowds—until 1910, when there were several accidental deaths ("Vanderbilt Cup Race Slaughter," blared the *Scientific American*). Auto manufacturers and professional drivers pulled out, deciding it was no longer safe, and the state legislature restricted auto racing on public highways. Auto racing shifted elsewhere, notably to the Indianapolis Speedway (1909). In 1915 the Sheepshead Bay Race Track, which had established the Futurity and the Brooklyn Handicap, shifted from horses to horsepower, remodeling itself as the Sheepshead Speedway. It briefly challenged Indianapolis for the "world's fastest course" title, but it only lasted four years and was later turned into a housing development.

The Long Island Motor Parkway was extended in 1911 to Lake Ronkonkoma in Suffolk County, and its principal rationale shifted from racing to revenue production (a dozen "toll lodges" were built along the route) and to suburban development. Boosters believed broad benefits would accrue to providers of (said *Automobile* magazine) "an uninterrupted route across the Island that, owing to its proximity to the metropolis, is destined to be the home of millions with business and social interests in New York City." It was in fact mainly used by tourists and rich New Yorkers buying up estates of old colonial families (like the Hewletts and the Hickses).

Vanderbilt's road was the pioneering instance of a quintessential Auto Age product: the limited-access highway. But its reliance on private financing was an anachronism, given the enormous costs of construction and maintenance, which could only be met by public involvement. So the first fully formed model of the genre was another New York road: the

Bronx River Parkway, whose development began earlier, in 1906, though it did not become fully operational until 1925.

It began as part of an ecological rescue mission. The growth of Westchester County had been accompanied by pollution of the Bronx River with residential sewage and industrial waste. In 1905 a Bronx River Sewer Commission was established to channel the effluent. And in 1906 a Bronx River Parkway Commission was created to protect the river's banks by nestling them within a linear ribbon park (à la Olmstead and Vaux). The park, in turn, was designed to include a parkway—a 40-foot-wide, four-lane, limited-access, publicly built, toll-free road. It would stretch over 15 miles from the south end of Bronx Park to a plaza at the base of the magnificent Kensico Dam, which had been finished in such high style in part because it was assumed affluent day trippers would motor out to see it. In addition to encouraging Sunday outings, the road stimulated auto commuting to and from Scarsdale, Mount Vernon, Bronxville, and New Rochelle, and exerted enormous influence on future highway construction, the spines of auto-civilization.

DESPITE THE NEW YORK ELITE'S INITIAL HAMMERLOCK on automobiling, this was one monopoly that proved impossible to sustain. After 1905 the luxury market was nearing the saturation point, and the rapidly expanding auto industry sought wider sales. Cars got cheaper, more rugged, and easier for people of middling incomes to buy and maintain—especially after the introduction of Ford's Model T in 1908. By 1915 there were roughly 70,000 autos licensed in the city; within five years the number tripled.

Anti-auto animus ebbed swiftly among the respectable middle class. The *Times* had long attacked autos as "devil wagons" and demanded a speed limit of 8 miles per hour to make them compatible with social uses of the street. But after 1905 the paper made a U-turn. It began blaming pedestrians for accidents and urging mothers to keep their children on the sidewalks. In the *Times*'s case, rethinking was facilitated by the advertising revenues the auto industry afforded. The editorial change was part of a larger tilt: for New York's middle class, the mandate of heaven was shifting from horse to car, and from public to private transport.

The auto was hailed by middle-class reformers concerned about pollution and public health. In 1908 Gotham's 120,000 horses deposited 60,000 gallons of urine and 2.5 million pounds of manure on the city streets every day. When steamy fresh, the dung attracted flies, which carried communicable diseases. When dry, it got pulverized by traffic, then floated up and hung in the air, ready for ingestion. In addition, roughly 15,000 dead horses had to be removed from the streets each year, the clatter of iron-rimmed wheels and horseshoes on cobblestones was deafening, and when huge Clydesdale horses panicked in traffic, their kicks packed a wallop and their bites threatened tetanus. Small wonder that enthusiasts longed for a horseless New York. They even believed (with *Scientific American*) that "streets, clean, dustless and odorless, with light, rubber-tired vehicles moving swiftly and noiselessly over their smooth expanse, would eliminate a greater part of the nervousness, distraction, and strain of modern metropolitan life." Even more exuberantly, Frank Munsey argued in a 1903 issue of his *Munsey's Magazine*, devoted to the auto, that cars were "the greatest health-giving invention of a thousand years," because "the cubic feet of fresh air that are literally forced into one while automobiling rehabilitate worn-out nerves and drive out worry, insomnia, and indigestion."

Middle-class car enthusiasts considered autos superior to public transport, in part because of the latter's defects. The trolley and street-railway monopolies had an unsavory public image; car companies carried no such baggage. Trolleys were dangerous; until forced

"The Close of a Career in New York," ca. 1900–6 (Detroit Publishing Co./Library of Congress Prints and Photographs Division)

to adopt pneumatic brakes in 1913, they caused more transit deaths than cars. And trolleys threw respectables together with their social inferiors; the poor, to their dismay, they always had with them. Genteel women in particular complained that their fellow riders were rude and smelly "bustle-pinchers"; a 1912 *Outlook* article decried groping by "coarse-grained, vulgar or licentious" males. Automobilists could avoid all these unpleasant proximities by retreating to a peripatetic private space.

Driving one's own car was not just a relative but an absolute good. It provided an exhilarating sense of autonomy, of independence. No longer bound to trolley tracks or regulated by timetables, the automobilist could weave around obstacles at will and go point-to-point from work to home. Auto owners could thus free themselves from the constraints that tethered working-class commuters, a sign of their superior capacity to shape their own destiny. Munsey noted that while a man who knew autos only from the outside might see them as "an invention of the devil," once inside, a "marvelous change of heart comes over him." The fledgling driver is soon "lost in admiration and wonder" as "the motion, the feeling of strength and power, the speed, and the obedience to the driver, thrill and delight him."[6] The ability to buy, maintain, operate, and appreciate such a machine testified to the owner's moral and tangible worth. The motorcar became a symbol of middle-class mobility, social as well as geographical.

THE ARRIVAL OF THE MIDDLE-CLASS CAR BUYER, and the rapid expansion of the auto market locally and nationally, reverberated throughout the city's various business sectors, as each came to terms with the possibilities and perils of the new phenomenon.

---

6. On the other hand, it was agreed that the aristocrats' rejection of street rules had generated chaos—the *Saturday Evening Post* coined the term "traffic jam" to describe it. Order was a value, too, so there was general approval when William Phelps Eno, a millionaire car buff, convinced the police commissioner to require slower traffic to stay to the right, faster traffic to pass on the left, and pedestrians to cross at corners.

The burgeoning auto industry needed investment capital, and powerful city financiers entered the new field, some enthusiastically, most cautiously. William C. Whitney, the strategist behind the Metropolitan Street Railway, plunged heavily, trying to set up a US Steel of autos. Whitney put his chips behind electric technology (which had worked so well for his streetcars), but overcapitalization and financial skullduggery punctured his enterprise, which deflated in 1907. In 1908 William C. Durant, the head of Buick, formed the General Motors Company as a New Jersey holding company, in an effort to vertically integrate manufacturers and suppliers. He sought financing from the House of Morgan but it declined, considering GM in particular and the industry in general too risky. Durant forged ahead, only to fall victim in 1910 to over-rapid expansion and insufficient reserves. When the firm nearly folded in 1910, he called in New York bankers to save it—J. & W. Seligman, the Central Trust Company, and Kuhn, Loeb—only to see them assume control and sideline him. Despite this, big New York capital remained tentative about the new industry. Similarly, though several insurance firms began to write auto fire and liability policies, by extending their horse-drawn policies, most shied away from car coverage.

Auto manufacturing rapidly centralized in the Midwest, though some New York entrepreneurs did enter the lists. The old (1810) Brewster & Company carriage-maker firm lost much of its traditional coaching business, but after 1905 it sidled into producing classy auto bodies for imported French (Delaunay-Belleville) and English (Rolls-Royce) concerns and even turned out its own line of fine cars. In 1910 business seemed brisk enough to warrant construction of a 400,000-square-foot, red-brick auto-body factory in Long Island City, facing Queens Plaza at the end of the Queensboro Bridge. By 1917 that neighborhood had emerged as an automotive center, with thirteen manufacturing, assembling, and service plants and twenty-nine accessory and parts concerns.

Gotham also contributed to the auto boom by marketing it. As noted in a 1917 issue of the *Hub* (the New York–based trade journal of American automobile manufacturers), the city was the country's "sales center," with "practically every motor car manufacturer in the country maintaining a branch office in this city." These were strewn along Automobile Row, the stretch of Broadway between Longacre Square and Columbus Circle, where the reconstituted carriage quarter reassembled. Shops that sold wagons, carriages, harnesses, and saddlery shut their doors. The American Horse Exchange (1885) came down in 1910. Meanwhile, tall towers were going up along the strip between 46th and 66th Streets, erected by companies including Benz, Buick, Fiat, Ford, General Motors, Lancia, Oldsmobile, Packard, Peerless, Renault, and Studebaker. Many of these were multi-purpose structures, like the ten-story 1902 Studebaker Building (at Broadway and 48th), which included offices, a factory, and a salesroom that in 1909 was displaying touring cars, suburbans, roadsters, runabouts, coupes, limousines, landaulets, ambulances, delivery wagons, 10-ton trucks, and "electric pleasure vehicles." Secondhand shops flourished, too, selling and shipping used cars to all parts of the country. And a vast range of auto supply stores sprang up to sell ignition systems, speedometers, batteries, carburetors, and tires. Often these, too, were created by substantial corporations. The B. F. Goodrich Building (1780 Broadway at 58th), which opened in 1909, had a tire showroom on the first floor and "the most complete automobile tire repair facilities in the United States" on the twelfth. Three years later Goodrich was overshadowed by the United States Rubber Company Building, whose twenty-story tower arrived virtually next door, at 1790 Broadway, where it loomed over Columbus Circle.

There were other items for sale (or rent) in the auto district, notably spaces to park one's car. Architect and auto enthusiast Ernest Flagg had tried designing a private solution to the storage problem. His own town house included an elevator that lowered his Packard to a base-ment garage complete with gas pump. But this was a wildly expensive approach, out of reach even for the majority of the greatly expanded Automobile Club of America. The ACA re-sponded by hiring member Flagg to build an eight-story clubhouse whose opulent French Renaissance façade on 247 West 54th Street (1907) enclosed a utilitarian garage that could house 300 vehicles—along with a library, a grill room seating 300, and accommodation for chauffeurs. Even so, demand for parking places rapidly outstripped supply, and in 1910 the club added an annex on 55th Street for 600 more cars, and threw in a Turkish bath to boot. But parking spaces were soon in demand from a far wider circle of middle-class automobil-ists, and more plebeian facilities were made available in over eighty publicly accessible ga-rages, many of them established by auto manufacturers, some decked out as grand civic buildings. In 1908 New York constructed its own municipal garage, the first in the country.

Repair work was another auxiliary trade that sprang up. Car owners complained about the quality of work done in garages. Taking advantage of the ignorance of the owners, mechanics charged high prices for shoddy work. So the ACA started a register of reliable chauffeurs and mechanics in 1902 and pushed the YMCA into starting a training school. By 1908, it had tutored 2,000, and the private New York School of Automobile Engineers had produced 1,500 graduates.

FOR ALL THESE MANIFESTATIONS OF AN AUTO BOOM, the intra-city movement of people and commodities remained dominated by rail-based transit—newly bolstered by the more or less simultaneous arrival of the subway—and by the dogged persistence of horse-drawn vehicles, though several equine domains now entered on a terminal decline.

The biggest blow had come with the electrification of trolleys. In 1900 6,000 horses had still been hauling streetcars, more than in all other US cities combined. Then, virtually over-night, these vehicles were deleted from the cityscape: in 1917 the last horse-drawn trolley stopped running along Bleecker Street, leaving the field entirely to electric trams.

Other horse-pulled vehicles in the city, notably the cab and the omnibus, also gave way to autos, with similar alacrity.

In July 1897 twelve silent and odorless electric hansom cabs had begun plying the city's streets, dispatched by the Electric Carriage and Wagon Company to do battle with horse-drawn hacks. They'd done well, and the fleet expanded to sixty-two in 1898, then a hundred the following year. But the electric vehicles were cumbersome, couldn't go faster than 15 miles per hour, and their batteries had to be recharged (a twenty-four-hour-long procedure) every 25 miles, making cruising for customers impossible. Electric hansoms did not catch on, and in 1907, when 300 cabs burned in a garage fire, the company went belly up. Horse cabs looked ready to recover lost ground.[7]

But in 1907 Harry Allen, a New York businessman incensed at being overcharged by a hansom cab driver, decided to start a taxi service that charged a fixed price per mile. Allen went to France, where, with capital provided by French, English, and Wall Street backers, he bought sixty-five shiny, red, gasoline-powered Darracq cabs, complete with "taxameters,"

---

7. At the turn of the century, electricity was thought ideal for city driving. Clean, comfortable, with no gears to shift, it was particularly favored by women. The New York Auto Show in 1901 featured 58 steam, 23 electric, and 58 gas models. In 1902 there were more steamers and electrics registered in New York than gas cars. This didn't last. Steamers might blow up. And electric cars could only go 20 miles before recharging, which took two to three hours. In 1905 there were forty-one places electrics could be charged in New York City but few in rural districts. Edison promised he would develop an improved storage battery, but failed. Given cheap domestic petroleum, this put gas ahead. The 1905 Auto Show featured 9 steam, 20 electric and 219 gas models.

and paraded them down Fifth Avenue to a hack stand in front of Harry Black's new Plaza Hotel. Allen's New York Taxicab Company prospered. Within a year he had 700 cabs on the streets, and these pushed out horse-drawn and battery-driven cabs alike. But labor problems laid him low. His uniformed drivers, who earned less than a dollar a day, joined the Teamsters Union and struck; Allen hired hundreds of strikebreakers; a violent war broke out, from which Allen's firm did not recover.

His rivals did better, thanks in part to growing middle-class demand, in part to a labor strategy that granted a fixed wage ($2.50 a day in 1913), and in part to developing a large fleet that had the muscle and resources to bribe its way into monopoly control of cab stands at key hotels, clubs, and restaurants. (Independents were reduced to cruising.) By 1912 the Morris Seaman Corporation owned about 60 percent of the 2,000 cabs in the city, and when it went under in 1916, the Yellow Taxicab Corporation came to the forefront. The day of the horse was done.

Horse-drawn omnibuses bit the dust, too, those few that had survived the electrification onslaught because their routes ran on elite streets whose residents had successfully fought off the introduction of rail transit—notably Fifth Avenue. Then, in 1907, the Fifth Avenue Coach Company introduced imported gasoline-powered De Dion-Bouton buses and scrapped its horses and stable, becoming the first urban motor bus line in the United States. Its green-and-gold double-deckers charged a ten-cent fare down to Washington Square—double the customary cost—and did so well that applications for bus franchises began arriving.

It was in trucking that horses failed to go gently into the night. Motor trucks did make an appearance. Institutions began deploying the new vehicles. Department stores, hospitals, and municipal departments (street cleaning, fire, health, docks, and public works) experimented with them. The Post Office used electric vans to collect and transfer mail among nineteen post offices in Manhattan and the Bronx. And for commercial long-distance hauling it was agreed that—in the words of a 1919 report on "the economic status of the horse"—using horses was "out of the question" given the truck's speed advantage. But inside the city, the horse still made economic sense. Trucks and wagons hauled immense granite blocks and marble columns for Grand Central and other massive construction jobs. In factory and warehouse districts they hauled manufactured goods to and from the docks. They also distributed products such as beer, baked goods, ice, hardware, and coal to local merchants using large 5-ton wagons. Merchants and retail businesses delivered goods such as milk and baked products directly to customers along scheduled routes. Department stores developed extensive delivery services based on large stables of horses, and express companies like American Express and Wells Fargo had their own fleets of horses and vans. In all these cases, horses were advantageous: they were less costly when stuck in traffic (which was often) than gasoline or electric trucks; they could negotiate cobbled streets, which punished trucks; and as they knew their routes, when and where to stop, they were partners as well as tools.

Nevertheless, the decline continued apace. In 1910 there were over 125,000 horses within the city limits; by 1920 the number had been cut by more than half. (In 1918 Barren Island received 600 dead horses, a considerable number, but nothing like the thousands that had arrived a decade before.) A reinforcing dynamic set in that made horse usage ever harder to sustain. Asphalt surfaces spread, to car fanciers' delight, but they were too slippery for horses. Neighborhoods were increasingly intolerant of stables because of perceived risks of disease and fire. Manure, once a valuable by-product of street railway stables, had now become a liability, its price declining because of competition from imported guano fertilizers.

Some stables were converted to auto housing, but others couldn't be—like the enormous Dakota Stables (on the southerly blockfront of 75th between Amsterdam and Broadway) whose ramps were too steep—and were torn down. Stables didn't disappear; indeed, some of the grandest were built after 1900, like the massive seven-story horse-hotel-cum-auction-arena between East 24th and 25th Streets, whose galleries seated a thousand spectators. But the six-story Tichenor-Grand Stable off Central Park West between 61st and 62nd, built in 1906, would prove to be the last of New York's great horse palaces.

Clearly, as an article in *Munsey's Magazine* in 1913 observed, the "horse has become unprofitable. He is too costly to buy and too costly to keep."[8] But if an auto future was rolling into sight, it was the city's spectacular rail-based system that made possible the era's massive relocation of the populace, which now poured into the wide open spaces of Greater New York.[9]

8. Yet one opinion survey of officials involved in horse shows, riding academies, and horse racing reported that the interest of equestrians in high-grade horses, especially riding and saddle horses, was increasing because "a wonderful horse holds the human interest much more than any mechanical exhibit could hope to do."

9. The future was also flying into sight. Almost immediately after the Wright Brothers first skimmed the air at Kitty Hawk, fragile wire-and-canvas airplanes were looping the loop out at Long Island aerodromes. But though planes were more startling than cars, at this time they had far less impact; even so, they served as a symbol of almost magical hopes to the younger generation.

10

Housing

OLD LAW, NEW LAW

In 1856 the New York state legislature launched a full-scale investigation of working-class housing in the slums of Manhattan. Its 1857 report found the great bulk of domiciles to be "without room sufficient for civilized existence." Some were so bad that "it is astounding that everyone doesn't die of pestilence." This galvanized the legislature into drafting the state's first housing code. It did not, however, get beyond the drafting stage. The prospect of regulation led builders and owners to raise an enormous hue and cry that forced the legislature to abandon the effort.

In 1867 the legislature authorized another investigation. Statistics were amassed. Fifty-two percent of Manhattan's tenements were found to be "in a condition detrimental to the health and dangerous to the lives of the occupants." This time the legislators passed the Tenement House Law, New York's first regulation of working-class housing. It required ventilation, one water closet for every twenty residents, and fire escapes, among other things. The law, however, was loosely worded and loophole ridden. For fire escapes, a wooden ladder would do.

In 1879, another investigation, another law. This one required every tenement bedroom to have a window opening directly onto a street, a yard—or an acceptable substitute. Like the 28-inch-wide air shaft created between two adjacent wasp-waisted buildings. Builders leapt to provide these "dumbbell" tenements—by 1900 there would be 13,600 of them below

Manhattan's 14th Street, 28,000 above. Landlords packed four families into each of the five or six floors, with each family (plus boarders) squashed into a three- or four-room apartment, whose "bedrooms" measured 7′ × 8½′. The air shafts—noisy with the quarrels of twenty-plus families, and noisome from the cooking odors of twenty-plus kitchens—became garbage dumps and firetraps, which shot flames up from one story to the next.

In 1890 journalist Jacob Riis's housing investigation—presented in *How the Other Half Lives*—warned the propertied classes that dreadful conditions in the tenement quarters had bred "a proletariat ready and able to avenge the wrongs of their crowds." These restless, pent-up multitudes "hold within their clutch the wealth and business of New York, hold them at their mercy in the day of mob-rule and wrath."

In 1894 the state established a Tenement House Committee. It investigated. It reported. Over 70 percent of Manhattan's population of roughly 1,800,000 lived in multi-family dwellings. There was terrific overcrowding, a high rate of disease, and a lack of accessible parks and playgrounds. The committee urged a policy of reform through demolition, asking that bad buildings be destroyed, thus creating open spaces for neighborhood parks. The Tenement House Act of 1895 authorized this slum clearance approach. It empowered the Board of Health to condemn buildings judged uninhabitable. But landlords and developers successfully challenged its new powers. Other reformers cautioned that simply subtracting low-rent housing from the market would hardly improve the situation.

In 1897 some reformers took heart from the charter establishing Greater New York, as it called for a commission to revise the building code. One of these optimists was Lawrence Veiller (pronounced vay-yay), who, after graduating from City College in 1890 (at age 18), had worked as a volunteer for the University Settlement and the Charity Organization Society (COS). During the mid-'90s depression, he had become convinced that squalid tenement conditions were created by greedy builders and landlords, and that it was "unquestionably the duty of the state" to rectify matters.

The state, alas, was often in bed with the profiteers, as Veiller discovered when he worked in the Building Department (1895–97) during Mayor William Strong's reform administration. There he learned firsthand how contractors, architects, and real estate developers, abetted by Tammany politicians, watered down some housing regulations and bribed their way past others. Veiller decided that it would take a dedicated permanent watchdog body "to secure the enforcement of the existing laws relating to tenement-houses." In particular, such an entity could start by putting pressure on the forthcoming Building Code Commission.

In 1898 Veiller took this idea to Robert W. de Forest, president of the COS. De Forest, a wealthy and well-connected lawyer, was director of a score of banks, railroads, and insurance companies. He was also, like his friend Theodore Roosevelt, a New York aristocrat (though of Huguenot, not Dutch, descent), and sensitive to his social responsibilities.[1] In December 1898 de Forest set up a COS Tenement House Committee to lobby for housing reform and placed Veiller at its helm.

---

1. Born in Gotham (in 1848) and raised in Washington Square, de Forest was a direct descendant of Jessé de Forest, leader of the group of seventeenth-century French-speaking Protestants from what is now Belgium who arrived in New Amsterdam in 1624 (though without de Forest, who had gone to Guyana and died there). After graduating Yale in 1870 and Columbia Law in 1872, Robert joined his father's law firm and married Emily Johnston, daughter of John Taylor Johnson, president of the Central Railroad of New Jersey. De Forest would go on to serve as general counsel for his father-in-law's firm for fifty years and become a very wealthy man.

When the Building Code Commission started work in January 1899, Veiller submitted a raft of recommendations. The reform community backed him. The City Club, Social Reform Club, Architectural League, and other charitable societies all testified. They were all ignored. Indeed, when the commission delivered its report to the municipal legislature in September 1899, Veiller declared that the building code had been moved "a distinct step backward." It permitted tenements to reach eight stories in height, if the first two floors were "fireproofed," and then permitted the installation of wooden dumbwaiter shafts—a serious fire hazard. Tenement fires were a major worry in the working-class districts. In March 1899 the Central Federated Union had demanded "publication of a list of all dangerous buildings" and insisted that "all the dangerous tenement houses should be included in the list." Protest availed nothing. The code, according to the *Times*, was "rushed through the Municipal Assembly by order of Richard Croker in defiance of the opposition of architects and members of the Tenement House Committee of the Charities Organization Society." In October 1899 Mayor Van Wyck duly signed on the dotted line.

Furious, Veiller set out to mobilize public opinion behind a campaign that would induce the state legislature to undo the work of the municipal authorities. Working "about 16 hours a day for months," he put together an exhibition whose general purpose, as he explained, was to prove that in New York "the working-man is housed worse than in any other city of the civilized world, notwithstanding the fact that he pays more money for such accommodations than is paid elsewhere." The show opened in February 1900 in the Sherry Building at Fifth Avenue and 38th Street. Photographs and cardboard models of the Lower East Side forcefully evoked

"Saving Lives at a Tenement-House Fire (An Actual Scene)," 1899. (New York Public Library, Art and Picture Collection)

"Model of Block on Lower East Side from the Tenement House Exhibition of 1900." *The Charity Organization Society of the City of New York Eighteenth Annual Report, from July, 1899 to June, 1900 Inclusive,* 1900. (Columbia University, Community Service Society Collection)

the choked reality. One display recreated in miniature a tenement block, bounded by Chrystie, Forsyth, Canal, and Bayard Streets, whose density level reached 1,515 per acre. Maps and charts correlated crammed conditions with tenant tuberculosis—and landlord profits. New York, Veiller summarized, was "the City of Living Death."[2]

Ten thousand visited the exhibition, the biggest on housing the city had ever seen. Theodore Roosevelt, then governor, attended and was impressed. "Tell me what you want," he told de Forest and Veiller, "and I will help you get it." What they wanted, and got, was New York State's establishment in 1900 of a Tenement House Commission, of which de Forest was made chair and Veiller made secretary. More investigation ensued, but Veiller went beyond cataloging horrors to suggesting solutions. The key problem, in his judgment, was the assumption that decent multi-family housing could be built, profitably, on a standard New York 25' × 100' plot. The dumbbell tenement was an inhuman failure because it accepted preposterous constraints. Like City Beautiful proponents, Veiller chafed at the grid.

Part of the solution, therefore, was to break with existing tenement design. For an alternative approach Veiller turned to Ernest Flagg, an architect who, for all his prestigious commissions and family links to powerful New York clans, concerned himself with working-class housing. In an 1894 *Scribner's Magazine* article—"The New York Tenement House Evil and Its Cure"—he had proposed merging four standard lots and erecting on the consolidated parcel a 100' × 100' structure, wrapped around a bright and airy central courtyard. Flagg's "light-court" plan, in essence, adapted Parisian living arrangements to New York conditions. Veiller now proposed a new housing code that outlawed the dumbbell and fostered Flagg's light-court, in effect eliminating 25'-lot construction from the mass market. He didn't stop there. His code also mandated minimum room sizes, required separate toilets in each apartment, and imposed stringent fire-protection measures. Owners of existing dumbbells would be required to cut windows into shrouded interior rooms, install water closets, add fire escapes, and illuminate dark hallways. All of this would be embodied in a state law. In addition, a municipal Tenement House Department would be created to ride herd on builders and landlords, bypassing the corrupt Building Department.

It took a struggle, but the Tenement House Law was passed in 1901. The proposed department was created, too, and reform Mayor Seth Low, now in possession of City Hall,

2. In the United States, Gotham was in a class by itself. The aggregate ratio of persons to inhabited structures in most American cities, where single family detached or row houses were the norm, was less than 7:1. Runner-up Chicago's was 9:1. But New York City, its multi-story tenements jammed with family members and enough boarders to carry the rent, weighed in at 20:1. In the North Atlantic world, only German cities, girdled by speculative land companies that refused to build till land values soared, outranked Gotham, averaging (by 1914) 33:1 in the biggest metropolises and hitting 76:1 in Berlin. In overall density per acre, however, the Lower East Side was number one on the planet in 1900, with the Tenth Ward out-peopling the Koombarwara District of Bombay.

"Air-Shaft Permitted by the Law Prior to 1901: 28 Inches Wide. New-Law Court: Substitute for Air Shaft 12½ Feet Wide, 25 Feet Long." *The Charity Organization Society of the City of New York Eighteenth Annual Report, from July, 1899 to June, 1900 Inclusive,* 1900. (Rare Book & Manuscript Library, Columbia University)

"Rear View of 'New Law' Tenement Houses," c. 1910. (Rare Book & Manuscript Library, Columbia University)

appointed de Forest as commissioner. He, in turn, promptly appointed Veiller as his first deputy commissioner.

The established interests did not meekly acquiesce. In 1902 and 1903 thirty-one bills were introduced to repeal or amend the legislation. They were promoted by a combination (in Veiller's words) of "the speculative builders, the material men, the institutions which made loans on such property, the architects who had to learn their trade all over again," and owners of existing tenements who were required to shell out serious money to make their houses comply with the law. In successfully fending off all such challenges, middle- and upper-class reformers had support from working people. Mass meetings were held all over the East Side, delegations waited on Mayor Low and Governor Odell, and a monster petition, signed by 40,000 East Side tenement dwellers, protesting against any change in the law, was sent to the legislature.[3]

The impact of the new order in lower Manhattan was contradictory. The Tenement House Law barred bad housing. But it didn't guarantee the production of good housing, at prices the poor could afford. Under the new rules, tenements cost more to put up, so landlords charged higher rents. This ensured that improved Lower East Side tenements would be reserved for an elite of manufacturers, skilled artisans, and shopkeepers. Most working people found that the reforms *reduced* the availability of cheap housing.

The existing housing stock, moreover, was being whittled away by the era's transportation improvements. In 1903, to celebrate the opening of the Williamsburg Bridge, the Board of Aldermen issued a commemorative booklet that took notice of the fact that 10,000 area residents had "already been displaced" and "been compelled to seek new homes." Additional demolitions to widen approach roads were expected to evict 5,000 more in Manhattan, 3,000 more in Brooklyn. The booklet offered a tip of the municipal hat to the departed: "This seems to be the occasion to make acknowledgment to the many thousands of our fellow-citizens who have thus submitted to inconvenience in the public interest."

"Inconvenience" was putting it mildly. To make matters worse, as the supply of awful but affordable housing was diminishing, demand was soaring—from the dispossessed, and from the impoverished immigrants pouring into the area. Landlords of dumbbell buildings saw their opportunity and took it, hiking rents by 20–30 percent. This triggered

Hester Street Jam-Packed. "In the heart of New York's ghetto, Collier's Weekly, January 24, 1903." (Art and Picture Collection, The New York Public Library)

---

3. The East Side advanced even more radical solutions. The 1901 platform of the Greater New York section of the Social Democratic Party included a public housing plank: "Tenement laws should be improved, the city itself to erect fire-proof tenement houses, with all needed provisions"—a recurrent demand of militants dating at least to the 1857 calls on the municipality to build low-income housing on city-owned land.

an outraged response in the spring of 1904, when several hundred Jewish residents of the Lower East Side, led by neighborhood women who well remembered the 1902 Ladies' Anti–Beef Trust boycott, called on tenants to "fight the landlord as they had the czar" by withholding rents. Drawing on established labor union language, they called their protests "rent strikes," their organizations "tenant unions," their non-cooperative neighbors "scabs." Union and socialist men formed a thousand-member-strong New York Rent Protective Association, modeled on the *landsmanshaftn* (mutual aid societies formed by Jewish immigrants from the same towns or regions). It provided small sums to recently evicted tenants. Under tremendous pressure the movement fragmented and collapsed, but by then many local landlords had rolled back rents, and the protest was widely deemed a success.

Three years later, the Panic of 1907 left tens of thousands on the Lower East Side unemployed and unable to pay rent. When evictions of families spread rapidly, housewives and young garment-worker women (notably shirtwaist maker and union activist Pauline Newman) organized a resistance movement. In December they sent notes to landlords explaining that because of "the present industrial depression," their husbands were "out of work" and couldn't pay rents, which had already "risen skywards" over the last two years. They demanded a reduction of 20–30 percent. One landlord who came to a tenant meeting and argued that "he had the right to ask whatever he wants for his merchandise" was shouted down, and others who proceeded with evictions were threatened with violence. The tenants picketed, marched, demonstrated, and canvassed for support. The Socialist Party provided organizational and financial backing. Settlement house leaders Lillian Wald and Mary Kingsbury Simkhovitch called for a program of rent control, a novel concept, arguing rents should be capped at 30 percent of a family's monthly income. The strike spread to Brooklyn and Harlem. Two thousand families won rent reductions. Landlords, however, won the

G. G. Bain, "East Side Eviction," ca. 1900–10. (Library of Congress Prints and Photographs Division)

backing of police and courts. After they secured three-day eviction orders for 6,000 families, the strike ended, leaving no institutional structure behind.

THE 1901 LEGISLATION MARKED A TURNING POINT in the history of housing in New York City. The flood of buildings that would be erected according to its specifications would become known as "New Law" tenements; those that had been constructed under the now superseded 1879 ordinance were branded "Old Law" tenements. Most New Law structures would arise out in the vast stretches of Greater New York that were rapidly being made accessible by the mass transit matrix set in place during the boom years. In time this would begin to address the hyper-concentration of the population. (In 1900 the Lower East Side—a scant one-eighty-second of the city's 305-square-mile territory—was home to one-sixth of its residents.) But much of the new housing would be beyond the economic reach of Old Law renters. How to ensure decent housing for them?

Veiller understood that regulation alone wouldn't address this issue, and he believed part of the problem lay in the process of production. To his mind the dumbbell had survived so long because it suited the needs of the speculative builders who dominated construction. These small entrepreneurs—often middle-class German, Irish, Jewish, or Italian immigrants—didn't have much capital. They borrowed funds, put up a few structures, sold them off, and started again. Veiller believed—like the corporate promoters then stoking the merger wave—that competition between small-scale entrepreneurs was inefficient and uncivilized. But if small builders were no longer to house the poor and laboring classes, who would?

MODEL HOMES

Some reformers believed corporate philanthropy was the answer. Concentrated capital could work on the requisite grand scale, and could afford to settle for moderate profits. As an example of what was possible, reformers pointed to the City & Suburban Homes Company (C&S), an enterprise launched in 1896 by housing activists (including Jacob Riis, Alfred Tredway White, Felix Adler, and Bishop Rainsford) and financiers (among them Cornelius Vanderbilt II, Isaac N. Seligman, Darius Ogden Mills, and the brothers W. Bayard Cutting and Robert Fulton Cutting). Inspired by the work of London philanthropists, who by that point had established more than thirty limited-dividend housing companies, City & Suburban Homes aimed to provide wage-earners with "improved, wholesome homes at current rates." It was capitalized at a million dollars (J. P. Morgan helped issue its stock), and its dividends were limited to 5 percent.

For its first venture the company had Ernest Flagg design the Clark Estate, a complex of six-story buildings on a site (West End/Amsterdam/68th/69th) given by Elizabeth Scriven (Mrs. Alfred Corning) Clark, heir to the Singer fortune, in exchange for shares in C&S. When completed in 1898, its 373 apartments each contained its own toilet, laundry, and tub.

In 1900 City & Suburban began constructing the First Avenue Estate, between 64th and 65th Streets. It offered middle-class features to a working-class constituency: broad central courts, apartments with light and ventilation, fireproofed staircases, central hot water and steam heat, gas fixtures and ranges, and built-in closets. When finished in 1915, the project covered the entire block between First and Avenue A (now York). It was complemented by the Avenue A Estate, another massive complex containing 1,200 apartments, which spanned 78th and 79th Streets between York and the East River, at the edge of Yorkville; when completed in 1913 it was the largest low-income-housing project in the world. C&S, as per its name, also urged "suburban" development. It built Homewood, a community of two-story brick-and-timber cottages, on a 530-acre tract in Brooklyn's New Utrecht (between 16th/18th Avenues and 67th/74th Streets), fifty-five minutes from downtown Manhattan. The company offered twenty-year mortgages (10 percent down and 5 percent interest) and provided life insurance policies to cover repayment in the event of a borrower's death. It supplied city gas and water, trees, hedges, sidewalks, and macadamized streets. And it barred saloons, factories, and tenements.

City & Suburban sought temperate, steadily employed tenants who could pay the average of ninety-three cents per room per week. It had no trouble filling its buildings with policemen, firemen, clerks, bookkeepers, salespeople, and dressmakers. The company ran a tight house. Each week, when the corps of agents collected rents and attended to maintenance, they also checked out each tenant's continuing desirability—watching for an "unkempt apartment or some other infraction of the rules." "The drunkard, the incorrigible, the criminal, the immoral, the lazy and shiftless," decreed C&S president Elgin Ralston Lovell Gould, were to be directed to public lodging. The associated Junior League Hotel, built with subscriptions by wealthy members, also insisted on a "morally healthy" environment.

Other model housing projects—some funded by individual millionaires—adopted similar policies.

Banker Darius Ogden Mills commissioned Flagg to build two lodging houses for single men. (Mills House No. 1 was on the south side of Bleecker Street, between Thompson and Sullivan; No. 2 was at Rivington and Chrystie.) Twenty-five cents bought a bed for the night in one of 1,500 tiny cubicles (facing either the street or an airy atrium). Residents had access to a smoking and reading room, a basement restaurant serving cheap meals, and self-service laundries. Tramps and objectionables were excluded, and the conduct of bachelor tenants was rigidly regulated.

Ann Harriman (Mrs. William Kissam) Vanderbilt funded the architecturally innovative Shively Sanitary Tenements on East 77th and 78th Streets (later known as the Cherokee Flats). The Phelps Stokes Fund underwrote the first philanthropic project for black tenants since the Workingman's Home in 1855—the Tuskegee on West 62nd Street (later acquired by C&S). And in 1905 former Carnegie partner Henry Phipps formed Phipps Houses with a million-dollar start-up grant, and it, too, erected model homes for African Americans (on 63rd Street, east of West End Avenue [1907], and West 64th, between Amsterdam and West End [1911]).

For all their innovations of design and management, such efforts made little dent in the need for affordable housing. By 1916 Manhattan's model tenements sheltered at most 18,000 people, and virtually none of the buildings were downtown where

Rendering, Courtyard, Phipps Houses. "Phipps Houses Model Tenement Number 1, Showing Front and Spacious Interior Court," 1906. (New York Public Library, Art and Picture Collection)

they were most needed. The problem was straightforward. These finely wrought projects generated dividends of 4–5 percent, often lower. Housing the middle and upper classes fetched returns of 5–10 percent, often higher. Even in the boom years of the early twentieth century, capitalists prepared to settle for less than the average rate of profit weren't thick on the ground.

A MUNICIPAL ROLE?

If neither small-scale nor corporate capital could or would produce enough low-cost worker housing, who might? Some reformers—especially the growing number who were attuned to European developments—thought public intervention was the answer.

In Britain, the 1890 Housing of the Working Classes Act gave local authorities the power to borrow funds for building low-cost homes. Glasgow and Liverpool each constructed more than 2,000 units, and the London County Council built 15,000. But like philanthropic housing, public housing was affordable only to the skilled and steadily employed, not the truly poor. And opposition by private interests held government construction, even in London, to less than 5 percent of the total housing stock. On the continent, Belgium and France established state banks that made inexpensive loans to non-commercial builders for sound worker housing. And Germany allowed social insurance funds to invest in non- or limited-profit development by working-class building associations. Frankfurt even bought land along its new streetcar corridors and leased it to co-operative building societies, which by 1914 had produced 7.2 percent of the city's homes.

These European forays into municipal housing proved barely thinkable in New York City, much less doable. The real estate industry vehemently opposed public initiatives. So did the courts. And so, for that matter, did leading reformers. Veiller, for all his belief in rigorous regulation, considered housing a commodity whose provision was best left to the market. Government competition with private capital was unfair. With its superior resources and access to cheaper credit, it would drive private enterprise out of the field. It was also fiscally unsound: given heavy immigration, meeting demand would entail colossal expenditures. And if the municipality *did* build homes, some do-gooders would undoubtedly insist that it also provide the poor with bread and other necessities they couldn't afford. Where would it all end but in socialism? Besides, Veiller added, government enterprises were inherently inefficient; public housing would destroy its occupants' "self-dependence"; and in a city where "government" meant "Tammany," municipal tenements would lead to mammoth corruption, as politicians stocked them with political supporters. Veiller was not averse to all European ideas—his own Tenement House Act had borrowed heavily from English regulatory practice—but he drew the line at public construction.

With even ardent critics of laissez-faire so opposed to municipal housing, small wonder it was a nonstarter—with one exception, due (albeit indirectly) to Jacob Riis. Back in 1896, when Riis and Roosevelt, then police commissioner, were making their midnight prowls, the duo passed a Church Street police station. Riis told TR how back in 1872, as a penniless immigrant, he had been forced to lodge there. He had left his dog outside in accordance with the rules. In the middle of the night, Riis awoke and discovered his mother's locket missing. He raised such a ruckus that he was escorted bodily to the street, where his dog attacked one of the police officers, who in turn killed it. Roosevelt was so outraged at this recital that he vowed he would ban police-station lodging within twenty-four hours—and did. As Riis later wrote: "The murder of my dog was avenged."

The dog's soul perhaps rested more easily, but the 10,000 men pitched into homelessness did not. The popular press ran cartoons of heartless men shivering outside closed police lodging houses. In December the city set up a sanctuary in a rented factory at 398 First Avenue—but for only 270 men and 47 women. Not until 1909 did the city erect a Municipal Lodging House at 438 East 25th Street, in a building designed to serve as a shelter. But this afforded rudimentary accommodations to only 1,000 people, a small percentage of the disabled, the dependent, and those temporarily displaced from the labor market. In economic downturns, shelter capacity quickly proved unequal to demand; in the crisis of 1914–15, estimates of those "with no fixed abode" ran to 60,000.

Housing for the down-and-out was left mainly to private enterprise or private charity. Cheap lodging houses multiplied on the Lower East Side, places where ten or fifteen cents bought a bug-infested bed or a canvas-string hammock, and two cents fetched a cellar chair. In 1909, according to *The Wretches of Povertyville: A Sociological Study of the Bowery*, the work of a New York physician, the area sheltered twenty-five thousand homeless men each night. By 1917 the Bowery had become a skid row, complete with a network of missions, Salvation Army Halls, flophouses, labor agencies, lunch counters, used clothing stores, cheap saloons, and pawnshops.[4]

FIGHTING CONGESTION

Clearly, neither building codes, model homes, nor public housing would halt the piling-up of people in the Lower East Side and other clotted communities. Quite the opposite: with an average of 90,000 immigrants pouring into the city each year, things were getting steadily worse. Then came the recession of 1907–8, which sent homelessness surging and triggered rent strikes. Clearly, fresh thinking was required.

It arrived, as if on cue, from the settlement houses—outposts of social reform dotted about the city, in which resident activists aided their poor and working-class neighbors in tackling a variety of social ills. Three of these activists took the lead in re-spotlighting the crisis of the slums. Lillian Wald ran the Nurses Settlement; in operation on the Lower East Side since 1893, it was incorporated in 1903 as the Henry Street Settlement, as by then it owned five buildings on Henry, between Montgomery and Grand. Florence Kelley, who had been living in and working out of Jane Addams's Hull House in Chicago, moved to New York in 1899, where she settled into the Henry Street Settlement, and became executive secretary of the National Consumers League (which brought consumer power to bear on labor issues). Mary Kingsbury Simkhovitch was headworker at Greenwich House, located at 26 Jones Street, between Bleecker and West 4th in Greenwich Village; established in 1902, it was one of the newest settlements.

As community organizers, their modus operandi was to analyze local needs by undertaking sociological and economic surveys, then publicize the results in an effort to rectify the situation. Hitherto they had focused seriatim on specific issues, like the terrible state of housing, health and child care, recreation and education, or wages and working conditions. But they now came to decide that these several problems were insoluble without confronting what Kelley called "the foundation problem of congestion." Heretofore she and her colleagues

---

4. The decline of the Bowery, once the grand allée of working-class New York, was not an overnight affair. From the 1870s to the 1890s many of the "legitimate" entertainment venues had drifted north and west to the Tenderloin, leaving behind those devoted to dispensing cheap drink. (By 1891 the Bowery and Park Row had one-sixth of the city's saloons.) Women, too, largely departed the scene (apart from prostitutes), leaving behind an increasingly male terrain. Commerce mostly evacuated the area; the new bridges bought a surge in pass-through traffic; real estate values sagged; the street hit the skids. Headlines took notice: "Slowly the Bowery Passes into the Shadow of Tradition"; "The Street That Died Young." But in truth the Bowery had been transformed: housing and feeding the down-and-out had become the new basis of its macro-economy.

had, she admitted, uncritically accepted "overcrowding as permanent" and dealt only with its results. "Why did we not see, years ago, that people who are crowded must remain poor, growing weaker and less capable of self-help from generation to generation?" It was time to focus attention on the "evils" of congestion itself—not the traffic congestion that preoccupied skyscraper restrictionists, nor the sidewalk congestion that troubled Fifth Avenue merchants, but the housing congestion that blighted the lives of residents.

In 1907, accordingly, Simkhovitch, Wald, Kelley, and a few like-minded colleagues such as the Reverend Gaylord S. White (headworker of the Union Settlement uptown at East 104th Street) formed the Committee on Congestion of Population (CCP). And in March, to take charge of figuring out what caused congestion and what could be done about it, they hired Benjamin C. Marsh as executive secretary and housed him at Greenwich House, the de facto headquarters of the CCP.

Marsh, the son of New England Congregational missionaries, had graduated from Grinnell College in Iowa, worked for the YMCA, fund-raised for overseas church missions, and done graduate work in economics at the University of Chicago (1899–1900) and the University of Pennsylvania (1902–5). By 1907 Marsh, 28 years old, had evolved a worldview that admixed social gospelism, Fabian socialism, and Henry George's single-taxism.

That summer the Committee on Congestion dispatched Marsh to study city planning and housing policies in Germany, France, and Britain, with the highlight of his trip being attendance at the Eighth International Housing Congress in London. Marsh was impressed by arguments that housing reformers should concentrate their efforts not in the center of cities but in the open fields on their fringes, and he was particularly taken with the initiatives of English and German municipalities along these lines. There was a lot of buzz, in particular, about two British demonstration projects—not of model housing, but of model communities. In 1903 Ebenezer Howard, a utopian socialist, had conceptualized what he called a "garden city," an experimental environment that combined country and city, factory and farmland, workplace and residence, and that retained (as per Henry George) any increase in land value for the working-class residents themselves. Architects Raymond Unwin and Barry Parker were selected to design the first model at Letchworth, in Hertfordshire, 34 miles out of London. (Tours of the town-in-progress were available to conferees.) The enterprise had gained instant international recognition, and only months before the London congress, in December 1906, a Garden Cities Association had been established in New York, by Christian socialist William Dwight Porter Bliss, to promote American spin-offs; it attracted many high-powered supporters but did not survive the crash of 1907. In 1905 Unwin had been recruited to design a garden suburb in Hampstead, on London's edge. The idea was to create a factory-less version of the garden city—a bedroom community from which workers would commute to central-city jobs—and Unwin's village of meandering streets, squares, and cul-de-sacs immediately became another imaginable alternative to tenement-packed quartiers.

Once back in New York, Marsh and the CCP leadership prepared an exhibition—inspired by Veiller's promotional methods, if not his analysis and program. It opened in March 1908 at the American Museum of Natural History, with presentations by nearly forty organizations, including the Municipal Art Society (now moving away from a narrowly aesthetic approach to planning after the 1907 Improvement Commission report's disappointing reception). Popularly known as the "Congestion Show," it featured a life-size mockup of a typical 12′ × 12′ tenement room; charts comparing death rates in different neighborhoods, with mortality closely correlated with density; diagrams documenting concentration of land ownership; and photographs from the Charity Organization Society, the Tenement House

Department, and the National Consumers League, graphically displaying the social consequences of congestion.

Most proposed solutions focused on dispersing residents from the city's core to its periphery, ideally by providing them with superior, healthier, and more affordable housing.
How this was to be accomplished remained somewhat vague. The City Club, taken with the
garden-city model, suggested relocating lower Manhattan's factories to land along outer-
borough waterfronts or transport lines, and then planting around them single- or double-
family houses, with parks and recreational facilities sited nearby. But the city had no power
to force factories to leave Manhattan, and no manufacturer would likely relocate without a
workforce and infrastructure already in place.[5]

There was widespread agreement that the expansion of mass transit was an indispensable
precondition for disaggregation, and widespread condemnation of August Belmont's then-
stubborn refusal to extend IRT service to the city's edge. "More Subways!" was a plank
around which a diverse set of players could rally, one reason that Henry Morgenthau agreed
to serve as honorary chair of the Committee on Congestion of Population. In 1905
Morgenthau had dissolved his alliance with Harry Black, formed his own Henry Morgenthau
Company, and plunged full tilt into real estate speculation, concentrating on properties along
the new transit lines in Washington Heights and the Bronx. The CCP's push for decongestion dovetailed perfectly with his desire to build up the outer boroughs, so he gave the group
free office space in one of his partially filled buildings, and pledged his name and $1,500 to
the cause.

Though Marsh and Morgenthau now worked together in harness, their visions for suburban development were markedly different. The socialist Marsh sought housing for workers
that would free them from the tyranny of landlords, while Morgenthau believed congestion
should be fought as "an evil that breeds physical disease, moral depravity, discontent, and
socialism." City & Suburban's E. R. A. Gould also believed home ownership would wean
workers from radical politics, noting that suburban proprietors tended to become "reflective,
careful, prudent, wedded to order and rational conservatism and usually turn a deaf ear to
specious isms." The *Real Estate Record and Builders Guide* agreed that dispersing the working class into freestanding cottages or two-family houses in Brooklyn would do far more to
"counteract anarchistic tendencies" than would "military or legislative influences." It wouldn't
eradicate the slums, but at least it would separate "the industrious and self-respecting poor"
from "the less regenerate people by whom they are surrounded."

Marsh, though content to enter a tactical alliance with Morgenthau, was convinced that
truly tackling congestion would require a profound reordering of the entire city-building
process, and of the larger framework of economic relationships—particularly those of land
and labor—within which it was nested. And that, in turn, would require expanding the power
of municipal government—in a manner akin to the various municipal ownership proposals
then being floated for city intervention in transit and utilities. Marsh wanted to enable cities
to plan their overall development, not merely scattered pieces of it.

He was confirmed in his convictions by a second sojourn in Europe during the summer
of 1908, and a sustained encounter with German municipal initiatives. After returning he

5. Edward Ewing Pratt of the New York School of Philanthropy followed up with a study of industries that had *already* moved to
the suburbs, which showed that many of their Italian workers moved along with them. Pratt suggested that perhaps private
philanthropic agencies could underwrite the costs of relocation. His *Industrial Causes of Congestion of Population in New York City*
(1911) also stressed the need for government to take responsibility for planning city development.

published *An Introduction to City Planning: Democracy's Challenge and the American City* (1909), the first treatise on the subject by an American, in which he suggested ways that Germany's reforms might be applied in an American (and specifically New York) context. In this compact book, and in the talks he gave at a huge City Planning exhibition held in 1909 at the 22nd Regiment Armory at Broadway and 67th (which his CCP and the MAS co-sponsored), and in a series of essays he churned out over the next few years, Marsh laid out, often bluntly, what was wrong and how to fix it.

His first proposition was that congestion of population was a consequence of "the high cost of land." Garden cities and suburbs on the periphery were nice ideas, but to be made affordable they had to be built on inexpensive land. If speculators got to the outskirts first, they would buy up farmland cheap, and quickly sell it dearer to other speculators, who would flip it again, and again, at each resale jacking the price higher, until it reached what was considered to be its highest future value, if put to its most profitable use. (Alternatively the first speculator, if as deep-pocketed as the Astors and Goelets, might simply hoard the land—doing nothing to increase its actual value—and wait for its price to soar as metropolitan development came ever closer.)[6]

The buyer who eventually developed the land had to do so in a way that would generate sufficient income to cover the extravagant cost of the land itself, as well as to produce a profit on the capital invested in building. This could be done either by constructing pricey housing for the affluent, or by throwing up New Law tenements, into which one could pack working-class tenants, making money through volume sales, not unit price. Tenants, in turn, if the rents were too high for their low-wage income, would be forced to pack in boarders, as they had done on the Lower East Side. And—voilà!—downtown congestion would be transplanted to the outlying areas.

The bottom line was that speculators *liked* congestion, as did subway and utilities magnates; it created bigger markets and higher profits. It was a fantasy, therefore, to think subway extensions alone were the solution—they could well be part of the problem, as the mere announcement of their pending arrival would unleash a speculative bidding war.

There were, Marsh argued, solutions to this conundrum. One was to have the city itself buy up land on its periphery before the speculators got there. Were the land kept cheap, by cutting out speculators' (unearned) profits, rentals could be kept low. Not only would this pull worker tenants to the periphery, but their mass exodus, he believed, would deflate land and property values in the center. Here the inspiration came from German cities, especially Frankfurt, which had bought up inexpensive undeveloped peripheral land, thus removing vast areas from the market. The government then extended long-term leases to building societies, which had pledged to build low-cost worker housing on the urban rim.

Marsh wanted New York to do likewise—get out to the Bronx and Queens and Staten Island ahead of "the land speculator or the grafting politician." Riis, too, argued that New York should buy up land "on the outskirts toward which the speculator is reaching, and to hold it lest he get his grip upon it." As Riis wrote de Forest in 1910: "We have built bridges and subways, but ahead of the surging crowd that seeks the open, is the real estate speculator, buying up the land and building tenements when there should be no tenements and is no need of them other than that which proceeds from his own greed."

---

6. Frederic C. Leubuscher, a single-tax activist, noted in 1914 that "the Astor estate owns about 500 acres of unimproved land in the Bronx, and it has a large sign there reading: 'Astor estate. Not for sale.' What does all this mean? Simply that these big estates and corporations are holding these lots until the increased population will allow them to unload at enormous profits."

Another solution was to levy a tax on unearned increases in land values. Again, Frankfurt seemed exemplary. In 1904 it imposed a tax that skimmed off speculative profits every time a title was transferred; by 1911 650 German municipalities were doing the same, though bitter opposition from property owners and imperial authorities kept such exactions to modest levels. Marsh also urged taxing undeveloped land heavily—following Henry George and the British Fabians—to force speculators to disgorge hoarded territory, either by building on it, or dumping it on the market, which, by boosting supply, would help depreciate the value of all land.

The most comprehensive solution that Marsh advanced, again drawing on urban German precedents, was not only to open up new low-cost land to development, but to establish some controls on *how* it was to be developed—indeed, how the entire city, center as well as periphery, was to be developed. Here the model was zoning, the imposition of legal restrictions on the use to which land could be put (encouraging or barring factories, permitting or precluding tenements) and the type of structures that could be built upon it (regulating the heights of buildings or coverage of plots). Frankfurt had zoned its entire territory back in 1891, primarily to defend bourgeois villa districts from encroachment by proletarian tenements. But zoning evolved into a device for setting aside districts for low-density, low-cost worker housing—banning tenements forestalled speculation based on garnering multistory rents—and for steering industrial development to districts near rail yards and harbors. Purposeful planning replaced market-driven mayhem.

Marsh argued for importing planning and zoning to Gotham, arguing that "a city without a plan is like a ship without a rudder." His ultimate goal was not mere efficiency, important as that was, but social justice. The city should plan its development—should struggle to enhance its legal capacity to do so, now hampered severely by the courts—for "the prime purpose of improving the homes of the working and professional classes of the city." The Bronx, Brooklyn, and Queens should be set aside. "The duplication of conditions in Manhattan, where we permit the poorer classes to be farmed out for exploitation by real estate speculators and tenement sweaters, must not be permitted in the other boroughs."[7]

Metropolitan planning, argued Kelley and Simkhovitch, could benefit from a dose of British thinking, too. If the city could preemptively purchase land on the edge to keep land cheap, and use zoning to nudge factories out of the center to industrial districts, then the garden-city and garden-suburb models might become practical. If working people were to be drawn to the rim, the new communities would have to afford at least the same quality of life and access to social services as did the central slums. After all, Simkhovitch argued in 1909, for all the misery and squalor of jam-packed neighborhoods, they also provided proximity to work sites, schools, churches, shops, cheap theaters, parks, child care, and health care—things that were important to working people. "The reason the poor like to live in New York is because it is interesting, convenient, and meets their social needs," she pointed out. "They live there for the reason I do; I like it." The best-laid plan was not much good "unless the people like it." To work, the new planned suburbs would have to be made city-ish.

MARSH AND HIS COLLEAGUES MADE REMARKABLE HEADWAY in rallying support for reforms that challenged very powerful interests. When he first came to New York City, Marsh had been introduced to Robert de Forest. He "looked at me," Marsh later recalled, 'with the

---

7. Marsh also wanted the city to seek the power of excess condemnation—the legal device that made Baron Haussmann's transformation of Paris fiscally feasible.

maddening tolerance of a wise old man for a well-intentioned young fool and said, "'If you touch the land problem in New York, you probably won't last here two years."' De Forest was pretty much on target, but it was startling how far Marsh got before being brought down (by De Forest, among others).

Marsh convinced Governor Charles Evans Hughes—who had opened the Congestion Show in 1908—to create a Commission on Distribution of Population, to ponder how to arrange a "more efficient placement of people." Mayor William Jay Gaynor followed suit, establishing a New York City Commission on Congestion of Population (NYCCCP), which was top-heavy with Tammany aldermen. Marsh was made the unpaid secretary of both. The municipal commission, after nearly a year of investigation and public hearings, reported in February 1911 that despite all the new laws regulating tenements, congestion had gotten worse. Strikingly, the group placed much of the blame for overcrowding on the concentration of city landownership in the hands of a few corporations or families. And it called for study of Marsh's proposal to increase taxes on land (discouraging speculation) and to reduce them on buildings (encouraging construction).

Partly this openness to new departures was a reflection of the patent need to do something to address recession-era unrest. Partly the NYCCCP rode the contemporary muckraking wave, which saw investigative journalists tackling housing issues as well as corporate and financial and political malfeasance. In July 1908 *Everybody's* published "The Tenements of Trinity Church" by Charles Edward Russell, exposing the church's unseemly harvesting of profits from its slum housing—notoriously squalid hatcheries of tuberculosis along Varick, Hudson, and West Houston Streets. Trinity doggedly fought each new improvement law, in one instance going to court rather than install tap water on each floor of a tenement. In the end, however, the church was forced to comply. And over the next several years it quietly pulled down blocks of tenements, though without ever confessing culpability.

The NYCCCP also had influential allies, like John G. Agar, president of the Municipal Art Society, who roundly declared that "improvement of the dwellings of the poor should be considered before the erection of monuments and statues and fine public buildings," and who pointed to the exemplary efforts of German municipalities in providing "better housing for the people."

None of this was music to real estate men's ears, nor those of the propertied in general. Charles Pratt, treasurer of Standard Oil, declined to appear before the Congestion Commission, saying, "I don't believe you know how radical that man Marsh is, or you wouldn't have anything to do with him." Morgenthau—owner of large amounts of undeveloped New York property—asked Marsh to withdraw his tax proposals, and when Marsh declined, Morgenthau quit the NYCCCP and booted it out of his building. De Forest wrote Riis that while Marsh had "lots of good intentions," he doubted his "practical judgment" and noted that his friends were leaping off the NYCCCP bandwagon.

Marsh, conversely, had no reliable base of mass support; the labor movement, which might have provided one, was focused on issues closer to the point of production. Inside the fledgling planning movement itself, Marsh was sidelined by a contingent of conservatives captained by Frederick Law Olmsted Jr. On the housing front, Veiller and de Forest formed a National Housing Association in 1912, which disavowed radical goals, particularly "the municipal ownership and operation of tenement houses." Marsh, convinced that "land speculators and bankers had captured the city planning movement," retired from the enterprise he'd done so much to kick-start. He did help form a Society to Lower Rents and Reduce Taxes on Homes (1913)—another Georgite vehicle to push for shifting taxes from buildings to

"Our Religious Landlords and Their Rookery Tenants." *Puck,* January 9, 1895.

land—and crusaded among tenants and apartment dwellers for support. Though his magazine (*Tenant's Weekly*) never took off—and a proposed referendum to allow a popular vote on changing taxation policy was blocked—Marsh was one of the first to see tenants qua tenants as a political constituency. When zoning was enacted in Gotham in 1916, it would be at the behest of large-scale developers, financial institutions, and department store magnates, not housing reformers, and it would extract from German municipal legislation only those elements aimed at stabilizing (and hopefully enhancing) real estate values, not diminishing them.[8]

Yet even without the fundamental reforms proposed by Marsh and his colleagues, by 1916 space-starved Manhattanites had embarked on a decongestion movement of their own. It would not be the planned and orderly relocation to outer-borough garden cities envisioned by housing activists, but a pell-mell, market-driven land rush that would produce, in a very short space of time, a wide variety of new communities, marked by a spectacular variety of housing forms and living conditions—including a virtual re-creation of the slum dwellings they'd hoped to leave behind.

WORKING-CLASS NEIGHBORHOODS: MANHATTAN, BROOKLYN, QUEENS

The private housing market failed to provide decent shelter for the unskilled or the unorganized, the unfortunate or the unemployed, the ill, the widowed, or the poor. It did

---

8. While it was not their primary focus, Marsh and the CCP agreed with the push to limit the heights of skyscrapers in the "office district below Chambers Street," on the grounds that the transit lines couldn't handle the huge numbers of commuters they created. But Marsh proposed a much tougher approach to restriction, and a much simpler one, too: "We must recognize that a skyscraper is a quasi-monopoly, just as a street privilege is, and should be paid for as is any other franchise." Accordingly, the city should tax buildings by the number of floors; the higher the building, the higher the tax.

much better, however, at serving skilled artisans, clerical workers, shopkeepers, small entrepreneurs, and city employees—those whose real wages increased during the boom years. They could, and did, cut loose from the Lower East Side, and the gashouse, industrial, and slaughterhouse districts along the Hudson and East Rivers, and find comparatively good and affordable housing elsewhere in Manhattan, or in other parts of the consolidated city.

While the decision to depart downtown was made at the individual or familial level, ethnicity and class tended to govern departure date and destination. The exodus of better-off British, Irish, and Germans, begun before Consolidation, accelerated after the turn of the century—in the case of Kleindeutschland, drastically and tragically so.

On June 15, 1904, the paddle-wheeled steamer *General Slocum* embarked from the East 3rd Street pier, its three decks filled to capacity with 1,331 passengers, overwhelmingly women and children. Members of St. Mark's Evangelical Lutheran Church (323 East 6th Street), linchpin of the dwindling German community, they were off on their annual excursion to celebrate the end of the Sunday school year.

Captain William Van Schaick was in command. He had a reassuringly excellent record. The safety equipment was also comfortingly sound—according to inspector Henry Lundberg, one of the complaisant, incompetent, and likely corrupt members of the New York Bureau of the United States Steamboat Inspection Service. Lundberg had recently taken a cursory look at the boat's 2,500 tattered Kahnweiler's Never-Sink Life Preservers, managing not to notice that the once-solid chunks of cork inside had turned to dust over the previous thirteen years. He signed off on the lifeboats, too, though they had been wired to the deck and were patently useless. It's not clear if he stuck his head in the forward compartment, housing the electric generator, and noticed it was filled with cans of kerosene and strewn with oily rags, wood scraps, dry hay, and other highly flammable objects; nor is it known if money changed hands to ensure his inattention.

The *Slocum* steamed up the East River and had reached a spot opposite 130th Street when a fire broke out—sparked perhaps by a tossed cigarette or overturned lamp—setting the ship ablaze. The captain panicked. Instead of immediately running aground on Manhattan, he headed a mile upriver to North Brother Island, streaming flames. As frenzied passengers were discovering their life preservers were lethal—waterlogged fill turned to mud, which dragged them to the bottom—the ship smashed onto jagged rocks, hurling hundreds into the cauldron below decks. Scores of other women, half-roasted to death, now threw their babies and themselves into the water. Despite heroic efforts by watermen, police, nurses, and doctors who rushed to the scene, 1,021 perished, the most lethal disaster in the history of New York to date.

Kleindeutschland now melted away. Countless relatives, friends, and neighbors of *Slocum* victims couldn't bear to remain where everything reminded them of those they'd lost. Their departure further eroded a community that had been diminishing since the 1890s. By 1910 Little Germany was largely history. Most migrants headed uptown to an already established beachhead in Yorkville (74th/89th/Third/East River), the Mitteleuropean haven of Germans, Hungarians, Czechs, and Slovaks.

African Americans also headed north, all but completing their exodus from "Little Africa" in Greenwich Village, though as late as the turn of the century, approximately 1,200 still lived on the streets and alleys near lower Sixth Avenue, or adjacent to the Minettas. And their flagship houses of worship still remained in place: Abyssinian Baptist at 166 Waverly Place, Mother Zion at 351 Bleecker. But blacks were on the march north—"The ambitious

"The Excursion Steamer General Slocum, Destroyed by Fire, and Beached on North Brother Island, Photograph by the *New York Tribune*." *Marine Engineering* 9 (July 1904).

Negro has moved uptown," one observer noted—and the two churches joined the exodus in 1904 and 1905, respectively. The great bulk now lived in the Tenderloin, whose boundaries, like most borders in Manhattan, were permeable, mutable, and on the move uptown. In the nineteenth century its perimeter had enclosed the territory between 23rd and 42nd Streets and Fifth and Seventh Avenues, with black residents densest in the lower 30s around Seventh. But by 1900 the influx of African Americans moving up from downtown had expanded the Tenderloin northward to 53rd Street, a frontier to which they staked a spatial claim by planting along it major institutions like churches and hotels. Propelled by a growth in population fed by immigration from the South and the Caribbean, and by the dislocation generated by the building of Penn Station, the community pressed farther north into the prominence called San Juan Hill.

The downtown Irish also headed north. Unskilled workers tended to go no farther than the Irish-German stronghold of Hell's Kitchen. This section of the Middle West Side—between 34th and 54th Streets, from Seventh Avenue to the Hudson River—had been settled by Irish and German immigrants in the mid-nineteenth century, and was dominated by their descendants. Residents labored in the district's docks, factories, and rail yards that saturated its western side, and crammed into the dumbbell tenements lining its eastern blocks. Better-off Irish, particularly building-trades workers and civil servants, headed farther uptown to Yorkville. And middle-class migrants leapfrogged up to Washington Heights, settling east of Broadway, where they melded with compatriots moving up Amsterdam Avenue from an earlier enclave around City College (at Convent Avenue and 138th Street).

For Jews and Italians, the most-traveled route out of lower Manhattan ran due north. Some stopped off in Yorkville, but most pressed on farther, to East Harlem. Italians fleeing super-dense Little Italy, centered on Mulberry Street, headed for the well-established uptown colony east of Second Avenue, between 100th and 115th Streets. By 1913 Italian East Harlem, with 75,000 residents, was gaining on Mulberry Street's 110,000, and with some blocks now equaling downtown's 700–800 per acre, locals began calling the uptown branch "*the* Little Italy."

Downtown Jews also poured into an established uptown ghetto, pioneered back in 1890 by 1,300 Poles. By 1910 nearly 100,000 more had moved into the blocks just west of Little Italy—from Madison Avenue to east of Third, from 100th to 125th Streets—supplanting Germans and Irish. East Harlem was now home to the second-largest concentration of East European Jews in the United States, and density levels at its core had hit 500–600 per acre.

Amid this Jewish quarter was a tiny congregation of Puerto Ricans, around Third Avenue between 100th and 110th Street, encompassing by 1916 perhaps fifty families of cigar workers who had moved up from downtown, joining Cubans who had been there since Martí's day. This nucleus of what the Spanish-speaking migrants called La Colonia Hispana or El Barrio would be a chief point of arrival of newcomers from Puerto Rico, whose numbers began to swell after 1917, when the Jones Act made islanders US citizens. By 1920 there were 7,364 Puerto Ricans in New York, a figure approaching the size of the hitherto-predominant Cuban and Spanish communities.

Like Little Italy, Jewish East Harlem was less an escape from the Lower East Side than a reproduction of it. Residents who rode the el northward took their cultural baggage with them. They swiftly recreated (or relocated) the old neighborhood's synagogues, *landsman-shaftn*, yeshivas, and theaters, and also its panoply of radical organizations—socialists, anarchists, labor unions, and Workmen's Circle branches.

The downtown migrants (and new arrivals fresh from Europe) found plenty of jobs in shops and factories and—by accepting lower wages than the unionized Anglos and Irish—elbowed their way into the construction trades then transforming the area. More pivotally, immigrant Jews began replacing the Anglo-, Irish-, and German American contractors who over the previous two generations had covered much of Manhattan with brownstone row houses and small groups of apartments. The old-timers fell by the wayside for several reasons. They were mostly small-scale operators, who had started as artisans and crossed over into becoming developers. But they remained individualistic, often not bringing even their sons into the business. Their finances were limited. They often borrowed from wealthy individuals and worked on a few small projects at a time. In the new century, the real profits were made in putting up the bigger, costlier, and riskier New Law dwellings. The traditional builders found it harder to borrow the requisite sums, partly as venture capitalists began investing directly in new development consortiums. Would-be immigrant entrepreneurs, on the other hand, had several things going for them. Up-and-coming "realestateniks" (as *Jewish Daily Forward* editor Abraham Cahan called them)—professionals, small tradesmen, and workingmen eager to invest their savings in houses and lots—plunged into the impromptu markets that sprang up during the building frenzy of the zeros. Harlem's Fifth Avenue and 116th Street "swarmed with Yiddish-Speaking real-estate speculators," Cahan wrote, "a gesticulating, jabbering, whispering, excited throng resembling the crowd of curb-brokers on Broad Street." Jewish builders thus had better access to capital. They were also able to hire cheaper labor from among semiskilled Jewish carpenters, masons, and painters who were nonunionized, having been excluded from the construction guilds. They also preferred to work for same-faith employers who might pay less but were willing to accommodate religious customs—letting workers off early on Fridays, for example. Finally, the Jewish contractors had greater staying power because they tended to set up family businesses. Julius Tishman, who arrived from Poland as a teenager in the 1880s, worked first in dry goods, opened an upstate department store, then recycled his profits into real estate, building his first six-story tenement at 519 East 13th in 1898. In 1909 his eldest son, David, who had been working with his father off and on for years, graduated from NYU Law School but, rather than heading off to professional pastures, joined his father (in 1912) as vice president of the now Julius Tishman & Sons; before the decade was out he had taken de facto control of the company.

IN THE YEARS AFTER THE DISASTROUS WAR OF 1898, though Spain had lost its imperial foothold in the hemisphere, its presence in New York increased significantly. The small Spanish community, dominated for decades by resident merchants of Iberian commercial firms, now acquired a substantial working class. After 1901 the Spanish Line offered direct service straight to South Street's Pier 8, at the foot of James Street, often carrying immigrants from Spain's northern coastal provinces of Galicia and Asturias, from where most ships set sail for America. Shipping was itself a major source of employment for Iberians, as sailors and stokers easily found work; by the 1910s the Marine Firemen's, Oilers', and Water-Tenders' Association (affiliated to the International Seamen's Union) had developed a substantial and powerful Spanish (and Portuguese) section.

Many of these newcomers hung their hats in Little Spain, a Hispanic neighborhood that crystallized, around 1900, in the northwest corner of Greenwich Village, near the Hudson River docks. West 14th Street was its spinal thoroughfare. Here, in 1902, Archbishop Michael Corrigan opened Our Lady of Guadalupe Church in a row house at 229 West 14th Street, between Seventh and Eighth Avenues, and established a "national" parish with the same name; it was the first one dedicated to serving Spanish-speaking Catholics of the archdiocese. Other institutions now arrived on the street, including Casa Maria (a Spanish settlement house run by the Servants of Mary), the Spanish Benevolent Society, St. Raphael's Spanish Immigrant Society, and the Spanish American Workers Alliance. Soon the surrounding blocks were home to bodegas (grocery stores), boardinghouses (and a Hotel Español), barbershops, taverns, and restaurants. Little Spain became a cultural magnet for Hispanic communities around the city. Puerto Ricans traveled down to buy food in Spanish shops on 14th Street, and the Basques around Cherry and Water Streets (near the Spanish Line's dock), though they had their own bodegas and restaurants, would head up to Nuestra Señora de la Guadalupe for major religious ceremonies, like getting married. Still, the influx was tiny in comparison to the torrent arriving from Southern and Eastern Europe: by 1920 there were only 14,659 Spanish-born residents in New York.

Farther down the Hudson shoreline from Little Spain, just south of the Washington Market, lay a small community of Arabic-speakers from the Ottoman province of Syria, who called themselves Syrians, though nearly 95 percent were from the district of Mount Lebanon, in today's Lebanon. Ninety percent were Christians, of either the Maronite, Melkite (Greek Catholic), or Greek Orthodox persuasions. (The First Melkite Church, known as the Syrian Church, was on Washington Street.) In 1904, out of a total population of 2,482, there were only 7 Muslims and approximately 100 Syrian Jews, including migrants from Aleppo and Damascus.

First to arrive (in the 1880s) were merchants who rented brownstones near the market and set up retail shops, as well as wholesale operations, which supplied a growing network of Syrian peddlers. By the 1890s there was a well-defined Syrian district (Rector/Greenwich/Morris/Washington). By the 1900s it boasted factories, import houses (notably of Oriental rugs), and a vibrant Arabic press.

Not far off, an embryonic Greek community was taking root. While most Greek émigrés to the United States came from rural communities, a small number of skilled fur workers arrived from Kastoria, an urban community in West Macedonia. Between 1904 and 1909

"Syrian Restaurant," ca. 1910–15. (Library of Congress Prints and Photographs Division, George Grantham Bain Collection)

they settled near the center of Gotham's fur business, then strung out along Broadway between Canal and Houston. In the next decade they followed the industry as it moved north and west toward 14th Street. By 1913 there were 20,000 Greeks in the city, and they had branched out into wholesaling food and flowers.

FOR ALL THE ATTRACTIONS OF MANHATTAN, a substantial contingent of Lower East Side refugees and new-wave immigrants opted for Brooklyn, rendered steadily more accessible by the opening of the Williamsburg (1903) and Manhattan (1909) Bridges and the extension of transit lines deeper into the borough. Here, as in Harlem, migration meant mass relocation rather than atomized dispersal—producing in some areas, notably Brownsville, what many opponents of Consolidation had feared: the Manhattanization of Brooklyn.

"Garden of Allah," ca. 1910–15. (Library of Congress Prints and Photographs Division, George Grantham Bain Collection)

In the early 1880s, Brownsville had still been a village of small farmers. Factories arrived in the 1890s, and between 1900 and 1915 thousands of Eastern European Jews streamed across the river or arrived direct from Europe. The population leapt from 10,000 in 1899 to 60,000 in 1904 to 92,000 in 1910 and to 169,000 by 1920 (including a small contingent of African Americans).

The rush to Brownsville lofted land values. Prices on some lots soared from $50 in 1907 to $3,000 in 1909. As in Harlem, a vigorous real estate market emerged. At a café on Pitkin Avenue, speculators bought and sold land and lodgings over cups of coffee. And, as in Harlem, the boom in Brownsville opened space for Jews to enter the construction industry. A host of small-scale contractors threw up New Law tenements in a helter-skelter (and often slipshod) fashion, cramming them into narrow blocks despite the ample availability of space in which to stretch out. By 1904 88 percent of the dwelling units were in three- or four-story tenements containing four or five families; by 1907, 96 percent were.

By 1916 Yiddish-speaking Brownsville, a Lower East Side offshoot, had replaced Harlem as the second-largest Jewish community in the city.[9] Sweatshops and factories had proliferated (many of whose owners were also refugees from Manhattan, seeking to escape government

9. By 1916 Brownsville and Harlem, along with Williamsburg and the Bronx, had been so successful in attracting immigrant Jews that only 25 percent of the city's Jewish population still lived on the Lower East Side. Put differently, between 1905 and 1915, over 60 percent of the East Side's Jews had left the premises.

inspectors and union organizers, usually without success). A cluster of transplanted institutions addressed social, cultural, ethnic, and religious needs. Pitkin Avenue provided a shopping-street-cum-promenade. Belmont Avenue hosted an open-air pushcart market. And Brownsville reproduced, as well, Manhattanesque levels of congestion. Though its New Law tenements were roomier, the tenants, mostly low-wage workers, still had to take in boarders to make the rent. As a result, there were blocks (in 1915) where population density hit 724 per acre. With congestion came social ailments, like high rates of TB. For those, like Marsh, who found Brownsville "only a little less murderous" than the East Side slums, it was a case study in misguided urban development.

Other Brooklyn working-class enclaves—strung out along the East River industrial shoreline from Greenpoint to Sunset Park—similarly bulged with new arrivals.

Poles flocked to work in Greenpoint's foundries, potteries, and gasworks, and settled into the community centered around St. Stanislaus Kostka's (1890), the largest Polish Catholic congregation in the borough. The Williamsburg Bridge brought substantial numbers of Yiddish- and Italian-speaking Manhattanites into Williamsburg and Bushwick. The Irish retained their Vinegar Hill stronghold on the rise overlooking the Brooklyn Navy Yard, and newcomers packed Sands Street boardinghouses to labor in the factories and power plants between the Brooklyn and Manhattan Bridges, and to work as maids and handymen for Brooklyn Heights brownstoners.

Farther south along the Brooklyn waterfront, a spin-off of Manhattan's Little Syria emerged around Atlantic Avenue, where the South Ferry docked. This convenient link, enhanced by the arrival of the subway in 1910, allowed for the emergence of a commuting community. By 1915 the so-called South Ferry colony, bounded by Joralemon, Boerum, Warren, and the waterfront, numbered over 2,000, and though it had developed its own institutions—Our Lady of Lebanon opened in 1903 at 295–297 Hicks—nearly all its members commuted to work in Manhattan's Syrian quarter.

Farther south, the Red Hook/Gowanus peninsula was dominated by the Irish, who worked the wharves, shipyards, gas tanks, and industrial facilities strung out along Buttermilk Channel, Gowanus Bay, and the Gowanus Canal. But an Italian presence was growing rapidly, radiating out from the Hamilton Ferry landing (next to the Atlantic Basin), heading inland along President and Union Streets. This territory remained an Old Law stronghold.

Brooklyn's expanding working class also pushed on into Sunset Park. Laboring men were drawn by expanding job opportunities along the burgeoning waterfront, in the adjacent manufacturing district, and on the Fourth Avenue subway construction project. Women found work in the area's garment shops.

The Irish paced this southern migration, with the Catholic Church buying up property and establishing parishes in undeveloped areas. Our Lady of Perpetual Help at 5th Avenue and 59th, which the Redemptorists opened in 1894, preceded the arrival of paved streets by fifteen years. The Italians, uncomfortable in Irish churches, formed their own; St. Rocco's, at 27th Street between Fourth and Fifth Avenues, was organized in 1902. So did the Poles—whose men worked in Green-Wood Cemetery or the Ansonia Clock Company, and whose women commuted to clean the new office buildings in lower Manhattan. They established Our Lady of Czenstochowa Parish in 1896 and built their own church, rectory, school, and convent between 24th and 25th Streets and Third and Fourth Avenues.

Sunset Park was also home to Norwegians and Finns. The former had been coming to Brooklyn since the 1870s and 1880s, when the triumph of steamships doomed their sailing villages. They clustered at first along the piers, near their jobs as sailors, shipbuilders, dockworkers, and harbor pilots. Then they moved up to the hills overlooking the harbor between 45th and 60th Streets and Fourth and Eighth Avenues. Here, between 1897 and 1913, they established a bevy of Lutheran, Reformed, and Methodist churches. The ethnic enclave—nicknamed the "Mysost-Kolonien" (meaning "Whey-Cheese Colony")—also attracted ship chandlers and ship brokers, merchants and professionals and artisans. Here the *Nordisk Tidende (Nordic Times)* was founded in 1891, as were Viking Leagues and Scandinavian Republican Leagues that denounced the "anarchistic social Darwinism" of American big business, and singing societies that performed Edvard Grieg compositions for male chorus.

Builders in Sunset Park produced a landscape of low-rise attached homes, which looked identical to the one-family homes of more prosperous neighborhoods. But many housed two families, who relied on boarders to help pay the rent. Still, it seemed that the farther away one got from the industrial waterfront belt, the more inviting became the range of housing opportunities for better-off working-class residents.

Finns were particularly innovative in this regard. Importing a predilection for cooperative ventures, members of the workingmen's societies and socialist clubs created the first co-operative housing venture in the city. In 1916 sixteen families came together to build a four-story apartment house on 43rd Street between Eighth and Ninth Avenues, in the center of Finntown (the blocks between 40th and 45th Streets and Fifth and Ninth Avenues). It was a mold-breaker less for its architecture than its financing and process of construction. The co-operators included carpenters and other building-trades craftsmen (bricklayers, plasterers, painters, and electricians), who agreed to pool their money and their skills and construct a domicile for use, not for profit. They set up a Housing Association, in which the tenants-to-be bought shares that entitled them to a permanent lease on their apartment, with legal ownership vested in the cooperative. The structure itself—modeled on worker housing in Helsinki—they called Alku I, meaning "beginning," and so it proved to be. It was followed up in 1917 by Alku II, then other apartment houses, and an array of cooperative businesses, including a grocery store, bakery, meat market, restaurant, poolroom, newspaper, and a garage, most concentrated on Eighth Avenue, between 40th and 45th Streets.

A SIMILAR RANGE OF HOUSING POSSIBILITIES EMERGED in working-class Queens. At the borough's industrial core, Long Island City remained the most densely packed area, as it absorbed many of those working in the new and nearby Degnon Terminal factory behemoths, like the plant of Loose-Wiles Biscuits. But there were roomier districts to the east, which, though emulating Manhattan by adopting a grid system, rather than an ambling garden-suburb streetscape, boasted superior quality options in tenement living—most notably in Ridgewood.

As newcomers (East European Jews and Italians) piled into Brooklyn's Williamsburg and Bushwick sections, most Germans pulled out, migrating across the Queens border to the adjacent high ground of Ridgewood. There they became commuters. They continued to work in Williamsburg breweries, ironworks, tin factories, and sugar refineries along the river, now newly accessible by mass transit. In Ridgewood itself a mini-city sprang up. In 1903 the area was still marked by wood-framed houses, a half-dozen breweries, and a few large farms; by 1908 it was all subdivided, gridded, and becoming covered with block after block of two- or three-story row houses. Between 1908 and 1914 New Law tenement buildings went up—hundreds of them—the overwhelming majority of which were erected by the G. X. Mathews Company.

Founded by German immigrant Gustave Xavier Mathews and his two brothers in Ridgewood in 1904, the company became famed for its Mathews Model Flats, a decided improvement over the warrens of Williamsburg and the Lower East Side. Each three-story, nicely detailed, yellow-and-amber brick building—the brick manufactured by B. Kreischer & Sons on Staten Island—included six separate railroad apartments (two families per floor), each with five rooms and a separate bathroom, each decently supplied with light and air. They were extremely popular in Queens. The Mathews brothers built hundreds more in Astoria, Woodhaven, Corona, Woodside, and Long Island City. Indeed, their company was the borough's most active builder, receiving 25 percent of the tenement house permits issued in Queens in 1911. In 1915 the New York City Tenement House Department was so taken with their model for affordable working-class housing that it exhibited the Model Flats at the Panama-Pacific Fair in San Francisco.

Queens in general grew briskly in the century's first decades. From roughly 150,000 residents in 1900, the population tally grew to 285,000 in 1910, and to 470,000 in 1920. In that year Long Island City was still the largest neighborhood, with 90,000 residents, followed by Ridgewood (70,000), Richmond Hill (50,000), Corona (40,000), Jamaica (40,000), Flushing (35,000), Far Rockaway (25,000), and Woodhaven (16,000).

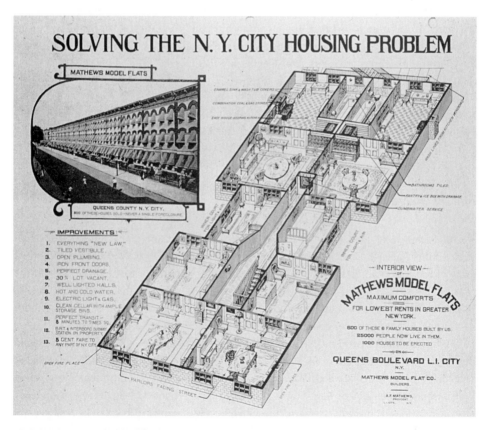

"Solving the N.Y. City Housing Problem: Mathews Model Flats." ca. 1905–15. (Courtesy Greater Astoria Historical Society)

"Bay Side Park, 3d Ward, Borough of Queens, New York City." ca. 1915. (Library of Congress Geography and Map Division)

But Queens's changes, while substantial, did not profoundly transform the nature of the borough as a whole, whereas during these same years, Consolidation engendered a truly spectacular metamorphosis in the mainland borough of the Bronx.

THE BRONX: INSTANT CITY

In the decades before Consolidation, much of the Bronx was a bucolic haven. Orchards and fields of plowed farmland alternated with wildflower-covered meadows, and woods filled with songbirds. Great estates blanketed the land—some dating to colonial days—on which gentlemen farmers raised trotters and prize cattle. Charitable institutions flourished on the Bronx's cheap acreage: at the New York Catholic Protectory's 114-acre plot in Westchester, the Christian Brothers taught orphans gardening, horse care, and craft skills.

Sprinkled across this terrain was a series of villages. Their residents lived in wooden cottages or frame houses with front porches. Many grew vegetables in rear gardens and kept their side yards stocked with pigs, cows, or chickens. Larger towns had an array of shops and services; smaller hamlets made do with a general store. People could also purchase necessities from the host of peddlers—Romani tinkers, scissor grinders, fishermen with shad from the North River—who traveled the dirt roads and the few macadamized highways.

Most villages, and their nearby employment opportunities, were dominated by a particular ethnic group.

"Birds Eye View of That Portion of the 23rd and 24th Wards of the City of New York, Lying Westerly of the New York and Harlem Railroad, and of the Grand Boulevard and Concourse Connecting Manhattan Island with the Park System North of the Harlem River," 1897. (Library of Congress Geography and Map Division)

Morrisania and Melrose were chiefly German. Villagers worked in the local breweries. (The Ebling and Hupfel firms chilled and aged their product in caves cut into hillsides along the Eagle Avenue escarpment.) They worshiped at local Lutheran and Catholic churches and shopped and amused themselves along Courtlandt Avenue—known as "Dutch [Deutsch] Broadway" for its German saloons, beer halls, and gymnastic and singing societies.

Highbridgeville, an Irish settlement since the building of the Croton Aqueduct, afforded work for railroad section hands, stevedores along the Harlem River docks, and gardeners on the nearby Ogden, Morris, and Archer estates. The Irish also settled in Woodlawn Heights, where they tended the cemetery; in "Irishtown," close to service positions in Riverdale's manors; and in Fordham, near jobs at St. John's College.

The densest Irish concentrations were in Mott Haven, the Bronx's most industrialized section. Here they labored in the Mott Iron Foundry, or in Stephens Coal Yard, or on the docks, railroads, and horsecars. (A substantial German minority worked in the many piano factories.) The community also sustained doctors, politicians, and magistrates who lived in decorative town houses on Alexander Avenue, known as the "Irish Fifth Avenue."

Getting around the Bronx was difficult. Since the 1860s horsecars had run infrequently (and on stormy nights not at all) from the Harlem Bridge along Third Avenue up to Fordham. During the routine delays, passengers would hop off to pick huckleberries, giving the road its popular name, the "Huckleberry Line." More horsecar routes were added in the 1870s and 1880s, eventually gridding the territory, but access remained rudimentary.

Then, in 1886–87, the elevated arrived. From its original terminus at 143rd Street, the el was extended up the Third Avenue corridor to 177th Street in Tremont (by 1891), next to Fordham (in 1900), and finally up to Bronx Park (in 1902). A nickel now afforded passage from the upper Bronx to South Ferry. Street-level railways also improved: in 1892 the Huckleberry Line was electrified; in 1900 it, and all Bronx surface transit, came under Whitney and Ryan's Metropolitan Street Railway, integrating Manhattan's and the Bronx's rail networks under one management. There was also service available on the New York and Harlem, through the Central Bronx, and on the New York, New Haven, and Hartford line, running along the elevation above the Bronx River.

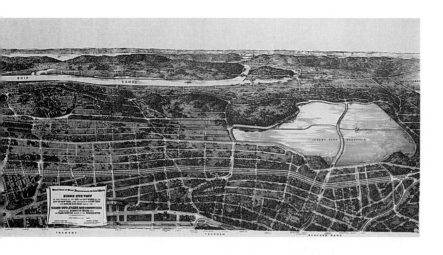

"Why Don't You Go to Williamsbridge to Live?" 1891. Bronx Museum of the Arts, *Building a Borough: Architecture and Planning in the Bronx, 1890–1940* (1986).

The new transport precipitated a lurch northward by working-class Manhattanites. The borough's population—which had numbered barely 17,000 in 1860—jumped to 89,000 in 1890 and shot past 200,000 by 1900. The vast majority of the newcomers settled along the route of the Third Avenue El. Mott Haven, Melrose, and Morrisania's vacant lots filled with brick row houses and dumbbell tenements. Densities soared to Manhattan levels.

This sudden surge sparked a battle for the future of the Bronx.

Since annexation in 1874, Manhattan's middle and upper classes had been grooming the North Side as a rural residential enclave. In the mid-1880s, the prototype suburb of Bedford Park—forty English Colonial villas with turrets, verandas, and all the modern conveniences—went up on 23 acres just north of Fordham.

To keep the borough green, and to forestall Manhattan-type development, downtowners and prominent Bronx estate owners got the state legislature (in 1884) to set aside the huge Van Cortlandt, Bronx, and Pelham Bay Parks, and to authorize three connecting parkways (Mosholu, Pelham, Crotona). In the southern, more built-up portions, Louis A. Risse, the

Park Department's chief engineer, called for a street plan organized around City Beautifulesque boulevards, traffic circles, and parks. Risse also proposed, in 1892, a Grand Boulevard and Concourse. This Champs-Élysées of the Bronx would run 4.5 miles, from 161st Street to Van Cortlandt Park, and carry bicyclists, pedestrians, and horse carriages on different roadways, all separated by traffic islands planted with shade trees. Traversing an elevated ridge, it would afford wealthy Manhattanites access to the new parks and their Queen Anne country manors.

This Olmstedian vision was strongly opposed by a coalition of North Siders who wanted to make the Bronx a city, not a suburb. The pro-development forces included brewers, factory owners, politicians, Irish and German residents seeking improved services, and—above all—those real estate brokers, builders, and estate owners who saw in the boomlet brought on by the Third Avenue El a harbinger of future bonanza profits. Leagued together in the North Side Board of Trade (1894) and led by Louis F. Haffen, the Bronx's first borough president, the North Siders demanded their territory be woven into the fabric of the Greater City.[10]

The city builders won. They had the Bronx remapped with an eye to the "vast population which in the near future must inevitably flow into these wards." Suburban curves were scrapped, and straight graded streets were imposed on the irregular terrain. The Grand Concourse, however, was retained—work started in 1902 and was completed in 1909—but the roadway remained suspended between visions. In 1909 it began a slow transition from greenway to highway when its outermost lanes were paved for autos, though cars remained rare, as did house construction of any sort. Not until 1918, when the Jerome Avenue subway was completed—the North Siders having lobbied loudly for mass transit—was this hilly part of the West Bronx swept into Manhattan-style urbanity, with villas giving way to apartments.

The Bronx demanded, and received, massive public spending for an urban infrastructure of sewers, docks, bridges, viaducts, water supply, schools, police stations, firehouses, and courthouses. They got home rule, too. Consolidation had made the Bronx a borough but not a county. By 1911 600 Bronx organizations had joined in lobbying Albany for county status, backed by the borough's first daily newspaper, the *North Side News*. With help from State Senator Franklin D. Roosevelt, this was achieved in 1914.[11]

The coming of the subways between 1905 and 1919 finalized the urbanists' victory. Building booms broke out along the four pathways. The IRT's Lenox Avenue line ran above ground along Westchester Avenue and Southern Boulevard to West Farms Square. The Broadway line crossed Spuyten Duyvil at Kingsbridge and carried on as an elevated to 242nd Street at Van Cortlandt Park. These were followed a decade later by the two branches of the new Lexington Avenue line. One ran up Jerome Avenue to Woodlawn (1918). The other rolled under 138th to Southern Boulevard, swung north under Hunt's Point, then emerged to run as an elevated over Westchester Avenue up to Pelham Bay Park (1919).

From roughly 1904 to 1916, the Bronx was in continual frenzy. In the old villages, as town lot prices skyrocketed from $500 to $5,000, modest frame houses were ripped down to make way for apartment houses. Rustic old farms near planned subway stops were

---

10. Haffen was a local boy, born in 1854 in Melrose, and educated at St. John's College and Columbia's School of Mines. After graduating in 1879 he worked as a civil engineer in the Far West, then joined the Parks Department in 1883. In 1893 he became commissioner of street improvements for the 23rd and 24th Districts—a body that wrested control over development from the Parks Department—and was elected borough president when that body vanished at Consolidation.

11. They got armories, too. The 105th Artillery Armory (1910) commanded Morrisania from the heights at Franklin Avenue and 166th Street. And in 1912, in a filled basin originally intended to be part of the Jerome Park Reservoir, state authorities erected the Kingsbridge Armory, perhaps the largest in the world, for the National Guard's 8th Coastal Artillery Regiment.

"Auction Sale of the Est. of Lewis Gouverneur Morris at Morris Heights, Bronx Borough N.Y. City,"
June 7, 1910. Bronx Museum of the Arts, *Building a Borough: Architecture and Planning in the Bronx,*
1890–1940 (1986).

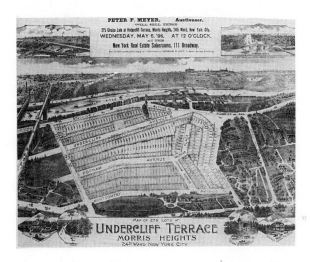

Map of 275 Lots at Undercliff Terrace, Morris Heights, 24th Ward New York City," 1896.
Bronx Museum of the Arts, *Building a Borough: Architecture and Planning in the Bronx, 1890–1940*
(1986).

almost torn apart by bidders. The borough's remaining great estates—the acreages of the
Morrises, Lorillards, Harpers, Pells, Ogdens, and Hoes—were snapped up by professional
speculative realty corporations, like Henry Morgenthau's and the American Real Estate
Company (AREC).

AREC, founded in the late 1880s, was a trailblazing developer, in that it accumulated
enough capital to operate on a huge scale, buying up massive tracts wholesale and then
either retailing pieces to smaller contractors (sometimes giving them building loans) or,
more novelly, undertaking the development itself. In 1899 AREC bought 86 acres of the old
Hoe and Simpson estates, on the south side of Westchester Avenue, for about $1 million.
Then work gangs demolished old mansions, felled ancient trees, blasted rock outcroppings,
stripped meadows, paved streets, laid sewer, water, and gas mains, and marked off roughly a
thousand building sites. AREC itself built and sold forty-two two-family homes and more
than fifty tenement houses, while auctioning off the remaining property to be developed by

other operators (Morgenthau being one). In 1909, for $1.5 million, the company bought 93 acres of the Watson estate (on the high ground north of Westchester Avenue and East of the Bronx River) and spent the next three years preparing the land. Then, in 1912, it auctioned off approximately 1,200 ready-to-build-on city lots to investors and operators. AREC rode the boom brilliantly, until the slump in real estate values after 1914, and some reputed financial shenanigans by AREC officers to offset their declining incomes, led them into bankruptcy by 1917.

"Ever Think of Living in the Bronx?" 1906. Bronx Museum of the Arts, *Building a Borough: Architecture and Planning in the Bronx, 1890–1940* (1986).

Morgenthau, heavily invested in Bronx speculations, enlisted the aid of J. Clarence Davies, the borough's preeminent real estate man. Davies was one of those who had pushed most vigorously for choosing an urban rather than suburban future. As he noted unambiguously in 1908, "The reason Bronx values are high today and will be higher in the near future is that many sectors are densely populated, and the density is growing." Davies himself had developed a highly lucrative brokerage by becoming the agent of choice for the great families selling off their holdings, and becoming an expert at reselling them. In Morgenthau he had someone who could provide capital in the requisite quantities needed to operate on a grand scale.

Swarms of construction crews raised row after row of brick one-, two-, and three-family homes and legions of New Law apartment houses "of the most modern and high-class type." Massive ad campaigns promoted the new uptown utopia. Throngs rolled in from Manhattan. The most Aladdin-like changes took place in the East Bronx, to which better-off working-class Jews streamed up from the Lower East Side and Harlem into the instant communities of Longwood, Hunt's Point, Southern Boulevard, and Crotona Park East. They were attracted to the four- or five-story walk-ups and the six-story elevator buildings by lower rents and superior amenities. Leon Trotsky, who for nearly three months in early 1917 was living with his family at 1522 Vyse Avenue (just east of Crotona Park), was one of many enthusiasts. "We rented an apartment in a workers district and furnished it on the installment plan," Trotsky recalled. "That apartment, at $18 a month, was equipped with all sorts of conveniences that we Europeans were quite unused to: electric lights, gas cooking range, bath, telephone, automatic service elevator, and even a chute for the garbage. These things completely won the boys over to New York."

Italians were also drawn to the Bronx in large numbers—both immigrant Sicilians and Calabrians, and the more affluent Italian Americans escaping Manhattan's slums. Fordham Manor (earlier a Lorillard estate, later called Belmont) was one popular destination. Workers building the Jerome Park Reservoir, the Bronx Zoo, and the subways flocked to apartments around the newly erected Our Lady of Mount Carmel Church on East 187th Street and near the shops along Arthur Avenue.

The herculean construction and massive demographic shifts utterly transformed the Bronx. From 100,000 in 1895 and 200,000 in 1900, the borough's population leapt to 431,000 in 1910, jumped to 650,000 in 1915, and climbed to 732,000 by 1920. Five years later, with over a million residents, the once quasi-rural countryside—and intended suburban community—had become, in its own right, the nation's sixth-largest city.

HOUSING THE MIDDLE CLASS: BROOKLYN, QUEENS

Greater New York's middle class had lost a potential paradise in the Bronx. Would it hold its own in Brooklyn? Or would the expansion of Brooklyn's working-class territory inundate the traditional bastions of the better-off, and turn the borough into a clone of Manhattan—the nightmare of those who had opposed Consolidation?

Brooklyn Heights, thanks in large part to its elevated topography, had remained a largely defensible stronghold, but even so, as the *Brooklyn Daily Eagle* reported in 1916, there had been "an invasion of the section by business and apartment houses." Other territories, too, were feeling the pressure. In fashionable Bedford, construction of mansions and brownstones tapered off as working-class Italians, Jews, and African Americans began spilling in from Williamsburg and Brownsville. Bedford would remain a genteel district, especially in its eastern reaches along Stuyvesant Avenue, but many of its businessmen and professionals began looking for better quarters.

Park Slope, too, was changing. The elegant brownstones along Prospect Park West still attracted the upper middle classes (and their retinue of Irish, Swedish, or African American servants). But by 1915 Irish and Italians were moving up the Slope from the Gowanus and Red Hook, into converted brownstones and new apartment houses. Still other buildings became boardinghouses for students, widows, and lower-middle-class clerks and salesmen. And subways were threatening a new mass migration. The Slope's cachet had slipped, and its posher inhabitants sought more exclusive pastures.

Just in time, new refugee Edens arose and beckoned. Not along the salubrious heights, or at the shoreline now so dominated by industry and commerce, but deep in the interior, on the enormous expanse of land that ran south and southwest from the old village of Flatbush—just below the high hills and ridges of Prospect Park—fanning out through the old townships of Flatbush, Flatlands, New Utrecht, and Gravesend, down to the sea, 6 miles away.

This vast glacial outwash, embracing a good chunk of Kings County, had been undergoing a steady transformation from country to city since the 1880s. In his 1884 history Henry Stiles had called Kings "one immense garden." But not because Brooklyn was, like the Bronx, an abode of gentlemen farmers. Brooklyn's gardeners were rigorously commercial ones, descendants of the Dutch agriculturalists who had been working the land for 250 years. Indeed, in the 1880s Kings (with Queens) County was the vegetable capital of the United States, doing a flourishing business trucking its goods to the markets of Brooklyn City and Manhattan, and picking up in return horse manure with which to fertilize its fields—a mutually profitable symbiosis.

Relations between city and country had been changing. The two burgeoning metropolises north of the terminal moraine—that "ridge of hills that long kept back the . . . tide of human life in the adjoining city," in the words of a contemporary Brooklynite—were steadily infiltrating the farmlands. Urban merchant princes established palatial country mansions. "Shrieking locomotives" and troops of "pleasure-seekers" invaded rural havens, bemoaned Gertrude Lefferts Vanderbilt in her *Social History of Flatbush* (1880), along with roughnecks who stole fruits and vegetables, set fires in the fields, and squatted on the commons. "The city has stretched out its hand," she said, "and the mark of the beast can usually be seen." Worse was surely on the way. The "first ripple of this rising [urban] tide has touched our borders," Vanderbilt observed, "and before long the sudden rush of some great wave will sweep away every trace of village life."

Vanderbilt understated the danger. The devil here was not some menacing external force but the seductive attraction of city-ness. Urbanity captured the hearts and minds of the younger generation, undermined their attachment to farming as a way of life, and rendered them vulnerable to the siren songs of the real ambassadors of the big cities—the modernizers, the improvers, and above all the real estate speculators (often drawn from their own ranks) who prowled their paradise with fists full of money.

Developers had been buying farmsteads here and there, converting them to batches of residences, as members of ancient families decided that living off the proceeds from selling their land was more appealing than growing cabbage. (The more industrious used the money to buy farms farther east on Long Island, or branch out into other businesses; one member of the Ditmas clan segued into the gas and electric field.) The pace of purchasing accelerated in the 1890s when buyers began making offers the farmers simply couldn't refuse, paying from $2,000 to $8,000 per acre for land that was yielding one-twentieth to one-eightieth as much in annual profits. Henry Meyer of the Germania Real Estate and Improvement

Brownsville, East New York, and the Empire Keystone Improvement Company. Excerpted from "Bird's-Eye View of Brooklyn," ca. 1908 (Library of Congress Geography and Map Division)

Company bought up and subdivided land from Vanderveers, Suydams, Cortelyous, and Lotts. His competitor Jere Johnson Jr., scion of a local farm family, had also shifted into development and over the course of a long career converted tracts into lots, some 200,000 of them, which he advertised vigorously in the big cities.

Johnson, who became president of the Brooklyn Real Estate Exchange, was also a vigorous advocate of Consolidation. And Consolidation, coupled with transport improvements that put Flatbush within thirty minutes of Manhattan, ushered in the wave of doom that Vanderbilt had predicted. A headlong rush to subdivide ensued, and by 1910 the city had enclosed and obliterated much of the country's remaining farmland. By 1905 the continued existence of a vegetable or dairy farm seemed anomalous; in 1913 the Brooklyn Botanical Garden established demonstration pea and tomato patches to teach local children where vegetables came from.

THE CITY HAD TRIUMPHED. Kings County had been de-agriculturalized.[12] But what kind of cityscape would replace the farms and fields? Brooklyn now confronted the same dilemma that had preoccupied the Bronx. City or suburb? Tenements or villas? In those territories closest to Prospect Park, villas carried the day.

---

12. At some cost. Curtailing its local supply of fresh vegetables had rendered it reliant on long-distance imports, which were more expensive and, given the cumbersome machinery of the Washington Market complex, often over the hill by the time they reached consumers. Also, eliminating agriculture ended the need for fertilizer, which rendered the presence of manure piles unprofitable as well as odiferous, and hastened the departure of horses from city streets, further reducing urbanites' contact with the animal kingdom and deepening the cultural chasm between country and city.

In 1898 real estate agent Dean Alvord purchased 50 acres of farmland from the Dutch Reformed Church, just northwest of the old village center at Church and Flatbush Avenues. Here he laid out Prospect Park South—installing utilities, planting Norway maples and Carolina poplars, and putting down paved streets with entranceways grandly marked by plaques reading "PPS" in bas-relief. Only then did he sell the plots.

Alvord offered something more appealing than location; he offered a homogeneous class environment. PPS was not for renters (tenements were not allowed), and the price of admission was relatively steep (including the cost of the land and of building a house). To ensure a scenographic uniformity, purchasers had to employ Alvord's chosen architect or get approval of their own plans. In short order, block after block of substantial freestanding houses sprouted, in a wild profusion of styles—Georgian, Tudor, New England Shingle, Swiss châlet, Roman temple, and Italian villa—all of them respectable. The personalized dwellings and orderly framework appealed to middle-class New Yorkers not yet prepared to give up the old dream of home ownership—a status now virtually unattainable in Manhattan.

Other subdivisions soon followed. Most lay to the south along the Brighton Line's path: Ditmas Park, Slocum Park, Manhattan Terrace, Fiske Terrace, Midwood Manor. Despite their imposing names, most were more modest than Alvord's original. They did, however, retain the concept of stylistic diversity within ordered unity, and the middle classes flocked to their single-family homes, set back from amply planted streets.

So enclaves could be established. But were they sustainable? What was to stop the proletarian migration then making its way south along the shoreline from penetrating the interior, especially as it was increasingly crisscrossed with transport lines running down to Coney Island? "How are we to prevent the invasion of crowded tenements and cheap apartments," worried the *Brooklyn Eagle* in 1914, "into regions now attractive for single houses?"

Some developers used covenants—restrictions embedded in the deed of sale—to guarantee middle-class stability. When James Lefferts decided to subdivide the family farm and establish Lefferts Manor (just east of Prospect Park, between Lefferts and Fenimore), he established restrictive covenants for each lot, requiring a single-family house, of brick or stone, set back from the street, worth at least $5,000. Covenants, however, were often time-limited, and when they expired, nothing could stop property owners from reaping huge profits by selling out to developers of apartments or businesses. Even where covenants ran in perpetuity, how could property owners halt development outside their neighborhood, which could soon surround and, in their opinion, degrade them?

For owners fearful of declining land values, the solution was clear: zoning. The 1916 law most famous for restricting the heights of buildings, and imposing land-use constraints, also created five "area districts," which mandated how much of its site a structure could occupy. These ranged from the A classification, mainly for industrial districts, in which buildings could fill their entire lot, through B and C designations, meant mainly for tenements, through D territory, which required substantial yards, to the ultimate status of E, intended for "villa districts" of detached single-family houses, on substantial plots, with a maximum of 50 percent coverage. Once the system was announced, a period of fierce lobbying followed, as actual or would-be upscale residential sections sought the E designation that would allow them to deploy the force of law to keep the market at bay. Ditmas Park petitioned for a change from C to E designation, the Brooklyn Heights Association pushed for greater protections, and the Zoning Commission, amenable to protecting middle-class enclaves, doubled the number of E zones, especially around Flatbush.

THESE BROOKLYN ENCLAVES HAD THEIR COUNTERPARTS in Queens, whose older suburban villages were being made increasingly accessible by rail. Richmond Hill was a case in point. Laid out in the 1870s by Albon P. Man, a New York lawyer, on 400 acres of farmland, Richmond Hill drowsed until the 1890s. Then the elevateds arrived (affording access to Manhattan along Jamaica and Liberty Avenues), a new Long Island Rail Road spur was run through its northern section, and sewers, electricity, and phone lines were installed. Richmond Hill blossomed. Its blocks of gambrel-roofed, front-porched, shingle-style houses, and its location just south of Forest Park (Queens's largest) attracted, among others, Jacob Riis. In 1907 Riis declined to join the City Club as he was now "living out in the country."[13]

These Queens and Brooklyn enclaves had something else in common. For all the efforts by developers to visually distinguish their middle-class projects from proletarian ones, both had one seemingly inescapable commonality, they were prisoners of the grid. One brand-new Queens development, Forest Hills Gardens, set out to challenge the tyranny of rectangularity by drawing on English garden-city precedents to fashion an entirely new model for suburban middle-class abodes.

Robert de Forest, whom Margaret Olivia Sage had appointed vice president of the Russell Sage Foundation, set out to develop a demonstration project that would avoid the "abhorrent rectangular city block" and "set an example to the growing suburban districts of New York...of how the thing can be done tastefully and at the same time with due regard for profit." The initial site was to have been near Jamaica, where the foundation bought a 48-acre parcel, planning to enlarge it later, only to discover that word of their sponsorship had leaked out and sent land prices soaring. The foundation turned instead to Cord Meyer, a German immigrant who after making a fortune manufacturing fertilizer went into real estate. In 1906 his Cord Meyer Development Company had broken ground for Forest Hills (named for its proximity to Forest Park), where he planned to erect 6,000 "high class residences" whose character would be guaranteed "by the adoption and enforcement of sensible restrictions regarding the class of buildings which can be erected within its limits." In 1909 the Sage Foundation bought 142 acres from Meyer, for a stiff $6,000 an acre. De Forest then hired landscape designer Frederick Law Olmsted Jr.—just back from exploring the model garden city of Letchworth—to lay out wide boulevards and winding local roads, breaking decisively with the grid. Architect Grosvenor Atterbury was taken on to design romantic Tudor houses, set on spacious tree-shaded lawns, and a charming (if synthetic) mock-English village square.

When the project was announced to the press, reporters assumed it was a philanthropic pilot intended to help solve the housing crisis of New York's working class—a well-known goal of de Forest's—and they pointed out that the project, given its location and likely cost, seemed hardly likely to help the poor and needy. De Forest admitted that "the cost of the land" would "preclude provision there for the day laborer"—Benjamin Marsh couldn't have put it any better—but insisted that the "Sage Foundation has not forgotten the laboring man" and declared it "may be ready to announce something for his benefit later on." It never did.

The foundation made its revised intentions clear in 1911, as the project neared completion. Forest Hills Gardens would *not* be a subsidized enterprise like City & Suburban Homes but rather, as its ads put it, a "high-class suburban residential community." Homes were to be

---

13. Man's sons would raise 300 houses in nearby Kew Gardens (also named for a London suburb), just to the east of Forest Park.

owned, not rented. References would be required from potential plot purchasers to ensure the community's "homogeneous and congenial" character. While no formal exclusionary policies were imposed, a press release made clear that the foundation believed the interests of property owners "would best be advanced and preserved if a certain amount of care were taken to avoid the forced association of persons not likely to have harmonious relations with each other." (Read: No Jews need apply.) Restrictive covenants controlling design of structures would be written into every sales contract, with prior approval required on a host of aesthetic issues.

Despite being a philanthropy, the Sage Foundation's housing project would be "conducted upon strictly business principles." De Forest was quite familiar with Ebenezer Howard's (and Marsh's) garden-city notion of returning income from improvements to the community as a whole. But he hadn't the slightest interest in challenging conventional real estate practice. On the contrary, he wanted to demonstrate to developers and builders that they could profit from purveying advanced European designs to middle-class New Yorkers. "There's money to be had in taste," he confided to Olmsted. In the end, however, though Forest Hills Gardens did indeed become an upper-middle-class enclave soon after it opened in 1912, when the foundation sold off its interests a decade later it lost money on the deal. Nevertheless, it had succeeded in demonstrating, once again, that splendid and sustainable single-family housing could be built in Gotham's suburbs, for those who could afford it.

APARTMENT LIVING IN MANHATTAN

Affordability was precisely the rub for those of New York's middle class—the overwhelming majority—who opted to remain in Manhattan. As the cost of a private town house soared from under $17,000 in 1889 to $64,000 in 1902, the number of single-family homes built each year plummeted from over 800 to fewer than 100.[14] From now on, middle-class Manhattanites would live in apartments. Legally speaking, "apartment houses" were indistinguishable from "tenements," the term New York City records applied to virtually any rental building with more than three units. Many middle-class families were therefore, officially, tenement dwellers. But in popular parlance, "tenement" was increasingly reserved for buildings occupied by working-class or poor tenants. "Apartment houses" sought to differentiate themselves by location, superior construction, stylistic embellishments, and functional amenities, but ultimately by the class composition of their occupants.

The number of multi-family dwellings multiplied rapidly, and after 1897, when height limits were loosened, such buildings also shot up in size. Residential structures of seven to fifteen stories became commonplace for the better-off. Housing, like so much else in New York, was agglomerating.[15]

---

14. By way of comparison, in Philadelphia, in 1900, 84.6 percent of the population lived in single-family houses, and only 1.1 percent occupied buildings that contained six or more families. In New York City, the figures were 17.5 percent and 50.3percent, respectively.

15. In 1885 New York State—in the interests of safety and health—had restricted the heights of residential buildings in Manhattan to a maximum of 70 feet on narrow streets, 80 feet on wider streets and avenues. This allowed commercial buildings, their heights as yet unrestricted, to soar ahead of their residential cousins, and also to outbid them for choice locations. (Hotels, however, were deemed commercial, and they joined the great leap upward.) In 1897 an amendment to the 1885 law loosened the constraints on residencies, allowing a maximum height of 150 feet—but no more than twelve stories (the average story was a little over 12 feet)—if the building was fireproof and had at least one passenger elevator. The 1901 Tenement House Act reimposed height limits, limiting residencies to one-third more than the width of the widest street on which they stood—a serious diminution—but allowed buildings fronting on 80-foot-wide cross streets to rise to ten stories, while leaving the maximum at twelve stories on 100-foot avenues. It also exempted hybrid apartment hotels from any restriction. Accordingly the great growth of twelve-story apartment houses would come overwhelmingly on Broadway and other broad avenues, and apartment hotel construction would bloom luxuriantly, though they seldom surpassed twelve stories in height.

Middle-class New Yorkers reconciled themselves to this prospect, and even came to celebrate it. By the 1890s they no longer saw apartments as a dangerous communal threat to privacy, or as a risqué ("French flat") peril to female morals, or as a hazard to class status (being insufficiently distinguishable from tenements). Genteel families had learned to feel "at home" in multi-family dwellings. Their cooperative character suited the temper of the times. A 1901 commentator argued that the New York apartment "follows a distinct tendency of this age of concentrated effort" in that "it eliminates the individual for the common good." Reformer Helen Campbell noted that apartment living brought cooperation—the secret of corporate success—to domestic enterprise.

A host of appealing features helped reconcile the middle classes to living stacked one on top of the other.

Apartments—the better ones—now came loaded with modern conveniences: all-night elevators, phones in each apartment, shower baths, filtered water. They also provided public spaces—lobbies, reception rooms, roof terraces, dining rooms—for genteel social interaction.

Apartments suited a wide variety of lifestyles. "Bachelor apartments" (for women as well as men) supplemented minimal personal quarters (a parlor, bedroom, and bath) with public places for entertaining. "Residential hotels" (the Iroquois, the Prince George, the Gotham) sent meals up in dumbwaiters. Studio apartments for artists (Hotel des Artistes, Central Park Studios) featured oversized windows.

Bachelor apartment, 1903. (Image No. 93.1.1.17661, Byron Company/Museum of the City of New York)

Apartments accommodated a great range of incomes. There were walk-ups and elevator buildings, rentals and co-ops, flats of two rooms or flats of twenty. In buildings of the highest class, doctors, lawyers, or businessmen could rent mammoth duplexes for $2,000–$10,000 a year. Seven-to-eleven-room apartments in more modest structures could be had for $600–$1,500 annually. Whatever the category, apartments (especially co-ops) ensured middle-class inhabitants like-statused neighbors; some promised explicitly to keep out "hooknosed tenants."

The designers of apartment interiors accommodated genteel values by segregating social, sleeping, and service spaces. Reception rooms—parlor, dining room, sitting room, and library—were clustered near the entrance. The family's private bedrooms were at the farthest remove, down a hall passageway. The kitchen and servants' quarters buffered the public and private territories.

Some residents dispensed with servants altogether, who were getting more expensive. Many of them, resenting the social stigma, the interminable hours, and the lack of independence, had opted for factory work over domestic labor, producing a shortage of maids, and driving up wages. The less affluent of the middle classes rapidly shed household help in these years: the number of servants per thousand families in New York dropped from 188 in 1880 to 141 in 1900 to 66 in 1920. One solution was to replace live-in workers with days-only workers, drawing increasingly on African American women; Bridget, the stereotyped full-time servant of the nineteenth century, increasingly gave way to Beulah, the part-time black maid of the twentieth. Apartment dwellers had yet another option: they could rely on workers hired by the building—laundresses, cooks, doormen, elevator operators, maintenance men. Apartment dwellers could also use machines situated in the basements and top floors (once the habitat of family retainers) to meet heating, refrigerating, and washing needs. The centralization and mechanization of housekeeping was particularly appealing to women. Ladies' household burdens were eased, making it easier to participate in city life.

There were also child-rearing benefits. Apartments, especially those with interior courtyards, helped keep children off the streets. A few even experimented with centralizing child care by hiring building nurses. But belief in women's mothering role set limits on this development. More generally, the ideology of family privacy, though weakened, remained strong enough to forestall full-scale collective living arrangements among the middle classes.

Externally, apartment buildings embodied a range of design vocabularies. Some came with bombastic French Baroque façades. Others featured a dignified Roman or Renaissance classicism. Most were now built as a unified ensemble rather than (as with the Dakota in the 1880s) a set of highly individualized fragments that allowed tenants to distinguish their part of the whole. All were sufficiently embellished to be readily distinguishable from tenements.

Apartment living had become progressive, even glamorous. The right kind of dwelling now certified social status. Moving out of a boardinghouse or tenement into an apartment building was a step up—particularly if it had the right address.

AFTER THE TURN OF THE CENTURY, the right address for tens of thousands of professionals, businessmen, and white-collar workers lay on Manhattan's West Side. The IRT, by making it easy to live north of 57th Street and work downtown, sparked a furious building boom. Large-scale developers raised hundreds of apartment buildings, usually ten to twelve stories tall and lavish enough to win over the respectable middle classes. They lined the area's prime crosstown streets (72nd, 79th, 86th, 96th, 106th, and 110th) and graced its avenues (Riverside Drive, West End, Central Park West, and Broadway—as "the Boulevard" was renamed in 1899).

Broadway's apartments were the grandest and most stylish. Developers vied to erect ever more spectacular structures along its route, rather as the steamship companies competed to launch ever more magnificent ocean liners.

The race began with the Dorilton (1902) at 71st Street, a voluptuously (some said floridly) detailed building, as bombastic as a Sousa march. In 1904 the Dorilton was eclipsed by the Ansonia, an apartment hotel a few blocks up Broadway financed by multi-millionaire William Earl Dodge Stokes. Having inherited *two* fortunes—Phelps, Dodge money from his father, Ansonia Brass and Copper funds from his mother—Stokes plunged into the booming real estate business. He obtained a block-long plot between 73rd and 74th Streets (part of the site of the old New York Orphan Asylum), and hired a French architect to confect a Belle Epoque Parisian apartment hotel. The ebullient seventeen-story Ansonia sported bulbous roofs, wrought-iron balconies, turrets, scrolls, brackets, cornices, and assorted satyrs. Its sumptuous units could accommodate families with their own servants in eighteen-room complexes for $625 a month.

The building—which took 240 employees to run—was as self-sufficient as the most vertically integrated corporation. Tenants got heat from its four steam boilers, electricity from its five dynamos, and—for those who dreaded New York's sweltering summers—air-conditioning from electric blowers in the basement, which circulated air over coils cooled by freezing brine, as done by cold-storage warehouses in the meatpacking district. Tenants also had

"Ansonia Apartments," ca. 1904. (Library of Congress Prints and Photographs Division)

"appliances for freezing artificial ice upon the spot" in their pantries. In the lobby, residents had a bank, a book stall, a cigar shop, a telegraph office, a doctor, a dentist, and a fountain with live seals. There they could take one of the seventeen elevators up to the seventeenth floor and eat in the English grill—they could also be served in their private suites—or continue on to the roof garden, where an orchestra played on summer nights. Or they could descend to the basement, with its garage (complete with repair shop), swimming pool, and Turkish bath.

Within four years, the title of "world's largest apartment house" passed to the Apthorp, a limestone-façaded megalith five blocks farther up Broadway commissioned by William Waldorf Astor. And it, in turn, lost the scepter to the mammoth Belnord (1908), another block-square Renaissance courtyard structure at 86th. Aside from these Broadway behemoths there were many others: the Belleclaire (1903), Manhasset (1904), Astor Apartments (1905), Hotel Marseilles (1905), Spencer Arms (1907), Van Dyck and Severn (1907), Alwyn Court (1908), and Astor Court (1916).

Other West Side avenues underwent a similar transformation. Around 1900 West End Avenue's charming three- and four-story houses began coming down, and by 1912 it had been transformed into a canyon of twelve-story structures. Central Park West, which had pioneered tall dwellings with the Dakota, underwent a second surge that didn't stop until buildings seven to twelve stories tall lined it almost continuously from 72nd to 110th Streets.[16] Riverside Drive retained a mansion-and-town-house character, except in its northern reaches at Morningside Heights. Here, on blockfronts bought up a generation earlier by the Astors, Goelets, and other investors, lavish structures rose, like the immense Hendrik Hudson (1907) at 110th, the stylish Strathmore (1909) at 113th, and the aptly named Colosseum (1910) at 116th, whose curved façade swept around toward the equally impressive Peter Minuit, Eton Hall, and Rugby Hall buildings on Claremont Avenue.

The building boom flowed northward into Central Harlem, following the projected pathway of the Lenox Avenue subway.[17] Between 1898 and 1904, Harlem experienced a land rush. Professional speculators formed syndicates that raised millions from corporate giants like Equitable and Metropolitan Life. Next they bought up the area's remaining undeveloped land from old Knickerbocker families. Finally they sold off the pieces to smaller investors, who contracted to builders, who covered Harlem's last vacant spaces with apartments and New Law tenements. In 1903–4, with the subway nearing completion, the fever also seized the German Jewish merchants and businessmen who had settled in the area since the 1880s, and even Russian immigrant workers, who now poured their modest savings into real estate speculation.

Elegant buildings went up along Lenox and Seventh Avenues, from Central Park North up to the 140s. The grandest of all was William Waldorf Astor's Graham Court (1901), an eight-story Florentine palazzo on Seventh between 116th and 117th Streets that was a close cousin to the Apthorp.

Middle-class Jews—the manufacturers, businessmen, and professionals Abe Cahan called "alrightniks"—flocked to these Central Harlem structures. They also drew clerks and

---

16. CPW became a site for major religious edifices. In 1897 Congregation Shearith Israel, the city's oldest Jewish congregation, settled into its newest home at 70th Street—a classical Corinthian-columned building that eschewed the once-favored Oriental or Near Eastern mode, now associated with Eastern Europeans. There was also the Ethical Culture Society Hall (1910) at 64th, Second Church of Christ Scientist (1900) at 68th, and the First Church of Christ Scientist (1904) at 96th.

17. It also followed the IRT's main line up into Hamilton and Washington Heights. (The road reached Dyckman Street and Fort George Hill in 1906.) The Riverside Drive viaduct (1901) over 125th Street also enhanced upper Manhattan's accessibility.

salespeople who worked in stores and offices in midtown, Yorkville, or Harlem itself. Among the arrivals were many newly prosperous Orthodox Jews, willing to sacrifice the Lower East Side's Jewish ambience for the amenities of middle-class life. One later commentator remarked that they considered the old neighborhood "more distant in their past than the Second Temple."

Edging their way westward, to avoid their proletarian brethren pouring into East Harlem, they soon occupied most of the new housing directly above 110th Street at Central Park. North of 125th Street and west of Fifth Avenue, however, supply outstripped demand. In 1906 the real estate market here crashed. Many apartments went begging. Rather than slash rents, Northwest Harlem real estate brokers would open their doors to African Americans, dramatically changing the complexion of the community. The outer limit of middle-class expansion had been established.

HOUSING STYLES OF THE RICH AND FAMOUS

The rich—those who *could* still afford private houses—went on a mansion-building binge during the boom years. Pulling out of their beleaguered downtown strongholds, they sidled up Fifth Avenue and occupied the Upper East Side.

As commerce infiltrated lower Fifth Avenue (below 59th Street) it lapped at the edges of Murray Hill, long a genteel citadel. Some fled; others held on tight. J. P. Morgan stayed imperiously put in his ample brownstone mansion at Madison and 36th. In 1906 he even commissioned Charles McKim to raise next door a Medicean library to house his vast collections. (In perhaps another indication of his determination to hold fast, he provided McKim an extra $50,000 to have the building's joints sealed as tight as the stones in the wall of the Erechtheum in Athens.) JPM also extended the Morgan family compound, providing a house for his daughter and son-in-law farther down 36th Street and purchasing another of the original Phelps Stokes mansions, at 231 Madison, for JPM Jr.

Farther north, the thick patch of Vanderbilts in the 50s began to thin out as hotels and retail stores invaded their precincts, converting Fifth Avenue into a busy, nerve-jangling thoroughfare. Here too the more stubborn dug in more deeply. John D. Rockefeller, ensconced since 1884 in an ostentatiously modest four-story brownstone at 4 West 54th, was joined in 1901 for a few years by his son JDR Jr. after his spectacular wedding to Abigail "Abby" Aldrich, daughter of the political potentate Rhode Island senator Nelson Aldrich. In 1912, at 10 West 54th, Junior built an immodestly gargantuan eight-story mansion, the tallest private home in the city. Junior also acquired other nearby houses and lots, widening the Rockefeller enclave. Standard Oil men remained rooted nearby, with Henry Flagler occupying the southeast corner of 54th Street and Fifth, and brother William Rockefeller the northeast corner. The Rockefellers were also busy building Kykuit (1913), a forty-room mansion in Westchester County overlooking the Hudson, a territory earlier staked out as Rockefeller country by William's 204-room Rockwood Hall.

But most in the lower Fifth Avenue vicinity decided to pull up stakes.

Some of the wealthy tried to open a new frontier on the West Side. Charles M. Schwab, US Steel's (and then Bethlehem Steel's) president, purchased another piece of the old New York Orphan Asylum site at Riverside Drive between 73rd and 74th Streets. Schwab bought it from Jacob Schiff, who had toyed with the idea of relocating there, until his wife vetoed the idea of living on the West Side, so far from her East Side friends. Schwab

"Aerial View of Schwab Mansion and Riverside Drive," 1907. (Image No. x2010.11.3082, Museum of the City of New York)

turned his block-square territory into a landscaped park, and erected thereon a seventy-five-room French Renaissance château. When completed in 1906, at a reputed cost of $7 million, it contained a private chapel, a state drawing room copied from the Petit Trianon, and a banquet hall for 1,500.

A few of Schwab's peers followed him across town. Singer heiress Elizabeth Clark had Singer architect Ernest Flagg design a mansion of white marble and red brick at 89th with sweeping river views (and a private colonnaded bowling alley). And Isaac Rice put up his Tuscan-style Villa Julia on Riverside Drive, one of roughly thirty freestanding mansions along the Hudson. But these were exceptions.[18]

Most of the super-rich stayed on or near Fifth Avenue, but pressed on north, to Lenox Hill—an area staked out by Havemeyers and Astors in the 1890s—and even higher, into the rugged reaches of upper Fifth Avenue, still an area of ragged farms, vacant lots, and squatter shanties.

The most prescient pioneer was Andrew Carnegie, who commissioned a sixty-four-room Georgian Revival mansion at the highest point on the avenue, between 90th and 91st Streets, which the Scotsman liked to call the Highlands of Fifth Avenue. Carnegie's presence (from 1902) established the area's fashionable character. So did his land policies. He purchased the territory to his north and south and sold it off only to buyers of whom he approved. One who passed muster was financier Otto Kahn. At 91st Street, he raised one of the largest private houses ever built in New York—a stunning Renaissance palace more faithful to Rome's Palazzo della Cancelleria than even the Villard houses had been.

By the 1910s Fifth Avenue, from Rockefeller to Carnegie, was congested with millionaires. So were the side streets of the 60s, 70s, and 80s that stretched east from Central Park.

---

18. J. P. Morgan's right-hand man, George W. Perkins, erected a neo-Georgian house on an estate in Riverdale (the Bronx). But he simply was joining an enclave of wealthy families, notably the Dodges, Delafields, and Pynes, who had been ensconced in great houses along the Hudson since the 1860s and 1870s.

They piled into mansions a scant few feet from the palazzo next door, and squeezed into town houses abutting their neighbors. The Upper East Side positively teemed with stockbrokers, department store owners, commercial bankers, mine owners, real estate moguls, railroad entrepreneurs, oil magnates, insurance executives—and the out-of-town monied coming to the Big City to make their mark.

Most of the era's movers and shakers roosted here: Henry Clay Frick (who purchased the site of the old Lenox Library and had Thomas Hastings build him a Louis XV palace-cum-gallery intended, Frick supposedly said, to make former associate Carnegie's home "look like a miner's shack"); utility entrepreneurs Thomas Fortune Ryan and his partner William C. Whitney (whose housewarming festivities in 1901 inaugurated the city's largest private ballroom); financiers Jacob Schiff, his son-in-law Felix Warburg, James Stillman, Percy Pyne, and Levi Morton; industrial magnates Henry Phipps and James B. Duke; publisher Joseph Pulitzer (in his soundproofed McKim, Mead & White mansion on 73rd Street); and corporate attorney and imperial proconsul Elihu Root.

Adding to the crush were the proliferating number of heirs and heiresses, the progeny of the New York rich, old as well as nouveau. The Upper East Side swarmed with little Pratts, Clarks, Vanderbilts, Ryans, Harknesses, Rhinelanders, Iselins, Cuttings, and Livingstons. William C. Whitney's son Payne had a sumptuously furnished marble palazzo. Stockbroker Lewis Gouverneur Morris resided in a gabled brick domicile. And a French Gothic concoction—with pinnacled dormers, gargoyles, and a moat—housed the last direct male descendent of Peter Stuyvesant.

Raising new town houses (or converting old brownstones) kept the city's leading architects busy. McKim, Mead & White, Delano & Aldrich, Carrère & Hastings, C. P. H. Gilbert, Grosvenor Atterbury, Ernest Flagg, and James Ware churned out structures in a profusion of historical styles that some found amusing. Charles Whibley, a visiting Englishman, was tickled by Fifth Avenue's jumbled-up juxtapositions. "Here you may find a stronghold of feudalism cheek by jowl with the quiet mansion of a colonial gentleman. There Touraine jostles Constantinople." Did the wealthy inhabitants perhaps "dress their parts with conscientious gravity," he wondered, "and sit down to dine with the trappings of costume and furniture which belong to their houses? Suppose they did," he mused on, "and suppose in obedience to a signal they precipitated themselves upon the highway, there would be such a masquerade of fancy dress as the world has never seen."

Some discerned more substantial issues in the prevalent mansion-itis. From the quasi-anthropological vantage point of Thorstein Veblen's *Theory of the Leisure Class* (1899) it seemed a form of class preening was at work, with the mansions displaying their owners' pretensions to cultural as well as economic hegemony. Others perceived insecurity rather than hegemony. Architectural and social critic Herbert Croly suggested (in 1902) that the New York millionaire was drawn to things with an "atmosphere of time and stability" because he wanted "to emancipate his children and his fellow-countrymen from the reproach of being raw and new; and consequently he tries in every way to bring to bear upon them historical and traditional influences." Aggressive and innovative in business, the Manhattan elite still seemed culturally timid, reliant on European models to certify status.

The elite's architectural choices were not, however, completely random. Though many continued to construct feudal strongholds—French châteaux or Italian palazzi—the drift was increasingly toward the plainer mansions of Georgian English or Colonial Federalist provenance. To keep up with the shifting styles, many East Side town-house owners purged their Italianate or Queen Anne brownstone façades and substituted neo-Georgian or neo-Federal limestone fronts.

Trends in interior decoration were still more decisive. In 1897 Edith Wharton (scion of an old New York family and a blossoming writer) collaborated with Ogden Codman Jr. (a "clever young Boston architect" in Wharton's words) in authoring *The Decoration of Houses*. Their manifesto denounced the "sumptuary excesses" of the 1870s and 1880s—the dark and elaborate furniture, the "smug and suffocating upholstery," the hideous clutter and bric-a-brac that had characterized the parlors of their youth and still infected many of the rich. The Vanderbilts, Wharton sniffed, "are entrenched in a sort of *thermopylae* of bad taste, from which apparently no force on earth can dislodge them."

Wharton and Codman's proposed alternative, gleaned from extensive European travels, was a return to the style of the eighteenth century (in either its Louis Seize or American Federal variants). They anathematized ornament, eclecticism, and profusion. They exalted lightness, formality, and symmetry (an instinct "more strongly developed in those races which have reached the highest artistic civilization"). True "style," they taught, derived not from gewgaws but from harmony of organization, unification of color, and an architectural exactitude gained only from careful study.

With Wharton's crisp prose, Codman's illustrations, and Charles McKim's endorsement, *The Decoration of Houses* soon achieved canonical status among New York (and Newport) Society. Codman himself (aided by Wharton's connections) reworked homes of the Vanderbilts, Rockefellers, and Morgans. Many of Fifth Avenue's drawing rooms and great halls—the settings for the period's balls, dinners, and receptions—owed much to their precepts.[19]

The Upper East Side mansions owed even more to the immense staffs who ran them. Like the new apartment houses, the great houses deployed state-of-the-art technology. But they relied far more on the valets, coachmen, footmen, cooks, nurses, lady's maids, parlormaids, chambermaids, scullery maids, and laundresses—supervised by butlers and housekeepers—who lived in parallel households (usually upstairs though occasionally downstairs), and did the washing, ironing, cooking, cleaning, and purchasing—from Third Avenue shops, if they didn't like what tradesmen's wagons brought to the kitchen door.

Fifth Avenue became famous (or infamous) throughout the country for its "Two Miles of Millionaires." Its mansions became part of a new street theater. In the 1860s, 1870s, and 1880s, the affluent had paraded before the masses in their coaching processions. Now—especially after 1905, when the Fifth Avenue Coach Company imported twenty-four French double-decker buses—the masses rolled past the rich.

FOR ALL THEIR NOTORIETY, THE MANSIONS PROVED EVANESCENT. Within a generation, nearly all would be pulled down. But the rich themselves would not be driven from the Upper East Side as they had been from Bowling Green, Bond Street, the various Squares, and the lower reaches of Fifth Avenue. This time they put down stronger roots.

---

19. Their ideas were popularized by Codman's protégé Elsie de Wolfe. Though she is sometimes called the first interior decorator, her book *The House in Good Taste* (1913) mainly rephrased *The Decoration of Houses* in a chattier, more personal style and with an air of practicality aimed at those "modern women who demand simplified living." Wolfe decorated Frick's second floor and, at Stanford White's urging, was engaged to design the rooms of the Colony Club. The new stylistic canon also served to draw a sharp line between class tastes. The middle classes who lagged behind, still hewing to Queen Anne excrescences of spindles and balconies, could now be condemned as ill bred.

They gathered their schools, clubs, and churches around them. Private academies like St. Bernard's, Brearley's, and Buckley were moved to the new uptown oasis. Clubs like the University, Union, Racquet and Tennis, Colony, Lambs, Knickerbocker, New York Yacht, Harmonie, Harvard, and Lotos were housed or rehoused nearby, in suitably monumental and "historical" structures. Houses of worship were relocated (St. Bartholomew's Episcopal was built anew on the site of the old F. & M. Schaefer Brewery) or rearranged (Phillips Presbyterian was merged with Madison Avenue Presbyterian and redesigned in austere neo-Gothic).

More significantly for the area's future, some of the very wealthy decided to emulate their working- and middle-class peers and adopt conjoint modes of living. Cautiously at first, then in growing numbers, the Upper East Side rich abandoned individual residencies for ultra-luxurious high-rise apartment houses. With only one flat, or at most two, per floor, these buildings afforded all the amenities of private houses.

The icebreaker, in 1910, was 998 Fifth, a twelve-story Italian palazzo erected by McKim, Mead & White just across from the Metropolitan Museum of Art. (In keeping with the East Side's more staid character, most of its tall buildings eschewed the exotic English and French names adopted across the park and stuck to numbers.) The grand luxe "998" housed a very exclusive clientele, once it had been rendered respectable by the arrival of Elihu Root, now Senator Root. He was coaxed into taking a floor there by Douglas Elliman, the enterprising rental agent for 998, who—seeing the senator as a loss leader—offered him a twenty-room $2,000-a-month apartment for only $1,250.

Because Fifth was crammed with mansions, underdeveloped Park Avenue attracted most of the new high-class high-rises.[20] After the trains running beneath it were electrified, eliminating the blasts of steam issuing from subterranean vents, luxury apartments went up between the 50s and the 90s. Many were commissioned by Bing & Bing, a real estate management firm founded in 1905. Among these was Warren and Wetmore's 903 Park, at 79th Street. With seventeen floors, 903 Park was the city's tallest apartment house; it boasted duplexes with twenty-four rooms and seven baths. By 1917 Park Avenue south of 59th Street was solidly lined with neo-Renaissance, neoclassical, or neo-Gothic towers, and most desirable uptown corners were similarly occupied (though much of upper Park Avenue in the 60s and 70s still retained the old mix of tenements, row houses, garages, and institutional buildings).

These pioneer towers helped anchor the rich. They minimized the tendency of the affluent to take wing, like startled geese, at the slightest intrusion of commerce or the lower classes. The density levels of their own kind provided a safety and stability they'd never known. They had spatially consolidated their class.

THE MANHATTAN RICH HAD ONE ADDITIONAL HIGH-RISE HOUSING OPTION: the spectacular grand hotels now opening up in their neighborhood.

One of the first of the seductive new venues was, fittingly enough for an era of mergers, the Waldorf-Astoria, an 1897 consolidation of two hostelries. In 1893 William Waldorf Astor had erected a thirteen-story hotel at Fifth Avenue and 33rd and named it after himself (a family tradition dating to John Jacob Astor's Astor House of 1836). One of his motives was to

---

20. There were some upper-class apartments on the West Side. Hearst, always the contrarian, rented a three-floor apartment atop the luxurious Clarendon on Riverside Drive at 86th Street. But he never became completely apartment-broken. Having crammed his triplex with tapestries, paintings, and statuary armor, he decided he needed more space still. When the landlord refused his request to lease the eighth and ninth floors as well, Hearst bought the building and redid the top five tiers as a unit, including a two-story bedroom, and a three-story baronial gallery fronting the Hudson.

annoy his Aunt Caroline (who lived next door) in retaliation for her having successfully defended her title as "*the* Mrs. Astor" against William's wife, Mary. Caroline indeed was forced to flee to a Hunt-designed château at 65th and Fifth, but her son John Jacob IV riposted by putting up the Astoria, an even taller hotel at 34th Street. Finally the feuding cousins concluded a merger, creating the Waldorf-Astoria, though a clause in the contract stipulated the two properties could be sealed off in the event of a falling out.

The Waldorf-Astoria—the largest hotel in the world (it filled the Fifth Avenue blockfront between 33rd and 34th Street)—provided far more than living quarters; it served as something of a community center for the city's elite. The management enticed Vanderbilts and Fishes to its elegant public rooms for their private entertainments, and to its mammoth ballroom for their major fêtes. The grand hotel allowed the rapidly expanding upper class to meet and socialize in quarters more commodious than most mansions could afford.

As the monied precincts shifted uptown, so did hotel construction. John Jacob Astor IV followed up his 34th Street triumph by commissioning the eighteen-story St. Regis (the city's tallest hotel) twenty blocks farther up Fifth at 55th Street. When it opened in 1904, the towering building took the palm as New York's finest, with its copper-crested mansard, bronze Art Nouveau elevators, forty-seven Steinway pianos, and a 3,000-volume library.

Certainly the St. Regis utterly outclassed the old eight-story, brick-and-brownstone Plaza Hotel (1890) three blocks farther up the avenue. So much so that one day in 1904, over lunch at Astor's new hotel, a group of men formed a syndicate to tear down the old Plaza and erect a new one. One of these players was Harry Black, of the United States Realty and Improvement Company; another was Bernhard Beinecke, a German immigrant butcher who had gotten rich supplying hotels and steamship lines, then moved on to command a Hudson River stockyard at 59th Street, and finally became a financier. A third participant was John Gates, who had been, successively, grocery clerk, salesman, barbedwire king, steel magnate and—after selling out to Morgan's US Steel—a fabulously wealthy speculative promoter.

The syndicate hired architect Henry Janeway Hardenbergh, designer of the Dakota, the Waldorf, and the Astoria, and he produced an eighteen-story French Renaissance masterpiece. From the day in October 1907 that it opened its crystal-and-bronze revolving doors (manned by doormen in black satin and yellow silk braid), the Plaza became the apotheosis of Edwardian elegance. Plaudits were showered on its French tapestries, Louis XVI furniture, gold-encrusted china, Savonnerie and Aubusson rugs (supplied by W&J Sloane), 1,650 crystal chandeliers, great marble foyer, magnificent Tea Room, ballroom paneled in yellow silk—and even its garbage destroyer, capable of rescuing accidentally rubbished silverware.

Ninety percent of the Plaza's suites were reserved for permanent guests—the earliest of whom included a Vanderbilt, a Harriman, a Jay, a Gould, and a Duke. They paid in annual rental roughly what it cost to maintain a Fifth Avenue mansion. In addition, the Plaza gradually usurped the Waldorf-Astoria's role as premiere venue for Society's most shimmering affairs.

SUMMER HOMES

One reason monied New Yorkers were drawn to hotel living was that for some of them the metropolis was only one stop on a perpetual grand tour. The very rich tended to be "in residence" only from around Thanksgiving Day through a week or so after New Year's, and again for part of March and April. The rest of the time they were on the move.

In January or February they might go south to their winter quarters, perhaps near Aiken in South Carolina, or on Jekyll Island off Georgia. After a spring stopover in the metropolis for shopping and dressmaking, it was off to Long Island for May and then (by steam yacht) to Newport or Bar Harbor in June or early July. After a strenuous summer of dinners, balls, and picnics—and perhaps a stint in August roughing it at their neo-rustic hunting and fishing lodges in the Adirondacks—they might go down to their summer cottages in the Berkshires (notably to Lenox) during September. The Horse Show brought them back to New York in November (apart from hunting excursions on Long Island) where they stayed for the Season of new plays and operas until the chill sent them south again. In some years, however, this rotational scheme might be scrapped altogether for a lengthy stay (six months or more) in Europe. For travelers such as these, camping out in a super-luxurious hotel was a convenient alternative to maintaining a full-scale Manhattan residence, its closing down and opening up being such a chore.

The super-rich did not stint on their out-of-town accommodations—in Newport, in Lenox, in the Adirondacks, in the Lorillards' Tuxedo Park in the Ramapos, or on Jekyll Island (hideaway of "One Hundred Millionaires," where the streets—Morgan Road and [William] Rockefeller Path—were named after residents.) But perhaps their most spectacular constructions were those on Long Island, the peregrination point closest to the city.

From roughly 1900 on—especially after William Kissam "Willie K" Vanderbilt II's auto races introduced them to the charms of the island's North Shore—the boom-era's top beneficiaries competed vigorously in building stupendous country estates. The "Gold Coast" that emerged, running from Manhasset to Huntington, was festooned with Belmonts, Dodges, Guggenheims, Kahns, Havemeyers, Morgans, Phippses, Whitneys, Woolworths, and Vanderbilts—and many, many others, whose names were less resonant, but who were able to ante up and join the game.

Their celebrity architects and designers produced a profusion of castles, villas, manors, and châteaux, usually replete with formal gardens. J. P. Morgan Jr. bought himself a Georgian revival estate in 1909, along with the 240-acre island off Glen Cove on which it sat; the only access was a medieval-style stone bridge with a twenty-four-hour guard (which would prove insufficient to block an assassination attempt in 1915). Frank Winfield Woolworth used $9 million worth of nickels and dimes to build Winfield Hall (1917), a fifty-six-room Italian Renaissance marble manor, also in Glen Cove, but on more firma terra. At Sands Point, the next peninsula over, Jay Gould's son Harry couldn't make up his stylistic mind; when he first bought the land in 1900 he commissioned a replica of Ireland's medieval Kilkenny Castle; completed in 1904, it was dubbed Castle Gould. Then Harry decided he didn't much care for the castle, so he switched to Tudor; a forty-room manor with an 80-foot tower was duly completed in 1912, only to be sold off in 1917 to Daniel Guggenheim. When Alva Belmont did her own Sands Point castle in 1917, she too insisted on medieval Irish but made sure her white stucco confection Beacon Towers was considerably roomier than Gould's relatively cramped quarters: hers had sixty rooms. Two peninsulas farther west, at Manhasset, gas and electric magnate Nicholas F. Brady's Tudor manor, Inisfada (Gaelic for "Long Island"), trumped Alva's, with eighty-seven rooms on 225 acres (and $6 million worth of furnishing); indeed, it was the fourth-largest residence in the United States. But it was Otto Kahn who won the mine's-bigger-than-yours sweepstakes. His Oheka Castle (an acronym for Otto Hermann Kahn), out at Cold Spring Harbor, was designed by Delano & Aldrich. It had 127 rooms, fifty baths, thirty-nine fireplaces, a dining room that seated 200, and a grand staircase inspired by the Château Fontainebleau in France; and its 443 acres were landscaped by the Olmsted

Brothers. It was rated the country's second-largest private residence (with George Vanderbilt's Biltmore, down in Asheville, North Carolina, retaining the number-one position).

The second front of this colossal patrician playpen was strung out along Long Island's southern shore. Here August Belmont Jr. raised racehorses on an 1,100-acre estate in North Babylon. Farther east, around Oakdale, at the head of the Connetquot River, which flowed into Nicoll Bay, another collection of multi-millionaires established estates. The elder William K. Vanderbilt (Willie K's father, the Commodore's grandson) had pioneered the area with his 900-acre Idle Hour estate back in 1879, and when it burned down in 1899 he replaced it with a 110-room version in 1901. Right nearby was the 2,000-acre Indian Neck Hall estate of Frederick Gilbert Bourne, president of Singer Sewing Machine (designed, of course, by Ernest Flagg), and Westbrook, the estate of financier, lawyer, and railroad man William Bayard Cutting. Farther east still was the colony at Southampton opened up by Gotham Society figures like Salem H. Wales, who back in the 1870s had built one of the first summerhouses and erected another one for his son-in-law, Elilhu Root, who became a regular.

In addition to these compounds, there were a host of convivial gathering spots, such as the Meadow Brook Hunt Club, the Meadow Brook Polo Club, the Shinnecock Hills Golf Club in Southampton (its Stanford White clubhouse perhaps the oldest in the United States), and the Piping Rock Club (Locust Valley, 1911), whose Colonial Revival architecture, said *Country Life* magazine, was "the sort of thing that George Washington would have built if he had the money."

Jews not being completely comfortable (or welcome) in many of these venues, the Guggenheims, Lehmans, Lewisohns, Loebs, Schiffs, Seligmans, and Warburgs often opted for the "Jewish Newport" in Monmouth County, running south along the Jersey Shore from Rumson through Sea Bright, Long Branch, Elberon, and Deal Beach to Allenhurst, just above Asbury Park.

This extravagantly peripatetic style was open to only the super-wealthiest. The run-of-the-mill rich didn't migrate with the seasons but contented themselves with summers in the country, or by the sea, in their own country estates or second homes.

The prosperous middle and moderately well-off laboring classes stayed closer to home, tethered by their lesser resources, opting for summer rentals, usually in ethnic enclaves.

Until the 1880s comfortable German-Jewish families had summered in the Catskills without incident. They would take the ferry from 42nd Street to the Weehawken depot of the Ontario and Western Railroad and journey northwestward to one of the hotels advertised in the railroad's magazine, *Summer Homes*. Then the season of anti-Semitism began. Many Catskill hostelries—as had those at Saratoga—announced that "Hebrews will knock vainly for admission." The response was to establish alternatives. In 1899 *Summer Homes* carried an insert promoting the Rock Hill Jewish Boarding House. It promised "good airy rooms," "scenery unsurpassed," and "Jewish faith and customs throughout."

In the next decade, more than a thousand farms were sold to Eastern European Jews, most along a 10-mile strip near Ellenville, New York. Nearly all the farmhouses were turned into summer boardinghouses, and the produce of the land used to feed the visitors. Some old-time Baptists and Methodists now referred to the area as "the Sheeny Mountains," and bouts of anti-Semitic vandalism erupted from time to time. But most local farmers were reconciled to the invasion by the booming demand for poultry, eggs, and vegetables.

Word of the mountains' delights spread rapidly. In 1904 Abraham Cahan ran a series on Catskills living in the *Jewish Daily Forward*. Tubercular patients in upstate sanitariums sent back reports about its health-giving qualities. Ads trumpeting "Pure Air. Pure Water. Pure Milk" captivated a people who divided their lives between tenement and sweatshop.

By the 1910s the Catskills were booming. Some of the larger establishments raised their prices, hired bands, and imported vaudeville entertainers. They sought

"The Catskill Mountains." *Puck*, July 25, 1906. (Library of Congress Prints and Photographs Division)

out and attracted a wealthier clientele of sweatshop owners, real estate speculators, successful merchants, cigar manufacturers, Yiddish-theater stars, doctors, lawyers, and dentists. Wives stayed the season; spouses came up on the weekend "husband train" or by auto. Singles of both sexes came, too. These stenographers, bookkeepers, and librarians usually spent a fortnight (they were known as "two-weekers") taking in the hotel dances and hayrides, looking for romance (often unsuccessfully, as there were twelve Jewish girls for every eligible boy).

There were also accommodations for those who couldn't afford hotels. These ranged downward from small boardinghouses (like one opened in 1913 by Galician refugees Selig and Malke Grossinger) to the *kuchaleyn* ("cook-alones"), where patrons slept in separate rooms of the farmhouse and shared an overpopulated communal kitchen, to the bungalow colonies (considered the slums of the Jewish Catskills), which consisted of wooden shacks behind the main farmhouse.

The Irish middling classes headed east to the Rockaways. This barely accessible peninsula of Queens County had earlier attracted well-to-do vacationers (Astors, Vanderbilts) and literary luminaries (Irving, Longfellow) after the Doric doors of the Greek Revival Marine Pavilion had opened in 1833. (It burned down in 1864.) Between the 1870s and 1890s, ferries from Canarsie, steamboats from Manhattan, and cross-bay rail service via an 1880 trestle bridge made the area more accessible and less fashionable. As the wealthy headed east toward the Hamptons, in came the Irish (and the Jews). Bungalows and tent cities sprang up; old hotels near Neponsit and Belle Harbor were converted to rooming houses; arcades and other amusements flourished in seaside towns called Seaside, Irish Town, and Averne. Much of this infrastructure, including nineteen hotels, was incinerated in a great 1892 fire, but surging demand for ocean access led to prompt rebuilding, indeed extra added attractions: Rockaways' Playland opened in 1901. Train service was electrified in 1905, making it even easier for working fathers to commute to the beaches on summer weekends to visit vacationing families in the hundreds of cottages that now rimmed the bays and coves.

The great mass of the populace, of course, stayed and sweltered in the summer heat. Apart from Sunday trips to various beaches and amusement parks, the only exemptions from August doldrums were those provided by the popular press, charities, and settlement houses. Since 1878 the *Tribune* had been running the Fresh Air Fund, activated originally by the *Evening Post*. It was soon joined by Pulitzer's *World*, which ran its own excursions taking poor kids to the country. In 1908–9 the Henry Street Settlement opened its first summer camps: Camp Henry for boys and Echo Hill Farm for girls. Catholics, the Young Men's Hebrew Association, Orthodox Jewish groups, the YMCA, the Association for the Improvement of the

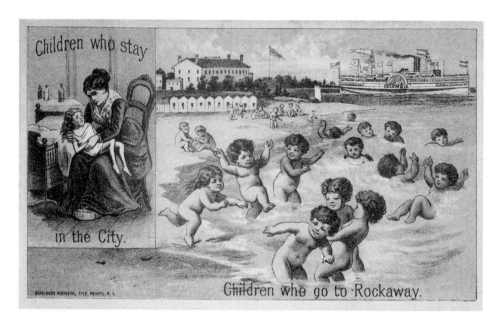

"Children Who Stay in the City — Children Who Go to Rockaway," ca. 1900. (Library of Congress Prints and Photographs Division)

"The Tent City at Rockaway," ca. 1903. (Library of Congress Prints and Photographs Division)

Condition of the Poor, and the Children's Aid Society all offered possibilities for tenement children to spend a few days or weeks in a clean, healthy, and "uplifting" environment.[21]

AS THE CITIZENRY MOVED OUT INTO THE LARGER CITY, their rehousing facilitated by the expanding transit latticework, Gotham's industrial and commercial sectors were also moving across the urban landscape, partly pursuing customers and workers, partly drawing clients and laborers along in their wake.

---

21. New Yorkers were as divided in death as they were in life. Society's upper crust came to favor Woodlawn Cemetery. Jay Gould was one of the first plutocrats interred there, and while the Four Hundred had shunned him in life, they soon joined him in death. Soon Belmonts and Goelets were commissioning McKim, Mead & White, Ernest Flagg, and other leading architects to design them suitable mausoleums. Here again fashion dictates shifted, and mortuary (like domestic) architecture tended toward classicism. Hebrews cultivated their own plots. Affluent German Jews like the Guggenheims turned to Salem Fields in Brooklyn's Cypress Hills. Many working-class Jews bought plots in Mount Hebron or Mount Zion through burial societies like the Workmen's Circle. Middle- and working-class Catholics turned to the cemeteries strung out along the glacial moraine on the Brooklyn-Queens border, the greatest number to Calvary in Maspeth and Woodside. The poor and destitute who died in Bellevue or on Blackwell's Island were laid out in the City Morgue. Those unclaimed after two or three days—perhaps 5,000–6,000 each year—were photographed and taken to the potter's field on Hart's Island.

11

Industrial and Commercial City

FACTORY TOWN

In 1913 there were, roughly speaking, 34,000 factories in New York City, in which some 700,000 men, women, and children labored, at a time when the total population was about 5,000,000. Gotham's industrial workforce was larger than Chicago's and Philadelphia's combined; larger than the combined factory population of Pittsburgh, Cleveland, Cincinnati, St. Louis, Detroit, Boston, Rochester, and Buffalo. This army of labor, coupled with $1.5 billion of invested capital, retained for Greater New York its status as the country's leading manufacturing center.

The city's industrial economy also remained the nation's most diverse, as evidenced by a 1913 listing, compiled by the Merchants' Association of New York, of manufactured goods in whose production Gotham ranked first among American cities. It included artificial flowers; blacking and polishing preparations; bread and other bakery products; boxes (cigar); boxes (fancy and paper); buttons; chemicals; clothing (men's); clothing (women's); coffins; confectionery; cooperage; copper, tin, and sheet iron products; cordage, twine, jute, and linen goods; engravers' materials; flags, regalia, and society emblems; food preparations; furnishing goods (men's); furs and fur skins (dressed); gas and electric fixtures, lamps, and reflectors; gas (illuminating and heating); gold and silver leaf and foil; ink (printing); jewelry; leather goods; liquors (malt); marble and stone work; millinery and lace goods; musical instruments, pianos, and organs; paint and varnish; paper goods; patent medicines and druggists preparations;

Cover, *Associated Manufacturers' Catalogue*, Spring 1916. (Smithsonian Institution, Warshaw Collection of Business Americana, National Museum of American History)

pens (fountain); photoengraving; pipes (tobacco); printing and publishing; smelting and refining; stereotyping and electrotyping; tobacco manufactures; toys and novelties; umbrellas and canes; and window shades.

According to a bulletin issued by the Federal Census in 1912, the total value of products manufactured in New York City in 1899 had been a little over $1 billion; by 1909, it had doubled, passing the $2 billion mark.

Gotham's manufacturing output had grown so vast and variegated because it had developed in interaction with other equally substantial and rapidly expanding economic sectors. Consider printing, the city's second-biggest industry. New York manufacturers produced one-fourth of the nation's printed matter because Gotham's expanding publishing industry was churning out books, magazines, and newspapers that needed printing, and the city's booming financial, corporate, and commercial sectors required an unending torrent of printed stocks, contracts, bonds, deeds, trust certificates, paper money, and the like.[1] These accelerating demands summoned ever more print shops into being, which in turn expanded the need for printing presses, printer's ink, and linotype machines; for the tools of the photoengraving, lithography, and bookbinding trades; and for production of typewriters, pencils, envelopes, letter files, paper clips, and paper—tons and tons of paper.

---

1. In 1909 1,953 publications (newspapers and periodicals) were produced in New York City; they had an aggregate circulation of roughly forty-four million readers.

The clothing industry—New York's largest—had been galvanized by the ongoing shift from home- and tailor-made garments to ready-to-wears, by the presence of an immense immigrant workforce and a deep pool of highly skilled artisans, by the growth of the city's network of wholesalers who soaked up product and distributed it to far-flung purveyors, and by a concomitant expansion of the city's retail outlets (notably department stores). The garment trade's growth stimulated in turn the local production of sewing machines, textiles, pins, needles, buttons, notions, paper patterns, and dyestuffs.

One of the greatest spurs to industrial development was the city-building project itself. The construction of skyscrapers, offices, hotels, warehouses, and residences demanded a steady supply of steam shovels, air compressors, boilers, elevators, sheet metal, iron pipes, brick, firebrick, cement, concrete, terra-cotta, roofing material, iron and steel shutters, steam and hot water apparatuses, plumbing supplies, and doors. The spectacular spread of tenements and town houses generated demand for household goods, duly supplied by metropolitan manufacturers of crockery, pottery, enamelware, metal kitchenware (brass, copper, nickel, silver), gas fittings, bulbs, iceboxes, artificial ice, chairs, furniture, cabinets, carpets, rugs, linoleum, paint and varnish, brushes, wallpaper, window frames, window shades, blinds, clocks, pianos, phonographs, and billiard tables; and, for final resting places, wooden or steel coffins, stone memorials and monuments. The residents themselves needed provisioning, which prodded the food-and-drink industry—already responding to the shifting of much food production from home to factory—to turn out more bread, biscuits, pies, cakes, candy, chocolate, chewing gum, pickles, fresh and cured meats, beer, milk, condensed milk, roasted coffee, and seltzer. This cornucopic outpouring of goods was sped on its way—to local, national, and international markets—by the city's enhanced rail and shipping networks, which, themselves being under construction, drummed up still more industrial production.

Twentieth-century manufacturing would be carried out on a new scale. While there were still many thousands of small plants and sweatshops—most manufacturers did *not* go through the corporate merger process—the era's distinctive features would be the mushrooming number of giant-sized factories (a thousand workers or more) whose owners *had* incorporated and tapped into the capital markets; and the emergence of quasi-cooperative ventures, in which a constellation of small- and mid-sized manufacturers would come together in king-sized congeries—from the same or different trades, in horizontal or vertical formats—to share costs of production and distribution. And while these Everests of production did loom over Manhattan's crowded manufacturing districts, they were more strikingly in evidence in the outer boroughs—as a tour of Gotham's early-twentieth-century industrial landscape makes clear.

TOURING THE INDUSTRIAL CITY

Staten Island, though still largely bucolic in 1900, had inherited a modest industrial sector from the nineteenth century, dating back to Factoryville (later West Brighton), a cluster of manufactories that had grown up around an 1819 dye works, and to Linoleumville (later Travis), which developed as the lengthened shadow of the 1873 American Linoleum Manufacturing Company. In 1880 there had been 100 manufacturing establishments, employing, all told, 1,557 persons.

The new century ushered in new developments, particularly at the western end of the island's northern shore, just across the water from New Jersey's industrial powerhouses—Bayonne (Standard Oil's refinery stronghold) and Elizabethport (where Singer was expanding its manufacturing base).

In 1905 Procter & Gamble purchased a 77-acre parcel at Howland Hook, where Kill Van Kull merged with the Arthur Kill. Its mammoth plant began operations in 1907, and soon its 1,500-strong workforce was producing a million cases of Ivory Soap each year. The firm added soap powder to its mix in 1912, and within a decade the complex had grown to twenty-eight buildings, spread over a 129-acre site, which so completely dominated its corner of the island that it got renamed Port Ivory.

Virtually next door, slightly to the east, lay another huge complex, the Milliken Brothers Company, established in 1887. The Milliken firm provided structural steel to, and served as construction contractor for, high-rises and bridges. The only structural steel plant in New York City, its 150 engineers and draftsmen and 2,500 workers fed the skyscraper boom, never more dramatically than in 1906, when it won the contract to erect and furnish structural steel for the Singer Building. Milliken also worked in other US cities, and in foreign countries: it established branch offices in London, Havana, Mexico City, Capetown, and Honolulu, becoming an early exporter not only of prefabricated steel components but of construction and engineering expertise. Its Staten Island base expanded steadily as the company invested in new equipment by issuing millions in bonds. But the firm overreached, and got caught out in the 1907 panic. It did manage to limp along in receivership for the next few years—it completed the Singer Tower but had to pass on Pennsylvania Station—before tumbling into bankruptcy in 1913; in 1917 its plant was absorbed into a shipbuilding complex being created by Wallace Downey.

Downey, a Nova Scotia–born marine architect, had moved to Brooklyn in 1880, had been apprenticed to a firm of shipwrights at the Erie Basin, and in 1892 had organized the firm of Townsend & Downey. In 1898 he set up a shipbuilding operation on Shooters Island, just offshore from Mariners Harbor (the neighborhood directly east of Howland Hook). Downey assembled an 1,800-man labor force that turned out a variety of ships, including substantial (9,000-ton) vessels for the federal government, and barges for its neighbor Standard Oil. Downey also did yachts, and he gained international attention when he built a schooner yacht, the *Meteor III*, for Kaiser Wilhelm II. It was launched in 1902 from Shooters Island by Alice Roosevelt (at the request of the German ambassador). Her father was in attendance as well, but the president was overshadowed by the presence of Prince Henry of Prussia, the Kaiser's brother, whom Gothamites fell all over themselves in welcoming—as the citizenry had once, for all its republican professions, gone wild over the Prince of Wales back in 1860.

Downey's firm went belly up in 1904, in part because of labor troubles with the boilermakers union. He worked on shipbuilding in Brooklyn for a time, and became a vigorous advocate for rebuilding America's merchant marine, urging a combination of government support (to offset state aid to European competitors) and standardized production techniques. In 1915 Downey returned to Shooters Island and founded Standard Shipbuilding, capitalized with $3 million, and rapidly installed new facilities capable of handling 12,000-ton ships. In 1917, now at the helm of a Downey Shipbuilding Corporation, he bought up the property and equipment of the defunct Milliken Brothers steelmaking operation, and installed there several 10,000-ton shipbuilding berths and steel plate furnaces, capable of turning out 100,000 tons of standardized steel steamships per year.

By then other large shipyards had entered the field—particularly along the northern shore but some, too, in Tottenville, a village on the southern end of Staten Island. Tottenville

"Townsend-Downey Shipbuilding Co.: Shipyard and Works, Shooters Island, Borough of Richmond, New York City. New York Office, 12 Broadway." *New York, the Metropolis: The Book of Its Merchants' Association and of Co-Operating Public Bodies*, 1902.

also hosted the Atlantic Terra Cotta Company. Atlantic's three gigantic cone-shaped kilns—forty-eight feet high—fired the clay panels used to clothe the steel bodies of many a Gotham structure, notably the Flatiron, the Plaza Hotel, and the Woolworth Building.[2] It was the largest producer of its kind in the world.

STATEN ISLAND'S INDUSTRIAL EFFORTS, though impressive, were small potatoes compared to Brooklyn's. Long a manufacturing power, the borough at the twentieth century's commencement would have been ranked fourth in the country had it still been a city. In the next two decades factories sprouted up and streamed in—some relocating from across the East River, others coming from the continent—all eager to be sited in New York City, the country's biggest market and premier base for exports and imports, but without paying Manhattan's higher land costs, or suffering its clotted traffic.

Brooklyn's ease of rail/sea connectivity was exploited to the fullest at Bay Ridge—the extreme southern end of the industrial belt that ran along the East River shoreline up to the border with Queens. There the Bush Terminal's private railroad, float bridges, piers, and warehouses maximized the ability of manufacturers-in-residence to receive raw materials and dispatch their finished product. Irving Bush provided more than that. He pioneered a new morphological model, which he called an "Industrial Colony," that gathered together disparate producers, of varied size, and provided them with accommodations and centralized services. Beginning in 1904 Bush built a series of immense factory-loft buildings—with open floors, each subdivisible to suit a manufacturer's changing needs: expandable if business boomed, contractable if sales diminished. Each firm was provided with port-to-factory service. Arriving raw materials were delivered to their building's elevator and hoisted to their floor. When the finished goods were ready, the Bush Terminal's freight department would dispatch a railroad car from the desired national line, load the shipment (free of extra charge), and haul it away to the outbound tracks using a Bush Railroad locomotive. These and other services attracted over 200 concerns, many of them light manufacturers—makers of clothing,

2. Also in the south, at Prince's Bay, lay the S. S. White Dental Manufacturing Company, a huge dental-supply factory that produced amalgams, fillings, anesthetic gas, dental chairs, drills, and cuspidors.

carriages, wallpaper, asbestos, window shades, paper boxes, and shoes—though some were more substantial, including several foundries, and the Tidewater Paper Company, whose mill produced 30,000 tons of newsprint paper each year. (In 1918 it was acquired by the *New York Times* to secure itself a private stash.)

Farther up the Brooklyn shoreline, in Red Hook, the New York Dock Company followed suit by erecting, in 1911–12, two immense factory structures on Imlay Street, just behind the Atlantic Basin (of which it had taken possession back in 1901). Each building, though only six stories tall, was 460 feet long and 80 feet wide. Designed for manufacturing, they were equipped with elevators providing access to railroad tracks below, to a float connection to Jersey Shore railroads, to a roadway accessible by motor truck, and to a dock from which product could be transferred (via company-owned lighters) to piers around the harbor.

Equally interesting developments were afoot farther up the waterfront past Brooklyn Heights, where the coast curved eastward under the Brooklyn and (after 1909) the Manhattan Bridges. The neighborhood had become firmly industrialized in the decades following the Civil War. Some of its pioneers, like the E. W. Bliss Company, whose roots ran back to 1867, had grown to enormous size. In 1915 the Bliss works at Adams and Plymouth employed 4,000 people (half of them machinists), who produced heavy metalworking machinery, drop hammers and other machine tools, sheet metal, dies, presses, and munitions (notably torpedoes).

Another long-standing player, the Edinburgh-born immigrant Robert Gair, had opened a paper-jobber business in Manhattan in 1864, then began manufacturing paper goods (like bags with square bottoms) on machinery he himself constructed. In 1879 Gair patented a machine for creating folding boxes, which became an indispensable component of packaging, rapidly replacing wooden crates, and which made his fortune. By the late 1880s Gair's firm had became the largest manufacturer of paper boxes in America and had outgrown its Reade Street factory. Wanting both more space and better access to shipping, Gair moved to Brooklyn, into a purpose-built brick building on Washington Street (between Water and Plymouth); another brick structure followed later on Adams. In 1904, when he was ready to

"Projectile Department Buildings." *Presses, Dies and Special Machinery Built by E. W. Bliss Co.*, 1906.

"Erecting Shop at Projectile Department." *Presses, Dies and Special Machinery Built by E. W. Bliss Co.,* 1906.

expand again, Gair struck out in a new direction and ordered up a building made of reinforced concrete.

The proposal originated with two young engineers, Henry Turner and DeForrest Dixon, who in 1902 bought the patent rights for a system of concrete construction. In 1903 they set up the Turner Construction Company, won their first major contract—casting the stairs and platforms of the IRT subway system—and persuaded Gair of concrete's superiority for factory buildings. Concrete would allow for large expanses of windows, thus increasing light and ventilation; it was vibration resistant and fire resistant (which would lower insurance costs); and it was easy to keep clean and vermin-free. The 1904 Gair Building No. 3, at 41–49 Washington Street (expanded in 1908 to encompass the entire block), was the biggest reinforced concrete structure built to that point. Gair went on to erect a network of buildings, culminating in One Main Street (between Water and Plymouth Streets). Built in 1914, the twelve-story structure, topped by a four-story clock tower, was the tallest reinforced concrete building on earth. By then the complex—its buildings linked by rail (the tracks laid in granite Belgian block paving), by underground tunnels, and by aerial bridges—was dubbed "Gairville," and it employed 1,702 people.[3]

Pressing east, the industrial trail passed through the Brooklyn Navy Yard, a major beneficiary in these years of Theodore Roosevelt's imperial project. The president had summoned up a series of battleships—shown off in the globe-girdling, muscle-flexing, 1907–9 voyage of the Great White Fleet. The armada was flagshipped by the USS *Connecticut*, a product of the Yard, as were subsequent battleships such as the *Florida*, *New York*, *Arizona*, *New Mexico*, and *Tennessee*.

---

3. Bush Terminal quickly followed suit. Its first factory loft (1904) had been of brick, but the twenty-five that followed, beginning in 1905, were of concrete, as were New York Dry Dock's behemoths at the Atlantic Basin. The fashion spread rapidly. New manufacturing centers, like the one at the Manhattan Bridge Plaza and running south along the Flatbush Avenue extension, almost invariably adopted the new approach. Or they upgraded to it: in 1917 the Sperry Gyroscope Company built an eleven-story concrete addition to its original building on Flatbush.

Robert Gair Company, "Fig. 5 – Completed Building," *Concrete Engineering* (September 1908).

Turning north again, the trail ran through Williamsburg's vast panoply of manufacturers, crowned by the Havemeyers' American Sugar Refinery (2,218 employees), and the Hecla Iron Works, on North 11th Street, which supplied iron stairs, railings, gates, canopies, and elevator cars for the Flatiron, the New York Stock Exchange, the Chamber of Commerce, and Grand Central, as well as producing the 133 kiosks of the original IRT line.

On and on the factory belt went, past Bushwick, with its great knitting mills and nationally famous breweries, past Greenpoint's jumble of manufactories (including the formidable rope-and-bagging American Manufacturing Company, more familiarly known as the Jute Trust, which in 1913 employed 968 men, 1,063 women, and 23 children), until it finally reached Brooklyn's outer edge at the hyper-industrialized Newtown Creek, where it crossed over into Queens.

LIKE STATEN ISLAND, QUEENS HAD A MODEST nineteenth-century industrial inheritance, which in 1904 amounted to 513 factories, 16,669 employees, and invested capital of roughly $93 million. Once plugged firmly into Manhattan via the Pennsy's tunnels, the Queensboro Bridge, and the new subway lines, its industrial sector shot forward. By 1916 its now 1,169 factories employed 63,964 and represented an investment of $323 million. And what the *Times* in 1917 called "New York's marvelous growth toward the east" was assured of abundant expansion space by the 1916 zoning law, which decreed 22,000 acres of Queens "unrestricted" (open to industrial development). That was 30 percent of the borough's land mass, an area nearly as large as the Bronx.

For all that, most new construction was at first shoehorned into the borough's long-established manufacturing district, Long Island City. As its great leap forward came a little after Brooklyn's, it overwhelmingly followed the latter in adopting the new fashion of concrete construction, taking it to new levels of gargantuanism.

Nowhere was this more evident than in the industrial park called Degnon Terminal, the brainchild of Michael Degnon, a contractor who had worked for the IRT and the Pennsylvania Railroad. In 1914 Degnon put together a 125-acre parcel that was very strategically placed. Just off Queens Boulevard, it had easy access to Manhattan over the Queensboro Bridge. It abutted the Sunnyside Yards, its point of entry to the Pennsylvania Railroad's East River tubes and the New York Connecting Railroad. It was also hard by Dutch Kills, an inlet from Newtown Creek, which linked his land to the East River and the harbor beyond. Degnon then filled in his territory, using material salvaged from his work on the East River subway tunnels. Next he dredged channels, built bulkheads, graded streets, installed sewers, and ran rails into the Sunnyside Yards (after obtaining a franchise from the Public Service Commission). Finally he announced his readiness to either sell or lease sections of his land to industrial concerns. Businesses could build on these (or have Degnon build for them) a factory of any size, from a four-story building to a plant covering several acres.

Starting off big, the Loose-Wiles Biscuit Company (manufacturer of Sunshine crackers) erected in 1913 at a cost of $2 million the largest concrete factory unit in the world (800,000 square feet)—the swiftly famous "Thousand Window Bakery." The ten-story building housed production, sales, and management, providing jobs for 2,500 people. (In 1914 Loose-Wiles topped its structure with a 586-foot-long electric sign, the largest in the world, whose four thousand bulbs, proclaiming LOOSE-WILES SUNSHINE BISCUITS, could be seen seven miles out at sea). Next, an entire block was taken up by the Ever-Ready Company, relocated from Manhattan's Hudson Street; it made electric lamps, batteries, meters, and auto supplies. These were followed by the American Chicle Company (of Chiclets gum) and the Packard Auto Company (one of the seventeen auto and truck plants and dozens of supporting factories that, paced by the venerable Brewster & Company, had set up shop in Long Island City). This Degnon-based ensemble produced a formidable skyline that soon became a proud emblem of the new industrializing Queens.

Loose-Wiles: Sunshine Biscuits. Night, ca. 1914. (Courtesy Greater Astoria Historical Society)

FOLLOWING THE NEW YORK CONNECTING RAILROAD out of Sunnyside Yards and over Hell Gate Bridge would have brought an industrial tourist to the South Bronx, center of the mainland borough's manufacturing since Jordan Mott had established his iron works on the Harlem River at 134th Street in 1828. The most intensive development had been at Mott Haven (particularly around Mott's Mott Haven Canal) and Port Morris, just to the east. This concentration continued in the new century, fostered by new transport developments. The 1904 subway line beneath 138th Street brought more workers to man-and-woman the local factories. The Harlem River and Oak Point Yards of the New York, New Haven & Hartford offered excellent freight rail connections, as did the Melrose Yard of the New York Central system. There was also an abundance of land coming on the market, as the subway-driven speculative boom engendered a divvying up and selling off of old estates. As a result, in 1909 there were 700 factories in the Bronx; by 1912 the number had more than doubled.

As elsewhere, local industry built on former strengths. The pre-Consolidation piano industry surged from only a handful to the sixty-three factories—forty-three of them in Mott Haven, south of 149th Street—that in 1919 were employing more than 5,000 people, and producing approximately 115,000 units. Some firms were big—Jacob Doll & Sons, at 100 Southern Boulevard (near 135th St) housed 650 employees in a seven-story structure covering an entire block. Many were smaller, particularly start-up firms, whose survival was aided by the presence of a large number of components suppliers and a substantial pool of skilled labor. Between them all, the Bronx had become the capital of the national piano (and player piano) trade, and its products were sold all over the world.[4]

Some old, established trades did languish, notably iron foundries: Janes & Kirtland (of Capitol dome fame) failed; the Mott Iron Works decamped for Trenton. But novel ones emerged, as brewer Jacob Ruppert entered the artificial ice business by building a huge plant at East 133rd—yet another "largest of its kind in the world" addition to the New York record books—which in turn boosted sales of the 5-acre De la Vergne Refrigerating Machine Works, at the foot of East 138th Street. (De la Vergne sold to the empire as well, dispatching product to Cuba and the Philippines.)

Industry also spread eastward, into the Hunt's Point peninsula. Again, transport was key. The opening of the IRT subway in 1904, particularly the Intervale Avenue station, and the 1908 upgrading of the New York, New Haven & Hartford's Harlem River branch, especially the Hunt's Point Avenue and Westchester Avenue stations (both designed by Cass Gilbert, then between his Customs House and Woolworth Building commissions), attracted new investment to the neighborhood.

The most remarkable entrant was a long-established Manhattan firm, the American Bank Note Company (ABN). After discussions with the New York, New Haven & Hartford about its considerable freight delivery needs, the ABN in 1908 bought the old (1832) Faile Mansion and estate, situated on the high ground just east of the Hunt's Point Avenue station. There the firm erected a huge arsenal-like factory, complete with crenellated tower, within whose secure portals printers, engravers, and a large supporting cast (1,500 in all) turned out stock certificates, postage and revenue stamps, bonds, checks, traveler's checks, lottery tickets, letters of credit, bank notes, and paper money for governments around the world,

---

4. Not that Queens wasn't still a major piano player. In 1901 Steinway & Sons opened a new factory on Ditmars Boulevard, less than a mile from its old building on Bowery Bay, where the dampness had prolonged the drying time of the wood, varnish, and glue, and the 1,100-person workforce had outgrown its capacity; in 1911 the booming business required the addition of another three stories. Sohmer and Company remained runner-up, with its 600-person factory (expanded in 1906) on Vernon Boulevard in Astoria.

American Bank Note Co., Mexican 100-peso bill, 1908.

particularly Latin America. Billions' worth of pesos, cruzeiros, coons, scures, gourdes, and pesos were shipped south for Mexico, Brazil, Costa Rica, Ecuador, Haiti, and Cuba.

FOR ALL THIS OUTER-BOROUGH FERMENT, the fact remains that in 1913 Staten Island had but 1 percent of Greater New York's industrial employees, the Bronx 4 percent, Queens 5 percent, and Brooklyn 22 percent, while Manhattan had 68 percent. And of the 36,000 factories in the entire city as of 1914, 24,866 were on the latter island. It is true that there was a *relative* slippage in Manhattan's primacy, as its share of metropolitan manufacturing employment slid from 73 to 61 percent between 1899 and 1919, but in *absolute* terms Manhattan's industrial workforce jumped 36 percent during those decades. There was a sharp drop-off in metalworking, woodworking, chemical, and refining industries, as bulkier businesses left in pursuit of cheaper land and better transport. These departures were more than offset by an explosion in the garment and printing industries, and by the stubborn geo-stability of manufacturers who needed access to the unparalleled richness of Manhattan's industrial ecology. The island offered the efficiencies of proximity to clients and customers, to skilled workers and business services, to competitors and parts suppliers, to specialists in virtually any process or product, to information about current fashions and markets, to wholesalers and retailers, to wharfs and warehouses, to hotels hosting buyers from every section of the nation, to unfathomable sources of commercial credit.

Manhattan manufacturing continued to flourish on the Middle and Lower West Sides, thanks to the conjunction of freight rail lines, working piers, and a deep pool of skilled and unskilled workers. Many West Side concerns were locally owned small and medium-sized firms that thrived amid the maelstrom of markets, warehouses, slaughterhouses, stables, coal yards, lumber yards, and gas plants. A 1911 survey of Hell's Kitchen factories found eighty-two metal works that between them employed a total of 1,845 workers, an average of twenty-two per shop. Midsized industrial outfits employed between 100 and 400 workers in plants making cordage, pianos, carriages, beer, soaps, dies, and chemicals. The sole exception to this modest-scaled industrial landscape was the giant Higgins Carpet Company, with 2,000 workers in its factory at Eleventh Avenue and 44th Street. Higgins had been a fixture in Hell's Kitchen since the 1870s. But in October 1900 the company pulled up stakes and moved to the Connecticut countryside, drawn by lower tax rates, smaller water bills, and the possibility of establishing a company town that would provide a more pliant labor force—a strike in 1899 had protested a speedup.

Despite Higgins's departure, some manufacturers in Manhattan, particularly those shifting from downtown to midtown, experimented with housing their corporate enterprises, or agglomerations of smaller producers, in the king-sized structures being adopted in the outer boroughs, though given scarce and costly land, they built taller rather than wider.

Manhattan's printers had long clustered around Printing House Square, just above and below the Brooklyn Bridge, near the big newspapers on Park Row, and the central Post Office in City Hall Park. Then the *Herald* departed for Herald Square, the *Times* lofted off to Times Square, and the new General Post Office opened on Eighth Avenue and 33rd. Some major entities did remain downtown—notably Press Publishing, the production arm of Joseph Pulitzer's *World*—but many printers headed off to a new district emerging in the blocks above and below the Penn Station/Post Office complex. Newly accessible by subway, the neighborhood was also home to a covey of book publishers that had flocked to the area (like Grossett & Dunlap at 26th, McGraw-Hill at 39th, Scribner's at 43rd). By 1913 several fifteen-story buildings, aimed at printing-trade clients, had been built on West 25th, West 31st, and West 33rd Streets. But the area's would-be anchor, erected in 1916, was a colossal twenty-two-story tower at 461 Eighth Avenue, occupying the entire west-side blockfront between 33rd and 34th Streets. The Printing Crafts Building was the largest structure in the country devoted to publishing and printing. Its second to eleventh floors were reserved for printing, binding, lithographing, electrotyping, engraving, and ink and paper companies; those above were primarily for offices, salesrooms, clubrooms, publishers' stockrooms, ad agencies, and graphic arts suppliers, though presses operated on the twenty-first floor, a testimony to the stability of the building's reinforced-steel framework.

As an instance of king-sized construction by well-heeled corporations, consider the baking and telephone complexes that rose up amid the welter of West Side manufactories that stretched south from Penn Station through West Chelsea, the West Village, and the area below Canal now known as Tribeca.

Back in 1890 eight large eastern bakeries had merged to form the New York Biscuit Company, which soon absorbed a dozen more firms. The company immediately began building a series of six-story bakeries on the east side of 10th Avenue between 15th and 16th Streets. At the same time, this New York conglomerate was going toe-to-toe with a Chicago-based consortium, the American Biscuit and Manufacturing Company. In 1898, in classic fashion, the two combatants backed away from their ruinous competition and merged, forming the National Biscuit Company, which supporters called Nabisco and opponents labeled the "Cracker Trust." With 114 bakeries and a capital of $55 million, the corporation transformed cookie and cracker manufacturing by introducing between 1898 and 1913 a string of new products, including Uneeda Biscuits, Barnum's Animal Crackers, Fig Newtons, Mallomars, Lorna Doones, and Oreos. Its bakery buildings multiplied as well, expanding eastward to cover most of the block from Tenth over to Ninth Avenue, and then pushing westward, toward Eleventh, culminating in 1913 with an eleven-story full-block structure between Tenth and Eleventh Avenues and 15th to 16th Streets. Taken together, the complex, with 21 acres of floor space, constituted the world's largest bakery, capable of producing, among other things, 6,375,000 biscuits a day.[5]

Eight blocks farther south lay the twelve-story Western Electric building, which covered most of the West/Washington/Bank/Bethune block; 463 West was its corporate address.

---

5. By 1912 an outer-borough contender, Ward Baking Company, had built two six-story bakeries, one in the Bronx (covering an entire block at Southern Boulevard and 143rd Street, the other in Brooklyn (at 800 Pacific Street near Vanderbilt Avenue). Advertised as "the first sanitary and scientific bakery in America," and a "snow-white temple of bread-making cleanliness," Ward had taken the industrialization of bread manufacture to new heights. Where in 1900 the largest bakeshops turned out 15,000 loaves a day, Ward's two plants together produced 500,000.

This far-west Greenwich Village plant represented a move uptown by the company—since 1881 the official manufacturing unit of the Bell Telephone System—from its original ten-story office and factory building at Greenwich and Thames Streets (1888–89), where it made telephones and transmitters, telegraph machines, and testing instruments. In 1897 Western Electric relocated to its new brick-and-terra-cotta building, four times the size of the downtown factory, and immediately became the largest manufacturer of telephone equipment in the world. By 1913, with day and night shifts totaling some 8,000 employees, it was probably the biggest plant in the city. In 1907 it also became home to the relocated Boston laboratory that had evolved from Alexander Graham Bell's original attic workshop. In 1911 Western Electric physicist Frank B. Jewett was set to work on inventing a "repeater" that would amplify signals weakened by transmission over transcontinental distances (New Yorkers could call no farther than Chicago). Gathering a small group of talented physicists, Jewett launched a vigorous two-front research program, seeking an immediate engineering solution (via improving the recently invented three-element vacuum tube) and doing long-term theoretical work that explored the basic science of electrons. After 1913, when manufacturing was whisked away to far larger quarters in Hawthorne, Illinois, the West Street building became AT&T's dedicated research and development center. By 1916, now home to a substantial body of engineers and scientists, it had become both research laboratory and invention factory.[6]

FINALLY, THE FACTORY TOUR ARRIVES AT THE CENTER of Gotham's industrial order, wherein dwelt the garment trade, a sector undergoing massive and profound transformation.

In the century's first decade, in response to the tripling each year of the amount Americans spent on ready-to-wear clothing, the industry doubled its capitalization and labor force. Before then mass production of clothing had been pretty much limited to men's coats and suits, but now the output of female ready-to-wear surged as women abandoned home- or tailor-made garments for factory-made dresses, undergarments, cloaks, coats, and—the central items of a sartorial transformation—skirts and shirtwaists (high-necked blouses of cotton or linen). Beginning in the 1890s the skirt-shirtwaist combination had become a fashion sensation—fanned by graphic artist Charles Dana Gibson's iconic magazine illustrations—as women opted for a chic but practical style, more suitable for the broadened spectrum of situations in which they were finding themselves. Ankle-length skirts enabled easier navigation of muddy streets, crowded stores, and factory floors. And shirtwaists seemed just the ticket for shopping, sports, and working in offices or manufactories.

After 1900—paced by waists—annual production of women's wear raced ahead of men's clothing output, virtually doubling it, while soaring past all other manufacturing sectors. By 1919 it bettered the combined output of printing, publishing, metalworking, and food production, and its workforce of 165,000 constituted almost one-sixth the city's industrial laborers. On a national scale, New York clothing production utterly overshadowed that of all other cities, with somewhere between 70 and 75 percent of the country's output, as measured by value, being produced in Gotham.

The metropolitan garment business was propelled to such preeminence by several factors. The city was the locus of dry-goods importers, so manufacturers had ready-to-hand the

---

6. One Manhattan trade *not* on the march north was the jewelry business. Despite being insistently nudged from below by the financial district expanding up William Street, high-end jewelry makers stayed obdurately put, hunkered down at Maiden Lane and Liberty Street, forcing the money men to flow around them.

Shirtwaists, 1902–1903. (Fashion Institute of Technology/SUNY, FIT Library Special Collections and College Archives, New York, NY, USA)

showrooms and warehouses of New England textile mills, importers of silks and woolens, and manufacturers of buttons and notions. It was the premier port of entry for Parisian fashions, and European cultural styles in general. And it was the chief point of arrival for the immense influx of Jewish and Italian immigrants, for whom work in the rag trade was among the best of a limited range of employment opportunities, and who themselves added hundreds of thousands to the already enormous market for inexpensive but stylish clothing.

At the same time the industry was undergoing such spectacular growth, its internal structure—and the structures in which it was housed—were undergoing their own (interlinked) transformation. The late nineteenth century had bequeathed the garment trade a trifurcated format. The "inside" shops were largely owned and run by German Jewish manufacturers, for whom employees worked directly, mostly in converted old cast-iron warehouses. "Home-work" referred to production by workers and family members who, in their tenement rooms, assembled clothing from cut cloth supplied by the manufacturer. "Outside" shops were established by middlemen contractors, chiefly Eastern European Jews, who received orders from manufacturers to "finish" garments, and hired laborers to do the work, either in their own homes or in small workshops. Locked in competitive combat to win these contracts, outside contractors bid as low as possible, then made their profits by "sweating" their vulnerable employees, forced to work long hours in miserable "sweatshop" conditions.

In 1892, alarmed by the tenement quarters' high rate of tuberculosis and other diseases, which health inspectors and labor reformers argued could be passed on to consumers, the New York state legislature had enacted the first of a series of laws to regulate manufacturing outside of factories. It forbade doing home-work in any room used for sleeping or eating (though it exempted immediate family members) and established a procedure for licensing tenements. These provisions were strengthened by later legislation that banned certain categories of home-work manufacture altogether, notably production of babies' and children's clothing. Home-work itself was not abolished. Indeed, in 1911 13,628 tenements were licensed for hosting home-work, and many others harbored it illegally. But regulatory constraints, coupled with the rise of an attractive alternative, helped drain the number of home-workers operating in authorized tenements from 21,000 in 1900 to 5,700 in 1915.

Most had decamped to mechanized factories, housed in new steel-framed loft buildings, far larger than the older warehouses on the streets south of Houston, where inside shops had clustered since the 1870s; ten to sixteen floors became the new normal. These structures—like the Printing Crafts Building or the megaliths at Bush Terminal and the Atlantic Docks—were intended to house multiple medium-sized factories. They were equipped with electricity, enabling manufacturers to replace foot-treadled sewing machines with long rows of power-driven Singers, as well as new-tech braiders, corders, seamers, binders, and improved cutting and pressing equipment, all connected by a drive shaft and flywheels to a single motor. Manufacturers liked these structures. Mechanization improved worker productivity; the lofts' 12-foot ceilings allowed for big windows, which admitted more daylight, which cut illumination costs; and the steel-framed buildings were deemed fireproof, or fire resistant, which lowered insurance costs.

Modernizing did not require relinquishing exploitative production relations. Manufacturers could incorporate sweating procedures by turning over inside space to outside contractors and leaving them to hire the machine operators, usually young immigrant girls; competition between such "inside contractors" could be counted on to force wages down. This format freed manufacturers to take on tasks previously done by middlemen—obtaining contracts from big retailers like department stores or mail order houses and buying materials directly from textile manufacturers. Gathering those threads in their hands not only saved money; it strengthened their hand against remaining outside contractors, driving many of them to come in from the cold and become employees. Centralization also pulled the workers out of external sweatshops and their own home-work apartments, from which they were simultaneously being squeezed by overcrowding and regulation. By 1913 56 percent of dress and waist workers worked in factories of 75 or more employees, and 27 percent labored in establishments of 100–200 workers.

Centralization did not lead to transformation of ownership patterns. The garment industry did not participate in the great merger movement. Clothing firms did not incorporate and issue stock. There was no "Consolidated Apparel" or "United States Women's Wear" among the hundred largest industrials in 1917. There were no titans of the rag trade to take a seat alongside the moguls of steel and oil. Partly this was because there were no significant cost savings to be wrung from the production process by doing so; indeed, the trade thrived on competition between multiple small contenders. Nor was there need for great injections of capital into what remained a labor-intensive industry. Also, the business was risky, vulnerable to sudden shifts in fashion. So most large firms preferred to spin off production to a variety of subordinate contractors, or specialized autonomous firms, a flexibility that allowed for rapid response to stylistic volatility.

Given the move to larger lofts, the garment district itself began to move. Housed since the 1870s in what today is SoHo, venturesome manufacturers and speculative builders drifted north, breaching Houston Street by the mid-1890s and establishing beachheads on Bleecker and Bond. By decade's end, with the return of prosperity after the 1893–97 depression,

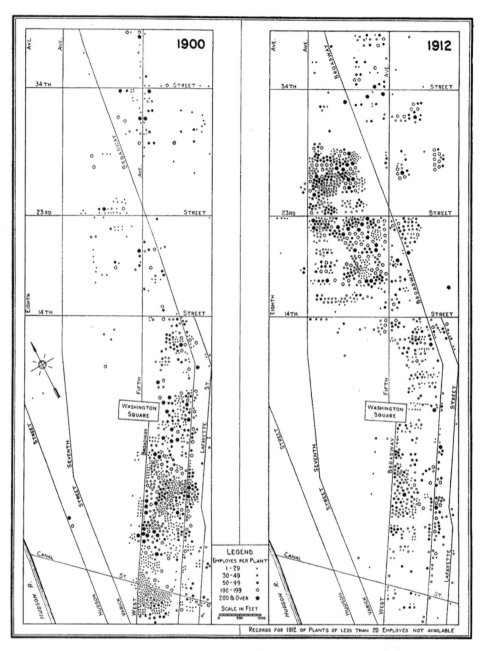

"Location of Plants in the Women's Garment Industry in the Area of Greatest Concentration in Manhattan,," 1900 and 1912, Committee on Regional Plan of New York and Its Environs, *The Clothing and Textile Industries in New York and Its Environs: Present Trends and Probable Future Developments*, 1925.

"Location of Plants in the Women's Garment Industry in the Area of Greatest Concentration in Manhattan,." 1917 and 1922, Committee on Regional Plan of New York and Its Environs, *The Clothing and Textile Industries in New York and Its Environs: Present Trends and Probable Future Developments*, 1925.

garment men (warehousers as well as manufacturers) advanced higher, into the blocks east of Washington Square, heading steadily upward toward Union Square.

Among these were one Joseph J. Asch, a furrier who also had a wholesale business down on White Street. By 1899 Asch had picked up some contiguous properties on Washington Place, among them No. 27 (the 1843 birthplace of Henry James[7]). After some complex real estate transactions, he was able to raise the eponymous ten-story Asch Building on the corner of Washington Place and Greene Street, a block east of Washington Square, completed in January 1901. In August its eighth floor was leased by Max Blanck and Isaac Harris, Russian-born Jewish immigrants who in 1900, hoping to cash in on the shirtwaist craze, had established the Triangle Waist Company in a loft building on Wooster Street, just south of Houston Street. They were pleased with their new quarters, which afforded them 9,000 square feet of usable space, thirty times the size of a typical sweatshop. They were acutely aware that bringing so many workers together in close communion made the duo more vulnerable to unionization and strikes, but they hoped that adoption of the "inside contractor" model, along with other precautionary measures, would forestall any such unfortunate developments. Triangle flourished. Within a few years, the growing company took over the ninth and tenth floors. In 1908 the partners' profit exceeded $1 million, and they were acknowledged as the leading shirtwaist makers of the city, perhaps the nation.

By then the garment district had swept north. Shirtwaist makers had plunged into Union Square around 1905—Tiffany's decamped from its 1870 building at 15 Union Square West in 1906, and it was rented out to needle-trade firms—then spread north and west of Broadway, across Fifth and into the blocks on either side of Sixth between 14th and 23rd (Ladies' Mile). By 1912 garment plants had forded 23rd and were halfway up to 34th Street. Some of the many loft buildings that went up were constructed by manufacturers themselves, turning to real estate development as a profitable sideline. Cloak and suit manufacturer Abraham E. Lefcourt launched into a building career by commissioning in 1910 a twelve-story loft at 48–54 West 25th Street, with his own factory on the bottom two floors. Admittedly all these were far from the Lower East Side tenement workforce, but the arrival of the subway system had mooted that problem, allowing garment workers to commute for a nickel each way. As a result, where in 1900 70 percent of women's garment workers had worked below 14th Street, by 1917 the situation was completely reversed, with 68.6 percent now working above it, closer to midtown.

THE CITY OF COMMERCE

Like its industrial quarters, Gotham's wholesale precincts were undergoing rapid structural and geographical changes. These were not easy to spot, given the obdurate rootedness of the city's central commercial institutions—the great commodity exchanges ensconced in massive palaces at the bottom of Manhattan Island. Nowhere did the established order appear more stable than at the base of Broadway, where sat the New York Produce Exchange (NYPE). Housed in George Post's colossal palazzo, it had loomed over Bowling Green since 1884, when it had replaced an 1861 incarnation, which in turn was descended from the Dutch-era market, just steps away, which Peter Stuyvesant had established in 1648, at which country farmers could display their "meat, bacon, butter, cheese, turnips, roots, straw, and other products of the farm."

---

7. Writing shortly afterward, in "New York Revisited," of discovering his birth house had been "ruthlessly suppressed," James recounted: "That was where the pretense that nearly nothing has changed had most to come in; for a high, square, impersonal structure, proclaiming its lack of interest with a crudity all its own, so blocks, as the right moment for its own success, the view of the past, that the effect for me, in Washington Place, was of having been amputated of half my history."

Two hundred and fifty years further on, at the dawn of the twentieth century, the scene in the NYPE's cavernous Exchange Room—it could accommodate 7,000 traders—might have seemed familiar to the earliest settlers. Here sellers spread out on tables samples of their wares—wheat, barley, oats, rye, buckwheat, corn, cornmeal, flour, oatmeal, hops, hay, straw, flaxseed, seeds, beans, pork, pork lard, beef tallow, greases, hams, and naval stores (turpentine and resin)—for buyers to examine. The scale and reach of the transactions were something else again. A buyer-broker might receive a cablegram from a firm in Liverpool seeking several thousand bushels of wheat and a shipload of dressed beef, at prices current or proposed. The broker would then head for the appropriate place on the huge floor—each trade (flour, grain, cotton oil) had its own location—and, after negotiations were completed, instructions would be telegraphed that set in motion the transport of goods from midwestern granaries and meatpacking plants to New York by rail, then by ship across the Atlantic. The whole process was closely overseen by market officials, who inspected the samples on offer, graded them according to established standards, and tested the cargo before it was dispatched to ensure it matched the sample. Should disagreements arise between buyers and sellers, they would be adjudicated by Exchange officials, whose goal was to guarantee that members paid for what they bought and delivered what they sold.

The trading pits, on the other hand, were bidding arenas, organized by commodity (wheat, lard, cotton oil, etc.), in which commission brokers shouted out puts and calls, making arrangements for *future* deliveries, betting on whether or not the price of the commodity would have risen or fallen by that time. The pits could be used prudently, to hedge against market uncertainties, or speculatively, to make a purely financial killing, perhaps by arranging a corner in wheat.

On the whole, however, Produce Exchange members came together for traditional reasons—to keep in touch with each other, to glean up-to-the-minute information about crops and prices, stocks of merchandise, and movements of produce. To do business, that is, more or less as it had been done for decades, if not centuries, except that now New York traders sat at the center of a global web of relationships of which their city was a critical node.

A similar combination of stability and growth marked the other exchanges planted around lower Manhattan, which had been doing business at more or less the same stands since the post–Civil War decades. The New York Cotton Exchange was at 60 Beaver, a few blocks from Bowling Green; the New York Coffee Exchange resided at 113–117 Pearl Street (in 1916 it added sugar to its business and its name); the Commodity Exchange and the Maritime Exchange were cheek by jowl on Broad Street. The Coal and Iron Exchange and the Petroleum Exchange were also downtown denizens. Only the New York Mercantile Exchange, which dealt in eggs and tubs of butter, was an outlier, opting in 1885 for 2–6 Harrison Street (at Hudson Street), closer to the West Side docks. That put them conveniently near the adjacent warehouse district, which in the 1900s and 1910s added new steel-framed storage structures, done up as neo-Renaissance palazzos, to the already thickly warehoused north-south conduits of Washington, Greenwich, and Hudson Streets and cross-cutting lanes like Hubert and Laight.

Yet for all this continuity, the 1900s and 1910s were by no means decades of business as usual in the wholesale sector. Once upon a time, when New York was the nation's unchallenged emporium, the great merchant trading houses had dominated the flow of commodities into and out of the city. Twice a year, buyers from country towns and southern plantations would flood the city's auction and wholesale houses, where the newest and biggest variety of goods imported from Europe and the Americas was on offer. The wholesalers were then the principal middlemen—"jobbers"—who facilitated the flow of commodities from manufacturers and farmers to the retailers who sold them to consumers.

Since the Civil War, the development of new means of transportation and communication had increasingly undercut the power of Gotham's middlemen merchants, by establishing alternate circuitries of sales. One of these was simply the rise of rival jobbers in the booming heartland cities, who bypassed New York wholesalers, buying directly from manufacturers or farmers, at home or abroad, and reselling the goods to their own region's rural stores and urban retailers. As these were wholesalers, just like those in New York, the structure of distribution remained the same; only the network geography changed. But emerging in the late nineteenth century were contenders of a very different caliber.

One set were mass retailers—chain stores, mail order houses, and department stores—who had the money and muscle to buy directly from manufacturers and sell directly to consumers. A second alternative involved big manufacturers establishing their own marketing and distribution networks and selling directly to their own affiliated retailers. A third group consisted of big manufacturers who established national brand names and employed advertising agencies to drum up demand among end-users, counting on that demand to pressure local retailers into stocking the desired product. While these end-runs around traditional wholesaling patterns would have dire consequences for New York's old-school merchants, they did not undermine the city's economic primacy, partly because so many of the novel approaches were launched and developed in Gotham itself.

Consider chain stores. Arguably the first step in this marketing revolution was taken in lower Manhattan during the Civil War, when George Francis Gilman and George Huntington Hartford affixed the name Great American Tea Company to five downtown stores selling tea and coffee, which they kept supplied from their five-story office-warehouse at 51 Vesey Street. They considered themselves simultaneously wholesalers and retailers—wholesalers who supplied their own retail network. Beginning an aggressive expansion campaign, replete with Barnumesque advertising, by 1865 they had twenty-six stores, all in lower Broadway and the Wall Street area. Soon they aimed higher and farther. In 1869, with the golden-spiked establishment of transcontinental rail service, they grandly renamed their operation the Great Atlantic and Pacific Tea Company and established outlets in other cities, beginning with Chicago in 1871. By 1878, when Gilman retired and Hartford (and his sons) assumed control, the firm boasted seventy stores, most in the Northeast and Midwest.

By 1900 the company had expanded its product line to include cocoa, sugar, and one-pound tins of baking powder—the first commodity sold under what would soon become a powerful brand name, not of a product but a store: A&P. Now the Hartfords set out to add more products—condensed milk, spices, butter—and morph their tea shops into grocery stores. This required a whole new scale of operation. A&P by then had 198 stores, but they were strewn over twenty-eight states, which meant many towns had only one or two outlets. Groceries (unlike coffee and tea retailers) required frequent resupply, and would become profitable only if they were fed by the kind of warehouse/outlet operation A&P had in New York.[8]

---

8. By now A&P had competitors, several of which were based on its own Gotham turf. By 1901 a chain operation named Grand Union owned 140 stores in New York, as well as 2,000 delivery wagons that serviced them from a huge warehouse in Brooklyn (Water/Front/Jay/Pearl); Grand Union also manufactured and packaged many of its goods, enough to require 50,000 cans and 180,000 cartons daily. Virtually next door was another wholesaler/manufacturer, Arbuckle Brothers, by now the world's largest coffee dealer. The Arbuckle firm did wholesaling—it imported beans from Latin America on its own ships—and manufacturing—it roasted its own coffee—and retailing—it filled, weighed, sealed, and labeled the ground coffee in (well-advertised) small packages that were shipped to retailers and consumers throughout the world. All this production and distribution took place in Brooklyn; Arbuckle warehoused his coffee and other goods in the Empire Stores, which he linked to his factory via a connecting railroad; and the surge in new-style wholesaling boosted neighboring manufacturing operations, like those of Gair's paper boxes, and the rope and twine of cordage makers.

"The Great Atlantic & Pacific Tea Co.'s A&P Pure Food Products." *Judge's Library*, January 1906.

So, in tune with the times, A&P incorporated in New Jersey in 1901 and generated $2.1 million of capital—a negligible amount for heavy industry, but quite enough to power a mighty expansion by the mass retailer. Between 1903 and 1912 the Hartfords began opening an average of one store every two weeks, upping their total to 480. In 1907 they started construction of a complex of concrete buildings (offices, warehouses, factories) on Bay Street in Jersey City, within walking distance of McAdoo's new under-river railroad to Manhattan. Here were produced dozens of items (coffee, baked goods, canned corn, stove polish), which were then packaged under the A&P label and shipped out to their national network. Raising more capital, the Hartfords went into hyperdrive, upping the store count to 1,817 by the end of 1915, then doubling it over the next two years. Clearly this was a new factor on the American scene, and indeed A&P (and rival chain operations) was condemned by independent grocers as a malevolent one, guilty of predatory pricing and destroying small family-owned businesses.

The grocery chains were matched by another operation that applied much the same strategy to selling dry goods, an industry even more vital to the city's traditional wholesale merchants. After Frank Woolworth established his five-and-dime business model in rural areas and small cities in the 1870s and 1880s, he took his road-tested act to Broadway. In 1887 he opened a buying office in New York to gather goods at wholesale prices for resale in his stores, set up a small office at Chambers and Broadway, and moved himself and his family to Brooklyn (buying a Bed-Stuy brownstone at 209 Jefferson Avenue). He and his associates opened more and more stores, in ever larger cities, finally entering Brooklyn in 1895 with an outlet on Fulton Street that drew thousands on opening day, and arriving in Manhattan in 1896 with a venue on Sixth Avenue and 17th Street, a direct challenge to Ladies' Mile department stores. Business boomed. In 1897 the family moved to the Savoy Hotel; in 1901 he commissioned a thirty-room marble château at 990 Fifth (and 80th). In 1911 he sought backing from J. P. Morgan for merging his chain with five others. Morgan turned him down, supposedly because he thought the low-end five-and-dime business beneath him. Woolworth turned to Henry Goldman, of Goldman, Sachs, which with Lehman Brothers had underwritten the initial public offering of Chicago's Sears, Roebuck in 1906, another novel marketer deemed beneath the dignity of the premier investment banks. Goldman arranged a re-incorporation that would bring 611 stores under one umbrella and then, with Lehman Brothers and Kleinwort, Sons & Co., arranged the sale of stocks, $15 million preferred and $50 million common; the common, issued at 55, went to 80 on the first day of trading. It was this infusion of funds for business expansion that allowed him to pay for the Woolworth Building out of his previous personal profits. In 1916 Woolworth employed the tower's architect, Cass Gilbert, to build him a Gold Coast mansion to replace one that had burned down. A year later a fifty-six-room Italian Renaissance behemoth had emerged on an 18-acre site, and it was there, in 1919, with his empire now encompassing a thousand stores, that Frank Woolworth died and was buried in Woodlawn Cemetery, in an Egyptian Revival mausoleum he had commissioned. A successful innovator indeed.

If chain stores were one way to outflank traditional wholesalers, direct sales by manufacturers was another. Companies that produced vast quantities of low-priced commodities, using high-priced equipment, were particularly taken with this strategy. Taking on marketing functions could also solidify a company's position in the industry, by raising the costs for would-be new entrants. Thus Duke's Tobacco Trust, whose Bonsack machines turned out more cigarettes than the extant smoker market could absorb, built its own sales network and advertised heavily. Chain operations like the United Cigar Stores were a collateral undertaking.

Big companies also had the capital to work closely with the expanding advertising industry, by mounting "campaigns" to bolster sales. J. Walter Thompson had long advocated that his emerging profession go beyond merely recommending media in which to place ads, to providing a full-spectrum service—studying a client's product line and that of his rivals, preparing copy and illustrations, and placing them in appropriate media. Thompson advised manufacturers to nationally advertise commodities "that you wish to compel retail dealers to keep in stock by inciting a demand therefor." In his *Advertising as a Selling Force* (1909) he argued that advertising would also enhance their position vis-à-vis jobbers and wholesalers.

Some, like Nabisco and Procter & Gamble, worked with agencies to establish strong ad-backed brands (Uneeda Biscuits, Ivory Soap), and used ads to generate consumer demand, but still relied on jobbers to handle the details of distribution to thousands of retailers. Others, like Ward Bakery, developed their own wholesale sales force, and deployed it, in tandem with ad campaigns, to pressure retailers into carrying their product. When Ward decided to tackle the New York market in 1911, shortly after an outcry over basement bakeries as being unhealthy breeders of disease, the company launched a campaign in print media and billboards touting its new factories as "Snow-white Temples of Cleanliness," where gleaming steel machines in white-tiled rooms produced "pure, white dough—aerated with pure, fresh air." As *"bread kneaded by hand or mixed by hand can never be made a truly clean sanitary product,"* ran one *New York Times* ad, Ward promised that "the human hand never touches dough or bread at The Ward Bakeries." Even its deliverymen would wear white gloves and use clean electric autos, not dirty horses. Then, backed by these omnipresent images, Ward's (immaculate) sales force descended on the city's retail grocery stores and walked out with orders for Tip-Top bread. In short order, one in every five bakery loaves eaten in Gotham came from Ward's Bronx and Brooklyn factories.

Industrial advertising not only strengthened the city's manufacturing base, but it helped grow and solidify New York's ad industry itself. As it became a settled belief that touting commodities was a job for specialists, the number of full-time copywriters in New York grew from half a dozen in 1891 to hundreds by Consolidation Day. And as agencies went beyond simply selling space in newspapers—J. Walter Thompson, for example, heavily promoted advertising in the new mass magazines (*McClure's* was a favorite)—the ad men increasingly moved out of the Park Row newspaper district (as had the printers, and some of the papers themselves). Several headed uptown, to Madison Square, at the base of Madison Avenue (Thompson to 44 East 23rd, the George Batten company to 11–15 East 24th). The agencies grew rapidly in the boom years, with Batten's going from fewer than 50 employees in 1905 to

126 in 1916. In 1911 the largest of them gathered together in the Association of New York Agents, which in turn dominated the movement that led to creation of the American Association of Advertising Agencies in 1917, the industry's first effective trade association.

THE CUMULATIVE EFFECT OF THE RISING REACH and power of mass retailers and ad-backed manufacturers was to make the old dry-goods wholesalers wither away. By the early 1900s many independent jobbing firms had been forced out of business. The dry-goods district—long clustered along Broadway between Duane and Canal, and on side streets like Franklin, Worth, and Leonard—began to shrivel. Some outfits moved uptown en masse and resettled into consolidated structures, as had the printers. In 1911 the eighteen-story American Woolen Company Building, on Fourth Avenue and 18th, became the new center of the woolen trade, while dealers in silk, ribbons, and notions rallied at the Mills and Gibbs Building, four blocks farther up Fourth at 22nd Street. In 1912 some 150 firms still at the old stand formed the Wholesale Dry-Goods Centre Association, in an effort to head off a wholesale exodus to Fourth Avenue and points north. In their campaign "for all hands to stick together," one of the strongest arguments was that H. B. Claflin & Co., the mightiest of their clan, was still holding fast at Church and Worth.

The Claflin firm had settled there in 1861, but its pedigree ran back to clipper ship days. Horace Brigham Claflin had begun operations in 1843 as a national distributor of imported and domestic lace goods, white goods, flannels, blankets, hosiery, shirts, underwear, shawls, hoods, scarves, and gloves. By 1865 his sales were held to exceed those of any other mercantile house in the world. Claflin had a rough patch during the Panic of 1873 but paid off every penny of his debts, further enhancing his gold-standard reputation. When the founder died in 1885, his son, John, took over the firm. The young Claflin, who had been educated in Gotham's public schools and at City College, was aware that times were changing, and he set out to keep up with them. In 1890 he converted the family enterprise into a corporation, capitalized at $9 million. To head off regional competitors, he expanded the wholesale business, opening up branch offices and warehouses across the nation. To keep up with the garment revolution, he added newly fashionable items: ladies' ready-to-wear, toilet articles, laces, hosiery, notions, jewelry, and household furnishings. To ward off the ad/manufacture nexus, he got into manufacturing—of sheets and pillowcases—and adopted his own brand names, which he advertised nationally, annoying some of his retailers by competing with them. But retail stores remained key to his wholesaling business, and he set out to control greater numbers of them, in order to guarantee outlets for his products. His initial strategy was simply to extend them liberal credit, which they were expected to use to buy their goods from Claflin & Co., and he did not press them too hard for repayment when times were bad.

Then he decided to actually acquire retailers, big ones. This required capital, lots of it. In 1900 financial capitalists had not yet become active in underwriting merchandising, but Claflin managed to land the biggest of them all, J. P. Morgan himself. After forming the Associated Merchants in 1900—which combined his own company with Ladies' Mile stalwarts Adams Dry Goods and James McCreery & Co.—the House of Morgan formed a syndicate that underwrote $20 million of shares. The conglomerate soon moved to take on board retailers in Baltimore, Buffalo, Newark, and Minneapolis. In 1909 Claflin and Morgan set up a still bigger holding company, United Dry Goods, which amalgamated the Associated Merchants crowd with the Lord & Taylor department store.

By 1914 Claflin's was indisputably the biggest dry-goods operation in the country, a wholesaler-retailer-manufacturer rolled into one. It was also indisputably bankrupt. It had collapsed not from any lack of earnings, but from having stood behind too many debts taken on by too many subordinate retailers, debts (it being a recessionary moment) that had been called in by nervous banks. Claflin turned over much of his fortune to cover the losses and sold off his Bronx estate to meet the claims of creditors. (It covered 500 city blocks and fed the borough's boom.) But the business never recovered. Mighty Claflin had struck out.

Preeminence now passed definitively from wholesalers to retailers. And for all the prestige and profits accumulated by the chain store kings, the city's crown jewels of commerce were its giant palaces of consumption, and they too were on the move.

DEPARTMENT STORES

Just before the turn of the century Henry Siegel, a Chicago-based retail magnate, set out to make his mark on New York City. On Sixth Avenue between 18th and 19th Streets, in the heart of Ladies' Mile, he had the Milliken Brothers (of Staten Island) erect Siegel-Cooper, the grandest department store in town. It was an instant success. On opening day in 1896 an estimated 150,000 jammed in to marvel at its White City architecture and the range of commodities it had consolidated under one roof.

Siegel-Cooper billed itself as "The Big Store: A City in Itself"—a clear case of truth in advertising. In addition to dry goods, it sold wines, groceries, hardware, and, in its huge pet department, dogs, cats, birds, lizards, monkeys, lion and panther cubs, and on one occasion an elephant. It had a bank and a barbershop, a jeweler and a drugstore, a telegraph office, post office, and doctor's office, a photography gallery, a manicure and hairdressing parlor, a nursery, and an agency for hiring maids. It offered restaurants and tearooms, exotic shows, edifying lectures, a pianist who demonstrated the latest Tin Pan Alley tunes, and an all-women

"Opening of Siegel and Cooper's Department Store," 1896. (Image No. x2010.11.8894, Museum of the City of New York)

orchestra that serenaded the grocery department. And Siegel had a genius for advertising, most spectacularly evident in his using the 7-million-candlepower searchlight mounted on the gold-domed central tower, to beam ads for the Big Store onto the underside of clouds; the images were visible within a thirty-mile radius of Gotham.

The arrival of the Big Store touched off a competitive building frenzy among retailers that rivaled the skyscraper race.

Hardest hit by Siegel-Cooper's state-of-the-art facilities was Macy's, still quartered in a ramshackle series of old buildings along 14th Street. Isidore and Nathan Straus, who had acquired complete ownership of the Red Star emporium in 1896, decided on a bold counteroffensive. The Strauses would follow the uptown movement of their carriage trade clientele, abandon Ladies' Mile altogether, and consolidate their holdings in a built-from-scratch super modern store.

In 1900, Isidore's sons, Jesse and Percy Straus, scouted out a location a mile north at 34th Street, where Broadway diagonaled its way across Sixth Avenue, forming Herald Square. A brilliant choice, it would place Macy's at the center of the extant transport web of electric trolleys and Sixth Avenue El, as well as align it with the uptown thrust of the in-progress IRT subway. The new store would be north of all existing department stores, except for Bloomingdale's at 59th and Third, situated in an entirely different retail district. Henry Siegel, his newfound primacy threatened, tried to abort this development by buying up the northwest-corner site at Broadway and 34th, but the Strauses simply built around his property.

The Strauses borrowed $4.2 million ($2.5 million of it from James Stillman's National City Bank) and hired the Fuller Company to erect the largest department store in the world. (Cozily, Stillman was a director of Harry Black's US Realty—Fuller's parent company—as was Henry Morgenthau, a friend of the Strauses.) Paul Starrett razed thirty-two buildings, including the palatial Koster & Bial's Music Hall (the former Manhattan Opera House), and in their stead erected a mammoth red-brick-and-limestone structure, wrapped around a million-plus square feet of floor space.

The move up from the 14th Street store, a Herculean affair, began on Tuesday, November 4, 1902. For three days 200 delivery wagons, loaded with merchandise, processioned north on Seventh Avenue to 34th, disgorged their contents, then cycled back down Sixth to load up again, the entire route patrolled by special guards and policemen.

When the doors were thrown open that Saturday, the entering throngs discovered the new Macy's was a model of luxury and modern efficiency. Burnished wood escalators accommodated 40,000 people an hour, while 18 miles of brass pneumatic tubing shot cash and sales checks about the store, eliminating the need for "cash boys." The store furnished almost any imaginable want: clothing, furniture, tools, food, drink, drugs, jewelry, cosmetics, sports equipment, music, books, devotional goods, and (after 1905) motorists' clothing and auto supplies. The store later offered a phone "pickup booth" in McAdoo's Hudson Terminal Building: tube commuters could place orders in the morning and pick them up on the way home.

Macy's move helped spark a massive migration of retailers, akin to that by the city's printers, wholesalers, and garment manufacturers. Some homed in on Herald Square itself. Gimbels, a Philadelphia firm, set up shop a block south in 1910 and raided Macy's staff for personnel, touching off a famous (and mutually profitable) feud. (Appropriately enough, Gimbels was built not by the Fuller Company but by its archrival, Thompson-Starrett.) But most Ladies' Mile stores chose to land a block east, nesting along Fifth Avenue.

In 1906 Benjamin Altman opened a monumental limestone palazzo between 34th and 35th, kitty-corner from the Waldorf-Astoria. Over the next decade, large retailers and smaller specialty shops followed suit. Best and Company moved to 35th, Franklin Simon to 37th,

Macy's, ca. 1908. (Image No. 93.1.1.18407, Byron Company/Museum of the City of New York)

Bonwit Teller and Lord & Taylor to 39th, Arnold Constable to 40th, Stern's to 42nd, Bergdorf Goodman to 50th, and Henri Bendel (a favorite of opera diva Geraldine Farrar) to the northern frontier at 57th Street.

Sprinkled among these anchor emporiums were the lavish palazzos of jewelers (Tiffany's in a Stanford White marble palace at 37th Street; Cartier's at 55th), art dealers (the Duveen Brothers at 56th), booksellers (Scribner's in Ernest Flagg–designed quarters at 47th), rug merchants and home furnishings (W. & J. Sloan, also at 47th), and toy stores (F .A. O. Schwarz, who moved to 31st in 1910). Gentlemen's firms favored Madison Avenue: Brooks Brothers relocated to 44th, and Abercrombie & Fitch settled a block farther north.

Ladies' Mile, outflanked, slid downhill. Siegel-Cooper declined rapidly. A desperate Henry Siegel embezzled a vast sum from the Big Store's bank. He was caught, arrested, tried, convicted, and jailed; the Big Store closed in 1917. While some grand-scale Sixth Avenue stores hung on for a time, Ladies' Mile began to look like a deserted village, and downtown commerce was increasingly abandoned to smaller entrepreneurs and pushcart vendors.[9]

By 1917 Fifth Avenue, once a genteel lane of residences and hotels, had become a bustling boulevard of cavernous bazaars. Now store managers, together with new marketing

---

9. With one major exception. In 1896 Philadelphian John Wanamaker took over A. T. Stewart's old Cast-Iron Palace at Broadway and 9th Street. A decade later, in 1906, he opened a towering annex, hoping the new Astor Place subway station (which afforded direct access to Wanamaker's basement) would make it profitable. It did. Wanamaker's would draw posh customers downtown for decades with ad campaigns, the finest imports, and lavish entertainments in its 1,500-seat auditorium (replete with organ).

The boroughs developed their own shopping centers. Fulton Street in downtown Brooklyn boasted Abraham and Straus. (In 1893 the Straus family had acquired part of Wechsler and Abraham, Brooklyn's leading department store, and renamed it.) Pitkin Avenue became the grand shopping promenade for the Yiddish-speaking community. In the Bronx, department stores and retailers clustered at the "Hub" (where 149th Street and Third, Willis, and Melrose Avenues conjoined), along Tremont Avenue from Webster to Third, and at McKinley Square. In Queens, Jamaica Avenue retained primacy of place.

professionals, invented myriad ways to entice middle- and upper-class women—80 to 90 percent of shoppers were female—into entering and buying.

Window displays flourished behind newly inexpensive plate glass. They offered scenes from current theatrical productions, thematic ensembles of furnished rooms, or outfits of clothing down to the last accessory. The job of display person became significant in these years; a single big store might employ dozens. Chicagoan L. Frank Baum, when not writing children's tales, founded the National Association of Window Trimmers to uplift "mercantile decorating" to the status of a profession. Baum also edited the *Show Window*, in which he promoted scores of tactics that might "arouse in the observer the cupidity and longing to possess the goods." Female mannequins, clad only in corsets and sexy undergarments, helped in this regard, generating crowds—but also scandalized protests from purity reformers. Santa Clauses became another draw during month-long Christmas extravaganzas. Santas not only proliferated but organized: by 1914 the Santa Claus Association, headquartered in New York City, had undertaken "to preserve Children's faith in Santa Claus."

More broadly still, the development of new merchandising strategies was underwritten by the emergence of schools and institutes devoted to teaching such skills, from decorative architecture to commercial design and display. Both Pratt Institute and Cooper Union offered commercial art programs after 1905. The Parsons School of Design, which had begun in 1896 as the art-oriented Chase School (after its founder, the painter William Merritt Chase), refocused itself after the arrival in 1904 of Frank Alvah Parsons, who urged that art and design be better linked to industry and commerce. The school proceeded to offer a series

Shop window, Simpson Crawford Company, 311 Sixth Avenue (between 19th and 20th Streets), 1905. (Image No. 93.1.1.1965, Byron Company/Museum of the City of New York)

of educational firsts—programs in fashion design, interior design, and advertising and graphic design. The latter was particularly apposite, as department store managers were advertising copiously in the metropolitan press (especially the Sunday papers), thereby providing the city's newspaper industry with a crucial income stream; vice versa, the big stores and big papers now settled into symbiotic and profitable partnership.

Once lured inside, women entered a festive arena of continuous spectacle, one that offered an escape hatch from parlor propriety into a glamorous world of public pleasure. A host of theatrical effects vivified the commodities on sale: brilliantly colored glass and lights (made possible by the new aniline coal-tar dyes), profuse flower displays, splashing fountains, resplendent live birds, and romantic settings (like Turkish bazaars) which (as at Coney Island) conjured up exotic lands. Everyday items became objects of desire whose acquisition could fulfill dreams as well as supply needs. The excitement, the sensory stimulation, the profusion and availability of goods, encouraged impulse buying in some, shoplifting in others.[10]

Service supplemented spectacle. Customers were pampered with amenities rivaling the luxurious appointments of a downtown men's club. These appealed to upper-class pretensions and allowed middle-class women to experience lifestyles of the rich. The emporium came to seem as much community center as store, a delightful place to socialize with friends.

It took a small army to keep these carefully crafted dream worlds in good working order. Already in 1898 Macy's had over 3,000 employees, as many as did most textile mills or steel plants, and by 1919 the total reached 10,000—fluctuating to twice that number during the holiday season. To an extraordinary degree, it was a female workforce. Women occupied all but the highest managerial ranks; almost one-third of the buyers for the store were women. The sales staff was overwhelmingly female. Given that it had been 88 percent male as late as the 1880s, this represented a transformation as thoroughgoing as that worked in the clerical staffing of skyscrapers. Native-born daughters of Irish, Italian, Polish, Russian, German, and Scandinavian working-class families flocked to the stores despite low wages, long hours, and high expenses for the requisite good clothing. Pink-collar selling was considered higher-status work than blue-collar manufacturing jobs. And National Consumer League pressure, new laws, and the managers' own need to cultivate a cheerful satisfied sales force eventually led stores to moderate brutal discipline and to improve wages and working conditions somewhat.

The department stores fitted into the city's macro-economy in a more fundamental way, by becoming linchpins of the fashion industry, of which Gotham was the American capital. It had long been the port of entry for Parisian creations and the home to pattern-book magazines (like the Butterick Company's *Ladies Quarterly of Broadway Fashions* [1867] and the *Delineator* [1873]), which passed along the latest designs for women to reproduce at home. By 1903, Butterick's pattern-manufacturing operation having become a huge global business, the company erected the sixteen-story Butterick Building at Spring and MacDougal, which contained the largest publishing plant in the city. With the explosion of the women's

---

10. The puzzling phenomenon of well-off women stealing things they could easily afford was explained, by doctors, as a form of mental illness—kleptomania. Male judges, lawyers, merchants, reporters, and popular humorists accepted this explanation as it accorded with their convictions about female weaknesses. (A 1901 Weber and Fields sketch reported that a Mrs. Tankton, a wealthy respectable woman, "has been told by her doctor that she had kleptomania and was taking things for it.") Women defendants pointed to the propaganda blitz to which they were subjected and counterattacked the stores, on occasion launching boycotts. Macy's inaugurated a formal protection department in 1902 and hired female store detectives as well as male. Edison's *The Kleptomaniac* (1905), essaying a radical class analysis, shows a banker's wife getting let off for shoplifting high-end goods, while a poor woman, who stole a loaf of bread for her starving child, gets sent to the slammer.

"R. H. Macy & Co., 34th St. & Broadway," 1913. (Image No. 93.1.1.1913, Byron Company/Museum of the City of New York)

Theatrical Poster, "Only a Shop Girl," ca. 1902. (Lebrecht Music & Arts)

ready-to-wear industry, New York became central to designing and marketing the garments it was producing.

Department stores were at the heart of the process. Heavily reliant on fashion's mutability to ensure continuing sales, they worked overtime to convince consumers (as a trade paper acknowledged) that "last season's coat, costume or hat is irretrievably out of date." At the same time they promoted that mutability by serving as launch vehicle for the latest styles. In the 1900s Wanamaker's, Macy's, and Gimbels held fashion shows with live models (many of them unemployed chorus girls) displaying imported gowns. By the 1910s, great spring and fall pageants with orchestras and special effects were commonplace. And though Paris set the style trends, American women waited to see which French novelties were adopted or rejected in Manhattan.

Fashion magazines evolved into agents and cheerleaders of this process. When *Vogue* magazine had launched in 1892, it was a small weekly, written "by society for society," for which "fashion" was a subordinate clause. It formally described itself as a "journal of society, fashion and the ceremonial side of life." In 1895 Edna Woolman Chase, age 18, came on board as a temp worker in the circulation department but soon became obsessed with the magazine's possibilities. Working her way up to becoming a fashion reporter, then managing

Circulation Department, Butterick Publishing Company, 1905. (Museum of the City of New York)

editor (1911), and eventually editor-in-chief (1914), she helped transform *Vogue* from a gazette of social activities to a magazine intended (as she put it) "to show the women in the rest of the U.S. what New York stores, dressmakers and milliners were offering and what the smart women of New York were buying."

Smart women in those years were adopting a new silhouette. In the late 1890s and early 1900s, the statuesque Gibson Girl had dominated fashion. Her figure was less voluptuous than the previous Lillian Russell shape but still large-bosomed and ample-hipped—corseted into an S-curve with bodice bloused over waistline, and skirt gathered over slightly protruding rear end. This look was in significant measure a New York rather than a Parisian fashion, the creation of illustrator Charles Dana Gibson. Though raised in modest circumstances in Flushing, Gibson, son of a salesman-turned-commercial-artist, became an associate of the New York aristocracy. Many of his drawings portrayed metropolitan society women at balls, the opera, the Horse Show, and on ocean liners. Commercial advertisers made the image omnipresent.

In the 1910s Parisian avant-garde designs recaptured the lead, especially those of Paul Poiret, who in 1908 began reinventing the female silhouette by abandoning the Victorian hourglass emphasis on breasts and hips, which highlighted a woman's maternal and reproductive aspects, and opting for a tubular, high-waisted, hipless look, reminiscent of the Napoleonic era's Empire style, which focused on legs, connoting mobility, youth, and a freer sexuality. Shortened skirts also made it easier to get around in motorcars, subways, on dance floors. Hats receded, too: the gigantic brim trimmed with ostrich or egret (and the longest hatpins in history) peaked in 1909–10.

New York's department stores heavily promoted Paris couturiers. Macy's and Gimbels imported their gowns each season and displayed them in elaborate fashion spectacles and window displays. Visits to the metropolis by reigning designers received lavish and adoring coverage—especially that of Poiret in 1913, whom a *Times* headline hailed this way: "The Man Who Revolutionized the Silhouette of Gowns, and Who Is a Many Sided High Priest of the Beautiful, Comes to Lecture in New York of His Art." *Vogue* and *Harper's Bazaar* vied for the rights to publish haute couture designs, and newspapers presented colorful fashion sketches. Poiret was pleased with the publicity, until he discovered that excellent knock-offs of his dresses were being hawked by Gotham manufacturers, for as little as fifteen dollars, within two weeks of their debut in Paris, sketches having been rushed to New York by fast steamer. Poiret returned to France in a rage reminiscent of Dickens's fury at discovering his latest novels were routinely peddled by Manhattan newsboys, sales from which he received not a penny's worth of royalties. With colleagues, Poiret launched the grandly named Syndicat de Defense de la Grand Couture Française, but it proved largely ineffective. Gotham had become a crucial transmission station for French design, an avenue of access to the American market to be cultivated, not condemned, whatever sins it might commit against the short-term bottom line.

DESPITE THEIR IMMERSION IN SUCH COMMERCIAL REALITIES, the great department stores cultivated the illusion of being a world apart from reality—utopian palaces of consumption in which glittering goods appeared as if by magic. Yet no sooner was Fifth Avenue established as a street of dreams than it was threatened with a rude awakening. Delegates from the grubby world of production, in the person of factory employees, had arrived unbidden and unwanted on their doorsteps.

COMMERCE V. INDUSTRY

While the Big Stores were leapfrogging to the 34th–57th Street strip, the manufacturing lofts that provided their goods were in hot pursuit, pushing north from 23rd Street, heading for (and in some cases slipping across) 34th Street, now elite Fifth Avenue's southern frontier. Where commerce and industry overlapped—along and adjacent to Fifth between 14th and 34th—they clashed.

Each workday at noon, thousands of garment workers poured onto the streets for their lunch break—just as affluent ladies were arriving, noon being the start of fashionable shopping hours. The busy streets made store access difficult—one had to push one's way through the crowds—with the obstacle made more disagreeable to some genteel female sensibilities by the composition of the crowd: working-class, immigrant, mostly male, and occasionally militant (this being a period of great labor upheavals in the garment trades, with Union Square next door being ground zero for protests).

The department stores had long been ambivalent about the working class—even as shoppers—and the ambivalence was mutual. The bazaars' atmosphere intimidated working people, who in any event had little time to browse and socialize, but they *were* attracted to sales. To separate "shawl trade" from "carriage trade," the stores moved their bargains to the basements (rather as Irish churches had relegated Italians to the lower depths). Now, however, those who actually produced the goods were crashing the consumption party, and the lunch-hour inundation of immigrant workers was threatening to drive off upscale customers.

In 1907, to protect the character and image—and hence the value—of what was being called the Bond Street of the New World, a Fifth Avenue Association (FAA) was formed by high-end retailers, the remaining wealthy residents, commercial-property owners, and real estate agents. From a founding membership of 37, it rocketed to 500 by 1910 and kept climbing. Its spokesmen argued that the factory lofts had "practically ruined" the stretch of Fifth between 14th and 23rd—had "utterly changed its former high-class character"—by disgorging "hundreds and thousands of garment workers and operators who swarm down upon the Avenue for the lunch hour between twelve and one o'clock," refusing to heed the educational leaflets, written in several languages, in which the FAA explained that "loitering" and spitting were bad for business. Some argued that loiterers, beggars, peddlers, and "agitators" were "now infesting Fifth Avenue at all hours of the day and night."

By 1916 such feelings were at the boil, the elite mood summarized by a *Times* story headlined "Menace to Trade on Fifth Avenue: The Garment Factory Invasion Threatens All

Retail Business to Thirty-Fourth Street. Much Talk but No Action." The most alarming claim about the uptown thrust was that even the 34th Street border was in danger of being breached, and that "if no restriction is put on this invasion we may confidently expect to see Fifth Avenue ruined for retail purposes as far north as Forty-second Street within ten years." This, a hyperbolic *Real Estate Record and Builders Guide* believed, would not only be the ruination of retailing and hoteling, but "New York City as a whole would receive a death blow." Less emphasized was the fact that when a district shifted from high-end retail to low-end manufacturing, the value of its property plummeted accordingly. The collapse of Ladies' Mile real estate values after the department stores' departure was an anxiety-provoking case in point.

Mere protestations had proved unavailing, it was agreed, because there were no legal mechanisms by which retailers could halt this advance. So businessmen turned cautiously to the idea of municipal intervention. When they did so, they discovered a host of potential allies—notably hard-pressed skyscraper developers—marching in the same direction. Just as the big builders were running up against the dilemmas posed by the free market in matters of height, the big stores were discovering its deficiencies in dealing with land use. The store owners, accordingly, became vigorous supporters of the campaign for a comprehensive zoning law that would establish use districts, especially one banning manufacturing near Fifth Avenue. They succeeded, and in 1916 the new law declared the rectangle formed by 33rd/59th Streets and Third/Seventh Avenues to be basically off-limits to manufacturing.[11]

The trouble was that the law was not retroactive. Manufacturers who had leased space in the restricted zone were "grandfathered" in. So even before final passage, the Fifth Avenue Association formed a subsidiary Save New York Committee, grimly determined to force such aliens to leave. At an organizational lunch meeting at Delmonico's in early 1916, representatives from department stores, shops, hotels, clubs, banks, and insurance companies were addressed by J. Howes Burton, the socially prominent textile dealer who sparkplugged the new committee. "Gentlemen," said Burton, "you are like cattle in a pasture, and the needle trade workers are the flies that follow you from one pasture to another, nagging you into abandoning one great center after another and leaving a trail of ruin, devastation, and bankruptcy up and down the length of the city." The way to free themselves from their tormenters, he explained, was to boycott any manufacturer—refuse to buy its shirts and skirts—who remained in the restricted zone after February 1, 1917. Burton assured the assembled dignitaries that this collective action would be perfectly legal (unlike boycotts undertaken by labor unions, which were strictly beyond the pale). The heads of Altman's, Gimbels, Lord & Taylor, Macy's, Saks—indeed, virtually every major department store in the city—signed on with alacrity. Big banks, mortgage houses, and insurance companies backed the expulsion edict by declaring they would lend no money to would-be developers or lessees of lofts in the proscribed area. Burton also sought support from the general public, running full-page advertisements in virtually every metropolitan newspaper, addressed to "Every One Who Has Pride in This Great City," announcing that Save New York intended to rescue Gotham from "unnatural and unnecessary crowding, from depopulated sections, from being a city unbeautiful, from high rents." The boycott proposal received universal support from New York's major daily newspapers.

---

11. The new law designated the restricted zone as a business section, open to retail development, and limiting manufacturing to 25 percent of a building's square footage, which allowed auxiliary uses but effectively barred garment manufacture.

Support was not quite unanimous. One real estate operator criticized the self-serving nature of the Save New York proposal, "which plainly on its surface will accrue to the benefit of one class of people and to the detriment of another." Opponents were also irritated by the hypocrisy of the retailers, who themselves had invaded Fifth Avenue, then a residential neighborhood, and now proposed "to dictate who shall and who shall not be allowed to sojourn in the land they have conquered."

To Burton et al.'s great surprise, the garment manufacturers were not among the dissidents. On March 8, 1916, only three days after the initial Save New York diktat was issued, the heads of several large manufacturing houses told the astonished committee they had called off negotiations for leasing quarters in the forbidden territory. And on April 2, 1916, a statement signed by more than 250 garment manufacturers declared they backed the Save New York campaign "as a matter of civic pride." (They chose not to underscore the fact that rents in the retail district were among the highest in the world for manufacturing space, and reasonable alternatives would be welcome.) In return for this easy triumph, Burton allowed as how those who already had their nose under the tent would not have to relocate until their present leases expired.

Where were the refugees to go? The Save New York Committee proposed herding them into a district just south of the new Penn Station, bounded by Sixth and Eighth Avenues and West 17th Street and West 31st Streets. Burton also raised the possibility of a new encampment in Long Island City, and the ever alert Degnon Terminal Company proposed constructing a $50 million "Garment City" (with homes for workers) on its territory, a project that would have looked rather like Bush Terminal.

The assembled garment manufacturers made acquiescent noises, but sent out their own search party to canvass the possibilities. They soon came up with what seemed a much better idea: the territory just *north* of Penn Station, in the streets above 33rd and the avenues west of Seventh (those being the frontiers of the forbidden zone). This terrain seemed ideally suited for hosting showrooms where they could receive out-of-town buyers. These would likely arrive at Penn Station and stay at the new Pennsylvania Hotel just across the street, which was in turn conveniently close to the theater district on Broadway. (The Metropolitan Opera was on 39th.) The neighborhood was also now plugged into the new Seventh Avenue subway line, which would allow workers from the Lower East Side, and even Brooklyn or the Bronx, to make their way to the factory floors. Freight trains and warehouses lay just to the west; the great department stores were only two avenues to the east. Best of all, the land was cheap—dirt cheap compared to Fifth Avenue—being part of the old Tenderloin district of tumble-down tenements dating to the Civil War, and home to an easily displaceable population of immigrants and African Americans.

Some garment-manufacturers-turning-developers, notably Abraham E. Lefcourt, had already targeted the territory. In 1914 the prescient Mr. Lefcourt had erected a building at 142 West 37th Street, just off Seventh Avenue, and he was now welcoming the industry with open arms. The organized manufacturers had a more ambitious agenda in mind. Rather than filter into the new territory in piecemeal fashion, they would occupy it collectively and decisively, turning it into a district as exclusively industrial as the newly captured midtown zone was securely in the camp of commerce.

In 1919 Saul Singer, a Russian immigrant who had risen from sweatshop worker to president of the Cloak, Suit, and Skirt Manufacturers' Protective Association, together with Mack Kanner, a leader of the dress trade, one of the two great branches of the ladies' garment industry, announced that a group of fellow manufacturers had organized a syndicate that would erect two giant loft buildings on the west side of Seventh Avenue, astride opposite corners of 37th Street. The northern one would be twenty-two stories tall, the southern one seventeen, and together they would offer 1.5 million square feet of floor space. The complex—grandly denominated the Garment Centre Capitol—was intended to be a comprehensive needlework-trade center. The ground floors would be rented to retail shops catering to locals; the second, third, and fourth stories would be leased as offices and showrooms, the latter quite ornate, as they were intended to make buyers feel cosseted while they viewed finished garments and dickered over prices; the top floors, as in other such industrial city megaliths, would be flexible spaces that could easily be partitioned for factory production. Two years later, when the Garment Centre Capitol opened, it was the largest single center for manufacturing garments in the world. The seventy companies housed within employed an estimated 20,000 workers.

In certain quarters, this whole enterprise seemed wrongheaded. Retailers and real estate brokers were pleased at the quick solution of an immediate crisis. But there were those who wondered if a better solution would not have been to have "removed the industry from the heart of the city entirely"—the Long Island City option, perhaps. After all, the *Real Estate Record and Builders Guide* mused, "if Manhattan loses as a manufacturing center, it is destined to gain enormously as a center of retail and wholesale trade," a vision of the future that readily embraced offices, hotels, and entertainment venues. Besides, wasn't Manhattan overcrowded? Wouldn't it be better to move not just the garment center but factories of all kinds to the industrial outskirts? Especially if—as though they were Pied Pipers—their employees would be sure to follow? But it was too late. "Seventh Avenue" was about to join the roster of synechdotal New York street names, as the impregnable domain of the city's largest industry.

PART THREE

CULTURES

George Luks, Cake Walk, 1915. (Courtesy of the Delaware Art Museum)

12

Acropoli

CONSOLIDATING CULTURE

In his 1903 essay "New York as the American Metropolis," critic Herbert Croly argued that while Gotham had established itself as the nation's preeminent center of industry and commerce, it was not entitled to claim the status of US "art metropolis" or to assert its "authoritative position" in matters "social and intellectual." New York certainly "offers unique opportunities for good Americans to make and spend money," Croly agreed, "but it has not yet become a city in which the finer and more constructive social and aesthetic ideals...have received any adequate expression."

There were several reasons for this. One was that the city's cultural sphere had not experienced the same "processes of definition and concentration" that had made its corporate sector so "well-organized, well-directed and efficient." Not, to be sure, that the "culture of a people" could be equated with the organization of its industries. "Consolidation in social and intellectual matters does not mean management from a central office by an artistic 'boss' or a 'captain of culture,'" Croly cautioned. Rather, "it means the existence of a communicating current of formative ideas and purposes" which "stamps the mass of its works with a kindred spirit and direction." If being the "social and intellectual metropolis of a country" meant being the center from which such a current radiated, New York wasn't there yet.

The unfinished state of cultural consolidation was due in part to the fissiparous nature of Gotham's upper class—less a tight-knit social formation, Croly thought, than "a set of cliques." New York Society was composed of (among others) a smart set, a literary set, a philanthropic set, a new millionaires set, and a set "that has not much money but has Knickerbocker, or other highly respectable ancestors."

But even as Croly wrote, many of Gotham's boom-era elite were consolidating and expanding the city's major cultural institutions—museums, zoos, libraries, universities, preservation societies, opera companies, and symphony orchestras. The New York rich, their bank accounts bulging with merger-era profits, piled onto the boards of venues like the Metropolitan Opera, the New York Philharmonic, and the Museum of Natural History and donated vast sums to house others in grand Beaux-Arts buildings—viz. the New York Public Library, the Metropolitan Museum of Art, the campus of Columbia University. These were the cultural counterparts of Grand Central Terminal, the New York Stock Exchange, and the Chelsea Piers—designed, often as not, by the same architects, and built by the same construction companies.

There was a variety of explanations for this surge into the cultural arena. Some of the elite focused narrowly on improving entities devoted in large part to the entertainment and edification of their own class; opera houses were places to play and preen. But the super-rich also sought to demonstrate that they cared about more than money. Editor E. L. Godkin had long ago suggested that "plenty of people know how to get money; but not very many know best what to do with it. To be rich properly is indeed a fine art. It requires culture, imagination, and character." This injunction had seldom been taken to heart by Godkin's contemporaries during Gotham's Gilded Age—the post–Civil War era of competitive accumulation and conspicuous consumption. In the early twentieth century Morgan and his peers, who in business prided themselves on having risen above the scramble of the marketplace, so in cultural affairs sought to display *richesse oblige* by creating temples of high culture—acropoli set above or apart from the hurly-burly.

Such culture work bolstered their international standing. New York, by their lights, was *their* city, and they wanted it to reflect their world-class ambitions, to become a capital of culture as well as commerce. Gotham's elites had been struggling to catch up with Europe's Joneses since at least the 1850s, building Crystal Palaces, or Bois de Boulognes, or whatever was fashionable in rival transatlantic cities. Now they would have the wherewithal to run neck and neck, even pull ahead. New York's consolidated cultural institutions, housed in monumental splendor, would proclaim the city's arrival on the global stage, as its triumph over Spain had announced its entry into the imperial sweepstakes. Gotham's haute bourgeoisie were still cultural subordinates, in that they remained intent on emulating Europe's aristocracy, but they could now do so on a scale that presented modern American capitalists as the rightful heirs and custodians of that ancient civilization.

On the home front, their institutions would also purvey that civilization to the city's lower orders. Croly had noted that another obstacle to New York's attaining cultural supremacy was the "unusual proportion of raw and unapproachable foreigners" in its population. To overcome this, Gotham patricians would launch a cultural offensive. Their acropoli, far from being defensive citadels, would be activist agencies, sending High Culture radiating downward and outward to elevate and uplift the classes and races crowded into the city's plebeian quarters. More precisely, this would be an effort by Northern and Western Europeans—the elite being nearly all Anglo Protestants or German Jews—to "civilize" Eastern European Jews and Southern Italians. Museums, libraries, and historic houses would transmit and inculcate approved aesthetic ideals and political values, thus assimilating and "Americanizing" the newcomers.

Or so they hoped. In truth, this vision would not work out quite as the English critic Matthew Arnold had imagined back in the 1880s and 1890s, when the high priests of Victorian culture still commanded considerable authority. Their writ would have trouble running in working-class quarters whose occupants, possessed of their own cultural and political traditions, proved far less malleable than elites had hoped. Indeed, influences could and did run in the opposite direction, as the perimeters of elite institutions proved surprisingly permeable. Not least because many private acropoli were crucially dependent on public funding or grants of land, their trustees had to come to terms with political actors, such as Tammany politicians, who marched to different drummers.

We begin with museums, several of which leapt into imperial splendor during the boom years, as wealthy trustees bankrolled global treasure hunts. Expeditions ranged from the canyons of Wyoming to the châteaux of straitened European aristocrats, from the Nile to the North Pole. Acquisitions poured into newly giantized repositories where the heaped-up treasures—oil paintings, totem poles, dinosaur bones—were put on display to amuse the elites, instruct the masses, and testify to the power and glory of the metropolis.

ART BY THE CARTLOAD

Art collecting was a passion of the Belle Époque rich. A brilliant collection displayed one's taste, sealed one's status. Gotham's millionaires competed with Russian grand dukes and South African gold magnates to snare the world's cultural riches. Some gobbled indiscriminately and got bilked accordingly. Most millionaires, however, were like the era's great steamships—convoyed safely into harbor by pilot boats captained by art experts.

New York City was a paradise for European dealers. Nineteenth-century arrivals like Knoedler, Goupil, Durand-Ruel, and Gimpel & Wildenstein had mostly clustered around Madison Square. They liked the proximity to Thomas Kirby's 23rd Street American Art Association, the nation's premier auction house, where older collections of art, antiques, books, and jewels got recycled. But as the super-rich drifted north, the art business (like the department stores) chased after them. And once the Plaza Hotel opened, the American Art Association itself held auctions there, signaling a definitive shift in the art trade's center of gravity.

In these sumptuous surroundings, dealers laid before their wealthy patrons the treasures in which they specialized. Henry Duveen and then his nephew Joe guided J. P. Morgan, Henry Clay Frick, Benjamin Altman, Otto Kahn, Elbert Gary, and William Randolph Hearst toward eighteenth-century English portraits, Dutch masterpieces by Rembrandt and Hals, and Italian painters of the early and high Renaissance. Paul Durand-Ruel catered to the minority of New Yorkers interested in the Impressionists, his superstar clients being Louisine Havemeyer and her husband, sugar king Henry (Harry) Osborne Havemeyer, who picked up Courbets, Manets, and Monets. The Havemeyers were also early devotees of Spanish old masters like El Greco, Velázquez, and Goya—Harry liked to say that after the war with Spain the United States should have demanded the Prado instead of the Philippines—and in the hyper-competitive collecting world, the couple were quickly joined by Frick, Altman, and Philip Lehman. American painters, however, were distinctly out of vogue, in contrast to the nineteenth century, when local city merchants had happily snapped up work by Hudson River School contemporaries.

These Medici did not patronize living artists. The turn-of-century collectors preferred their paintings as pedigreed as possible, as they did with the tapestries, jewel-encrusted books, gilded altarpieces, and the decorative arts in general that constituted the vast bulk of their purchases. Given the flood of forgeries that now issued from underground ateliers, the role of dealers like Joe Duveen, and authenticators like connoisseur Bernard Berenson, grew ever more important.[1]

---

1. The authentication process was not without its own perils. Duveen struck an under-the-table deal with Berenson, paying him a percentage (first 10 percent, then 25 percent) to certify that Italian old masters were as advertised, while Berenson collected another fee from the purchaser for his supposedly "independent" judgment. Still, for all the finagling in this wild and wooly market, the vast majority of purchased goods seem to have been legitimate.

Many moguls supplemented gallery purchases with their own shopping expeditions to Europe. Morgan roamed widely and bought lavishly, with awe-inspiring speed. A discerning collector, he acquired hundreds of individual masterpieces in a dozen media—including paintings, porcelains, tapestries, exquisitely carved ivories, medieval reliquaries, and illuminated manuscripts. What he particularly enjoyed doing—mirroring his business methods—was collecting other men's collections: "What's the use of bothering about one little piece when I might get them all?" There was also method in his obsession, as he moved deliberately from one field of acquisition to another: "I have done with the Greek antiquities," he informed his sister. "I am at the Egyptian."

The New Yorkers' shopping trips and bidding wars produced an incredible inflation in prices. In 1901, with the previous record for an artwork being $65,000, Morgan paid $400,000 for a Raphael altarpiece Madonna; then Frick coughed up $500,000 for a Gainsborough, Kahn paid over $400,000 for a Hals, and when Joe Duveen purchased the entire Rodolphe Kann collection for $4.5 million, Morgan plunked down half of that for the right to pick the thirty best items.

As treasures poured across the Atlantic, protests arose from the governments of drained countries and from hopelessly outbid dealers and museum directors.[2] These were briskly dismissed. In 1906, on the occasion of a Titian being scooped up and sent Gothamward, a *Times* editorial ("New York: The Art Magnet") admitted that "American collectors are the terror of foreign curators of museums," and understood why countries like Italy and Greece were insisting that "these things shall remain at home." But the Europeans should just grow up and face facts: as they "cannot afford to pay the market price," the only way they might block art transfers would be to seize private property, and that, of course, would be unthinkable. Stanford White was blunter. Reproached for importing art treasures, he rebutted that "in the past, dominant nations had always plundered works of art from their predecessors." Now, he said, "America was taking a leading place among nations and had, therefore, the right to obtain art wherever she could."

The only barrier to an even greater flow of imports was on the US side. An 1897 Revenue Act had imposed a 20 percent tariff on incoming works of art, daunting even for Morgan. While working to overturn it, the banker kept the vast bulk of his purchases at Prince's Gate, his London quarters, and loaned the overflow to the Victoria and Albert Museum. Finally, with help from Robert de Forest, Joseph Choate, and Elihu Root (then serving in the US Senate), Morgan got a clause inserted in the Payne-Aldrich tariff (1909) that abolished duties on works of art over one hundred years old. (In 1918 the New York corporate lawyer and art collector John Quinn would successfully get the duty on modern art repealed as well.) In the next five months an estimated $50 million of art sailed across the ocean blue. Morgan moved more deliberately, but in 1912 he began packing up his collections (under the eye of a customs inspector specially imported from the Port of New York) and would ship 351 cases' worth across the Atlantic.

The tremendous influx created a space crisis. Most millionaire collectors—Collis P. Huntington, the Havemeyers, Thomas Fortune Ryan, Edward S. Harkness—parked acquisitions in their grand town houses strung out along upper Fifth Avenue, but they were

---

2. The British were particularly infuriated. With the crisis of the aristocracy continuing—great landowners were increasingly unable to compete with US mass-produced agricultural products—they were forced to sell off ancestral holdings and their contents. But just as long-hidden-away treasures were seeing the light of day, many were whisked across the Atlantic, English buyers proving unable to keep them in the country.

"The Magnet," *Puck* (June 21, 1911). (Everett Collection Inc/Alamy Stock Photo)

beginning to feel the strain. Down at Murray Hill Morgan was having his own problems, as his swelling holdings overflowed his Madison Avenue basement, a warehouse on 42nd Street, the attic of the Lenox Library, and his bank's vaults down at 23 Wall. In 1900, accordingly, he bought the property adjoining his house on East 36th and drafted Charles McKim to design a library for his once and future collection. McKim came up with an Italian Renaissance palace, based on the Villa Medici, and he also borrowed from the Greeks—specifically the Erechtheum in Athens—using the (costly) technique of fitting marble blocks together without binding material. Morgan settled in during 1905–6 and gave charge of the contents to Belle da Costa Greene, a formidable 26-year-old, light-skinned African American woman passing as white. (She attributed her olive complexion to a confected Portuguese grandmother.) As J. P. Morgan's librarian, and ofttimes his representative at auctions, Greene became one of the most powerful players in the roiling art market.

Morgan had few rivals when it came to building personal galleries, but in some respects he was outclassed by Archer Milton Huntington, the stepson of Collis P. Huntington, the railroad magnate. Young Huntington, never interested in taking over the railroad business, had discovered his true calling when he first encountered Hispanic culture on a visit to Mexico City in 1889, when the family dined in Chapultepec Castle with Huntington père's business associate Porfirio Díaz, for whom he was building the Mexican International Railroad. Archer now set out with "feverish eagerness" to accumulate Hispanica, from Latin America as well as the Iberian peninsula. And after Collis's death in 1900 he devoted a goodly portion of his inheritance to amassing the greatest such collection outside of Spain. To house and display it, he founded in 1904 the Hispanic Society of America (with Díaz among the luminaries on the board). He then purchased sections of the former estate and game preserve of John James Audubon, ornithologist extraordinaire. It was there, on a plot running west from Broadway between 155th and 156th Streets, which overlooked Trinity Cemetery to the south and was handily accessible via the new subway station at 157th, that he opened his Hispanic museum in 1908. In February 1909 Huntington mounted an exhibition of Valencian painter Joaquín Sorolla's work, his first in the United States, which was a spectacular success, drawing 160,000 uptown in its first four weeks.

Huntington was just getting started. On his capacious acropolis—which he named Audubon Terrace—he orchestrated construction of an entire cultural complex. The Hispanic Society would be joined in short order by the American Numismatic Society (of which he was president), the American Geographical Society, the American Academy and National Institute of Arts and Letters, and Nuestra Señora de la Esperanza (Our Lady of Hope). The latter was the brainstorm of the widow of Spain's consul-general in New York, who suggested Huntington pair a Spanish Catholic church with his Hispanic Society. Though a Protestant, he liked the idea and donated the land to Cardinal Farley, along with $50,000 to build on it. The archdiocese's second Spanish-language church opened in 1912.

Huntington still wasn't finished. He got in touch with George Gustav Heye, an equally obsessed collector, who had founded (on paper) a Museum of the American Indian. Heye had purchased a Navajo hide shirt in Arizona in 1897 and begun buying Indian artifacts piece-meal. In 1901 he entered investment banking and got in on the merger boom. By 1903 he was in a position to start buying large archaeological collections of objects fashioned by indige-nous peoples throughout the Western Hemisphere. He also began traveling and collecting items himself, as well as sponsoring important excavations in Mexico and Ecuador (in 1906). By 1916 he had 58,000 objects, and—his various temporary facilities overwhelmed—he de-lightedly took Huntington up on his offer to build a permanent home on the Audubon Terrace platform.

AS IMPRESSIVE AS WERE THESE PRIVATE INITIATIVES, they were dwarfed by the city's great museums, which were able to draw on public financing.

The most grandiose museological vision was Brooklyn's. Before Consolidation, the local gentry—determined to trump Manhattan's Metropolitan Museum—laid plans to have the Brooklyn Institute of Arts and Sciences (BIAS) erect what would come to be called the Brooklyn Museum. It would collect and display *everything*, dwarfing even London's Victoria and Albert. To house this three-dimensional encyclopedia, they commissioned McKim, Mead & White to build the largest such building in the world—a 1,500,000-square-foot colossus along Vaux and Olmsted's Eastern Parkway. In the waning days of municipal independence, the City of Brooklyn had undertaken to finance, own, and maintain the building, with the private-sector BIAS operating the museum and creating its collection. Ground was broken in 1895. The first section opened in 1897, three months before Brooklyn was to turn into a borough. By then the city was virtually broke. There seemed little likelihood of further construction—unless Consolidation brought access to Manhattan's money, as its advocates promised it would.

To Brooklyn's delight, Greater New York delivered. Almost immediately the consoli-dated city issued $300,000 in bonds to finance the second section. In 1902–3, it came up with $450,000 for the third and last section of the front façade, which was completed in 1906–7. The city also agreed to aid BIAS in creating an adjacent 50-acre Botanic Garden (1910), with a Kew Gardens–style greenhouse (1917), also designed by McKim, Mead & White. And under the same joint aegis, BIAS in 1899 founded the Children's Museum, the first of its kind in the United States, in an old mansion near the intersection of Brooklyn and St. Mark's Avenues. In addition to supporting all this construction work, New York supplied roughly $70,000 each year for maintenance, supplementing donations gleaned from private funders.

But such donations steadily slackened as Brooklyn's rich—in limited supply compared to the massed millionaires of Manhattan—found borough boosterism ever less compelling.

Here was the downside of Consolidation: it was clear to affluent Brooklynites that if they wanted to make their mark on the greater city's cultural scene, they would have to play in the big leagues across the river. Public funds for construction also tapered off, leaving less than a quarter of McKim's planned vastness completed.

The greater city's appropriations for the museum's maintenance did continue to increase, in part because the trustees invited the borough's expanding populace, providing a wealth of programs that enticed the increasingly diverse citizenry to the museum, thus developing political support for its continued existence. There was an irony here, as the institution had been originally intended by the Anglo-Protestant elite to serve Brooklyn's upper- and middle-class Anglo-Protestants, presumed, before Consolidation, to be the heart and soul of the city of homes and churches. That overstated self-image was challenged in the century's first decades. Between 1900 and 1920 the number of Protestants inched up from 606,000 to 708,000. But the Jewish presence shot up from 161,000 to 604,000, and Catholics swelled from 399,000 to 899,000, driving the Protestant percentage down from 51.9 percent to 33.4 percent. And while Director Franklin Hooper complained about the "immense influx of people representing a lower grade of civilization," the institution shifted focus and justification, offering exhibits and lectures that reflected the increasing diversity of its audience, even tackling controversial issues such as "the Negro Problem in the South" or "Trade Unions." It also appealed for funding on the grounds that it was "now open more hours than any other museum in the world." In 1910 300,000 visitors stopped by.

THE METROPOLITAN MUSEUM OF ART ALSO RELIED HEAVILY on municipal support. In the nineteenth century, the city had underwritten its first building and covered crucial operating expenses, especially after the trustees had learned the hard way that delimiting working-class visitations, notably by staying closed on Sundays, was not the best route to the public purse, especially when Tammany was holding the strings. The museum cultivated its municipal connection. In 1905 the mayor and parks commissioner were named ex officio members of the board. The museum expanded the number of free-access days, provided educational programming, allowed New York public school teachers to bring classes, and appealed for taxpayer support on the basis of booming attendance (500,000 visitors in 1900, 700,000 in 1915). Several city administrations agreed and raised annual contributions for operating expenses (from $95,000 in 1900 to $200,000 in 1909), while authorizing massive layouts for building expansion.

With the bulk of these costs covered by the city, the Met trustees could concentrate on acquisitions. As the merger boom took off, donations from its leading beneficiaries became progressively more generous. Morgan, a longtime trustee, took the lead with a quantum leap in giving during 1902. In that year a banker and Chinese ceramics collector named James A. Garland died. In 1893 Garland, having run out of room to house his treasures, had loaned 2,000 porcelains to the Metropolitan, which hoped he would convert it to a gift, but when the will was read no such bequest had been made. Henry Duveen bought the lot for $500,000; Morgan immediately purchased it for $600,000 and left it on deposit with the Met.

In 1904 Morgan became president of the board.[3] It was already a prestigious body, heavy with old- and new-monied, and Morgan proceeded to fill vacancies with the likes of iron magnate Henry Frick, banker George Baker, architect Charles McKim, Standard Oil heir

---

3. Seconded by the indefatigable and omnipresent Robert de Forest, to whom Morgan entrusted most of the administrative responsibilities of the museum. De Forest—the son-in-law of John Taylor Johnston, the Metropolitan's first president—had been on the board since 1889.

Edward Harkness, and the first Jewish trustee, George Blumenthal, the head of Lazard Frères, making the Met board the richest and most exclusive club in the city. Henceforth when museum foragers overspent their budget, Morgan simply announced the deficit and went around the table collecting pledges until it was erased.

Donations of art works poured in, too. If a mansion was jammed (as with Garland's ceramics) or a purchase didn't work out (as when in 1907 Louisine Havemeyer decided her Manet *Dead Christ with Angels* was "impossible to live with"), one could ship it up Fifth Avenue to the Met. Bequests became routine. The childless Rutherfurd Stuyvesant, Peter Stuyvesant's direct descendant, and a trustee of long standing, bequeathed his massive armor collection in 1909. And the similarly heirless Benjamin Altman, nudged by his lawyer (and Met trustee) Joseph Choate, bequeathed nearly a thousand objects, valued at $15 million, when he passed on in 1913.

The Met became a formidable purchaser in its own right. Morgan himself led annual expeditions, moving with his retinue through London, Paris, Aix-les-Bains, Monte Carlo, Rome, and Venice. Some of the acquisitions were matters of impulse, but increasingly the museum's procurements were driven by scholarly curatorial concerns. The Met sought not individual unrelated masterpieces but objects that, grouped into a sequence, would illustrate the evolution of "art" itself.

There were occasional tussles over what (or when) art was. For Morgan and most trustees, older was better. He established an Egyptian Department in 1905 and financed excavations near Cairo (1907), in the Libyan desert (1908), and (from 1910) at Luxor, site of the ancient city of Thebes. Each summer he (and Harkness, another major benefactor of the Egyptian Department) went out to Luxor on private *dahabiyehs* to watch tomb sculptures, wall paintings, jewels, and pottery be dug up and packed off to New York City.

Others pushed for more modern works and made some progress despite strong headwinds. When Roger Fry, a Met scholar-adviser nearly as credentialed as Berenson, bought Renoir's *Madame Charpentier and Her Children* in 1907, indignant trustees nearly fired him. In 1913, when the curator of paintings recommended purchasing a Cézanne landscape, de Forest and others fought the idea but were overruled. *La Colline des Pauvres* became the first Cézanne to enter a public collection in the United States. The gates remained barred against contemporary American artists.

The sheer quantity of arriving artwork—whatever the provenance—threatened to overwhelm the premises. Even before Morgan's presidency, the Met trustees had decided on an expansion program. Richard Morris Hunt had devised a grand master plan that would envelop Vaux and Mould's old red-brick Gothic buildings in a vast new limestone structure fronting on Fifth Avenue. In 1895 the city appropriated $1 million for it, and when Hunt died that year, completion of the first portion—the majestic Great Hall, a neoclassical entrance pavilion—was turned over to his son, who finished it in 1902.

In 1904, amid another space crunch, the museum invited McKim, then designing Morgan's library on East 36th Street, to add four classical wings to Hunt's centerpiece—the first two extending northward up Fifth Avenue, for which the city authorized the sale of $1.2 million worth of New York City bonds. By 1907, with all the initial appropriation committed, the state legislature authorized a payout of $750,000 a year for ten years, which made possible completion of the entire Fifth Avenue façade. Even before completion, the new galleries were spoken for. The Egyptian collection alone would fill ten of them.

By 1911 the trustees felt confident in insisting that "our Museum no longer appeals merely to 'the upper classes,' the educated, the cultured, the rich. It has entered the life of the people."

FOSSIL PHILANTHROPY

The American Museum of Natural History across the park was an even bigger people-pleaser. Though begun as a rich men's toy, it contained much the public could play with. It had taken some time, however: for years after it opened in 1877, few had boarded the horse cars heading up the still-undeveloped West Side. Nor was low attendance offset by scientific repute. Its curators published virtually nothing. But in 1881, the Natural History Museum had been taken on as the special cause of its new president, Morris Jesup. A multi-millionaire from his merchant banking and railroad securities work, Jesup retired in 1884 to devote himself to his various philanthropies.

The American Museum became the major recipient of most of Jesup's still-phenomenal energy, and a good deal of his phenomenal fortune: he pumped in $450,000 during his lifetime, left another $1 million at his death, and his wife bequeathed $5 million more. Jesup also rallied the rich, particularly wealthy sportsmen, to provide not only money but exhibits. Members of the Boone and Crockett Club (a society of big game hunters founded by Teddy Roosevelt in 1887) were intrigued by curator Joel Asaph Allen's ambition to have the museum contribute to ongoing debates over evolution. As assembling large collections was considered the way to study variations in species, Allen proposed to amass and exhibit examples of the country's big game animals in a North American Mammal Hall. The requirements of science dovetailed nicely with the sporting trustees' desire to possess and exhibit animal trophies. Guns at the ready, they headed out west in 1888 on the first of a series of collecting expeditions that would, by the end of the 1890s, make the institution's corpus of birds and mammals second only to the Smithsonian's.

Jesup also began to make good on the museum's public outreach mission. In 1888 the museum abandoned its Sunday closing policy, prompted by Mayor William Russell Grace's refusal of money for a new wing, in response to incensed protests at the closed-door policy. But once the trustees gave in, Tammany politicians, especially local leader George Washington Plunkitt, persuaded the city council and state legislature, during the 1880s and 1890s, to pour almost $5 million into wing after wing of the burgeoning structure.

As at the Metropolitan Museum of Art, the city's underwriting of construction, operation, and maintenance freed the trustees to acquire and manage the collections. Also as at the Met, these were uniformly super-rich Anglo-Protestants—until 1910 when the then president looked about for "an agreeable Hebrew, because the Zoo, the Metrop.[olitan Museum], the Public Lib. have all done so, and our atti[tude] is becoming conspicuous." (Felix Warburg of Kuhn, Loeb was the chosen one.) The trustees' support was generous—Morgan gave $650,000—if occasionally reluctant. Cleveland H. Dodge wrote in 1914: "I firmly believe in the fiduciary responsibility of the owners of capital so here is my check. Only do I wish those Indians had not made so many pots." What was particularly appealing was the museum's ability to combine popular exhibits with the advancement of science. And that admixture was in large measure the doing of two antipodal individuals—the difference between their biographies being surpassed only by the great divide between their ideologies.

HENRY FAIRFIELD OSBORN, LIKE ARCHER HUNTINGTON, had been born into a wealthy railroading family—his father was president of the Illinois Central—but had no wish to continue in the family business. He lived the club life expected of a patrician millionaire, being active in the Century, Metropolitan, and University, as well as the Boone and Crockett, and was considered by many to be insufferably pompous and pretentious. Yet where natural science was concerned he was passionate and professional. After getting a Princeton BA in geology and archaeology in 1877, the 20-year-old Osborn participated in his first paleontological expedition in 1877–78, out in the wilds of Wyoming and Colorado. He went on to study anatomy with Dr. William Welch at Bellevue and Physicians & Surgeons, and comparative anatomy with Thomas Huxley in London. He then taught at Princeton during the 1880s, and moved to New York in 1891 to become professor of biology at Columbia and to head the Department of Vertebrate Paleontology at the museum.

Seeking answers for problems in Darwinian theory, he began sending fossil-hunting expeditions out west each summer, to accumulate a complete record of the vertebrate life of North America. These scientific concerns also proved to be crowd-pleasers.

In 1897 one of the western expeditions discovered dinosaur skeletons. Osborn hired Barnum Brown, known as "Mr. Bones" for his ability to almost sniff out fossils, and sent him off to Wyoming. In 1898 Brown began shipping back carloads of bones—30 tons in all—free of charge (courtesy of the Erie railroad). In 1899 another 20 tons followed, including the elements of a magnificent brontosaurus (whose right thigh bone alone weighed 570 pounds). In 1902 a Montana expedition uncovered a previously unknown meat eater; Osborn would christen it *Tyrannosaurus rex*.

"Mounting Brontosaurus skeleton forelimb," 1904. (Image No. 17506, American Museum of Natural History Library)

Back at Central Park West the bones were not allowed to lie in drawers, inarticulated and inarticulate. Instead Osborn dramatized his science for trustees and public. He found a young artisan who devised a technique for boring through fossil bones, making it possible to mount freestanding skeletons. In 1905 the brontosaurus, nearly 70 feet long and over 15 feet tall, was installed in the new Hall of Fossil Reptiles. It reaped a nationwide bonanza of publicity for the museum. So did novel displays like Frank Chapman's Hall of North American Birds (1903), the first to use dioramas setting stuffed specimens amid backdrops of artificial plants, flowers, rocks, and trees. In 1907 the museum was visited by more than half a million, and the city willingly contributed $160,000 for its maintenance.

IN 1896, FIVE YEARS AFTER OSBORN'S ARRIVAL, Jesup hired Franz Boas to be assistant curator of ethnology and somatology.

Born in Westphalia in 1858, Boas was an assimilated German Jew; though his grandparents had been observant believers, his parents were religious skeptics. While Boas did not proclaim his Jewishness, he refused to convert to Christianity, vocally opposed anti-Semitism, and carried a facial scar from a duel fought to punish an anti-Semitic slur. He also came, he said, from a "German home in which the ideals of the revolution of 1848 were a living force." He believed in equality of opportunity, freedom of inquiry, and openness to the socially excluded.

Boas got a doctorate in physics from Kiel University in 1881 but moved into geography. German geographers were then divided over what caused the wide variation in human societies. Many argued that the physical environment was the principal determining factor; others, that diffusion of ideas through migration was more important. In 1883 Boas went to Baffin Island in northern Canada to research the impact of the environment on native Inuit migrations.

After living and working closely with the "Central Eskimos," Boas had a revelation. "I often ask myself," he penciled in his Arctic diary, "what advantages our 'good society' possesses over that of the 'savages' and find, the more I see of their customs, that we have no right to look down upon them." It was apparent that the Eskimo "enjoys as well the beauties of nature as we do; that he expresses his grief in mournful songs, and appreciates conceptions." Boas had come to believe in the mental equality of Eskimos and Europeans, indeed of all humanity.

This was a revolutionary assessment. The version of evolutionary theory then fashionable among most anthropologists—the profession to which he now found himself drawn—presented the human saga as a glorious climb up from apehood through dark savagery to various levels of white civilization. Peoples stuck in lower levels were simply biologically incapable of rising higher.

Boas whaled away at this concept of a "presumed hierarchy of racial types." There were, to be sure, enormous variations in condition and custom among the world's peoples, but these were the products of geography and history, not biology. Each society had evolved its own "culture"—a term theretofore generally understood as the private possession of "cultured" individuals but which Boas in the 1890s used in the plural. These "cultures," moreover, were quite capable of transformation. Boas didn't argue that all cultures were equal—he reserved the term "civilization" for societies with the highest levels of technical achievement and humane values—but rather that the condition of "savages" was the end result of millennia-long vagaries of war and disease, habitat and migration, not immutable racial inferiority.

Franz Boas demonstrating a Kwakiutl *hamtasa* dance, 1895. (National Anthropological Archives, Smithsonian Institution)

Back in Germany, alienated by growing anti-Semitism and nationalism, Boas in 1887 decided to emigrate to New York. With the assistance of his uncle Dr. Abraham Jacobi, a prominent member of the city's German Jewish community, he took a position as assistant editor of *Science*. From 1888 to 1892 he taught at Clark University, then from 1892 to 1894 took the post of chief assistant to Harvard's Frederic W. Putnam, who was supervising the Department of Ethnology and Archaeology at Chicago's Columbian Exposition. During these years he also made a series of field trips to the Pacific Northwest Coast on behalf of various organizations, and (between 1886 and 1896) produced over 150 publications.

In 1896, when Boas was named Putnam's assistant—Putnam having accepted the direction of anthropology at the American Museum of Natural History—he was also given a parallel appointment at Columbia University. Boas quickly proposed that Jesup finance a long-term expedition to survey and compare cultures in Siberia, Alaska, and the northwest coast of Canada, to test the theory that the Indians of North America had migrated from northeastern Siberia across the Bering Strait. Jesup, intrigued, backed the Jesup North Pacific Expedition (1897–1902), the biggest-ever in the history of anthropology. In 1897 Boas left New York for British Columbia. While exploring coastal Indian myths, he also shipped back handsomely carved artifacts to the museum—masks, a war canoe, giant totem poles (for which he paid one dollar per foot)—which he would arrange in the new Hall of Northwest Coast Indians.

Jesup also backed more heroic and dashing expeditions, like the search for the North Pole. In 1894 Lieutenant Robert Peary of the Navy Civil Engineers Corps had gotten stranded in Greenland, and his wife won Jesup's financial assistance in getting the ship home. Peary thanked Jesup by naming a glacier after him. Jesup now got Peary released from active duty (with help from American Museum trustees) to permit him to explore the Far North full time.

In the fall of 1897 Peary's Arctic steamer *Hope* returned from northwestern Greenland and moored in Brooklyn, at Dock Street. Twenty thousand bought passes and trooped on board to view its dramatic cargo, the largest meteorite ever discovered. It was then unloaded by a 100-ton floating crane at the Brooklyn Navy Yard, floated by barge to the 50th Street pier, and hauled to the museum by a block-long team of twenty-eight horses. The publicity was wonderful.

So too, at first, was the attention given by crowds and press to the other cargo Peary had brought back from the arctic, six Polar Eskimos, who, it was explained, were there to help arrange the collection of tools, tents, sleds, kayaks, and clothing, displayed on the *Hope*'s deck, for the American Museum of Natural History.

Less pleased at the arrival were museum officials, including Boas. He had suggested to Peary it would be splendid if one adult Inuit would agree to convey and clarify the artifacts' uses and cultural meanings—information of the "greatest scientific importance." He hadn't, however, planned on three men, one woman, and a girl and boy (the latter, Minik, being the 8-year-old son of Qisuk, one of the men). Boas chided Peary and tried to arrange return passage, but he managed to do so for only one of the men. The others were housed in the museum's basement, where they soon found the temperature oppressive and contracted tuberculosis. They were treated in Bellevue, but all died, except for Minik. The boy pleaded for a proper burial for his father, using the traditional rites only he as an Inuit could give. The curatorial staff wanted to preserve Qisuk's body for study—research that would be impossible if his remains were buried. So they staged a fake burial, by lantern light, for Minik's benefit, and the bones, returned from Bellevue, were held for analysis. Years later, a now-adolescent Minik discovered the ruse and pleaded to be given his father's bones for burial, but the museum refused, a decision an exposé in the *World* turned into a scandal. (By then Boas was no longer at the museum, though he rather cold-bloodedly stood by his original decision.)

In 1903 Putnam resigned, and Boas was promoted to curator, now with real authority to participate in long-term planning. This led to battles with Jesup over the nature and purpose of the institution's exhibition methods. There were a variety of museological disagreements. Jesup thought Boas's displays were overspecialized, confusing, and unattractive to the museum's patrons and visitors. Boas, though he agreed on the need to appeal to both general and advanced audiences, refused to reduce displays to the lowest level.

Then there were the differences in interpretive strategy. As early as 1887 Boas had critiqued the US National Museum in Washington for grouping together tools, weapons, and ornaments by function rather than provenance, then arranging them in sequence based on ascending degree of technological sophistication, to demonstrate the presumed stages of civilizational evolution. Boas argued the focus should be shifted from an object's external form and function to its meaning(s) within a specific cultural context. A throwing stick should be grouped not with other sticks from other areas but with other objects—baskets, fish hooks—produced by the same cultural unit. And he wanted to eschew exhibits based on evolutionary schemes, in favor of providing a historical context for assembled artifacts.

At a higher level still, Boas had proposed that the main object of "ethnological collections" should be "dissemination of the fact that our civilization is not something absolute, but it is relative, and that our ideas and conceptions are true only so far as our civilization goes." To do so, museums would have to show "how far each and every civilization is the outcome of its geographical and historical surroundings."

Jesup, in contrast, favored arrangement by fixed categories—either function (house life, industries, personal adornments) or material (stone, wood, clay)—and in 1905 had facilitated, over Boas's head, such an arrangement of the Peruvian collection. At the big-picture level, Jesup, being an optimistic evolutionist, sought to have the museum illustrate "the advance of mankind from the most primitive form to the most complex forms of life."

Boas pushed back, urging displays to persuade visitors "that our people are not the only carriers of civilization, but that the human mind has been creative everywhere." This was out of sync with Jesup's desire to show, in the case of less developed societies, just "how primitive and crude is the life of the people."

Boas came to believe that the kind of anthropology he wanted to pursue might better be done in a university setting, and in 1905 he resigned, shifting to full-time work at Columbia. It was just as well he did, as in 1908 Jesup died, and his place was taken by the even less sympathetic Osborn, who had nearly left in 1906 to head up the Smithsonian, but been persuaded to stay by his uncle J. P. Morgan. On taking the reins Osborn told a colleague, "Between ourselves, much anthropology is merely opinion, or the gossip of the natives. It is many years away from being a science. Mr. Jesup and the Museum spent far too much money on anthropology."

Osborn would continue on his own path and preside over a major expansion of the institution. In 1909 he hired Carl E. Akeley to create more habitats. Akeley, a famous Chicago taxidermist, had perfected lifelike techniques for mounting animals by modeling them in clay (later papier-mâché) and draping skin over the model. He had first gained public renown by stuffing Jumbo the elephant, P. T. Barnum's 6-ton super-attraction, after it got run down by a speeding freight train in Ontario in 1885. Barnum, typically, turned disaster into profitable opportunity. Shamelessly claiming Jumbo had died heroically trying to save a baby elephant, he hired Akeley to mount the carcass and launched Jumbo on a postmortem career. Akeley's real ambition—characteristically for the age—was to stuff and display not individual elephants but a whole herd of them. He got his first chance in 1910 when his hunting partner Teddy Roosevelt killed one, which he mounted, and in 1912 plans for a full-scale African Hall were approved, which would come to fruition in the next decade.

Osborn was pleased with the popularity of his exhibits, but he had higher goals than mere entertainment. In addition to exploring evolutionary science, he wanted the museum to be a "positive engine" for the "propagation of socially desirable views." He believed that it could be a vital agent in the education of new immigrants. "Nature," he argued in 1908, "teaches law and order and respect for property." Nature, however, was far away from New York's poor. Hence his institution's worth: "If these people cannot go to the country, then the Museum must bring nature to the city."

THE BRONX ZOO

An even more spectacular importation of nature flowered in the Bronx, when Teddy Roosevelt's Boone and Crocketteers headed out west, not to fetch bones but to "bring 'em back alive." The idea originated in 1894 with new club member Madison Grant, a young Wall Street lawyer.

Grant had been born in 1865 in his grandfather's Murray Hill town house, scion of a long line of colonial magistrates, revolutionary patriots, and Civil War heroes. His mother was a descendent of Jessé de Forest, the Walloon Huguenot who in 1623 had recruited the first band of New Amsterdam settlers; his father, a distinguished surgeon, traced his roots to the first Puritans in New England. Wealthy, if not astronomically so, the patrician Grants afforded Madison private tutors, study abroad, a Yale BA, and a Columbia Law degree. In 1890 he opened his own office next to the New York Stock Exchange. Grant had no interest in, or need for, a law career. He much preferred socializing and shooting.

He joined the Union, Knickerbocker, University, Down Town, and Tuxedo and "was regarded as a typical society and club man," according to his close friend Henry Fairfield Osborn, whom Grant, eight years younger, lionized, considering Osborn's bearing not pompous but patrician. Indeed, Grant and Osborn became socially (and ideologically) inseparable. In 1892 the two worked to found the Society of Colonial Wars, a typical ancestor-required patriotic society (Elihu Root was an early recruit), aimed at perpetuating the memory of the men who "were in truth the founders of this nation."[4]

---

4. They would also found, in 1906, the Half-Moon Club, modeled on the Royal Geographical Society, for New York aristocrats with an interest in science and adventure. Members (including architect McKim, physicist Michael Dodge, and businessmen J. P. Morgan Jr. and Cleveland Dodge) would hold periodic dinners in the Council Room of the University Club, to listen to a talk by an explorer or scholar.

Grant's other avocation was hunting big game all over the North American continent. In 1893 he was admitted to the Boone and Crockett. He quickly became a close friend of Theodore Roosevelt, then the club's president—not surprising, given that they both hailed from old Gotham families, were raised blocks away from one another, spent summers on their respective Long Island estates, were both interested in natural history, and camped often in the Adirondacks.

In 1894 Grant published an article, "The Vanishing Moose," in the *Century Magazine*, in which he expressed concern that the animals were being overhunted. He urged a preservation effort to save them from dying out, on the admittedly self-interested grounds that extinction would deprive Grant and his friends of targets—a "save now, kill later" policy. With TR's support he rallied the Boone and Crockett members behind him, thus turning it from a mere social organization into a conservation society. Its first big victory was winning passage of the Park Protection Act of 1894, which defended Yellowstone National Park (1872) not only from overenthusiastic sportsmen but, more tellingly, from voracious mining interests, real estate speculators, fur companies, and mass-market hunters.

At the same time, Grant began to think of providing a different kind of sanctuary for beleaguered fauna—an urban zoological park—which could also educate the public about the fact that iconic animals (like the buffalo) were facing extinction. In this park the goal would be "to secure herds—not merely individuals—of each of the large North American quadrupeds" and place them in surroundings resembling their natural habitats.

The idea appealed to his confrères. They had long been game to pit themselves against the wilderness, to toughen their manly fiber and prove their mettle. Grant's approach—game preservation—would allow them to be protectors as well as predators. It would underscore their sportsmanlike eastern superiority to the western commercial hunters then rampaging systematically through the great herds. Animal conservation also fitted nicely with the corporate elite's preference for long-term rational planning, over competitive capitalism's short-term, short-sighted rapacity. (Grant would go on to help form many varieties of conservation groups, including a Save-the-Redwood League.) A zoo also appealed to New York gentry, men like Philip Schuyler and John L. Cadwalader, as a way to save part of Old America—the "heritage which was our fathers."

Republican William Strong's 1895 installation as mayor provided an opening to win essential city support, and TR got Grant (and Elihu Root) to lobby Albany for state backing as well. Grant created a New York Zoological Society, appointing the distinguished banker and former vice president Levi Morton as president, but retained the reins of power in his hands—and those of Henry Fairfield Osborn, whom he made chair of the executive committee. (Osborn returned the favor, putting Grant on the Natural History board and giving him considerable authority to appoint new trustees, which led to an extensive overlap between the two boards.)

To win municipal and state acceptance, Grant and Osborn argued that just as London's zoo—replete with specimens from around the planet—testified to Great Britain's position as a colonizing power, so a local counterpart would certify the greatness of imperial New York. "We are *fifty* years behind the big cities of Europe!" Osborn exhorted. "This thing really *must* go on!" In 1897 the city agreed. It authorized the Zoological Society's use of 261 acres (all of Bronx Park south of Pelham Avenue), and pledged ground-clearing and maintenance funds, which by 1910 would amount to $1.9 million. For its part, the society promised to pay for buildings, animals, and the salaries of zoo employees, whose hiring would remain in the society's hands, not those of Tammany Hall. It was required to admit the public free of charge five days a week and to demonstrate, within three years, that it had $250,000 in hand. Grant and Osborn called on the usual suspects—Morgan, Rockefeller, Carnegie, Whitney, Huntington, and Vanderbilt, et al.—and accumulated the funds with time to spare. They also selected William T. Hornaday, a Buffalo taxidermist turned conservationist, to be the director. (In fact, it would be a troika directorate, as the Zoological Society's chiefs remained very much hands-on.)

The Bronx Zoo opened to the public in November 1899 and was immediately and immensely popular. In 1900 over a half million visited; in 1903 a million; by 1914, 2 million. The number of animals soared, too, hitting 5,000 in 1909, making it the biggest in the world. Better still, accolades from abroad accounted it the most beautiful and most animal-friendly as well, thrilling Grant and Osborn.

There had been some bumps on the road. Breeding herds on Bronx ranges proved difficult. Buffalo died of grass poisoning; moose and caribou failed to adapt to the environment. The original free-range vision of barless enclosures became subordinate to a set of elegant and expensive buildings (1899–1911) grouped around a ceremonial court (an exact mockup of the Chicago Fair's). Here the quadrupeds dwelt in high style—lions in Beaux-Arts baroque, primates in neo-Greco quarters, the elephants in Roman and Byzantine splendor.

They also had to overcome a difficult contretemps, of their own making, when in the fall of 1906 they added a human being to their collection. In 1904 the St. Louis World's Fair had imported representatives of various "races" from around the planet and displayed them in simulations of their natural habitats. The scout the fair dispatched to Africa, an explorer-missionary named Samuel Verner, brought back an Mbuti pygmy named Ota Benga whom he had rescued from slavers in the Congo. In St. Louis Benga helped build an "authentic" native African village. After the fair, Benga returned to Africa, but when he learned Verner was going back to the United States for at least a year asked to come along. When they landed in New York in August 1906, Verner hustled over to the zoo to sell a chimp to Grant and Hornaday and asked the officials if he could leave Ota Benga in their care for a few weeks while he attended to business out of town. They agreed, put him up in the museum, and for a while employed him in helping out with chores at the zoo. But on September 8 they encouraged him to enter an empty cage in the Monkey House, so that (said Hornaday) "he might show visitors how they did things in Africa." Crowds gathered swiftly to see the 4'11" "savage," who was encouraged to bare his filed teeth and charge the bars, giving visitors a frisson of fright. The news hit the papers. Thousands came to see. The keepers added an orangutan, a parrot, and some bones, to evoke darkest Africa, and posted a specimen label. Crowds laughed uproariously and compared him with the orangutan, which was not far off from what Grant and Osborn deemed their scientific purpose—suggesting Benga was something of a link between man and ape, and thus evidence of evolution; they wanted visitors (said Osborn) to acknowledge their kinship with the animal kingdom. Black ministers protested the "degrading exhibition." They called on Mayor McClellan to halt it. He refused. The ministers then confronted Grant in his Wall Street office. Sniffing bad publicity, he agreed to end the encagement but kept Benga in the zoo, where thousands chased him around the grounds all day. This continued until Verner returned and arranged Benga's transfer to the Howard Colored Orphan Asylum in Brooklyn.[5]

---

5. In 1916, balked in an effort to return to Africa, he committed suicide.

"Ota Bengi," ca. 1915–16. (GL Archive/Alamy Stock Photo)

For all their interest in enlightening the crowds they'd summoned up, the zoo troika were uncomfortable with the masses of visitors trampling about what they half-considered to be their own fiefdom; they saw them more as interlopers than guests. Everything the visitors did was annoying, starting with calling the New York Zoological Park a zoo. The trio insisted it be called by its full name. *"There is no "Zoo" in Bronx Park!"* Hornaday prissily wrote the New York papers; the term was "undignified," "offensive," "injurious," and "inexcusable." Grant also refused to permit cameras, partly so that visitors couldn't snap animals in the act of doing something indecorous; a string of mayors requested he rescind the ban; he turned them all down.

More disturbingly, the grounds of their animal City Beautiful were festooned with discarded newspapers and peanut shells, the litter being clear evidence that "the present horde of unsuitable immigrants are utterly unfit to govern themselves." In 1908 the zoo sent a manifesto to seventeen city papers "formally declaring war on the rubbish-throwing habit." It lost. In 1914 Hornaday was still railing at "low-lived beasts who appreciate nothing and love filth and disorder."[6]

This irate juxtaposition of ordered citadel with disorderly citizen was not merely a distempered and petty outburst; it was a synecdoche for the larger fury that Grant felt at his city's seeming inundation by immigrants. The Rubbish War took place at the crest of a demographic tsunami, which between 1900 and 1908 had brought over 6 million newcomers onto American shores—one-quarter the number that had arrived since the founding of the Republic. Grant's classical education told him that Rome had fallen when it opened the gates to inferior races. Perhaps, he obsessed, it was native-stock humans he should be preserving, rather than moose and bison.

It was around 1908 that Grant switched his attention from mammology to anthropology. He began delving into the European literature that studied the impact of "race" on human society. He quickly accepted as gospel that the putative unity of the human species was delusory, an artifact of Adam and Eve religiosity. Instead humanity was divided into inferior and

---

6. The nearby New York Botanic Garden faced similar problems. Incorporated in 1891 by officers who included Cornelius Vanderbilt II, Andrew Carnegie, and J. P. Morgan, it was modeled on the Royal Botanic Garden at Kew, outside London. In 1902 a conservatory and museum were erected on the Bronx Park site. The goal, again, was to combine scientific scholarship with public outreach. Columbia University botanist Nathaniel Lord Britton wanted to make it a venue for botanical science, and mounted a series of expeditions that cataloged the flora of the Western Hemisphere, including the new colony of Puerto Rico. The city's civic elite wanted an urban space that might exert a salutary moral influence on attendees, but some soon found it had become a bit *too* public. On sunny weekends, hundreds arrived hourly, drawn from crowded tenements to the cool hemlock forest. Some were so taken with it that they stayed the night. At times long lines of newly washed clothes could be seen drying in the sun near the Bronx River.

superior races (black, yellow, white), arranged in an ascending hierarchy that culminated in a trio of white Caucasian subsets—Southern European *Mediterraneans*, Central European *Alpines*, and, at the top, Northern European *Teutons* (though Grant was an early advocate of replacing that term with *Nordics*). When in doubt, one could sort out people's race by measuring their skulls and calculating their cephalic index—a ratio of maximum head width divided by maximum (front to back) head length—a presumably infallible (because immutable) indicator.

Grant's studies of the likes of race theorist Arthur de Gobineau also persuaded him that—historically—once a racial group established its dominance, it began to decline, because it engaged in miscegenation with the lower orders, diluting its racial purity, and was dragged down to its inferior's degraded level (if not below). From Houston Stewart Chamberlain, another racialist writer, he learned that Jews were particularly capable of bringing down their superiors; they infected the bloodstream of Indo-Europeans as if they were poisonous germs. From the work of Sir Francis Galton he adopted eugenics as a solution to the problem of preserving purity—either positively, by expanding the supply of the good breed, or negatively, by preventing bad stock from reproducing itself. (Alcoholics, gamblers, paupers, and criminals could be selected out of the population by sterilization). The arrival of Mendelian genetics, he believed, provided a solid basis for arguing that positive measures wouldn't work. Education, for example, couldn't improve the genetically inferior. While the merely bigoted imagined that the repellent morals and customs of Polish Jews on the Lower East Side could be transformed over time, "scientific racists" knew this was a fantasy. Only removing those bearing inferior germ plasm from the reproductive stream would do. The duo would accordingly align themselves with the eugenicist leader Charles Davenport, who joined the Zoological Society in 1904; indeed, they would make the museum a headquarters of Davenport's movement.

Grant emerged from his immersion in this literature filled with dire forebodings about the implications for the future of his beloved New York City. As he now saw it, Gotham's native Teutons were being overwhelmed by arriving Alpines and Mediterraneans, and if history repeated itself—if the superior stock intermingled with the inferior—a racial cataclysm loomed. In 1916 Grant would summarize these worries in a book entitled *The Passing of the Great Race*. In it he warned that "in the city of New York and elsewhere in the United States there is a native American aristocracy resting upon layer after layer of immigrants of lower races." These lower races were hereditarily impervious to uplift. Worse, the Nordic races who had built America were being overwhelmed by "a large and increasing number of the weak, the broken, and the mentally crippled of all races drawn from the lowest stratum of the Mediterranean basin and the Balkans, together with hordes of the wretched, submerged populations of the Polish Ghettos." Perhaps it was time to realize that unregulated immigration was as dangerous as unrestricted capitalism? Perhaps the doors should be slammed shut before New York tumbled into a "racial abyss"?[7]

---

7. Ironically, the development of genetic analysis moved the biological sciences swiftly away from Grant and Osborn's morphological approach, relegating much of their focus on tracing evolution through studying old bones to the margins of the field. Osborn, like Grant, would try to move with the times. In 1908 Osborn had announced that "paleo-anthropology" would be the new "top priority" at the museum, and in 1915 he came out with *Men of the Old Stone Age*, which argued that in the Paleolithic Era inferior Neanderthals had been supplanted by physically and mentally superior Cro-Magnons, who, alas, had then been invaded and replaced by the inferior Teutons, Mediterraneans, and Alpines. It served as a prequel to Grant's analysis of the current scene; together the two volumes constituted a history of the white race.

For most of Grant's elite peers this was as yet too dark a vision. There were, surely, grounds for alarm, but there was sufficient optimism among the city's upper echelons to believe that the newcomers could be safely absorbed into the body politic. One way to do this was to inculcate in them a feeling of civic patriotism, by acquainting them with the city's history. Curiously, the institution that might have best been entrusted with this task, an entity situated literally across the street from the Museum of Natural History, had virtually no interest in assuming that educative burden.

WIELDING THE PAST

The New-York Historical Society (NYHS), founded in 1804, was one of the oldest cultural institutions in the city. By the early twentieth century it had amassed a rich collection: the library contained 100,000 volumes; the gallery had 987 paintings. But it was not inclined to share these treasures with the public. Society officials, led by Librarian Robert Kelby, refused to open on Sunday—"We go to church on Sundays," he harrumphed—or in the evenings, which meant most working people could not attend. The institution didn't *have* to let the masses in, because it hadn't sought the governmental support that would have mandated a more open-door policy. Indeed, its trustees boasted that with the exception of a grant from the legislature back in 1827, they had *never* requested public funding, relying entirely on private contributions and membership fees to finance their operations. Most recently, they had successfully erected a grand new headquarters on Central Park West between 76th and 77th Streets—its central wing opened in 1908—with support from old-monied New Yorkers, and some newer-monied as well, notably J. P. Morgan and George W. Vanderbilt. Since the building had not received municipal funds, there was no need to change its admission policies. NYHS disinterest in visitors was reciprocal. The largest exhibit in 1909 attracted a mere 2,000 viewers, and only 15,000 came by in all of 1910, a year in which the Brooklyn Museum attracted over 300,000.

In truth this was the way most members wanted it. They were happy with the NYHS being more private club than museum. It was a place where filiopietistic lectures and exhibits helped them snuggle into the city's past, *their* past, not something they cared to share with immigrant masses. Behind their imposing doors they could control the past as they could not control the present. There the huddled elite could breathe free the air of "Old New York," a quasi-fictional construct confected by congenial antiquarians, whose books rolled reassuringly off the presses—texts like *A Little Colonial Dame: A Story of Old Manhattan Island* (1898) by Agnes Carolyn Sage, Charles Hemstreet's *Nooks & Crannies of Old New York* (1899), Charles B. Todd's *A Brief History of the City of New York* (1899), Rufus Rockwell Wilson's *New York: Old & New: Its Story, Streets, and Landmarks* (1909), or Hugh Macatamney's *Cradle Days of New York, 1609–1825* (1909).

Henry Collins Brown, a particularly zestful chronicler, added a visual dimension when he produced the *Book of Old New-York* (1913), a volume of antique prints amassed by private collectors, interspersed with "Delightful Memories of Bygone Days by Men Still Living." In 1916 he revived the long-defunct *Valentine's Manual* and began issuing annual compendiums of miscellaneous lore concerning Gotham's past. Brown mingled charming reminiscences of his boyhood city with self-confessedly romantic, sentimental, and nostalgic reflections on earlier eras. His books, wrote one reviewer, marshaled the memories of old New York in the easiest of prose, for the pleasure of the city's best people. And if Brown eschewed what he called the "sordid and squalid side of New York" in favor of "the beautiful," he was not alone in screening out unpleasantries like slavery, poverty, criminality, or war.

Relishing New Yorkiana was by no means restricted to the pedigreed; indeed, it became yet another appetite of the financial elite, who snapped up rare vintage engravings of Gotham as if they were Titians or dinosaur bones. Brown's 1913 book tapped into the holdings of J. P. Morgan, Robert de Forest, A. Van Horne Stuyvesant, Robert Goelet, and Henry Morgenthau, among others. And they, in turn, had been inspired by the project of the Society of Iconophiles, launched in 1894 by William Loring Andrews, a member of the Grolier Club. The Iconophiles set out to produce a "visual biography" of the city by issuing a series of engraved views of Gotham and prominent New Yorkers. Each volume was to be issued in a limited edition of 101. The first volume, containing just twelve images, was *The Journey of the Iconophiles around New York in Search of the Historical and Picturesque* (1897). In the same year, Andrews produced his own more ambitious *New Amsterdam, New Orange, New York: A Chronologically Arranged Account of Engraved Views of the City* (1897).[8]

Andrews's book was an inspiration for the era's most spectacular such project, launched in 1908, when Isaac Newton Phelps Stokes began preparation of *The Iconography of Manhattan Island*. Stokes had feet in both monied camps. The Phelps and Stokes families had planted their respective family trees in New York in the eighteenth century, but had also been deeply engaged in the industrial and financial transformations of the nineteenth and twentieth. Isaac (born 1867) was the eldest son of multi-millionaire Anson Phelps Stokes, whose Phelps, Dodge mining interests spanned the hemisphere from Arizona to Chile. Isaac and his brothers were partners in the Phelps Stokes Estates, which invested in Manhattan real estate, helping produce a combined family fortune estimated at $40 million.

Isaac opted for a professional over a business career. After studies at the École des Beaux-Arts (1894–97), he founded an architectural firm with the son of writer William Dean Howells. The duo quickly won a competition to build the Eldridge Street headquarters of the University Settlement (into which his brother James Graham Phelps Stokes would then move, as a resident teacher, and there fatefully cross paths with Rose Pastor). Through family friends E. R. L. Gould and Robert de Forest, Stokes got into model housing and tenement reform, while also designing apartment houses and residences for the affluent.

He had long been interested "in a desultory sort of way" in buying "views of Old New York," but his enthusiasm was stoked in 1908 by a visit to the home of Richard Townley Haines Halsey, a successful stockbroker and Americana collector, where Stokes was mesmerized by a 1796 Saint-Mémin engraving, "View of the City and Harbour of New York, taken from Mt. Pitt, the seat of John R. Livingston, Esq." The scene, a pastoral panorama as seen from Livingston's porch fronting on Grand Street, surveyed what a century later would be the Lower East Side, and it pulled him irretrievably into the past; he would even come to repeatedly dream "delightful" dreams of wandering through just such bygone landscapes. Stokes immediately settled on a plan, taking off from Andrews's volume, of collecting maps, plans, views, and documents of Manhattan from the seventeenth century to 1909. He would then publish them in an exquisite "little book on Old New York," on finest-quality "Japan paper." It would constitute a storehouse of Manhattan facts and images, with "special reference to its topographical features and to the physical development of the island." He was

---

8. The era was marked, as well, by scholarly collecting of documents, in which New York State continued to play a role, issuing such compilations as the *Ecclesiastical Records of Colonial New York* (6 volumes, 1901–5), and the *Minutes of the Common Council of the City of New York, 1675–1776* (8 volumes, 1905)—and just in the nick of time, too, as on March 29, 1911, a tremendous fire ravaged the State Library in Albany, destroying 450,000 books, 270,000 manuscripts, and the entire catalog—nearly one million cards burned.

soon inducted into the Society of Iconophiles. The first of what would turn out to be six volumes, collectively weighing in at 39 pounds, appeared in 1915.

The *Iconography* was narrative-free and bereft of interpretive strategy. It was rather like the grid in facilitating a plot-by-plot, blow-by-blow record of demolitions and constructions—a real-estate-developer's-eye view.[9] Yet it was also suffused with antiquarian longings. As he would recall in later autobiographical musings, "We cannot escape a feeling of envy, mingled with regret, when we consider how calm and peaceful life must have been in those charming little old eighteenth- and early nineteenth-century towns...how different from that which we lead to-day!" Nor were the volumes aimed at a wide public. The sets were printed in limited editions and prohibitively priced. In this the *Iconography* resembled the holdings of the New-York Historical Society (from whose collections it drew liberally); it was really for the cognoscenti, not the hoi polloi.

In 1917 NYHS insularity provoked an in-house protest from member May King Van Rensselaer, descended on both sides from old and prominent New York families. She, too, had authored an ancestral study, *The Goede Vrouw of Mana-ha-ta at Home and in Society, 1609–1760* (1898), but her history of colonial women had a feminist edge. ("No one in Nieuw Amsterdam dreamed of insisting that a woman's place was in the home," she snorted.) At the annual meeting, the formidable Van Rensselaer stunned the assembled members by blasting Librarian Kelby for making the society into "an old man's club." It was "a deformed monstrosity filled with curiosities, ill-arranged and badly assorted." It was "dull," "uninteresting," "moribund," "dead." She criticized, too, the lack of outreach to immigrants. "It is our duty, if we should hope to assimilate these new peoples without danger to our society and civilization, to make them over anew. We must teach them the background of history of our country. The New York Historical Society can supply the straw to make bricks from the foreign mud and water."

IN THE ABSENCE OF HISTORICAL SOCIETY LEADERSHIP, others had stepped forward to celebrate and promulgate the city's past (or an Anglo-Dutchified version of it). A mix of genealogical societies and progressive reformers had set out to convince New York's polyglot peoples that they were part of an organic entity, one to which they owed a civic obligation. The approach was summed up in the motto of the City History Club: "We must know a thing before we can love it."

The City History Club (CHC) was founded in 1896 by Catherine Abbe, a society matron who belonged to the Colonial Dames of America and cofounded the League of Political Education, a pro-suffrage group. Abbe recruited a distinguished board that combined members of prominent old New York families—Van Rensselaers, Roosevelts, Van Dusens—with top civic leaders and academics. The goal was to awaken an interest in the city's traditions, "such educational work [said its 1897 charter] being for the improvement, uplifting, and civic betterment of the community." Its programs were directed by Dr. Frank Bergen Kelley,

---

9. There were other, more pecuniary ways a developer-collector might view such images. Clarence Davies, the prominent real estate broker who marketed the Bronx's early subdivisions, amassed a major collection, which he used as a sales tool. His eureka moment, quite unlike Stokes's, came when he spotted in a store some prints that depicted "farm land and a cottage at Fifth Avenue and Forty-second street," at that point worth a fortune. "I was selling real estate in the Bronx," he recalled, "and it occurred to me that these old prints were the finest arguments I could have. They showed the growth and changes in Manhattan in a few years and I bought them to show to clients, in order to stir their imagination as to what was going to happen in the Bronx."

Davies might have mentioned that the prints themselves were becoming lucrative investments, as the massive demolitions then under way were generating a tremendous demand for prints of threatened or vanished properties. In 1910 the *Times* reported: "Never before have such high prices been paid for good material illustrative of the growth and progress of the metropolis."

who headed the History Department at the prestigious Columbia Grammar School, itself an ancient (1764) Gotham institution. "Knowledge of city history would do much to bind together the hod-carrier and the millionaire," Kelley affirmed in *Municipal Affairs* in 1899, "for the former learns thereby that he has an equal share with the latter in the greatness of the city."

The CHC published historic guides, a newsletter, and a student newspaper, printed essays on city history, sponsored a lecture series, maintained a traveling history library, took school children on walking tours, and offered New York City history classes. Kelley recruited young, upper-middle-class women—from the same background as settlement house workers—to teach these courses. The volunteers had to take a two-year training course in city history, studying the seventeenth and eighteenth centuries in their first year and the nineteenth in their second. Kelley handled their instruction himself, though occasionally bringing in guest lecturers (on the order of Theodore Roosevelt). After finishing, the women received teaching kits (handbook, reading materials, maps, pictures) and fanned out across the city to convey their new knowledge. In 1896 there were 7 such classes; by 1902, 108.

As it was a fundamental club purpose "to help the immigrant's child and the child of generations of loyal Americans alike to feel the duties of social service and the privileges and responsibilities of being 'citizens of no mean city,'" the CHC scheduled courses at places like settlement houses, church missions, industrial and truant schools, the Hebrew Institute, and the Working Girls' Club. One annual report noted proudly that a group of Italian girls was taking a course at the Italian Library on Mulberry Street.

"Father Knickerbocker Making Good Americans of the Children of All Nationalities," ca. 1919. (Irma and Paul Milstein Division of United States History, Local History and Genealogy, The New York Public Library)

A SIMILAR MIX OF PATRIOTIC SOCIETIES AND PROFESSIONALS set out to preserve remaining relics of the colonial era and convert them into historic shrines.

In 1897 the Colonial Dames of the State of New York coaxed municipal authorities into leasing the 1748 Van Cortlandt Mansion to them for restoration. The unpretentious country house, cobbled together out of fieldstone, had remained in the family until 1889, when it was deeded to the city, after which it had slumbered peacefully in its meadow in Van Cortlandt Park. The Dames now filled it up with Dutch and English household furniture and implements, and laid out a Dutch garden, replete with canal.

The Daughters of the American Revolution—rivals of the Colonial Dames, and a bit put out by the suzerainty the latter had attained in the Bronx—persuaded the city to purchase (in 1903) what came to be called the Morris-Jumel Mansion, the upper-Manhattan vantage point from which Washington had directed the Battle of Harlem Heights.[10] In 1904 the Daughters—"emulating [the *Times* noted] the business methods of Directors in large trusts"—merged several chapters into a Washington's Headquarters Association, which won the right to operate the mansion as a museum. That same year their male counterparts in the Sons of the Revolution purchased Fraunces's Tavern (recently threatened with demolition), hired an architect, had the lower-Manhattan building—scene of Washington's farewell to his officers—restored to its presumed eighteenth-century condition (it having been burned and rebuilt several times in the nineteenth), and opened it (in 1907) as a museum and Sons headquarters.

Structures like these, it was believed, had an almost magical ability to transform youthful aliens brought within their walls. Colonial Dame Justine Van Rensselaer Townsend explained in 1900 that the "Americanizing of the children—by enlisting their interest in historical sites and characters has a great significance to any thinking mind—the making of good citizens of these many foreign youths." Good citizenship meant, among other things, accepting constraints on political activity; one speaker urged the Sons to educate the working classes "out of all these crass and crazy notions of popular rights . . . into a true understanding of American liberty as handed down by our Fathers."

Preservation also attracted support from professionals and top businessmen. In 1895 Andrew Haswell Green, who had helped save City Hall from demolition, launched the city's first formal preservation and conservation group, called (after a name trim in 1901) the American Scenic and Historic Preservation Society (ASHPS). Unlike the Daughters, Dames, and Sons, the society didn't require prospective members to demonstrate genealogical bona fides. Nor was the organization focused on recycling patriotic narratives. The ASHPS was pretty much an all-male operation, run by a score of activists, many of them also core players in the Municipal Art Society, the Fine Arts Federation, and the National Arts Club. It had a full-time secretary—the historian Edward Hagaman Hall—and J. P. Morgan supplied a small endowment. (His son, Jack, and associates George Baker and George Perkins would serve on the board.)

Green wasn't into promoting nostalgic reveries for "Old New York," but he was disturbed that the hyper-competitive land market was destroying remaining traces of the city's past. Objects and places of "historic value," he argued, "should be rescued from the grasp of private speculation and preserved for public enjoyment"—and public edification. Historic sites, he believed, "lift us above the pettiness and the selfishness of common affairs, enlarges the scope of our being, and brings us into touch with . . . all that is sublime, noble and generous." The city was dotted with buildings wherein had been enacted dramatic events that could serve as "inspirations to lofty undertakings," but "such landmarks are too rapidly yielding to the obliteration of time, and to preserve them is a sacred duty."

The larger issue here was that capitalist urbanism was undermining civic patriotism. This was of course a very old concern. In 1856 *Harper's Monthly* had declared that New York was notoriously the "least loved of any of our great cities. Why should it be loved as a city? It is never the same city for a dozen years together. A man born in New York forty years ago finds nothing, absolutely nothing, of the New York he knew." The velocity of transformation in the early twentieth century left the nineteenth century's turnover rate looking turtlish. In

---

10. At the time it had been known as the Jumel Mansion, but this was deemed problematic by the patriotic set, as Mme. Jumel had been a lady of doubtful virtue, even before her brief marriage to the even more doubtful Aaron Burr, and "Morris" was their name of choice; but "Morris" came with its own baggage, he having been a Tory during the Revolution. The eventual double attribution perhaps diluted the difficulties.

1907 Henry James decried the city's "restless renewals" that dehistoricized its landscape and left its citizenry marooned in a provisional present. By 1913 critic James Huneker could argue: "In our town memories like rats are chased away by the ever-rising flood of progress. There is no room for ghosts or landmarks in New York." It was the rending of the social fabric by unchecked development that led the ASHPS to argue, in 1912, that "in the midst of the many changes in our fluid city we need some permanent landmarks to suggest stability."

Landmarks proved hard to preserve. Green had originally conceived of his society as something akin to Britain's National Trust, a body that would receive bequests and donations of patinaed properties, which when networked together would constitute, in effect, a disaggregated museum. But precious few properties came its way, and the ASHPS had to settle for allying with genealogical organizations in campaigns to pluck a handful of brands from the burning. It was even more disconcerting to discover how often their efforts came up short. In 1908, I. N. Phelps Stokes, R. F. Cutting, and R. W. de Forest, among others, were aghast to learn that the vestry of Trinity Church had decided to shutter St. John's Chapel, having decided that pecuniary gains from redeveloping the site would outweigh its value as cultural heritage. Preservationists organized a petition drive of those (primarily Episcopalians) who revered "the ancient monuments of our city, and believe in the uplifting power of venerable traditions and accumulated effort"; the signatories included President Roosevelt, Elihu Root, J. P. Morgan, George McAneny, and Seth Low, among many others; Trinity paid them no heed.

In a sense St. John's played the same role as did the Equitable Building: in the latter case powerful interests failed to block construction; in the former they failed to halt demolition. There was, however, a crucial difference. Where the Equitable struggle led to passage of the Zoning Act, in the case of St. John's and other historic properties, preservationists proved unwilling to use the law to protect vulnerable structures. Not only was such legislation deemed an unacceptable intrusion on private property rights, but it might have hampered the breakneck building boom over which they themselves were presiding—a boom that was not only profitable but thrilling. Even so dedicated an antiquarian as William Loring Andrews, who deeply deplored the destruction of Old New York, told his fellow Iconophiles in 1913: "The rebuilding of this city as it is going on with breathless rapidity before our eyes, is a Titanic work, and I am glad that I have lived to witness it. I only hope that a few of the narrow, crooked lanes in the lower part of the city, with their antiquated buildings...will outlast my time." The best preservationists could hope for was to create a few historical zoolettes, within which some representatives of the past—yet another endangered species—could dwell in safety, protected from the snarling real estate market just outside the bars.

IF PRESERVATION WAS TOO BLUNT (OR TOO SHARP) AN INSTRUMENT, how to address continuing elite concerns that the city lacked historical ballast, that it needed devices for impressing arriving immigrants with the achievements of those who had preceded them? To some extent the gap was filled by placing markers and erecting statues—tangible reminders of a now-dematerialized past. Private and public initiatives installed historical tablets at places like the sites of Fort Amsterdam and the Battle of Harlem Heights, raised statues of patriots like Nathan Hale, and underwrote Stanford White's Prison Ship Martyrs' Monument (1908), a granite column in Fort Greene Park that loomed over the remains of some of the 11,500 Revolutionary War prisoners who had died on British ships in nearby Wallabout Bay. The new Hall of Records at Chambers and Centre Streets (1906), which housed $4 billion worth of real estate titles, had its exterior festooned with sculptures, including two allegorical groups (symbolizing Manhattan in Dutch and Revolutionary times), and eight statues of historic New York leaders (selected by the Municipal Art Society): James Duane, Cadwallader Colden, Peter Stuyvesant, Phillip Hone, De Witt Clinton, Caleb Heathcote, David DeVries—and Abram Hewitt, the only contemporary figure on whom the sponsors could agree. Hewitt had just died, in 1903, and the statue was in effect his memorial. It was not, however, a selection that pleased most immigrants: Hewitt, a nativist, had believed "America should be governed by Americans."

In the end, neither statues, tablets, shrines, museums, nor books of prints were deemed a sufficient response. So history-minded New Yorkers came up with an astonishing alternative. They sponsored a colossal pageant—the Hudson-Fulton Celebration—involving millions of people and millions of dollars, devoted to nothing less than generating a great "historical awakening" in Gotham.

It began small, with the ancestral Holland Society noting in 1901 that the three-hundredth anniversary of Hendrick Hudson's discovery of his river was coming up in 1909, and wouldn't it be nice to have a celebration? In 1902 a Hudson Tri-Centennial Association set up shop, with J. P. Morgan and James Stillman among the organizers, but it proposed only to build a Hudson Memorial Bridge. Also that year, Dr. George Frederick Kunz, of the American Scenic and Historic Preservation Society, urged a World's Fair as the proper commemorative vehicle. It was in 1905 that Robert B. Roosevelt, the president's uncle, gathered together all of the above, plus a gaggle of genealogical societies and powerful civic leaders, who then prevailed on Mayor McClellan and Governor Higgins to appoint a 150-person committee to explore possible forms a commemoration might take. This Celebration

"Hall of Records Statuary," 1906. (Library of Congress Prints and Photographs Division)

Commission, on learning of another Hudson River anniversary in the offing—the centennial of Robert Fulton's first steamboat voyage in 1807—quickly effected a merger. The Hudson-Fulton Celebration it would be.

The Celebration Commission, at first merely unwieldy, soon swelled to an impossible 1,500 (everybody who was anybody wanted to get in on this). So they elected a hundred-man board of trustees to run things, which in turn elected fifteen vice presidents—princes of the city including J. P. Morgan, William Rockefeller, and Andrew Carnegie. The eventual million-dollar bill would be footed by the state (48 percent), the city (24 percent), and individual and corporate donors.[11]

These massed worthies rejected the exposition model, and indeed (as the event's chronicler Edward Hagaman Hall recounted) "the most careful pains were taken to avoid anything of a commercial tincture."[12] Instead this was to be an educational affair whose festivities, Hall reported, were "designed to create an historical awakening." Partly this was again a matter of catching up with the Joneses—in this case Massachusetts and Virginia—given that New York's "questionable modesty in refraining from exploiting her own history" had led to a "very general ignorance of the full part played by our Colony and State in our national history." Yet as the celebration's deeper purpose was "to promote the assimilation of our adopted population," it would purvey historical information to the masses, because dissemination of such knowledge "serves to bind a people together, make it more homogeneous and give it stability."

Here the organizers drew on tactics developed by playground and holiday reformers. Playground activists had begun introducing historical skits, games, and dances into their prescribed programs. Brooklyn's vacation schools enacted "Father Knickerbocker's Birthday" celebrations that were designed, said their supervisor, "to entwine the beautiful story of our city about the hearts of our charges."[13] These efforts caught the eye of groups intent on reforming civic holidays—outfits like the Safe and Sane July Fourth movement. This Russell Sage Foundation–supported group called for municipally sponsored celebrations that would eschew fireworks and involve immigrants in a way that generated a sense of common citizenship. What emerged was the historical pageant—participatory public rituals, organized around historic themes.

Hudson-Fulton week would have many parts, but the one that adopted the pageant model most thoroughly was Children's Day, when nearly a million youngsters were shepherded to parks around town, dressed up in historic garb or ethnic costume, and encouraged

---

11. There were a host of collateral events, paid for by separate sponsors, some with significant cultural ramifications. The Metropolitan Museum of Art mounted two theme-related shows, one of Dutch paintings from Hudson's day, one of American fine and decorative arts from Fulton's. The old-master offering was widely hailed as demonstrating the depth of New York's holdings, with its 149 paintings (20 Hals, 5 Vermeers, and a whopping 34 Rembrandts)—contributed by the likes of Morgan, Frick, George Gould, Louisine Havemeyer, and Benjamin Altman (whose contributions, newly purchased from the Duveens in London, had been rushed across the Atlantic). But it was the assemblage of Americana, overseen by Met secretary de Forest, that proved truly pathbreaking. De Forest had borrowed the furniture, silver, pottery, and textile collection gathered by H. Eugene Bolles, a wealthy Boston lawyer, partly to test whether putting "industrial arts" in a museum setting could win public acceptance. (The Met owned not a single piece of American furniture.) It was a great success. After it closed, de Forest persuaded Olivia Sage to purchase all the nearly 900 objects and donate them to the museum; soon he began planning an American Wing.

12. An overstatement: yes, advertising was banished from all official literature (though tons of ads sprouted on the margins), but the organizers worked closely with hotel men and railroad executives to transport and house the enormous influx of visitors—an estimated million-plus attended the week-long core events—giving a tremendous boost to the fast-rising tourist industry. It was a source of great satisfaction that the burgeoning stock of hotels and the new subway lines proved able to accommodate the crush. September 30, 1909, was the biggest day ever for the IRT, which handled two million passengers.

13. Similarly, Anglo-American Maypole dances in Central Park incorporated ethnic dances to foster immigrant inclusion.

to express their cultural predilections: young Norwegians mounted a mini-parade with a Leif Ericson float; Syrian and Russian girls whirled and twirled in traditional folk dances. African American children were not similarly encouraged, though some of their families dated to Dutch days, and instead were garbed as Indians or Japanese. Education Day was more directive. Pupils in classrooms and auditoriums across the city partook of programming that drew on the now decade-long experience of the City History Club—performing in history plays, enacting living tableaux, debating historical topics, writing historical essays, and fashioning historical arts and crafts.[14]

The main Hudson-Fulton attractions were the Naval Parade (with war ships from many nations on hand, more than had ever been assembled in one place), and the Great Historical Pageant, both of which were strictly top-down and meticulously planned affairs. To fulfill the charge of bringing "visual instruction" in history to "New York's foreign-born population," the commission deployed "moving tableaux." For the aquatic display, pageant masters arranged for replicas of Henry Hudson's *Half Moon* and Robert Fulton's *Clermont*. For the street festival, designers constructed fifty-four gigantic floats that graphically illustrated "memorable scenes in the history of the City and State for public education and entertainment." Scaled for a skyscraper city, they were the largest ever made—32 feet long and up to 40 feet high—and their preparation took a full year. Most floats dealt with events or genre scenes from the years of Anglo-Dutch supremacy. ("A Dutch Doorway," "A Colonial Home," "The Destruction of the Statue of George III," "Washington's Farewell"). A few touted civic achievements of the early-nineteenth century. ("Erie Canal," "The Delivery of Water to New York from the Croton Reservoir," "The Old Volunteer Fire Department"). The caboose of the procession was a gigantic "Father Knickerbocker Receiving" the immigrants.

Father Knickerbocker's reception of the immigrants was ambivalent. The floats were overwhelmingly Anglo-Dutch in orientation. The French—a revolutionary ally—got four. The Italians got one, a re-creation of Garibaldi's home on Staten Island. The Germans received zilch, but they won a starring role in yet another parade, on Carnival Day.[15] The historical characters on the floats were impersonated by college students, descendants of old families, and members of "the leading patriotic and hereditary societies." In an effort to "include representatives of as many as possible of the nationalities composing the cosmopolitan population of the State, so as to make them feel that the heritage of the State's history belonged to them as well as to those more distinctively American," about twenty phalanxes of citizens of African, Bohemian, Danish, Dutch, English, French, German, Hungarian, Irish, Italian, Norwegian, Polish, Scotch, Swedish, and Syrian descent were invited to serve as "escorts" to the floats—to be the foot soldiers of the procession.

Nothing went quite as planned.

As an estimated 4 million spectators along the banks of the Hudson River gasped or giggled, the *Half Moon*'s crew lost control of their vessel and rammed it into the *Clermont*'s

---

14. The club itself produced a 420-page *Historical Guide to the City of New York* (1909), compiled by Frank Bergen Kelley, that drew on a series of twelve Excursion Leaflets, drawn largely from original sources, that had been published over the preceding thirteen years by members of the club. Kelley divided these itineraries into sixty walks, each about two hours in duration, that collectively covered all five boroughs, and were accompanied by maps, vintage illustrations (sometimes paired with contemporary photographs), and references to the extensive number of historical tablets that had been put up around town by various genealogical societies and the American Scenic and Historic Preservation Society.

15. Indians were represented by seventy real Iroquois—men, women, and children in "picturesque native costumes"—who were secured from the Indian reservations. Jews did poorly (apart from Hebrew-school children); indeed, the commission managed to hold the opening ceremony on Yom Kippur, an oversight for which they apologized several days later.

port quarter, shattering twenty feet of rail and battering their own prow. On shore, the enormous floats lurched and wobbled through the streets, with occasionally disastrous consequences, as when the "Statue of Liberty" lost its torch. Some floats broke ranks, muddling the tidy chronological order: the "Croton Reservoir" strayed ahead of "Nathan Hale."

More alarmingly, the Knickerbocker tableaux mingled promiscuously (and hilariously) with the ethnic associations. The French Society ambled alongside "Dutchmen Playing the First Game of Bowls on Bowling Green" while belting out "The Marseillaise." The Poles, the Bohemians, and the Friendly Sons of St. Patrick Hibernians got jumbled up with the Iroquois. The arrival of the Anglo-colonial floats was heralded by a contingent of Syrians wearing red fezzes. The good-natured crowds huzzahed all and sundry (though reserving most applause for the immigrant brigades). Flustered officials deemed it a fiasco.

Still more alarming was the successful effort by the city's Italian community to muscle its way into the proceedings, winning a far more visible presence than the sponsors had intended to allot them. This was not about boosting their parade presence—they weren't out to merely garner another float or two; rather they mounted a challenge to the celebration's central raison d'être.

Carlo Barsotti, publisher of *Il Progresso*, together with his fellow Italian American *prominenti*, had already demonstrated a determination to claim public space in Gotham back in 1892, when they had won the right to erect a statue of Columbus atop a 27-foot-high column at the prime location of Central Park West and 59th Street, soon to be named Columbus Circle. Barsotti had next used his newspaper as a tool to raise funds and mobilize political support for getting Garibaldi into Washington Square (1898) and Verdi into a mini-park at Broadway and 73rd (1907). But then, with planning for the hullabaloo in full swing, Barsotti demanded to know what all the Hudson fuss was about, given that Giovanni da Verrazzano, a Florentine in the service of France, had arrived on the scene more than fourscore years before the English explorer in the service of Holland had shown up. Rank discrimination, Barsotti charged, and he demanded a prominent piece of real estate—in City Hall Park, no less—for a statuary tribute to the true discoverer. The Art Commission, cultural bastion of the Anglo-Protestant establishment, was able to quash that siting but had to give ground on the larger issue, especially given the professions of multi-ethnicity voiced by Hudson-Fulton dignitaries.

So Barsotti got Battery Park—which would be a high-visibility location during the celebration—and on October 6, 1909, 25,000 Italians from 250 Italian societies in the city marched down Fifth Avenue from 23rd Street, past 200,000 of their cheering compatriots, who then repaired to Battery Park, where the statue was duly unveiled, with Hudson-Fulton and municipal officials on hand to pay tribute. (Historian Hall couldn't resist pointing out in his official chronicle that Verrazzano had only entered the harbor, *not* the river, and that "no beneficial results ensued from his brief stay," whereas Hudson had "opened it up to civilization, and made his knowledge useful to all mankind.")

This vexing ability of newcomers to work their way into established strongholds was on display elsewhere in the city, notably at a set of acropoli dedicated precisely to the production of useful knowledge.

UNIVERSITIES

New York's colleges had drowsed through much of the nineteenth century. In their halls, the city's merchant sons had studied the classics and picked up class credentials before proceeding on to apprenticeships in their fathers' firms. As the rise of the corporate economy rendered this kind of training obsolete, reformers sought to divert academic vessels into new waters. Colleges, it was thought, should become universities. They should start churning out the lawyers, accountants, and managers needed to run the national firms headquartered in New York. They should produce original research, especially in the useful sciences, rather than piously pass on received Christian "truths." They should let students take career-oriented electives rather than force-feed them a traditional and irrelevant canon. But academic and theological conservatives retained their hammerlock. New Yorkers drifted away. Even those simply seeking polish could get a better shine at Harvard, Yale, or Princeton. Then came a fin-de-siècle revolution that catapulted New York's leading colleges into a new era, ensconced them in dramatic new acropoli, and revamped their relation to the city.

COLUMBIA'S METAMORPHOSIS WAS PARTICULARLY STRIKING. Seth Low had begun its transformation on becoming president back in 1889. Low had moved on two fronts. He tried to enhance Columbia's civic role by inaugurating public lectures and forging a series of links to other cultural institutions. And he bolstered professional training by gathering law, mining, medical, and teaching programs into a consolidated organization in 1896. The institution's designation as "Columbia University in the City of New York" signaled both its broadened scope and public involvement.

Low underscored Columbia's new status by abandoning the old midtown campus. Charles McKim was brought in to lay out a new one on the site of the old Bloomingdale Asylum up on Morningside Heights. In 1894 McKim master-planned a City Beautiful acropolis. The university's various parts were physically grouped together—in White City fashion—around a pantheonic Low Library (for which Low contributed $1 million, reputedly one-third of his fortune), and a formal court punctuated by *Alma Mater*, sculpted by Daniel Chester French.[16]

In 1901 Low ascended to the mayoralty, and Columbia's presidency passed to Nicholas Murray Butler, not a businessman or man of wealth but a professional educator and administrator. Butler, born in 1862, had grown up in Paterson, New Jersey, where his father manufactured carpets. He attended public schools, then Columbia College (Class of 1882), then stayed on to earn a Columbia PhD in 1884 with a dissertation on Kant's philosophy of education. After studies in Paris and Berlin (where he befriended Elihu Root), he began teaching philosophy at his alma mater in 1886. He also offered free public lectures on the science of education, which attracted hundreds of students, overwhelmingly female teachers in the public school system. Butler tried to get a course in pedagogics included in the curriculum, but the trustees refused, seeing it as a Trojan Horse intended to circumvent their ban on coeducation.

In 1887 Butler accepted the presidency of a philanthropic organization developed by Grace Hoadley Dodge called the Industrial Education Association, which promoted manual training for poor and working-class children. Butler converted it into the New York College for the Training of Teachers (it would be renamed Teachers College in 1892), and also pushed for an affiliated children's school (Horace Mann) where teachers-in-training could practice

---

16. Barnard College migrated, too, from its original 1889 home—a rented brownstone at 343 Madison Avenue—to a new campus on 119th–120th Streets, the gift of Mary E. Brinckerhoff, Elizabeth Milbank Anderson, and Martha Fiske. Brinckerhoff, Milbank, and Fiske Halls were built in 1897–98. And in 1903 Barnard received the three blocks south of 119th Street from Anderson, who had purchased the former portion of the Bloomingdale Asylum site from New York Hospital. Physical proximity aided efforts by the college and its male supporters to force Columbia into conceding partial integration into the larger university system. Die-hard trustees mounted a rear guard action against coeducation, but the gender wall was proving permeable.

Morningside Heights, 1908. (Roger Viollet/Getty Images)

their craft. Both institutions moved up from Greenwich Village to Morningside Heights, on 120th and 121st Streets (between Broadway and Amsterdam), and affiliated with the university. Over the next two decades, Teachers College morphed into a massive complex (over 5,000 students in 1911), its transformation sped along by substantial donations from the Dodge, Macy, Milbank, Rockefeller, and Vanderbilt families.

The education project launched, Butler resigned (in 1891) to become the first dean of Columbia's new Faculty of Philosophy. In 1901 Low left to run for mayor—an elevation that the ambitious Butler (a rising figure in the Republican Party thanks to his friendship with Root and Roosevelt) did everything in his power to promote—and in 1902 Butler was chosen for the top job.

Soft-pedaling Low's civic ideals, Butler concentrated on making Columbia an academic mega-institution. A consummate consolidator—Morgan would offer him a railroad presidency—Butler in 1911 arranged an alliance between the College of Physicians and Surgeons (the university's medical school) and Presbyterian Hospital (which would provide medical students with clinical experience). In 1912 he launched the Graduate School of Journalism that Pulitzer had proposed and paid for. In 1916 he opened a School of Business that offered courses in accounting, banking, real estate, insurance, foreign trade, business organization, and corporate finance.

All this cost money, and Butler worked assiduously to convince the super-rich that New York needed a souped-up Columbia, not just to train its professionals, but to keep pace with European metropoles. "Every city which, because of its size or wealth or position, aims to be a center of enlightenment and a true world-capital," he argued in his inaugural address, "must be the home of a great university." The boom-era response was gratifyingly substantial: donations and bequests climbed from the $5.4 million harvested in the 1890s, to $16.5 million in the century's first decade.

By 1915, between the college and the professional schools, there were over 16,000 students enrolled, making it the biggest university in the country—the US Steel of higher education.[17] And Butler ran it like a CEO. In 1903 he told an assistant he wanted the presidential office organized like "a large business corporation downtown." That meant gaining better control of the workforce, via a top-down bureaucracy. In 1905 he got the trustees to terminate the tradition of faculties electing their own deans; these now became part of management, appointed by and answerable solely to the president. This did not sit well with many in the professoriate, notably James McKeen Cattell, a renowned experimental psychologist, who stoutly defended traditional faculty prerogatives (notably in his 1913 book *University Control*), and more or less denounced Butler as a despot. The president came close to firing Cattell, but former president Seth Low, still a member of the board of trustees, opposed this, and Butler backed off, and bided his time.

He also wanted the faculty to toe his political line. Butler was a conservative Republican who broke with Roosevelt when the latter lurched leftward. When the equally conservative John Burgess retired in 1912 as dean of the Faculty of Political Science, Butler made it clear that "no person with progressive or liberal views would be acceptable" as his replacement. On the other hand, he wanted scholars with king-sized reputations, and accepted the presence of professors with whom he disagreed, if they enhanced Columbia's standing. He welcomed John Dewey to the Philosophy Department in 1904, though he had little interest in pragmatism, and opposed Dewey's ideas on progressive education. He bore with Charles Beard, even after the historian published his *Economic Interpretation of the Constitution* (1913), a book that shockingly suggested the Founding Fathers had allowed economic self-interest to influence their shaping of the Constitution, an approach that smacked of muckraker charges that the United States Senate was in the pocket of millionaires. And Butler stuck it out with E. R. A. Seligman, even though the famous economist supported government regulation in the interest of working people, favored the imposition of a progressive income tax, and accepted and sheltered students like Isaac M. Rubinow, a member of the Socialist Party and an advocate of social security—though at least Seligman himself was no socialist.[18]

Arguably the most radical of all was Franz Boas, yet it had been Butler who back in 1895, when still dean, had recommended to President Low that Columbia hire him as he was "one of the most competent Anthropologists now living." He had also assented to Boas's proposal that Columbia consolidate the various anthropology professors, scattered about the university, into one department and put Boas in charge of it. Then this first PhD program in anthropology in the United States became a launching pad for assaults against the racial "science" promoted by such respectable figures as Henry Fairfield Osborn, an old friend of Butler.

In 1911 Boas gathered together ideas he'd been advancing since the 1890s and published a magisterial summary, *The Mind of Primitive Man*, that hammered home his theses: "Savages" didn't differ in mental capabilities from "civilized" people. "Race"—a term that should be reserved for biologically based subdivisions of the human species—accounted for

---

17. The speed of development was manifested in the rapid obsolescence of Low's library. When it opened it could accommodate 450,000 books, a capacity second only to the Library of Congress. As it only had 215,000, and was (in 1896) acquiring only 12,000 a year, it looked to be serviceable for decades. But the explosion in numbers of students and range of fields soon overwhelmed it; in 1910 architectural critic Montgomery Schuyler passed along the catty comment of a French friend that it had become a "library de luxe and not de books."

18. Radical students like Rubinow, Max Eastman, Matthew Josephson, and Randolph Bourne found the intellectual atmosphere exhilarating: "Ideas," Josephson remembered, "were sprouting up through the bricks at Columbia."

certain physiological features, notably skin color, but was worthless for explaining the vast variety of the world's peoples. The behavior of any human collectivity was attributable to its culture—the distillate of its historical experience—and cultures were transmitted socially, not bequeathed biologically, hence were mutable.

In 1912, challenging his opponents on their own ground, Boas demonstrated, via a bravura piece of old-style, empirical, physical anthropology, that even their beloved cephalic index, the supposedly infallible indicator of racial type, could be influenced by the environment. As reported in his *Changes in the Bodily Form of Descendants of Immigrants*, part of a massive study authorized and financed by the United States Immigration Commission, Boas and thirteen assistants calculated the height-to-width head ratio of 17,821 New York City immigrants and their offspring. He proved that the skull shapes of children born to Italians and Jews who had been in the United States for ten years had *changed* from the norm of children born in their respective old countries—altered by a relatively brief immersion in a different environment. Madison Grant ridiculed (without refuting) Boas's findings—a potentially mortal threat to elite pretensions to biological superiority—by asserting that "speaking English, wearing good clothes, and going to school and to church, does not transform a negro into a white man." And Grant predicted that "we shall have a similar experience with the Polish Jew, whose dwarf stature, peculiar mentality, and ruthless concentration on self-interest are being engrafted upon the stock of the nation."

Butler had his own problems with Polish Jews. Columbia was building classroom and dormitory buildings with names like Hamilton, Livingston, Kent, and Hartley—drawn from the honor roll of Anglo-Protestant New York history—but many of those *using* these buildings sported Polish or Russian surnames. The subway had made Columbia accessible to public high school graduates (55 percent of whom were Jews in 1910). All *too* accessible, worried Butler, a (discreet) anti-Semite. In 1902 John Pine, a close ally on the board, wrote Butler that "you know as well as I, that we are in danger of being overwhelmed by the number of Jewish students who are coming to us, and who are certain to increase in number." The problem as Pine saw it—and Butler concurred—was that Columbia was losing its Christian (Episcopalian) identity (Seth Low's fault, for having ended mandatory chapel attendance), and getting a reputation as "a 'Jew college.'" This wasn't helping fund-raising, Butler fretted, noting that even trustees were shipping their sons elsewhere in the Ivy League.[19] Butler didn't want Protestant students, destined as they were for social, economic, and political leadership, to be bothered by contact (or intellectual combat) with Jews. Not *all* Jews were beyond the pale, to be sure. As College Dean Frederick P. Keppel wrote in 1910, "The Jews who have had the advantages of decent social surroundings for a generation or two [read: affluent German Jews] are entirely satisfactory companions." The problem was the pushy Lower East Siders who, "fired with ambition," had become grinds, overachievers, and were "not particularly pleasant companions."

Butler and his associates wrestled with how to screen out undesirables—bring back chapel? require physical exams? impose quotas?—but all methods raised legal, moral, or public relations difficulties. In 1910 Butler proposed refurbishing Columbia's Christian credentials by offering university facilities for an Episcopal Convention—an offer he would not extend to Jewish organizations—but pesky Seth Low objected again, declaring it was to the university's credit that it "makes no discrimination against the Jews, either in its faculty or

---

19. Butler successfully kept Jews off the board, sighing in 1913 that Adolf Lewisohn, who had given substantial donations, would have made a fine trustee, "if he had been born a Methodist."

its student body," and that unless the offer was extended to all it should be extended to none. Besides, he pointed out, the trustees had raised no objections to receiving gifts from Jewish philanthropists; didn't consistency require refusing their money in the future? Faced with a potentially embarrassing Low resignation from the board, Butler backed down again. In 1914 he tried another tack, suggesting that admission criteria be expanded beyond exam results by adding interviews: "I suggest treating the candidate for graduation," he wrote Keppel, "as one treats a candidate for admission to a club, that is, having his personal qualifications examined." But nothing worked. By 1918 roughly 25 percent of Columbia's entering class was Jewish.

What *did* mitigate the "Hebrew problem," at least in a relative way, was something Butler had long promoted—the emergence of a citywide division of higher academic labor. Columbia, in Butler's schema, would turn out Wall Street lawyers, corporate executives, national statesmen, and school administrators, while leaving the more mundane tasks of producing accountants, neighborhood lawyers, and public school teachers to New York University (NYU) and the City College of New York (CCNY). If all went well, the flow of immigrants would be diverted away from his acropolis.

NYU—AS THE UNIVERSITY OF THE CITY OF NEW-YORK BECAME KNOWN IN 1896—was unreconciled to its assigned role; it had higher ambitions. Under Henry Mitchell MacCracken—chancellor from 1891 to 1910—it undertook its own acropolization. Having decided that their old Washington Square location had gotten too commercialized and industrialized for a proper undergraduate experience, MacCracken in 1891 purchased the bucolic forty-acre Mali estate on a sparsely settled Bronx bluff overlooking the Harlem River. MacCracken called in Stanford White to design a group of buildings. White fashioned a classical campus centered—as did his partner McKim's plan for Columbia—around a Roman-rotundaed library (Gould Memorial, as funds were provided by Helen Gould Shepard in memory of her father, Jay Gould) and supplemented by a colonnaded Hall of Fame. By 1903 the University Heights campus had 280 students, including both dorm residents and commuters. (It was seventeen minutes by train from Grand Central.)

Until 1911 the Bronx branch retained its Protestant (Presbyterian) identity. "It is hardly to be expected," MacCracken declared, "that the intellectual activity of either the Catholic or Jewish population will ever find its expression in Columbia or in New York University." Then the university opened a pre-med program uptown, which drew large numbers of mostly Jewish students, triggering petitions by those of "older American stock" that a 20 percent quota be imposed. Administrators responded by introducing a more selective admission policy that would "modify the composition of the student body as to permit Americanizing influences to work more freely and efficiently."

Downtown, however, NYU proceeded in exactly the opposite direction. MacCracken, like Butler, was into developing professional schools, and these remained in Washington Square. The old University Building (wherein Samuel Morse had developed his telegraph) was demolished and replaced by a ten-story loft structure. This Main Building was not all that different from the Asch Building just around the corner, but where the latter's top floors housed the Triangle Shirtwaist Company's factory, the former's contained graduate and professional schools. NYU downtown would soon embrace a law school; a School of Pedagogy; a School of Commerce, Accounts, and Finance; and a Graduate School of Business Administration, sited farther down-island, on Trinity Place, convenient to its Wall Street clientele.

Downtown there were no restrictions, the doors were flung wide open, and students poured in—older men and some women, part-timers, and, of course, large numbers of immigrants, particularly Russian Jews. Many of these enrollees in the professional schools also needed or desired access to liberal arts courses but weren't keen on trekking up to University Heights. So a Collegiate Division was added to the Washington Square complex, and when its enrollment shot past that of the Bronx campus, it was upgraded, becoming in 1914 the full-fledged Washington Square College. By 1917 surging downtown growth had driven NYU's overall student population up to 9,300, of whom roughly half were Hebrews. Ironically, it was the tuition income generated by students drawn to the hyper-urban atmosphere of Greenwich Village that kept the secluded but deficit-ridden University Heights acropolis afloat.

THE BOOM-ERA TRANSFORMATION OF NEW YORK ACADEMIA was perhaps most profound at City College. At century's end Gotham's public-sector free-tuition college was still at its old Gothic Revival stand on 23rd Street and Lexington, teaching Latin and Greek to sons of middle-rank merchants. Ten of eleven bailed out before graduating and hustled off directly to careers in business or the professions. A group of would-be modernizers, active since the 1880s, had made scant progress. They blamed the board of trustees—chosen by the city's Board of Education—for a lack of the substantial resources needed to install an up-to-date elective system.

At the turn of the century a group of militant alumni—bankers, lawyers, and corporate managers—seized control. They got the legislature to create a separate board of trustees and put them on it. They also wangled an increase in funding levels and brought in a young and progressive president, John H. Finley, who eased out conservative faculty, brought in PhD'd instructors, and promoted scholarship over Christian piety. The trustees also employed architect George B. Post to design a new campus. Using Manhattan schist salvaged from subway construction sites, he fashioned a cloister of Oxbridge-type buildings, set atop the dramatic promontory overlooking St. Nicholas Park (1907). The new campus, said Finley, was intended to be "the Acropolis of the City, its sacred enclosure," akin to "the crowned hill of ancient Athens."

The new CCNY *welcomed* immigrant students. When sons of affluent German Jews had first entered back in the 1870s and 1880s, the environment had been inhospitable. Fraternities excluded Jews, anti-Semitic incidents abounded, and the air was heavy with Protestant moralizing. Now, in 1904, Finley abolished required daily attendance at chapel and vigorously embraced ethnic heterogeneity (going so far as to visit students in their tenement neighborhoods). Given the changed tenor, the free tuition, the unique evening college, the fresh new curriculum, and the strong links to the expanding public school system (graduates of the new high schools were specially welcomed), immigrants jumped on the IRT and headed uptown in droves. By 1919 78 percent of CCNY's students were Eastern European Jews. So were 38.7 percent of the students at Hunter College, as the Normal College—the municipally financed counterpart of CCNY devoted to training teachers—was renamed in 1914, in honor of its first president.[20]

---

20. Though more and more students were Jews, very few Jews were students. In 1913 the entire graduating class of City College numbered 209. This in a city whose Jewish population was almost a million. CCNY students, moreover, were usually drawn not from the working class, but from the small-business class, where parents could afford to forgo children's wages. Educational achievement was more the result of economic advance than the cause of it.

CCNY, it was said, had become the Jewish University of America. But there was a catch. Lower East Siders had to check radicalism, unionism, religious orthodoxy, or Yiddish culture at the campus gate. The Anglo-Protestant values of CCNY's administrators and faculty suffused the curriculum. (As late as 1920, Bernard Baruch was the only Jewish trustee.) Conservative economics and "scientific" racism were staples of the curriculum. The new CCNY and Hunter College aimed to provide an escape route from the slums to the professions. Along the journey, it was hoped, those future lawyers, accountants, engineers, businessmen, civil servants, and, especially, teachers in the city's school system would adopt the values of elite Americanizers.

IN WRESTLING WITH THEIR RELIGIO-ETHNIC COMPOSITION, Columbia and NYU made far less fuss about Catholics than they did about Jews. There was less need, Catholics having conveniently withdrawn into their separate collegiate institutions, which were in turn fed by their separate parochial school system.[21]

St. John's College transformed itself into a university in 1904. It took its new name from the old manor (later village) of Fordham, where Archbishop Hughes had established it threescore years before. At its collegiate core the institution remained much the same. The Jesuits eschewed the elective system, rejected vocationalism. They did, however, embrace add-ons: a law school, a medical school, and (after 1916) a School of Sociology and Social Service, intended to supply Catholic charities with social workers.

Catholic women's higher education expanded as well. The old Academy of Mount St. Vincent north of Riverdale, run by the Sisters of Charity, became the College of Mount St. Vincent in 1910. And Manhattanville College—founded in 1841 as the Academy of the Sacred Heart—was chartered in 1917 as a degree-granting institution.

The archdiocese also augmented institutions aimed at reproducing Church cadre. To supplement the work of St. Joseph's Seminary up in Dunwoodie (Yonkers), Archbishop Farley established the preparatory Cathedral College, next to St. Patrick's, in 1903. It would produce the great majority of diocesan priests for the city.

THE CITY'S OTHER LEADING DENOMINATIONS FOLLOWED SUIT.

At the turn of the century, the Jewish Theological Seminary (JTS) revived. Started in 1886 by a handful of rabbis and laymen who wanted to produce an Orthodox but

---

21. Columbia, NYU, and CCNY, whatever their internal wrangling over religious composition, did not have formal requirements that required a denominational affiliation of trustees, faculty, or students, as did other institutions, notably Catholic or evangelical Protestant ones. The division between secular and sacred education was dramatically deepened by an Andrew Carnegie intervention.

In 1905 he set up the Carnegie Foundation for the Advancement of Teaching (CFAT), which granted funds to colleges to pay for professors' pensions. There were, however, significant strings attached. The CFAT board—Butler, who had developed close ties with Carnegie, sat on the Executive Committee—set criteria of eligibility for Carnegie's largesse. A proper college had to have at least a $200,000 endowment (later raised to $500,000), have strict entrance requirements (which led to wholesale changes in high school curricula throughout the country), and have at least eight departments, each headed by a PhD. Most crucially, to be eligible a college had to be nondenominational, and impose no sectarian requirements.

This wrought a revolution. Colleges jumped for Carnegie's money, abandoning the old order. Emergency sessions of boards of trustees throughout the country quickly changed charters that had been considered inviolate. The trustees had little choice. With Carnegie money, colleges could attract the best faculty, and pension off entrenched older classics-oriented professors, making way for younger elective-oriented faculty. Without it they might go under. The impact on many Protestant colleges was stunning: either they dropped their denominational affiliations or, with their religious banners nailed to their masts, were relegated to provincial status for lack of funds. Catholic institutions had the wherewithal to survive without Carnegie money. It was a stunning demonstration of the power that could be wielded, albeit indirectly, by the New York–based foundations. John D. Rockefeller's General Education Board would be similarly influential.

English-speaking rabbinate, it never won support from Eastern Europeans; they regarded it as an "uptown" institution. Then Jacob Schiff and his Reform colleagues at Temple Emanu-El (including Daniel and Simon Guggenheim, Leonard Lewisohn, Louis Marshall, and Mayer Sulzberger) stepped in to reorganize it. Though opposed to orthodoxy, they thought JTS might produce a milder variety of rabbi—more decorous, less socially embarrassing—who would help in Americanizing the new immigrants. In 1902 they brought in Solomon Schechter, a great rabbinical scholar and historian from Cambridge University, to run the institution. Schiff also paid for a building on Morningside Heights at 123rd Street, between Amsterdam and Broadway. The Orthodox community, in the event, remained skeptical of Schechter's program (classes were taught in English, not Yiddish), and preferred Rabbi Isaac Elchanan's Theological Seminary (1896). JTS then took on an unanticipated life of its own. Its graduates would help lay the foundation of Conservative Judaism, a new denomination, midway between Orthodoxy and Reform, that upheld some traditional rituals but abolished others, notably the separation of sexes.

In 1910 the Union Theological Seminary also moved to Morningside Heights, to a Collegiate Gothic quadrangle (120th/122nd/Broadway/Claremont). Founded by Presbyterians in 1836 as the New York Theological Seminary, it had moved in 1881 from University Place and 8th Street, to Park Avenue (between 69th and 70th), before relocating uptown with the aid of a million-dollar contribution from Daniel Willis James in 1905. The senior member at Phelps, Dodge (he was Anson Greene Phelps's grandson), James was prominent in New York banking, mining, and railroad circles; he made the gift in appreciation of the 1904 decision to put the seminary on a nondenominational, ecumenical, but still liberal Protestant basis.[22]

BY 1918 THE CITY'S ACADEMIC LANDSCAPE had been reconfigured. New university complexes, perched predominantly on heights and ridges from upper Manhattan to the lower Bronx, would seek to generate the new knowledge and train the new personnel New York would need in the new century. But on the checklist of cultural institutions required of a world-class metropolis, a substantial gap remained—a system of public libraries—which the civic elite now endeavored to fill.

LIBRARIES

In the pre-Consolidation decades, New York's libraries had slipped into somnolence. The musty and forbidding Astor Library on Lafayette Place attracted few users; even its wealthy sponsors backed away from it. Only a select clientele made their way up Fifth Avenue to the Lenox Library (between 70th and 71st). There were specialized libraries that met specialized needs (the Bar Association, the Academy of Medicine, the New-York Historical Society). And private subscribers could pay for access to private libraries (the General Society of Mechanics and Tradesmen Library, the New York Society Library, and the Mercantile Library Association, rehoused since 1891 in its own eleven-story building on Lafayette between Astor and 8th). But New York City had no large central collection comparable to the vast treasure houses of Paris, London, and Washington—or even those of Boston and

---

22. The General Theological Seminary stood pat, theologically and geographically, hewing to its Episcopalian roots and its Chelsea location on Clement Clarke Moore's former apple orchard (20th/21st/Ninth/Tenth).

The fortifying of denominational institutions was accompanied by early efforts at historical examination, as in the Reverend John Talbot Smith's *The Catholic Church in New York: A History of the New York Diocese from its Establishment in 1808 to the Present Time* (1905) and Samuel Oppenheim's *The Early History of the Jews in New York, 1654–1664* (1909).

Chicago. If a great library was (as widely believed) an indispensable attribute of a "capital of civilization," the metropolis was not up to the mark.

The first sign of impending salvation had appeared in 1886 when bachelor Samuel Tilden died, leaving the bulk of his estate to a trust charged with establishing a great library. When a family lawsuit reduced the funds available to a mere $2 million, a sum insufficient to complete the project independently, trustee Andrew Haswell Green, then promoting municipal consolidation, proposed using Tilden Trust funds to underwrite a merger of existing institutions. In 1895, after intensive negotiations, "The New York Public Library, Astor, Lenox and Tilden Foundations" (NYPL) was born.

The NYPL drew its trustees uniformly from the city's upper crust. Bankers, industrialists, and corporate lawyers (Carnegie, Morgan, Root, Harkness, Payne Whitney) mingled with pedigreed scions like Philip Schuyler, great-grandson of Alexander Hamilton. There were no writers, librarians, or scholars. Nor, at first, any Catholics or Jews. Nor representatives of labor or the left.

The trustees had two goals: first, to efficiently consolidate the component collections into a scholarly research facility that would rival the British Museum. And second, to house the mammoth collection in a peerless central structure that would settle any question about New York's world-class status on the library front.

They entrusted the first task to John Shaw Billings, the famed physician-cum-bibliographer who had created the monumental Surgeon General's Library and its *Index-Catalogue* and *Index Medicus*. Appointed director in 1896, the vigorous and commanding Billings swiftly reorganized and cataloged the 400,000-odd volumes of the old Astor and Lenox facilities.[23] He also amalgamated the substantial contributions that now poured in from assorted societies, corporations, government bodies, and individuals.

The second task was trickier. The NYPL didn't have sufficient funds to build a megastructure, nor to buy the land on which to put one. So John Bigelow, the library's first resident, turned to the city for help. He asked the municipal government to underwrite construction costs and donate land. Specifically, he requested Reservoir Square, the site on Fifth Avenue and 42nd Street where sat the 44 foot-high, vine-covered, and now superfluous Croton distributing reservoir. Its size and location would make it possible (the trustees told the mayor) "to erect a library building, dignified, ample in size, visible from all sides, with uninterrupted light, free from all danger of fire, in no respect encroaching upon the existing Bryant Park, and which will be an ornament to the City."[24]

The request raised a question: What quo would the city get for its quid, beyond an ornament? If New York was to pay for library facilities, shouldn't it get a guarantee that (in the *Tribune*'s words) "the plain, everyday workingman can derive some benefit from them"? The city's Socialist Party certainly thought so, and would ask the municipality "to improve the free library system."

The NYPL projectors hadn't contemplated much public outreach. Bigelow envisioned his central research facility as serving the "literary and contemplative class." What one trustee called the "inferior business" of circulation had, after all, never been central to the old Astor and Lenox Libraries: though on paper they'd been open to the public, their restricted hours and general incivility had effectively kept workers out.

---

23. The Lenox was sold off to Henry Clay Frick, who, in 1912, would have Carrère and Hastings erect his mansion thereon. The Astor was sold off in 1920 to the Hebrew Sheltering and Immigrant Aid Society.

24. Much of the library's foundation would consist of stone taken from the reservoir's walls and basins.

THE REMAKING OF NEW YORK

THE VIEW SOUTHWARD FROM FIFTH AVENUE AND FORTY-SECOND STREET, BEFORE THE
DEMOLITION OF THE MURRAY HILL RESERVOIR

THE PRESENT VIEW SOUTHWARD FROM THE SAME POINT, SHOWING THE PUBLIC LIBRARY
AND MANY TALL OFFICE-BUILDINGS AND LOFT-BUILDINGS

"The View Southward from Fifth Avenue and Forty-Second Street, before the Demolition of the
Murray Hill Reservoir." "The Present View Southward from the Same Point, Showing the Public
Library and Many Tall Office-Buildings and Loft-Buildings." Hugh Thompson, "The Remaking of
New York," *Munsey's Magazine*, September 1912.

The task of bringing books to the populace had been left to several private agencies. In 1880 a group of well-to-do women and men, drawn from the Protestant and professional elites, had incorporated the New York Free Circulating Library. A first branch was purchased on Bond Street in 1883; a second (on Second Avenue and 8th Street) was provided in 1884 by *New Yorker Staats-Zeitung* editor Oswald Ottendorfer and well stocked with German-language materials and a German-speaking staff. From 1887 on, municipal funds began to flow alongside an increasing river of private contributions, and by 1901 the system had eleven branches and a Traveling Library, and it loaned over 1.5 million volumes annually. In addition, the Aguilar Free Library, founded in 1886 by philanthropic Jews, was equally successful and similarly purposed: it aimed at "uplifting the mental and moral tone of a class that woefully lacks refining influences." Catholics ran the Cathedral Free Circulating Library, B'nai B'rith sponsored the Maimonides Library, Episcopalians offered the St. Agnes Free Library, and various settlement houses added to the stock of available literature-for-loan.

Despite their growing subsidies from the city, most of these were hard-pressed to meet the voracious popular demand. People read more, a practice underwritten by compulsory schooling, and publishing-industry productivity had lowered prices and expanded the range of titles. The city wanted to consolidate and organize these separate bodies into a central circulating system, under NYPL auspices. The trustees agreed to do so, albeit reluctantly, in return for city support for the reference library.

In 1897 the NYPL announced an architectural competition. The specifications for the 42nd Street building combined exacting functional requirements with an insistence that it be "one of the chief monuments of the city." John Merven Carrère and Thomas Hastings won with a grandly conceived monumental design that mixed French Renaissance and classical styles. The choice was surprising, as while the young men—former draftsmen in McKim's office—had done some private residences and hotels, they'd tackled nothing on this scale.

The cornerstone was laid in 1900, and the Department of Public Works began construction. It would take a decade. Partly this was due to the great scale of the project: over a half-million cubic feet of white marble were brought down from Vermont quarries to raise the foot-thick façade. Partly, too, Carrère and Hastings, fastidious about details, demanded refined workmanship.

The library opened in May 1911, two months after Carrère was killed in an auto accident. A great crowd attended the dedication, which featured President Taft, Governor Dix, Mayor Gaynor, and Cardinal Farley. The guests walked up the great Fifth Avenue terrace, past Edward C. Potter's stone lions, and on into the main rotunda. Agog, they took in its marble vaults, pillars, and arches. They mounted the marble staircases—marveling at the ornate ceilings and sculptured drinking fountains—to the superb main reading room with its carved tables. They descended again, via ingenious scissor staircases, to the Central Circulation Room, dominated by a 30-foot-high cast-iron and glass domed ceiling.

The next day, when the library opened for business to the general public, less visible marvels were revealed. The first call slip was deposited (requesting a Russian-language study of Nietzche and Tolstoy). It traveled down via an innovative system of brass pneumatic tubes to multi-tier steel stacks (the biggest in the world) where pages retrieved the book and sent it, by lifts and conveyors, on up to the reading room—in seven minutes flat. This was a triumph of circulation as great in its own way as the Pennsylvania tubes or the new subway system.

"A Sectional View of the New York Public Library. The seven tiers of stacks in which many of the books of the New York Public Library are shelved. Elevators transfer the books to the room above as they are called for." 1911. (New York Public Library, Art and Picture Collection)

By 1919 the reference library was drawing seven times the readership of the British Museum. The problem, however, was that this didn't add up to a significant percentage of the city's population. The new library, magnificent as it was, was still, in the European mode, aimed at scholars and business users far more than the general public.

What had happened to the idea of branch libraries?

The city had bludgeoned most of the old free libraries into merging with the Circulation Department. They had not wanted to lose their identity, or give up their power, but the city's threat to cut or eliminate their subsidies forced their surrender.[25] But now there was no money available for buildings. The 42nd Street structure had cost $9 million, well over the original estimate, and the goal of a series of branches throughout the consolidated city seemed doomed.

Enter Andrew Carnegie. The steel baron had long argued that rich businessmen must offset the diminution of opportunity wrought by the rise of corporations, lest the thwarted poor turn to revolution. The ideal solution would be to underwrite the creation of new "ladders upon which the aspiring can rise." Free libraries appealed to the bookish Carnegie, who had begun funding them in 1881, first at his Scottish birthplace of Dunfermline, then in Pennsylvania cities and towns where Carnegie's steel works were located. While he didn't require that his gifts bear his name, he wasn't displeased with publicity that might refurbish an image badly tarnished by the bloodletting he and Henry Clay Frick had inflicted on the workers at Homestead. As Mr. Dooley drily observed: "Ivry time he dhrops a dollar it makes noise like a waither fallin' down-stairs with a tray iv dishes."

On March 12, 1901, a day after the sale of his steel business to J. P. Morgan was made public, Carnegie put his money where his ideas were, in a spectacular way. He offered to contribute $5.2 million toward building sixty-five branches on city-purchased sites: forty-two for Manhattan, the Bronx, and Staten Island; twenty for Brooklyn; and three for Queens. The NYPL would then equip and operate the libraries, on lease from the city, which would cover ongoing maintenance costs. (The Brooklyn Public Library contracted separately with Carnegie for its branches.)

Over the next decade, leading architectural firms (like Carrère & Hastings and McKim, Mead & White) churned out branch buildings, most of which followed a standardized plan that was classically severe, more ceremonial than invitational. Nevertheless, they were enormously successful. Neighborhood residents eager for knowledge and advancement crowded into these structures, some of the first tangible fruits of the new Consolidation. Circulation figures soared steadily. By 1913, at 8 million volumes borrowed annually, they were the highest in the world.[26]

That same year, Vladimir Ilyich Lenin, then in European exile, got his hands on the 1911 annual report of the New York Public Library, and the revolutionary's jaw dropped. In a scathing piece he promptly penned for *Pravda*, Lenin contrasted library practices in Gotham with those in "Holy Mother Russia." "Instead of regulations, discussed and elaborated by a dozen committees of civil servants inventing hundreds of formalities and obstacles to the use of books, they see to it that even children can make use of the rich collections; that readers can read publicly-owned books at home; they regard as the pride and glory of a public library,

---

25. Some of the resistance was rooted in gender concerns. Women had founded and served on the Free Circulating Library board, but the NYPL's Circulation Department was run by men.

Some objections were theological. The Catholic archdiocese had exercised strict control over the Cathedral Library's selection process, to minimize potential harm from "dangerous books." Archbishop Corrigan, not wanting to give up this power to an all-Protestant board, rejected a merger with NYPL. Later, compromises were arranged. Corrigan died in 1902, and his successor, Archbishop Farley, was more conciliatory, especially after the trustees gave a seat to a Catholic—Farley himself. This brought a turnaround in 1904.

Other holdouts included the libraries of Brooklyn and Queens. The consolidated Greater City had forced the two boroughs' libraries to merge into a Brooklyn Public Library and a Queens Borough Library, respectively. But the two systems refused to go the next step and merge with the NYPL, partly out of concern for their already diminishing cultural identities. The city-owned Brooklyn library remained autonomous and laid plans for its own central facility at Flatbush Avenue and Eastern Parkway.

26. The total was further boosted by the Traveling Library Office, which in 1910 circulated over a million volumes from 802 stations (schools, playgrounds, precinct houses, factories, hospitals, churches, and department stores). There was also a Library for the Blind.

not the number of rarities it contains, the number of sixteenth-century editions or tenth-century manuscripts, but the extent to which books are distributed among the people, the number of new readers enrolled, the speed with which the demand for any book is met, the number of books issued to be read at home, the number of children attracted to reading and to the use of the library." And the numbers were astounding! "In the course of the year," he reported, "the library was visited by 1,658,376 people. There were 246,950 readers using the reading-room and they took out 911,891 books." Lenin did not fail to note that the first book requested was in Russian, but what really amazed him was that "the request for the book was handed in at eight minutes past nine in the morning. The book was delivered to the reader at nine fifteen....Almost eight million (7,914,882 volumes)," he continued in dazed amazement, were issued to readers at home, "400,000 more than in 1910." Imagine the effrontery of these people, he said, dripping furious irony, "making these gigantic, boundless libraries available, not to a guild of scholars, professors and other such specialists, but to the masses, to the crowd, to the mob!...Such is the way things are done in New York," he concluded. "And in Russia?"

In Gotham itself, success brought unanticipated consequences. The intention of most librarians, like most schoolteachers, was to uplift their patrons, to wean them from bad fiction and bad habits. Like public school classrooms, libraries were strictly ruled, proper etiquette enforced. The central system, guarding public morals, scrutinized book selection to screen out "indecent" literature. (George Bernard Shaw's *Man and Superman* was kept off the open shelves as undesirable for young people, generating a scornful response from Shaw, and much ridicule in the press).

Condescension and Anglo-Saxonizing did not long survive the daily contact with crowds of eager immigrants. Like the settlement workers, librarians came to respect their patrons, to celebrate their cultures, to provide books in their languages. Particular branches took on the coloration of their neighborhoods: the Webster Library carried Czech materials; the Seward Park Branch on East Broadway featured Russian and Hebrew literature; Rivington Street provided Yiddish, Rumanian, and Polish works, and Chatham Square started a Chinese-language collection. The librarians stocked muckraking books like Upton Sinclair's *Jungle*—not what Americanizers had had in mind. More and more the branches functioned as community centers, offering clubs, exhibits, and festivals that celebrated ethnic holidays. The imaginative and humane services offered to children—from kids' rooms to storytelling sessions—brought the system worldwide fame.

The New York Public Library thus reflected the ambitions of its diverse progenitors and varied constituents. For wealthy businessmen it offered status and services. For professionals it offered scholarly resources. For librarians it provided an opportunity to uplift and serve immigrants. For working people it offered a communal and individual resource, now (thanks to city backing) transformed from charity into essential municipal service.

OPERA

To all appearances, the Metropolitan Opera House at 39th and Broadway—newly redecorated by Carrère and Hastings in gold and maroon—was utterly dominated by the city's upper-upper class. The Diamond Horseshoe's coveted boxes glittered with representatives of mercantile, industrial, and financial capital. The Astors chaired a Knickerbocker contingent. Alice (Mrs. Cornelius) Vanderbilt II captained her clan with ritual flair, entering Box Three in mid-opening-aria, humming off-key through each successive act, and departing in

Metropolitan Opera House, New York, Which Seats 3200 Persons
LHJ Nov 1, 1910

"Metropolitan Opera House, New York, Which Seats 3200 Persons," 1910. (New York Public Library, Art and Picture Collection)

mid-finale. And Box Thirty-Five, at the imperial center of the Horseshoe, was occupied by the magisterial Pierpont Morgan. Society's stars seemed to twinkle fixedly in the Metropolitan's firmament.

Appearances misled. The Astor-Morgan-Vanderbilt conglomerate ruled, but it did not, exactly, reign. For one thing, musical decisions were increasingly delegated to Jews. In their collective incarnation as the Metropolitan Opera and Real Estate Company, the all-Protestant box holders owned the building. The business of actually staging operas they contracted out to a (profit-seeking) production company. In 1903 they signed a deal with Austrian Jewish impresario Heinrich Conried. His candidacy had been advanced by Henry Morgenthau, with backing from Jacob Schiff and Daniel Guggenheim, but Morgenthau, aware the lease would not likely be awarded to such an group, won the support of James Hazen Hyde (a power at Equitable Life Assurance), who in turn attracted sponsors from the Vanderbilt, Goelet, and Whitney families and thus ensured attainment of the lease. Schiff declined an offer to be on the operating company board but suggested instead his partner Otto Kahn. Hyde applauded and approved, as both he and Kahn were musical sophisticates, attuned to European currents, and had similar ambitions for the city's cultural development.

Conried—in effect a hired hand—was no threat to Anglo-Protestant hegemony. Otto Kahn was another story. The very cultivated, very dapper, and very rich Kuhn, Loeb partner, at first merely one of Conried's backers, grew ever more prominent in the Metropolitan's affairs, partly through timely infusions of cash (as when he made good the touring company's losses in the San Francisco earthquake in 1906), and partly by slowly buying out other investors until by 1908, as majority stockholder, he was in all but complete control.

That ultimate power remained in box-holder hands was forcefully demonstrated in 1907 when Conried mounted *Salome*. Already controversial for its Oscar Wilde libretto and Richard Strauss score, it touched off a major scandal when the opening-night crowd was treated to the sight of Salome lasciviously fondling the severed head of John the Baptist. The *Tribune*'s revulsed critic summarized audience reaction—"starting eyeballs and wrecked nerves"—and described in detail the "moral stench with which *Salome* fills the nostrils of mankind." Anthony Comstock demanded authorities close the production, but J. P. Morgan was way ahead of him. Thundering against the obscene and profane spectacle, Morgan summoned an emergency meeting of the Real Estate Company, which peremptorily ordered Conried to drop *Salome* forthwith. Its opening night proved its last. The embarrassed Kahn conveyed to the offended Strauss his dismay at the "totally inappropriate religiosity of Morgan" but was in no position to challenge box-holder prerogatives.[27] Even after he gained control of the operating company, Kahn refrained from trying to buy a box of his own, all too aware that Diamond Horseshoe anti-Semites frowned on being joined by Jews. For all Kahn's contributions to the Met, and despite his wealth, polish, and assimilationist attendance at St. Thomas's Episcopal Church, he, too, was under the ban. Even later, when he was finally (in 1917) allowed to buy Box Fourteen, he refused to occupy it, a riposte as pointed as his bitter witticism that "a 'kike' is a Jewish gentleman who has just left the room."

Even as they guarded the gates against Jews, the box holders began accommodating Italians—as singers, composers, and conductors. Partly this was due to their disaffection from German opera, the Wagner craze of the 1880s having definitely cooled. Before coming to the Met, Conried had produced operettas and German-language plays at William Steinway's Irving Place Theatre, and the Wagner-shy Real Estate Company had warily stipulated that no more than 40 percent of Conried's performances could be in German. And while this transformation in taste was a response to contemporary European musical developments—notably the rise of *verismo*, a realist movement in opera—it was also to some degree a response to changing demographic conditions in the city. The sway of German opera in New York had been not unconnected to the market power of the quarter-million (and very musically inclined) Kleindeutchlanders. And after the turn of the century, the growing presence of Italians, many of them strongly oriented toward opera, helped swing Gotham's musical compass from Bayreuth to Milan.

On November 23, 1903, opening night of the Conried group's first season at the Met helm, the young Neapolitan tenor Enrico Caruso debuted as the Duke of Mantua in *Rigoletto*. Reviews were mixed. Some critics objected to his "Italian mannerisms." The *Times* sniffed that the "frenzied 'bravos'" he inspired came from "his compatriots who were present in large numbers." But Caruso's vocal opulence and bubbling amiability soon conquered New York Society. Mrs. Payne Whitney invited him to sing at a fashionable soirée, and soon Mrs. Vanderbilt, Mrs. Belmont, and Mr. Schwab were paying enormous fees for his private performances. In the next few years he became the most popular singer at the Met, and the best-known opera star in the United States.

Caruso identified strongly with New York's Italian community. He ate in its restaurants, printed his caricatures in *La Follia* (a magazine read widely in the Italian colony), gave benefits for Italian hospitals and settlements. When in town his various hotels—first the Majestic,

---

27. In fact, Morgan—no puritan—had previously okayed the opera. But Conried had incautiously invited stockholders to a dress rehearsal, at which event Morgan's daughter Louisa Morgan Satterlee, appalled by the spectacle, convinced her father to change his mind.

then the York, the Savoy, and finally the Knick-erbocker—were besieged by *paisani* attracted by his down-to-earth style and his well-known willingness to help down-on-their-luck compatriots.

Caruso's associations also rendered him suspect to the hefty contingent of New Yorkers who looked down on Italians, especially with the crisis of Black Hand criminality in full swing.[28] This became glaringly clear on a November day in 1906 when the singer strolled over to the Central Park Zoo. He was in the monkey house when a woman began screaming, "You loafer! You beast!" and claimed he had pinched her buttocks. Caruso was arrested, charged with disorderly conduct at the Arsenal, and tried the next day at Yorkville Police Court, where he was declared guilty and fined ten dollars.[29]

The "Monkey House Scandal" hit the headlines. Caruso was shrilly denounced as a vile foreign seducer of American womanhood. Hate mail demanded his deportation. Deeply depressed,

Enrico Caruso, in Costume, ca. 1908. (Library of Congress Prints and Photographs Division)

and ravaged by blinding headaches, Caruso dreaded his next Met appearance. When he took the boards in *La Bohème*, some hissing broke out. But then—from the Italian battalions in the gallery—came an explosion of frantic applause and cheers, quite drowning out the catcalls. The bulk of the orchestra and parterre patrons joined in, giving Caruso a dozen curtain calls, and afterward in his dressing room the singer sobbed in gratitude: "New York still loves me."[30]

They loved Puccini, too. *La Bohème* came to the Met in 1900, *Tosca* had its US opening there in 1901, and in 1907 Conried brought Puccini himself to New York—just in time to receive enthusiastic acclaim for the January premiere of his *Manon Lescaut* and to supervise the Met's first production of *Madama Butterfly* in February. (Caruso, whom Puccini had given a leg up early in the singer's career, took the composer window-shopping, dining with Italian American friends, and driving around town.) Though the opera flustered some with its "carnality," *Butterfly* got a standing ovation. Four years later Puccini was back, viewing rehearsals for his 1910 opening of *La Fanciulla del West*, and by that time his works, together with those of others in the Italian repertoire (Mascagni, Leoncavallo) dominated the Met's stage. They appealed partly for their *verismo*—the degree to which they portrayed (one critic wrote) the "rhythms of everyday hearts...the experiences of the common people"—and

---

28. Caruso himself was blackmailed by extortionists sailing under the Black Hand flag.

29. Despite the guilty plea, and Caruso's undeniably amorous nature, there are plenty of grounds for suspecting a frame-up, either on the part of the female complainant and arresting officer—a duo who had worked together on previous occasions—or by a zealous press agent of a rival company that had failed to talk Caruso into deserting the Met.

30. Luckily, that public was clueless about the complex reality of Caruso's love life, else things might have gone differently. In the mid-1890s he'd begun living openly with a woman who was married but separated from her husband, and with whom he had two children. US newspapers, however, presented her as his wife. And even when she left him in 1912, and sued him on various grounds, it was barely reported in America, though it was a sensation in Italy. Another scandal was thoroughly covered, however, when in 1918 he eloped with Dorothy Park Benjamin, whose father, a distinguished and wealthy attorney, refused permission to marry a slum-born Neapolitan, no matter how famous.

Geraldine Farrar (left) and Louise Homer in *Madama Butterfly*, in the presence of the composer. Metropolitan Opera House, February 11, 1907. (Metropolitan Opera Archives)

partly for their melodiousness, the way people could sing or hum them, or play them on the piano. Caruso too combined a democratic ordinariness—no airs and graces for him—with a voice that was lyrical but manly.

The Met was fortunate to have Kahn, Caruso, and Puccini in its corner, because at the beginning of the same 1907 season in which the composer scored two back-to-back triumphs, a rival opera company emerged, and from a most unlikely quarter. In December 1906 Oscar Hammerstein, a cigar manufacturer turned theatrical entrepreneur, opened the Manhattan Opera House at 34th Street (between Eighth and Ninth), scant blocks south of the Met.

Hammerstein, born in 1847 to musically inclined German Jewish parents, grew up in Berlin, where he was enrolled (aged 12) in a conservatory, and developed a passion for grand opera. After his mother died, he ran away from his harsh father, and arrived in New York in 1863. He found work in a Pearl Street cigar factory, then opened one of his own, then began inventing and patenting cigar-making machinery that proved extremely profitable. Hammerstein parlayed his earnings into Harlem real estate and—bitten by the theatrical bug—designed and built the Harlem Opera House. A series of other theaters followed; most of them flopped, but some proved colossally successful. He now dedicated his eighth venue, the Manhattan Opera House, to giving the Met a run for its money.

With Barnumesque flair, Hammerstein advertised himself as an operatic populist. "I'm the Little Man Who'll Provide Grand Opera for the Masses," he declared. The 3,000-seat house—no grand entrances, many inexpensive tickets—underscored his intention to eschew the "fashionable" in favor of "society in the broad sense"; it was for people interested in music rather than aristocratic display. The Manhattan's opening night (December 3, 1906), indeed its entire first season, was a smash success, drawing *both* the subway-arriving, ordinary-garbed masses *and* the carriage-arriving, begowned and bejeweled classes. The Metropolitan, meanwhile, lost money for the first time in years.

The Met struck back. Managers and singers were informed that any dealings with Hammerstein might endanger future relations with Conried. The operating company prevailed on Puccini's Italian publisher to give it exclusive performing rights to all the maestro's operas. And it played its Caruso card repeatedly. Hammerstein retaliated by embracing modernist opera and enlisting Mary Garden, the greatest singing actress of the period, whose

Pelléas et Mélisande climaxed his sensational second 1907–8 season; Debussy was so pleased he sent personal thanks to the impresario. Again, the Met lost a substantial sum.

Now seriously alarmed, Kahn (who had personally covered the previous season's losses) and his fellow directors turned to Europe for reinforcements. To take charge of German opera, Gustav Mahler was brought in. Mahler had ruthlessly renovated the Vienna Court Opera, where he'd been musical director since 1897. He'd demanded thirty to forty rehearsals (at the Met, one was par for the course), dismissed singers and orchestral players to make way for new talent, and freely reinterpreted composers' scores to freshen them up. Offered a substantial salary, Mahler arrived in Gotham in December 1907 and opened the Met's season in January 1908 with a revitalized *Tristan and Isolde*, followed shortly by a superb *Don Giovanni*.

Overall artistic control, however, was handed to Italians. In 1908 Kahn brought in a new musical director, Giulio Gatti-Casazza, direct from Milan's La Scala; he would transact the Met's business entirely in Italian. Accompanying Gatti-Casazza was conductor Arturo Toscanini, a man of Napoleonic force and vision, who was given charge of the French and Italian repertoire. Like Mahler, Toscanini found the Met lacking in discipline, and he fought to instill higher standards. He also set out to master the performers. The Parma-born son of a tailor and sometime Garibaldi redshirt had no patience with prima donnas. At one rehearsal, Geraldine Farrar, the company's exciting new soprano, ordered him to follow her lead as she was the star. He replied: "The stars are all in the heavens, mademoiselle. You are but a plain artist, and you must obey my direction." Farrar exploded but eventually gave in, their reconciliation so complete they soon commenced an affair.[31]

Toscanini also tried disciplining the Met's audience. He barred latecomers and forbade talking during a performance—constraints that fell heavily on the chattering upper classes. He also tried to abolish mid-performance encores—a tradition upheld, the *Times* noted in 1909, by "the Italian contingent"—which could double the length of an evening. Here he was less successful. Organized claques resisted being transformed from participants into spectators.

The two companies now prepared for battle, scouring Europe for new productions, foraging for new stars as collectors canvassed for Rembrandts and Goyas. On October 31, 1908, forty singers engaged to appear at either the Met or Manhattan arrived on the French liner *Lorraine*, with both Hammerstein and Gatti-Casazza at the pier to meet their respective talents. The Met opened its 1908–9 season in November 1908 with *Aida* (Toscanini conducting), followed in December with *Tristan* (Mahler at the podium). Hammerstein, having broken the Met's exclusive grip on Puccini, opened with *Tosca* to a packed house. Subsequent Manhattan triumphs featuring Nellie Melba and Luisa Tetrazzini were capped, most spectacularly and pointedly, by resurrecting the stifled *Salome* in January 1909, with a bloodcurdling performance by Mary Garden.

The opera war, with its competitive flood of productions and aggregation of stars, generated feverish excitement but was wildly costly. Part of the problem was that each company embarked on an imperial expansion, seeking to outflank the other in an ever-widening hinterland. Hammerstein opened a 4,100-seat house in Philadelphia in late 1908, began buying

---

31. This encounter smacks of the apocryphal, especially as it comes in many varieties. Another version of the duet has Farrar saying, "Maestro, you must conduct as I sing, for I am a star," and Toscanini replying, "You a star? Just remember, when the sun shines, you don't see the stars!" All the scripts, however, point to the same forceful assertion of conductorial authority—the rights of management over labor—and in this he was firmly backed by financier Kahn, who argued that "however great the individual artists, the greatest artistic successes can only be accomplished if there exists a spirit of willing cooperation with, and submission to the Management, and a recognition of the necessity of centralized authority, together with mutual confidence and good will." Within a short time the "star-cast" house had been transformed into a smooth running repertory enterprise.

Opening night: *Aida*, act 2, scene 2. Metropolitan Opera House, November 15, 1908. (Metropolitan Opera Archives)

land in Brooklyn and Cleveland for new theaters, and sent touring companies to Boston, Pittsburgh, Baltimore, Washington, Montreal, Quebec and Toronto—road shows that were critically acclaimed but financially draining. Gatti-Cassaza likewise pulled out all the stops for the 1909–10 season: the Met gave 359 performances of forty-two operas and twenty-five dance works in Baltimore, Boston, Brooklyn, Chicago, and Philadelphia, plus Paris and ten other cities. It was costly for the Met, too—Gatti-Cassaza announced a hefty quarter-million-dollar loss on the season—but the operating company had deep pockets: Kahn's, and he covered the deficit.

Hammerstein's pockets, on the other hand, were close to empty, partly because of his aversion to the Horseshoe elite; when super-rich (and anti-Semitic) Clarence Mackay offered to underwrite the Manhattan's expenses, the impresario told him "to go to hell." By 1910, near insolvency, Hammerstein decided that "the operatic war is suicide." Via his son, he entered into secret negotiations with Otto Kahn. The banker quite admired Hammerstein, and while he could simply have waited for the cigar-chomping impresario to topple into bankruptcy, he personally funded a $1.25 million buyout, in exchange for Hammerstein's agreeing to produce no operas of any kind in New York, Boston, Philadelphia, or Chicago, for a decade. Kahn's generosity, to be sure, also reestablished the Met's monopoly position, which the Kuhn, Loeb consolidator promptly bolstered by setting up an operatic cartel, via an interlocking directorate between the Met and houses in Chicago, Philadelphia, and Boston.[32]

---

32. In Brooklyn, after the old Brooklyn Academy of Music (BAM) burned in 1903, local gentry, fearing cultural subsumption by Manhattan, supported raising the most complex cultural center since Madison Square Garden. Herts and Tallant won the competition to design the new BAM, and their creation, which opened in 1908, on Lafayette Avenue in fashionable Fort Greene, housed an opera house, concert hall, lecture hall, and ballroom, all linked by a lobby and vast foyer. But BAM became not a rival but a venue for the Met. The gala inaugural evening, which featured Farrar and Caruso in Gounod's *Faust*, began a series of annual full-season engagements by the Met, as well as visiting orchestras, performers, and lecturers.

"The Metropolitan Opera is not now, and never was, an 'opera trust,'" Kahn would insist in 1914, and indeed Hammerstein's attempt to renege on the deal, alleging it violated the Sherman Antitrust Act, was thrown out by the courts, which ruled that opera did not constitute interstate commerce. But the feeling would persist in New York that a bevy of Wall Street bankers and lawyers had battered down a game "Little Man's" challenge to a corporate colossus, and that the city's operatic scene was the worse off for his defeat.

At almost the same moment, a similar contest was under way on the terrain of symphonic music, one that would have a more ambiguous outcome.

SYMPHONY

City elites had long considered the New York Philharmonic Society a thorn in their cultural side. New York's oldest musical institution had been founded in 1842, primarily by German musicians, as a cooperative venture. The performer-owners selected their own repertoire, elected conductors for annual terms, promoted the concerts, and divided the box-office receipts. It had no permanent home, so the company had to rent space in Carnegie and other halls, which cut into profits. As there were no guaranteed salaries, most of the musicians counted on other steadier employment for their bread and butter, which meant they frequently missed rehearsals to meet other (remunerated) obligations and often missed performances as well, forcing the orchestra to hire substitutes. By the 1908–9 season only fifty-seven musicians were registered as members of the society, of whom only thirty-seven played consistently in an orchestra of a hundred men.

The same elites who were working to upgrade Gotham's standing as a cultural center fumed at an arrangement they deemed self-evidently inefficient, a point painfully underlined by the annual arrival of the touring Boston Symphony—a superbly professional outfit single-handedly underwritten by Henry Lee Higginson in the manner of an Esterhazy prince. The wealthy New Yorkers made sporadic efforts to upgrade the orchestra. In 1902 Andrew Carnegie accepted the presidency and, with other *affluenti*, engaged well-known conductors, which improved attendance, but not enough. Wealthy patrons offered to subsidize its transformation into a full-time salaried orchestra, but only if the society abandoned its cooperative format, and the Philharmonic's older hands, committed ideologically to their democratic tradition, and committed personally to holding on to their positions, rejected the offers. Growing competition from touring groups and Walter Damrosch's New York Symphony Orchestra, coupled with hard times during the Panic of 1907, forced them to capitulate when a consortium of the mighty made them an offer they could no longer afford to refuse.

Mary Sheldon, the politically savvy wife of George R. Sheldon (president of the United States Trust Company and longtime treasurer of the Republican National Committee), pulled together a group of guarantors (Carnegie, J. D. Rockefeller, Morgan, Pulitzer, Ryan, Belmont, Louisine Havemeyer, Mary Harriman, Minnie [Mrs. Samuel] Untermyer, and others culled from "the best families in the city") who agreed, in 1909, to provide $90,000 in annual operating expenses, for each of the next three years, which would include guaranteed salaries for the musicians. There were conditions: orchestral democracy must give way to control by a board of millionaires and society ladies; the season must expand from eighteen to forty-six concerts; the superannuated should be retired and the remainder subjected to the dictates of discipline and efficiency. The most stinging requirement transferred power to a conductor—appointed by management, not elected by workers—who together with the funders would have complete control over both programming and personnel.

The first conductor of the new order would be Gustav Mahler. Mary Sheldon had been courting Mahler—who had not been thrilled about sharing turf with Toscanini—and in March 1909 he signed a contract with the guarantors. At the end of the bruising 1909–10 opera season he abandoned the Metropolitan for the Philharmonic, though not without some trepidation, as he believed the orchestra (so he wrote Bruno Walter) was "untalented and phlegmatic"; rescuing it looked to be "uphill work."

Mahler proved effective but troublesome. Yes, he did work vigorously on reconstituting the Philharmonic, and won critical acclaim for his interpretations. Annoyingly, he didn't stop at transforming the orchestra; he set out to transform the audience, too. "It will be my aim to educate the public," he told a reporter, and in his determination to uplift New Yorkers who were wedded to an untaxing romanticism, he laced his programs with austere renditions of Beethoven, and heavy doses of moderns like Bruckner and Strauss. Attendance tapered downward. When the wealthy patrons complained—uplift was for *other* people—the irritable conductor brooked no interference.

Mahler's exalted notion of his independence was swiftly pricked. In February 1911 he was forced to accept a humiliating veto over his scheduling. When he fell gravely ill shortly afterward—he conducted for the last time on February 21—his wife, Alma, blamed the patrons: "You cannot imagine what Mr. Mahler has suffered," she told an interviewer in May, after they had returned to Europe. "In Vienna my husband was all powerful. Even the Emperor did not dictate to him, but in New York, to his amazement, he had ten ladies ordering him about like a puppet." Alma smudged the lily here—perhaps understandably, as Gustav was then at death's door and would expire a few days later.

But the transformation had been wrought. In 1911 the patrons and matrons handed the Philharmonic's baton to the affable and efficient Joseph Stransky. That same year, Joseph Pulitzer died, leaving half a million dollars to the Philharmonic, if it became a permanent orchestra, reduced prices, and kept its programs "not too severely classical." Stransky chucked Bruckner for Liszt, Wagner, and Dvořák (all Pulitzer favorites). Soon the crowds were standing room only.

New York's elite seemed to have come up with an ideal arrangement for running performance-based cultural institutions. Rejecting orchestral democracy, vocalist autonomy, conductorial autocracy, and European-style state subsidy, they settled instead on rule by an oligarchy of millionaires. It worked well enough at Carnegie Hall and the Metropolitan Opera House, where Gotham's corporate elite more or less held sway. When they attempted to create an equivalent institution for the theater, however, they ran up against their limits.

THE NEW THEATRE

The idea of creating a repertory company for both drama and music originated with Heinrich Conried. In 1906 he proposed launching a "legitimate" theater, a New York equivalent of Louis XIV's Comédie Française, which would "cultivate, develop, and elevate the public taste." This "New Theatre" would present world-class works—Shakespeare, Molière, Goethe, Ibsen, Sophocles—and mount operas (drawing on the Met's singers) that were not suitable for the Metropolitan's enormous space. It would also establish schools for teaching drama and music, employ actors and singers, and set up endowment and pension funds.[33]

---

33. Conried was inspired by the theatrical companies supported by the city's enormous German community, which mixed Shakespeare, Schiller, and Goethe with problem plays (Ibsen, Shaw) and farces; their staging and acting were "superlatively good," far better than the work turned out by commercial impresarios. Conried himself was coming out of this background.

Kahn immediately climbed on board. Enlisting Walter Damrosch to help with planning, he assembled a company of twenty-eight leading actors, and pulled together a familiar set of incorporators from the city's corporate pinnacles—among them Astor, Belmont, Cravath, Frick, Gary, Huntington, Hyde, Mackay, Morgan, and Stillman. William K. Vanderbilt was to be president, Otto Kahn treasurer. Most were connected with the Met—and the Met's anti-Semitism. Fearful that the incorporation plan would "let all the Jews in town into the thing," and that they "would swamp it in no time," a showdown ensued. ("The Jew question came up point blank," according to cofounder Eliot Gregory.) Kahn allowed as how "I have not the same prejudice against Jews as I am one. But I agree for the success of this enterprise it will be better to have only one or two boxes sold to Jews." Schiff, Speyer, and Kahn would be the chosen people.

Carrère and Hastings won the architectural competition to design the playhouse, and produced a Beaux-Arts structure, bigger than the White House (but smaller than their New York Public Library then under construction); it filled Central Park West between 62nd and 63rd Streets. The $2 million theater offered 2,300 seats and a ring of private boxes (which immediately sold out at $25,000 each). It was sumptuously appointed—glittering chandeliers, thick carpets, palm gardens on the roof, Connemara marble everywhere—an obvious knock-off of the Metropolitan. The invitation-only dress rehearsal on November 6, 1909, drew a scintillating Met-style crowd by car and carriage. After Morgan dedicated the theater to "the services of the drama and the citizens of New York," the principal speakers—Governor Hughes and Senator Root—hammered home the governing principle that the New Theatre would be "run for the sake of art only and not in any way for the sake of profit." Because it was a philanthropic venture, Root averred, it would be able to present "what is best upon the stage," whereas "the requirements for profit may demand a lower standard." Hughes agreed that encouragement of the arts "cannot be left simply to the incentive of cupidity." Happily "men of means" would now provide productions that would never be staged if left to "those who were impelled purely by commercial consideration." These philanthropists would also purvey an art that reflected life—not its "abnormality" but rather its "wholesome currents," those in which "goodness ever predominates and progress is ever sure." The New Theatre would "promote the refining influences of life," and "its influence will permeate the community in a wholesome manner."

With this leaden mantle draped around its shoulders, the company sailed into action, days later, with *Antony and Cleopatra*, and promptly sank. The playhouse itself was plagued with terrible acoustics and sight lines, and was far too large for its intended repertory. Its putative audience failed to fill the hall for the uninspired offerings, and the site was too distant from its real audience base. (Central Park West was no Fifth Avenue.) By January the private boxes were all but empty. Kahn picked up the bills and soldiered on, attempting to attract "the intelligent public" to what Hughes had called "the people's theatre," making cheap seats available to agencies like the Association for Improving the Condition of the Poor, the Rand School, and the Women's Trade Union League. Nothing worked. The house limped along, running up enormous bills, until Morgan decided to cut the consortium's losses. ("Get rid of it," he decreed.) In 1911, renamed the Century Theatre, it was leased to producers of spectacles and musicals.

Postmortems focused on the mismatch between intention and venue. American producer Henry Miller suggested that "you can't uplift the theatre in a gilded incubator," and Kahn came to agree. The project had "needed air, [and] plain fare," he said ruefully, but instead "we stifled it with heavy golden raiment; we fed it on a diet seasoned with 'society' ingredients." As Shakespearean actor and company member E. H. Sothern tersely summa-rized this line of thinking: the New Theatre "was doomed to fail because it was built not for the masses but for the classes."

The critics were on to something, but they hadn't quite gotten to the nub of things. It wasn't just that ordinary New Yorkers were spurning Official Theater, but rather that at that very moment they were flocking by the millions to an alternative entertainment industry, one organized not by wealthy Anglo-Protestants and affluent German Jews seeking uplift, but by working-class Jewish, Italian, and Irish entrepreneurs seeking profits, and who were perfectly prepared to accept the public on its own terms. The locus of this raucous new world of com-mercial culture, which lay quite outside the purview of the city's gentility, was a mile to the south of the New Theatre, and just to the north of the Metropolitan Opera house, at the heretofore undistinguished juncture point where Broadway crossed paths with 42nd Street.

13

Show Biz

TIMES SQUARE

In the early 1890s Broadway's brilliantly illuminated river of theaters and nightspots ribboned up to 42nd Street—and winked out. Northward lay the dimly gaslit flats of Longacre Square, home to horse-ware dealers by day and footpads by night. Named (back in the 1870s) after London's livery district, the Longacre was still dominated at its upper end by carriage manufactories (Brewster, Studebaker), by the Vanderbilts' enormous American Horse Exchange, and by ancillary outfits like harness stores, repair shops, blacksmiths, and stables. Stinking of manure and dangerous after dark, the district stood athwart the uptown drift of Gotham's entertainment district. First-rank "legitimate" institutions, like the Metropolitan Opera and Casino Theatre, weren't found above 39th Street, and even the Tenderloin district, Broadway's raunchy sidekick, hadn't gotten farther north than the brothels lining 39th and 40th.

Longacre's major landholders were content with this status quo. Back in 1803 the Astors had bought a 22-acre farm, that ran west from Broadway (between 42nd and 46th) to the Hudson, and they were prepared to let most of the property lie fallow until a tide of profitable development reached it. "Nothing could be done in that section," the *Real Estate Record and Builders Guide* recalled, "until the large estates which owned nearly all the avenue property showed a disposition to either improve, lease or sell their holdings." Their decision, said the trade journal, had in effect drawn a "dead line" across the Longacre's southern border. "No one was supposed to cross that line."

Then, in 1895, Oscar Hammerstein transgressed. At that point in his career, the would-be operatic tycoon had just recovered from the failure of his initial challenge to the Metropolitan's supremacy. In 1892 he had opened his first Manhattan Opera House, on 34th Street between Broadway and Seventh Avenue, only to have it fall victim to the mediocre productions he'd come up with. To ward off bankruptcy Hammerstein went into partnership with Messrs. Koster and Bial, two brewers who had been running a vaudeville house on 23rd Street and wanted to move to larger premises farther uptown. In 1893, accordingly, Hammerstein's opera house became Koster & Bial's Music Hall, with himself installed as manager. He soon revealed a flair for vaudevillian fare, scoring his first big hit with the exceedingly well ripped Eugen Sandow, whose strongman act was managed by the 24-year-old Chicagoan Florenz Ziegfeld. But Hammerstein fought all the time with his quarrelsome partners and finally, in 1895, sold them his interest in the Herald Square enterprise. With the proceeds, and a $900,000 loan from the New York Life Insurance Company, he boldly leapt to Longacre.

There, on the east side of Broadway, between 44th and 45th, Hammerstein built the Olympia Music Hall, a ten-story-tall entertainment complex. Inspired by Stanford White's Madison Square Garden (1890), he gathered three different venues under the Olympia's capacious roof: the Music Hall for variety acts, the Lyric Theatre for opera and musical comedy, and the Concert Hall. Done up lavishly in Louis XIV, XV, and XVI, the triplets could collectively seat 6,000. On the roof itself, following the well-established summertime practice of shuttering indoor theaters, made intolerable by New York's stifling July-August heat, he opened a woodland garden, replete with real trees, and real swans a-swimming on a 40-foot lake. The limestone extravaganza was topped off—in best Barnumesque fashion—with an electric sign that blazed out Hammerstein's name, piercing the gloom of Longacre, grandly staking out his claim.

The Olympia proved to be *slightly* ahead of its time. Overhead was high and profits were low, due partly to problematic programming (Hammerstein, dearly wanting to be seen as a serious composer, routinely inflicted vanity productions on steadily dwindling audiences), partly to popularly priced ticketing (fifty cents afforded access to all theaters), and partly to the 1890s depression. As a result, New York Life foreclosed in 1898, and the debt-laden Olympia was auctioned off and broken up into its constituent parts.

In 1899, however, with the return of flush times, the scrappy impresario bounced back, opening the Victoria Theatre at the northwest corner of Seventh and 42nd, for a fraction of the Olympia's cost. This time Hammerstein's mix of musical comedies, dramas, and variety acts proved profitable from the get-go, enabling him (in 1900) to build the Republic right next door, intended for top-flight theatrical presentations. Finally, on their combined roof-tops, he confected Paradise Gardens—a miniature Dutch village replete with working wind-mill, quaint clay cottage, rustic bridge over a pond, and open-air farm where milkmaids and their swains tended ducks, chickens, and two real cows.

Hammerstein's success was followed by something of an Oklahoma land rush into Longacre, propelled by long-pent-up demand, fueled by prosperity, and galvanized, cru-cially, by the 1900 signing of the construction contract for the first subway. Soon August Belmont's IRT roared into the district, depositing an express stop at its bottom (42nd) and a local at its top (50th). At the same time, publisher Adolph Ochs abandoned Printing House Square, and had Harry Black and Paul Starrett erect a new *New York Times* building atop the 42nd Street station, just across Seventh Avenue from Hammerstein's Victoria. To highlight the arrival of the city's second-tallest skyscraper (the Park Row Building being still the reigning champion), Ochs and Belmont got Mayor McClellan to give Longacre a name-lift in April 1904. And in December, to celebrate his paper's relocation to what was now officially Times Square, Ochs threw a monster New Year's Eve street party. Merrymakers poured into the still-dim square by the thousands, courtesy of the new subway, and when fireworks were lobbed aloft at the midnight hour, the giant tower lit up from base to dome—"it seemed almost as the building was aflame," wrote one observer—and the throngs below greeted the arrival of 1905 with cowbells, whistles, horns, and huzzahs, inventing a tradition.

Over the next decade, New York's show business surged north. Old institutions were uprooted and transplanted to Times Square (rather as the giant department stores were being migrated from lower Sixth to upper Fifth), and new ones, some the product of world-historic technological revolutions, piled pell-mell into its booming precincts. Land values shot up. The Astors relaxed their century-long grip, became developers themselves. The district erupted theaters and vaudeville houses, ornate restaurants and intimate cabarets, premier hotels and fancy brothels, massive office buildings and major motion picture theaters. Electrified marquees blazed out the names of the galaxy of talent that poured onto the boards and screens but were soon overshadowed—perhaps not the right word—by the gigantic electric signs that bloomed on the rooftops above them, posting illuminated advertisements on the nighttime sky.

Longacre Square had simply vanished, and not in name only. The horse-based businesses—themselves under assault from car-based rivals—either expired, trotted away to more peripheral pastures, or converted to auto outlets and sidled farther up Broadway. Low-rent rooming houses were erased, and replaced by upscale apartment hotels. The transformation wrought in this roughly sixteen-square-block area was more swift and profound than anything occurring anywhere else in the booming city, even including lower Manhattan's skyscraper district—a clear sign that the district's development was engaging the city's core commercial and cultural energies.

NEW YORK HAD LONG BEEN THE COUNTRY'S PREEMINENT ENTERTAINMENT METROPOLIS, and it now rolled that status over into the new century. Central to retaining its supremacy was the consolidation and centralization of its major branches, in a manner akin to—though not identical with—contemporary developments in finance, commerce, and industry. The directing spirits were different: the Protestant elites then fashioning the corporate world were less often drawn to the entertainment business, leaving it instead to a variety of ethnic entrepreneurs. These show biz men wrought changes in the way entertainment commodities were *produced*, but focused even more on restructuring the manner of their *distribution*. They fashioned and financed specific institutions, like vaudeville houses, legitimate theaters, nickelodeons, phonograph parlors, music-publishing houses, amusement parks, and motion picture palaces. But more crucially they established consortiums, corporations, chains, and circuits—the booking agencies, theatrical syndicates, patent-pooling arrangements, and composers associations that controlled the networks, run out of New York, whose business it was to deliver shows, songs, dances, and films to "the Road"—a.k.a. the USA.

This reconfiguring would affect every Gotham neighborhood, engendering a terrific expansion in the number and size of local entertainment venues—notably on Coney Island, Times Square's incandescent counterpart on Brooklyn's southern shore—but it was Times Square that emerged as New York's densest pleasure ganglion. And while it's tempting to pin Longacre's virtually overnight transformation on the IRT, mass transit facilitated the

"New Year's Fireworks at the Times Building, Times Square." *New York Times*, January 1, 1905.

upheaval, but didn't generate it. The primal driving force was the expansion, consolidation, and centralization of the theatrical industry. "There's No Business like Show Business," the song has it, but this was something most entertainment entrepreneurs wanted desperately to change. They eagerly sought to reproduce the kind of market domination achieved by their peers in manufacturing, commerce, and finance. And to a remarkable degree they did just that, with major consequences for the wider city.

BROADWAY

In the summer of 1896, six men sat down to lunch at the Holland House Hotel (Fifth and 30th). Over entrees, they hammered out a plan to monopolize the country's theatrical business. Free enterprise, they agreed, was making a mess of things. The conferees proposed to fashion a smoothly running machine out of the currently disjointed order. Like Rockefeller and Morgan, they would squelch competition, impose rationality, and make huge profits in the process.

Plays were customarily put together—overwhelmingly in New York City—by producers. These men found a script, raised money, assembled a cast, collected scenery and costumes, and rented a theater. If the show did well in the metropolis, the producers offered their property—duly certified as "Direct from New York"—to theater managers around the country. Each summer managers would come to New York to book shows for the coming season—rather as country merchants had once arrived to inspect wholesalers' clothing or hardware offerings.

In practice, glitches developed. Theater managers booked two or three attractions for the same night and took whichever showed up first. Producers scheduled the same performance in two cities on the same night and went where pickings looked best. The attendant chaos had been mitigated somewhat in the 1880s, when both sides had organized. Theater managers formed "circuits" and offered their collective venues, connected by convenient rail links, as a joint package. Producers turned to booking agents who assembled a group of plays and offered to fill a theater's entire season. But rivalries between and among bookers and circuits kept the system unsettled.

The Holland House diners—all booking agents and producers—were ideally positioned to remake the industry. Charles Frohman was the undisputed king of Broadway producers (and a famous starmaker: Ethel Barrymore and Maude Adams were among his luminaries). He also dispatched plays to theaters around the country. Also at table were Frohman's greatest rivals, Abraham Lincoln Erlanger and Marc Klaw, who dominated bookings throughout the South. They and the others now pooled their resources and created the Theatrical Syndicate. They set about regulating the flow of product out of New York and into the nation's theaters, demanding in return a percentage of each house's annual profit. Those who balked were muscled into acquiescence. If a theater didn't play ball, the Syndicate denied it shows or, worse, established a rival playhouse that offered superior productions at cut-rate prices until the holdout came to terms or shut up shop. Producers who didn't cooperate were frozen out of Syndicate theaters. Actors who signed with non-Syndicate producers were blacklisted. By 1904 it owned, leased, or controlled the bookings of more than 500 theaters, including all but two or three of the first-class houses in New York. In that same year, Klaw looked back at the founders' near-decade of work and pronounced it good: "The Theatrical Syndicate has brought order out of chaos," he declared, and "legitimate profit out of ruinous rivalry."

There was considerable truth to this claim, but—as with market domination achieved by oligarchs in other industries—their tactics had also generated vigorous opposition. The muckraking press denounced the Syndicate as yet another arrogant Trust, though in this instance the vilification sometimes took on an anti-Semitic quality—as when the *Dramatic Mirror* called the Syndicate a "Shylock combination." And indeed, the Syndicate was not the usual patrician Protestant operation: all its members were Jews—immigrants or the sons of immigrants. The theater business attracted Jews precisely because Protestant magnates wouldn't touch it—too risky, too risqué. Largely frozen out of the corporate and professional world, Jews found the stage appealingly open to talents.

Some of the moguls exacerbated their bad press with maladroit public relations. The paunchy, bulldog-faced Erlanger underlined his imperiousness by collecting Napoleana and putting his hand in his vest whenever interviewed. But basically the Syndicate shrugged off journalistic invective. They did, however, take note of moves by the few remaining independent producers—men like Hammerstein and David Belasco—to impede their drive to monopoly.

Hammerstein stayed stubbornly independent—partly a matter of personality, partly the distaste of maverick entrepreneurs for methodical organization men. Nor was he pleased that his beloved Olympia's constituent parts had fallen into Syndicate hands. (They'd renamed the Lyric the Criterion, reincarnated the Music Hall as the New York Theatre.) Hammerstein was able to resist Syndicate threats and blandishments because his Victoria, repositioned in 1904 as a full-time vaudeville house, was making pots of money with acts supplied by William Morris, the city's biggest independent agent of vaudeville talent. Hammerstein's Republic Theatre, however, the "legitimate" house next door, did prove susceptible to Syndicate pressure. Deprived of access to dramatic actors, or to the profits of the Road, the house became unsustainable. But rather than bend the knee, Hammerstein leased the Republic to David Belasco, an independent of another sort.

If Erlanger fancied himself the Napoleon of show business, Belasco claimed to be its high priest. The long-haired San Franciscan dressed the part: though Jewish, he wore black vestments and a collar turned back to front. After moving to New York, Belasco had developed a formidable reputation in the 1880s and 1890s as a playwright, stage manager, and producer, and had become deeply resentful of the Syndicate. Control of Hammerstein's theater, which he promptly renamed the Belasco, allowed him to spurn their pressure. Belasco, after all, could write much of his own material, draw on an established network of stars and pupils, and obtain capital from investors impressed by his track record. With his own playhouse he could hunker down outside the Syndicate's reach, and concentrate on perfecting his art, developing hyper-realistic scenery and startling effects, and writing plays that were spectacularly successful. (Puccini fell in love with two of them—*Madame Butterfly*, *Girl of the Golden West*—and made them into operas.) Belasco was the rare bird who could ignore the Syndicate, or even excoriate it. He particularly delighted in lambasting Erlanger—"the thugger, the slugger and the bulldozer of the trust." But Erlanger, equally, could afford to ignore Belasco.

The real threat to the Syndicate came from a trio of Jewish brothers who, while posing as anti-Trust warriors, aimed to replicate its success. Sam, Levi (Lee), and Jacob (J. J.) Shubert were sons of a Lithuanian peddler who, in 1882, had fled pogroms to the safe haven of Syracuse, New York. Little Sam—he was five feet four—went to work in the theatrical business, a world which had fascinated him ever since (at age 10) he had played a bit part in a Belasco road production that had come to town. Beginning as a ticket taker at the local

Opera House, at 15 Sam had become its treasurer. Then, with backing from a Syracuse clothier, he built a theater in Rochester and went on to acquire a circuit of upstate houses.

Dapper Sam had bigger ambitions. He wanted to be an impresario like Belasco and Frohman and produce shows on Broadway. So in March 1900 Sam and Lee entrained to New York, offered fealty to the Syndicate, leased the Herald Square Theatre, and hosted a smash-hit melodrama (with the young Lionel Barrymore attracting attention in a minor role). Next the Shuberts began acquiring or leasing theaters; by 1903 they controlled six, including the Casino, the temple of musical comedy. They also assembled houses out in the country, to the rapidly growing consternation of Klaw and Erlanger.

Then the Shuberts issued a more frontal challenge. In 1902 Klaw and Erlanger had commissioned noted theater architects Henry B. Herts and Hugh Tallant to build them a flagship playhouse on the south side of 42nd Street, near Seventh Avenue, directly across from Hammerstein's Victoria and Belasco's Belasco. Both were École des Beaux-Arts graduates and well aware of current European trends. In designing the New Amsterdam, they drew on the Art Nouveau style then sweeping Parisian boulevards. It opened October 26, 1903, to great acclaim. The problem was that precisely two weeks earlier, the Shuberts had opened *their* brand-new flagship theater, the Lyric, also to much applause, and also on 42nd, indeed, just across the street.

That tore it. The Syndicate issued an interdict, demanding all producers and actors boycott Shubert theaters on pain of being banned from Syndicate houses. Sam responded by calling for an "Open Door" policy (a term then being used by the US government in demanding equal access to Chinese markets). He urged theater owners, producers, and Broadway stars to join in liberating the theater from tyrannical Syndicate rule.

In 1905 the Shuberts' counteroffensive was momentarily derailed when Sam was killed in a train wreck. But Lee and J. J. carried on. They also incorporated the Shubert organization, something the Syndicate had not done. This gave them more stability and made them better able to bring in outside investors. By now the Shuberts had outgrown their upstate financial backers. They began relying on wealthy New Yorkers, like big-league attorney Samuel Untermyer, whose clients included leading Jewish financiers, and Andrew Freedman, an IRT subway insider, an associate of the House of Morgan, and someone well wired into Tammany Hall.

Banding together with Belasco and other independents, the Shuberts carried the theatrical war to the Syndicate. In a coup de théâtre, they announced a Sarah Bernhardt tour for the 1905–6 season, and when the Syndicate promptly (and foolishly) blacklisted her, the Shuberts put her on in city halls, second-class houses, even tents, and were hailed as trust busters. Huge crowds rallied to see the Divine Sarah (now 60), and help give the loathed Syndicate a black eye.

In 1906 the Shuberts strengthened their position considerably by assuming management of the largest theater on earth. The Hippodrome was the brainchild of Frederick Thompson and Elmer Dundy, amusement park impresarios who (in 1902) wrought a revolution down in Coney Island, and set out to do the same for Broadway. What New York needed, they believed, was a theater for its middling classes, the sort of people who wouldn't go to a low-end vaudeville house but couldn't afford two-dollar orchestra seats in "a fancy Broadway theatre among a lot of overdressed people." As this was potentially a huge untapped audience, the duo was able to win financial backing from Harry Black's United States Realty Corporation, which underwrote the $1.5 million cost of constructing the enormous structure on Sixth Avenue between 43rd and 44th.

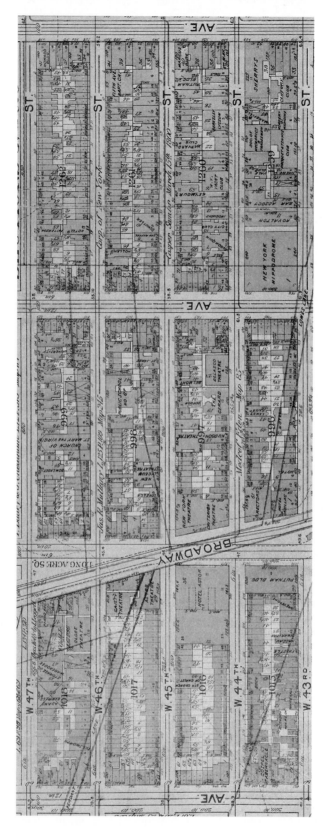

G. W. Bromley and Walter S. Bromley, "Plate 20: Bounded by W. 47th Street, E. 47th Street, Lexington Avenue, E. 36th Street, W. 36th Street, and Eighth Avenue," 1911. (New York Public Library, Lionel Pincus and Princess Firyal Map Division)

Amazing as was its gargantuan Moorish exterior, the Hippodrome's cavernous interior (seating 5,200 normally, 8,000 in a pinch) was still more so. Not only could its vast stage—twelve times larger than any theater on Broadway—handle a thousand performers at a time, or host an entire circus complete with elephants, but it was full of marvelous machinery. Like a 750,000-gallon water tank, 96 feet long and 14 feet deep, which did service as a lake or river, and could be raised or lowered on pistons; the *Engineering Record*, which normally stuck to reviewing bridges and such, lauded it as a "mechanical triumph of high order." Submerged semicircular conduits allowed for rapid movement of people and animals on and off stage, as when a cavalry charge raced from stage right to stage left, then circled beneath the audience to reemerge stage right, creating the illusion of an unceasing flow. Its initial production, in April 1905, was a triumphant success. In its first year, 3 million attended performances. Nevertheless, given the stupendous upkeep costs, the investors weren't making money. So in 1906 they fired the founders and turned management over to the Shuberts, who soon had it clearing nearly a million a year, without sacrificing immensely popular spectaculars—like onstage auto races, or naval engagements fought in the humongous tank.

In 1907 the Shuberts suffered a setback. They and other independents had been instrumental in winning a grand jury indictment of Klaw and Erlanger for conspiring to restrain trade, in violation of local antitrust laws. But though they (and Belasco) offered testimony about how their businesses had been hurt by Syndicate practices, the New York County Court of General Sessions ruled that plays were not commodities and that producing them was not a form of trade; hence restraint of trade was not possible (or actionable) in the industry. This greatly encouraged the Syndicate, which even began dreaming of expanding overseas. Klaw and Erlanger went so far as to propose incorporating a $100 million global syndicate to take control of the theaters of Germany, England, and France, a project punctured by the Panic of 1907.

So the Theater War went on, indeed expanded, triggering a building boom as the Shuberts struggled to multiply the number of outlets under their control—rather as the great railroad corporations had expanded (and duplicated) rail services. Nowhere were the repercussions greater than in New York City, the hub of the entire system. Because the contending parties needed products certified by metropolitan critics and audiences, they vied to build or lease ornate theaters to serve as showcases. The Shuberts, playing catch-up, were most prolific. They leased the Vanderbilts' American Horse Exchange (at Broadway and 50th), overhauled it, renamed it the Winter Garden, and opened it in March 1911 with Broadway newcomer Al Jolson. (Within a month he was a star.) In 1913 they erected the Sam S. Shubert Memorial Theatre, with Sam's picture in the lobby, on 44th between Broadway and Eighth Avenue. Just in back of it they put up the Booth, fronting on 45th. To provide private carriage access to both, they cut a small lane through the block, creating Shubert Alley. Clustered around this core would emerge the Bijou, Broadhurst, Morosco, and Plymouth. Nor did the brothers restrict themselves to Times Square; their houses soon included the Majestic at Columbus Circle, the Lincoln Square at West 67th, the Yorkville on East 86th, and the West End at 125th.

The building boom was further stoked by independent producers who needed a showcase of their own if they were to survive outside the Syndicate. Daniel Frohman (Charles's brother) moved uptown from the Lyceum at 23rd (demolished in 1902) to a new Lyceum at 45th (opened in 1903), a small Herts and Tallant theater with a monumental neoclassical facade. Belasco built the Stuyvesant on West 44th in 1907, changing its name to the Belasco in 1910 when he abandoned his eponymous 42nd Street venue. And Charles Dillingham had Carrère & Hastings build the Globe on Broadway and 46th in 1910.

By 1919 forty-five theaters had gone up in and around Times Square. Along with the playhouses, the industry's auxiliary businesses had drifted northward from Union Square: costumers, scenery makers, lighting companies, wigmakers, photographers. Soon the area was filled with rehearsal and tryout spaces, producers' and agents' offices, theatrical publishers and newspapers, boardinghouses for aspiring (and retired) performers, and houses of worship that catered to the theatrical community as well as to Hell's Kitchen parishioners.

By then there had been massive defections from the Syndicate on the part of regional circuits, and the Shuberts far surpassed it in number of theaters owned, leased, or booked. Most of the Holland House diners had died or retired, and while Erlanger would keep the remains of the Syndicate going awhile longer, it had clearly been hooked off the stage. But from the city's perspective, its passing was of little moment, as its successor, the Shubert Organization, had solidified metropolitan control of the national theatrical industry—it controlled more than 75 percent of the theater tickets sold in the United States—and had grounded it even more firmly in Times Square.

VAUDEVILLE

Like the Shuberts, vaudeville entrepreneurs Benjamin Franklin Keith and Edward Franklin Albee found the Syndicate an irresistible act to follow. Keith and Albee were New Englanders, long based in Boston where, in the 1880s, they'd been industry innovators. Their "continuous vaudeville" enhanced attendance by having eight or nine acts performed in a row, with each sequence repeated four to six times daily, from ten in the morning till ten at night. This eliminated downtime and allowed patrons to drop in and leave whenever they chose. They also established a theatrical "circuit" that coordinated the movement of acts between different houses in Boston, then between different cities in New England. In 1893 they extended the Keith Circuit—Keith got top billing, but Albee was the real organizer—down to New York, taking over the Union Square Theatre at 58 East 14th Street. They thus invaded the domain of Tony Pastor, Gotham's grand old man of vaudeville, whose 14th Street Theatre was just a block farther east, near Third Avenue, at number 143, the structure he shared with Tammany Hall.

Pastor, whose career as performer-manager dated to the era of minstrelsy and P. T. Barnum, was arguably the inventor of vaudeville. Back in the 1870s and 1880s he had cleaned up his male-oriented "variety" show, scrubbing away raunchy acts (which peeled off into burlesque) while adding those "catering to polite tastes"; he also made his theater comfortable for women and children by banning drinking, smoking, prostitution, and male rowdies. Keith (a Catholic) and Albee (an Episcopalian) had followed suit, even more rigorously, scrutinizing the content of acts line by line, and pledging audiences that "nothing shall be given which could not with perfect safety be introduced to their homes." Not for nothing did vaudevillians refer to the Keith theaters as the Sunday School Circuit.

Unlike Pastor, Keith and Albee were empire builders, and in 1900 they took the lead in forming the Association of Vaudeville Managers (AVM), which brought together managers of sixty leading vaudeville theaters, from Boston to San Francisco. The duo hoped the consortium would end damaging competition between theaters, organize the booking and circulation of performers more efficiently, and tamp down the pay of actors who had "taken advantage of the sudden growth of vaudeville and the subsequent brisk demand for acts to inflate their salaries."

The central office was established in New York, in the St. James Building, at Broadway and 26th.

B. F. KEITH'S
NEW UNION SQUARE THEATRE.

Performance Continuous from 1.30 to 10.30 P. M.
(Doors open at 1 o'clock P. M.)

598TH CONSECUTIVE WEEK
– OF –

Refined and High-Class Vaudeville,
COMMENCING MONDAY, AUGUST 28, 1905.

SPECIAL NOTICE.—Positively no fees of any kind are permitted in this theatre. Patrons are respectfully requested not to disobey this rule, as we desire all our patrons treated alike, and this becomes an impossibility where fees are given for courtesies extended by our employees. Everything is free after you purchase your ticket, and the encouragement of our fee-nuisance disarranges our system of extending courtesies and makes it impossible for all of our patrons to receive the attentions which are due them.

Acts are run only in the order given when function to do so and are subject to change without notice. It should also be noted that the order in which they are placed in the programme does not necessarily indicate the value of acts.   SEE STAGE SIGNS.

A   Overture   KEITH'S ORCHESTRA—Emil Katzenstein, Director.
March—"The Gridiron Button"..........................Ernest Hall

B   Stereopticon   Miscellaneous Subjects.

C   Charles and Katherine Gibson   Presenting their Serio-Comic Playlet, "THE BURGLAR'S KIT."

D   Great Chick   The Wizard of the Wheel.

E   The Alpha Trio   Comedy Hoop Jugglers.

F   Jack and Bertha Rich   Refined Talking and Dancing Duo.

G   Charles Serra   Creator of his Original and Unique Gymnastic Act on the White Column.

H   Halladay and Leonard   Kings of Irish Comedy

I   William Bonelli and Company
— IN —
"THE PINK WIDOW."
By Brandon Hurst.
CAST
Reginald Rackett..........................William Bonelli
Judy Downeast............................Lonnie Deane
Modena West.............................S. S. Wiltsie

**J   First Appearance in Vaudeville.
Klekko and Fravoli**   Selections from "Trovatore."
(Late of Metropolitan Opera Company.)

K   Ellis-Nowlan Trio   Eccentric Comedy Acrobats.

**L   Innovation Extraordinary,
The Great Lafayette**   In Remarkable and Astounding Protean Changes, Presenting a Series of Novelties New to Art Theatre going Public.

M   Cliff Gordon   The German Politician.

N   The Great Lafayette   AND HIS TRAVESTY BAND
Presenting Humorous Impersonation of the World's Noted Musical Directors.

O   Keith's Motion Pictures (The Kinetograph)
Showing an Excellent List of Interesting and Humorous Subjects.
MR. KANYOUSPELLIT AND HIS AIRSHIP.
PLAYMATES.
THE GAY WASHERWOMEN.
THE WONDERFUL ALBUM.
MODERN BRIGANDS.

ENTIRE CHANGE OF PROGRAMME WEEKLY

RED LIGHTS INDICATE EXITS.

Programme printed, published and controlled by Frank V. Strauss & Co., 108-114 Wooster Street, New York.

"B. F. Keith's New Union Square Theatre: 598th Consecutive Week of Refined and High-Class Vaudeville," August 28, 1905. (Smithsonian Institution, Warshaw Collection of Business Americana, National Museum of American History)

Like Klaw and Erlanger, Keith and Albee had to deal with managers who preferred to remain independent. Men like F. F. Proctor, who controlled five New York venues and was a highly successful practitioner of continuous vaudeville: his slogan was "After Breakfast Go to Proctor's, After Proctor's Go to Bed." Or Percy Williams, who had thirteen theaters in the city and was particularly strong in Brooklyn. And then there was the dapper Oscar Hammerstein, resplendent these days in Prince Albert coat, striped pants, silk top hat, and Vandyke goatee, who was doing a bang-up business at the Victoria. Hammerstein eschewed the "drop in anytime" approach, more appropriate for local neighborhoods, and presented just two shows a day, each four to five hours long, aimed at people who traveled to Times Square on mass transit. Nor were all Victoria acts squeaky clean; indeed, the house retained much of the raw character of the older male-oriented variety houses, especially after Oscar turned over management to his son Willie, who was given to bawdy or sensational acts— exotic dancers, Jack Johnson (the black heavyweight champ), a pair of women murderesses he billed as the Shooting Stars. The Hammersteins also encouraged their discerning audience to rowdily express approval or disapproval: "You can put on a whistler or any old kind of act at Keith's and they shout themselves hoarse over it," said Oscar, "but here they know what is what."

In 1906 Albee tightened the screws on Hammerstein and the other holdouts. (By then Keith had begun to lose interest in the business, and by 1909 he'd withdrawn completely.) He set up a United Booking Office (UBO), also at 26th Street, and now decreed that member circuits across the country could no longer hire performers on their own; they had to take whatever acts were dispatched from New York. Houses that didn't book through the UBO would be blacklisted. Over the next year, subject to heavy pressure, Williams, Proctor, and even Hammerstein fell into line, though the latter extracted a promise of exclusive rights to midtown Manhattan vaudeville. William Morris, the independent agent who had been supplying acts to the dissidents, drawn from his extensive network of talent, was now driven out of business (though only for the moment). By 1907 virtually every major manager in the eastern United States was booking through the UBO. Martin Beck's Orpheum Circuit, which controlled big-time vaudeville west of the Mississippi, coordinated with the consortium in an informal way. The UBO regime exempted small-time houses, run by local promoters like Marcus Loew or William Fox, who offered small-time acts, at lower ticket prices, to neighborhood working-class markets.

For a moment in 1907, the UBO was menaced by a potentially dangerous rival, when the Theatrical Syndicate and the Shuberts, hitherto mortal enemies, joined in incorporating a United States Amusement Company, capitalized at $100 million, a potential US Steel of vaudeville. Klaw and Erlanger had decided to enter Keith/Albee territory, and they convinced the Shuberts that both would benefit if together they broke the UBO's power. But the novice vaudevillians proved no match for Albee, who ruthlessly blacklisted actors who dared jump ship, and with the panic-led collapse of the larger economy, the allies backed off, their retreat sweetened by a $250,000 payoff from Albee in exchange for their commitment to keep out of vaudeville for a decade.

From then on it was pretty much smooth sailing for the UBO, its constituent circuits, and the outlying small-time impresarios, and the city experienced a decade or so of rampant construction. By the end of the 1910s, New York was saturated with vaudeville halls. In Manhattan they glissandoed upward from downtown venues like Loew's Delancey (at Suffolk and Delancey) and Keith's Jefferson on 14th Street through a dense string of venues along upper Broadway (ten theaters went up between 59th and 110th in 1911–12 alone); and on to a dense cluster of stages in Harlem: the Regent (at 116th, whose façade by prolific theater architect Thomas Lamb recalled the Doge's Palace in Venice), Hurtig & Seamon's (at 125th, later the Apollo), the Gotham (also 125th), the Alhambra (at 126th), and the Audubon, at 166th (another Lamb confection, complete with ballroom).

The outer boroughs were equally well represented; performers used to touring the continent by rail joked that they could now ply the Subway Circuit. Brooklyn was blanketed with theaters. Vaudevillians who wanted to assemble a Kings County route could have started at the Manhattan Beach or New Brighton in Coney Island; headed up to the B. S. Moss Flatbush, the Prospect, and the Bushwick; played the Bedford or the Fulton; hit the Strand or the Orpheum, cheek by jowl on Fulton; and finish farther north at the Novelty in Williamsburg, or at the Greenpoint. Bronx actors could have hop-skipped their way up from the National or the Bronx (both at the Hub) to the Boulevard, then the McKinley Square, before winding up at the Crotona and the Tremont.

The center of the industry remained rooted in Times Square, especially after one last competitive rumpus in 1913, when Martin Beck, master of western vaudeville, decided to come east and plant an outlet for his Orpheum Circuit right in the middle of Manhattan. Shredding the gentleman's agreement he'd made with the UBO, Beck commissioned construction of the Palace, an eleven-story office-building-cum-luxury-theater, on Broadway between 46th and 47th Streets. Not only was this a frontal challenge to Albee; it also violated Hammerstein's UBO-guaranteed monopoly on Times Square vaudeville. But even before it opened on March 24, 1913, an infuriated Albee had upended Beck's plan. By means that remain murky, Albee forced Beck to hand over three-quarters of the building's ownership and to settle instead for the right to choose which acts the Palace would book, drawn only from the slate of UBO-approved performers. Not only did Albee wrest away control of Beck's theater, he made it the center of his own empire, moving both Keith Circuit and UBO headquarters to the theater's sixth floor.

In short order, the two-a-day offerings at the Palace were rivaling those at Hammerstein's Victoria, thanks to star turns by Ethel Barrymore and Sarah Bernhardt (now 70, and making her debut on a vaudeville stage). Albee had paid the always cash-strapped Hammerstein $200,000 to relinquish his exclusive rights. But in 1914, his son Willie died of Bright's disease, aged 42, and Oscar—demoralized and ill—decided to pack it in. In 1915 he sold off the Victoria. Now the Palace would be the Valhalla of Vaudeville, and soon "playing the Palace" would become synonymous with big-time success. (Albee, characteristically, forced acts who wanted to perform there to take a pay cut.)

As in the theater world, New York's Times Square had become the capital of the national vaudeville scene. When B. F. Keith died in 1914, one obituary called the UBO organization he and Albee had created "probably the greatest consolidation of money and power in the entertainment world"—and declared it an entity that "ranks with the most important of America's industrial combinations."

OF RATS AND ACTORS

Before attaining the summit of their respective industries, both Keith/Albee and Klaw/Erlanger had to battle labor activists as well as rival capitalists.

The Association of Vaudeville Managers' unilateral move to reorganize the industry in 1900 was not well received by vaudeville's acting class. Keith and Albee claimed their new order was advantageous for workers, as it guaranteed them forty weeks of employment a year.

But the job security came at a stiff price. Actors had to accept whatever routing and salary was offered them, they could no longer work for any producer who sought to hire them, and they had to kick back 5 percent of their wages to the middlemen. Also, "continuous vaudeville," with its repetition of acts, greatly increased their workload, while "clean vaudeville" subjected them to censorship. And given that managers were allowed to cancel acts at will, a privilege denied the workers, their supposed job security was seriously compromised. Perhaps most disturbing was the sudden subordination to autocratic administrators and businessmen. As Groucho Marx recalled his dealings with Albee, actors were ushered into his private lair, where "the Ol' Massa" sat behind a desk "about eighty feet long, or so it seemed," and the poor player had to "humbly listen while Albee informed him what his salary would be for the coming season."

Their response came swiftly. No sooner was the employer consortium created than performers founded an employee association, called the White Rats. It was modeled on the Grand Order of the Water Rats launched in 1889 by London's music-hall artists. The primary organizer, George Fuller Golden, was a vaudevillian (monologues were his specialty) who had joined the Water Rats while working in England. Golden and the seven other initiators, all men, were alarmed by what they saw as the emergence of a "gigantic vaudeville trust" that would undermine their manly independence. Seeing themselves as a band of brothers, and the Rats as a cross between fraternal organization and skilled labor union, they barred women from membership, despite the significant female presence in the trade. Within a year the White Rats—"white" being an accurate adjective given that blacks were also barred— had enrolled hundreds of clowns, magicians, acrobats, and dancers, both regular troupers and top acts like George M. Cohan and Eddie Foy.

In February 1901, a thousand members strong, the Rats struck the AVM. Members boycotted syndicate theaters, closed some houses, and won substantial sympathy from press and public (including managers Tony Pastor and the duo of Koster and Bial). Benefit performances on behalf of striking actors were hugely successful, with audiences shouting, "Down with the trusts." After a few weeks, the managers rescinded the 5 percent commission requirement, and the Rats called off their walkout, then held a victory benefit at Koster & Bial's. The rejoicing was premature. The AVM had made a (temporary) concession but retained control of the industry. When the Rats opened their own cooperative booking office, it worked poorly, as Keith and Albee controlled the theaters and could woo stars with fabulous salaries and threaten lesser souls with blacklisting. The 5 percent commission was reinstated. Soon the Rats dwindled in numbers, and the coast was clear for instituting the United Booking Office, with its even more onerous controls, like requiring job applicants to swear they were not Rats. "All my life actors have been gypping me," Albee gloated. "Now I am going to gyp them."

Then the Panic of 1907 hit Broadway—hard. Plays failed, road companies collapsed, and by mid-November an estimated 3,000 actors were unemployed. But hard times also sparked a revival of the Rats, paced by a British music-hall performer and militant trade unionist named Harry Mountford. Having been active in a strike against London theater managers, and subsequently blacklisted, Mountford relocated to New York City. Invited to help reorganize the White Rats, he threw himself into the work, and by 1910 membership had climbed to 11,000, a headquarters had been established on West 46th Street, a sister organization (the Associated Actresses of America) had been launched, and Mountford had obtained a charter from American Federation of Labor (AFL) chief Samuel Gompers that made the Rats exclusive bargaining agent for all thespians.

IN THE MEANTIME, "LEGITIMATE" ACTORS HAD EMBARKED on a more hesitant response to the emergence of the Theatrical Syndicate in 1896. Some actors had been shocked into protest—chiefly stars who felt they had lost control of the profession to a group of commercial philistines—but their efforts at organizing were hampered by debates over the appropriate response. It was one thing for vaudevillians to tie up with the AFL; they were seen (and looked down upon) as rough-and-tumble performers defined as much by physicality as by artistry. It was similarly fine for stagehands—the manual laborers who had worked around the clock for maybe fifty cents a day—to have come together in 1894 when the National Alliance of Theatrical Stage Employees was chartered by the AFL. But stage players aspired to high-culture status, and while it was acceptable to come together in fraternal or professional associations, anything that smacked of labor organizing seemed to threaten their standing as artists. Broadway actors were also more deeply divided among themselves than were the vaudevillians, as the star system afforded immense prestige and vast salaries to a handful of players at the top, but only meager rewards to the far greater number of performers who eked out a living at its base.

Still, in 1913 an uneasy alliance was cobbled together between headliners, seeking to recover their accustomed autonomy vis-à-vis theatrical entrepreneurs, and common players, for whom job insecurity was the abiding issue. Together they established the Actors' Equity Association (AEA). At first it leaned toward a strictly professional identity, but management intransigence—the Shuberts rejected the AEA's call for a standard theatrical contract—tilted the balance toward greater militancy.

Nevertheless, when in 1915 Harry Mountford sought to explore a White Rats–Actor's Equity alliance, looking toward industry-wide action, the AEA balked. AFL rules allowed only one union per trade, and Equity members refused to take a back seat to vaudevillians; the cultural gulf was too wide and deep. Instead they urged Gompers to revoke the Rats' charter and transfer it to a new umbrella organization. Mountford resisted, and Gompers refused. But the AEA's obvious warming to unionism alarmed the Shuberts and led them to a more conciliatory stance. They offered to settle outstanding grievances. The AEA, believing the Shuberts were acting in good faith (a belief of which they were soon to be disabused), shelved their plans to affiliate with the AFL.

The Rats, left to their own devices, went ahead in 1916 with a general strike against the UBO. It ended in catastrophic defeat, and the near-total disintegration of the organization. For the moment, both Albee and the Shuberts—perched in their Times Square offices three blocks apart—were left in untrammeled possession of their respective theatrical fields.

TIN PAN ALLEY

Some members of the songwriting trade—the third leg of Gotham's show biz—may have dreamed of establishing the kind of control achieved by their theatrical counterparts, but the popular music business remained competitive. What it did become was more industrialized and more centralized in New York City.

The sheet music business had taken off dramatically in the 1890s in tandem with the spread of vaudeville houses. Performers who had been used to writing their own ditties couldn't keep up with the booming demand for fresh material. Increasingly they turned to professional songwriters. Households eager to sing these latest tunes and play them on their parlor piano sent sheet music (and piano) sales surging. The enormous profits that some hit tunes earned for existing publishing houses drew a slew of new ones into the business.

Overwhelmingly these were established in Gotham. Previously there had been some regional diversity in the trade, but rarely after 1900 did a national hit originate in any city other than New York. Indeed, after the turn of the century, the nation's popular musical course was effectively steered from one single block in Manhattan. By 1909, when journalist Monroe Rosenfeld wrote a series of articles about the popular music business for the *Herald*, the industry's geographical center had shifted from Union Square to 28th Street between Sixth and Broadway. This one strip housed at least twenty-one music firms at one point or another, including nearly all the major ones. On his visit there, the din of pianists displaying their musical wares reminded Rosenfeld of tin pans clanging; hence "Tin Pan Alley."

"Tin Pan Alley," 28th Street between Fifth and Sixth Avenues, ca. 1905.

Overwhelmingly the new firms were established by thoroughly assimilated, American-born, middle-class German Jews. There had been a smattering of other ethnic houses, but by 1910 most of them had disappeared. The industry was now led by men such as Louis Bernstein, Leo Feist, Max Dreyfus, Charles K. Harris, Edward Marks, Jerome Remick, Maurice Shapiro, Ted Snyder, Joseph Stern, and the three Witmark brothers, Isidore, Julius, and Jay. The reasons for their success were many. Germans had brought a profound musical tradition with them from the old country, and established a powerful presence in other branches of American music (operas, symphonies); popular songs were yet another outlet for their talents. Many had worked as salesmen before going into publishing: Isidore Witmark had sold water filters; Stern, neckties; Marks, notions; Feist, corsets; Dreyfus, picture frames and ribbons. Salesmanship trained them in cultivating novelty, responding rapidly to shifts in consumer tastes and desires, and in general for selling music as they had once hawked dry goods.

In the new century, Alley publishers transformed songwriting into an industry, comfortably mixing art and commerce. It was widely agreed, as the *Music Trade Review* argued in 1910, that "songs may be properly classed with the staples, and are manufactured, advertised, and distributed in much the same manner as ordinary commodities." In that same year, the *New York Times* characterized Tin Pan Alley as a group of "popular song factories"—a bit hyperbolic, but the publishing houses indeed developed a sharper division of labor and a higher level of professionalism in these years. At the top of each house, the publishers embodied the managerial ethos sweeping through the business world in general. They oversaw a growing cadre of staff songwriters, who provided a steady supply of standardized musical products in a few general categories—parlor ballads, show songs, dance tunes—altering them slightly to generate a sense of novelty, much as fashions were shifted in the rag trade. One notch down were the arrangers, who tailored a piece of music to the needs (and available instruments) of a particular performer or group.

Paired with this production team was a promotional crew, devoted to getting songs into circulation. "Pluggers" were the key players here, as they had been for a long time, energetic young men who would pick up freshly minted sheet music in the morning, then spend the day and night performing the pieces, or cajoling others into doing so. As in the past, they would make the rounds of the city's restaurants, cafés, dance halls, hotels, parks, elevated trains, baseball games, and political rallies. But increasingly they interfaced with large enterprises, like department stores such as Siegel-Cooper and Macy's, which established music counters where publisher reps would give song demonstrations. And in the core vaudeville business, it was no longer a matter of corralling individuals and singing their wares at them but of plugging into the now nationally organized vaudeville networks.

Tin Pan Alley firms grew rapidly in the 1900s, from one-room operations into substantial concerns. Each publishing house now needed a suite of demonstration rooms, maybe even a small auditorium, in which vaudeville artists who stopped by before setting out to troop cross-country could have lyricists and accompanists teach them new numbers, fitting song to singer on the spot. Firms also required rooms for house arrangers, libraries, stock rooms, band and orchestra departments, shipping departments, sales departments, and publicity departments.

Publishers needed more space. They also needed to stay close to the northwardly migrating theater district, to which their fortunes were so closely tied. So during the 1910s Tin Pan Alley, too, decamped and headed up to Times Square, with most of the majors settling into new quarters throughout the West 40s, and many small-to-medium-sized firms clustering in the Exchange Building at 145 West 45th Street.

IN THE SAME YEARS THAT THE MUSIC-WRITING BUSINESS BURGEONED, notably in the boom decade of 1897 to 1907, a cognate music-recording industry emerged and surged, though it wasn't at first clear to Alley publishers whether it was friend or foe.

In 1877 Edison had invented a device that could record and play back sound. It was a primitive affair—a strip of tinfoil wrapped around a revolving drum—and produced results that were barely audible. Yet it was miraculous, and seemingly bursting with possibilities for development. The Wizard put it aside, though—too many other inventions on his plate, notably the electric light—and it lay there for nearly ten years. Only when other inventors began coming out with improved versions did he turn back to it, in 1886, and he soon came up with both a better technology (removable wax cylinders) and a potentially profitable use (as a dictating machine).

In 1888 he set up the North American Phonograph Company to lease Edison machines to regional subsidiaries. In 1889 a group of Washington, DC, businessmen incorporated as the Columbia Phonograph Company, hoping to market Edison products to federal government offices. The equipment proved unreliable, bankruptcy loomed, and to stay afloat, the company began producing and selling pre-recorded musical cylinders, notably marches played by the Washington-based United States Marine Band. The purchasers were entertainment-oriented entrepreneurs who began placing coin-operated machines, equipped with multi-tube listening attachments, in saloons, amusement parks, ice cream parlors, drugstores, and soon in arcades devoted to such mechanical contraptions. These ventures were spectacularly successful—in Gotham hundreds of arcades would blossom—convincing Columbia, and even Edison, that the future of the technology lay in recording music, not dictating memos.

The mounting demand spurred growth (in the early 1890s) of small recording studios like the New York Phonograph Company (257 Fifth Avenue), which captured local vaudeville acts on cylinders. Edison and Columbia, which remained in the forefront, soon realized that if there were a way to enable people to play back cylinders in their own homes, the resulting profits would dwarf those reaped in public venues. By 1896 Edison had developed a sturdy spring-driven device for home use, and set up a new firm, National Phonograph (at Broadway and 26th), to market both cylinders and the new twenty-dollar machines manufactured in West Orange, New Jersey. Columbia followed suit and by 1897 was selling a rival model for ten dollars. The low-priced phonographs and the lifting of the depression touched off a boom in the fledgling industry.

Columbia now decided to move to New York, where sales were strongest and content providers most plentiful. In 1897 the company set up executive headquarters on the fifteenth floor of the Tribune Building (154 Nassau Street) and placed sales outlets and a recording studio near Tin Pan Alley; its machines were produced at a plant in Bridgeport, Connecticut. By 1900 Columbia had opened offices across the country, and in Paris, Berlin, and London as well. Along with Edison's National, it was poised to dominate the industry.

Then both were upstaged by a newcomer with a technological edge. Back in 1888 Emile Berliner, a young German immigrant, had invented a simpler way to record sound by using flat discs rather than cylinders; he had taught himself the necessary physics studying at night in Cooper Union's library. In 1894 Berliner persuaded a group of businessmen to back formation of a United States Gramophone Company. To solve certain technical problems Berliner turned to Eldridge R. Johnson, a gifted machinist who owned a small machine shop in Camden, New Jersey. Johnson made and patented many improvements in Berliner's disc technology. In 1901 he absorbed Berliner's operation and incorporated it as the Victor

Talking Machine Company. In 1903 Victor and Columbia, which had also switched to discs, agreed to pool patents and cross-license products; Edison stubbornly stuck to cylinders and fell behind. The two corporations thus emerged as the principal powers in the industry, Victor based in Camden, Columbia in New York City (where in 1913 it would move to the new Woolworth Building).

The duo continued their competition, but now primarily on the terrain of musical content, and here Victor pulled ahead, though it had to come to New York to do so. Johnson decided to delineate his brand by associating it with Old World Culture and Serious Art. In 1903 he established Red Seal Records, which at first featured eminent European concert artists, recorded abroad by Victor's UK affiliate, and then, in 1904, stars from New York's Metropolitan Orchestra, preeminently Enrico Caruso. The company signed the great tenor to an exclusive contract, paying him by far the largest fee accorded any recording artist up to that time. Then it captured his magnificent voice in a small Recording Laboratory in Carnegie Hall's Annex (soon relocated to larger quarters down on 28th Street, near Tin Pan Alley). In 1906 Caruso did a duet with Antonio Scotti—"Solenne in quest'ora" from Verdi's *La Forza del Destino*—which sold in awesome numbers. By 1907 Nellie Melba, Emma Eames, and Geraldine Farrar were also Victor artists. To trumpet the association, Victor erected a huge illuminated facsimile of Nipper, its trademark quizzical-looking dog ("His Master's Voice"), above the legend "The Opera at Home," on the roof of an office building just south of the Metropolitan, illuminated by more than a thousand light bulbs.

Geraldine Farrar, facing left, with right arm on Victrola, as Carmen, ca. 1915. (Library of Congress Prints and Photographs Division)

Victor also vigorously advertised the Red Seal series in more conventional print media, promoting it as "music of the highest class," hence worthy of a higher class of patron (particularly those who could afford a higher price point). The machines that played these wonderful discs were also touted as an aid to uplift, worthy of replacing the piano in the parlor. This claim was given added force in 1906 when Victor introduced the Victrola, which replaced the large protruding horn that had mesmerized Nipper with one concealed in a handsome wooden cabinet, making it an appropriate piece of parlor furniture, fit (said the ads) for "the best class of people."[1]

Not to be outdone, Columbia quickly arranged to record several Metropolitan stars at its own 26th Street studio, and played catch-up on machine design. However, it never managed to match the Victor Company's high technical and artistic standards, much less its Caruso contract, and it settled into the number-two position in the high-culture field. Columbia would parlay its New York location into a flourishing business recording Tin Pan Alley tunes, eventually forcing Victor, which had required pop artists to trek to Philly or Camden, into expanding its presence in Gotham.

IT MIGHT BE SUPPOSED THAT NEW YORK'S MUSIC PUBLISHERS were delighted by the arrival of the new recording industry, which was, in large measure, playing their songs. The problem was that they weren't being paid for such usage. Worse, they had no legal recourse. The law barring unauthorized reproduction of copyrighted material referred only to making copies of their printed sheet music. Phonograph companies contended that as their discs were not "copies" of sheet music, they owed the composers nothing. The publishers took their case to Congress, with the Witmarks leading the campaign to update the copyright code. The recording industry, led by Columbia and Victor, strongly opposed any changes. The publishers won, and the 1909 Copyright Act required manufacturers to pay royalties to composers and publishers for "mechanical reproductions" of their work.

A similar battle broke out over live performances of copyrighted music in ballrooms, dance halls, restaurants, hotels, and theaters. Publishers demanded royalties. Institutions and musicians argued they had sufficiently compensated publishers by purchasing their sheet music—for pennies—and could do as they pleased with their possession. In October 1913 a small group of publishers and songwriters met at Luchow's German restaurant (110 East 14th Street) to form a trade organization. Called the American Society of Composers, Authors, and Publishers (ASCAP), its goal was to license its members' works en masse to subscriber organizations (hotels, restaurants, etc.). After its formal founding in February 1914, at the Hotel Claridge in Times Square, many of Tin Pan Alley's firms joined right away. One of ASCAP's principal founders, Victor Herbert, sued Shanley's Times Square restaurant for playing his songs without permission or payment. In 1915 Judge Learned Hand ruled against Herbert in the US District Court for the Southern District of New York, finding that people went to Shanley's for the food, not the music. In January 1917 the US Supreme Court reversed him, with Justice Oliver Wendell Holmes Jr. finding that music was indeed part of what drew paying customers—that's why Shanley's provided it—and as the purpose of playing was profit, publishers and composers were entitled to royalties.

---

1. Phonographs began to displace parlor pianos, and the piano industry (a substantial one in Gotham) riposted with automatic player-pianos, an intermediate form, for which one purchased piano rolls.

AT THE SAME TIME THAT THE CITY'S THEATRICAL, MUSICAL, AND VAUDEVILLIAL sectors were in full transformational swing, a brand-new medium arrived in town. It seemed at first a minor addition to the entertainment menu—the basis for a novelty industry that would fit comfortably if marginally into the established order. Then, suddenly, that industry began to expand, and with tremendous speed. Then it consolidated, and centralized, and became a colossus. Then, even more astonishingly, just as it was on the point of being acknowledged as the fourth full-fledged jewel in Gotham's show biz crown, this shooting star kept soaring, shot out of the city's sight, and was gone.

MOVIES

On April 23, 1896, crowds flocked to Koster & Bial's Music Hall on 34th Street to see "Thomas A. Edison's latest marvel, the Vitascope." The Vitascope proved to be a machine that projected moving images on a twenty-foot screen set in a gilded frame. Six shorts were shown. The *Umbrella Dance* was performed by two showgirls. *The Monroe Doctrine* attacked British meddling in Venezuela. But the hit of the screening was *Rough Sea at Dover*—a "view of an angry surf breaking on a sandy beach near a stone pier," which, the *Times* reviewer observed, "amazed the spectators." At the end there was "vociferous cheering" and "loud calls for Mr. Edison." The great inventor was uncharacteristically silent. Appropriately so, as the Vitascope was in fact not his creation but that of Thomas Armat, the man working the projector.

Despite the false advertising in this instance, Edison had indeed been active in the nascent motion picture industry. During the late 1880s and early 1890s, while inventors in the United States, Britain, France, and Germany raced to perfect cameras and projectors, Edison had roughed out a possible approach and set his assistant William K. L. Dickson to implementing it. Working in the new Edison lab in West Orange, New Jersey, roughly fifteen miles west of Manhattan, they developed a working Kinetograph (camera) and Kinetoscope (peep-show playback machine). In 1893 they began making mini-films in a tar-papered studio, with a retractable roof that they called the Black Maria, after police vans of the day.

In April 1894 Edison rigged up twenty-five Kinetoscopes with nickel slot attachments. He sold ten of them to two entrepreneurs, who opened the Holland Brothers' Kinetoscope Parlor in 1155 Broadway (at 27th Street). For twenty-five cents patrons could peer into five of the machines, each running short strips with titles like *Blacksmiths*, *Cock Fight*, and *Wrestling*. Crowds came, and soon the male-oriented penny arcades along the Bowery, 14th, and 125th Streets were setting peep shows alongside their coin-operated phonographs, muscle-testing apparatus, and fortune-telling machines.

To meet growing demand, the new Edison Manufacturing Company turned out Kinetoscopes, and films to view with them. Throughout 1894 assorted vaudeville celebrities (Buffalo Bill, strongman Eugen Sandow, Spanish dancer Carmencita) ferried over from Manhattan to appear before Dickson's camera. Edison, a fight fan, arranged the filming of bouts, including one with Gentleman Jim Corbett. The expanding catalog also included soft-core items like *Hot Stuff*, *Here's Married Life*, and *Scenes in a Massage Parlor*.

Having to squint into machines on a one-by-one basis curtailed audience development. By 1895 the novelty had worn off, and demand and profits were tapering downward. The obvious next step was to move from peep shows to projectors, which could throw the images up on a screen, allowing for simultaneous mass consumption. But Edison's lab failed to crack some critical technological problems. So when inventor Armat showed up with his working

Vitascope, Edison agreed enthusiastically to mass-produce the projector, supply its purchasers with films, and wrap it in his Wizard's mystique by advertising it as "Edison's Vitascope." Yet even as his team moved toward its Koster & Bial demonstration, news arrived that on December 28, 1895, the Lumière brothers' hand-cranked Cinématographe had astounded a Parisian audience, projecting scenes of a train pulling into a station and workers leaving a factory. Scooped, the Edisonians worked furiously to one-up the Parisians. After the Vitascope's belated debut in April 1896, they produced a portable camera, brought it to Herald Square on May 11, shot the locale from a second-story window, and the following week added the footage to their Koster & Bial playlist, allowing those inside the 34th Street house to see the bustling streetscape just outside.

Meanwhile, vaudeville-meister B. F. Keith, not to be outdone by his uptown K&B competitor, struck a deal with the Lumières. On June 29, 1896, his Union Square Theater gave the Cinématographe its first American outing, to great acclaim. In November the Lumières established their own agency in Gotham, and began supplying Keith theaters with a touring service that included use of a portable camera-projector, the services of a technician, and a weekly allotment of filmlets, heavy on scenes shot in foreign lands. Keith soon broke with the Lumières, believing their projector was rapidly becoming outmoded, given its incompatibility with the Edisonian standard adopted by most US and English filmmakers. Keith, however, turned not to Edison himself but to the Wizard's former assistant William Dickson, who had gone out on his own, tinkered away, and come up with a superior projector. Dickson and associates also established a New Jersey corporation, American Mutoscope (eventually renamed Biograph); this allowed them to tap substantial capital pools and to start selling rival machines—produced in a plant in Hoboken—and rival films as well.

Soon Edison and Biograph (and Vitagraph, a newcomer created in 1897 by two young English immigrants) were slugging it out on the New York skyline, each production facility perched atop the sunlit roof of a tall Manhattan tower.

Edison had quickly realized his New Jersey studio was irksomely far from performers—as well as suppliers of backdrops, costumes, props, etc.—so he built a glass-enclosed studio on the roof of 41 East 21st Street that opened for business in February 1901. There, with Edwin S. Porter in charge of production, the Edison Manufacturing Company began cranking out films, including Porter's twelve-minute blockbuster *The Great Train Robbery* (1903). Short on space, Edison opened another studio in 1907, at Decatur Avenue and Oliver Place, on the periphery of Bronx Park, a perfect site for outdoor shooting; by 1908 it was producing a film a week.

Vitagraph opted for the top of the Morse Building, at Nassau and Beekman, where in 1897 it shot its first film, appropriately titled *Burglar on the Roof.* In 1905, also in need of expansion, it relocated to a large tract in Flatbush (at East 15th and Locust Avenue).

The first studio of the Biograph Company was constructed (in 1896) on the roof of 841 Broadway at 13th Street in Manhattan. Quite similar to the Black Maria that Dickson had designed for Edison, the contraption was mounted on circular tracks to facilitate a hot pursuit of the sun. In 1906 the company moved indoors, to a brownstone at 11 East 14th Street, where it became the first studio to use all artificial light. This was made possible by the timely invention in 1901 of the mercury-vapor lamp by Peter Cooper Hewitt, son of former Mayor Abram Hewitt, and grandson of industrialist-inventor Peter Cooper. In 1912 Biograph switched to a still newer New York invention, the carbon-arc "Klieg lights" manufactured by the Kliegl Brothers Universal Stage Lighting Company. Just off Times Square, at 240 West

Thomas A. Edison, Inc., "What Happened on Twenty-Third Street, New York City," August 21, 1901. (Library of Congress Motion Picture, Broadcasting and Recorded Sound Division).

50th Street, this collateral enterprise was handy to the Broadway theaters, especially Belasco's, which, like the fledgling film factories, made creative use of the new technology.

In the recession year of 1908 Biograph took on an unemployed actor, David Wark Griffith, who a year later directed a picture for them, beginning a brilliant career as cinematic innovator. (He was soon hailed as the "Belasco of the Screen.") Griffith had an eye for talent, and in 1909 he hired a teenaged fledgling Broadway actress named Mary Pickford. Soon Lillian and Dorothy Gish, Lionel Barrymore, Mabel Normand, and Mack Sennett were bustling in and out of the 14th Street studi, or (after 1913) Biograph's new Bronx location up at 807 East 175th Street in Tremont. Griffith and other filmmakers also loved the woods, hills, meadows, and marshes of northern New Jersey, and often ferried crews across to Fort Lee.

By 1907 an annoyed Edison found himself confronting not only Biograph and Vitagraph but a host of newly popped-up local and national film production companies and, even more disturbingly, powerful European firms, notably Pathé Frères and Gaumont in France. (Of the 1,092 films released in the last ten months of 1907, only 364 were American made.) The market was being flooded. Profits were imperiled. "Ruinous competition" had again reared its ugly heads, and Edison was determined to lop off enough of them to tame the unruly industry. His weapon of choice—unlike those deployed by brother monopolists Keith, Albee, Klaw, Erlanger, and the Shuberts—was to force his major competitors into a cartel by barraging them with lawsuits charging infringement of one or another of his patents on motion picture technology. Exhausted by endless litigation, six leading firms (including Vitagraph) agreed to pay to use Edison technology, and Edison, in return, agreed he would grant no other company (including Biograph) a license, which hopefully would drive the smaller fry (and Biograph) out of business altogether. The goal, an Edison lawyer admitted bluntly, was to "preserve the business of present manufacturers and not to throw the field open to all competitors." Biograph counterattacked by buying the patent for a key piece of camera technology, forcing Edison (in December 1908) to allow it inside the charmed circle, wherein all patents were shared.

In January 1909 the resulting Edison Trust (formally the Motion Picture Patents Company) laid down the following diktat: henceforth only Trust members would be permitted to make movies, and these could be no longer than one reel (thirteen to seventeen minutes in length), and ideally would be both uncontroversial and uncomplicated. Giving performers screen credit was verboten (lest an actor gain a following that might lead to "unreasonable" salary demands). Violators would be sued for unauthorized use of Trust-patented cameras. And to double-lock the door against outside intruders, Eastman Kodak, which held the patent on raw film stock, joined the Trust, and agreed not to sell the indispensable celluloid to non-members.

The Trust also announced a reorganization of distribution, making use of its patents on projectors. Licensed producers could no longer sell their films to "exchanges," as the key distributors were then called, but only rent to them. The exchanges, in turn, could re-rent only to theater owners who had been licensed by the Trust and had agreed to show only licensed films (this would bar most European producers). Any distributor or exhibitor that broke the rules would be blacklisted, denied access to future films.

If the Trust could enforce these rules—and its patents entitled it to federal support in doing so, support it supplemented by hiring thugs to disrupt unlicensed shoots—then it would have achieved a near-total monopoly on the barely-out-of-the-cradle industry, achieving the kind of centralized (and by its lights rationalized) control won by its theatrical and vaudeville counterparts.

In the event, however, it triggered the birth of a brand-new crop of competitors—the industry refused to remain pruned—and they appeared from an unexpected quarter. Virtually all Trust insiders had entered the film business from the production side; many had been involved in the actual invention of movie hardware. And they were also, with few exceptions, Anglo-Protestants. The new crowd came out of the distribution side. They had focused on the construction and cultivation of movie audiences. And they were also, with virtually no exceptions, Jews.

EDISON, BIOGRAPH, THE LUMIÈRE BROTHERS, AND OTHER EARLY PRODUCERS had relied on New York's top-flight vaudeville halls to showcase their wares. Managers like Keith and Albee, Koster and Bial, or Hammerstein and Proctor simply slipped films into their potpourri of acts. But very quickly other more dedicated outlets emerged, notably the city's penny arcades, which at first had hosted peep shows. With the arrival of projectors, some arcade owners closed off the back of their amusement parlors, set up a screen, rented chairs, and charged five cents to watch movies. Start-up costs were cheap and overhead low—especially as the Board of Aldermen decided these "nickelodeons" were "common shows," not theatrical performances; hence licenses would cost $25, not $500. By 1910, it cost $2,500 a week to run a theater but only $500 to operate a nickelodeon.

High profits attracted new investors. One was Adolph Zukor, a Hungarian-born Jew who had immigrated to New York in 1889 at the age of 16. Zukor apprenticed with a furrier, became a sewer and then designer of fur pieces, moved to Chicago, where he started up his own Novelty Fur Company, made a small fortune, opened a New York branch, and in 1900 resettled back in Gotham. In 1903, when the wealthy and impeccably tailored young man was living comfortably on 111th Street and Seventh Avenue, in German Jewish Harlem, a cousin convinced him to back an arcade on 125th Street. It did so well that Zukor opened his own—the Automatic Vaudeville theater, downtown on 14th Street—and when it cleared $100,000 the first year, Zukor liquidated his fur business and opened more arcades.

One of those who invested in Zukor's growing arcade empire was a friend, Marcus Loew, who had grown up desperately poor on the Lower East Side, and whose road to riches had been rockier than Zukor's. He too had worked in the fur trade, but when he opened his own business it failed; he then turned to sales, then opened another venture, and it also failed. "It is a pretty sentiment to think industry always brings success," he would say, "but it is a fallacy." Then Loew discovered New York real estate speculation and climbed rapidly out of poverty. When Zukor moved back to Gotham in 1900 and (at Loew's suggestion) settled across the street, Loew began investing in his friend's arcades. He did well, then in 1904 started his own chain, the People's Vaudeville Company, beginning with an arcade on 23rd Street and rapidly expanding to a score or more. Deciding that movies, not peep shows, were the wave of the future, Loew began converting arcades into nickelodeons. Now it was Zukor who followed suit, transforming his Automatic Vaudeville's second floor to a 200-seat theater, and transforming himself into a motion picture exhibitor.

Others followed the same path. William Fox, like Zukor a Hungarian Jew, had peddled stove black, hawked lozenges in Central Park, cut garments, and risen to foreman of a clothing firm. In 1903 he acquired a penny arcade in Brooklyn, installed a 150-seat movie theater on the second floor, hired a barker to attract patrons, cleared $40,000 on a $10,000 investment in the first year, set about acquiring others, and by 1908 owned over a dozen.

Thanks to the efforts of exhibitors like Zukor, Loew, and Fox, nickelodeons spread rapidly through the tenement districts. By 1907 there were 200 in Manhattan alone, one third of them below 14th Street. By 1908, there were over 600 in the five boroughs, and they daily drew over 300,000 people, overwhelmingly of working-class background.

The nickelodeons were more accessible to immigrant communities than any other form of commercial culture. They were cheap. Their silent product, open to multi-lingual audiences, appealed especially to recent arrivals. (The native-born still preferred vaudeville.) The storefront theaters were close to home, bunched conveniently on principal shopping blocks. Open from noon to late evening, their fifteen- or twenty-minute programs were short enough for housewives to see during the day, kids to catch after school, and factory workers to take in on the way home. Evenings and Saturdays, whole families came.

The nickelodeons were extensions of the street and community, their presence advertised by garish lights, gaudy posters, and perhaps a barker or phonograph. Unlike at stuffy uptown theaters, seats were not de facto segregated on class lines. And unlike at the raunchy male arcades, between a third and half of the attendees were women. The atmosphere was informal, convivial. There was no set schedule; crowds came and went. Kids tramped the aisles selling peanuts and popcorn. The audience munched, gossiped, cheered, sang along with the piano player's accompanying rendition of sentimental songs.

Working-class patrons were drawn by cinematic fare tailored to their cultural and political proclivities. Some films jabbed at bankers, landlords, and politicians. Others pushed at the boundaries of propriety, portraying street-smart career girls flirting with men in offices, at dancing academies, and at Coney Island. Nickelodeon films often mocked middle-class morality and poked fun at reformers (including women who advocated political equality and a blurring of gender roles).

SLOWLY WORD SEEPED UP TO RESPECTABLE MIDDLE-CLASS OPINION MAKERS—clergymen, editors, civic reformers—about what was going on in these ghetto nickelodeons. They reacted with astonishment and alarm. A vast enterprise had sprung up virtually without their knowledge and utterly without their sanction. And almost everything about it was worrisome.

The nickelodeons were dangerous. Critics pointed (quite properly) to the fire hazards presented by crowded theaters. But what troubled them at least as much was cultural flammability: unsupervised youth, lured by lurid posters, mingling promiscuously in the intimate darkness.

The films themselves were even more dangerous. Their too-often anti-authoritarian and sexually subversive content might warp vulnerable minds, exacerbate social tensions, unleash primitive passions.

Guardians of tradition raised a hue and cry against film manufacturers and exhibitors. In 1907 the Children's Aid Society had a nickelodeon proprietor arrested for showing *The Great Thaw Trial* to a house packed with schoolchildren. A court agreed that Biograph's graphic recounting of the Stanford White scandal impaired their morals and fined the exhibitor $100. Comstock and Parkhurst pressed for more vigorous action. Finally, on Christmas 1908, after a balcony collapsed in an overcrowded Rivington Street nickelodeon, police closed every movie house in New York, and Mayor McClellan revoked all their licenses.

The infant industry was too strong to be throttled in its cradle. Led by William Fox, the exhibitors obtained a court injunction allowing them to reopen. New regulations were imposed, requiring improved safety and the chaperonage of children under 16. But calls for controls over content were turned back.

Despite their success, producers and exhibitors knew it was folly to buck the city's formidable cultural establishment. And some, already dreaming of reaching a wider middle-class market, actively sought the elite's imprimatur. So, in a preemptive strike, they asked for censorship. In March 1909 they requested the People's Institute, an adult education center at Cooper Union, to ride herd on the industry.

It was a shrewd move. The People's Institute was a reasonably sympathetic group. True, it had warned that movies were "potentially too great an influence of popular attitudes to be left unsupervised." But the organization clearly believed the medium a legitimate form of popular recreation and one with great potential for education and uplift.

The institute assembled ten leading civic organizations—mostly wealthy Anglo-Protestant or German Jewish in composition—to sponsor a Board of Motion Picture Censorship of New York. Months later, in June 1909, it reorganized as the National Board of Censorship, admitting to larger ambitions. Sponsors included the Public Education Association, Federation of Churches, Women's Municipal League, Society for the Prevention of Crime, Neighborhood Workers Association, and City Vigilance League.

The principal producers, newly assembled in the Trust, bowed to New York's massed respectability. They agreed to submit all films for censorship and to finance the board's work. Soon a screening committee of volunteer ladies was snipping away all footage deemed obscene or vulgar, brutal or blasphemous. By October 1909 an estimated 85 percent of all movies shown in the United States had first passed muster with a handful of metropolitan mandarins.

New York, it seemed, had established an absolutely monopoly on the new medium, far more thoroughgoing than earlier controls on information flow established by publishers, editors, and wire services. Yet rather than protesting this arrogation of authority, many in the country complained that the board's standards were too lax. The censors seemed too influenced by the "complicated, liberal and abnormal life" of New York City. The board (and the industry) resisted calls for a crackdown. Demands for state censorship grew (in tandem with calls for prohibition of alcohol). Crackdown proponents took heart from a 1915 Supreme Court ruling that First Amendment protections did not apply to movies. For the moment, however, bowdlerizers were held at bay.

AT THE SAME TIME EXHIBITORS WERE ACCOMMODATING MIDDLE-CLASS OPINION as to content, exhibitors were seeking to entice the middle class as consumers, building bigger and more comfortable venues in which to seat them, and producing films that would appeal to them as proletarian fare did not.

Marcus Loew began buying or leasing theaters that the Shuberts had found superfluous, or refurbishing down-at-the-heels burlesque houses, and then offering a mix of vaudeville and one-reelers. Zukor invested heavily in Loew's project, and in 1910 the two merged their operations and incorporated as Loew's Consolidated Enterprises, capitalized at $5 million, with Zukor becoming treasurer. When in 1911 the firm took over a vaudeville chain that agent William Morris had put together, Loew's made the newly acquired American Music Hall (260 West 42nd) the company's headquarters, joining the other entertainment moguls based in and around Times Square.

William Fox, too, began taking over established second-string vaudeville houses, and expanding the percentage of stage time allotted to movies. In 1907 Fox also opened a new wing of the industry by forming the Greater New York Rental Company. One of the first film distributors in the country, it bought films and rented them out to the growing number of nickelodeons and theaters.

Fox's midwestern counterpart was Carl Laemmle, an 1883 immigrant from Germany. He spent his first ten years, mainly in Chicago, bouncing from one low-wage job to another; then put in twelve years in Oshkosh, managing a clothing store; then, in 1906, after being fired for seeking a raise, he moved back to Chicago and opened a nickelodeon. The nickels rolled in, he expanded into film distribution, and by 1909, with his Laemmle Film Service now one of the nation's biggest, he moved to New York to be nearer his source of films.

Nineteen nine, however, was when the Edison Trust announced it was taking over film distribution, and independents like Laemmle, Fox, Zukor, and Loew, would henceforth have to play by its rules. The Trust underscored this by establishing in 1910 a General Film Company, which began systematically buying out the exchanges and folding them into a giant centralized distribution machine. Most went along or quit the business.

The New York Jews did neither. Laemmle was livid, Fox was furious, and both vociferously denounced the "film octopus," branding it a wicked and tyrannical monopoly that would stunt the industry. They had cultural as well as commercial objections. Most of the Anglo-Protestants in the Trust had other entrepreneurial avenues open to them, but the Jews in the movie trade believed they had found a rare pathway to success, a path gentile monopolists were now threatening to block. And more than their careers were at stake. They also believed the Trust was being incredibly shortsighted in insisting the industry stick to short standardized films. As exhibitors, in close, everyday communion with young, ethnic, urban, working-class moviegoers, they knew there was a growing market for longer-story films. (Directors in some Trust companies, like Griffith at Biograph, felt the same, and believed their style was being cramped by the Trust's assembly line mentality.)

What to do? The Trust and the General seemed to have a lock on the industry. For the Jewish exhibitor-distributors the answer seemed obvious. They had to go rogue, become outlaws, by continuing to serve as distributors and, more boldly, by entering production themselves.

In 1909 Laemmle founded the Independent Moving Pictures Company. Its whimsical acronym (IMP) figured heavily in Laemmle's advertising campaign, whose logo was a mischievous devil wielding a pitchfork, presumably intended for the Trust's plump posterior. Setting up studios at 111 East 14th and in Fort Lee, New Jersey, across the Hudson, Laemmle brought out his first picture in October 1909, a self-described "classy" dramatization of Longfellow's *Hiawatha*. Edison and company now dispatched Trust squads to harass IMP film crews, and Trust lawyers to bring suit after suit against Laemmle—289 of them between 1909 and 1912. IMP prospered, partly by giving star billing to performers, which helped lure away publicity-starved talent from Trust companies (IMP stole away Biograph's "Biograph girl"), and from the Broadway stage as well. In 1912, after a complex series of mergers, IMP morphed into what would be soon be called Universal Pictures.

Fox, too, refused to hand over his chain of theaters to the Trust. Instead, in 1912, he filed a civil antitrust action against the Motion Picture Patents Company, then lobbied the Taft administration to follow suit, which—needing to burnish its antitrust credentials in an election year—it did. While the ensuing court battle dragged on, Fox plunged into production. (His first movie, *Life's Shop Window* [1914], was shot in Fort Lee.) In 1915 he established the Fox Film Corporation.

Zukor followed a different route from Fox and Laemmle's but also wound up entering the production side of the trade. For some time Zukor had been interested in wooing refined middle-class audiences, expressing a desire to "kill the slum tradition" in movies. Partly this was an entrepreneurial strategy—adopted from predecessors like Barnum, Pastor, and Keith—aimed at expanding his market and hence profits. It also fit his personal assimilationist agenda: Zukor was leaving Jewishness behind and had been a Republican since he'd heard Bryan's Cross of Gold speech in Chicago in 1896. The way to entice "the better class," he believed, was to replace short, action-packed melodramas with lengthier narratives and suaver acting—imitating bourgeois forms like the novel or legitimate stage, as French and Italian producers were doing. By 1912 he crystallized this into a formula, scribbled down during a subway ride: "Famous Players in Famous Plays." And when he learned that a US distributor had purchased the American rights to a 1911 French film that perfectly embodied this vision—*Queen Elizabeth*, starring Sarah Bernhardt—he immediately purchased them, for a whopping $35,000. With this property in hand, he set up the Famous Players Film Company, opened an office in Times Square, and convinced prestigious Broadway producer Daniel Frohman to bestow instant legitimacy by signing on as managing director.

Well aware that to screen the Bernhardt vehicle he would need permission from the Trust, he asked Frohman to personally intervene with Edison, who indeed was finally persuaded that making movies more artistic was a step in the right direction. When Edison sent Zukor to the head of the Motion Pictures Patent Company for a final OK, Zukor was told that *Queen Elizabeth*, which ran forty minutes and gave Bernhardt star billing, did not fit the Trust's format, and that "the time is not ripe for features, if it ever will be." Now Zukor had reached the same Rubicon as had his compeers, and just as resolutely crossed it. Renting Frohman's posh Lyceum Theatre, he invited leading figures from Gotham's theatrical and social scene, who, lured by the combined cachet of Bernhardt and Frohman, showed up en masse to the opening on July 12, 1912. They responded enthusiastically. So did the masses who flocked to its follow-on run at Loew's theaters all over town.

Convinced his formula was economically viable, Zukor rented an old armory at 221 West 26th Street for a studio, hired talent from the New York stage (coaxing John Barrymore to cross media lines), and lured famous players from rival filmmakers (in 1913 signing Mary Pickford, who bounded to superstardom, with Zukor doubling then quintupling her salary as she rose, making her the world's highest-paid actress). Capping his drive to marry New York's film and theatrical industries, in 1914 he persuaded Charles Frohman, Dan's elder brother and Broadway's premier producer, to ally his interests with those of Famous Players and grant Zukor the right to cinematize all the plays he controlled.

Zukor's success inspired competition. Jesse Lasky, a vaudeville producer, borrowed money from his brother-in-law Samuel Goldfish (later Goldwyn), a Polish-born glove salesman, and started the Lasky Feature Play Company. In short order he had hired Cecil B. DeMille, a stage director with virtually no film experience, signed David Belasco and the rights to his plays, and begun acquiring celebrity performers (including Caruso).

Biograph hopped on the bandwagon by contracting with Klaw and Erlanger to film their successful plays in its new state-of-the-art Bronx studio, but Griffith, displeased at the cinematically static format, departed on the last day of 1913 to Mutual, another newcomer.

In 1914 both Lasky and Famous Players signed a distribution deal with a start-up company, Paramount Pictures Corporation, launched as a way for independent producers to bypass Edison's General Film throttlehold. In 1916 Zukor maneuvered a three-way merger of his Famous Players, the Lasky Company, and Paramount, with the combined enterprise eventually taking the name of its distribution wing. At decade's end, having integrated production and distribution, Zukor decided to shoot for a film-business trifecta by reaching out to control exhibition as well, on a scale far beyond anything achieved by William Fox. To do so he turned to Kuhn, Loeb's Otto Kahn, asking for and receiving his help in floating a $10 million offering of Paramount stock. Zukor's goal went beyond achieving the kind of vertical integration obtained by counterparts in the industrial corporate economy. He was after Wall Street validation as well. "If we got it," Zukor argued, "motion pictures would be regarded as an important industry." Kahn agreed, though he insisted on placing Kuhn, Loeb representatives in key positions.

Zukor was now well placed to replace the now-defeated Edison combine (as the Shuberts had the Syndicate). Not only had the Trust been unable to keep independent producers and distributors from multiplying at a fantastic rate, but in 1915 the courts had finally upheld the Fox-instigated federal antitrust suit begun in 1912, finding Edison's combines guilty of conspiring to restrain trade. The tattered Trust and bypassed General Film were ordered dissolved; by 1917 both were history; and in 1918 the Edison Manufacturing Company itself discontinued production and sold off its studios.

BEFORE EDISON DEPARTED THE STAGE, HIS EFFORTS at monopolizing the industry had left an indelible mark—or rather erasure—on New York City's entertainment complex. While some Trust opponents had stood and fought, most had cut and run, moving their operations to a suburb of Los Angeles whose distance from Edison's East Coast base, and nearness to Mexican havens, made it more difficult for the Motion Picture Patents Company to arrange injunctions and subpoenas. Perhaps of more importance than the border's proximity was the reluctance of the West Coast Ninth Circuit Court of Appeals to enforce Edison's claims. In 1910 Laemmle's Independent Motion Pictures had begun doing some production in Los Angeles; in 1912, when IMP morphed into Universal, the company began shifting production efforts westward; and in 1915, Laemmle opened the world's largest motion picture production facility, Universal City Studios, on a 230-acre farm in the San Fernando Valley, though he himself would not leave New York for another decade.

Not all the blame for this cinematic exodus can be laid at Edison's door. Trust members, too, had tested the western waters. In the winter of 1909–10 Griffith had taken a Biograph crew to southern California, returning to New York in the spring. Directors were drawn by the year-round sunshine, the warm weather, the varied topography. And Los Angeles—a notoriously anti-union city—appealed to the industry's entrepreneurs: labor costs for set builders and seamstresses were half New York's. By 1913, with the eager cooperation of local business and real estate interests, production companies were flocking to Hollywood; by the mid-1910s there were seventy in the vicinity.

Though much of the industry hatched in New York now flew away, not everyone left town. Famous Players did open up a Hollywood studio in 1915, but Adolph Zukor retained his East Coast operation, using the West 26th Street armory until it was destroyed in a 1915 fire, then camping out in a riding academy on West 56th and a renovated theater on West 44th. But finally, at the end of the teens, Paramount departed Manhattan and struck out for greener pastures—in Queens. Zukor's decision to consolidate operations in one enormous studio complex in Astoria was facilitated by an expansion of subway service to the neighborhood, making it an easy twenty-minute ride from Times Square (and only a fifteen-minute jaunt by auto over the Queensboro Bridge, which opened in 1909). Assembling a 140,000-square-foot tract (Sixth/Seventh/Pierce/Graham), he erected a structure that could accommodate twenty production units working simultaneously and installed ultramodern equipment, including an innovative lighting system.

Zukor wasn't alone in resisting Hollywood's charms—Vitagraph continued to produce silents successfully at its Brooklyn studio (though the company did open a second front in Santa Monica in 1911)—but on the whole New York holdouts fared poorly. Not only did the Edison Company collapse; so did its former archrival Biograph. Bereft of Griffith (and the actors who departed with him), it irised into oblivion, shooting its last films in 1916, then lived on for another decade by reissuing old movies and leasing its Bronx studio.

STILL, THE METROPOLIS WOULD CONTINUE TO HOST one major film industry function (in addition to finance, of course: many studios would maintain executive offices in Gotham to be near their bankers). As home to the nation's premier movie market, center of its advertising and magazine trades, and headquarters of its theatrical and vaudeville businesses, New York emerged as the movies' showcase city. Just as distribution of stage commodities to the Road was a journey that began with—was often contingent upon—a successful New York opening, so the baptismal applause of Gotham crowds and critics was deemed a crucial precondition for sending reels of celluloid off on their cross-country rounds, even if they'd been manufactured in California.

A proper sendoff required a proper setting, and here the needs of the increasingly nationwide distribution system meshed with the efforts of New York producers to develop ever grander theaters. Zukor and others had long sought to reach the middle classes. One route involved making feature films. The other centered on providing a new way to screen them.

Respectable people wouldn't step foot in a nickelodeon. Exhibitors calculated they might be enticed to buildings designed in some currently fashionable style. Economics, too, dictated larger buildings: nickelodeon profits relied on short films and quick turnover; lengthy programs would require increasing capacity and raising prices.

Enter the movie palace.

Encouraged by a city ordinance expanding seating limits from 300 to 600, exhibitors had begun raising more substantial structures for working-class audiences. Now designers developed a deluxe version for a more affluent constituency.

First came the Regent Theatre on Seventh Avenue at 116th Street. Thomas Lamb's exuberant tile-faced building, chock-full of columns and arches, was a luxurious movie-ready house. At first the target community of Germans and Jews stuck to vaudeville, and the theater floundered. So management sent out a distress call to Samuel L. Rothapfel. (He later dropped the *p*.) Roxy (as he became known) had come to the attention of B. F. Keith after he'd transformed (in 1908) the back room of his father-in-law's tavern in Forest City, Pennsylvania, into a nickelodeon that consistently ordered more films from New York distributors than did far bigger venues. Keith brought Roxy to New York to upgrade the movie portions of his vaudeville productions, and then, in 1913, the theatrical makeover man moved on to raising the Regent's internal image to the standard of its exterior. He added a curtain, printed programs, hired a staff of well-drilled and uniformed ushers. He installed a large orchestra (in pointed contrast to nickelodeon pianos) and insisted the music match the mood of the film. With the Regent's fortunes revived, Roxy was called downtown for a repeat performance.

In 1914 nickelodeon owners Mitchell and Moe Mark decided to build the Strand Theatre, designed to be a model for "moving picture palaces." After surveying houses in Europe and the United States, the Marks brothers purchased the site of the old Brewster Carriage manufactory at 47th and Broadway, hired Thomas Lamb to build a 3,000-seat hall, and hired Roxy to give it class. Ornamental plasterwork festooned the walls, ceilings, and elaborate lobbies. Gilt and marble were everywhere. Crystal chandeliers, artworks, rich carpeting, and royal restrooms added grace notes. Roxy arranged special lighting, uniformed ushers, and surrounded the onstage orchestra with a garden, complete with active fountain. The projection booth was capable of screening a nine-reeler without interruption. The Strand was comfortable and sanitary. No peanut vendors would tramp the aisles. There would be no community sing-alongs. Would the better-off bite?

Indeed they did. Some of the best (and best-dressed) people in town showed up on opening night, Saturday, April 11, 1914. The *Moving Picture World*'s reporter noted the "long procession of handsome autos" dropping off "prosperous-looking theatergoers," many of them in evening dress, and described many in the lobby as "an animated edition of 'Who's Who in Society.'" The *Times*'s drama critic compared the turnout favorably with season-opener crowds at the opera and the Horse Show. For their delectation, Roxy laid on patriotic tableaux vivants, operatic interludes, and the Strand Topical Review, a form of newsreel that amazed the audience with scenes from that day's baseball game. And yet for all the Strand's cachet, the Marks—determined to fill those 3,000 seats—offered a wide spectrum of prices, charging only fifteen cents for balcony seats during weekday afternoons.

Other palaces followed, and Roxy migrated with them. In 1916 he was engaged to manage the sumptuous new Lamb-designed Rialto at the northwest corner of Seventh Avenue and 42nd Street, replacing Hammerstein's Victoria vaudeville venue—an augury of things to come. Commissioned by the owners of Mutual Film—Crawford Livingston and Felix Kahn (Otto's brother)—the Rialto was totally committed to movies. It had no stage. The screen was mounted directly on the back wall. It was advertised as "the Temple of the Motion Picture." The owners were so pleased with its success that they leased the site of an old garage at the northern end of the Square and in 1917 opened the Rivoli (again engaging Messrs. Lamb and Roxy).

Neither the Rialto nor the Rivoli was originated by Zukor, but in 1919 Paramount purchased a controlling interest in both of them, as part of his plan to make the company a dominant force in exhibition. From then on, the two were frequent sites of opening-night galas for Paramount releases, just as the Capitol (1919, Broadway and 51st)—the next Lamb/Roxy collaboration—would become the flagship of Marcus Loew's chain of theaters.

The movie biz had arrived, big-time, in Times Square, culminating a development that had begun on 34th Street, gathered force on the Lower East Side and in the outer boroughs, and finally taken the center by storm.

John Sloan, "Movies, 5 Cents," 1907. (© 2017 Delaware Art Museum/Artists Rights Society (ARS), New York)

NIGHTLIFE

By the late teens, the center itself had blossomed into something considerably more than the sum of its theatrical-vaudevillial-cinematical-musical parts. As Times Square boomed, it developed an ambience unlike that of any other place in the city. A spectacular nightlife emerged, rooted in the symbiotic relationship between enterprises in which professionals entertained audiences and those in which audiences—quite novel audiences—largely entertained themselves. These amateur performance spaces—where throngs of locals and tourists came to see and be seen—first took the form of ornate restaurants, some newly fashioned, others drawn uptown in the migrating Rialto's wake.

From the late 1890s on, a series of ethnic promoters (French, Swiss, Irish, German, Basque, and Jewish) began opening midtown dining establishments usually named for themselves: Shanley's, Rector's, Bustanoby's, Churchill's, Reisenweber's, and Murray's Roman Gardens. Many of these impresarios, who once had run oyster saloons and beer gardens, now competed to outdo one another in lavish meals and refined French cooking, served up in ever more eye-popping venues, which attracted an ever more diverse array of customers.

Shanley's was first into the Square, hard on Hammerstein's heels. It was the third in a sequence of restaurants first launched when Thomas J. Shanley, of County Leitrim, had opened one at Sixth Avenue and Twenty-third Street, aimed at Ladies' Mile shoppers. Then, with his six brothers, Shanley opened another in the old theater district at Broadway and 30th Street, which attracted actors and theater patrons. Then, in 1896, the brothers infiltrated the Longacre, settling on the west side of Broadway between 42nd and 43rd Streets. Shanley's enormous dining room, which featured lobsters, chops, and broiled kidneys, drew a largely male sporting crowd, heavy on Tammany politicians (it was a favorite uptown haunt of Big Tim Sullivan) and Irish contractors, but it also drew judges, merchants, authors, playwrights, and newspaper men. Retired gunfighter Bat Masterson, now a sportswriter for the *Morning Telegraph* (boxing was his beat), could be found most nights in the Grill Room, spinning yarns of the Old West.

Rector's cast a wider net. Charles Rector had been running an enormous and hugely successful seafood restaurant in Chicago when in 1899 he moved back to New York and opened a place at Broadway and 43rd/44th, anticipating, correctly, that theaters were about to inundate the Longacre. Rector's two-story yellow façade featured the Square's second electric sign (a huge winged griffin) and the city's first revolving door, which whirled patrons into the one-hundred-table ground floor (with seventy-five more available one flight up). The food was first rate—Charles had sent his son George to Paris, where he'd studied at Le Cordon Bleu and worked at the Café de Paris and the Marguery. ("I brought Paris to New York," George would say, "and improved it by the transplanting.")

What pulled in patrons, however, was the carefully crafted atmosphere. Rector modeled the interior on elite East Side establishments, principally Delmonico's and Sherry's, whose latest incarnations faced one another across Fifth Avenue (at 44th Street). His dining room featured Belfast linen, waiters in full evening dress, and silverware embossed with his griffin logo. But Rector made his place more raffish, more theatrical, as befit the neighborhood. The mix of East and West Sides worked. His place drew the show biz crowd (actors, producers, playwrights, critics) and the sporting and gambling crowd, but also the more daring of the old-monied, along with peacocky new millionaires given to flashing their bankrolls. After-theater diners flocked to Rector's opulent stage set, the leading roles played by wealthy men and Broadway beauties, who would enter arm in arm, their reflections ricocheting in the floor-to-ceiling gilded mirrors, and make their way to table as the orchestra played hits from the star's (or starlet's) latest show.[2] It was a place to celebrate wealth and success—on the stage, in business, at the track or at the polls—and the images of celebrants were caught and transmitted to a vast public by a hungry press. Rector's was the subject of endless feature stories, gossip items, even theatrical productions—like the 1909 musical comedy *The Girl from Rector's*, which ran for a year in Weber's Music Hall, then took to the Road. All this free publicity helped make it the best-known nightspot in the United States.

Imitators rushed in. They were known in popular parlance as Lobster Palaces, as per George Rector's boast: "I found Broadway a quiet little lane of ham and eggs and left it a full-blown avenue of lobsters and champagne." By 1906, the *New York Times* reported, an estimated 8,000 people were dining nightly in their neighborhood.

The Lobster Palaces offered high style as well as fancy food. Most adopted aristocratic French architecture—the style traditionally beloved by the New York rich. Rector's was done up in Sun King. So was Maxim's, where waiters, doormen, and pages were decked out in satin knee breeches, silk stockings, and powdered wigs.

"The Girl from Rector's," 1910.

Others opted for the classical Roman forms newly voguish in this imperial-minded era. In 1908 John Murray, a seasoned restaurateur, opened Murray's Roman Gardens at 228 West 42nd Street (between 7th and 8th Avenues, a few doors down from the Syndicate's New Amsterdam). Murray's advertised its interior as being modeled on Caesarean Rome, "the period of the Imperial city's greatest opulence," and its main dining room reproduced the garden of a villa in Pompeii (helpfully identified for patrons as "the Newport of Rome").

Luxury levels escalated rapidly. Murray, after opening his Roman Gardens, almost immediately put together a consortium—the grandly named United States Realty and Restaurant Company, evoking Harry Black's corporate colossus—and announced plans to transform the eight-story Hotel Saranac (1874), which occupied most of the tract from Broadway to Seventh Avenue between 41st and 42nd Streets, into a restaurant, the Café de l'Opéra, whose staff of 750 would seat and serve five thousand diners, making it the largest in the world. One competitor, on hearing the size of the planned restaurant, predicted failure, as "New Yorkers only want to go to places where they can't get a table." The prediction proved accurate, though the collapse wasn't due to ease of access. Despite what the *Times*

---

2. The cast of men-about-town included raffish millionaire industrialists (Diamond Jim Brady), dapper financiers (Otto Kahn), successful professionals (Stanford White), adventurous scions of merchant or corporate families, notables from the entertainment, sporting, and underworld scenes, and wealthy first-generation immigrants barred from opera boxes. They shared a pursuit of "aristocratic" pleasure. They rejected the restraints of bourgeois home life for a realm of "continental" freedom and sought glamour as much as sex. (Lobster Palace owners maintained public gentility, though some permitted trysts in private dining rooms.)

reported as an investment of $4 million—$1.25 million of it for interior decoration alone, including a reproduction of the great staircase of Persepolis, a gigantic Assyrian silk rug, and an immense painting of the fall of Babylon—the designers committed some elemental faux pas. The distance between the kitchen and the tables was so great that food arrived cold, and patrons were *required* to wear evening clothes. Within a year of the 1909 opening, the Café de l'Opéra was in trouble. An old pro, Louis Martin, was brought in to rescue it. He deep-sixed the dress code, relocated the kitchen, and rebranded it as the Café Louis Martin. But it never really took off, and in 1913 Martin withdrew. A final remake/rename (now as the Café de Paris) was a bust. Bankrupt by 1914, it was razed the following year.

There were plenty of nighttime alternatives, though, and among the most successful were the grandly theatrical hotels erected by the deep-pocketed William Waldorf Astor and John Jacob Astor IV, the feuding cousins who had hyphenated their hostelries into the Waldorf-Astoria in 1897.

In 1904 William raised the ten-story Hotel Astor, its lobby invitingly open to Times Square crowds on Broadway's west side between 44th and 45th Streets, for a reported cost of $7 million. Over half of the space was used for banquet halls and ballrooms whose thematic interiors resembled period-piece stage sets. There was a Pompeian billiard room, a Flemish smoking room, and—in a bow to the Astor pedigree—an Old New York lobby, with wall murals by William de Leftwich Dodge depicting scenery from "Ancient and Modern" Gotham. On the roof was a garden with a miniature waterfall and illuminated walkways that provided sensational views of the Hudson. Not to be outdone, cousin John followed up with the Hotel Knickerbocker (1906), at 42nd Street and Broadway. It featured Sun King décor, the world's longest bar, a Maxfield Parrish mural of Old King Cole, and tenants like Caruso, Farrar, and Scotti, pleased by its proximity to the Met.[3]

The most dramatic gathering place, however, was out in Times Square itself, whose wattage had been steadily increasing since Adolph Ochs threw his first New Year's Eve street party at the end of 1904. The neighborhood had still been dim then—apart from Hammerstein's and Rector's electric signage—so much so that Ochs had had to set up large gas lanterns for the assembled merrymakers to keep back the gloom until, at the witching hour, the building itself became a pillar of light and sent fireworks exploding into the sky. In 1907, when the city banned fireworks for safety reasons, Ochs came up with an alternative ritual, one that looked backward to "ball drop" technology. As in other seaports, a ball was lowered each day, precisely at noon, from a tall building (in New York it was the Western Union tower), allowing ships in the harbor to synchronize their chronometers. The *Times*'s version involved lowering a lighted ball, precisely at midnight, which triggered an electric sign that spelled out "1908."

The real future of outdoor lighting had arrived at the Square's *northern* end back in 1904 when—on the roof of a low building at 47th between Broadway and Seventh—two giant illuminated disembodied hands began clinking glasses high in the sky, an ad for Trimble's Whiskey. It was the handiwork of Oscar J. Gude, New York's maestro of exterior advertising. The German American Gude, born in New York in 1862, had started work as a sign hanger and bill poster, moved up to become head of a soap company's advertising department, and in 1889 opened his own billboard business. (In 1894 he became the first to put up ads in els.) Soon Gude had offices nationwide devising aggressive marketing campaigns for firms like

---

3. Less grand, but crucial to the emerging Times Square infrastructure, was the series of apartment hotels that now arose along side streets, like the Algonquin (1902) at 59 West 44th, for those who aspired to, were engaged in, or had retired from theatrical careers.

Quaker, Bull Durham, and Uneeda. His big breakthrough came in 1900 when he was hired by food magnate H. J. Heinz to erect a fifty-foot green-bulbed pickle on the wall of the Cumberland Hotel at 23rd and Fifth (soon to be replaced by the Flatiron Building). The whimsical phallus was a sensation, it drew crowds, and Gude realized he was onto something. He also understood that the pickle's effectiveness was partly place-related, being adjacent to Madison Square, which allowed for long sight lines—as did the new Times Square.

It took a while. After 1904 nearly every business in the Square added electric signs, but these were at first small-scale affairs, on the buildings' façades, designed to be seen by passing pedestrians and to attract them within; they were old-fashioned trade signs rendered in new-fangled glass bulbs. Gude, however, aimed higher. He went not to firms who did business in the Square itself but to national companies seeking to peddle a product, and he persuaded them to target the growing number of entertainment seekers shuffling in and out of the entertainment zone. A properly placed electric sign, Gude argued, bypasses the brain, goes straight to the retina, and there "forces its announcement on the vision of the uninterested as well as the interested passerby." With clients in hand, he then convinced building owners to rent their rooftops, often for princely sums. Then he and his designers set to crafting aerial ads, utilizing such key technological breakthroughs as "flashers"—less flashily, "commutators"—which allowed groups of connected bulbs to be turned on and off in sequence, simulating movement, and also rheostats, which allowed the lights to be dimmed or raised. Both were invented by William J. Hammer, a pioneering electrical engineer who had worked for Edison in Europe. With these tools O. J. Gude & Co. created gargantuan cartoon-like figures: acrobats, babies, horses, vaudeville actresses. These figures moved, engaged in actions, enacted mini-narratives (like those of the mini-movies in nickelodeons): a girl walked a tightrope; boys boxed in their shorts; a polo player whacked a ball. And all this was in the service of hawking the most prosaic commodities: bran flakes and beer, cigarettes and chewing gum, gloves, shoes, underwear.

There was nothing prosaic about the impact. The signs were delightful, mesmerizing, awe-inspiring: "an enfevered phantasmagoria," wrote British author Arnold Bennett on a 1912 visit to the Square. Fountains of sparkling White Rock Table Water gushed into basins

"Showing Polo Player on Horse's Back in the Act of Striking Ball. Both Figures in Motion. Red, Green, and 'White' Lamps Used." H. J. Mahin, "Light—Its Relation to Electric Signs," *Good Lighting and the Illuminating Engineer*, November 1912.

seven stories down. An electric acrobat performed stunts on an electric tightrope stretched a full block from Seventh Avenue to Broadway. The Heatherbloom Girl had her petticoat whipped about by gusts of electrical wind and rain, revealing a naughty glimpse of leg. A mastodon kitten played with a ball of Corticelli silk thread and got all tangled up. And in 1917, atop the Putnam Building—a block-long office building on the west side of Broadway between 43rd and 44th erected by the Astors in 1909—the Wrigley Spearmint Chewing Gum company, having rented the roof for $100,000 a year, had Gude construct the biggest sign on earth (Wrigley seeing it as a weapon in his war with the Chewing Gum Trust). *Eight* stories high (the building itself was only six) and two hundred feet long, with 17,500 white and multi-colored lamps (inspected daily), it featured six animated Spearmen who went through a series of twelve calisthenics, which the public promptly dubbed the "Daily Dozen."

Gude's company put up roughly twenty of these "spectaculars," as they became known in the trade, between 1904 and 1917, each more amazing than its predecessor. Gude wasn't the only game in town, though. In 1910 a Dayton, Ohio, sign man enacted the chariot race from *Ben-Hur* above the Normandie Hotel: wheels spun, drivers cracked whips, legs galloped, and tails waved, while on the street below a special squad of police kept immobilized gawkers moving. Strauss & Company, an old gas-lit marquee manufactory actually located in the Square, went electric and in 1909 built a sign for the Casino, featuring showgirls riding in a pony cart that undulated from side to side. The arrival of the movie palace brought in new specialists, one of whom in 1916 constructed a façade sign that had a spinning pinwheel set off animated rockets that shot up sparks that spelled out R-I-A-L-T-O, above which a giant eagle slowly beat its wings. But the new landscape—the new art-and-commerce form itself—was overwhelmingly Gude's accomplishment.

Heatherbloom Petticoats, electric sign, n.d. (Image No. AAA0109, Outdoor Advertising Association of America Digital Collection, Duke University)

He didn't please everybody. The Municipal Art Society (MAS), given its City Beautiful–Parisian aesthetic, viewed the helter-skelter placement around town of billboards, placards, and posters—the spectaculars' predecessors—as a form of visual pollution. In 1902 the MAS had launched an anti-billboard campaign, the nation's first, calling for revision of the city building code to regulate their placement, a proposal that included banning them from rooftops. The corporation counsel declared that restricting the use of private property on purely aesthetic grounds would be an unconstitutional "taking" of property, and would require compensating owners for lost income. The MAS then settled for a modest restriction, imposing a 10-foot height limit, a constraint that was simply ignored until it too was declared impermissible.

Then the spectaculars arrived. Not surprisingly, the MAS consigned the "gaudy electric signs" to "the deepest circle of billboard hell." It was okay to use strings of light to outline façades, especially of important civic spaces. Chicago's 1893 White City, after all, had glowed in the dark. But the carnivalesque Midway Plaisance style of flashing colored lights, strewn like litter across the landscape, evinced no orderly overall design and was anathema. (These signs' occasional vulgarity, as in the case of Miss Heatherbloom's petticoats, or the Canadian Club ginger-ale bottle that exploded open, bawdily covering its tip with froth, only made matters worse.)

In the early 1910s, accordingly, the MAS squared off against the new menace, mobilizing not only civic reformers but the powerful Fifth Avenue Association, which was mortally afraid that the electric virus would infect their high-toned allée. Against them were arrayed the Broadway Association and the tourist industry, which had already noted that Times Square signage was hugely popular with vacationers and conventioneers. The sign makers and their business backers triumphed, though the Fifth Avenue worthies would later win a special exemption that outlawed "projecting and illuminating" signs on their turf, from Washington Square to 110th Street, and the 1918 Zoning Commission ruled billboards to be a "nonconforming" usage in residential neighborhoods. In effect, big electric signs wound up restricted in most of midtown, with the exception of wide-open Times Square, which only intensified the unique appeal of its glittering domain.[4]

Drawn to these dazzling lights and manifold delights, crowds swarmed into the new entertainment zone. The IRT ferried in residents from uptown, downtown, Brooklyn, and the Bronx. The refurbished Grand Central and Penn Station ushered in pleasure-bent suburbanites from Long Island, New Jersey, and Westchester. And the great ocean liners deposited tourists from around the world at its Hudson River doorstep, all eager (as was George M. Cohan) to give their regards to Broadway and all the gang on 42nd Street. Times Square had become a gigantic Kleig-lighted stage set on which vast numbers trod the boards. Perhaps 50,000 had attended Ochs' first New Year's Eve party in 1904/5; by 1910 it was estimated that between 300,000 and 700,000 tromped through the Square every twenty-four hours. As a total entertainment package, Times Square was unmatched anywhere on earth.

With one exception. During the same years the Square was shooting to global preeminence, another patch of New York real estate, perched on Brooklyn's southern shore, was achieving an equal degree of worldwide fame as a locale dedicated to the pursuit of happiness. Even their respective origin stories, which revolve around an almost overnight transformation from darkness to dazzle, had interesting parallels, though Coney Island's pleasure industry was of far longer standing, and its sun-drenched beach could hardly be characterized

---

4. A similar battle raged in London over illuminated sky signs in Piccadilly Circus, where their development lagged behind New York's, as the forces of resistance were much stronger.

as dim. But to many the honky-tonk character of Coney's western reaches was the moral equivalent of Longacre's forbiddingly unlit terrain, and the island's reincarnation as a respectable and astoundingly popular entertainment zone—a transformation that also had consolidation and electrification at its core—was analogous to the transmutation of dodgy Longacre into visitor-friendly Times Square.

CONEY ISLAND

West Brighton in the 1890s had been a wide-open working-class playground. Artisans and laborers rode mass transit to West Brighton's taverns, saloons, beer gardens, mechanical rides, shooting galleries, freak shows, dance halls, gambling dens, and brothels that lined the (other) Bowery and Surf Avenue. During the city's broiling summers the beach itself drew enormous numbers. Brooklyn plants often closed (or their employees refused to work) in excessive heat, and Greenpoint iron founders, Wallabout Bay shipyard workers, and Kent Avenue sugar refiners headed for the shore.

Many clergymen, educators, and civic reformers had not been happy with West Brighton (a.k.a. "Sodom by the Sea"). Under Boss John Y. McCain's protection, most anything had gone. McCain got sent up the river to Sing Sing in 1894, but it seemed to make no difference. The civic bourgeoisie then organizing city consolidation dreamed of bringing the outlaw island under control, perhaps by turning the depraved resort into a City Beautiful public park, with rides and amusements giving way to lawns and pristine beaches. The Association for Improving the Condition of the Poor called for making Coney "a moral and physical sanitarium." An opportunity emerged when a series of fires ravaged West Brighton. Reformers urged the newly consolidated city to purchase the area between Ocean Parkway and Sea Gate and construct therein a seaside sanctuary.

The plan was defeated—in part because East River bridges, subways, sewers, and school buildings claimed city funds. But mainly it failed because a new breed of professional showmen, also bent on redeeming Coney's corrupt image, got there first. Using tactics familiar in the corporate world, they consolidated the island's amusement industry into thematic "parks," utterly transforming the resort.

In the summer of 1893, George Cornelius Tilyou had gone to the Chicago Fair, where he observed the immensely popular Midway Plaisance with a professional eye. George helped manage a vaudeville theater in Coney Island, and his parents ran a small hotel there. He decided to emulate the Midway's success in New York. His first move was to build a smaller edition of Chicago's Ferris wheel, followed by other mechanical rides he scattered throughout West Brighton. Then, taking a leaf from Captain Paul Boyton, who in 1895 had built an enclosed fairground called Sea Lion Park to house his collection of aquatic attractions, Tilyou gathered his rides together and surrounded them with a fence that allowed him to bar unsavory sideshows and disreputable visitors. Tilyou opened his compound (which ultimately spread over fifteen acres) in 1897. He called it Steeplechase Park, after a racetrack ride on which patrons jockeyed mechanical horses along iron rails.

Visitors entered Tilyou's carnival through a plaster archway entrance surmounted by a huge (and vaguely diabolical) "Funny Face." Inside, a series of scary-but-safe rides encouraged patrons to shed propriety, at least temporarily. ("WILL SHE THROW HER ARMS AROUND YOUR NECK AND YELL? WELL, I GUESS, YES!") In the Barrel of Fun—an enormous slowly revolving cylinder—men and women tumbled atop one another. At the Blowhole Theater, compressed-air jets shot up from iron grates, sending hats and skirts flying; once past it, patrons turned to laugh at the next victims. In the Tunnel of Love, small boats rocked their way on shallow water through a blackness that provided ghetto dwellers an unaccustomed degree of privacy. Tilyou's simple formula turned patrons into participants, and allowed them normally forbidden pleasures.

In 1902 Tilyou invited Frederic Thompson and Elmer Dundy to reconstruct in Steeplechase a spectacular ride they had created for Buffalo's Pan-American Exposition in 1901, where Tilyou had seen it. The two were professional showmen by now, but the Ohio-born Thompson had been studying architecture when he visited the Chicago Fair back in 1893 and been converted to the amusement business. Thompson proved particularly inventive at designing ride environments (his first being a Heaven and Hell experience that was a hit at an 1898 Omaha exposition). In Buffalo, he teamed up with Nebraskan Dundy to work on "A Trip to the Moon," a ride he'd conceived in 1899–1900 while living in New York and taking courses at the Art Students League. Visitors entered an enormous airship, with flapping wings, that ingeniously produced the sensation of leaving Earth and flying over Buffalo and Niagara Falls, then zooming through space to the Moon, where they were greeted by Moon People, who offered canapés of green cheese.

"A Trip to the Moon" was the smash hit of Tilyou's summer 1902 season, when 850,000 made the lunar journey. (Such voyages were in vogue that year; H. G. Wells had just serialized *The First Men in the Moon* in *Cosmopolitan* during 1901, and now Georges Méliès brought out his fantastical fourteen-minute film *A Trip to the Moon*, which was promptly pirated by Edison and widely distributed in New York and the nation.) Thompson and Dundy now decided to make "Trip" the core of their own rival fun fair. But they had a far grander vision than Tilyou's in mind: instead of simply corralling disparate rides into an enclosure, they would construct a total environment as enticing as any of its components. They proceeded to lease Captain Boyton's old (and ailing) park, as well as some adjacent properties. Then they cleared most of their 22-acre parcel, borrowed $700,000 from John Gates and other super-rich habitués of Coney's racetracks, and began building Luna Park.

Thompson banished Beaux-Arts formalism from his design. Using plaster and lath, the same materials used in Chicago's classical White City, he swirled up a flamboyant profusion of towers, minarets, and domes—1,221 assorted spires in all. Thompson stood City Beautiful precepts on their heads, eschewing disciplined civic monumentality for an architecture of voluptuous excitement. After dark, Luna turned into a shimmering city of light; its towers, outlined with a quarter-million electric lamps, etched a blazing skyline in the night air.[5]

The 45,000 who poured in for the May 1903 opening found two kinds of experiences awaiting them.

One set of rides copied the Steeplechase formula, but on a grander, more capital-intensive scale and at an accelerated tempo. Industrial devices were adapted to create a technology of pleasure. Coal cars used in mining shafts became roller coasters; the flip-flap railway mirrored the elevated; Shoot-the-Chutes shot two-person boats down a steep incline into a shallow pond. The machines overwhelmed their passengers, creating a feeling of anarchic release, and then

---

5. By 1907 Luna Park was illuminated by 1,300,000 lights. Some found the "Electric City by the Sea" a disequilibrating experience. One critic said, "The place seemed a burning mirage, twisting itself into fantastic shapes that whirled and spun and teetered bewilderingly." But the flood of light was also hailed for bringing order to a previously "dim and dismal place," notorious for its criminality. This thesis was advanced most ardently by the Brooklyn Edison Company, which supplied the power (for $5,600 a week). Electricity, it boasted, had transformed "the entire moral and material character" of Coney: "Under its benign rays the possibilities of crime are reduced to a minimum and its searching gleam finds out the perverted and the false and mercilessly exposes it."

"Luna Park at Night, Coney Island," ca. 1903–6. (Library of Congress Prints and Photographs Division)

safely restored order. Rides of a minute's duration whisked, spun, and jolted people off their feet. They also legitimated the display of affection in public; one even mimicked the motions of the tango. The success of these machines generated a spin-off industry for New York. Makers of mechanical devices like the Razzle-Dazzle, the Tickler, and the Whip—men like William F. Mangels and LaMarcus A. Thompson—shipped their products around the world.

Luna also offered a series of artfully crafted illusion-rides. These simulated travel, through space and time, for visitors who seldom left their neighborhoods. The most popular was the original "Trip to the Moon," now slightly revised from its original Buffalo incarnation, with Airship Luna IV lofting its passengers over Coney Island and Manhattan's skyscrapers before whisking them to their rendezvous with the Moon People. A "20,000 Leagues under the Sea" ride simulated a journey from Luna Park to the North Pole, encountering mermaids and Eskimos on the way.

Luna also offered more ground-level but equally exotic destinations. Guests could visit a Delhi marketplace, complete with gilded chariots, trained elephants, dancing girls, and regiments of soldiers; one could play raja or ride on camels. Other shows recreated famous disasters, like the Johnstown Flood of 1889, or the Fall of Pompeii (with regularly scheduled eruptions from "Mt. Vesuvius"). At "Fire and Flames" a four-story building was repeatedly set ablaze. While patrons applauded, heroic firemen doused the flames (offering, at no extra cost, reassurance about Gotham's ability to avert the disasters that had ravaged their past). An even greater peril was warded off at "War of the Worlds," where patrons, assembled in a battleship-shaped amphitheater, watched as a forty-ship fleet (of electrically controlled

"Loop the Loop," 1903. (Library of Congress Prints and Photographs Division)

models), drawn from the combined navies of Germany, Britain, France, and Spain, launched an attack on New York harbor. "Fort Hamilton's" huge guns fired on the invaders still five miles away; a return volley blew up one of the defending bastions with a thunderous roar, startling the visitors; but then, in the nick of time, Admiral Dewey's American fleet showed up and sank every last one of the enemy.

Luna Park was an instant success. It inspired instant competition.

William H. Reynolds, a former Republican state senator, was a real estate promoter; he had founded the Brooklyn suburb of Borough Park. Reynolds now set out to create a more upscale amusement park aimed at the kind of respectable people who purchased his homes. Gathering investors, he assembled $3.5 million and in 1904 raised Dreamland, on the seaward side of Surf Avenue.

Where Thompson had rejected the Chicago Fair's aesthetics, Reynolds enthusiastically embraced them. He used every City Beautiful strategy he could think of—spacious grounds, wide and imposing avenues, splendid lagoons and plazas. He made every building snowy white and festooned them with a million electric lights. Dreamland's 375-foot Beacon Tower, with 100,000 lights of its own, could be seen thirty miles out to sea.

Apart from its emphasis on classical respectability, Dreamland was Luna's clone. It had its own vertigo-inducing machines, a simulated aerial ride ("Flight over Manhattan"), and its own disaster spectacles, which quadrupled the number of firefighters and threw in an "End of the World" to boot. Dreamland also offered ersatz travel—like a boat ride through the Canals of Venice. More uniquely, it had incubators in which premature infants, brought from

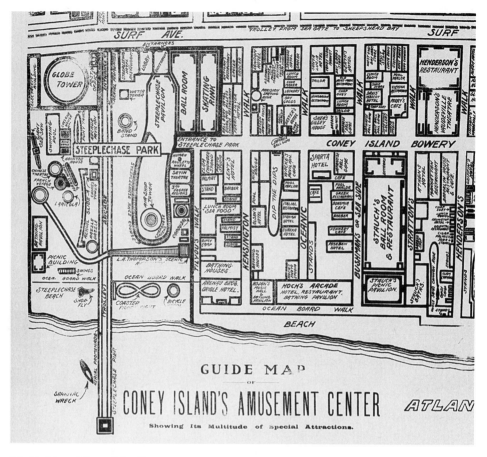

"Guide Map of Coney Island's Amusement Center," *Brooklyn Daily Eagle*, May 19, 1907.

city hospitals, were nursed to health before visitors' eyes, and a Lilliputian village scaled to size was occupied by 300 little people.

IN NOTHING FLAT, CONEY ISLAND BECAME THE MOST POPULAR RESORT on the planet. The size of the crowds was astonishing. Once a turnout of 22,000 at a baseball stadium had been thought remarkable. In 1904, with all three parks open, over 500,000 turned out on Sundays, and on some occasions over a million.

One key to this success was transport. Like Times Square, with which it rose in tandem, Coney was a mass transit hub. Nickel trolley cars rolled down Brooklyn's avenues; the Luna Park Express from the Brooklyn Bridge took thirty-two minutes; steamship companies ran excursion vessels at fifteen to twenty-five cents per round trip. (Boats left the Battery hourly for Dreamland's steel pier.)

Publicity was another ingredient. Five-cent magazines popularized Coney as an antidote to daily life. Mass-marketing techniques helped: street posters, coupons in the *World*, billboards on Lower East Side buildings. Patrons spread the word by using the postcards distributed free to visitors. This new medium was first approved for use in 1898; in the summer of 1907 the Brooklyn Post Office processed over a million cards each week.

The new Coney had breadth of appeal. It drew both sexes. Like "clean vaudeville," Luna advertised itself as "The Place for Your Mother, Your Wife, Your Daughter and Your

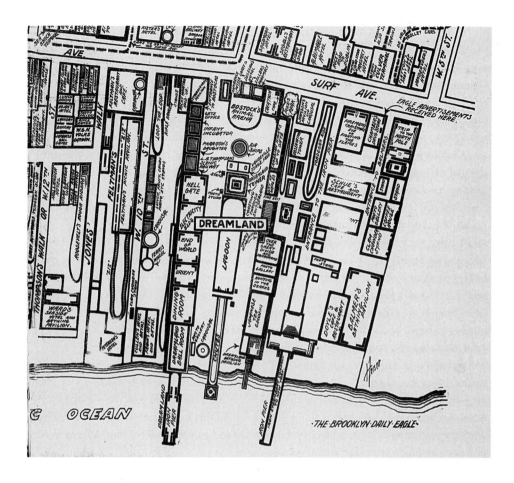

Sister." It also encouraged a playful mixing of women and men. It tapped all social classes. Laboring families might manage outings only once or twice a summer, but young men and women came out more often. More affluent white-collar workers—salesmen, clerks, tradesmen, and secretaries—came in greater numbers. Steeplechase Park's rides attracted a greater percentage of working-class patrons. Higher-priced Luna and Dreamland lured a more middle-class clientele. (When Dreamland failed to match Luna's popularity its promoters decided they had made it *too* classy.)[6] Coney's rise also spelled decline for other working-class venues. Trips to old-fashioned picnic grounds (already being displaced by residential and commercial development) were replaced by jaunts to Steeplechase and Luna Park; by 1910 there were only ten left in Manhattan and the Bronx.

The phenomenon of the new Coney commanded attention. Journalists, critics, photographers, painters, and civic reformers followed the crowds to the booming parks and tried to grasp their significance.

---

6. The amusement parks' success overwhelmed the gentry bastions on the east end of the island. Brighton and Manhattan Beach hoteliers had kept their distance from plebeian West Brighton, but the enormous numbers down the beach started an exodus of the wealthier to more exclusive resorts. This became a headlong flight when the Sheepshead Bay, Gravesend, and Brighton Beach racetracks were shut by reformers. The owners of the Manhattan Beach—mostly New York and Boston financiers—closed the hotel and built Manhattan Beach Estates, an exclusive year-round residential community. The Brighton Beach, owned by leading Brooklyn citizens, became the Brighton Beach Gardens apartments.

Overall, respectable opinion was delighted. Sanitized amusements had triumphed over the unsavory old order of saloons, dancing girls, freak shows, and whorehouses. The new mass-leisure entrepreneurs bowed to the precepts of genteel culture, as did the impresarios of respectable vaudeville. They provided wholesome entertainment to a heterogeneous audience and profited by doing so. They had discovered, one critic wrote in 1904, that "not only can Coney Island be good, but that goodness pays, and pays handsomely."

Others thought Coney a gift horse whose teeth merited closer inspection.

Genteel observers deplored its suspension of conventional proprieties, its subtle subversions of class and sexual decorums. The rides sanctioned a surrender of repression. Mixed bathing revealed more body than respectability deemed tolerable. The atmosphere of gaiety, abandon, and revelry undermined genteel values of sobriety, industry, and ambition.

A few radical analysts suggested just the opposite. Coney didn't endanger New York's social order; rather, it provided the metropolis with a giant safety valve, a mechanism of social release and control. In this reading, Coney's putatively carnivalesque attractions were deeply fraudulent. Carnivals had for centuries offered temporary alternatives to the prevailing economic and social order; they had turned the world "upside down." But Coney didn't subvert (even briefly) the existing order, it mirrored it. Attendees were offered and consumed scientifically managed and industrially engineered experiences. They were turned into articles on a movable assembly line. The only things turned upside down were the patrons.

Leisure reformers took a different tack. They condemned Coney as a species of exploitation. Industrial workers—fatigued and frustrated by factory work and stresses of ghetto life—deserved refreshment and renewal. Instead, cynical profiteers took the popular craving for amusement and exploited it for private gain. Coney's proprietors were like brewers, brothel keepers, and the managers of dance halls and gambling dens: they offered perversions of play rather than purposeful recreation.

From these tiny (but influential) ranks came revived suggestions for razing the existing parks and restoring Coney to its "natural" state. Such proposals got absolutely nowhere. Until 1911, when they received an inadvertent boost.

On the opening day of the 1911 season, the lighting system in Dreamland's Hell Gate ride short-circuited. The sparks started a fire. It spread rapidly, fanned by the strong sea breezes. The fake firemen of "Fighting the Flames" took to their heels. When the real ones arrived—over thirty-three companies responded to the first double-nine alarm in the city's history—they didn't do much better. Lions, elephants, and gorillas ran amok, enveloped in flames. Most of the park was destroyed. Reynolds didn't rebuild. He advised the city to take the land and make it a park.

Luna, too, experienced a decline, albeit not such a drastic one. Dundy had died in 1907, and Thompson had suffered personal setbacks; in 1912, after Luna's fire insurance policy was canceled in the wake of the Dreamland disaster, he went bankrupt. New management added rides but lacked Thompson's flair. The park ran down. Pigs replaced elephants on Shoot-the-Chutes; old towers toppled or burned and were not replaced. The arrival of the movies, cheaper, closer to home, and utterly novel, took its toll. Luna survived, as did Steeplechase, aided by the expansion and upgrading of rail service, and continued to draw millions of visitors each summer season. And local problems didn't dim its national and international luster: by 1912 Luna Parks had blossomed across the country—from Scranton to Seattle, Detroit to Denver, Chicago to Charleston, and by 1916 the roster of cities containing their own Luna Park included Berlin, Buenos Aires, Cairo, Melbourne, Mexico City, Paris, Rome, St. Petersburg, and Tokyo.

14

Popular Cultures

New York's entertainment entrepreneurs pumped cultural commodities into an arterial system that nourished cities and towns across America. But who produced the songs, plays, and vaudeville routines that Gotham packaged and distributed to the Road? To a remarkable degree they were manufactured in New York.

The city, to be sure, continued to perform its traditional role as cultural entrepôt, so some of what was shipped westward was imported European goods. Thus Gotham remained the port of entry for English comedies of manners, naughty French farces, opulent Viennese operettas, or serious dramas by Ibsen and Shaw—which, after getting their initial staging on Broadway, were then conveyed by New York producers to the nation's theaters and concert halls, rather as New York bankers funneled European capital to the nation's industries.

Gotham also attracted talented individuals from around the country—ragtime pianists, playwrights, songsters, writers, filmmakers, inventors, actors, and producers who were drawn to its jobs, its capital, its enormous internal market, its amplification systems (critics, publicity organs, theatrical circuits, music publishers, recording labs, film studios), and its status as Gateway to the Road. This influx of creative people deepened the pool of artists with whom one could collaborate or clash, and the resulting excitement enticed still others. The city's culture industry thus achieved critical mass and momentum, becoming almost self-perpetuating (though filmmakers did hive off to Hollywood).

But the bulk of the city's offerings were home-brewed in a different way. They were products of a cultural fermentation bubbling up from Gotham's effervescent streets. The comic routines that survived the vaudeville hook, the million-seller tunes turned out by Alley songsmiths, the glamorous revues that knocked 'em dead on Broadway—all grew out of an interaction between New York's changing social ecology and its booming culture industries.

Three such intersections were particularly significant in the century's first two decades: those between ethnicity and the vaudeville business; between race and the music business; and between gender and the dancing business.

Gotham's theatrical generativity owed a great deal to the fact that its populace was grouped into massed ethnic enclaves. Many of these communities were big enough and cohesive enough to sustain original-language drama. Some of these plays were imported from the home country: national masterpieces (modern or traditional), or the classics of other countries, presented in translation. A second set of dramatic works were made-in-Gotham explorations of enclave life itself—presented in the vernacular, performed in neighborhood playhouses, meeting halls, and cafés, before audiences overwhelmingly of the same ethnicity as the playwright.

The city's ethnic communities also served as source material for English-language vaudeville, which relied heavily on comic skits purporting to capture the nature and experiences of enclave residents. These routines were written *about* ethnic communities, not *by* or *for* them. Between English-language vaudeville and enclave-supported or enclave-generated theater yawned a gulf whose width and depth varied with the ability of any particular enclave to control the way it was represented (or misrepresented) to the wider city. This will become evident by comparing theatrical productions coming out of Gotham's German, Yiddish, Italian, Hispanic, and Chinese communities with those generated for the English-language vaudeville stage.

The second intersection of culture and commerce involved the city's African American enclave and the music business, whose relationship was peculiarly contradictory. On the one hand, the intensity of turn-of-the-century racism undermined black New Yorkers' already limited ability to control their own representation. On the other, the city's black community had nurtured a cultural product—ragtime music—that white businesses (Tin Pan Alley publishers, record companies, the theatrical and vaudeville circuits) realized was extremely valuable. A group of strategically placed black composers and performers attempted to seize on the opening this situation afforded to scale the heights of the culture industry, hoping also to contest its deep-dyed racism—a project that, for a time, achieved a remarkable degree of success.

A third interplay between cultural mores and profit-making enterprise revolved around the growing desire of many women and men to engage in leisure-time behaviors that pressed against the constraints of propriety, and the simultaneous emergence of novel entertainment venues—notably dance halls, Parisian-style revues, and cabarets—that catered to such desires. These new practices and institutions in turn provoked resistance from self- appointed guardians of traditional gender arrangements. These critics had little feel for the emancipatory dimension of the new culture. They were riveted rather by its drawbacks and dangers— the cynical profiteers hawking shallow pleasures, the multiple exploiters lurking in the forest of alluring freedoms. They sought to shore up weakening cultural levees by privately patrolling the amoral marketplace and encouraging the municipal government to do likewise.

Each of these three arenas witnessed a series of conflicts and compromises out of which came both modest adjustments in the city's cultural landscape, and a set of brilliant entertainments, some of which grabbed the attention of the world.

STAGING ETHNICITY

From the mid-nineteenth century on, immigrants arriving from Germany quickly established professional theatrical companies, adaptively reusing English-language houses whose patrons had moved elsewhere. The Stadttheater, which had opened in 1854 in the former Bowery Amphitheatre at 37–39 Bowery, appealed to both working- and middle-class audiences by presenting a mix of classics and operettas, along with melodramas and farces. When the German community itself moved uptown in the 1880s, so did its theaters, which now became more specialized, tending to concentrate on either "highbrow" or "lowbrow" presentations, in the parlance of the times.

In 1888 Amberg's German Theatre opened at Irving Place and 15th Street, in Union Square's Rialto district. In 1893 Amberg's was taken over by theatrical manager Heinrich Conried, who renamed it the Irving Place Theatre. For the next decade, the Conried-trained repertory company offered polished performances of classical German drama (Goethe, Schiller, Lessing), along with Shakespeare and French masterpieces in translation, and works by distinguished modern playwrights (notably Ibsen)—up to sixty-five productions a year. Conried, widely hailed by English-language drama critics as the German American Belasco, was hired away to manage the Metropolitan Opera in 1903, and his calls for scaling up his repertory approach led to the 1909 Otto Kahn–backed New Theatre misadventure. The Irving Place Theatre continued on in a highbrow vein until 1918, with support from German American elites, notably piano manufacturer William Steinway and restaurateur August Luchow (whose establishment was half a block away).

Meanwhile, a few blocks to the south, an alternative approach was assayed at the Germania Theatre, a former church, located in Astor Place on 8th Street between Broadway and Fourth Avenue. In 1894 it was leased by Adolf Philipp, an actor and singer from the Hamburg stage who had been recruited by Amberg to come to New York in 1890, then decided, age twenty-five, to manage his own theater. The Germania initially tried the classics, too, but when they didn't draw enough of an audience, Philipp decided to write and produce musical *Volksstücke* (folk plays), "showing German-American life" in New York City. Set in Kleindeutschland, Philipp's plays poked affectionate fun at the community and its habits, and featured neighborhood locales. His shows—like *Der Corner Grocer aus der Avenue A*, *Der Pawnbroker von der East Side*, and *Geheimnisse von New York* (Mysteries of New York, 1900)—included acts entitled "Grünhörner auf Island" ("Greenhorn on Island") and "Ein Tag auf Coney Island" ("A Day on Coney Island"). "The Germans in New York want something typically American," Philipp said, "only they want to understand it"; therefore he was giving them "American musical comedy in German" (though he tossed in bits of pidgin English, to help newcomers navigate their way into the city's linguistic mainstream).

Eschewing Conried's high-culture aspirations, Philipp hewed instead to an unabashedly commercial dynamic: "I do not work for glory, only for cash," he declared, and he got what he was after. During his decade at the Germania he had one box-office hit after another, with *Der New Yorker Brewer* racking up a sensational 856-night run. In 1902 the Germania was razed to make way for Wanamaker's and the Astor Place subway station. Philipp now took his show on the road, to Germany, where he scored an even bigger success: *Der New Yorker Brewer* ran 1,300 times in Berlin. In 1907 he leased a theater in Yorkville, where much of the German American community had resettled, and offered similar fare, in some cases simply reformatting earlier plays, *Der Butcher aus der Erste Avenue* becoming *Der Butcher von Yorkville*.

Philipp argued that his work was more popular with Gotham's Germans than what was on offer at Conried's Irving Place: "I believe they prefer it to high-brow drama or even comedies by the leading German authors." It was probably safer to say that his *Volksstücke* appealed to a different (and, yes, larger) segment of that community, more plebeian than patrician, without suggesting a head-to-head, either-or confrontation; Kleindeutschland was large enough to comfortably sustain two radically different theatrical styles.

IN THE JEWISH COMMUNITY, which had largely occupied the Lower East Side territory from which the Germans had withdrawn, theatrical politics were considerably more contentious.

Yiddish theater, born in Romania in 1876 and imported to New York in 1882, had by the 1890s moved from the tiny meeting halls where it had first taken root, to proper theaters, often bequeathed them by departing German companies. The three principal Yiddish houses, all on the Bowery, were the Windsor (formerly the Stadttheater), the People's, and the Thalia. (Originally the 1826 Bowery Theatre, it became a German house in 1879, then a Yiddish hall in 1891, after having oscillated between German and Yiddish the preceding two seasons.)

The growing Yiddish-speaking population adored the theater—a blessed relief from harsh ghetto realities. Yiddish playwrights offered sad and nostalgic evocations of shtetl life that played on immigrant homesickness. Or they presented historical and biblical dramas, chock-full of spectacular displays of Jewish heroism. They also produced melodramas of daily life in New York—tales of wayward wives, drunken husbands, cruel landlords, and children who married "no-goods"—along with comedies portraying greenhorn blunderers that reminded "regelah Yehnkee" audiences how far they had come from Ellis Island. Whatever the fare, plebeian audiences were enthusiastic participants, yelling out their approbation or outrage at the action—in a manner reminiscent of antebellum Bowery audiences, though minus the physical rowdiness.

Yiddish plays also tended to interpolate bits of stage business that didn't necessarily move the story but generated a larger-than-life "theatrical" experience. As one journalist noted in

People's Theatre, *Der Griner Boher* (The Green Boy), 1905. (New York Public Library, Dorot Jewish Division)

1901, "Jewish theatre-goers demonstrate great enthusiasm for couplets, dances, jokes, acrobatic stunts, and funny scenes which belong to vaudeville." Yiddish actors shunned understatement. They shouted, cursed, whispered, wept, and wallowed in schmaltz. The great and flamboyant stars—Boris Thomashefsky, Sigmund Mogulesko, Bertha Kalich, and the princely Jacob P. Adler—inspired not only up-and-coming Jewish actors but uptown practitioners as well: John Barrymore and Isadora Duncan were among those who came to study and admire these performers.

Noticeably absent from the ranks of admirers were the Russian Jewish socialist intellectuals, like Abe Cahan of the *Jewish Daily Forward*, who regarded themselves as the immigrants' cultural as well as political mentors. They considered what was on offer in Yiddish playhouses to be *shund* ("tripe" or "trash"), stupid and stupefying entertainment, and they were not shy about letting the community know of their displeasure. As socialists they promoted instead a realist theater, whose plays would raise audience members' awareness of social ills and trigger a demand for change.[1]

Cahan's great ally in his campaign was Jacob Gordin, a Russian writer who arrived in New York in 1891 and began writing for the socialist *Arbeiter Zeitung*. Jacob Adler prompted him to try his hand at playwriting. Gordin's *The Jewish King Lear* (1892), set in mid-nineteenth-century Vilna, with Adler in the lead, was his first great success; he would also rework Tolstoy, Hugo, Ibsen, and Schiller for local consumption. Gordin's plots were naturalistic treatments of the experience of Eastern European Jewry and New York's immigrant Jewish community, and by the early 1900s he was held in high esteem by a considerable swatch of the East Side's public. In 1903 the first theater built specifically for the Yiddish stage opened—the Grand Theatre at 257 Grand (and Chrystie)—with Jacob Adler as artistic director.

Shund, however, had never gone away; indeed, it drew far more patrons than did realist fare. Worse—from Cahan's perspective—*shund* was now being challenged by the even "trashier" offerings of Yiddish music halls, which began popping up on the Lower East Side in 1901. Situated at first in the back rooms of saloons, they featured bawdy songs, titillating dances, and broad humor. (These were places where references to the wife of the tsar as the "tsardine" brought down the house.) By 1906 most of the important streets on the Lower East Side had a glaring electric sign that announced JEWISH VAUDEVILLE HOUSE or JEWISH MUSIC HALL, and they appeared in Brooklyn and the Bronx as well. Some were substantial venues: the Grand Street Music Hall (at the Bowery) could seat more than a thousand spectators. Cahan and his crowd thundered against the new menace—a "crime against decency"—and insisted that attending music halls wasn't the kind of Americanization he'd been thinking of. Nevertheless, thousands of Jewish workers and their families attended regularly, partly because music-hall tickets were one-third the price of regular theater seats, but mainly because most patrons were seeking diversion rather than edification. According to a contemporary observer, "The audience does not consider the music halls a holy place or a 'temple' of art. . . . No one comes here to use his brains, to search for criticism or learn about morality."

The newest wave of immigrants, who poured into the area after the 1903 Kishinev pogroms, had an additional problem with Gordinian theater. They could appreciate realism, but only if it spoke to their own experience as a persecuted minority, not if it was anti-nationalist and pro-universalist. Gordin's earlier plays had been appealing on ethnic grounds, but his

---

1. Writers around the Orthodox press agreed that theater should educate the audience but had a different lesson plan in mind, urging plays that celebrated Jewish virtues and national identity.

later ones, which attacked traditional Jewish morality, provoked bitter dissent, another reason that from 1903 until his death in 1909 his influence declined sharply.

Even the work of a Yiddish writer of world stature couldn't buck these trends. In 1906 Sholom Aleichem, having fled the pogroms, resettled in Gotham, hoping to earn his living writing plays. At first the Yiddish and American press greeted him as a celebrity. But he began making patronizing remarks, announcing he would elevate the American Yiddish theater to a European level, and alienated the left-wing *Forward* crowd by aligning himself with the conservative *Tageblatt*. Still, actors like Adler and Thomashefsky vied for a Sholom Aleichem script, and in February 1907 each opened a play by the master. Only to see both flop: each closed in two weeks. In the summer of 1907, disappointed and resentful, he departed for Europe.[2]

Still-heavier seas lay ahead for the uplift variety of Yiddish theater. In 1905 the nickelodeons had begun arriving on East 14th Street and the Bowery (Zukor's being one of the first), and their cheap seats became all the more attractive during the 1907–8 recession. By 1908 there were well over thirty movie theaters on the Lower East Side, and their competition cut deeply into the theaters' box office, at just the time the Hebrew Actors' Union (founded in 1899 by Joseph Barondess) had won a raise in pay that made it impossible for the houses to raise ticket prices. In 1909, to the shock and fury of the Cahan forces, the Grand Theatre— Adler having been unable to keep the house afloat with reruns of early Gordin plays—was taken over by Zukor and Loew. Cahan railed against this sacrilege, and movie houses in general, calling for a boycott, but the Jewish masses paid no heed.

In an effort at a comeback, Yiddish theater entrepreneurs opened up a new front at Second Avenue, hoping to draw on a more affluent catchment area. First in the field was Kessler's Second Avenue Theatre, which opened in 1911 at East 2nd Street. It was followed next year by the National Theatre, two blocks to the south, just across Houston Street.[3] The 1,700-seat National occupied the street level of an eight-story building constructed by real estate broker Louis Minsky, who had called in the theater and movie palace architect Thomas W. Lamb to design it. Minsky also commissioned a rooftop theater for the building—the National Winter Garden—with seating for a thousand. The downstairs venue was a legitimate Yiddish playhouse, managed jointly by Adler and Thomashefsky, but it remained to be seen if it could withstand the torrent of *shund* and Jewish vaudeville and movies—to say nothing of what was transpiring upstairs.

The National building was actually Louis Minsky's second venture into the theatrical business, of which as an orthodox Jew he thoroughly disapproved. In 1909 Minsky's son Abe, and Abe's friend Charlie Steiner, had talked Louis into buying a building at 143 East Houston Street, between Forsyth and Eldridge Streets. Once a Dutch church, then a German one, then a boxing hall, under Abe and Charlie it became the Houston Street Hippodrome, a music hall seating 299, that combined Yiddish and English vaudeville with movies. Yonah Schimmel's knish shop, which in 1910 opened nearby at number 137, served as snack bar. But when Louis got word that some of the films his son was showing were rather racy—with

2. In 1914, in poor health, Sholom Aleichem returned to New York. There he signed a contract to write for the newspaper *Der Tog* (The Day), which assured him a fixed income, and he returned to literary projects. But in the summer of 1915, he was crushed by news of his son's sudden death, and in 1916, when living in the South Bronx (968 Kelley Street), he fell ill and died. His funeral attracted hundreds of thousands of mourners—Cahan was pallbearer—a demonstration of the scope of New York's Yiddish-speaking population.

3. When the Irving Place Theatre (at 15th Street) ceased operation as a German house in 1918, it was taken over by actor-manager Morris Schwartz, who had been performing at Kessler's, and reopened as the Yiddish Art Theatre. It would later move to Second Avenue at 12th Street.

titles like *The Butler and the Upstairs Maid*—he exiled Abe from the enterprise. (A few years later Steiner expanded it to 600 seats and renamed it the Sunshine Theater.) Abe, meanwhile, had been given the rooftop National Winter Garden just down the street, which he and his brother Billy used to screen the newer, more respectable, four-reeler feature films. In 1917, however, facing declining box-office returns, the Minskys executed a sharp change of direction, baldly announced by a sign downstairs: BURLESQUE AS YOU LIKE IT—NOT A FAMILY SHOW.

GOTHAM'S ITALIAN THEATRICAL LANDSCAPE WAS ALSO RICH AND COMPLEX, though more fragmented than its German and Yiddish counterparts. Around the time Yiddish theaters were emerging in the 1880s, amateur Italian theatrical clubs were sprouting in *caffé concerti* in the Italian colonies. Small, informal affairs, they usually charged no entrance fee and made their profit selling liquor. On a small stage at the rear, performers entertained customers with Italian songs, skits, and sometimes full-length dramas. In Little Italy, these *caffés* included L'Eldorado (24 Spring Street), Villa Vittorio Emanuele III (109 Mulberry Street), and Villa Giulia (196 Grand Street); Ferrando's Music Hall was a little farther away, in Greenwich Village (at 184 Sullivan Street.)

Soon formal theater companies emerged, including Il Circolo Filodrammatico Italo-Americano of New York, at 88½ Mulberry, and La Compagnia Comico-Drammatica Italiana, which began in the back of the Banca Sessa, a combination bank, travel agency, and Italian bookstore at 40 Union Street, in the heart of South Brooklyn's largely Neapolitan community. The Compagnia was founded by Guglielmo Ricciardi, who also ran the Grand Eden Caffé, which opened in Italian Harlem in 1900 (on First Avenue between 111th and 112th). Newsboys and bootblacks and grown-ups too beelined for the Sicilian puppet shows at the Teatro delle Marionette, and to Pulcinella farces at La Compagnia Napoletana.

By 1900 the city's Italian community boasted an analogue of Conried and Gordin—Antonio Maiori, a tragedian who established the Teatro Italiano, a tiny 24 Spring Street venue, to host performances of his Compagnia Comico-Drammatica Italiano di Antonio Maiori e Pasquale Rapone. Occasionally Maiori was able to rent space in some of the bigger Bowery houses, such as the People's Theatre or the Thalia, which were primarily occupied by Yiddish companies. Sometimes Maiori and Jacob Adler would share a theater, alternating performances of the same play (Italians on Friday and Saturday), using the same sets and costumes, with billboards blazoning the joint production done half in Italian, half in Yiddish. Maiori's goal was to introduce immigrants to European classics (translated into Italian or regional dialect), and also to "the best of Italy's national stage repertoire, and not just the Southern one." This proved a hard act to sell to mostly southern immigrants. Overall, he considered the project a failure, certainly when compared to the accomplishments of other ethnicities. "All the Colonies, even the Chinese, have their National Theatre," Maiori lamented. "I hoped that ours could also start up with one through my sacrifices but I was soon disillused [*sic*]."

Where the city's Italian playwrights and performers shone was in intra-enclave theater, which focused on portraying life in New York. Eduardo Migliaccio, one of Italian American theater's most famous performers, immigrated to the United States in 1897 and got a job in a Mulberry Street bank writing letters for illiterate immigrant clients to relatives in Italy. He also began writing *macchiette coloniali*, closely observed character sketches of community members. Adapting the commedia dell'arte tradition to his needs, Migliaccio performed under the name of Farfariello, and his impersonations (there were more than 250 of them) amounted to a collective portrait of Gotham's Italian American community. The sketches ranged widely, including the drunk, the priest, the undertaker, the mafioso, the radical, and the capitalist, and even his friend Enrico Caruso. He did female impersonations as well: the East Side schoolgirl, the nanny, the anxious bride, the modern woman. The heroes of his highly realistic urban ethnography were the proletarians—quick-witted greenhorns who were poor, honest, and hardworking street vendors, laborers, rag pickers, organ grinders, tailors, and construction workers.[4] And his favorite targets were the *prominenti*, the overzealous national-istic presidents of Italian American associations who were forever marching in parades, making speeches at banquets, and shouting *Viva l'Italia!*—even as they pushed Americanization and took a condescending attitude to the Italian language and regional dialects.

The *prominenti* were also the target of more pointed darts thrown from the left. Many Italian socialist and anarchist clubs had amateur dramatic societies affiliated with them— Filodramatiche rosse—which were imbued (said the magazine *La Follia* in 1907) with the goal of "spreading the modern ideals of social justice and brotherhood through the theatre." Among these were the Filodrammatica dell'Unione Socialista (1905), L'Avvenire [the Future] (1907), and the Circolo Enrico Ibsen (1907). The playwrights were mostly amateurs who wrote in their spare time, as were the actors who performed the works in social clubs, in cafés, at picnics, or (on weekends and holidays) in hired halls like the Manhattan Lyceum, the Thalia, Webster Hall, and the People's House. The money collected on these occasions was used to benefit their affiliated radical groups, newspapers, and political prisoners.

Riccardo Cordiferro, the most popular and prolific of the radical playwrights, was also a poet, journalist, and activist. He had emigrated from southern Italy in 1892, first to Pittsburgh, then to New York, where he founded the humor weekly *La Follia*. Cordiferro wrote lectures, too; one of his best-known—the forthrightly named "Capitalist Tyranny and Proletarian Solidarity"—was first read aloud in 1907 at Palmer's Hall in Brooklyn before an assembly of striking Italian barbers. Cordiferro's plays ridiculed and vilified those he consid-ered the community's oppressors—bosses, priests, and the aforementioned capitalists. Exposing the arrogance and corruption of *prominenti* who got rich by contracting out unskilled workers' labor, he mocked the honorific titles—*cavaliere, commendatore*—lavished on them by the Italian government.

IN THE 1890S SPANISH-LANGUAGE THEATER didn't just have a political wing, it was entirely political—an offshoot of the Cuban war against the Spanish Empire. Amateur and semipro-fessional shows were performed at political gatherings to promote the independence move-ment and raise funds for the struggle. With the war's end, Spanish-language theater—after a benefit performance in 1899 to raise funds for a Martí sepulcher—seems to have vanished. It reappeared in 1916 when Manuel Noriega, a Spanish comic actor-singer, arrived in Gotham. Noriega, who had debuted in Mexico City in 1904, came to the city via the Havana stage. An enthusiastic promoter, he founded the Compañía Dramática Española, which put on Spanish *zarzuelas* (operettas) and *sainete* (one-act comic sketches). Urged on by *La Prensa*, Puerto Rican *tabaqueros* packed in to see Noriega's 1918 debut at the Amsterdam Opera House (West 44th near Ninth). For a time his troupe flourished. He expanded it, hiring Cuban, Spanish, and Mexican actors, and adding works from Galicia and Catalonia, along with Cuban blackface skits. In 1919 he partnered with some businessmen to lease the Park Theatre

---

4. In one sketch a worker says: "What a big city, New York. When I saw the palaces rising up to the sky I told myself I must have gone to Paradise, without having noticed. But when I saw men who were working in a deep pit, between water and dynamite and all sorts of pipes . . . it dawned upon me that they must have been summoned to hell."

at Columbus Circle. Rebaptizing it El Teatro Español, he set out to make it the city's Hispanic house: "It is the intention to make the Park a bit of the mother country," Noriega told the *Times* in April 1919. But being seriously undercapitalized and poorly managed, the project collapsed, and Noriega, after floating his company from one rental theater to another for two years, vanished. The still tiny (and diverse and scattered) Spanish-speaking communities did not have the critical mass to sustain an enclave theater.

THE CHINESE COMMUNITY, EVEN SMALLER, had similar difficulties, though it had the advantage of being repeatedly visited by touring Cantonese opera troupes, from China and Hong Kong, which made their way across the continent after performing in San Francisco. First to arrive was the Most Sublime Company, which opened in 1889 at the Windsor Theatre on the Bowery, when its nearly fifty actors staged *The Faithful Vassal*, a play set in the early-seventeenth-century Tang Dynasty.

Chinatown got a company of its own in March 1893 when Chu Fong, a wealthy English-speaking merchant, imported thirty actors from California and rented a large warehouse basement on Doyers Street for a theater. He quickly ran afoul (as Yiddish houses often did) of the city's Sabbath laws, which prohibited theatrical performances on Sunday—the only day on which the Chinese laundrymen scattered around the metropolis came together in Chinatown. Chu Fong would argue, as had impresarios since Barnum, that his Sunday shows were "sacred concerts," not profane amusements. He was nevertheless arrested, tried, and released after witnesses testified that in Chinese culture plays were religious ceremonies, which explicated

Stafford Mantle Northcote, *Chinese Theatre, NYC*, 1900, Oil on Linen (Object No. 78899d, New-York Historical Society)

moral precepts and were performed in temples. He was arrested again, and again, until he gave up in 1897. The enterprise was taken over eventually by Charlie Gong, whom reporters christened "the Frohman of Doyers Street." He carried on with classic Cantonese opera, which was enlivened by interludes of farce and acrobatics. There does not appear to have been a Chinese Farfariello who addressed life in New York. Charlie Gong carried on until he closed down in 1909, after his house got caught in the crossfire of a tong war. It would be another fifteen years before theater would return to Chinatown.

TO LEAVE AN ENCLAVE THEATER AND ENTER AN AMERICAN VAUDEVILLE HOUSE was to move from three-dimensional portraits to two-dimensional caricatures. Vaudeville entrepreneurs had no interest in complex characterizations, à la Farfariello or Philipp. They wanted instantly graspable stereotypes (generally negative ones)—cartoon images that reduced enclave residents to their presumed essential core: Jewish cheapskates, drunken Irishmen, stiletto-wielding Italians, black chicken thieves. These images were conveyed by ethnic impersonators. Their routines parodied the city's assorted peoples, affecting their clothing and mimicking their speech—with heavy stress laid on the ways in which recent immigrants murdered the English language. Vaudeville ethnics were often presented in a demeaning way, but never a scary one. They were meant to be amusing, not threatening. Vaudeville was ethnicity played for laughs.

Male stock characters were the comics' chief stock-in-trade.

Stage Germans were fat, stolid, beer-loving fellows, given to boozy buffoonery. The "Dutch" act of Joe Weber and Lew Fields—"Dutch" being an Americanization of "Deutsch" (German)—featured knockabout slapstick humor (choking, shaking, and eye poking), along with malapropisms and assorted other manglings of English, as in this classic bit of thickly accented Weber and Field business: "Mike: I am delightfulness to meet you. Myer: Der disgust is all mine. Mike: I receivedidid a letter from mein goil, but I don't know how to writteninin her back. Myer: Writteninin her back! Such an edumuncation you got it? Writteninin her back! You mean rotteninin her back. How can you answer her ven you don't know how to write? Mike: Dot makes no nefer mind. She don't know how to read."

The stage Italian wore a sack suit with short trousers, a blue shirt, and a red bandanna neckerchief, had a small black mustache, sported brass earrings, and perched a black slouch hat atop his black wig. He answered to names like Antonio Spaghetti or Tony Macaroni and was a genial (if ignorant) fellow—easy-going (not to say indolent), ready with a joke and a song. He was also, however, hot-blooded, quick-tempered, and capable of flaring in a moment into murderous knife-wielding rage.

The stage Hebrew often came attired in a long black frock coat, baggy pants, oversized shoes, and a derby hat pulled down over the ears. He had a protuberant hook nose (fashioned with the aid of nose putty), he spoke in a thick Yiddish-English dialect, and he embodied a variety of anti-Semitic stereotypes. For one, he was physically unclean. (In one 1910 monologue, philanthropist Jacob Schiff sends New York newsboys to Coney Island once each summer for a swim. At the beach, "little Ikey Epstein was just getting into the water when Mr. Schiff says to him, 'you look pretty dirty.' 'I know it,' said Ikey, 'I missed the train last year.'") For another, he was ethically dishonest. In his various incarnations as a pushcart peddler, an old-clothes dealer, or a pawnbroker, he was driven by a concern for money. (One common shtick involved neighborhood Shylocks setting fire to their small businesses to collect on the insurance.) He was not, however, as in European representations of Jews, a blood-sucking agent of the devil; the vaudeville Jew was ridiculous, not menacing.

Stage Chinese ("chinks") wore "coolie" costumes—baggy blue shirts and pants, the traditional dress of laborers from southern China. White actors donned short-cropped wigs with queues, applied yellowface greasepaint, outlined their eyes with India ink to create a slanting effect,; affixed a mustache and goatee if portraying an elderly male, and added five-inch fingernail sheaths if playing a sinister character. They spoke in pidgin English or outright gibberish. Musical accompaniments, like "Chinatown, My Chinatown" (1910), described essential accouterments: "Pigtails flying here and there . . . pipe dreams banish ev'ry care."

The stage blacks' signifiers were airlifted in straight from minstrelsy, a suitcase full of rural-based attributes—childlike, hapless, ignorant, lazy. Jim Crow shirked work, lived by stealing chickens and watermelons. Vaudeville added in characteristics of the urban Zip Coon, who was addicted to gambling, drink, sex, and violence. The blend produced a near-perfect inversion of the ideal American, with each virtue replaced by its corresponding vice. Again, though one might imagine a slight frisson of danger to be inherent in this depiction, the characters were presented in a humorous way, never generating fear or rancor.

All these stereotypes were migrated wholesale to other media. Movies appropriated vaudeville's plots and stock characters—conniving Jews, quarrelsome Irishmen, treacherous Mexicans, shiftless blacks—and vaudeville's comic routines were reenacted in recording studios for transfer to disks.

The handy thing about stereotypes from a manager's point of view was that vaudeville conventions allowed pretty much anyone to play any ethnic group. Put on the right accent, the right clothing, and the right color greasepaint—sallow for Jews, red for Irishmen, olive for Sicilians—and you were in business. Don blackface—an even older convention—and you could safely indulge the more indecorous forms of humor. There were limits, to be sure; very rarely were blacks allowed to don whiteface (though wearing yellowface was acceptable). "Actual" ethnics were thought to have something of an edge in presenting their own people's stereotypes. Joe Welch, a Jewish performer, perfected in the late 1880s a woeful doppelgänger who would enter, face the audience at center stage, stare at them with a sorrowful look for a full half minute, then come out with his winning opener: "Maybe you tink I'm heppy?" David Warfield was renowned from the mid-1890s on for his "famous Hebraic Specialty," which involved creating comic characters like Isidore Nosenstein. Warfield was Jewish but didn't look it (blue eyes, sandy hair, modest nose); nor did he practice it. Underlining the distinction between his life and his role, Warfield stressed "the care and time I have given to studying the quaint Russian types which come to this country from southeastern Europe." He liked to plunge "into the very heart of the East Side" to talk with locals, and on occasion test his characterization by donning makeup and "passing" as a Hebrew on Hester Street. "This Jew of mine has no prototype in life," he admitted, but "is a sort of composite character absorbed through general observation."

What did audiences make of all this? It depended on the audience, which varied with the venue. High-priced Keith houses drew more American-born, middle-class crowds; working-class immigrants headed for the cheap seats at the local Loew's. Anglo-Protestant attendees—a fair number of whom were anxious about the vast influx of immigrants—had concerns assuaged by their vaudeville representation as bumbling newcomers. Whites could feel similarly comforted by the reaffirmation of their convictions about the inferiorities of black, brown, and yellow peoples. Middle-class attendees who had limited experience with real immigrants or colored folk often tended to accept the stereotypes on offer as actual reflections of urban reality (especially when backed by claims of expertise).

How did immigrants in the audience respond to stage denigrations of immigrants? Often, it seems, they chortled with recognition at the simulated identities—at least those of other groups. Stereotypes could seem useful, after all, as they provided instantaneously identifiable markers that could help in navigating the city's complicated cultural landscape. You knew, or thought you knew, with whom you were dealing. Stereotypes of one's own people, where the gap between representation and reality was apparent, might be greeted with greater ambivalence. Much depended on tone and style; skits that were affectionate in nature might be well received, especially if they were cleverly done, and those that traded in largely obsolete images (Jewish peddlers in the 1910s) might seem merely dated, even stir nostalgia for the old neighborhood in those who'd moved away.[5]

Outrightly demeaning portraits were something else again, and such performances were subject to attack—and revision, or even cancellation, if an enclave could muster sufficient muscle.

In the case of Germans, the *New Yorker Staats-Zeitung*—catering to its respectable middle-class readers—frowned severely on the stereotyping of the Dutch act's stage German: "We German-Americans do not laugh at him." Nor did they like Philipp's work at the Germania. And it's telling that when Weber and Fields, who broke up their act in 1904 at the height of their popularity, attempted a comeback in 1912, it didn't fly.

In the Jewish community, organizations emerged that set out to rid the vaudeville stage of entertainers who caricatured and maligned Jews. The Chicago Anti-Stage Ridicule Committee was first in the field, joined in 1914 by the powerful Associated Rabbis of America, whose members advised their congregations to shun theaters where something was being said or done that could feed religious hatreds. Any theater manager in Williamsburg contemplating engaging a put-down Jewish comic who had been denounced by the rabbis would think twice before doing so.

Sometimes the images were redrawn inside the vaudeville hall itself. In 1907 squads dispatched by the Ancient Order of Hibernians and the United Irish Societies of New York booed, hissed, and hurled eggs and vegetables at the Russell Brothers, comics they believed portrayed Irish servant girls in a bigoted way. Within a year of having been driven from the stage of the Brooklyn Orpheum and then Hammerstein's Victoria, both had retired. Even Edward Harrigan, of the once wildly popular Harrigan and Hart, lost favor with the many Irish who had risen into the respectable middle class. No longer recognizing themselves in Harrigan's characters, they rejected the stage Irishman image, even when presented sympathetically.[6]

In 1916, in Yorkville, a largely German audience was chuckling at a film supposedly set in Puerto Rico that featured half-savage boys and half-naked women being enlightened by a Yankee hero. Some Puerto Ricans in the audience protested the trashy portrait, explained the cultural situation on the island, and won a round of applause from the Germans.

The audience-feedback mechanism, however, didn't work too well if the audience in question hadn't much political clout or was seldom in the vaudeville hall itself—blacks being

---

5. Stereotypes could also evolve naturally with their real-life models. Thus Irish caricatures shifted from the greenhorn hod carrier of the 1880s to the East Side "Mick" of the 1900's (a contractor, politician, or policeman). And Hebrew impersonator Barney Bernard (himself Jewish) replaced the Jewish frock-coated-and-bearded peddler with a more contemporary-looking Jewish businessman, the bald and bespectacled Abe Potash in the Potash and Perlmutter routine (from 1913), though he retained the thick Yiddish accent.

6. Ironically, there were those in the Irish community who feared that the 1911 tour by the Irish Abbey Theatre, with its impending performance of Synge's *Playboy of the Western World*, might jeopardize their newfound respectability and political influence, and it was denounced as immoral and anti-Irish.

often barred by cost or custom. Nor did the city's African American community have its own enclave theater—it hadn't since the African Grove in the 1820s. With comics thus meeting minimal resistance to racist images, they had little inducement to refrain from making blacks the chief butt of jokey disrespect. Yet it was that community that leapt over the vaudeville scene altogether and set its sights on remaking black representations on Tin Pan Alley, and the legitimate Broadway stage itself.

RAGTIME

With the passing of the 1890s depression, Tin Pan Alley songsmiths were ready for something new. New York publishers could still get mileage from sentimental ballads—tearjerkers like "Hello Central, Give Me Heaven, for My Mama's There" (1901)—but audiences in boom-time America seemed eager for something less lugubrious. Some tunemakers responded with songs that were sunnier but essentially cut from the same cloth—"In the Good Old Summer Time" (1902), "On a Sunday Afternoon" (1902), and "Wait 'Til the Sun Shines, Nellie" (1905). But more dynamic fare was on hand, notably that produced by song-and-dance man George M. Cohan.

Cohan was not a native New Yorker, but he became the personification of Broadway. Technically he hailed from the Irish slums of Providence. In fact he grew up on the Road. With his vaudevillian family, young George (beginning at age 8) barnstormed America's variety halls and county fairs. In the 1890s the Four Cohans broke into the big time with an engagement at Keith's Union Square Theater. George, who had written songs for the group, now took his material around the Tin Pan Alley houses. In 1894 the Witmarks brought out his first published piece. By 1898 jaunty George was a 20-year-old phenomenon—a songwriter of some standing and a brassy, straw-hatted performer who drew top billings.

In 1901, after a dispute with B. F. Keith, he quit vaudeville to write musical plays. His *Little Johnny Jones*, produced on Broadway in 1904 by Abe Erlanger, featured two smash hits—"The Yankee Doodle Boy" and the New York anthem "Give My Regards to Broadway." Other enduring numbers quickly followed, notably a rouser called (at first) "You're a Grand Old Rag" (then altered to "Flag" in response to objections). Cohan's music was brash, and so was he. Cocky and frenetic, he called everybody "Kid," jabbed them in the ribs, thumped them on the chest. His aggressively patriotic lyrics reflected the country's new imperial swagger. In a way, they reincarnated old-fashioned Bowery B'hoy jingoism, with its Irish-American scorn for the English and local Anglophile elites. Cohan was a latter-day Big Mose, a strutting Yankee Doodle boy who waved Old Glory and made the Eagle scream. Post–Spanish–Cuban–American War audiences, tired of spoonfed gentility, relished his all-American energy. "Speed! Speed! And lots of it!" was his motto, and his rapid-fire songs and dances were a great fit for a fast town like New York.

Gotham's drama critics weren't so sure. This flashily dressed son of immigrants, spouting up-to-the-minute slang, was perhaps okay for the vaudeville stage, but Broadway? Cohan was well aware they thought him an ill-mannered upstart—an "impudent, noisy vaudevillian, entirely out of place in first class theatres." They soon made their peace with him because he proved both a consummate professional and a canny businessman. Cohan mastered every aspect of the theater: he danced, managed, acted, sang, choreographed, cast, financed, composed, directed, and produced. He set up his own publishing house to hawk his songs' sheet music. Klaw and Erlanger erected the Gaiety Theatre for him in 1909; in 1911 he moved to his own house, the George M. Cohan at Broadway and 43rd. His formula proved fabulously successful. By 1914 he had made over $3 million and moved to a house in Great Neck.[7]

ANOTHER NEW MUSIC ARRIVED IN THESE YEARS, one that departed even more radically from the traditional canon. It was called ragtime. Like Cohan's music, it seemed emblematic of modern times—a rhythmic reflection of the peppy new century, and one that drew its energy from the city streets. Tin Pan Alley publisher Edward B. Marks said that "the best songs came from the gutter." But ragtime didn't just steam up from the pavements. It represented a complex blending of musical practices. At bottom, however, it was essentially black music filtered through white minstrelsy.

"Ragged time" described the syncopated, polyrhythmic piano music played in the saloons and brothels of the black sporting districts of St. Louis and other midwestern cities. Syncopation—"a disturbance or interruption of the regular flow of rhythm"—gets created most often by stressing a note that is not on the beat, producing, as it were, "off-beat" music. Ragtime was surely that, and in its sharp break with the conventional lay the secret of its infectious appeal.

The first master of the form was Scott Joplin, a pianist and composer born just after the Civil War. He was the son of a railroad laborer—a former slave, who played the violin—and his wife, a domestic, who played the banjo and gave Scott a rudimentary musical education. Growing up in Texarkana, Texas, he studied classical piano free of charge with a sympathetic German Jewish music professor. In the late 1880s he became an itinerant ivory tickler, playing in brothels and saloons throughout the South. In 1894 he established a base in Sedalia, Missouri, where he began writing rags. In 1899 John Stark, a local piano dealer who published sheet music as a sideline, brought out Joplin's *Maple Leaf Rag*, paying the composer fifty dollars, plus (most unusually) royalties of one cent per copy. The initial printing of 400 took a year to sell, but then sales accelerated rapidly (by 1909 half a million had been bought), which led Stark to open an office on New York's Tin Pan Alley in 1905. Joplin followed in 1907.

By then Joplin's music, and ragtime in general, had long preceded him, carried to Gotham by a host of traveling black pianists. There it had taken firm root—along with the cakewalk, its associated dance form (ragtime being irresistibly danceable). An ebullient strut—done with the body bent way, way back, elbows out and wagging, legs kicking high—the cakewalk seems to have originated as a parody dance, fashioned by southern slaves to mock their masters' approach to social dancing.

Both music and dance came to roost in the city's closest approximation to an African American enclave: the black section of the larger Tenderloin that they shared with the Irish and other immigrants. Though the bulk of the population had moved north of the 40s, as far as San Juan Hill in the 60s, in the early 1900s the lower Tenderloin (the 20s and 30s) still contained many black-owned poolrooms, honky-tonks, dance halls, brothels, gambling dens, and saloons—many of which featured ragtime pianists.

Ike Hines's Professional Club, which had relocated from its original home in a Greenwich Village basement to 118 West 27th, was an early port of entry for the new music. Hines's place was a center of black Gotham's sporting life. Its walls were covered with lithographs or photographs of famous colored boxers, jockeys, stage celebrities, and political figures (prominently

---

7. Despite his meteoric rise, Cohan at first retained his early pro-labor sympathies. When George Fuller Golden, first president of the White Rats union, contracted tuberculosis, Cohan gave him $10,000 to move west to get well. When Golden was dying, he left word to have his ashes sent to Cohan to scatter from the top of the Statue of Liberty. Sterner tests of Cohan's labor politics lay just ahead.

Frederick Douglass). Its back room—which featured Hines-hired pianists and bands, along with ambitious hoofers practicing their song-and-dance routines—drew bohemian blacks and hip whites. So did Barron Wilkins's Little Savoy at 253 West 35th Street, where professional players, singers, and dancers competed for steady work, and jam sessions gave up-and-comers a chance to shine; here, too, whites joined the basic black audience, as slummers, regular patrons, or possible clients.

Though some whites were intrigued, many found the new music too daring. They were bothered by its popularity in brothels and dance halls. When there were lyrics, they seemed crude and vulgar. Some said ragtime "suggested the ardor of the saloon, the smell of the backyard and subways." It seemed less American than African. It was, in short, too black.

White pop-music businessmen, however, knew a hot property when they heard one—and Tin Pan Alley, on West 28th, was in easy earshot of the Tenderloin clubs. They also understood that to make even such limited transgressions of musical propriety respectable, they had to cover them with a kind of aural whiteface. So they added lyrics—songs with lyrics sold far more copies than did plain instrumentals—whose words were drawn from the Negrophobic minstrel tradition. What emerged was "coon songs," snappy, lightly syncopated ragtime ditties that recycled minstrelsy's familiar tales of happy, rural darkies stealing chickens and gorging on watermelon and added accounts of impudent, urban, razor-wielding coons (an image update of sorts). By packaging together lyrics calculated to be hilariously funny with music guaranteed to be exciting listening, Alley publishers had produced a commodity with which white consumers could feel perfectly comfortable. Listening to lyricized ragtime simultaneously affirmed their racial superiority while allowing them to experience, through the energy of the music, the kinds of passions they officially condemned.

Virtually all the Tin Pan Alley firms trafficked aggressively in coon songs—especially the Witmark brothers, several of whom had been minstrel performers themselves. Songsmiths cranked out numbers like "The Gentlemen Coons' Parade," "The Coon Musketeers," and "Dat Famous Chicken Debate ('Resolved, That Stealing Chickens Ain't No Crime')," in which shiftless "no account niggers" and their sensuous "wenches" ceaselessly swilled whiskey, munched watermelons, and rolled dem bones. The sheet music usually featured a grotesque caricature on the cover. By 1910 well over 600 coon songs had been produced, with total sales in the millions of copies; in 1906 "If the Man in the Moon Were a Coon" alone sold over 2.5 million. These offerings were the industry's leading and most profitable product.

Coon songs were overwhelmingly written and sung by whites. May Irwin, a blond-haired, blue-eyed, popular vaudeville actress became Broadway's most famous "coon-shouter" after belting out a showstopper about a "razor-toting nigger," in the premiere of *The Widow Jones* (1895); she secured her reputation the following year with the smash hit "All Coons Look Alike to Me."

There were also African Americans who actively participated in producing and promoting these songs. Indeed, the author of "All Coons" was a black songwriter, Ernest Hogan, though Isidore Witmark, who published it, later took credit for some of the lyrics. The song's success propelled Hogan to the top of New York's growing vaudeville star system. When the African American press denounced the song as epitomizing the demeaning nature of coon songs, Hogan, an old pro who'd worked in minstrel shows for most of his career, was mystified, unable to understand the unfavorable reaction.

Hogan was caught in a generational shift. A cohort of younger African Americans—some New York bred, most newly arrived—wanted to shake free of the minstrel tradition. On the other hand, black music and dance, as presented by white performers, were suddenly hot.

This opened up a possible opportunity for them to work as professional entertainers. But they would have to cater to commercial demand as determined by white producers, publishers, and audiences. It looked like they could either do coon songs or resign themselves to invisibility.

Black musicians and performers, in a difficult spot, decided on a dangerous strategy. They would slip into the straitjacket of coonery—burnt cork and all—and even demand access to the coon song parade on grounds of their authentic blackness. Then they would attempt to escape from their bonds, Houdini fashion, by subverting minstrel stereotypes from the inside, thus gaining control of their own representations. The danger, of course, was getting stuck inside the stereotypes, perhaps even reinforcing them.

The lead in this enterprise was taken by group of exceptionally accomplished black performers and songwriters, most of whom migrated to Gotham, seriatim, from cities of the South and West. Encountering one another in Tenderloin venues, they would join forces and attempt to ride the coon song phenomenon not only into Tin Pan Alley, but into Broadway itself.

THE FIRST TWO OF THIS COHORT TO ARRIVE, and its eventual pacesetters, were Bert Williams and George Walker, two vaudevillians who had been slowly working their way toward New York. Williams, a West Indian, had been born in 1874 in Nassau, capital of the Bahamas. His father moved the family first to Florida and then to California, where Bert had hoped to study engineering at Stanford University but couldn't raise the money. Instead, having had some youthful experience as a barker for a medicine show, he joined an integrated traveling minstrel troupe and in 1893 set out to play western lumber and mining camps. Along the way he met and teamed up with George Walker—born in 1873, raised in Lawrence, Kansas, his father a hotel porter. Together they fashioned a city-slicker-and-country-bumpkin routine. Walker played the strutting urban dandy—clever, streetwise, an agile dancer. Williams was the shuffling, slow-witted but good-natured sad sack, perpetually down on his luck. Their repartee borrowed much from minstrelsy, and their sequence of jokes and songs ended with a cakewalk. The two took their act on the road with a traveling medicine show, made their way to Chicago, and then, in 1896, arrived in Gotham. There they were included in a Victor Herbert farce, which flopped, but not before Williams and Walker had been praised in the press.

They now decided to stay in New York and work the vaudeville circuits. Needing an edge against the stiff competition, the duo billed themselves as the "Two Real Coons," the only ones capable of doing proper Negro delineations. As Walker explained later, he and Williams had been amused at watching corked-up whites try to pass themselves off as blacks and had decided "we would do all we could to get what we felt belonged to us by the laws of nature"—a tricky maneuver, as it meant accepting there was indeed an essential black nature, thus reinforcing racist stereotypes.

On the other hand, it worked. They got a contract for a forty-week run at Koster & Bial's and were written up in an October 1896 review as "colored performers, who are coming rapidly to the front." By December they had moved to Proctor's at 23rd Street, where their version of the cakewalk drew tremendous attention. Next it was on to gigs at Tony Pastor's and at Hammerstein's Olympia's roof garden. Their production grew steadily grander. In January 1897 they added two "dusky maidens," one of whom, the 17-year-old, Manhattan-raised Ada Overton, would become the leading choreographer of the Williams and Walker Company; with fame, and marriage to George, she would change her name to Aida Overton Walker. By February they had taken on "a score of celebrated high-steppers," and their amplified

"Bert Williams And George Walker Portrait," ca. 1902. (Donaldson Collection/Getty Images)

rendition of the cakewalk made them the rage of Manhattan—certified in March by the *New York Dramatic Mirror* as being "in the front rank of the top liners."

They also began to organize. The duo took rooms at the Marshall Hotel at 127–129 West 53rd Street (between Sixth and Seventh) and immediately threw their doors open "to all colored men who possessed theatrical and musical ability and ambition." Their goal, Walker recalled, was to provide a space where "all professional colored people could meet and exchange views and feel perfectly at home." Soon the building became "the headquarters of all artistic young men of our race who were stage struck."

More an elegant rooming house than a formal hostelry, the Marshall consisted of two converted four-story brownstones. A large dining room on the first floor, complete with piano and four-piece orchestra, provided one of the few upscale restaurants in New York at which blacks could dine. The basement drew house bands from around the city to jam during lunch hours, and hosted more formal performances every night. Within the safe space of the hotel, performers could entertain friends and colleagues, including white theatrical folk from nearby Broadway come to mingle with their black counterparts. Principally, however, it was a place where black performers came to talk—the "main question talked and wrangled over," one participant remembered, "being always that of the manner and means of raising the status of the Negro as a writer, composer, and performer in the New York theater and world of music."

Out of these conversations emerged a vibrant network of African American artists, several of whom moved into the Marshall or took rooms in nearby theatrical boardinghouses.

"Ada (Aida) Overton Walker, Half-Length Portrait, Facing Left," 1912. (Library of Congress Prints and Photographs Division)

Several had had advanced musical training but been balked in finding work commensurate with their skills and talent.

Will Marion Cook, born in DC, where his father was dean of the Howard University Law School, studied violin at the Oberlin Conservatory, at the Berlin Hochschule für Musik, and in 1894 with Antonin Dvořák at New York's National Conservatory of Music. Convinced that despite all his training he'd never win access to the white musical world, Cook turned his back on classical music and opted for pop, declaring that "the Negro in music and on the stage ought to be a Negro, a genuine Negro," rather than waste time imitating what "the white artist could always do as well, generally better." In 1896 and 1897 he made numerous visits to New York, where he met Williams and Walker, and decided to try his hand at composing musical shows.

The Johnson brothers—James Weldon and John Rosamond—were born in Jacksonville, Florida, where their mother, a public school teacher and musician, first introduced them to classical music. J. Rosamond went on to train at the New England Conservatory of Music in Boston; James, though he'd studied piano and guitar, opted for letters and the law. In 1899 the two collaborated on a musical and went to New York to seek a producer; they failed to find one but met Cook, Williams, and Walker and got bitten by the theatrical bug. They returned to DC, where in 1900 they wrote "Lift Ev'ry Voice and Sing," which would become a virtual African American anthem, and in 1901 they made their way back to New York, determined to break into show biz. Moving into the Marshall, they began to make contact with potential collaborators.

One of these was Bob Cole, a Georgia-born composer, director, and performer who lived two doors down from the Marshall and stopped by most nights. Cole had studied music at Atlanta University, then gotten into vaudeville as a composer and song-and-dance man. In 1894 he'd moved to New York to start his own theater troupe. Cole's goal was to have blacks write and control their own shows. He also aimed to abolish audience segregation: "No divided houses—our race must be seated from the boxes back."

James Reese Europe, born in Mobile, Alabama, in 1880, grew up in Washington, in an elite black household. His father had a comfortable government position, and his mother was a classically trained pianist. Young James became proficient in the violin and piano and began to think of a career in music. In December 1902 he traveled to New York, violin in hand, only to discover that Gotham orchestras weren't into hiring black men. Fortunately his brother, John, had preceded him and gotten a regular job playing piano at the Little Savoy, so James began to accompany him on the mandolin, then got gigs as a piano player himself. In 1903, as soon as he "could afford to eat in its dining room," Europe moved into the Marshall, where he made the contacts that enabled him to shift into show conducting.

Black theater critics also gathered at the Marshall. Through the pages of the black press, notably the *New York Age*, news of its emergence as a vital African American cultural center was dispatched to a national black audience, which in turn accelerated the arrival of aspiring musicians and performers from around the country.

THE FIRST INITIATIVE TO FLOW OUT OF THIS CONCATENATION of talent, energy, and ambition was undertaken by Bob Cole, who organized a production company and concocted *A Trip to Coontown*, the first full-length, non-minstrel theatrical show to be written, produced, stage-managed, and owned by African Americans. Cole had wanted a Broadway venue. But a former employer, enraged he'd gone out on his own, organized a boycott against him by the city's top-rank stages. When *Coontown* opened in the fall of 1897, it could find accommodation only in third-rate theaters. Turnout was good, word got around, its success grew, and finally Klaw and Erlanger's Syndicate stepped in, broke the boycott, and allowed Cole to open in April 1898 at their Third Avenue Theatre. It wasn't quite Broadway, but it was a respectable house, and *Coontown* did well there, and on the road, and at later engagements in Gotham. Cole wasn't thrilled about the content, which didn't break sufficiently with coonery buffoonery or racist lyrics, but he saw it as a step toward a theatrical future that would include "dramas of Negro life" written by "Negroes themselves."

Next up was Will Marion Cook, who in 1897 set to work on a full-scale musical comedy that would have an all-African-American cast explore the cakewalk craze. Cook summoned to his aid the poet Paul Lawrence Dunbar, also living in DC, where he was clerking at the Library of Congress (though he made frequent trips to New York to meet publishers and hang out at the Marshall). Dunbar's 1896 book of verses *Lyrics of Lowly Life* had been hailed by William Dean Howells, and Dunbar was then writing poems hyper-attuned to the constraints of a racist culture, like "Sympathy" ("I know why the caged bird beats his wing / Till its blood is red on the cruel bars"). In short order the two produced *Clorindy, or the Origin of the Cakewalk*, which proved a critical breakthrough.

Prior commitments prevented Williams and Walker from accepting Cook's offer to be the lead performers, so *Clorindy* starred comedian Ernest Hogan (who had moved into the Marshall with his younger colleagues). The trick, again, was gaining access to a theater. Cook aimed high, shooting for Broadway, and managed to get his foot, if not in the door, then on the roof of a premier showcase, the Casino Theatre. After repeated turndowns, he'd shown up uninvited with his entire chorus and wowed the roof garden's booking agent. The July 5, 1898, opening-night audience was wowed as well, cheering for ten minutes straight at the end. "Negroes were at last on Broadway, and there to stay," Cook exulted. "Gone was the uff-dah of the minstrel! Gone the Massa Linkum stuff! We were artists and we were going a long, long way."

An associated effort at shuffling off stereotypes was undertaken by Marshall confrères Bob Cole and the Johnson brothers, with their target being Tin Pan Alley. Rejecting the repellent coon song as "rough, coarse, and often vulgar," the trio began writing romantic numbers, hitherto taboo for blacks: "We try to write in our songs the finer feelings of the colored race," Cole told the *New York Times*. Rosamond took their case to Alley publisher Edward Marks: "We want to clean up the caricature," Johnson told him (rather as Irish, German, and Yiddish counterparts were attempting to do in vaudeville). Marks's house—Joseph W. Stern & Co., named for Marks's partner—was happy to oblige, consummating a deal in 1901 that rapidly expanded its list of African American composers and soon made it the country's number-one publisher of black music. (One key to their alertness was Bill Tyers, an African American whom the firm had hired around 1897 as staff arranger, editor, and orchestrator—the first black to hold such a position. Tyers became a critical link between the world of black musicians and the white music-publishing industry.) The Witmarks, not to be left behind, signed a contract for the songs from Cook and Dunbar's *Clorindy*. These proved to be wise business decisions: in 1901 six of the seventeen songs that sold over 100,000 copies were composed by blacks.

Their leverage enhanced, Cole and Rosamond Johnson pressed their advantage. In 1902 they put together their own vaudeville act, stripped of stereotypes. Both dressed in white tie and tails. Johnson played classical works on the piano; then the pair performed an art song (sung in German by Cole); then they offered a selection of Cole & Johnson songs. In 1903 Klaw and Erlanger, ever alert to new possibilities, signed them to a three-year composing contract for a regular salary and royalties.

In 1903 the Marshall circle reached for the brass ring. Williams and Walker pressed for a Broadway theater for their next show, *In Dahomey* (music by Cook, lyrics by Dunbar). The script tossed more stereotypes over the side and chose as its setting an African country notable for its resistance to French colonization. They convinced producers—the Hurtig Brothers and Harry Seamon—to invest $15,000 in the elaborate production and got Klaw and Erlanger to grant them access to their New York Theatre (once part of Hammerstein's old Olympia)—though the Syndicate bosses refused to suspend the color line. When African Americans rushed to see the first-ever all-black show on Broadway, they were relegated to the gallery.

Still, Walker and Williams were ecstatic. "Broadway!" Williams crowed. "And Williams and Walker! Williams and Walker! On Broadway! At last! Hallelujah!" And it just got better. Audiences and critics cheered. The Hurtigs and Seamon reaped impressive profits. The show went to London, where in June 1903 King Edward VII commanded a performance, and the English nobility—mesmerized by *Dahomey*'s spectacular finale (when fifty couples cakewalked up and down the stage)—lined up to engage Aida Walker to give them private dance lessons.

Now the Marshall circle moved even more boldly, aiming to get a bigger piece of the business action they themselves were generating. In 1904 Williams, Walker, and others involved with *In Dahomey* set up the Attucks Music Publishing Company, named to honor Crispus Attucks, the black casualty of the Boston Massacre of 1770. In 1905 Will Marion Cook, James Reese Europe, and others founded the Gotham Music Company, and later that year the two companies merged into the Gotham-Attucks Music Company, setting up shop on the same street as Tin Pan Alley's white-owned firms, first on 28th Street and later on 37th. Williams and Walker songs were mainstays in the company's catalog—above all Bert

Williams's signature song, "Nobody," which was no coon song but rather a wistful human lament with which almost anybody of any race could identify. The firm's sheet music was also notable for avoiding "darky" caricatures on its covers.

Walker and Williams plowed ahead with new productions, pouring the bulk of their earnings back into their company to pay actors, writers, musicians, and stagehands. This made them heroes in the African-American community. The *New York Age* commended Walker for "providing positions for colored writers, composers and performers—positions paying large salaries"—and hailed him as "the commander-in-chief of the colored theatrical forces."

In 1906 *Abyssinia* opened at the Majestic Theatre, Williams and Walker again setting their show in an African country, this time the only one to keep itself free from Euro-imperial rule. In 1907 Bob Cole and the Johnson brothers staged *The Shoo-Fly Regiment*, an all-black operetta, with James Europe conducting, set in the Philippines during the Spanish-American War. Its black male leads were brave and patriotic, and its black women had serious romantic roles, crumpling another Broadway taboo. In 1908 Williams and Walker's *Bandana Land* opened on Broadway, their most lavish production to date.

The Marshall crowd, it seemed, had pulled it off, had boarded and seized Broadway. All that remained was to formalize their informal network by establishing an organization of the "colored theatrical forces." Black thespians being barred from outfits like the Lambs and the Players, Walker, Williams, Cole, Europe, Rosamond Johnson, and others inaugurated (in 1908) an equivalent club and called it the Frogs, after Aristophanes's comedy. Bert Williams was elected its first president.

AND THEN IT ALL FELL APART, WITH SICKENING SPEED. In 1909, while touring with *Bandana Land*, George Walker fell ill and was forced to retire; he died in 1911, the victim of incurable syphilis. Bob Cole committed suicide in 1911, after a period of massive depression. Collective projects died as well. Black productions vanished from Broadway. Gotham-Attucks went under that same year.

There are a variety of possible reasons for this reversal of fortune. Some of it could be chalked up to the vagaries of mortality, the losses magnified by the fact that the circle had a limited bench, so replacements of Cole and Walker's quality were hard to find. The cohort's supply of capital was limited, too. Gotham-Attucks had always been hard-pressed to compete with large publishing houses like Joseph Stern, and songsters had drifted away, leaving it vulnerable to being taken over and milked dry by a crooked "song shark." Some individual blacks left to make their way in the white profession—Williams became a solo performer, Cook an orchestral conductor—though this seems more a consequence than a cause of the larger project's demise.[8]

---

8. Scott Joplin's fate was a sad one. In 1907 Joplin had followed John Stark, his publisher, to New York City. There he set up an office, on West 29th Street, and set about composing and arranging ragtime pieces, while dropping in from time to time at the Marshall and the Tenderloin Clubs. By the end of 1909 he'd brought out twelve new rags, some released by Stark, others by Stern. By then he'd moved on to his great project, the production of an African American grand opera. In 1910 Joplin finished *Treemonisha* and brought it around to publishers. Every one turned it down; a 230-page opera score by a black man seemed an impossibly heavy lift. In 1911 Joplin had the score printed, at his own expense, then struggled to get it produced. No dice. Nor did he attract support from the African American theatrical network, possibly because after 1910 it was considerably frayed. Finally, in 1915, he managed to arrange a bare-bones vocal performance in a rented Harlem theater—no costumes, scenery, dancers, or orchestra, just a singer, accompanied by Joplin at the piano. Again, not a ripple of interest, from any quarter. The disaster seems to have broken his spirit, though it's hard to be sure, as his body and mind were broken, too, ravaged by syphilis. In 1916 he was committed to Manhattan State Hospital, where, after suffering horribly, he died the following year, aged 48.

It's possible that the novelty of the post-minstrelsy all-black shows had simply worn off. The music biz, like the rag trade, was susceptible to sudden shifts in fashion. Yet in 1910 rag-time—though not coon songs—was on the point of an explosive growth in popularity, one that would see it listened (and danced) to by far more white folks than ever before. They would, however, be listening primarily to a new generation of *white* musicians, who had been clamber-ing their way up the bars of the jungle gym that had been constructed by Tin Pan Alley entre-preneurs, and now burst upon the scene. Overwhelmingly, those new performers were Jewish, and their city seedbed was not the black Tenderloin but the Yiddish Lower East Side.

IN 1892 RAMPAGING COSSACKS BURNED THE RUSSIAN VILLAGE of Temun to the ground. Moses Beilin, cantor at the local synagogue, fled to America with his family of nine, arriving on the Lower East Side in 1893. Unable to find work cantoring, Baline (as his name became) worked as a kosher meat inspector and then as a house painter, while his spouse became a midwife. When he died in 1901, Israel, his 13-year-old son, left school to hawk papers, carry tele-grams, and sew collars to help support the family. In 1902, believing himself a net drain on the Baline household economy, "Izzy" left home altogether and headed for the Bowery. There he became a freelance singer and self-taught piano player, moving from one sawdust saloon to another, putting across dialect-comedy ditties to hookers and Tammany politicians, the coins they tossed him providing just enough for that night's slat bed in a local flophouse.

At sixteen, Izzy tried plugging songs for Tin Pan Alley publisher Harry Von Tilzer (his first point of contact with the professional music world). He sat in the gallery at Tony Pastor's, disguised as a paying customer, and applauded furiously when Von Tilzer's coon songs were sung. The job didn't last, and he went back to the saloon circuit. There his spirited renditions of Cohan songs like "Yankee Doodle Boy" and "Give My Regards to Broadway"—and his own salacious parodies of current hit tunes—brought him to the attention of Bowery tour-master Chuck Connors.

Connors led uptown slumming parties through Chinatown's supposedly sin-drenched streets. A prime stop on his tour was "Nigger Mike" Salter's ritzy new Pelham Café at 12 Pell Street. Nigger Mike (in fact a dark-complected Russian Jew) drew a mixed crowd of gang-sters, cops, and politicians to his dance-hall-cum-bar. In 1904, at Connor's recommendation, he gave Baline an 8:00 p.m. to 6:00 a.m. singing-waiter job, for a regular wage plus tips. Izzy did well. He got hold of the latest Broadway songs by traveling up to 28th Street to get free copies from the Leo Feist Publishing Company. "They made a Bowery busker," he recalled, "feel like a real professional singer."

He also wrote some snappy numbers of his own—mainly dialect songs that mocked Italians, blacks, and Jews with equal abandon. In 1907 he took one of these uptown to Tin Pan Alley. It was a "wop" dialect song called "Marie from Sunny Italy" that he'd written in collabora-tion with the Pelham's pianist. When Joseph Stern & Co. published it, he had them put his name down on the sheet music as I. Berlin, stepping away from his ghetto background and fashioning a public persona. Distancing himself still further, he moved to the Union Square area and began wearing fashionable suits, with ties and celluloid collars.

In 1909 Berlin produced his first hit, "Sadie Salome, Go Home," which played with elite foibles and immigrant anxieties. In the aftermath of the Metropolitan Opera's banishment of *Salome*, lascivious versions of the banned Dance of the Seven Veils had sprouted on the city's vaudeville stages. Berlin's song (written with lyricist Edgar Leslie) poked fun at Fifth Avenue bluenosery while playing upon Lower East Side fears about the seductions of urban life. Sadie, a nice Jewish girl, goes vaudeville and does the offensive dance. This shocks her very

"Sadie Salome Go Home!" 1909. (Buyenlarge/Getty Images)

kosher boyfriend, Mose, who implores: "Don't do that dance, I tell you Sadie / That's not a bus'ness for a lady! / 'Most ev'rybody knows / That I'm your loving Mose / Oy, oy, oy, oy— where is your clothes?"

"Sadie" sold 3,000 copies, enough to land Berlin a job as staff lyricist with the Waterson & Snyder publishing house, climbing up another rung. Ragtime songs were the craze, and he cranked them out by the dozen. His lyrics, like the routines of vaudeville comics, roamed the ethnic landscape, purveying the usual stereotypes. His songs—"Sweet Marie, Make a Rag-a-Time Dance with Me," "Yiddle, on Your Fiddle, Play Some Ragtime," "Abie Sings an Irish Song," "Oh How That German Could Love"—were becoming known on Broadway, getting interpolated into the period's loosely plotted shows.

None of this quite foreshadowed the staggering success of "Alexander's Ragtime Band" (1911). Despite its name, there was hardly a trace of ragtime in it. Nor was it a coon song, though the name Alexander signaled coonery, as it was thought comically grand for a black man. Instead of a black-faced caricature, Waterson & Snyder's cover art showed a white-faced bandleader. The song's enormous success—by the end of 1912, it had sold over 2 million copies—suggested that after a decade of gingerly experimentation, white Americans were ready to follow Berlin's clarion injunction to "Come on and hear!": to take in rambunctious ragtime directly, the whiteness of the performer obviating the need for a racist filter.

Berlin, an Alley neophyte only a few years earlier, was now crowned Ragtime King. Waterson & Snyder made him a partner. Suddenly in great demand on the vaudeville stage, he played Hammerstein's Victoria in Times Square. His greatest honor came when the Friars Club threw him a party where George M. Cohan, Broadway's reigning superstar, lauded the "Jew boy that had named himself after an English actor and a German city." Berlin, said

Cohan, had successfully negotiated the transition from the ghetto to the Alley: he "is uptown, but he is there with the old downtown hard sell."[9]

Like Cohan, Berlin became a businessman. In 1914 he left Waterson, Berlin & Snyder and opened his own publishing house, the Irving Berlin Music Company, setting up shop in the Exchange Building (145 West 45th Street), part of the latest Tin Pan Alley. That same year, he joined Cohan, Herbert, and others in forming ASCAP (the American Society of Composers, Authors, and Publishers), to ensure members would earn royalties for performances of their songs. And those performances reached a new pinnacle, also in 1914, when Broadway producer Charles B. Dillingham produced *Watch Your Step*, with the entire score composed by Irving Berlin. At a stroke he was catapulted to the top of the theatrical world—looming over it, said *Variety*, "like the *Times* building does in the Square."

Just as the African American presence was waning on Broadway, Berlin had planted syncopated music based on African American rhythms more firmly in the soil of American musical life. Some saw this as theft; there were rumors that Berlin had a "colored boy" squirreled away somewhere who was composing his songs. It is certainly true that Berlin was deeply indebted to those musicians who first cultivated ragtime, a debt he acknowledged. And it's also true he refashioned that music, filtering it through his own cultural heritage, making it more acceptable to Euro-American taste. This too was not unprecedented, as Berlin also acknowledged, in "Alexander's Ragtime Band" itself, in a passage that musically quoted Stephen Foster—"And if you care to hear the Swanee River played in ragtime"—where he suggested the ability of modern music to absorb and extend what had preceded it. When Berlin got an Alley office of his own, he put up a framed portrait of Foster, another white songwriter who had adapted black music and subjects in complex ways.

There was perhaps a deeper black-white issue involved here. It's possible that one reason that coon songs and the Marshall circle's decade-long run on Broadway both came to a relatively abrupt end around 1910 is that it was just around that time that whites began to feel more comfortable about incorporating sexuality into their own culture. Urban whites were breaking free of traditional confinements, and ragtime—increasingly taken neat, without the protective coating of racist lyrics—provided the accompanying sound track.

This larger shift in gender arrangements was an immense and complex development, and one that would trigger resistance to shifting standards of acceptable behavior for men and women in public. One theater of operation in this culture war would be the Broadway stage, where representations of female sexuality became more daring, while remaining deeply traditional in being about women performing for the pleasure of men. A far more contested, significant, and diversified struggle—with key combat zones being the city's dance halls and cabarets—was fought over the acceptability of women's seeking pleasure for themselves.

CHORUS LINE

In 1900 the Florodora Sextette danced their way into Broadway history at the Casino Theatre. They evinced no particular acting or singing ability. They mainly glided about the stage in fashionable outfits, carrying parasols and getting sung to. Their claim to fame was a new kind of beauty. At 130 pounds, these brunettes were far slimmer than traditional chorines (those

---

9. Very uptown: Berlin bought his mother a home in the Bronx in 1913 with his royalties, and he himself relocated to Jewish Harlem, at West 112th Street, then moved again in 1912 to the Chatsworth, a high-status apartment building at Riverside Drive and 72nd.

in Billy Watson's Beef Trust weighed in at 180), and at 5'4" were more petite than the statuesque Gibson Girl.

Their gamine good looks caught on. Boosted at first by standing ovations from Yale students, they went into self-sustaining orbit when Broadway men-about-town—raffish millionaire industrialists (Diamond Jim Brady), dapper financiers (Otto Kahn), successful professionals (Stanford White)—began showing up night after night, inundating the girls with bouquets, money, and jewels, and whisking them from stage door to Lucullan après-theater Lobster Palace suppers, or to more intimate encounters in private hideaways. What fixed them in the Broadway firmament was that all six married millionaires. A Cinderella mystique—Horatio Algerism for women—now attached itself to the Casino's chorus (and by extension others). Their success, blared in Sunday supplements, drew an endless series of new recruits.

For every chorine whose favors to wealthy playboys (or casting directors) were rewarded with marriage, stardom, or creature comforts like autos, jewels, furs, and apartments, there were hundreds, thousands, whose lives belied the Cinderella myth. Most young women of the Broadway chorus lines lived a precarious existence, their wages only marginally higher than those available to other female workers, and their shelf life considerably more limited. Few lasted more than four or five seasons on the Broadway stage—producers having little use for them once they hit their early twenties—and fewer still graduated to important theatrical roles. Most simply left to get married or to work as domestics, factory hands, or laborers in the booming sex trades. (Brothels were all too ready-to-hand in the theatrical district.) Even "success" could prove problematic, as high-profile model and Florodora Girl Evelyn Nesbit discovered after her 1905 marriage to multi-millionaire Harry Kendall Thaw, who turned out to be a deranged sadistic monster.[10]

Still, the chorus line was a job; they needed a job; and the number of available jobs was increasing rapidly as producers and choreographers began deploying platoons of girls in their musicals. No one did more to expand demand than Florenz Ziegfeld Jr., who created a whole new girl-centric vehicle by Gothamizing the Parisian "revue."

"Flo" Ziegfeld was born in 1867 to a family of German Chicagoans, his mother Catholic, his father Lutheran. In 1893, during the Columbian Exposition, his father—founder and

---

10. Previously Nesbit had had another ambiguous "success" when in 1901 she had been seduced (perhaps raped) by Stanford White at his secret studio at 22 West 24th Street. The details are murky, given Nesbit's varying accounts, but as she was sixteen, and the age of consent was eighteen (having been raised from ten in 1895), the legal situation was clear. White was a voluptuary who collected beautiful teenage girls as he did precious artworks, though he tired of them quickly. He'd largely left Nesbit's life by the time of her marriage, but Thaw, who in addition to having "ruined" his now-wife had blocked him from Gotham's best clubs. Thaw—with a perseverance reminiscent of the Marquess of Queensberry's pursuit of Oscar Wilde a decade earlier—sought out Anthony Comstock and demanded he expose White and his friends as "moral perverts," but the old zealot could find nothing *currently* untoward in White's behavior, nor could the detective agency Thaw hired to spy on the architect. Nesbit may, or may not, have egged on Thaw's mania with "the Beast" (as they both referred to White)—sorting out this mare's nest of a triangle seems impossible—but matters came to a head on June 25, 1906. White was seated by the stage of the theater atop his creation Madison Square Garden, watching a new musical, *Mam'zelle Champagne*, when, as the chorus sang the closing number, "I Could Have Loved a Thousand Girls," Thaw walked over and shot him three times in the head.

In the trial that followed, the yellow press portrayed the murdered White as the guilty party, a fiendish satyr and corrupter of innocence who deserved what he'd got. ("Stanford White, Voluptary [*sic*] and Pervert, Dies the Death of a Dog," headlined *Vanity Fair*.) So fiercely did the anti-White publicity blaze that most of his friends said nothing in his defense, lest they get burned as well. There were many particular reasons behind this lynching of a dead man, some of which raise larger issues. Both upper-class feminists and middle-class moralists bristled at the exercise of class and patriarchal privileges by the likes of White. This was an old story, long characteristic of New York nightlife. Wealthy sports had cruised working-class neighborhoods in the 1830s, and blue bloods had picked up girls at Harry Hill's in the 1870s. But cavorting in Times Square was not like slumming in the urban underworld. It was a spectacularly public form of play, a high-profile break with propriety. Rector's was denounced by some as a "palace of sin," and the postmortem assault on White's reputation may have partly been a way of staking out the limits of the permissible.

director of the prestigious Chicago Musical College—opened a nightclub (the Trocadero) that would provide visitors to the fair with a classical music venue. When attendance limped, he asked his son to vitalize the operation, the younger Ziegfeld having garnered some entertainment experience working with Buffalo Bill's Wild West Show. Flo signed up a variety of vaudeville routines, notably the strongman act of German-born Eugen Sandow, whom he brought in from New York City. Displaying an unsuspected genius for advertising, Flo promoted Sandow as the "Strongest Man on Earth," dressed him in skimpy briefs, applied white powder till he looked like a Greek statue, then invited the grand dames of Chicago Society to come feel his man's muscles. The show was a great hit, and afterward Ziegfeld took Sandow back to New York for a run (in January 1894) at Koster & Bial's, where he democratized the act by inviting any and all ladies in the audience to come up onstage to touch and feel. Again Sandow was a sensation. Edison had him out to perform for his Kinetoscope in March, and soon his physique was on display at peep shows across the country.

In 1895 Ziegfeld parted company with his beefcake attraction and set out to break into Broadway. He decided to revive a previously successful play by finding a sexy new actress to star in it. In 1896 he went on a scouting mission to London, seeking a female counterpart to Sandow. It was there, at the Palace Music Hall, that he caught the act of a Gallic singing comedienne, Anna Held, a ravishing coquette who knew how to flirt and dress and was loaded with *le charme*. Though Held was already booked for the coming season at the Folies-Bèrgere in Paris, Ziegfeld offered to buy out her contract and pay her the then-staggering sum of $1,500 a week to appear in his production, to open that October. She agreed happily, and Ziegfeld rushed back to Gotham to whip up a storm of publicity.[11] The show flopped—Held wasn't cut out for operettas—but Ziegfeld, now her manager, lover, and soon-to-be common-law husband, got her a star billing at Koster & Bial's. Here Held shone, performing both coon songs and her own material. Next, Ziegfeld segued her from vaudeville to the Broadway stage, where in shows like *The French Maid* and *The Parisian Model* she danced and sang sultry songs like "Won't You Come and Play wiz Me?" She broke the Casino's box-office record in 1901 and went on to star in hit after hit, replacing Lillian Russell as the darling of the theatrical world. (And the bête noir of ministers like the Reverend Dr. Madison J. Peters, who in 1906 denounced Held for "pandering to the animalized and depraved passions of a sin-slaved public," and fretted that "New York is becoming more wickedly Parisian than Paris.")

Held now encouraged further Parisianization by convincing Ziegfeld he ought to develop an entertainment that would be part Folies-Bèrgere and part a "revue," a format with which New York had had some experience. In 1894 an American producer had created *The Passing*

---

11. Amid the torrent of manufactured news was the soon-to-be famous "milk bath" stunt. After arranging the complicity of a Long Island dairy farmer, who had a retail outlet in Brooklyn, Ziegfeld "leaked" word that Anna had contracted for a delivery of 40 gallons every other day, in which to bathe (the supposed secret of her flawless complexion). *And*, that said milkman was in the process of suing her for nonpayment of a $64 bill, for 320 gallons she claimed were insufficiently fresh and lacking in the essential creaminess. Miss Held, the story continued, was hoping to settle out of court, milk baths being "too peculiar to be discussed in public." Every newspaper in town ran this bit of hokum, though in its coverage the *Times* did raise an eyebrow, drily referring to her as "the much advertised French singer." But it ran the story, and the follow-up, when the annoyed milkman revealed the whole thing was a fraud—nary a drop had been delivered—and he'd only agreed to have his name used, not to have his milk maligned. This, plus a completely fabricated story, which was nevertheless run by the New York press, about how Held heroically stopped a runaway horse on the Speedway and saved a magistrate's life, elevated Ziegfeld to Barnum-class status as a master of ballyhoo.

Held's knack for publicity rivaled and perhaps excelled Ziegfeld's, most notably in passing herself off successfully as a native Parisian. In truth she'd been born in Warsaw, the daughter of a German Jewish glove maker and his French wife. When anti-Semitic pogroms swept Poland in 1881, the family had fled to Paris and, after he died in 1884, to London, where Anna and her mother lived with relatives. There, thanks to her command of Yiddish, Anna got work in Jacob Adler's theater company. Later she returned to Paris, where her vivacious personality, rolling eyes, eighteen-inch waist, and naughty songs made her a major star in the city's finest cafés.

Show, a mix of songs, dances, and comedy sketches, held together by a running commentary on current political, social, and theatrical events. Where vaudeville assembled distinct acts by disparate troupers, the review (as it was still spelled) used one set of performers to present tailor-made text, music, and lyrics. Other reviews followed, like *In Gayest Manhattan* (1896), which similarly created a novel unity of mood.

So Klaw and Erlanger were not leaping blindly when they agreed to produce the first *Follies* (named after a contemporary column, "Follies of the Day," written by the show's librettist). They leased Ziegfeld the roof garden atop their New York Theatre, which he redecorated

"There's One in a Million Like You: Song Hits of the Ziegfeld Follies," 1912. (The New-York Historical Society/Getty Images)

and renamed the Jardin de Paris. The *Follies of 1907*, a summertime diversion, was organized loosely around an imagined visit by a reincarnated John Smith and Pocahontas to modern New York. It poked fun at current doings—spoofing the Met's *Salome* scandal, throwing in not just the Dance but a fake police raid. It presented topical skits about Roosevelt and Rockefeller, Caruso and Comstock. It hailed the car craze with a song, "I Think I Oughtn't to Auto Any More." And it laid on girls—fifty of them, called "the Anna Held Girls"—in a lavish and mildly racy way. It was enormously profitable, and the next edition, the *Follies of 1908*, was staged down in the theater itself.

In the *Follies of 1910*, Ziegfeld folded in a Jewish and black presence, in the persons of Fannie Brice and Bert Williams, giving the Parisian-themed show more of a New York flavor.

Born Fania Borach in 1891 to Jewish-immigrant parents who had settled on the Lower East Side, Brice was largely raised by her mother, Rose, who had left her husband, who gambled away the money Rose made running a saloon. A chronic truant who dropped out in the eighth grade, Brice took aim at a career in show business. In 1906 she won an amateur-night contest at Keeney's Theatre on Brooklyn's Fulton Street. In 1907, still Fania Borach, she landed a spot in a Cohan production, *The Talk of New York*, only to be fired before it opened when Cohan realized that while the gangly 16-year-old could sing, she couldn't dance. Lowering her sights, she began working as a chorus girl on the less demanding burlesque circuit, changing her name to Fanny Brice in an effort to seem less Jewish, and thereby expand her job opportunities. In 1909 she landed a spot in another burlesque show, *The College Girls*, by claiming she had a specialty number up her sleeve, which in fact she hadn't. Desperate, about to be exposed and probably fired, she went to Irving Berlin, whom she had befriended back when she'd been song plugging at a nickelodeon. Berlin offered her his new number, "Sadie Salome, Go Home," and sang it for her in a Yiddish accent. Though Brice didn't speak Yiddish, she could do a passable vaudeville-style Hebrew impersonation, which, together with her very funny parody of the Seven Veils dance, brought down the house. Ziegfeld caught her act as a "Yiddisher Salome" at the Columbia Theatre in April 1910, and it was as a Jewish comedian that Ziegfeld took her on board.[12]

Also in 1910, Ziegfeld offered the now-partnerless Bert Williams a leading role in that year's *Follies*. This was unprecedented, startling. Williams was by this point a theatrical luminary, to be sure, but no black man had ever been offered such a major part in an all-white show. Indeed, some cast members threatened to quit if he was taken on. Ziegfeld responded: "Go if you want to. I can replace every one of you, except the man you want me to fire." They stayed, and so did Williams—though that first year Ziegfeld kept him offstage whenever white women trouped on; for the *Ziegfeld Follies of 1911*, the restraints were lifted. Williams now embarked on a spectacular second career as a comedy headliner, one that earned him a salary equal to that of President Taft. This provoked a nasty sour-grapes attack from the Shuberts, who years before had sought to add Ziegfeld to their stable, only to see him sign with Erlanger. In 1912 a Shubert-controlled magazine declared that all "self-respecting Caucasians" were "revolted by the commingling of negro men and white women on the stage," adding that Ziegfeld had proven himself someone who would go "to lengths to which no others would demean themselves."

---

12. Brice—herself a second-generation Jew—would follow David Warfield in immersing herself in the ghetto to improve her grasp of Yiddish. In a 1912 article she claimed she spent two or three weeks in the ghetto each summer, "listening, imitating, bargaining, quarreling—using every opportunity for a new trick."

As the decade unfolded, the *Follies* shed some of its "review" quality. Ziegfeld still constructed stage sets depicting metropolitan scenes: the 1911 show reproduced the girders of the recently redone Grand Central Station. And he still deployed comedians—Williams, Brice, Eddie Cantor, W. C. Fields, and Ed Wynn—who offered parodies of New York celebrities like Caruso, Hearst, Twain, and Carnegie. One new comic, Will Rogers, dressed in a cowboy outfit (though he was in fact a Cherokee), and twirled a lariat while riffing on the day's news. But increasingly, the role of the comic was to mark time while the showgirls changed costumes. And the costumes slowly drifted from the outrageously lavish to the simply outrageous.

Ziegfeld girls were chosen out of thousands auditioned for their slender silhouettes and non-threatening, non-provocative, girl-next-door sensuality. Once on board they tapped, kicked, and paraded about the stage: as taxicabs, with FOR HIRE signs on their shoulders; as warships, depicting the fleet in review; as birds (heavily feathered ospreys, lovebirds, cockatoos, and peacocks); as girls, dressed in sequins, beads, furs, and rhinestones; as girls, dressed apparently in nothing at all (though in fact wearing fleshings). His more soft-core numbers kept the girls motionless and aloof, hewing to the accepted fiction that if it didn't jiggle, it was Art.

Ziegfeld's recipe was unbeatable, though competitors tried, notably the Shuberts. In 1912, J. J. opened the first *Passing Show* in their new Winter Garden Theatre. Over the next few years they offered broad sketches and snappy songs and debuted new comic and performing talents, like (in 1918) a brother-sister dance team called the Astaires. ("Both dance with zest and apparent joy in the doing," said the *Times* reviewer.) The Shuberts' biggest discovery, Al Jolson, never did a *Passing Show* but was a sensation in the Winter Garden's opening production, *La Belle Paree* [1911]. But the emphasis at the northern end of Times Square was the same as that at the south: J. J. assembled *eighty* chorus girls and constructed a long runway that ran out into the audience, allowing closer inspection of the Shuberts' chorines—slimmer, younger, nuder.

In 1913 Ziegfeld nailed down his primacy by moving the *Follies* to the Art Nouveau auditorium of the Syndicate's New Amsterdam citadel, and he soon put its magnificent stage and modern equipment to spectacular effect. In 1915 Ziegfeld hired Viennese architect and interior decorator Joseph Urban, whose shimmering sets and exquisite lighting gave the show a svelte elegance. Much of the cost was underwritten by financier friends like Otto Kahn and Vincent Astor, many of whom had girlfriends in the show—a reminder that while the sumptuous sets, high-fashion outfits, steep admission price, cautious direction, and elegant women ("There are chorus girls and chorus girls," as one Ziegfeld press release put it) had lofted the *Follies* far above working-class, girly-show burlesque, even branded it a respectable heterosexual entertainment for the "best people," it was, in the end, about male gazing—and not just looking, but hooking up, as Brooklyn-born chorine Marion Davies discovered in 1915 when (the married) William Randolph Hearst came to call.[13]

MANY UPPER-CLASS WOMEN WERE SICK OF THEIR HUSBANDS' well-publicized philandering in Times Square Lobster Palaces. They were tired of postponing dinner parties until 8:15 so their mates (and sons) could stop off on the way home to visit kept chorus girls. They were also bored with the parties themselves—empty, etiquette-laden affairs. So wealthy women decided to loosen some cultural corset strings.

---

13. When he first spotted her she was in Irving Berlin's new musical, *Stop! Look! Listen!*; a few months later she was tapped by Ziegfeld for the *Follies of 1916*.

After 1900 the rambunctious Mamie (Mrs. Stuyvesant) Fish began throwing parties—in her new Stanford White–designed mansion (25 East 78th) and her "cottage" in Newport—that broke most rules of decorum. She didn't separate men and women after dinner. She parodied the entertainments put on by her stuffier peers, as when her visitors arrived to discover the "guest of honor" was a monkey in white tie and tails. She invited theatrical celebrities like John Drew or Ethel Barrymore to dine, not simply entertain.[14]

Here Mamie was playing catch-up ball. The rise of stars as media celebrities had precipitated something of a crisis of cultural authority for the city's social elite. Americans were turning elsewhere for standards of taste and value, and actors were capturing much of the attention once given Mrs. Astor's Four Hundred. Popular magazines and Sunday supplements now offered illustrated features on the lives of stage and screen players—their homes, vacations, personalities, and incomes—in the way they had once breathlessly chronicled Fifth Avenue affairs. Society—or its sharper heads like Mrs. Fish—sensed this usurpation and strove to regain cultural authority, partly via association with the newly powerful.

Upper-class women also partied more in public. The Fishes, Vanderbilts, Sloanes, Astors, and Mills held extravagant events in East Side venues like Sherry's and the Plaza. At the Waldorf-Astoria, hordes of curious tourists and ordinary New Yorkers began thronging the corridors, hoping for a seat in the Palm Room, where they could mingle with the social, financial, and theatrical elite. Crowd control became a problem, until the Waldorf's gatekeeper, Oscar Tschirky, hit on the (then-novel) idea of setting up a red velvet rope to filter access. Though it turned out that this *increased* demand: "It seemed that when people learned they were being held out," Oscar recalled, "they were all the more insistent upon getting in." The rotogravure sections of the Sunday papers provided a substitute experience, publishing images of the rich at play—their lavish dinners, their clothes, their yachts, their polo ponies—for the millions to gape at, cluck over, and dream about.[15]

Restless Fifth Avenue women also increasingly challenged the constraints being so publicly flouted by their men on Broadway, and gander gadabouts found themselves confronted with increasingly saucy geese. Elite ladies began smoking cigarettes in public, making up their faces with powder puffs and lip rouges in public, flirting with men in public, and drinking in public at the Ladies' Bar at the Café des Beaux-Arts on 40th Street and Sixth.

But all these breaches of propriety were as nothing compared to those that became apparent around 1911 when Knickerbocker blue bloods—women as well as men—began to twist, shake, and leap about shamelessly in public, as if they had contracted a virus, which in a way they had—an infectious cultural virus that had first been spotted several years earlier in the city's working-class quarters, when the Great Dance Craze struck New York.

---

14. When actress Marie Dressler told Mrs. Fish that she would boast to her mother of having dined with her, the socialite replied she would be "proud to tell my children that Marie Dressler dined with me."

15. Some of New York's finest families actively sought publicity, in some cases staging events that were guaranteed to draw public attention. In 1903 the tycoon C. K. G. Billings, newly selected head of the New York Equestrian Club, threw a dinner at Sherry's for thirty-six male guests, who were ushered into a dining room that had been dressed up as an English country estate, with imitation grass and burbling brooks. There waiters dressed as if for a fox hunt invited the attendees to hop on horses that had been hoisted up by elevator. Once mounted, they dined from tray-tables attached to the saddle, and sipped champagne, through lengthy straws, from bottles tucked in saddlebags. The press ate it up.

EVERYBODY'S DOIN' IT

Dancing had long been a community affair in working-class Gotham, restricted to family functions, or to balls sponsored by unions, radical groups, fraternal lodges, and mutual aid societies. These were intergenerational and supervised affairs. Young women came with parents or approved escorts.

In the early 1900s a rival form emerged. Social clubs began holding unchaperoned dances open to the public. Extensively advertised, they drew crowds of 800 or so to rented neighborhood halls. By the 1910s local sites couldn't meet the surging demand for space. Commercial dance palaces opened in the city's pleasure zones (including Times Square and Coney Island) and served a citywide, multi-ethnic clientele.

The steamy dance halls drew masses of young women. After working hours, servants, stenographers, salesgirls, and seamstresses shed their shirtwaist-and-skirt regalia and donned gaudy eye-catching outfits that, like Bowery fashions of the past, copied and parodied elite styles. Then they headed for the bright lights and syncopated music—on their own or with female friends, looking for fun, romance, a husband. In the halls, no introductions were necessary. Any man could ask any woman to dance. Some women didn't wait to be asked.

These were not their parents' waltzes, polkas, or folk dances. Partners held each other tightly, cheek to cheek, body to body. "They're spoons on each other," wrote one observer. They twisted and spun about—went "spieling"—a sharp departure from the graceful and refined waltz. After 1905 even more outrageous dances arrived, from the brothels of San Francisco's Barbary Coast and from southern black jook joints. Dancers doing the Turkey Trot, Bunny Hug, Grizzly Bear, and Texas Tommy mimicked animal movements or pressed their loins together in mock intercourse.

Nor was all the intercourse mock. Women made dates, and sometimes had sex, with men they met on the dance floor. Yet they weren't prostitutes (and indeed were known as "charity girls" for refusing to accept money). They coupled for pleasure, or in exchange for being treated to evenings on the town.

THE WORKING-CLASS DANCE HALL PHENOMENON appalled a set of middle- and upper-class reformers, partly out of simple prudery (though prudery was seldom simple), and partly from being attuned to the potential for exploitation of vulnerable young women who had slipped free of community or familial control/protection. Some were particularly worried that commercial dance halls might become stalking grounds for procurers who would seduce or shanghai innocent girls into full-time prostitution. They began to investigate the situation.

At the forefront of these concerned activists was Belle Lindner Israels, a Harlem-born German Jewish settlement worker who headed the Committee on Amusements and Vacation Resources of Working Class Girls. In the summer of 1908 the committee, consisting of five members of the Council of Jewish Women, undertook a study of seventy-three New York dance halls, and in 1909 Israels began to publicize their findings. In press conferences, speeches, and articles like "The Way of the Girl" (in the *Survey*), she charged that the halls tolerated "reckless and uncontrolled" dances, thus providing the "opportunity for license and debauch" of young women.

Her proposed remedies were milder than some. There were those who argued all dance halls should be shuttered. Israels opted for regulation over prohibition; for cleaning up, not closing down. Her committee put together a model bill for the New York State legislature that would limit or ban the sale of liquor, exclude under-16s unaccompanied by a parent or guardian, require the presence of state-appointed chaperones to keep out "undesirables," arrange for proper introductions, and veto inappropriate dance steps. She won support from powerful members of Gotham's intellectual, social, financial, and political worlds—particularly their distaff sides, like the wife of City Club president George McAneny and a daughter of J. P. Morgan. The *New York Times* chipped in with favorable coverage.

Brewers, dance hall owners, and immigrant groups fought back. One senator denounced the "untiring energy of those who desire to interfere with the pleasures of the citizens of New York." Mayor William Jay Gaynor warned Israels "not to be too strict," noting that he himself had gone to dances when young, "and I am quite sure that I am none the worse off. We must not be too straight-laced in this world." Nevertheless, in June 1910, he went along with a compromise bill that required licensing of dance halls, mandated regular inspections by health and fire department officials to ensure they conformed to safety regulations, and barred liquor from being sold on the premises (though the latter provision was left to private groups like Israels's to enforce). The Committee on Amusements also sponsored its own dance halls, at which supervisors permitted only old-fashioned steps and promoted folk dancing as a wholesome alternative.

All this availed little. The dance craze not only gathered force but jumped class lines, barreling into Society around 1911. Suddenly the graceful teamwork and clockwork regularity of nineteenth-century waltzes and cotillions were history, replaced by the seeming anarchy of gyrating couples vigorously pursuing individual pleasure. Unshackled patrician youths grabbed one another and began gliding, dipping, hugging, and jerking, as they Turkey Trotted and Grizzly Beared to ragtime rhythms. (Irving Berlin's "Everybody's Doin' It Now" was an unofficial anthem: "See that ragtime couple over there / Watch them throw their shoulders in the air / Snap their fingers / Honey, I declare / It's a bear, it's a bear, it's a bear / There!") Or they indulged in the sensuous tango, an exotic import from the brothel quarter of Buenos Aires.

The craze spread, grew more public. Heretofore, society ladies had danced in private (if they danced at all). Alice Roosevelt, the president's exuberant daughter, had scandalized Newport by doing the hootchy-kootchy (a belly dance), but only in Grace Vanderbilt's home. Now Mamie Fish gave dancing parties at Sherry's where black bands played ragtime and adventurous Society couples experimented with the tango and the Texas Tommy. Then, to facilitate mushrooming demand, a new dance-dedicated institution popped up—the cabaret.

Cabarets were begat by Lobster Palaces, or more precisely, their patrons. Customers who had just come from a blood-stirring Broadway play, replete with cakewalking couples, descended on their favorite Times Square venue in carriages and taxis, determined to emulate what they'd just witnessed. Many of Rector's clients demanded that tables be swept away to give them leg and elbow room. "All they wanted to do was dance," an astonished George Rector recalled.

Fiercely competitive, the city's restaurants, theaters, and hotels now hired orchestras and entertainers and carved out spaces for floor shows in which professional dancers demonstrated the raffish new steps and diners then tried them out. In April 1912 Murray's Roman Gardens inaugurated a postage-stamp-sized dance floor, with a twelve-piece orchestra and a Turkey Trot show, followed by dancing until 4:00 a.m.; by 1915 Murray's had escalated to a revolving circular platform, thirty feet in diameter. Theater owners converted their roofs: the Shuberts opened a Palais de Danse atop their Winter Garden; Klaw and Erlanger riposted with a Jardin de Danse on the New York Theatre's roof; Ziegfeld launched a Midnight Frolic at his New Amsterdam Theatre, with inter-table telephones and a dance floor on which chorus girls and top acts from the *Follies* cavorted close to patrons, who were encouraged to join in. At the major hotels, smooth string ensembles and strolling troubadours gave way to full-fledged dance orchestras, hired at considerable expense.

Places like Rector's, Bustonoby's, and even the Plaza began offering afternoon tea dances from three to five ("thés boozants," Rector wisecracked). Young women could drop in while purportedly shopping; unsuspecting parents or working husbands need never know. To provide instruction for the uninitiated and partners for the unescorted, the venues hired young immigrant men to tango and Bunny Hug with the clientele. Maxim's took on one Rodolpho Alfonzo Raffaeli Pierre Filibert di Valentina d'Antonguolla (or Rudolf Valentino, as he now styled himself), to squire female customers around its hastily constructed dance floor. Valentino had arrived from southern Italy in 1913, and after a spell working as a gardener or busboy, and sleeping on a bench in Central Park, the 18-year-old had been informed by a friend that far better positions were available, given that Valentino was a splendid dancer and possessed of dark good looks.

The dance craze was a potential bonanza for black musicians, too, a much-needed one, as the demise of black musical theater after 1910 had left many out of work. At first, they were not able to capitalize on the possibilities. Barred from the whites-only Local 310 of the American Federation of Musicians, African American performers had no central place where employers could contact them, much less any ability to bring collective leverage to bear on contract negotiations. Worse, being (perforce) non-union, they were precluded from working alongside union musicians, which further diminished opportunities. Employers in the know could pass word about job openings to barbershops, saloons, or poolrooms where music men hung out. A more organized approach began to emerge when musicians-in-waiting began gravitating toward the Marshall Hotel to trade information and wait for calls, but this, Jimmy Marshall made clear, was not a viable long-term solution. Nor was the practice by some hotels and restaurants of pressing into service the musically proficient from among their own black employees—the hundreds of nearby Tenderloin residents who walked up to Times Square to work as busboys, waiters, dishwashers, or bellhops. These men were encouraged, after their regular shift, to play ragtime in the dining rooms (for no pay, just tips), while remaining hidden behind screens or palm trees so as not to alarm white dancers by their proximity.

Black Broadway veteran James Reese Europe set out to rectify this situation. In 1910 Europe founded (and became first president of) the Clef Club, a central hiring place, hangout, and booking agency for Gotham's black musicians, located just across 53rd Street from the Marshall. By limiting admission to seasoned professionals, it also guaranteed employers access to quality performers, and soon it had enough muscle to establish standard contractual terms of work and pay. It was an immediate success: the city's major hotels and restaurants rushed to hire Clef Club musicians, and so did Society matrons seeking entertainers for private parties.

To draw further attention to the organization, Europe assembled its top musicians into a 100-piece Clef Club Symphony Orchestra. Working with Will Marion Cook, J. Rosamond Johnson, and other veteran composers and performers, Europe arranged for a Concert of Negro Music—including ragtime, blues, and plantation songs—to be held at Carnegie Hall on May 2, 1912. For this performance, segregated seating was suspended. The capacity crowd responded with stormy applause; repeat performances were held in 1913 and 1914, and Victor arranged the first-ever recording of an all-black band. The Carnegie Hall concerts burnished the Clef Club's credentials to a high gleam, and won for black musicians a virtual monopoly of the dance craze business in the city; members were even engaged to play at

"James Reese Europe and the Clef Club Band," 1914. (Schomburg Center for Research in Black Culture, Photographs and Prints Division)

private parties in London and Paris and on private yachts at sea. They now earned the highest salaries of any musicians in New York, higher than those of their white counterparts.

THE MUSIC MANIA WAS NOT WITHOUT ITS CRITICS. Press and pulpit lashed the new dances. Hearst's *American* lambasted the "disgusting and indecent dance known as the Turkey Trot." The *Sun* called them a "reversion to the grossest practices of savage man." Complainants hammered away at the venues, too. The mix of respectables and demimondaines was troubling. "People of position have taken to frequenting the restaurants where dancing is the attraction," wrote the gimlet-eyed Broadway flaneur Julian Street in 1913, and in doing so created "a social mixture such as was never before dreamed of in this country—a hodge-

podge of people in which respectable young married and unmarried women, and even débu-
tantes dance, not only under the same roof, but in the same room with women of the town."

Even more disturbing was the physical interaction of upper-class women with lower-
class men. The tea dances were exposing innocent girls (or married women) to sinister and
sensual foreigners—"tango pirates"—who would rob them of wealth or virtue. The flap over
tango pirates flipped older plebeian anxieties about aristocratic seducers; now upper-class
female vulnerability to the virile charms of working-class men looked to be the Achilles' heel
of class solidarity.

Worse still was a blurring of the color line fostered by the music itself. Paul Lawrence
Dunbar had slipped a sly line into *In Dahomey* that read: "When dey hear dem ragtime tunes /
White fo'ks try to pass fo' coons." This was precisely what critics feared. The dance craze was
being propelled by black music, made more dangerous by having been stripped of its protective racist lyrics. Opponents feared ragtime's rhythms were introducing into white culture
the bacillus of African Americans' presumed primitive sexuality and lack of bodily restraint,
threatening an epidemic of moral degeneracy.

The deepest worry of all was the possibility of dance-driven sexual congress between
white women and black men. The Committee of Fourteen, a civic activist organization primarily dedicated to rooting out organized prostitution, took time out to hunt down and snuff out
institutions that facilitated interracial sex, a practice they believed would undermine the city's
social and racial order. Not surprisingly, the committee zeroed in on the Marshall Hotel.
Though the Marshall was patently no whorehouse, undercover agents that the committee repeatedly dispatched documented what was no secret: whites were welcome on the premises.
Investigators noted direly that white women had been seen dining and dancing with blacks like
James Reese Europe and George Walker. The committee's chief demanded that Jimmy
Marshall eliminate race mixing, on pain of being denounced as a disorderly house and getting
his liquor license revoked. Though integrated places of leisure were perfectly legal under New
York's laws—indeed, as an infuriated W. E. B. Du Bois, the city's leading African American
civil rights activist, pointedly reminded the committee, it was *discrimination* that was illegal—
Marshall was forced to agree (in October 1912) to inaugurate internal segregation, including
a separate street entrance "*exclusively* for colored people" and a separate room for dancing
"*exclusively* for my white patrons only." He also promised that "performers will not be allowed
to sing vulgar and suggestive songs."

In 1913 the cabarets themselves came under fire—all of them—with the fusillade directed
by the municipal government itself. Mayor Gaynor was normally a staunch libertarian, and
indeed had long been a famously caustic critic of zealous reformers like the Reverend Parkhurst.
But two of his daughters had eloped with men met at cabarets, and Gaynor also had his eye on
a gubernatorial run for which he would need reformers' support. So the mayor now startled the
city by launching a crusade to end the "lascivious orgies going on in these so-called 'respectable
places.'" Many Lobster Palaces and cabarets possessed an all-night liquor license, which enabled them to sell drinks round the clock. The mayor now revoked all such licenses and directed
Police Commissioner Rhinelander Waldo to shut down any liquor-serving venue at 1:00 a.m.,
even if at that hour it was supplying only food, not drink. In his letter to Waldo, which was released to the press, Gaynor declared: "The people who patronize such places after the regular
closing hour of 1 o'clock are not, as a rule, decent people. They are vulgar, roystering, and often
openly immodest. They get intoxicated, behave boisterously, and indulge in lascivious dancing
in rooms devoted to that use." Days later he announced his intention to bar objectionable
dances from venues around the city and to outlaw tea dances altogether.

The proprietors of places like Shanley's, Maxim's, and Murray's protested vigorously; the manager of Louis Martin's told the mayor, "It is a mistake to try to run New York City like a village." The owner of Healey's Restaurant (on Broadway and 66th) halted liquor service at 1:00 a.m. but refused to lock his doors, indeed encouraged his clients to refuse to be evicted. Hundreds of patrons filled his restaurant to display their solidarity. Gaynor had the police briskly override resistance, slugging and clubbing protesting male patrons and tossing them in patrol wagons. "This all-night guzzling and vulgarity," Gaynor proclaimed, "is at an end in New York forever, I hope."

His optimism was premature. The next night, not only was the house full again, but a crowd of 3,000 thronged the street outside. Among the resistants, to the mayor's dismay, was New York district attorney Charles Whitman, whom Healey had invited to witness what the DA now agreed was "atrocious brutality." Not only did Whitman announce he would refuse to prosecute those whom the police had hauled away—arguing that the mayor had no legal right to close down a place obeying the liquor curfew, much less lay a hand on its patrons— but a magistrate ordered the arrest of police officers who had participated in the raid. Gaynor backed down. The ban on all-night liquor would remain in effect, but there would be no more raids. Some venues quickly circumvented the restrictions by establishing special private rooms—open after hours to "members" only—thereby inventing the "night club." And after Gaynor died weeks later, in September 1913, from the lingering effects of the attempt on his life, his successor, Mayor John Purroy Mitchel, himself a dancing man, quickly reversed course, moving the curfew to 2:00 a.m. and then liberally handing out a new round of all-night licenses, overriding protests from press and pulpit.

Gaynor's campaign had an impact, nonetheless. To counter ongoing criticism from the likes of Mrs. Israels, some cabaret owners banned unescorted women and hired floorwalkers to keep several inches of cool air between overheated dancers. The assault on cabarets also prompted a modest tactical retreat by some highly placed Society ladies, who were not about to be deprived of their newfound dancing freedoms but were persuaded that to counter the clamor, the dance craze "needed an uplifting influence to bring dignity to it." One of their biggest allies in this pursuit was a couple named Vernon and Irene Castle.

In 1910 Vernon Castle, a British immigrant actor, married Irene Foote, a willowy beauty born to middle-class parents in New Rochelle. In Paris the following year, they made a splash demonstrating America's new dances (to the strains of "Alexander's Ragtime Band"). There they were spotted by Elisabeth Marbury, a leading literary agent and dramatic producer, and Elsie de Wolfe, former actress and theater owner and pioneering interior decorator. Both were impressed by the Castles' ability to step down the voltage of high-powered dances, thereby serving as cultural transformers. As Irene explained: "We get our new dances from the Barbary Coast. Of course, they reach New York in a very primitive condition, and have to be considerably toned down before they can be used in the drawing-room. There is one just arrived now—it is still very, very crude—and it is called "Shaking the Shimmy. . . . It's a nigger dance, of course." The Castles took such raw material and smoothed, slowed, and simplified the steps. They eliminated leg-revealing dips. They deleted hops, flounces, and twists. They banned excessive body contact. When finished, they had bowdlerized it into something respectable New Yorkers could see as graceful and romantic—something the *New York Times* pronounced fit to dance, explaining that where before it had "smacked strongly of the Dahomey-Bowery-Barbary Coast form of revelry," it had "been trimmed, expurgated, and spruced up until now it is quite a different thing."

Marbury became the duo's agent and introduced them to New York's rich. Society women soon clamored for private lessons or attended small demonstration classes held at Sherry's or the Plaza. Vanderbilts, Astors, Goulds, and Garys relied on the couple. Hearst whisked them up by limo to the Clarendon, where they taught him the latest steps. Marbury also helped them establish a dance school—Castle House—at which Society's daughters could learn the steps "without being exposed to the discredited elements." She, de Wolfe, Anne Morgan (J. P.'s daughter), Mamie Fish, and Almira (Mrs. William) Rockefeller helped set them up operations across from the Ritz-Carlton on Madison at 46th Street and themselves chaperoned and served tea to the dancers.

So handsomely certified, the Castles became a New York industry. They opened their own cabarets—Sans Souci, in a Times Square basement; Castles in the Air and Castle Club, both in the Shuberts' 44th Street Theatre; and Castles by the Sea, in Luna Park. They set up licensed instruction ballrooms across the country. They published an instruction book. They supervised a series of Victor-produced dance records, and families across America began cavorting in their parlors to Castle-approved rags from their Victrolas. Charles Dillingham featured them in *Watch Your Step*, his smash-hit musical about the dance craze, with Irving Berlin providing the ragtime score.

Irene also helped advance the shift in female fashion commenced by the Florodora Sextet, Anna Held, and the Ziegfeld Girls. Irene bobbed her hair, smoked cigarettes, wore men's riding pants. Her thin, supple physique, youthful girlish image, and calls for freer fashions were featured repeatedly in top women's magazines. Dancing, she said, demanded dispensing with corsets, tight shoes, and heavy petticoats that "trussed [women] like fowls for the roasting." By 1913 the *World* declared that Irene's silhouette had supplanted the Gibson Girl's.

FOR ALL THEIR CASUAL REMARKS ABOUT "NIGGER MUSIC," the Castles' closest comrade-in-arms was none other than James Reese Europe. They met, most likely, at a 1913 Mamie Fish affair, at which Europe's Society Orchestra was providing the music, and the Castles were providing the dance steps (Mamie's friend Marbury having recommended them). They clicked immediately. The Castles, who had been unable to find (white) backup musicians who could play ragtime properly, engaged him as their personal accompanist. Henceforth all their contracts would stipulate that Europe's orchestra be hired as well.

This quickly provoked opposition. In January 1914 the couple was invited to dance at Hammerstein's Victoria. Vernon insisted Europe's group be included. The (white) musicians union—fearful that blacks would take over Broadway as they had the hotels, restaurants, cabarets, and private parties—refused to allow them in the orchestra pit. The Castles refused to dance without them. In a compromise, Local 310 allowed Europe's orchestra to play from seats on the stage. But the compromise was really a capitulation, as it broke the barrier against African American musicians in first-class venues. Given the tremendous popularity of Clef Club players, the local opted to allow blacks inside the union tent, lest their competition from outside bring the tent down altogether; Europe joined, and advised his colleagues to do likewise.

Europe did more than provide backup for the Castles' various engagements and clubs; he was their musical collaborator, composing hit numbers for them like "Castle House Rag" and the "Castle Walk," while also keeping them abreast of the latest developments in African American music. Fascinated with the work of W. C. Handy, a young black composer, Europe suggested the Castles come up with a new dance step that would work well with Handy's "Memphis Blues." Between them—and drawing also on steps Vernon had seen in African American clubs—they created the slower-tempoed, less staccato Fox Trot,

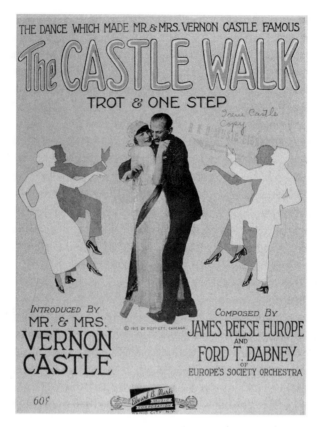

"The Castle Walk: Trot & One Step," 1914. (Baylor University, Crouch Fine Arts Library)

which became wildly popular in cabarets, especially after Irene performed Irving Berlin's "Show Us How to Do the Fox Trot" in *Watch Your Step*. The fox would soon sweep turkeys and grizzlies aside and dominate American dance floors—another instance of New York's calling the national tune.

GOTHAM'S CABARETS, HAVING GOTTEN PAST THE SPEED BUMP erected by the Gaynor/Israels forces, continued to serve as crucibles for musical entertainments that reflected and accelerated the city's taking leave of Victorian-era constraints. In doing so, cabarets drew particularly on Jewish and African American innovators, as had Ziegfeld's *Follies* and the Castles' various establishments. At the cutting edge of new developments was Reisenweber's, up at Columbus Circle, the northernmost outpost of cabaret country.

Reisenweber's was built on the southwest corner of 58th and Eighth, on the site occupied from 1855 by the Halfway House tavern for wayfarers on the Bloomingdale Road. By 1900 it had become a building with a dozen dining rooms and a staff of a thousand. When owner John Reisenweber's son-in-law Louis Fischer took over in 1905, he reorganized it into a multi-level entertainment center. By 1917 it featured a ground-floor restaurant, popular with producers and actors working at the nearby Park Theatre; a second-floor cabaret, the 400 Club (as in Mrs. Astor's Four Hundred, i.e., exclusive); the elegant third-floor Paradise Room (whose costly and lavish revues led to imposition of the city's first cover charge, of twenty-five cents); the fourth-floor Hawaiian Room (for aficionados of the hula wing of the dance craze); and a rooftop garden.

In January 1917 the 400 Club featured an all-white quintet, most of them second-generation Italians, who called themselves the Original Dixieland Jass Band (ODJB). Their music was an up-tempo instrumental offshoot of ragtime, marked by a greater degree of syncopation and raucous improvisation. The ODJB men had picked up the style in New Orleans, absorbing it from black musicians with whom they had played in integrated brass-band parades. Their own band had taken final form in Chicago in 1916, and it was there and then that Al Jolson caught their act. Jolson raved about them to his New York agent, who booked them into the Paradise Room at Reisenweber's. After a two-week run there, they settled into the 400 Club, where their combination of a firm backbeat with a wildly abandoned sound broke with ragtime's semiformal quality and drew high-spirited dancers, along with appreciative reviews.

Columbia now invited them to its Woolworth Building studio to make a record, but when they arrived, on January 31, 1917, their unrestrained style, and the pandemonium created in the confined space by the mix of clarinet, cornet, trombone, piano, and drums, simply overwhelmed the capabilities of Columbia's equipment, and the session was aborted. The band then took its act to Victor, which leapt at the opportunity to outdo its rival. On February 26 the ODJB went to Victor's new recording studio, on the twelfth floor of 46 West 38th, where savvy engineers solved the technical difficulties by using multiple recording horns, set at varying distances. They proceeded to successfully record two of the group's most popular songs, the "Livery Stable Blues" (which managed to work in animal sounds, including a whinnying horse), and the "Dixieland Jass Band One-Step," a frenetic dance number. The wildly anarchic music—promoted in the press as "a brass band gone crazy"—was an overnight sensation. Sales soon rivaled Caruso's.

Jazz—the *ss* was largely replaced by *zz* the following year—had arrived in Gotham.

"Sophie Tucker and Her Kings of Syncopation at the Hippodrome," ca. 1916–17. (New York Daily News Archive/Getty Images)

ALSO THE FOLLOWING YEAR, ON JUNE 13, 1918, vaudeville headliner Sophie Tucker started a six-week gig at Reisenweber's, which turned into a ten-month run. So enthusiastic was her reception that for the next five years Tucker alternated vaudeville tours (in New York and on the Road) with lengthy stays at the 400 Club, which from 1919 on became known as the Sophie Tucker Room. Tucker's success was a tribute to her personal talent and perseverance, but also to the way she drew upon and wove together Jewish and African American performance styles, while also moving to the forefront of those challenging conventional notions of sexual propriety.

Tucker—originally Sonya Kalish—was born in 1884 during her family's escape from Russia to America. The Yiddish-speaking Orthodox family eventually settled in Hartford, Connecticut, and opened a kosher restaurant, where Sophie helped in the kitchen, and sang Tin Pan Alley hits for the customers. Wanting out, she eloped with a boy from the neighborhood and gave birth to a son, but her husband proved unwilling to support the family, and she found herself back in the kitchen. In a bold move, much bad-mouthed in her traditional community, she decided to leave her baby with her sister, find work singing professionally, and support her family from afar.

In 1906 she headed down to New York, where, rejecting an offer to perform on the Yiddish stage, she began singing in beer gardens and rathskellers, visiting Tin Pan Alley (where she befriended Berlin) to get fresh material. In 1907, learning that producers and booking agents scouting for talent came regularly to Chris Brown's Amateur Night at the 125th Street Theatre (at Third Avenue), she traveled uptown for a tryout. Brown heard her stuff and said she could go on. Knowing that his audiences were quick to boo and catcall performers off the stage, and seeing Tucker's size (she weighed in at a hefty 160) and looks (not at all up to Ziegfeld standards), Brown called out to his assistant: "This one's so big and ugly the crowd out front will razz her. Better get some cork and black her up. She'll kill 'em." She did indeed knock 'em dead, and a booker immediately signed her up for a tour on a small-time vaudeville circuit. She asked if she could lose the black, but was refused. Indeed, she was billed as a "World-Renowned Coon Shouter."

In 1908 Tony Pastor put her onstage in blackface. She was a big hit and got written up in *Variety*. In 1909 she toured with a famous burlesque troupe, the Gay Masqueraders, during which Marc Klaw caught her act in Holyoke and offered her a singing spot in the upcoming *Follies of 1909*, opening in June. She again asked if she could work without blackface; Klaw said no. While waiting for the opening, she was hired to do her usual routine at a theater in Boston, where her appearance was widely advertised. On arrival she discovered her luggage was lost, including her black-up kit; the manager said to go on anyway, he didn't think she needed it. She strode to center stage and stunned the crowd by saying: "You-all can see I'm a white girl. Well, I'll tell you something more: I'm not Southern....I'm a Jewish girl and I just learned this Southern accent [i.e., 'stage black' dialect] doing a black-face act for two years. And now, Mr. Leader, please play my song." Coming offstage, after her act had met with thunderous applause, she declared: "I'm through with blackface. I'll never black up again."

She did, of course, for her *Follies* debut, which was to consist of three songs of her own choosing (Berlin picked them out for her), for which she was allotted six minutes, and also a specialty number with Tucker as a blackface "Jungle Queen." The glittering opening-night crowd roared for encores and kept her on for three more songs. This enraged top-biller Nora Bayes, who demanded Ziegfeld fire her; he tried to appease his headliner by cutting Tucker's stage time down to the one specialty number; Bayes departed anyway and was replaced by vaudeville's hottest star, Eva Tanguay, who promptly insisted on taking over Tucker's song; Ziegfeld reluctantly went along, and Sophie was sacked. (He later apologized.)

She was nevertheless a star. She began to dress the part, in glamorous sequins and ostrich feathers. William Morris became her agent and promoted her vigorously. In 1910 she surged into high-class vaudeville. Morris also arranged recording dates; between 1910 and 1911 she made ten wax cylinders for Edison. Her income soared; remittances home would buy her parents a house and send her brother to NYU Law. She toured extensively, played Hammerstein's Victoria in 1912, in 1913 was signed by the Keith Circuit, and in 1914 reached the summit when she played the Palace.

As Tucker climbed in status, her act began to evolve. She finally dropped blackface altogether, and though she continued for a time doing coon songs, by 1913 she was no longer billed as a coon shouter. This was perhaps hastened by her dawning recognition—after touring the South and meeting a good many African Americans—that the "Negro impersonations" she'd been doing were gross distortions. "I realized how far away I and other performers were from the real thing," she told an interviewer in 1909. "The conventional stage representation," she now understood, was "a descendent from minstrel shows, and that which I considered a real impression of a living race was nearly all a stage creation."

Tucker ditched racist lyrics but held on to a black sound. People who heard her recordings were convinced she was African American. She also worked closely with black composers, notably Shelton Brooks, who in 1910 wrote what would become her signature song, "Some of These Days"; a major hit, it sold over 2 million copies in the next few years, and she gave him fulsome and repeated credit.[16] She would also become the first woman to record the blues, performing W. C. Handy's "St. Louis Blues" in 1917.

At the same time, Tucker deepened the Jewish dimension of her act, interpolating Yiddish expressions, including ethnic-themed material like "The Yiddishe Rag," and regularly introducing herself as a Jewish girl who'd begun her career singing in a kosher restaurant.

The key new element in her act was her projection of an aggressive female sexuality. Deploying her powerful brassy voice, she belted out songs—like "That Loving Soul Kiss" (1911)—that conveyed the message that women had sexual desires and the right to satisfy them. She also flaunted her zaftig body; the gyrations that accompanied her 1910 rendition of the "Angle Worm Wiggle" got her arrested (on the Road) on charges of obscenity. She also challenged conventional relations between males and females, playing up her own status as an unruly woman. "Some of These Days" was directed at a man who has jilted a woman. Hurt but defiant, she refuses to pine after her lost love, but instead announces, "You're gonna miss me, honey / When I'm far away." She proceeds to hop a train and leave town—saying, "I'll go too, / And show him two can play this game." The man changes his mind and returns but finds only an empty house.

Possibly even more startling was Tucker's willingness to joke about sex. One of her songwriters had early on suggested that her unfashionable girth in a slimmed-down Ziegfeld era, and lack of sex appeal (she was not a beauty by the standards of the day), gave her a rare opportunity to sing about sex "without offending or enticing anyone." She could put over lyrics that would seem smutty coming from a sexy girl, and make them funny. She began regularly including verbally sophisticated double-entendre songs in her act, beginning with an old

---

16. Her 1911 recording of "Some of These Days" gave a great boost to Brooks's career; she would go on to successes like "Darktown Strutters' Ball (I'll Be Down to Get You in a Taxi, Honey)," which was recorded by the Original Dixieland Jazz Band in 1917.

whorehouse number, "There's Company in the Parlor, Girls, Come on Down"; innocents in the audience found it mildly amusing, certainly unobjectionable, while those in the know were rolling in the aisles.[17]

When she joined the Keith (Sunday School) Circuit, however, she ran up against Edward Albee. At her debut performance, she included her risqué "Who Paid the Rent for Mrs. Rip Van Winkle When Rip Van Winkle Was Away?" Albee demanded she drop it. She did, rather than lose a fabulously recompensed position, but when William Morris suggested she consider Reisenweber's, as the new cabarets were more receptive to her kind of material, she agreed, becoming one of the first vaudeville headliners to cross over.

By 1919 Sophie Tucker, master of virtually all New York's commercial entertainments, was at the vortex of a cultural whirlwind that was transforming the city's gender, sexual, ethnic, and racial arrangements. "Everybody Shimmies Now," she sang in 1919, referring to the newest hottest dance craze, but she might well have been describing Gotham's efforts to shimmy off fifty years of cultural confinements.

---

17. See also "I Wonder Where My Easy Rider's Gone."

15

Seeing New York

On any given day in 1912, somewhere between 100,000 and 200,000 out-of-towners visited New York—a floating population the size of Indianapolis or Kansas City. Many came on business. Since the Erie Canal era, commercial travelers had been flocking to Gotham to buy and sell. Their numbers had grown throughout the nineteenth century as the great port became a booming manufactory and merchandise mart. In the early twentieth century, commerce, like so much else in the city, expanded to gargantuan levels, with the metropolis becoming a vast bazaar. Giant trade shows attracted tens of thousands of out-of-towners to ever bigger venues, like the colossal new Grand Central Palace (1911), which superseded an earlier (1893) version. The new Palace, a thirteen-story tower on Lexington between 46th and 47th, was conveniently adjacent to the reconstructed Grand Central Terminal. Its massive multi-floored exhibition spaces quickly became home to Gotham's huge annual exhibitions—the Auto, Electrical, Real Estate, Flowers, Dogs, Cats, and Poultry Shows.

In 1912 the Grand Central Palace hosted New York's first-ever Travel and Vacation Exhibition, an indication that tourism had become yet another Big Business. This was a relatively recent development. For most of the nineteenth century, Americans affluent enough to afford a vacation had headed mostly for the mountains, or warm spring health spas, or seaside resorts. Cities hadn't appealed as tourist destinations, especially those deemed dangerous or wicked; most, in any event, were inconveniently far away. Rural resistance had been slowly worn down, however, by special trips to the great urban expositions, which cosseted country visitors: Philadelphia's (1876), Buffalo's (1889), Chicago's (1893), Atlanta's (1895), St. Louis's (1904), and New York's. Gotham had been quickest off the mark with its version of London's Crystal Palace back in 1853–54, and had followed up with Washington's Inauguration Centennial (1889), the Grant's Tomb Dedication (1897), the welcome home accorded Admiral Dewey (1899), and the Hudson-Fulton Celebration (1909), the latter attracting more than a million out-of-town guests.

Rural and small-town Americans began to perceive New York as an appealing vacation destination even when there was no World's Fair–type attraction on offer, in part because

Gotham began promoting itself as a tourist mecca. The Merchants' Association of New York, founded in 1897, suggested that commercial travelers consider extending their stay in the city so they would have time to pursue pleasure as well as profit. To facilitate this, the association prevailed on railroads to offer excursion rates, if purchased through their organization. Metropolitan merchants also campaigned to convince country counterparts to bring their wives and children along on business trips. Promotional literature aimed at spouses particularly touted Gotham's department stores—thereby drawing big retailers into the emerging tourist industry complex—and by 1912 the *New York Times* reported of visiting buyers and merchants that "fully one-half of them bring part of their families with them." New York also coaxed extended stays from those who once had simply passed through on their way to Europe. The boom years' prosperity, coupled with decreasing costs of Atlantic steamship travel, racheted up the numbers vacationing abroad. On any given Saturday in June, the *Times* reported in 1912, of the 5,000 people who would walk up North River gangplanks, two-thirds had arrived from the heartland, days ahead of their departure, "to see the city and finish their shopping."

It had also become easier to get to Gotham. Rail travel had gotten smoother as competing lines consolidated into extensive networks; by 1906 the New York Central and Pennsylvania Railroad systems encompassed lines originally owned by 200 companies. Travel

"Seeing New York from the Head of the Statue of Liberty." "It's a Fine Place to Visit, Yes—But I'd Hate to Live There." *Everybody's Magazine,* December 1916.

time dropped. Gotham was now eighteen hours from Chicago, three days from San Francisco, with comfortable Pullman Palace sleeping cars available to ease the journey. Railroads began marketing eastern cities to western vacationers.

WHEN VISITORS ARRIVED, a vastly increased and diverse array of accommodations awaited them. City directories in 1890 had listed 128 hotels in the city, including many little ones. By 1912 there were more than 200 substantial venues (those with fifty or more rooms) and a class of behemoths that boasted hundreds of units, in some instances over a thousand. The latter barrier had first been broken by the Astor cousins' Waldorf-Astoria. Its success, plus the growing ranks of wealthy locals and incoming tourists, spurred developers to construct more skyscraper hotels, putting to use a building type at first reserved for offices.

There were several distinct hotel districts. One was Fifth Avenue between 34th and 59th, a stretch from which the super-rich had been removing themselves and resettling higher up Fifth between 59th and 90th, the new Millionaire's Row. As they departed, their places were taken by elegant department stores, jewelers, dressmakers, milliners, and purveyors of silver-ware, china, and art, all scurrying northward to stay close to their clients, in the process re-making Fifth Avenue into (as a contemporary put it) "what Regent and Bond Streets are to London, the Rue de la Paix to Paris, the Unter den Linden to Berlin, [and] the Ringstrasse to Vienna." It was here, at 55th Street, that John Jacob Astor IV erected the eighteen-story St. Regis (1904), intended as a hyper-refined retreat where Society could hold its functions, high-end tourists could perch, and mansion-less millionaires could winter, secure in the knowledge that their accommodations were "as luxurious as the most expensive private house in the city." A challenger rose across the street in 1905 when the Gotham Hotel opened, nine-teen stories tall, but in 1908, having been denied a liquor license because it was too close to a church (the Fifth Avenue Presbyterian), the Gotham went bankrupt. More formidable was the cluster of competitors four blocks north at 59th Street and the southeast corner of Central Park, including the New Netherland (an earlier William venture), the Hotel Savoy, and Harry Black and associates' eighteen-story second edition of the Plaza Hotel (1907).

The second locus was Times Square, where the dueling Astors had constructed the Astor and the Knickerbocker. Less snooty than the Waldorf-Astoria or the St. Regis, the Astor was considered more congenial for commercial travelers, prosperous middle-class tourists, con-ventioneers en masse, and civic celebrants. Its banquet hall seated 500; its 35,000-square-foot kitchen was yet another "largest in the world"; and it boasted the latest modern conveniences: air-conditioning, smoke detectors in every room, and a "crematory" to incinerate hotel trash. It was so popular that Astor doubled its size in 1910, pushing its bedchamber count over the 1,000 mark, definitively surpassing his cousin's Knickerbocker, which had but 556. But the 42nd Street venue, its manager insisted, was the more affordable—"a Fifth Avenue Hotel at Broadway prices."[1]

The third and newest set of caravansaries, which rose up around the two great railroad depots, was aimed particularly at tourists and business travelers.

Those near Grand Central were part of the New York Central's Terminal City complex, a massive and interlocking collection of skyscraper hotels and office buildings, most designed

---

1. For all their East Side/West Side differences in style, Broadway and Fifth Avenue were scant blocks from one another. So a hotel like the Algonquin (1902), on 44th Street between Sixth and Fifth Avenues, had one foot in the theater district (the Hippodrome [1905] was on the Sixth Avenue corner), and one in the more fashionable quarter (Sherry's and Delmonico's were on opposite Fifth Avenue corners).

After the Theatre at the Knickerbocker

Advertisement, Hotel Knickerbocker. *Town and Country*, January 3, 1914.

by Warren & Wetmore, the terminal's architects. The Biltmore (1913) was the first to go up. At twenty-four stories the reigning hotel height champion until 1919, it was nestled up against Grand Central's western flank, from 43rd to 44th Streets between Madison and Vanderbilt Avenues. The 1,000-room structure had its own arrival station within the terminal, with elevator access to its lobby (whose clock quickly became a rendezvous point). Occupying the terminal's eastern flank was the Commodore Hotel (1919), sited on the northwest corner of 42nd Street and Lexington Avenue and named after "Commodore" Cornelius Vanderbilt. Its twenty-eight stories snatched the height record from the Biltmore, and its 2,000 rooms doubled the Biltmore's inventory, allowing the Commodore to proclaim itself the world's largest hotel; for good measure, it declared its lobby the world's most spacious.

The room count title was immediately wrested from the Commodore's hands by a giant summoned into being by Penn Station. The twenty-five-story Hotel McAlpin (1912) had claimed the status of world's largest when it had opened its 1,500-room building on Herald

Square, at the corner of Broadway and 34th, but the McAlpin—and now the Commodore—
were alike outdone by the Hotel Pennsylvania (PEnnsylvania 6-5000). Designed by the station's architects, McKim, Mead & White, it was placed directly across from the station's
Seventh Avenue entrance (between 32nd and 33rd Streets). The twenty-two-story building
saw the Commodore's 2,000 and raised it 200. It also included swimming pools, Turkish
baths, and a 4,000-volume library; and it employed a staff of up to 2,000.

These gargantuan hotels were not trolling for society types; public rooms were smaller
and less lavish. Nor were they seeking affluent tourists bent on long-term stays; ample suites
gave way to single rooms designed for rapid turnover. These high-volume hostelries aimed at
visiting businessmen and short-stay tourists. By editing out the costly flourishes of luxury
hotels, they were able to offer state-of-the-art amenities for relatively low prices.

The new hotels also aimed at the rising number of female professionals and business
women coming to town, and the growing ranks of middle-class New York women living apart
from their families. This market inspired creation in 1903 of the memorably named Hotel
Martha Washington. Located at 30 East 30th Street, it was founded specifically as a female-
only accommodation, its 416 rooms serving both transient guests and permanent residents.
The McAlpin followed suit by reserving an entire floor for single women, with a separate
female-staffed check-in desk on that level. The tradition of refusing admission to "unaccompanied" women—presumed to be prostitutes—was crumbling.

HOTELKEEPERS TOOK THE LEAD in forging the kind of coordinated "tourist industry" long
since put in place by Europeans (most enviably by the Swiss) but sorely lacking in Gotham.
When in 1911 the New York Hotel Association (1878) called for a campaign to advertise the
city as a summer resort in Sunday newspapers throughout the South and West, it sought
contributions to a $100,000 kitty not only from railroads and retailers but from steamship
lines, banks, exchanges, restaurateurs, the Chamber of Commerce, and the Merchants'
Association. It also called for establishing the kind of convention and visitors bureau that
existed in hundreds of cities and towns throughout the country, each ardently pursuing con-
ventioneers and tourists. It was not right, thought the hoteliers, that Chicago had broad-
shouldered its way into becoming the leading US host city for convention and trade association meetings, while New York seemed not to care about expanding visitation levels and was
widely deemed not only indifferent but inhospitable.

The Merchants' Association took up the challenge and in 1913 created a subsidiary
Convention Bureau, which vigorously pursued commercial and professional associations,
doggedly nailing down one after another—chemical engineers, insurance underwriters, dentists, rotary clubs, hardware dealers, and the National Education Association (which alone
provided 50,000 conventioneers). The bureau trumpeted Gotham's innumerable commercial
and touristic assets and stressed that no city in the country could match its hotel facilities:
—48,000 rooms with baths, and another 60,000 without, but up to convention standards. It
had significant success: where in its founding year New York had hosted 289 conventions, in
1914 it garnered 371; in 1915, 442; and in 1916 it topped 500, surpassing Chicago for the first
time, and adding 300,000 visitors to the year's total.

NEW YORK'S OUTREACH INITIATIVES had something going for them that none of its rivals
could match. As the media capital of the country, Gotham transmitted an endless stream of
information to the hinterlands, much of it featuring the city itself—in effect, free advertising.
The metropolis, as a commodity, had been "pre-marketed," and from multiple platforms.

National magazines, the major metropolitan newspapers, and city-based syndicated columnists wrote reams of Gotham-centric text, recounting the amazing events that were transpiring in the booming city, and describing the bountiful flow of one wonder after another—new skyscrapers, bridges, ocean liner docks, subways, museums, libraries, parks, schools, universities, water supply systems, foreign quarters, hotels, theaters, movie houses, mansions, and millionaires.

From the late 1890s to about 1905, the fledgling New York–based film industry generated hundreds of "actualities"—(very) short movies shot by Edison or Biograph in which cameras were taken out of the studio to locations around town. At first, movie men simply plunked their tripods down on city streets and ground away, producing hundreds of filmlets—like *Herald Square*, *Skyscrapers*, *Central Park*, or *Hotels*—that provided static views of famous metropolitan features. Edison offered *New York in a Blizzard*, a spellbinder two minutes and fifty-eight seconds long, in which the camera panned slowly from right to left, taking in Madison Square Garden, scrutinizing Broadway, gawking at the Fifth Avenue Hotel, and finishing with a westward gaze down 23rd Street.

Soon the cameras were on the move, capturing more animated marvels. They rattled along underground on the new subway; were taken up to high-beam construction sites and down into train-station excavation digs; were carried aboard East River boats to record passing skyline views. They snared scenes of immigrants arriving at the Battery from Ellis Island, pushcart venders arrayed on Hester Street, shoppers on 14th Street, crowds jostling along Broadway, skirts flying at the Flatiron, horse-drawn sleighs in Central Park, thrill seekers at Coney Island, firemen in action, and panoramas viewed from the tops of skyscrapers. These boosterish civic portraits were complemented by views of more exotic (or underworld) venues. In Edwin Porter's *How They Do Things on the Bowery* (1902), big-city women lured country rubes to ruin, drugging their drinks and stealing their money, while *Panoramic View of the Ghetto*, *The Bowery*, *Chinatown*, and *Tenderloin at Night* offered safely cinematic slumming tours.

When the drama of watching people scurry across 34th Street while dodging trolleys wore off, and directors turned to spinning stories to capture viewers' imaginations, the fledgling industry became less tethered to its urban location. But New York still figured prominently in the multi-reelers, not only as backdrop but as subject. Thus the crime-film genre was launched on a wave of narratives about Gotham gangsters, as in Griffith's *Musketeers of Pig Alley* (1912), George Tucker's *Traffic in Souls* (1913), and Raoul Walsh's *Regeneration* (1915), which were shot on location and cast real Bowery thugs as extras.

New York City was itself US cinema's first great subject, and Gotham-saturated images were screened at theaters and nickelodeons throughout the country, fixing the city ever more firmly in the national imagination and doing wonders for its booming tourist industry.

Similarly, Tin Pan Alley poured out a profusion of New York–themed songs and sheet music ("Give my Regards to Broadway," "Sidewalks of New York"). Broadway not only staged New York dramas (*45 Minutes from Broadway*), which then went on the Road, but the theatrical industry itself was news: the doings of the stars of stage (and screen), most of whom still lived and worked in Gotham, were avidly followed in the *New York Dramatic News*, *New York Dramatic Mirror*, and *New York Clipper*. The "society pages" of Pulitzer's *World* and Hearst's *Journal*, and gossip magazines like *Town Topics*, carried analogous information about Fifth Avenue affairs. Ladies' magazines (like the *Delineator*) relayed the latest word on fashions. The publishing industry brought out New York novels by the likes of Theodore Dreiser and Edith Wharton (as well as white slavery "exposés" like the *House of Bondage*, which went through sixteen editions in two years).

Tourists helped spread the Gotham gospel simply by sending picture postcards back home to relatives, friends, and neighbors. A postcard craze had struck the nation after 1898 when the government reduced postage rates to a penny; in 1905 an estimated billion cards were dispatched in the United States. Dozens of small New York printers used new halftone technologies to turn photos into mailable missives, with a hefty percentage carrying images shot in New York.[2] Most focused on what were emerging as iconic structures and locations: the Woolworth tower and the New York Stock Exchange, the Aquarium and Madison Square Garden, the great hotels and terminals, Chinatown and "the Ghetto," Coney Island, Times Square, the Statue of Liberty, and the ever-rising Cathedral of St. John the Divine.

RESPONDING TO ALL THIS STIMULUS, tourists poured in from the continent to "do" New York. But how? What to see, and how to see it?

One possibility was to avail themselves of a new tourist-industry amenity, the motorized guided tour. In 1897, according to the American Sight-Seeing Car and Coach Company's in-house history, the firm's founder had launched on the streets of Denver the "FIRST CAR ever operated for the purpose of showing any city to strangers." By 1903 its "sight-seeing conveyances" were rolling about cities across the country and had "become as much a part of the traveler's itinerary as a railroad ticket or a berth in a sleeper." Given their "superb guide service," they were "less observation cars than schools of instruction, whereon the intelligent public learns fully, quickly and completely the salient points of interest concerning every city."

In 1906 their "Seeing New York" open-air electric coaches departed from the Flatiron Building, daily and Sunday, at 10:00 a.m. and 4:00 p.m. (Later there'd be hourly service.) Each conveyance had an "expert lecturer" perched up front, megaphone in hand, coxswain style, prepared (for a fee of one dollar) to illuminate one of two itineraries.

The two-hour "Uptown Trip" traveled north on Madison and then Fifth to 90th Street, then into Central Park and out again at Seventh and 110th, then west to Cathedral Heights (past the St. John construction site) and on to Riverside Drive, thence north to Grant's Tomb—the general's relics still having great drawing power, second (in monuments) only to the Statue of Liberty—and then, after a stop at the delightful Claremont Inn virtually next door, south on Riverside Drive and Broadway back to Madison Square.

The "Downtown Trip" would head south along Fifth, then east on Waverley to Broadway, south to Wall, and east to Broad (there pausing for a ten-minute stop at the New York Stock Exchange), then on to South Street, then wend its way to and up the Bowery and Fourth Avenue, looping around Union Square and up Broadway back to the beginning. Evening tours of Chinatown and the Bowery were available every night at 8:30. All tours ended at the Post Card Store on 946 Broadway, opposite the Flatiron, where photos of the tourists and their fellow "rubberneckers," whose collective portrait had been snapped at departure, would be available for purchase (twenty-five cents), along with souvenirs of their New York visit.[3]

---

2. In 1895 several of the major printers and lithographers merged into American Lithographic Company, 52 East 19th Street, which by 1900 had consolidated most of these firms' facilities into a single plant.

3. The company also offered a circumnavigation of Manhattan on board a yacht that departed from the Albany Day Line Pier at the foot of West 22nd and headed south, rounded the Battery, sailed up the East River to Spuyten Duyvil, then returned to the Hudson via the Harlem Ship Canal.

American Coach inspired new automobile competitors, who offered more or less the same services, and several equine-dependent operators adapted to the motorized age. The Fifth Avenue Coach Company phased out its dilapidated horse-drawn stagecoaches and by 1907 was running only hybrid gas-and-electric, London-style, double-decker busses along the avenue. Popular with

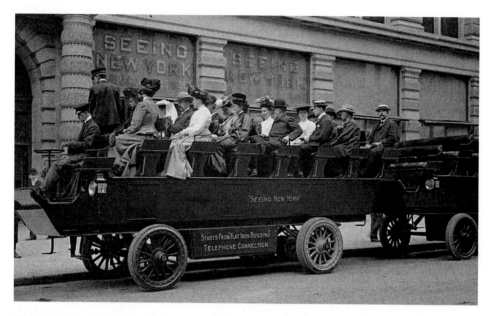

Photograph, Detroit Publishing Co. (Library of Congress Prints and Photographs Division)

GUIDED TOURS FREED TOURISTS from worrying about logistics and security; it was as if they were on a metropolitan safari. But this mode of seeing also insulated visitors from more leisurely and intimate encounters with locals and localities. Which is why most visitors preferred to strike out on their own, navigating their way through the city's streets, armed only with a guidebook, of which a wide variety was available.

One of the first on offer was a fifty-page section on New York City in Baedeker's 494-page *United States with an Excursion into Mexico* (1893). This was the first time the venerable German firm, which had been publishing its authoritative raspberry-red guidebooks since 1832, had turned its attention from Europe and the Middle East to the North American continent. Though the book had been occasioned by Chicago's Columbian Exposition, the host city rated only six pages of coverage. Gotham continued to get premier treatment in the three subsequent editions (1899, 1904, 1909), but locals wanted a volume they didn't have to share with other cities, much less another country.

Appropriately enough the Merchants' Association, perhaps New York's leading promoter of tourism, stepped up with *New York, the Metropolis: The Book of its Merchants' Association* (1902). Unfortunately for the tourists, it was more about the subtitle than the title. After a cursory high-altitude survey of cultural, social, and governmental institutions (useless for groundlings), it got down to business—its members' businesses—and launched into a prideful listing of virtually every transport, mercantile, financial, and real estate concern in the city. Each was supplemented with photo engravings (1,200 in all) of the firm's headquarters building (exterior and interior views) and pictures of each company's president (and vice president, and second vice president) in all their mustachioed, goateed, muttonchopped, or

millionaire-watchers, they made their way from 88th Street down to Washington Square. In Central Park, horse-powered carriages continued to clip-clop around its six-mile circuit, allowing stopovers at the Met and Natural History Museums, but were now supplemented by "electric wagonettes."

full-bearded glory, along with assessments of the worth of each business in the relevant coin of its realm—capital, deposits, stock price, dividends, value of exports or imports, or real estate valuations per square foot ($325 was the current peak). Really a self-congratulatory panegyric, akin to an annual report, it hardly spoke to the needs of tourists.

Perhaps in recognition of this, and in response to many requests, the Merchants' Association came out four years later with a short, slim *Pocket Guide to New York* (1906), presenting just the unadorned facts out-of-town buyers, and even resident members, needed to navigate their way about the city. It consisted entirely of lists, including the location of streetcar, elevated, and subway stops, hotels and hack stands, railroad offices, piers, ferry landings, municipal offices, banks, consulates, monuments, museums, colleges, schools, parks, hospitals, race tracks, stadiums, and automobile sight-seeing businesses. A handy and portable reference tool—but it provided only directions, no evaluations.

This sort of thing was all too common, thought Cromwell Childe, author of *New York: A Guide in Comprehensive Chapters*, published in 1903 by the *Brooklyn Daily Eagle*. "Most guides do not 'guide,'" he complained, but instead "present merely masses of undigested facts, many of these of little or no interest, compiled generally by writing 'hacks.'" Offering his guide as an antidote, Childe began by supplying new arrivals with inside tips on getting taxis. Explaining that hackmen were prone to overcharge, and warning that "strangers who are not acquainted with distances" will find it "difficult to bargain without disputes," he urged visitors to stick to their train station's official railroad cabs, which were "quite reliable." Other helpful hints were aimed at tourists presumed to be of moderate means. The traveler might consider booking into one of the great hotels, but only for one night, to get a sense of the "gorgeousness of metropolitan hotel life," then switch to "one of the medium priced hotels, or better still some boarding house in the centre of the city." Childe was also full of opinions: about which churches "should emphatically be visited," which theaters (including Yiddish and Italian ones) offered the most "brilliant dramatic performances," which floor of the Natural History Museum featured "a splendid scene of moose in the woods." He also explained to would-be millionaire-watchers that most of the rich actually lived not on Fifth Avenue (and then usually fewer than two months a year), but rather on side streets and Park or Madison. Therefore tourists who turned out for the Fifth Avenue post-church "Sunday parade," expecting to catch a glimpse of top-hatted Croesi and high-fashion ladies, would likely wind up mostly watching one another.

Where Childe arranged his material by topic (shopping, finance, waterfront), leaving his readers to assemble their own itineraries, Julius Chambers, author of *Seeing New York* (1906), opted for a geographical approach, taking his readers by the hand (metaphorically) and walking them up, say, Broadway (the city's "spinal column"), from the Battery to City Hall Park, disbursing chiefly historical commentary as he went. Other walks had other foci, but always the writer was forcefully directing the walker's attention ("Do not fail to notice...") or interjecting vigorous opinions (the statues in Madison Square "are not remarkable" and indeed all "ought to be removed"). Chambers's authoritative tone probably stemmed from his long journalistic career in New York City, including a stint as managing editor of Pulitzer's *World*.

If some books admitted to blemishes, others stuck to bellows of affirmation, like the *Standard Guides* issued by the Foster and Reynolds Company. Its handsomely illustrated *New York, the Metropolis of the Western World* (1910, reissued 1917) made this explicit in its opening paragraph. "In describing New York," it insisted, "none other than the superlatives will suffice," and then proceeded to lard them on: Gotham's skyscrapers were "among the modern wonders of the world"; its Fifth Avenue mansions were "among the most luxurious of the dwellings of man"; its hotels were "peerless in size and appointment." And yet "great and surpassing as the city is, each year adds to its material greatness and commanding influence," so much so that it was certain that from today's "Metropolis of America" was "emerging the city of the future which shall be the Metropolis of the World."

While few guidebooks could match Foster and Reynolds's products in braggadocio, the genre in general displayed an understandable tendency to accentuate the positive. The boom era's sunny surveys were a far cry from the gloomy urban reportage of the 1860s through the 1890s, which had included, even featured, the city's darker side—books like Matthew Hale's *Sunshine and Shadow in New York* (1869), Jacob Riis's *How the Other Half Lives* (1890), and *Darkness and Daylight; or, Lights and Shadows of New York Life* (1892). The latter was written by city missionary Helen Campbell, whose "labors among the lower classes," her publisher explained, had "brought her face to face with squalor and misery among the hopelessly poor." *Darkness* would recount her visits to "wretched tenement districts, where the horror of the life that is lived by human beings herded together by thousands is well-nigh incredible." Her harrowing assessment, the publisher insisted proudly, would be "presented without any attempt to tone it down." Quite the contrary, it was accompanied by a warning that "one who undertakes to 'see life' in the haunts of vice and crime in New York, especially by night, takes his life in his own hand, and courts danger in many forms."

Such a melodramatic approach was obviously ill suited for the tourist trade and soon fell out of fashion, though some guides continued to advise viewer discretion. One such, *The Gate to the Sea* (1897), admitted that visitors might want to "see a little of the seamy side of metropolitan life, in order that the impression of the city shall be true," but suggested that a little slumming went a long way. "See the tenement districts of the East and West Side, the crowded, squalid, noisy, ill-smelling, dirty barracks, where families pay as much in two years for a room as would give them a home of their own in the healthful country. Here vice and crime abound; here the death-rate is high; here are ignorance, drunkenness, filth, insolence. The effect is depressing and a very short visit suffices."

But far more often the city's "foreign quarters" were now presented as well worth a visit. They were cast as portals into exotic cultures, which should be explored in an anthropological spirit. It had become something of a fad at World's Fairs, especially since Chicago's in 1893, to set up ethnic villages wherein "representatives of living races in native garb"—imported from around the world (Javanese, Samoan, Dahomeyan)—were resettled into simulacra of their "native habitats." Visitors could wander through these spaces and observe up close these backward (but interesting!) ways of life, which contrasted so sharply with their own go-ahead modernity. At Omaha's 1898 event, a Philippine Village allowed American fairgoers to inspect some "savage" human trophies of their recently acquired empire.

At Coney Island's amusement parks, visitors were soon being treated to similar ethnographic exhibits. But New York could offer something better still, whole neighborhoods into which tourists could enter for a ramble. The city's "foreign quarters" were now deemed "picturesque"—an aesthetic category, born in late-eighteenth-century England, which referred to landscapes that were neither regular and classical, nor wild and savage, but somewhere in the middle—irregular or rugged, but in a pleasing way, a scene ideal for contemplation, for being made into a picture. Gotham's "ghettos" and "colonies" were now portrayed as "charming," "quaint," and "delightfully picturesque." It seemed amazing that these Old World subcultures survived in the heart of New York, the country's most forward-looking city. This was credited by Cromwell Childe to the fact that while many recent arrivals adopted American ways, newcomers "keep the 'quarters' filled and their traditions and customs alive." No longer deemed dangerous, Gotham's congested and impoverished districts were now hailed for providing splashes of local color—though not all colors were included in the ethnic rainbow. Guidebooks touted Italian, Jewish, Syrian, Hungarian, Polish, Bohemian, Greek, Finnish, etc., etc., communities, but were all but totally silent about the "Negro quarters." The Tenderloin did, in fact, draw some adventurous visitors to interracial ragtime joints, but via word of mouth, not the printed page.

DANGER COULD BE ALLURING, to be sure, if experienced in very modest doses. Chinatown's reputation as a center of violence (tong wars, white rowdies) and vice (opium dens, gambling hells, brothels) was not entirely undeserved. But the scene was changing in the 1900s and 1910s, as Chinese merchants (restaurateurs, curio shop proprietors) sought to drive out vice-economy competitors and make the Doyers-Mott-Pell territory safe for middle-class tourists. Sophisticates signed on for Seeing New York's 8:00 p.m. tour, which drove them to Chatham Square, then took them by foot to prearranged stops at the opera house, a joss house, and an Oriental restaurant for a chop suey supper. Such visitors might well have perused beforehand Julius Chambers's respectful and knowledgeable pages, in which he noted, for example, that the "great sheets of fiery, red placards" at the joss-house door were "Chinatown's bulletin board," and that "during the recent war between Japan and Russia, this spot was thronged every hour of the day" as "the Chinese recognized the importance of that contest to their mighty Empire." A far cry from the usual racist tropes.

Some frisson-seeking tourists, however, stubbornly continued to patronize lowlife lobbygows (guides) like Chuck Connors, who marketed the old seamy-side image by arranging visits to fake opium dens. Such suckers were increasingly mocked for their gullibility. *The Deceived Slumming Party*, a 1908 movie from Biograph (directed by and costarring D. W. Griffith), showed some tourists being fleeced at a supposed opium joint. A putative slave girl addict pretends to commit suicide, the "police" show up, the slummers fork over cash to avoid further involvement, they depart, and (as the moviegoers see) the "police," the "tour guide," and the "dope fiends" then split the take. Nevertheless, the New York Police Department, fearing that women in the real slumming parties might be enticed into returning on their own, in 1910 slapped a midnight curfew on the neighborhood and forcibly removed all non-Chinese found there after that hour. Police officials also pressured the sightseeing companies into suspending their midnight tours. The clampdown crippled restaurateurs, who protested vigorously that their establishments were "honorable and respectable businesses, catering to a respectable class of people only." But the reformer representations of Chinatown as full of hidden dangers guaranteed it would retain its "seamy" edge a while longer.

IN ADDITION TO THESE WIDE-SPECTRUM INITIATIVES, there was a host of guidebooks and organized tours published or mounted by specific institutions—among them the New York Stock Exchange, Coney Island, the *New York Times*, and Wanamaker's department store. Hands down the most popular were those offered by Gotham's soaring skyscrapers. Of the three successive holders of the "world's tallest" title—the Singer Building (1908), the Metropolitan Life Tower (1909), and the Woolworth Building (1913)—only the last included an observatory as a integral element, to be promoted in its own right. The Singer tower used its fortieth floor for publicly accessible viewing, as Met Life did its fiftieth, but Frank Woolworth had had grander ambitions ever since he visited the Eiffel Tower in 1890 and learned from its French operators that returns from admission tickets had underwritten much of the cost of the structure. In 1911 Woolworth, with his project under way, told a reporter that a tower observatory would be a crucial part of the design, intended to appeal to "the millions who visit the city for business or for pleasure." In 1916, over 100,000 visited his building, from more than sixty countries. Each received a booklet entitled *Above the Clouds and Old New York: An Historical Sketch of the Site and a Description of the Many Wonders of the Woolworth Building* (1913), which traced the uses to which its plot of land had been put since New Amsterdam days.

NOT UNTIL 1916 DID A VOLUME ARRIVE that matched Baedeker's breadth and depth. Indeed, *Rider's New York City and Vicinity, including Newark, Yonkers and Jersey City: A Guide-book for Travelers*, by Fremont Rider (and associates), avowedly took *Baedeker's United States* as its model. But where its predecessor had given only 60 pages to Gotham (compared to the 400- or 500-page tomes the firm lavished on Paris and London), *Rider's New York* devoted 506 pages to a capacious and meticulously laid-out survey. Rider was an editor and writer but foremost a librarian. He had attended New York State Library School but left before graduating in order to work with his teacher, mentor, and hero, Melvil Dewey (whose biography he would write), on a revision of the latter's decimal classification system. His training in the orderly assembly of information marked Rider's rigorous effort to grasp New York in its entirety.

He began his introduction with concise but thorough overview essays: General Description, Geography and Geology, History, Public Administration, Business, Charitable Work and Social Investigation, and General Notes on the Life and Customs of New York. Then he attended to "Information for the Prospective Visitor" (Passports, Customs, Time, Climate, Money, Expenses). Next came "Preliminary Information" on accommodations and travel: Hotels, Restaurants, Urban Travel (with subcategories for rail and water), Postal Facilities, Theaters, Concerts, Sports, Clubs, Shops, Churches, Libraries, Newspapers, Physicians, Banks, and Consular Offices.

Then it was on to "Planning a New York Visit." He began with a caution. "The most tireless sight-seer cannot hope to cover the sights of Greater New York, even in a most cursory way, in less than from two to three weeks, and only then by devoting practically all the daytime to sight-seeing, uninterrupted by shopping or social intercourse." This reservation registered, Rider proceeded, after laying out a suggested two-week itinerary that would "aid the visitor in covering the principal points of interest with a minimum loss of time," to add an abbreviated five-day plan and a one-day whirlwind tour. (The latter was actually proffered as a way to reconnoiter the territory in advance of a full-fledged campaign, but time-pressed tourists might well have pressed it into service.)

Rider then provided more fine-grained ways of deciding what was truly important. These included a "List of New York's Principal Attractions"—sixty-four items organized under eleven subcategories: Drives, Parks, Harbor, Views, Engineering Feats, Notable Buildings, Famous Hotels, Museums, Universities, Historic Mansions, and Churches (classified by location and denomination). Finally Rider, again acknowledging his debt to *Baedeker's*, promised to indicate "especially noteworthy" sites with an asterisk, and the "extraordinarily" so with two.

After presenting a solid bibliography of relevant works of history and fiction, it was on to the guide proper. Here boroughs were the organizing principle (though Queens didn't make the cut), along with the peripheral urban centers referenced in the title. The most

ILLUSTRATIONS, EXCEPT-
ING TWO, MADE FROM
PHOTOGRAPHS BY
J. C. MAUGANS, NEW YORK

A TELE-PHOTO VIEW OF THE
OBSERVATION GALLERY

THIS BOOK WAS DESIGNED
AND MADE BY THE
THOMSEN-ELLIS COMPANY
BALTIMORE AND NEW YORK

Woolworth Building. "A Tele-Photo View of the Observation Gallery." *The Cathedral of Commerce: The Highest Building in the World,* 1918. (Museum of Science and Industry, Chicago/Getty Images) interesting classification decision was Rider's division of Manhattan into three parts, not the usual two, categorizing the territory bounded by 14th and 59th Streets as "Midtown New York." This was a novel usage in the guidebook canon, though since 1905 the *New York Times* had been referring to its now-surrounding neighborhood as the "midtown business district." In its Downtown Manhattan section, *Rider's* gave the Lower East Side relatively short shrift: "This excursion involves a rather long walk through narrow, sordid streets, teeming with an overcrowded population, but it is picturesque and quite safe for strangers."

Rider's also passed along information about aspects of the cultural context that impinged on tourism. Tipping, for instance. Writer and humorist Julian Street, in a 1912 article called "Welcome to Our City," described an arriving middle-class couple being besieged sequentially by a Pullman porter, station porter, taxi driver, carriage starter, bellboy, valet, porter, maid, theater ticket scalper, brush boy, barber, washroom attendant, headwaiter, waiter, hatcheck girl, doorman, and another taxi driver—all of whose outstretched palms they crossed with silver, resentfully but anxiously, lest they be perceived as tightwads. (The aggrieved husband is "one of custom's cowards," who on his deathbed will tell his wife, "Don't forget to tip the undertaker.") *Rider's* cut though such self-pity, noting briskly that "the hotel attendants are paid low wages and expect to supplement them by gratuities. If one is staying at a large hotel fees must be counted as a part of the daily expenses."

Rider also underscored changes in mores affecting women travelers. He mentioned the Martha Washington and the McAlpin's all-female floor but added that in all large hotels near Grand Central, women arriving unescorted in the evening were received "without parley." More broadly still, "it may be stated that the old bugaboo of women being refused admittance to hotels on this score no longer obtains in large hotels in New York City." True, he qualified, in some of the smaller ones "the naive supposition still lingers that a woman who comes to a hotel at night without a man can hardly be respectable," and therefore he suggested that "it would be best to telephone from the station to avoid the possibility of this annoyance." There'd be no such trouble at the major hotel restaurants, or indeed most ordinary eating establishments, he affirmed happily, which now "consider a woman's money as good as a man's." On the issue of female smoking, however, he was more cautious. "A certain number of New York restaurants, especially of the semi-bohemian sort, now permit women to smoke," but the practice "is not allowed in the best restaurants." Nevertheless, "tourists should understand that the presence of women smoking does not imply that the restaurant in question lacks respectability."

RIDER'S ESTABLISHED THE GOLD STANDARD FOR GUIDEBOOKS. Still, it had its limits. Like all the genre, it stuck to describing and ranking institutions and localities and did not convey to potential tourists what it *felt* like to be in Gotham. A notable exception to this relatively dry, matter-of-fact approach was essayed by Rupert Hughes, whose vivid *The Real New York* (1904) cross-pollinated guidebook and novel by mixing fact and fiction. Hughes was a prolific writer of short stories, magazine articles, poems, plays, art and music criticism, and novels; later he would enter the movie business, as did his nephew Howard Robard Hughes Jr., and concoct or inspire many film scripts. Influenced by the novels of Henry Fielding, Hughes set out to display all aspects of New York life, as Fielding had done for London.

Real New York introduces a series of characters who are visiting the city from out of town and have met cute on the inbound train. One is a midwestern cleric come to gather material for a sermon on "The Modern Babylon Where Mammon Alone Is God." Another, a Chicagoan, has conversely come to sample the fleshpots of Gotham, which he's sure won't hold a candle to those of his raucous hometown. Another is a young woman from San Francisco, on her way to Paris to study painting, and planning to skip New York altogether as "everybody says there's nothing worth seeing," that "it's just a big, ugly commercial town," that "everybody who lives there thinks only of money and excitement." There being "no artistic atmosphere" there, she sums up, it's "the *Quartier Latin* for me." A Bostonian similarly holds forth on "what a horrible hole New York is, after all—nothing but commercialism, no Copley Square architecture, no music, no 'Pops,' no Kneisel Quartet, no Back Bay, no Faneuil Hall, no decent beans, no culture." And a visiting English aristocrat compares New York with London, which he believes patently superior in all imaginable ways.

These deluded souls are confounded by a crew of Gothamites, principally Gerald De Peyster, a deep-dyed New Yorker (a supposed descendant of Abraham De Peyster), ably seconded by a savvy metropolitan newspaper reporter, and a poet who, as a disciple of Whitman, believes the city's the best and greatest in the world. The latter group proceed, in a whimsical manner, to disabuse the former of their misapprehensions, not by *telling* but by *showing*—by seeing New York with a cinematic eye. Thus *Rider*'s reference to the Woolworth Building's aerie is *informative*: "The Observation Gallery[*] is open 9 a.m. to 5 p.m. Tickets (50 cents) may be obtained at the news-stand at the Barclay St. entrance. Six express elevators, running at a speed of 700 feet per minute, the fastest electric elevator service in the world, take the visitor to the 56th floor, from which a shuttle elevator runs to the gallery." But Hughes's description of a visit there is *evocative*: "Joyce led them to the elevators and chose an express. The door slammed shut, and the elevator man made an extra fast start for the benefit of the visitors. As the car shot upward at the rate of 700 feet a minute, both Silas and Sally sat down hard, or rather the car brought their feet up against their spines with a jolt. They looked scared and rose with difficulty. They had experienced one of the newest sensations science has given to man."[4]

The characters are tissue thin, and occasionally De Peyster gets taken over completely by his inner tour guide and starts spouting facts and figures, but the city itself is limned in convincing detail, and the armchair tourist gains access to places that in other guidebooks are either absent or represented solely by an address.

The New Yorkers take their acquaintants out on the town, where they have adventures and misadventures, after which all the doubters are converted. The minister demands to see the squalor of the Five Points, about which he's heard so much, and finds "to his unutterable regret" only "a clean and prosaic group of solid buildings all devoted to business, except the Five Points House of Industry and the Five Points Mission," which as they arrived "was making its weekly distribution of free footwear to poor children." After several such experiences he heads home, saying, "Wonderful city, New York"; it "seems entirely devoted to the works of charity and the cultivation of all the virtues. I am going back to Terre Haute to do what I can to make my city imitate the ways of New York." The Chicagoan, meanwhile,

---

4. In Hughes's telling, once atop, the Woolworth tourists gazed out at a "view that Cheops might have envied for all his pyramid. The map of the region was as plain as from a balloon. To the west the Hudson, here called the North River, flowed into the bay, and across its crowded current the Jersey cities rose, and far back of them one could see to the Orange Mountains. In the bay a huge 13,000-ton ocean liner was pushing out and another edging in. Liberty rose in all her pride; round her were anchored the tramp steamers of the coast, the unloaded ones showing a wide margin of red hull, the others weighted deep with merchandise for South America and the Indies.... To the north lay, mile on mile, the multitudinous roofs of Manhattan, clear-cut under the clear sky in the clear air. Mute at this distance, its streets were ravines, its infinite towers peaks crowded together to the dim crag of the Flatiron, and on, on beyond." Shifting into booster mode Hughes adds: "Not the least of the triumphs of the city's Board of Health has been its crusade in favor of hard coal. Joyce alone, from his soft-coal smudge of Chicago, could rate at its true value the absence of black clouds of smoke. So far as the eye could reach the air was undefiled of soot."

having been arrested in a police raid on a poolroom, and nabbed again at an illegal prizefight, and been floored by knockout drops at a low dive, goes home to what he now realizes is his tame hometown. And Myrtle from San Francisco is wooed by De Peyster—he takes her to the opera and bohemian haunts—and in the end she abandons all thoughts of Paris and agrees to wed her New York escort. (Their vows are exchanged, in the novel's climax, while they are stranded by a storm inside the crown of the Statue of Liberty..

Hughes did not shy away from depicting poverty; far from it. De Peyster takes Myrtle to a "cluster of ramshackle structures bounded by Cherry, Catharine, Hamilton and Market Street," and explains (channeling Veiller) that "this one block of six acres, which a farmer would count hardly big enough for a pasture, houses a city of more than 3,000 persons; on each acre there is an average of 478 men, women and children living a prairie-dog life. All of the tenements are full of the gloom and uncleanliness of overcrowded dens. The worst of them is called the Ink Pot; it has front and rear tenements and the rooms are plague spots where tenant after tenant has died of consumption." At this point "De Peyster offered to show Myrtle the inner miseries of these repellent exteriors, but she was sick of ugliness. She had devoted her life to the beautiful, and she fled from its opposite as from toads and slime."[5]

IN A 1916 *EVERYBODY'S* ARTICLE, " 'It's a Fine Place to Visit, Yes—But I'd Hate to Live There,' " the well-known columnist and wit-about-town Franklin P. Adams assailed tourists who spent their visit carousing in midtown, making the rounds from theater and opera to Lobster Palace and cabaret, and then assumed that they had experienced (and overdosed on) the essence of Gotham. Such drop-ins, he growled, had "no right to generalize about New York from a hasty glance at a few New York blocks." But when the veteran journalist tried to imagine what an *informed* takeaway overview of the metropolis might be, he came up empty. "I do not know New York," Adams admitted. "I can not interpret it. I do not know what its 'message' is. New York is too large to know. Too many things are simultaneously true of it." Cromwell Childe thought much the same: "New York is now so great that it has become like London, no one knows it completely."

But if the city was too big for anyone to wrap his or her mind around, it might still be possible, claimed Edward Hungerford, to discern critical components of what might be called its "personality." Hungerford, another seasoned journalist (*Herald, Sun, Brooklyn Eagle*) and publicist (for railroad corporations), argued this in his collection of sketches bundled together as *The Personality of American Cities* (1913). And in his chapter on Gotham he advanced a series of characteristics he believed essential, and perhaps unique, to the early-twentieth-century city. Other commentators did the same, and from the welter of their various observations emerge several key descriptive words, among them "flux," "crowds," "speed," "rude," "nighthawks," and "cosmopolitan."

---

5. In this section, Hughes has De Peyster break into an anti-Semitic aria, whether in an effort to display conventional Fifth Avenue bigotry or, more likely, simply evidencing his own prejudices on that score, but it's a complex rendering. He applauds the cultural taste and accomplishments of the brilliant men and fascinating women of Gotham's wealthy Judaic circles (and "its gilded youth—someone called them the *Jewnose doree*"), and he hails "its lower middle class" with "its music-halls, its theatres, its decent fare." But "in its lowest stages," he avers, "it furnishes New York with its most repulsive elements," those who "cling to the brawl and stench of the Ghetto, with its horrible streets and its more horrible tenements." For all this, Hughes paints a sympathetic portrait of Jewish victims of the ghetto economy. "Father, mother, the sons, the daughters and the little children turn and baste and work the buttonholes and stitch and hem hour after hour, winter and summer, cold season or hot. In the corner, perhaps, squats an old, old man. His eyes are weak and his trembling fingers drive the needle often into his own flesh, but still he sews. He is racked with a consumptive's cough, but still he sews ... . At night he sleeps with coats and trousers for coverlets. At early light he is sewing again; and the endless seam goes on, interrupted only by the spasms of coughing, coughing, coughing."

NEW YORK AS THE CITY OF CEASELESS CHANGE was one of the oldest tropes wheeled out by Gotham-watchers, but between the nineteenth and twentieth centuries its polarities got reversed. In 1856 *Harper's Monthly* had lamented that Gotham was "never the same city for a dozen years together. A man born in New York forty years ago," said the magazine wistfully, "finds nothing, absolutely nothing, of the New York he knew." But in 1902 its descendant, *Harper's Weekly*, saw this as grounds for exultation. "The man who has not seen New York in ten years would not know it to-day," boasted an article called "New York, the Unrivalled Business Centre," and "the man who sees it day by day is astonished almost every hour by the wonderful changes that are springing up before him. He rubs his eyes in looking at them."[6]

Indeed, "the amazing transformation that is going on in New York City," *Harper's* continued, "is like unto nothing the world has ever seen. Not only has the outward appearance of the lower part of the old city been changed completely within a decade, but day by day some magic process startles the eye and dazzles the brain.... The city is simply bursting its bonds. It is as if some mighty force were astir beneath the ground, hour by hour pushing up structures that a dozen years ago would have been inconceivable." That "mighty force" was commerce: "The primary cause for the upbuilding of the new New York is the uncounted prosperity of the United States"—a great change "since the dark days" of the 1890s depression—and that prosperity, "centred in the giant metropolis," was pulsing through the city as "an electrified current of financial strength that is charged with an energy unknown before in the field of human endeavor."

This energy was in turn manifested in human behavior. "New York has many historical associations, many beautiful and costly buildings, and its museums of art and science are unrivaled in America," *Rider's* noted. "Yet what the visitor will chiefly remember is none of these, but the rush and surge of the city streets, the thronging crowds, the high tension of life, the motley cosmopolitanism, that altogether make New York unparalleled by any other city on earth."

This judgment was echoed by another urban analyst, John Charles Van Dyke, who argued in his *The New New York: A Commentary on the Place and the People* (1909) that "the omnipresent interest of New York—to New Yorkers themselves as well as outsiders—is the passing throng, the great flux, the moving mass of people on the streets," along with "the roar and rattle and clang that seem to accompany the movements of that mob of humanity!" "What causes this never-ending ebb and flow of human currents up and down the avenues and through the cross streets?" Van Dyke wondered. "What is the initial force that sends wave after wave of humanity hither and yon each morning and evening, and makes of New York a city of almost perpetual movement?" His answer: "Undoubtedly the motive power comes from commerce, trade, traffic,—what is commonly called 'business.'" The "enormous buildings, the roar of traffic in the streets, the babel of tongues, the glare of lights, the strident screech of car wheels, speak the business character of the city as the hum of a top its spinning motion. If there is one feature of the city predominant above all others it is its life, its vitality, its tremendous energy kept forever in action by commerce."

---

6. Guidebook creator Fremont Rider agreed that "no great city on earth is in so constant and rapid a state of flux as New York," but grumbled about the consequences for his profession. Where a guidebook to Rome "may stand without revision for a dozen years or a score of years with tolerable complacency," he observed enviously, a New York guidebook half as old "would be most annoyingly out of date." Indeed, he confided, during the three years his volume had been in active preparation, some parts of it had "been rewritten and actually reset three times, while other changes in the text have occurred literally on every page, up to the moment of closing forms."

Hungerford agreed but stressed the specific contribution of the city's topography, with the enormous workforce having to make its daily way from distant upper Manhattan, Brooklyn, and Jersey to downtown and midtown's tall towers, by traveling through constricted streets. Every morning, "this flood of humans pour[s] out of the ferry-house and the railroad terminals, up from the subway kiosks and out from the narrow stairways of the elevated railroads," into the "narrow downtown streets" which "congest, again and again" as the "sidewalks overflow and traffic takes to the middle of the streets." Van Dyke concurred: the crowd heading to work "follows the sidewalks, fills them full to the curbstones, and winds on over gratings, around upright showcases, along iron steps, intent upon arriving at a certain place at a certain hour, and not intent upon anything else. Obstructions, such as packing-cases being loaded on a truck, or a belated ash-man rolling a barrel across the sidewalk, divert the throng, but does not stop it. It turns out into the street, goes around, and then resumes its accustomed flow....You move with it and at its set pace, other-wise someone will be treading on your heels. In fact, to do as the crowd does, is almost compulsory."

THE FLOW AND FLOOD DIDN'T END with the rush hour ebb tide of commuters heading home; Gotham was a 24/7 town. "Before the dawn," as Hungerford put it, "metropolitan New York is astir. As a matter of far more accurate fact she never sleeps. You may call her the City of the Sleepless Eye and hit right upon the mark. For at any time of the lonely hours of the night she is still a busy place. Elevated and subway trains and surface cars, although shortened and reduced in number, are upon their ways and are remarkably well filled." The *New York Times* had spotted this phenomenon nearly a decade earlier. It had been borne in on them by virtue of their new location at Broadway and 42nd Street. A January 8, 1905, story headlined "New York That Never Sleeps" reported that "day and night, for every second of the twenty-four hours, the tide of human life ebbs and flows" in "that section of the great city adjacent to Times Square." Thronged in the sunlit daytime, it was jammed as well in the midnight hours. After dark, New Yorkers and tourists poured into "the huge human whirlpool"—drawn by the brilliant electric signs, illuminated shop windows, theaters, blazing cafés and barrooms, exclusive gambling dens (like Arnold Rothstein's), and Lobster Palaces that remained open until 3:00 or 4:00 a.m. These nighthawks—"men and women who seem to get most pleasure out of life between sundown and sun-up"—kept midtown hopping until the milkman made his rounds.

Business, too, was being transacted, particularly (said the *Times*) on 33rd Street between Broadway and Fifth, a.k.a. "Uptown Wall Street," a "new financial section growing uptown." Here brokers from downtown houses set up branches in midtown hotel suites where they met out-of-town customers, eager to transact business after the NYSE had closed for the day. They would wait up to get the opening prices on the London exchange and place orders in advance to be executed first thing the next day.

NIGHT AND DAY, NEW YORKERS MOVED FAST. Hungerford noted that subway riders jampacked their way into the cars, putting up with a crowding that would not be tolerated elsewhere. Indeed, you "can ask a New Yorker about it half an hour after his trip down town, sardine-fashion, and he will only say: 'The subway? It's the greatest ever. I can come down from Seventy-second street to Wall street in sixteen minutes, and in the old days it used to take me twenty-six or twenty-seven minutes by the elevated.' There is your real New Yorker. He would be perfectly willing to be bound and gagged and shot through a pneumatic tube like a packet of letters, if he thought that he could save twenty minutes between the Battery and the

Harlem River." If the train comes to a stop in the subway or on the elevated, "instantly a hundred windows go up and a hundred heads are thrust out, each one anxious to know what the delay is about." It is the same on the rivers, where ferry pilots often forge ahead in the fog, heedless of cross traffic, and people on the decks murmur approbation. "That is the proper spirit. No stop for anything. A collision? Well,—they would rather run that risk than get to the office late."

RUDENESS WAS AN OFFSPRING OF SPEED. Rupert Hughes acknowledged that the "chief fault in New York found by strangers is the impoliteness of the people. A majority vote would probably give New York the disgrace of being the most impolite city in the world." Hughes argued, however, that it was "not the bad manners of uncouth boors" but rather the defensive mechanism of those who live too crowded lives. New Yorkers didn't own houses, not even single floors. They were so crammed in with one another that they found their "only way of getting privacy is by mentally withdrawing themselves from the crowd that is packed about them." That was also why "New Yorkers do not know even the names of people in their own apartment house or next door." It was "the conditions and not the people that are impolite," he concluded.[7]

Van Dyke focused elsewhere. The throngs on the ferries, subways, and elevateds were, he agreed, "not over-polite." While there were "men who get up invariably to give their seats to women, and others who always apologize for crowding or jostling a neighbor," there were many "who do neither the one thing nor the other." But this was attributable not so much to "want of manners" as to "thoughtlessness." They were simply "not thinking about their neighbors. They have their minds fixed on the day's work and are quite unconscious of anything in their surroundings, except the time that is being made."

BUT AMONG THE VARIOUS DESCRIPTORS OF GOTHAM, pride of place went to "cosmopolitan," a term applied almost universally by guides and commentators. Their ur-text was Whitman's celebration of the city's "many-sided and many-colored life," his declaration that New York was the "City of the world! For all races are here, All the lands of Earth make contributions."

Cromwell Childe followed suit: "No city of the world is more cosmopolitan, has so many peoples, such a shouldering together of nations." The Merchants' Association noted it was the "agglomeration of all sorts and conditions of humanity" that "makes New York the most cosmopolitan of cities." Gotham, wrote Julius Chambers, was "the most cosmopolitan assemblage of mankind upon the face of earth. Here is spoken every language of the habitable globe. Most Christian of towns, here are preached and practiced nearly all forms of religion: the Mohammedan has his mosque, the Jew his synagogue, the Confucian his joss-house, the Buddhist his shrine, the Mormon his chapel, and the Russ his Byzantine altar."

Rupert Hughes's De Peyster lectured the out-of-towners that "the word cosmopolitan was invented for us. Rome in her palmiest days never knew what wideworldliness was compared with New York." It "would be hard to find an important race that has no representation in New York. The city has become a congress of nations, in permanent session." There were, he pointed out, "whole districts of New York where hardly a sign is in English; the

---

7. For some, an alternate solution to overcrowding lay across the East River. Thus Hungerford mentions a wealthy woman who bemoans the inability of even prosperous New Yorkers "to live in a detached house," but when he cautiously ventures, "There is Brooklyn?" the woman declares with withering scorn: "No New Yorker ever goes publicly to Brooklyn unless he is being buried in Greenwood cemetery."

Postcard. "Cosmopolitan New York. 'Chinatown.' In Mott Street." Raphael Tuck & Sons' 'Oilette' [Regd.] Postcard 6601, ca. 1906.

Postcard. "'Cosmopolitan New York.' The Ghetto. — Remnants." Raphael Tuck & Sons' 'Oilette' [Regd.] Postcard 1737, ca. 1904.

Postcard. "'Little Italy.' — Garlic Venders [*sic*]." *Cosmopolitan New York*, Raphael Tuck & Sons' Postcard Series 1014, ca. 1904.

legends are in Italian, Hebrew, German, Russian or French. To ride up Broadway and read the names of the merchants on a single building is a startling revelation of what a multiplex civilization is ours. In London and Paris, while there are foreign bits, the general impression is of uniformity," but "in New York irregularity alone is regular." Most remarkably, he suggests that the origin of the "wealth of beauty" one sees on the sidewalks was "perhaps best sought in the mixed blood of the Americans; this mingling of races not only seems to redound to vivacity of mind and charm of mien, but it brings about an unending variety of feature, complexion and personality that forbids a New York street scene any of that cloying monotony of type that marks the other boulevards of the world."

Thus did Gotham's tourism industry, by hailing the everyday street-level internationalism of New York City, make its own small contribution to an evolving ideology that treated cosmopolitanism as a civic and social and cultural virtue, in sharp contradistinction to the simultaneously evolving alternative, advanced by New York cultural consolidationists, increasingly abetted by eugenicists and "race scientists," that recoiled from heterogeneity, and demanded the imposition of ethnic uniformity.

PART FOUR

CONFRONTATIONS

Emma Goldman (1869–1940) Russian-born anarchist making a speech in Union Square, New York, 21 May 1916, urging direct action. (Pictorial Press Ltd/Alamy Stock Photo)

16

Progressives

THE AGE OF REFORM

In his 1903 essay "New York as the American Metropolis," critic Herbert Croly argued that Gotham would not truly merit that lofty title until it paid as much attention to its social infrastructure as it did to its financial and industrial affairs. There were some promising signs this was happening. The city, Croly noted, had recently set about "improving the sanitary and economic position of the poor, by defending them against the most poisonous of their surrounding influences"—the 1901 Tenement House Act being a case in point. And efforts were afoot "to bridge the gulf between the rich and the poor" by "inculcating among the better-to-do the desirability and the habit of coming into some personal relations with their poorer fellow-citizens."

Croly was onto something. Since the political protests of the 1880s and the depression spawned upheavals of the mid-'90s, some of the "better-to-do" had been descending on New York's working-class quarters, determined to improve their residents' lot. Over the next decade or so, their ranks would swell. Tramping through immigrant neighborhoods, or actually settling down inside them, would come a host of settlement house residents, visiting nurses, social scientists, social gospelers, social workers, professors, doctors, researchers, teachers, ministers, rabbis, and priests. Most of their initiatives were funded by private donations from the affluent, some of whom also established "personal relations" with the poor.

As a group, these women and men optimistically believed that New York could be transformed into an efficient, humane, and harmonious community. They asserted that a city capable of Pharaonic-class construction projects could and should and would build a social order that was free (or reasonably so) from disease, ignorance, poverty, corruption, and crime.

There were two wings of this phalanx—middle-class professionals and wealthy businessmen—and they approached their joint project from somewhat different angles.

Many of the middle-class reformers—the ones on the front lines, who daily witnessed appalling conditions—stressed that the beneficiaries of their interventions were the New Yorkers most damaged by the existing order; they couched their efforts as a pursuit of social justice.

Many of the bankers, executives, and corporate lawyers who financed these shock troops regarded social ills as impediments to profit. Disease cost them man-hours, illiteracy depleted human capital, poverty bred unionism and socialism, corruption wasted tax dollars. They knew that great private enterprises could not be raised on a weak civic base. They believed New York needed to undertake social improvements to ensure a favorable climate for business, and to deflect demands for more radical change.

Despite these differing emphases, the two wings had much in common. Many businessmen were also driven by an ethically based sense of civic and moral obligation, and many professionals accepted the legitimacy and value of corporate capitalism. The partners-in-reform tended to come from similar religious backgrounds, being chiefly Anglo-Protestants or German Jews, and to share similar cultural attainments—the professionals being well-bred and highly-educated sorts, whom their elite backers could see socially (admittedly on rare occasions) without embarrassment. Many, moreover, had come to know one another personally, through shared service in New York's interlocking directorate of charitable, educational, and civic organizations.

The reformers also had common perspectives on the city's social and economic landscape. All too aware of New York's vast extremes of wealth and gross disparities of condition, they nevertheless believed that while classes were inevitable, class *struggle* was not; it was possible, they thought, to establish a civic community that did not eliminate classes but (as Croly put it) bridged the gulf between them. Their goal was to alleviate bad conditions without radically altering relations of power and property; they sought both social reform and social stability.

The two platoons were alike, as well, in tending to be paternalist (or maternalist) in their "face to face" dealings with the masses. They were more comfortable doing good *for* the less advantaged than in doing it *with* them, though some reformers did move beyond sympathy to solidarity.

The bulk of reformers shared an antipathy for the competitive economy and its enabler ideology, laissez-faire government. They agreed that the free-for-all, socially heedless marketplace in goods and labor must be regulated, and the state brought in to mitigate the myriad social problems spawned by the chaotic economic order. Corporate Morganizers and their professional allies saw eye to eye on this, with the former hard at work wringing competition from the economy, and the latter peopling the ramparts of an emerging regulatory state. Government, however, had to be efficiently administered. This required breaking Tammany's grip on power, and turning political decision making over to public-minded businessmen, advised by experts in the social, political, and economic sciences. And while some in the propertied class groused and grumbled about taxes, and insisted the chief mark of successful governance was lowering its cost, most elite reformers were prepared to help foot the bills.

But an overweening state was something else again. Most in this reform community were opposed to socialism, which they tended to equate with coercive, even tyrannical statism. And unlike socialists, they believed they were up against what social welfare advocate Edward T. Devine called "more or less isolated . . . conquerable evils"—child labor, tuberculosis, crowded tenements—rather than a "bad system." These ills could be remedied piecemeal, Devine believed, "even while private property and wages and profits remain in evidence as essential features of our industrial system."

For some, particularly in the business reformers' camp, concern about socialism was more visceral; they were haunted by the specter of its burgeoning cultural clout and growing political muscle. The National Civic Federation, a big-business group seeking to ameliorate labor-capital conflict, warned of "the menace of Socialism as evidenced by its growth in the colleges, churches, newspapers," and others feared "The Rising Tide of Socialism," as suggested by the election across the country of numerous Socialist mayors and public officials. Many of the reformers' interventions to aid the casualties of capitalism were intended to curtail the advances of socialism.

In an effort to pinpoint their political location—lying somewhere between laissez-faire and despotic statism—many of the reform cohort adopted the label "progressive." A fuzzy term, it eschewed commitment to a specific political line, in favor of situating its users at the cutting edge of history. But fuzziness had its uses. For one thing, those who accepted the tag distanced themselves from dogmatism; there were no hard-and-fast theoretical or programmatic positions to defend or proclaim; the label conveyed open-mindedness and up-to-dateness. "Progressive" was also a capacious descriptor, under whose big tent could comfortably gather some of the Morganizers (already convinced they were surfing history's wave), and most of the professionals (whose mastery of modern sciences entitled them to similar vanguard status).

In truth, the term wasn't as vague as it seemed, for it had a referent in developments in Europe, the real league leader in social activism, with whose accomplishments American progressives were eager to catch up. Since Bismarck's efforts in the 1880s to outflank Germany's socialists by providing state-run social insurance, European governments of varying political persuasions had set in place a broad variety of social policies aimed at providing some security against the volatility of capitalist economies. Germany, England, and France (among others) had legislated a host of programs to insure working people against the devastating effects of workplace accidents, ill health, old age, and unemployment—any of which could plunge a wage-earner into pauperism, as most workers lived from payday to payday, with virtually no cushion to tide them over should a crisis interrupt their income stream.

These safety net programs were not fashioned by each nation in isolation. Rather, as US social activists discovered, industrialized countries were engaged in a vigorous international conversation, with each tracking the others' policy experiments, attending expositions that showcased the latest reforms, and collectively debating their relative efficacy at regularly convened international conferences.

American progressives—noses pressed against the future—believed the US was being left behind. "Progress," it seemed, was now happening elsewhere. The nation had long prided itself on the superiority of its democratic institutions to those of aristocratic or monarchical Europe, but on the social legislation front, the Old World had seized the lead from the New. Many Americans clung to their conviction of superiority, but cosmopolitan New Yorkers were culturally predisposed to believe there was much to be learned abroad. Gotham, after all, had for centuries been the first port of call for Europe's ideas, as well as its people and capital, and the city had been striving to keep up with the Joneses (a.k.a. London and Paris) since at least the 1840s.

So local progressives edged out into the bustling transoceanic traffic in reform ideas, policies, and legislative devices. The most energetic went to Europe to see for themselves how social insurance schemes worked in action. New York's Institute of Educational Travel helpfully offered a sixty-five-day "Civic and Social Tour," which arranged visits to the Imperial Insurance Office in Berlin, vocational schools in Munich, cooperatives in Copenhagen, municipal housing in Liverpool, public milk stations for mothers of infants in Paris, public baths in London, and public pawnshops in Brussels, among other stops. Armchair analysts could subscribe to *Social Service: A Monthly Review of Social and Industrial Betterment*, put out by the Gotham-based American Institute of Social Service, which set itself up as a "clearing house" for social policy ideas from around the world.[1] Or they could peruse the *Survey* magazine, a New York forum for social policy debates. Or they could turn to muckraking journals like *Everybody's Magazine*, which in 1905 sent Charles E. Russell around the world to collect examples of social advance, or Benjamin O. Flower's *Arena*, which overflowed with reports from "foreign experiment stations abroad." The goal of these foragers, wrote Frederic C. Howe, a leading interpreter of progressive Europe to American audiences, was to "assemble the achievements of Germany, England, Switzerland, and Denmark, and present them as a demonstration of constructive democracy, of the kind of a society we might have if we but saw the state as an agency of service."

New Yorkers did more than import plans; they fashioned their own. Given the absence of a strong European-style national state, or a powerful (and uncorrupted) municipal government, the progressives created an array of private "nonprofit" institutions—leagues and think tanks and committees and commissions—to tackle particular problems (child labor, the tuberculosis pandemic, workplace accidents, failing schools). Analysts researched them, discerned their causes, designed solutions, and then mobilized public support, lobbying for legislation, bringing court cases, and waging political battles to win the backing of municipal or state governments. Many were single-issue entities, focused on specific efforts—to curtail child labor, regulate women's work, establish social insurance, alleviate poverty, reorganize public and private health care, or restructure the city's school system. Yet they also cooperated with one another. They developed interlocking, overlapping memberships. They jointly held conferences, created journals, developed funding institutions. Collectively, they created one of the nation's most advanced social policy complexes.

The process was facilitated by physical proximity. Not only were these progressives co-resident in Gotham, but their network radiated outward from a very specific neighborhood—Gramercy Park. A tranquil enclave of the well-to-do, it was situated just a few blocks north of its opposite number, Union Square, famed for tumultuous working-class demonstrations. Even more precisely, at the very center of the reform matrix sat the purpose-built United Charities Building (UCB), a seven-story Renaissance/Romanesque structure (by R. H. Robertson), at 105 East 22nd Street (corner of Fourth Avenue). Built in 1893, the UCB

---

1. The institute actually went a step further. In another indicator of New York's new sense of imperial responsibility for shaping civilization on a global level, it took on the task of serving as a relay station, transmitting the latest European and US "social and industrial betterment" programs to "backward" continents now being absorbed into the new industrial order. Their peoples were not prepared for what was about to hit them: "multitudes thrown out of employment by machinery, the increasing congestion of cities, the springing up of festering tenement houses, the exploitation of little children, struggles between capital and labor, and a swarm of other evils which follow industrial revolution." Hopefully, places like Siam, Syria, and Buenos Aires might be enabled to avoid the mistakes of their predecessors.

"The New Building for the United Charities of New York City, Corner Twenty-Second Street and Fourth Avenue." (Library of Congress Prints and Photographs Division)

was the brainchild of Wall Street banker and philanthropist John S. Kennedy, who deeded it to the Charity Organization Society and the Association for Improving the Condition of the Poor—the city's two largest Protestant charitable relief agencies—and two smaller entities. Rental space was then offered at a 20 percent discount to bona fide betterment organizations, which flocked in like homing pigeons. Among these were groups soon to be widely known: the National Consumers' League, the National Child Labor Committee, the National Housing Association, the New York School of Philanthropy, the Methodist Federation for Social Service, the Commission on the Church in Social Service of the Federal Council of Churches, and the *Survey* magazine. In 1897, bulging with the benevolent, the building was expanded—its mansard roof taken down and three new stories added—and in 1915, again strapped for space, a four-story addition was erected next door.

Others in the progressive camp clustered nearby. Two doors down was the Institute of Social Service. A block to the north was the American Association for Labor Legislation. The Institute of Educational Travel was a bit to the west, at Madison and 23rd. A bit to the east, at Second Avenue and 21st Street, lay the United Charities Building's Jewish counterpart, the United Hebrew Charities Building (1899).

Even closer, just down the block, was the headquarters of the Russell Sage Foundation (RSF), a useful proximity as the foundation became a major funding source for the progressive network headquartered in the UCB. When in 1912 the RSF discovered there was no available rental space for it in the United Charities Building, Olivia Sage decided to gift the RSF its own headquarters, and up went a nine-story Italian Renaissance structure (by Grosvenor Atterbury) at 22nd and Lexington Avenue, steps away from the UCB.

New York's buzzing reform hive not only kept abreast of European developments, but worked in tandem with corresponding circles across the United States, most significantly those in Chicago and Madison, Wisconsin. Gothamite progressives also joined nationwide discussions as members of the National Conference of Charities and Corrections, the country's leading collection of social welfare experts. (De Forest served as president for a time.) And it was out of these collective conversations and connections that the New York progressive community would come to play a crucial role in the 1912 formation of a national Progressive Party, which would run ex-president Theodore Roosevelt as a third-party challenger.

WHILE GRAMERCY PARK WAS THE HEADQUARTERS of New York progressivism, the front lines ran through the settlement houses and churches located in working-class communities, situated precisely at the intersection where Herbert Croly had spotted the "better-to-do" coming into "personal relations with their poorer fellow-citizens."

SETTLEMENTS AND SOCIAL GOSPELERS

Gotham's settlement house movement had grown dramatically since Stanton Coit opened the Neighborhood Guild on the Lower East Side (at 146 Forsyth Street) back in 1886, during the turmoil surrounding Henry George's labor-backed mayoral campaign. Coit had been inspired by London's Toynbee Hall, which in 1884 had been established in a destitute neighborhood, by an Anglican rector, as a community center where university men could live and work among the poor. In 1891 Coit's Neighborhood Guild, now renamed the University Settlement, defined its goal as bringing "men and women of education into closer relations with the laboring classes in this city for their mutual benefit." The University Settlement project, headed by Seth Low, then president of Columbia, was taken up by the metropolitan elite. Among those contributing to the 1898 construction of its four-story home on the Lower East Side (at 184 Eldridge Street) were John D. Rockefeller Sr., James Speyer, James Stillman, Felix Warburg, Otto Kahn, August Belmont, William Schermerhorn, and John S. Kennedy. Members of the governing council included (by 1904) the likes of Elihu Root and Jacob Schiff.

"The University Settlement Society owes $75,000 on its new building, and the following subscriptions have been made to pay this debt," 1899. "An Important Piece of University Settlement's History," *New York Social Diary*, September 26, 2012.

College grads lined up to become residents, including men of wealth like James Graham Phelps Stokes and William English Walling.[2] The residents, assisted by scores of volunteers, administered clubs, lectures, a day nursery, a kindergarten, a library, a public bath, a purchasing co-op, an employment bureau, a gym, and a bank. Nearly a thousand local children and adults came every day to avail themselves of these services.

The University Settlement also studied its neighborhood. Researchers wrote papers for a quarterly publication on various aspects of local life—"the candy store as a social influence"—but focused mainly on community problems: the role of ill health, or overcrowded housing, or economic downturns, in impoverishing working-class families. This investigatory role was emphasized by Robert Hunter, installed as headworker in 1902. A scion of a prosperous manufacturing family in Terre Haute, Hunter opted for social activism, motivated by the impoverishment he'd witnessed during the '90s depression. After graduating from Indiana University in 1896, he became an organizing secretary for the Chicago Bureau of Charities, and a resident of Hull House and then of London's Toynbee Hall, before arriving at Eldridge Street. In 1904 he published *Poverty*, a pioneering sociological study based on his experiences in Chicago and New York settlement houses.

THE UNIVERSITY SETTLEMENT'S FEMALE COUNTERPART, the College Settlement (1889), had also flourished since it had opened three blocks away, at 95 Rivington Street. It attracted scores of young, idealistic, mostly college-educated women—some quite affluent—in search of meaningful work. And it offered a similar basket of programs, including music classes, social, athletic, and mothers' clubs, a public bath, and a playground. These residents, too, were assisted by part-time volunteers, one of whom, in 1903, was the niece of President Theodore Roosevelt. Though she had helped her father serve Thanksgiving dinners to newsboys and assisted her uncle in decorating Christmas trees for children in Hell's Kitchen, College Settlement work was 19-year-old Eleanor Roosevelt's first serious contact with poor people. She was brought to Rivington Street by fellow debutante Mary Harriman (daughter of Edward and Mary Harriman). In 1901 Harriman, a Barnard freshwoman determined to go beyond social teas, had founded a Junior League for the Promotion of Settlement Movements. "We were just a group of girls anxious to do something helpful in the city where we lived," Roosevelt later recalled. She signed on to teach calisthenics and dancing to local children. Daringly for a woman of her class, she took the Fourth Avenue streetcar downtown by herself, but at times was escorted home after class by her courting cousin Franklin Roosevelt, who had never before directly encountered tenement conditions.

---

2. Stokes was a scion of one of New York's wealthiest families. His great-grandfather had founded Phelps, Dodge. His father, Anson Phelps Stokes, was a banker and real estate developer. His uncle William Earl Dodge Stokes had just built the Ansonia. He himself had extensive mining and railroad interests out west. But he had also inherited the family's liberal strain—best evidenced in his aunts Caroline and Olivia, who founded the Phelps-Stokes Fund to give money to American Indians, African Americans, and slum residents of New York City. Young James Stokes worked for the YMCA, then joined Hartley House, then the University Settlement, where in 1903 he met Rose Pastor, a Jewish former factory girl, now a journalist and settlement worker. The 1905 marriage between a Protestant millionaire and a Yiddish Cinderella generated enormous press coverage, which drew additional attention to the settlement.

Walling was an out-of-towner. Born in 1877 to an affluent Episcopalian family in Louisville, Kentucky, he studied with Thorstein Veblen at the University of Chicago and, on graduation in 1897, joined Jane Addams's Hull House, Chicago's premier settlement. Though he'd received a bequest that brought him $10,000 a year, he became a socialist, got a job as a factory inspector, and in 1902 moved to New York, where he joined the University Settlement. In 1906 Walling, too, married a radical Jewish woman, Anna Strunsky. Her family had emigrated from Russia to New York in 1886, and relocated to San Francisco in 1893. She became a socialist at age 16, studied at Stanford, befriended Emma Goldman, became a writer (encouraged by fellow socialist Jack London), and worked with Walling in supporting the Russian Revolution of 1905, joining him in St. Petersburg to cover the story. They married the following year in another headline-making event. ("Girl Socialist Wins Millionaire," shouted the *San Francisco Call*.)

ONE OF THE BIGGEST SUCCESS STORIES was the Nurses' Settlement on Henry Street, established in 1893 by Lillian Wald and Mary Brewster. Wald, born in Cincinnati in 1867, was raised in Rochester, where her comfortable and assimilated German Jewish family had moved in 1878. Inspired by a nurse who had treated her mother, Wald relocated to Gotham in 1889 to study at New York Hospital's School of Nursing. After graduating in 1891 she worked for a year at an orphan asylum, then enrolled in Elizabeth Blackwell's Women's Medical College. In 1893 she volunteered to teach home nursing to immigrant women. The course was offered by the Hebrew Technical School for Girls, an institution underwritten by Betty (Mrs. Solomon) Loeb—the second wife of Kuhn, Loeb's cofounder—and other wealthy female members of Temple Emanu-El. Stunned by the suffering and poverty of her immigrant working-class students, Wald decided to move to the Lower East Side permanently and become what she called a "public health nurse."

She and Mary Brewster, a nursing school classmate, stayed for a time at the College Settlement on Rivington Street. Then, in 1893, they established the Nurses' Settlement in Spartan rented rooms on Jefferson Street, from which they visited patients in their homes, for little or no money. In 1895 Betty Loeb and her son-in-law Jacob Schiff bought the two women a building at 265 Henry Street, and they renamed their operation the Henry Street Settlement. There they fashioned an attractive community space, one markedly free of the patronizing attitude that sometimes marred resident-local relations. Wald's respect for her neighbors was widely reciprocated. Jacob Schiff's philanthropy, too, was unusually sensitive,

Lillian Wald, ca. 1893–95.

guided as it was by the Jewish tradition of *tzedakah*. This required that the giving of aid flow from a sense of obligation, not self-aggrandizement, and it mandated face-to-face relations with recipients. Schiff and his family ate regularly with Lower East Siders at the Henry Street Settlement, and he thanked Wald for helping him "better understand the life of those who have to struggle."

Henry Street would offer a variety of social services to the neighborhood, but its special contribution was the spectacular expansion of its visiting nurse program. Wald opened branches around Manhattan and the Bronx for Italian, Hungarian, and African American communities. The project attracted prominent nurse-residents, including Lavinia Dock, former superintendent of the Johns Hopkins University School of Nursing. Their numbers grew from 27 in 1906, to 47 in 1910, to 100 in 1917, during which year they made 250,000 home visits, reaching more patients than were treated at Mount Sinai, Presbyterian, and New York Hospital put together, and achieving a significantly better recovery rate from basic diseases like pneumonia.

IN 1902, MARY KINGSBURY SIMKHOVITCH opened Greenwich House, the first settlement of the new century. Like others in the movement—many of whom came to the big city from smaller out-of-state communities—Simkhovitch was "drawn to the idea of plunging into life where it was densest and most provocative." Born Mary Kingsbury, daughter of the city clerk of Newton, Massachusetts, she graduated from Boston College in 1890, taught Latin in a local high school, then did a year of graduate study (1895–6) at the University of Berlin. There she met her future husband, Vladimir Simkhovitch, a Russian-born economics student

A visiting nurse on a Lower East Side tenement rooftop, ca. 1920. (MPI/Getty Images)

(and later professor at Columbia). She attended mass meetings addressed by Wilhelm Liebknecht, a founder of the German Social Democratic Party. And she traveled to London to observe the International Socialist Trade Union Congress, where she heard speeches by Jean Jaurès, Sidney and Beatrice Webb, and Labour movement organizer Keir Hardie.

Back in New York Simkhovitch joined the College Settlement, and boned up on her new neighborhood by studying Yiddish and reading the stories of Abraham Cahan. In 1898 she left to become headworker of a start-up, the Friendly Aid House, sponsored by the All Souls Unitarian Church, but soon decided it was really a mission rather than a settlement house, which she defined as "a group of people who have had educational and social advantages," who decide to live in a "neglected neighborhood" in order "to understand the problems of the wage-earner" and "in cooperation with its neighbors to work out the best sort of

Mary Simkhovitch, ca. 1901–7. (The Tamiment Library & Robert F. Wagner Labor Archives)

neighborhood life possible." With the aid of reformers (like Jacob Riis and Felix Adler), church-men (like the socially minded Episcopal bishop Henry Codman Potter), and philanthropic bankers (like patrician financier and Citizens' Union chair Robert Fulton Cutting), she set out to establish her own operation. Helped by Frances (Mrs. J. Pierpont) Morgan, who pre-sented the fledgling operation with its first check, she purchased a former longshoremen's boardinghouse in the heart of Greenwich Village, at 26 Jones Street. The super-packed block was home to 1,400 people—Irish, Italians, African Americans, and twenty-three other na-tionalities—one reason she announced that Greenwich House would adhere to "no creed but that of a common humanity." Like Wald, Simkhovitch learned to respect and sympathize with local residents. "We knew not only poverty and crime," she recalled, "but also the intel-ligence and ability and charm of our neighbor." And Greenwich House quickly set to inves-tigating local conditions, with an eye to becoming an agent of community transformation.

BY 1908 A SCORE OF SETTLEMENTS WERE SPRINKLED AROUND TOWN—including, on the Upper East Side, the Union Settlement on East 104th and the East Side House on East 76th; on the West Side, Hartley House on West 46th and the Hudson Guild on West 25th; and in Brooklyn, Maxwell House on Concord Street and the Greenpoint Settlement on Franklin Street. This network would serve as a crucial infrastructure for progressive reformers, not least because the settlements, to an unusual degree, encouraged the participation of women. There were roughly equal numbers of male and female headworkers at the principal settle-ments, but women averaged twenty-four years of service in the movement, men only eight. Some of this was due to the greater opportunities available elsewhere for male professionals, but it was also true that women were attracted by the settlements' communal intimacy. Only a very small percentage of female headworkers married, most forging instead intense per-sonal relationships with female coworkers, fashioning networks that would sustain them in their reform efforts. Also, given the outlawry of female suffrage, settlements were one of the few institutions through which middle-class women could exercise political power.

In addition to developing strong in-house bonds, the settlements established lateral connections, beginning in 1900, when Simkhovitch and Hudson Guild headworker John Lovejoy Elliot formed the Association of Neighborhood Workers to "effect co-operation" and promote "movements for social progress." In 1907 the Brooklyn Neighborhood Association followed suit.

The settlement houses were welcoming, too, in their nonsectarianism: they rejected proselytizing, which distinguished them from the evangelical Protestant missions that had long irked their intended targets, especially Catholics and Jews. True, many houses were launched by particular religious denominations, overwhelmingly Protestant ones—the East Side House was a project of wealthy Episcopal laymen, and the Union Settlement was started by alumni of Union Theological Seminary—but none included religious instruction in their programs.

There was, however, a cognate movement, led by the so-called Institutional Churches, which admixed social service with spiritual practice. Partly this development was inspired by the settlement houses, partly it was driven by declining membership as parishioners moved away, and partly it emerged in tandem with Gotham's social gospel movement, whose goal was to establish the Kingdom of God on earth.

SINCE THE 1880S, DOWNTOWN PROTESTANT CHURCHES had been retreating northward as Catholic and Jewish immigrants advanced uptown. Some, however, chose to stay and make themselves useful to newcomers by providing settlement-style programs along with denominational services. This movement expanded in the depressed 1890s, as poverty stalked their parishes. By 1897, according to an article entitled "The Progress of the Institutional Church," some dozen Protestant establishments in New York City were pairing humanitarian work with religious outreach.

Episcopalian churches had pioneered, notably St. George's, on East 16th Street at Stuyvesant Square, its once-fashionable parish now in decay. Rather than pack up and follow its congregants uptown, the vestry of lawyers, bankers, and businessmen, led by senior warden J. P. Morgan, had invited (in 1883) an innovative young rector to direct outreach efforts to the poor. The Reverend William S. Rainsford had begun by making the church less daunting for those with low incomes. He abolished pew rentals—removing the brass nameplates—and made all seats free; Morgan personally replaced the lost income. Then Rainsford developed settlement-style community services, on which the church spent more than $3 million by 1899. These included a program of home visitations that provided care and communion. One beneficiary was Tammany boss Richard Croker's mother; in gratitude, Croker made sure sanitation men kept Stuyvesant Square tidy, and a police patrol kept it safe on Sundays. By 1906, when Rainsford stepped down, the number of St. George communicants had skyrocketed to 4,000, and it had become the largest and most active Episcopal parish in the United States.

Fashionable Grace Church, nearby at Broadway and 10th Street, joined the Institutional movement. Rector Henry Codman Potter started up workingmen's clubs, day nurseries, kindergartens, and other social programs. In 1896 the church set up its own Grace Church Settlement at 413 East 13th. Potter would continue to support the movement during his years as Gotham's Episcopal bishop (1887–1908).

Farther north, at Madison and 44th, St. Bartholomew's, another Episcopal congregation, received nearly $400,000 from the Vanderbilt family to build a five-story parish house (at 205–208 East 42nd), which opened in 1891. Its chapel ministered to new arrivals in the tenements of the East 40s and 50s, providing diverse forms of worship in several languages, including Near Eastern ones, to serve immigrants from Turkey, Syria, and Armenia. It also provided space for classes, social clubs, a working girls' summer home, a medical and surgical clinic, a gymnasium, a laundry, a print shop, a loan association, and an employment bureau.

Not all Episcopalians were on board with this approach. The wing that emphasized individual spiritual growth wondered pointedly what social programs had to do with religion. Yes, people were packing the pews, but to what avail, if they were there seeking services rather than salvation?

Baptists were similarly divided on this score, though they could choose from three alternative approaches rather than two. As a working-class denomination, there were fewer rich coreligionists to sponsor Institutional-style social welfare programs—with one whale of an exception. Since the 1880s, when John D. Rockefeller, a devout Baptist, had transplanted his family to New York—and almost immediately escorted them to the Five Points slum to witness the needy at first hand—Rockefeller had subscribed to the Institutional Church approach. In particular, he had underwritten the ministry of Edward Judson, pastor of the Berea Baptist Church at 117 West 15th Street, who aimed at poor Italian immigrants. Judson won Rockefeller over to his vision of building a religious center that would unite elements of both church and settlement, a plan spectacularly realized in 1893 with construction of the Judson Memorial Church (in honor of his missionary father) on Washington Square. Given Rockefeller's resources, the architect called in was Stanford White, who confected an

Italianate structure, to attract Italian immigrants, with an adjoining Judson Hotel, to bring in revenue. Not only did the church offer medical, educational, and recreational services alongside worship and religious instruction; it aimed to bridge the gap between the immigrants of the South Village and the aristocrats of Washington Square North. It soon became apparent, however, that the established rich were none too keen on rubbing shoulders with the immigrant poor. Funding dried up, and even Rockefeller cut off direct support in 1910, though principally because he had concluded that "scientific philanthropy" required giving on a "wholesale," not a "retail," basis, so he shifted his support to the New York Baptist City Society, which administered numerous church projects, with Judson Memorial only one of its beneficiaries.

There were plenty of Baptists who opposed such Institutional Church programs, and stuck to the old-time religion, centered on confession of sin and rebirth in Christ. There was, however, a third, social gospel wing of the denomination, which argued that Institutional Churches didn't go far enough. One of the principal founders of this movement, Walter Rauschenbusch, had undergone a spiritual-political conversion when serving between 1886 and 1897 as pastor of the Second German Baptist Church in Hell's Kitchen. Early on he raised funds for a new church structure at 407 West 43rd. (Rockefeller made a handsome donation.) But the omnipresent daily reality of widespread suffering—squalor, crime, malnutrition, disease (the "children's funerals" gripped his heart)—all exacerbated by the 1890s depression, had led Rauschenbusch to shift his energies from saving individual souls, to advancing an agenda for social justice. His New York apartment became headquarters for the Brotherhood of the Kingdom, an association of Baptist ministers who agreed that establishing the Kingdom of God was "not a matter of getting individuals to heaven, but of transforming the life on earth into the harmony of heaven."

In 1897 Rauschenbusch was offered a position on the faculty at Rochester Theological Seminary, and there, in works like *Christianity and the Social Crisis* (1907), *Christianizing the Social Order* (1912), and *Theology for the Social Gospel* (1917), he deepened the critique he'd developed in Gotham. Baptists, he argued, and indeed most Protestants, focused too much on individual sin, and not enough on what he called "institutionalized sinfulness." Evil could be embedded in "suprapersonal entities" like capitalism or militarism, or "lodged in social customs and institutions" and potentially "absorbed by the individual from his social group." Rauschenbusch urged Baptists to press for improving the lives of the working poor, lest by inaction they become complicit in perpetuating an unjust social order. Baptism itself should be reframed as "not a ritual act of individual salvation but an act of dedication to a religious and social movement."

THIS DIVISION BETWEEN SUPPORTERS OF A SOCIAL GOSPEL, an Institutional Church, and evangelical individualism was replicated in other Protestant denominations, notably Presbyterians and Methodists.

The Presbyterian mainstream was heavily traditional, but for a time it gave considerable leeway to the Reverend Charles Stelzle, who argued that social regeneration and individual evangelism were equally important, indeed complementary. This conviction grew from his own experience of living in both worlds at once.

Stelzle, born in the Bowery to German immigrant parents in 1869, grew up on the Lower East Side and became a journeyman machinist and trade unionist. He also developed a religious calling and became a minister. Then he set about trying to bridge the two pursuits. In 1903 he got Presbyterian authorities to establish a Department of Church and Labor, and to put him in charge. The department collected and disseminated to churches data about working conditions in their neighborhood. It also encouraged establishment of "industrial parishes," in which each congregation accepted responsibility for the welfare of workers in a particular factory. And it aided those parishes in starting workshops and employment bureaus, while also arranging noontime devotional meetings at "their" factories.

Stelzle arranged for unions and local ministerial associations to exchange fraternal delegates; he himself went to the 1905 American Federation of Labor convention as an official representative of the Presbyterian Church. He wrote a regularly syndicated column that by 1907 ran in over 300 US labor periodicals. And in 1910 he founded the Labor Temple, repurposing an old Presbyterian church at the southwest corner of Second Avenue and 14th Street, one of the many whose congregations had fled the neighborhood as it filled up with immigrants, vaudeville houses, saloons, and brothels; even superstar revivalist Dwight Moody had failed to draw an audience in this quarter.

Stelzle succeeded—with a blend of traditional evangelism, settlement-style social services (including Sunday evening movie screenings), and an open forum on economic, social, and political issues of the day. The Labor Temple was staunchly pro-union—Stelzle supported strikes and backed campaigns to abolish child labor and improve working conditions—while repudiating violence, class struggle, and socialism. Emma Goldman denounced him as a "tool of the capitalistic class," but Italians, Jews, Poles, and Slavs turned out in record numbers, seven days a week, 150,000 annually.

Stelzle proved *too* successful. A large percentage of New York Presbyterians tended to sympathize with management's side in industrial disputes. Conservatives found Stelzle insufficiently attentive to orthodox doctrine, too friendly to socialists, too enamored of sociology, too willing to legislate social betterment. Wealthy businessmen cut back on donations, Stelzle's budget was slashed, and in 1913, seeing the writing on the wall, he resigned as director of the Department of Church and Labor.

IN THE METHODIST WORLD, THE SALVATION ARMY—Wesleyanism's most prominent evangelical organization—was arguably more socially oriented than any Institutional Church. Since the 1880 arrival in New York of the British Salvation Army's scrappy vanguard, intent on winning souls among thieves, prostitutes, gamblers, and drunkards—the *un*deserving poor—the Army in Gotham had been deemed of dubious respectability. This began to change as it steadily expanded its commitment to providing material as well as spiritual sustenance. Salvationists moved into tenement districts and provided assistance to neighbors in need: sending out ice carts in summer and coal wagons in winter; providing free breakfasts to poor schoolchildren; setting up soup kitchens, rescue homes, hospitals, shelters, orphanages, and workingmen's hotels for the desperate or incapacitated. More innovatively, the Army created "salvage brigades" run by down-and-outers who were able and willing to work. Going door to door, they picked up middle- and upper-class castoffs—clothing and furniture that was then offered to the poor at minimal prices, and paper and rags that were sold off to junk dealers.

In the new century, the Army combined and expanded its operations, establishing "industrial homes" that, under one roof, simultaneously provided lodging, food, recycling work, and evangelistic activities. Between 1904 and 1913 the number of these relief institutions surged, and their size swelled. The Army's first industrial home had been a converted, run-down milk depot. But in 1907, at a cost of $130,000, it built a seven-story industrial home at 535 West 48th Street that accommodated 175 men, who staffed the twenty-two salvage wagons that rumbled out each day. In 1913 the Army opened the ten-story tall Booth Memorial Hotel at 223–225 Bowery, which had 611 cubicle rooms.

All these initiatives took money, big money, which their familiar nineteenth-century fund-raising methods—like setting out red kettles staffed by bell-ringing Army lassies on sidewalks to collect loose change at Christmas time—could no longer provide. So the once pugnaciously plebeian operation cultivated relationships with prosperous patrons. Casting their peaceful version of spiritual warfare as a bulwark against the bloody revolution supposedly sought by anarchists and socialists, they successfully rebranded themselves, morphing from ragtag religious missionaries into respected providers of social services—particularly after 1904, when Evangeline Booth, the founder's daughter, was appointed commander of the Army in the United States. Booth's speeches dwelt on her great love for the poor, though she herself dwelt among the rich. Her upstate estate abutted that of banker Felix Warburg, and her summer retreat at Lake George was close to another friend, Adolph Ochs, owner of the *New York Times*, a paper once harshly critical of the Salvationists, but no longer.

But if the Army could portray itself, with considerable justice, as a supporter of the poor, it was not an advocate for transforming the economic order from which their poverty flowed. For all its fire-and-brimstone rhetoric, it proposed no Social Gospel Kingdom of God on earth, nor did it provide settlement house progressive critiques of working conditions. With its spiritual efforts focused on saving individual souls, its social values stressing traditional

Commander Evangeline Booth, Salvation Army, ca. 1915–20. (Library of Congress Prints and Photographs Division, George Grantham Bain Collection)

virtues like hard work and sobriety, and its material outreach increasingly financed by middle-
and upper-class money, it was squarely on the side of the status quo. Booth had no qualms
about underlining this, noting in a 1913 *War Cry* article ("Why the Capitalist Should Help
the Salvation Army") that her troops turned out "honest, sober, consistent, to-be-depended-
upon working-men." Those in power—the press, politicians, and business leaders—had no
reservations about warmly lauding such work.

Beginning in 1899 the new collaboration between the Army and the wealthy was institutionalized with the inauguration of a spectacular annual Christmas Dinner, held at Madison
Square Garden or the Grand Central Palace. Thousands of affluent contributors assembled
in the upper tiers, from which they looked down upon the thousands of recipients of their
largesse who filed in to be served, at long tables festooned with linen and china, a splendid
holiday banquet by Army soldiers and officers. The *Times* reported that the "well-fed and
prosperous" patrons "looked on in happy sympathy" as a band played and the poor ate.
Some, to be sure, watched the feasting hordes with a jaundiced eye, and "whispered and
pointed at poorly clad men and women who ate ravenously or smiled when a piece of turkey
was surreptitiously slipped into a capacious pocket." Though these extravaganzas were criticized by some in the charity movement as overindulgent or exploitative, the banquets were
popular with the patricians, pleased at the visual ratification of a social order so tidily divided
between benevolent elites and grateful beneficiaries.

THE REAL SOCIAL GOSPEL METHODISTS WERE SOMETHING ELSE AGAIN. Far stronger than
Presbyterian counterparts like Charles Stelzle, they won control of the levers of denominational power and committed much of organized Methodism to rejecting business as usual.

Salvation Army Christmas dinner. Spectators and benefactors look on from Madison Square
Garden's seating gallery, n.d. (Library of Congress Prints and Photographs Division, George
Grantham Bain Collection)

The theology of Baptist Rauschenbusch resonated with particular force among Methodists. In December 1907 a group of socially active Wesleyan clergymen, denominational executives, educators, and businessmen formed the Methodist Federation for Social Service (MFSS). Headquartered in the Methodist Book Concern building at 150 Fifth Avenue, it called attention to the Panic-exacerbated suffering among the working class and urged re-formation of an economic system based on competition and selfishness. More specifically, it drafted a document that laid out public sector interventions that might protect exploited workers. Months later, in the spring of 1908, the General Conference of the Methodist Episcopal Church—the largest branch of American Methodism—adopted the MFSS draft as its "Social Creed." The social gospel had captured its first denominational citadel.

This, it turned out, was just the beginning. In December 1908 a conference was held in Philadelphia at which the latest in a long series of ecumenical efforts by mainline Protestants came to fruition. Representatives of twenty-nine denominations—including Methodists, Presbyterians, Congregationalists, Reformed, Quakers, Moravians, and Baptists (Rauschenbusch among them)—agreed to set aside doctrinal differences and join forces by establishing the Federal Council of Churches of Christ in America (FCC). This was a confederation, not a consolidation; indeed, its constitution forbade the body from trying to adopt a common religious creed, lest the ensuing struggle shatter the organization back into denominational slivers. But it was deemed perfectly acceptable to unite around social issues; indeed, it was a way to cement their solidarity. Accordingly, the FCC adopted almost verbatim the Methodists' Social Creed, and issued it as the Social Creed of the Churches. In 1912, it was readapted and supplemented at a conference in Chicago, whose delegates represented 17 million church members. Organized Protestantism had come out unreservedly for the abolition of child labor, the regulation of the conditions of work for women, suppression of the "sweating system," reduced hours and a living wage, workers' old age pensions, the protection of workers from dangerous machinery and occupational disease and "the hardship of enforced unemployment," "the conservation of health," the "fullest development of the child by education and recreation," and "the abatement and prevention of poverty." The Kingdom of God, indeed![3]

The national headquarters of social gospel Protestantism were established in New York City, at first, in 1908, in the old Bible House on Astor Place. By 1914 the FCC had joined the betterment throng at the United Charities Building on 22nd Street.

JEWS DIDN'T DO SETTLEMENT HOUSES OR INSTITUTIONAL SYNAGOGUES, though the Educational Alliance (1889) embraced elements of each. The Alliance didn't have live-in residents, but its daytime staff administered a host of social programs—clubs and gyms, concerts and classes, public baths, a 12,000-book library, a reading room, and a roof garden—that in 1903 drew 300,000 to the yellow brick building at 197 East Broadway. The Alliance wasn't non-sectarian; indeed, it was explicitly aimed at Jews, and in 1900 even opened a People's Synagogue on the premises. Nor was the Alliance into "cooperation with its neighbors"; it was into remolding them. The Alliance had been created by wealthy uptown German Jews, panicked that the en masse arrival of Eastern European Jews, given to either Orthodox religiosity or radical

---

3. The assembled Protestants also noted "with deep regret the increasing prodigality on the part of irresponsible men and women of large possessions. We would point out the intimate relation between reckless display of wealth and the revolutionary and defiant attitude of the multitude who feel, rightly or wrongly, that it is at their expense."

politics, might undermine their hard-won but precarious social respectability, perhaps even trigger a new round of anti-Semitism. Their proposed solution was to Americanize their coreligionists as speedily as possible. The Alliance's first fifteen years, therefore, featured crash courses in civics and English and etiquette, while bluntly barring Yiddish from the premises. In the face of widespread and vocal immigrant resentment, the patriarchs slowly gave ground. Lectures in Yiddish were permitted. The synagogue offered Orthodox services in Hebrew as well as Reform versions in English. And though it never became an outright supporter of the labor and progressive movements, the Alliance did become an advocate for Lower East Side improvements.[4]

A Jewish version of the Institutional Church awaited the arrival on the scene of Rabbi Stephen Samuel Wise. The Budapest-born Wise (1874), son and grandson of rabbis, had been brought to New York as an infant and reared in a traditional German Jewish household. After starting studies at City College and completing them at Columbia (BA, 1892), Wise was appointed (in 1893) to a rabbinical position at the conservative Congregation B'nai Jeshurun (then at Madison and 64th). He stayed six years, though with increasing discomfort, as his own inclinations were trending liberal. Then there was his support for Zionism, which put him even more at odds with his congregation. In 1897 Wise helped organize the Federation of Zionist Societies of Greater New York and Vicinity, which led to formation of the nationwide Federation of American Zionists, incorporated (and headquartered) in New York. On an organizing tour out west, Wise was offered and accepted a post in Portland, Oregon, where he had the freedom to hone his own rabbinical style. Modeling himself on the Hebrew prophets, he spent far more time than did conventional rabbis in preaching, exhorting, and seeking to quicken the conscience of his congregants. Increasingly this involved taking stances on public issues, and Wise got deeply involved with Oregonian struggles to abolish child labor, clean up corrupt politics, and expand workers' rights. He also blossomed as a superb orator.

In December 1905, at the age of 32, Wise was invited by Temple Emanu-El trustee Louis Marshall to apply for appointment as rabbi of the preeminent center of Reform Judaism. Marshall, a distinguished corporate lawyer, shared the traditional lay view of rabbis as a special kind of employee. This was anathema to Wise, but he headed east anyway to give a trial sermon. Provocatively he spoke out against immoral business practices, a shoe that might have fit some in his New York audience. Nevertheless, a committee of trustees told him in camera that they were inclined to offer him the position and wanted to know what his conditions were. He said he would need to be free to speak his mind in the pulpit. Marshall made clear the Emanu-El pulpit was "subject to and under the control of the Board of Trustees." Wise replied he would not be "tethered and muzzled" and would accept no "humiliating conditions." Instead, he asserted, "as a Jewish minister, I claim the right to follow the example of the Hebrew prophets, and stand and battle in New York . . . for civic righteousness." Pushing the point home, he told Marshall to his face that if his law firm represented the

---

4. The Brooklyn Hebrew Educational Society—in Brownsville at Hopkinson and Sutter Avenues—followed a similar trajectory. An 1899 initiative of the Baron de Hirsch Fund and A&S department store magnate Abraham Abraham, the Americanization and uplift focus of its early activities was refashioned, under immigrant pressure, to suit the mores of the local community, and it eventually came to attract 360,000 visitors each year.

Though the professionalization and secularization of social work continued apace, the tradition of synagogues and churches offering volunteer services retained vitality. The United Hebrew Charities assigned districts to sisterhoods of congregations that, like the Central Synagogue on East 101st Street, provided direct relief and also ran kindergartens and taught settlement-style classes.

Equitable Life Assurance Society before Charles Evans Hughes's investigating committee, "I would in and out of my pulpit condemn the crimes committed by insurance thieves." Turning to copper baron Daniel Guggenheim, he declared that "if it ever came to be known that children were being employed in your mines, I would cry out against such wrong." That tore it for the committee (though Jacob Schiff, who rather liked the candidate's brashness, suggested he take the job and then "tell them to go to hell—and I'll back you up"). Wise had now alienated himself, probably on purpose, from the group he disparaged as the "Fifth Avenue aristocracy" (despite his marriage to the German Jewish heiress Louise Waterman). But he had dramatically raised his personal profile in the Jewish and the wider metropolitan communities.

Wise now moved back to New York and set out to create a Free Synagogue, one that would give his prophetic inclinations free rein. First he lined up financial support from real estate baron Henry Morgenthau Sr. A millionaire, but not of the inner Emanu-El circle, Morgenthau was drawn on principle to Wise's approach, having been an early adherent and underwriter of Felix Adler, with whose Ethical Culture movement the planned Free Synagogue had much in common. Then, from January to March 1907, Wise gave a series of lectures at the Hudson Theatre, outlining some key proposals—the abolition of Torah readings, the establishment of Sunday morning services (for the many Jews who had to work on the Saturday Sabbath), and, most forcefully, his intention to place the pursuit of social justice at the core of his teachings. These talks were followed in April by a large gathering at the Hotel Savoy, at which now-President Morgenthau told potential supporters: "The Free Synagogue is to be free and democratic in its organization; it is to be pewless and dueless." And, for the moment, homeless, though in a matter of months, Wise began holding services at Carnegie Hall, establishing his new institution as a highly visible alternative to Emanu-El.

In December 1907 Wise established a Social Service Department, the first of its kind in a contemporary synagogue, as German Jews had separated out charitable operations from theological ones over the previous generation. It was true that most important synagogues still featured a Sisterhood for Personal Service, in which women of the congregation did volunteer work among the poor. The trend of the times, however, was toward the professionalization of social work, and Wise kick-started this by hiring experts to provide social services to Jewish patients in hospitals.

Wise also dipped a toe in the settlement and Institutional Church waters, when he established a downtown branch of the Free Synagogue, at the invitation of Lillian Wald. While Wald's Henry Street operation was rigorously nonsectarian, she did believe Lower East Side Jewish youth should be given an opportunity to experience Reform Judaism, which had virtually no presence in the overwhelmingly Orthodox (or secular) neighborhood. Jacob Schiff had thought the same and offered Wise $50,000 to set up shop downtown, but Wise declined, saying he wouldn't offer services "subventioned by the well to do" to people who hadn't invited him. Wald was another matter. She had been largely responsible for building Clinton Hall—an "East Side Waldorf," the *Times* noted on its opening in 1904. The five-story building (plus roof garden) at 151–153 Clinton Street boasted restaurants, meeting rooms, billiard parlors, a wedding chapel, and a 750-seat auditorium—affordable spaces in which settlement clubs and labor unions could meet without having to resort to the back rooms of saloons. At *her* urging Wise began offering Saturday evening services, a religious school, a club program, and a forum on topical issues; Wise's eloquent English attracted downtown crowds, though few converts to Reform. Settling in for the long haul, in 1911 he purchased a number of brownstones on West 68th Street as the site of a permanent home, and established branches in the Bronx (1914), Washington Heights (1917), and Flushing (1918).

THE CATHOLIC CHURCH HAD INITIALLY BEEN RELUCTANT to endorse settlement houses, partly because they might undercut the primacy of parish priests, more so because the existing ones seemed to be hotbeds of secularism and radicalism—"mere roosting places," one critic sputtered, "for frowsy anarchists, fierce-eyed socialists, professed anti-clericals and a coterie of long-haired sociologists." But slowly the Church came to see them as possible solutions to its own demographic problem, the still substantial reluctance of Italian immigrants to seek the ministrations of churches or attend parochial schools. There were even fears that settlements—which despite their professed non-sectarianism were considered by most Catholics as basically Protestant initiatives—were siphoning off their core Irish parishioners. Some priests began urging Catholics to take the field. The Reverend James B. Curry, pastor of St. James's Parish in lower Manhattan, argued in 1898 that a settlement "with a prudent administration under Catholic auspices" would help win new adherents.

As if on cue, the first such settlement arrived that year, courtesy of a lapsed Protestant, Marion Lane Gurney, who in conjunction with the Episcopalian Church of the Redeemer had founded the Church Settlement Home. When she converted to Catholicism in 1897 she was picked by the pastor of the newly established St. Catherine of Siena Parish to establish St. Rose's Settlement (1898) at 257 East 71st Street. Gurney hoped that its combination of religious education and social activities (neighborhood visitations, a library, cooking and sewing and English classes) would attract local Italians. And it did: by 1904 roughly 3,500 Italians, chiefly of "the artisan and mechanic class," were using St. Rose's, which prompted a move to bigger quarters, and the addition of still more services. The Madonna House (1910), run by the Sisters of our Lady of Christian Doctrine, was more decidedly Catholic, preparing children and adults to receive the sacraments, and arranging baptisms, first communions, and confirmations. Yet it too offered clubs, a day nursery, and home visits to the sick.

By 1910 there were half a dozen Manhattan settlements aimed at Italians (as well as the Casa Maria on 14th Street for Spanish-speakers, organized in conjunction with Our Lady of Guadalupe church), and four more in Brooklyn, grouped in a Catholic Settlement Association.

Unlike the initial set of settlements, the Catholic variants stressed spirituality, not social change; they did not generally engage in lobbying for civic reform or better living and working conditions. There was, nevertheless, a strong progressive surge by lay Catholic organizations that took their cue from *Rerum Novarum* (1891)—the now generation-old encyclical of Leo XIII on the "Rights and Duties of Capital and Labor." Leo had devoted most of his missive to excoriating socialism, denying the inevitability of class struggle, and proposing the Church draw rich and poor together. But he was utterly clear that "working men have been surrendered, isolated and helpless, to the hardheartedness of employers and the greed of unchecked competition"; that their situation had been worsened by the "rapacious usury" practiced by "covetous and grasping men"; that with the concentration of capital "a small number of very rich men have been able to lay upon the teeming masses of the laboring poor a yoke little better than that of slavery itself"; and that to thusly "misuse men as though they were things in the pursuit of gain, or to value them solely for their physical powers—that is truly shameful and inhuman."

New York's progressive Catholics were not into political reform—their relations with Tammany Hall dictated otherwise—but they supported almost all the social justice planks.

In 1907 the American Federation of Catholic Charities promised to "encourage all reasonable endeavors of workingmen by organized effort to promote their moral and material well-being" and to "heartily support any legislation beneficially regulating labor hours, factory conditions, etc." In 1910 a new entity, the National Conference of Catholic Charities, convened largely at the urging of New York Catholics, blamed urban poverty mainly on bad industrial conditions. Monsignor William J. White, superintendent of Catholic charities in Brooklyn, urged "a war on the causes of poverty whether that cause is a disease germ lurking in a dark corner or a merchant prince grown rich on defrauding laborers of their wages." New York Paulist Father Joseph McSorley told the delegates that as working people would "not submit much longer to the rules that now control the distribution of wealth," Catholic laymen should be ready to guide the discontented "along legitimate ways" and "prevent violent revolution" by "wise and just reform."

Among these reforms, the first to gain serious political traction was the campaign to abolish child labor.

CHILD LABOR

In 1899 Florence Kelley—a gale-force woman—blew in from Chicago.

Kelley had been born in the Germantown area of Philadelphia in 1859; her father was William "Pig Iron" Kelley, a radical Republican congressman, abolitionist, and champion of labor. (He taught his daughter to read using a book depicting the brutality of child labor in British brickyards.) After graduating from Cornell in 1882—having written her senior honors thesis on the history of child labor laws—she studied at the University of Zurich. There she joined a circle of émigré Russian and German radicals, enrolled in the German Social Democratic Party, and befriended Friedrich Engels and translated his *Condition of the Working Classes in England* before moving to New York in 1886. In 1891, fleeing an abusive marriage, she took her three children to Chicago. There she became a resident at Jane Addams's Hull House, where she undertook pioneering surveys of labor conditions. In 1893 she won appointment as Illinois's first female chief factory inspector, responsible for enforcing labor legislation she had drafted and lobbied to enact. To better battle employers' resort to the courts, she earned a law degree from Northwestern in 1895. Her career blocked by a shift in the political wind, she accepted an offer in 1899 to come to Gotham and head the staff of the new National Consumers' League (NCL). On arriving, she headed straight for Lillian Wald's Henry Street Settlement, settled in, and dove into organizing.

The National Consumers' League grew out of the Consumers' League of New York (CLNY), founded by Josephine Shaw Lowell and others in 1891. Despite its name, it wasn't a conclave of consumers but an effort to mobilize consumers on behalf of the city's miserably paid and treated department store workers. Deploying a reverse boycott strategy, stores that agreed to improve conditions were put on a so-called white list, which the league then published in Gotham newspapers. In 1898 the CLNY—now directed by Maud Nathan—joined forces with consumer leagues in Boston, Philadelphia, and Chicago to establish a national organization, headquartered in the United Charities Building. Kelley was imported to run it, with the assistance of Pauline Goldmark, a recent Bryn Mawr graduate.

Kelley's first goal was to beef up existing child labor laws. As she'd observed in 1890, "Wherever the capitalistic method of production prevails there is child slavery, and wherever there is child slavery we find ... some pretense of restrictive legislation." This was certainly the case in New York. Back in 1885 manufacturers had beaten back a bill that would have barred children under 12 from their factories, threatening to leave the state if it passed, while arguing that widowed mothers needed their children's earnings (which indeed they did, given the minuscule wages they received). But in 1886, confronting increased pressure from an aroused labor movement and the state medical society, the legislature had passed a factory law that forbade employment of children under 13; an 1889 amendment prohibited night work, and another in 1900 notched up the legal age to 14, and limited 14–16-year-olds to ten hours a day. The laws, however, had cavernous loopholes, and the initial regulatory apparatus consisted of two inspectors (with no office) charged with scrutinizing the state's 42,739 manufacturing establishments and their 629,869-strong workforce. The statutes were a grim joke.

Kelley went into action. First she mobilized the settlement network. Wald and Simkhovich got the Association of Neighborhood Workers to establish a New York City Child Labor Committee (NYCCLC). Kelley prevailed on Robert Hunter, head resident at University Settlement (and an old Chicago colleague) to chair it. Then she brought on board social gospel churchmen Lyman Abbot and Bishop Potter, along with Felix Adler, newly appointed as professor of social and political ethics at Columbia; Dr. Abraham Jacobi, professor of pediatrics at Columbia; William Maxwell, New York City's superintendent of schools; and a representative from the Central Federated Union. To raise funds for a campaign, Hunter called in the deep-pocketed and well-connected J. G. Phelps Stokes and William Walling from the University Settlement, and they in turn appealed successfully to upper-class businessmen (chiefly bankers, who did not, like manufacturers and department stores, depend on cheap child labor), netting Kuhn, Loeb's Jacob Schiff and Paul Warburg, and Title Guarantee and Trust's Valentine Everit Macy. With funds in hand they set up shop in the Sohmer Building at Fifth and 22nd, one block from the UCB in the Gramercy Park neighborhood where Kelley had her office.

Declaring that the problem of child labor had "escaped attention in the general movement for improvement in industrial conditions of this city," the committee set out to chart the "extent of this evil." Kelley hired a full-time investigator, Helen Marot, who, during the summer of 1902, aided by settlement residents, teachers, and union members, prowled through factories, tenements, and the streets, amassing statistical evidence of the widespread presence of underage children in the city's workforce.

Written up in persuasive prose by Josephine Goldmark, Pauline's younger sister, who was then working as a tutor at Barnard College, the 1902 report made clear that the great boom was chewing up the city's children. In the factory sector, they were victims of dangerous and unshielded machinery, especially as they had less stamina than adults: tired operators of "corner-staying machines" in box-making plants had their hands crushed; child twine makers feeding flax into a twisting machine had their fingers sliced off. Rules about night work were ignored: 10-year-olds employed in Jersey brickyards got up at 3:00 a.m. to row across the Hudson from home to work. Child street workers were omnipresent. An estimated 4,000 newsboys hawked their wares after picking them up at 4:00 a.m. They were joined by peddlers, bootblacks, errand boys, and messengers, who had their own vulnerabilities. Delivery boys, after ending their day at 3:00 a.m., slept in their wagons, and occasionally froze to death. Investigators surveying tenement workrooms discovered droves of 10-year-olds laboring from dawn till deep into dark, pulling bastings or assembling artificial flowers.

Data in hand, the NYCCLC mobilized organizations of clergy, doctors, educators, philanthropists, charity workers, businessmen, and women's clubs. It hired a press agent to supply papers and magazines with pathetic case histories accompanied by photographic evidence. It noted that new psychological theories suggested premature work imperiled

Lewis Hine, "Bowery Bootblack," 1910. (National Archives and Records Administration)

development. It argued that rather than building character and developing job skills, child labor foreclosed mobility: stunted in mind and body, deprived of schooling and skills, these children were doomed to lives of perpetual drudgery.

This formidable lobbying effort pounded Albany legislators. Manufacturers and store owners battled back. But employer resistance had weakened somewhat. Manufacturers found the labor market newly awash in adult immigrants—nearly as cheap as tot workers, and more efficient. Department stores discovered that pneumatic tubes, cash registers, and telephones made messengers and cash boys less essential. So restrictionists carried the day. In 1903 a series of state laws banned children under 14 from manufacturing plants, strengthened proof-of-age requirements, held employers responsible for the presence of any underage employees, restricted 15- and 16-year-olds to a nine-hour day, expanded the force of factory inspectors; extended factory regulations to department stores, business offices, telegraph offices, restaurants, hotels, and apartment houses, and extended regulation to embrace street trades (prohibiting boys under ten and girls under 16 from selling papers on the street, and requiring a permit for 10–14-year-olds, who had to stop work at 10:00 p.m.). It was an impressive legislative triumph for a rookie organization. President Roosevelt sent congratulations.

The factory legislation proved to be relatively effective, but in the sphere of street trades and tenement work, widespread evasion and ineffective enforcement vitiated the new regulations' effectiveness. Policemen were reluctant to drag unlicensed peddlers or newsies into Children's Court. It took a complaint from Lillian Wald about children hawking chewing gum at an el entrance to produce the arrest of nineteen youngsters. And within days the gum pushers had swarmed back to their accustomed posts. Some enforcement slack was taken up by the Gerrymen (as kids called agents of the Society for the Prevention of Cruelty to Children, after its president, Elbridge Gerry). These private policemen would swoop down on a group of bootblack boys playing cards or tossing pennies, grab one, and get him

Lewis Hine, "Newsboys and Newsgirl. Getting Afternoon Papers. New York City," 1910. (National Archives and Records Administration)

committed to some reform institution on charges of gambling or vagrancy. (Hence the popular child's taunt, "The Gerrymen will getcha.") They "protected" child actors with special vigor—being easier to nab—and drove the likes of 10-year-old Milton Berle from Broadway theaters to neighborhood halls.

More serious was the evasion of laws regulating home/sweatshop work. In 1906 the New York City Child Labor Committee hired Mary van Kleeck to check up on conditions. Born in 1882—her father was an Episcopalian minister—van Kleeck had developed her interest in social issues when she served as president of Smith College's Association for Christian Work. After graduating in 1904, van Kleeck worked as a fellow at the College Settlement on Rivington Street, combining her social gospel and social science proclivities. In 1906 she turned her attention to underage workers in tenements. They weren't hard to spot—one needed only to follow little children carrying large bundles of unfinished garments, or boxes containing materials for making artificial flowers. Her report, published in 1908 as *Child Labor in New York City Tenements*, confirmed the failure of the regulatory approach. Van Kleeck blamed the intense competition in the garment trades that made utilization of child labor profitable to manufacturers—in 1907, making, counting, and bunching 1,440 artificial flowers fetched only eighty cents—but nevertheless, given miserable adult wages, still a necessary contribution to the worker's family economy. She also noted the difficulty of policing the vast number of possible work sites. The Labor Department required that tenement houses obtain licenses if homework was done on the premises; by 1911 13,268 buildings had registered, but the roughly 80,000 that remained unlicensed no doubt harbored vast numbers of home workers, who were not likely to be apprehended. When reformers pressed for an outright ban on tenement manufacturing, businessmen's resistance stiffened, and—despite the support of Governor Hughes—their campaign was beaten back.

Lewis Hine, "Home Industry," 1910. A woman and her children making artificial flowers. (Granger Historical Picture Archive)

Lewis Hine, "5 P.M. Making dolls legs for Campbell Kids. Cattena family, 71 Sullivan St., 5th floor front," 1912. (Library of Congress Prints and Photographs Division)

One response was to escalate their efforts to the national level. In 1904, at a mass meeting in Carnegie Hall, a National Child Labor Committee (NCLC) was launched (and headquartered, all but inevitably, in the United Charities Building). When it was officially chartered by an act of Congress in 1907, a majority of the fifteen members of the board of directors were New Yorkers: Felix Adler (chair), Florence Kelley, Paul Warburg, Lillian Wald, Jacob Schiff, Robert de Forest, Edward Devine, Homer Folks, and, Rabbi Stephen Wise.

The campaign produced another flood of investigations and reports, whose theme, as John Spargo said in his *The Bitter Cry of the Children* (1906), introduced by Robert Hunter, that "this great nation in its commercial madness devours its babes." In 1908 the National

Lewis Hine, "Little girl conversing with a Campbell Kid. See photos showing where they are made," 1912. (Library of Congress Prints and Photographs Division)

Child Labor Committee hired a full-time documentary photographer, Lewis Hine. A Wisconsin native, Hine was thirty and teaching at New York's Ethical Culture School, where he encouraged his students to use photography as an educational medium. In 1904 he took them to Ellis Island to capture the immigrant experience. In 1906 Hine became staff photographer of the Russell Sage Foundation, tasked with capturing life in the steelmaking districts for a survey of Pittsburgh. In 1908 he quit his teaching job and became an investigative photographer for the National Child Labor Committee, traveling around the country exposing the working conditions of children in all types of industries. The Edison Company chipped in with *Children Who Labor* (1912), filmed in cooperation with the NCLC; in the last scene (according to the silent movie's narrative insert) CHILDREN RAISE HANDS TO UNCLE SAM FOR HELP.

But Uncle Sam wasn't immediately forthcoming. The NCLC did encourage other states to follow New York's lead, and with considerable success. A stack of new statutes were enacted—thirty in 1911 alone. Calls on the federal government ran into strong opposition from southern cotton manufacturers and coal mine operators, who in turn got the putatively moderate National Civic Federation to back off from investigating child labor. Nevertheless, the NCLC won passage of a federal child labor law in 1916, and again in 1919, only to have both declared unconstitutional by the Supreme Court.

The judiciary would prove a stumbling block as well in the campaign to protect women workers, but here the New York progressives would engineer a signal breakthrough, winning a landmark victory, albeit one laced with ambiguities.

WOMEN'S WORK

In the early 1900s, at the same time the child labor campaign was getting under way, investigators were fanning out across the city to observe the situation of working women—garment workers, salesgirls, laundresses, maids—and collect masses of hard data on wages, budgets, health, employment, and living standards. Most of the witnesses were college-educated women, based in settlement houses or supported by groups like the Consumers' League and the Russell Sage Foundation. Their dispatches from the labor front mixed sober statistics with sensational vignettes and captured the city's attention.

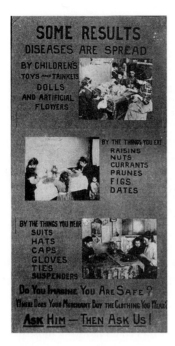

Lewis Hine, Exhibit Panel, "Some Results: Diseases Are Spread," ca. 1913. (Library of Congress Prints and Photographs Division)

Lewis Hine, Exhibit Panel, "Home Life," ca. 1913. (Library of Congress Prints and Photographs Division)

Lewis Hine, Exhibit Panel, "He Is a Messenger Boy," ca. 1913. (Klotz Gallery)

Lewis Hine, Exhibit Panel, "Homework Destroys Family Life," ca. 1913. (Library of Congress Prints and Photographs Division)

Maud Nathan's Consumers' League of New York continued to focus on women in department stores. Investigators—including 19-year-old Eleanor Roosevelt, who in 1903 joined the CLNY and accompanied more-seasoned researchers on inspection tours—discovered that workers clocked sixty hours a week for pittance pay, that behind the glittering stores lay filth-ridden quarters for employees, that sexual harassment was commonplace.

Maids had it worse. In 1902 Frances Kellor arrived in New York, fresh from graduate school in Chicago, and quickly put her research skills to work. With funding from the Women's Municipal League, Kellor investigated the city's domestic employment agencies, disguised variously as applicant-maid or would-be employer. She uncovered rampant exploitation of immigrant and black women, who were fleeced outright, shanghaied into brothels, or shuttled into long-hour, low-wage, heavy-labor jobs. Kellor blew the whistle in vivid stories for the *Tribune* in 1903, and in 1904 a serious treatise: *Out of Work: A Study of Employment Agencies*.

In 1905 Mary van Kleeck, still at the College Settlement, undertook a study of *Women in the Bookbinding Trade*. After she and her investigators interviewed 201 women workers and their employers, she painted a grim picture of dismal working conditions, irregular employment, and hours that often stretched through the night till daybreak—notwithstanding a law specifically forbidding such all-nighters, which had been passed in 1899 and amended in 1903. The statute stated that female factory workers could not work more than sixty hours a week or labor "before six o'clock in the morning, or after nine o'clock in the evening of any day." In 1906 van Kleeck researched an article entitled "Working Hours for Women in Factories," demonstrating that at least 5,000 Gotham manufacturers blithely ignored the law and that twelve-, thirteen-, and fourteen-hour days were commonplace.[5]

Then the law barring night work for women was wiped away altogether. In 1907 the New York Court of Appeals considered a bindery company's challenge to the statute. The state's highest court was notorious for advocating the "freedom of contract" doctrine. The doctrine took it as given that both parties to any labor contract (say, an immigrant Polish scrubwoman and United States Steel) were equal in the eyes of the law. Therefore, if the worker was willing to work for ten hours a day—or twenty should she so desire—and the corporation was willing to hire her, for whatever wages they settled on, the state had no right to interfere with their mutual agreement. Accordingly, since 1878 the court had consistently ruled that any restriction on male laborers' hours was utterly unconstitutional. Now, in *People v. Williams*, it held that, as there was no evidence demonstrating "it is more harmful for a woman to work at night than for a man to do so," the law restricting female laborers was equally null and void.

To counter this reasoning, Florence Kelley wheeled out gender notions of compelling cultural power. Women were *not* physically equal to men. Frailer than males, their health and reproductive capacity were easily eroded by protracted workdays. The nation—and even businessmen—had an interest in protecting those who produced future citizens and workers. Ideally, fathers should be paid a "family wage" so mothers could stay home and raise their children. But as long as women *did* work, the state was justified in safeguarding them.

To accumulate the evidence needed to demonstrate that females had a greater need for protection, Josephine Goldmark, now the National Consumers' League's research secretary,

---

5. Van Kleeck also noted that many of the 130,000 women working in more than 39,000 factories in New York City stood all day at work, operated dangerous machines, worked in air laden with steam or dusty fiber, in dark, dirty, ill-ventilated rooms, and, under pressure, at a high rate of speed.

produced a study demonstrating that night work was physically depleting for women, and exposed them to moral danger (for example, the risk of being attacked while walking home). The Russell Sage Foundation also entered the fray and, in direct response to *People v. Williams*, gave van Kleeck a special grant in 1907 to study the deleterious effects of night work. Should the occasion arise, the progressives would have data ready to back up their legal arguments.

The occasion arose in 1908, this time at the level of the Supreme Court. Back in 1905, in *Lochner v. New York*, the high court had struck down a New York statute mandating, for bakers only, a ten-hour maximum day and a sixty-hour maximum week, on health grounds. The court decided it was in fact a labor law attempting to regulate the terms of employment, and was therefore an "unreasonable, unnecessary and arbitrary interference with the right and liberty of the individual to contract."[6] Now the case of *Muller v. Oregon* was on its docket. In 1903 Oregon had passed a law barring females from working in a factory or laundry more than ten hours a day, claiming that the parties were *not* equal, so the state could exercise its police power to protect its citizens. Curt Muller, the owner of a laundry, was convicted of violating the law; he appealed to the Oregon Supreme Court, which rejected his plea, and the case was lofted up to the US Supreme Court.

Kelley and Goldmark undertook to defend the Oregon statute, and first approached Joseph H. Choate, a pillar of the New York bar, asking him to prepare an amicus curiae brief. Choate dismissed them out of hand, saying he could not understand why "a great husky Irish woman should not work in a laundry more than ten hours a day" if she wanted to. The corporate attorney knew perfectly well what was at stake: if the court allowed *any* restriction on the "liberty of contract" to stand, other restraints—on hours, working conditions, even wages, and for men!—might follow.

Kelley and Goldmark now approached Louis Brandeis, a Boston lawyer who also happened to be Josephine's brother-in-law, and he agreed to submit a brief on behalf of Oregon. Of the voluminous document, only two pages dealt with legal issues. The rest, compiled by researchers working under Goldmark's supervision, provided an annotated compendium of social science and medical studies and reports on European practices all aimed at demonstrating the "special susceptibility to fatigue and disease which distinguished the female sex, qua female." Brandeis argued that "overwork" undermined female "moral fibre" and reproductive capacity, and that therefore the law was justified by the state's compelling interest in protecting women's health. The court sustained this position, arguing that it was in the "public interest" to "preserve the strength and vigor of the race." The court also insisted the ruling did not dismantle the barriers to intervention on behalf of males that it had erected in *Lochner*.

Kelley and Goldmark were ecstatic, but not all progressives welcomed the decision. Critics worried that sex differences, and in particular women's childbearing capacity, had been used as a basis for restricting women's rights as workers—subordinating their individual needs to the presumedly higher needs of the family. Mary van Kleeck, for example, argued that women needed legal protection, all right, not because they had inborn weaknesses or family obligations that precluded market work, but because women were hyper-exploited, their wages being lower than those paid males for equivalent work. Particularly dismayed,

---

6. In a dissenting opinion (the case was 5–4), Justice Oliver Wendell Holmes Jr. claimed the majority had based its ruling upon laissez-faire doctrine, "an economic theory which a large part of the country does not entertain," adding that "the Fourteenth Amendment does not enact Mr. Herbert Spencer's Social Statics."

indeed infuriated, were the many women printers who found themselves unemployed because they could no longer accept night work. In 1915 they founded a Women's League for Equal Opportunity, whose first president declared bitterly that "welfare legislation, if persisted in, will protect women to the vanishing point."

The potential for splitting reform ranks aside, the Consumers' League victory in *Muller v. Oregon* cleared the constitutional way for legislation restricting the hours of women wage-earners. The Russell Sage Foundation gave the NCL a grant to widely distribute the so-called Brandeis Brief—more properly, the Brandeis-Goldmark Brief—and by 1913 twenty-four states had such laws on their statute books. Maddeningly, New York was not among them. Despite the judicial breakthrough in Washington, Kelley found her legislative forays stymied in Gotham. The New York Consumers' League campaigned year after year for a maximum fifty-four-hour work week for women but was balked repeatedly by businessmen and Tammany politicians. Gathering data and mobilizing public opinion did not, at least for the moment, translate into sufficient political muscle.

Nor did reformers get anywhere with efforts—as van Kleeck and Father John A. Ryan, a Catholic economist, had urged—to win passage of minimum wage legislation. The facts of female hyper-exploitation were not in question, thanks to another round of research. The Greenwich House–based Caroloa Woerishoffer went undercover to study steam laundry workers, and the Russell Sage Foundation helped Louise C. Odencrantz survey Italian women in factory jobs. Their common findings: miserable wages, wretched working conditions, recurrent unemployment.

Analysts also demolished a common justification for pittance pay often deployed by employers: that women worked only for pocket money, spare change for personal luxuries; hence there was no urgency about giving them equal pay. Louise B. More, another Greenwich House operative, trashed that thesis in *Wage-Earners Budgets: A Study of Standards and Cost of Living in New York City* (1907). Her study of 200 Greenwich Village families headed by longshoremen, porters, and factory hands demonstrated that only the income of working wives (and children) kept these households above subsistence level. Or didn't: given that women's wages were generally half those paid men, it was difficult for families to get by even when women did work. Robert C. Chapin's *The Standard of Living among Workingmen's Families in New York City* (1909) demonstrated that while $800 per year was needed to stay afloat, a large proportion of the working poor families he studied made under $600. And what if there was no male income to supplement? Katherine Anthony's *Mothers Who Must Earn* (1914), an RSF-backed analysis of Irish and German Hell's Kitchen families, found that one-third of the households were *headed* by females, usually widows supporting children. It was widely noted, too, that meager female incomes made prostitution a desperation alternative.

Hence the campaign for a minimum wage. Kelley herself was converted to the idea at the international Consumers' League congress in Geneva in 1908, where representatives of the British National Anti-Sweating League, on the verge of bringing Australian-style minimum wage boards to Britain, urged the delegates to follow suit. Back in the States, Kelley—still flushed with the victory in Oregon—got the local league to launch a campaign in 1910. Not only did the business class attack the notion; so did Samuel Gompers's American Federation of Labor, fearing that de jure floors might become de facto ceilings. Or worse, that recompense levels imposed by government-run "wage boards" might become a substitute for collective bargaining—indeed, "a condition akin to slavery." In the end, judicial intervention put the quietus to any hopes for a minimum wage.

Only one small provision for guaranteeing a minimum (very minimum) income for a small (very small) subset of women squeaked its way through the maelstrom of opposition, and its survival was wrapped up with a ferocious battle within the reform universe over how to deal with the poorest of the city's poor.

POVERTY WARS

The steamboat *Thomas S. Brennan*'s route ran from the Department of Public Charities' pier at the foot of East 26th Street, adjacent to Bellevue Hospital, up the East River to Blackwell's Island. There it deposited its passengers—Gotham's "insane, feeble-minded, sick, infirm and destitute persons"—for consignment to one or another of Blackwell's stony institutions. The poor but healthy were dispatched to the old Almshouse (1848), two barracks-style buildings that dominated the central part of "the Island" (as it was universally known), across from 70th Street in Manhattan. At the end of the century, these dilapidated and unsanitary quarters—no running water, sewage dumped into adjacent sinks—housed 2,700 unfortunates, hundreds of whom slept on the floor.

The *Brennan* also ferried men and women who'd been condemned to the Penitentiary or the Workhouse, picking them up from holding pens along the pier where they'd been temporarily caged. Since 1896 these institutions had been under the purview of a separate bureaucracy, the Department of Corrections, with the Workhouse reserved for those found guilty of lesser offenses, like "vagrancy," the crime of being poor in public.[7] The aged (1855) structure was another scandal: its masonry cells had no toilets, only pails; there was no provision for outdoor exercise, and virtually none for the industrial work that was supposed to impart skills and improve character.

The *Brennan*'s sister boat *Fidelity* made runs way up to the potter's field on Hart's Island, in Long Island Sound off the Bronx coast, transporting there unclaimed bodies from the City Morgue, also on the 26th Street pier. Like the Almshouse, the Morgue was under the jurisdiction of the Charities Department, as was the first Municipal Lodging House (1896) a few blocks away at 23rd Street and First Avenue, intended to terminate the old practice of housing the homeless in verminous police station basements. It was a decidedly temporary refuge: those who sought to stay more than three nights in succession were taken to court, committed as vagrants, and shipped off to the Island. Space was often in short supply, especially during economic downturns; in 1908 many of the unemployed homeless, turned away from the full-up Lodging House, were bedded down in the Morgue.

The Charities Department oversaw a host of other public institutions. These were scattered around the East River islands complex (Blackwell's, Hart's, Randall's, Ward's), and sprinkled throughout the outer boroughs (the Kings County Almshouse in Flatbush; the Richmond County Poor Farm near New Dorp, where residents grew vegetables). But Charities' budget was insufficient to pay decent salaries to its 2,000 employees, or afford decent care to its 9,000 inmates. This didn't bother those who believed wretched conditions would ward off freeloaders and keep taxes low, but it troubled those who thought inmates deserved humane treatment.

Some improvements got carried out during the Strong administration, in the mid-1890s, but a major overhaul awaited the mayoralty of Seth Low, who in 1901 appointed

---

7. If a man abandoned his wife or children, and was unwilling or unable to pay for their support, he could be committed to the Workhouse for up to six months.

Homer Folks as the department's commissioner. Folks was ideally qualified. Born in Michigan in 1867, he had studied at the University of Michigan and Harvard and, after debating between a ministerial or a teaching career, accepted a post as general superintendent of the Children's Aid Society of Pennsylvania. In 1893 he moved to New York City to become executive secretary of the State Charities Aid Association (SCAA), a watchdog agency set up in 1872 by the activist Louisa Lee Schuyler, great-granddaughter of Alexander Hamilton. SCAA volunteers visited and inspected public institutions housing New York's poor and sick, then nipped at the heels of the State Board of Charities, demanding improvements in the generally deplorable conditions. Folks became a consulting expert. In 1900, at the request of General Leonard Wood, military governor of Cuba, he'd studied the island's charity needs, and drawn up legislation establishing a network of insular institutions. In 1901 he reorganized those of New York City, adding buildings, plumbing, bathhouses, recreational facilities, and improved menus (hitherto basically bread and coffee), and in 1903 decreed a name change, with the Almshouse rechristened the New York City Home for the Aged and Infirm.

SINCE 1693, GOTHAM HAD ACCOMPANIED SUCH "INDOOR RELIEF"—almshouses—with "outdoor relief"—grants of food, fuel (coal or firewood), clothing, even cash, that were provided to the impoverished in their homes. This form of aid had been abruptly cut off in the midst of the 1870s depression, at the urging of welfare reformers, who were appalled by rising expenditures, which they had no doubt were rooted in deceit and corruption. They were also convinced that handouts would only make the recipients dependent on more handouts, turning the poor into paupers, unable ever to regain their footing. Equally troubling was the possibility that paupers might come to demand such support as a right.

The calls for a shutdown of outdoor relief had been led by the long-established Association for Improving the Condition of the Poor (AICP) and the recently established State Charities Aid Association, and effectuated in the legislature by anti-Tammany Republicans. The Board of Aldermen had protested, saying there were "more needy and deserving poor in this city than ever before in any one winter, rendered so in consequence of the general prostration of business." But the commissioner of charities and correction forged ahead, and indeed took steps to ensure that indoor relief remained an unenticing alternative. "Care has been taken," he noted, "not to diminish the terrors of this last resort of poverty, because it has been deemed better that a few should test the minimum rate at which existence can be preserved, than that the many should find the poor-house so comfortable a home that they would brave the shame of pauperism to gain admission to it." When churches and private philanthropists stepped up to offer emergency shelter and soup kitchens, the AICP, appalled at this "outgush of morbid sympathy," had urged an end to such scattershot benevolence as well. Charity should be governed by a time-honored axiom: as most poverty stemmed from individual moral and character defects (probably hereditary), relief should be dispensed only to the deserving—cautiously, grudgingly, "scientifically."

In 1882, however, convinced that despite the AICP's best efforts too many private charities were still "encouraging pauperism and imposture," Schuyler's SCAA associate Josephine Shaw Lowell launched the New York Charity Organization Society (COS), modeled on a London group that worked to curtail indiscriminate almsgiving. Over the next decade, Lowell presided over a thoroughgoing amalgamation of Protestant philanthropic organizations and families, creating what some snarkily called the "Charity Trust," which from 1893 was housed in the United Charities Building. To block multiple handouts, COS established a central registry and accumulated data on the "dependent and disreputable classes." By the mid-1890s it had compiled files on 170,000 families or individuals. Fortified with facts, it could now sift and classify applicants, channel the worthy or incapacitated poor to the Almshouse or public hospitals, dispatch cheats and vagrants to the Workhouse, and send "friendly visitors" to those deemed deserving.[8] Even the worthy rarely received material aid, however. Instead, the volunteers, usually well-to-do women, sought to help the poor become better stewards of their unfortunately limited resources, instructing them on budgeting, housekeeping, cooking, and child care.[9] The focus was kept relentlessly on rehabilitating individuals rather than improving their environment.

The 1870s and 1880s generation of charity workers had had their certitudes shaken by the monstrous impact of the 1890s depression. The plunging of hundreds of thousands of patently willing workers into unemployment raised widespread doubts that character deficiencies could satisfactorily explain widespread joblessness. Even the most adamantine moralizers—even Josephine Shaw Lowell—were shocked into considering the possibility that poverty had structural, even systemic roots. In 1898 one COS worker reported (with remarkable precision) that only 32 percent of the impoverishment of families in his district "was the result of their own faults, while 68 percent was due to causes beyond their control."

The COS also had to deal with a disturbing backlash against its own ruthlessness. Its tight-fisted behavior had come to seem less "scientific" than mean-spirited, stingy, cruel, Scrooge-like—especially when contrasted with the open-handedness of the Salvation Army or Tammany Hall. Worse, the bad press alienated old-fashioned philanthropists who thought that efficiency was getting the better of charity; it turned off potential donors and interfered with fund-raising.

The response was twofold. There was a distinct drift into the progressive camp, as evidenced by Lowell's organization of the New York Consumers' League and de Forest's role in winning tenement legislation. By 1907 de Forest was arguing that the COS should focus on "removing or minimizing the causes of poverty," rather than merely bestowing temporary relief on the impoverished. The society had rebranded itself as a more socially minded institution.

The other thing it did was to polish up its "scientific" credentials by professionalizing charity work. This new approach became identified with a new face, that of Edward T. Devine, who had been brought on as general secretary in 1896. Unlike de Forest (who remained as president), Devine boasted academic credentials. The Iowan had earned a doctorate in economics from the University of Pennsylvania in 1889, and in 1896, along with his COS appointment, he was made a professor of social economy at Columbia. While not prepared to break entirely with moralistic explanations of poverty, Devine clearly found them old-fashioned. Under his leadership, COS too embraced research, teaming up with Columbia students to study income, health, and housing. Their data confirmed settlement

---

8. The COS reserved its heaviest firepower for an all-out, mid-depression assault on "professional beggars," whom they saw as their most devious opponents, dedicated tricksters out to deceive good-hearted New Yorkers into opening their wallets. Undercover COS agents nabbed hundreds of these (presumed) fakers, and had them committed to the Workhouse as vagrants—699 of them in 1895—having gotten the commissioner of correction to keep such miscreants locked up for three months rather than the customary five days. More, COS asked the police to take over this responsibility and station plainclothes officers near theaters, clubs, and hotels, prepared to pounce. It also urged the legislature to set up a farm colony where such beggars "would be obliged to work, and would acquire habits of thrift and industry."

9. Though primarily a Protestant initiative, the COS had a Jewish counterpart in the United Hebrew Charities, organized even earlier, in 1874, which was similarly upset with indiscriminate giving to the "thriftless and indigent" and called for cooperative scrutiny of the putatively "distressed."

worker findings: unemployment, industrial accidents, sickness, low wages, and high rents far overshadowed character defects as explanations for poverty. Even urban vices were "more largely the results of social environment than of defective character," Devine opined, in his *Misery and Its Causes* (1909). He also aligned the organization with progressive activism by working with the National Child Labor Committee and by helping turn the COS in-house magazine, *Charities and the Commons*, into the *Survey* magazine.[10]

In another professionalizing move, de Forest, in his capacity as chairman of the COS Committee on Philanthropic Education, launched (in 1898) a six-week summer course in "applied philanthropy." The goal was to provide the formal training that would demarcate "social work" as a profession. Within three years it had become the Summer School for Philanthropic Workers. In 1904, with help from board member J. P. Morgan, it was renamed the New York School of Philanthropy, its course of study lengthened to a year. Devine, appointed as director, would guide the institution's development while remaining general secretary of the COS. Between 1907 and 1917, de Forest (president of the Russell Sage Foundation) channeled half a million dollars to de Forest (president of the COS), enabling the now New York School of Social Work to offer a two-year program.

This new social work movement mixed old and new philosophies, vigorously upholding individual responsibility of the poor for their own fate, while insisting on the need to improve social conditions. "Caseworkers," said Devine (the first to use that term), should be taught to view their "clients" as "having an objective economic or social problem," and to understand that the caseworker's job was to change the client's problematic environment, or enable the client "to wend his or her way through it." In practice, the emphasis fell on the latter approach, which the new profession called the "retail" rather than "wholesale" method. Emphasizing the need for a client to adapt to society rather than vice versa—a modernized version of friendly visitation—became the basis of the emerging profession.

ALL IN ALL, THE CHARITY ORGANIZATION SOCIETY had engineered a successful remodeling, dropping much of its alienating rhetoric, and emerging as a professional philanthropic organization. With indoor relief upgraded, outdoor relief banned, and wildcat benevolence curtailed, the interlocking outfits that composed the Charity Trust—COS, AICP, SCAA, RSF—were masters of Gotham's charity domain.

With one glaring exception: the overwhelming majority of the city's private charitable institutions were not under their control, but were run by Irish Catholic women religious. Indeed, Catholic philanthropy was expanding in size and strength year by year, to the dismay of the charity workers, under whose nonsectarian skins beat Protestant hearts, and to their great chagrin, as they had been partly responsible for what they considered an unfortunate state of affairs.

In the 1840s and '50s, Archbishop John Hughes had created New York's parochial school network in response to Protestant proselytizing in the public schools. In the 1860s and 1870s, Catholic religious congregations and lay volunteers had created a constellation of charitable

---

10. In 1905 de Forest created a COS Publication Committee "to get at the facts of social conditions" and consolidated *Charities* with a Chicago journal, the *Commons*, and made Devine editor. When *Charities and the Commons* published much of the RSF-sponsored Pittsburgh Survey, it was renamed again, in 1909, as the *Survey*, and in 1912 Paul Kellogg, who had directed the Pittsburgh investigation, became editor. Kellogg had given up a job as city editor on a newspaper in his home town of Kalamazoo, Michigan, to come to New York, where he became a resident of Greenwich House, and acquired social research expertise through working on the new-model COS publications. *Survey*, with an immense subsidy from the Russell Sage Foundation, became the country's leading periodical for social workers and social reformers.

institutions that included foundling homes, asylums, and orphanages, overwhelmingly run by Irish Catholic nuns. This network, too, was a defensive measure—in this instance a response to the rise of the Protestant "child-saving" movement. Starting during the '50s inundation of Famine Irish, and accelerating after the fearsome Irish-driven Draft Riots, Protestant organizations—led by Charles Loring Brace's Children's Aid Society—began deporting thousands of poor Catholic children from their depraved New York environment to homes in rural America, where (hopefully) they'd be born again as middle-class Protestants. Catholics, perceiving this as a mortal threat to their community, began constructing institutions in New York City in which to house, and protect, their most vulnerable children.

This troubled Protestant charity activists, though the new infrastructure seemed modest in scope. Then the situation changed dramatically. In 1875—in the midst of their assault on outdoor relief—Protestant reformers had won passage of a so-called Children's Law, which prohibited the placement of youngsters (aged 2–16) in public poorhouses and required the removal of those already there. The law had been intended partly to spare them Almshouse horrors and partly to separate them from their parents. It was axiomatic to Lowell, as it had been to Brace, that the best way to break the cycle of pauperism was to remove children from "bad" family influences. The new law required deserted and desperate mothers, if driven to enter the Almshouse, to relinquish their children to private orphanages, which would then be granted per capita allotments from the state to support them. The problem was that Catholic lobbyists, backed by their Tammany co-religionists, had managed to tack on a last-minute rider to the law, stipulating that all needy children must be placed in institutions "governed or controlled by officers or persons of the same religious faith as the parents of such child, as far as practicable." At first few thought this would be of great moment. But the establishment of a public revenue stream enabled Catholic child-caring institutions to provide a safety net for the thousands of impoverished children who were victims of the 1870s depression and the cutoff of outdoor relief.

After 1875 the number and size of Catholic institutions exploded. By the turn of the century, subsidized shelters included St. Joseph's Asylum (750), the Roman Catholic Orphan Asylum (802), the Institution of Mercy (1,010), and the New York Catholic Protectory—with 3,220 children, the largest such institution in the country, and perhaps the world.[11] All in all, by 1900 nearly 20,000 children were being housed in Catholic institutions, and women religious in effect controlled most of Gotham's welfare system.[12] So unique was this arrangement that it became known as the "New York system."

Appalled by this development, Protestant charity workers, led by Lowell and Folks, set out to curb or reverse it. When Folks became commissioner of public charities in 1901, he won greater authority over private agencies receiving public funds and hired hundreds of inspectors to reevaluate the per capita commitments each year, aiming both to lower public

---

11. Jews had a much smaller network, in part because they lacked access to a large pool of unpaid female labor. The Hebrew Orphan Asylum of New York (1860)—whose 1884 building at Amsterdam Avenue between 136th and 138th Streets had a capacity of 1,755 children—and the Hebrew Sheltering Guardian Society (1879) both received Children's Law appropriations, but as they were forced to rely on paid staff, the public monies never covered costs.

12. Though overwhelmingly run by working-class women, the Catholic charities had a small male middle-class component: the New York City Council of the Society of St. Vincent de Paul, founded in 1848. The Vincentians did parish relief work, visited Catholics confined on Blackwell's and Randall's Islands, and had their own thousand-plus orphanage on Staten Island. The society was led by Thomas Maurice Mulry, who ran a construction company and was closely connected to Tammany. Being male, he was widely regarded as the "voice" of Catholic charities in New York between 1895 and 1915. Mulry proved far more given to compromise with Protestant reformers (he was close to Homer Folks) than were the Catholic sisters, who were locked in combat with Protestant women over who would control the city's welfare system.

costs, and reduce the institutional population. But the New York system itself handily survived such administrative challenges.

On the ideological front, Folks and other Protestants began arguing that huge institutions were a "grave error" because their regimented environment throttled "individual initiative," leaving their charges unprepared for responsible citizenship in a democracy. The place to raise children was in a family, Folks argued, and therefore "children of worthy parents or deserving mothers should, as a rule, be kept with their parents at home." Given the assumption that most poor families were neither "worthy" nor "deserving," the solution—which came readily to the mind of a former official of the Children's Aid Society—was to place children of the unworthy in foster homes. The government could then redirect its payments to foster parents, simultaneously slowing the flow of funds to big institutions. The COS and AICP jumped on board this retro policy bandwagon and set up home placement services.

Catholic institutions contested this new/old wisdom. They argued that placing children in foster families was cruelty incarnate, as most of the orphanage inmates were not orphans. Poor parents, hard-pressed, often committed their children to the care of the nuns until able to reclaim them, in effect using the institutions as free (and same-faith) boarding schools. Parents who sent their kids off in hard times often wanted them back when better times arrived. One official calculated that the average child spent only eighteen months in his institution, and that 75 percent returned to their parents or close relatives. The institutions also insisted their services were unavoidable: given the poverty of the city's recent Catholic immigrants, there just weren't enough Catholic foster parents to go around, and shipping their children off to Protestant households, as in days of old, was no longer in the political cards.

With (chiefly female) Protestant and Catholic activists at loggerheads over the proper child-saving model, a third group of activists, led by (chiefly female) secular settlement workers entered the conversation.

The settlement workers preferred homes to institutions, but suggested it was the child's *real* mother, not foster parents, who should get assistance, and it should come directly from "the citizens of the state, not the subscribers to the charities." This financial aid, moreover, should take the form of non-demeaning of-right grants, which they called "pensions," suggesting they were rewards to which women were entitled for their meritorious service as mothers, a socially vital employment.

Here again there were European precedents on which to draw, but there were homegrown examples as well. Pensions for Civil War veterans and their families had expanded in scope and liberality as the war itself receded into the past. Encouraged by the Republican Party, to its great political profit, the program swelled until by 1893 nearly a million (primarily northern, middle- or working-class) Americans were receiving benefits, with the collective tab accounting for an astounding 41.5 percent of federal spending. And these payments were not begrudged—as were "outdoor relief" payments to the poor—as pensions were considered to have been "earned" though honorable service to the country.

Even closer to home, there was a well-established practice of paying pensions to New York's public sector workers. Back in 1857 Gotham had become the first US city to pension its employees, when the legislature established a fund for the relief of policemen injured in the performance of duty, and for their dependents in case such injury resulted in death. Pension funds followed for firemen in 1866, for teachers and health officers in 1894, for City College professors in 1902, and then, in one swoop, all citywide employees in 1911. These usually granted half pay after twenty or twenty-five years of service, 85 percent of the costs being born by the city, through direct appropriations, or sale of bonds. Most of these were not actuarially sound, and by the time of the Mitchel administration (1914–17) many were on the point of collapse, but even that pinch-penny regime didn't dream of abolishing them, rather restoring them to fiscal health by requiring reserves be built up to meet liabilities.

Mary Simkhovitch, Lillian Wald, and Florence Kelley borrowed the language of pensions from these widely accepted government programs, hopefully borrowing their legitimacy as well. Then they set out to pass a mothers' pension bill and swiftly received backing from multiple sources: the Association of Neighborhood Workers (the settlement houses' umbrella organization); reformers like Frederic Howe and Rabbi Stephen Wise; the American Federation of Labor, alarmed at the growing number of women being forced into the workplace, putting downward pressure on men's wages, and threatening male jobs; some charity institutions (particularly Jewish ones), which broke with the scientific philanthropists and began giving regular monetary aid; and key newspapers like Pulitzer's *World* and Hearst's *Journal*.

The White House Conference on the Care of Dependent Children, held in 1909, came out strongly against institutions, except as an emergency backup system, and even then only in modified form, broken up into smaller, more family-like clusters. Declaring that "home life is the highest and finest product of civilization," the conferees stated that "except in unusual circumstances, the home should not be broken up for reasons of poverty, but only for considerations of inefficiency or immorality." Then, in a carefully hedged endorsement of mothers' pensions as a way to deal with the poverty dimension, they resolved that "children of parents of worthy character, suffering from temporary misfortune and children of reasonably efficient and deserving mothers who are without the support of the normal breadwinner, should, as a rule, be kept with their parents, such aid being given as may be necessary to maintain suitable homes for the rearing of the children." The source of that aid—from either "public relief" or "private charity"—was left up to local communities (a fudge that reflected the presence of both Wald and Folks, champions of the opposing views).

In the next few years, one state after another began passing mothers' pension laws. Illinois started, in 1911, and by 1913 seventeen more states had joined the list. New York, usually first off the mark, was not on it, due chiefly to the ferocious opposition of the private Protestant agencies, deeply threatened by the attack on their hegemony. "Who are these sudden heroes of a brand new program of state subsidies to mothers?" demanded Edward T. Devine of the Charity Organization Society, the most vocal antagonist. These handouts were simply the wolf of "outdoor relief" tricked out in "pension" sheep's clothing. Reciting chapter and verse from the anti-social gospel for the umpteenth time, Devine declared that government was incapable of learning the lessons of scientific philanthropy, that its revival of direct relief would breed official corruption and political interference, that giving recipients cash merely tempted them "to spend money recklessly or foolishly," that handouts would lead to a "pathological parasitism" that would "inevitably create a new class of dependents," and that the putative "pensions" would substitute an impersonal bureaucratic dole for the "individualized care" only caseworkers could provide. Worse, pensions would transform charity into entitlement, with all-too-predictable consequences. Mothers' pensions are the "entering wedge towards State socialism," a COS vice president said. Today, money for widows. Tomorrow, "old age pensions, free food, clothing and coal to the unemployed and the right to be given work." "It is not American" he sputtered; "it is not virile."

Settlement workers lashed back at the "bureaucrats of philanthropy" for blocking pensions. In 1913 a Commission on Relief for Widowed Mothers (run by the assistant headworker of the University Settlement) denounced COS and the social workers who "dominate the New York School of Philanthropy and the Russell Sage Foundation" for selfishly usurping responsibilities that properly belonged to government. It was nonsense to claim public officials couldn't administer aid wisely. A crowd of midwestern states had already implemented successful mothers' aid programs.[13]

Some opponents fell away. In 1912 Folks, assessing the political winds, announced that "more harm is being done at the present time by inadequate relief of widows by private societies than could possibly be done by a system of outdoor relief for widows properly administered." But COS hung tough, battled on. Then, in 1914, as the pension bill entered the legislative arena, the privates overplayed their hand.

In January John Purroy Mitchel took office as mayor. Though a staunch Catholic, he was ardently anti-Tammany, and his Fusion campaign had been supported by some of the most powerful Protestants in the city, including the leaders of the Charity Trust. As payback, Mitchel appointed John Adams Kingsbury as his commissioner of charities. Kingsbury had been Folks's number two at the SCAA from 1907 to 1911 and then general director of the AICP until his recruitment to public service. Determined to intensify city scrutiny of the congregate institutions, and hopefully dismantle the New York system altogether, Kingsbury ordered a full-scale investigation of the privates. The ensuing report cited twenty-four organizations—twelve run by Catholic women—for failure to meet standards. Charges included long hours of hard labor imposed (especially on girls in institutional kitchens and laundries), "beds alive with vermin," antiquated methods of discipline and punishment, and "educat[ing] the children in little more than religious matters." In one location, 200 children were said to be sharing the same toothbrush and cake of soap. The *New York Times*, which had battled the New York system for years, called the revelations "shocking, almost incredible." "Worse than anything in 'Oliver Twist,'" echoed the *New York World*.

Kingsbury's report also accused State Board of Charities inspectors of being either incompetent or in collusion with the institutions. Devine had already opted for the second explanation, having called the New York system the creation of "a well organized Catholic interest, whose power and influence with the public officials is such that they dare not deny them anything,"

Catholics from Cardinal Farley and Auxiliary Bishop Patrick J. Hayes on down detected "a nasty anti-Catholic animus" in Kingsbury's inquiry, which they believed was intended to discredit their organizations and bring down the New York system. The diocese responded with a campaign of self-defense. Hundreds of thousands of pamphlets were printed and distributed on church steps each Sunday after mass. Mitchel was denounced as a betrayer of his own faith. Kingsbury and his fellow social scientists were accused of operating a "highly-organized agency of paganism." "The Church is from God," parishioners read. "Modern sociology is not."

Kingsbury, suspecting a criminal conspiracy to thwart his initiatives, got the mayor's permission to have the police install wiretaps on the telephones of several prominent Church spokesmen. The police listened in on more than a hundred conversations, which were indeed filled with fulminations against the Charity Trust. When the taps story leaked, an uproar ensued. Civic and religious groups from all corners demanded Mitchel's impeachment. The mayor justified the eavesdropping as an effort to prove the Catholic Church was attempting

---

13. Vitagraph's *The Silent Plea* (1914), produced in conjunction with Sophie Irene Loeb of the New York State Commission for the Relief of Widowed Mothers, backed the campaign for widows' pensions, and was intended to influence the legislative debates.

to seize control of the city government. The governor launched an investigation. A grand jury indicted Kingsbury. He was later acquitted. But he hadn't done his cause any good. Indeed, even the AICP dropped its resistance to the proposed pension bill, though the COS struggled on till the end.

Which came in 1915, with passage of the watershed Child Welfare Act. The law embodied a compromise between the three contenders.

It allowed the city to set up a local Board of Child Welfare—bypassing Tammany Hall—that would grant allowances directly to widowed mothers with children. Despite the term "pension," and the argument that the payments were compensation for "meritorious services in bearing children and rearing them through infancy," it was patently clear that the decades-long ban on public "outdoor relief" had been broken, a development pregnant with possibilities.

On the other hand, the state imported wholesale all the strictures that the most "scientific" philanthropist could have wished for. First, it extracted a tiny fragment of the impoverished population on grounds of its presumptive virtue: not all poor "mothers" were eligible, or even "deserted" mothers (fathers could pretend to leave, then pick up their wife's pension payment and head for the saloon), but only "widowed" mothers, those whose formerly employable husbands were stone-cold dead. Second, the aid was directed at the children, not the mother, and it terminated once the youth(s) reached 14, the age of employability. Third, they were to be subject to ongoing surveillance. The law required that a board representative visit each recipient at least every three months. These field investigators could terminate allowances if the mother: neglected or abused her child, showed signs of "intemperance, wastefulness, or of misconduct," failed to keep her home and kids "clean and orderly," used tobacco, didn't attend church, had extramarital affairs, or tolerated lodgers whose behavior was "such as to bring the widow into disrepute." The state was to be as meddlesome and overbearing and sexist as the unfriendliest of friendly visitors had ever been.[14] Fourth, the sums dispensed were niggardly in the extreme, never reaching a level sufficient for the widow to support her family without resorting to other sources of aid.

The task of setting it up was handed to Harry Hopkins, a man known in both settlement and social work camps. Hopkins had been raised in small-town Iowa; his harness-maker father was a Bryanite, his mother a Social Gospel Methodist. He came to New York in 1912, after graduating from Grinnell College (where he took courses in Applied Christianity) and joined the Christodora House settlement at 147 Avenue B (on Tompkins Square). Next he worked at the AICP under Kingsbury, rising by the fall of 1914 to supervisor of relief on the Lower East Side. The next year he followed Kingsbury into the Mitchel administration. As executive secretary of the Board of Child Welfare, Hopkins worked fast, handing out allowances to 1,567 widows, with 4,915 kids, in his first year; the average per child was $7.99.

Catholic charities were not addressed in the new law, which was a victory of sorts, as it left their institutions intact, though not untouched. In 1915 Governor Charles Whitman had established a state commission to investigate Kingsbury's charges, and appointed City Club president Charles H. Strong to run it. After extensive hearings, Strong rejected as overblown the depiction of the Catholic child-caring institutions as "unfit for human habitation" but conceded that at least some of the institutions were indeed "a scandal and a public disgrace."

---

14. The standards were in some respects more stringent than those established a century earlier by the Ladies Society for the Relief of Poor Widows in New York City (1797). Those ladies would aid a woman who presented evidence of either her husband's death, or his twelve-month absence, and would strike her from the list only for "intemperance, promiscuity, begging, dancing, selling liquor," or living in a disreputable neighborhood.

And while Strong concluded that the New York system was too strongly entrenched to be dismantled, it did trigger a move toward diocesan centralization on the part of Auxiliary Bishop Hayes, in an effort to ensure compliance with public regulations and to guarantee the steady flow of per capita payments to Catholic institutions. He also set out to professionalize the caregivers, establishing the Fordham School of Social Service in 1916, and began to shift control from the nuns to Catholic laywomen trained in social work methods.

HEALTH

As of Consolidation Day, New York's public health sector had earned a worldwide reputation for successful battles against communicable diseases, and for having developed the biggest public hospital network in the United States. In the new century, the city would open fresh fronts in the epidemiological wars, and medical progressives would expand the array of public health services New York provided its citizens, at times triggering resistance from private sector practitioners.

What had put Gotham on the global map was the work of Dr. Hermann Biggs, who had taken the bacteriological breakthroughs of Robert Koch in Germany and Louis Pasteur in France and applied them in public health campaigns. During the 1892–93 cholera crisis, the Health Department had established a Division of Pathology, Bacteriology, and Disinfection under Biggs's direction. His laboratory had examined the feces of suspected infectees for traces of the cholera spirillum, and confirmed or refuted questionable diagnoses. Biggs's exams were credited, together with prompt and widespread interventions by the Health Department, with helping save the city from the horrific epidemic that for weeks had killed 2,500 a day in Russia. Only nine lives were lost in New York.

In 1894 Biggs, who kept in close touch with bacteriological developments in Europe, learned while visiting there of a brand-new diphtheria antitoxin. Immediately he sent orders back to his associate Dr. William Hallock Park—one of the country's few trained bacteriologists—to begin mass-producing it in New York. In 1895, after the antitoxin halted an epidemic at the Infant Asylum on Randall's Island, Biggs had begun giving it away free to doctors for use with poor patients. The serum brought an immediate and spectacular decline in mortality rates.

Consolidation in 1898 allowed the Health Department to deepen its infrastructure and extend its regulatory sway to the entire metropolitan population. In 1901 Biggs was elevated to chief medical officer of the department, where he would work in conjunction with Commissioner Dr. Ernst Lederle, also appointed in 1901, and with Dr. Park, who would develop what became known as the Bureau of Laboratories. The first municipal diagnostic lab in the United States, it was also pioneering in including a research component and establishing a link with academic scientists at New York University, facilitated by Park's joint appointment as professor of bacteriology. Backed by reform and Tammany administrations alike—Dr. Biggs having successfully treated Boss Charlie Murphy for typhoid—the department's annual budget soared to $3 million by 1910, and its 2,500 employees instituted a series of preventive campaigns.

Among the first targets were the diarrheal diseases, including dysentery and typhoid fever, which were major killers of children. Victims usually died from eating spoiled food (common in households that couldn't afford ice) or from drinking germ-laden milk. Since the anti-swill milk campaigns of the 1850s and 1860s, producers and wholesalers had invented new ways to adulterate their product. Filthy conditions, warm temperatures, and the lengthy trip from cow to consumer rendered the product lethal.

In the 1890s Nathan Straus, the philanthropist, had halved the death rate in the city's Infant Asylum by using pasteurized milk. He then built his own pasteurization plant on East 3rd Street and opened eighteen milk stations around the city that sold the milk for pennies, or gave it away to the penniless. Lillian Wald's Henry Street Settlement helped expand this program, and then in 1911 the Health Department entered the field. By 1914 it was running fifty-five municipal milk stations, the product handed over free of charge, the only requirement being to bring a clean pail with which to take the milk away.

The Health Department also regulated producers. It inspected dairies within city limits and destroyed sick cows. It arrested retailers who adulterated milk. It blocked sales by outside dairies whose product didn't meet standards. And in 1912 a vigorous campaign by Park's Bureau of Laboratories led to the requirement that all milk entering the metropolis be pasteurized. In the Mitchel administration, documentaries explaining all this—like *The Production and Handling of Milk*—were projected on tenement walls. The department also scrutinized the food supply. In 1898 fifty food inspectors conducted over 4,200 chemical analyses, made a million inspections, and condemned 9.6 million pounds of food.

Attacking germs from another direction, the city introduced chlorination and filtration of the water supply, after New Jersey had blazed the way. Dr. John T. Leal, a physician trained in bacteriology, was health officer for Paterson, in which capacity he had used solutions of chloride of lime to disinfect homes where scarlet fever, diphtheria, and other communicable diseases had been found. Leal was also aware of European efforts to chlorinate water supplies—in 1893 in Hamburg, Germany; in 1897 in the town of Maidstone, England; and in 1905 in Lincoln, England, to fight a typhoid fever epidemic. In 1908 Leal crossed the Hudson to the New York office (at 170 Broadway) of the country's premier sanitary engineer, George Warren Fuller, famous for his work in filtration. Fuller devised a chlorine feed system that successfully disinfected the Boonton Reservoir, which supplied Jersey City. In 1910 Gotham followed suit. In 1912 a *New York Times* headline announced: "Croton Water Free of Typhoid Germs."

But the real adversary was tuberculosis, in 1900 the leading cause of death among adults in New York City. A terrible and drawn-out disease, its advancement was marked by bloody sputum, a hacking cough, chills, night sweats, emaciation, paleness, copious expectoration, and lung hemorrhage. It had been known since Koch's discovery in 1882 that TB was caused by the tubercle bacillus. It was known to be communicable. It was known that sunlight helped kill the germs, that being run-down increased one's chance of catching it, that there was no known cure. A poor New York neighborhood—where people crowded together in dark and unsanitary tenements and factories, wherein they worked for an exhausting number of hours—was a happy breeding ground for tuberculosis. The only known treatment for the disease consisted of reversing such causal conditions: providing the patient with medical and nursing attention, bed rest, isolation, clean and sunny and well-ventilated surroundings, and perhaps opium to relieve the pain of lung hemorrhage—options out of reach of workers and the poor. Biggs set out to make this possible.

The first step was to get clear on what they were up against, which meant finding and registering everyone already infected. In 1894 Biggs had the Health Department require mandatory reporting of TB victims by all health care institutions, and recommend voluntary notification by private doctors. He also set up facilities where doctors could drop off sputum jars with samples taken from suspected infectees, which would then be sent for free bacteriological inspection to the department's lab, with an analysis forwarded to the doctor next day. Biggs soon found, however, that many doctors were refusing to comply. In part their concerns were selfless. They knew patients were terrified of being branded a carrier, fearful of being sent to hospitals, and the doctors felt that reporting would violate professional confidence. But many simply found outside interference in their affairs intolerable, and a fair percentage still refused to believe TB was contagious.

So in 1897 Biggs had the Board of Health amend the sanitary code to *require* notification. This aroused bitter antagonism and furious resistance. In 1898 the medical societies went to the state legislature to have the board stripped of its power to deal in any way with tuberculosis, a campaign beaten back with some difficulty. Over the next decade, as the evidence (and some leading doctors) bore out Biggs's position, most came around on the issue, but it would not be the last clash between public and private medicine.

With accurate data now coming in, Biggs plotted all known or suspected cases on maps of the city, finding a striking (though not surprising) concentration in poor neighborhoods. Next he established a special corps of medical inspectors who visited the premises, collected samples, and sent them to Park's lab. In 1902 janitors and landlords were required to report the death or departure of any tenant "consumptives," so that inspectors could come and remove bedding, rugs, and clothing for steam disinfection, and if necessary renovate or close the apartment. In 1903 the department established a corps of public health nurses, who visited patient homes to monitor their progress, and educate them and their family members about proper isolation techniques. If hygienic measures were disregarded, nurses could recommend that patients be transferred to an institution.

Before 1902 there was no separate municipal facility for "white plague" victims. Most were scattered among the contagious wards of Bellevue, City, Metropolitan, Willard Parker, and the Almshouse hospitals. Often these were so jammed that many patients had to sleep two to a bed. In 1902 Commissioner of Public Charities Homer Folks carved out the country's first municipal tuberculosis infirmary, repurposing three buildings of the Metropolitan Hospital. In 1903 a tuberculosis pavilion was opened to treat and isolate victims at Riverside Hospital. Founded on Blackwell's Island in 1856 as (James Renwick's) Smallpox Hospital, Riverside had relocated in 1885 to the then uninhabited North Brother Island. Various pavilions and tents had been hastily constructed to segregate different quarantinable victims of smallpox, scarlet fever, typhoid, diphtheria, even leprosy. The 1903 TB pavilion was a detention facility designed for patients who resisted measures required to stem the spread of the disease.[15]

Gotham also opened public sanatoria, sunlit structures bathed in fresh air. In July 1906 the City of New York Municipal Sanatorium was established at Otisville, upstate in Orange County, some 75 miles from Manhattan in the Shawangunk Mountains. And in 1913 Sea View Hospital came on line near Four Corners, Staten Island, one of the highest points between Maine and Georgia. A $4 million complex of twenty buildings, Sea View had 763 beds available for tuberculosis patients, most of whom were relocated from tenement houses around the city.

A crucial component of the war on TB was educating the general public about the disease. Here the Health Department made common cause with the Committee on the Prevention of Tuberculosis, set up in 1902 by the Charity Organization Society, along the

---

15. Riverside's most famous patient was Typhoid Mary (Mary Mallon), a woman who tested positive as a typhoid carrier in 1907. Feeling perfectly healthy, she refused all medical treatment. Because she cooked for a living, she was confined, as a lethal menace, to Riverside for three years. When released in 1910, she was told to report back every three months. She disappeared. Then an epidemic broke out. It was traced to Mallon. In 1915 she was taken to Riverside and kept there until she died in 1938.

"Staten Island—Seaview Hospital—[Hospital for the Treatment of Tuberculosis]," 1913. (New York Public Library, Irma and Paul Milstein Division of United States History, Local History and Genealogy)

lines of its Tenement House Committee. A collaboration between leading physicians and social activists, the committee included Biggs (who chaired) and Commissioner Lederle, along with Lillian Wald, Robert de Forest, Homer Folks, and Edward Devine. Possibly the first mass education campaign directed at a single disease, it promulgated the message that TB was communicable, preventable, and curable. It deployed a panoply of measures, including lectures, pamphlets, exhibitions, lantern slides, stereopticons set up in the parks in summer, and Red Cross films shown in schools, factories, and churches. These efforts zealously trumpeted the importance of hygienic behavior, and warned particularly about the possibly lethal consequences of spitting. Placards prohibiting the practice went up in subway cars, trolleys, and ferryboats, and were backed up with arrests by the sanitary police.

In this campaign there were no miraculous breakthroughs, but steady progress brought the TB death rate (per 100,000) down from 2.79 to 1.94, though the absolute number of victims rose slightly, given the exploding size of the population.

ALSO DURING THE 1900S AND 1910S, the city's sprawling public hospital system got a makeover.

The municipal hospitals, which were required to accept every patient who applied to them, provided basic services to the aged, dependent, and sick poor, especially those who lacked relatives to care for them at home. But the majority of patients, as *Charities* magazine observed, were "working men and working women who by reason of illness or injury are temporarily prevented from earning a living." A 1907 survey of occupant occupations included housewife, cook, actor, soldier, salesman, coachman, metal polisher, waiter, domestic, janitor, longshoreman, brakeman, manicurist, bricklayer, painter, and blacksmith. As the numbers subjected to the vagaries of the metropolitan economy grew, so did the strain placed on the complex of municipal institutions.

At the center of this complex was Bellevue Hospital, still at East 26th Street on the water's edge, where it had relocated in 1816 in search of more salubrious quarters than the City Hall area, where it had been established in 1736, as the second-floor infirmary of the Workhouse and House of Correction on the Commons. In 1900 Bellevue boasted an excellent staff of doctors, attracted by the opportunities to practice surgery and medicine on the city's unfortunates. The facilities, however, were a disgrace. Repeated exposés uncovered inhumane conditions and rampant corruption. The main building—the gloomy former Almshouse (now eighty-five years old)—was abominably overcrowded. The pavilion for the insane was far worse. Awful quarters and wretchedly low wages for the support staff of orderlies, engineers, painters, clerks, cooks, maids, laundry workers, porters, laborers, ambulance drivers, scrubwomen, and maintenance men ensured a turnover rate of 40–50 percent a month, and terrible treatment of patients.

In 1902 a group of reformers led by Bellevue physician Dr. John Brannan pushed to insulate the institution from patronage and graft. With support from Mayor Low, they extracted it from the Department of Public Charities and gave it to an independent mayor-appointed Board of Bellevue and Allied Hospitals (B&AH)—the latter including Fordham in the Bronx, Harlem in upper Manhattan, and Gouverneur on the Lower East Side. The new trustees (with Brannan as chair) bludgeoned the Board of Estimate into funding new facilities, and the city committed itself to spending $8 million. In 1904 McKim, Mead & White, no less, were retained to prepare a grand master plan for a complex of buildings, on the order of the firm's Columbia University campus way uptown. Most of them were actually built—though funding tapered off during the 1914 downturn, leaving the 1816 Almshouse as the anachronistic centerpiece. The B&AH board also upgraded its Allied components; by 1906 Fordham Hospital had moved to a new, half-million-dollar, city-erected home on Southern Boulevard and Crotona Avenue, amid the Bronx's healthful public parks.

Institutions remaining under the Department of Public Charities umbrella fared less well. Metropolitan, City, and Central Neurological, all on Blackwell's Island, and the Brooklyn institutions of Kings County, Coney Island, Greenpoint, and Cumberland remained overcrowded. And the specialty hospitals on Randall's Island—for infants, children (over 2 and under 15), and "feeble-minded, idiot and other children" in the nomenclature of the day—had been marked by unwholesome food, inadequate nursing, and unsanitary surroundings.[16] But with the arrival of Homer Folks to the commissionership, all these got a substantial upgrading. New equipment was installed (including X-ray machines), laboratories created, the nursing staff expanded, steam heating added, and various abuses of patients abolished (including the minor but vexing requirement at Metropolitan that patients stand and salute when the superintendent passed through the wards).

---

16. The treatment of the insane was the worst. In 1839 the New York City Asylum for the Insane had opened at the northern end of Blackwell's Island; jammed to overflowing, it was repeatedly expanded, but never kept pace with new arrivals. Better facilities were constructed on Ward's Island, which since 1847 had hosted the State Emigrant Refuge, a mammoth hospital complex for the sick and destitute immigrants then pouring into the city. The city began shifting patients from Blackwell's to Ward's in the 1870s, but many remained in horrific circumstances, as exposed by undercover journalist Nellie Bly in 1887. The ensuing uproar precipitated an eventual takeover by New York State, which led to closure of the Blackwell's asylum and the absorption of its patients on Ward's, utilizing buildings of the old immigrant complex. In 1899 the now Manhattan State Hospital, with 4,400 patients, was the largest psychiatric institution on earth.

Many of the Health Department's new ventures brought services directly to neighborhoods and homes. Since 1876 the department had been sending a Summer Corps of doctors into the tenement districts each July and August. The physicians, roughly fifty in all, treated sick children, advised mothers on infant care, and looked out for violations of the sanitary or health laws. Lillian Wald's suggestion of building on this precedent was taken up by Dr. S. Josephine Baker—a Poughkeepsie-born graduate of Emily Blackwell's Woman's Medical College—who in 1902 had begun working as a Health Department inspector. In June and July of 1908 Baker helped set up an experimental district wherein she and her colleagues ran a saturation education program, aimed at teaching mothers about infant and child care. When it produced an immediate and spectacular drop in the mortality rate, the department quickly established a new Division of Child Hygiene, the first government agency in the world devoted exclusively to children's health, and appointed Baker its director. In addition to building up the school inspection, school nurse, and milk station programs, Dr. Baker sent public health nurses to homes of expectant mothers before, during, and after childbirth. They gave instruction on child care and feeding, distributed pamphlets, and referred the sick to voluntary agencies. The division also opened sixty-eight Baby Health Clinics. The impact was dramatic. From 1908 to 1917 New York City's infant mortality rate fell from 129 to 88.8 per 1000 births.

Baker also worked with New York's midwives, who in 1909 delivered 40 percent of all babies born in the city. Male obstetricians—their great professional rivals—blamed the city's high maternal mortality rates on midwives' ignorance and ineptitude (as well as their gender) and hoped to drive them out of business. As most midwives, though experienced, were indeed medically undereducated, hence vulnerable, Baker (in 1911) persuaded Bellevue to set up a free six-month course, whose successful completion would be a prerequisite for the public registration system she also established. Many women signed up, notably immigrants who could not afford nursing school, and the School of Midwives' students and staff provided free prenatal care and home deliveries to thousands of women.[17]

Another of the city's public health programs promoted personal hygiene—a prescription difficult to fulfill in tenement districts where, as of 1897, 97 percent of families did not have access to bath rooms. Even if a building provided water, it had to be procured from a dilapidated communal sink and lugged up several flights of stairs—one reason that, according to settlement worker Henry Moskowitz, "many tenants do not bathe more than six times a year, and often less." The 1901 tenement codes mandated that each new apartment include a private water closet and running water, but left out private baths as an unessential expense.[18]

During summers, millions of New Yorkers had used one of the fifteen free "floating baths" maintained by the city along the Hudson and East Rivers. But these had become subject to growing pollution from sewage dumping. Beginning in 1902 they were slowly phased out; by 1914, abolished altogether.

---

17. The city also came to the aid of Lillian Wald's Visiting Nurse Service. Despite its having almost 30,000 patients under care, New York had never funded the institution, requiring Wald to spend an increasing amount of her time fund-raising. When John Purroy Mitchel's administration took office in 1914, Jacob Schiff petitioned the mayor, urging that Wald's work "should receive an allowance from the municipal treasury." Finally, in 1917, the Board of Estimate inserted a $25,000 line in the city's budget.

18. Many in the middle classes had the effrontery to claim poor tenement-class hygiene was a sign of moral failure, while their own cleanliness and pleasanter smell was proof of their superior refinement and personal responsibility. "Have you ever stood near an Italian or Greek street vendor, or have you ever been within five feet of a low-class Polish Jew?" asked one writer for *Health* in 1902. "If so, the stench arising from their unwashed bodies must have turned you sick!"

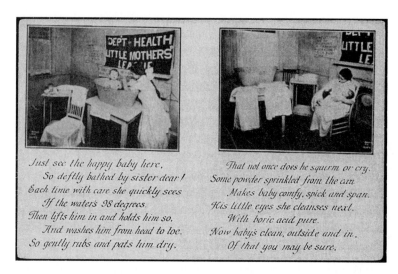

Just see the happy baby here,
So deftly bathed by sister dear!
Each time with care she quickly sees
If the water's 98 degrees.
Then lifts him in and holds him so,
And washes him from head to toe.
So gently rubs and pats him dry.

That not once does he squirm or cry.
Some powder sprinkled from the can
Makes baby comfy, spick and span.
His little eyes she cleanses next.
With boric acid pure.
Now baby's clean, outside and in.
Of that you may be sure.

"Postcard Distributed by the Bureau of Child Hygiene," ca. 1910. (Image No. x2011.34.3837, Museum of the City of New York)

Interior, River Bath House. "Recreations and Hobbies: Swimming," 1905. (New York Public Library, Irma and Paul Milstein Division of United States History, Local History and Genealogy)

The public clamored for replacements. The city responded with indoor bathhouses. Here they followed the pioneering initiative of Simon Baruch, a German-born doctor who in 1891 successfully urged the Association for Improving the Condition of the Poor and the Baron de Hirsch Trust Fund to build a German *Volksbad* (People's Bath), in which patrons could wash themselves under "rain baths," a.k.a. "ring showers." After Consolidation New York took over the task of replicating Baruch's successful model, making $200,000 available for construction, beginning with the Rivington Street Baths (1901). Over the next thirteen years, at least twenty-five municipal baths were built in four of New York's five boroughs. Though most were placed in immigrant neighborhoods, they were usually done up in high

Free-Floating Bath House, New York Harbor. Waldman, *Heartbeat*, 81.

style; the one at Avenue A and 23rd Street (1906) was modeled—appropriately enough—on ancient Rome's Baths of Caracalla.

The city also constructed public toilets. By 1907 New York had provided eight, most of them near public markets. In the next year alone they were used by nearly 10 million. These "comfort stations" were touted as promoting not only cleanliness but temperance. In their absence men with bursting bladders dropped into saloons, and after utilizing the facilities often bought a glass of beer on their way out. (Men were six times as likely to use the public facilities as women, who tended to favor the elaborate versions available in department stores.)

By 1914 New York was envisioning still bolder projects. Mayor Mitchel appointed Dr. Sigismund S. Goldwater as health commissioner.[19] Goldwater, since 1902 the distinguished superintendent of Mount Sinai Hospital, set out to expand preventive medicine. He created a Bureau of Public Health Education, a Bureau of Food and Drugs, a Division of Statistical Research, and a Division of Industrial Hygiene to study and supervise industrial hazards. He also tightened the Sanitary Code and enforced it throughout the city's tenements, factories, and food establishments.

Even more daringly, Dr. Goldwater extended free municipal medical care from infants and children to needy adults. In November 1914 he established a permanent Health Department presence in the slums. He began with experimental Health District No. 1—twenty-one Lower East Side blocks housing 35,000 people, mostly Russian and Austrian Jews. Health workers stationed there compiled medical records on all residents, established close working relations with the community, and produced dramatic improvements. Next Goldwater expanded the program to the entire borough of Queens. And he proposed a Bureau of Adult Hygiene that would offer physical examinations to every resident of the city.

19. Sigismund Shulz Goldwater, known to friends as S. S., was born in New York in 1873, into a middle-class German Jewish family. He attended Columbia, took a leave to study philosophy in Leipzig University, and decided there to go into public health. On returning to Gotham, Goldwater enrolled in the University and Bellevue Hospital Medical College (an 1898 merger of NYU's and Bellevue's teaching institutions), from which he got his MD degree in 1901. Beginning a medical internship at Mount Sinai, he asked instead to be sent to Europe for a year to study the administrative practices of the continent's great hospitals. In 1902, aged 29, he returned to assume daily management of Mount Sinai.

Goldwater also intended to grow the public hospital system, though this initiative never came to fruition, partly checked by hard times, partly resisted by a group who believed its interests would be hurt by it: private-sector doctors.

NEW YORK CITY'S PHYSICIANS HAD COME A LONG WAY since the mid-nineteenth century when they had been widely distrusted, even despised. In the 1890s, though still struggling to differentiate themselves from homeopaths, osteopaths, chiropractors, and Christian Scientists, they had found their prestige enhanced by the triumphs of scientific medicine (though in truth the great bacteriological breakthroughs, while boosting their diagnostic capabilities, did not add much to general practitioners' curative toolbox). Increasingly, in the 1900s, leaders of the profession—the physicians ensconced at the top medical schools, best hospitals, and biggest university research departments—came to believe that the greatest obstacle to further enhancement of the professional status of doctors was . . . other doctors.

From their perspective the city, indeed the country, was plagued with an "oversupply" of physicians—too many doctors competing for too few patients. Some of their concerns were about money. In 1904, the president of the American Medical Association (AMA) noted forthrightly that "overcrowding was steadily reducing the opportunities of those already in the profession to acquire a livelihood." Low income in turn hampered attainment of a properly "professional" status. The income "of many a medical man who has spent years in acquiring a medical education," noted one observer in 1903, "is often less than that of an ordinary mechanic." The *Journal of the American Medical Association* (*JAMA*) said (in 1901) that while juxtaposing medicine and industry was "not a dignified comparison," it had to be admitted that "the same principles of political economy apply in a measure to both. Overproduction in either has its bad effects, and we have not the recourse of foreign markets enjoyed by the ordinary manufacturer."

The wellspring of this "oversupply" was the medical schools. While there might be "room for nearly 3300 new doctors each year," *JAMA* argued in 1901, these "doctor-factories" were spouting out about 6,000. Not only were graduates too abundant; many were poorly trained, according to the new tenets of scientific medicine. Many had been taught at "proprietary" medical schools, small for-profit institutions set up by doctor-professor-entrepreneurs, who relied on traditional amphitheater lectures, rather than providing laboratory training or an opportunity to work with patients. Also troubling, these institutions encouraged entry into the profession of just the kind of people status enhancers were trying to exclude. In 1903 an AMA official disdained "these sundown institutions" (i.e., medical schools that offered night classes), which enabled "the clerk, the street-car conductor, the janitor and others employed during the day to earn a degree."

More troubling still, the oversupply led to an unseemly scramble for business, leading newly hatched doctors to step outside of, and thus imperil, the fee-for-service community.

One place new MDs turned was the city's dispensaries and the outpatient clinics of hospitals, venues where the poor and newly arrived immigrants could go to receive free care. Fledgling physicians seeking diagnostic experience and potential future patients would often work in these part-time, often without pay, dispensing medicine to huge numbers: in 1915, 92 of Gotham's 106 dispensaries and outpatient departments treated 2.2 million patients, and about 3,000 of the city's 8,000 doctors were working there.

Established practitioners were deeply opposed to dispensaries. "Vast sums of money are wasted yearly on worthless and undeserving persons," grumped Dr. George Frederick Shrady, one of the city's foremost physicians. Others were sure that many dispensary patrons were in fact freeloaders, who could bloody well afford to patronize regular doctors. Under pressure, some dispensaries employed social workers to weed out the undeserving—whose numbers turned out to be inconsequential. But the focus on keeping people out heightened the odor of charity that wafted from the institutions, giving them their reputation as "medical soup kitchens." Patrons were alienated, too, by the quality of the service. Patients often waited hours for hasty and superficial exams.

Other overproduced MDs preferred to work for "lodges," a practice that mandarins considered an even bigger threat to the profession's fee-for-service model. In the city's working-class quarters, residents tried to cushion themselves and their families against the always lurking possibility of impoverishment, by forging a multitude of independent mutual-aid associations, based around place of origin (*landmanschaftn*) or affinities of language, politics, or religion. In 1917 there were 528 such societies in New York, together embracing 69,555 members. These fraternal organizations (overwhelmingly male and given to masculine rituals) were organized in democratically structured clusters—lodges—whose most common aim was to provide members with burial benefits, and thus avoid the ultimate disgrace of pauperism: consignment to the potter's field on Hart's Island. As time went on, many added other functions, ranging from rudimentary forms of health insurance to acquisition of a common cemetery. They also leagued themselves in national organizations, spreading insurance risks over ever larger people pools. Branches of these national bodies were also present in large numbers in New York. In 1917 B'nai Brith had 19 lodges and 2,100 members; the Arbeiter Ring (Workmen's Circle) had 240 lodges with a combined membership of 25,000; and Brith Abraham, the country's largest, had 354 lodges, with 90,000. All in all, Gotham had 982 lodges with 162,012 members.

By the turn of the century, an increasing number of these societies were adding to their menu of services treatment by a doctor, usually a young and recent graduate. The physician was paid an annual salary, determined by the size of lodge membership, in return for providing basic primary care and sometimes minor surgery. Participants paid about two dollars a year—roughly equivalent to a laborer's daily wage—and were entitled to vote on whether a prospective doctor would be selected. In 1915, Commissioner Goldwater noted, a lodge practice had become "the chosen or established method of dealing with sickness among the relatively poor." In that year, on the Lower East Side alone, 500 physicians were catering to Jewish societies.

Fee-for-service doctors—mandarins and general practitioners alike—were utterly appalled by what they called the "lodge practice evil." It turned independent professionals into hired hands. Submitting to election was degrading. And it was costly. The AMA denounced the "ruinous competition" that, one opponent predicted, would depress fees to levels "comparable to those of the bootblack and peanut vendor."

Happily, the critics realized, both lodges and dispensaries could be undermined by drying up the supply of impecunious doctors. Just as corporations were then struggling to restrict "ruinous competition" and "overproduction," the AMA set out to diminish the supply of doctors by constricting the number of medical schools. At the same time, they would raise the scientific standards (and status) of the profession by requiring medical schools to dramatically upgrade their curriculum. In 1904 the AMA set up a Council on Medical Education (CME), which—after examining English, French, and German approaches, as well as that of Baltimore's Johns Hopkins, the US gold standard—proposed requiring significant premedical education for admission; then a year of physics, chemistry, and biology (preferably at an affiliated university); then two years of laboratory science (anatomy, physiology, pathology, and pharmacology); followed by two years of clinical work in a teaching hospital. This five-year plan aroused furious opposition from the proprietaries, who couldn't possibly meet such standards, and from homeopathic schools, who would refuse to even if they could. To overcome this resistance, in 1908 the CME asked the Carnegie Foundation for the Advancement of Teaching (526 Fifth Avenue) to survey American medical education. President Henry Pritchett, a staunch advocate of medical school reform, chose educator Abraham Flexner to conduct the investigation, which confirmed the CME's assessment and recommendations. This in turn helped win enactment of state licensing laws that put teeth into the suggestions. The 1910 publication of the Flexner Report transformed medical education, scything away most proprietaries (including most of those run by and for women and blacks) and homeopathic schools. In 1904 there were 160 MD-granting institutions, with more than 28,000 students. By 1920 there were only 85, educating only 13,800. Just what the doctors had ordered.

THIS SEA CHANGE DID MORE THAN DRY UP THE POOL OF PHYSICIANS—sending dispensaries and lodge medicine into a long and terminal tailspin—it transformed the entire private sector of organized medicine. The AMA/Carnegie approach strongly urged hospitals, medical schools, and universities to consolidate into giant "medical centers"—entities that would combine and coordinate their component parts, tied together by a mutual commitment to scientific medicine. Their belief in the efficacy of size and centralization dovetailed nicely with the reigning ideology of the corporate merger movement then at high tide. As one doctor proclaimed: "Concentration in all matters is a law of modern development."

Reconfiguring the medical landscape, it was well understood, would be an expensive proposition. Constructing well-equipped laboratories, expanding hospitals, and paying highly trained teachers, researchers, and practitioners would require tapping the resources of industrial philanthropists, especially those committed ideologically and materially to consolidation.

In 1901 John D. Rockefeller Sr. launched the Rockefeller Institute for Medical Research, which would become a central pillar of the city's medical scene. Since 1897 his chief philanthropic adviser, Frederick Gates, had been warning him that Gotham's physicians and medical establishments were on the whole hostile to basic biomedical research. Rockefeller, always interested in creating organizations that rose above short-term considerations and adopted long-haul perspectives, began cautiously with a $200,000 planning commitment. In 1903 he donated $660,000 to purchase the old Schermerhorn farm, which had been in the family since 1818. The thirteen-acre tract ran from Avenue A (now York Avenue), where cows still grazed, to a forty-foot-high rocky bluff overlooking the East River, between 64th and 68th Streets. (The city granted permission to close off 66th, and would later do the same for 64th, 65th, and 67th.) More Rockefeller infusions got laboratory buildings erected, residents and staff hired, and research in pathology, bacteriology, physiology, and pharmacology commenced. By 1914 Senior had poured $12,500,000 into the institute, finally giving New York City the equivalent of France's Pasteur Institute (1888) and Germany's Robert Koch Institute (1891). The institute's influence and accomplishments would be enormous, not only because of the investigations carried out at the East Side institute but from the grants it gave to researchers, overwhelmingly those based at elite university medical schools.

Other philanthropists concentrated on pushing particular institutions into joining forces. George F. Baker, president of the First National Bank and a longtime member of the Board of Governors of New York Hospital, prodded it into affiliating with Cornell Medical

College in 1912 by making the merger a condition for his giving a $250,000 donation. In tying the knot, New York Hospital was following its great rival, Presbyterian Hospital, which the year before had allied with Columbia University's College of Physicians and Surgeons, encouraged by Standard Oil heir Edward Harkness, who kicked in $1.5 million to underwrite the merger. Cornell Medical College, which itself had been established in 1898 with a $4 million fund supplied by Oliver H. Payne (oil, steel, and tobacco magnate), got the right to name half the hospital's medical staff and gained access to ward patients for its own faculty and students.

Often the upgrading of scientific standards went hand in hand with the latest uptown migration of hospitals. Under the direction of Dr. Goldwater, Mount Sinai had departed its outmoded facilities at Lexington and 66th and struck out for northern pastures at Fifth and 100th. In 1904, when the 456-bed, ten-pavilion hospital opened, it included up-to-date clinical and research facilities, funded by the Lewisohn family and others. In 1913 the proliferation of specialized departments prompted construction of additional housing.

New York Hospital decided to cohabit with Cornell, aiming to move north together into a purpose-built joint facility just above the Rockefeller Institute on the East River, between 68th and 70th. This would concentrate in one enclave a hospital, a research facility, and a university medical school, at a location just across from Blackwell's hospitals. It would take more than fifteen years, and many more millions, before its new quarters would open for business. But already in 1911, a *New York Times* survey of leading members of the profession found a widespread belief that such consolidations would soon allow Gotham to seize the crown from Baltimore and, indeed, to establish itself as "the foremost medical centre of the world."

THE REFOCUSING OF PRIVATE HOSPITALS on the educational and scientific aspects of medicine worked an internal transformation in their functioning and clientele. For the previous two centuries, the mission of religious and charitable hospitals had been the same as that of the public institutions: tending the sick poor. They were not, for the most part, places for cures. Hospitals and medical practice had little to do with each other.

The rise of scientific medicine changed all this. Hospitals—rendered newly antiseptic— became preferred sites for surgery. As more high-tech equipment was brought to bear, it became less and less convenient, or even possible, for surgeons to operate in private homes and apartments. Hospitals offered physicians the technical resources needed to practice modern medicine—without turning them into hired hands. Hospitals provided technical (usually female) assistants who accepted their authority. They enabled doctors to see more patients in a shorter time. Hospitals were transformed into physicians' workshops.[20]

While the construction of new facilities was often underwritten by corporate philanthropists, paying for the ever higher operating expenses was an ongoing problem. To come up with the funds, hospitals reached for upscale patients.

Upper-class New Yorkers had theretofore entered hospitals only during acute crises. To make their institutions more appealing, boards turned them into virtual hotels. Roosevelt Hospital advertised a new private patients' pavilion designed to appeal to "those of the most cultivated tastes." Architect Ernest Flagg, commissioned to build the new St. Luke's Hospital

---

20. Young doctors would flock to posts in the newly reorganized hospitals, further reducing the numbers interested in pro bono dispensary work. Interns and residents could get their clinical training at the hospital, and enjoy access to the scientific and technical equipment dispensaries couldn't afford.

(1896), modeled his magnificent structure on the Luxembourg Palace; private rooms with fireplaces awaited paying patients. For the middle classes the hospitals invented the "semiprivate room"—affordable, yet stripped of the connotations of indigence and failure.

As the percentage of paying patients, attended by doctors of their own choosing, leapt upward, the number of charity cases, treated by hospital staff, declined dramatically. Some proposed jettisoning the poor altogether, but administrators refused. Medical students and interns needed the poor to practice on. And if they were shunted off to municipal hospitals, tax exemptions might get revoked, charitable donations might dry up. That would require raising rates for private rooms. Besides, the city subsidized treatment of the indigent. In 1906 New York purchased almost a million days of care from private hospitals.

Still, with new reserves of cash, and free from the public hospitals' take-all requirement, the privates could pick and choose their patients. They could and did turn away those with morally reprehensible ills (like venereal disease) or chronic contagious diseases (to keep their mortality numbers low). Sometimes the privates would evict patients at death's door, passing them to a municipal institution on very short notice. ("No hospital likes to increase its death-rate," one journalist observed.) Sometimes the receiving public hospital would lateral the expiring patient to another public hospital, a practice that Homer Folks clamped down on when he was put in charge. Of course, only the poor were subjected to this grim game of musical beds, as one outraged reformer underscored when he demanded of hospital authorities: "Open your books and show me one man of wealth who has ever been transferred!"

The private hospitals could bar entire categories of doctors, too. Some Protestant institutions banned non-Anglo doctors. This perpetuated tribal medicine, which theoretically had no place in a secular "scientific" regime. Young Italian doctors, and patients fearing denial of last rites, turned to small Catholic institutions sustained by the unpaid labor of nursing sisters. Jewish doctors who were denied residencies, and Jewish patients who were fed non-kosher food, had access to alternatives in the expanded Mount Sinai and, up in the Bronx, the transplanted Montefiore Hospital (its migration to Norwood arranged by President Jacob Schiff, who routinely spent Sundays visiting its patients).[21]

THE PUBLIC SUPPORT OF THESE PUTATIVELY PRIVATE INSTITUTIONS let doctors have their cake and eat it too. Their hospitals adopted a market orientation but were inoculated against the full impact of market forces. The subsidized citadels also provided doctors and hospital administrators with a power base, assisting them in efforts to roll back public-sector interference with their prerogatives and profits. New York's public programs were challenging the way health care was delivered to children and women and were threatening to do so for the entire population. Doctors had not beaten back capitalist medicine to succumb to municipal socialism. Hence the various forays against particular public initiatives.

Doctors opposed Biggs's diphtheria inoculation program. At first, wary of the speed with which an unproven program was being rushed into practice, they opposed testing itself. When reassured by the plummeting death rate, they (and local druggists) directed their ire at the Health Department's sell-off of surplus antitoxin at low prices. The city had entered into "business competition with its citizens," they complained. In 1902 a thousand

---

21. There were tribes within tribes, too. Orthodox East European downtown Jews were reluctant to travel up to German Jewish Mount Sinai, where there were none of their background on staff and Yiddish was a lingua non grata. In 1890 a group of Lower East Side Orthodox created Beth Israel, originally a combination lodge/dispensary, which by 1902 had transmuted into a 115-bed hospital.

physicians and druggists petitioned Mayor Low to halt the sales. He did so, enabling private labs to produce the antitoxin at a higher price, contributing to a dramatic expansion of the pharmaceutical industry.

Doctors fought mandatory tuberculosis reporting as an infringement on their turf, and only a concerted counter-mobilization had stopped them from banishing the Health Department from the war on TB.

Doctors opposed S. Josephine Baker's child hygiene clinics. It was okay for school inspectors to uncover problems. But opening free clinics to *treat* the problems robbed physicians of customers.

Doctors denounced Goldwater's planned public health expansion, declaring it would be "ruinous to the business of the medical practitioners of the city." The Society of Medical Jurisprudence warned that the health commissioner was committing New York City "to a policy of Socialism." After Goldwater left office in 1915, the city's nose-and-throat clinics for children were shut down, a step applauded by the Public Health Committee of the New York Academy of Medicine.

And in 1916, in their most sweeping intervention to date, doctors set out to beat back a proposal to establish a state-run system of health insurance—and in this campaign they would have a variety of powerful allies. The plan would have provided benefits including surgical, medical, and nursing care, hospital stays and treatment, medical supplies, cash payments in lieu of lost wages, maternity coverage for female workers and the wives of male workers, and a funeral benefit. It did not offer universal coverage; it left out the unemployed, the self-employed, agricultural workers and domestic servants (i.e., African Americans), the elderly, the permanently disabled, and workers making over $100 a month (i.e., skilled and unionized labor). It was not a charitable handout; it was a compulsory contributory insurance program, with the premiums coming 40 percent from employers, 40 percent from employees, and 20 percent from the public till.

The proposal—rooted in Germany's compulsory sickness insurance law (1883) and its British descendant of 1911—had been advanced by the American Association for Labor Legislation (AALL), the chief importer of European social insurance innovations in the 1900s and 1910s. Founded in 1906, the AALL was an organization of social scientists from leading US universities—notably Columbia, Princeton, Wisconsin, and Yale—that was heavily stocked with German-trained progressive economists. New Yorkers played key roles, especially on the funding side, with 65 percent of AALL income (in 1912) coming from twenty-one contributors, including John D. Rockefeller, Elbert Gary, Felix Warburg, Madeline Astor, and Anne Morgan. From 1908 the national office was housed in the Metropolitan Tower, later shifting to larger quarters at 131 East 23rd Street.

AALL members were for the most part socially minded defenders of capitalism, worried about the tension between rapid industrialization and preindustrial social and legal institutions. Its first major initiative—replacing the old-fashioned way of dealing with industrial accidents—had been a great success. Common law principles and "freedom of contract" jurisprudence had made it virtually impossible for employee casualties to successfully sue their employers. (Workers were held by the courts to have freely assumed the risks of whatever job they'd signed on for.) The AALL's plan—modeled on the British Worker Compensation Act of 1897—argued that as accidents were an inevitable part of the industrial order, and often as not due to employers scrimping on safety measures, their costs should be socialized and borne by employers as well as employees. Organized labor supported the shift from adversarial to bureaucratic proceedings because unions usually got hammered in the courts. And business signed on because obstreperous juries occasionally awarded fat damages, which had driven up insurance costs, making prearranged and strictly delimited payouts a less expensive option. Accordingly, when the AALL helped Governor Hughes draw up a bill, it was passed in a relative jiffy, and New York State's Worker Compensation Act of 1910 became the first significant piece of social insurance legislation in the United States.[22] Within three years, twenty-one more states had followed suit.

In 1912 it seemed to the AALL that a health insurance bill would be the logical next step toward catching up with Europe, where such coverage was all but universal. The prime mover was board member Isaac Max Rubinow. Son of a wealthy Russian Jewish textile merchant, Rubinow emigrated from Moscow to New York in 1893, at age 17, graduated from Columbia College in 1895, got an MD from NYU Medical College in 1898, and began practicing medicine on the Lower East Side, an experience that got him thinking about alleviating social as well as personal distress. Learning about Germany's social insurance schemes, he abandoned medicine, studied part-time at Columbia's School of Political Science, and co-directed a monumental two-volume study of European workmen's insurance systems in 1908–9 that was published in 1911, the same year Britain passed its National Insurance Act.

Rubinow was a socialist—he had joined the Socialist Party of America at its founding in 1901—and had declared himself dedicated to "radically changing our social institutions." He accepted, however, the need to work for interim improvements, and counted himself a reformer. Still, he insisted he wasn't a "progressive," as they were not true reformers: "A new patch on an old hole—that is as far as their social vision goes. Social reformers, indeed! Social conservators—that is more accurate." Nevertheless, his short-term policy proclivities were closely aligned with those of the progressives with whom he worked.

Rubinow and his AALL colleagues' optimism about their model bill's chances of success was due in part due to their conviction that they, as detached experts, were offering a rational (and Euro-tested) plan, whose virtues would be as rapidly acclaimed as their solution to the industrial accident problem had been. Big mistake. When hearings on their bill took place in March 1916 they were startled—more so than they should have been—at the storm of opposition that bore down on them, starting with that of the medical profession.

Doctors were not a unified bloc. There were significant differences between the institution-based physicians, and the individualistic fee-for-service general practitioners, but on the issue of compulsory health insurance, there was a clear convergence of opinion. Representatives of the Society for Medical Jurisprudence, the Medical Society of the County of New York, and the New York State Medical Society, testifying in opposition to the legislation, pronounced the schema as the "lodge practice evil" writ large. It would subject doctors to state control, condemning them to a loss of income, and deprive the citizenry of the right to choose their own physicians. They also objected bitterly to having been cut out of the drafting process, and declared that the doctors involved in fashioning the bill were not representative of the state's medical men—Rubinow being a non-practitioner and a socialist, Goldwater being a public health physician and probably a crypto-socialist.

---

22. In 1909 Hughes had established a Commission on Employer's Liability and Causes of Industrial Accidents, with AALL president and Columbia professor Henry Seager among its members, and Crystal Eastman as secretary. Eastman, daughter of two upstate congregational ministers, had graduated from Vassar in 1903 and moved to New York. There she lived and worked at Greenwich House while studying for an MA at Columbia (1904) and a law degree at NYU (1907). In 1907–8 she investigated labor conditions for the Russell Sage Foundation's Pittsburgh Survey, published her key results in the AALL journal in 1909, and in 1910 came out with the authoritative *Work Accidents and the Law*. Eastman was principally responsible for drafting the legislation.

Insurance companies lined up to denounce the bill, especially those, like Metropolitan Life and Prudential, which sold "industrial insurance" to working people, going door to door to collect their weekly premiums. These policies were not really health insurance plans; they offered only the crucial funeral benefit, and each brought in only pennies in profit. But there were a lot of pennies at stake—in 1911 those two companies alone had 24.7 million policies in force in the United States—and they believed, not unreasonably, that the AALL's inclusion of death benefits in their plan was aimed squarely at them. (The reformers could hardly have been ignorant of the likely response, given the AALL's office location on the sixteenth floor of Met Life's tower.) Accordingly, they and other firms lobbied vigorously against the bill. The Great Eastern Casualty Company told its agents that the bill portended "the end of all Insurance Companies and Agents and to you personally the complete wrecking of the business and connections you have spent a lifetime building and the loss of your bread and butter"—arguments that found ready ears among the many insurance agents who were members of the state legislature.

The fraternal lodges were equally opposed, convinced that state health insurance would swiftly put them out of business.

Organized business was dead set against. The New York State Chamber of Commerce testified in opposition. The Real Estate Owners' Association of New York City said the measure was "as insane as anything that ever emanated from the wildest lunatic asylum in the country." It would force property owners to pay tax increases of perhaps 50 percent, and, given the no doubt consequent rise in rents, they predicted the "manufacturing element will move en masse over to New Jersey if this bill is passed." The National Manufacturers' Association found the bill "devilish in principle and foreign in ideals"—a reference to its "Germanic" origins—and branded it "class legislation" in the sense that it told working men, "You are not capable of taking care of yourself; you are dependents of the State." The National Civic Federation concurred, arguing that as the British act of 1911 threatened "to destroy the virile elements of the English character," so too, if New York followed suit, it would lead to "an insidious undermining of working-class honor."

Gompers agreed. The American Federation of Labor chieftain argued that as the bill assumed workers were unable to look after themselves, it was "repugnant to freeborn citizens," and a threat to workers' "independence of spirit and virility." "Sore and saddened as I am by the illness, the killing and maiming of so many of my fellow-workers," Gompers said in attack on social insurance, "I would rather see that go on for years and years, minimized and mitigated by the organized labor movement, than give up one jot of the freedom of the workers to strive and struggle for their own emancipation through their own efforts." The labor movement, moreover, had already made considerable efforts along these lines. Many AFL affiliates had sickness benefits of their own (though often actuarially shaky), and the bill would be of no use to his members, as most earned more than the maximum allowed income of $1,200 per year.

Gompers harbored a profound distrust of government. And government had given him plenty of grounds for wariness, given the state's cozy symbiosis with capital, as expressed in anti-union legislation and adverse court decisions. Nor did Gompers trust the professor-dominated AALL. (He resigned his honorary vice presidency in 1915.) It had not solicited opinions from labor leaders, nor included worker representatives in the drafting process, and had arrogantly assumed labor would approve whatever the AALL came up with. Beyond resentment at this particular slight lay a more visceral animus, rooted in his fine-tuned sensitivity to clashing class interests. "The welfare workers, the social uplifters, the social legislative enthusiasts" all belonged, he said, to "that class of society that is very desirous of doing things for the workers and establishing institutions for them that will prevent their doing things for themselves and maintaining their own institutions." Nor were they doing this out of the goodness of their hearts, but rather out of self-interest. Their plan, after all, would put workers under the control of government boards, which would be run by middle-class professionals. They were creating positions and empires for themselves and were, he calculated, out "for revenue only." If in fact progressives actually *believed* what they said—that they were only "disinterested outsiders" concerned solely with the public interest—then that was an even *more* compelling reason not to trust them.

Gompers, however, was not representative of Gotham's labor movement. Pauline Newman, a garment worker organizer who had helped establish union health benefit plans and clinics, noted that skilled worker unions represented less than 10 percent of the US workforce, and she urged the legislators to forget for the moment "the organized small minority and think of the great mass of unorganized workers." The New York State Federation of Labor, defying Gompers, offered enthusiastic support for the AALL bill. And others trooped to Albany to testify on its behalf, those whom Gompers might have called the usual suspects: the Russell Sage Foundation, the AICP and COS, the Consumers' League and the Socialists, and the public health physicians, including the Health Department commissioner.

These were not enough. The doctors' revolt, the resistance of business, the mobilization by insurance agents, the opposition of Gompers—all combined to strangle the proposed health insurance bill.

Nevertheless, public health programs and environmental reforms had served the city well, providing it with a great triumph at the most basic of levels. In 1890 New York's death rate had been 27.2 per 1,000. By 1900 it had tumbled to 20.1. And by 1914 it had nose-dived to 13.4—the lowest ever recorded—making New York one of the healthiest of great cities.

SCHOOLS

Since at least 1888, Nicholas Murray Butler, then president of the New York School for the Training of Teachers, had been obsessed with transforming Gotham's public school system, which he loathed as passionately as he hated the Board of Aldermen, and for much the same reason: it decentralized power and put it in the wrong hands.

Overall, administrative and policy-making duties were the domain of a lay, mayorally appointed Board of Education, assisted by a lone (and subordinate) professional, the superintendent of schools. But the board delegated much of its authority to appointed neighborhood-based trustees—five in each of the city's twenty-four wards. It was these ward trustees who hired teachers (subject to the superintendent's approval), determined promotions, appointed and advised school principals on curricula and administration, selected sites for new schools, and let contracts for their construction, supply, and repair.

Butler thought this preposterous, a primitive holdover from the days when each neighborhood had its own watchmen and volunteer fire company. Localism facilitated Tammany grafting. It let immigrants (and Catholics) control the curriculum. It fostered bad (excessively democratic) management, which was doubtless responsible for the city's overcrowded schools, underqualified teachers, rampant truancy, and growing juvenile delinquency.

Butler proposed a plan to wrest the schools back from the brink. He would abolish the local trustees altogether, revamp and downgrade the Board of Education, and hand most management authority over to experts—professional educators—who would standardize the schools' curricula and administer affairs from a central office. Run the schools the way the great corporations ran their businesses: *that* would get them back on track.

Butler, Wall Street lawyer Stephen H. Olin, and a close circle of advisers (chiefly corporate attorneys, including legal leviathan Elihu Root) put together a coalition of school reformers, which included upper-class businessmen and professionals, settlement workers, institutional church leaders, good-government reformers, and Protestant charity organizations. In 1894 they linked up with the Fusion campaign of Republicans and anti-Tammany Democrats and, after putting William Strong in City Hall, submitted a bill to the state legislature calling for centralization of the system.

In Albany, Butler's forces encountered stiff resistance. School administrators, teachers, labor unions, Catholic and Jewish organizations, neighborhood ethnic and business associations, and Tammany Hall all supported the existing decentralized system. Butler's opponents pointed out that most ward trustees were not "ignorant Tammany heelers." They were, rather, well-educated and middle-class merchants, lawyers, doctors, and real estate brokers; the majority were Republicans or independents. True, some had struck corrupt deals with contractors, developers, and textbook promoters, but Butler never dug up a major scandal.

Decentralizers warned against replacing the ward trustees with an "educational bureaucracy." Once reform-minded "Anglomaniacs" were no longer accountable to local parents, they would impose their culture on children. Or, more precisely, on other people's children. For the offspring of wealthy reformers—as their opponents noted caustically—were not *in* the public system. Indeed, rich New Yorkers were busily renovating and expanding their network of private schools.[23] Mass meetings denounced Butler's proposals. One hundred thousand petitioned to maintain "the people's schools." And in April 1895 the bill was scuttled.

Butler and Olin immediately redoubled their efforts. In early 1896 they organized a Committee of One Hundred for Public School Reform. Of these, forty-nine were Wall Street lawyers (thirty-one of whom were officers of national corporations), and eighteen were bankers (including partners from the House of Morgan and Kuhn, Loeb). Ninety-two of the members were listed in the Social Register; fifty-eight were members of the City Club. Also on board were doctors, academics, publishers, and, as before, representatives from Protestant philanthropies, institutional churches, and settlement houses, many of which had pioneered programs they now wanted the public school system to adopt. Society ladies, too, embraced the cause. The Women's Committee of Good Government Club E (the Goo-Goos' Gramercy Park branch) had morphed in 1895 into the Public Education Association, led by Butler and author Mariana Griswold Van Rensselaer. With Butler's guidance, Van Rensselaer penned a series of editorials that Pulitzer published in his *World*, and she also mobilized prominent women's organizations to lend their credentials to the campaign.

In February 1896 Butler again introduced a school reorganization bill, which called for erasing the ward trustees so thoroughly that "the very name ceases to exist." This time, with

---

23. Collegiate and Trinity, which moved to the Upper West Side, were joined by a score of others (including Trinity's new sister school, St. Agatha's [1898]). Others relocated to the millionaire district across Central Park, where the Protestant elite favored St. Bernard's, Buckley, and Brearley (which occupied new McKim, Mead & White quarters at Park Avenue and 61st in 1912). Also: Mrs. Reed's, Miss Spence's, the Misses Ely's (for girls); Cutler School, John Browning's school (for boys); and Dr. Sachs (one for each).

In terms of pedagogy, the upper classes opted for more child-centered alternatives. There was considerable interest in the approach of Maria Montessori after *McClure's* ran a major story on her work in 1911, though it was set back in 1914 after publication of a critique by an influential Teachers College philosopher of education, William Heard Kilpatrick.

such formidable backing from the city's über elite, upstate Republicans acquiesced, overriding another outpouring of downstate protest. The new law, as amended by charter revisions in 1901, rearranged the educational landscape. Ward trustees indeed vanished. Official authority was vested in the central Board of Education. Real power passed to a new Board of Superintendents, headed (from 1898 to 1918) by Butler's ally William H. Maxwell.

Maxwell, in contrast to his backers, was a Scotch-Irish immigrant. In 1874, as a young man of 22, he had come to the United States hoping to teach. Stymied by lack of a ward boss patron, he turned to educational administration. By 1887 he had worked his way up to being superintendent of Brooklyn's schools. A decade later, now sternly imposing in frock coat and walrus mustache, he was chosen to consolidate the revolution Butler had begun.

Maxwell's first hurdle was the system's decrepit physical plant. Most school buildings were dark, foul-smelling, verminous, and noisy (often adjoining els). They were also jammed. As of Consolidation, Greater New York's schools handled 500,000 children, twice the number of twenty years earlier. Each arriving steamer swelled the pupil population further (attendance was now mandatory until age 14). By 1905 classrooms of seventy were commonplace. Tens of thousands attended half-day sessions. Thousands more were simply turned away.

Maxwell launched a building boom. The Board of Education's talented in-house architect C. B. J. Snyder designed monumental H-block structures that ingeniously maximized the limited light and air available in cramped tenement districts. Many were built in the Dutch (occasionally Flemish) Revival mode, and named after famous old New York families (Clinton, Cooper, Morris), to impress immigrants with the solidity of established institutions. Snyder's PS 165, at 108th/109th, east of Broadway, was modeled on the Hotel de Cluny. Jacob Riis called it a "palace for the people"; Lewis Mumford, who attended third grade there in 1903, remembered it as "prisonlike."

De Witt Clinton High School, Tenth Avenue between 58th and 59th Streets, ca. 1900. (Image No. x2010.7.1.112, Wurts Brothers/Museum of the City of New York)

By 1915 the city had erected thirty-eight new structures—especially in the Lower East Side, Brownsville, and the Bronx. Scores more had been remodeled and enlarged. But school registration had more than kept pace. Enrollment had soared by 60 percent to nearly 800,000 pupils. Almost 100,000 still went part-time.

Maxwell also expanded the teaching staff. By 1914 it more than doubled to 20,448. Increased size brought novel headaches. Maxwell and Butler's vision of a consolidated system included strict control of the labor force. They wanted to bring scientific management to education, diminish teachers' say in teaching, and reduce even principals to closely watched employees. But the mostly female teachers proved unexpectedly obstreperous. They objected to their pay. In 1900 starting teachers averaged $504 a year, less than stable hands or elevator boys made. They also objected to wage discrimination: male teachers were paid considerably more than identically qualified females.

In 1906 Kate Hogan, a Manhattan seventh-grade teacher, organized the Interborough Association of Woman Teachers. By 1910 three-fourths of the female teachers had signed on. Shattering their reputation for docility, the women ignored board gag orders, sought and gained allies among the unions, women's clubs, churches, and civic groups, and won a 1911 law requiring equal pay for equal work. Next the teachers went after the board's requirement that women (though not men) who married must resign. They got it reversed. Administrators then dismissed wives who became mothers (though not husbands who became fathers). In 1915 the teachers got that overturned, too.

FOR ALL THEIR DISAGREEMENTS OVER WAGES AND WORKING CONDITIONS, Maxwell and the teachers concurred on the schools' primary mission.

The core curriculum, newly standardized throughout the consolidated city, remained essentially what it had been for a century. It aimed to impart rudimentary literacy, moral virtues (punctuality, industriousness, orderliness, and obedience), and familiarity with American institutions. The school, Maxwell argued, should be "the melting pot which converts the children of the immigrants of all races and languages into sturdy, independent American citizens."

Thousands of respectable middle-class teachers agreed. These Anglo-, Irish-, and German American young women peered at their immigrant charges across an immense cultural divide. Some sought to establish a sympathetic rapport, but most had little appreciation for their pupils' cultures. They approached the task of molding them into American shape with varying degrees of white-gloved prejudice.

Teachers demanded cleanliness—scrubbed faces, well-starched collars and aprons, and polished shoes (a huge drain on harried mothers). They exacted silence. Children sat staring rigidly forward. Corporal punishment, though technically forbidden, was employed, especially the practice of washing out mouths with soap (which particularly dismayed Jewish parents as the soap used was not kosher). Teachers also relied, as had their predecessors, on mechanical rote learning. Lessons were recited in unison or seriatim. One critic watched as pupils jumped up, shouted their answer, and sat while the next one rose. They bobbed up and down so quickly and mechanically that "the class presented the appearance rather of a traveling pump handle than of a large number of human beings."

Many educators demanded Anglo-conformity. One official called for an "absolute forgetfulness of all obligations or connections with other countries because of descent or birth." Popular textbooks, like Columbia professor David Saville Muzzey's *American History* (1911), lauded Anglo-Saxons as the real Americans and painted other "races" in stereotypically

"Italian Pupil," ca. 1910–15. (Library of Congress Prints and Photographs Division, George Grantham Bain Collection)

inferior terms. "Foreignness" was deemed a badge of shame, either out of the belief that deracination was essential to success and civility, or from simple antipathy to immigrant cultures.

For all their determination to teach proper English, the schools had trouble reaching those who spoke only Yiddish or Italian. Authorities were reluctant to authorize using foreign tongues in teaching. Though some innovative programs were established—special classes for overage children and non-English-speakers—these reached only a small percentage. Many newcomers were dumped into the earliest grades, regardless of age. Left back year after year, they languished (or went truant) until old enough to get working papers.

These difficulties were compounded by equating correct speech with patriotism. A flag salute designed by George T. Balch, a Board of Education official and author of *Methods of Teaching Patriotism in the Public Schools*, required students to stand with their right arms outstretched and slightly elevated, palm down, while pledging "One Country! One Language! One Flag!"[24]

The new immigrants were ambivalent about the core curriculum. Many happily accepted the invitation to assimilate. But few wanted to deny their origins in the process. Responses varied by group.

---

24. The legal stance toward non-English–speaking minorities, however, remained one of tolerance. As in most European countries, there was no attempt to stop the private life of a minority language so long as it didn't challenge the public supremacy of the national tongue.

"Jewish Pupil," ca. 1910–15. (Library of Congress Prints and Photographs Division, George Grantham Bain Collection)

Some Eastern European Jewish parents were pained to find their children rejecting Yiddish for "refined" English. Yet many accepted this as part of becoming educated in America. A passion for learning, rooted in faith and history, helped override reservations. So did the discovery that the education in New York was both open and free. They knew that they would never go back to Europe, and that education was a key to moving forward. German Jews encouraged their efforts: the Baron de Hirsch Fund ran an English-as-a-second-language program to prepare young immigrants for the public schools.

Not all Jews acquiesced. Some insisted their children supplement public schooling with religious instruction. In 1914 perhaps 25 percent of New York's elementary-aged Jewish children went to congregational schools (for children of synagogue members), hedarim (private Hebrew schools), melameds (private tutors), and Sunday schools. Though many people commented on the brightness and eagerness of Jewish students, on the whole they were not so different from other ethnic children. Poverty, lack of English, disease, parental neglect, child labor, and malnutrition led to many being left back. The majority of Russian Jewish children dropped out at or before the legal school-leaving age. Swedish, German, and English immigrants did much better. Nevertheless, the Jewish commitment to public education remained overwhelming.

Catholics were more divided.

Italian peasants had never considered education a route to opportunity. Only 57.4 percent of Lower East Side Italian families were even partly literate (compared to 85.8 percent of Jewish immigrants). An old Mezzogiorno proverb ran "Do not make your child better than you are." Many Italians planned only a temporary stay; schooling seemed extraneous. Many were extremely poor; children's wages seemed essential. The school system also antagonized the *contadini*, with their fierce family loyalty, by making children ashamed of their shawl-wearing mothers. Americanized youth were "less respectful and obedient and more independent." Worst of all, daughters could more readily evade parental supervision. Italian pupils, faced with such home-front disapproval of schooling, floundered badly.

Leonard Covello, himself an immigrant, tried to alleviate the conflict between New York's educational institutions and Southern Italian mores. A 1911 Phi Beta Kappa Columbia graduate, Covello in 1915 designed a bilingual, bicultural educational program. First in private clubs and then at De Witt Clinton High, Covello taught Italian American students the Italian language and acquainted them with their own culture. Using language as a bridge rather than a wedge between home and school overcame parents' suspicions of prolonged education. But Covello made few inroads with fellow educators. The public schools would long consider use of Italian a badge of inferiority.

Italian parents were, accordingly, open to alternatives. They found a growing Catholic parochial school system eager to recruit them. In 1884 American bishops, meeting in Baltimore, had underscored their insistence that Catholic parents send their children to Church-run schools. New York archbishop Michael Corrigan heartily agreed. He argued that Catholic schools sheltered pupils from Protestant zealots while simultaneously making it easier for foreigners to enter American life. Parochial school teachers knew their pupils' language, did not equate patriotism with fluency in English, and built upon family, ethnic, and religious traditions. At the same time, they were flag-wavingly patriotic, and their school-books and curricula taught diligence and deference as vigorously as any public school.

Corrigan reached out to the Italians. He added Italian parishes, staffed them with Italian priests, and opened Italian-speaking schools. When he died in 1902 his policy was continued by another Irish prelate, John Murphy Farley, the new head of the Archdiocese of New York. Despite such overtures, only a minority of Italian parents chose Church schools. Most couldn't afford the tuition. Others resented the anti-Italian prejudices of the Irish nuns who ran them.

The latter problem, of course, was no hindrance to Irish parents. A near-majority sent their children to parochial schools. Their finances had improved, so they could afford to, and they felt comfortable there. But even the Irish were divided. Many in the aspiring middle class favored the public schools. So did workers who supported the radical priest Father Edward McGlynn's battles with the "ecclesiastical machine." Both groups saw the city system, now purged of the grossest forms of anti-Catholic bias, as the likeliest passport out of the ethnic ghetto.

When it came, however, to the possibility of providing public funds to support Jewish and Catholic schools—as the state had accepted the funding of Jewish and Catholic charities—the Protestant establishment remained adamantly opposed. When the idea was broached in the 1894 state constitutional convention, delegate Elihu Root got on his rhetorical high horse. Recalling that his ancestors had "left their English homes in the reign of Charles the First, to escape that controlling force of Church and State united," he demanded the convention guarantee that "never in this state of ours shall be repeated that union of Church and State." Specifically the conclave should declare that "the money of the state shall not be used in aid or maintenance of any school or institution of learning wholly or in part under the control or direction of any religious denomination, or in which any denominational tenet is taught." And so it did.

EDUCATIONAL REFORMERS BELIEVED PATRIOTISM AND LITERACY WEREN'T ENOUGH to prepare pupils for the realities of the larger city. They needed "schooling for life." This battle cry meant different things to different wings of the movement.

Businessmen wanted city youths prepared for the job market. A proper curriculum would introduce pupils to the requirements of the industrial and commercial world, and prepare them to step directly into the occupational structure.

Charity workers proposed "preventive social work." Increasing the length of the school day would keep children off the street and away from their slum homes longer. This would allow schools to contest the impact of incompetent families and vice-ridden communities. Put "under the influence of educated, refined, intelligent men and women," one reformer argued, poor children would "be elevated and lifted out of the swamp into which they were born and brought up."

Settlement workers opposed derogation of Old World cultures. Lillian Wald, for one, warned against detaching the child "from the traditions which are his heritage." The practice diminished parents in their children's eyes. It contributed to family breakup and juvenile delinquency. Immigrant communities should be involved in the life of schools. And dull drills should be replaced by practical and stimulating courses that would ready children for work and an active citizenship.

A radical version of this latter vision was advanced by John Dewey, a Columbia professor of philosophy newly arrived in New York (in 1904) from the University of Chicago. Dewey had been closely associated with Jane Addams's Hull House settlement, and active in Chicago's educational reform movement, having set up an experimental Laboratory School at the University in 1896. In New York he was similarly engaged with the work of Wald's Henry Street Settlement. And while he was primarily engaged in philosophical battles during his first decade in Gotham, he did publish work on educational issues, culminating in his *Democracy and Education* (1916).

The point of education, Dewey believed, was not to reproduce the environment but to change it. In traditional societies, bent only on perpetuation, it made sense for the young to be brought up in (even coerced into) the ways of their elders. But modern (and certainly American) societies were in constant flux, and rather than repressing the natural questioning and curiosity of their young, schools should encourage them in exploring new ways of seeing the world. Education should be less about transmitting a fixed body of knowledge than about cultivating a spirit of experimental inquiry. This was especially vital in democratic societies, which Dewey believed should cultivate democratic dispositions. Schools— certainly "progressive" schools—could do this by themselves becoming exemplary social institutions. This meant abandoning rigid discipline, cultural orthodoxy, and the cultivation of a passive acceptance of authority, in favor of preparing children for a role in reshaping their communities.

Some of these pedagogical goals were complementary, others completely contradictory, but all envisioned greatly expanding the range and content of schooling. With so many powerful forces demanding educational intensification, Superintendent Maxwell embarked on ambitious changes, often by adopting and integrating programs that had originated in the private sector.

Kindergartens had been long in gestation. Felix Adler, and the German community in College Point, Queens, had inaugurated free kindergartens in the 1870s. Settlement houses, discovering their popularity with working mothers, rapidly expanded their number. The city experimented with them in 1893 and soon incorporated them en masse. By 1913 virtually every elementary school in New York had a kindergarten.

Special education classes were similarly transferred from settlement house to public school auspices. Henry Street's Elizabeth Farrell had worked out creative approaches to teaching the handicapped; in 1906 the Board of Education created a separate department and put Farrell in charge. The Association for the Aid of Crippled Children opened private classes on Avenue B in 1899; by 1910 the board ran forty-eight throughout the city. A friend of Wald's began teaching the "retarded" in 1902; by 1909 there were eighty-six classes for "children of retarded mental development" in the city system.

The board also took over settlement-initiated social service programs for school children. Wald and Simkhovitch urged school lunches to offset poor diets. Superintendent

"N.Y. Schools Opening," ca. 1910–15. (Library of Congress Prints and Photographs Division, George Grantham Bain Collection)

Maxwell took this up enthusiastically, as he did calls for providing baths and medical examinations. In 1906 Henry Street also set up study rooms—refuges from crowded tenements, street noise, poor lighting, bad ventilation, family fights, and absence of privacy—and stocked them with books and texts suggested by the local public school.

Some programs the school system had pioneered itself. New York City had provided evening adult education classes since the eighteenth century. The Public School Society had taken them over after 1823 and passed them to the new Board of Education in 1842. By 1898 the consolidated city was offering nighttime schooling to 50,000, a figure that doubled by 1907. Particularly popular were courses—often initiated by immigrant associations—that taught English. The Board of Education also offered a lecture program for adults. Talks, many in foreign languages, dealt with science, literature, history, art, and geology. In 1909 nearly a million people attended at least one.

ANOTHER SIGNIFICANT TRANSFORMATION IN NEW YORK SCHOOLING dealt with its relation to the sphere of play.

After school, children fled its ordered precincts and plunged into the streets—for many progressives, their great nemesis. Close behind them, notebooks in hand, trailed investigators hired by the Russell Sage Foundation or various settlement houses, tabulating youthful activities. Some seemed relatively innocuous. Girls on stoops and sidewalks played potsy, jumped rope, bounced balls, talked, and danced to the music of itinerant performers. Boys played stickball on the street itself, using broom handles and rubber balls; fire hydrants, lampposts, or manhole covers served as bases. New asphalt streets rendered dirt games like marbles and knives difficult but facilitated "skelly," which involved flicking checkers or bottle caps with thumb and forefinger along the smoother surfaces. Others hung out in the candy stores ("Cheap Charlies") that multiplied in the first years of the century until they were more numerous than saloons. Here kids talked boxing, baseball, and girlfriends/boyfriends, bought sweets for a penny, and patronized the new (1907) gumball machines.

Some forms of amusement were more disturbing. Boys stole from pushcarts and ice trucks. They hitched rides on the back of wagons and streetcars. They chased ambulances and fire engines. They lit bonfires. They fought with stones and snowballs. They played tag on roofs or competed at spitting or pissing from one roof to another. They congregated in street-corner semicircles to shoot craps.

Preteens who found the block too confining roamed to the river for a swim. (Willie Sutton, born in 1901, swam back and forth from Brooklyn through the floating muck.) Such travels led to violence when kids traversed defended turf. The warning-cum-greeting "What streeter?" often presaged a beating. Blacks in white neighborhoods risked serious bodily injury. Jews in Irish slums could get "cockalized"—thrown to the ground, pants opened, circumcised penis spat and urinated upon to accompanying shouts of "Christ killer."

Settlement workers, educators, clergymen, and assorted "child-savers" feared the streets, both their real dangers—like the new automobiles that killed hundreds—and, even more, the autonomy they afforded children. In sharp contrast to the schools, the streets seemed beyond adult command. Anarchy reigned. Bullies flouted rules. Gambling, rough-housing, and petty thievery were accepted. Even innocuous games appeared unstructured, unsupervised (though in fact young children were subject to lively surveillance from mothers in tenement windows overhead, older sisters on the stoops and sidewalks, and local shopkeepers).

Reformers believed moral and political relationships were learned in play. Given street-afforded license, kids would grow up bad. "If we let the gutter set its stamp upon their early days," Jacob Riis warned in 1904, "we shall have the gutter reproduced in our politics."

The antidote to the street was the supervised playground.

Settlement houses had opened rudimentary play spaces in the 1890s. In 1898 the Outdoor Recreation League (ORL), founded by Lillian Wald and Charles B. Stover and housed in the College Settlement, opened the city's first outdoor playground in Hudsonbank Park (at West 53rd Street), whose sand gardens, running track, and equipment were supervised by Hartley House's headworker.

Playground proponents insisted the city take over and expand these programs. An 1898 University Settlement report argued: "Waterloo was won in part on the playing fields of Eton said Wellington; good government for New York may partially be won on the playgrounds of the East Side." In 1902 the city assumed responsibility for the nine ORL playgrounds created to date. And in 1903 Seward Park became the first municipal park in the country to be equipped as a playground.

The Board of Education had its own play program. In 1895 Riis got the City Council to require that new schools be built with adjacent open-air playgrounds. Then settlement workers complained that once summer (or evening) came, the schools and their facilities sat empty. At their urging, in 1898, the Board of Education established "vacation schools." These offered daytime courses, evening recreational centers, and playgrounds (124 in 1912) supervised by directors of "unsoiled" moral character. A typical vacation day's play schedule began with marching, flag salutes, and patriotic songs; moved through organized games,

G. G. Bain, "Maypole Dance, Central Park, New York," 1905. (Photo Researchers, Inc./Alamy Stock Photo)

gymnastics, free play, drills, folk dancing, and the good citizens' club; and ended with singing, marching, and another round of flag salutes.[25]

In 1903 Maxwell and Luther H. Gulick organized the Public Schools Athletic League to arrange sporting contests between schools. Gulick, the Honolulu-born son of an American Bible Society missionary sent out to civilize the natives, abandoned a planned career of religious proselytizing for the kindred one of promoting physical education. After a decade of YMCA work he became director of physical training for New York's public schools.

Gulick believed team sports developed the "corporate conscience" required by the "complex interdependence of modern life." Self-sufficient craft work was out, cooperative factory labor was in. Street play reeked of primitive laissez-faire values, but team sports promoted conformity without obliterating individuality. Children who played together would work together.

Andrew Carnegie, John D. Rockefeller Sr., and Solomon Guggenheim agreed. With their financial support, the Public Schools Athletic League got off to a rousing start. Its opening meet, held in Madison Square Garden, included over 1,000 elementary school competitors. By 1907, with over 100,000 participants, it had become the largest program of organized athletics in the world.

In 1906 Gulick and others founded the Playground Association of America (PAA) to spread the New York gospel to the country. (Crucial funding would come from the Russell

---

25. English country dancing, imagined as the recreation of a pure Anglo-Saxon peasantry, allowed the "gaiety of youth" to find expression, without the sort of "dangerous expression" such exuberance was taking in cabarets and dance halls. Maypole festivities—an alternative to May Day parades—gathered enormous numbers of girls for orderly festivities. A Folk Dance Festival in Van Cortlandt Park assembled 2,500 in 1899; by 1914, 8,000 danced around a hundred maypoles in Central Park's Sheep Meadow while 15,000 looked on.

"Public Schools Athletic League, Meeting, Central Park, June 1913." Left to right: Theodore Roosevelt, Gen. George Wood Wingate, William Vincent Astor, Gustavus Kirby, Solomon R. Guggenheim. (Library of Congress Prints and Photographs Division, George Grantham Bain Collection)

Sage Foundation.) Honorary President Theodore Roosevelt wrote in the organization's magazine, the *Playground* (1907), that cities must find "some other place than the streets" for children to play "if we would have our citizens content and law-abiding."

Members were ecstatic about playgrounds' ability to produce "more loyal as well as more efficient citizens." One PAA director noted in 1907 that Tompkins Square Park, where once "the rally to the red flag" had been commonplace, was now "the scene of games...and other forms of patriotic play." Another suggested that six weeks of playground interaction between Jews and Italians so reduced animosities that "they did not know whether they were Jews or Italians."

Wishful thinking. In truth, fewer than 10 percent of the city's children used the playgrounds regularly. Many who did were middle-class kids, the same sorts drawn to the YMCA or the Boy Scouts. (The latter, an English import, set up national headquarters at 124 East 28th Street in 1910). Working-class youths, though drawn to the equipment and facilities, tended to balk at adult supervision and opt for the freedom of the streets.

WHILE SETTLEMENT WORKERS WORRIED ABOUT PLAY, businessmen fretted about work. Corporate managers had made great strides in wresting control over skills training from union-dominated apprenticeship programs. Now they needed an alternative. From the 1880s and 1890s prominent businessmen and business organizations—including J. P. Morgan, J. D. Rockefeller, Frank Vanderlip, the Chamber of Commerce, and the National Association of Manufacturers—had been pushing the public schools to offer vocational courses in industrial and commercial skills. They had warned that Germany's schools, which channeled pupils found unsuited for university studies into technical and vocational courses, were producing efficient workers, giving German competitors an edge in the "world's race for commercial supremacy."

Butler's Teachers College, which itself grew out of the manual training movement, embraced the corporate argument. So did settlement workers—though some worried that "vocationalism" might be abused. "If this movement becomes a tool in the hands of employers merely to produce more effective workers," Mary Simkhovitch warned, "public funds are being diverted from the proper function of creating citizens, to that of creating an industrial army." There was, however, widespread agreement that youths who left school after compulsion ended at age fourteen were being left without training that would prepare them for anything other than unskilled, dead-end, miserably paid jobs. Most reformers believed that only vocational programs could provide the skills needed to climb the economic ladder. What kind of education to offer, and whom to offer it to, were questions that took on increased salience when the public system began opening high schools—institutions aimed at the 14–17-year-old age bracket.

There had been a sprinkling of such secondary schools before Consolidation, notably in the outer boroughs. Flushing High School (1875) had been the first, though tiny and transitional. Brooklyn's paired Girls' High (1885–86) at 475 Nostrand and Boys' High (1891) at 832 Marcy had been the first to be purpose-built as high schools. In the new century, at Butler's urging, the Board of Education launched several such institutions, housing each in a grand Snyder structure. In 1906 De Witt Clinton High School for Boys occupied a massive Flemish Revival Snyder building at Tenth Avenue and 58th Street—with seventy-eight classrooms, the largest in the United States. Wadleigh High School for Girls (1902) settled into a Harlem space at 215 West 114th (named after Lydia Wadleigh, who had fought for free education for girls). Morris High School (1904) flourished in another showpiece, a huge English Collegiate Gothic at 166th Street and Boston Road in the Bronx. And on Staten Island, Snyder's Curtis High School opened on Hamilton Avenue in 1904. Later, several of the older and overcrowded high schools were Snyderized—receiving upgrades or add-ons designed by the master—among them Girls' High (1912), Flushing High (1912–15), and Erasmus Hall High, the latter done incrementally, with two new sections completed in 1906 and 1911. By 1914 twenty-three New York public high schools were in operation.[26]

Maxwell saw these schools as key steps on New York's educational stepladder that climbed "from the gutter to the university." They were aimed at preparing students for college or teacher-training institutions. But the high schools seemed more a barrier than a pathway. Fewer than 6 percent of high-school aged youths went in, and in 1906 74 percent of these dropped out. Critics claimed this proved the irrelevance of the traditional curriculum for immigrants and demanded "suitable" vocational courses. It was unwise, argued Dean James Earl Russell of Teachers College, to school the masses as one did the classes, as academic courses promoted dreams of professional status, and there weren't enough such jobs

---

26. Partly in response to this surge of public high school construction, the Catholic Church expanded its secondary school education offerings beyond its many private academies (most run by the Jesuits, De La Salle Brothers, and Sisters of Charity), which many parents could not afford. In 1905 the Cathedral School at East 50th Street added upper-level grades; in 1910 these split off to form Cathedral High School, the first in the archdiocese. In 1914 the Jesuits opened the (tuition-free) Regis High School for boys at 55 East 84th. And in 1915 the first multi-parish school, St. Peter's, was erected on Staten Island, at Richmond Terrace, staffed by the Christian Brothers and Sisters of Charity.

to go around. Maxwell disagreed. Students dropped out for economic reasons, he said, and he warned that closing off escape routes from poverty might well generate leveling measures.

A compromise was arranged. The leading high schools remained primarily academic institutions. They drew in the children of professionals and white-collar workers for whom private prep schools were out of economic or social reach but who had enough resources to postpone entering the workforce a few extra years. They also attracted the children of tradesmen, contractors, minor officials, and artisans or workers who aspired to escape from manual labor and saw a high school diploma as the ticket to white-collar work.

At the same time, separate "technical" or "manual training" high schools were established, like the High School of Commerce (1902) at 155 West 65th, the first to be devoted exclusively to commercial education. More industrial-oriented institutions included the Manual Training High School (1904) in Brooklyn at Seventh Avenue (between 4th and 5th Streets) and the Vocational School for Boys (1909) at 138th and Fifth, where skilled workmen instructors taught woodworking, plumbing, electrical trades, sheet metal work, machine tool use, printing, and bookbinding, and offered a two-year program for those who couldn't afford four years out of the workforce. The ne plus ultra of the genre, Stuyvesant High School, was established as a "manual training school for boys" in 1904 and was rehoused in 1907 in a $1.5 million Snyder extravaganza at 345 East 15th Street. Here, using the latest equipment, courses in drafting, printing, woodwork, plumbing, foundry work, and electrical wiring were offered to boys who wanted to work in machine shops, electric light and power plants, or the chemical departments of manufacturing or packing establishments. Stuyvesant grads were positioned as well to go on to higher technical institutions or even college, which the school facilitated by offering courses in geometry, chemistry, physics, English, American history, civics, and industrial and commercial law.

The city also provided equivalents for teenaged girls. The Manhattan Trade School for Girls had started in 1902 as a private institution, offering courses in dressmaking, millinery, machine sewing, and other aspects of the needle trades; in 1910, now at 209–213 East 23rd Street, it was taken over by the Board of Education. The Girls' Technical High School, also dating to 1902, developed in a different direction. Many working-class households had been sending daughters to factories so their brothers could go on to college and the professions. But with the expansion of white-collar work, Jewish and Italian girls became valuable resources themselves. Hence the success of Girls' Tech's latter-day incarnation as Washington Irving High School, to which it changed its name when it moved into a colossal Snyder building at 40 Irving Place in 1913. There it immediately drew 6,000 girls, most from Jewish East Side tenements. While the school did prepare these students for careers as dressmakers, milliners, bookbinders, and library assistants, and while it did offer college prep courses for those aiming to teach, its specialty was turning out the clerks, bookkeepers, and secretaries needed by the growing number of small Jewish businesses. To counter fears that vocational education would undermine students' eventual roles as wives and mothers, the curriculum included an apprenticeship in domesticity. Courses in marriage, baby care, personal hygiene, and household sanitation taught students how to speak, behave, and dress properly. A set of model stairs even allowed girls to learn the ladylike way to climb them. Wiseacres renamed it "Washing and Ironing School."

THE EMERGENCE OF THIS VOCATIONAL SECTOR TROUBLED SOME, like John Dewey, who had wanted industrial and academic studies to be integrated in the same institution. Like-minded critics feared vocational students were being funneled (at public expense) into the existing industrial regime, without having been equipped with the broader intellectual wherewithal that might have allowed them to critique that order, as was essential for a democracy. Reserving a broad liberal arts education for the elite, Dewey thought, while mainly providing workers with narrow technical training, would exacerbate not mitigate class divisions. Which makes it all the more remarkable that Dewey believed he'd discovered an ideal and actually existing approach to education, which had been devised by the biggest corporation of them all.

In 1906 the United States Steel Corporation founded Gary, Indiana, as a factory town in which to house the workers of its gigantic new plant, the Gary Works. In 1908 Gary hired William Wirt, who had been a student of Dewey's at the University of Chicago, to design the new town's school system from scratch.

First Wirt lengthened the school day to eight hours and the school year to twelve months. Then he divided the student body into two "platoons," one of which would study academic subjects, moving every hour from one subject-specific classroom (history, math) and teacher to another, while the other platoon rotated between non-academic spaces, some of them pre-vocational (science labs, forges, carpentry or print shops, on the order of those at Stuyvesant High), some of them geared to the fine arts (music studios, drawing rooms), or to physical education (the gyms), or to play (the school's playgrounds and ball fields), or to specialized lecture/screening spaces (the auditoriums). Halfway through the lengthened day the platoons would swap pathways, which halved the number of classroom seats needed at any one time, in effect doubling the school's capacity, and allowing it to accommodate twice as many students. (In the evenings, the schools were used for adult education classes or for events organized by community groups.) In addition, the students would "learn by doing," chiefly by helping skilled workers maintain the school itself. Domestic science would involve helping cooks run the school kitchen; skills learned in carpentry class would be further developed by helping adult carpenters build desks and chairs. Lastly, the school would draw upon the resources of the wider community—visiting museums, taking in concerts, touring factories.

Dewey was enthralled by this "work-study-play" approach—not surprisingly, as Wirt, his former student, had set out to demonstrate the practicability of his teacher's pedagogical ideas. Dewey applauded the Gary experiment in his *Schools of Tomorrow* (1915) for expanding education into the community, combining intellectual and practical work, and overcoming the dualism between the vocational and the academic. He arranged for further publicity by having Randolph Bourne, a former Columbia student and ardent disciple, dispatched by a New York journal to write about Gary. Bourne, who believed that conventional schools had "become as autocratic and military as the industrial" sector, was enchanted by his visit, hailing the school for producing not just workers but "critical citizens."

Someone else's interest was piqued by the Gary Plan—Gotham's newly elected mayor, John Purroy Mitchel—and he traveled out to Indiana in June 1914 with a coterie of New York educational officials to have a look. Mitchel professed interest in various aspects of the experiment, but what really grabbed his attention was the super-efficient utilization of classroom space.

Mitchel was hard up against an escalating school crisis. He was being prodded by bankers, lawyers, and other efficiency-minded businessmen who were appalled at the percentage of the municipal budget devoted to the school system, and the amount of money that had been expended during the McClellan and Gaynor years on the massive school construction program. In response, Mitchel adopted a "pay as you go" requirement for all capital expenditures, meaning new schools would have to be paid for out of current revenues. In the event, during Mitchel's mayoralty he would spend even less than the Board of Estimate authorized (only $5 million out of $17 million) for new sites, buildings, or alterations. Given that previous expenditures had failed to keep up with the rapidly growing school-age population, overcrowding and part-time classes could only get worse, and fast.

In this context, the mayor and Public Education Association watchdogs were thrilled with the prospect of vastly expanding the existing system's capacity. True, Gary-type schools needed a significant outlay of funds to build the labs and shops and playgrounds the platoon system required—equipping fifty schools would cost around $7 million. But eliminating part-time schooling in the conventional way, by erecting more buildings, would run to $42 million, so adopting the Gary Plan could be cast as an efficient response to the crisis. Given that its programming would also please the progressive education critics, "work-study-play" definitely seemed worth trying.

Wirt was hired as a consultant, and experiments were assayed in two overcrowded schools, one in the Bronx, one in Brooklyn, both of which were deemed successful. So was an expanded trial in twelve additional Bronx venues. Then in September 1915 the city comptroller recommending extending the approach to all congested schools. But by then a countercurrent had set in, largely of Mitchel's own making.

Given that the plan involved a 20-percent increase in teachers' working day, and an extension of the school year from forty to forty-four weeks, it might have been deemed wise to win the instructional staff over to the proposed new system. Instead Mitchel—already on record as believing that teachers were overpaid—announced that there would be no recompense for working extra hours, meaning effectively a cut in pay, and that the savings from installing the Gary Plan would allow him to cut the teaching force by 10 percent. When teachers objected, he attacked their character and motivation. Dewey complained that the administration had "presented its most brutal face" to the city's teachers. It also seemed to some critics that "study" and "play" had dwindled from the plan. The *New York Globe* lamented that "more and more, it becomes a device for reducing school costs and less and less a plan for enriching the educational opportunities for the children."

The Gary Plan's addition of a pre-vocational component to elementary schools raised concerns among some parents and students that the effort was really intended to shuttle working-class children into the blue-collar labor force, rather than on to college and the professional world to which a degree was deemed a passport. Tammany Hall—preparing for a comeback campaign against the Fusion Mitchel administration—held countless community meetings drumming up opposition to a corporate-spawned system "which aims to make our public schools an annex to the mill and factory." Superintendent Maxwell, citing some assessments that found Gary-type schools less successful at imparting basic skills, also advocated a more cautious consideration. Some unions switched to the anti-Gary column. And in October 1917 thousands of students (most under fifteen years of age, many of them Jewish) went out on "strike" against Garyized schools. Often accompanied by angry mothers, they launched demonstrations around the city, day after day, notably in East Harlem, Yorkville, Washington Heights, Williamsburg, and Brownsville. At one mass meeting a mother shouted: "We want our kinder to learn mit der book, der paper unde der pensil und not mit der sewing and der shop." Five thousand children marched through the streets, in some cases hurling rocks through school windows, hoisting banners reading "Down with the Gary System!" and "2-4-6-8-Whom do we not appreciate? Gary!" Even Teddy Roosevelt chided Mitchel for not having consulted with parents, and better explained the proposed changes, instead of jamming them down their throats. Having been transmuted into a major issue in the upcoming mayoral campaign, the fate of this reform would be settled at the ballot box.

BEFORE 1912 EDUCATIONAL REFORM, AND EFFORTS TO tackle health care, poverty, social insurance, and women's and children's labor—the whole panoply of initiatives grouped together under the "progressive" rubric—had been waged, for all their considerable overlaps in personnel and perspective, as single issue campaigns. But in that climactic year, an effort was made to assemble all the piecemeal efforts, in New York and throughout the country, into a single political movement, and Gotham progressives would be smack in the center of that campaign.

A BULLY MOOSE

On June 18, 1910, Teddy Roosevelt had returned to New York with blood on his hands and blood in his eye. In the spring of 1909 he had turned the White House over to William Howard Taft and gone off to Africa to kill and collect animal specimens (eventually bagging over 11,000 of them). Emerging from his eleven-month expedition, he had continued on to Europe for a grand tour. Then he sailed home to assault his successor.

President Taft had taken up TR's antitrust crusade, but all too enthusiastically. Instead of simply regulating the giant corporations, he was dismantling them—a retrograde strategy in Roosevelt's opinion.

Nor had Taft Republicans tackled the country's social problems, as British, German, and French politicians were doing. On his British visit, TR had been enormously impressed by the proto-welfare-state being established by David Lloyd George's New Liberal Party. England had already enacted workmen's compensation (1906) and old age pensions (1908) and was about to extend unemployment and health benefits to all citizens, along with establishing minimum wage requirements, public employment exchanges, and progressive land, inheritance, and income taxes on the rich to pay for it all. Their party, wrote New Liberal Winston Churchill in 1908, had "become acutely conscious of the fact that political freedom, however precious, is utterly incomplete without a measure of social and economic independence." The New Liberals had broken definitively with the laissez-faire Gladstonian tradition and, as the politically canny Roosevelt couldn't help noticing, had been amply rewarded at the polls.[27]

By contrast, Roosevelt worried, Republican stand-pat-ism was driving America leftward. Socialist Eugene Debs had drawn record support in the post-panic presidential election of 1908. Unless government addressed capitalism's defects, people would soon be following "every variety of demagogue and wild-eyed visionary."

So in 1910 Roosevelt decided to undertake a multi-state speaking tour with an eye toward snatching the Republican nomination from Taft and blocking its seizure by Robert "Fighting Bob" La Follette, who, as governor of and then senator from Wisconsin, had emerged as leader of the nation's insurgent progressive forces. La Follette, a consistent opponent of "vast corporate combinations" and their grip on the political process, had been promoting various forms of direct democracy, labor law, and social policy, in conjunction with an intellectual cohort of social scientists at the University of Wisconsin.

Over the summer of 1910, in preparation for his tour, Roosevelt read Herbert Croly's *The Promise of American Life* (1909), which cast the contemporary political scene, in peculiarly American terms, as a battle between Hamiltonianism and Jeffersonianism. Jefferson's

---

27 In Germany, Roosevelt had talked with Wilhelm II about social insurance, and in an address at the University of Berlin declared, "When in America we study labor problems and attempt to deal with subjects such as life insurance for wage-workers, we turn to see what you do here in Germany."

vision of limited government had been appropriate for the pre–Civil War decades, Croly argued, when small farmers and local businesses could be safely left alone to pursue individual wealth. But it was no longer realistic in an era of giant corporations. Now a strong Hamiltonian hand was needed to protect the citizenry from big business's consolidated economic power, and its concomitant ability to dominate the political arena. Not that Croly wanted the corporations broken up—the new economic order was far superior to the dog-eat-dog regime it had largely replaced—but they had to be reined in. The Sherman Anti-Trust Act should be repealed, he thought, and replaced with a National Incorporation Act, which would authorize the oversight and, if necessary, the nationalization of corporations. A strong central government could also "regulate the distribution of wealth in the national interest" by imposing an inheritance tax, and practicing "constructive discrimination" on behalf of poor and working-class Americans.

The man Croly thought could best serve as the people's tribune was his fellow New Yorker Theodore Roosevelt, who "may be figured as a Thor wielding with power and effect a sledge-hammer in the cause of national righeousness." This was catnip to TR, who thanked Croly for helping clarify his ideas. Borrowing his term "New Nationalism" (in preference to Lloyd George and Churchill's "New Liberalism"), he took Croly on as consultant and friend, and hit the road to test-drive his message before a national audience.

On August 31, 1910, he told 30,000 assembled citizens of Osawatomie, Kansas, that "the citizens of the United States must effectively control the mighty commercial forces which they have themselves called into being." This did not mean breaking up the corporations: "Combinations in industry are the result of an imperative economic law which cannot be repealed by political legislation. The effort at prohibiting all combination has substantially failed. The way out lies, not in attempting to prevent such combinations, but in completely controlling them in the interest of the public welfare." A Federal Bureau of Corporations should be set up to ride herd on the consolidated companies, but because there could be "no effective control of corporations while their political activity remains," the government had to first curtail their political power. The key to that was regulating campaign finance. "Corporate expenditures for political purposes," he explained, "have supplied one of the principal sources of corruption in our political affairs," and it was therefore "necessary that laws should be passed to prohibit the use of corporate funds directly or indirectly for political purposes." More broadly, the corporate class must itself be curbed. "The absence of effective State, and, especially, national, restraint upon unfair money-getting has tended to create a small class of enormously wealthy and economically powerful men, whose chief object is to hold and increase their power." One way to diminish that power would be to enact both "a graduated income tax on big fortunes" and "a graduated inheritance tax on big fortunes, properly safeguarded against evasion and increasing rapidly in amount with the size of the estate." In addition, "the officers, and, especially, the directors, of corporations should be held personally responsible when any corporation breaks the law."

Roosevelt's Osawatomie proposals left Taft aghast and much of the business world in an uproar. "His new doctrine is more and worse than rank Socialism," shrieked one editorialist; it "is communism at the limit." But TR pushed ahead, challenged Taft in a series of primaries in late 1911 and early 1912, and won nine out of twelve. (La Follette won two, Taft one.) The bulk of the delegates, however, were not chosen in primaries but by conventions, which party machines ruled, and they were overwhelmingly pro-Taft. At the Republican convention in Chicago in June 1912, Elihu Root commanded the president's forces—despite his longtime friendship for Roosevelt he put preservation of the party above personal loyalty—and he skillfully nailed down Taft's renomination. New York was awarded the vice presidency, but when Old Guard conservative James S. Sherman died a week before the election, Nicholas Murray Butler was designated as his stand-in, having also broken with his old friend Roosevelt, appalled by his lurch to the left.[28]

Roosevelt and his supporters now bolted the Republican Party and created a new entity, the Progressive Party. In August, also in Chicago, 2,000 delegates met to acclaim him as their candidate. Their platform—entitled a "Contract with the People"—while drawing on a variety of sources, owed less to Karl Marx than to Gotham-based social activists and businessmen.

The social and industrial planks of the Progressive platform had arrived in a ready-made bundle, the outgrowth of a decade of struggle, and of three years of deliberation by the National Conference of Charities and Correction (NCCC). Its assembled activists had been talking for some time of the need for a national movement, perhaps even a political party, one that would unite all the varied reform groups. In 1909 the NCCC had assigned to its Occupational Standards Committee, chaired by Paul Kellogg, the task of formulating an industrial social justice program. Kellogg was perfectly placed for the task, being a settlement worker, leading social researcher, and skilled writer and editor; his successor chairs, Florence Kelley and Owen Lovejoy (secretary of the National Child Labor Committee), were equally experienced veterans.

In June 1912 the Occupational Standards Committee issued a comprehensive program, endorsed by the NCCC, that it called "Social Standards for Industry"—quite similar to the "Social Creed of the Churches" promulgated that same year by the social gospelers of the Federal Council of Churches. It called for an eight-hour day, a six-day week, abolition of tenement manufacture, establishment of occupational health and safety standards, prohibition of child labor, regulation of women's employment, and provision of federal insurance against accidents, illness, unemployment, and old age. These were all reforms either in effect or long promoted in New York City.

When the NCCC adjourned, a group of Manhattanites—including Kellogg, John Kingsbury (of the AICP), Samuel McCune Lindsay (former director of the New York School of Philanthropy), and Homer Folks (of the State Charities Aid Association)—headed to Chicago to the Republican convention. There they presented their platform, which was rebuffed, and cheered Roosevelt, who was also rebuffed. In mid-July, back in New York, where the fledgling Progressive Party was preparing for its August convention, Kellogg, Kingsbury, and Henry Moskowitz (head resident at Madison House) traveled to Oyster Bay and presented their planks. Roosevelt adopted them wholesale and assigned the New Yorkers key roles in drafting the new party's platform. Belle Lindner Israels was ecstatic. In TR, she wrote Lillian Wald, "social reform has the services of America's first publicity man and our ideas will become common currency."

At the Chicago convention, in addition to industrial initiatives, the Progressives committed themselves to corporate, income, and inheritance taxes, a federal department of public health, women's suffrage, the direct popular election of United States senators, recall of judicial decisions and elected officials, and "the protection of home life against the hazards of sickness, irregular employment, and old age through the adoption of a system of social

---

28 In a 1911 Chamber of Commerce speech, with Morgan, Rockefeller, and Carnegie in attendance, Butler declared that Roosevelt would "change our representative republic into a socialistic democracy." He also defended the corporation, pronouncing it as "the greatest single discovery of modern times, whether you judge it by its social, by its ethical, by its industrial, or in the long run ... by its political effects. Even steam and electricity are far less important than the limited liability corporation, and they would be reduced to comparative impotence without it."

insurance adapted to American use." In seconding Roosevelt's nomination, Jane Addams declared that "the new party has become the American exponent of a world-wide movement toward juster social conditions, a movement which the United States, lagging behind other great nations, has been unaccountably slow to embody in political action." More than simply advancing a wish list of social engineering projects, the gathering was swept by religious fervor, the delegates breaking repeatedly into choruses of "Onward, Christian Soldiers." (Even New York's Progressive gubernatorial candidate, Oscar Straus, sang along.) The social gospel sentiment was fueled by Roosevelt, whose speech to the convention he called his Confession of Faith, the peroration of which was climaxed by his roared-out conclusion: "We stand at Armageddon, and we battle for the Lord."

The fired-up reformers now charged enthusiastically into campaign work. The party set up national headquarters at the Manhattan Hotel (42nd and Madison); the Republicans took space in the Times Building; and the Democrats moved into the Fifth Avenue Building (at 23rd Street). The roll call of Bull Moose activists—so-called because TR, queried about his health, snorted that he was as healthy as a bull moose—was a roster of familiar faces and some new recruits, including Mary E. Dreier, Homer Folks, Learned Hand, Stanley M. Isaacs, Belle Israels, Paul Kellogg, Frances Kellor, John Kingsbury, George Kirchwey, Samuel McCune Lindsay, Walter Lippmann, Owen Lovejoy, Henry Moskowitz, Maud Nathan, E. R. A. Seligman, Mary Simkhovitch, Joel Spingarn, Lillian Wald, and Walter Weyl. They worked as candidates, speechwriters, and ward organizers; they did research and publicity and fund-raising. Most were well educated and white collared, which pleased Roosevelt, who hoped "that in this movement for social and industrial justice and betterment the lead may be taken by those among us to whom fate has been kind, who have themselves nothing material to gain from the movement, and not by those who are sullen with a sense of personal wrong."

THE BULL MOOSE PARTY ALSO ATTRACTED A STRATEGIC (and distinctly un-sullen) stratum of New York City businessmen, led by George Perkins, the former New York Life executive and J. P. Morgan partner. Like others in a small but significant segment of corporate leaders, Perkins backed Roosevelt because TR accepted the giant firms' right to exist. More specifically, Roosevelt as president had blessed Morgan firms as being good, unlike Rockefeller firms, deemed wicked. And it had been President Taft's move in 1911 against United States Steel and International Harvester, two companies Perkins had been instrumental in assembling, that had precipitated his own revolt. More broadly, Perkins believed that corporations could live with Roosevelt's regulatory approach. Insurance companies and public utilities had managed quite nicely, after all. And government supervision was far preferable to either laissez-faire competition or state-directed socialism.

Perkins actually considered himself an "exponent of real and justifiable Socialism." In a lecture entitled "The Modern Corporation" he gave at Columbia in 1908, he had advanced the usual Morgan line. Competition was cruel, wasteful, and outmoded; cooperation was humane, effective, and modern; giant conglomerates offered standardization, efficient marketing, better research, steadier employment, higher wages, and the ability to flatten business-cycle curves by holding to fixed prices. But Perkins followed this logic further than Morgan did, by suggesting that corporations had acquired a public character and should welcome federal regulation. Indeed, he saw no difference between "the United States Steel Corporation, as it was organized by Mr. Morgan, and a Department of Steel, as it might be organized by the government." He felt equally comfortable with governmental supervision of labor conditions and supported social insurance programs. He could have called, but didn't, his preferred system Corporate Socialism or, following Hillquit, State Capitalism.

Perkins became Roosevelt's right-hand man. He chaired the party's executive committee, ran the national headquarters, and contributed over a quarter-million dollars to the Bull Moose campaign (earning the sobriquet "Dough Moose"). Equally munificent was publisher Frank Munsey, US Steel's largest stockholder.

THE COMBINATION OF NEW YORK CITY FUNDING, a New York City brain trust, a New York City headquarters, and a New York City candidate gave the Progressive Party a decidedly Gothamesque air. But while many Progressives were New Yorkers, most New Yorkers were not Progressives.

Though TR had indispensable support from key corporate executives, most businessmen and editorialists feared his program, especially his attack on the courts, which were seen as a bulwark against radical change. The *New York Sun* called the Progressive platform "a manifesto of revolution" that would create a "monstrous socialist despotic state." Most city-based captains of industry supported Taft.

Most city voters supported Woodrow Wilson. The Democratic candidate stoutly defended the little man and small enterpriser, contending that trusts foreclosed opportunity. Wilson's intellectual spear carrier, his equivalent of TR's Herbert Croly, was Louis Brandeis, who argued that competition and equal opportunity for small businesses was at the heart of American democracy. (Croly, in truth, had little sympathy for small business, declaring that "whenever the small competitor of the large corporation is unable to keep his head above water, he should be allowed to drown.")

Pointing to Perkins, Wilson accused the Progressives of being big-business puppets, and Roosevelt of being the corporations' front man, who would give companies free rein under the guise of regulating them. TR countered that he would "use the whole power of the government to protect all those who, under Mr. Wilson's laissez-faire system, are trodden down in the ferocious, scrambling rush of an unregulated and purely individualistic industrialism." But he had been maneuvered into seeming to support trusts, not a winning hand in 1912.

Wilson's campaign rhetoric also alarmed many on Wall Street, though he did have supporters there, if not in the highest circles. William Gibbs McAdoo, the expatriate Georgian who had built the Hudson River Tubes, was among the first to judge Wilson essentially safe; he would become secretary of the treasury. McAdoo also brought in other New York money men, notably Henry Morgenthau, who chaired Wilson's campaign's finance committee.

McAdoo also spotted Edward House, another southern expatriate, who'd been living in New York since 1902. (He'd settled into the Hotel Gotham, on Fifth Avenue at 56th Street.) "Colonel" House (the title was purely honorific) hailed from Texas, where he'd been a wealthy businessman (plantations, banks, railroads), and a kingmaker in the state's Democratic Party. Bored with Texas politics, he'd been looking for a national-level candidate to back, and McAdoo drew him into Wilson's quest for the Democratic nomination. In October 1911 Wilson called on the Colonel in his rooms at the Gotham. The two men hit it off immediately. With the nomination in hand, meetings came more frequently. In September 1912 House moved to an apartment in Murray Hill, at 145 East 35th Street, where he put Wilson up when the candidate came to town. Visits became even more frequent after the election, with House emerging as the president-elect's closest adviser, a one-man transition team. Wilson would often stay with the Colonel, talking appointments and policies late into the night (or catching a Broadway show, light comedies preferred).

Wilson offered House any cabinet post he wished (except for State, reserved for Bryan), but the Colonel declined, preferring the more influential position of informal consigliere. At times he traveled down to Washington, where he'd often stay in the White House, but he preferred to remain in Gotham as Wilson's man in New York (a special direct telephone line was set up connecting East 35th Street with 1600 Pennsylvania Avenue) and behind-the-scenes ambassador to Wall Street. Just before Wilson's inauguration in March 1913, House, on February 26, conferred with financial and corporate chieftains, among them Henry Davison (of Morgan), Otto Kahn (of Kuhn Loeb), and Henry C. Frick. At Wilson's instruction, the Colonel assured them that the incoming president was not going "to make an attack on business." House explained, privately, that Wilson's public campaign "utterances" were "idealistic" efforts to "raise the moral stamina of the nation, and were not for the purpose of writing such sentiment into law." The tycoons, House reported, were "like a lot of children whose fears must be quieted. They must be told there are no bears around to hurt them."

Nationally, Wilson had won with a plurality of 42 percent to Roosevelt's 27 percent, Taft's 23 percent, and Debs 6 percent. In New York City, Wilson had led the field with 47.3 percent, TR nailed down second place with 28.5 percent, Taft followed with 19 percent, and Debs got 5.1 percent. Progressives were not disheartened. They had pulled off an amazing feat in a scant three months. They were convinced that the election of 1912 was the beginning of a new political era. Looking ahead, the party organized a National Progressive Service

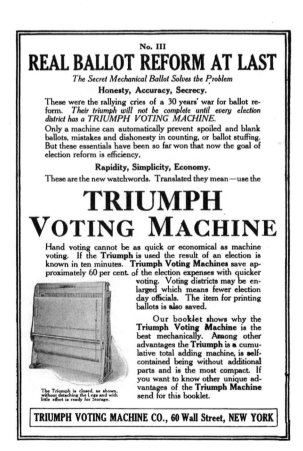

No. III
REAL BALLOT REFORM AT LAST
The Secret Mechanical Ballot Solves the Problem
Honesty, Accuracy, Secrecy.
These were the rallying cries of a 30 years' war for ballot reform. *Their triumph will not be complete until every election district has a TRIUMPH VOTING MACHINE.*
Only a machine can automatically prevent spoiled and blank ballots, mistakes and dishonesty in counting, or ballot stuffing. But these essentials have been so far won that now the goal of election reform is efficiency,
Rapidity, Simplicity, Economy.
These are the new watchwords. Translated they mean—use the

TRIUMPH
VOTING MACHINE

Hand voting cannot be as quick or economical as machine voting. If the **Triumph** is used the result of an election is known in ten minutes. **Triumph Voting Machines** save approximately 60 per cent. of the election expenses with quicker voting. Voting districts may be enlarged which means fewer election day officials. The item for printing ballots is also saved.

Our booklet shows why the **Triumph Voting Machine** is the best mechanically. Among other advantages the **Triumph** is a cumulative total adding machine, is self-contained being without additional parts and is the most compact. If you want to know other unique advantages of the **Triumph Machine** send for this booklet.

The Triumph is closed, as shown, without detaching the Legs and with little effort is ready for storage.

TRIUMPH VOTING MACHINE CO., 60 Wall Street, NEW YORK

Advertisement, Triumph Voting Machine Co. "Real Ballot Reform at Last: The Secret Mechanical Ballot Solves the Problem." *Survey* 29 (February 1, 1913).

(NPS), under Frances Kellor, to educate the public on progressive policy proposals and assist legislators in drafting progressive legislation. Run out of New York, the service enlisted a host of metropolitan talent, including John Dewey, Jacob Riis, Paul Kellogg, Henry Moskowitz, John Kingsbury, and Lillian Wald.

But even as the social activists organized enthusiastically, they saw ominous signs that the Progressive Party was fracturing along the business/activist fault line that from its beginning had divided Progressives into two wings. Increasingly, Roosevelt leaned ever more heavily toward the Perkins faction: "Defeat has thrown him clear back into the lap of the most conservative counselors of our party," Kingsbury decided early in 1913, and he "[has] become suspicious of the whole social worker crowd." Many of the latter began drifting away. Some turned toward the Democrats, as the Wilson administration showed signs of being amenable to some of their programmatic concerns. A fair number downshifted to municipal politics and accepted significant posts in Mitchel's mayoral regime. And in 1916, when the Old Guard Republicans, seeking reconciliation, nominated New York's moderately progressive ex-governor Charles Evans Hughes, Roosevelt refused the Progressive Party's nomination, rejoined the Republicans, and stumped for Hughes, and the nationwide political project collapsed. The city's progressive *movement*, however, soldiered on.

THAT MOVEMENT WAS MORE CAPACIOUS THAN THE PLANKS of the Progressive Party might suggest. At the city level, concerns over social order loomed large. Crime was on the rise. Progressives called for cracking down on violent street gangs, and on Black Hand or Mafia extortionists who leeched off the immigrant working- and middle-classes. Professionalizing police work was a reform that won supporters up and down the class scale. But there were social reformers and their elite underwriters who went beyond tackling unquestionably criminal activities—murder, robbery, blackmail—to attempting to criminalize working-class activities that clashed with middle- and upper-class conceptions of a proper social order.

Where the progressives pursued better housing, improved health care, greater access to education, and safer working conditions, those who might be characterized as "repressives" aimed at suppressing saloons, clamping down on gambling, outlawing boxing and horse racing, curtailing prostitution, prohibiting alcohol and drug use, banning "improper" dancing, muzzling movies, and censoring "obscene" books. They sought to criminalize behaviors they grouped under the category of "vice," especially as they were abetted by and in turn strengthened a corrupt Tammany Hall.

If the public faces of emancipatory progressives were settlement house workers, visiting nurses, muckraking journalists, and social gospel clerics, repressive progressives appeared in the form of vigilantes, censors, scientific criminologists, undercover snoops, eugenicists, and prohibitionists.

Yet while there were some individuals—funders and reformers—who worked exclusively in one or the other of these phalanxes, many more operated simultaneously in both. Convinced that laissez-faire was pernicious in politics and economics, they considered it equally appalling in culture and morals. For all their differences, progressives were linked by a readiness to use the state to impose what they believed to be a decent moral and economic order.

17

Repressives

GANGS OF NEW YORK

The shooting started in Livingston's Saloon, at the northwest corner of First Avenue and 1st Street, at 9:30 in the evening of September 16, 1903. As reinforcements piled in from the contending gangster armies—the Monk Eastmans and the Five Pointers—the battleground began drifting south of Houston Street. Combatants blazed away at each other from behind pillars of the Second Avenue El, which at that location ran along Allen Street. Bullets ricocheted here and there. Storekeepers barricaded themselves in. Tenement dwellers laid low in their rooms. Finally, after four hours, the fighting reached a crescendo with a furious fusillade beneath the Rivington Street station—"revolvers," the *Times* reported, "flashing on all corners." At around 2:00 a.m. the cops finally broke it up, and ambulances began ferrying the dead and wounded to Gouverneur Hospital and Bellevue's morgue.

Commentators groped for an appropriate metaphor. "They shot up the town in regular Wild West style," said one of the on-scene detectives. The *Times* suggested that lawless East Side gangs had "set up in New York City a feud code like that of the Kentucky mountains." It is true that in some respects the so-called Battle of Rivington Street resembled western gunfights or Appalachian vendettas, or, closer to home, the turf wars fought by their own ancestors—pre–Civil War gangs like the Bowery Boys and the Dead Rabbits. But there were significant differences.

For one thing, these twentieth-century contenders drew on contemporary immigration streams. The Five Pointers—a host of young thugs led by the dapper Neapolitan Paulo Antonio Vaccarelli (a.k.a. Paul Kelly)—was a predominantly Italian outfit. It controlled the blocks between City Hall and Union Square, from Broadway to the Bowery. Just to the east lay the preserve of a horde of chiefly Jewish toughs, the Eastmans, named after their ferocious commander, Monk Eastman. Their writ ran from the Bowery to the East River, within the same latitudinal bounds as their rivals. There were, to be sure, still gangs composed of older immigrant stock, notably Irish, such as the West Side's Hudson Dusters of Greenwich Village, and Gophers of Hell's Kitchen; and the East Side's Car Barn Gang (in the shadow of its eponymous structure at 97th and Second) and Gas House Gang (around the great red tanks at Avenue C and East 19th Street). But Jews and Italians occupied the cutting edge.

The gangsters of the early 1900s, moreover, were full-time crooks. Their nineteenth-century predecessors mostly had day jobs and hung out together only after hours, their primary motivations being comradeship and collective security. Essentially *criminal* entities first emerged with the river pirates (like the Daybreak Boys) of the 1850s and 1860s; more professionalized versions came along in the 1870s and 1880s with outfits like the Whyos. The 1900s gangs did still band together around commonalities like ethnicity and residence, and occasionally fought to ward off intrusions by aliens, but they were primarily intent on defending not homes but preying grounds. Much of Manhattan and sectors of the outer boroughs had been carved up into sharply demarcated kingdoms whose resident gangsters controlled the exclusive right to mug, burgle, pickpocket, extort, kidnap, and murder therein.

This helps explain why the new gangs were also more violent than their vanished forebears. Where the Roach Guards and Plug Uglies of yore had mostly fought with teeth, fists, clubs, and brickbats, their twentieth-century counterparts sported blackjacks, brass knuckles, stilettos, bludgeons, and often two revolvers apiece. Some of this was a matter of keeping up with evolving mayhem technology. But violence was now also a means to pursue or secure market share, as well as avenge perceived slights to group honor.

Violence was a commodity, too. The gangs furnished rent-a-goons to manufacturers out to break strikes, to unionists seeking to stomp scabs, to gamblers and brothel-keepers wanting protection or seeking to wreck rival establishments, to politicians wanting to blackjack opposition voters away from the polls. Slashings, maimings, bombings, murders—all were available for a price, often laid out quite precisely, as in a 1911 bill of fare that offered "Slash on the cheek with a knife...$1 to $10; Shot in leg...$1 to $25; Shot in arm...$5 to $25; Throwing a bomb...$5 to $50; Murder...$10 to $100 and up." Violence was also essential for enterprises like extortion. Gangsters offered "protection" to small-fry criminals, gamblers, and madams operating in their territory and levied tribute on local shopkeepers, urging them to buy tickets to gangland balls, a request they'd have been ill advised to refuse.

Finally, the new-model gangs appeared to be much larger than their antecedents. Claims were bandied about that rival ganglets had consolidated into vast agglomerations, containing a thousand members or more. This seems dubious. Though a few forward-looking sorts dreamed of transcending competition, as many industrial capitalists had, the Eastmans and Five Pointers are more accurately seen as loose confederations of criminal clans that really came together only once a year, on Election Day. And, unlike corporations, which could outlive their founders, gangs were constantly coming unglued through the assassination of their leaders, with the torch not so much passed to a new generation as wrested from the Old Guard's cold dead hands. Still, turn-of-the-century gangs, particularly the Jewish ones,

Monk Eastman. *New York World-Telegram,* December 27, 1920. (Library of Congress Prints and Photographs Division)

sustained a rough-hewn continuity, even underwent a certain development, as a genealogy of the Eastmans suggests.[1]

Edward "Monk" Eastman, the progenitor, was a holdover from the previous century's style of gang leader. Brawny and tough, he was a chieftain who led his men into battle, as with the Rivington Street affray, where he'd been on the scene pumping lead. He was born in 1873 to American parents—his mother, Mary Ellen Parks, apparently of English descent; his father, Samuel Eastman, a wallpaper hanger, from an old New Hampshire family. Both, perhaps, were Methodists; probably neither was Jewish (which Monk is conventionally assumed to have been, given the ethnicity of his followers). His first occupation, as listed in the 1900 census, was "Salesman, birds"—though a better characterization might have been "Thief, birds," as the stock of the pet shop he opened on Broome Street was largely stolen; indeed, his first arrest, in 1892, had been for purloining pigeons. Monk soon moved up to breaking and entering, for which, in 1898, he was sentenced to three months on the Island. When he got out he became a "sheriff" (bouncer) in Charles "Silver Dollar" Smith's saloon at 64 Essex Street (between Broome and Grand). He soon earned a reputation as a fierce street

---

1. Not all professional criminals traveled in packs. Skilled craftsmen of crime, in particular top-notch bank robbers, continued to freelance, though the ranks of these independents diminished as financial institutions successfully deployed private security forces and high-tech protective devices, like the robber-roaster in City Bank.

fighter, whose hard-punching, club-swinging, ear-biting, eye-gouging style left its mark on his victims—as they left theirs on him, leaving him with a scarred, battered, and usefully intimidating visage.

Eastman soon graduated to similar duties at the far larger New Irving Dance Hall (214 Broome), where the clientele leaned heavily to gangbangers and prostitutes, over whom he and his assistants kept order with bludgeon, blackjack, and brass knuckles. His assistants came to constitute the nucleus of his gang, which he headquartered in a dive on Chrystie Street, just off the Bowery. To this core group he recruited youthful Jewish criminals: pickpockets who worked weddings, funerals, and Yom Kippur services; "goniffs" (thieves) who stole and fenced clothes and furs from the neighborhood garment industry; pimps who ran Jewish girls; and tough guys—*shtarkers* in Yiddish—whose contributions were of the muscular/murderous variety. The Eastmans were prepared to hire out individuals or small groups as bodyguards, lookouts, runners, touts, doormen, debt collectors, etc.—for poolrooms, racetracks, saloons, brothels, gambling dens, etc. They were also proficient shakedown artists, whose methods ranged from upsetting the pushcarts of peddlers who didn't pay up, to attacking the employees (and destroying the stock and buildings) of stores, restaurants, or factories that failed to come across. The casualties of these operations were trundled off to the accident ward at Bellevue, in such numbers that the ambulance drivers started calling it "the Eastman Pavilion."

Crucial to Eastman's rough dominance over his growing horde was his status as the interface with Tammany Hall. Monk had attained this position by working for Silver Dollar Smith (né Finkelstein), who in addition to owning a saloon was a potentate in the Lower East Side Democratic Party, providing Irish pols with an entrée to the growing Jewish electorate. Smith began relying on Eastman to help scare up votes. And when Smith died in 1899, the powers that be, centrally Big Tim Sullivan, turned to Eastman for assistance. Assistance meant providing "repeaters" prepared to fulfill Tammany's injunction to "Vote Early and Vote Often." At six o'clock on election mornings, ten to fifteen of Monk's hoods were first in line at every polling place in the district, after which they'd move on to the next, and the next, collectively casting a substantial number of ballots. Should any poll watchers be rash enough to challenge a repeater's credentials, Eastman sluggers would beat them to a pulp. Should overzealous cops arrest a repeater (283 were so detained in 1903), Sullivan provided him with bail money, usually forfeited, especially as the gangsters gave phony names. And should someone actually go to trial, sharp Tammany lawyers would be on hand to represent him, often before a complicitous Tammany-appointed magistrate. This symbiotic relationship—the gangsters providing votes, the politicians providing protection—had been foreshadowed in the 1830s, but back then gangsters had unquestionably been mere hired hands. The scale of voter fraud in the twentieth century—it was the massive Election Day turnout that gave plausibility to membership claims in the thousand-plus range—elevated the status of gangster go-betweens like Monk closer to parity with Tammany chieftains, close enough to begin to worry the likes of Big Tim.

The Five Pointers had a similar origin story. Paolo Antonio Vaccarelli, born in New York in 1876, became a bantamweight prizefighter in the 1890s, and, as was de rigueur, assumed an Irish *nom de boxe*, Paul Kelly. In 1901 he organized the Paul A. Kelly Association at 24 Stanton Street, which mixed sporting, political, and illicit activities, and later opened his own saloon at 57 Great Jones between Lafayette and the Bowery, named the New Brighton Dance Hall (a.k.a. the Little Naples). Kelly had an altogether different style than plug-ugly Monk's. A dandy, he wore expensive threads and brilliantined his hair. He spoke four languages and was well versed in classical literature. But the ex-pugilist could break bones and wield a knife or gun with the best of them, essential skills for acquiring the street cred required of a gang leader.

Like Monk's crowd, Kelly's collection of Italian thieves, thugs, and pimps was a confederation of mini-gangs. Again, the Tammany connection was crucial to group cohesion. Sullivan, an equal opportunity employer of gang muscle, first turned to Kelly's outfit for help in an intramural fight, the 1901 Democratic primary in the Second Assembly District. Tim's man in that race was Tom Foley, who was challenging the Old Guard incumbent Paddy Divver. Kelly's army of Italian repeaters and sluggers overwhelmed Divver's own shock troops, and Foley won three to one. Having proved his mettle, Kelly was granted the Tammany seal of approval: the Big Feller became an honorary member of the Paul Kelly Association, and authorized the hanging of his portrait in Kelly's dance hall headquarters.

When it wasn't Election Day, the two gangs remained bitter rivals and roiled the East Side with their constant combat. Tammany, reliant on both sides, felt obliged to mediate, arrange truces, and demarcate territory. In 1903 Alderman Tom Foley sponsored a peace conference on Staten Island, at which he stressed the counterproductive nature of violent street brawls, and threatened to withdraw protection if the gangs didn't kiss and make up. They did, at a chowder ratification feast at New Dorp on Staten Island. But embarrassments continued—the vendetta dynamic kept overmastering the business-mindedness—and in the end Tammany made good on its threat and brought Monk's leadership years to a close.

In February 1904 Eastman and a colleague were leaving a Times Square saloon on 42nd Street at Sixth Avenue, at three in the morning, when they noticed a well-dressed young drunk, fresh from carousing at Rector's. Unable to pass up the opportunity for a quick mugging, they drew their guns. It turned out that the young man's prominent father had hired two Pinkertons to protect his wayward son. They intervened, and a running gun battle erupted, Monk sprinting away along 42nd Street while returning fire, until at Broadway he was laid low by a policeman's nightstick. Usually such a spot of bother would have been smoothed over by Tammany. This was too over the top, and Pinkertons couldn't be bought off as cops could, so Monk was left to twist in the wind. Consigned to the Tombs, Eastman was tried, found guilty of felonious assault, and in April sentenced to ten years in Sing Sing. He received the court's permission to postpone his trip up the river until he could find someone to tend his now 500 pigeons. That accomplished, he was taken north from Grand Central, with a crowd of 5,000 on hand to gawk or bid farewell.

This precipitated the gang's first succession crisis, which was eventually settled when 20-year-old Max "Kid Twist" Zweifach successfully killed or intimidated his rivals. The Kid, who dressed like a prosperous young banker, brought a bit of order to the gang's affairs, regularizing the shakedowns of legitimate businesses. Innovatively, he started up a quasi-entrepreneurial sideline, manufacturing a celery tonic that he then compelled all small refreshment and confectionery stores in his territory to buy. After ruling for four years, in May 1908 the Kid was shot and killed at Coney Island by Louie "the Lump" Poggi, a member of the Italian Five Points Gang.

Next up was Zelig Zvi Lefkowitz, who also ascended by violence, though in his case fisticuffs proved sufficient. Zelig was born to Russian Jewish parents in 1888. His father was a successful tailor, but the son, at age 12, opted for pickpocketry. In 1901, caught by passersby as he attempted to snatch an old lady's purse, he was sentenced to eighteen months in the ancient House of Refuge (1824), located since 1854 on Randall's Island. In April 1906 he was nabbed ripping off a passenger on a subway platform and sentenced to a term in Sing Sing,

G. G. Bain, "Tombs Prison," n.d. (Library of Congress Prints and Photographs Division)

where he immersed himself in reading Dickens. Out again in 1908, he returned to picking pockets, until November 1910, when he single-handedly beat up three fearsome desperadoes and was elevated to leadership (and renamed "Big" Jack Zelig) on the strength of his martial prowess. His reign was marked by violent assaults on Italian gangsters operating in Jewish territory. Partly this was a matter of business—fighting off Italian pimps seeking to recruit Jewish girls, or Italian robbers holding up Jewish gambling houses. But he was also hailed by respectable opinion for service to the community, as when his men protected Jewish passengers being harassed on streetcars. After a successful two-year run, Zelig was murdered in October 1912 by an Italian gangster, under murky circumstances, while on an outing at Coney Island.

Zelig was succeeded by Benjamin "Dopey Benny" Fein (né Feinschneider). Dopey was by no means dumb, though he did look doped up, which he wasn't, but rather suffered from an adenoidal infliction that gave him a heavy-lidded look. His father was a tailor, but Benny preferred picking pockets or stealing packages from delivery wagons. After two brief terms in Blackwell's gloomy old Workhouse (1852) for theft, he joined the Eastmans, rose in the hierarchy, and in 1912, fresh from a stint in Sing Sing, won the top slot, in part because of his special expertise in an emerging gangster profit center.

His predecessor Zelig had expanded what had been in Monk's day a peripheral enterprise: intervention in labor conflicts of the Lower East Side garment industry. Struggling unions, confronted with management-hired professional strikebreakers like James Farley and Pearl Berghoff, began to turn to Jewish gangs as counterweights. Zelig had been politically sympathetic—his sister Ida worked in a shirtwaist factory—and Fein too declared, "My heart lay with the workers." But with labor conflict heating up after the 1907–8 recession, it was a lucrative leaning as well. As Fein later reminisced, his first job as a "gangster for hire was to go to a shop and beat up some workmen there." His employer, a union official, paid him $100, and $10 for each man hired. He got a brigade of sixty men together, divided them into squads, passed out pieces of gas pipe and clubs, and beat up the scab workmen. "I was always busy after that."

Fein led his own troops into battle. On one occasion he had his nose broken fighting scabs at a Brooklyn factory. (He charged an extra $30 to have it repaired.) And he had a sharp eye for talent; his gang included future underworld luminaries Waxey Gordon, Lepke Buchalter, and Gurrah Shapiro. But his real métier was organization. He took the business to a whole new level by arranging a retainer deal with the United Hebrew Trades (UHT), whose lawyers drew up contracts stipulating weekly wage and price lists for protecting picket lines, attacking scabs, or wrecking nonunion shops. This arrangement broke down in 1914 after Dopey, having been arrested for efforts on the UHT's behalf, felt inadequately supported by the union leadership in his hour of need. So he cut a deal with the district attorney, trading his release for a full and detailed accounting to a grand jury of his strong-arm work (he'd kept meticulous records), which led to the indictment of eight labor leaders, including the UHT president. The labor movement rallied to the UHT's defense, correctly seeing the proceedings as an attempt to break the union, and in October 1915 the officials were found not guilty. Yet the UHT hadn't denied the facts of the charge, and had indeed more or less justified hiring gangsters as a necessity-dictated response to employer violence. Despite their short-term victory in the courts, the long-term consequence was that racketeers had become embedded in the union movement, though, for the moment, only as subordinate hired hands. Not Dopey Benny, who soon retired and became a successful garment businessman.

FEIN HAD ALSO BEEN A PIONEER IN ATTEMPTING TO ESTABLISH pacts of cooperation between rival criminal concerns in the nascent labor racketeering industry. Such efforts had proved unavailing, partly because savvy employers turned to hiring Italian gangsters to protect their strikebreakers. Indeed, on one occasion in 1913 mobsters on opposite sides of the picket line had exchanged gunfire outside Feldman's hat-frame factory on Greene Street.

By that time the Italian Five Points Gang had long since passed out of Paul Kelly's hands. Back in 1905 violent dissension had broken out among his followers, and the gang had fractured along its internal lines of cleavage. Two attempts had been made on Kelly's life. (First he was knifed in the back; later he was shot three times.) He survived but prudently retired from the field, leaving the schismatics "Big" Jack Sirocco and Chick Tricker to assume ownership of the Five Points Gang banner.

Kelly himself moved uptown to the safer precincts of the Italian colony in Harlem, and by 1909 he'd effected a lateral career move, as portentous as Dopey Benny's insertion of Jewish gangsters into the garment industry. Kelly became an organizer and strike leader for the Garbage Scow Trimmers' Union, then the only New York local affiliated with the International Longshoremen's Association (ILA). In 1915—having reassumed the name Vaccarelli—he was made a vice-president of the ILA. And in 1916 he oversaw a waterfront strike, in which management claimed he used gangsters to threaten recalcitrant members. If true—and Vaccarelli protested that he'd gone legit—it marked the arrival of Italian gangsters on the waterfront.

By then the Five Pointers had largely faded away, replaced in the world of Italian criminality by two new distinct (but often confused) underworld phenomena—one not really an organization at all, but rather a modus operandi, the other an American variant of an infamous Mezzogiorno secret society.

IN SEPTEMBER 1903 NICOLA CAPPIELLO, a wealthy Brooklyn contractor, received a letter, signed by the "Mano Nera" (the Black Hand), demanding $1,000, and warning that refusal to pay would lead to his house being dynamited. When the money was duly proffered, another $3,000 was asked for. At this point, Cappiello went to the police, and one Biaggio Giordano of Sackett Street was arrested.

Though the Cappiello case was one of the first instances in which the term "Black Hand" was introduced, the incident itself was only the latest instance of what had become since 1901 an avalanche of blackmail attempts in the Italian colonies of Manhattan and Brooklyn. Hundreds of wealthy Italians—doctors, bankers, storekeepers, opera singers (notably Caruso)—received letters threatening to kidnap their children, bomb their property, or kill them, if they didn't pay up. "Sunday at ten o'clock in the morning," read one such, "at the corner of Second Street and Third Avenue, bring three hundred dollars without fail. Otherwise we will set fire to you and blow you up with a bomb. . . . I sign the Black Hand." These missives were often adorned with coffins, skulls, daggers dripping blood, and handprints affixed in thick black ink. Nor were they empty threats. A wave of bombings and kidnappings broke out in Italian neighborhoods, and by 1904 Gotham was in the grip of a full-fledged panic. "The city is confronted with an Italian problem," one paper fretted that year, "with which at the present time it seems unable to cope."

The sensationalist press (and Italian language papers, too), seeking to explain the outbreak of violence, pushed the argument that a single criminal society—"perhaps the most secret and terrible organization in the world"—was behind the rampage. "THE BLACK HAND DOES EXIST!!" shrieked a 1906 *Tribune* story that attributed to the shadowy organization hundreds of extortions, dynamitings, and murders. The police and some Italian *prominenti* ridiculed the notion, and indeed the Black Hand soon proved to be not a centralized organization but a disparate crew of parasites, individuals working alone or in small-scale partnerships. The letter-writing practice was probably inspired by extortion rings common in Sicily since the end of the 1890s.

That the villains were operating severally and not jointly didn't make them easier to catch.[2] Nor were the perpetrators always strangers; they might be former friends and business associates, at times even the "victims" themselves—as when failing merchants employed arsonists to assume the guise of the Black Hand and burn down their premises for the insurance money. Nor did one have to be Italian to love the tactic. One group of Jewish extortionists, who specialized in threatening stable owners with poisoning their horses, styled themselves the Yiddish Black Hand Association.

AMID THE UPROAR OVER THE BLACK HAND CRIME WAVE came news that a different kind of menace might have arrived in New York. In July 1902 a corpse was discovered at the foot of 73rd Street on the Bay Ridge shoreline. The victim, eventually identified as one Giuseppe Catania, a Brooklyn grocer, had been beaten savagely, his throat slit from ear to ear, his body then doubled over and sewn up inside a potato sack. Immediately it was noted in the press

---

2. As one victim, a landlord, recounted: "The Black Hand come and demand $7,000. I tell them to go to hell. They try to blow up my house. I go to the police and fight them as well as I can. They set off another bomb; two, three, four, five bombs. My business is ruined. My tenants leave, all but six of 32 families. I have $1,000 interest coming due next month that I cannot pay. I am a ruined man. My family live in terror day and night. There is a policeman in front of my house, but what does he do? Only my brother Francisco and myself can watch with my wife and children, who dare not go out. How long must this endure?" It was, he noted, "an extremely difficult thing to catch a Sicilian bomb planter in the act," as it was easy to slip his stick of dynamite with a long fuse under the front stairs, ignite the fuse, and quietly slip away. He might have added that dynamite was readily to hand at innumerable construction sites around the city, where Italians were the primary labor force.

FACSIMILE OF A TYPICAL BLACK HAND LETTER, WHICH, TRANS-
LATED, READS:

This is the second time that I have warned you. Sunday at ten o'clock in the morning, at the corner of Second Street and Third Avenue, bring three hundred dollars without fail. Otherwise we will set fire to you and blow you up with a bomb. Consider this matter well, for this is the last warning I will give you.

I sign the Black Hand.

"The Black Hand." *Everybody's Magazine*, September 1908.

that the murder had all the earmarks of a Mafia-style execution. But no one could prove who did it; no one was even accused of the crime.

Then, on April 14, 1903, another grisly discovery turned up. A scrubwoman passing by a lot at East 11th Street and Avenue D noticed a 3-foot-high barrel that on closer inspection, to her horror, proved to have a corpse crammed within. It had been doubled over, and its throat slit from ear to ear, all but severing the head from the body.

With remarkable dispatch its identity was discovered—one Benedetto Madonia, a recent arrival from Sicily—and police asserted again, more vigorously this time given the similarity to the Bay Ridge murder, that it looked like the Mafia had come to town. Reputable Italians were quick to deny any such thing as the Mafia even existed, and if it did, it certainly wasn't in New York City.

In fact, both sides were correct; Sicilian mafiosi had indeed arrived on the Gotham scene, but not the feared criminal syndicate itself. The perpetrators of the "Barrel Murder" (and probably the Catania killing) had actually arrived a decade earlier, in the person of one Giuseppe Morello, known as "the Clutch Hand" because of his deformed right hand. Morello hailed from the village of Corleone (Lion Heart), south of Palermo, where as a youth he'd been initiated into a Mafia family of which his stepfather was a prominent member. Morello began his life of crime as a cattle thief, then moved into counterfeiting. In 1892, when the Corleone police issued a warrant for the 25-year-old's arrest, he fled to New York. He was followed six months later by his wife, mother, sister, stepfather, stepsister, and three stepbrothers (Nicola, Ciro, and Vincent Terranova). The Morello-Terranova clan settled down on East 116th in Harlem's Little Italy, where there was already a small colony of Corleonesi. Morello had not been dispatched by Mafia central headquarters to set up a Gotham branch office of the Italian secret society; he was just a bad guy on the lam, though one who bore with him cultural seeds that would germinate and flourish in New York.

At first, actually, Morello had tried to go straight. But the '90s depression had blown in shortly after he had, and there was almost no work to be found. The Morellos went south, found jobs on a Louisiana sugar plantation, then sharecropped in the Texas cotton fields. They returned north in 1896 with sufficient savings to open an ornamental plastering business. Morello worked alongside his stepfather and then, with more ambition than business

"Photographs Taken at Police Headquarters To-Day of the Twelve Men Arrested on Suspicion of Being Involved in Barrel Tragedy." *Evening World*, April 16, 1903.

acumen, struck out on his own, setting up, in turn, a coal basement, a saloon on 13th Street, another on Stanton Street, and a date factory, all of which failed.

In 1899, his money mostly gone, Morello returned to his counterfeiting roots. Installing a small printing press at 329 East 106th Street, he turned out badly printed five-dollar bills, on poor-quality paper, replete with spelling errors. These were then put into circulation by some Irish "queer-pushers," who bought the phony bills at a discount and passed them off on bartenders and shopkeepers in the wider city—successfully, until they were caught and arrested in 1900. Morello himself was hauled in, though, having maintained an arm's-length distance from the pushers, he was let go for lack of evidence.

Convinced he needed confederates of assured loyalty and efficiency, Morello decided to organize a gang of his own, and between 1900 and 1903 he assembled New York's first Mafia family (a.k.a. *cosca*—artichoke—after the tightly knit relation of its constituent leaves). The thirty or so men (including Madonia) were all related by blood or marriage, recruited from Corleone, or recommended by bosses in Sicily; in this sense only did his group constitute a transatlantic tentacle.[3]

Morello's most important recruit was the Palermo-born Ignazio Lupo, a Mafia-connected man who had fled to New York in 1898 to escape arrest for the killing of a rival in the wholesale grocery business. Lupo soon hooked up with Morello, whose stepsister he married in 1903, and became known throughout the Italian community, somewhat redundantly, as Lupo the Wolf (Wolf the Wolf). He set himself up as an importer of oil, cheese, wine, and lemons, and built an impressive chain of wholesale grocery stores, the largest being at 210–214 Mott Street in Little Italy. One of the secrets of his entrepreneurial success was that he browbeat Italian retailers into buying his goods by threatening to bomb their buildings. The grocery business also dovetailed nicely with counterfeiting, as he and his associates could now send plates to Italy, print the currency over there, then smuggle bills back inside olive oil cans.

In January of 1903 members of the gang, in possession of counterfeit money, were arrested in Yonkers. Morello and Lupo, fearing that Madonia might prove a squealy wheel, dispatched him in a pastry shop basement, then trucked his embarreled mutilated body to a public place where his corpse would advertise the fate that awaited betrayers. The two men were arrested for Madonia's murder—and both were also suspected of Catania's (Lupo having been the last person seen with him alive)—but in the end they were reluctantly released for lack of evidence.

The Morello gang now laid off counterfeiting, and carried on with their distinctive mix of straight and crooked projects. With the city economy booming, and the Italian quarter receiving some of the benefits, Morello entered the construction trade, incorporating the Ignatz Florio Co-Operative Association of Corleonesi to erect tenements in the Bronx and sell them to better-off Italian immigrants. The gang also engaged in extorting other enclave businesses—coal, ice, artichokes, chickens—by imposing regular weekly payoffs ("skiming the cream off the milk without breaking the bottle," as one mobster put it). Morello also returned to horse thieving—stealing and reselling the animals after changing their appearance, trimming their manes and docking their tails at an equestrian chop shop.

Then came the 1907 recession. It hit Little Italy hard. Twenty-five banks in the community failed, costing 12,000 customers their life savings. Hundreds of small businesses

---

3. Apparently by coincidence rather than plan, Don Vito Cascioferro, one of the Sicilian Mafia's most powerful bosses, happened to be living in New York in this period. He'd arrived in September 1901 and would spend two and a half years in Gotham, during which time he was often seen in the company of Giuseppe Morello. Clearly there were at least individual links between Palermo and the fledgling New York Mafia.

went to the wall. One of the casualties was the Ignatz Florio Co-Operative Association, which by 1908 had defaulted on its obligations. Lupo's grocery business, too, toppled into bankruptcy. To escape his creditors, Lupo left town and situated himself upstate, in Ardonia, New York. It was there he and Morello decided to get back in the counterfeiting game, and in December 1908 they press-ganged an immigrant Italian printer into restarting operations.

Their handiwork was soon spotted by William Flynn, head of the New York office of the Secret Service, a branch of the Treasury Department, nine-tenths of whose manpower and budget were then devoted to catching counterfeiters (especially in New York, the money center). Flynn—an efficient and persistent sleuth—nailed Morello, Lupo, and more than thirty associates. In January 1910 they were tried and convicted in New York's Southern District federal court (still located in the Post Office building in City Hall Park). The judge gave Morello not the usual two-to-three-year sentence but twenty-five years at hard labor. (On hearing this the Clutch Hand collapsed in a dead faint.) He gave Lupo thirty. The gangsters organized a "fund-raising campaign"—terrorizing East Harlem peddlers, merchants, and bankers into coughing up cash to hire Bourke Cochran, a high-priced Tammany-connected lawyer, to handle their appeal, but it was dismissed in 1911.

With Morello and Lupo behind bars in an Atlanta federal penitentiary, the Terranova brothers, Ciro, Vincent, and Nicholas (aged 23, 25, and 21, respectively) took over. But they proved unable to dominate the expanding Italian underworld: partly because they'd lost so many of the original Morello gang due to death, defection, and incarceration; partly because they were not as ruthless as Morello and Lupo.

They were challenged on two fronts. One new contender consisted of recent immigrants from Naples who established in Brooklyn two branches of the Camorra, a secret society even older than the Mafia. The two groups, one on Navy Street near the Navy Yard, the other down at Coney Island, began muscling local merchants into switching protection payments to them rather than the Terranovas. In 1916 they went after the East Harlem mafiosi directly, inviting Nicholas Terranova to a dinner to discuss possible joint ventures, where they wined, dined, then murdered him. The Harlem Mafia gang and the Brooklyn Camorra gangs now embarked on an all-out war. Bodies piled up. In the end, a disaffected Camorra member turned state's evidence and confessed to a litany of murders, which led to the arrest, trial, and lengthy incarcerations of key Camorrans, in effect eliminating them as a serious contender for mob dominance in New York.

The Sicilians were another story. Newcomers continued to pour into Gotham in the 1910s, most of them from towns other than Corleone. The criminally inclined among them were aware that, as outsiders, if they signed on with the Terranovas they'd never be trusted with real authority. Plus it was a huge city, with plenty of elbow room in which to establish rival *cosche*. New formations crystallized, one led by Nichola Schiro, composed of recruits from the small port town of Castellamare del Golfo, and another run by Salvatore D'Aquila of Palermo, whose big-city members believed themselves superior to backcountry bumpkins. The Terranovas remained in the running, however, and the Mafia, though now divided into four or five families, had arrived, big-time, in New York City.[4]

---

4. There were also signs they established a rudimentary machinery for avoiding endless warfare between them. Some former participants, notably mobster memoirist Nicola Gentile, state that a Council of senior bosses from around the country existed, as did a larger General Assembly (150 men at times), which could elect capos, and debate proposed hits on rogue mafiosi. In this emergent system of cities, New York had primacy of place, notably in its right to select the Boss of Bosses, a chair whose first occupant was Morello. But the degree of effective authority these entities could muster remains unclear.

TONGS SERVED A MULTITUDE OF FUNCTIONS and embraced a variety of constituencies, which gave them considerable strength and stability. Tongs were—more or less simultaneously—business and trade associations, fraternal and benevolent societies, welfare and social service agencies, criminal and political confederations, self defense organizations and secret societies. Though rooted spatially in their tiny micro-domains, they were linked to networks of similar entities throughout the United States and in China.

There were two principal tongs—the On Leong and the Hip Sing—each with a different class base. The On Leong, led by Tom Lee (self-styled "Mayor of Chinatown"), was a merchant-based tong whose members included some of the most prestigious and powerful businessmen in Chinatown, owners of restaurants, stores, and import-export firms; indeed, "On Leong" was often translated as "Chinese Merchants Association." The On Leongs also regulated illegal enterprises, like gambling halls, opium dens, and brothels, and handled the payoffs to police and politicians such businesses entailed. They kept in Tammany's good graces by turning out the few existing Chinese registered voters on Election Day, which ensured protection by (and from) the police officers at the nearby Elizabeth Street Station. Their base of operations was on Mott Street.

The Hip Sings, headed by Mock Duck, ruled over Pell Street, which T-junctioned into Mott. Their base was in the Chinese working class—overwhelmingly laundrymen, who worked in shops throughout the city—and their criminal income stream included profits from smuggling people and opium from China. What the Hip Sings lacked in elite resources and political connections, they made up for by flaunting their facility with violence, based on the ferocious reputation of their West Coast comrades, and the presence among their own ranks of numerous *boo how doy*, a.k.a. highbinders, a.k.a. hatchetmen (from their weapon of choice). These salaried assassins were versatile figures, handy for kidnapping rivals, providing security for other tong members, and diverting some of the vice industry's extortion payoffs from On Leong to Hip Sing pockets. For a time the elite tong considered these losses an acceptable business expense, partly as the scary *boo how doy* did keep overall extortion payoffs flowing. But in 1899, after Mock Duck arrived in town from San Francisco, the number-two operation began pushing for half of number one's profits. Given that the Chinese were tightly contained in Chinatown, there was no way the On Leong could compensate for such a Manhattan loss through outer-borough gains. Chinatown crime was a zero-sum economy. Full-scale combat was unavoidable.

The tong wars that began in 1899 were an on-again, off-again series of clashes—isolated shootings, stabbings, and hatchetings, raids and counter-raids, gun battles in the street—that went on for much of the century's first two decades. The On Leong hired their own professional killers, and the Hip Sing brought in reinforcements from California. In one peak moment, on August 6, 1905, tong members blazed away at one another inside the Chinese Theater at 7 Doyers Street; the affray made national headlines. The wars were interrupted by spasmodic episodes of peace, one in 1906 brokered by the Chinese emperor's representative, the Chinese consul, and a barrage of lawyers, police, and political figures. The contenders agreed to divide gambling profits, which had been driven down by years of combat, and crackdowns by police and vice reformers, but, as in the mainstream business world, such efforts at restraining competition often came unglued.[5]

---

5. At times the rivals subordinated their differences to larger agreements, notably their joint backing of the republican movement fighting to overthrow the Qing (Manchu) dynasty. In December 1911 both tongs pledged financial support for the revolutionary forces—"We have buried the hatchet in the breast of the Manchu dynasty," said "Mayor" Tom Lee. And on January 1, 1912, both sides hailed the establishment of the Republic of China by hoisting its new flag, saluting a painting of its new president, Dr. Sun Yat-sen, and setting off thousands of firecrackers.

COPS AND ROBBERS

Faced with rampant and violent criminality, the moral reformers (like Parkhurst and Moss of the Society for the Prevention of Crime and the City Vigilance League), the businessmen and professionals of the Ci.ty Club, and various elected and appointed city officials, argued that criminals' customary immunity from arrest stemmed from Tammany's willingness to protect gangsters in exchange for Election Day services and a share of their ill-gotten gains. The machine was able to do this, reformers believed, because police hiring was decentralized and commercialized: precinct inspectors and captains owed their bought-and-paid-for jobs to Tammany district leaders. The first step on the road to reforming the corrupt criminal justice system, therefore, would be to centralize and professionalize the department. This approach was pursued for the better part of twenty years, with forward movement depending on whether reformers or Tammany controlled City Hall.

At the formation of Greater New York, the various borough forces had been folded into a single New York Police Department (NYPD). Unfortunately for the reformers, Tammany won the first post-Consolidation election, and the four-man Board of Police Commissioners handed the office of chief of police to the notoriously corrupt Big Bill Devery. In 1901, however, Theodore Roosevelt, in his last days as governor, signed legislation that replaced the four-man commission with a single commissioner, and abolished the office of police chief, putting paid to Devery's career (though he and Tammany wangled a short reprieve, ended definitively when Seth Low took office on January 1, 1902).

The Low administration set in motion plans for a Central Police Headquarters at 240 Centre Street (between Broome and Grand), a baroque City Beautiful structure pointedly designed to "impress both officer and prisoner...with the majesty of the law"; it would open for business in 1909. For the new top-cop spot, Low opted for a military man, Brigadier General Francis V. Greene, who had commanded the second Philippine Expeditionary Force. Greene, not surprisingly, opted for a military approach to law enforcement. To deal with gang violence, he decreed what might be called a "stop and club" policy.

After the September 1903 Rivington Street shootout Greene told the press: "There will be no more of that kind of lawlessness if I can help it. There is entirely too much of it." To execute his get-tough approach he turned to Max Schmittberger, the cop whose crucial testimony before the Lexow Committee had implicated high-level police officials. Hated by Tammany and fellow officers, he'd been in the doghouse ever since. Now Greene promoted him to inspector, the department's highest rank, and made him his strong right arm.

Schmittberger and his men stormed Paul Kelly's Stanton Street headquarters, cracking Five Pointer skulls with locust nightsticks (less prone to splitting than hickory or oak), then demolishing the premises. "You cannot deal too severely with these men," Schmittberger explained. "We will attend to the other gangs in a similar way." And indeed a pounding of the Eastmans followed hard upon, with Monk himself taken down the following year. Schmittberger, aware these thrashings didn't have much lasting effect, argued that court complicity made it impossible to break up the gangs permanently. "We have arrested them time and time again," he complained, "but the Magistrates let them go." Reformers duly put judicial reform on their to-do lists.

Tammany returned to power in 1904 with Mayor George McClellan, whose choice for commissioner was William McAdoo (no relation to William Gibbs McAdoo), a former congressman and assistant secretary of the navy. In his two-year term (1904–5), McAdoo undertook several important initiatives. One was to send Detective Sergeant Joseph Faurot to study

Joseph "Joe" Petrosino, ca. 1904–9. (Granger)

fingerprinting in London, where Scotland Yard had used it for several years.[6] Another was to establish an Italian Squad.

Italian *prominenti*—many of them victims of Black Hand extortion—had been calling loudly for more Italian police. They argued, with some justice, that little was being done to deal with murders and dynamitings in the Italian quarters because most Irish cops didn't much care what Italians did to one another, and the few who did lacked the language and community connections essential to effective policing. So in September 1904 McAdoo set up a special squad containing all the Italian-speaking detectives on the force—all six of them, later trickled up to thirty—and gave its command to Detective Sergeant Joseph Petrosino, later elevated to lieutenant.

Petrosino, born in Padula, south of Naples, had been brought to the United States in 1873, at age 13. He had assiduously worked his way up from shoeshine boy to foreman on garbage scows to the city Sanitation Department (one of Waring's White Wings), then joined the police in 1883. Petrosino was only 5'3"—he wore lifts in his shoes—but was well muscled, fearless, and shrewd. In an effort to keep their identity secret, Petrosino and his men avoided headquarters and operated for a time out of his two-room apartment. But there were so few of them that their faces quickly became known. Indeed, established gangsters set up something of a reverse rogues' gallery and pointed out the not-so-undercover operatives to newly arriving crooks. The semi-secret branch made hundreds of minor arrests but won few

6. Faurot spent two years in this endeavor, but on his return in 1906 McAdoo's successor had no interest in the newfangled notions. He pressed on, compiled his own fingerprint file, and in 1908 solved a murder case using the new technology. But the department remained leery until, in 1911, Faurot proved its value with a bravura courtroom demonstration that led to the first conviction in New York City on the basis of fingerprint evidence.

convictions, witnesses being hard to come by as they had little reason to believe the police could protect them.

In McClellan's second mayoral term he replaced McAdoo with General Theodore A. Bingham, a retired army engineer. He would serve as police commissioner from 1906 to 1909.

For Bingham, crime in Gotham was almost entirely a corollary of immigration. As he explained in "Foreign Criminals in New York," an article he published in 1908 in the *North American Review*, immigration had brought to the city's shore "the predatory criminals of all nations," along with their squabbles—"the feuds of the Armenian Hunchakist, the Neapolitan Camorra, the Sicilian Mafia, the Chinese Tongs, and other quarrels of the scum of the earth." Collectively, he estimated, 85 percent of the criminal element were "of exotic origin."

Half this total, he adjudged, were "Russian Hebrews," who preferred crimes against property. "They are burglars, firebugs, pickpockets and highway robbers—when they have the courage." But though the Jews were numerically predominant, "the Italian malefactor is by far the greater menace to law and order," as "while the great bulk of these people are among our best citizens, there are fastened upon them a riff raff of desperate scoundrels, ex-convicts and jailbirds of the Camorra and the Mafia."[7]

Bingham admired the "rigorous punitive supervision" to which such "banditti" were subjected in Italy (one reason, he thought, they relocated to Gotham in the first place). Emulating that approach, he authorized aggressive street patrols in immigrant communities, and ordered police to keep nightsticks in their hands at all times, with which to dispense rough justice. One Brooklyn cop recalled the method for dealing with pimps: "A strong punch in the jaw, a sharp rap of my lead-laden night stick taught them to stay clear of my beat."

But the police swung their clubs indiscriminately. They cracked the skulls of drunks; they arrested people for violations of minor regulatory ordinances, like improper garbage disposal. They clubbed boys for playing ball on Sunday and threw them into verminous cells. In 1909, of the 11,000-plus children taken into custody, nearly half were charged with trivial violations—flying kites, building bonfires, playing shinny (street hockey), splashing under hydrants.

Bingham's seeming determination (noted one critic) "to put the town under martial law," along with his "autocratic and severe" style, generated protests from a wide variety of quarters.

He angered the German Jewish establishment with his suggestion that Jews, who constituted 25 percent of the city's population, contributed 50 percent of its criminals. Stung by his article, they dissected his figures and demonstrated that after subtracting petty "crimes" like peddling from pushcarts without a license, or violating Sunday closing laws, Jews accounted for only 16 percent of the city's felonies. Bingham was forced to agree, and retracted his accusation.[8]

---

7. Frank Moss, of the Society for the Prevention of Crime, held much the same view. The Lower East Side, he wrote in his *American Metropolis*, was "filled with a polyglot wriggling compound, in which are some of the basest and most despicable of humanity's scum. It is a foul, writhing mixture, and it exhales a poisonous miasma that is as evident as any east side smell and far more dangerous to the city." He did, however, think that Jews, not Italians, were the more serious menace, as "the criminal instincts that are so often found naturally in the Russian and Polish Jews come to the surface here in such ways as to warrant the opinion that these people are the worst element in the entire make-up of New York life."

8. Though they easily refuted the wilder claims about Jewish dominance of the underworld, the German Jewish elite had to admit that Jewish criminality was a real problem. The newly minted Kehillah, a federation of Jewish organizations spurred into being by Bingham's charges, didn't demand the commissioner establish a Jewish version of the Italian Squad—the department had already expanded to include over 200 Jewish cops. Instead, the Kehillah created a parallel police department, the Bureau of Social Morals, which hired private detectives to investigate the Jewish underworld and then report their findings to the NYPD.

Bingham also angered the Italians with his indiscriminate rousting and abusing of ordinary immigrants. *Il Progresso* complained bitterly of the *brutalità dei poliziotti*—and also of false arrests, attempted shakedowns, and outright thefts. Bingham scathingly rejected such charges, and officers rarely got even the slightest punishment.

It didn't help Bingham's standing with Italians that, incautiously, he had sent Lieutenant Petrosino to his doom. Hoping to use a provision in a 1907 immigration law that allowed deportation of aliens if it could be proven they were wanted by the law in their country of origin, Bingham dispatched Petrosino with a list of several hundred Italian criminals whose records he was to bring back to the United States. Details of his mission made their way into the press, some of them blabbed by Bingham, and on March 12, 1909, Petrosino was assassinated on a street in Palermo—the four bullets in his back partly the result, it appears, of collusion between New York and Sicilian mafiosi.[9] His body was brought back to Gotham, and a requiem mass held in old St. Pat's, after which a huge procession, including over 3,000 members of the NYPD, accompanied Petrosino to his grave in Calvary Cemetery, as an estimated 200,000 lined sidewalks and windows along the route.

Bingham's list of enemies was further swelled when powerful Tammany chieftains realized that efforts to curtail police abuses would be highly popular on the Lower East Side. Big Tim Sullivan accordingly sponsored a bill in the state legislature in 1909 that would have banned police use of blackjacks or brass knuckles, claiming he sought to disrupt "a rule of armed terrorism" in his district. Commissioner Bingham denounced the plan and ensured its defeat.

Bingham also alienated the police rank and file. The Patrolman's Benevolent Association (PBA) had won an eight-hour day, with three shifts replacing the old two-shift system (under which police were on duty for thirty-six hours at a stretch), though Bingham yanked this victory away from them. They were also upset by his tying promotions (or demotions) to the number of arrests an officer achieved. And many of the department's foot soldiers were demoralized by the corruption for which they were lambasted by press and pulpit, though most of the graft lined their superiors' pockets. The PBA wanted to strengthen civil service provisions, which would curtail Tammany's influence. Bingham wanted to concentrate further power in the commissioner's hands, and in this he was backed by most reformers, who feared unionization more than corruption. The police mounted protests, like refusing to patrol on the third (night) shift, and raised a fund with which to lobby Albany against Bingham's centralization scheme—to no avail.

Bingham's anti-union animus was not restricted to the PBA. He also kept up a full court press against labor unions and radicals. On his watch, police notoriously sided with employers by protecting strikebreakers and arresting union picketers. And in 1906 an Anarchist Squad began harassing and arresting radicals, barring them from meeting halls and blocking distribution of papers like Emma Goldman's *Mother Earth*.

In the end, Bingham's most dangerous adversary proved to be William Gaynor, at that point still a justice of the New York State Supreme Court. Gaynor had long criticized police abuses from the bench, especially assaults on "those whose rights and liberties ought to be jealously guarded, namely the weak, uninfluential, and friendless, whose protection should be the chief aim of government." Then he went public with his critique, challenging the

---

9. The hit was widely believed to have been carried out on orders of Don Vito Cascioferro but set in motion by the then-at-large Morello gang; Lupo was reported as having said, "Some credit is due us though the Palermo gathering will get most." No one on either side of the Atlantic was ever charged with the killing.

treatment of one George Duffy, a Brooklyn milkman, who had been seized as "a suspicious person," held overnight, photographed, and then released without charges. His photograph was nevertheless added to the now over 13,000 images in the department's rogues' gallery, supposedly reserved only for those convicted of a crime. Police detectives accordingly continued to harass Duffy, at times arresting him on sight. Gaynor urged Bingham to remove Duffy's picture. Bingham refused. The judge published a letter censuring the commissioner and calling on the mayor to remove him. Bingham tried to justify his position by maligning the milkman as a "degenerate." Mayor McClellan, already alarmed at the volume of complaints about his commissioner, ordered an investigation of the Duffy affair. It supported Gaynor's charges. McClellan told Bingham to expunge the photo, to establish a procedure for investigating allegations of malfeasance, and to fire several officials. When Bingham balked, McClellan fired him for insubordination.

This dramatic turn of events proved mere prelude to a far bigger upheaval, when Boss Charlie Murphy, more than ever convinced that playing to popular resentment of police harassment was now a winning electoral card, chose Gaynor himself to run as Tammany's candidate for mayor, and Duffy's defender coasted to victory in 1909.

When he took office in 1910, Gaynor ordered a sharp change of course. He prohibited police use of clubs on citizens except in defense of their own lives, encouraged people to come forward with complaints of police brutality (some showed up at City Hall with bashed and bleeding heads), and instructed commanders to give all such charges immediate attention and, if the accused were found guilty, to dismiss them summarily. He also barred warrantless raids, removed photos of all non-convicted from the rogues' gallery, and ordered the police to issue summonses for petty offenses in lieu of arrests. By the end of his first year in office, total arrests had dropped from 220,334 in 1909 (compared with 111,000 in London despite its much larger population) to 170,681 in 1910 and to 153,768 in 1911. He also ordered the force to remain neutral in industrial disputes and to respect the rights of strikers. (Moonlighting as management muscle was put off-limits, too.) Socialist and other dissenting orators and demonstrators were to be tolerated so long as they remained orderly. The mayor also responded to the police rank and file's complaints, restoring the three-shift system and ruling that vacancies on the force be filled from the civil service eligible list in strict numerical order.

Reform opinion, however, soon shifted against Gaynor. Parkhurst's Society for the Prevention of Crime, the City Club, Republicans, anti-Tammany Democrats, and the Hearst papers declared he'd "gone too far" and turned soft on crime. Most of their animus was directed at his refusal to wage war on "vice" (e.g., refusing to arrest Sunday drinkers), but they also charged that the police were handcuffed, that street gangs were running rampant, that criminals were flocking to the "wide open" city. In short, New York was being inundated by a full-fledged "crime wave" (a relatively recent coinage). Manhattan's recently elected district attorney, Charles Whitman, a Republican and no friend of Gaynor, encouraged a grand jury investigation in March and April 1911 and assigned reform zealot Frank Moss, whom he'd appointed first assistant district attorney, to aid it. The grand jury heard contradictory assessments about a supposed increase in holdups and robberies, and varying responses to charges that demoralized police were backing away from confronting gangs lest they violate departmental edicts. In May the panel decided no indictments were warranted but asserted there were some parts of the city in which "gangs of hoodlums" were not being properly restrained, and in such areas plainclothes policemen "should have a freer use of their clubs."

A complementary anxiety was triggered by a Coroner's Office presentation at the end of January 1911 of data on recent Manhattan homicides. It found that the number had risen sharply from 110 in 1909 to 185 in 1910.[10] (The latter figure had nearly included the mayor himself, given the assassination attempt in August.) This report reinforced growing worries on the part of Tammany politicians that gang violence was getting out of hand, even *their* hands. In response, Big Tim Sullivan introduced a bill into the state senate in 1911 making it a misdemeanor to possess pistols, blackjacks, bludgeons, brass knuckles, stilettos, dirks, daggers, slungshots, or sandbags without a permit, and a felony to have one of these on one's person. Gun manufacturers made a fuss, but Sullivan overrode resistance by noting that respectable opinion was firmly on his side, specifically citing Jacob Schiff, John D. Rockefeller Jr., Nathan Straus, the Merchants' Association, the City Club, and the NYPD. Indeed, "the only thing they found bad about the bill," Sullivan wryly informed the senate, "was that Tim Sullivan introduced it." The law went into effect on September 1, 1911, and became a model for gun-control legislation across the country. Policemen cheered, as the Sullivan Act increased their leverage over gangsters. They could now plant guns on miscreants and then arrest them for carrying concealed weapons; smart mobsters had their suit pockets sewn up, and had their aides or womenfolk tote their revolvers.

Faced with such widespread criticism of his constraints on clubbing, Gaynor made a partial retreat. First he picked a new police commissioner, Rhinelander Waldo, scion of an old New York clan. A West Point graduate, Waldo (like Greene) had fought in the Philippines against rebel Moro tribesmen, first in the 17th Infantry, then as an officer commanding 250 natives of the Philippine Constabulary. The *Times*—having recounted how Waldo had imposed "order" on "gangs of brigands"—expressed confidence in May 1911 that he could "handle his job here on Manhattan Island as well as he handled his job out on Mindanao Island."

In July, Waldo established an undercover Special Squad of men known for their fighting abilities and assigned them (unofficially) to beat up gang hoodlums and roust street-corner roughs. The squad's command was assigned to Lieutenant Charles Becker, who, being 6'2" and weighing 200 brawny pounds, seemed well qualified for the post. Becker, born in 1870 to German American parents, had grown up poor on a farm in the Catskill foothills of rural Sullivan county. In 1890 he'd moved down to the Lower East Side's German district, where he worked at various odd jobs, including a stint as a bouncer at a beer hall off the Bowery. In 1893 he joined the NYPD, having saved up the $300 required to grease his way into office. He swiftly made it back, by becoming a protégé of graft-master Alexander "Clubber" Williams. After Williams's fall, Becker's career was becalmed until, in 1911, he was chosen by Waldo to take back the streets, and he and his Special Squad (popularly known as the Strong-Arm Squad) waded vigorously into work.

First they tackled the Car Barn gang, a vicious crew from the East River docks, that had not only carved out a domain bounded by 90th/100th/Third and the river, but had taunted the police by posting placards reading: "Dead line for cops, by order of Mayor Gaynor."[11] Worse, they had beaten up and in one instance stabbed officers who entered their territory. Becker now smashed his way into their headquarters, clubbed them into submission, and arrested the lot. Next he went after the Gophers of Hell's Kitchen; then, what one reporter

---

10. There was a similarly sharp rise in the numbers issued by the Department of Health (larger because they included, e.g., "justifiable" homicides). These increases appeared steep to contemporary observers, but were well within normal fluctuations of New York City's nineteenth- and early-twentieth-century homicide rate, which ranged from 3.0 per 100,000 to 6.0.

11. The well-understood reference was to the 1880 declaration by Chief Inspector Thomas Byrnes, then head of the police department's detective bureau, that henceforth Fulton Street was to be considered a "Dead Line," south of which criminals (of the blue-collar variety) would not be tolerated, thus establishing a protective cordon around the Wall Street community.

Police Lieutenant Charles Becker, ca. 1912. (Bettmann/Getty Images)

referred to as "the Negro toughs of San Juan Hill." Waldo also provided the squad with a sixty-man auxiliary force they dispatched around the city, dispersing or arresting rowdies who at ferry landings, street corners, and train stations molested women and extorted money from passersby. Within a few weeks, Becker and his men were princes of the city, the subject of lavish press attention. "The Strong Arm Squad a Terror to the Gangs," the *Times* exulted. "The Rowdies Who Make Trouble Get a Dose of Their Own Medicine."

The next administration completed the "restoration of nightstick rule." Mayor Mitchel formally revoked Gaynor's anti-clubbing decree and set out to suppress the gangs at all costs. "I hope the police will use their clubs on every gunman on whom they can lay their hands," he declared. By 1916 the larger outfits had been broken up into smaller criminal groups. Mitchel's police commissioner, Arthur Woods, claimed (overly optimistically) that "the gangster and the gunman are practically extinct."

Woods's term (1914–17) was about more than clubbing. Unlike many of his recent predecessors, Woods, from a wealthy Boston family, was not from a military background. After graduating from Harvard he taught English literature at Groton (to young Franklin D. Roosevelt, among others). Later, with help from his friend Jacob Riis, he shifted careers and worked as a police reporter on the *Evening Sun*. There he got interested in police reform, and in 1907 Bingham had appointed him a deputy commissioner, whereupon he went to England at his own expense to study the methods of Scotland Yard.

When Mitchel made him commissioner, Woods set about professionalizing the NYPD, now 11,000 strong. He established a well-equipped detective college; created specialized units for homicide, robbery, pickpocketing, etc.; opened a Training School for Police, which not only taught modern methods of policing but suggested alternatives to clubbing and shooting; and encouraged college graduates to join the force. Woods emphasized crime prevention. Believing that much criminal activity was due to bad environment—terrible housing, bad jobs, social neglect—he sought to enlist the police in solving community problems (and improving the NYPD's image). Working with philanthropic organizations, he established community relations programs; cops visited schools, formed a Junior Police force, set up a Committee for the Relief of the Unemployed, and found jobs for hundreds of ex-prisoners. To reduce the temptation to graft, he set up a loan fund for police with financial problems.

Mitchel and Woods also maintained Gaynor's tolerance of unions, socialists, and anarchists—insisting on police neutrality and permitting public protest meetings. In 1914, after an anarchist bomb intended for John D. Rockefeller (in revenge for a massacre of miners in Ludlow, Colorado), accidentally exploded in a Lexington Avenue town house, Woods also created another specialized unit, the Bomb Squad, principally intended to infiltrate and disrupt domestic radical groups. In 1916 it was revealed that in recent years police had tapped 350 phones, including those of labor unions and churches.

VICE AND VIGILANTES

The furor over how to police street gangs and secret societies did not exhaust the public conversation about crime in Gotham. Far from it. The debate over proper procedures was a narrow one. It was about *how* to combat such malefactors, not *whether* to do so. No one defended gangsters' crimes—murder, kidnapping, extortion, burglary, and street thuggery. Nor, apart from the perpetrators, were there many who stood to gain, even indirectly, from such crimes being committed. Their depredations were not only against the law, but against public opinion. There was almost universal agreement that some kind of policing was desirable. The discussion was about means, not ends.

There were other forms of behavior—prostitution, gambling, and the consumption of drink and drugs being the chief instances—that were to one degree or another defined as crimes, though their criminality was contested by significant portions of the general public. These disagreements gave rise to a far broader and more contentious conversation, not about crime but about criminalization, about whether or not certain behaviors *should* be outlawed. This was a discussion about ends, not means.

The debate was driven by a reform community that, taken as a whole, was opposed to this triad of activities, which they grouped together under the general category of "vice." Reformers seeking a crackdown on long-tolerated social behaviors were happy that vice had been criminalized. Many, believing its various incarnations merited even stronger legal condemnation, pushed to enhance state sanctions, up to and including outright prohibition. In the meantime they took it upon themselves to spur enforcement of existing laws whenever they believed the police and courts were unable or unwilling to do so. Some activists engaged in direct action campaigns, and proudly assumed the label "vigilante"; others proceeded more cautiously, clamping down on vice using legal, political, and even commercial means.

The circle of vice reformers was relatively small but extremely influential. It was drawn principally from civic elites—bankers, corporate executives, men and women of property and pedigree—and from a wide range of professionals, notably clergymen, settlement workers, lawyers, academics, journalists, physicians, social workers, and even some politicians (primarily upstate Republicans). Motivations varied—businessmen feared disorder, evangelicals battled sin—but their commonalities tended to outweigh their differences, and they often pulled together. When they did, the reform coterie was capable, at particular junctures, of mobilizing support from other social sectors for an assault on a particular vice.

Beyond this reform circle lay the vast majority of the population who were more or less content with the status quo, or who wanted to *loosen* legal constrictions. Many New Yorkers were to one degree or another actively involved in the vice economy: as consumers—people who paid for sex, drank on Sundays, bet on horses; or purveyors—prostitutes and pimps, barkeeps and brewers, bookies and casino operators; or enablers—policemen and magistrates who were paid to look the other way. This massive congeries of constituencies could also be mobilized, on occasion, particularly by Tammany politicians, to oppose further criminalization, or even to push for decriminalization of one or another of the three vices.

Because criminalization (or decriminalization) could be enacted only by duly constituted authorities (federal, state, or municipal), disagreements over commercialized vice perforce spilled into the political arena. Indeed, uproars over prostitution, donnybrooks over gambling, and battles over drink and drugs would become hallmarks of the era.

PROSTITUTION

In 1902 the anti-brothel Committee of Fifteen published its final report, *The Social Evil*, and disbanded. Finally, its members believed, a reform government had come to power that would take up their fight against prostitution in Gotham. Seth Low had won the 1901 mayoral election; even better, the new district attorney was their ally William Travers Jerome— the activist judge whose "brass checks" campaign had just wrested many voters away from Tammany. But in short order it became apparent that despite a series of Jerome-led raids on brothels, the supply of prostitutes continued to grow, in tandem with expanding demand.

In most of the burgeoning immigrant enclaves, males continued to dramatically outnumber females. The ratio ran from 30:1 in the Chinese community down to 56:44 in the Jewish quarters. True, native-born white women outnumbered native white men, but the latter postponed marriage longer than did their female counterparts, and thus helped swell the bachelor population. Camped out in boardinghouses or tenement rooms, this army of single men—joined by philandering husbands and tourists on the town—generated a voracious demand for commercial sex.

Prostitutes seemed to be everywhere, bolder and brassier than ever. Gaudily dressed ladies of the evening perambulated the Bowery, soliciting men to join them in cheap hotels and nearby lodging houses. In the Jewish quarter, particularly on Allen Street, whores swarmed on every corner, sat on stoops, lolled wantonly out of windows beckoning passersby. (As one resident recalled, if a woman hailed you as you walked down Allen Street, "you knew she wasn't calling you to a *minyan*.") Over on Mulberry and Elizabeth Streets, Italian women held sway. In Chinatown, white Irish prostitutes sold sex to Asian men on Mott Street. Along Second Avenue and St. Mark's Place, German women marched two or three abreast, grabbing potential patrons. Along Greene and Wooster black women *en déshabillé* issued blandishments from bagnio windows. To the north, French hookers worked Washington Square Park. At Gramercy Park, Lexington Avenue was thronged by prostitutes.

"The city is being rebuilt," former police commissioner McAdoo observed in 1906, "and vice moves ahead of business." South of Houston, sex workers, displaced by manufacturing, pushed northward, as their client base drifted uptown along with the hotel and theatrical district. The Tenderloin, long the city's premier commercial sex center—its de facto red light district—spilled over into the new Times Square area and beyond. By the early twentieth century, Broadway between 27th and 68th Streets was a 2-mile parade ground for white prostitutes, and Seventh Avenue (the "African Broadway") was crowded with black women selling sex. The Tenderloin's side streets were lined with brothels, often clustered by race or ethnicity. At 242 West 40th Street, as Adam Clayton Powell Sr., pastor of the block's Abyssinian Baptist Church, noted in 1908, "harlots would stand across the street on Sunday evenings in unbuttoned Mother Hubbards soliciting men as they left our service." French bordellos had clustered at West 39th Street but by 1901 had relocated to 43rd Street between Seventh and Eighth, where almost every house was a brothel. The old brownstones that William B. Astor had built west of Broadway, from West 44th to 47th, now filled up with dozens of bordellos, drawn by the booming theatrical and restaurant trades. Up on West 59th Street, at the district's northern end, whores in four-story flats had sex with windows wide open while kids lined up on roofs of neighboring buildings to enjoy the view.

Enterprising sex workers seized on new transport opportunities. They solicited passengers on subway platforms and rode the rails into new uptown markets on the Upper West Side, territory from which they'd been previously barred by concerted clerical and property-owner resistance. By the teens, they were solidly entrenched in Morningside Heights and Manhattanville, with a particularly dense concentration at "Little Coney Island" (a popular strip of hotels, saloons, and dance halls on 110th Street, where, a hundred feet overhead, the Ninth Avenue El rumbled east along Suicide Curve before swerving north over Eighth Avenue), and in Hamilton Heights and Harlem—notably alongside the luxurious apartment houses lining Seventh and Lenox Avenues north of 130th. By 1915 some argued that Harlem had surpassed the Tenderloin as Sin Central.

In the outer boroughs, prostitutes clustered wherever males prevailed—around the Brooklyn Navy Yard; near the docks at Hamilton Avenue, or on Union Street—as well as in old established haunts like Coney Island. The automobile fostered the development of "road houses" in Far Rockaway and Rockaway Beach, though some of these catered as much to premarital as commercial sex. The new machines facilitated the automobiling class's pursuit of pleasure: J. P. Morgan's chauffeur told vice investigators his employer routinely hired prostitutes, "conveying his kept women to an apartment he maintained in Westchester County." Farther afield, the excursion boats to Albany and New Haven were notorious for the blatant behavior of onboard purveyors of sexual services.

As alarming to reformers as was this very public, very in-your-face upsurge of the sex trades, so too was the new scale of organization adopted by some of its developers. Motche Goldberg, "King of the Vice Trust," had started out in the 1890s with one girl; by 1912 he had a controlling interest in eight houses, staffed by 114 women, and was raking in $4,000 a month. The notorious Max Hochstim organized a syndicate that owned twenty-one houses in the Tenderloin. Hertz, the city's most famous madam, started out as a visiting prostitute, making house calls. Then she took the stake she'd accumulated renting out her own body and opened her own brothel on First Street. She kept expanding until she controlled a chain of houses and hotels. Investing her profits in real estate, she became extremely wealthy, and moved to Borough Park, where she lived in splendor. Jewish procurers even established (and in 1896 incorporated) the Independent Benevolent Association (IBA), a 200-member cross between a trade association and mutual aid society. The IBA provided death benefits and burial plots in Flatbush for those the Jewish community had anathematized and disinherited, though some reformers worried that it had morphed into something truly worthy of the title "Vice Trust."

The most troubling phenomena were the so-called Raines Law hotels, whose existence was not only appalling, but grating, as it was the result of a reform initiative gone terribly wrong, a classic case of unanticipated consequences. The Raines Law of 1896 had prohibited saloons and taverns from selling liquor on Sundays (their busiest day by far, being the workingman's only day of rest), or between one o'clock at night and six in the morning. The law, however, exempted hotels—defined as establishments with ten or more bedrooms—thus constraining the hoi polloi without inconveniencing a higher class of drinkers.

Or so they thought. Almost immediately, hundreds of bars, especially in the immigrant quarters, surrendered their saloon license, closed off the back room or second floor, partitioned the space into ten "bedrooms," and took out a hotel license. Now, not only could patrons guzzle 24/7, but proprietors could and did rent out the "bedrooms" to prostitutes. As license fees were a lucrative source of income for the state government, Albany handed them out with abandon. By 1905 there were over a thousand Raines Law hotels in Manhattan and the Bronx alone, and they were extremely profitable. Where a well-run brothel took in $20,000 annually, an operation like the sixteen-room National Hotel off 14th Street handled 240 couples a day and brought in over $200,000 each year. Reformers had handed the sex biz a vast new infrastructure.[12]

CONFRONTED WITH WHAT THEY CONSIDERED to be a sex-drenched cityscape, the reformers went back to work. In January 1905, three years after the Committee of Fifteen had folded its tent, concerned members of New York City's commercial, clerical, and civic sectors caucused to consider strategy; this led to a City Club–sponsored organizing conference, which launched the Committee of Fourteen for the Suppression of Raines Law Hotels (C14).[13]

How to proceed? It was not enough to say, as did the Reverend Parkhurst, that they would "fight the devil" with the "incisive edge of bare-bladed righteousness." Not their style. "We are not a society of vice crusaders," declared the C14's chairman, the Reverend John Peters, rector of St. Michael's Episcopal Church (Amsterdam and 99th). The group renounced any intention of trying to prohibit prostitution. As the energetic executive secretary, Frederick H. Whitin, insisted, "certain things must be recognized," among them that commercial sex was an inevitable fact of big-city life. But prostitution could and should and would be brought under control.

The trick, Peters explained, was to recognize that "the social evil in New York is an elaborate system fostered by business interests" and that "what must be fought is not vice per se, but vice as a gainful business." The point where Raines Law hotel operators were most vulnerable was their indispensable need of a liquor license. So the C14's first move was to get the state legislature to pass a law in 1905 that permitted citizens (i.e., themselves) to insist that the Excise [Tax] Department inspect any establishment suspected of non-compliance with hotel construction regulations. If violations were found—a partitioned "bedroom" with

---

12. It wasn't only fleabag hostelries that became de facto whorehouses. Some of the best hotels in town tolerated lobby solicitation by well-dressed women, and some well-known restaurants provided spaces for their patron's less licit proclivities. Luchow's, a favorite haunt of actors, singers, artists, and politicians, kept twenty-five bedrooms at the ready upstairs. Another troubling venue emerged with a mass conversion of massage and manicure parlors into what one reformer called "disorderly houses, frequently of the most perverted kind."

13. Among the founders and early members were Lawrence Veiller, secretary of the City Club; settlement worker Mary Simkhovitch; social investigator Frances Kellor; banker Isaac N. Seligman; William Jay Schieffelin of the Citizens' Union; Rabbi Pereira Mendes of Shearith Israel; Ruth Standish Baldwin of the New York Probation and Protective Association; publisher George Haven Putnam; and former police commissioner William McAdoo.

no window, or walls thinner than the law required—the Excise Department was required to revoke the license, after which the Buildings Department was required to order the ex-hotel to cease serving liquor forthwith, with the NYPD as designated enforcers. The committee dispatched investigators to gather evidence and initiated proceedings, only to have Tammany-dominated city magistrates dismiss the cases, or even grant injunctions against police interference. Worse, the law itself was quickly declared unconstitutional.

Back to the legislature they went. A tighter statute was enacted, which passed judicial muster, and the number of revocations, fines, and closings mounted. This gave them another card to play. To get a license, an alcohol retailer had to pay a $1,200 fee to the state, and take out an $1,800 bond from a surety company. This was an astronomical expense for would-be saloonkeepers, which is why most of them signed an exclusive contract with a brewery agreeing to serve only their brand, in return for which the brewery would front the money for fee and bond—or more: often the brewery provided the building and bar fixtures, making saloonkeepers in effect renters rather than owners.

Brewers and surety companies were not only substantial organizations, but were joined together in industry-wide associations. The C14 realized that if they could come to an understanding with these groups, they could skip dealing with one retailer after another. They succeeded. In 1906 the major surety associations, whose members had begun to lose serious money on license revocation fines, agreed to put together a blacklist, drawn up in conjunction with the committee, of proprietors deemed too risky to ensure. Almost overnight this forced roughly 500 Raines Law men to surrender their hotel licenses and either go back to being saloonkeepers or go out of business.

Then the C14 cut a deal with the State Brewers' Association (SBA), which represented 95 percent of the city's brewers, who collectively controlled 80–90 percent of Gotham's more than 11,000 saloons. The brewers had long tolerated or abetted commercial sex, which boosted profits. Now the industry was worried about the rising strength of outright prohibitionists, who sought to ban the sale of alcohol itself. To ward off this challenge, they sought to burnish their credentials as responsible and civic-minded businessmen. So a deal was struck, formalized in an April 1908 agreement signed by SBA president Colonel Jacob Ruppert. The C14—using their army of undercover agents—would identify "disorderly" establishments; brewers would pressure the managers to mend their ways, and cut off the flow of beer if they didn't.

For the committee the ultimate test of "disorderliness" was prostitution, of which the presence of unaccompanied women was deemed prima facie evidence. Many immigrant cultures, however, the Irish and German in particular, considered it perfectly acceptable for women to be in commercial leisure venues without male companions. But the C14 and their secret snoops—overwhelmingly white, native-born, middle-class, and Protestant—believed that unaccompanied women went to such places for one reason only: to solicit men. More broadly still, investigators were instructed to look for "tell-tale signs" of immorality—females who smoked, swore, or wore too much makeup—then mark them down as the equivalent of whores, and label the establishment "disorderly." If unattached women showed *no* signs of being debauched or immoral, then they must be hapless innocents, badly in need of protection, which the committee, like Belle Israels and her dance hall task force, was happy to provide. The C14 forced saloonkeepers to sign promissory letters agreeing to bar unescorted women at night, along with other activities the members found offensive, like dancing. They also forbade mixed-race parties, as at the Marshall Hotel, determined to police racial as well as gender boundaries.

Then, just as they were making quiet, behind-the-scenes progress in tackling the "social evil," the perils of prostitution exploded onto the front pages.

IN 1909, *MCCLURE'S* PUBLISHED "The Daughters of the Poor: A Plain Story of the Development of New York City as a Leading Center of the White Slave Trade of the World, under Tammany Hall." The article, by muckraker George Kibbe Turner, claimed that Jewish sex traffickers were enticing women into "white slavery," consigning them to whorehouses around the city, or exporting them to the rest of the country, and "the four corners of the earth."

Turner argued that the practice dated to the 1880s, when great numbers of single young Jewish men began arriving on the Lower East Side. Jewish entrepreneurs recognized the profit potential in providing these bachelors with affordable "fifty-cent prostitution." Soon "Jewish commercial acumen" had developed the business "to great proportions," under the protection of Irish politicos at Tammany Hall. At first, given the relative paucity of Jewish girls, procurers had fetched poorly paid mill girls from industrial towns in New England and Pennsylvania. But the mass arrival of Jewish women changed all that, and soon the sex merchants had filled their local brothels with local girls, and begun exporting them "by the hundred" to the South African gold and diamond fields, to Shanghai and Australia, to Alaska and Nevada and the banks of the new Panama Canal, sending them to camp-follow the armies of labor. They reaped fabulous profits, according to Turner, and plowed them back into building gambling hells and Raines Law hotels in Gotham, all the while establishing ever more centralized organizations to oversee the business, outfits like the Independent Benevolent Association. When their Tammany protectors got defeated in 1901, and business was temporarily disrupted, the sex wholesalers extended their operations to US cities. "Several hundred New York dealers" arrived in Chicago and set up a red light district there, Turner declared, stocking it with "between seven hundred and fifty and a thousand Jewish girls from New York"; hundreds more dealers flocked to San Francisco, Los Angeles, Seattle, Boston, New Orleans, organizing and importing, until half the prostitutes working in the United States had started their careers in Gotham, and the city had become the "chief center of the white slave trade in the world."

This perfervid description of the rapid rise of a new industry, with the city its global headquarters, was seriously overheated. Yes, there was a significant expansion in the number of prostitutes, though the business had been a substantial one since at least the 1820s, and it's not clear—there are no reliable per capita comparisons—how much of the increase was simply a function of population growth. And there were no doubt instances of female sex workers being shipped (or traveling on their own) to mining camps out west, just as padrones were dispatching male laborers to dig in them. But the notion that the structure of the business in any way resembled a giant corporation—a US Sex, replete with branch offices throughout the world—was seriously wrongheaded.

Turner was, however, perceptive about another kind of change taking place in the prostitution racket. In the previous century, he noted, "so far as it had management, it was entirely a woman's business," but "during the past six or seven years," he suggested, "the trade of procuring and selling girls" had been "taken from the weak hands of women and placed in control of acute and greedy men." These were the "pimps," or, as they were more decorously called, "cadets": young Jewish men, often members of gangs like Monk Eastman's, who hung around places poor girls congregated—factories, employment offices, dance halls—and seduced them into the trade. "These lonely and poverty-stricken girls," Turner argued, "ignorant and dazed by the strange conditions of an unknown country, are very easily secured by promise of marriage, or even partnership." The pimps—having "intimate connections with the political machines of the slums"—were in a position to provide the girls protection from the police and courts. And while a pimp might "sell" his girl or girls to a brothel, those female-headed and relatively safe houses were being driven out of business by reformers. As sex workers shifted into hotels, apartments, or the streets, protection of their persons (and procurement of customers) became new necessities, which the pimps provided, in return for a hefty share of their earnings. "The boy of the slums has learned," Turner suggested, "that a girl is an asset which, once acquired by him, will give him more money than he can ever earn, and a life of absolute ease." It was, he concluded, "the appearance of the Jewish pimp, a product of New York politics, who has vitiated, more than any other single agency, the moral life of the great cities of America in the past ten years."[14]

The *McClure's* piece triggered an outpouring of white slave literature. Between 1909 and 1914 tracts and magazine stories tumbled from the presses, purveying salacious tales of abductions in which immigrant girls were surreptitiously drugged, placed in captivity, and sold into a life of sexual servitude.[15] Titles included "Graphic Accounts of How White Slaves Are Ensnared and a Full Exposition of the Methods and Schemes Used to Lure and Trap Girls" and "Fighting for the Protection of Our Girls: Truthful and Chaste Accounts of the Hideous Trade of Buying and Selling Young Girls for Immoral Purposes." Reginald Wright Kauffman's novel *The House of Bondage* presented the story of a girl being drugged by a "thickly accented German Jew" who then "robbed" her of her virginity and sold her to a madam; *Bondage* went through fourteen editions in two years and was followed by a film version. Movie producers made fortunes working the genre. *The Traffic in Souls* netted a staggering half-million dollars during its first run. *Smashing the Vice Trust*, *The Exposure of the White Slave Traffic*, and *The Inside of the White Slave Traffic* were also boffo at the box office. *Inside*, which premiered in December 1913 at the 2,000 seat Park Theatre on Columbus Circle, routinely turned away hundreds of would-be patrons, despite running five shows daily. After the film was pilloried by pulpit and press, the police raided the Park, confiscated the reels, and arrested the entire staff while the crowd shouted in protest. The next day there were *eight* screenings, and *thousands* jammed the sidewalks.[16]

The white slave craze served a variety of functions. Its core conviction—that most prostitutes were passive victims of male treachery, entrapped or coerced into the business—allowed believers to avoid confronting the reality that most prostitutes "chose" the profession, albeit from a bleak basket of survival strategies that they found even more unpalatable. Blaming a few villainous white slavers, almost invariably foreigners, was easier than confronting and contesting the conditions that produced such straitened options. It also comforted those worried about the era's loosening of constraints on women, as the moral of many white slave stories was that females who stepped out of traditional roles invariably came to a very bad end. And for many male readers and viewers, white slavery melodramas provided an

---

14. Though fixated on Jews, Turner did take some notice of their Italian counterparts, who he believed labored at a disadvantage. Italian families, he suggested, kept closer watch on their daughters than did Jewish families, who often sent girls to work so that sons could be sent to study. Balked in New York, the "young Italian laborers who return to Italy every year for the winter … induce young peasant girls to accompany them back to America under promise of marriage. When they arrive here, they are satisfied to give up the girls to the dealers in New York upon payment of their passage money and a small bonus."

15. Turner didn't buy this plot line: "The tale of drugging is almost invariably a hackneyed lie —the common currency of women of the lower world, swallowed with chronic avidity by the sympathetic charitable worker."

16. The Lower East Side, the presumed locus of the trade, drew audiences to goggle at plays ground out by Yiddish theater hacks, with titles such as *White Slaves*, *The Sinner*, and *Love for Sale*.

opportunity to wallow in soft-core porn without embarrassment, as they came packaged as uplifting exposés of evil. (This was reminiscent of the way some antebellum abolitionist tracts had been snapped up by readers attracted less by their politics than their lurid accounts of wicked masters flagellating helpless slave girls.)

The reform community that had been struggling to control prostitution was of mixed mind about the white slave hoopla. On the one hand, it certainly brought massive public attention to the issue. On the other, its approach was so overwrought and sensationalized that it tended to bring the issue into disrepute. It was left to a new recruit to their cause to throw some cold water on Turner's work without extinguishing the flames he'd kindled.

In 1910 John D. Rockefeller Jr. reluctantly agreed to serve as foreman of a grand jury impaneled to investigate the truth or falsity of the claim, advanced by Turner and others, that New York was the center of a vast and highly organized white slave trade. The call came at a turning point in Junior's life. He had just decided to retire from Standard Oil, and from all his other corporate directorships (save one, a Colorado mining concern). He'd been convinced by a recent Standard Oil corruption scandal that if he stayed in the corporate world he would be unable to hew to the high moral standards he'd been professing to his pupils in the Young Men's Bible Class at the Fifth Avenue Baptist Church, off and on, for the previous fifteen years. Rockefeller's announcement that he was shifting from business to philanthropy came, moreover, just at the moment he acquired the wherewithal to do so, as Senior had finally begun transferring significant sums (eventually totaling half a billion dollars) to the 36-year-old Junior's control.

The choice of Rockefeller was probably a stratagem on Tammany's part. Fearing that Turner's accusations might damage their prospects in the next mayoral election, the politicians thought the shy and prudish young man would go through the motions quickly, and provide a clean bill of health. Instead, Junior—determined to break out of Senior's shadow— threw himself and his considerable resources into a six-month-long investigation, which called in hundreds of witnesses.

In the end, the big takeaway was the grand jury's declaration that "we have found no evidence of the existence in the County of New York of any organization or organizations, incorporated or otherwise, engaged as such in the traffic in women for immoral purposes," and, specifically, that intense scrutiny of the Independent Benevolent Association had uncovered "no evidence that the association as such does now or has ever trafficked in women." The grand jury simply hadn't bought Turner's big-picture analysis; he'd been interviewed and been unable to back up his wilder charges.

Less noticed was the considerable overlap between Rockefeller's findings and Turner's focus on Gotham's pimpdom. "A trafficking in the bodies of women does exist," the grand jury went on, though it was "carried on by individuals acting for their own individual benefit," not by sinister syndicates. These "creatures" were able, "with promises of marriage, of fine clothing, of greater personal independence," to "induce girls to live with them and, after a brief period, with threats of exposure or of physical violence, force them to go upon the streets as common prostitutes and to turn over the proceeds of their shame to their seducers, who live largely, if not wholly, upon the money thus earned by their victims." Violence was part of the way they sustained control and increased productivity—the pimps "ill-treat and abuse the women with whom they live and beat them at times in order to force them to greater activity and longer hours of work on the streets"—but even more chilling was the observation that though they operated individually, the pimps cooperated in foreclosing escape routes for women inclined to flee, it being "an unwritten law among these men that the authority of the individual over the woman or women controlled by him is unquestioned by his associates to what ever extreme it may be carried." The grand jury might have added that given pimps' pull with police, women who wanted to break free could hardly count on cops to rescue them.

Rockefeller suggested future police sweeps should focus on pimps, not prostitutes. He also urged the city to establish a commission that would investigate prostitution in other US and European cities, along with their methods of policing it. When it became clear the municipality had no interest in doing so, he decided to consider establishing one himself. To test support for such an initiative—which would also be Junior's debut on the city's stage—he embarked on a listening tour, seeking advice from over a hundred prominent citizens: "lawyers, physicians, business men, bank presidents, presidents of commercial organizations, clergymen, settlement workers, social workers, labor leaders and reformers," as he put it, with clerics all but lost among the secular leaders.

Based on this canvass, Rockefeller decided to create a permanent organization, one that "would go on, generation after generation, continuously making warfare against the forces of evil," not in a "sensational or hysterical" way but rather in the "spirit of scientific inquiry." Not for Rockefeller the vice raids of Parkhurst and Jerome, or the hyperventilated exposés of Turner. Rather the goal would be to gather reliable information that would provide a solid base from which to launch future campaigns. In March 1911 Rockefeller, together with Kuhn, Loeb's Paul Warburg and Senior's personal counsel Starr Murphy, organized the Bureau of Social Hygiene (BSH). The name itself signaled a shift from the rhetoric of social purity to that of public health, and suggested it would do for the city's social order what the Rockefeller-supported Bureau of Municipal Research was doing for the city's government.

The bureau's first move was to commission George Kneeland to undertake a study of prostitution in New York City. Kneeland had been one of the Committee of Fourteen's investigators from 1908, had moved to Chicago to run its Vice Commission, and returned to Gotham at Rockefeller's behest. Deciding that the best way to find out how the sex business operated was to interview the women engaged in it, he hired a female investigator who compiled personal histories of 1,106 prostitutes, mostly streetwalkers. He also arranged with Katharine Bement Davis, superintendent of the State Reformatory for Women at Bedford Hills, to question 647 prostitutes who had been committed there from New York City. Bureau representatives also visited 142 brothels spanning the spectrum from fifty-cent houses to ten-dollar venues.

Kneeland's investigators counted the women they encountered, a total of 14,926. Of these, 6,759 worked the streets, while the remainder labored in parlor houses (brothels), tenement apartments, hotels, saloons, or massage parlors. He estimated that 15,000 was a reasonable estimate of the total number of non-clandestine, full-time professionals operating in Manhattan; previous estimates had ranged from 25,000 to 100,000. Kneeland's study exploded other pieces of conventional wisdom, too. Where Turner had stressed the prominence of immigrants, the Bedford data showed that American-born whites constituted 62.75 percent of the cohort, and American-born "colored" women 13.14 percent, while foreign-born women contributed only 24.11 percent. Turner had harped on the Jewish component, but Kneeland's statistics put their proportion at 19 percent, to Catholics' 41.1 percent and Protestants' 38.9 percent (the latter figure including almost all the African American women). And where many spoke of the prevalence of "ruined" country girls, out of the 491 American-born women, 404 were born in cities, and of these, 59.2 percent were born in New York City.

Commissioner Katharine Bement Davis, Blackwell's Island, ca. 1910–15. (Library of Congress Prints and Photographs Division, George Grantham Bain Collection)

Perhaps the most interesting statistic of all was that of the 647 Bedford inmates, only 2 said they'd been coerced into the business. White slaves were notable for their absence.

Instead the women advanced a variety of reasons for having entered the trade. Family troubles were a big issue. Many spoke of parental abuse, or neglect, or alcoholism, or generational conflict between immigrant elders and American-born daughters, or simply the daily damage wreaked on families by chronic poverty. Others told of husbands and lovers who abused or deserted them, or in some cases actually pushed them into the business, becoming their pimps.

Money was the biggest issue. Many of those sampled simply couldn't support themselves, or their babies, or sometimes their parents, not only because they couldn't find work (or were precluded from working by health or other issues), but because the jobs they could get—and many had had regular employment—simply hadn't brought in enough income. The ranks of the surveyed sex workers included former department store salesgirls, retail store clerks, office workers, stenographers, telephone operators, actresses, schoolteachers, milliners, nurses, dressmakers, waitresses, chambermaids, factory workers, and domestic servants. Some had fled dangerous or demeaning working conditions. "I was tired of drudgery as a servant," said one ex-domestic, adding, "I'd rather do this than be kicked around like a dog in a kitchen by some woman who calls herself a lady."

For most it was the bottom line that counted. Kneeland analyzed the wages they'd earned in their former occupations and found they varied from $3 to $15 weekly, the majority having received $6, $7, or $8. In what he admitted was a "startling" contrast, the receipts from soliciting varied from $26 to $76 per week, with the average being closer to the higher figure. In stark opposition to the image of debauched and imprisoned victims propagated by the white slave narratives, were the women like one who said, "I loved the excitement and a good time, easy money and good clothes." Others enjoyed breaking with the constraints of proper female behavior; as one put it, "I was born bad and actually enjoy the life." Such sunny recollections didn't dwell on the life's unquestionably dark side—physical abuse, venereal disease, jail time, declining earning capacity, and ostracism from family and community.

Though Kneeland noted the centrality of poverty as a motivating force, he couldn't quite bring himself to draw systemic conclusions. Others did. Settlement workers stressed the conditions that drove women to prostitution, and advocated wages-and-hours legislation. Feminists saw prostitution as a rotten fruit of the double standard, and sought to corral male sexuality. Socialists said "white slavery [was] the result of industrial slavery," and called for emancipation. And Emma Goldman, one of the few to flag the racial obfuscation in the "white slavery" term itself, asked: "What is really the cause of the trade in women? Not merely white women, but yellow and black women as well," and she answered bluntly: "Exploitation, of course; the merciless Moloch of capitalism that fattens on underpaid labor, thus driving thousands of women and girls into prostitution."[17]

This was not an assessment to which John D. Rockefeller Jr. was drawn. Instead of allying with socialists, anarchists, unionists, and feminists, who called for workplace or legal reforms, or clerics, who urged a war on sin, Rockefeller cast his lot with the medical community, who sought to suppress the trade to improve public health. Abraham Flexner, the physician Rockefeller commissioned to investigate European prostitution, put it this way: "Civilization has stripped for a life-and-death wrestle with tuberculosis, alcohol and other plagues. It is on the verge of a similar struggle with the crasser forms of commercialized vice."

New York's physicians had entered the fray after an alarming 1901 investigation found near-epidemic levels of venereal disease, attributed to male patronage of prostitutes, with innocent wives and children among the greatest sufferers. The doctors also denounced Parkhurstian moralizers for sustaining a dangerous conspiracy of silence about VD. Syphilis and gonorrhea were simply not discussed in polite circles. When the *Ladies' Home Journal* ran articles on the subject in 1906, it lost 75,000 subscriptions. Hospitals refused to admit patients with infectious venereal diseases. Some argued VD should *not* be eradicated, but left unchecked as a deterrent to immorality. Such attitudes, doctors like Prince Albert Morrow insisted, didn't protect purity, they spread disease.

Dr. Morrow, a professor at Bellevue Medical College, kept in touch with the latest European developments in the field and publicized the perils of VD in *Social Diseases and Marriage* (1904). In 1905 he organized the American Society of Sanitary and Moral Prophylaxis. It proposed to combat prostitute-propagated disease by educating young men in the benefits of continence—diminishing demand for illicit sex rather than suppressing its supply. By 1910 Morrow's society had attracted many civic reformers—including Felix Adler, Robert de Forest, Homer Folks, Charlotte Perkins Gilman, Seth Low, E. R. A. Seligman, and Upton Sinclair—but the great majority of its 700 members were physicians from New York City.

---

17. Not only radical women could cut to the heart of the matter: former police commissioner McAdoo pointed in 1906 to "the horrors of the sweat-shop, the awful sordidness of life in the dismal tenement, the biting, grinding poverty, the fierce competition, the pitiful wages for long hours of toil under unwholesome conditions, physical depression, and mental hopelessness [which] are all allied with the temptation to join that better-clad, better-fed, and apparently happier but awful army whose steps take hold on death." And Mayor Gaynor snapped: "For a man to pay a woman three dollars a week and then accuse me and say there are too many prostitutes in the city of New York is infamous."

The medical community recoiled, however, when Hermann Biggs, chief medical officer of the Department of Health, got the city (in 1911) to authorize construction of a pavilion at Riverside Hospital, on North Brother Island, to treat severe VD cases. He also had VD put under the Board of Health's required reporting plan (in 1912), and tried to establish community clinics to treat the disease. The doctors defeated this (in 1913), squelching public care for patients who might otherwise pay private physicians for treatment. So Biggs turned to Rockefeller, who provided the initial funding that got a Health Department diagnostic clinic up and running. The clinic conducted tens of thousands of bacteriological tests, and hired a medical adviser to inform the sick about the nature of venereal diseases. It did not provide treatment, instead handing out a list of private physicians. Nevertheless, the medical profession remained hostile, and the social stigma attached to venereal disease slowed further progress.[18]

Rockefeller now set about merging the social hygiene and social purity organizations working on prostitution and VD. Being his father's son, he believed that "whenever existing organizations working along similar lines can be combined, such combination is in the interest of economy of management and efficiency in operation." He shotgunned a wedding between the American Federation for Sex Hygiene, the American Vigilance Association, and the American Purity Alliance, which (in 1914) produced the American Social Hygiene Association. This conglomerate became a central player, along with the Bureau of Social Hygiene and the Committee of Fourteen (which Rockefeller also underwrote, providing one-fourth its budget), launching a final offensive against prostitution in New York City.

John D. Rockefeller Jr., ca. 1915. (Library of Congress Prints and Photographs Division)

18. In 1901, Rockefeller Senior founded the Rockefeller Foundation for Medical Research. Joined by Hermann Biggs, the institute became one of the leading centers of medical research in the world, and Rockefeller contributed over $12.5 million to the facility by 1914.

IT HAD LONG BEEN THE CASE THAT HIGHLY RESPECTABLE PROPERTY OWNERS had no qualms about renting space to sex purveyors, though they tended to use agents as intermediaries, which allowed them to feign ignorance. In the twentieth century the temptation of securing affluent tenants continued to attract men like Hamilton Fish Jr. who, using a complicated trail of leasing arrangements, rented space to Jacob Hertz, whose wife, Rosie, was the best-known madam in New York. Reformers argued (as did contemporary zoning proponents) that uses of private property that caused harm to neighbors, could be subjected "to the proper exercise of the police power." In 1914 the social hygienists coalition won passage of legislation that penalized the owner of a building used for prostitution by barring the structure's use for *any* profitable purpose for an entire year. (Peters of the Committee of Fourteen allowed as how district attorneys were as yet reluctant to use their new authority, though he believed reformers had "made real estate more conscious of its responsibilities.")

In 1915 reformers won an amendment of the Code of Criminal Procedure that outlawed all forms of prostitution—not only those transacted in streets and tenements. This was done by expanding the definition of "vagrant" to include any person "who is a common prostitute who has no lawful employment whereby to maintain herself" or—in line with Rockefeller's proposal to focus on pimps—anyone who "offers to secure a female person for the purpose of prostitution, or for any other lewd or indecent act," or who loiters "for the purpose of inducing, enticing, or procuring another to commit lewdness, fornication, unlawful sexual intercourse or any other indecent act."

With these prosecutorial tools in hand, the Mitchel administration swung into action. At Kneeland's suggestion, Rockefeller authorized the Bureau of Social Hygiene's investigators to funnel information (gathered in pursuit of "scientific" ends) to Police Commissioner Woods, who "acted upon it fast as it has been turned in." The police department managed to reduce the number of vice resorts from 1,831 in 1912 to 303 in 1917. Brothels, in particular, were hit hard. Where BSH investigators had counted 142 parlor houses in 1912, a vice survey in 1917 discovered only three such establishments. With the 1916 arrest of Lucy Rogers, a Tenderloin madam for thirty-six years, the C14 concluded that the "old-fashioned resort, where prostitutes sat around waiting...practically has been eliminated in New York City."

This is not to say that prostitution was eradicated. It shifted location and modes of outreach. Streetwalkers abandoned the major boulevards for side streets. Former brothel-based prostitutes became "call girls," using the telephone to do business out of the public eye, or relied on pimps to steer johns to their apartments. Others advertised in the *Herald*'s personals columns (known by newsmen as "The Whores' Daily Guide and Handy Compendium"). Yet within a dozen years, reformers had ended decades of high-visibility prostitution in New York City. Commercial sex had become a furtive, clandestine enterprise.

GAMBLING

At the century's start, gambling was widespread in Gotham.

There were two broad types: gambling on games of chance (cards, dice, numbers) and gambling on sports events (principally horse racing). Within each type, a spectrum of institutions served gamblers from different classes.

In the first category, elites gambled, as they had for many decades, in elegantly appointed casinos. Like other entertainment venues, these were migrating uptown. The premiere casino-meister was Richard Canfield, who had opened his latest gaming palace in 1899—the Saratoga Club, at 5 East 44th, just next door to the latest incarnation of Delmonico's.

Canfield's was awash in white mahogany and Spanish leather, Chinese porcelains and Chippendale furniture, and oils by Canfield's friend James McNeill Whistler. His casino attracted corporate titans, financiers, and Society players, figures like Reggie Vanderbilt and John Bet-a-Million Gates. Wagers of $1,000 at faro or $5,000 at roulette were routine. Canfield's major competitor was the House with the Bronze Door, at 33 West 33rd, owned by a syndicate of gamblers headed by Frank Farrell, a Tammany-connected former saloon-keeper. At Farrell's place, patrons played roulette, baccarat, pinochle, and poker in similarly sumptuous surroundings. The interior decoration, including the eponymous door (imported from Italy), had been arranged by Stanford White.

These venues were illegal, and they paid off police and politicians to avoid trouble with the law.

Equally illegal were the low-end versions of casinos available to the working class, like the Lower East Side stuss parlors where immigrants played a New York variant of faro. Also forbidden were the even more accessible "policy shops"—estimated in 1902 to number between 800 and 1,000—where poor folk in neighborhoods throughout the city could bet on numbers. Wagers ranged from a penny to twenty-five cents, with bets being placed on combinations whose names were drawn from the racing world, like Gig, Saddle, Horse, Cross-saddle, or Capital Cross-saddle; some of the latter could pay out a hundred dollars on a penny bet. Players often placed their wagers (as people had for decades) with the assistance of a "Policy Players' Dream Book" that assigned numbers to types of persons, objects, or situations that appeared in a dream.

Policy shops, being illegal, were often hidden or disguised—nestled perhaps in the back room of a barbershop, or made up to look like a florist's or a cigar store. From there runners carried bets to the headquarters of their circuit—the biggest impresarios ran circuits of twenty to a hundred shops—where bookkeepers and clerks processed the bet, and later dispatched runners back with the payoff on any winning numbers. These were usually derived from the outcome of a horse race, or picked in a putatively blind drawing (though the numbers were often massaged to minimize payouts).

THE SECOND KIND OF GAMBLING OPERATION WAS TIED more directly to racetrack outcomes. Here the difference between the venues catering to different classes was crucial. The well-to-do usually bet at the track itself, while the less-well-off wagered in off-track venues. The critical distinction was not location but legal status. Betting at the track was legal; betting off-track was not, even if the off-track wager was placed on the exact same horse, running in the exact same race.

This state of affairs dated to the 1887 Ives Act, which had barred horse-race gambling throughout New York State, then exempted betting done at tracks. The law's provisions reflected the strength of a political alliance between "sporting" members of normally antagonistic cohorts—city elites and Tammany politicians. The Ives exemption was challenged in 1894 by reformers, partly on grounds of corruption (fixed races being commonplace). But trackmen and Tammanyites again joined forces and saved the exemption by setting in place a regulatory apparatus that admixed private and public components—the Jockey Club (1894) and the State Racing Commission (1895).

The Jockey Club, established and presided over by August Belmont II, was the lineal descendent of the American Jockey Club founded by August Belmont I back in 1865. As with its predecessor, the club's members were drawn from the cream of New York Society, old money and new (John Jacob Astor IV, Cornelius Vanderbilt II, J. P. Morgan, et al.).

The Jockey Club established track rules, licensed jockeys and trainers, appointed judges and stewards. The State Racing Association—also chaired by Belmont II—regulated and supervised the sport overall, licensing tracks and cracking down on corruption.

Under these arrangements, New York racing entered a golden decade, coterminous with the 1898–1907 boom years, during which it secured its position as national center of the sport. Gotham had the most outstanding tracks, the biggest crowds, the largest purses, the finest Thoroughbreds, and the leading media (from sporting weeklies to Western Union, which transmitted racing results to fans and gamblers near and far).

Big money poured into building magnificent racecourses, modeled on premiere European versions. When Jerome Park Racetrack closed in 1889—its Bronx site slated for drowning by a new reservoir—it was swiftly replaced by the Morris Park Racecourse (1889), also in the Bronx. Operated by the Westchester Racing Association (headed by Belmont II), it became a favorite playground of the city's super-rich. That lasted until 1904—when the Morris Estate, from whom the WRA was renting the land, decided to sell it off for development (property values were soaring with the impending arrival of the subway). The WRA soon found an alternative site—a 666-acre tract in the hamlet of Elmont, in the town of Hempstead, just outside city limits. There they built the opulent Belmont Park, a $2.5 million enterprise that boasted a complex of five racecourses (including a superb 1.5-mile oval), a 12,000-seat grandstand, 200 acres of stables, and a lavish clubhouse with balconies where members could quaff mint juleps while viewing the races.

Belmont II aimed unashamedly at the city's classes, not its masses, as had Belmont I, famous for asserting that "racing is for the rich." On opening day in 1905, Society responded en masse, filling five acres of parking lots with their automobiles. Practically no laborers and very few skilled workmen attended Belmont in distant Elmont, 20 miles from Times Square, an hour's ride by train. Spectators were predominantly businessmen, professionals, and small entrepreneurs (grocers, butchers, saloonkeepers) whose time was their own.

But the working classes had more accessible options. Apart from established venues like Brighton Beach (1879), Sheepshead Bay (1880), Gravesend (1886), and Aqueduct (1894), there was the new Jamaica Race Course, thanks to Tammany's Big Tim Sullivan. As had Boss Croker before him, Sullivan owned a stable of Thoroughbred racehorses (one of them named The Bowery), in partnership with gambler Frank Farrell and others. In 1901, he and Farrell, together with developer W. H. Reynolds (soon to erect Coney Island's Dreamland), organized the Metropolitan Jockey Club, which bought a 107-acre site near Jamaica, on which they built their track, which opened in 1903. Easily reachable by train from Long Island City, and by el or trolley from the Brooklyn Bridge, the Jamaica became known as the "People's Track."

At all these racecourses, gambling was *legal*. Designated areas were set aside where dozens of little groups clustered, each composed of a bookmaker and his clerks. They would chalk up on slate boards the odds they were offering, handling bets as high as $25,000. The most reliable were members of the Metropolitan Turf Association, a.k.a. "the Mets." Tracks charged the bookies a fee for access, and the income from gambling constituted a substantial portion of their profits.

STILL, MOST NEW YORKERS DIDN'T GO TO ANY TRACK. Too far, too expensive; no time, no money. But many did gamble on races at neighborhood venues called poolrooms. In 1900 there were over 400 in Gotham, some independent, some part of a circuit. (One of the biggest networks was run by gambling mogul Frank Farrell.) Poolrooms offered the excitement and immediacy of a horse race without the horses. Arriving punters would check out the blackboard where horses and odds were posted. Then they'd hand over their money (off-track bookies accepted smaller bets than did the on-track Mets) and get a card with the horse, its odds, and the amount of the bet written on it; then they'd lounge about on the dozens of chairs and benches provided and socialize, perhaps shoot some pool. Then came the race, covered in real time by Western Union, which wired reportage direct from trackside.

Poolrooms were illegal. So, like policy shops, they adopted various evasive strategies (in addition to requisite payoffs.) Customers might be required to provide a password. Or the rooms might be disguised. Female-friendly places might be tricked out as millinery shops or dressmaking parlors. One ingenious venue posed as a restaurant. Patrons would sit at a table, be handed by a "waiter" a "menu" with betting odds scribbled in the margin, then place their "order," pay their tab, and be handed their profits as "change" if they won.

But *why* were they illegal? Or, put differently, why was at-the-track betting *not* illegal? Why, as poolroom keepers complained, was there "one law for the rich and another for the poor"? One rationale advanced by defenders was that the rich could afford to lose, whereas "wage-workers, salaried men, and boys" might tumble into "destitution." An associated justification fretted that gambling "tends to destroy character and take away the incentive to individual effort by holding out a constant hope of making money without work." More blunt still was the suggestion—as in a 1905 piece for *Cosmopolitan* entitled "The Delusion of the Race-Track"—that poolrooms were "trap-doors into hell," through which losers might fall into "that desperate state of mind in which accounts are falsified, tills tapped, pockets picked and the black-jack of the highwayman wielded." The argument that gambling debts might lead to embezzlement certainly resonated with employers. Saks, Macy's, and Siegel Cooper all forbade employees from betting on races. There were broader concerns, too, fears that addicted public officials would betray their trust, husbands forget their duties and vows, gaming wives forsake their families.

These concerns were not absurd. Gamblers could indeed find themselves in over their heads, with all the dire consequences outlined by critics, but there was precious little evidence that the problem was widespread. Nor despite the shrill invective of pieces like "The Pool-Room Vampire and Its Money-Mad Victims" was there any sign that dropping some pennies at a neighborhood poolroom was wreaking havoc among the city's working classes.

What seems more at the core of the anti-gambling animus—certainly that of those who had criminalized poolrooms, casinos, stuss parlors, and policy shops—was the belief that Tammany politicians and corrupt policemen were making fortunes helping gamblers evade the law, and that these profits helped the Tammany machine stay in power. Reverend Parkhurst and Frank Moss claimed that Big Tim and Frank Farrell ran a secret, highly centralized "Gambling Commission" that charged would-be gaming establishments $300 to open, and $100–$300 a month for ongoing protection, with rake-offs totaling perhaps $3 million a year. The assertion was probably overstated (in the way that claims about "vice trusts" and "white slavery" were overblown), but there's no doubt that Tammany potentates like Sullivan could and did offer protection to gambling operations. Still, there was something perversely circular about such complaints: if reformers hadn't criminalized gambling in the first place, cops and politicians would not have been able to profit from end-running a law that didn't exist. If reformers truly wanted to hit the grafters in their pocketbooks, then *de*-criminalization might have been the better way to go.

Instead, from 1902 on, reformers launched a ferocious assault on gambling, spearheaded by District Attorney Jerome. Joining up with private vigilante groups and NYPD squads operating directly out of central headquarters, Jerome initiated raid after raid on casinos and

"Watching the Tape or Watching the Wheel—What Is the Difference Morally? If it is legal to gamble in Wall Street, why isn't it legal to gamble in the West Forties?" *Puck*, August 28, 1912.

pool halls alike (no class favoritism for him). These assaults accelerated when General Greene became police commissioner in 1903 and made arrests on an unprecedented scale. Two raids in Greenwich Village netted 140 prisoners (90 men and 50 women). Shortly thereafter, over 200 were rounded up at the establishment of "The" Allen, a prominent poolroom operator. And one evening in late June officers staged a series of "axe and ladder" raids on six pool-rooms and arrested 578 men, including ten off-duty policemen. While a few of the arrestees were named in warrants, the great bulk were taken in for "disorderly conduct," helping swell the grand total of such arrests that year to 70,000, the most in the city's history.

Some vigilante groups went hunting on their own. In 1901 vice crusader F. Norton Goddard, who had inherited a $12 million estate from his New York merchant father, organized an Anti-Policy Society devoted to tackling the numbers shops. His men smashed in doors, sending hundreds of bettors fleeing through the streets, and then, revolvers drawn, arrested shop owners at gunpoint. In June 1902 Goddard got the state legislature to make possession of policy paraphernalia (betting slips, bookkeeper records) a crime, punishable by a year in jail. Goddard tracked down Al Adams, a "Policy King" millionaire, and got him sent to Sing Sing. He also dragged hundreds of poor players into court and, when challenged, defended the practice (in May 1903) on the grounds that the policy shop was "one of the chief causes of destitution" in the city, and his goal was "to abolish it absolutely and keep it abolished." In June 1903 he declared victory, and was hailed, at a Hotel Savoy dinner in his honor, by speakers including Jerome, Greene, and Moss, before an audience that included Robert de Forest, William Baldwin, Jacob Schiff, and Otto Kahn—all of whom joined in singing "For He's a Jolly Good Fellow."

Then-Justice Gaynor did not join in the jollity. Indeed, in a January 1903 article, "The Lawlessness of the Police of New York," he'd specifically denounced reforming morals "by the policeman's club and axe" as "pernicious and dangerous." When a vice squad smashed into a poolroom, arrested people, seized records, and chopped up furniture—all without a warrant—Judge Gaynor scored it as "mob violence" and set the gamblers free. "Racing horses for stakes may be bad, but unlawful arrests are worse," Gaynor argued, adding, "History teaches that we have more to fear from arbitrary power than from all species of gambling combined." If the police would stay "out of doors" and stick to keeping an "out-ward order and decency," "the immense system of blackmail" would be instantly destroyed.

Rather than consider de facto decriminalization, reformers doubled down and set about criminalizing the last remaining oasis of legal gambling. Jerome began promoting a ban of on-track wagers in 1906, but his campaign went nowhere until it was picked up in January 1908 by Governor Charles Evans Hughes, then being boomed as a possible Republican pres-idential candidate to succeed Roosevelt, and hoping to heighten his appeal in the heartland. Finding little enthusiasm among state legislators, Hughes set out to mobilize public opinion, relying particularly on upstate Methodist ministers. He also picked up support in the me-tropolis, from the City Club, the Woman's Municipal League, the New York Federation of Churches (a nondenominational Protestant association), and the New York Board of Jewish Ministers (who denounced the "injustice" of permitting "the rich man to enjoy pleasures which are made a crime to the poor"). These downstate supporters coalesced in a Citizens' Anti-Racetrack Gambling League.[19]

19. They picked up press support, too—from the *Times* on the conventional grounds that "thousands" of young men had been "ruined," that gambling profits flowed to "evil resorts," and that gamblers themselves were "generally objectionable citizens." The *World* hoped suppression might lead to the halting of *all* gambling, notably speculation on Wall Street.

The Jockey Club mounted a vigorous resistance to what was called the Agnew-Hart bill. Belmont and company hired lawyers and lobbyists, who argued that suppression would violate personal liberties, encourage contempt for a law that would surely be evaded, and perhaps bring down racing itself, destroying the massive investment New Yorkers had made in it. Closure, they said, would throw thousands of track-related employees out of work, along with thousands more working in stables and breeding farms. It would also wipe out roughly $50 million in property values, be a blow to city tax revenues, and hurt the bottom line of transport and tourist industries.

The bill was defeated, but Hughes mustered all his political capital (giving up on most of his other agenda items) and in June 1908 managed to drive the Agnew-Hart law across the finish line. Opponents had managed to insert a loophole in the legislation that allowed oral betting, putatively aimed at legitimating informal wagers between friends, and some bookies managed to carry on, calculating the changing odds in their heads, but most found it impossible to master the technique. The Mets disbanded. Track profits and attendance sagged through 1909. And in 1910 opponents delivered a knockout blow, passing a law that made officers of racing associations criminally liable—subject to jail time—if bookies were found operating at their tracks, even without the directors' knowledge or approval.

In 1911 all of New York's tracks shut down. Some were converted to other uses or sold off for redevelopment. Racing in Gotham seemed dead.

But trackmen continued to struggle in the courts. And in 1912 a state supreme court ruling held that track directors would be liable only if they had foreknowledge that bookies were at work. In 1913 jubilant track owners reopened, though stripped of professional gambling, and some never recovered, including Gravesend, Brighton, and Sheepshead Bay.

BOXING, TOO, SEESAWED BETWEEN LEGALITY AND CRIMINALITY in this period. The sport had been outlawed since the 1880s, and police had routinely broken up major fights, even John L. Sullivan's bouts at Madison Square Garden. By the early 1890s the sport's national center had shifted to New Orleans.

In 1896 Big Tim Sullivan got the state legislature to pass the Horton Act, which permitted sparring matches in buildings owned by athletic associations. The sport revived overnight. Big-time contests flourished again: in 1899 a crowd of 10,000 men (no women allowed) flocked to the Coney Island Athletic Club to watch Jim Jeffries win the heavyweight championship title.

The next year, 1900, upstate Republicans made a comeback. Denouncing boxing's brutality, its unruly crowds, and its association with gambling and Tammanyites, they repealed the Horton Act. Boxing was driven back to saloon back rooms and offshore barges or to bouts in fake "membership clubs" like Sharkey's (opened at 127 Columbus Avenue by a retired fighter), where patrons joined for the evening, and every handbill described contestants as "Both Members of This Club." Again Tammany pols made common cause with elite sportsmen. In 1907 Frank Farrell established the National Sporting Club, whose "boxing entertainments" at Lyric Hall (42nd and Sixth) were restricted to 300 blue chip members from the corporate, commercial, sporting, theatrical, and elite club worlds.

In 1911 it was the Democrats who bounced off the ropes. They passed the Frawley Act, which legalized ten-round professional boxing under the supervision of a State Athletic Commission. Now the sport flourished in the city, and by 1914 most of the country's principal prizefights were being held in Gotham.

The glory years ended in 1917 when reformers repealed Frawley and banned boxing altogether.

WHILE BOXING AND RACING LURCHED FORWARD AND BACKWARD, baseball surged steadily ahead. Reformers loved baseball. They thought it clean and wholesome. It embodied middle-class values. It taught individualism *and* teamwork. Ladies' Days welcomed women, their presence thought to foster decorum. Immigrants could attend without fearing loss of face through ignorance: it was easy to learn the rules and feel part of a great American ritual. And the games were generally free from disorderly crowd behavior and, indeed, from much of the blue-collar working class itself. .

Blue laws kept ballparks closed on Sunday, working people's day off. Team owners and politicians fought this, and so did reformers who argued baseball was far preferable to other amusements. But Sabbatarians held the line, and Sunday games were raided by the police. During the week, games started at 3:30 p.m. This gave Wall Streeters and their white-collar employees a half hour to arrive—the market closed at 3:00—while effectively excluding immigrant laborers and operatives. Some manual workers did make it to the parks, mainly artisans who worked half-Saturdays or had unusual shifts. These attendees sat in the cheap seats—the "bleaching Boards"—separated from the more respectable sorts, surveilled by private police.[20]

Ironically, this idyllic pastime, whose genteel virtues were celebrated in the 1908 Alley ditty "Take Me Out to the Ball Game," was run by the very machine politicians and traction magnates so loathed by reformers. Between 1895 and 1902 the New York Giants (originally the Gothams) were controlled by Andrew Freedman, financier and intimate associate of Boss Croker. Even after Freedman sold out to John T. Brush, a successful clothing merchant from Indianapolis, Freedman remained a minor stockholder, and the Giants remained a Tammany team. With the management of John J. McGraw, and the pitching of Christy Mathewson, the Giants became the most profitable team in organized baseball. In winning six National League pennants between 1904 and 1917, the club generated $100,000 to $150,000 a year for its owners. Success also provided opportunities for honest graft, notably in construction.

Until 1888 the Giants had played in a double-decked wooden structure just north of Central Park on 110th Street (between Fifth and Sixth). It was called the Polo Grounds for the equestrian uses to which its owner, newspaper tycoon James Gordon Bennett, had once put it. During Harlem's expansion a street was cut through it. The Giants shifted to another wooden stadium built in 1890, 2 miles to the north in Washington Heights (on a plot of land once part of John Lyon Gardiner's seventeeth-century farm, now owned by James J. Coogan, Manhattan's borough president; hence Coogan's Bluff). In 1911, when the stands burned down, Brush decided to rebuild in fireproof steel and concrete. The newest Polo Grounds resembled a Roman stadium, complete with friezes depicting martial shields and garlands. The design was in keeping with City Beautiful aesthetics and with the need to compete with grand new entertainment sites rising around the city. When formally dedicated in 1912, the monumental horseshoe-shaped grandstand was the largest in the United States.

The Giants' success stemmed in part from their hammerlock on the Manhattan market. Freedman had stymied all attempts by would-be rivals to get an American League franchise. He used his real estate clout to block efforts to buy potential playing sites, and he used his political clout to threaten having streets cut through any sites he *didn't* control. His monopoly

---

20. Workers had other venues available. At Big Tim Sullivan's monster picnics, Irish crowds played and watched baseball (along with football, bowling, and Gaelic football), and unions sponsored amateur baseball teams.

"Polo Grounds, View from Coogan's Bluff," 1909. (Library of Congress Prints and Photographs Division)

"Polo Grounds During World Series Game," 1913. (Library of Congress Prints and Photographs Division)

was broken only when the American League finally realized it had to cut a deal with equally powerful forces. In 1903 it gave a franchise to a syndicate owned by Tammany's Bill Devery (the former police chief) and poolroom king Frank Farrell. Now things happened fast.

The new owners secured a rocky site at 165th and Broadway. Though it was isolated, the subway was scheduled to arrive next year. Then they paid the local district leader $275,000 to excavate the site and erect Hilltop Park, a flimsy wooden edifice. Lastly they fielded their new team, the New York Americans (unofficially called the Highlanders, in a reference to their ridge-top location overlooking the Polo Grounds below Coogan's Bluff).

Unfortunately, the club lurked unprofitably in the second division for a decade. Then Hilltop Park was torn down in 1913 for apartment buildings, forcing the team to rent space at the Polo Grounds. Devery and Farrell lost heart. In 1915 they sold out to Jacob Ruppert Jr., a power in Tammany and a brewer inspired by the prospect of increased sales. Under his control, the Highlanders—rechristened the New York Yankees (another nickname that had crept into popular parlance)—would go on to better things.

Across the East River, the Dodgers were on the move again. Brooklyn's National League club had removed from South Brooklyn out to East New York, but when crowds failed to materialize at this distant site, the club moved back to the old neighborhood (in 1898) and into a new Washington Park (at Fourth Avenue between 1st and 3rd Streets). Rising attendance, fueled by an inter-borough rivalry with the Giants, soon outstripped the field's capacity. The new president and principal owner, Charles Ebbets, scouted around for a new location. He found one in 1908 on a craggy piece of land on Crown Heights' lower slope. It was known variously as "Ginney Flats," after an Italian shanty settlement, or "Pigtown," for the squatters' garbage pit where farmers fed their porkers.

On its face, an unlikely place. But Ebbets recognized the potential of a spot just east of Prospect Park and midway between Bedford and Flatbush, home to a burgeoning middle class. The area was accessible to 90 percent of Brooklyn's populace via nine local trolley lines, and the subway provided easy access from Wall Street. Over the next four years, Ebbets secretly bought up 1,200 parcels of land. To pay for his acquisitions and the cost of erecting a stadium, he sold half the club's stock to local, politically connected Irish contractors. Ebbets Field opened on April 5, 1913, on which occasion the home team happily beat the Yankees, 3–2, thanks in part to the promising performance of a young outfielder from Kansas City named Charles Dillon (K. C.) Stengel.[21]

If gambling and corruption were less associated in the public mind with baseball than with racing and boxing—though results of games were wired to poolrooms for off-stadium betting—the structural and business underpinnings of the sport were deeply interlaced with both, as would become all too evident when links were exposed between organized baseball and organized gambling, particularly in the person of one Arnold Rothstein.

---

21. Amateur sports—notably tennis and golf—were happily beyond the reach of politicians and gangsters. Lawn tennis became the quintessential game of middle-class suburbs. Open to both sexes, it provided a way to meet partners who, though not introduced via one's family, were certain to be of comparable social position. Golf appealed to professional and business men. Played on large, expensively constructed, and well-maintained pieces of real estate, by members of clubs that excluded socially and financially unacceptable outsiders, golf provided open air exercise and satisfied social needs. (Business needs as well: the formation of United States Steel took final shape on the links.) Golf, of course, was allowed on Sunday.

Country clubs, which had flourished since the 1880s, provided—in addition to golf and tennis—polo, steeplechasing, and riding to hounds (though often chasing not a fox but an aniseeed bag). They were liveliest in spring and fall, before and after Society went to the country and Newport. At least a score ringed New York: Meadowbrook Hunt and Rockaway Hunt (near Hempstead), the Westchester, Ardsley, Suburban, Tuxedo, Staten Island Golf, Staten Island Cricket, Crescent Athletic (Bay Ridge), and the Marine and Field (Bath Beach). Not all were exclusively for the rich, and for the less affluent, there were public golf courses in Van Cortlandt Park after 1895.

Ebbets Field, ca. 1914. (Image No. ARC.202 v1973.5.1801, Brooklyn Photographs and Illustrations, Collection of the Brooklyn Historical Society)

"Casey Stengel, full-length portrait, standing, facing left, wearing sunglasses, while playing outfield for the Brooklyn Dodgers," ca. 1915. (Library of Congress Prints and Photographs Division)

IRONICALLY, THE RAIDS AND CLAMPDOWNS THAT FINISHED off established casino operators (like Canfield) and first-rank bookmakers (like the Mets) opened the door to a new generation of gamblers. Most of them were Jewish—counterparts of those rising in the entertainment industry—and most relied on backing from Irish pols like Sullivan. Among the most promising of the young men to whom Big Tim gave a leg up were two soon-to-be household names, Arnold Rothstein and Herman Rosenthal, though their trajectories couldn't have been more different.

Arnold Rothstein's grandparents fled Russian-ruled Bessarabia to New York, where in 1856 Arnold's father, Abraham, was born, on Henry Street. He became a highly successful cotton-goods dealer, and by 1882, when Arnold arrived, the family had moved to the Upper East Side. The Rothsteins were Orthodox Jews—his older brother had trained to be a rabbi—and in 1895 Arnold was bar mitzvahed at B'nai Jeshurun synagogue on Madison Avenue between 64th and 65th. But uptown respectability was not for him. By 1898 the 16-year-old had dropped out of Boys' High School and, while working as a stock clerk in his father's dry-goods establishment at 94 Greene Street, was drawn inexorably to the nearby Bowery scene. Rothstein frequented pool halls there, including one run by Tim Sullivan's cousin Florrie. Rothstein's skill at shooting pool brought him to the Big Feller's notice, and Sullivan enlisted him to help connect with his Yiddish-speaking constituents. Rothstein also discovered a mathematical aptitude—he was able to instantly calculate odds and payoffs in his head—and decided to become a professional gambler, taking an entry-level position as a bookmaker's runner. Big Tim supported him in this ambition, telling him (so it's said, perhaps apocryphally) that being a "smart Jew boy" he would do well in gambling because "that business takes brains."

Rothstein became a regular at the Hesper Social and Political Club at 111 Second Avenue (between 6th and 7th Streets), founded around 1900. Dominated by the Sullivan clan, the Hesper brought together professional gamblers and professional politicians, for poker parties and annual fund-raising balls. By 1902 he was working for himself, making book on horse races, ball games, elections, and prizefights, and gambling on his own (mostly craps and poker). In 1904 he began what became annual visits to Saratoga for the summer racing season, where he remained a second-tier bookie, as the Mets excluded him from their ranks. Later, when Agnew-Hart barred written bookmaking, and the Met bookies faltered, Rothstein's aptitude for numbers stood him in good stead.

As the decade wore on he began operating in the booming new Times Square area, again with Sullivan's help. The Tammany chieftain was co-owner of the Metropole, a six-story hotel at 149 West 43rd, near the corner of Broadway. It had an all-night liquor license, was a favorite with theater people, gamblers, and gangsters, and had poker tables upstairs which Sullivan turned over to Rothstein to run. He also ran a floating crap game that moored on Monday afternoons in the property room of Hammerstein's Victoria, right around the corner. But Rothstein's ambition was to run his own place, something on the order of Richard Canfield's now defunct Saratoga Club, and in 1909 he was able to launch a casino in a three-story brownstone at 106 West 46th (just off Sixth); he and his new wife lived on the top floor. He was soon attracting high-rolling millionaires, partly because Big Tim's protection meant raids were scarce (and tipped off in advance when they happened), but also because Rothstein was now socializing in the Times Square venues frequented by his target client base. He became a regular at Rector's, a familiar at Delmonico's, a constant and elegantly attired figure at Jack's and Shanley's. He hung out with major players in the Broadway scene (Ziegfeld, Berlin, Jolson, Brice), journalists like Herbert Bayard Swope, then a reporter on the *Herald*, and wealthier patrons who might be up for a visit to Rothstein's nearby establishment. In

1910 steel magnate John Gates's son, Charley, dropped $40,000 on roulette and faro in the house on 46th Street; in 1913 Percival Hill, of the American Tobacco Company, was parted from $250,000 on the premises.

ROTHSTEIN THUS PIONEERED WHAT BECAME A MAJOR MIGRATION of Jewish professional gamblers from the Lower East Side to midtown. Others in the cohort included Bridgey Webber, who in early 1911 opened a faro house at 117 West 45th; Harry Vallon (born Valinsky), who moved from place to place; and Bald Jack Rose (né Jacob Rosenzweig), so called for being bereft of hair, eyebrows, or lashes. But it was Herman Rosenthal who was soon to be front page news.

Rosenthal had arrived in Gotham in 1879, age five, also from Bessarabia, with his parents and siblings. As a lad he ran with an East Side boy gang, became a competent (if pint-size 5'3") street fighter, and caught the eye of Tim Sullivan, who became something of a mentor. Through Sullivan, Rosenthal got a spot as a Tammany district captain, then also a series of jobs—runner for a local poolroom, manager of a small craps game, off-track bookie in Far Rockaway, and then overseer of a chain of Second Avenue poolrooms including the gambling concession at the Hesper Club. Rosenthal prospered as a downtown bookie, despite being generally reputed to be (as one critic put it) "a flashy, greedy, loudmouthed braggart." His fortunes turned downward in 1909, however, when he attracted the attention of District Attorney Jerome, who began repeatedly raiding his premises, smashing them up until they could no longer reopen. Rosenthal decided to try his luck uptown, and with a loan from Sullivan he leased a brownstone at 104 West 45th, fitted it up in deluxe fashion, and opened for business in November 1911—only to have the local precinct captain come round and demand a thousand dollars down, and a thousand a week to stay in business. When Rosenthal refused, the cops smashed their way in and axed his equipment to splinters.

Rosenthal was now up against two big problems. The first was that Big Tim Sullivan had taken ill (with what would prove to be a terminal case of syphilis), and while he would come in and out of crisis over the next two years, his power, and hence his ability to protect his protégés, had begun to wane. The second was that Mayor Gaynor, who in July 1911 had responded to the outcry over gang outrages by unleashing Lieutenant Charles Becker's Strong-Arm Squad, now decided to join the crackdown on gambling, but to do it differently. Rather than relying on crooked precinct cops (like the ones who put the bite on Rosenthal), he established two other special squads run directly out of City Hall. Then, in October 1911, Becker's squad having gotten gangsterdom under control, Gaynor had Commissioner Waldo redirect the lieutenant's energies into the war on gambling. For the next nine months, between October 1911 and July 1912, the three strong-arm squads launched more than 200 raids and made 898 arrests. New York's newspapers gave the campaign major league coverage, singling out the heroic Lieutenant Becker for particular praise (thanks in part to Becker's having hired his own press agent).

What neither the public nor Waldo nor Gaynor knew was that their fair-haired Becker, the reformers' hero, the prince of the city, had gone rogue. The opportunities for graft had been just too tempting—as they had once been for his mentor Clubber Williams, who on being transferred to the Hell's Kitchen vice district had famously rejoiced that after years of settling for chuck steak he planned to pig out on tenderloin. Becker was in a strong position to demand protection money from New York's gamblers, in return for not raiding them, though he couldn't offer ironclad guarantees; he had to take orders from Waldo or Gaynor. Still, he could always torpedo a case by "losing" crucial evidence, and indeed charges were dropped against 800 of the 898 arrested, with the remainder receiving either suspended sentences or inconsequential fines. Making hay while the sun shone, Becker managed to rake in an estimated $1.8 million in his nine-month run. While most of this had to be parceled out among complicitous police and politicians, in a year when his salary was under $1,700 Becker managed to deposit $59,000 in just one of the fifteen accounts he opened and to pay cash for a house in Williamsburg.

It was slowly borne in on Herman Rosenthal, sitting amid the ruins of his casino, that the go-to person for protection was no longer Sullivan but Becker. So, according to Herman, at the end of December 1911 he cut a deal with the lieutenant, making him a (very) silent partner. Becker, Rosenthal later claimed, actually loaned him the money with which to reopen, to be repaid, along with protection money, out of profits. On March 20, 1912, the refurbished club opened for business.

It lasted less than a month. Almost immediately Gaynor and Waldo were bombarded with anonymous letters, almost certainly penned by jealous gambler-competitors, calling attention to Rosenthal's brazen defiance of their campaign. The mayor and commissioner demanded Becker raid the place. Becker told Rosenthal he would have to appease his bosses. No way! said Rosenthal; he was paying good money precisely to prevent such raids! Becker said he'd give Herman advance warning, even reimburse him for the damage. Rosenthal declared that if Becker raided him, the gambler would blow the whistle on the hero cop's crooked operations.

On April 15, 1912, Becker raided anyway, smashing up the custom-made gaming tables. Worse, Waldo assigned a round-the-clock police guard to keep the place locked down.

Rosenthal—furious, indignant, and desperate (big debts, no income)—decided to complain to the Manhattan district attorney. This was now Charles Whitman, a relatively obscure Republican magistrate who had succeeded Jerome in 1910. Having set his sights on the governor's chair, he needed to make a big splash as DA. Whitman listened to Rosenthal's tale of woe about how Becker, his silent partner, had gotten greedy and, no longer satisfied with his rake-off, was harassing him with raids. Whitman found the assertions about Becker's corruption interesting but too vague, too uncorroborated. Not surprisingly, no other gamblers proved willing to admit they'd been paying off Becker. Indeed, the gambling fraternity, who detested Rosenthal anyway, were appalled at Herman's whining, which was bringing decidedly unwanted attention to their affairs.

Now even more enraged, Rosenthal tried to see Commissioner Waldo, then Mayor Gaynor. Both refused to hear him out.

So Rosenthal went to the press. On Friday, July 12, Rosenthal had a long conversation with reporter Herbert Bayard Swope, who had recently begun working at Pulitzer's *World*. Swope was the paper's expert on Gotham's underworld, which he knew reasonably well. A man-about-town, Swope loved to gamble, was a regular at gaming houses, had been best man at Arnold Rothstein's wedding, and was a friend of Sullivan, Foley, and Boss Murphy. Swope was perfectly prepared to believe the worst about Lieutenant Becker. And he had already established a mutually beneficial relationship with DA Whitman, trading favorable publicity for exclusives.

So the next morning, Saturday, July 13, the *World* published an affidavit in which Rosenthal laid out his charges, without naming names. Swope followed this up the next morning, Sunday, July 14, with another Rosenthal affidavit, this one naming Becker. With the press now in full cry, and Swope pushing Whitman to seize the moment (to advance both their careers), the district attorney that very evening invited Rosenthal to his uptown town house for another informal chat. At the end of it, he told Herman to come to his office the next morning, at 8:00 a.m., when he would interview him formally, and immediately seek a grand jury indictment of Becker.

It is generally agreed that this is what happened next: gambler Bald Jack Rose hired four members of Big Jack Zelig's gang—Jacob Seidenshner (a.k.a. Whitey Lewis), "Lefty" Louis Rosenberg, Harry "Gyp the Blood" Horowitz, and (a multi-cultural addition to the basically Jewish outfit) "Dago Frank" Cirofici—for a job whose exact parameters remain unclear. Bald Jack also rented a gray Packard from an agency that called itself the Boulevard Taxi Company, which supplied getaway cars for fifty dollars an hour to robbers and other gunmen in need of wheels. The gangsters then cruised uptown to the Metropole Hotel at 43rd Street, wherein Herman Rosenthal, fresh from his evening interview with DA Whitman, was excitedly reading the *World*'s headline coverage of his charges. Just before 2:00 a.m. Rosenthal was called outside, and he went, emerging into the sultry summer night to meet his doom in the form of a volley of bullets fired by the four hoods across the street, which killed him instantly. (Whether his walking out was simply stupidity—and Herman was not the brightest bulb in the chandelier—or whether, as some hypothesized, he'd been expecting a payoff that the gambling community had promised in return for his leaving town that evening, was never determined; there were also theories that the gangsters had been deputed only to beat up, or perhaps kidnap, the squealer but had gotten carried away.) Whatever Herman's motivation or their instructions, the deed was done, and the gunmen now drove off. They were quickly

"Gangs and Gangsters as They Pass from View" *Sun Magazine Section*, July 20, 1919.

tracked down—having neglected to cover up or switch their license plate—and the car company fingered Bald Jack as the renter. Rose—and his confederate gamblers (including Webber
and Vallon)—soon confessed their responsibility, but claimed that Becker made them do it,
as he was determined to shut Herman up forever.

Becker denied all. Gaynor and Waldo at first defended him and the NYPD. But the
reform community jumped on the case, scenting a golden opportunity to capture the mayoralty and the governorship, maybe even topple Tammany Hall for good. Wealthy reformers
hired Burns detectives to circumvent any NYPD obstruction of Whitman's investigation,
which was run out of a suite they rented for him at the Waldorf. (Contributors included
William Jay Schieffelin of the Citizens' Union and JDR Jr., who sent a check for $5,000 to
help "end graft in New York.") The sleuths soon dug up evidence galore of Becker's nine-
month orgy of payoffs—the bank accounts, the house in Williamsburg—and fed it all to
Swope, who blazoned it in the *World*. The firestorm of bad publicity seriously undermined
the former hero in the court of public opinion, though no evidence whatsoever was advanced
that Becker had ordered the hit, apart from the testimony of Rose and his fellow gamblers,
given in exchange for immunity from prosecution for a capital crime.

The reformers raised their sights, holding public meetings to whip up hysteria over the
corrupt "System" of criminals, cops, and politicians that, they charged, had usurped the
government of Gotham. It appears likely that at this point Boss Murphy, fearing the ailing
Big Tim's involvement with the midtown gamblers might come to light as well, giving the
crusading Republican DA a hook on which to hang Tammany itself, decided to let Becker take
the fall. The case was tried before Justice John W. Goff, one of the reformers' inner circle;
he'd been chief counsel for the Lexow investigation and worked closely with Jerome and
Moss. The trial began October 5, 1912. Rose was the key witness. Sullivan's name never came
up. Goff more or less directed a verdict of guilty and, on October 30, imposed a sentence of
death. Becker appealed and won a retrial. The appellate court issued a blistering rebuke of
Goff's prejudicial behavior and more or less asserted the prosecution's case rested entirely on
perjured testimony. But in 1914 Becker lost round two, the trial presided over by Judge
Samuel Seabury, and the death sentence was confirmed. In April 1914 the four actual killers
were executed. In November Whitman won the gubernatorial election, taking office in
January 1915, just in time to deny Becker's last-ditch appeal for clemency. NYPD Lieutenant
Charles Becker was electrocuted in Sing Sing's death house, on July 30, 1915, for a crime
with which he almost certainly had nothing to do. In the interim between Rosenthal's death
and that of Becker, the mayoralty passed from Gaynor to John Purroy Mitchel, with the latter's triumph due in no small part to the uproar over the Rosenthal assassination. Arthur
Woods, the new police commissioner, was deputed to clean house. He also accelerated axe-
and-revolver raids on gambling establishments, indeed insisted that every man netted in
such roundups be arrested (reversing Gaynor's policy) and hauled off in a patrol wagon.
Deprived of Tammany's and the NYPD's protection—the scandal, election loss, and police
reforms having badly eroded their capabilities on this score—Gotham's gamblers (like its
prostitutes) went underground.[22]

---

22. Not Rothstein, though. He just moved on to bigger and better things. By 1914 he had amassed so much money that he became
a bookmaker for bookmakers, something like a reinsurer who sells insurance to insurance companies seeking to manage risk. Not
that he gave up gambling, but noting the difficult post-Rosenthal climate he phased out his West 46th Street operation and opened
a more opulent casino in affluent Hewlett, in Nassau County. (He hired the entire staff of Sherry's for the opening.) Then he
glided up to Saratoga Springs, where his idol Richard Canfield had long operated the Club House (which John Morrissey had
started up back in 1871), and opened Brook Casino, the most luxurious gambling palace in the country.

It was at this moment that the repressive progressives' war on drink and drugs—the third leg of the anti-vice trifecta—was coming to its momentous conclusion.

DRINK

In 1903 there had been roughly 7,000 licensed saloons in Manhattan and the Bronx, 3,800 in Brooklyn, and hundreds more throughout the other boroughs—not counting the many "speak-easies," as unlicensed venues were known. Bars were particularly in evidence along major commercial arteries (like Third and Eighth Avenues between 14th and 125th Streets), and on neighborhood street corners. In the 15th Assembly District (43rd/53rd/Eighth/the Hudson) almost half the ninety-two corners were occupied by saloons, with sixty-six others scattered along the blockfronts.

Their density was thickest in working-class districts, jumbled in among the factories, shops, and tenements, and they were central to workingmen's public social life. Male workers would pack saloons at break time, when they could get a free lunch with a five-cent beer, and at nightfall, on their way home from work, when they'd belly-up to the bar, four or five deep, and talk over the day's doings, wrangle over sports, debate political issues, and treat one another to rounds of beer. With their bright lights and polished fixtures, the saloons offered an enticing contrast to wretched workplaces and cramped tenements, but they were more than simply sites of masculine camaraderie. They were places to pick up information about employment possibilities—Italian men frequented President Street venues to drink wine and play cards while waiting for news about incoming ships and possible dock work—and were often pressed into service as impromptu strike headquarters in times of labor upheaval. They

"Ernest Roeber & His Saloon." (Library of Congress Prints and Photographs Division)

helped new immigrants adjust to an often bewildering environment, while providing established ethnic fraternal organizations, and political parties of all stripes, with meeting and entertainment spaces in their back rooms or second stories. Saloons, in their thousands, provided the infrastructure for New York's plebeian male culture; they were sinews of working-class and ethnic solidarity.[23]

But when Gotham's middle- and upper-class vice reformers gazed out on the saloon-strewn landscape they saw only, in the words of a Brooklyn Baptist minister, "the breeding place of criminals and spawning place of vice."

They drew up a lengthy indictment. Saloons were linked in an unholy trinity with whorehouses and gambling hells, as their spaces provided bases for betting and prostitution. The product they peddled was hazardous not only to morals but to health (cirrhosis) and safety (drunken workers could get mangled by machinery). Drink could drive imbibers down the road to personal perdition, alcoholism costing them jobs and families (as recounted in decline-and-fall narratives such as "The Story of an Alcohol Slave," a *McClure's* article from 1909).

Vice reformers of an anti-monopolist bent argued that saloons were props to, and products of, concentrated corporate power. In the spirits world, they stressed the impact of the Distilling Company of America (a.k.a. the Whiskey Trust)—a consolidation of former competitors established in 1899. Headquartered in New York, it controlled more than 90 percent of US liquor production, and its lobbying arm, the National Liquor League, was accused of wielding undue political influence on behalf of, in the words of the *New York Globe*, "a parasitic class which has battened on human weakness." In the more diversified beer business, conversely, critics cited "wolfish competition" among top-tier firms as being responsible for the rampant multiplication of saloons and deplored "the terrible and undisciplined commercial forces which, in America, are fighting to saturate the populations of cities with alcoholic liquor."

The barroom was also the bulwark of Tammany Hall. Not only did profits from payoffs feed the machine, but the saloon was an integral part of the organization's workings. It provided spaces for party meetings and a base of operations for repeaters and sluggers. And Tammany's top leadership—Sullivan, Foley, Murphy himself—had all launched their careers through the saloon or the liquor trade.

Perhaps most important, if most diffuse, was the reformers' conviction that the matrix of city saloons sustained a class and ethnic male culture whose rowdiness and resistance ran counter to the sobriety and discipline that reformers and employers believed essential to civic order and business efficiency.

BUT WHAT TO DO ABOUT IT? New York's reform community was divided as to the relative merits of regulation versus repression.

---

23. These were decidedly male spaces partly because men wanted it that way, and partly because the reformers themselves (i.e., the Committee of Fourteen) reinforced gender barriers, forcing saloons to bar unescorted women. As a result women stood in an ambiguous relation to barroom culture. Breadwinners' wages, defined as personal, afforded them entrée to commercial sites of public recreation, but their expenses there, including treating, constituted subtractions from the family budget, which might or might not be offset by the benefits that accrued to bar-goers (information about jobs). But it blocked women from benefits—like the five-cent bowl of soup and glass of beer—that were available to men. And it in effect precluded them from access to a leisure space and time that was separated from work. Their workday was far longer than men's, and their pleasures, like doorstep gossiping, were limited to the home. Even family outings—picnics, parties—involved a considerable amount of work. These generalities varied in practice with ethnic groups.

Initially the preferred approach was temperance, not prohibition; moderation, not abstinence. The key proponent of this strategy was yet another numerical association, the Committee of Fifty to Investigate the Liquor Problem. It emerged in 1893 as the voice of eastern urban corporate elites and affiliated professionals—social scientists, charity agents, settlement workers, medical researchers, and clergymen. The committee was headquartered in Gotham, and New Yorkers figured prominently in its work, among them banker Jacob Schiff, industrialist William E. Dodge Jr., lawyer James C. Carter, railroad director William Bayard Cutting, and merchant and mayor Seth Low.

The Committee of Fifty began with the premise that while there was indeed much to fear from drink, the movement to moderate or preclude its use suffered from hyperbolic rhetoric. The "cause of temperance," it argued, "has been much obstructed by intemperate speech and exaggerated statement." The committee advocated a more sober approach. Its principal goal would be "to secure a body of facts which may serve as a basis for intelligent public and private actions." It divided its members and staff into four task forces, which over the 1893–1903 decade examined the physiological, economic, legislative, and social aspects of the issue. Their collective conclusions were summarized in *The Liquor Problem*, a 1905 volume produced by John Shaw Billings, director of the New York Public Library.

The physiology subcommittee concluded that alcohol was not a poison, that it was not true that "a single glass of beer is a step to a drunkard's grave," that total abstinence was not necessary for health, and that a drink a day was well within "the limit of judicious use."

The economic subcommittee found that alcohol nevertheless had deleterious social consequences. Twenty-five percent of US poverty, it suggested, was due to drink, and intemperance was a factor in nearly 50 percent of American crime. Social problems were often "due very directly and obviously to a very prominent fault of the individual" rather than to economic and social arrangements—a perspective shared with opponents of gambling who pinned poverty on personal irresponsibility.

Turning to solutions, the legislative subcommittee studied "dry" states, where advocates had been able to outlaw alcohol altogether, and concluded that such "prohibitory legislation" worked only where an overwhelming majority of the public supported it. When it was imposed on unwilling populations, it engendered an extremely damaging and dangerous corruption of the legal and criminal justice system. And it spawned "habitual lawbreakers schooled in evasion and shamelessness"—in some instances provoking entire municipalities to "complete and successful rebellion against the law."[24] Where virtual unanimity was absent, the subcommittee proposed a cautious program of regulating and constraining saloons by constricting their hours of business, barring them from opening on election days and Sundays (workingmen's only day off), banning sales to minors or habitual drunkards, and boosting the cost or limiting the number of licenses. They also sought to make saloons less appealing—"as devoid of social attractions as a dry goods store"—by forbidding pool, cards, dice, boxing, cockfighting, and not only prostitution and single women but pictures of naked ladies.

On the other hand, the committee astutely grasped that saloons were about more than serving liquor—they satisfied a "thirst for sociability." Its fourth subcommittee therefore explored possible substitutes for the barroom—like "temperance saloons" equipped with

---

24. There could be a political backlash to such strategies, too, as Committee of Fifty member Low discovered the hard way, when he won the mayoralty in New York and set his police commissioner, General Greene, to cracking down on violations of the liquor law. In Greene's first full year, 1903, city magistrates heard over 5,400 liquor law cases, up from 1,800 in 1902. This cost Low the votes of the large and influential German community, which, given its strong tradition of Sunday drinking, felt singled out for harassment, and contributed to the defeat of his reelection bid.

reading rooms, billiard tables, and nonalcoholic drinks. These would be run by the state or, better, wealthy philanthropists, along the lines of the chaperoned and alcohol-free dance halls proposed by Belle Israels.

Virtually none of its regulatory program came to pass, however, except for the Raines Law initiative, which proved a calamitous failure, and saloon culture flourished unabated in Gotham. This afforded an opening to the Committee of Fifty's nemesis—the Anti-Saloon League, whose name bluntly signaled its intentions.

THE LEAGUE HAD ITS BEGINNINGS IN OHIO, in 1893, with the formation there of a state body. In 1895 it federated with other state organizations that had sprung up in its wake, creating the Anti-Saloon League of America (ASL), which set out to ban the trafficking or consumption of alcohol, and thus obliterate saloons. The ASL was at first largely dependent on the moral energies of evangelical Protestant churches. Its top leadership was overwhelmingly ministerial; its anti-drink ideology was promulgated chiefly from the pulpit. But it quickly leavened its religious appeals with secular assaults on liquor industry plutocrats and politicians. ("If we wish to purify politics, the saloon must be destroyed.") And it advanced utopian predictions about the social as well as moral benefits that would accrue from banning demon rum. Eradicating drink, it proclaimed, would banish crime, poverty, and disease virtually overnight.

The ASL rapidly professionalized its operations, establishing a paid staff of lawyers, statisticians, researchers, and publicists. It became a pressure group, a lobby devoted to a single issue. State leagues didn't field candidates, instead backing those of either party who would vote as they wished, and drafted laws for legislators to pass. To pay for all this they

"Sunday Morning Scenes in Foul Bowery Dives." *Evening World,* March 13, 1899.

expanded their fund-raising capabilities, harvesting many small contributions, and increasingly large ones from the business world, notably some very substantial donations made by the Ohio-raised Baptist John D. Rockefeller Sr.

ASL organizers arrived in New York in 1899 and established a New York Anti-Saloon League, which they incorporated in 1905. But their task seemed hopeless. To the drys, wets seemed omnipresent, omnipotent. The wet community included the obvious beneficiaries of an untrammeled flow of alcohol: saloonkeepers, brewers, the liquor industry, and Tammany Hall; the hotel industry, the restaurant and theatrical trades, and the racetrack and gambling interests; and the wealthy imbibers ensconced in their gentlemen's clubs. But there were many other New Yorkers, they discovered, whose hackles were raised by prohibitionist premises.

Mayor Gaynor voiced one widespread sentiment when he flatly rejected even partial prohibition as chimerical. "To prevent all of the people of this city drinking on Sunday is an impossibility," he declared, "and every sane man knows it, and I am not willing to be a hypocrite for one minute about it." He also resented the movement's class bias. On Sundays, he noted, the rich "swig whisky and wine all day" in their clubs on Manhattan's Fifth Avenue or Brooklyn's Eighth Avenue; surely the working men who drink in the back room of a Bowery saloon "have as much right to [do] that as others."[25]

There were religious dissenters as well. The Methodists, Baptists, and Presbyterians who were the chief supporters of the anti-saloon movement found themselves up against Episcopalians, Lutherans, Catholics, and Jews. In 1902 Bishop Henry Codman Potter of the Episcopal Diocese of New York took a strong stand against the "doubtless often well-intentioned zeal which seeks to make men and women virtuous and temperate by a law of indiscriminate repression." The Central Conference of American Rabbis, the principal organization of Reform Jewish clergymen, similarly denounced prohibitionist advocacy. It was a movement "born of fanaticism [and] disregard of the actual needs of life," the rabbis declared, and it was fueled by "the ambition of ecclesiastical tyrants." They urged liberal Jewish leaders to go on record as believing that their "conception of religious ethics does not condemn the moderate use of alcoholic beverages."[26]

While some progressive reformers were drawn to prohibition, attracted in part by its anti–Whiskey Trust stance, others repudiated it. Columbia professor Charles Beard criticized the prohibitionists as "moral enthusiasts," and Herbert Croly rejected the "misdirected effort" of these "purifiers" who were gripped by "illiberal puritanism." Even George Kibbe Turner, who argued in his "Beer and the City Liquor Problem" (which appeared in *McClure's* almost simultaneously with his 1909 white slavery diatribe) that the "city saloon" was "the greatest single corrupting force of the past fifty years in this country," thought it a "ridiculous optimism to expect it to be cured by any one method at a single stroke."

---

25. Anti-Saloon League undercover investigators confirmed this distressing truth about the Gotham elite's disregard for a law they pressed on others, when they reported that liquor flowed freely on Sundays at hotels like the Waldorf-Astoria and the Knickerbocker, the Belmont, and the McAlpin.

26. Jews had affirmative reasons for rejecting prohibition as well as defending themselves against Christian zealots. Eastern European Hasidim regarded liquor as a soul-elevating substance, and celebratory events were occasions for copious drinking, though habitual drunkenness was accounted a decidedly un-Jewish trait. Jewish women enjoyed evenings at "coffee saloons," which, unlike typical ethnic saloons, were not a homosocial environment but included women as customers and participants in the spirited political and cultural debates that characterized these venues. And there were particular economic interests involved: Sam Schapiro, an immigrant from Galicia, established the first kosher winery in the city, which eventually occupied nearly an entire square block on Rivington Street. (He used Concord grapes of mediocre quality, rendered potable by adding large quantities of sugar, leading to the long-standing perception among American Jews that kosher wine must be sweet.)

The vast majority of the membership of the American Federation of Labor (AFL), even those inclined to temperance, also opposed prohibition. Some did so because it would destroy their jobs—brewery workers, bartenders—and others because they resented business-backed bluenose meddling in their private affairs (though the AFL never actually fought against it, heeding Samuel Gompers's injunction to avoid political issues not directly connected to workplace.)

Socialists, too, opposed the ASL (Germans being particularly influential voices), arguing that alcohol was being made the scapegoat for problems created by the capitalist order. Though some did argue that precisely because economic and social problems caused most drunkenness, socialism would inaugurate a reign of sobriety, partly by diminishing demand, partly by nationalizing the liquor industry and thus reducing the profit-driven push to peddle alcohol.

Prohibitionists also discovered that even when a congenial administration held municipal power, the ban on Sunday drinking proved (as the Committee of Fifty had warned) impossible to enforce. Between May 1907 and April 1908, with Commissioner Bingham at the helm, the NYPD raided 2,026 saloons and arrested 2,857 people, but when the culprits came before the Tammany-inflected courts, only 5 of them received any punishment of the slightest consequence. A 1908 report showed that over 5,000 out of 5,820 saloons in the Bronx and Manhattan were serving alcohol on Sundays in flat defiance of law. Worse yet, in 1910 Mayor Gaynor went so far as to tell saloonkeepers they could safely violate Sunday blue laws if they kept their shutters drawn.

Given this inclement climate the ASL was prepared to be flexible, to make tactical alliances with activists who didn't accept their notion of a solution. Anti-Saloon League leaders were thus active in establishing the Committee of Fourteen in 1905, even though the C14 favored a "clean up, not close down" strategy. The ASL was even willing to accept deal-with-the-devil relationships with brewers' associations in order to achieve regulatory gains.

This meant that in 1914, after a dozen years of effort, there were 13,000 licensed saloons in Gotham. In fifteen years, the New York ASL had gotten exactly nowhere.

ELSEWHERE, HOWEVER, THE PROHIBITIONIST FORCES HAD BEEN MARCHING from triumph to triumph. The key to success proved to be the adoption of a "local option" strategy. In several southern and midwestern states the ASL had been able to prevail on the legislature to allow individual towns and counties to vote in "no license" laws. They had succeeded partly because they played the democracy card, and partly because most state legislatures were undemocratic, with country voters given more electoral weight than their city cousins. Then local referendums were held, county by county, shutting down rural saloons, bypassing and surrounding urban centers. Next they won passage of statewide legislation that required the cities to go dry, though many just ignored the law. Then, in 1913, the ASL won passage of the federal Webb-Kenyon Act, which tightened the noose on recalcitrant cities by banning interstate shipment of liquor into states that had declared themselves dry; prohibitionists even mustered the votes in Congress to override President William Howard Taft's veto. Now, flushed with success, the movement opened a drive to impose prohibition on the entire country, in one fell swoop, by amending the US Constitution. If they could get it through Congress—and their veto override had just demonstrated their capacity to muster two-thirds of both houses—the odds were good that three-quarters of the state legislatures would ratify.

While not essential to this arithmetic, moving New York from soaking wet to merely damp would be an enormous spur to the national campaign. So in 1914 the Anti-Saloon

League decided to send one of its top guns to Gotham. William H. Anderson had been head of the Maryland ASL for the previous seven years, during which time he'd managed to close more than a thousand saloons in Baltimore, nearly half the city's total. "From now on," he said on arriving at local headquarters in the Presbyterian Building at 156 Fifth Avenue, "the attention of the National Anti-Saloon League will be directed toward New York as the liquor center of America."

Anderson was no hatchet-wielding Carrie Nation; he was a conservatively dressed, 40-year-old lawyer, and he presented his agenda as being "distinctly progressive," aimed at "health and industrial efficiency." But Anderson could play hardball, too; indeed, he proved an aficionado of dirty tricks. Soon after arriving he tried to frame the Speaker of the New York State Assembly, circulating rumors he had taken bribes from liquor interests, producing a bogus letter of support from a fictitious dealer as evidence. The Speaker won that round, but Anderson kept punching, above and below the belt. In 1915 he demanded Governor Whitman remove Mayor Mitchel and Police Commissioner Wood for failing to enforce the Sunday closing laws. Again, he failed in his stated objective but succeeded in making the liquor question a central issue in state politics.

Anderson's principal tactic was to call for a bolder version of the local option strategy used so successfully elsewhere. He urged the state legislature to allow not only towns and counties to vote on whether or not to allow saloons on their soil, but urban election districts as well. This would enable drys to nibble away at wet supremacy, neighborhood by neighborhood, even in New York City. This was cast as a democratic move, which it was, though, again, its passage relied on a gerrymandered legislature that made the vote of one upstate, native-born, likely bone dry, Republican farmer equivalent to the votes of seven Democratic, Irish American, working-class wets from Hell's Kitchen. This precipitated a three-year-long struggle, which grew nastier as it went on, with Anderson striking out at the Catholic Church and falsely reporting to 300 newspapers that a secret "slush fund" had been established by "liquor interests" to bribe New York legislators into voting against his legislation. Protestant ministers—downstate as well as up—rallied behind the Anderson proposal (including such notables as the Reverend Henry Sloane Coffin of Madison Avenue Presbyterian). So did the Republican governor, Whitman.

When passage appeared likely, many Gotham businessmen redoubled their opposition, both those long in the trenches, like the hotel industry, and newly aroused commercial and real estate interests. The prestigious Broadway Association opposed the bill because, as one member said in April 1917, "the success of hundreds of pieces of real estate on Broadway is dependent on the sale of liquor." In the end (May 1917) the law was passed, but opponents had been able to tack on an amendment that allowed New York to hold a special referendum to decide whether or not the provisions of the law should apply to it; if the local option was voted down, the matter could not be put before the voters again for five years.[27]

But if the city had dodged a bullet, it now confronted a cannonball. In November 1917 Governor Whitman proposed a referendum on New York's declaring a statewide prohibition. At the same time, the struggle in Congress over national prohibition reached a climax on December 18, 1917, when Congress voted to submit the Eighteenth Amendment to the states, half of which were already in the dry column.

---

27. The referendum on whether to allow local referendums was to be held in April 1918, but only if voters equal in number to one-quarter of the total vote that would be cast in the upcoming fall 1917 mayoral election signed a petition asking for it.

Aridity had spread beyond the South and Midwest and edged into the urban Northeast. Inside Gotham itself some in the corporate community, who were not direct beneficiaries of the liquor trade, began to swing round to support desertification, which, after all, promised businessmen a more efficient workforce, fewer industrial accidents, lower insurance payouts, expanded consumer purchasing power for non-alcoholic commodities, less pressure for wage increases, and a more orderly society. It also seemed the kind of reform that much-maligned corporations could safely back, thus restoring some of their tarnished legitimacy. Among those who now signed on to prohibition were Judge Gary of US Steel, V. Everit Macy (president of the National Civic Federation), and Frank Vanderlip of the National City Bank— joining longtime advocate Rockefeller Senior, who with Rockefeller Junior had lavished $350,000 on the cause since 1900. On the very day Congress voted to submit the amendment to the states, New York ASL chief William Anderson wrote the elder Rockefeller that "in light of what your money made possible...we trust that you will feel repaid for your investment."

This was to exaggerate Rockefeller's importance (as the obsequious grantee was doubtless aware). There had been a more general shift in upper-class attitudes, and a similar reorientation among middle-class ranks, too, in part because the tumultuous strikes and radical gains of the previous few years had made repression of working-class culture a more appealing strategy, in part because the outbreak of war in Europe had roused similar anxieties about ethnic enemies within. And even if New York City had remained universally wet, the dry surge that a year hence (January 1919) would win passage of the Eighteenth Amendment, would have been impossible to halt. In the war on drink, Gotham had been utterly outflanked.

In these same years the city had been a central actor in still another prohibition struggle, a war on drugs, whose outcome—the criminalization of previously legal narcotics—would be equally satisfactory from the reformers' point of view.

DRUGS

In the two Opium Wars of the mid-nineteenth century Britain had forced China, at gunpoint, to accept imports of a drug it had barred, giving new meaning to the term "market penetration." By 1900 China was consuming 95 percent of the world's opium crop—to British India's great profit—and over 16 million Chinese were regularly smoking the poppy product. As the armies of Chinese contract laborers moved out onto the planet, they took the practice with them.

Since at least the 1870s, businessmen in New York's Chinatown had been selling opium pellets, and providing pipes and places wherein to smoke them. These opium "dens" (or "dives" or "joints") were the resorts of Chinese laundrymen and laborers, who on Sundays would come to Doyer, Pell, and Mott Streets to smoke and socialize. Some were addicts, but many were not, partly because the smoking process—ritualized and complex—limited ingestion.

The dens were illegal. In 1882—the year in which the federal Chinese Exclusion Act was passed—the New York state legislature had made it a misdemeanor to operate a venue where opium was sold or given away, or to smoke opium therein. Violators, if convicted, were subject to a $500 fine and/or three months in the penitentiary. As a result, proprietors turned to the tongs for protection, and the syndicates took charge of paying off cops and Tammany politicians.

The tongs also controlled supply. There was no law against the importation, manufacture, or sale of opium, but imports were subject to federal taxation. In 1883 the levies on opium prepared for smoking (i.e., destined for recreational use), were set much higher than the tariffs on crude opium or processed morphine to be used for medical purposes, principally as painkillers, having come into wide usage during the Civil War's carnage. An 1887 follow-up law specifically barred Chinese from importing opium at all.

The result was smuggling on a massive scale to evade the tax—a time-honored tradition in the port of New York. Much of it was organized by the tongs, whose networks stretched back to China. As ever, smuggling spurred ingenuity. In one instance, cattle shipped from Hong Kong had had their horns removed, fitted with an inner thread, filled with crude opium, and then screwed back into place. However it reached the West Coast, the opium was often refined in British Columbia, conveyed eastward through Canada, then smuggled south across the border into Vermont or northern New York. This cross-border work was undertaken by French Canadian women, African American railway porters, or Irish American men—anyone other than Chinese Americans, who, under the terms of the Exclusion Act, would be deported if caught. Once the goods reached US soil, they were transferred to various front companies, which assembled shipments in nearby towns, like Burlington, then sent them down to Gotham, c/o some innocuous address, usually a Chinese laundry in lower Manhattan.[28]

In the 1890s Chinatown's opium dens were considered exotic and picturesque by middle- and upper-class commentators. Tourists came to gawk at them. Slummers who wanted to safely experience the seamy side of urban life could hire "lobbygows" (tour guides) like reformed roughneck Chuck Connors to escort them around. Connors, who worked closely with Chinatown merchants, could arrange to visit a den, though more often he conveyed naïve tourists to a faked version thereof, complete with a staged knife-wielding scuffle between "opium crazed" Chinese fighting over a "slave girl."[29]

In the 1900s, however, opium dens came to seem less amusing than threatening. An elaborate demonology evolved that suggested iniquitous Chinese were foisting sin and addiction on virtuous American women. Anti-miscegenationist novels, plays, and movies portrayed lecherous orientals using opium to lure white girls into virtual captivity (a version of the white slavery panic that also gripped the city). Often in these melodramas—like *A Raid on a Chinese Opium Joint* (1900) or *The Heathen Chinese and the Sunday School Teachers* (1904)—the police arrived in the nick of time to save the innocents from shame and degradation.

The hysteria was considerably magnified in 1909 when the murdered body of a white woman was discovered, stuffed inside a trunk, in a Chinese man's apartment. She proved to be 19-year-old Elsie Sigel, a Christian missionary worker who was the granddaughter of a Civil War general. She had been having an affair with the apartment's renter, Leon Ling, a Chinese male of "Americanized dress and manners." Ling became the primary suspect but, though he was at the center of a nationwide manhunt, was never apprehended nor proven guilty. The press had a field day with the Chinatown Trunk Mystery, though the murder hadn't happened in Chinatown, but at 782 Eighth Avenue, just off Times Square. In fact, the ensuing hullabaloo was driven in part precisely by the ubiquity of the Chinese presence throughout the city. A paranoid conviction took hold that many of their hand laundries and

---

28. There were other routes, too. The On Leong tong was heavily involved with the international "coolie" trade, and fare reductions were offered those willing to smuggle. Indian opium also traveled via the Dutch East Indies and the Philippines to Cuba, and then to New York, smuggled ashore by seamen. Large quantities of opium and codeine also arrived from Europe; one long-running and profitable supply line was organized by stewards aboard the North German Lloyd liner *Kronprinzessin Cecilie*.

29. Such frisson-seeking tourists were increasingly mocked for their gullibility. *The Deceived Slumming Party*, a 1908 movie from Biograph (directed by and co-starring D. W. Griffith), showed some tourists being fleeced at a supposed opium joint. A putative slave-girl addict pretends to commit suicide, the "police" show up, the slummers fork over cash to avoid further involvement, they depart, and (as the moviegoers see) the "police," the "tour guide," and the "dope fiends" then split the take.

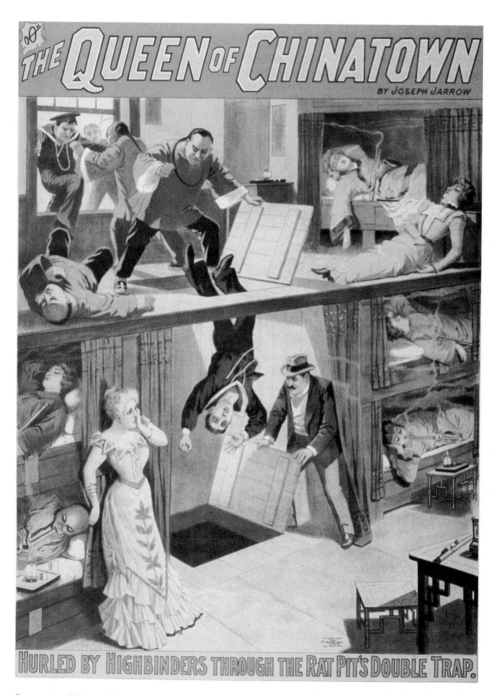

Promotional Poster, "The Queen of Chinatown by Joseph Jarrow," 1899. (Library of Congress, Performing Arts Poster Collection)

chop suey restaurants were actually fronts for hidden opium dens, their proprietors intent on ensnaring white women in their webs. In several instances would-be lynch mobs raised a hue and cry at suspected venues. In Chinatown itself, the police—on orders from Captain Michael Galvin of the Elizabeth Street Station—forced 200 white women who had been residing in Chinatown, some working as prostitutes, some cohabiting with Asian men, to vacate the area unless they possessed marriage licenses.

The anxieties attached to the spread of opium use grew as the drug leaked out into the wider urban underworld, becoming popular among prostitutes and gang members, and among those on the fringes of show business and the sporting life. Stephen Crane had argued as early as 1896 that actors, showgirls, racetrack touts, and gamblers were drawn to the drug and that "the greater number of smokers [were] white men and white women." Opium dens became popular in the Tenderloin and Times Square areas, and not only with lowlifes; one house on 46th Street near Seventh Avenue was reserved exclusively for wealthy hophead gentry.

YET FOR ALL THESE FEARS ABOUT MORAL CONTAGION rippling out from Chinatown, the spread of narcotics in New York (and the country) owed far more to the solidly Anglo-Saxon pharmaceutical industries than to putatively vicious Asiatics. And the typical American opium user (and addict) in the early twentieth century was not a Chinese man, or a white gangster, but a middle-aged, middle-class white woman.

Opium, after all, was a highly successful painkiller, indeed one of the few effective methods available to medical practitioners. Doctors and druggists accordingly prescribed opium—and opiates, too, derivatives like laudanum, codeine, and morphine—for pain relief (particularly of menstrual cramps), diarrhea, coughs, and a wide variety of ailments. But many people couldn't afford doctors, or didn't trust them. They turned instead to the booming patent medicine industry, which churned out syrups, tonics, and pills advertised intensively as affording relief from a staggering number of ills (including squalling infants).[30] Many contained opiates (and alcohol). They could be found in every drugstore or purchased anonymously from numerous mail order catalogs. As a result, opium addiction spread most rapidly among genteel native-born whites, who discovered too late that many patent medicines were habit forming. Addiction, in turn, created a demand for medicines that could detox victims. One such arrived in 1898 when Germany's Bayer Company introduced heroin. Hailed by the medical profession as a non-addictive analgesic, it was advertised as a "most remarkable remedy" for opium habitués. New studies would eventually demonstrate heroin's own addictive properties, but meanwhile it was heaped by drug companies into cough syrups, asthma remedies, and sedatives.

IF THE TONGS WERE PIKERS AS PURVEYORS, compared to the patent medicine industry, the latter, in turn, depended for its supplies on legitimate importers or manufacturers of medicinal opiates. Overwhelmingly these were located in New York, which for over a century had been the headquarters of the US pharmaceutical trade.

One of the leading wholesale importers and distributors, Schieffelin & Co., had been founded back in 1794, and it was presided over in the 1900s and 1910s by William Jay Schieffelin, a great-grandson of John Jay. The company imported drugs from Europe and manufactured its own in a Bronx laboratory on Southern Boulevard. McKesson & Robbins (M&R) was another major player. It dated its founding to 1833, when it began importing and selling therapeutic drugs and chemicals to stock the medicine chests of merchant vessels, and in 1855 it became one of the first New York firms to manufacture them. In the early 1900s M&R persuaded several well-established wholesalers to become its subsidiaries, and the

---

30. "Patent" is a misleading descriptor; these nostrums weren't patented (which required proof of novelty) but trademarked (though registration was still unusual), or branded, as we would now say, and reliant more on the emerging advertising industry than on the legal system to make their mark in the marketplace.

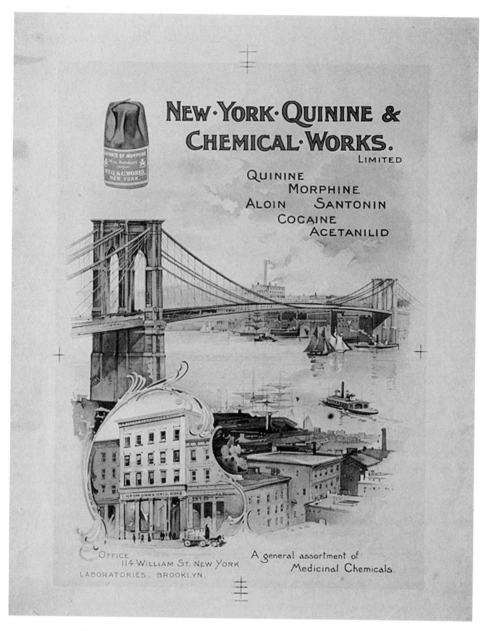

Advertisement, New York Quinine & Chemical Works Limited. "Quinine, Morphine, Aloin, Santonin, Cocaine, Acetanlid," ca. 1890–1900.

consolidated firm became the country's leading distributor of pharmaceutical products. A spinoff from M&R—the New York Quinine and Chemical Works—concentrated on manufacturing; it turned out opium and morphine, among other items, in its Williamsburg lab. And a leading rival, E. R. Squibb, founded in 1858 in Brooklyn, had its lab nearby; the *Squibb Materia Medica* for 1906 offered opium and laudanum for sale.

The giants of the German chemical industry were a presence as well. E. Merck of Darmstadt marketed its morphine through the port of New York. In 1891 it opened an American branch, Merck & Co., which in 1903 established manufacturing facilities just across from Staten Island, in Rahway, New Jersey. Bayer—developer of heroin and aspirin—used Schieffelin & Co. as its US representative; other European firms turned to import outfits like Lehn & Fink.

Gotham thus became by far the largest drug distribution center in the United States. In 1907 the combined manufacturing and wholesale branches of the city's pharmaceutical trade were annually buying and selling $100 million worth of drugs and chemicals.

At around the same time, the patent medicine industry, which packaged and advertised various drugs for mass sales, was reaching the peak of its capacity. And while there were nostrum dealers throughout the United States, this business, too, had had a long and important presence in New York City. Back in 1881 industry leaders, led by Gotham-based Charles Crittenton, the largest dealer in the country, had established the Proprietary Medicine Manufacturers and Dealers Association, devoted to mitigating competition and stabilizing prices. Its managers often worked hand in glove with those of the National Wholesale Druggists Association (of which William Jay Schieffelin was a pillar and, from 1910, president) and the National Association of Druggists. Any retailer found selling medicines at cut-rate prices was likely to find his supply line severed by one or another of these behemoths, which is why the troika was often referred to collectively as the Drug Trust.

OPIATES WERE NOT THE ONLY PSYCHOACTIVE DRUG PROMOTED. Cocaine, opium's great rival, was of more recent vintage, dating to 1884 when Dr. Karl Köller of Vienna announced he'd been able to anesthetize the surface of the human eye with a solution of cocaine hydrochloride. Days later, Dr. T. R. Pooley, a New York ophthalmologist, confirmed cocaine's marvelous properties as a topical anesthetic, and the following year Dr. J. Leonard Corning, a New York neurologist, discovered its usefulness as a spinal anesthetic; a patient could now read the paper while a surgeon cut off a leg.

Gotham rapidly became the center of cocaine import and manufacture. In 1905 the city's pharmaceutical companies imported over a million pounds of coca leaves, and between E. R. Squibb, McKesson & Robbins, New York Quinine, and Merck, the dollar value of cocaine sales made it one of the industry's five highest-grossing products.

Cocaine rapidly made its way onto the patent medicine bill of fare. Many of the earliest products capitalized on its utility as an anesthetic—toothache drops, hemorrhoid remedies, and corn cures, in the form of an ointment or a solution, were highly popular—and its properties as a vasoconstrictor and bronchodilator made it seemingly ideal for the relief of, and even cure for, sinusitis and hay fever. Items like Dr. Agnew's Catarrh Cure, made by New York's Anglo-American Medicine Company, came in a cocaine solution that could be sprayed into the nose, or as a powder admixed with sugar of milk (lactose) that could be snuffed.

Recreational and self-enhancement products also poured onto the market in the 1880s. Metcalf's Coca Wine was advertised as a valuable tonic for "public speakers, singers and actors," and also athletes, "who have found by practical experience that a steady course of coca taken both before and after any trial of strength or endurance will impart energy to every movement." Coca-Cola, which arrived in 1886, was described as the "ideal brain tonic." Other formats included cocaine cordials, coca cigarettes, and cocaine solutions for those who preferred injection (as did Sherlock Holmes, who favored a 7 percent solution, as Dr. Watson related in *The Sign of Four* (1890), six years before Dr. Freud ended a twelve-year-long involvement with cocaine.

Cocaine production soared roughly 700 percent between 1890 and 1902, in which year wholesaler Schieffelin foresaw a bright future for pharmaceutical chemists, given the new wonder drug. Cocaine, like heroin, was even marketed to opiate addicts experiencing withdrawal symptoms—Parke-Davis announced its product would "free the victims of alcohol and opium habits from their bondage"—but its own addictive capabilities, and other deleterious effects, were recognized relatively quickly, chiefly by doctors, partly because they were among the earliest users.

These downsides didn't prevent cocaine from becoming a popular drug of choice among recreational users. It began spreading through the white underworld, the practice frequently acquired in brothels, where prostitutes introduced customers to cocaine's pleasures, or in street gangs, where members were alerted by their fellows. The Hudson Dusters were particular aficionados—"dust" being one common synonym for cocaine in the emerging drug culture. Others were "coke," "snow," and "blow"—the latter from "having a blow," after a mode of ingestion in which the consumer put cocaine powder in a glass snuff bottle whose stopper had two holes for tubes; the user put one in the nose, the other in the mouth, and then blew.

Cocaine began cutting into opium use. It was less risky to ingest as it gave off no powerful odor, its equipment was far more portable than opium's elaborate rigs, and it did not have to be used in fixed locations well known to the police. It was also more addictive, not being subject to the elaborate and time-consuming smoking rituals, and users were not nested in social settings where others might constrain overuse. The resulting overindulgence could lead over time to physical deterioration and social dysfunction. Heavy users of cocaine might become paranoid, even violent—unlike hop-heads, who just tended to nod off. Addicts began turning up at Bellevue's Psychopathic Ward, and some hospitals set aside "cocaine wards" in which "coke drunks" could detox. Soon a new figure of fear was conjured up, the "cocaine fiend," who might run amok, steal, even kill to support his habit, someone akin to a carrier of a contagious disease, worthy of permanent quarantine. "The vicious user of a drug whose sole excuse is the seeking for new sensations," argued Dr. John Van Doren Young, secretary of the Medical Society of the County of New York, was someone who needed "restraint by law in order that he may not become a menace to the public weal and a care for the public charities." Indeed, such people should be "confined in properly equipped institutions," Young believed, "where they can eke out the remainder of their miserable existence as living examples of the dangers to which these habits lead."

Dr. Young's hyperbolic response was not typical of his profession, and even he insisted that his strictures did not apply to respectable members of the community who, through "innocent and ignorant" consumption of patent medicines, had contracted a drug habit. Most physicians, led by the American Medical Association (AMA), joined the movement to bring patent medicine manufacturers to heel, a drive sparkplugged by muckraking journalists. In 1905 *Collier's* began running a series by Samuel Hopkins Adams entitled "The Great American Fraud." Adams attacked the manufacturers of "cocain-[*sic*] and opium-bearing nostrums" as a "shameful trade that stupefies helpless babies, and makes criminals of our young men and harlots of our young women." The AMA published Adams's series as a book and distributed it widely. Other attacks on the pharmaceutical industry followed, denouncing its profit-motivated failure to reveal that it added dangerous drugs to its products. These assaults helped win passage in 1906 of the Pure Food and Drug Act, which required that the presence of morphine, opium, cocaine, or cannabis be clearly indicated on the label.

The following year, New York State entered the lists with a much tougher piece of legislation, initiated not by the city's drug reform community, but by a Catholic priest and a Tammany politician. Father James B. Curry was pastor of St. James' Church, at 32 James Street, just off the Bowery. He'd noticed that several young men of his parish had gotten addicted to cocaine. Curry got in touch with State Assemblyman Alfred Emanuel Smith

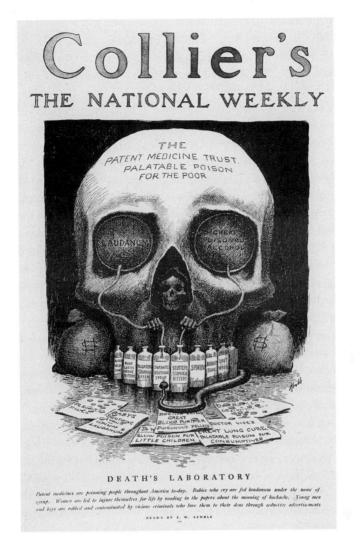

"Death's Laboratory—The Patent Medicine Trust." Cover, *Collier's*, June 3, 1905. (Food Collection/ Alamy Stock Photo)

(a Tammany stalwart and a former St. James altar boy). Smith immediately drew up a proposed Anti-Cocaine Law and in March 1907 got Albany to pass it, despite opposition from patent medicine companies and wholesale druggists. Smith's law made it illegal to sell cocaine in New York State without a prescription, trusting physicians and pharmacists to limit access to responsible (non-recreational) users. The law also required that items like Dr. Agnew's Catarrh Cure, if sold in New York, bear labels announcing that "this preparation, containing among other valuable ingredients, a small quantity of COCAINE, is, in accordance with the New York Pharmacy Act, hereby labeled POISON." Pressured by muckrakers, legislators, and pharmaceutical industry leaders like Schieffelin who were concerned about their profession's public image, patent medicine manufacturers rapidly deleted cocaine from their product lists.

The new unavailability of drug-inflected remedies, coupled with the growing reluctance of physicians to prescribe cocaine, and of pharmacists to fulfill such prescriptions, pushed addicts or recreational users into the arms of rogue retailers, who would prescribe, or fulfill, almost anything if the price was right. Other balked users turned to street salesmen—"peddlers"—who stepped in to fill the breach. In August 1908 the *Times* noted that since passage of the "Smith Anti-Cocaine" bill the previous year, "peddlers, unmoral creatures of the underworld, have sprung up to ply a thriving trade in dispensing the drug among the victims of the habit." Seventh Avenue between 28th and 33rd Streets was now known as "Poison Row," an ironic nod to the new labeling requirement; Third Avenue from 12th to 16th was more forthrightly denominated "Cocaine Row." The peddled products, however, were generally of lower quality and higher price, which drove some straitened addicts to thievery to meet the steeper cost, or led them to switch to cheaper or more accessible drugs, like morphine and heroin.

In 1909 Congress passed the Smoking Opium Act, which banned the "importation and use of opium for other than medicinal purposes." Violators could be fined up to $5,000 and imprisoned for up to two years; mere possession of smoking opium was deemed sufficient to warrant conviction "unless the defendant shall explain the possession to the satisfaction of the jury." The bill sailed through Congress, in part because it had been proposed and written by Secretary of State Elihu Root, as part of a diplomatic offensive that aimed to expand US penetration of the Chinese market.[31] Also, there was virtually no opposition to the measure because smoking opium was associated with the Chinese, gangsters, and prostitutes, because American pharmaceutical firms had little financial interest in its importation, and because banning it didn't threaten the interests of physicians or pharmacists.

The 1909 act proved effective, albeit in some unanticipated ways. It finished off the opium dens, as intended, but this forced some smokers into private apartments (just as the extirpation of brothels gave rise to telephone-and-apartment sex). It drove others to switch to snorting or shooting up morphine or heroin, practices considerably more dangerous than smoking opium. It also led to an increase of what was called "bootlegging." At a 1911 congressional hearing into the importation and use of opium, one legislator asked invited witness William Jay Schieffelin: Wasn't it true that "the more restrictions you put around [illegitimate use] the more you drive it away from legitimate druggists into the hands of what you call bootleggers?" Schieffelin replied that he certainly hoped so—"I would like to see it entirely driven into the hands of bootleggers," leaving the drug industry free to "only sell them for legitimate medicinal purposes, and have nothing to do with supplying the victims of the habit." A 1912 story in the *World* suggested he might get what he'd wished for. It estimated that in the previous year underground suppliers had smuggled in large amounts of opium from Canada, in the process netting themselves a profit of roughly $3 million.[32]

In 1914 pressure from reformers helped win passage of the Harrison Narcotics Tax Act, which required "all persons who produce, import, manufacture, compound, deal in, dispense, sell, distribute, or give away opium or coca leaves, their salts, derivatives, or preparations" to register with the federal government and keep meticulous records of all their narcotics-related transactions. Nonregistered dealers—such as street peddlers—could now be imprisoned for

---

31. The United States had called for an international conference at which Western countries would pledge support for China's long-standing efforts to block the influx of opium that Britain had engineered decades earlier. Root hoped the show of goodwill would help overcome Chinese resistance to affording American capital greater access to China's economy. As the Shanghai Conference was about to get under way, Root belatedly realized that the US itself had no laws on its books proscribing opium use, so he hurriedly arranged for such a measure, in order, as he put it, "to save our face" at Shanghai.

32. One bootlegger who did not prosper in this profession was Monk Eastman, who had been paroled from Sing Sing in 1909. Monk returned to his old haunts, only to find that his former gang, now under new management, had zero interest in restoring him to power. So he turned to opium, using it, selling it, and—or so claimed the police when they busted him in 1912—manufacturing it without a license, and it was for the latter offense that he served an eight-month stretch in the Blackwell's Island Penitentiary.

five years.[33] Middle-class users could still get their supply from doctors and pharmacists, so quality remained high, dosages controlled, and drug deaths rare. Working-class addicts, however, including growing numbers of Italians, Middle Easterners, and Asians, were forced into a thriving black market, wherein prices climbed ever higher.

That market, in turn, relied for supplies on "dope doctors," unscrupulous druggists, smugglers, importers, and gangsters who ransacked Gotham's many drug company warehouses. By the end of the 1910s heroin (taken on its own or in combination with other chemicals) had solidified its position as New York's drug of choice.[34] In 1919 it was estimated that perhaps 90 percent of America's heroin addicts lived within 180 miles of Manhattan.

BY THAT TIME, THE REFORMERS WHO HAD BEEN FIGHTING crime and vice for two decades could look back with a certain amount of satisfaction. The alliance of corporate elites, professional experts, and Protestant clerics had gone a long way toward cracking down on hitherto tolerated behavior and imposing their vision of a righteous civil society on Gotham's unrulier citizens. They had shut down Raines Law hotels, shuttered many brothels, blown the whistle on white slavers, and driven streetwalkers underground; they had axed pool halls, raided gambling casinos and policy shops, terminated on-track betting, banned boxing, and helped execute a crooked cop; they had forced saloons to clean up their act, helped put opium dens out of business, forced the pharmaceutical industry to detoxify home remedies, and tightened restrictions on drug traffickers; they had gone a long way to cleaning up the police department, had splintered the big street gangs, had helped enact gun control, and had made serious inroads on Tammany's grip on political power. True, there were some remaining trouble spots—the new phenomenon of labor racketeering, the expansion of drug peddling, the novel presence of mafiosi and Black Handers and pimps, and the obdurate resistance of saloons to Sunday drinking laws. But now, with a national prohibition amendment hurtling toward ratification, it looked like the millennium might finally be at hand.

---

33. By that standard young Salvatore Lucania got off lightly. Born in Lercara Friddi, near Palermo, in 1897, he'd been brought to New York in the spring of 1907, his family settling in at 265 East 10th Street (between First Avenue and Avenue A), in a predominantly Jewish neighborhood. After years of chronic truancy he left school for good in 1911, aged 14, and took a job as a shipping clerk in a hat factory. After a few months he decided he'd "rather be dead," and left conventional employment behind as well. The teenager picked pockets, burgled some apartments, shot craps, and with a ganglet of cronies extorted money from Jewish kids on their way to school. But noting the number of addicts in the neighborhood, he went into the drug-peddling business, for which he was arrested in June 1916 (giving his name as Charles Lucania) and sentenced to a year, of which he served six months.

34 When New York opened up a narcotics clinic on Worth Street in 1919, of the first 3,262 patients treated, 6 were there for a cocaine problem, 41 for a mix of morphine and heroin, 42 for morphine and cocaine, 305 for cocaine and heroin, 690 for morphine, and 2,178 for heroin alone.

18

Union Town

LABOR DAY

There was something both comfortably reassuring and curiously antiquated about the 1907 Labor Day parade.

Despite a torrential downpour—hundreds of umbrella vendors did a brisk business—25,000 turned out to march, an imposing demonstration of organized labor's municipal presence. The usual formidable array of unions was on hand: the many varieties of building-trades workers, printers, and teamsters; also the pattern makers and actors, telegraphers and longshoremen, butchers, pavers, coopers, bakers, bagel makers, bartenders, cigar makers, metal polishers, and horseshoers—to name but a few. Many were accompanied by floats on which working craftsmen displayed their skills and products.

The parade was a tendril in time. Coming on the twenty-fifth anniversary of the first Labor Day celebration, which had wound around Union Square back in September 1882, it conveyed continuity. Many of the unions present in 1907 had taken part in that earlier demonstration. Many were themselves older still: the horseshoers union dated to 1874, the carpenters and joiners to 1867, the bricklayers 1865, the cigar makers 1864, the coopers 1864, the plasterers 1862, the pavers 1860, the molders 1859, the hatters 1854, the stonecutters 1853, and the typographical union to 1850 with roots back to 1809. Indeed, the 1907 parade did not look fundamentally different from civic street celebrations of the eighteenth century, like the Grand Federal Procession of 1788 hailing the Constitution, in which thousands of New York artisans—blacksmiths, bakers, ship joiners, peruke makers, sixty-odd trades in all—paraded with the floats and banners of their craft.

This continuity was somewhat odd. Why, in an industrial era, were labor's organizations so redolent of the preindustrial world? Was this evidence of stability? Or an inability to respond to changing times? And why, at the moment when myriad business competitors were merging into giant corporations, was organized labor still splintered into hundreds of often rivalrous units, and getting more fragmented with each passing year? In 1898 there were 440 labor entities in Greater New York; by 1904 there were 670.

The building trades were particularly fissiparous. Unions representing the men constructing Gotham's skyscrapers, bridges, and tunnels, or building its tenements, apartment houses, and mansions, were grouped loosely into the categories of "outside" and "inside" workers. Outside organizations included the unions of the Housesmiths and Bridgemen, the Caisson Workers, Compressed Air Workers, Tunnel Bracers, Rockmen and Excavators, Rock Drillers and Tool Sharpeners, House Shorers, Derrickmen, Double-drum Hoisting Engineers, Portable and Hoisting Engineers, Pipe Caulkers and Tappers, Steam Pipe and Boiler Coverers, Boilermakers, Sheet Metal and Stamped Ceiling Workers, Tin and Sheet Iron Workers, Metal Roofers, Mosaic and Encaustic Tile Layers, Marble and Enamel Mosaic Workers, Stone Cutters, Bluestone Cutters, Brownstone Cutters, Granite Cutters, Marble Workers, Marble Polishers and Rubbers, Cement and Asphalt Laborers, Asbestos Workers, and Elevator Constructors (among others). Inside workers included Carpenters and Joiners (joiners being cabinetmakers), Steam and Hot Water Fitters, Decorators, Electrical Workers, Bricklayers, the Laborers' Protective Union (largely aides to bricklayers), along with Plumbers, Painters, Plasterers, and Paper Hangers.

There were advantages to this micro-division of labor. New unions could bud out rapidly in response to new developments. But there were serious drawbacks, too, most notably the jurisdictional squabbles that broke out between unions over the right to perform particular tasks—and to receive the dues of those who performed them. Often these were triggered by the development of new building materials or products that transgressed customary trade boundaries. The emergence of reinforced concrete as a cheaper alternative to brick work touched off a conflict between the Bricklayers, the Plasterers, and a start-up outfit of Cement Finishers. Metal doors appeared. Should they be installed by the ironworkers who made them, or the carpenters who traditionally erected doors? Who was to wire the new electric elevators—the Electricians or the Elevator Constructors? Should the new thermostats be installed by plumbers or gasfitters? Would the Mosaic and Encaustic Tile Layers get control of the latest type of ceramic tile, or would it be the province of the Marble and Enamel Mosaic Workers?

There were also struggles between unions that did the same work but whose members were of different ethnic background or political persuasion. There were territorial conflicts, too, some of them artifacts of the city's consolidation, like the rivalry between the Journeymen Pie Bakers Union of Greater New York, and the Pie Baking Employes' [sic] Union of Brooklyn. And there was straight out head-butting between virtually identical entities, as with the war between the United Brotherhood of Carpenters and Joiners, the Amalgamated Society of Carpenters, and the Amalgamated Wood Workers; or that between (and among) the seven competing marble worker locals, the Bridge and Stone Curb Setters, and the International Association of Pavers, Rammermen, and Flag Layers.

These rival claims were not merely rhetorical; they led to jurisdictional strikes, with one or another of the contending unions calling out enough workers to shut down entire building sites. Hardly a week went by without major projects being interrupted. Indeed, strikes against fellow workers vastly outnumbered strikes against employers.[1]

And yet, during the boom years, these craft outfits were able to win or preserve significant benefits for their members. In part this was because labor leaders, only too aware of the unseemly wrangling in their ranks, did try to bridle competition. They did so not by *merging* the unions into larger structures—adopting, say, an industry-wide form of organization—but rather by establishing or strengthening *confederations*, which then attempted to mitigate clashes between fractious members, without infringing on their local autonomy.

Some of these bodies were at the level of a trade—like the United Board of Building Trades, a 1902 creation that merged the hitherto antagonistic bodies that had been representing inside and outside unions.

At the citywide level, the largely German and socialist-leaning Central Labor Federation merged in 1899 with the largely Irish and non-socialist Central Labor Union, forming the Central Federated Union (CFU), a group that by 1902 claimed to represent 140,000 members of Gotham's workforce. The CFU aimed to adjudicate jurisdictional disputes and encourage allied action against employers, such as sympathy strikes or boycotts, when so requested by embattled unions.

At a national level, intercity confederations emerged to foster united action between geographically dispersed locals—like the International Association of Bridge and Structural Iron Workers of America formed in 1897 (the use of "International" usually signifying that one or more Canadian unions had come on board).

Over and above all these was the American Federation of Labor, which by the new century had effectively vanquished its major rivals (notably the Knights of Labor), and become the overarching umbrella for citywide, craftwide, and nationwide bodies, and for the constituent locals below them, which retained their separate identity and authority.

These supra-local confederations were able to smooth over some but by no means all jurisdictional conflicts. Indeed each was riven by its own internal divisions, and spats broke out between the different levels as well. In 1903, for instance, New York ironworker locals refused to ratify a nationwide contract negotiated by the international union, effectively sinking it. And in the 1907 Labor Day parade the citywide CFU and the craftwide United Board—which hadn't been seeing eye to eye on political issues—split into two contingents and marched in opposite directions: the CFU unions headed south on Fifth Avenue from 59th Street, and a half hour later the building-trades unions headed north on Fifth from 60th.

Nevertheless, the confederation model enabled much of New York labor to hold its own against much of New York capital, in large part because, in the manufacturing sector, capital was nearly as fragmented as labor. It's true that corporate giants were beginning to make their presence felt in the local economy, but most employers in the manufacturing sphere remained small in scale and highly competitive. This state of affairs gave confederated unions considerable leverage in negotiations over wages, hours, and working conditions, and allowed them at times to establish "union shops," in which employers agreed to hire only union members.

Manufacturers, to strengthen their own hand, also formed federations—of building contractors, brewers, jewelers, printers, publishers, and express companies (among others)—which

---

1. The city's teamsters finessed some of this by organizing themselves into non-overlapping bodies, named after what they hauled in their carts, cabs, and trucks; thus there were Milk, Meat, Ice, Wholesale Grocery, Wholesale Flour and Feed, Coal and Asphalt, Department Store Merchandise, Furniture and Storage Warehouse, Paper, Street Cleaning, Private Ash, Grease, Bone, Building Material, Lime and Cement, Lumber, and Funeral locals.

then squared off against the allied craft unions. The clash of contending constellations became the characteristic format of economic combat during the boom decade. These battles could take quite different forms, as a look at warfare in the construction and the printing trades makes clear.

BUILDERS AND PRINTERS

No group was closer to the heart of the city's skyscraper and infrastructure boom than the ironworkers. The men who bestrode the steel skeletons rising in Manhattan, and the great bridges being flung across the East River, were an individualistic devil-may-care lot. The "Cowboys of the Skies" were famed for their physical courage in the face of great danger. Collectively they were as timid as their individual behavior was bold. Their Housesmiths'[2] and Bridgemen's Union (H&B) traced its origins to an 1864 entity, which had collapsed and revived several times, most recently in 1894. In 1896 it joined the newly constituted International Association of Bridge and Structural Iron Workers of America, becoming Local No. 2. But the H&B remained weak and ineffective, its members making between $1.75 and 2.50 for a ten-hour day while their counterparts in Chicago were clearing $4.00.

Things began to change in 1896 when Local 2 elected a new "walking delegate." Walking delegates were full-time employees of a union who walked from site to site making sure their union's rules were being enforced; if they weren't, the officials were empowered to shut down a job on the spot. Local 2's new walking delegate—or "business agent," as the position was coming to be called—was ironworker Sam Parks. He had arrived in Gotham in 1895 from Chicago, where he'd been working for the Fuller Company, and when Fuller opened up its New York operation it brought Parks east as a foreman.

A skinny but broad-shouldered Irishman, Parks was one tough hombre. He'd been an itinerant laborer—lumberjack, coal heaver, sailor, railroad brakeman—before becoming a high-steel worker, and he set out to expand the H&B membership using a mix of argument and muscle. Going from site to site, accompanied by a forbidding-looking crew (whimsically called the "entertainment committee"), and a pet bulldog (wryly named Arbitrator), Parks adopted the following approach: "In organizing men in New York I talked with them at first nice and pleasant, explaining how they could be better off in a union. Bosses began to learn that I was about and pretty busy; and they had men stationed about to 'do' me. But they could not keep me off a job. I sneaked up ladders and elevator shafts, stole up on beams, waited for the men on cellar doors where they ate dinner. Some did not believe unions would be good for them; and I gave them a belt on the jaw. That changed their minds. Lots of men can't be moved by any other argument."

Within three months, virtually all of New York's 4,500 (mostly Irish) ironworkers had joined up. Parks then deployed similar methods to maintain his authority inside the union, unleashing his rib-cracking adjutants against any who dared challenge him at meetings in Maennerchor Hall on East 56th Street—a leadership strategy with echoes of the way would-be New York gang chieftains like Monk Eastman were attaining their dominance.

Parks's power expanded exponentially when he gained control of the United Board of Building Trades. Composed of business agents from all thirty-nine constituent unions, it represented in 1902 roughly 60,000 construction workers, and was authorized to call

---

2. Despite the implied domestic scale and venue of the term "housesmith," in this era it meant a worker who erected iron or steel structures.

sympathy strikes that could and did shut down even the biggest of projects. Parks, a deft tactician, launched strike after strike, targeting contractors one at a time. In the middle of New York's frenzied skyboom, builders bowed to his demands rather than halt a project, especially as contracts were commonly on a cost-plus basis, so builders could easily pass the financial burden to owners. By 1898 his campaign had raised the wage level to $2.50. He then jacked it up to $3.20 by 1900, to $4.00 in 1902, and to $4.50 by 1903, when he announced, "We are going to get five dollars, and then we'll stop"—as, after all, "capital has some rights."

Given such a track record, his men adored "Fighting Sam" Parks, declared him their Moses, and forgave him his heavy-handed methods. They forgave him too—at first—for transforming their collective strikes into an instrument for his personal enrichment. Parks began threatening work stoppages to extort cash from contractors. If an employer refused to ante up, "Fighting Sam" would order his men to down tools, often without providing a reason, and they forthwith did his bidding. "I know what Parks is doing," said one union man, "but what do I care. He has raised my wages. Let him have his graft!"

In March 1902 he told Nels Poulson, president of the huge Hecla Iron Works in Williamsburg—then producing ornamental ironwork for the Flatiron, Stock Exchange, and Chamber of Commerce buildings—that Hecla had to cough up $1,000. When Poulson summarily rejected the demand, Parks shut him down, throwing 1,200 men out of work for a week, and costing the company $50,000. When Poulson finally agreed to a meeting, Parks told him bluntly, "You can go to work when you pay Sam Parks," and doubled the bribe-price. Poulson proffered a check for $2,000, which Parks incautiously accepted, a move he would come to regret.

Employers also bribed Parks to overlook violations of contract clauses, or to call strikes against their competitors. It was widely noted in New York construction circles that during Parks's reign Harry Black's Fuller Company never suffered a major job action, and it was commonly assumed that Parks remained (clandestinely) on the Fuller payroll.

By 1902 Parks was king of the building trades and a leading figure in Gotham's union movement. On Labor Day that year, he was appointed grand marshal of a 35,000-strong building-trades parade, replete with floats and thirty-six bands (including the 69th Regiment Fife and Drum Corps, the Catholic Protectory Band, and the American Federation of Musicians' Band). Parks himself, mounted on a white horse, rode at the front of his nearly 5,000 Housesmiths'and Bridgemen's Union members, all attired resplendently in red blouses, white hats, and blue trousers. And, as the *New York Times* noted approvingly, "the usual mottoes to be seen in socialist parades calling for the downfall of the capitalistic system were conspicuously absent."

In 1903, however, drunk on power or driven by greed, Parks went on a rampage. That spring he ordered hundreds of strikes, ruined many small builders, and threatened to pull all 60,000 men out if employers didn't come up with 10–20 percent increases (and commensurate compensation for himself). When some workers balked, Parks unleashed his bulldog and bully boys. The resulting shutdowns cost his men $3 million in lost wages.

The offensive provoked a concerted response from employers. In May 1903 nearly 800 of them met. Representatives from nearly every major building firm in the city were present (with the exception of the Fuller Company), and from most of the existing craft combinations as well. Those on hand included the Master Carpenters' Association, the Employers Association of Architectural Iron Workers, the Electrical Contractors Association, the League of Heat and Cold Insulation, the Iron League Erectors Association, the Metal Ceiling Association, and the Parquet Flooring Association. The meeting voted to form the Building

Trades Employers Association (BTEA) and selected as president Otto M. Eidlitz, who had inherited his father's highly reputed construction company—it had built J. P. Morgan's residence and the Metropolitan Opera House. The assembled employers vowed to force the unions to accept an arbitration plan that would sidestep the walking delegates. Parks got the United Board to reject the plan, but only by a 19–16 vote. His star was losing altitude.

The employers next went to the politically ambitious District Attorney Jerome, who was making a name for himself as a crusader against corruption. On being shown the cashed $2,000 check—Poulson had had it framed—Jerome arrested Parks for extortion and sent him to the Tombs. There he was immediately bailed out by his cigar-chomping, 250-pound friend "Big Bill" Devery. The former Tammany district leader, former right-hand man of Boss Croker, and former chief of the New York Police Department, had repeatedly eluded conviction on charges of bribery and extortion. Big Bill had broken with Boss Charlie Murphy and was planning an independent run for mayor; he hoped a grateful Parks would deliver union votes.

In June, the ironworkers, rebuffing Jerome's charges, reelected Parks as walking delegate of Local 2. Three days later, Parks led forty business agents around the city, pulling men off construction jobs. In August, Parks went on trial for extortion; he was convicted and sentenced to two and a half years, but his lawyer, arguing that bad publicity had made a fair trial impossible, won him a new trial and temporary freedom. Released just as Labor Day rolled round again, Parks was once more selected to lead a building-trades march. Yet when he clambered aboard his white steed, many of his once-loyal H&B members were missing in action, despite his threat to fine any who didn't join his "vindication parade." Worn down by the constant strikes, many of the high-steel men were prepared to sign the arbitration agreement employers were proposing and get back to work. Parks refused and called more strikes, but now his troops ignored him. At the end of October, he was again convicted and dispatched to Sing Sing, where he would die, in 1904, of tuberculosis. That same year, in a deal struck between the iron workers' International and the new employers' association, Local 2 was extinguished and its members scattered among four new locals. The erasure of Local 2, the passing of Parks, and the inauguration of arbitration procedures were clear wins for the builders. But they didn't have enough muscle to reverse the gains the unions had already won. The union shop, higher wages, and shorter hours remained in place.

PARKS'S PATH WAS NOT UNIQUE. While he was the most flamboyant, others proved more efficient in their corruption. Lawrence Murphy, treasurer of the Stone Cutters Union, extracted $200,000 worth of bribes, primarily from the Stonecutters Association of Brooklyn, a haul that was split between the union's six principal officers (enabling one to buy a farm in Scotland), though fives and tens were doled out to members. At his trial in July 1903, Murphy's defense was that a) such extortion had become commonplace, and b) it was really just a "fine" exacted from employers for having used non-union labor in the past. These gambits went nowhere, and Murphy was dispatched to the slammer. Murphy's and Parks's takings, moreover, would soon pale before the accumulations amassed by Robert Brindell, an official of the carpenters union who would get control of the building trades and pull in a cool million before he too was sent up the river.

The phenomenon attracted the attention of muckrakers, who began to call Parks and the others "labor bosses," arguing they were an analog of the political bosses who ran Tammany Hall, and of the corporate bosses who ran the economy. Lincoln Steffens, in *The Shame of the Cities* (1904), suggested "there was no essential difference" between "the corruption of a

Cover, *McClure's Magazine*, November 1903. (Library of Congress Prints and Photographs Division)

labor union, a bank, and a political machine," and "none between a labor boss like Sam Parks, a boss of banks like John D. Rockefeller, a boss of railroads like J. P. Morgan, and a political boss like Matthew S. Quay." Ray Stannard Baker had a different take. In a 1903 *McClure's* article ("The Trust's New Tool—The Labor Boss"), he argued that corrupt labor leaders were in the end creatures of big capital and, specifically, that Parks was really an agent of Harry Black's Fuller Company, a proposition with which DA Jerome agreed.

Such high-altitude reflections on the nature of union corruption seldom essayed systematic comparisons between different types of labor organizations, and thus couldn't account for the stark differences between the ironworkers and, say, the printing trades, differences that were clearly apparent closer to the ground.

JUST AFTER NEW YEAR'S DAY OF 1906, when the New York Typographical Union No. 6 joined a nationwide printers strike for the eight-hour day, one of the strikers announced: "We printers are gentlemen, and there'll be no Sam Parks methods with us."

The printers union indeed had a very different organizational culture from Parks's outfit, rooted partly in the structure of the printing trade, and partly in their organization's century-long history in Gotham. The New-York Printers Union (1850)—itself a descendant of the New York Typographical Society (1809)—was one of fourteen associations that in 1852 had

American Type Founders Co., 1902. (Image No. 93.1.1.194, Byron Company/Museum of the City of New York)

created the National Typographical Union (which became the International Typographical Union [ITU] in 1869). At that founding 1852 convention, a lottery was held to assign locals a number. The New York group, drawing number six, became Typographical Union No. 6—soon known familiarly (probably because it was the largest and strongest local) as "Big Six."

Originally Big Six had included all the trade's craftworkers, but as new technologies came along in the 1880s and 1890s, their practitioners spun off into separate organizations—creating unions of electrotypers, photoengravers, pressmen, lithographers, and bookbinders. This left the Typographical Union primarily representing typesetters who worked for newspapers, magazines, publishing houses, and job shops (which printed small batches of customer-specific orders). The various printing trades nevertheless retained a strong tradition of cooperative unionism, and in 1894 formed a federation—the Allied Printing Trades Council—to counteract fragmentation. The printers also evolved a system of internal democracy that offered a stark contrast to the caudillismo structure of the building trades under Sam Parks. Big Six had two internal political parties—the Administration and the Anti-Administration (the first favoring moderation, the second militancy)—which were formally organized, published weekly papers, and held primary elections to nominate local candidates for direct election by the membership.

In 1899 the ITU finally obtained the nine-hour day in book and job work (for which they had first called in 1887). And in 1904 it announced that after January 1, 1906, eight hours would constitute a day's work, and employers who refused to grant it would be struck.

At this the employers dug in their heels. They too had a long collective presence on the New York and national scene. Employing printers had formed the Typothetae (Ancient

Greek for "to put or set") of New York City in 1865. In 1887 a national organization of proprietors and master printers—the United Typothetae of America (UTA)—had been organized to resist the ITU's demand for a shorter working day. It also celebrated the glories of the printing craft; its first president was Theodore De Vinne, a renowned printer and a founder of Gotham's Grolier Club, dedicated (said its charter) to "the study, collecting, and appreciation of books and works on paper, their art, history, production, and commerce."

Though staunch believers in their absolute right to run their businesses, most employing printers had pragmatically negotiated with unions, until 1904, when a growing number of local Typothetae were swept up in the open-shop movement, which called for repudiating existing agreements that required shops to hire only union members. When confronted with the ITU's call for an eight-hour day, they opted for a showdown.

On December 30 New York Typothetae–affiliated printers posted notices declaring their shops open; the men regarded this as a lockout and set up pickets. The New York Typothetae, having amassed a war chest, now advertised for strikebreakers, from whom "loyalty to employers is expected," and set up headquarters in an old school building at 67 West 10th Street, where they established sleeping and eating facilities for those the strikers called "scabs" or "rats," but employers preferred to call "freemen," as having thrown off the union yoke.

Big Six set up its strike headquarters in Webster Hall on East 11th Street, and workers chipped in to build a very substantial strike fund; the union would end up spending $762,485 in strike benefits.[3]

Some shops began deserting the Typothetae and signing contracts with the union almost as soon as the strike began; the mighty Harper Brothers gave in on January 4. Others hung on, counting in part on winning public sympathy when the strikers resorted to violence. So sure were the employers of impending mayhem that they hired a corps of photographers to take pictures of pickets assaulting strikebreakers, and retained a squadron of lawyers to be ready to prepare cases against union malefactors. They were chagrined to discover, as they admitted to the press, that the "strikers, instead of resorting to violence, are buying off our men." Pickets would approach a strikebreaker and "in a courtly and gentlemanly way" point out the benefits of unionism, offer him free membership in Big Six (which would entitle him to strike pay of twelve to fifteen dollars a week for doing nothing), and provide a cash payment for transport back home. This approach, the employers complained, "completely disarms him, and he falls an easy victim to their blandishments."

In mid-January the electrotypers and stereotypers went out in sympathy. So did the waiters and cooks who'd been hired to cater to the strikebreakers housed on West 10th Street: "We won't serve non-union meals for non-union printers," they declared.

By the fall of 1905 other leading houses had yielded, though the struggle dragged on for almost two more years, until by late 1907 nearly all the major New York shops, including that owned by the secretary of the New York Typothetae, were running on an eight-hour schedule, using only union workers. Worse, from the UTA's perspective, given its rule that any employer who gave in to the union had to resign from the association, the group lost nearly half its members. In 1908 it quietly removed that rule from its books. The lockout had been a total rout.

---

3. It helped that in 1890 newspaper publishers withdrew from the United Typothetae and formed the American Newspaper Publishers' Association; this meant that the ITU, which continued to represent compositors in both wings, was able to draw on support from newspaper workers.

BANG THE BELL, JACK, I'M ON BOARD

Such successes were more the rule than the exception during the merger wave years of 1898–1904, as skilled workers parlayed their advantageous position into union shop contracts. With union membership a passport to higher wages, shorter hours, and better working conditions, craftsmen surged into the many unions chartered by the American Federation of Labor. Nationally, AFL membership leapt from 250,000 in 1897 to over 2,000,000 in 1904. In Greater New York, the number of union members went from 125,429 in 1898 to 254,719 in 1904.[4]

A union card wrought demonstrable improvements in a skilled worker's standard of living. His pay packet allowed him to move to better housing in a better neighborhood, provide his family with more food and clothing, buy a small insurance policy, and perhaps rent a summer cottage. His shorter hours meant more leisure time in which to enjoy Gotham's multiplying popular entertainments.

These attainments were precarious. Craftsmen were vulnerable to the vagaries of the business cycle, or to seasonal fluctuations, or to accident, illness, and death, any of which could diminish or eliminate the breadwinner's earnings, plunging his family back down the social slope, their slide unchecked by any safety net. These were old familiar threats.

And there were new vulnerabilities, ones that stemmed from the inability or unwillingness of unions and their federations to confront some of the era's central dynamics: the merger movement and the corporatization of the economy; the attendant growth of factories; the deskilling of work via new technologies that enabled employers in many branches of industry to replace skilled craftsmen with semi- or unskilled workers; the tidal flow of immigration that dramatically increased the availability of such semi- or unskilled workers; and the political mobilization of capital, large and small, to blunt or halt the unionization drive.

In responding to these dynamics, union leaders from AFL president Samuel Gompers on down basically opted for a purely defensive strategy—to circle the wagons, protect what they'd won, and avoid reaching out to new constituencies. The approach and its consequences are evident in the history of Gompers's own union, the Cigar Makers International Union (CMIU) which Gompers had joined in 1864, its founding year, at the age of 14.

There were then but two locals, his own No. 15, the English-language one, and Local No. 10, for German-speakers; both were limited to skilled hand rollers. The 1870s brought the introduction of the cigar mold, a mechanical press that enabled manufacturers to break down the skilled craft into two stages, bunch making and rolling, the first of which was assigned to unskilled recent Bohemian immigrants who worked out of tenement apartments for lower wages. In 1874 Gompers took the lead in organizing a new union, more socialist minded, and more willing to try organizing the tenement workers; it joined the CMIU as Local No. 144. A disastrous strike in 1877 led him to retreat to a craftsmen-only stance. Tenement workers were barred; women and the semiskilled were excluded in practice by high dues. In the early 1880s the CMIU tried to put the "tenement trash" out of business by having the state outlaw home-work (in 1884), though stressing the compassionate aspects of shutting it down because it was (as it was) dangerous and unhealthy (the arguments that

---

4. In 1897 Gompers moved the AFL's national headquarters to Washington, and moved himself there as well. The New York headquarters were at 25 Third Avenue, near Cooper Union.

moved Teddy Roosevelt to win passage). But the courts declared the new law unconstitutional, and Gompers and his colleagues retreated to their parapets.

In the 1890s competition steadily increased. In addition to tenement work, some manufacturers shifted production to factories that had as many as 500 employees. These made a cheaper product—five-cent cigars, which undercut the CMIU shops' ten-cent version—lowering costs by hiring women. By 1900 one-third of the industry's workforce was female, with some factories composed entirely of women. These workers soon developed a cohesive solidarity and challenged managerial authority; however, they perforce remained non-union, because skilled males were unwilling to accept them as allies. Partly this was because (the men claimed) women were really temp workers at heart. As they intended to get married and leave the labor force, it was a waste of time and money to try to organize them. Partly it flowed from the masculinist culture that suffused the trade: craftworkers drew collective strength from their manliness, their fraternal loyalty, their mastery of a trade, their traditional work practices—a Samsonite strength they feared Delilahs would shave off. Rather than open their doors to women workers, and thus tackle head-on the vast changes in their industry, they promoted legislation that would limit women's presence in the workplace, in the name of protecting them. None of this forestalled the ongoing erosion of membership, with Gompers' old Local 144 among the hardest hit.[5]

Nevertheless, Gompers remained convinced he had chosen the right path, or at least the best available. The AFL's brand of craft unionism had weathered the economic storms of the 1890s, where that of its great rival the Knights of Labor had not. The AFL membership in the 1900s was skyrocketing. Why break hard-won contracts and stage sympathetic walkouts or launch general strikes to help the unskilled? Why try to organize the unorganized? Even if he had been inclined to do so, the fact remained that the AFL's membership consisted overwhelmingly of skilled workers, and if Gompers wanted to keep his position at the apex of organized labor, it would not be prudent to antagonize them. Hence "*sauve qui peut*," not "solidarity," came to be (metaphorically) inscribed on labor's banner. Which is one reason that AFL affiliates at the turn of the century embraced fewer than 20 percent of the working class. It was an archipelago of the organized in a sea of those left to their own devices.

READ ETHNOGRAPHICALLY, ORGANIZED LABOR CONSISTED OF A CHAIN of Northern European islands in a sea of Southern and Eastern Europeans.

The members of craft unions were overwhelmingly first- or second-generation Americans of British, German, and Irish descent, with the last group most heavily represented in labor's leadership. Each of these nationalities had its ranks boosted by new arrivals during the boom years, but these add-ons were as naught compared to the influx of Italians

---

5. Cigar rollers were hardly alone in not squarely confronting technological deskilling. Softstone cutters were seriously affected by the introduction of the stone planer, which allowed one man with a plane working limestone, brownstone, or bluestone to replace seven or eight hand workers. The unions responded by forbidding use of the machine in the city's stoneyards, where cutting had traditionally been done. But this only led contractors (after 1900) to order precut stone directly from quarries, which did use the machines, costing the union even more jobs. That, plus competition from concrete and terra-cotta, started a long slide in membership, with softstone cutters dropping from 25,000 to 10,000 between 1900 and 1915.

Printers proved more adroit. Rather than trying to block the introduction of typesetting machinery, Big Six won management approval for requiring that linotype operators had to be compositors (a reasonable demand, as it required printers' skills to realize the machines' maximum potential) and also guaranteeing compositors the right to learn the machines when introduced. In addition, displaced compositors were to be recompensed for being deprived of their work. Thus Big Six workers retained their strategic position in the production process.

from the south and Sicily, and Jews from Russia, Poland, and Austria-Hungary. In 1900 there were very roughly just under 500,000 Jews in New York City; by 1910 the number had more than doubled, to just over 1 million. For Italians the equivalent figures went from just over 200,000 (1900) to just under 525,000 (1910). Their respective percentages of Gotham's total population (which was about 3.5 million in 1900 and 4.8 million in 1910) went from roughly 15 percent to 25 percent (for the Jews) and roughly 6 percent to 11 percent (for the Italians).

One AFL response to these numbers was to call for raising the drawbridge against the rising tide. Gompers, once firmly opposed to immigration restriction, now moved to embrace it, condemning Asiatic arrivals most vigorously but also moving toward promoting broader restrictions. "We are not going to let [the Caucasian] standard of living be destroyed by negroes, Chinamen, Japs or any others," he said in 1905. New York's Central Federated Union lobbied for including Southern and Eastern Europeans in that "others" category. And individual unions—shoe workers, painters, paperhangers, plumbers, gas fitters, hotel and restaurant employees—adopted higher initiation fees and required citizenship papers, in order to screen out African Americans and new immigrants.[6]

Yet despite their wariness about the danger of demographic submersion, Irish labor leaders, in particular, could take comfort from the fact that their compatriots in church and state continued to hold their own. The hierarchy of the city's Catholic Church was overwhelmingly Irish, as were the upper echelons of Tammany Hall, and though each institution confronted a mass of new players in its respective sphere (Italian Catholics, Jewish Socialists), they were clearly in no immediate danger of losing their grip on power.

The reassuring presence of Irish prelates and politicians offered more than merely models for Irish labor leaders to emulate, as they provided actual support for craft union organizers—on condition that they reject their former radicalism. Irish unionists had been in the forefront of the third-party Henry George campaign and the eight-hour movement of 1886, in alliance with radical Catholics like Father Edward McGlynn. But McGlynn had since been silenced and exiled by the staunchly conservative Archbishop Michael Corrigan. And during his reign—and that of his successor, John Murphy Farley (archbishop from 1902, cardinal from 1911)—the city's hierarchy, paced by papal encyclicals, argued that while it was okay to join conservative unions, Catholic unionists should raise only moderate demands, avoid strikes, and stoutly contest any lurches toward socialism. Even liberals like journalist Patrick Ford (whose *New York Irish World* included the words "Industrial Liberator" in its full title) now opposed strikes and justified social reforms as bulwarks against socialism. At the same time as the Church was shepherding Irish workers into AFL unions, it was helping push them back into the Tammany fold, by insisting they avoid radical political parties. And Tammany rewarded such fealty by entrenching Irish men and women in public-sector positions (police, fire, rapid transit, schools), and by providing public works jobs for Irish building-trades contractors and unskilled laborers.

This new trinity—of the AFL, the Democratic Party, and the Catholic Church—strengthened the conviction of each constituent group that it could hold its own against demographic inundation. But its parochial metropolitan allies were not much help in fending off attacks on labor by the powerful economic actors who now appeared on the national scene.

---

6. The charge that immigrants were undermining AFL unions was misplaced, as labor statistician Isaac Hourwich demonstrated in a 1912 study, as newcomers moved into rungs on the occupational ladder that craftworkers had abandoned, and rarely were AFL strikes broken by unskilled immigrants.

OPEN-SHOP WARRIORS

One reason employers acceded to union demands during the merger wave was that business was booming, and they preferred giving essential workers a bigger slice of the era's burgeoning pie to having the flow of profits interrupted by strikes. But businessmen were nevertheless alarmed by the growth of unions in their industries, the enhancement of the AFL's national power, and the emergence in 1901 of the Socialist Party. Fearing that prerogatives and profits, while not menaced now, might be so in the near future, they mobilized to halt labor's advance.

In 1895 the National Association of Manufacturers (NAM) had been organized in Cincinnati by a collection of midsized manufacturers, many of them proprietors of single-plant family firms that they had inherited from their fathers or grandfathers. The NAM's constituency was concentrated in the industrial corridor stretching from St. Louis to Boston, but the state with the largest number of active members was New York, with Gotham home to a substantial percentage of them.

NAM companies had not gone through the corporate transformation. They were still locked in competitive struggle, their profit margins slender. Union demands could conceivably not just thin their wallets but sink their businesses, or so they complained. Also troubling was the public backing of labor's cause, as evidenced by widespread support for the 1902 coal strike.

So, in the new century, the NAM declared war on unions.

First it launched an ideological offensive. In an effort to change the conversation from miserable workplace conditions to the illegitimacy of unions, it denounced labor organizations as mini-despotisms that violated individual liberties, first and foremost NAM members' own. "Closed shops"—the term they preferred to "union shops"—contravened "the inherent right vested in the employer to control his property and conduct his business," which included the rights to "fix the terms and conditions" of employment, to "employ whom he desires," and to "refuse to employ whom it pleases him." NAM also portrayed itself as defending workers. Unions denied employees "the individual right to dispose of their labor as they see fit—a right that is one of the most sacred and fundamental of American liberty." Members joined a union "not because they sympathize with its purposes, but because they fear the consequences of not yielding to its tyranny," given that non-members were deprived of access to employment. NAM favored the "open shop," which, because it did not require employees to join a union, would expand job opportunities, and leave each worker "free" to cut the best deal he or she could with management. The unions rebutted that "closed shop" was a misleading term because any qualified non-union worker could enter a union shop through the union door. But this riposte was less than convincing, it being no secret that craft unions had excluded 80 percent of the workforce, on grounds of skill, race, gender, and national origin—not that NAM had the slightest interest in organizing the unorganized.

Their ideological line in place, the NAM leadership swept into action. One arena was the courts. Using common law doctrines on property rights, they obtained injunctions from sympathetic judges that hamstrung strikes, blocked boycotts, and helped check the AFL offensive; union recruitment peaked in 1904. The NAM also argued that the AFL was a monopoly—labor's equivalent of Standard Oil—hence subject to the Sherman Anti-Trust act. In NAM's view any action aimed at raising wages, shortening hours, or improving working conditions should be construed as a conspiracy to restrain trade, and declared illegal under

Sherman; it also demanded individual union members be held personally liable for any financial judgments against their organization. A series of Supreme Court decisions made clear that the courts were indeed inclined to cripple, perhaps even annihilate, workers' organizations. These culminated in the 1908 Danbury Hatters decision in which the justices held that Sherman *did* apply to unions, that a successful nationwide boycott of a hat manufacturer constituted an illegal restraint of trade, and that individual union members *were* personally liable for damages levied against their union.

In 1906, with this legal trend already painfully clear, the AFL abruptly reversed course and entered the political arena. Gompers had long believed, not without reason, that party politics was a corrupt snakepit, and that even if labor won passage of a favorable law, the courts would overturn it, or it wouldn't be enforced. Better for labor to rely on itself and fight at the point of production, where it was strong, rather than the halls of Congress, where it was not. Now that capital was using the state to strip labor of its economic weaponry, labor had to muster its political potential and fight back. This did not, Gompers insisted, mean organizing a labor party, as British trade unionists and socialists had just done in 1900, and as New York activists urged doing now, but rather backing whichever candidate would promise to support labor's platform. In 1906 the AFL-drafted "Labor's Bill of Grievances" was ignored by both President Roosevelt and the Congress. And in 1908, when Gompers tried again, the Republican Party (in which the NAM had a strong presence) cold-shouldered him. The Democrats did endorse labor's demands and received the AFL's endorsement in return, but William Jennings Bryan lost the election.

The NAM was not content with such judicial and electoral victories, however. It sought victory as well on the economic field of battle. The NAM called on member businesses to repudiate unions, tear up existing contracts, and declare their factories "open." This hard line represented a sharp break with past practice. Many manufacturers had mobilized in trade associations not to fight with unions but to negotiate with them from a stronger position. Now the NAM's fervent open-shop ideologues dangled before them the possibility of obtaining unchallenged mastery of their businesses. It had been NAM that in 1904 nudged the Typothetae's employing printers into responding to the Typographical Union's call for an eight-hour day by reframing the struggle as resistance to union "tyranny." Annoyingly, from the warriors' perspective, the employers had buckled, and the NAM-inspired confrontation had been a bust. But its campaign was only beginning.

LET'S MAKE A DEAL

Bigger capital took another tack on labor relations. In 1900 it founded its own organization, the National Civic Federation (NCF). It was essentially a conclave of bankers, industrialists, and corporate executives who occupied the commanding heights of the American economy, far above the foothills where most NAM businessmen roamed. By 1903 nearly one-third of the 367 American corporations with a capitalization of more than $10 million were represented.

Though initiated by Chicagoans, and national in membership, the NCF was headquartered from 1901 in Gotham, at 281 Fourth Avenue, and was top-heavy with New Yorkers. And though the first president, Mark Hanna, hailed from Ohio, he was succeeded by Manhattanites August Belmont (1904–7), Seth Low (1908–16), and Alton B. Parker (1916–26). Major funding for the project was provided by Andrew Carnegie, J. P. Morgan & Co., United States Steel, Metropolitan Life, and Kuhn, Loeb. George Perkins (then a Morgan partner), Frank Vanderlip, Elihu Root, Isaac Seligman, Cornelius W. Bliss, Oscar

S. Straus, James Speyer, George B. Cortelyou, Charles Schwab, John B. McDonald, and Elbert Gary all played important roles.

The NCF had far more Morgan people than Rockefeller people. JDR Sr. was personally more akin to NAM types, being an unrelenting opponent of organized labor, whose members he believed sought "to do as little as possible for the greatest possible pay." In 1903 Senior came into control (with George Gould) of Colorado Fuel and Iron, an assemblage of Western mills and mines. In response to an organizing drive by the UMW in 1903–4 the Rockefellers took an intransigent stance, Junior telling CFI's president: "We are prepared to stand by in this fight and see the thing out, not yielding an inch. Recognition of any kind of either the labor leaders or union, much more a conference such as they request, would be a sign of evident weakness on our part."

The NCF's goal was to overcome the competition between labor and capital, as its member corporations had overcome the competition between capital and capital. The corporate managers then transcending the archaic practices of business buccaneers hoped to replace primitive workplace slugfests (strikes and lockouts) with modern mechanisms for arbitrating disputes. NCF leaders believed that two forces were impeding attainment of industrial stability. To their left, socialists and radical unionists denied corporate legitimacy and stirred worker antagonism. To their right, the NAM's smaller-scaled (and smaller-minded) businessmen sowed needless discord by denying union legitimacy and prodding employers to reject negotiation.

The NCF concern about instability extended from the economy to the polity. In 1904 Elihu Root told Union League Club members: "Never forget that the men who labor cast the votes, set up and pull down governments," and that "continued opportunity for enterprise, for the enjoyment of wealth, for individual liberty, is possible, only so long as the men who labor with their hands believe in American liberty and American laws." Later that year Theodore Roosevelt, echoing Root (as he so often did), wrote his attorney general that unless the Republican Party could "show the wage-worker that we are doing justice," some day it would "go down before a radical and extreme democracy with a crash which would be disastrous to the nation."

The key to regularizing labor relations and forestalling radicalism was to reach an accommodation with respectable and moderate labor leaders like Samuel Gompers. NCF official Ralph Easley's draft declaration of NCF principles made it clear that the big corporations were ready to deal with unions that were "guided by proper rules and governed by judicious and conservative leaders," especially if they would agree not to interfere "with the employment of non union unskilled labor in any department." Big capital was willing to recognize and reward representatives of skilled labor, if they jettisoned radicalism and abstained from organizing the unorganized.

This extended olive branch was quickly grasped by Gompers, who gladly accepted the position of first vice president of the NCF. And why not? The organization's program coincided with his own analysis and inclination. He believed giant corporations were here to stay and were all-in-all a progressive force. He thought big capital was more efficient, able to generate more wealth, and could thus afford to be less antagonistic to organized labor. He shared the corporate sector's opposition to antitrust laws (especially after they were turned against labor). And he was of course more than willing to take up cudgels against socialists and radicals—he'd been doing so for years—and after one particularly vigorous assault in 1903, the NCF printed a picture of him captioned "Socialism's Ablest Foe." It helped, too, that Gompers knew many NCF leaders personally, having worked with them in New York City; as VP he would hobnob happily with capitalist luminaries like Carnegie, Belmont, and

Vincent Astor, at grand fêtes in the Hotel Astor. Thus big labor and big capital struck up an alliance, and Gompers, together with his corporate confrères, set out to preach the advantages of negotiation to employers, and the virtues of restraint to employees. This alliance was attacked from both flanks. The NAM was enraged at NCF accommodationism, and socialists denounced Gompers as a class collaborationist. Socialist members of the Central Federated Union objected particularly to labor leaders wining and dining with NCF nabobs, with one irate cigar-maker unionist fulminating about their "sitting beside capitalists and smoking non-union cigars."

Yet for all the professions by corporate NCF-ers of their willingness to work with labor unions, they proved deeply reluctant to do so in their own enterprises.

Their corporate headquarters in downtown Manhattan were thoroughly union-free zones. True, attaining this happy state hadn't required a NAM-style war. The absence of unions was a collateral benefit of the feminization of their office workforce. Clerking in nineteenth-century Wall Street countinghouses had been an all-male affair. The twentieth brought a tremendous expansion of white-collar office work, whose enormous costs managers kept down by hiring the public-school-trained daughters of the city's Anglo, German, and Irish working classes. By 1920 corporate offices were staffed largely by women, and nearly one-quarter of New York's female workforce was employed in clerical jobs. Most of these women considered their positions a huge step up—in working conditions and social status—from those of factory workers and domestics. And male clerical workers offered little resistance to feminization, partly because tasks like typing had never been encoded as "men's work," hence couldn't be considered as "lost" to their gender; and partly because senior male clerks and bookkeepers became supervisors of female workers, willingly accepting reorganization of the corporate office in exchange for an elevated place in the new hierarchy. Neither men nor women, therefore, were inclined to protest their improved situation by promoting unionization.[7]

But the similarity between NCF and NAM attitudes really became apparent whenever NCF members had to deal with union efforts to organize their industrial enterprises.

HARDBALL

The ranks of the NCF elite included several executives of US Steel, notably Elbert Gary, the company's president and chairman, and George Perkins, J. P. Morgan's man on the board of directors. Both were stout defenders of the NCF's commitment to working with unions. Yet in June 1901, immediately after the corporation was created, the board, behind closed doors, laid down a different line, declaring itself "unalterably opposed to any extension of union labor." Subsidiaries were accordingly instructed to sign agreements at already unionized mills but to oppose any new agreements at currently unorganized plants.

The board's chief focus of concern was the Amalgamated Association of Iron, Steel, and Tin Workers (AA). The remnant of the skilled steelworkers union that had been crushed at Homestead by Carnegie and Frick had established a foothold in the tin-works sector and represented 10,000 of the mega-firm's 160,000 employees. Aware that the formation of US Steel threatened it with definitive ruin, the union decided to make the first move. It demanded

---

7. A "secret meeting" of New York typists and stenographers was called in 1904 to discuss unionization, but the attempt did not succeed. In 1908 the Women's Trade Union League, a middle-class support organization, set up a Bookkeepers and Accountants Union, but WTUL organizers found that office workers "do not feel that they are 'wage earners' but have a notion that they are professionals and, therefore, it would be degrading to join a union." This was matched by male unionists' complementary conviction that women clerical workers were unorganizable, a self-fulfilling prophecy.

recognition of the union shop throughout the empire, ignoring Gompers's advice that this was an utterly unrealistic goal, given that only 6 percent of the workforce was currently unionized. The NCF arranged a meeting with Morgan and Schwab. The banker declared he wasn't hostile to organized labor, and indeed preferred to regularize relations. However, he bluntly refused to accept the establishment of closed shops where they didn't already exist.

The Amalgamated called a general strike, but the craft union proved unable to rally the largely unskilled immigrant workforce. The AA seemed oblivious to the fact that the skills needed to manufacture steel had shrunk, and that a rigid craft union couldn't stir the mass of those it had scorned. As one union member wrote: "The self-centered aristocratic Amalgamated Association looked with contempt upon the unskilled workers and the manufacturers took advantage of the situation." Back to the wall, the union requested sympathy strikes by railroad and coal-mining unions, which Gompers refused to authorize. Utterly outmatched, the AA surrendered in September, on humiliating terms (arranged via the NCF) that included a guarantee it would not even *try* to organize any non-union plant. Over the next several years, the steel company shuttered its unionized mills, depleting the union through attrition, and by 1909 had ousted it from all their plants.

THE US STEEL DE-UNIONIZATION CAMPAIGN had been smoothly executed, but others in the NCF were prepared to employ rougher methods.

In February 1904 August Belmont, president of the Interborough Rapid Transit Company (IRT), became president of the National Civic Federation. In September, unions representing workers of the former Manhattan Elevated Railway company, which the IRT had taken over in 1903, protested the conditions being imposed on them by their new employer. When negotiations failed to resolve the issue, they voted to strike. Belmont, a major underwriter of the national Democratic Party, was anxious to avoid bad publicity in the weeks just before the presidential election, so when his NCF proposed arbitration, Belmont agreed. A deal was worked out, and the unions signed a three-year contract.

In 1905, with the election over, and the subway up and running, conflict broke out again between the IRT and local members of the Amalgamated Association of Street and Electric Railway Employees and the Brotherhood of Locomotive Engineers. The workers threatened a walkout, which the nationals' officials and Gompers himself repudiated, as it violated the contract they'd signed. Belmont's term as NCF president was just ending. He asked its labor members if it wouldn't be a mistake to reelect him, as "we may have a strike and it would embarrass you, the National Civic Federation, and the Interborough." Gompers assured Belmont that labor's leadership was behind him and there would be no strike. On March 7 the New York locals announced a strike, though said they would submit to arbitration. When the company refused, the system's 7,000 men walked off the job, effectively shutting down the subway.

Yet within hours, Belmont had it more or less operational again.

In preparing for this showdown Belmont had turned to James Farley, the so-called King of the Strikebreakers. Farley had gotten into the scabbing business during Brooklyn's great trolley strike of 1895. After several years of strikebreaking around the country, in 1902 he had opened his own agency in New York, specializing in defeating streetcar strikes. He received annual retainers from companies in twoscore cities, giving them first call on his services, which included access to a hard core of 600 or so experienced railwaymen who, though scattered across the country, were available for handsomely paid service at a moment's notice. A consolidationist of sorts, Farley required a contracting company to give him complete control of the strike scene, rather than recruiting (as was usual) from a half-dozen competing detective and employment agencies, with chaotic results. Farley quickly compiled a success-ful record. According to a 1904 profile by muckraker B. T. Fredricks in *Leslie's Magazine*: "In no single case where he has responded and taken hold of capital's end of a fight with labor, has labor won the fight." Farley himself insisted he had no animosity to unions, that scabbing was purely a business proposition for him. The *New York Herald* agreed. "Farley," the paper declared, "has created a new economic force—the professional strikebreaker."

In preparation for the 1905 IRT showdown, Farley had begun assembling an alternate labor force of motormen, engineers, firemen, conductors, and ticket choppers, and the guards to protect them. He brought in 400 street railway employees from Chicago, a bevy of electric railroad experts from Richmond, Virginia, and assorted laborers from New England, marshaling them at the Pennsylvania Railroad station in Jersey City. He also recruited New Yorkers at the 34 Dey Street IRT employment office, including a group of seventy-five ex-pensively dressed student volunteers from Columbia College (including many of its top athletes), who had converged on the office singing rah-rah college songs. Then he began shipping his troops, who would eventually number about 5,000, to the uptown point of impending conflict.

On March 6 a sidewheeled steamboat carrying a thousand or so strikebreakers departed Jersey City at dawn and looped around lower Manhattan and up the Harlem River, passing under bridges jammed with crowds jeering "Scab!" and "Bums!" and throwing vegetables, tin cans, and stones, until at dusk the boat arrived at the 145th Street pier of the subway yards, where it disgorged its cargo, who were then escorted by Pinkertons to temporary bar-racks in the power station at 147th and Seventh, the repair shops at 147th and Eighth, and the terminal at 145th and Lenox.

An hour after the strikers left their cars, Farley assumed command, running the IRT out of his Broadway office, using telephones and a string of messenger boys to communicate with his troops. (A reporter mentioned August Belmont to a strikebreaker, who responded, "Who the —— is Belmont? Farley's runnin' this road.") The trains ran poorly, and there were huge tie-ups, but they ran, and so the strike was broken. In four days the workers were back on the job—except for the two-thirds who had been fired, with many of their positions transferred to Farley men. The rehired one-third had their seniority clocks reset to zero, thus starting anew at reduced wages; this gambit alone netted the company a million dollars a year in saved salary.

Belmont paid Farley $300,000 for his services.

Some NCF leaders were embarrassed. Was this what capital/labor comity looked like? Did the corporate world's improvement on NAM's approach to labor relations amount to being rich enough to hire an army of professional strikebreakers? They asked Belmont to permit IRT employees to organize. He refused. Gompers supported him. It was imperative, Gompers believed, that labor demonstrate to capital that in the AFL they had a trustworthy partner that would live up to agreements and clamp down on wildcatting.

Yet wildcats among the skilled workforce were as nothing compared to the oceanic labor upheavals breaking out among the unorganized immigrants in the two major ethnic groups then pouring into the city—southern Italians and Eastern European Jews.

ITALIANS

There were many skilled craftsmen among the new Italian arrivals, especially in the building trades (masons, carpenters, painters, glaziers), though few joined unions in New York. For some—the birds of passage who were planning on earning money quickly and then returning home—this was a matter of choice, as spending money on union dues, or losing money due to strike participation, seemed patently counterproductive. Those who *were* inclined to join a union soon discovered that the Anglo/Irish/German workers who controlled organizations like the Bricklayers and Masons, or the Carpenters and Joiners, had effectively barred the door to Italians. "American workers," *Il Progresso* complained, "are reserving for themselves the union and holding the foreigner at arms length." *Il Proletario*—started in 1896 by immigrant socialists—also bitterly denounced AFL unions for their restrictive policies and, more fundamentally, for dividing workers into competing craft units rather than uniting them in industrial unions. Only when a craft union ran into trouble did it relent, as when the Bricklayers and Masons Union, finding itself undercut by Italian masons working for Italian contractors, agreed to charter an Italian local in 1901, after having refused to do so for eleven years.

In any case, most Mezzogiorno newcomers were not skilled workers but young men straight off the farm, who flowed into Gotham's pool of common laborers—garbage workers, ditch diggers, sewer layers, hod carriers, snow shovelers, and subway excavators. To get these jobs, greenhorn Italians turned not to unions but to *padroni*, labor brokers: either small-time operators, who found work for individuals and small groups; or larger ones, who supplied substantial contractors; or the biggest and wealthiest, who were employed by corporations. Many Italian laborers were dispatched in gangs to work in distant states on railroads and mines—where they often found themselves victims of fraud and abuse. However, most of the 60,000 adult Italian males who in New York as of 1897 relied on the *padrone* system as their pipeline into the labor market, were sent to sites around the city, often as strikebreakers. (Farley and others turned to *padroni* to supply some of their requirements.)

Most Italian men took what work they could find, under whatever conditions were offered, as without unions or essential skills they had little leverage vis-à-vis employers. Sometimes, when conditions became unbearable, or wages flagrantly exploitative, they erupted in spontaneous unorganized revolts, lashing out at *padroni* or contractors, as had been the case with the uprising of Croton Aqueduct workers in 1900. But on occasion during the boom years, tentative and fragile alliances were made between organized labor and Italian workers (usually with the militant backing of their communities), producing hybrid forms of protest.

In 1901 the various craft construction unions working on building the subway hammered out a collective agreement with the employing subcontractors gathered in the Contractors' Protective Association—though without consulting the unskilled Italian laborers who were doing most of the work. As the latter's discontent grew, Tito Pacelli, a minor official of the masons union, and Herman Robinson, the New York representative of the AFL, founded two AFL locals in 1903—one for the Rockmen, the other for the Excavators—both of which were welcomed into the citywide Central Federated Union (CFU).

The new outfits demanded better wages and hours, and wanted to go on strike to get them, even though it would violate the labor-management agreement, to which they had not been a party. Robinson backed them, saying they were getting $1.25 a day, "wages no American can live on," and the CFU should authorize their strike, thus putting the muscle of the craft unions behind the unskilled Italians' cause. Delegate Staunton of the Electrical Workers objected. Robinson's talk of defending "American standards is all rot," he sputtered. The Italians weren't citizens but "dagoes," some of them "scum of the earth," who wanted "to make as much money as they can and then hurry back to Italy." Besides—the ultimate putdown—they were "unskilled men." There was a loud outcry at this, with

Delegate Donnelly of Big Six protesting that "some of our ancestors started here with a pick and a shovel, and it comes with bad grace from us to look down on people who start where our ancestors did." In the end the CFU endorsed a strike.

Hundreds of Italians poured into the two unions, and when the strike was launched, on May Day 1903, 5,000 men downed picks and shovels and came out for a two-dollar eight-hour day. On May 2, in a huge show of community support, an estimated 20,000 paraded through the East Harlem Italian quarter in solidarity.

The day after that, the contractors turned to *padroni* and ordered up strikebreakers, threatening to import blacks from the South if needs be. "If the niggers come here," Pacelli responded, "we won't do them any harm, but we will parade by them and they will all get so frightened that they will all run away." On May 4 violence broke out all over city. Crowds of strikers marched to various subway construction sites and assaulted strikebreakers—Italians as well as African Americans—driving them off with rocks, knives, and pistol shots. When police were rushed to the scene to protect the scabs, the crowds clashed with them, too: one riot at Lexington and Franklin Avenue in Brooklyn massed 1,000 workers; another in Brownsville, 2,000, with Italian women very much in evidence.

On May 7 the CFU—getting antsy at the turmoil and duration of the strike—arranged an agreement with the subway contractors that the men would return to work and the dispute be submitted to arbitration. Pacelli signed off on the deal. But at a mass meeting in Brommer's Park on East 133rd Street, 8,000 strikers (out of the 15,000 now in the two unions) voted not to go back until they achieved their goal. On May 8 the assembled official delegates of the two locals concurred, vowing to stay out for six months if need be, spurning the advice of the citywide labor leadership. Now the CFU withdrew its support. Head IRT contractor John B. MacDonald accelerated his replacement of Italian strikers with blacks and Irish and other Italians; the police redoubled their protection efforts; more violence against scabs ensued, with the *New York Times* denouncing the unions' "Mafia methods"; some Italians began drifting back to work, though a contingent of 3,000 went off to other states, promising to send back half their wages to support the strike, until finally, on June 15, it was called off and the men went back to work at the old rates. The unions carried on, winning some small concessions in the next few years, but went bankrupt in the 1907 downturn when the membership, with no strike in prospect, refused to continue paying dues.

IN 1903, ITALIAN LABORERS HAD DEMONSTRATED that unskilled workers could, with skilled-worker backing, obstruct a giant construction project—the subway system—that was promoted by powerful interests including millionaire businessmen and the municipality itself. In 1907 Italian longshoremen took on still more powerful forces, this time with no craft union backing. Thanks to their new centrality to the waterfront workforce, and a sudden and startling alliance with traditional ethnic and racial rivals, they came close to shutting down the Port of New York.

At the apex of Gotham's waterfront economy were the great European shipping companies—Cunard, North German Lloyd, et al.—enormous enterprises backed by their respective governments. Laissez-faire America, stingy with its subsidies, had long since dropped out of the race to dominate international commerce. (In 1897 only 8 percent of US exports traveled in US-registered ships). Only J. P. Morgan's International Mercantile Marine (IMM) conglomerate offered the possibility of a comeback, as evidenced by his credible showing in the ocean-liner size-and-speed race.

For all their rivalries, the transatlantic shippers—and the smaller firms that dominated the coastal and Caribbean trade—had one thing in common, the need to unload and load cargoes with maximum speed and minimal cost. The new municipal piers, docks, and warehouses had boosted the Port's efficiency, but what kept it profitable was the low-wage labor of perhaps 40,000 longshoremen. (New York employed more than half the dockworkers in the country; the nine Chelsea Piers alone often employed more than did entire cities.) Most shipping companies filled their needs by turning to highly competitive stevedore contractors, who drove *their* costs down by fostering competition within the workforce between ethnic groups and individuals.

Over recent decades, dockworkers of different nationalities had carved out sections of shoreline whose piers they dominated and whose nearby neighborhoods were peopled by their landsmen. The Irish ruled the Chelsea Piers, home to many of the great transatlantic liners, and dominated the adjacent West Side community. Germans clustered on the New Jersey side, near the deep-sea shippers of Hoboken. Poles had a grip on the piers near their Greenpoint enclave. And concentrations of Anglos and Africans, Scots and Scandinavians were to be found throughout the Port.

Italians—the fastest-growing segment of the workforce—prevailed along Red Hook and the East River, where coastwise companies had their berths. They had gotten a foothold during the late 1880s when shippers recruited them, via *padroni*, to break strikes by the Irish or to undertake jobs others didn't want, like hauling coal or unloading tarantula-laden banana boats around Coenties Slip. Meant to be temps, the Italians had dug in and held on to occupational and residential niches, and by 1907 were nearly one-third the longshoring fraternity.

As employers played these ethnic groups off against one another, they also fanned competition between individuals. Longshoremen were hired as casual laborers, one job at a time. "Job security" was a contradiction in terms on the waterfront. Men gathered with their baling hooks at pier heads each morning in "shape-ups," each seeking to convince the hiring boss to pick him out of those assembled. Given the tremendous oversupply of dockworkers—there were usually at least three longshoremen available for each job—corruption followed as the night the day, with workers signaling their willingness to kick back a portion of the day's wages, in exchange for access to the job. Wage rates on some docks could go as high as those for tunnel work—thirty cents an hour was average—but given the intermittent nature of ship schedules, one could go for days, even weeks, without working at all.

Longshoring was dangerous as well as sporadic. The abundance of labor power obviated the need for expensive investment in capital equipment. At a time when European ports had turned to traveling cranes, New York had not a single one. Why bother? There were plenty of hands and backs to haul the sacks of potatoes (180 pounds), coffee (200), flour (280), and sugar (320); the average man handled 3,000 pounds per hour. Given the lack of inspections or safeguards, and the relentless demand for speed—the bigger the boat, the costlier it was to idle—the rate of accidents (often fatal) from fast-moving slings, of hernias and gnarled hands and crippled backs from lugging great weights, of lung disease from fumes and dust, was breathtaking. Such costs were borne by workers and their families, and there were always replacements available.

The only thing that might have impeded the smooth functioning of the Port was unionization. Gotham longshoremen had been banding together to improve their situation since the strike of 1836, but such efforts had been repeatedly beaten back. Among the landmarks of defeat were the failed confrontations of 1874 and 1887, and most recently the fiasco of 1898, when Britain's Dockers' Union had sent over an organizer, who successfully put together a large multi-ethnic association, only to have it fall apart after a union official absconded with the treasury. The rank and file quickly regrouped and reincorporated as the Longshoremen's Union Protective Association (LUPA)—reviving the title (minus an *A*) first used in 1864 by the Alongshoremen's Union Protective Association of New York City. Most members were Irish and German, but as it grew—very slowly—it embraced some Italians as well. By 1907 President Patrick Connors' 3,100 men—a tiny proportion of the waterfront workforce—were organized in five branches in Manhattan, seven in Brooklyn, and three in Hoboken (including two Italian locals, one each in Brooklyn and Hoboken). When the Brooklyn Italians asked to be represented by an Italian-speaking business agent, the Irish LUPA leadership refused, and the Italians split off, obtaining a separate state charter.

On Monday, April 29, 1907, a group of 400 African American workers quit work at the Mallory Steamship Company. They'd been taken on as strikebreakers back in the 1890s and stayed on ever since, and now demanded a raise from twenty-five cents an hour to the prevailing thirty. The line quickly hired Italians to replace the blacks. An old story. But then things veered from the usual script.

On Wednesday, May 1, at least 6,000 Italian longshoremen held a Primo Maggio (May Day) rally, starting at Bush Terminal, to protest abusive treatment from foremen (wages weren't yet on their agenda), then paraded north waving red flags and those of various countries, urging/forcing others to join them as they went. After marching through the Atlantic Dock they crossed to Manhattan, then, from Battery Park, flags still flying, headed in two columns up the Hudson and East Rivers, each demanding dockworkers throw down their hooks and join them. In the next days the still-disorganized strike spread to other coastal lines, and then jumped to the transatlantic piers (at Fulton and Vesey) of the American and Red Star lines, both part of J. P. Morgan's IMM consortium, and to the French Line (at Pier 42, Morton Street).

On May 5 leadership passed to LUPA when the English-speaking union endorsed the strike (though by just one vote), and set up headquarters in the Brunswick Saloon at West and 11th Streets, just across from the Cunard piers. Their now formal demand was for an across-the-board ten-cents-an-hour increase to forty cents (sixty cents for night and overtime work) and recognition of the union. An infectious surge of solidarity raced through the harbor. Workers of all nationalities and races, fed up with the entire waterfront system, not just their low wages, rushed to enroll in LUPA. Seven thousand Italians jammed Brooklyn's Prospect Hall and surrounding streets, wildly cheering speeches by strike leaders and signing up en masse. Roughly German workers went out in Hoboken. By May 10 the walkout had reached every corner of the Port and was estimated to include at least 30,000 longshoremen. It was, Hearst's *Evening Journal* reported enthusiastically, the "largest strike of any single trade ever in New York."

Also on the tenth, the heads of the thirty biggest steamship companies met, agreed to make no concessions, and appointed a committee to hire and transport scabs. It turned not to Farley, who was preoccupied with strikes in San Francisco, but to one of his disciples. Pearl Bergoff (his mother had wanted a girl) opened up a Vigilant Detective Agency in 1905, then in 1907 shifted its name and focus to the Bergoff Brothers Strike Service and Labor Adjusters, with an office in the Shubert Building at 39th and Broadway. Bergoff turned to *padroni* who funneled him Italian strikebreakers, rented a tug from the Moran company to ferry 400 blacks north from Newport News, lined up 200 men from cheap lodging houses in Philadelphia, and relied on thugs from Monk Eastman's gang to ride herd on the assembled scabs. J. H. Thomas, president of Morgan's IMM, announced with misplaced confidence, "We are getting plenty of men to do the work and expect the strike will soon be broken."

Some of these men hadn't known there was a strike in progress, and deserted almost on arrival. Others—overwhelmed by the work itself, which they did poorly and slowly and with a high rate of accidents—accepted LUPA's offer to pay their return fare home. And those who hung in were hit with a wave of violence as crowds of strikers—wielding clubs, stones, blackjacks, brass knuckles, monkey wrenches, iron bars, knives, and guns—sought to drive the strikebreakers from the piers, or intercept them before they arrived and settled in to live on the docks where, protected by the police, they would load and unload.

Riots broke out all over port, growing steadily in scale and intensity. When a fleet of tugs unloaded a mixed lot of roughly 1,000 scabs at the Williamsburg shore near Metropolitan Avenue, they were met by 10,000 longshoremen and neighborhood supporters, augmented by 2,000 striking sugar refinery workers from the Havemeyer plant nearby, who now joined forces with the dockworkers. A massive all-day battle ensued that ended badly for the scabs.

"Guarding Williamsburg Sugar Plant," ca 1910. (Library of Congress Prints and Photographs Division)

"Deputies Guard Williamsburg Sugar Plant," ca 1910. (Library of Congress Prints and Photographs Division)

Given this kind of community-backed resistance, the shipping lines were unable to fill more than a third of the striker-vacated positions, and then only with workers whose productivity was extremely low. Soon a million tons of undelivered freight had piled up on the piers. European exporters were told to ease off on westbound shipments. And Custom House statistics on the total value of US exports from the Port dropped from $13,400,000 for the week ending May 11, to $6,400,000 for the week ending May 18.

The shippers, while admitting the "obstinacy" of the strikers, nevertheless held firm, convinced they had the resources to outlast them. The strikers, for their part, turned aside pleas to modify their demands. These came from Ralph Easley of the NCF, from Mayor McClellan, from Catholic prelates, from Irish American leaders in the Central Federated Union, and from Gompers of the AFL (with which LUPA was not affiliated).

Finally, on May 27, the employers made a tentative offer of thirty-five cents. The strikers, reading this as a sign of weakness, rejected it out of hand, holding out for forty. Their own resources, however, were dwindling rapidly. At the beginning, some branches had paid strike benefits, covered rent and groceries, handled the fines of those arrested, laid out money for the gasoline and crew of launches used to battle the strikebreakers out on the water, and provided return fares for decamping scabs. Now their financial fuel ran out.

Meanwhile, the companies had come up with a new strategy: they required the sailors on incoming ships themselves to load and unload cargoes, protected by Bergoff's muscle and police escorts. The value of exports U-turned upward. Some strikers began drifting back to work, though at least 20,000 remained out. On June 2 the union agreed to take the deal that been offered, but now the companies, whip firmly in hand, took it off the table. The strike continued, deflating slowly, punctuated by clashes here and there, until June 13, when at a meeting in Hudson Hall (at the corner of Hudson and Leroy), Connors threw in the towel. "The companies were too strong," he said, in tears.

Many strikers were bitterly resentful, having lost over a million dollars in wages, only to return to the same pay scale and conditions—and many, during the panic and depression that followed hard upon defeat, joined the massive return exodus to Italy. Those who stayed, and refused to give up on unions altogether, left LUPA and joined the AFL-affiliated International Longshoremen Association (as it renamed itself in 1908), which established an Italian local in 1910.[8]

THE SUBWAY STRIKE OF 1903 AND THE WATERFRONT STRIKE OF 1907, like the garbage workers strike later in 1907[9]—in all of which Italians played the foremost role—forcefully called into question the AFL's *strategic* premise that only skilled labor had enough clout to contest capital. If unskilled or semiskilled workers mustered sufficient numbers, militancy, and communal backing, there were sectors in which they could have considerable impact, especially when allied with skilled workers in an industry-wide initiative. At the same time, these strikes demonstrated the wisdom of AFL's *tactical* insistence on careful preparation, amassing of resources, establishing attainable goals, and developing alliances—the sorts of things Big Six printers had done in 1904—because while spontaneous mass uprisings were spectacular, without an organized ground game they lacked staying power. If there was a way to combine the discipline of pure and simple unionism with the passionate energy of a general strike backed by wider communities, labor might enhance its chances in its jousts with capital. Something very like this was emerging in Gotham's Jewish quarter during these years.

JEWS

The Jewish labor movement in New York had a very different backstory from that of the Italians. Italian arrivals were preponderantly young men fleeing economic deprivation, who had the option of returning "home," hence less incentive to build institutions for the long haul. The Jewish migration consisted of entire families and communities in collective flight from pogroms and pervasive anti-Semitism. They were not going back; their home was here.

---

8. Before leaving the waterfront, an update on the longshoremen's aquatic colleagues. Sailors had been among the first workers in New York to organize. Indeed, "strike" was a nautical term, borrowed from the striking—lowering—of sails. In 1802 white and black seamen had paraded along the docks "with drums beating and colors flying," demanding merchants and shipowners raise the basic wage. They had also been among the earliest to fail: the 1802 strike collapsed when its leaders were jailed. A century later, sailors (and stokers, who shoveled coal into the ship's engines) were still working and living below decks, in appalling conditions, for twenty-five dollars per month, minus the chunk taken in advance by crimps who—like *padroni*—landed them (or shanghaied them into) their positions. Sailors in the early twentieth century were, as of old, subject to corporal punishment and could be arrested for quitting a ship, and their strikes could be defined as mutiny, meaning summary execution. In 1897 the Supreme Court ruled that the Thirteenth Amendment outlawing slavery and involuntary servitude didn't apply to seamen. No wonder that in 1911 striking seamen marched through Gotham handing out a statement declaring in three languages that "we are held in more abject slavery than the Negroes of the South before the Civil War." When finally worn out, the luckiest old salts retired to Sailors' Snug Harbor; the less fortunate wound up on Blackwell's Island. Their latest organizational gambit was the Atlantic Coast Seamen's Union (1889), ineffective until 1892 when it joined in federation with West Coast, Gulf Coast and Great Lakes unions in the National (soon International) Seamen's Union. Under Andrew Furuseth, its Norwegian émigré leader, the ISU affiliated with the AFL and hewed to a craftworker approach, at a time when the old nautical skills were becoming obsolete, so its organizing drives were only modestly successful. On the other hand, Furuseth's focus on the political arena garnered significant results in 1915 when, with help from Wisconsin's Senator La Follette, he won legislative liberation from some of the ancient legal shackles.

9. At the end of June, Department of Street Cleaning employees—the 750 drivers who loaded residential trash cans onto their horse-drawn trucks, and the 1,200 street sweepers, both mainly unskilled Italian laborers—allied with the teamsters and struck, with CFU support. As garbage piled up, and fears of an epidemic mounted, the department's commissioner turned to Bergoff the "labor adjuster." He brought in black strikebreakers who, as in the longshore and subway affairs, were met with violent attacks by armed strikers and hailstorms of bricks hurled from rooftops by their womenfolk. Finally the men went back, pending arbitration, and the commissioner was fired.

And what a home! The Jewish community, augmented by immigrants, took over much of the Lower East Side, making it the largest enclave of Jews in the world outside the Pale of Settlement. Its relative ethnic homogeneity gave it an internal coherence that was further enhanced by being the locus of the ready-to-wear garment trade, the economic base that sustained the community. The interweaving of work sites and residences gave the area the feel of a one-industry company town, nestled within the giant metropolis. And being largely under the community's control, it gave the Jews an unprecedented sense of security, feeding their perception of New York as a place of collective liberation, an assessment kept green by memories of collective oppression.

This did not mean there were not sharp internal cleavages. The community was fractured along lines of religion, politics, place of origin, and, most of all, class. Proximity and a common culture could heighten as well as mitigate struggles between workers and bosses—or in this fragmented industry, between many, many disaggregated workers and many, many competitive bosses.

Perhaps the most critical difference between the evolution of Jewish and Italian labor stemmed from the arrival on the Lower East Side of a sizable cadre of immigrant radical Russian Jewish intellectuals who took up the task of forging a labor movement out of a vast and newly minted Jewish working class.

The would-be organizers had an initial communication problem, however. Few of the Russians could talk to their fellow workers, most of whom spoke Yiddish, a derivation of Middle High German admixed with elements of Slavic and Hebrew that was the daily language of village Jews in the Pale. It was a language that radicals (and "cultured" Jews in general) had always considered a mongrel "zhargon," an unwieldy and unworthy vehicle for conveying serious thoughts. But the radicals proved to be quick studies. In April 1885, together with some Galicians and Hungarians, they created the first Yiddish-speaking socialist group, the Yidisher Arbeiter Fareyn (Jewish Workers' Association). In 1886 they threw themselves into the strike movement and the Henry George campaign. In 1887 they established a Yiddish-speaking branch (Section 8) of the Socialist Labor Party (SLP). And in 1888 Section 8 intellectuals, working with SLP officials and the United German Trades (UGT), established the United Hebrew Trades (UHT). This ethnic labor federation, explicitly modeled on the UGT, now set out to organize Yiddish-speaking Jews in every branch of industry, to provide them with "mutual protection against the oppression of capitalism."

From its frail initial base of three Jewish unions, totaling a scant eighty members, the United Hebrew Trades grew rapidly, thanks to a group of organizers that included Morris Hillquit, at that point a 20-year-old shirtmaker, in-country only since 1885. Hillquit became one of the United Hebrew Trade's Johnny Appleseeds. Over the next few years these young men were whirlwinds of activity, building (with the aid of German predecessors) one union after another—training cadres of activists, addressing rallies, leading strikes and boycotts, negotiating contracts. By 1892 the UHT claimed forty unions, including locals of waiters, bookbinders, upholsterers, carpenters, architectural ironworkers, typographers, bakers, and Yiddish actors. About a quarter were garment unions—including the 1889 United Brotherhood of Tailors (of ready-made, not custom, clothing) and the makers of pants, knee pants, shirts (Hillquit was a member of the Shirt Makers' Union), children's jackets, buttonholes, suspenders, and caps; and pressers, too. The Operators' and Cloakmakers' Union was the biggest of the bunch, with 7,000 members, piloted by a UHT-designated leader, the flamboyant 24-year-old Joseph Barondess; its growth had been boosted by success in beating back an employers' lockout in 1890, with strong community support in the form of parades, demonstrations, and mass meetings. The relative absence of strikebreakers was likely an artifact of this powerful communal consensus.

In 1890, at the height of this organizing surge, the radicals launched the *Arbeiter Zeitung*, a weekly workers' paper in Yiddish. With funds contributed by German unions, the Russians established a publishing cooperative to run it, modeled on that of the *New Yorker Volkszeitung* (the Socialist Labor Party's paper, founded in 1878). The paper was an instant success, in part because of the heightened militancy (hence receptivity) of Jewish workers that year, in part because of the role that well-known strike organizers like Hillquit played in the paper's creation, in part because it began to give the community a linguistic coherence that complemented its demographic and economic cohesiveness, and in part because of its colloquial and accessible style, the doing, principally, of Abraham Cahan, perhaps the city's first professional Yiddish journalist.

Born in 1860 in Lithuania, Cahan came from learned stock. His grandfather had been a rabbi, his father a melamed (an elementary-level Hebrew teacher, a distinctly lesser status), and he at first studied for the rabbinate, in part to restore the family's standing. But in the heady revolutionary times Cahan lost his religious enthusiasm, became an atheist, and embraced Russian culture and politics. While studying to become a teacher he joined an underground reading group and, fearing arrest in the 1881 post-assassination roundups, fled to New York in 1882.

Cahan took jobs in a cigar and then a tin factory, and was drawn to a Russian socialist discussion group, set up by German Social Democrats to attract Russian Jewish immigrants to the cause. The Propaganda Verein did draw crowds to its lectures, but Cahan suggested these would be much larger if held in Yiddish. His advice was accepted, and he himself was invited to inaugurate a lecture series in Yiddish. Hugely successful, it brought him attention but not income, being volunteer political work. So he taught himself English, began giving lessons to other immigrants, then, in 1883, got a position teaching English in an evening school of the Young Men's Hebrew Association, which allowed him to quit factory work. In the next years he wrote articles about the Lower East Side for American newspapers, joined the Socialist Labor Party, worked with the UHT, and became a contributor to and eventually editor of the *Arbeiter Zeitung*.

In that literary pulpit Cahan translated his popular speaking style into written form, using familiar Jewish terminology to explain principles of socialism and unionism. As "Der Proletarishker Maggid" (the Proletarian Preacher), he offered a wildly popular weekly "Sidra"—a radical version of the sermon on the weekly Torah portion heard in synagogues on the Sabbath. In these epistles he compared the tribulations of Jewish immigrants in New York with those of biblical characters, and raised hopes of deliverance from oppression. Neither Cahan nor most of his readers were religiously inclined, but drawing on religious traditions allowed him to provide readers with an ethical-political underpinning, a moral purchase point from which to condemn workplace exploiters.

For all their promises of a redemptionist future and their fervent talk of class war (in Cahan's debut speech he had urged his audience to charge up Fifth Avenue with axes and swords), the radicals also focused on near-term objectives: winning union recognition and obtaining the eight-hour day. Hence their ambivalent relations with the American Federation of Labor, and vice versa. The UHT leaders, though displeased with Gompers's anti-socialist stance, were practical men. Aware that the AFL was the most powerful labor organization around, they presented their new unions to the national body for koshering with a charter. And Gompers, though displeased with a labor federation organized not on craft but on ethnic lines, and given to windy messianism to boot, was a practical man, too. He accepted UHT locals as a vehicle for introducing the new immigrants to the American labor movement.

This détente became harder to sustain after Daniel De Leon rose to power in the Socialist Labor Party, with which the UHT unions were *also* affiliated. De Leon attacked the AFL (and all ameliorative reformers) as impediments to socialist revolution. In 1895 he set up a rival Socialist Trade and Labor Alliance, and called on AFL workers to desert their unions and join his new ones. Some in the UHT movement supported this strategy, but most rejected it as a "dual unionism" that undermined organized labor. They also objected to De Leon's centralizing (not to say autocratic) insistence that the SLP leadership control the UHT unions and the *Arbeiter Zeitung* as well. So when Eugene Debs formed the Social Democratic Party of America in 1897, Cahan and fifty or so comrades jumped ship. They also created the *Forverts* (*Forward*) that year, borrowing its name and political orientation from *Vorwärts*, the Berlin organ of Germany's Social Democratic Party. The following year Cahan left the *Jewish Daily Forward*, as it became known, to work with Lincoln Steffens on the *Commercial Advertiser* and learn the ins and outs of the New York newspaper business. Then he returned in 1903 to help build the *Forverts* into a powerful institution, its circulation passing the 100,000 mark by 1910.

The Jewish labor movement had emerged as a multi-pronged decentralized affair. There were the Yiddish-speaking branches of the Socialist Party—itself the product of a 1901 merger between Debs's Social Democrats and a new set of breakaways from DeLeon's SLP (which now shrank into irrelevance). There were the United Hebrew Trades and its flotilla of unions, which withdrew from the SLP's dual-union federation and bonded more closely with the AFL. Hillquit's Yiddish socialists also moved into the AFL, swearing themselves to subordinacy; Gompers tolerated them for their organizing prowess. There was the Arbeter Ring (Workmen's Circle), a mutual aid society founded by New York shop workers in 1892 that admixed socialist politics and union activism with provision of benefits and services to members. The society went national in 1900, opened its doors to anarchists, social democrats, independent radicals, and progressive Zionists, enrolled women as full-fledged members, and became the movement's largest organization. Finally there was the *Forverts*, which reported on and promoted the work of all the others.

THAT WORK DID NOT GO SMOOTHLY, especially for Jewish unions in the garment industry. They proved to be as chronically unstable as the industry itself. Membership seesawed—rising during a strike, dropping when the struggle was over. Strikes, in turn, followed the industry's seasonal rhythm. Workers piled into a union at the beginning of the busy season, when they had the leverage to strike for and win immediate improvements; then they piled out in the slack season, when that leverage evaporated, allowing bosses to ignore or circumvent whatever gains had been won. Immigrant workers saw unions as ad hoc formations, not permanent institutions.

Some organizers argued that the solution was to create industrial unions, which would bring together skilled and unskilled workers, and use their combined power to achieve a superior bargaining position and maintain institutional stability. There was only one actual example of such a union in the city, however, and its tribulations highlighted the obstacles that lay in the path of such an approach, given the craft-based culture of the union movement.

The exception to the rule was the United Brewery Workmen, founded in 1886 by German socialists, who were convinced, as participant-historian Herman Schlüter wrote in 1910, that the tendency of the union movement was toward "consolidation into large and

Lewis Hine, "Old Man Carrying Garments, Delan[c]ey St.," 1912. (Library of Congress Prints and Photographs Division)

efficient organizations," because the "organization of capitalist employers…compel[s] the workingmen to unite their small trade unions into larger associations." The United Brewery Workmen included all who worked in the industry. Its ranks encompassed brewers, maltsters, distillery workers, engineers, firemen, coopers, bottlers, beer drivers, and laborers. This led to a complicated relationship with the AFL. Gompers had given the brewers a very wide jurisdictional charter in 1887, a decision he came to regret as craft-based unions (coopers, teamsters, firemen) began demanding the brewers union be broken up and its members redistributed to their organizations. In 1907, when the brewers union refused to spin off its constituents, Gompers revoked its charter, which led to major protests, and the charter's restoration in 1909, albeit with a narrowed jurisdiction.

One way to explore the possibilities of industrial unionism while circumventing opposition was to form proto-industrial unions—umbrella organizations that were alliances of the skilled and unskilled, rather than outright mergers between them. This format was taken out for a trial spin in the two major branches of the garment industry, the production of men's and women's ready-to-wear, with mixed results.

IN THE MENSWEAR DIVISION, the United Garment Workers (UGW, 1891) claimed to embrace all workers, from the skilled, male, Irish and German cutters at the top to the unskilled, female, Jewish basters and finishers at the bottom. In fact, each segment of the trade organized separately, with the cutters—the only ones with indispensable skills—becoming very much primus inter pares, while the women's unions were excluded from union shop provisions where they'd been won. The cutters were also a conservative lot politically, and the executive board, under their sway, denounced the United Hebrew Trades as "a disruptive socialistic influence upon the American labor movement." This did not sit well with the socialist Russian and Polish operators of the United Brotherhood of Tailors, a United German Trades affiliate and a United Hebrew Trades creation.

Only once, when the open-shop drive instigated by the National Association of Manufacturers menaced their own position, did the cutters deign to ally with the tailors. In April 1904 the New York Clothing Manufacturers Association (local branch of the National Association of Clothiers) declared its intention to pry open the United Garment Workers' closed (union) shop. The manufacturers were eager to remove this obstacle to taking advantage of the oversupply of cheap semiskilled labor, the number of Russian tailors being "thicker than the hair on a dog," according to the *Daily Trade Record*, a menswear industry publication, which added: "There is not a boat that comes to these shores that does not bring a thousand possible tailors." The UGW responded with strikes: first by the cutters, with AFL blessing; then the United Brotherhood of Tailors signed on; then a general strike was launched. Within weeks, "all branches of the ready-made tailoring industry" in New York were out, more than 50,000 in all, the great majority of them Jewish men, though perhaps 10 percent were Jewish women and there was a contingent of Italian women as well, plus the Irish and German cutters. Unity proved insufficient in this instance, and after six weeks the strike was lost, a powerful blow to the prestige of the union, which now began to fracture along predictable lines. Finally, in 1907, when the New York branch of the United Brotherhood of Tailors called an organizational strike, and the United Garment Workers leadership ordered workers back to the job, then sent scabs to replace those who had refused, the organization fissured, with the head of the UBT announcing his union (which he called "the Jewish tailoring element") was leaving the UGW.

THINGS WENT ONLY MARGINALLY BETTER IN THE WOMEN'S-WEAR TRADE. In 1900 survivors from the Cloakmakers Union that had been established by the United Hebrew Trades a decade earlier called for a national industrial organization. At a meeting that June in the Labor Lyceum—a center for workers' classes, lectures, rallies, and social gatherings at 64 East 4th Street—unions from New York, Newark, Philadelphia, and Baltimore merged to form the International Ladies' Garment Workers Union (ILGWU), declaring it open to all workers regardless of skill or nationality. Nevertheless, it set up an internal structure of separate unions based on trade or job classification, an approach similar to that adopted by the United Garment Workers. In sharp contrast to the UGW, however, the preamble to the ILGWU's constitution trumpeted another goal—to "organize industrially into a class-conscious labor union politically represented . . . by a political party whose aim is the abolition of the capitalist system." Lest there be any doubt about to whom they were referring, they passed a resolution of friendship for the Socialist Party, and encouraged members to engage in political activity. This was one reason the AFL leadership, though it granted the ILGWU a charter right away, excluded it completely from all governing bodies.

Much the same internal divisions now emerged in women's wear that had plagued men's. The cutters local rose swiftly to the top of the pecking order. Like its United Garment Workers counterpart, it was composed largely of native-born English-speaking Irish and German men and soon gathered into its fold older entities like the Gotham Knife Cutters' Association, and the Manhattan Knife Cutters' Association. The cutters—politically conservative and worried about the influx of immigrant radicals—held themselves aloof from their supposed brothers and sisters.

At the bottom of the heap, the Ladies' Waist Makers Union, composed largely of teenage girls who manufactured shirtwaists (blouses), were left to fend for themselves. In 1903 their local conducted a strike and gained 800 members, "all enthusiastic," but as soon as the strike was over the enthusiasts vanished, leaving the union at the edge of insolvency. Appeals for financial aid sent to the International proved fruitless. (It was having its own troubles.) In 1905 the waist makers were thrown out of their rented hall on Eldridge Street (being $600 in arrears). They relocated to smaller quarters in 206 East Broadway, big enough for their membership of ten, which a year later had dwindled to six. After which they disbanded, covering their charter with a black cloth, and sneaking away to avoid the landlord. They'd be back soon, though, with a new charter: Local 10 resurrected as Local 25.

Meanwhile, the ILGWU itself approached the brink, primarily due to wrangling between cutters and the tailors. The former had joined to get some additional help from a supporting cast of semi- and unskilled workers, but when the latter asked for help in return, the cutters refused to subordinate their interests to those of the less-skilled immigrants. As John Dyche, secretary-treasurer of the ILGWU, said in 1905, "The ill-will between the cutters and the tailors in our own trade is accentuated by the differences of language, race and religion," and in 1907 it got worse. When the General Executive Board ordered a strike on behalf of the tailors, the cutters bluntly refused to comply, which led to the temporary revocation of their charter, and nearly destroyed the organization.

But by then, as a by-product of horrific events occurring thousands of miles away, a new wave of militant workers was pouring into New York. In a few short years they would drastically transform labor relations in the city.

19

Radicals

JEWISH RADICALS

On Easter Sunday of 1903, in the town of Kishinev in southern Russia, churchgoers—having been reminded by their priests of who had killed Christ, and further maddened by rumors that a Christian child had been ritually murdered and her blood mixed into the Passover matzoh, rumors amplified by a profoundly anti-Semitic press—charged out of services and began slaughtering Jews. Crowds, eventually some 20,000 strong, disemboweled, beheaded, and crucified at will. Some victims had nails driven into their skulls. Children were killed alongside their parents. A baby was used to break windows. Block after block of houses and shops was burned. For nearly two days, the police stood by. Hundreds were killed and wounded, fifteen hundred buildings destroyed.

It was only the beginning.

As pogroms began erupting in villages and cities throughout the Pale of Settlement (the western region of Imperial Russia to which Jews were confined), resistance was spearheaded by the Bund (shorthand for the General Union of Jewish Workers in Lithuania, Poland, and Russia). In 1893, inspired in part by what the 1880s generation of Russian émigrés had accomplished in New York, a group of Vilna revolutionaries had started organizing Jewish workers, both to win better conditions in sweatshops and workshops, and to channel Jewish radicals into the movement to overthrow both czar and capitalism. Other Jewish socialist groups arose, and in 1897 they united to form the Bund, which launched a wave of strikes in industrializing cities like Vilna, Bialystok, and Minsk. Confronted with conservative forces that were also anti-Semitic, they increasingly demanded civil and political rights for Jews as a secular, non-territorial "nation" within a post-revolutionary Russian state. After Kishinev, the Bund became the main organizer of a Jewish self-defense movement to combat pogrom perpetrators. Leading strikes and demonstrations, it grew into a popular (but underground) movement with roughly 30,000 cadre and vast numbers of supporters.

In 1904 the czar initiated a war against Japan that quickly proved disastrous. Blame for that misadventure also fell upon the Jews, and pogroms intensified. But the failed war also strengthened Russia's broader revolutionary movement, which in 1904 organized a series of powerful strikes across the country, a campaign in which the Bundists played a prominent role. Then, in January 1905, in St. Petersburg, a peaceful procession of unarmed workers, led by Father Georgii Apollonovich Gapon, bearing a petition to the czar, their "little father," was shot down in front of the Winter Palace, with an estimated thousand killed or wounded.

After "Bloody Sunday," Russia erupted in full-scale revolution. Workers struck; students boycotted classes; minority populations rose against Russian imperialists; peasants attacked landlords' estates; middle-class liberals demonstrated; unrest emerged in the military. Bundists played a major role in the 1905 Revolution, arming themselves, erecting barricades, and mobilizing tens of thousands of Jews in some sixty cities to join strikes and demonstrations.

Counterrevolutionary forces, paced by the Black Hundreds (ultra-nationalist supporters of the czar), focused their wrath on the opponents of autocracy, particularly Jews. From February through mid-October 1905, some fifty-seven pogroms broke out in the empire. All-Jewish corps did their best to defend their communities against attacks by mobs, and in Lódz, during a June 1905 uprising, roughly 350 Bundists died in pitched street battles with czarist military forces.

Then, in the fall of 1905, an immense general strike by factory workers, artisans, small businesses, and white–collar workers paralyzed the entire country, forcing the government to issue the October Manifesto, which promised civil liberties—even to Jews—and an elected legislature (Duma) with substantial powers. These concessions provoked a violent reaction by Russian monarchists and assorted right-wingers (including the now-state-backed Black Hundreds), who directed much of their firepower at Jews. In November 1905 alone, there were more than six hundred pogroms, including a ghastly rampage through Odessa that left 800 dead and 5,000 wounded. Atrocities abounded. Jews were hurled out of windows, pregnant women raped and their wombs cut open, infants slaughtered in front of their parents. (In one instance pogromists hung a woman upside down and arranged the bodies of her six dead children on the floor below.) These horrors were but part of a maelstrom of repressive violence by the state and its outrigger death squads against liberals and radicals. The crackdown, in turn, provoked a vast wave of left-wing assassinations of government officials; close to 4,500 were killed or wounded between 1905 and 1907.

Slowly, counterrevolution gained the upper hand. Military and police assaults made strikes and demonstrations all but impossible. Pogroms climaxed in June 1906 when troops joined anti-Semitic rioters and battled Jewish defense forces for control of the streets of Bialystok. After three days of carnage, in which nearly a thousand Jews were killed or wounded, the back of the resistance movement, like the larger revolutionary thrust, was broken. Having regained control through force of arms, the czar rescinded reforms, first gutting the Duma's power by assigning himself and the nobility full veto power and then, in June 1906, dissolving it altogether. By the fall of 1906, with all hope lost, and mop-up repression continuing, many

Bund self-defense group mourns three comrades, Ukraine, 1905. "The Rise and Fall of the Jewish Labor Bund," *Jewish Currents*, Autumn 2013.

revolutionaries, Bundists included, joined the massive migration of Russians heading west to exile in the great industrial cities of Europe and the United States, particularly New York City.

GOTHAM HAD BEEN GLUED TO EVENTS IN RUSSIA. Developments between 1903 and 1906 were monitored closely and responded to all but instantly. Czarist atrocities were greeted with mourning, protests, and financial support for revolutionaries. The lead was taken by the city's Eastern European Jewish community—many of whom had fled to New York in the 1880s to escape earlier pogroms—and by its German Jewish elite. Powerful gentile figures were concerned as well, many having come to view Russia as a backward autocracy that oppressed its people and was worthy of condemnation.

As pogroms spread across the Pale after Kishinev, anxious families seeking word of their relatives' fate followed the stories headlined in the left-wing Yiddish press, and in Hearst's *Journal* and *American*, the publisher having hired Michael Davit, the Irish nationalist, to conduct on-site and in-depth interviews. In May a left-wing rally at Cooper Union, addressed by Abraham Cahan and Joseph Barondess among others, denounced the atrocities. Uptown, a committee was established to raise funds for relief of massacre victims; it included Jacob Schiff, Emanuel Lehman, Joseph Bloomingdale, Isaac Seligman, Isidor Straus, and Daniel Guggenheim; by June it had gathered $100,000. At the end of May, a group of Christian civic leaders, led by corporate attorney Paul Cravath, held a protest meeting at Carnegie Hall; speakers included former mayor Seth Low, ex-president Grover Cleveland, and Archbishop John Murphy Farley.

A similar campaign, though on a grander scale, followed the October 1905 pogroms. Again, Lower East Side leftists were first in the field. Thirty thousand constituents of seventy-two organizations, most of them connected with the socialist movement, marched from Rutgers Square to Union Square, singing "The Marseillaise" and toting red anti-czarist banners (RUSSIAN ATROCITIES HAVE NO EQUAL IN THE WORLD'S HISTORY). In November, uptown Jews arranged a gathering at Temple Emanu-El, representing most segments of New York Jewry, which established the American Committee for the Relief of Russian Jews, with Oscar Straus as chair and Jacob Schiff as treasurer. The German Jews' insistence that relief funds also be made available to gentiles annoyed the Russian radicals, but they did not walk out. By early December over a million dollars had been raised in the United States (almost half from Gotham) and forwarded by the Rothschilds in London to Baron Gintsburg in St. Petersburg, who, with the consent of the czarist government, transferred the funds to local relief committees.

Also in November 1905 an ad hoc gathering of prominent radicals, who styled themselves the New York Group of Socialist Revolutionaries, took the lead in establishing the Jewish Defense Association (JDA), to raise money to buy weapons to send to self-defense forces in Russia. So militant was the moment that non-socialists joined the gun-running as well, and in an ecumenical gesture, Judah L. Magnes was made the organization's chair. Magnes, a young but fast-rising Reform rabbi—he would soon be appointed associate rabbi at Emanu-El—took it as his mission to bridge the gap between uptown and downtown Jews. The JDA called for a mass meeting on November 26, 1905, at the Grand Central Palace (on Lexington between 43rd and 44th). Six thousand filled the space and heard Magnes's exhortation "to rise as heroes."

A far bigger event took place on December 4 when at the JDA's initiative a huge parade of mourning was organized. Taking the form of a cortege, replete with muffled drums and funeral marches, tears and lamentations, the procession—125,000 strong—wound through the Lower East Side, its tenements and shops draped in black, before an equal number of onlookers. At one point 6,000 Brooklyn Jews, having prayed in front of half a dozen synagogues, marched across the Williamsburg Bridge and joined their East Side brethren.

GOTHAM ALSO WELCOMED REVOLUTIONARY VISITORS, come to America to seek political and financial support. Their path was smoothed by local organizations like the American Friends of Russian Freedom, which arranged dinners and scheduled lectures, first in New York and then on a multi-city circuit. The settlement houses were another important conduit, sponsoring conferences that brought together influential Americans and visiting Russians. Lillian Wald's Henry Street operation was particularly active, as was the coterie of residents (Walling, Stokes, Hunter, and Ernest Poole) at the University Settlement. And socialists, anarchists, and industrial unionists hosted their Russian counterparts.

Bundists were the first to arrive. Their initial representatives disembarked in 1903, and were followed in 1904 by a full-scale delegation, whose visit was highlighted by a Jacob Adler presentation of Jacob Gordin's drama *The Bundist* at the Grand Central Palace. That fall Catherine Breshkovskaya came to town. Babushka ("Little Grandmother"), as she was known, had been found guilty in 1878 of spreading "revolutionary propaganda" and sentenced to twenty years at hard labor in Siberia. In 1901 she joined with Alexander Kerensky and others to form the Socialist Revolutionary Party (SR)—their major plank called for land confiscation and redistribution to the peasants—and then toured the world making speeches and raising money. Breshkovskaya bunked with Emma Goldman, who also acted as her interpreter, and she worked out of an SR office on Clinton Street that had been set up by recent immigrants. Lillian Wald arranged receptions for her at Henry Street, and in late December the Friends of Russian Freedom sponsored her speech at Cooper Union, attended by several thousand. In January 1905 Abe Cahan arranged for University Settlement resident Ernest Poole to interview Babushka in the *Outlook*, and her denunciations of the regime were ratified two weeks later when Bloody Sunday hit the headlines. (Hearst's *American* ran author Maxim Gorky's personal account of the massacre.) Poole now rushed to Russia to cover the revolution firsthand (he also smuggled in funds to aid the cause), along with other muckrakers—in St. Petersburg he bumped into S. S. McClure. Sailing in the opposite direction was the famous theatrical producer Paul Orleneff, and his troupe of actors. With the aid of producer Charles Frohman, assisted by prominent members of New York society like Ava Lowle (Mrs. John Jacob) Astor and Anne Harriman Vanderbilt, Orleneff mounted Russian social protest plays, which attracted widespread attention, and strengthened local revulsion against the czarist regime. In the spring of 1906, with the counterrevolution gaining, Bundist leader Gregory Maxim arrived in New York, and was squired from speech to speech by labor lawyer and Socialist Party stalwart Meyer London; Maxim raised $10,000, some of which was used to purchase weapons from a manufacturer in Cleveland.

NEW YORK WELCOMED FAR MORE THAN DELEGATIONS. The years of upheaval, and those of defeat, set in motion a vast exodus of Jews from the Russian Empire to the United States. Numbers are very imprecise, but historical demographers believe that between 1904 and 1917, roughly 1.2 million Jews entered the country. It also seems clear that the pogrom years generated the heaviest flow—approximately 100,000 a year came between 1904 and 1907—with the peak influx, roughly 150,000, coming in the crackdown year of 1906.

While many of these passed through Ellis Island and on to the continent, those who terminated their travels at the mouth of the Hudson were numerous enough to more or less double the Jewish population of New York. In 1900 just under 500,000 Jews had lived in Gotham. By 1910 a little more than a million were in residence (roughly 540,000 of who lived on the Lower East Side). By 1914 the total hovered around 1.4 million. By all accounts New York contained the biggest Jewish population of any city in the world.

An indeterminate but large and significant percentage of these newcomers had been involved in the labor and revolutionary movements. In New York, as in Russia, they were of varying political persuasions, and often at loggerheads. But most of the radical arrivals were committed to socialism (often in its strict class-war form) and to Jewish nationalism (often centered on self-defense), admixed in varying degrees to produce different political blends.

The largest and most visible on the local scene were the Bundists, who hit the ground organizing. Even while absorbed in events in Russia, they began establishing footholds in their new city, forming clubs, mutual aid societies, and landsmanshaften. By 1906 fifty-two of these groups—totaling 3,000 members—had coalesced in a Central Union of Bundist Organizations. And even as they continued to focus on events in their homeland, they were soon drawn into Gotham's internal Jewish politics: first, by altering the balance of power between the uptown Jews and the downtown cohort of which they were now vociferous members; and second, by challenging what they perceived to be the naïveté of city socialists vis-à-vis the "Jewish question."

AT THE HEIGHT OF THE CRISIS, the uptown and downtown class-and-ethnic communities had somewhat smoothed over their notoriously prickly relations, in order to jointly succor their Russian coreligionists and help combat their anti-Semitic foes. But the tensions over issues of class and culture were hardly extinguished. Abe Cahan, editor of the *Jewish Daily Forward* and a leading spokesperson of the downtown community, made it emphatically clear that while he was prepared to cooperate with the uptown elite during the emergency, dealings between Jewish employers and employees were and would remain antagonistic: "They cannot be brothers," he insisted. The Bundist newcomers were in complete agreement; class struggle, not cooperation, was and should be the default mode. Many in the elite agreed. Indeed, some worried that arms dispatched to the Bund in Russia would be used to attack not czarist forces but Jewish factory owners. Good-hearted contributors to self-defense funds should realize they might well be financing "the warfare of Jew against Jew."

Even in supposedly joint enterprises like the Jewish Defense Association, downtowners couldn't help but notice that in their great march through lower Manhattan, upper- and middle-class Jews had been very thin on the ground. The parade also had demonstrated a new willingness to perform their culture in public, marching with Star of David flags alongside those of the Republic, underscoring their differences with the assimilationist elite.

The antagonisms came to the fore in 1906, when Rabbi Magnes suggested transforming the ad hoc Jewish Defense Association into a permanent body that could represent the collective interests of New York's Jewry. What form would it take? Many downtowners favored a democratically elected representative body—a congress—that could legitimately speak and act on the community's behalf. But when Magnes broached the proposal to the Temple Emanu-El mandarins, he was swiftly rebuffed. Emanu-El board member and corporate attorney Louis Marshall had gone along with the JDA, even contributed $500, but the notion of a democratically organized body, in which he and his associates could be outvoted, was anathema. Oscar Straus, Macy's co-owner and the first Jew ever appointed to a cabinet post, also believed that "ability rather than democracy" should be the basis of any American Jewish organization. "The arrogant assumption of the so-called East Siders that numbers give wisdom," Judge Mayer Sulzberger chimed in, "ought to be treated as nil." Accordingly, participation in a downtown-uptown coalition was vetoed. Instead, a committee of five headed by Sulzberger appointed a group of fifty (with Marshall, Schiff, and the Emanu-El group at the core), which in November 1906 named itself the American Jewish Committee.

Magnes tried again in 1908, when Police Commissioner Bingham charged that most criminals in New York were Jews. The immediate issue was dealt with swiftly, and Bingham was forced to issue a retraction, but Magnes argued that a permanent body was wanted to deal with such issues as they arose. Again Marshall feared a democratic organization would be captured by radicals given to "indiscreet, hot-headed and ill-considered oratory," and perhaps actual "mischief making." Magnes, who shared elite reservations about excessive democracy, nevertheless insisted that the American Jewish Committee needed a credible popular mandate if its voice was to be authoritative. Magnes's solution was to structure the "New York Kehillah" as a federation of hundreds of Jewish organizations—synagogues, societies, schools, lodges, mutual benefit groups, charitable associations—so many that no one faction would be able to dominate the whole. The Kehillah could then proceed, in time, through working together, to "wipe out invidious distinctions between . . . 'uptown' Jew and 'downtown' Jew, rich and poor." In 1909 the Kehillah was established. Invidious distinctions remained. Real power was placed in the hands of an elected twenty-five-person executive committee, which would become a subsection of the American Jewish Committee. In addition, only US citizens could be elected as delegates, and political activity within the organization was banned. Radicals and socialists were in effect disfranchised. And the idea of a congress instead of a committee would continue to percolate.

BUNDISTS AND OTHER RADICALS ALSO ENHANCED THE POWER of the downtown Jewish community by piling into the various component institutions that collectively made up the city's socialist movement. They joined the trade unions that the United Hebrew Trades had fostered, particularly those in the needle trades, where many newcomers turned to find work. They also enrolled their various self-help organizations as chapters in the Arbeter Ring (the Workmen's Circle)—19,000 people joined in 1909 alone—and helped expand its compass. They bought and read the socialist press, helping boost circulation, and Bundist intellectuals joined the staffs of major Yiddish publications. Yet even as they became ardent participants in Gotham's socialist movement, infusing it with new energy, they also emerged as powerful critics of some of its ruling assumptions.

Since the 1880s New York socialists had been firm believers in internationalism, by which they meant transcending narrow national identities in the interest of forging working-class solidarity. The Marxist precept—"Proletarians of all countries, unite!"—was fundamental for them; it had figured prominently in the Communist Manifesto of 1848. Morris Hillquit and Abe Cahan—predominant political and cultural leaders of New York socialism—were accordingly firmly hostile to nationalism, including Jewish nationalism. For politician Hillquit this dictated a policy of refusing to allow ethnic federations with national orientations to exist semi-autonomously within the Socialist Party. For editor Cahan, this meant encouraging his Jewish socialist readers to rise above their provincial culture and to assimilate, become more American.

IN THE POLITICAL SPHERE, though the city's socialist unions, self-help groups, and media outlets were growing, New York's Socialist Party, supposedly the flagship of the collective fleet, was in a state of arrested development. Its German roots were showing. Two-thirds of the membership was German American, reflecting its origins in the Socialist Labor Party. Most members were middle-aged, and most were skilled workers (primarily from the building, cigar, and tailoring trades). There were few factory operatives, and negligible numbers of unskilled laborers. In fact, its membership numbers were negligible: its Manhattan branches in 1904 had but 922.

Aware of Engels's scathing critique of German American socialist parties as being too isolated from the larger currents of American politics, Hillquit took steps to grow the party and overcome its marginality. He did so not by reaching out to new immigrant industrial workers, but by forging links with English-speaking middle-class radicals and American Federation of Labor craft unionists. The Socialist Party itself, which Hillquit and Eugene Debs had formed in 1901, was an alliance between New York skilled workers and Debs's heartland industrial laborers. Hillquit had also joined forces with Gompers's AFL—affiliating with its largely native and skilled-worker membership, and tailoring party policies to suit the federation's leadership.

Hillquit also worked hard to recruit the disaffected bourgeoisie, writing extensively for middle-class magazines and engaging in dialogues with progressives. And it worked: the Socialist Party attracted a contingent of middle-class professionals and intellectuals committed to social change and political reform. Newcomers arrived from the city's literary, journalistic, artistic, legal, ecclesiastical, medical, social work, and settlement house circles. Some of the party's attraction to reformers lay in its increasing de-emphasis on class struggle, and its heightened attention to the inefficiency and corruption of the existing order. New York–style socialism and progressivism had much in common, and it was relatively easy to coax people across the porous border. In 1907, at an International Socialist Congress, Hillquit boasted that "in the United States, probably more than anywhere else, socialism is recruiting adherents from the better situated classes of society."

HILLQUIT NOT ONLY RECRUITED INDIVIDUALS; he helped create institutions.

In 1905 he supported formation of the Intercollegiate Socialist Society, dedicated to promoting socialist ideas on college campuses. The brainchild of writer Upton Sinclair, it was organized at a meeting that September in a loft over Peck's Restaurant at 140 Fulton Street. A prestigious body of participants was gathered, headed by the writer Jack London, and including Florence Kelley and Clarence Darrow, J. G. Phelps Stokes, and William English Walling. By 1912 there were forty-three chapters in operation, organizing lectures and discussions and distributing socialist literature.

In 1906 the Rand School for Social Science opened its doors. It had been in the works since 1901 when Hillquit and Christian Socialist minister George Herron organized the American Socialist Society, with the goal of founding a workers college. They found a backer in Herron's wealthy mother-in-law, Caroline Sherfey Rand, who'd been a supporter of social gospel and Christian Socialist movements. On her death in 1905 she left $200,000 to Herron and her daughter, Carrie, who used it to endow the Rand School of Social Science. Among its initiators was Columbia professor Charles Beard, who had helped organize Ruskin Hall, a workers college, while a graduate student at Oxford. While not officially a member of the Socialist Party, Beard supported the school's goal of tutoring actual or would-be Socialist Party and labor union organizers, as well as journalists and civil servants, in socialist theory and applied social science. The school would also offer adult education courses in US history, science, philosophy, drama and the arts, and English grammar, plus classes in public speaking (an important skill for organizers to master). It opened in 1906 with ninety students in a brownstone at 112 East 19th Street. Hillquit taught "The History of Socialism"; Beard offered "Industrial Capitalists and Wage-Workers" and "Development of New Class Antagonisms"; visiting lecturers included Beard's Columbia colleagues John Dewey, James Harvey Robinson, and Franklin H. Giddings, as well as prominent women activists like Florence Kelley and Charlotte Perkins Gilman. By 1917 the school had outgrown its headquarters, and the Socialist Society bought a six-story building, recently vacated by the YWCA, at 7 East 15th Street, just off Union Square. Dubbed the "People's House," it featured a reference library, a public reading room, and the largest radical bookstore in New York City. In 1918 about 1,500 students, many of them socialist workers, enrolled for one or more classes.

Yet another outreach project was the establishment in 1908 of a daily English-language socialist newspaper—the *New York Call*—with editorial offices at 6 Park Place. Muckraking journalist Charles Edward Russell was taken on as associate editor, having recently joined the Socialist Party.

MIDDLE–CLASS AND AFFLUENT RADICALS MAY HAVE LENT the Socialist Party prestige, but they didn't boost its sagging electoral fortunes. The party's cool rationalistic appeals didn't ignite the mass of Jewish (much less gentile) workers. Reform votes went to William Randolph Hearst, whose municipal ownership campaigns stole much of the Socialists' thunder. Those in search of rudimentary social services or patronage turned to Tammany. When Hillquit ran in 1906 for Congress from New York's Ninth District, which included the heavily Jewish Lower East Side, he lost to the incumbent, Henry Goldfogle, a Jewish Tammany man, who was also endorsed by Hearst. When Hillquit squared off with Goldfogle in 1908, he again ran a poor second.

Part of the problem was that the party made barely any outreach to the immigrant social-ists then crowding into the city. The Bundists organized political clubs and asked they be allowed to join the party as an autonomous, Yiddish-speaking federation. They were rebuffed. Other foreign-language groups similarly sought to connect but were turned away, though in 1906 the national party allowed a Finnish federation of over 2,000 members to affiliate, requiring them to pay extra dues and accept non-voting status. Not until 1912 would the Socialists allow autonomous ethnic- or language-based—"national"—subdivisions to become full participants in party decision making. To the degree that this posture was deemed to follow from "internationalist" premises, it proved remarkably self-defeating.

More offputting still, and hard to reconcile with any brand of "internationalism," Hillquit knuckled under to AFL nativism. In an article on immigration written in 1907, he declared that "the majority of American socialists side with the trade unions in their demand for the exclusion of workingmen of such races and nations as have not yet been drawn into the sphere of modern production, and who are incapable of assimilation with the workingmen of the country of their adoption, and of joining the organization and struggles of their class." Hillquit claimed to oppose exclusion by race or nationality (though he argued that Chinese and Japanese workers were "altogether unorganizable") and was opposed only to mass immi-gration (especially if arranged by capitalists) that might weaken American workers and lower their standard of living. But as the AFL claimed all new immigration had this effect, Hillquit's position was in practice exclusionary. And while Hillquit signaled that Socialist opposition to immigration was really focused only on Asians, his criteria for exclusion were chillingly open-ended: "Just what races are to be included in this category is a question that can only be decided from time to time with reference to the particular circumstances and conditions of each case." This enraged and alienated many New York immigrant socialists and infuri-ated party chieftain Eugene Debs, who denounced Hillquit's capitulation to the AFL, calling it "utterly unsocialistic, reactionary, and in truth outrageous."

ON THE CULTURAL FRONT ABE CAHAN ALSO HEWED to an anti-nationalist line, particularly in the case of Jewish nationalism. The editor hoped the new immigrants would assimilate rap-idly into a larger working-class culture. The socialist goal should be "to erase all boundaries between Jew and non-Jew in the labor world." His own role, and that of the *Forward*, was to help the masses transcend their own allegedly parochial culture, and also bring their children up in the American manner: "We should especially not raise our children so that they will grow up to be foreigners in their own birthplace."

Most critically—and here he agreed with the uptown German Jews—Cahan wanted to wean his readers from Yiddish, a backward medium destined for elimination. Back in the 1880s, he and other Russian-speaking intellectuals had needed to employ Yiddish, the spoken language of nearly all Eastern European Jewish immigrants, in order to organize Jewish workers. It was justified as a short-term concession, necessary only until the immigrants learned English. Thus, in a feat of linguistic jujitsu, Cahan would use his Yiddish newspaper to undermine Yiddish, helping readers acculturate to American ways from a comfortable and familiar platform. Cahan was perfectly placed to do this, having mastered American popular journalism during his stint working for Lincoln Steffens at the *Commercial Advertiser*. Once returned to the *Forward*'s editorial chair, he cut back on lengthy theoretical essays and instead zeroed in on daily life in the Jewish quarters, recounting Hester Street doings in eminently readable Yiddish. Cahan's reporters churned out snappy, at times lurid copy about scandals, gangsters, and prostitutes, as well as covering real estate and baseball news. A Yiddish

Pulitzer, a Hebrew Hearst, Cahan crusaded for popular causes, backed strikes, ran single-column short stories, and offered an advice column—"A Bintel Brief" (Bundle of Letters)—that answered readers' puzzled queries about American ways and dispensed counsel on love and work, manners and morals. (Political morals, too: "I am a Socialist and my boss is a fine man," wrote one. "I know he's a Capitalist but I like him. Am I doing something wrong?")

The paper took off, but its soaring circulation presented Cahan with a conundrum. Having in effect proved that American issues could be dealt with in Yiddish, he had in effect extended the "zhargon's" shelf life. In seeking to leave Yiddish culture behind, Cahan managed only a rousing reaffirmation of it.

IT WAS PRECISELY THIS POLITICAL AND CULTURAL DILEMMA to which the incoming Yiddish-speaking socialists addressed themselves. Fresh from the hellish urban battlefields of the Russian Empire, they found the "internationalism" of the New York Socialists naïve, wrong-headed, and counterproductive. They argued forcefully that socialists could (and should) affirm the kind of demand for Jewish cultural autonomy that had emerged in response to the anti-Semitic pogroms. More broadly, they believed there was no inherent contradiction between nationalism and internationalism. It was perfectly possible to hold nationalist sentiments without inflating national feelings to such a degree that it would blur class consciousness or degenerate into chauvinism.

The chief theoretician of this suggested reappraisal was Chaim Zhitlovsky, a Social Revolutionary Party official who had accompanied Babushka on her trip to New York in 1904, then stayed on for eighteen months, then returned permanently in 1914. A deeply learned philosopher and historian with heavy-duty revolutionary credentials, Zhitlovsky quickly established himself on the socialist scene with a series of brilliant lectures and debate performances, presented in an elegant Yiddish that few in New York had ever heard. He was not a Bundist, as he differed with them on a variety of issues, but back in Russia he had inspired their early (pre-Kishinev) amalgamation of socialism and nationalism.

Zhitlovsky distinguished between internationalism and socialist assimilationism (which he called "cosmopolitanism"), the latter being a utopian desire to amalgamate all nations into a universal and undifferentiated humanity. In practice, cosmopolitanism meant the absorption of small and weak national groups into larger, more powerful ones; it really amounted to national chauvinism disguised as universalism. Zhitlovsky also opposed nationalist "separatists" who rejected the conception of a common humanity. There was indeed a "general human culture"—observable in the sciences, humanities, and arts—but it arose from mutually enriching exchanges between nations. The true meaning of internationalism was, accordingly, not denying national differences in the name of an abstract universalism, as New York's socialists were wont to believe, but rather aiding the cultural development of individual nations in cooperation with others.

What, he asked, was a nation? Bucking conventional definitions, he denied that nationhood required command of territory or attainment of political independence. It was, rather, a cultural construct formed out of shared historical experience; its component parts were a common language, religion, literature, folkways, feelings of group solidarity, and in the case of the Jews a heritage of oppression. A nation, therefore, was any substantial group of people who, over many generations, had worked out their own take on cultural questions common to humanity and elaborated their own distinctive forms of creativity.

By these lights, the Yiddish-speaking Jews of the Russian Empire constituted a nation, as they were a people bonded together by a shared history and culture, even though they controlled no state. It was incumbent on socialists to speak up for such a nation when it was threatened with oppression. This was the message Zhitlovsky had brought to the Bundists in Russia, and it was under his influence that in 1903 they had demanded "national cultural autonomy" for Russian Jews.

This was also the message Bundists brought to New York. Socialists could and should foster both internationalism and Jewish national (but nonchauvinist) culture. In Gotham, Jews were threatened not by anti-Semitism but by assimilationism. The best way to combat this was by cultivating secular Yiddishkayt—Jewishness—crucially by strengthening the Yiddish language. Zhitlovsky agreed with Cahan that actually existing Yiddish was an under-developed medium, but the solution was to develop it, not abandon it. He proposed elevating the Jewish vernacular to the status of a national language, capable of handling scientific and artistic creativity as well as any of the great European languages.

Was such a flowering of *Yidishe kultur* possible in the United States, where expectations of assimilation were the norm? Zhitlovsky, for one, thought yes—and where more likely than in New York City? When Yiddish cultural nationalists looked around them in Gotham they saw an enormous and densely clustered Yiddish-speaking population; a flourishing Yiddish press, theater, and imaginative literature; and a degree of freedom of expression utterly unknown in Russia.

Cahan, Hillquit, and their colleagues weren't buying this. They denied it was possible to build a new Jewish culture in Yiddish; nor could such a culture withstand the pressures and allure of the English-speaking city that surrounded it. Yes, it was necessary, they believed, to aid Jews under fire in Europe, and perhaps to modify somewhat their anti-national stance in New York, but how far one could go in that direction without succumbing to national chauvinism, and undermining proletarian solidarity in the city, remained a debatable question.

There was, however, one thing on which the youthful Bundists, the Old Guard socialists, and the assimilated German Jewish elite could all agree: that Zionism was an understandable but ultimately insufficient, even inappropriate, response to anti-Semitism.

WHEN ZIONISM HAD BEEN LAUNCHED AS A POLITICAL PROJECT back at the turn of the century, most New York Jews, like most American Jews, had opposed it. Certainly there was wide-spread sympathy for the rivulet of Russian émigrés that had trickled into Palestine, then part of the Ottoman Turkish Empire, fleeing the pogroms of the 1880s. But the 1897 establishment of a political movement—embodied in the World Zionist Organization (WZO)—was viewed more dubiously. Its progenitor, the Viennese Jewish journalist Theodor Herzl, whose 1896 pamphlet *The Jewish State* made him a leading spokesperson for the Zionist cause, believed that anti-Semitism was universal and inescapable. Diasporic Jews could find peace and safety only in a territorial nation of their own, and the First Zionist Congress in Basel (1897) decreed that nation belonged in Palestine, the Jewish people's ancestral home.

This did not sit well with the many New York Jews who had found their promised land in the United States. Certainly the highly assimilated and wealthy German Jews of the American Jewish Committee rejected the notion. Calling for a homeland in Palestine would expose them, they believed, to a charge of divided loyalty, even disloyalty. It would also undercut their preferred focus on guaranteeing the right of Jews to live as free and equal citizens of any country in which they chose to dwell, rather than huddling in a ghetto-nation, especially one in such a barren and "Oriental" spot. Theologically, moreover, the Reform wing of American Judaism, of which they were prominent members and supporters, had long insisted that Jews were *not* a nation but a religious community. Indeed, the Central

Conference of American Rabbis had specifically said back in 1885 it did not expect a return to Palestine or the resurrection of a Jewish state.

Nor did the Cahan and Hillquit sector of the socialist movement see eye to eye with Herzl. Devoted as they were to proletarian internationalism, they considered Zionism a nationalist diversion from the class struggle.

Zhitlovksy and the Bundists similarly argued that the practical problems facing the Jewish masses had to be confronted in the countries where they lived, rather than by exodus, certainly not to Palestine, which would never be capable of receiving anything but a small percentage of the endangered populations. In addition, a Jewish state would be as vulnerable as any European or American power to falling into national chauvinism.

Zhitlovsky, in particular, objected to Herzl's grand strategy of inserting a Jewish state in an already occupied territory, its existence guaranteed by the major European imperial powers in return for it serving the collective interest of those states. "We should there form a portion of a rampart of Europe against Asia, an outpost of civilization as opposed to barbarism." Among the states to which Herzl appealed for backing was the czarist regime in Russia. In August 1903, just months after Kishinev, Herzl met with leading government officials, who offered support for the Zionist project if Herzl would rein in the Russian Jewish revolutionaries. Herzl asked Zhitlovsky to help him—a request predictably refused—and called on his followers in a Russia knee deep in blood to behave "calmly and legally." This enraged many of his left-wing followers, already unhappy about his intention to perpetuate some form of capitalism in the future Jewish state. Many now broke away and joined the socialist Zionist movement, Poale Zion (Workers of Zion), which dreamed of creating a classless society in Palestine. Zhitlovsky was among the many who thought this an escapist fantasy.

From yet another direction, many of Gotham's Orthodox Jews dissented from political Zionism, partly from concern at its secular focus, partly because they considered the effort itself borderline sacrilegious, as one Zionist fund-raiser learned at an East Side synagogue. "Young man, you are going against God's will," an elderly congregant chided. "If he wanted us to have Zion again, He would restore it again without the help of the so-called Zionists. God doesn't need apprentices. Please go schnorr [wheedle] somewhere else and let us lament in peace, like good Jews."

Nevertheless, it was in New York City that US Zionism took (shallow) root, and almost immediately. In July 1898, one year after the founding conference in Basel, a hundred delegates representing a mix of small, mainly East Side educational societies, synagogue organizations, and fraternal lodges met at the B'nai Zion Club on Henry Street and formed the Federation of American Zionists (FAZ), which affiliated with Herzl's WZO and endorsed the Basel program. As their respected titular leader they chose Richard Gottheil, a Columbia professor who studied Semitic languages and had authored a *Jewish Encyclopedia* article on Zionism. To do the real work, they drafted, as organizational secretary, a Gottheil student, Rabbi Stephen Wise, who had recently met Herzl and been converted to the cause. Wise would stay on until 1902, when he left for a pulpit in Portland; Jacob de Haas, a protégé of Herzl himself, ran things over the next three years, and when he retired in 1905, Judah Magnes took over until 1908, when he departed to assume the presidency of the New York Kehillah. Despite this capable leadership, for its first decade the FAZ remained a fringe affair, marginal to the city's Jewish life, much less to Jewry's national or international stages.

Even more marginal was the Poale Zion Party, which made its appearance in New York in the early spring of 1906, having emerged in Russia before and during the Revolution, when Zionist-inclined workers who refused to belong to the same organizations as their employers established autonomous societies. But even Zionism of the socialist variety—denied patronage or support by the *Forward* socialists or the larger labor movement—remained but a tiny current in Jewish life in Gotham.

FINALLY, IN THIS SURVEY OF EARLY-TWENTIETH-CENTURY NEW YORK'S radical Jewish political geography, come the Jewish anarchists, another group that Jewish socialists of whatever persuasion (and certainly the uptown elite) considered beyond the pale.

Gotham's Jewish anarchists had limped into the twentieth century. Their preeminent journal, the *Fraye Arbeter Shtimme* (Free Voice of Labor), had shut down for much of the 1890s, its worker supporters having been laid low by the depression. The Pioneers of Liberty, the first US anarchist group, formed in New York in 1886 to support the Haymarket martyrs-to-be, faded away in the aftermath of member Alexander Berkman's botched 1892 attempt to assassinate Henry Clay Frick, in response to his crushing of the Homestead strike.

Then, with the return of prosperity, and energizing visits by leading international anarchists (Peter Kropotkin lectured in the city in 1897 and again in 1901), the movement reignited. The *Free Voice of Labor* was resurrected in 1900, under the editorship of Saul Yanovsky, and there was an efflorescence of newspapers, journals, pamphlets, and books, which flowed from enterprises like the Germinal Publishing Association of Brooklyn (which brought out Kropotkin's work in Yiddish), to bookstores like Max Maisel's on Grand Street (which offered Yiddish translations of Thoreau and Wilde, as well as anarchist theoreticians like Errico Malatesta). Anarchist circles emerged, which organized picnics, excursions, concerts, and theatrical performances for the benefit of their various papers and journals.

The community was energized by events in Russia. It supported Kropotkin's organization of aid to Russian anarchists, welcomed their visits to New York, and then, in 1907, after defeat, organized an Anarchist Red Cross, headquartered in Gotham, which organized "prisoner balls" to raise money to send clothing to comrades jailed in Russia. New York anarchists also raised funds to support the efforts of the California-based Ricardo and Enrique Flores Magón to overthrow the Mexican dictatorship of Porfirio Díaz.

Nonetheless, the anarchist movement and Emma Goldman, its most well-known figure, were operating under a very dark cloud in the aftermath of the assassination of President McKinley in 1901 by Leon Czolgosz, who when asked about his motive replied, "I am an anarchist, a disciple of Emma Goldman. Her words set me on fire." He insisted, however, that he had acted alone and had no accomplices—and indeed he belonged to no anarchist group and had only met Goldman briefly—insisting that "I done it all myself. Emma Goldman...did not tell me to kill McKinley." Efforts to implicate her fizzled for lack of evidence. But an anti-anarchist furor ensued, and anarchists were hunted, arrested, and persecuted throughout the country. In New York the offices of the *Fraye Arbeter Shtime* on Henry Street were trashed by an angry crowd. Editor Saul Yanovsky was cornered and beaten in a neighborhood restaurant, though he had repudiated the assassination, as had the bulk of the anarchist movement, including even the still-in-jail Alexander Berkman. Yet Goldman, who had asked, "Am I accountable because some crack-brained person put a wrong construction on my words?" nevertheless vigorously supported the assassin, portraying him as "Brutus" and casting McKinley as "President of the money kings and trust magnates." This enraged the American public and many of her comrades, who were appalled by the crime, and who were suffering from a repression that was swiftly enacted into law.

During his first message to Congress, on December 3, 1901, President Roosevelt said that anarchists "should be kept out of this country, and if found there they should be promptly deported to the country whence they came, and far-reaching provisions should be made for the punishment of those who stay." While his proposal was under consideration, New York State moved first, passing a 1902 Criminal Anarchy Act that prohibited people from lecturing, writing, or disseminating literature promoting the doctrine that organized government should be overthrown by force or violence. In 1903 the federal Alien Immigration Act (widely known as the Anti-Anarchist Law) followed suit. It barred from entering the country "anarchists or persons who believe in or advocate the overthrow by force or violence of the Government of the United States or of all governments or of all forms of law, or the assassination of public officials."[1]

Tagged as a terrorist, Goldman was driven from public life. She was heckled and insulted when spotted at public events, was monitored intently by the police, had trouble finding work and lodgings, and heard rumblings that she might be subject to abduction or attack. Dropping out of active participation in the anarchist movement, she went into seclusion and neither gave speeches nor wrote for the anarchist press. She adopted the pseudonym "Mrs. E. G. Smith," which enabled her to earn money as a nurse, tending to patients on the night shift. In 1904 she opened up a "Vienna scalp and facial massage" parlor (on Broadway and 17th Street). She also worked at home, making dresses on her sewing machine, though homes were hard to hold on to, as landlords were loath to rent to the infamous anarchist. She moved from one tenement to another, from lower Manhattan to Harlem, until at the end of 1902 she settled in a sixth-floor, three-room, walk-up apartment at 210 East 13th Street (between Second and Third), where she would remain until 1913.

Then the revolutionary winds blowing in from the east revivified her spirits and resuscitated her reputation. In 1904 she played hostess and translator to arriving Russian émigrés, notably Babushka. In 1905 she became manager and interpreter for Orleneff's visiting Russian troupe. And in 1906, with funds raised by a benefit performance Orleneff put on for her in gratitude, she founded a journal, originally entitled the *Open Road* in a nod to Whitman, a favorite anarchist poet, and then (the name having been taken by another publication) *Mother Earth*. From its first issue in March 1906, it was successful enough to allow her to shutter her massage business, and when Berkman was released from prison later that year he joined Goldman and took up editorial duties.

The journal advocated and explained anarchist theories—spreading the gospel of "direct action" in opposition to socialist parliamentarianism—but was relatively ecumenical, opening its pages to a wide variety of radicals, and publishing articles on drama, literature, birth control, civil liberties, and the "social war."

To fund the journal, whose finances were always creaky, she began lecturing widely—in the city, around the country, and abroad. She was quite successful as a public speaker, though always the cloud followed her. In Gotham, she was the particular target of Police Commissioner Bingham, who spent his 1906–9 tenure building a "secret service" within the force, to crush Black Hand blackmailers (expanding the 1903 Italian Squad) and deal with political crimes, relying on the state's Criminal Anarchy Act for authorization. Bingham's men harassed and arrested anarchists, barred them from meeting halls, and blocked distribution of *Mother*

---

1. This came against a backdrop of successful assassinations. In 1881 radicals killed the czar; in 1894, the president of France; in 1897, the prime minister of Spain; in 1898, the empress of Austria; in 1900, the king of Italy; and then, in 1901, the US president.

Earth and other journals. When Goldman arranged a masquerade ball at Webster Hall (119–125 East 11th Street) on November 23, 1906, fifty policemen raided the fund-raiser, tore off people's masks, and forced the owner to close the hall.

It was much the same on the road, with repeated arrests (though never a conviction) for revolutionary anarchism, but she still managed to talk on a wide variety of subjects. She also kept a travel diary, whose accounts, printed in *Mother Earth*, provided a running chronicle of radical activities in the United States. Because of these endeavors Goldman and Berkman became the best-known Jewish anarchists in the country, though neither was typical of the Jewish anarchist movement. Nor did she often address Jewish issues. Goldman recalled that Chaim Zhitlovsky "never tired urging upon me that as a Jewish daughter I should devote myself to the cause of the Jews." She replied that she could not, as she "had become aware that social injustice is not confined to my own race." Goldman also criticized Jewish anarchists in the United States and Canada for being "still too Jewish, I fear, to really appreciate the great necessity of a wide-spread agitation in the language of the country they live in." And indeed, her primary focus was on popularizing anarchism among native-born American workers and intellectuals, though she continued to deliver some lectures in Yiddish.

Goldman was also interested in teaching children, and in 1911 she and Berkman co-founded the Modern School, initially on St. Mark's Place, later up in Harlem, at East 107th Street and Park Avenue. It was informally known as the Ferrer Center, named after and inspired by the Barcelona anarchist educator who promoted libertarian and secular schools, until he was executed by the Spanish monarchy in 1909. Goldman, like Dewey, saw the public schools as a "veritable barrack, where the human mind is drilled and manipulated into submission," and, following Ferrer, the Modern School opted for encouraging individual development.

The Ferrer Center also housed an adult education component, whose students were mostly Jews, though with a sprinkling of Italians, Greeks, Scots, and English radicals. The center provided evening lectures, experimental theater performances, and classes in painting, music appreciation, physiology, and psychology; the main-floor auditorium was packed nearly every day of the year. The offerings were not wildly different from the fare available at the settlement houses, though the presence of radical intellectuals and activists like Margaret Sanger, Jack London, Upton Sinclair, Clarence Darrow, Elizabeth Gurley Flynn, and Lincoln Steffens made it distinctive.

ITALIAN SOVVERSIVI

The huge migration of Italians to the United States dwarfed the exodus from Russia's empire; indeed, as early as 1898 it surpassed the migration level of any other nation on earth. The numbers rose swiftly in the 1880s and 1890s, then leapt spectacularly upward in the 1900s and 1910s. Where annual Jewish arrivals maxed out at 100,000, and that only during a few peak years, 100,000 was the *minimum* metric for Italians, with the annual influx breaking the 200,000 barrier in 1903, 1905, 1906, 1907 (at 285,731 the record setter), 1910, 1913, and 1914. Overall, between 1900 and 1909—the year when a record-breaking 2,111 walked down the gangplank of the liner *Ultonia*—nearly 2 million Italians arrived. And keeping up the blistering pace, another million came on board between 1910 and 1914.

Approximately 95–98 percent of these millions disembarked in the Port of New York, and while eventually many went back—between 1901 and 1920 over half the Italian immigrants repatriated themselves—many settled down in Gotham, enough to double the Italian presence in the city. From a modest 44,230 in residence in 1880, by 1900 the combined foreign born and children of foreign-born parents in the five boroughs had risen to 225,026. By 1904 that figure had shot up to 382,775, and by 1910 to 544, 449 (of which 340,765 were foreign born). For Italians, New York had become the largest settlement in North America, though they were scattered about the giant metropolis in more than twenty-five Italian districts, ranging in size from 2,000 to 100,000.

THE FORCES THAT SET SO MANY ITALIANS IN MOTION were in some degree similar to those driving the Jewish exodus—political insurrection and massive state repression—but the Italians were also up against wrenching economic transformations, especially in the Mezzogiorno (the south and Sicily) from where the great bulk of migrants came. Beginning back in the 1870s, the region had suffered from the loss of buyers for their wine and fruit, with cheap Florida oranges flooding into markets they'd formerly dominated, and from the undercutting of regional industries and artisanal crafts by imported manufactured goods. Add in declining grain prices, depletion of the soil, destruction of vines by phylloxera, a rapid increase in population, and the spread of malaria and cholera, and you had a recipe for widespread misery. All this was exacerbated by the ability of the dominant landowning and industrialist classes to pass along the costs of crisis in higher rents, lower wages, and higher taxes.

The whirlwind of social and economic change set workers and peasants in Italy's deep south to agitating and organizing on an unprecedented scale. Between 1889 and 1894, the Fasci Siciliani dei Lavoratori (Sicilian Workers Leagues), a popular resistance movement

Lewis Hine, "Italian Family Looking for Lost Baggage, Ellis Island," 1904. (New York Public Library, Miriam and Ira D. Wallach Division of Art, Prints and Photographs)

sparked by young socialist intellectuals, grew to include artisans, industrial workers, *contadini* (peasants), *mezzadri* (sharecroppers), and *braccianti* (day laborers), until it boasted a membership of more than 300,000, with branches in most Sicilian towns. They adopted the term *fasci* (*fascio* literally means "bundle") because while anyone can break a single stick, it's vastly harder to break a bundle of sticks.[2] Leagued together—often in conjunction with the recently established Italian Socialist Party (1892)—the Fasci launched strikes against great landowners and sulfur-mine owners, demanding lower rents, higher wages, lower taxes, a revision of land leases to undercut the power of the *gabellotti* (rural entrepreneurs allied with the Mafia), the establishment of model contracts for agricultural workers and sharecroppers, outright land redistribution, and hours, wages, and child labor laws. When ruling Sicilian elites stonewalled, protests escalated, miners struck, farmers seized land, and violent urban crowds demonstrated for jobs and burned down tax offices. The Sicilian elite convinced Rome to suppress the Fasci. Forty thousand troops were sent to the island, where they killed scores, perhaps hundreds, in street clashes and summary executions. Military tribunals handed down harsh sentences, and thousands of militants were imprisoned on the desolate islands off the southern Italian and Sicilian coasts. The Fasci was outlawed, the socialists suppressed, working-class societies dissolved, press freedom suspended.

The state also put down urban working-class upheavals in Naples, Rome, and northern cities. In Milan in 1898 unarmed crowds, protesting the high price of bread, marched toward the city center. They were met with point-blank musket and cannon fire that killed between 150 and 400 and wounded perhaps 1,000. King Umberto I decorated the commanding general for his "brave defense of the royal house," making many Italians molten with fury. To avenge those massacred, anarchist Gaetano Bresci, an Italian-born silk worker who had moved to Paterson, New Jersey, in the mid-1890s, returned from the United States and assassinated Umberto in 1900. (It was in fact Bresci, not Goldman, who inspired Czolgosz's killing of McKinley the following year.) Upheavals continued into the new century, as did periodic waves of repression, which together with the ongoing economic crisis propelled vast numbers into exile in France, Switzerland, the Argentina, and the United States—notably to New York City.

GOTHAM APPEALED PARTICULARLY TO MEZZOGIORNO ARTISANS AND INDUSTRIAL WORKERS. They saw New York as a place where they might ply their trades. Farm workers or miners were more likely to head into the North American continent. In 1910 an Immigration Commission survey of southern Italians in New York City found that only 31 percent had worked on the land. And indeed, many did get work as tailors, shoemakers, barbers, bakers, carpenters, cabinetmakers, ironworkers, stonemasons, grocers, printers, and waiters—as well as, for a small number, physicians, attorneys, journalists, and intellectuals—though the majority of Italians, of whatever background, worked as laborers. A 1916 study of the occupations of Italian fathers of children born in New York revealed that 50.4 percent were laborers and that the next four largest categories were *artigiani*: tailors (5.4 percent), barbers (5.3 percent), shoemakers (2.9 percent), and carpenters (2.1 percent). Only a minuscule 1.2 percent and 0.7 percent were listed as "professional" and "clerical."

By no means were all these newcomers radicals—many were simply in flight from terrible conditions—but a significant minority of those from Sicily, the Abruzzi, Campania, Calabria,

---

2. See also the anatomical term "fasciae," meaning dense connective tissues, containing closely packed bundles of collagen fibers.

and other southern regions were displaced militants, with strong ongoing ties to homeland activists. They did not check their politics at the Golden Door. Rather they made New York a center of Italian American radicalism. This was a diffuse category, as its members included socialists, anarchists, and syndicalists, who were often at each other's throats over theoretical issues, but who were nevertheless remarkably similar in their perspectives on, and activities in, the city. Soon, indeed, they adopted an all-embracing term to capture this commonality, calling themselves: the *sovversivi* (the subversives).

LIKE ARRIVING BUNDISTS, THE *SOVVERSIVI* BEGAN BY ORGANIZING THEMSELVES into scores of mutual aid societies (*società di mutuo soccorso*) and political circles (*circoli politici*) of varying persuasions (principally socialist or anarchist). These oases of radicalism became centers for education, recreation, political discussion, and labor organizing. The *sovversivi* rented meeting halls and created libraries, schools, food co-ops, orchestras, theater troupes, and choral groups. Women were active in this movement, though seldom in positions of high visibility and influence. At the local level, however, many did participate regularly in political as well as social and recreational activities. These groups backboned a subculture within the greater Italian community.

The *sovversivi* established newspapers and magazines. Generally published weekly or biweekly, they featured articles and editorials devoted to political ideology and movement activities, along with news of local, national, and international workers' strikes, peasant rebellions, government repressions—anything that dramatized the exploitation of the working class by capitalism and the state, and popular resistance thereto. But the *sovversivi* press also presented poetry and installments of plays or novels, and announcements about lectures, concerts, and theatrical performances. Conversely, the theatrical presentations bolstered press and party. In Antonio Maiori's playhouse, anarchist papers were sold during intermission, while Riccardo Cordiferro wrote and acted in plays with a socialist message. The circles in turn supported the papers by throwing fund-raising events, like picnics in public parks, which in turn helped integrate and sustain the radical communities.

The political and cultural ideas they disseminated were at variance with the traditional beliefs held by most of the city's Italians, and were put forward precisely to challenge conventional opinions. In a larger sense, they proposed themselves as alternative leaders of New York's Italian *colonia*, in opposition to the ruling elites that had established control of the community over previous decades. In this effort they resembled the 1880s generation of arriving Russian Jewish intellectuals, though they were starting from scratch, there being no cohort of established radicals who could provide the kind of leg-up assistance that German socialists had extended to arriving Jewish socialists.

The sworn enemies of the *sovversivi* were an interlocking directorate of capitalists, clerics, and representatives of the Italian state. They denounced the *prominenti*—wealthy *padroni* and *banchisti* (labor brokers and bankers)—who had attained their prosperity and status, so the *sovversivi* asserted, by exploiting their working-class countrymen. They excoriated the rich publishers of Italian-language daily newspapers—like Carlo Barsotti and his *Il Progresso Italo-Americano*—for criticizing Italian workers when they struck for higher pay, and for using their newspapers as recruiting agencies for strikebreakers. They attacked the Italian Consulate in New York, exposing its corrupt bureaucrats who fleeced Italian workers in need of assistance. They reserved their strongest invective for the Catholic Church. The *sovversivi* despised all priests as opportunistic allies of the rich and powerful, whose real mission was to keep the Italian masses ignorant and subservient. They were well aware that priests were powerful and articulate competitors for the support of working-class Catholics. Again, the *sovversivi* were at a disadvantage compared to Jewish radicals, who faced no such challenge from rabbinical elites, who had largely abandoned civic leadership to the left, in part because they'd been unable to reproduce the kind of authority they'd had in Europe, where rabbis could be official representatives of Jews to the state, whereas the Catholic Church had deep institutional presence and power in Gotham.[3]

The rich and powerful returned their hatred, and the resulting class antagonism in the Italian community was a naked one, unmitigated by the necessity of joining forces against an outside danger, as uptown and downtown Jews had done, to some degree, to aid czarist victims. Elites had their own ways of enlisting support in the *colonia*, in addition to bestriding the access routes to employment. *Prominenti* and clergy encouraged formation of patriotic societies, often named after Italian heroes or members of the royal family, and these sponsored banquets, balls, picnics, and parades to celebrate the national holidays of La Festa dello Statuto (Constitution Day) and XX Settembre (the incorporation of Rome into the kingdom). The colonial press published special issues on such anniversaries, extolling the virtues of the king and queen and the glories of Italy, and at the events themselves consular officials bestowed medals, while priests offered blessings, and the members of the societies, usually common laborers, dressed up in the elaborate uniforms of *carabinieri*, generals, and admirals, adorned their chests with medals, and marched behind a brass band playing the Italian national anthem.

Such religio-patriotic manifestations were anathema to the radicals, who ridiculed the elite's pretensions. They were also enraged by religious processions, in which Italian workers carried statues of saints through the streets and pinned hard-earned dollars on them. Again they responded with mockery and spoofs of the saints' supposed miracles. More compellingly, in an acknowledgment of the popularity of such practices, they contested nationalist-clerical hegemony over the immigrant masses by creating a counterculture. Their socialist clubs and anarchist groups were themselves alternatives to religious and patriotic societies. On Sundays, attendance at lectures and cultural events substituted for attendance at Mass. More innovatively, they published their own calendar of holidays, the *Almanacco Sovversivo*, to replace that of the Church. Rather than celebrate saints' days, the calendar noted anniversaries in the history of revolutionary movements, such as the fall of the Bastille, the Paris Commune, the assassination of King Humbert I, the birthdays of such as Marx and Bakunin, and, most formidably, Primo Maggio—May Day—as a workers holiday that embodied the aspirations of the international socialist movement.

THE *SOVVERSIVI* WOULD WIN ONLY OCCASIONAL AND EPHEMERAL VICTORIES in this internal class war, partly because they were up against powerfully entrenched forces, but partly, too, because their own ranks were riven by fierce doctrinal quarrels between socialists and anarchists—over ends (rival visions of the good society) and means (contending ways of attaining it).

---

3. The *sovversivi* appear not to have explored the possibility of alliances with radical Catholics in the mold of Father Edward McGlynn, who had allied publicly with Henry George in the election of 1886. It's true that McGlynn and radical Catholic allies had lost that round to Church conservatives—Archbishop Michael Corrigan had effectively squelched him—but supporters remained. When McGlynn died in 1894, his funeral was attended by about a hundred Catholic priests and many of the city's Protestant pastors, while tens of thousands filed by his coffin in his old parish of St. Stephen's. The intra-Church battle continued after his death. McGlynn was buried in Calvary Cemetery, Queens, but when supporters commissioned a life-sized bronze statue of him, and the archdiocese refused to allow it to be placed on his grave, they bought land in nondenominational Woodlawn Cemetery and erected it in the Bronx.

As to ends: the socialists advocated collective ownership of the means of production, to be managed by a democratic republic of workers and workers' councils; whereas anarchists, believing that power corrupts, refused to trust any state, even one run by socialists, and preferred that a decentralized federation of communes and workers' associations manage production and distribution.

As to means: *parliamentarians* advocated that workers, massed in a socialist party, capture state power at the polling place, while *syndicalists* urged workers to organize not in parties but in industrial unions, which would win democratic control of their workplace by direct action—strikes, boycotts, sabotage (slowdowns, etc.)—and then use their accumulated economic power to reorganize the political sphere.

There were many points of overlap between the ends. Anti-capitalism was central to both. And while socialists did see a major role for the state during the transition to socialism, they believed that in some (admittedly hazy) distant future it would fade away. But the differences in means—matters of style as well as principle—loomed larger. Socialists tended to favor parliamentary means, and anarchists opted for syndicalist modes of action, though there were innumerable possible combinations of the two that muddied the binary clarity of the distinction.

In terms of ethnic preferences, Jewish radicals tended to favor the socialist-parliamentarian model, while Italian radicals tilted toward an anarcho-syndicalist approach. There were several reasons for the Italians' preference, starting with the difficulties Italian socialists had in interfacing with their American, Jewish, and German socialist counterparts.

In 1902, following the advice of a visiting Italian Socialist Party leader, several dozen socialist *circolos* and workers' organizations came together to form the Federazione Socialista Italiana (Italian Socialist Federation, or ISF), to coordinate their activities and resources. By 1906 the ISF had eighty affiliates with more than a thousand members. It had also designated an official newspaper, *Il Proletario*, which had been started in 1896 by a local *circolo* in Pittsburgh, then moved, via a stint in Paterson, to New York in 1898. But it quickly became clear to the ISF members that Hillquit's Socialist Party would not welcome them with open arms, given its coolness, on "internationalist" grounds, to incorporating language- or ethnic-based federations (though in fact the New York party was predominantly Russian and German). The Italians also considered Hillquit's stance on immigration restriction to be xenophobic, a concern exacerbated by the party's dogged alliance with Gompers's American Federation of Labor. The AFL had long been averse to recruiting Italian workers, though after 1900 it had reluctantly begun to make room for skilled Italian craftsmen in appropriate AFL craft unions (carpenters, bricklayers, masons, barbers), fearing their competition if left outside the tent. But most Italians were laborers or factory workers, hence of no interest to Gompersian unionists. Virtually all the New York *sovversivi*, accordingly, loathed the AFL.

The bad feelings were mutual. AFL leaders abhorred the Italian radicals and countercharged that Italian workers were notoriously wary of trade unions, hence difficult to organize, and that Italian strikebreakers were the docile servants of capital. It was true that, given the situation of Italian workers, many found union membership irrelevant. They were, after all, an extremely mobile population, apt to move about the country in search of employment and, given their sojourner mentality, likely as not to return to Italy at any moment. It was equally true that many Italian workers found the socialists' electoral strategy unsuitable. As late as 1910, after all, fewer than 25 percent of Italian immigrants were naturalized and eligible to vote, and many of those had little interest in American affairs. All in all, most Italians were less into a long-haul accumulation of power at the polls than obtaining an immediate payoff at the workplace.

The ISF leadership, recognizing this state of affairs, sidled away from socialist parliamentarianism toward anarcho-syndicalism, a drift reflected in the evolving orientation of *Il Proletario*. In 1904 the ISF leadership chose a new editor, Carlo Tresca, himself a recent arrival from the Abruzzi. Born in 1879, Tresca, though a scion of a landed gentry family, embraced socialism with fiery militancy, its appeal to him more visceral than intellectual; it "awakened my combative spirit," he said. He joined the Italian Socialist Party, edited a socialist paper (which soon reaped libel charges from local priests), and organized strikes for the railway workers union. By 1904, his outspoken advocacy of violent revolution having convinced police he was a dangerous subversive, he decided to avoid an impending prison term by relocating to the United States.

On arriving in New York, Tresca resided with his doctor brother Ettore Tresca, at 53 Bayard Street, near Mulberry Park in Little Italy. He soon found the city overwhelming and alienating and relocated to Philadelphia, where there was a higher percentage of fellow Abruzzesi. Assuming the editorship of *Il Proletario*, he refocused it on fighting the Italian American elites—the "Camorra (Mafia-like) colonials" he called them—and promoting a shift to direct-action industrial union syndicalism. Having grown increasingly anarchistic, he resigned in 1906 and began publishing his own paper, *La Plebe*.

One of his successors at the helm of *Il Proletario*, Arturo Giovannitti, was born in 1884, also in the Abruzzi, and was also temperamentally a rebellious middle-class youth. Unlike Tresca's, however, the origins of Giovannitti's radicalism were to be found in America. He migrated to Canada at age 16, studied English and theology at McGill University, and worked at a Presbyterian mission for Italians in Montreal. In 1904, after receiving a call to take charge of a Presbyterian mission for Italians in Brooklyn, Giovannitti moved to New York and continued his religious studies at Union Theological Seminary. His exposure to the poverty of Italian immigrant workers—and he himself was often unemployed, forced to sleep on a bench in Mulberry Park—shifted him to a more secular response. By 1907 he had joined the lower Manhattan section of the Italian Socialist Federation, and two years later he joined the editorial staff of *Il Proletario*. His journalism denounced the humiliations visited on the city's "dagoes." He also began publishing verses in its pages in 1908, and in 1911 was elected general director of the paper, by which time, partly under the influence of Tresca, he had ardently embraced syndicalism.

ITALIAN ANARCHISTS DID NOT HAVE TO WORK THEIR WAY into syndicalism; it was the gospel of the dozens of anarchist groups that by the 1910s had emerged in lower Manhattan, and of those in every Italian neighborhood in the city, and across the Hudson in New Jersey.

Most were composed of southern Italians, but they included others as well. In Brooklyn, Sicilian anarchist shoemakers and garment workers organized, with their Cuban, Spanish, Puerto Rican, and Russian coworkers and neighbors, a *circolo* called Club Avanti, located at 210 Humboldt Street. It sponsored lectures on peace, religion, sexual and family questions, women's emancipation, nationalism, imperialism, major immigrant strikes, the Mexican Revolution, the problems of political prisoners in Italy, and current events in general. It also offered classes in Italian, the natural sciences, and "social questions"; published a small newspaper, *La Luce*; sponsored a theatrical group; and cooperated with Jewish and Spanish-speaking groups in the neighborhood.

One of the biggest anarchist entities was in Paterson, New Jersey, where Pietro Gori, one of Italian anarchism's foremost leaders, had established Il Gruppo Diritto all'Esistenza (Right to Exist Group) and founded its associated paper, *La Questione Sociale*, during a yearlong lecture tour of Italian communities in 1895–96. It was composed mostly of northern Italian textile workers, with smaller numbers of French, German, Dutch, Spanish, Greek, Austrian, and Belgian immigrants, most of whom worked in the city's silk mills, and they agitated for formation of an industrial union.

Paterson continued to attract eminent visiting anarchists, including the polar opposites Errico Malatesta and Luigi Galleani. Malatesta, who visited in 1899–1900 and edited *La Questione Sociale* (*LQS*) while he was there, was the leader of the so-called organizational anarchists, who wanted to form a revolutionary workers' movement. Galleani, who was on the Paterson scene from 1901–2, was the leading exponent of anti-organizational anarchism, which rejected labor unions as well as political parties, considering them both crucibles of authoritarianism. Galleani preferred to rely on spontaneous direct action, which for him included terrorist violence. (King Umberto's assassin, Gaetano Bresci, had been a member of the Right to Exist Group and had worked on *La Questione Sociale*, and Galleani applauded his attentat.) In 1902 Galleani helped precipitate a mass strike in Paterson, during which he was shot and wounded in a clash between police and strikers. He escaped to Canada but slipped back across the border using a pseudonym, settled down in Barre, Vermont, an anarchist stronghold, and in 1903 founded and edited *Cronaca Sovversivi*, which became the principal rival to *La Questione Sociale*, publishing among other things Emma Goldman's writings and reporting on her activities.[4] He also fashioned a cult of personality around himself that Malatesta, for one, considered as itself authoritarian.

ALL THESE *SOVVERSIVI*, OF WHATEVER STRIPE, remained on the margins of city life, lacking substantial connections to left or labor organizations, until suddenly, out of deeply American soil, sprang up a radical organization with which Italian socialists and anarchists alike could and did establish links of solidarity.

On June 27, 1905, in Chicago, William "Big Bill" Haywood gaveled to order the Continental Congress of the Working Class. Out of this conclave sprang the Industrial Workers of the World—a.k.a. the IWW, or the Wobblies, or the One Big Union. Its blistering manifesto announced that "the working class and the employing class have nothing in common." Indeed, "between these two classes a struggle must go on until the workers of the world organize as a class, take possession of the earth and the machinery of production, and abolish the wage system."

The Wobblies rejected the Socialist Party's patient parliamentarianism. Governments were hogtied by special interests. Best to bypass them, use the mass strike to achieve economic democracy, and replace the state with workers' councils.

The Wobblies also rejected racism and the politics of exclusion. The One Big Union was open to all, men and women, blacks and whites, and, most assuredly, the new immigrants. There were, as Big Bill put it, "no foreigners in the working class."

They rejected genteel (and socialist) culture, too. The irreverent songs of Joe Hill—"You'll get pie in the sky when you die"—broke with conventional moralizing. The IWW appealed to outsiders, rebels, romantics.

And, most critically, the Wobblies rejected craft unionism. They set out to organize entire industries, including unskilled workers. They rejected the AFL's approach, in which "one group of workers is led to believe that it is superior to and can get along without the aid

---

4. In 1908 the *LQS* was suppressed by direct order of President Roosevelt for propagating "anarchist crimes." In June, however, the anarchists resumed publication under a new masthead, *L'Era Nuova*.

of the less skilled or poorer paid workers in the same industry." Given that the AFL was unwilling to organize the unorganized—the 35 million workers in the United States without union protection—the IWW would take up the task, making initiation and dues low enough for poorly paid workers to join up. It would openly challenge the AFL's right to speak for American workers, dismissing Gompers and his men as (in Daniel De Leon's words) "labor lieutenants of capitalism." Down the road, when the workers of all races and nationalities had come together to take possession of the factories and mines, the warehouses and offices, the Wobblies would run the economy for the benefit of all.

New York's Socialists and AFL leaders alike found the IWW insufferable and intolerable, and they attacked it savagely. It was disruptive. It organized dual (competing) unions. It terrified the established order and made organizing more difficult. The only good thing about it was that it seemed mainly to afflict the West.

Then it blew into town, courtesy, to a considerable degree, of the local Italians. The IWW was proposing anarcho-syndicalism on a grand scale, and it electrified the *sovversivi* of New York and New Jersey. Paterson's Right to Exist Group immediately invited IWW organizers to come and address its members, and in March 1906 signed on as the first foreign-language local. Also in 1906 the socialists in the ISF, who had been inching steadily toward the anarchist position, now jumped over the remaining distance and, urged on by the likes of Tresca and Giovannitti, declared themselves Wobbly affiliates (later they would make IWW membership mandatory for all in their organization). Emma Goldman's *Mother Earth* reported on IWW doings, and she believed the union's arrival had generated great interest in anarchism, but she at first kept her distance, unsure where its volatile mixture of previously contending forces would lead.

At first the New York IWW was more talk than action. The Wobblies set up several locals in the garment industry and combined them into an industrial union, Local 59, of which cloak makers, pressers, white-goods workers, and ladies' tailors became branches. Many of these new members were Italians, pulled from local AFL unions, in effect creating a dual unionism that divided the ranks but stirred a spirit of militancy. The Wobblies also launched workplace agitations in Italian neighborhoods of Brooklyn, especially in shoe factories. But they had barely begun to fight when the Panic of 1907 led to their near-demise; a proper test of their capabilities would await an upswing in the economy.[5]

THE IWW ALSO PUT DOWN ROOTLETS IN LESS FERTILE SOIL. In 1907 Mayor McClellan boasted: "There are Russian Socialists and Jewish Socialists and German Socialists. But, thank God! there are no Irish Socialists!" This was basically true, though not completely accurate. The city had spawned an Irish Socialist Federation—complete with its own green and white banner with the slogan FAG AN BEALACH (Clear the Way) situated on a field of harps and shamrocks. This oddity was in part the creation of Tom Flynn and his remarkable daughter Elizabeth Gurley Flynn.

Tom Flynn was an Irish rebel, a socialist, and an itinerant civil engineer. His wife, Annie Gurley, was a professional tailor, a feminist, and tired of the family's constant peregrinations. In 1900, Annie took her four children, including 10-year-old Elizabeth, to New York City. She settled in the Bronx, eventually at 511 East 134th Street, in a cold water flat overlooking the Harlem River, while her husband came and went as his work dictated.

---

5. It's possible that the IWW and *sovversivi* lauding of "direct action" might have helped spark the great dock strike of 1907. It was, after all, a spontaneous uprising by thousands of Italian longshoremen, and it began at a Primo Maggio rally.

Elizabeth grew up amid Irish revolutionists, feminists, socialists, and anarchists. She blossomed early as a public speaker. Her debut talk, "What Socialism Will Do for Women," was given in the winter of 1906 at the Harlem Socialist Club. That summer Flynn began soapboxing near Times Square and at the corner of Seventh Avenue and 128th Street. The press extolled her youth and dramatic appearance—long black hair, white shirtwaist, red tie—even when they rejected her opinions. Theodore Dreiser in *Broadway Magazine* called her "An East Side Joan of Arc." Broadway producer David Belasco wanted to make her an actress. The police wanted to throw her in jail, and did, but she was soon discharged and again frequenting radical meetings.

In 1907, with her father and other Irish American members of the Socialist Labor Party, Elizabeth set out to establish an Irish Socialist Club. This attracted the attention of organizer James Connolly, who had moved from Ireland to New York in 1903 and was agitating for Ireland's freedom while organizing the docks for the IWW. (He worked for a year out of a Wobbly office at 60 Cooper Square.) Connolly proposed to the Flynns a more ambitious project, a language-based Irish Socialist Federation, associated with Ireland's Socialist Party; it was launched, in a minor way, in March 1907. In January 1908 he began publishing the *Harp*, designed to attract Irish into the American working-class movement while also supporting opposition to British rule in Ireland. It remained a marginal enterprise, and Connolly moved on to other projects, but not before he'd recruited Elizabeth Gurley Flynn into the IWW (Mixed Local No. 179). She soon took off on a cross-country speaking trip and until 1912 would lead the peripatetic life of a Wobbly jawsmith.

Elizabeth Gurley Flynn addressing striking silkworkers, IWW Strike Headquarters, Paterson, 1913. (Granger)

"Berkman, Union Sq., May 1, '08." Alexander Berkman, center. Banners include: the Industrial Workers of the World; the Irish Socialist Club; in Yiddish, "Poale Zion, New York, 1907"; "NY Branch of the Bund of Lit. Pol. & Russia;" "Unity Club, *Sempre Avanti*: Socialism In Our Time." (Library of Congress Prints and Photographs Division, George Grantham Bain Collection)

UPRISING IN THE NEEDLE TRADES

In 1903 17-year-old Clara Lemlich and her family arrived in New York City, part of the first wave of pogrom refugees. They had deemed the horrors of Kishinev to be uncomfortably close to their Ukrainian hometown of Gorodok, and indeed Clara's birthplace would experience its own pogrom in 1905. Lemlich's father, an Orthodox Jewish scholar, was not a rebel, though he had long been angered by Russian anti-Semitism, particularly the refusal by Gorodok's only public school to enroll his daughter. He'd responded by forbidding her to learn Russian, the language of the oppressor. But it was also the tongue of radicals and towering writers, so the teenager studied it on the sly, feasting on Tolstoy, Gorky, and Turgenev, and the revolutionary tracts provided clandestinely by a sympathetic neighbor. By the time her family emigrated, she was a committed rebel.

Two weeks after disembarking, Lemlich went to work in a Lower East Side shirtwaist shop—she'd been a seamstress since she was 12—and was appalled by the conditions. Over the next few years she honed her skills, becoming a relatively well paid draper (nearly as important to the production process as were cutters). She also continued her studies. She devoured the Russian collection at the Chatham Square (33 East Broadway) branch of the New York Public Library, joined a free night school on Grand Street, and after the Rand School opened began taking classes in Marxist theory.

In 1906, she later recalled, she joined a group of "class conscious girls" in helping resurrect Local 10 of the International Ladies' Garment Workers' Union. The local, aimed at organizing shirtwaist makers, had disbanded the previous year for lack of money and members. Now, reorganized as Local 25, and operating from the same rented headquarters at 206 East Broadway, the executive committee of the ILGWU—majority male but with a strong female contingent, including Lemlich—set out to organize the overwhelmingly female waist makers. By the end of the year, however, they had signed up a mere thirty-five or forty members—roughly one in a thousand of those eligible.

Partly this was because they received only modest assistance from the parent ILGWU, which, though founded in 1900 by Jewish socialist intellectuals, had not yet found its own footing. Local 25 got even less support from its grandparent institution, the American Federation of Labor. AFL president Gompers had encouraged and chartered the ILGWU, envisioning it as a confederation of garment-trade craftworkers, but he regarded it warily because it backed political action through the Socialist Party.

Male labor leaders looked askance at a local dedicated to organizing women. Females, they believed, were indifferent to union appeals because few teenage seamstresses saw themselves as permanent laborers. Since these women worked only between girlhood and marriage, the thinking went, their hearts were not in organizing the factory, but in leaving it, and devoting themselves to home and hearth—which was just where male unionists wanted them. Working-class men's ambition was to earn enough to keep their wives at home, as middle-class men did.

Women's work was also unskilled labor—not an AFL forte. It was one thing to mobilize skilled cutters. It was quite another to organize readily replaceable seamstresses. Success might require sympathetic walkouts, and male craft unionists had little interest in endangering their hard-won contracts.

There was another reason the AFL failed to back women-oriented initiatives with more than the occasional good word. Most female industrial workers were Jews and Italians. Most AFL leaders and members were Anglo-American, Irish American, or German American, often a generation or more in-country. They were, with varying degrees of prejudice, unsympathetic to newcomers.

The ILGWU leadership was similarly ambivalent, despite the centrality of women in the industry they were organizing. The cutters local at the top of the pecking order was, like the AFL leadership, composed largely of native-born English-speaking men. Politically conservative and worried about the influx of immigrant radicals, the cutters, who tended to show up at work wearing frock coats and high silk hats, held themselves aloof from their supposed brothers and sisters.

Women workers were thus triply damned—on grounds of sex, skill, and national origin. The AFL not only refused to court them; it often spurned their advances. This created a leadership vacuum. To the AFL's dismay, the task of organizing the new immigrant workforce would be taken up by the immigrant workers themselves, with Russian radicals, including women like Lemlich, in the forefront.

ONE OF THE EARLIEST SIGNS OF A NEW MILITANCY came in 1907, when the Reefer Manufacturers' Association—reefers being children's cloaks—reneged on its 1904 recognition of ILGWU Local No. 17 as bargaining agent. The bosses refused to renegotiate the existing contract, and announced an open-shop (union-free) policy, only to quickly discover they were up against a new breed of worker. As reefer making required relatively little skill, it had attracted the newly arrived and hard-pressed Russian immigrants, many of them Bundist veterans of the now-failed revolution. When a committee of manufacturers came to a shop on Walker Street, near Broadway, to hang up a sign announcing their new policy, one worker who had arrived in New York only seven weeks earlier declaimed in Lithuanian Yiddish: "We will reckon with you, you bloodsuckers who live off the toil of the workers, you who live in luxury while we die of hunger and starvation! You may battle us, you may starve us, but we will never surrender! We will die on the barricades first!" Climbing up on one of the pressing tables, fist upthrust, he perorated: "Down with the bosses, down with the capitalist system, long live the union, ... liberty or death!"

Twelve hundred workers went out on strike. Pickets were thrown up. Strikers marched through the streets singing "The Marseillaise." Workers from other branches of the trade, and other industries altogether, union and non-union alike, flocked to the scene to offer support. Crowds of the strikers' Lower East Side neighbors engaged in mass picketing (and kept watch at nights). The employers hired strong-arm men; the union countered with battle-hardened members. Police attacked the strikers; Abe Cahan denounced the cops as Cossacks in the *Forward*, and the citywide CFU complained as well.

And Local 17 won. The manufacturers agreed to a union shop, a fifty-five-hour workweek, and an arbitration board and promised that henceforth they would provide materials and equipment to the workers—the requirement that they bring their own sewing machine having been highest on the list of complaints.

The reefer makers' victory made a deep impression on Gotham's garment workers, but it didn't shelter them from the economic hurricane that blew in later in 1907. The deep recession of 1908 devastated the women's clothing industry and its unions. Many firms offered partial employment at reduced wages or folded altogether, and many ILGWU locals collapsed.

Yet taken as a whole, New York's working class had developed a complex infrastructure of craft unions, federations, newspapers, fraternal and benefit societies, and political organizations—a base from which to challenge the city's industrial arrangements. A new generation of hard-edged militants—Russians, Italians, Austrians—had arrived to carry on their predecessors' struggle and to further cultivate a radical working-class culture. Some progress had been made (admittedly limited and fleeting) toward overcoming internal divisions—between unskilled and skilled, between those of different nationalities, races, and religions, between women and men. There had been heartening signs of mass support from various communities for organizational efforts by their workers, and evidence that general strikes could make important contributions to union victories, especially if yoked to traditional craft-based protests. Transformations of the production process—mechanization, electrification, centralization— notably in New York's garment industry, were drawing workers out of their hard-to-organize scattered tenement sweatshops into packed factories that facilitated the sharing of grievances and collaboration for action. There were problems aplenty—ongoing divisions, union corruption, judicial assaults, attacks by coordinated capital—but all in all a combustible mixture had been assembled, awaiting only the right spark to ignite it.

BY MID-1909 THE ECONOMY HAD REVIVED and the waist industry was booming again, with more 500 blouse factories employing upwards of 40,000 workers. The shifting locus of manufacturing from small sweatshops into big factories accelerated as loft-based businesses used power-driven machinery to churn out goods in ever greater quantities, spurred by the simultaneous expansion of demand from the rapidly developing department stores. By 1913 56 percent of dress and waist workers would labor in factories with 75 or more employees, and 27 percent in plants of 100 to 200.

In some ways, these new outfits provided superior working conditions. Their new loft buildings were more sanitary, better lit, and airier than the grungy tenement shops. But the owners now sought to maximize the profitable use of fixed capital—plant, machines, materials, energy—and to do so, they needed continuity and stability in the production process, which to them meant, above all, control of the workforce. So the larger businessmen were devotees of regimented management. The clock was king. The foremen regulated and accelerated the pace of work, sweeping away impediments to maintaining high-volume throughput. They enjoined workers to silence, forbade them to lift their heads from their machines, required them to eat at their Singers. Forewomen followed girls on toilet breaks, nagging them to return. Seamstresses were locked in to prevent pilfering, subjected to galling inspections, hit with arbitrary fines. Wages and hours were similar to those in sweatshops. The average work week was fifty-eight to sixty hours. Men's wages, though low, were 40 percent higher than women's, and neither women's nor men's wage level had been raised from the recent recession's lows. Plus, for all the "modern" rationalization, primitive authoritarian abuses like sexual harassment and cheating on pay continued, as did the seasonal nature of the industry, with its long idle periods of no pay at all. Worst of all was the subordination to the clock/machine regime, and its attendant dehumanization of the "operatives." "It is a regular slave factory," Lemlich wrote. "Not only your hands and your time but your mind is sold." Workplace tyranny, sixty-hour weeks, and ever-faster machines generated strain, fatigue, and ever-increasing anger. Now, in their growing numbers, the workers discovered the strength to resist.

IN THE SUMMER OF 1909 THE NUMBER OF ILGWU LOCALS swelled to sixty-three, embracing 16,000 members, many of them Bundist militants. And then a trio of strikes erupted, one after another, each targeting one of the biggest businesses in the industry, each linking up with Local 25.

Late in July 200 workers walked out of the Rosen Brothers shop, a large shirtwaist factory at 33 East 10th Street, and asked Lemlich's local and the United Hebrew Trades (UHT) for assistance. Management refused to negotiate, and instead hired strikebreakers to attack the

Clara Lemlich, ca. 1910. (Courtesy of the International Ladies' Garment Workers' Union Archives, Kheel Center Collection, Cornell University)

picket lines. Strikers fought back. Tammany police intervened on the side of the owners, but again, as during the reefer strike, nightsticks and jail time didn't do the trick. The strikers held their ground. After a five-week struggle, with the busy season looming, anxious owners capitulated, giving the workers a 20-percent hike in piece rates and granting union recognition. This was the first significant victory for Local 25. News of its success shot through the garment district. Workers streamed into the union. Strike fever spread.

In September 1909 150 women marched out of Louis Leiserson's factory at 26 West 17th Street, led by Lemlich, it being her current place of employment. Leiserson was widely known around lower Manhattan as a socialist himself, a self-styled friend of the workers, though now he reneged on a promise to hire only union members. Instead he turned to strikebreakers. One enterprising firm, the Greater New York Detective Agency, sent letters to the leading shirtwaist factory owners that summer, promising to "furnish trained detectives to guard life and property, and, if necessary, furnish help of all kinds, both male and female, for all trades"—in other words, provide both scabs and the muscle to protect them. The gangsters quickly sussed out who were the leaders—Lemlich had been addressing street-corner meetings in English and Yiddish. On Thursday, September 9, several men attacked her as she made her way home from the Leiserson picket lines, inflicting a savage beating that broke six ribs and confined her to a hospital bed for weeks.

On September 27 Local 25 escalated. It tackled the Triangle Waist Company, the largest blouse-making operation in New York. In busy seasons, over 500 were at work on the eighth, ninth, and tenth floors of the ten-story building at 23–29 Washington Place, at the corner of Washington Place and Greene Street, half a block east of Washington Square. The Triangle's shipping plant bundled, boxed, and dispersed 2,000 garments per day, sometimes more, a million dollars' worth of waists per year. Owners Max Blanck and Isaac Harris had become rich. They lived uptown in neighboring town houses, Harris on West 101 Street, Max and Bertha Blanck with their six children just around the corner on West End Avenue.

It was Blanck and Harris who precipitated the clash. They organized a company union and declared that any workers who tried forming their own union would be fired, and when a group of Triangle employees caucused with Local 25 and United Hebrew Trades officials, the owners axed 150 of those involved, locked out all 500 workers, and the next day advertised for replacement workers. The local had little choice but to declare a strike. Picket lines mushroomed. Triangle hired "sluggers" to insult, harass, and beat them up. Downtown gang leader Johnny Spanish took a couple of his men—including veteran bruiser Nathan Kaplan—and went after Joe Zeinfield, chairman of the Triangle strike committee, pounded him to a pulp, and left him in the gutter. This was by now a standard script. But Blanck and Harris gave it a new twist when, on October 4, 1909, shortly after dawn, a dozen or so young women were picketing when a battalion of Bowery prostitutes came marching up the street, followed by a group of strikebreakers. The sex workers now beat up the garment workers, after which the police, who monitored the factory entrances as a favor to Blanck and Harris, arrested the picket girls for assault.

The strike was not going well.

Then an alternative to targeting individual firms emerged. On October 1 the Neckwear Workers' Union declared a general strike. The term meant a simultaneous strike by all workers against all shops in one branch of the industry, such as cloaks or dresses—not the enormous citywide, countrywide phenomena of Russia's 1905 revolution. Most of the 7,000 neckwear strikers were poor, young, Russian Jewish recent immigrants, roughly three-quarters of them women or teenage girls, with no savings to sustain them through the loss of their abysmal wages. Yet they refused to give in, and after twelve days succeeded in winning significant concessions. The socialist *Call* hailed the general strike as a model that might be replicable elsewhere.

Local 25 agreed. By mid-October, it appeared to its leadership that unless something similarly drastic was done, the strikes at Leiserson and Triangle would be lost. The local and the UHT began to contemplate a general strike. It was a daunting prospect. The local had grown somewhat—it now had approximately 500 members—but had only four dollars in its treasury. On October 21, Lemlich and her colleagues lofted a trial balloon, proposing a general strike. Over the next weeks 2,000 more joined the union. But ILGWU general secretary-treasurer John Dyche and AFL chief Gompers, seeking to puncture their balloon, refused to back the plan.

Triangle and other big manufacturers took steps to deal with a general strike, should it materialize. Triangle shifted some production to factories outside of New York—Blanck and Harris had established plants in Yonkers and Philadelphia—or subcontracted with smaller shops that had already settled to fill fall orders. In early November the Triangle owners circulated a letter to all shirtwaist manufacturers suggesting formation of an Employers Mutual Protective Association.

For its part, Local 25 appealed for help to the Women's Trade Union League (WTUL)—and got action.

THE WTUL WAS INSPIRED BY A BRITISH ORGANIZATION OF THE SAME NAME, founded in 1873. Its founders had been inspired by two Gotham-based female labor organizations, the Women's Typographical Union, and the New York Parasol and Umbrella Makers' Union. The British WTUL mobilized middle-class and wealthy women to support union organizing by working-class women. In 1897, while visiting England, socialist William English Walling had come across the organization and thought the United States should have one of its own. In 1903, together with Mary Kenney O'Sullivan, a union organizer he'd met when both were residents at Chicago's Hull House, Walling broached the idea at the annual convention of the AFL in Boston. A group of unionists and settlement workers took up the project and organized the national WTUL. On returning to New York, Walling organized a Gotham branch with the aid of the settlement house community. (Wald was an officer; Walling's University Settlement hosted its meetings.) To pull the operation together he turned to Leonora O'Reilly, the Irish factory worker who had been making inter-class connections since she had cofounded the Working Women's Society back in 1886. In 1903 she was head resident at Asacog House, a Brooklyn settlement, and was teaching at the Manhattan Trade School for Girls.

Once the capable O'Reilly came on board as the New York WTUL's vice president, Walling moved on to other projects, and the top slot was given to Mary Dreier, the Brooklyn Heights–born heir of an affluent German American businessman. Dreier had studied at the New York School of Philanthropy and dabbled in progressive good works before being drawn to the WTUL's more robust approach. She helped recruit other middle- and upper-class "allies," including the extremely rich Alice and Irene Lewisohn, daughters of the copper magnate.

This heterogeneous band of sisters got off to an awkward start. Between the allies and the unionists yawned a cultural gap as wide as the stretch between First and Fifth Avenues. Their uplift efforts (art appreciation classes at the Met) and insensitive gaffes (scheduling conferences on Yom Kippur) rankled. The allies romanticized labor, seeing paying jobs as an escape hatch from dependent femininity. Unionists saw work as unappealing drudgery, best escaped into marriage. Many allies rejected marriage and lived instead in a network of woman-centered friendships. They found it hard to relate to "giggly girls whose sole interest in life was boys and how to attract them." Working-class members, in turn, often found their partners overbearing; in 1906 O'Reilly resigned (temporarily), citing an "overdose of allies."

Slowly, most allies shed ladylike attitudes and conventions. They joined worker members in setting up unions, holding meetings at factory doors, launching strikes, walking picket lines, and organizing consumer boycotts. To guard against Lady Bountiful dominance, a majority of seats on the executive board were reserved for unionists. This led to outreach efforts, particularly by O'Reilly, who brought in strong working-class organizers, among them, most notably, Rose Schneiderman.

Schneiderman, born in a Polish shtetl to Orthodox Jewish needle workers, had been brought to Ludlow Street in 1890 at the age of eight. Two years later her father died, pitching the family into destitution and Rose into an orphanage, until her mother pieced together the funds to rescue her. Rose worked as a department store cash girl for $2.16 a week until in 1898 she got a job paying twice as much, lining caps in a factory. In the winter of 1903, the now 21-year-old Schneiderman organized her shop for the United Cloth Hat and Cap Makers, another of the unions founded and run by socialist Jews. In 1905, having led a successful cap maker strike, she was invited to join the WTUL. Soon the petite (4'9") dynamo with the flaming red hair was a familiar sight on East Side soapboxes. In 1908 German Jewish philanthropist Irene Lewisohn offered Schneiderman funds to finish her schooling. Schneiderman refused the scholarship on the grounds that she could not accept such a privilege when most working women lacked any kind of education. However, she did accept Lewisohn's amended offer to pay her a salary to organize working women, and in 1909 became chief organizer for the New York WTUL, operating out of headquarters at 43 West 22nd Street.

Lemlich, a regular at Socialist Party meetings, had become friends with O'Reilly and Schneiderman, also socialists, and it was to them that she turned for help, and it was they who responded. In late October, the WTUL began sending well-to-do allies to witness harassment at the picket line, and accompany arrested girls to Police Court, where they bailed them out or paid their fines. None of this was covered in the mainstream press. But on November 4, when Mary Dreier, the WTUL's wealthy chieftain, visited the Triangle picket line at quitting time, the constabulary hauled *her* away. On learning her identity, a horrified policeman blurted: "Why didn't you tell me you was a rich lady? I'd never have arrested you in the world!"

Suddenly the press was startled into attention. The arrest of Mary Dreier was front-page news in the mainstream papers: Pulitzer's *World*, Sulzberger's *Times*, Hearst's *American*, and others. The *Times*'s first coverage of the strike now reported (on Dreier's word) that "last night was only the latest of a series of outrages" that had been perpetrated by the police for months. Her arrest, moreover, came just two days after the November election, in which it was decided that as of January 1, 1910, William Jay Gaynor, a vigorous critic of police violence, would replace hard-nosed George McClellan in the mayor's seat. Tammany boss Charles F. Murphy, noting the bad press, leashed the police, at least for a time.

Shirtwaist workers poured into Local 25. Membership hit a thousand. Seizing the moment, its leaders called a meeting at Cooper Union to discuss an industry-wide walkout. An overflow crowd, attracted by brochures in Yiddish, Italian, and English, packed themselves into the Great Hall on November 22. For two hours, a procession of speakers—Sam Gompers, Mary Dreier, socialist lawyer Meyer London, United Hebrew Trades head

Samuel Gompers addresses shirtwaist workers at Cooper Union, November 22, 1909. (Brown Brothers/ Cornell University, ILR School, Kheel Center for Labor-Management Documentation and Archives)

Bernard Weinstein, *Forward* editor Abe Cahan, and Benjamin Feigenbaum, a popular *Forward* writer and the meeting's chair—hemmed and hawed about the dangers of embarking on an ill-prepared general strike. After two hours, a frustrated Lemlich demanded the floor. To shouts of encouragement—she had tremendous standing with the crowd for her struggle at Leiserson's and her prior years of organizing—Lemlich made her way to the front. There the impassioned 23-year-old declared, "I am a working girl, one of those who are on strike against intolerable conditions. I am tired of listening to speakers who talk in general terms. I am one who feels and suffers from the things pictured. I move we go on a general strike!" Two-thousand-plus women surged to their feet, cheering, stamping, waving hats and hand-kerchiefs, shouting their approval. Chairman Feigenbaum, taken aback, demanded: "Do you mean faith? Will you take the old Hebrew oath?" At this he moved to Lemlich's side and thrust her right arm into the air—two-thousand-plus right arms shot up as well—and the assembled throng repeated (in Yiddish): "If I turn traitor to the cause I now pledge, may this hand wither from the arm I now raise."

By noon the next day, 20,000 women had swarmed out of 500 shirtwaist shops in Manhattan and Brooklyn. Within days another 10,000 joined them. Crowds besieged the ILGWU office at 151 Clinton Street, and other hastily hired halls, to enroll in Local 25 and line up behind the strike's demands: a fifty-two-hour week; uniform wages, standards, and prices; the abolition of subcontracting; improved safety conditions; and, above all, union recognition and the union shop, to guarantee adherence to concessions.

The ILGWU and WTUL put together a disciplined organization, raised funds, arranged pickets, gained publicity, and provided legal services. The *Forward*, the UHT, the Workmen's Circle, and the Socialist Party also provided important logistical and financial and emotional support. Morris Hillquit became the ILGWU's attorney and made rousing speeches to shirtwaist makers.

"Going out for Better Conditions," 1909. (Cornell University, ILR School, Kheel Center for Labor-Management Documentation and Archives)

Small manufacturers caved quickly, settling on the union's terms. But the large-shop owners dug in, hired scabs, and fought back. Pleasant autumn gave way to severe winter. Thousands of young women walked the line in subfreezing temperatures. Employers stepped up proxy violence. Fist-swinging "gorillas" and "schlammers" mauled the girls, again assisted by prostitutes from the Allen Street red light district. McClellan, still in office, unleashed the police. Patrol wagons waited till the thugs were finished, then hauled away the badly beaten girls. As peaceful picketing was perfectly legal in New York, the police charged over 700 strikers with loitering, disorderly conduct, or prostitution. (They were, after all, walking the streets, and "shamelessly" at that.) Labeling strikers "whores" aimed to strip them of respectability and exact a price for stepping out of place.

The judicial response was also overwhelmingly anti-striker. At first the justices imposed fines and set high bail requirements, only to have the WTUL come up with the requisite funds. One judge remarked peevishly that it was "perfectly futile for me to fine them" as "some charitable women would pay their fines," and setting bail was to no avail as "the women of this town are all frantic to go bail." Accordingly, he declared, "I am going to commit them to the workhouse." One magistrate announced that he would convict strikers just for using the word "scab": "If these girls continue to rush around and cry 'scab' I shall convict them of disorderly conduct. There is no word in the English language as irritating as the word 'scab.'" Others pontificated on the sanctity of private property, and one theologically muddled judge,

"Girls Who Served on Blackwell's Island and Were Cheered Last Night," 1909. (Cornell University, ILR School, Kheel Center for Labor-Management Documentation and Archives)

W. H. Olmsted of Special Sessions, informed a 16-year-old girl: "You are on strike against God and nature, whose prime law it is that man shall earn his bread by the sweat of his brow." The WTUL solicited a comment on this from George Bernard Shaw, who cabled back: "Delightful mediaeval America always in the intimate personal confidence of the Almighty."

The union, WTUL, and socialists made police repression a major issue. In mid-December 10,000 strikers rallied at Bowery and Rivington Street, heard Rose Pastor Stokes speak, then trooped down the Bowery carrying banners (with slogans like THE POLICE ARE FOR OUR PROTECTION, NOT FOR OUR ABUSE) to City Hall, where they petitioned McClellan to rein in the cops. He promised to investigate but did nothing.

Slowly, remarkably, for perhaps the first time in New York's history, a mass labor uprising in the streets began to win support from the city's mandarins—or, more precisely, from their wives and daughters. With the wealthy "allies" of the WTUL serving as critical link, a startling array of upper-class women signed up to champion the strikers' cause and raise money for their support.

Feisty Alva Belmont, the former Mrs. Vanderbilt and, since 1908, the spectacularly wealthy widow of financier and subway heir Oliver Belmont, arranged weekly motor parades: rich suffrage supporters ferried strikers through Lower East Side streets to publicize the struggle. Her Political Equality League (a suffrage organization) hired the mammoth Hippodrome for a huge "women's rally" at which, on December 5, 8,000 suffragettes, unionists, and socialists wildly applauded speakers who denounced manhandling of strikers.

More remarkable still was the involvement of Anne Morgan, J. P. Morgan's daughter. Miss Morgan had in preceding months become increasingly involved in campaigns to improve workplace conditions, working through the conservative National Civic Federation. Now she sought out Rose Schneiderman, got a briefing about strike goals, then told her friends—a coterie soon labeled the "Mink Brigade" that included Arabella (Mrs. Collis) Huntington, Josephine Sykes (Mrs. Henry) Morgenthau, and Helen Taft, the daughter of President Taft—that "the girls must be helped to organize." Morgan arranged for Rose Schneiderman and Clara Lemlich to address Colony Club socialites, who then passed the hat to aid the strikers. With Alva Belmont and Lina (Mrs. Nathan) Straus, she promoted an immensely successful mass meeting at Carnegie Hall on January 2 that rang with denunciations of police persecution. On the stage that night were twenty strikers who had served time in the work-house, under a sign that read THE WORKHOUSE IS NO ANSWER TO A DEMAND FOR JUSTICE.[6]

This puzzling development—summed up by a *Times* banner as "The Rich Out to Aid Girl Waistmakers"—is more explicable in light of the city's larger political economy. The patri-cian ladies and their husbands were not, after all, directly involved in the garment industry. They had little in common—fiscally or culturally—with the swarm of Russian Jewish entre-preneurs, those whom Abe Cahan called "cockroach capitalists." Their wealth and position (when not simply inherited) rested on national corporations, major banks, corporate law firms, or giant retail outlets. They saw the garment business as an example of lunatic compet-itive capitalism. They had no sympathy for the crude exploitation to which free enterprise drove its practitioners, especially when the resultant unrest menaced civic stability. In addi-tion, the shirtwaist girls seemed particularly piteous. Wealthy allies were drawn to appeals that stressed the strikers' poverty, youth, helplessness, femininity, and victimhood. Protecting them from cruel employers and brutal policemen seemed noble and unthreatening. Editorialists fell into line with this class consensus, the *World*, the *American*, and the *Post* enthusiastically, the *Times* grudgingly.

On the other hand, there were limits. At Carnegie Hall, Morris Hillquit and Leonora O'Reilly had given impassioned speeches addressing the December 23 rejection by the union of an employer-proposed settlement, because despite concessions on wages and hours the offer withheld union recognition. Hillquit had insisted on the importance of a union shop—"the crux, the very heart" of the uprising of the shirtwaist workers. Only through the union, he declared, did labor have any power—it was "the last barrier between [the owners'] greed and the workers," and if the union were weakened, "the same old conditions of virtual servi-tude would be restored in the shop." Some of the assembled affluent were shocked by what they considered the extreme—even revolutionary—tone of Hillquit's speech, and by Leonora O'Reilly's defense of it. The next day, Anne Morgan issued a statement criticizing Hillquit and O'Reilly for preaching "fanatical doctrines of socialism." And though she said she would continue to support the strikers, she stepped back from the forefront, and the mainstream press stepped down its coverage.

The strike ground on through a particularly brutal winter, hundreds of small firms sign-ing with the union, the major ones remaining unyielding. The last few thousand strikers from the holdout firms continued to receive support from some of the wealthy backers. Alva Belmont remained faithful, as did Inez Milholland, daughter of the progressive millionaire John Milholland, who built a network of pneumatic tubes under Manhattan to speed mes-sages among businesses; she was arrested one frozen January evening on the Triangle picket line. And enthusiasm for the uprising remained high on college campuses. Mainly it was the Lower East Siders who kept up the struggle, mounting small but frequent fund-raising events: benefits at the Yiddish theater of Boris Tomashevsky, flickering films at Jacob's Moving Picture Theater, performances at the Third Street Vaudeville House, and balls, teas, dances, and recitals. Waist workers whose shops had already settled collected dimes for their still-striking colleagues. The UHT called on all Jewish workers to donate a half-day's wages to the cause. But by the beginning of February strike resources were nearing depletion.

In addition, workers were facing division in their own ranks.

---

6. The previous week, the same girls had received floral tributes at a WTUL-sponsored reception at Arlington Hall (12 St. Mark's Place), with Leonora O'Reilly noting that despite efforts to besmirch the girls' reputations, "in their case imprisonment was not a degradation."

A quarter of the shirtwaist makers were Italian, but very few had walked out. Many even signed up as scabs, replacing Jewish strikers. Incensed unionists excoriated Italian girls as father- and priest-ridden serfs. The fury of Jewish strikers was understandable, but their analysis was misplaced.

Italian families were, to be sure, intensely patriarchal. Young women were closely chaperoned to preserve chastity and marriageability. *Mia moglie è mia proprieta* (My wife is my property) was a southern Italian saying. Male family members escorted seamstresses to and from the factories and—often strikebreakers themselves—directed them to cross picket lines. Behind family patriarchs stood Italian community groups—*prominenti*, papers like *Il Progresso*, and priests who preached Pope Leo XIII's dictum: "To suffer and to endure, therefore, is the lot of humanity." At the Triangle and other shops, indeed, Italian priests from conservative Catholic parishes were invited into the factories to explain the workers' obligation to be obedient. And bosses did everything they could to divide workers along ethnic lines.

While many Italian women did consider themselves as subordinate members of a family unit (and many Jewish families were similarly patriarchal in their assumptions), this hardly dictated docility. It hadn't stopped tens of thousands from participating in the great agricultural strikes in southern Italy during the 1890s. Nor had it inhibited the mass and militant participation by Italian women textile workers in multiple strikes: in 1897 in Manhattan, Brooklyn, and Paterson; in 1903 in Astoria; in 1907 in Harlem. In 1909, virtually simultaneously with the shirtwaist strike, they participated in a month-long IWW-led walkout just across the river in Hoboken. And these were only a few of the many actions reported by the Italian-language *sovversivi* press.

Italian women did not join the 1909 strike en masse for several specific reasons. First, all Italian workers were wary about the ILGWU, which was, after all, an affiliate of the AFL, which had excluded most Italian workers (along with other semiskilled and unskilled laborers). The ILGWU itself had not made any significant effort to include them; nor had more than a few socialists reached out to Italian fathers who had themselves been spurned by unionists, and who often made less than their daughters, their poverty making them unwilling to forgo critical income. Nor had attempts been made to enlist liberal or radical Catholic clergy. Finally, Local 25, like the strike itself, was an overwhelmingly Jewish affair. The local's roots ran back to the United Hebrew Trades; meetings were conducted in Yiddish, late at night, and deep in the Jewish quarter; even the stirring launch at Cooper Union had been climaxed by the assembled throng taking "the old Hebrew oath," in Yiddish.

There were also structural inequalities and antagonisms built into the garment trade itself. Italian women entered the industry at the bottom, doing home-work for threadbare wages. They collected bundles of partly constructed flowers, feathers, and clothes from subcontractors and then, with the help of their children and other kin or neighbors, finished the products in their tenement rooms—lining garments, sewing on buttons, trimming threads, pulling bastings by hand, pasting on petals, inserting pistils into stems: tasks that did not require any particular training or skill and hence were the lowest paid; the work was known as "the Italian women's trade." The garment unions saw home workers as a threat to factory workers, who could not compete with the low wages home finishers accepted. Rather than attempting to organize the overwhelmingly (95 percent) non-English-speaking Italians, the largely Jewish unions sought to outlaw tenement work, which alienated their potential allies.

The 1909 strike provided a crash learning experience. Within days of the uprising, the Italian Socialist Federation and the Socialist Party belatedly sent out teams of organizers to mobilize Italian women garment workers. Rose Schneiderman began to work with a priest in

Brooklyn to identify potential leaders among the workers. The ILG and WTUL recruited Arturo Caroti, a Wobbly organizer of the Hoboken strike and administrator of *Il Proletario*, to aid the process. Alva Belmont included the Italian socialist leader Publio Mazzella in the Hippodrome proceedings, and he reminded the gathering that "for the first time in the history of the Italian labor movement in this city an Italian speaker has been asked to speak at such a meeting as this." Another socialist, Salvatore Ninfo, the leading Italian official in the ILGWU, worked with WTUL volunteers to promote participation. Ultimately, Italians would make up somewhere between 6 percent and 10 percent of the shirtwaist strikers, while Eastern European Jews, who were two-thirds of the shirtwaist labor force, made up three-quarters or more of the strikers.

INTERNAL DIVISIONS AND DECLINING RESOURCES led the ILGWU to call off the strike on February 15, 1910, short of total victory. The biggest manufacturers, notably Triangle, had refused to grant union recognition. But the gains were impressive. Employers gave ground on fewer hours (dropping from sixty to fifty-two, with overtime remunerated at time and a half) and higher wages, and even the recalcitrant shops—including Leiserson and Triangle—no longer prohibited union membership. Local 25's rolls had rocketed to over 20,000, making the hitherto marginal ILGWU a powerful and centrally important labor organization in the city. The dramatic demonstration of what solidarity could accomplish swiftly reverberated through the needle trades.

ON JULY 7, 1910, HARD ON THE HEELS OF THE "UPRISING" OF THE WAIST MAKERS, came the "Great Revolt" of New York's ladies' cloak makers. Workers, socialists, and radical intellectuals had pressed the ILGWU to keep the momentum going, and in December 1909, even before the shirtwaist strike had ended, the cloak makers' leadership began making careful preparations for their own general strike. Intent on ensuring unity of action, and presenting a disciplined and orderly common front, the cautious ILGWU leaders centralized control of the strike in their hands, and adopted as their goal the winning of an industry-wide settlement—not the shop-by-shop approach Local 25 had followed. At a June 28 Madison Square Garden packed-house rally, Gompers, Cahan, Dyche, London, and others urged the rank and file to act strictly in concert, with no premature walkouts or wildcat strikes. Five days later the membership voted to authorize a general strike, 18,771 to 615. At 7:00 a.m. on July 7, all went off like clockwork, with no chaos or confusion as in the more spontaneous 1909 walkout, and by midafternoon 75,000 were on strike, 90 percent of them men.

The 1910 strike was different in several significant ways from its predecessor.

Thirty to forty percent of the striking tailors were Italians. This time a welcome mat had been rolled out. The union started an official weekly paper, printed in Yiddish, English, and Italian. Salvatore Ninfo and Arturo Caroti were appointed key strike organizers. They and the WTUL worked to convince families and priests of the value of unions. Italian men, impressed by the shirtwaist victory and the outreach campaign, swung behind the new upheaval. At one mass meeting they declared they "would not be the knife in the hands of the bosses, whereby the Jewish workers would be stabbed in the back." Italian women were visible and active participants, attending union meetings and joining picket lines, often with their children at their side.

The financing was more secure this time around, and less dependent on the largesse of the affluent. Not only did the Socialist Party hurl itself into strike work, mobilizing street meetings, parades, and demonstrations that brought thousands of East Siders into the garment district streets, but it also, with the Workman's Circle, the UHT, and the Central Federated Union of New York (CFU), among others, worked on raising a strike fund. The *Jewish Daily Forward* and the *Call* kept the community abreast of the developments, and by September they had accumulated an incredible quarter of a million dollars.

Police harassment was less in evidence. The recently elected Mayor Gaynor believed that "labor has as much right to combine for its protection as capital has to combine for its protection."[7] When Gaynor was shot in the August assassination attempt, Acting Mayor Mitchel continued his policy, instructing the police commissioner to be "absolutely impartial as regards the strikers and strikebeakers."

Capitalists did indeed combine for their protection. A few days after the July 7 launch of the strike, a few hundred manufacturers met at the Hoffman House (Broadway and 24th), formed a protective association, and chose Julius Henry Cohen as legal counsel. This association, however, revealed a crucial but hitherto unconfronted division within the ranks of the employers. The smaller manufacturers worried that if the union won an industry-wide pay standard, requiring substantial raises, they might not survive. Some believed that the big employers were determined to use the strike to drive the little ones out of the industry.

They were right.

The leading manufacturers—Americanized German Jews—were ready to cut a deal. As heads of highly capitalized firms with strong connections to mass retailers, they had come round to the position embraced by corporate leaders, that competition was a chaotic and destructive menace. But unlike the Morgans and Rockefellers, they were in no position to control a highly fragmented industry where shoestring entrepreneurs flourished (Cahan's "cockroach capitalists"). Perhaps, they calculated, the unions could stabilize production, standardize wages and hours, and eliminate cutthroat competition.

Still, there were limits. They had no intention of acquiescing in the cloak makers' demands for a closed shop (in which every employee had to be a member of the union). Nor would the union negotiators abandon that goal. (Meyer London represented the strikers.) Efforts to bridge the gap failed, one after another. Then the idea emerged of calling in an impartial arbiter. The man selected was Louis Brandeis, the Boston attorney who had championed the ten-hour day for women. Brandeis devised an industry-wide settlement—a Protocol of Peace—that provided higher wages, fewer hours, improved work conditions, and— the key that unlocked a settlement—a "preferential shop" that required management to hire union labor in preference to unorganized workers. The proposed truce would require combatants to hang up their weapons: workers surrendered their right to strike, employers relinquished the lockout, and both agreed to submit disputes to arbitration, with the critical deciding vote being given to a non-governmental representative of "the public." Protocolism, Brandeis argued, would avoid both laissez-faire capitalism and socialism by ushering workers into "constructive" unions, which would bargain with "responsible" manufacturers, using a system of labor relations that excluded the state.

This seemed just the ticket to the big manufacturers and the union leadership, and to Hillquit socialists who hailed the achievement of ordered rationality in the industry. But it was opposed by many of the smaller businessmen, and it was contested by many radical rank-and-filers, often affiliated with the IWW, who objected to signing away the right to strike.

---

7. Gaynor took quite a different tack with city workers. In November 1911 teamsters in the Street Cleaning Department struck for abolition of night work. Declaring he would not tolerate union members or labor agitators, Gaynor dismissed 1,872 men and hired replacements for the entire force.

Militants on both sides were prepared to go to the mat, when Jacob Schiff and Louis Marshall—who worried that the good name of the Jewish elite was being imperiled by the conflict—entered the conversation and nudged manufacturers back to the bargaining table. At the same time, employers won issuance of an injunction that prohibited the picketing of cloak factories, and Acting Mayor Mitchel revoked his directive ordering police neutrality. On September 2, 1910, with both sides now feeling the heat, a deal was struck. The union dropped the closed-shop demand but accepted the "preferential" shop. Management agreed to a fifty-hour week and double-pay overtime, as well as to the abolition of inside subcontracting and of charging workers for electric power. A Joint Board of Sanitary Control would maintain shop standards, a Board of Grievances would settle minor disputes, and a three-man Board of Arbitration would sort out major ones. Hitherto incendiary and disruptive disputes would be transmuted from moral or political calls to battle into technical issues that could be peaceably resolved by administrative means—a quintessentially progressive notion.

The settlement, big manufacturers thought, might bring about what they'd been unable to achieve by themselves: stability, efficiency, and enhanced profitability. Standardizing wages, hours, and working conditions would take away the ability of unscrupulous smaller manufacturers to undercut them. Competition, their bête noir, would be curtailed. The union would supply efficient workers, and ensure continuous production by halting wildcat shutdowns led by irresponsible radical immigrant workers, in effect policing its own members for the benefit of the industry. This stability, union officials believed, might diminish rank-and-file democracy, but in the long run would benefit workers by protecting them from competition-driven exploitation, and by providing reasonable and steady improvements in pay and conditions.

All this assumed that a benevolent partnership between capital and labor was possible—an assumption about to be sorely tested.[8]

TRIANGLE AND TAMMANY

Shortly after 4:30 p.m. on Saturday, March 25, 1911, a fire broke out in the Asch Building, on the northwest corner of Washington Place and Greene Street. "The entire eighth floor was spouting little jets of flame from the windows," wrote a *World* reporter on the scene, as if "surrounded by a row of incandescent lights." Suddenly, what looked like a bale of dark dress goods shot from the flames and plummeted 110 feet to the cement sidewalk below. Horrified onlookers looked down, discovered it was a young woman, looked up, and saw girls crowding the window ledges, their hair and clothing all aflame. Then it began raining bodies.

The eighth floor, like the ninth and tenth, was home to the Triangle Shirtwaist Company, the outfit that had successfully beaten off union organizers during the great strike of 1909. The place was a tinderbox. A ton of cotton scraps—flammable as paper—lay strewn in bins, on tables, across floors. A dropped cigarette butt or unextinguished match ignited them. Fire fed on hanging paper patterns, oil in sewing machines, piles of shirtwaists. (Blanck and

---

8. This kind of accommodation was hailed, in principle, by National Civic Federation corporations but rejected when their own interests were at stake. In October 1910 express company drivers struck against seventeen-hour days and five-to-ten-dollar weeks. They took on not small-fry capitalists but national corporate firms. The Adams Express Company operated over a hundred steam railroads, electric lines, and steamboat and stage lines. The American Express Company had immense capital reserves, and its influential directors also sat on powerful railroads. Major merchants and department stores depended on them. When Mayor Gaynor barred police from protecting scab drivers, the companies hired private police and rammed shipments through. When Gaynor recommended concessions, companies refused point-blank and held out until beaten strikers returned without gains.

"Photograph of Fire Fighters at the Triangle Shirtwaist Factory," March 25, 1911. (National Archives and Records Administration)

Harris had rejected a sprinkler system as too costly.) It raced up narrow wooden staircases in drafty wells, roared into workrooms on other floors.

Crazed with fear and pain, workers panicked. (Despite a history of fires in Blanck and Harris factories, the owners had refused to waste time on fire drills.) Twenty-five crawled into a cloakroom; they were found burned to death, their faces raised toward a small window.

On the top floor, seventy or so hoisted themselves through the skylight and escaped across the roof to an adjoining building. In the pandemonium below, hundreds fought for access to the two stairways only to find several doors jammed—or locked. (It had been

"In Compliance with Law? The fire escape that ends in midair must be abolished." *New-York Tribune*, March 28, 1911. (Cornell University, ILR School, Kheel Center for Labor-Management Documentation and Archives. Trianglefire.ilr.cornell.edu.)

common practice to lock the doors on the Washington Place side, to prevent pilfering, said Blanck, who tested the locks every time he passed.) Others made their way to elevators until fire consumed the hallways.

Some—to their misfortune—reached the single fire escape. The ladder ended 5 feet above an enclosed courtyard, which rapidly filled with smoke. Those who got down nearly smothered before firemen battered in from the outside. But the ladder quickly collapsed, dumping girls eight full floors, impaling them on an iron spike fence below.

With all avenues foreclosed, some chose death where they stood: two bodies were found with arms clasped around each other's neck. Others (a survivor reported) feared above all being burned beyond identification. They began to jump. Within fifteen minutes, forty-seven women leapt into space, streaming flames, crashing through firemen's nets, splattering blood, and setting terrified fire horses lunging.[9]

---

9. "One girl after another fell, like shot birds, from above, from the burning floors," the poet Morris Rosenfeld wrote in the *Forward*'s special edition, published that night.

The police laid out the burned and mangled bodies at an impromptu morgue on the Municipal Charities Pier at East 26th Street. That day or during the following week, 146 died, the youngest being 14.

"The Morgue Is Full of Our Dead," read the *Forward's* banner headline. Cahan followed up with a searing editorial, published in the *Forward* two days after the fire. "The entire neighborhood is sitting shiva. Every heart is torn in mourning. Who is the Angel of Death? Who is the thug? Who is the mass murderer? Must we again say it is that gluttonous ravager of humans— capital?!...The blood of our victims screams out at all of us. The souls of our burned ones demand we must compel our cloistered government to fulfill its duty."

On Sunday afternoon, April 2, the ILGWU, Consumers' League, and Women's Trade Union League held a massive meeting at the Metropolitan Opera House (Anne Morgan covered the cost), dedicated to compelling government action. The Grand Tier boxes were reserved by the rich, who arrived in autos at a special side entrance. Orchestra seats were filled by middle-class New Yorkers chiefly from the Upper West Side. The galleries were jammed to overflowing with East Side workers. The first speakers included David Greer, the Episcopal bishop of New York, Rabbi Stephen S. Wise, and Jacob Schiff, all of whom advocated establishing a citizens' committee to push for legislation imposing fire safety regulations.

Referring to the outpouring of aid for the victims' families from innumerable civic organizations, and the diversity of attendees in the Opera House that evening, Bishop Greer

"The Ruins of the Triangle Shirtwaist Factory," 1911. (Science History Images/Alamy Stock Photo)

observed that "this calamity causes racial lines to be forgotten, for a little while at least, and the whole community rises to one common brotherhood."

That assessment was challenged by Rose Schneiderman, the "little red-headed girl," one observer noted, with "fiery red hair, and blazing eyes," who was on stage representing the Women's Trade Union League. "I would be a traitor to those poor burned bodies," she began, in a soft voice that could barely be heard in the huge pin-drop-silent opera house, "if I came here to talk good fellowship." The voice quickly gained strength. "We have tried you good people of the public—and we have found you wanting. . . . This is not the first time girls have been burned alive in this city. Every week I must learn of the untimely death of one of my sister workers. Every year thousands of us are maimed. The life of men and women is so cheap, and property is so sacred! There are so many of us for one job, it matters little if one hundred and forty-odd are burned to death. We have tried you citizens!" Schneiderman repeated. "We are trying you now, and you have a couple of dollars for the sorrowing mothers and brothers and sisters by way of a charity gift. But every time the workers come out [on strike], the strong arm of the law is allowed to press down heavily upon us. . . . I can't talk fellowship to you who are gathered here," she concluded her indictment. "Too much blood has been spilled. I know from my experience it is up to the working people to save themselves. The only way is through a strong working-class movement."

Three days later, on Wednesday April 5, 1911, that movement took to the streets in a silent funeral procession; 120,000 men and women marched, in a drenching rain, from various locations on the East Side and Brooklyn. The columns assembled in Washington Square, then marched up Fifth Avenue, with Schneiderman in the front row, past crowds estimated at well over a quarter-million people. Black bunting covered hundreds of buildings; the crowds, dressed in black, held black umbrellas aloft. It was, the *American* noted, "one of [the] most impressive spectacles of sorrow New York has ever known."

WORKING-CLASS MILITANCY SEEMED ALL THE MORE THE RIGHT ANSWER to those who followed the trial of Max Blanck and Isaac Harris. Manhattan District Attorney Charles Whitman, whose famed prosecution of NYPD Lieutenant Charles Becker would come one year later, was angling for a big case that could set him on the road to the governorship. On April 12,

"Demonstration of Protest and Mourning for Triangle Shirtwaist Factory Fire of March 25, 1911," April 5, 1911. (National Archives and Records Administration)

1911, Whitman ordered the Triangle owners arrested and charged with manslaughter. (Locking employees in during working hours was against the law, though only a misdemeanor, but if it led to a death, it warranted the more serious category.) Whitman decided the duo couldn't be charged with greater crimes, as they had, after all, fulfilled their legal obligations: the building, if not its contents, had proven fireproof.

Investigators digging through the rubble of the fire located the Washington Place lock in question, which was clearly shown to have been in locked position during the fire. This seemingly damning piece of evidence was but a minor hurdle for Blanck and Harris's attorney, the hugely expensive superstar lawyer Max Steuer, Tammany Hall's principal legal counsel, and Big Tim Sullivan's personal defender. When the trial finally began on December 4, 1911, Steuer mounted a brilliant defense and, coupled with crippling instructions by the judge to the jury, got his clients acquitted in three weeks flat. (Late in the summer of 1913, back in business at another location, Max Blanck was arrested again, and charged again with locking a door during working hours at his new factory. Blanck's explanation was identical to the one he gave at the manslaughter trial: his employees would rob him blind if he didn't lock them in. Finding him guilty, the judge ordered him to pay a fine of twenty dollars, then apologized to the defendant for so doing.)

Outrage at the verdict was redoubled when it transpired that the Triangle Kings had taken out an insurance policy on the goods in the factory that was far in excess of their total value. After the fire, they filed claims approaching their maximum coverage, an amount far more than their documented losses, and collected more than $60,000. This came out to a profit of $445 per dead worker, a sum scarcely diminished by their settling the twenty-three individual suits brought against them—for $75 per life.

Though Blanck and Harris were not accused of arson, there were plenty of eyebrows raised, given that the partners had been suspiciously fire-prone ever since they opened their Asch Building operation in 1902. Their fires (and those of many others) tended to come at the end of the busy season, when manufacturers were often burdened with unsold inventory that—given the abrupt fashion changes decreed by Paris—they'd never be able to unload. The fires also tended to come before dawn or after hours, so there were no human casualties. A 1913 *Collier's* series of muckraking articles about New York's commercial arson industry noted that in 1911, after fashion sentinels had discerned signs that Paris was tilting against shirtwaists, an epidemic of fires in shirtwaist factories had broken out. The *Insurance Monitor*, a leading trade journal, suggested that the atmosphere was "fairly saturated with moral hazard," i.e., the fires were deeply suspicious.

Blanck and Harris were known to be "rotten risks" for their incendiary history and hence paid some of the highest premiums in town. But the rot was widespread and systemic. Manufacturers took out insurance from brokers, who, as they collected a percentage of every sale, fared better when premiums were high. The brokers then protected the big fire insurers by dividing the riskiest policies into small shares, so that no one company bore the brunt. (Those who refused got cut out of more lucrative deals.) The big companies, in turn, simply raised their premium rates so that even after shelling out for big losses, they maintained a healthy balance sheet. With profits being made all around, no one had any incentive to make buildings safer, except, of course, the workers, and they weren't consulted. Quite the opposite: safer buildings meant lower rates, and therefore smaller commissions and smaller profits, while headlined catastrophes reaped a harvest of new policies. As a result, though by 1911 fireproofing technology was in widespread use elsewhere, firewalls, fire doors, fire stairs, and, most of all, automatic sprinklers were scarcely to be found in New York factories. A study done in 1910 found just one garment shop equipped with sprinklers, out of more than a thousand factories surveyed. This was perfectly consistent with the needs of that glutton, Capital. If many manufacturers (and brokers and insurers) considered arson a routine and profitable part of doing business, it would hardly be in their interest to make their factories fireproof.

DESPITE ROSE SCHNEIDERMAN'S INSISTENCE THAT ONLY WORKING-CLASS ACTION could deal with fire-ridden death traps, those assembled at the Opera House voted to press for legislative redress. Columbia professor E. R. A. Seligman underscored this call: "The Legislature will recoil from its task and will continue to shrink from it until driven by an insistent public opinion."

Within days, a Citizens' Committee on Safety was appointed and tasked with going to Albany to demand change. Ex-president Roosevelt had been asked to chair the body, but he demurred, suggesting instead a protégé of his, Henry Lewis Stimson. Also at TR's suggestion, real estate mogul Henry Morgenthau was made treasurer, and social activist John Adams Kingsbury became secretary. The board of directors was chosen from the ranks of labor unions, social and settlement workers, professional firefighting experts, and philanthropists. It included Anne Morgan, Lillian Wald, Rabbi Wise, William J. Schiefflin, and Henry Moskowitz, who had been appointed a "public" representative to the garment industry's Protocol-created Joint Board of Sanitary Control. Financier Robert Fulton Cutting put up $10,000 to get the ball rolling. By mid-April the committee had set up shop in the United Charities Building.

Putting together a team of volunteer lawyers and engineers, the committee sponsored a crash survey that quickly and amply demonstrated the ubiquity of dangerous workplace conditions. Thus armed, Stimson and his colleagues met with Governor Dix and won his approval for urging a legislative response. This meant passing the ball to Charlie Murphy, the man who with Tammany's electoral triumph of 1910 had become the master of both branches of government. And Boss Murphy was no friend of reform.

But Murphy was no fool, either. He understood that the labor uprisings had altered New York's political landscape and put him in a difficult spot. For decades—since the days of Henry George and Abram Hewitt—Tammany had talked labor but acted management. Some mainstream Democrats had condemned even Governor Hughes's mild reform proposals as socialistic. In 1909, however, there had been only 30,000 unionized workers in Gotham; by 1911 there were a quarter million. The hitherto feeble Socialist Party now had a mass base. Needle workers could scour shops and neighborhoods for votes and provide Election Day muscle to beat back Tammany thugs. In 1910 the party had tapped Meyer London, the hugely popular counsel to the ILGWU during the Great Revolt, to replace Morris Hillquit as the Socialist candidate for the Ninth Congressional District seat. With London, the party was also opting for someone who would begin appealing to Jews' ethnic loyalty as well as their radical convictions, something London was perfectly positioned to do, having been an early and staunch backer of arriving Russian revolutionaries, particularly the Bundists. Hillquit, on the other hand, in his 1908 campaign had made clear that he would not be "the special representative of the alleged special interests of this district"—which is to say, the Jews of the Lower East Side. London lost his initial outing but garnered a third more votes than Hillquit ever had.

No one in Tammany was more alive to the party's peril than Big Tim Sullivan, the boss of the Lower East Side, who saw his Irish and German electoral base shrinking by the day. In March 1911 Sullivan tried to get Murphy to use his newfound power to bolster the party's standing with Jewish voters by having the legislature appoint as United States Senator the deeply admired Isidor Straus, the Macy's magnate and philanthropist. (He'd been a founder of the Educational Alliance.) Murphy considered it, but in the end opted for a respected Irish judge.

Murphy proved obdurate on yet another matter of considerable interest to the city's Jews. The 1910 Democratic electoral victory had emboldened Florence Kelley to press again for a maximum-hours law for women and children. She turned over the mission of tackling the state legislature to a recent recruit to the Consumers' League, Frances Perkins. The Boston-born Perkins had been converted to social work as a student at Mount Holyoke (1898–1902), where she read Riis and heard Kelley lecture. After graduation she took up settlement work in Chicago's Hull House, investigated employment agencies' role in fostering prostitution in Philadelphia (during which time she became an ardent socialist), and undertook graduate study at the Wharton School. In 1909 she moved to Gotham. Living in settlements, Perkins surveyed undernourished youths in Hell's Kitchen for the Russell Sage Foundation, got a master's degree in political science from Columbia (in 1910), and then joined Kelley in the Charities Building as head of the Consumers' League's New York office. Her work there focused on studying conditions in laundries and cellar bakeries, workplace fire hazards, child labor, and working women's long hours and low wages.

In January 1911 Perkins went to Albany to lobby for a fifty-four-hour law for women. It seemed a promising moment, given Democrats' control of the legislature. All looked to be going well, but that summer, after the Triangle horror, to which she had been an eyewitness, Perkins went back up to check on the bill's progress. It was explained to her by a friendly insider that the putative party of labor, on orders from Boss Murphy, would bottle up the bill. Why? It turned out that the Huyler brothers' candy factory, notorious for its grim and dangerous working conditions, sat in Murphy's own district, and they were major contributors to the party's campaign chest. The Bloomingdale retail interests were also opposed to having the state restrict their right to employ salesgirls for long and grueling shifts, particularly at holiday time. Tammany, it seemed, would remain a roadblock to reform. This was about to change.

The pressure from the Stimson-headed Committee of Safety, and the general uproar in the city over the 146 corpses, led Murphy to a fateful decision. He okayed formation of a Factory Investigating Commission (FIC) that would examine working conditions around the state and propose legislative measures to improve them. The FIC was given unprecedented powers—to subpoena witnesses and documents, to elect its own members, to employ experts, and to change its own rules. The Tammany legislature whisked up the requisite bill. Tammany governor Dix signed it into law on June 30, 1911, three months after the fire. And to ensure

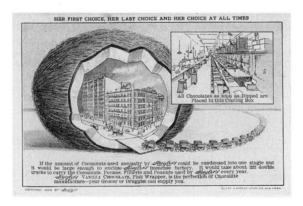

Advertisement, Huyler's Candy. "Her First Choice, Her Last Choice and Her Choice at All Times," Gelter & Kappes Lithograph Company, 1909.

that its recommendations would be given great weight, it required that the majority of the commissioners be members of the legislature—though room was found for representatives of "the public," notably Mary Dreier and Sam Gompers. Most important, Murphy gave the FIC's presidency and vice presidency to Albany's most powerful legislators—the heads of the assembly and the senate, respectively, Alfred Emanuel Smith and Robert F. Wagner.

AL SMITH'S NEW YORK ROOTS RAN DEEP. His maternal grandparents arrived from Ireland in 1841 on a Black Ball Line vessel. They raised six children, including Catherine Mulvhill, Al's mother. His father's family—of mixed Italian and German descent—had arrived in the 1820s. Alfred Emanuel Smith Sr. had been a volunteer fireman, served in the "Bowery Boys" regiment during the Civil War, and gone on to own a two-horse carting business. He met Catherine at St. James's Church and married her in 1872. The following year she gave birth to Al in their four-story South Street home in the shadow of the emerging Brooklyn Bridge.

Al grew up with the bridge. His mother kept him well scrubbed and respectable, a member of the neighborhood's decent laboring folk, at arm's length from the drifters and sailors who frequented the portside district's docks, boardinghouses, and 600 saloons. She had help from the church. St. James's was the largest Roman Catholic parish in the city. Monsignor John Kean offered his parishioners an array of institutions. In 1880 Al was enrolled in St. James's Parochial School, run by the Christian Brothers. He joined a youth group, served as altar boy, took elocution classes. Despite such extensive buffering from disreputability, he picked up a street urchin's racy slang and quick tongue.

The family's hard-won position swiftly unraveled when his father got sick. The Smiths moved to cheaper quarters. Al did odd jobs. In 1886 he peddled the *Leader*, Henry George's newspaper, while his father voted the straight Tammany ticket for the last time. After her husband's death, Catherine worked at an umbrella factory to keep her children from the orphanage. When her strength gave out she rented a basement room from their landlady and sold candy and groceries. It didn't bring in enough money. So in 1888, at 14, Al left school (before graduating from eighth grade) and went to work.

He chased trucks, relaying pickup and delivery notices to drivers. He worked at a kerosene firm. He clerked two years at the Fulton Market for twelve dollars a week and all the fish he could eat. He lugged pipe at the Davidson Steam Pump Company in Brooklyn.

In his spare time, he donned a derby and a dapper suit and haunted the city's theaters. He loved Bowery shows, roared at Harrigan and Hart, and took to the boards himself at the St. James Lyceum Company. A natural mimic and gifted improviser, he dreamed of a career in acting. But he found his true vocation at Tom Foley's saloon, where the burly former blacksmith held sway as Tammany leader of the Fourth Ward. Smith's errand-running was rewarded in 1895 with a white-collar job. For the next eight years he served subpoenas for the commissioner of jurors. During that time he wooed and won Miss Catherine Dunn, the daughter of a Bronx building contractor. The inter-borough commuting, conducted via the Third Avenue El, ended with marriage in 1900. The couple settled down at Peck Slip.

In 1903 Foley handed Smith the Democratic nomination for an assembly seat, a choice duly ratified by the voters. In 1904, just 30, he went off to Albany. He worked hard, learned fast, earned respect, and won reelection year after year. The press and upstate squires liked the "Assemblyman from the Bowery," a superb debater who told funny stories. The Citizens' Union reformers warily praised his support for some of Governor Charles Evans Hughes's measures. More importantly, Smith pleased Charlie Murphy, with whom he dined regularly at Delmonico's. In 1910 Murphy selected him to lead assembly Democrats, and the following

Charles Murphy (left) and Alfred E. Smith, 1916. (Library of Congress Prints and Photographs Division, George Grantham Bain Collection)

year to help run the FIC, a task he took up with alacrity, as many of his constituents had been Triangle fire victims.

That same year, Boss Murphy catapulted another youngster to power in the senate. Robert Wagner's family had arrived in New York from Germany in 1886, when he was nine years old. His father worked as a janitor in a succession of Yorkville tenement houses. Bobby went to public school, sold papers, delivered groceries, and peddled candy in Central Park. After graduating from Townsend Harris High School in 1893 he studied, free, at City College while working part-time as a bellhop at the New York Athletic Club. On graduating in 1898, he enrolled at New York Law School, finished with honors in 1900, was admitted to the bar, and formed a law partnership. For rendering campaign services to Tammany's Algonquin Club since his college days, Wagner was rewarded with a Tammany nomination (and consequent election) to the legislature in 1904.

In Albany, Protestant Wagner shared a dingy hotel room with Catholic Smith; they struck up a friendship. But Wagner's career was interrupted the next year when he was defeated by a Hearst-backed candidate. Jolted into awareness of the progressive tenor of the times, Wagner made a comeback as a Tammany reformer. Murphy bumped him over to the senate, then (in 1911) bumped him up to majority leader—at 33, the youngest in senate history.

IN OCTOBER 1911 THE FACTORY INVESTIGATING COMMISSION, with the "Tammany Twins" at the helm, began studying New York's working conditions—holding public hearings, examining witnesses, making on-site inspections. Wagner and Smith took their lead investigator, Dr. George Price, from the Joint Board of Sanitary Control. Frances Perkins arrived on loan from the Consumers' League to help out, and she in turn brought in more investigators, including Rose Schneiderman and Clara Lemlich. During the next two months Price sent his team of investigators into nearly 2,000 factories, covering twenty industries. (Perkins, fresh from the defeat of the fifty-four-hour bill, made sure to dispatch investigators to examine conditions in candy factories.) The commission met most Saturdays to discuss issues and strategies, and by year's end it had proposed fifteen new laws. Eight of them were enacted.

In the spring of 1912 Perkins resubmitted the fifty-four-hour law to the legislature. Murphy, not prepared to put all his eggs in the reform basket, arranged to have the bill killed without his fingerprints showing—Wagner was assigned this duty—at the behest this time not of candy makers but of canneries. State Senator Big Tim Sullivan came to Perkins's aid. "Me sister was a poor girl," he told her, and "I feel kinda sorry for them poor girls that work the way you say they work." Murphy split the difference: the bill became law, though it exempted canneries.

Fresh from this victory, Perkins was escalated (in June 1912) to executive secretary of the Committee of Safety. From this perch she worked closely with the FIC, housed across the street, on another round of investigations and another volley of legislative proposals. This time twenty-six out of twenty-eight became law. The year 1913 proved another good one for reform—the fifty-four-hour law was broadened to include cannery workers—a function of the 1912 election, in which many Old Guard Republicans were defeated by Roosevelt's Progressive Party candidates, eliminating some of the staunchest opponents of reform. By year's end, virtually every safety issue revealed by the Triangle fire had been addressed. Automatic sprinklers were required in high-rise buildings. Fire drills were mandatory in large shops. Doors had to be unlocked and had to swing outward. Fire escapes were mandatory. Other laws set lighting and ventilation standards; imposed occupancy limits; banned smoking; required washing facilities; ordered daily removal of flammable rubbish; barred children under 14 (with a physician's certification of age required); outlawed tenement-house manufacture of infants' apparel, children's toys, and food products; and forbade female labor between 10:00 p.m. and 6:00 a.m. To enforce the laws, the Factory Commission pushed through a complete reorganization of the state Department of Labor. This blizzard of legislation gave New York the most rigorous labor code of any American state.

Most employer organizations resisted many of these changes. They insisted they were 100 percent in favor of saving employee lives, but argued that the state had gone too far. By requiring "cumbersome and costly" upgrades, the new laws, said a spokesman for the Associated Industries of New York, would drive "manufacturers out of the City and State of New York." Factory owners weren't the only unhappy ones. Under the March 19, 1913, *Times* headline "Realty Men Protest. Albany Measures for Fire Prevention Regarded as Oppressive," the Realty League explained that "many owners will be so financially embarrassed by the great expenditure made necessary thereby that great numbers of buildings would be forced into foreclosure or otherwise sacrificed." George W. Olvany, special counsel to the Real Estate Board of New York (REBNY), declared this was already happening.

"Thousands of factories are migrating to New Jersey and Connecticut in order to be freed from the oppressive laws of New York State," he said, adding that "the owners of real property are becoming terrified by the number of laws which have been enacted.... You can no longer distinguish the real estate owner by the smile of prosperity, because his property is now a burden and a liability instead of a source of income. To own a factory building in New York City is now a calamity." The REBNY Board of Governors resolved that the FIC laws were "unnecessary for the proper protection of life," were "depreciating the value of real estate," and "should be so modified as to relieve property owners of needlessly burdensome requirements and unnecessary expense." Real estate broker Charles F. Noyes raised the shrillness level a notch higher, demanding that the legislature "relieve real estate from the terrible yolk [sic] of oppression which has been throttling it." The United Real Estate Owners' Association added to the list of gored oxen the city's "life insurance companies, savings banks, and all lenders of mortgage money." Still another casualty was certain to be the municipal treasury, because "factories will be driven from the city, labor will be compelled to accompany them, factories, tenements, and small houses will become tenantless with the final result of demoralization in tax collections by the city." Finally, at the exalted altitude of political economy, Laurence M. D. McGuire, president of the Real Estate Board, declared that "the experience of the past proves conclusively that the best government is the least possible government, that the unfettered initiative of the individual is the force that makes a country great and that this initiative should never be bound."

To which the Factory Investigatory Commission responded: "Notwithstanding all the talk of a probable exodus of manufacturing interests the commission has not found a single case of a manufacturer intending to leave the State because of the enforcement of the factory laws." The FIC suggested that employers must understand "that the health of the workers is of paramount importance to the state, which not only has the right but is bound to take measures that workers be properly safeguarded in the course of employment." Al Smith's response to the hubbub—a puzzled note to Frances Perkins—was more revealing of the underlying disagreement: "I can't see what all this talk is about," he wrote her. "How is it wrong for the State to intervene with regard to the working conditions of people who work in the factories and mills? I don't see what they mean. What did we set up the government for?"

THE OLD DEMOCRATIC PARTY WAS CLEARLY CHANGING—a transformation punctuated by the passing of Big Tim Sullivan, one of its bulwarks. By 1912, with his East Side barony now overwhelmingly Jewish and Italian, Sullivan had largely withdrawn from ward affairs, and he spent less and less time at old Bowery haunts. In July he was shaken by the murder of an associate, gambler Herman Rosenthal, and by the subsequent investigations into Bowery rackets. Sullivan began experiencing delusions of persecution and bouts of manic depression. In September, with the Becker trial looming, he had a complete nervous breakdown. In 1913 he was confined to a sanitarium, then remanded to his brother Patrick's country house in the Bronx. One night in August, while playing cards with male nurses, he slipped away and disappeared.

Two weeks later, a patrolman at Bellevue's morgue was taking a last look (as required by law) at bodies about to be shipped off to Potter's Field. Pausing before one mangled corpse, he peered more closely, gave a start, and exclaimed: "It's Big Tim, God rest him!" Sullivan had apparently been run over by a train and lain unidentified in the Fordham morgue before being sent downtown for final disposal.

Big Tim's funeral at Old St. Patrick's was one of the most impressive ever seen in New York City. Eight priests held a solemn requiem mass before friends, city officials, and a horde

"Sullivan Funeral—Bowery," September 15, 1913. (Library of Congress Prints and Photographs Division, George Grantham Bain Collection)

of weeping constituents who flowed out into the streets. Seventy-five thousand lined the Bowery for his funeral procession. Twenty-five thousand accompanied the casket to the gravesite at Calvary.

Obituaries stressed Sullivan's beneficence to the poor and unfortunate. And Big Tim *had* been spontaneously (as well as calculatingly) generous. The bottom line was that in Sullivan's heyday Tammany Hall stood for party philanthropy and public laissez-faire, while at the time of his death the Democratic Party, pushed from the left, was becoming an exponent of government-backed labor and social reform. The irony was that Sullivan, in championing Frances Perkins and Florence Kelley's fifty-four-hour law, had helped usher in the new order.

WOBBLIES AND SOCIALISTS

On January 12, 1912, the Great Hall at Cooper Union was jammed with an audience come to hear two of the country's leading leftists debate contending modes of radical action. On one side of the stage loomed Big Bill Haywood, the six-foot, 250-pound, barrel-chested, broad-shouldered, one-eyed, Stetson-hatted spokesman of the Industrial Workers of the World. On the other, the bantamweight Morris Hillquit—labor lawyer, union organizer, historian, theoretician, skilled debater, and cofounder of the Socialist Party.

The drama of their jousting lay partly in their antithetical personal styles. Haywood, a man of the West, liked to present himself as an outlaw cowboy, barroom brawler, and rebel incarnate, come east to taunt the milquetoast socialists of the big city. Hillquit, polished and suave, was as comfortable and capable of holding his own in the clubs and parlors of the metropolitan elite as he was addressing crowds from soapboxes in Union Square. But their contrasting styles were, more importantly, congruent with their tactical prescriptions for socialist and labor organizers. Haywood was a standard-bearer for "direct action," the launching of massed battles for control of the means of production, be they mines, forests, or factories, and a continuous shop-floor resistance to exploitation, if needs be by "sabotage"— by which he meant not blowing things up but rather minute observance of rules, purposive mistakes, a "withdrawal of efficiency." Hillquit was the parliamentarian, calling for a long and orderly march through the political institutions, patiently mobilizing electoral support with an eye to capturing power at the polling place.

Haywood was an industrial unionist. His IWW favored organizing all the workers in an industry "as the capitalists have assembled them"—consolidating labor the better to counter consolidated management. The Wobblies would also dissolve distinctions based on craft, ethnicity, gender, or race. Creating democratically run industrial unions was not simply a tactic; such institutions, in their openness and inclusiveness, were a prototype for the socialist commonwealth of the future. Not surprisingly, Haywood rejected Hillquit's strategy of working closely with Samuel Gompers's federation of craft unions—little "job trusts," Haywood thought, dedicated to protecting a small and privileged minority of the labor force. He urged the Socialist Party to spurn the AFL and instead make common cause with the Wobblies.

Hillquit agreed that industrial unions were preferable to craft guilds—a prime goal of the New York Socialist Party, after all, had been to organize great swathes of the garment industry—but he argued that Haywood exaggerated their efficacy: "A mere change of structural forms would not revolutionize the American labor movement as claimed by our extreme industrialists." More to the point, the AFL was a huge fact on the ground. It was the most powerful extant organization of the working class (admittedly only a small percentage thereof), and it behooved the socialist movement to work inside it to raise members' political consciousness. Hillquit's prognosis was quite optimistic: the party, he believed, was making major inroads in the AFL. Within five years, he predicted, the rank and file (though perhaps not the obdurate leadership) would be voting socialist and backing a socialist agenda.

This aspect of the debate shaded into a more contested assessment of the *value* of presumed electoral gains. Haywood was at times dismissive of political action. Indeed, he told his audience of New York leftists they shouldn't be sitting around waiting for the next election but should be out in the streets aiding the laundry workers then currently on strike. But Haywood also liked telling audiences, "I'm a two-gun man from the West, you know," and then pulling out his IWW card from one pocket, and his Socialist Party card from the other, both equally crimson. Capturing municipal power, he allowed, could be immensely helpful to union organizers by getting local police off their backs. He himself, moreover, had run on the Socialist Party ticket for governor of Colorado in 1906 (while in jail), and actively campaigned for Socialist leader Eugene Debs in the 1908 presidential election, traveling with him around the country. Debs, for his part, had declared in a 1911 article that the economic organization of the working class was ultimately more important than the size of the Socialist vote, for only if workers were organized and disciplined at the workplace could they "hold what is registered by the ballot."

Hillquit also believed in a two-gun movement, with separate but equal political and trade union arms. Through the United Hebrew Trades, he had long since put that preachment into practice. Still, the two debaters had very different understandings of how labor organizing should be practiced. Specifically, Haywood took Hillquit to task for having urged Gotham's garment workers to sign the Brandeis Protocol in 1910. Giving up the right to strike—labor's principal weapon—struck Haywood as madness, a species of unilateral disarmament in the class struggle. The IWW opposed *any* kind of contractual relations between labor and capital, including setting down the terms on which a strike had just been settled, as that would diminish militancy and lead to dangerous complacency.

For Hillquit, however, the establishment of orderly and industry-wide labor relations was a great step forward for the working class, as it struck a systemic blow against competitive capitalism and its counterpart—primitive hand-to-hand combat at the factory door. The Protocol represented a détente with capital, to their mutual short-term benefit, and served labor's long-haul strategy of eventually using its political arm to pluck the economic fruit that corporate capital was ripening. While Hillquit imagined workers would win power through the ballot box rather than the picket line, he didn't think that capital would simply acquiesce in being outvoted. In a debate two weeks after his debate with Haywood, this one with the US attorney general, Hillquit was asked by his opponent how the Socialists planned to make good on their promise of nationalizing the railroads, canals, telegraph and phone companies. They "might be acquired by purchase," Hillquit responded, "or perhaps the people would declare civil war and confiscate them."

For Hillquit, Haywood's encouragement of shop-floor radicals—who in defiance of the Protocol had been staging wildcat walkouts, usually in a pas de deux with management-rights diehards imposing speed-ups or pay cuts—was symptomatic of a still larger difference between them, this one verging on the existential. Haywood on occasion waxed eloquent about force and violence being the workers' ultimate weapon and trumpeted a disrespect for capitalist "law and order." Not two weeks earlier, in a speech from the same Cooper Union platform, Haywood, referring to the vast numbers of miners who had died in preventable accidents or violent suppression of strikes, called them victims of capitalist law and capitalist government and asked his audience: "Do you blame me when I say that I despise the law? (tremendous applause and shouts of 'No!')...I am not a law-abiding citizen," he'd insisted, "and more than that, no Socialist can be a law-abiding citizen." Rather it was "our purpose to overthrow the capitalist system by forcible means if necessary."

Hillquit was appalled by Haywood's effusions because he was sure they would alienate the middle and "respectable" working classes whom Hillquit had been cultivating so assiduously. Americans on the whole, he believed, *were* law-abiding citizens. The democratic United States was not despotic Russia. Workers had the ballot. Revolutionary violence was unnecessary, indeed counterproductive. Haywood (Hillquit argued) was spouting anarchist doctrine, and therefore little better than a terrorist.[10]

The real problem for Hillquit was that Big Bill wasn't shouting from outside the tent; the IWW camel had gotten much more than its nose inside the Socialist apparatus. Days before the January Cooper Union debate, in December 1911, there had been an election to fill the seven seats of the national executive committee. Hillquit had received the fourth-highest number of votes. But Haywood had garnered more and come in third. Not only did this rankle Hillquit personally—a founder of the party being outvoted by an upstart—it demonstrated that a substantial portion of the membership was prepared to contest Hillquit's parliamentarian focus and pro-AFL strategy. An unnerving sign of what such disaffection might lead to had been made manifest back in April 1911 when the Italian Socialist Federation—captained now by Arturo Giovannitti, who had also assumed editorship of the

---

10. Debs, too, thought Big Bill had crossed the line: the class struggle, he now wrote, was not guerrilla warfare; such talk should be left to the anarchists. The IWW insisted it did not believe in dynamite; that was an anarchist tactic. Hillquit ignored such protestations. Haywood hadn't exactly fostered comradely feelings, having taken a personal swipe at Hillquit by noting pointedly that "for all the ages agone" lawyers "have been the mouthpieces of the capitalist class."

ISF's paper, *Il Proletario*—voted in convention to declare itself a wholesale backer of the IWW. Worse still, Wobbly membership was made mandatory for ISFers.

Hillquit was determined to drive the IWW out of the party before it dragged the organization down in the court of public opinion. It was time, he thought, to do battle for the soul of American socialism. And then, suddenly, events dictated a postponement.

IN ATTENDANCE THAT JANUARY 1912 DEBATE DAY in the Great Hall were Wobbly activists Giovannitti, Elizabeth Gurley Flynn, and Joseph James Ettor, and it was there, to Ettor, that a message was delivered from Lawrence, Massachusetts, sent by textile workers with whom he'd been organizing the mills for some time. The message said they were at that moment walking off their jobs by the thousands, and would he please come north post haste and take direction of what was turning out to be an enormous general strike?

The mass of the Lawrence mill workers led desperate lives. Two-loom technology had sped up the pace of production, which expanded output per worker, which in turn allowed mass layoffs and led to lower wages for remaining employees, less than nine dollars a week for fifty-six hours of labor. Many families survived on bread, molasses, and beans. Out of every 100 men and women who worked in the mills, 36 died by the age of 25.

On January 1, 1912, a new Massachusetts labor law had reduced the workweek to fifty-four hours for women and children. Mill owners promptly lowered wages, precipitating the walkout, with Polish women leading the way, shouting, "Short pay, all out!" Most of the operatives were immigrants—with Italian, Québécois, Slavic, Hungarian, Portuguese, Polish, and Syrian being the largest of the two dozen resident nationalities. Most of the skilled jobs were held by native-born workers of English, Irish, and German descent. A few hundred of the latter paid dues to the AFL-affiliated United Textile Workers (UTW). A few hundred of the former—particularly militant Italians—had signed up with the IWW.

Joe Ettor, the Wobblies' man on the scene, was born in 1885 in New York City, the son of an immigrant Italian laborer family. His working life began at the age of 12, with jobs as a newsboy, railroad waterboy, lumber-mill saw filer, barrel maker, shipyard worker, and cigar maker. In 1906 Ettor went to work for the IWW as an organizer. Fluent (and inspirational) in Italian, English, Polish, and Yiddish, he traveled the country, organizing coal miners, steelmakers, and shoe factory workers in Brooklyn. He was well prepared—together with Giovannitti, whom he quickly summoned to his aid—to pull together the multi-ethnic strikers of Lawrence, all 25,000 of them. The two New Yorkers suggested forming a strike committee of two representatives from each nationality in the mills, and it was this international body that would make all major decisions, translating its minutes into twenty-five languages. The strikers organized mass picket squads, tied up all the mills, and issued demands for a 15-percent increase in wages for a fifty-four-hour workweek, double time for overtime, and no discrimination against workers for their strike activity.

The UTW did its best to break the strike, urging skilled workers to stay on the job. In this it was staunchly backed by the AFL, as Gompers loathed the IWW. But many mutinied, notably the German weavers, and joined their comrades on the picket line.

The mill owners struck back. On January 30 both Ettor and Giovannitti were arrested on a flagrantly trumped-up charge of murder (of a young girl most likely shot by the police). The governor called out the militia (with bayonets fixed) and declared martial law. The IWW sent in Haywood and Flynn. Big Bill, whatever his penchant for violent hyperbole when addressing parliamentary socialists, proved a staunch advocate of nonviolence on the picket line. Violence "wins nothing," he told the press. "We have a new kind of violence—the havoc

Joseph Ettor (left) and Arturo Giovannitti "Seated, in Handcuffs," 1912. (Library of Congress Prints and Photographs Division, George Grantham Bain Collection)

we raise with money by laying down our tools." The capitalists, Haywood assured the thronged strikers, "could not weave cloth with bayonets."

In February, with the strike dragging on through a difficult winter, some Italian Socialist Federation strikers called Haywood's attention to a practice long used in Italy to mitigate pressure on striking parents who were worried about feeding their children, by sending them out of starvation's way. Elizabeth Gurley Flynn took charge of arranging an exodus of malnourished and raggedly dressed children down to New York. A committee arrived from Gotham, led by Margaret Sanger, a trained nurse and Socialist Party member who had begun working with the Wobblies, to check on the health of the first group of 119 children to be trained down. On February 17 the contingent arrived at Grand Central Station, where they were met by 5,000 ecstatic supporters. They took the children to the Labor Temple on East 84th Street, where they were fêted and fed, examined again by fifteen volunteer doctors, then turned over to their eager and thoroughly screened hosts, who carried them on their shoulders to their respective el stations.[11]

Two more caravans departed without incident in ensuing days, but the fourth one, scheduled to leave on February 24, turned out to be decisive for the strike's outcome. So terrible had been the negative publicity that had befallen the elites of Lawrence, that the police

---

11. Sanger described the scene at Grand Central in the February 18 *New York Call*: "Thousands of men and women stood waiting for the little ones to come, and many had been waiting since early in the afternoon, so when at last they did appear in the evening their enthusiasm knew no bounds. Shouting, cheering with tears in their eyes, hundreds of these men broke through the ropes. Tearing off their own coats they wrapped them around the cold and ragged little bodies, placed them upon their shoulders, and marched on with the throng. Everywhere were men with tears streaming down their faces, tears of joy and gladness at this wonderful demonstration of working class solidarity; at this glorious slap in the face to capitalists in general, and charity organizations in particular; at this great fact that no matter what our nationality or creed, no matter what our methods of gaining our goal, the working class will take care of its own. Italian men carried Polish children, German men carried Italian children; Scotch, English, Polish, Italians and French, were one and all carried upon the shoulders of class-conscious men, who felt only that every child was a workingman's offspring, and as such has to be tended and cherished."

The children of the Lawrence strikers, marching in New York. "Lawrence, Mass Strikers Parading in N.Y.C.," 1911. (Library of Congress Prints and Photographs Division, George Grantham Bain Collection)

ham-handedly tried to abort further departures. Boarding the train, they dragged children away from their mothers, clubbed all and sundry, and threw the women in jail, precipitating an enormous nationwide uproar. The *New York Tribune*—no fan of the IWW ("a gang of outside agitators," it harrumphed, who had "seized" the city)—was exasperated beyond measure with the Lawrence authorities, declaring their actions "as chuckle-headed an exhibition of incompetence to deal with a strike situation as is possible to recall." And indeed, the mill owners' position rapidly became unsustainable. The US Congress held embarrassing hearings. President Taft weighed in. Pressure mounted until, on March 12, the employers accepted all the demands. Not only that, but mills throughout New England followed suit, giving raises to some 250,000 employees. Ettor and Giovannitti, however, remained in prison. Carlo Tresca was dispatched to Lawrence to organize a campaign to win their freedom.

TO HILLQUIT'S DISMAY, HAYWOOD AND HIS COLLEAGUES now returned to Gotham as heroes, indeed as national celebrities. Suddenly the IWW and Italian Socialist Federation had leapt to the forefront of the labor movement. As Haywood told a New York audience, the Lawrence uprising was the "greatest strike" in US history, not because of the numbers involved, but because "we were able to bring together so many different nationalities," and because "it was a democracy." This was clearly not the moment to excommunicate him, especially as the Socialist Party itself had helped out during the affray. What Hillquit did manage to do, when the party met in convention weeks later, in May 1912, was to win amendment (after a terrific internal struggle) of the party's constitution to allow expulsion of any member "who opposes political action or advocates crime, sabotage, or other methods of violence as a weapon of the working class." A gun had been locked and loaded.

IN THE MEANTIME, ALSO IN MAY 1912, seeking to build on its success in Lawrence, the IWW set out to tackle Gotham's hotel and restaurant trade. Of the 75,000 men and women who worked in that rapidly expanding sector, only 2,000 were organized, most of them bartenders, members of a clannish AFL craft union, not open to new applicants. The rest were mostly immigrants, poorly paid, who worked days that could last up to eighteen hours. The Wobblies formed the International Hotel Workers' Union (IHWU), which embraced not only waiters but cooks, oyster men, chambermaids, dishwashers, scullery maids, busmen, bartenders, scrub women, porters, and bellhops. Haywood and other fiery orators—including some Socialist Party members like Rose Pastor Stokes—addressed recruits at Bryant Hall, under the Sixth Avenue El at 42nd Street. On May 7 150 waiters at the Hotel Belmont (across from Grand Central) took off their white aprons and marched from the dining room to the picket line. By month's end, 18,000 had joined them. Organizers walked into establishments just as the lunch or dinner service was about to begin and blew three blasts on a whistle. The staff promptly vanished. Nearly all the big hotels were hit, as were dozens of restaurants, some long established, others lately sprung up in the Times Square area—Delmonico's, Sherry's, Shanley's, Churchill's, Louis Martin's, and the Plaza, Astor, Knickerbocker, Savoy, St. Regis, and Waldorf-Astoria. The demands were modest: a salary of ten dollars for a six-day, sixty-hour week, with overtime pay of fifty cents an hour (twenty-five cents for busboys).

The unexpected revolt stunned employers, but they rallied quickly. Proprietors refused to recognize the IHWU—"I'll close my place first," said George Rector—and combined to combat it. They fired large numbers of union men, recruited African Americans from southern hotels and college students as strikebreakers, hired private security, and received police assistance. Tempers flared. A crowd of waiters from Delmonico's and the Savoy charged into the New Netherlands Hotel at 59th and Fifth, determined to drag out still-working staff, only to be driven off by police with drawn guns. Despite violent harassment from hired guards, and pro-management decisions from the judiciary, the strike continued. The Socialist Party stepped in to help out, sponsoring a mass rally at Carnegie Hall, and donating the proceeds of a special strike edition of the *New York Call*. Then the organized employers announced they were conceding wage hikes for loyal employees, while remaining dead set against union recognition. Militants urged holding out, but with resources ebbing, many drifted back to work; the strike lost momentum, and the conflict was called off on June 25, 1912. The IWW had found Gotham hotels a tougher nut to crack than Lawrence mills. There was talk about trying again in the fall, the busiest time, rather than the ill-chosen spring season.

IN THE MEANTIME, ON JUNE 20, 1912, the socialists had called out *their* troops and tackled the city's rapidly growing fur trade. In that year there were about 10,000 fur workers in the shops then centered around Houston, Wooster, Spring, and Greene. Seventy percent were Jews, 30 percent a mélange of Germans, Greeks, Italians, French Canadians, Bohemians, and Slovaks. These were poisonous work sites. Dyes rotted fingers while dust ate at eyes and lungs. Of every ten, two had tuberculosis, two had asthma, and four suffered from other occupational diseases. Life insurance companies refused to issue policies to fur workers.

A small union, set up in 1904, had had little impact, but now, inspired by garment worker breakthroughs, it issued a call for a general strike, and was supported by the United Hebrew Trades. Over 7,000 workers turned out, their walkout from 400 shops generaled by Jewish and Italian socialists. Meyer London served as legal adviser. The bosses combined and brought in gangsters who slugged picketers with glass bottles and iron bars, wounding over 200. Police arrested four times that number. Judges consigned dozens to the Workhouse.

"Socialists in Union Square," May 1, 1912. (Library of Congress Prints and Photographs Division, George Grantham Bain Collection)

Despite this, on September 8, after twelve weeks of no income, employers granted most demands (though not the closed shop). Merrymakers jammed Lower East Side streets, tooting horns and rattling noisemakers.

TWO MONTHS LATER, ON NOVEMBER 5, 1912, the presidential election bolstered Hillquit's electoral strategy. Eugene Debs pulled in nearly a million votes, 6 percent of the total, coming in fourth but also coming on strong. And while many Socialists complained that the Progressives had eaten their lunch, the fact that many of Teddy Roosevelt's roughly 4 million ballots (27.4 percent) had been cast for a platform so akin to their own was also grounds for celebration. Even the winning Democrats, whose 6-million-odd votes (41.8 percent) put Wilson in the White House, had tacked toward the Socialists on some issues.

NOVEMBER 1912, HOWEVER, ALSO BROUGHT GOOD NEWS for direct-action proponents. Carlo Tresca had been working for months to liberate Ettor and Giovannitti, organizing mass demonstrations and walkouts, establishing a legal defense fund, and mobilizing rallies across the country and in Europe (including every major city in Italy). Italians of all classes and political persuasions, usually at loggerheads, rallied to this cause. Giovannitti in particular became a folk hero, in part for the string of poems he published from prison. When works like "The Walker," about his jail experience, came out in September, critics compared them favorably with Whitman and Wilde, earning him the title of "The Poet of the Working Class." After making powerful speeches in court, Ettor and Giovannitti men were finally acquitted, on November 26.

On November 30, Ettor arrived back at Grand Central. (Giovannitti was ill and didn't travel.) Haywood and a reception committee met him at the platform, then ushered him outside to a waiting crowd of thousands. They hoisted the "Little General" aloft and carried him down Fifth Avenue, bands playing "The Marseillaise," to Union Square, where thousands more awaited him. Haywood presented him with a huge floral arrangement in the shape of an axe and a torch, the iconography (Haywood explained) representing the destruction of capitalism, and the enlightenment of labor through which that destruction was to be accomplished.

The next afternoon, December 1, 5,000 crammed another welcome-home rally for Ettor, this one at the Harlem River Casino (127th and Second Avenue), under Socialist Party auspices. During a hell-raising speech, Haywood apparently told the wildly cheering crowd (though there are clashing versions of what he said) that "direct action is the shortest way home especially for women, foreigners, negroes, and disfranchised free American citizens"; that labor should use every weapon at hand, even sabotage; that the fact that there were no "political Socialists" in jail in the United States, while there were "almost 100 industrial Socialists behind prison bars," suggested the IWW approach "was more effective in making itself felt by the capitalist class." At another meeting during that week Haywood moderated this somewhat, noting that "I do believe in political action, because it gives us control of the policeman's club," adding that political action was of great educational value.

Ignoring the latter qualifications, Hillquit pounced. On December 3 the New York party moved to demand Haywood's expulsion. On December 14 a recall referendum was approved. When the nationwide balloting closed on February 26, 1913, with 25 percent of the membership having participated, the vote was 22,000–11,000 for removing Haywood from office. The bulk of the recall vote came from New York, Massachusetts, Pennsylvania, and Wisconsin; the pro-Haywood ballots came mostly from western states. Many of the party's New York intellectuals protested, including William English Walling, J. G. Phelps Stokes, Rose Pastor Stokes, and Margaret Sanger, but to no avail. Haywood resigned. Tens of thousands of Wobbly-Socialists followed him out the door. (Estimates conflict, but the lowest seems to be 15 percent of the membership.)

WHILE THE BATTLE OVER HAYWOOD WAS STILL IN PROGRESS, during January and February 1913, the IWW took another crack at winning recognition for the International Hotel Workers' Union, this time with Tresca and Flynn taking the lead, though Haywood, Ettor, and Giovannitti were participants as well. They launched round two without warning on New Year's Eve. A crowd of strikers arrived at the doorstep of the Hotel Astor on 44th Street, ablaze with festive Times Square revelry, and proceeded to smash its windows with bricks and stones, and do battle with hired guards.

Each day a different set of targets was hit, with whistle blasts calling out cooks and busboys alike, succeeding often (but not always) in shutting down dining establishments. But again the hoteliers held firm, firing strikers en masse, bringing in replacement workers, hiring private muscle, pressuring the city into unleashing the police.

At Bryant Hall rallies, the Wobbly leaders debated escalating to a general strike against the entire industry; the 5,000 IHWU members voted 10–1 to do so, but the leadership hesitated, given the forces arrayed against them. One advising caution was Jacob Panken, the prominent socialist attorney who was serving as legal counsel for the IHWU. On January 24 Panken was urging strikers to take their grievances to the polls and vote for the Socialist Party. Tresca, in the audience, climbed on a chair and cut him off, shouting in his halting English: "Fellow-workers, a strike, dat is not a course of lectures, but a fight!... Dis man, he talk about politic, he talk about election, while scabs betray our cause. I say we march in mass formation right away out of here and picket all hotels. I say we stop talking. I say we act. I say we win dis strike!" Two thousand unionists surged out behind him, their first stop the Knickerbocker Hotel at Broadway and 42nd Street, whose proprietor had discharged his entire staff of 286 waiters that afternoon. The strikers shouted "scabs" at those working inside and broke windows with umbrellas and rocks. Private guards hired by the Hotel Men's Association fought back with blackjacks and night sticks. Then Tresca and cohort moved on to the Belmont Hotel on Park Avenue at 42nd Street, where they shattered the lobby windows. Guards counterattacked by hurling rocks down at Bryant Hall strike head-quarters from the el platform at Sixth Avenue and 42nd. During the tumult, an outnumbered band of police grabbed Tresca, put a gun to his head, and threatened to kill him if the strikers did not retreat, which they did.[12]

Hotel managers blamed Mayor Gaynor for the violence, given his order restraining police from abusing citizens; one told the press he longed for the days of Clubber Williams and Big Bill Devery, cops who "knew how to suppress strikes." The next day police lines went up around the major hotels, and cops repelled striker assaults, nightsticks flailing freely. The hotel owners, denouncing IWW "hooliganism," dug in. Flynn and Tresca now advised the workers, whose strike-fund cupboard was bare, to call off the walkout. On January 31, 1913, after a last round of window smashing, the union threw in the towel.

Those middle- and upper-class New Yorkers who had backed the Wobblies at Lawrence—their sympathies having been enlisted by the pitiable children—were never going to be enthusiastic about immigrant workers interrupting their accustomed pastimes in their own hometown, but striker violence (albeit against property not persons) made it easier to dismiss the workers' legitimate complaints. The socialists joined the chorus of critics. Lawyer Panken refused to defend arrested strikers, even though the IHWU had retained him for that purpose, telling union officials: "Go to Tresca for counsel. He will teach you how to throw stones and stay out of prison."

Few hotel workers believed anything positive had been accomplished. Hundreds had lost their jobs to non-union replacements, and hundreds more were reemployed only on condition that they tear up their union cards. Conditions and wages remained the same as before the strike. Many were bitter. Months later, the union expelled all IWW members from its ranks. All in all, the second hotel strike was a major setback for the Wobblies.

ON FEBRUARY 25, 1913, THREE WEEKS AFTER THE END of the hotel strike, and one day before Haywood was removed from his Socialist Party position, silk workers launched a mammoth strike in Paterson, New Jersey, about 20 miles west of Manhattan. Unlike Lawrence's work-force, Paterson's had a lengthy tradition of labor militancy, dating back to the arrival of German silk weavers in the 1860s and 1870s, and seasoned northern Italian, Russian and Polish activists in the 1890s and 1900s. Their 1913 demands were the usual ones, but with a particular focus on management's upping the number of looms per worker from two to three or even four, which generated resistance not to the introduction of new machinery per se, but to the distribution of profits that accrued from increased productivity.

---

12. During the melee the contents of Tresca's coat had spilled out, including a little volume of Browning's *Sonnets from the Portuguese* that Flynn had given him, inscribed "Elizabeth to Carlo." The press blazoned the adulterous affair, forcing Tresca to choose between his wife and his lover; he moved in with Flynn and her family at 511 East 134th in the Bronx. In April 1914 he moved his newspaper, *L'Avvenire*, from Pittsburgh to Harlem (2205 Third Avenue), becoming a preeminent member of the New York *souvversivi*.

Paterson's pugnacious mill owners had long been preparing for a showdown. Since the turn of the century they had been opening up factory annexes in eastern Pennsylvania, employing coal miners' wives and children, among whom union traditions were attenuated or nonexistent, "so that labor trouble in one place will not control the whole industry," as one owner put it. They had also been substituting women and children for militant craftworkers in Paterson itself and had arranged for a totally pliable police department to replace its more even-handed predecessor. They were determined that Paterson not become another Lawrence.

The strikers got off to a strong start by arranging an unprecedented alliance between craft and unskilled workers, then between the diverse ethnic groups, the latter taking form as a multi-national strike committee. Within two weeks 25,000 had walked out of 300-plus mills. Buoyed by the example of Lawrence, the strikers invited IWW veterans of the Massachusetts affray—Haywood, Flynn, Tresca, and other Gotham residents—not to run the strike but to address and inspire mass meetings. Indeed, when Haywood showed up on March 7, he observed approvingly that the silk workers had gotten things up and running "without relying much on outside help," and insisted to reporters seeking "responsible" leaders to interview that shop-floor committees were in charge.

Nonviolence was the order of the day—for workers, not employers. Even when private detectives hired by the Wiedemann Silk Dye Company opened fire on picketers, killing one bystander, Tresca's eulogy at the victim's funeral cried out for vengeance—*"Sangue chiama sangue!"* (For blood you must take blood)—no retribution was in fact exacted. The Paterson police had been arresting people from day one, on the slimmest of grounds, or none at all. Flynn, among the first to be held, told the chief of police he was abusing his authority; he didn't disagree and candidly replied, "You may have the rights, but we have the power." Approximately 1,850 workers were incarcerated during the course of the strike; Tresca himself was nabbed at least five times. What ultimately won the strike for the mill owners—despite the near-total lockdown of Paterson factories—was less their control of the police, courts, local media, and most respectable opinion than their ability to shift orders to their plants across the state line. The Wobblies realized the danger and went beyond oratory to organizing strikes in Pennsylvania towns, but novice unionists were coaxed back to work with modest raises. This allowed owners in Paterson to grind down even the most militant, as they exhausted their savings and credit with store owners. In July the strike fell apart as workers, literally starved into submission, stampeded back to the mills, settling for whatever deal they could get.

"Paterson Silk Strike, IWW Leadership," 1913. From right: William D. "Big Bill" Haywood; Adolph Lessig; Elizabeth Gurley Flynn; Carlo Tresca; Patrick Quinlan. (Wayne State University, Walter P. Reuther Library)

Haywood's health now failed—he'd been involved in multiple strikes at the same time as Paterson's—and since he was dead broke, his supporters took up a collection to pay his doctors' bills. Obituaries were premature—he recovered after a few months of rest—but predictions of the Wobblies' demise were closer to the mark. Though the IWW would retain strength out west and shortly have a last hurrah in New York City, it never recovered from this defeat. Italians, in particular, deserted the syndicalists and jumped on the socialist bandwagon, which was rolling from one victory to another.

THE UNITED BROTHERHOOD OF TAILORS (UBT), a socialist-minded union founded in 1889 by the United Hebrew Trades, was the principal union of Gotham's men's clothing industry. The UBT was eager to emulate the success of the city's ladies' garment workers. But it was held in check by its parent organization, the United Garment Workers (UGW), which the AFL had anointed as the sole national bargaining agent for tailors. Run by and for skilled cutters, who were native born or children of Americanized immigrants, the UGW's top leadership was elitist, nativist, anti-Semitic, and corrupt. It had zero interest in organizing the mass of immigrant tailors in the big cities, partly because the majority of men's clothing was produced in Appalachian factories that turned out huge quantities of standardized, style-free work clothes, like overalls. (New York didn't dominate menswear as it did women's.)

The UBT, which had received a substantial infusion of seasoned Bundist refugees, was chafing under this absentee overlordship, and in May 1911 it began to plan for a citywide general strike of the trade. Facing a fait accompli, and nudged by the UHT, which strongly supported its offspring, the UGW reluctantly gave passive consent. The preparations went on through 1912, with substantial assistance from the UHT, the Socialist Party, the *Jewish Daily Forward*, the Women's Trade Union League, and settlement workers like Lillian Wald. On December 30, 1912, the strike was launched. Over 60,000 workers responded immediately. By mid-January 100,000 men and women had walked out. The leadership stressed above all the need for maintaining discipline and order—this was, strikers were told, "a small social revolution" but "not a riot." Discipline was impressively displayed on January 13, 1913, when 85,000 marched in an immense parade from Rutgers Square to Union Square, red flags admixed with red-white-and-blues, marching bands belting out "The Marseillaise" over and over. Even the police—whom Mayor Gaynor had under tight leash—were impressed by "the orderliness of the crowd."

Fifteen nationalities had a significant presence in the march, and the strike itself, but the great bulk were Jewish (roughly half) and Italian (about a third). The vigorous Italian participation (including a substantial proportion of women) marked a dramatic transformation since 1909, with the strike leadership now embracing Italian socialists like the Sicilian-born brothers Frank and August Bellanca. August, in turn, invited the participation of a friend of his, Fiorello La Guardia. Born in Greenwich Village in 1882, to an Italian father and an Italian Jewish mother, La Guardia had been working since 1907 as an interpreter for Croatian, Italian, and German arrivals at Ellis Island, while studying law nightly at NYU. On getting his degree in 1910, he began representing immigrants threatened with deportation—impoverished Italians referred to him by friends on Ellis Island—and then took on tenants with complaints against landlords, and workers who'd been cheated by bosses. Having made his mark as a people's attorney, he sidled into politics, speaking at fraternal associations, writing for ethnic papers, and joining the Republican Party (as a stalwart of the regulars: he supported Taft, not Teddy, in 1912 and was rewarded with a district captaincy). Still, in December 1912 he plunged into the garment strike, not only bailing out arrestees but marching on picket lines and addressing hundreds of meetings, in both Italian and Yiddish, attired in distinctive cowboy hat and string bow tie, a nod to childhood years spent in Arizona, where his father had been an army bandmaster.

La Guardia was among the many who were enraged when the United Garment Workers leadership, backed not only by Gompers but by the UHT and Abe Cahan as well, tried to short-circuit the strike (which was running low on resources) by coming to an arrangement with the association of large manufacturers, without consulting the rank and file. The deal they cut stopped well short of the agreed-upon demand for union recognition. On March 1 15,000 infuriated UBT militants stormed the *Forward*'s headquarters. (Cahan and the UGW blamed the IWW, but the tailors were self-motivated.) The settlement was repudiated, and the strike lasted three more weeks, with La Guardia, Meyer London, and Jacob Panken negotiating a more satisfactory solution.

But the UBT had had enough; the following year its members broke with the UGW, and a special convention, held in Webster Hall, formed the Amalgamated Clothing Workers of America as an independent union, setting up shop at 32 Union Square East (an office tower at 16th Street to which the ILGWU had moved from its original Waverly Place headquarters). A furious Gompers branded the Amalgamated a renegade and illegitimate entity, but the other Jewish unions, for all their loyalty to the AFL, recognized it as a bona fide organization. It quickly became a powerful new player on the metropolitan labor scene.

For president the Amalgamated chose Sidney Hillman, a Lithuanian-born radical, who in 1903, at age 15, had joined the Bund and embarked on labor organizing and revolutionary work. In 1904 he led a May Day demonstration in Kovno and was arrested. In jail he was brutalized by czarist police and introduced to Marx, Lassalle, Bebel, and Kropotkin by his fellow prisoners. Hillman took part in the great mass strikes of the 1905 Revolution and was jailed again. He became an organizer for the Menshevik wing of the Russian Social Democratic Party, whose members were less inclined than Bundists toward a Jewish nationalism. (They stressed the "worker" in "Jewish worker.") By the time he finally fled the counterrevolution, Hillman was a dedicated labor organizer and political leader.

Arriving in New York in August 1907, in the middle of the panic, unemployed and virtually penniless, he accepted a friend's invitation to go to Chicago, where he found menial work at miserable pay. An activist during a 1910 garment strike, Hillman linked up with members of Chicago's progressive elite. In January 1914 he moved back to Gotham, taking up residence in Wald's Henry Street settlement and taking on the position of chief clerk of the International Ladies' Garment Workers' Union, overseeing grievance procedures established by the Protocol, which were increasingly ignored by small manufacturers and militant workers alike. Months later he was drafted by the Amalgamated, packed with Bundists and Italian Socialists, becoming, at age 28, the youngest head of an international union in the United States. Hillman would set about establishing a position midway between the IWW and AFL, a radical syndicalist and socialist industrial union that would also make concerted efforts to build solid contracts, stable treasuries, and lasting locals.

THE MULTI-YEAR MAELSTROM OF RADICAL ORGANIZING immensely strengthened the complex of institutions affiliated with the Socialist Party. To underscore its heightened visibility on the city's political landscape, it constructed Gotham's first socialist skyscraper. In October 1912 Abe Cahan and his *Jewish Daily Forward* colleagues formally inaugurated their ten-story building at 173–175 East Broadway, across the street from Rutgers Square and Seward Park. Though every inch a conventional Beaux-Arts structure—replete with terra-cotta, marble columns, and stained-glass windows—the bas-reliefs on its façade uniquely featured the figures of Karl Marx, Friedrich Engels, and Ferdinand Lassalle, founder of the first German labor party. This workers' tower, appropriately, rose in competition with a capitalist edifice, the equally Beaux-Arts Jarmulowsky Bank Building, which opened virtually the same day, two blocks away, at Canal and Orchard. Local lore holds that when the Jarmulowsky forces learned the *Jewish Daily Forward* building would overtop their own, they added a fifty-foot cupola, thus winning the class struggle on the Lower East Side skyline. If true, however, it proved a short-lived victory, as the bank went belly up in 1914.

The *Forward*'s was a working building. In 1912 its three new Hoe presses in the basement churned out 132,000 copies of the *Forverts* each day, 150,000 on Sundays; by 1914 it was selling 200,000 daily and rapidly gaining ground on the major metropolitan papers. But the building was far more than a printing plant. It was a major political and cultural center of the city's Jewish socialist and labor movements. Like the United Charities Building up in Gramercy Park, it gathered under one roof a congeries of related and interlocking organizations. Among those to whom it leased out office space were the equally flourishing United Hebrew Trades (in 1909 it had had 5,000 workers assembled in 41 unions, but in 1914 its 111 affiliates claimed a quarter-million members) and the equally bustling Workmen's Circle, which had shot from fewer than 1,000 in 1900 to more than 50,000 by 1914.

The other geographical locus of city socialism was up at Union Square, where the great garment unions were headquartered—both the ILGWU, which was intimately intertwined with the *Forward* complex, and the new Amalgamated, which maintained a certain distance from the Cahan-Hillquit matrix. This vast expansion of organized labor in one of New York's leading industries gave the socialist movement a firm economic base. Adding to this the Rand School, the Intercollegiate Society, benefit societies, local branches, schools, summer camps, choirs, restaurants, theaters, and publications meant that Gotham now had a socialist complex that rivaled those of the largest European socialist parties, except for attaining power at the polls.

Here the Socialist Party continued to lag—political muscle not keeping pace with economic influence. Partly this was the result of its own internal divisions, such as those that led to the split and expulsion of 1913. This loss of membership was partly made up by a shift in party policy concerning the ethnic federations. Finns, Italians, Bohemians, South Slavs, Poles, Scandinavians, and Hungarians had been authorized to form foreign-language federations since 1910 but constrained in their intra-party impact. In 1912, however, the party allowed them to function as autonomous subsections. Joining a federation now brought automatic full membership in the Socialist Party itself.

These entities, newly attractive, brought a nationwide influx of 20,000 before the year was out, and arriving immigrants continued to replace departing American members with increasing speed. The changes wrought were qualitative as well as quantitative, mostly notably in the case of the establishment in July 1912 of the Yiddish-language Jewish Socialist Federation (JSF), whose initiators and the majority of members were Bundists. The JSF was politically more to the left than the *Forward* and the UHT, and more "Jewish" as well, given that the vigorous cultural nationalism of the Bundist intellectuals was still foreign to the Old Guard's traditional cosmopolitanism. But the establishment of new mechanisms for recruiting members beyond the Socialists' traditional constituencies began to enhance the party's performance at the polls.

In 1912 Socialist voters numbered 33,000 (giving Eugene Debs 11 percent of New York's presidential vote). And in the bellwether Lower East Side congressional district, Meyer

London further closed the gap with Tammany's candidate in 1912, appealing to Jews' ethnic loyalty as well as their radical convictions. Then the garment uprisings and JSF support gave him a mass base. And in 1914 ILGWU troops helped send London to Congress, breaking Tammany's grip on Jewish voters.

Citywide possibilities seemed to be opening up as well. In 1913 Charles Edward Russell ran for mayor of New York City on a platform whose planks included a resolution that every foreigner who had been in the country one year, and had declared his intention to become a citizen, be permitted to vote; that property held by religious bodies, or for speculative purposes, no longer be exempt from taxation; that city employees should have the right to strike; that city magistrates be elected; and that women should have the right to vote. Russell tripled the number of Socialist votes garnered in the last mayoral election, boosting the party's percentage from 2 percent to 5 percent, a modest but all things considered a heartening state of affairs.

THE ARMY OF THE UNEMPLOYED

And then the economy lurched downward. During the fall of 1913, the number of people pitched into unemployment rose steadily. By the winter of December 1913–March 1914, the Association for Improving the Condition of the Poor (AICP) estimated 325,000 were jobless. Homelessness soared as well. Social workers compared the resultant suffering to that of the Panic winter of 1907–8, only worse, as it was exacerbated by ferocious weather. Back-to-back snowstorms and below-zero temperatures left a trail of frozen bodies on the city's streets.

A survey of responses to hard times illuminates the political landscape.

Missions, restaurants, and civic-minded groups organized emergency breadlines for immediate relief. In mid-January 1914 the one run by the Bowery Mission (at No. 227) contained at times a thousand hungry men and boys, the line stretching up the Bowery from just above Rivington to just below Houston. On the homeless front, the *New York Evening Mail* raised funds for the relief of families on the verge of eviction.

The big organized charities (like the AICP) found their own resources taxed to the limit, and beyond, but they nevertheless disapproved of such do-gooder measures, fretful that freeloaders might stand on line for hours to snatch an undeserved roll and coffee.

Mayor Mitchel's reform administration, which took power in January 1914, acknowledged the unemployment crisis and accepted that joblessness was "a problem for the city administration." Its proposed solution was to create, in February, a City Bureau for the Unemployed. It undertook to coordinate the work of the 725 licensed job-placement agencies in the metropolis, in order to bring "the manless job and jobless man together." But the problem wasn't inefficient distribution of labor market information. There just weren't enough manless jobs for all the jobless men. And when the bureau trumpeted at the end of March that it had found work for 3,973 of the unemployed, it transpired that 3,646 of these jobs consisted of shoveling snow. Proposals were made for building public works, thus creating good jobs at union wages. Mitchel rejected them, saying, "It is not a function of Government directly to provide employment for those out of work."

The administration was more proactive in responding to homelessness. The Department of Charities doubled the 750-bed capacity of the 1909 Municipal Lodging House on East 25th Street. And while the shelter had well-known shortcomings—bullyings, beatings, thefts, and communicable diseases—as the only port in the storm it was quickly crammed to bursting. For the two-month period of December 1913–January 1914 it housed 93,807, compared to the previous winter's 37,780. Yet when some suggested converting the city's many armories into mass shelters, Charities Commissioner John Kingsbury demurred. "Such action," he argued, "would only bring more unemployed to this city and further complicate the situation." Besides, too much assistance would foster indigence. "Relief, like cocaine, relieves pain," he explained, "but it creates an appetite."

As the Mitchel administration was enamored of social science expertise, it decided to contribute to the conversation about the causes of joblessness by interrogating Municipal Lodging House residents. For two weeks in March 1914, Kingsbury had thirty specialists—ten physicians, ten sociologists, ten psychologists—and a contingent of stenographers, interview 143 subjects. They were asked if they had deserted their wives, or been convicted of a crime. They were required to recite the days of the week forward and backward. They were examined and measured by the doctors. "When the work is finished," Kingsbury promised, "we expect to know the who, the what, and the why of the unemployed problem."

This risible claim was dismissed by, among others, the editors of the *New York Herald*, who pronounced themselves as sick of "sociological investigators" as they were of "professional agitators." But there were in fact investigators (and agitators) who probed "the who, the what, and the why" more deeply and provided more compelling assessments and solutions.

Progressive social scientists, attuned to European developments, argued that inquiries should focus not on the unemployed, but on unemployment. In 1909, William Beveridge had argued this case in *Unemployment: A Problem of Industry*, and in 1911 the British enacted the first unemployment insurance program. This approach crossed the Atlantic and was picked up by the political economists, sociologists, lawyers, social workers, and businessmen reformers gathered in the American Association for Labor Legislation (AALL). When unemployment shot up in late 1913, the AALL issued a call for the First National Conference on Unemployment, which met in Gotham on February 27–28, 1914. Delegates from fifty-nine cities discussed causes, mulled the European solutions, and urged state and federal action. Unemployment insurance was the favored fix, partly as it neatly complemented the other AALL proposed reforms—social insurance programs to deal with industrial accidents, ill health, and old age. The conference also advocated free, state-run employment agencies.

Church activists followed suit. An interdenominational Unemployment Committee of the Churches of New York endorsed the AALL proposals and lobbied Albany for free employment agencies and unemployment insurance.

The city's radicals were divided.

The Socialist Party's platform called for "immediate government relief of the unemployed by the extension of all useful public works." Those hired were to be "engaged directly by the government under a work day of not more than eight hours and at not less than the prevailing union wages." In addition to fashioning a federally underwritten jobs program, Washington should "lend money to states and municipalities without interest for the purpose of carrying on public works," such as building highways and public schools. In addition, socialists and many unionists called for government-run employment agencies, unemployment insurance programs, appropriation of funds to feed and clothe the needy, and, in general, undertaking "such other measures within its power as will lessen the widespread misery of the workers caused by the misrule of the capitalist class."

Anarchists scoffed at such reformism and urged direct action. "The problem of unemployment cannot be solved within the capitalist regime," Alexander Berkman declared. "If the unemployed would realize this, they would refuse to starve; they would help themselves to the things they need. But as long as they meekly wait for the governmental miracle, they will be doomed to hunger and misery."

One who declined to wait was a young man, Frank Tannenbaum, situated politically on the cusp between the anarchists and the Wobblies. Tannenbaum, born in Austrian Galicia in 1893, had been brought to the United States by his family in 1905. His father eked out a living upstate as a subsistence farmer, with Frank as his primary labor supply. In 1906 he ran away to New York City, where he rented a room in a Bowery tenement and supported himself as a dish-washer, an elevator operator, a busboy (at the Stock Exchange Luncheon Club), and a waiter (in which capacity he helped organize the IWW waiters industrial union). In his spare time Tannenbaum attended evening classes at the Ferrer Modern School, came to know Berkman and Goldman, and helped them out with publishing *Mother Earth*. He also got acquainted with Carlo Tresca. In 1913 Tannenbaum lost his busboy position. Unable to find a job and unable to pay the rent, he took to sleeping in flophouses and parks, where he watched "men pick bread out of garbage barrels and wash it under a street pump so that it might be fit to eat."

In January 1914, at a general meeting of all IWW locals to discuss responses to the unemployment crisis, the 21-year-old Tannenbaum piped up with a proposal that he'd worked out with other Ferrer School students. "New York City is full of churches," he explained. "We will march to one of them and go to bed. If they don't like it, they can lock us up and then we can sleep in jail.... We must get some food, too. In this city there is plenty of bread and provisions. We have a right to as much as we can eat." The point of this initiative—in addition to food and floor space—was to insert the unemployed into the conversation about unemployment, as active agents, not passive supplicants.

On the evening of February 27, 1914, the same day on which AALL professionals con-vened their unemployment conference, Tannenbaum led an "army of the unemployed" to the Baptist Tabernacle at 164 Second Avenue at 14th Street, where the men entered during services and demanded shelter. The next night, 600 strong, they entered the Labor Temple, just around the corner at 14th and Second, and received food and lodging. On March 1 they assembled at First Presbyterian, on Fifth Avenue at 12th Street, where they were given twenty-five dollars with which to buy provisions. On March 2, responding to an invitation published in that morning's *World* by the pastor of St. Mark's-in-the-Bouwerie, at Second and 10th, 240 were served bean sandwiches and coffee in the Parish House, with journalists in attendance. Tannenbaum welcomed the presence of the press, saying, "At last we have a chance to let the city know what we want." We're "members of the working class," he explained. "Everything in this city was created by our hands or the hands of our brothers and sisters. We have a right to a share in every house and in every man's loaf of bread. What's more, we are going to make the city give it to us or take it by force.... A hungry man," he added, "knows nothing about law when he is starving."[13]

Addressing his troops, he said, "Men, don't accept charity." What they wanted was work, though not for fifty cents a day, but rather three dollars for an eight-hour day—"union wages and union conditions." Don't go to the Municipal Lodging House, he urged, which aside from being "not fit for a dog" required users to stand in line until one o'clock, then drove them out at four. Don't go to the missions, either, he exhorted: "Don't become men who are converted every night for the sake of a place to sleep."

---

13. Here Tannenbaum drew upon the well-known theology of Cardinal Henry Edward Manning, whom Emma Goldman was fond of quoting. "The obligation to feed the hungry springs from the natural right of every man to life," Manning argued, "and to the food necessary for the sustenance of life. So strong is this natural right that it prevails over all positive laws of property. Necessity has no law, and a starving man has a natural right to his neighbor's bread." In fact, there were no instances of forceful appropriation by Tannenbaum and his men on those snowy nights, no violence or disorder. Though the "army" was showing up at church doors by the hundreds and demanding to be taken in, none of the clerics reported feeling threatened.

Frank Tannenbaum addressing unemployed workers, March 21, 1914. (Bettmann/Getty)

If Tannenbaum was seeking the city's attention, he got it. The churches, by and large, were supportive; in the next frigid weeks, hundreds of the unemployed were given succor—food, shelter, or both—at the Church of the Ascension, St. Luke's (on Hudson Street), St. Paul's Chapel, St. George's (a.k.a. "Morgan's Church"), and Brooklyn's Plymouth Church, whose pastor, Dr. Newell Dwight Hillis, was active (along with John Haynes Holmes, Monsignor D. J. McMahon, and ten other prominent clerics) in organizing the Unemployment Committee of the Churches of New York. Much of the press, however, was rabidly opposed. The *New York Sun* said it was "better to club and shoot" the IWW bands of "vicious outcasts" and "honest dupes," to stop them from taking possession of New York. The *World* called the army "a criminal menace." The *Times* denounced the "defiance of law and order" and urged the police be called in.

Which, on March 4, they were. When Tannenbaum and 300 of his men arrived at St. Alphonsus, a German Catholic church at 312 West Broadway, they were refused entry, and twenty patrol wagons were called in to carry off Tannenbaum and 190 others. Tannenbaum was arrested for "inciting to riot." The charges were later dropped, as even the *Times* admitted the unemployed had been peaceful, but Tannenbaum was found guilty of "unlawful asembly" and sentenced to a year in jail (time he spent reading volumes of Nietzsche, Tolstoy, Kropotkin and Marx, delivered to him by Lincoln Steffens, and leading demonstrations against revolting conditions in the penitentiary.)[14] The police now forbade all further open-air meetings, clubbing and arresting as vagrants Wobbly speakers in Rutgers Square.

---

14. On his release, Tannenbaum wrote a powerful series of exposes for the *Masses*, which cost both the warden and the correction commissioner their jobs.

In response, Goldman and Berkman called for a mass demonstration on March 21 in Union Square, to protest Tannenbaum's incarceration, and accelerate anarchist involvement in the anti-unemployment movement. The socialists held aloof, as did Wobbly chieftains (like Big Bill Haywood), who were wary about the anarchists' penchant for at least verbal violence, a brush with which they did not want to be tarred.[15] Goldman, while militant, counseled a broader and nonviolent campaign. "March down to the Mayor," she cried. "March down to the police. March down to the other city officials. Make them tell you what they are going to do to give you food and shelter. Go to the churches, go to the hotels and restaurants, go to the bakeshops, and tell them they must give you something to keep you from starving." After the rally she, Berkman, and Tresca invited the demonstrators to join them in a march up Fifth Avenue to the Ferrer Center at 64 East 107th Street, where food would be dispensed, and shelter provided for about 250 people that night. Two thousand men and women tromped boisterously but peacefully uptown, jeering "Down with the parasites!" as they passed the Waldorf-Astoria, and "Down with the Church!" as they reached St. Patrick's Cathedral, though they maintained silence when marching by Mount Sinai Hospital, out of respect for the sick. That "incendiary woman," the *Times* fulminated in response, "should be placed under lock and key and left there."

INCENDIARY WOMEN HAD BEEN AT THE FOREFRONT of building a radical, militant, multi-national, and class-conscious movement—both as massed participants powering the great garment strikes and as inspirational and organizational leaders, like Lemlich and Goldman, O'Reilly and Pastor Stokes, Schneiderman and Flynn. They would be equally militant in building a movement to dismantle the multiple barriers blocking the way toward equal rights for women.

---

15. Two days before the assembly, on March 19, the socialists had sponsored a symposium on the unemployment issue. They had just resolved to petition Mayor Mitchel to push for state passage of an unemployment insurance law, when the meeting was invaded and broken up by 300 Wobblies, incensed that while sympathetic clerics had been invited, no IWW protesters or anarchists had been included.

20

Bending Gender

GORKY

On April 10, 1906, Maxim Gorky's ship docked at the North German Lloyd pier in Hoboken. There the famous author was greeted by thousands in a reception so tumultuous that it reminded the *New York Times* of the one accorded Hungarian revolutionary Lajos Kossuth back in 1852. Immensely popular in the States for his writings and his resistance to czarist despotism, Gorky had come to raise money for revolution in Russia. Metropolitan luminaries including Mark Twain and William Dean Howells planned gala receptions, mass meetings, a White House visit.

Gorky was whisked to a suite at the Hotel Belleclaire at 77th and Broadway. For the next few days the city was his. Twain hailed him at a literary stag dinner. He was driven by auto through Central Park, taken to Grant's Tomb, dined at the St. Regis, treated to a circus at Madison Square Garden. A front-page headline read "Gorky Amazed at New York's Greatness."

On Saturday the fourteenth, the *World* bannered a very different story. Acting on a tip from the Czarist Russian embassy (and out of fury that Gorky had granted an exclusive to Hearst's *American*), Pulitzer's paper reported that the woman traveling with the distinguished visitor was not Madame Gorky, but "an actress," one Maria Andreyeva (who was indeed a star of the Moscow Art Theatre as well as a leading figure, with Gorky, in the Lenin-led Bolshevik wing of the Social Democratic Party).

Maxim Gorky, front-row center with moustache, and Mark Twain. Dining at the A Club, 1906. (Granger)

Brutal ostracism followed. The Belleclaire bounced the pair. Gorky and Andreyeva were then checked into the French-themed Lafayette-Brevoort Hotel, downtown on Fifth Avenue between 8th and 9th Streets, supposedly a more sophisticated venue, popular with visiting Europeans. But early that evening the couple was ejected again. They were then transferred to the Rhinelander Apartments just across the street, a seemingly safe harbor, and went out for a night on the town. They returned, after midnight, to find their luggage piled up in the lobby.

The two were finally given refuge at the A Club, virtually next door at 3 Fifth Avenue, between 8th Street and Washington Square. The A Club was a cooperative rooming house, recently established in an old mansion by a collection of socialists and settlement workers. As most were writers of one sort or another, the club was also something of a literary watering hole. (Twain, then living nearby at 21 Fifth, was a frequent visitor.) The residents were also ardent supporters of the 1905 Revolution, and indeed the club was a principal sponsor of Gorky's trip.

Members had gotten advance word from Russia that Gorky would be traveling with Andreyeva and had tried to dissuade him, knowing the temper of the town, but he indignantly refused to reconsider. He had, after all, been living with Andreyeva since he and his wife had separated some years before—amicably but illegally, as the Orthodox Church refused divorces to men in the revolutionary camp—and in Russia theirs was considered a respectable common-law marriage. At first, A Clubbers had managed to convince the New York press to sit on the story, lest they short-circuit what promised to be weeks of juicy high-profile coverage of Gorky's US tour. But the Czarist Russian embassy was bombarding editors with pictures of Gorky's "deserted" wife and child, and the New York *Herald*'s publisher, James Gordon Bennett Jr.—now in his sixties and living in Paris with a young Russian countess—was reported to have ordered an exposé. So Pulitzer went with the story, and the A Clubbers' worst fears were instantly realized.

Doors slammed all over Manhattan, as against a carrier of moral plague. Meetings and dinners were canceled. Twain resigned as Gorky's chief promoter. President Roosevelt refused to see him. In Boston, a Faneuil Hall rally was called off by organizers after they received the "horrid news," lest the pro-revolutionary movement, by association, alienate "all Americans who love decency."

Gorky found shelter at a private home on Staten Island and occupied himself crafting a revenge essay, "City of the Yellow Devil." From the harbor, Gorky wrote, "the city seems like a vast jaw, with uneven black teeth. It breathes clouds of black smoke into the sky and snuffles like a glutton suffering from his obesity." The monstrous metropolis, Gorky fancied, gorged on its citizens. They were sluiced along, via the streets' deep gutters, "somewhere into the heart of the city where, one imagines, there must be a vast bottomless hole, a cauldron or a pan, into which all these people pour and are boiled down into gold."

Having gotten that off his chest, Gorky got out and about, giving talks chiefly to socialist supporters in Brooklyn and Manhattan—including two speeches at Lower East Side theaters backing Morris Hillquit's congressional campaign—and also to leftist rallies in Chicago, Philadelphia, and Boston. Some distinguished intellectuals stood by him. Professor John Dewey and his wife gave a tea party in honor of Mme. Andreyeva at their 431 Riverside Drive apartment, attended (to much tut-tutting) by some of Dewey's Barnard students. And his Columbia colleague sociologist Franklin Giddings wrote a bitter article denouncing Americans for having "morally and socially lynched two distinguished visitors." But by and large the embargo held. *Outlook* magazine deplored Gorky's "disregard for the sacredness of the family." *Harper's Weekly* considered the affair "evidence of the irresponsibility which lurks at the bottom of the mind that is capable of accepting the socialistic programme." And the *Presbyterian* suggested that Americans had best "realize that worse things for Russia might be in store than having a Czar for a ruler." The opprobrium in turn had calamitous consequences for Gorky's fund-raising drive: the hoped-for million-dollar harvest dwindled down to a mere $10,000. When he departed in October 1906 only a handful came to see him off.

Twain, uncomfortable at his role, blamed Gorky for ignoring local mores. "Custom," he argued, "is built of brass, boiler iron, granite," and "facts, reasonings, arguments have no more effect upon it than the idle winds have upon Gibraltar." Rightly or wrongly, he said, "laws are sand, customs are rock. Laws can be evaded and punishment escaped, but an openly transgressed custom brings sure punishment." But Gorky's reception did not signal a moral machinery in good working order. Quite the opposite. By the early twentieth century, traditional gender conventions were in serious disrepair and under serious attack. Gorky's treatment was a skirmish in an emerging war over manners and morals—a nationwide struggle in which New York City would be a crucial battleground.

NEW WOMEN

In the mid-nineteenth century, middle- and upper-class gender ideals had prescribed that men and women occupy separate spheres of action—men running business and politics, women raising children and governing the household. These Victorian ideals were not universally adopted, much less lived up to. But as goals, they achieved a measure of acceptance, particularly among members of their own social circles, in which husbands commonly had enough wealth or income to forgo their wives' earning power, which was in any case limited. Many working-class men also strove to attain "respectability." Craft unionists and socialists alike demanded a "family wage," ample enough to keep their wives at home. Only if their income fell short, which it did for many, would husbands reluctantly acquiesce in sending their daughters and spouses into the workforce.

Over the second half of the nineteenth century, the gap between prescription and practice had grown steadily wider. Middle-class women had gained access to higher education, and then, diplomas in hand, had challenged the formal barriers that had kept the professions—medicine, law, engineering, architecture, business management, college teaching, and the ministry—as male-only preserves. Some women did pass through professional school gateways and on into careers, though ongoing masculine resistance kept their numbers in check. Women had also been contesting the double standard, revising family law, managing economic resources, building female-run institutions, and engaging in politics (despite being barred from the polls).

The twentieth century's opening decades witnessed major developments in Gotham's macro-economy, changes that drew vast numbers of women into the workforce. This quantitative phenomenon was of such magnitude that it wrought a qualitative transformation in the metropolitan gender order—in fact if not yet in ideology.

"Concerning the American Girl: Do you really think, my clerical friend, that the old ideals were better than these?" *Puck*, January 6, 1904. (Library of Congress Prints and Photographs Division)

While women's progress in traditionally all-male professions remained incremental, professions already coded female—notably teaching and nursing—grew rapidly, responding to the immigration-driven boom in school creation and the parallel growth of hospitals and public health care agencies. The opening up of new positions drew in large numbers of public-school-trained daughters of the Anglo, German, and Irish lower middle class.

In a similar way, the creation of skyscraper-headquarters by the proliferating national corporations, and the collateral mushrooming of business service industries, generated a tremendous demand for office workers. Clerical positions had hitherto been a male

RICAN GIRL.
old ideals were better than these?

preserve, but the corporations opted for cheaper female labor. Male holdovers from the old regime were mollified by making them supervisors of the new army of women stenographers, typists, bookkeepers, copyists, file clerks, secretaries, receptionists, and telephone switchboard operators. Female entry into the white-collar workforce was further eased by the fact that many of the new positions were associated with new technologies, ones that hadn't yet been sex-typed. As a result, when the corporations brought in women, men couldn't complain their territory was being invaded. The new technologies quickly assumed the gender of their users—secretaries were called "Miss Remingtons" after the typewriters they used—helping to lock in the job category as female. Giants like Metropolitan Life recruited from the ranks of non-immigrant, unmarried women—successfully, as these jobs usually paid better than factory work, and were considered of higher status. (New hires in the Met Life Tower were dignified as "Metropolitan Belles.") As a result, where in 1880 a negligible number of clerks or bookkeepers had been female, and in 1900 a modest 7 percent of Gotham's working women were employed in such positions, by 1920 their portion had leapt to 22 percent.

The city's flourishing culture industries also opened up multiple opportunities for women workers. Publishing underwent a phenomenal growth. Old family-run institutions swelled in scale, and new entrants crowded into the print marketplace, which collectively produced a torrent of books, newspapers, and magazines (including scores of labor and radical publications). This increased the demand for copy editors, illustrators, reporters, headline writers, ad writers, executive secretaries, and sometimes even literary or newspaper editors. The print boom also generated a demand for copy, and a concomitant willingness to pay freelance writers for features, short stories, poetry, and reviews. The theatrical industry blossomed, with vaudeville, movies, and the legitimate stage providing work for bevies of singers, actresses, comics, chorus girls, dancers, costumers, and makeup artists. The fashion industry created jobs for ad writers, store buyers (checking out the latest Parisian styles), designers (the Society of American Fashions was formed in 1912), editors of fashion magazines, and proprietors or employees of import firms, millinery shops, dressmaking houses, and cosmetic companies.

Sales and service positions surged with the enormous expansion of department stores and retail outlets. Female recruits flocked in, despite wages being low and work conditions difficult, because wages were somewhat higher and conditions somewhat better than in manufacturing, and pink collars commanded somewhat greater respect than did blue ones. Waitressing slots soared, too, as boardinghouses (which had served meals) gave way to rooming houses (no meals, no kitchenettes), sending throngs through the doors of lunchroom chains (Child's,

Remington opened to women the doors of business life

"Remington Opened to Women the Doors of Business Life," ca. 1911. (Hagley Museum and Library)

Dennett's, Horn and Hardart). These spread rapidly throughout the city, relying on waitresses rather than the traditional (and better paid) waiters.[1]

Huge numbers labored in the manufacturing sector—by 1910 27 percent of New York State's industrial labor force was female. Women were especially prominent in the garment industry, but many others held down light assembly and operative jobs—artificial-flower making, box making, confectionary dipping, bookbinding—a response to steeply rising demand for consumer goods.

The transfer of household tasks (baking bread) to commercial concerns (mammoth bread factories) continued apace. Functions coded as wife-like, such as cleaning, were increasingly provided at an industrial level. Steam laundries hired women to wash and iron for private households and commercial-scale enterprises such as hotels. Charwomen scrubbed floors in offices and theaters, work that was arduous and ill paid. And sex in the patriarchal household was supplemented by professional sex workers housed in apartments and hotels.

The one occupational stratum that shriveled was live-in maids, another instance of the exodus of labor from the home. The percentage of New York City women wage-earners engaged in paid household labor (servants and laundresses) dropped from 32.7 percent in 1900 to 12.9 in 1920. In 1900 there were 141 servants and 22 laundresses per 1,000 Gotham families; by 1920 the numbers had shrunk to 66 and 8. Given the plethora of new employment opportunities, white women were able to flee domestic servanthood, which they found degrading (subject to petty tyranny and sexual harassment) and constraining (leaving them with virtually no time of their own). Second-generation Irish, German, and Scandinavian girls refused to follow in the footsteps of their first-generation forbears, for whom service had been an acceptable entry-level job. Immigrant Jewish, Polish, and Italian women were equally disinclined to don a maid's uniform. Black women, given their drastically narrower range of employment opportunities, perforce occupied a steadily increasing share of domestic labor's steadily declining ranks. A complement of servants became the prerogative of wealthy families, while middle-class women, for the first time in generations, were forced to do the bulk of their own housework, and raise children without full-time help.

AS YOUNG WORKING WOMEN SPENT MORE AND MORE TIME outside the household, they began to feel increasingly at home in the wider city. They rode the streetcars to their jobs, ate out in lunchrooms, went shopping. And after a day in the factory, shop, office, or department store, they headed out into the night, ready to sample the delights on offer in Gotham's commercial entertainments.

Such forays were possible because they now had a little money in their purses. How *much* money varied with their income and with their families' class, race, ethnicity, and personal finances. Some girls turned over their pay envelopes to their parents unopened. Others negotiated for what percentage they could keep for personal use. Others still, made enough to leave the family nest altogether, moving into cheap rooming houses, or into apartment buildings for single working women, like the Windemere on 57th and Ninth.

If working-class parents worried about their daughters slipping away from daytime parental or community supervision, they fretted all the more about their evening excursions, watching them sally out, dolled up in fancy dresses, costume jewelry, cosmetics, and elaborate

---

1. In 1898, the Child brothers, ready for aggressive expansion, incorporated the Childs Unique Dairy Company, with a capitalization of $1 million and the stated intention to "establish and operate restaurants in New York City and elsewhere." Several officers of Standard Oil were investors in the chain.

pompadours. Maidenly decorum was definitely not the order of the night. Intermingling with men was. "If you want to get any notion took of you," observed one working girl, "you gotta have some style about you." Unchaperoned couples on prearranged dates or on-the-spot pickups did the Grizzly Bear in dance halls, took in risqué music hall shows, cavorted in the back rows of nickelodeons, climbed into Coney Island rides that sent girls' skirts flying, played kissing games at social clubs, and engaged in more vigorous forms of intercourse with the opposite sex. The jokes told at these venues, one snoop reported, contained "unmistakable hints of things indecent," and the songs were "suggestive of everything but what is proper." Then there was what was up on screen. As one whimsical newspaper reported: "For the first time in the history of the world it is possible to see what a kiss looks like. . . . Scientists say kisses are dangerous, but here everything is shown in startling directness. . . . The real kiss is a revelation. The idea has unlimited possibilities."

The role cash played in all this was particularly worrisome to some reformer observers. Given their lower incomes, women might be able to come up with carfare or the entrance fee to a dance hall, but they relied on men to pick up the tab for drinks and tickets. Some men assumed they were entitled to sexual favors in return, and some women were prepared to entertain the idea, if they liked the guy. Conversely, one investigator observed, those who had "puritanic notions" fared ill. But most thought the notion that "treating" was a form of prostitution was wrong-headed. As one waiter at a restaurant with a dance floor observed, "Girls could be gotten here, but they don't go with men for money, only for [a] good time." Premarital chastity and circumspect behavior were far from passé, though many working girls hewed to a more relaxed definition of respectability, one that included engagement in premarital sexual activity.

A similar pushing at the boundaries of the gender order followed shortly in the ranks of among middle-class women. Like chicks pecking their way out of confining shells, youngsters edged their way into previously forbidden venues—restaurants, cabarets, and dance halls. Their mothers began to find wifehood and motherhood not as fulfilling as *their* mothers had. With the household no longer the sole source of identity and power, they questioned traditional virtues of submission and sacrifice and asexuality. Indeed, the ideal of sexual restraint began to seem harmful, while sexual indulgence claimed more cultural cachet.

Middle-class "New Women"—a term that began to gain currency in the mid-1890s—increasingly sought greater personal satisfaction from married life, and their unwillingness to tolerate unsatisfactory unions contributed to rising divorce rates. Some refused to marry at all. By 1910, though 90 percent of all US women were married, more than half the graduates of women's colleges were not. Alumnae who did tie the knot did so later and had fewer children (or none at all). Middle-class fertility rates in general did not drop sharply, but they did continue their century-long downward glide. In big cities like New York, perhaps two-thirds of white middle-class families had no more than two children, and roughly 15–20 percent were childless.

The emergence of the New Woman and the "bachelor girl" did not escape public notice. It was a social phenomenon, not just a statistical one. Reams of magazine features and popular romances, often written *by* New Women, dwelt on the new feminine restlessness and limned the women who longed to work, to have careers. Such challenges to the inherited gender order, in preachment and practice, were painfully palpable to cultural conservatives.

BACKLASH

In 1905, the year before Gorky's visit, President Roosevelt sounded the alarm. In a series of shrill speeches, he attacked middle-class New Women for self-indulgently pursuing careers and failing to breed enough babies. This perceived rebellion against motherhood, their primary social responsibility, disturbed a commander in chief then embroiled in the Philippines. If the United States was to attain imperial supremacy, TR believed, it had to win "the warfare of the cradle." America's women, the moral equivalent of soldiers, had a "duty" to spawn large broods. Shirkers stood condemned of "viciousness, coldness, shallow-heartedness."

Poor breeders were also slackers in a demographic war at home. Yankees were being outbred by fecund ethnics; they were committing "race suicide." Families of "better stock" should raise at least six children. Birth-dodgers should be made "the object of contemptuous abhorrence by healthy people."

Roosevelt firmly believed that the altruistic female world of home and family was an essential counterweight to the competitive, selfish male world of business and politics. "The whole fabric of society rests upon the home," as he put it. If women abandoned their roles as moral custodians, they might bring down not just a class, or an empire, but civilization itself.

Those like Roosevelt who feared the old gender order was either collapsing or mutating in monstrous directions set out to shore it up, to reverse the tide of change by exhortation, and by an expansion of moral policing and vigilantism, of which the brouhaha over Gorky and Andreyeva was a part. In 1905 New York's Committee of Fourteen had been set up to stamp out the brothel, that escape hatch for men that threatened the family, and it was in 1906, the year the Russian couple were checked into and shoved out of the Belleclaire, that the committee obtained passage of a law requiring hotels be declared prostitute-free before obtaining a liquor license. It was in 1905 that Dr. Prince Albert Morrow organized the New York Society of Sanitary and Moral Prophylaxis to combat the spread of venereal disease, and it was in 1906 that this initiative backfired, as stories about the syphilis and gonorrhea epidemics were *themselves* considered indecent. And it was in 1906, with Gorky still in town, that Stanford White's murder led to another "moral lynching," though the victim was the dead man, not his killer, and White's serial seduction of young women was a far more serious offense than any committed by the writer.

All this furor over sex and morals gave new heart to Anthony Comstock. Now in his sixties, he and his Society for the Suppression of Vice had been zealously throttling all public discussion of sexual matters for three decades. In the new century, surfing the backlash, he expanded his reach from pornography to high art. In August 1906, with Gorky still on the scene (though consigned to Coventry by polite society), Comstock arrested the 19-year-old receptionist of the Art Students League of New York (ASL) on 57th Street. She herself was impeccably respectable, but she gave him a free catalog that contained three images of nudes. He then seized all 2,500 copies of the issue. In an early warning sign that he was falling out of step with a substantial portion of middle-class opinion, many in the press cracked wise about his latest crusade. Stories made sarcastic reference to "the Purifier" and countered his accusations of obscenity with contrary readings from art experts, including the head of the Metropolitan Museum. Comstock gave a bit of ground, saying that while allowing the catalog "in the home, where it may suggest impure thoughts," was unthinkable and punishable, nevertheless, if "they keep their nude pictures in the studios, where they belong, we shall not molest them." His comment on a visit to the Art Students League's galleries suggested that even such a sanctum might yet prove insufficiently sacred to keep him at bay. He'd been aghast to see there "young people enjoying the pictures of two unclothed human beings." ASL students struck back, hanging the vice hunter in effigy and lampooning him in sketch and sculpture. But Comstock still had his supporters—the *New York Times* agreed such material shouldn't be available through the mail—and he still had

Insignia, New York Society for the Suppression of Vice. (Granger)

the law on his side. (It was, after all, *his* law.) In the end, to get him to drop the charges, the ASL was forced to burn the books.[2]

This backlash against deserters from traditional values—and the treatment accorded Gorky should be understood in this context—rolled on during the next few years. In 1908 came Belle Lindner Israels's campaign to sanitize dance halls, in the name of protecting women from possible exploitation; hyper-attuned to the possible dangers of commercial entertainment venues, she missed the liberatory dimension that made them so attractive. And 1909 marked the beginning of the moral panic over white slavery, the widespread fear that women were being seduced or kidnapped into brothels around town or sold abroad. Again, while some sex trafficking occurred, its extent was wildly overstated, partly due to anxiety over shifting sexual mores, partly perhaps to scare venturesome daughters back home.

There were nightmares, too, about the ability of new employment opportunities to weaken or even sever marital ties and lead wives, not just daughters, to join the exodus from the household, leaving the patriarch to his own devices. In a 1909 article, Columbia psychology professor James McKeen Cattell argued that women working "away from home, which is such a marked development of modern and especially of American conditions, obviously tends to prevent marriage, to limit the number of children and to break up the family." Worse: should married women come to "prefer the money they can earn and the excitement

---

2. Comstock had sufficient clout to make even J. P. Morgan think twice about crossing him. In 1906 Morgan backed off buying and importing Degas's *Le Viol* (The Rape), explaining that it "would be open to objections from the Comstockians, and that we ought not at present to face that particular music."

they can find in outside employment to the bearing and rearing of children," they would be in a position to "conveniently leave their husbands should it so suit their fancy."

IN 1909, ALL THESE PANICKED DEFENDERS of a weakened regime encountered something new, an articulate assault on the premises and proponents of the old gender order. The inchoate disaffection of hundreds of thousands who had voted with their dancing feet now gained a voice.

The voice belonged to Emma Goldman, anarchist analyst of the Victorian gender order, who began by arguing that "Victorian" was a misnomer, off target by roughly 200 years. What dissenters were up against was "Puritanism."

On May 24, 1909, Goldman gave a talk at the Café Boulevard, at 10th Street and Second Avenue. It was packed with a capacity crowd composed of members of the Sunrise Club (a discussion group), and a substantial contingent of the New York Police Department, armed with nightsticks, ready to break up the anarchist's lecture as they had her talk on Ibsen the day before. She began by taking George Bernard Shaw to task, though he was a favorite author of hers, for a remark he'd made after Comstock had alerted the New York police to the content of his play *Mrs. Warren's Profession*, the latest "filthy production" from "this Irish smut dealer." Shaw had riposted that "Comstockery is the world's standing joke at the expense of the United States. Europe likes to hear of such things. It confirms the deep-seated conviction of the Old World that America is a provincial place, a second-rate country-town civilization after all." Goldman quite agreed with Shaw's attack on what the writer had called the "Puritanism of the Comstocker." But she thought it was a bit much—indeed was "sheer British jingoism"—to point to America as the homeland of Puritanic provincialism. It was quite true "that our life is stunted by Puritanism, and that the latter is killing what is natural and healthy in our impulses," yet it was equally true that "it is to England that we are indebted for transplanting this spirit on American soil."

She then embarked on a historical exegesis of Puritanism—"its reign of terror in England during the sixteenth and seventeenth centuries, destroying and crushing every manifestation of art and culture"; and the establishment in the New World by the Pilgrims of *Mayflower* fame of a "reign of Puritanic tyranny and crime," enforced by "the ducking-stool and whipping-post." Contemporary Puritans no longer employed the thumbscrew and lash, Goldman allowed, but they had no need for instruments of torture given that Comstock—"the autocrat of American morals"—had established a "system of espionage" that "puts to shame the infamous Third Division of the Russian secret police." Like a thief in the night, "he sneaks into the private lives of the people, into their most intimate relations." The "almost limitless capacity of Puritanism for evil is due to its intrenchment behind the State and the law. Pretending to safeguard the people against 'immorality,' it has impregnated the machinery of government and added to its usurpation of moral guardianship the legal censorship of our views, feelings, and even of our conduct." Clearly, "the privacy of the mails, in fact, our most intimate tastes, are at the mercy of this inexorable tyrant."

Women were the biggest victims. "Absolute sexual continence is imposed upon the unmarried woman," a suppression of "natural sex desires" that produces "neurasthenia, impotence, depression and a great variety of nervous complaints." Married women, on the other hand, were supposed "to bear children, irrespective of weakened physical condition or economic inability to rear a large family." Women who refused—contraception being absolutely prohibited ("the very mention of the subject is considered criminal")—were accordingly forced to undergo abortions, which, "given the secrecy in which this practice is necessarily shrouded," could be deadly. Puritanism "exacts thousands of victims to its own stupidity and hypocrisy." Not even in the domain of the czar, she concluded, was "personal liberty daily outraged to the extent that it is in America, the stronghold of the Puritanic eunuchs."

Goldman's voice was a powerful and coherent one. Reframing the conversation, she called to the dock not the New Women but the male English Puritans and their Anglo-American descendants (who were her real targets). Coming out of a dramatically different cultural tradition, and drawing politically on a libertarian version of anarchism (with American as well as European roots), her opinions were strongly grounded, and she had the means of propagating them, via her widely read magazine (*Mother Earth*) and her annual nationwide lecture tour. The question was, would there actually be a conversation, or would the forces of order succeed again in silencing her and other voices of protest?

There would indeed be a conversation over the next few years, principally because Goldman would be joined in tackling the wobbling gender order by a cadre, then a crowd, of cultural rebels dedicated (among other things) to contesting "Puritanism" and all its works. A community would emerge, spatially rooted in its own enclave, a secured base of operations to which would flock recruits from around the country. This community of cultural activists would call for jettisoning old gender constraints and forging new ways for women and men to be together. These reformers would be dedicated not to slamming doors, but to throwing them open, and in the name of freedom of speech and the emancipation of women they would directly combat the use of the state to support the old order. Like the movement for sexual revanchism, the movement for sexual revolution would flourish in New York City.

IT TAKES A VILLAGE

Before there was an enclave, there was the idea of an enclave—a liberated zone from which assaults could be launched against the surrounding status quo. The model was "Bohemia," a name that had gotten attached to the Sorbonne student quarter on the Left Bank of the Seine in Paris, when artists, writers, musicians, actors, and journalists clustered there in the 1840s. Bohemians were mostly young and mostly poor; their cultural style was unconventional, their cultural politics oppositional.[3] After the community was celebrated in Henri Murger's collection of short stories *Scènes de la vie de bohème* (1851), the term was picked up in 1850s New York—already into keeping up with cultural developments in European capitals (not just parks and Crystal Palaces). It was applied mainly to the habitués (including Walt Whitman) of the rathskeller Charles Pfaff opened in 1855 at 653 Broadway, just north of Bleecker Street.

This mini-movement petered out in the 1860s. But in the 1890s bohemianism was again the rage in Europe and, perforce, in Gotham, too. George du Maurier's novel *Trilby* (serialized in *Harper's* in 1894) enthralled New Yorkers with its account of Parisian studio life; Robert W. Chambers, a Brooklyn-born, Beaux-Arts trained illustrator, wrote about Left Bank living in *In the Quarter* (1894); Clyde Fitch's play *Bohemia* brought Latin Quarter tales to Broadway in 1896; Puccini's *La Bohème* (1896) captivated Metropolitan Opera–goers in 1900.

Such bohemianism as New York had yet mustered wasn't rooted in a single place. In the 1890s various swarms hived around disparate nightspots. Midnight parties at Luchow's, a German restaurant at East 14th and Irving Place, attracted the circle of musicians, writers,

---

3. They were called bohemians because of their lifestyles' supposed resemblance to that of wandering Gypsies, the Romany people who were erroneously supposed to have come from Bohemia.

painters, and newsmen gathered around James Huneker, the city's most multi-faceted cultural critic, who reviewed European and local musical, theatrical, and literary developments for the *New York Sun* and assorted magazines. Others were aficionados of the French-themed Mouquin's, at Sixth Avenue and 28th Street. Still others clustered in gathering places just south of Washington Square, like Maria's, at 146 MacDougal, between West 3rd and 4th Streets, where in 1892 Marietta Da Prato had opened a boardinghouse with a convivial cellar restaurant. Patrons offered one another music, poetry, monologues, and repartee, accompanied by Italian food and red wine; one novel described the scene as "quite two hundred Bohemians in one huge lump."

The whole enterprise was more than a bit self-conscious and shallow, vulnerable to spoofs like Howells's *The Coast of Bohemia* (1893). But the fin-de-siècle craze was also a sign that genteel culture was faltering and alternate sensibilities stirring.

Then, in the early 1900s, New Yorkers discovered to their amazement that a real Latin Quarter had materialized in Manhattan, a community packed with literary societies, theaters, lecture halls, discussion groups, and cafés where students, artists, scholars, and writers argued passionately late into the night about philosophy, literature, and politics. This was no secondhand imitation of a legendary Paris, however, but the supremely authentic Lower East Side. And the denizens debating the relative merits of Gorky, Zola, Tolstoy, Gogol, Chernyshevsky, and Whitman, or arguing vigorously over anarchism, socialism, Zionism, and free love, were not wannabe bohemians but Russian Jews.

The "discovery" of this new Lower East Side, largely unknown to the wider city, was due in considerable degree to a series of organized expeditions commissioned by Lincoln Steffens. In 1897 Steffens assumed the post of city editor at the ancient *New York Daily Commercial Advertiser* (1797), a paper seemingly at long last on its last legs. He set out to refurbish it by exploring Gotham in a way that would allow his middle-class readers to see the sprawling metropolis with fresh eyes. To do so, he needed reporters who could vividly describe "the beauty in the mean streets of the hard, beautiful city." Eschewing old-school reporters, Steffens hired a crew of Ivy League graduates, particularly from Harvard, who'd been recommended by their English professors as people who knew how to *write*.

His first pick, Hutchins Hapgood, proved an inspired choice. Hapgood hailed from Alton, Illinois, where his father was an affluent manufacturer. From 1889 to 1892 he studied at Harvard, then got a master's there in English, did graduate work in Berlin, and taught English at Chicago before signing on with Steffens in 1897. Disdaining "the limitations of respectability," Hapgood plunged into the city's underworld, writing perceptive and uncondescending pieces about criminals, prostitutes, and Bowery bums.

Increasingly he turned his attention to the Lower East Side, thanks in large part to another sterling Steffens hire, Abe Cahan, who in 1897 had left his post at the *Jewish Daily Forward*. Cahan, too, was assigned to roaming the larger city, but he also directed Steffens's and Hapgood's attention to the revolutionary developments in his home quarter. The paper's only Jew began ushering his Anglo-Protestant colleagues into Yiddish theaters and squiring them around the coffeehouses, translating, explaining, in effect constructing a portal between two dramatically different worlds. Not all residents looked kindly on these visitations. One Romanian Jewish writer, Konrad Bercovici, who was entranced by the Lower East Side and given to introducing outsiders to local venues, roused the ire of a *Forward* writer: "He brings his friends to look at us as if we were animals in a zoo. Let him get a job with a sight-seeing car and wear the uniform and cap of a guide."

Hapgood (and Cahan) developed a way of seeing that broke drastically with the conventions that had governed such reporting since Riis had laid them down in his *How the Other Lives* (1890). In Riis's model—itself descended from the sunshine/shadow literary tradition—the intrepid reporter ventured into dangerous or exotic terrains to bring back evidence of the residents' poverty and squalor and ignorance, with the benevolent aim of rousing comfortable readers to political action on behalf of the downtrodden. The downtrodden themselves were depicted as easy-to-grasp stereotypes, not far removed from vaudeville caricatures.

Hapgood, however, provided respectful individual portraits of Jewish peddlers, sweatshop tailors, street hustlers, religious scholars, and members of the "educated class of Ghetto women"—lawyers, doctors, and authors—who believed women should be on the same footing as men. And he sought to convey the neighborhood's stunning level of intellectual attainment and cultural sophistication. By 1902, when he collected his pieces in *The Spirit of the Ghetto*, Hapgood was comparing the Lower East Side—with its "excitement in ideas and an enthusiastic energy for acquiring knowledge"—to Renaissance Florence. The notion of bringing the blessings of civilization to the natives never entered his head. Quite the opposite, he saw the newcomers not as objects of pity but agents of redemption. He hoped their vigorous Russian culture might reinvigorate New York's tired literary establishment, still mired in the English and French traditions Gotham's elite had favored for at least a century.[4] Steffens himself was infatuated with the Lower East Side. Praising Jewish immigration as the great hope of New York, he told his readers he considered himself "almost a Jew." He nailed a mezuzah on his office door, and every year on Yom Kippur spent the whole twenty-four hours fasting and visiting synagogues around the city.

STILL, ADMIRABLE THOUGH THE LOWER EAST SIDE BOHEMIA MIGHT BE, it belonged to others. Those (chiefly Anglo–Protestants) who were attracted to the notion of an enclave community needed something of their own. The A Club was a step in that direction. Established in the wake of the 1905 Revolution, it had deliberately opted for proximity to the roiling Lower East Side scene. Helen Todd, the wealthy settlement worker who bankrolled the purchase, said they took the house at 3 Fifth Avenue "because it is only a short distance from the 'ghetto.'" The proximity was political as well as physical. The members were deeply involved with the Russian cause, and functioned as something of an American press bureau for visiting revolutionaries, most notably Gorky.

The club was both a political and social community, recalled resident Mary Heaton Vorse: "It was the first time," she wrote, that "I had been in a large group of like-minded people who questioned the system under which they lived." Everyone was "a Liberal, if not a Radical—and all for Labor and the Arts." Most of the women who lived at the A Club between 1906 and 1910 participated in actions by the Women's Trade Union League.

The cooperative living arrangements were also unusual—the club housed both singles and married couples, and hosted an informal running salon, with artists and writers constantly dropping by, along with visiting radical celebrities, like labor organizer Mother Jones.

---

4. One had to be open to the possibilities, of course; some were led to water but refused to drink. When in 1906 Yiddish theater luminary Jacob Gordin took Henry James on a tour of Lower East Side cafés, where patrons spoke in accented, ungrammatical English, James considered the venues to be "torture-rooms of the living idiom." This "Hebrew conquest of New York," he felt certain, would permanently maim the language. James did admit that the intermingling of tongues might produce an "'ethnic' synthesis"—the "Accent of the Future"—which "may be destined to become the most beautiful on the globe and the very music of humanity." But it wouldn't be the English he deployed in his novels.

Vorse fondly remembered "the mutual kindness and the gaiety of our household." It was, she felt, "a completely successful and civilized experiment in communal living."

The A Club, half a block north of Washington Square, would prove a stepping-stone into Greenwich Village, the neighborhood that would emerge as New York's Bohemia.

SINCE WINNING EXEMPTION FROM THE GRID BACK IN 1818, Greenwich Village had maintained its independent ways. Manhattan's northward development, balked by the area's tangled streets, had flowed around and past it, leaving behind a quiet backwater. But by the turn of the twentieth century each of the area's four predominant communities was undergoing transformation.

The most dynamic was the Italian colony south of Washington Square. It had long been a modest enclave of northern Italians, particularly immigrants from Genoa, but in the 1890s and 1900s, southern Italians arrived by the thousands. They crowded into the five-and-six story tenement buildings that rapidly replaced the one- and two-family homes on Bleecker, Thompson, and Sullivan. And they went to work in the commercial and industrial establishments that sprang up—notably factories producing clothing, boxes, candy, and artificial flowers. Our Lady of Pompeii, the Italian-language parish founded in 1892, was centered in a church of the same name at 210 Bleecker Street, under the leadership of Father Antonio Demo. The church had originally been built in 1836 for the Unitarian Universalists, then purchased in 1883 by the African American Roman Catholic congregation of St. Benedict the Moor, which sold it to the Italian congregation of Pompeii, which took possession in 1898.[5]

The church's peregrination mirrored a larger transition—from Little Africa to Little Italy. The local black community, which dated back to Dutch days, had grown by migration from lower Manhattan before the Civil War, then from southern states after the end of slavery. As late as the turn of the century, approximately 1,200 blacks lived on West Village streets and alleys near and along lower Sixth Avenue, or on South Village streets in or adjacent to the Minettas (Lane and Street). And in 1900 their flagship houses of worship still remained in place: Abyssinian Baptist at 166 Waverly Place and Mother Zion at 351 Bleecker. But blacks were on the march north to the Tenderloin and San Juan Hill—"The ambitious Negro has moved uptown," one observer noted—and the two churches joined the exodus in 1904 and 1905, respectively.

The Irish community—descendants of the famine generation and post–Civil War immigrants—remained in situ, west of Sixth Avenue between Leroy and West 14th Streets. It was still largely a working-class population—truck drivers, longshoremen, factory workers, blacksmiths, and day laborers, along with female seamstresses and domestic servants—but it included a stratum of professionals and small businessmen, the classes connected to the masses by county societies, Tammany clubs, and the Catholic Church, particularly St. Joseph's on Sixth Avenue.

Many of the wealthy Anglo-Protestant patricians who lived in the sumptuous town houses that lined Washington Square North and several blocks of lower Fifth Avenue—dismayed by the arrival of tenements, factories, and Italians—gathered up their churches

---

5. When Mary Simkhovitch opened Greenwich House at 26 Jones Street in 1902, the largest ethnic group on the block was Irish American, about 40 percent. Another 25 percent came from other Western European countries, mainly Germany, France, and England. African Americans and Italians were found in almost equal numbers, about 12 percent each. The remaining 10 percent or so of Jones Streeters were either third-generation Americans or immigrants from Liberia, Algeria, Hungary, Turkey, Russia, China, and the West Indies.

and fled to newer elite districts above 14th Street. But a substantial number of substantial New Yorkers stayed put, among them Robert de Forest and his wife, Emily Johnston de Forest (No. 7 Washington Square North); Mayor George B. McClellan Jr., who lived next door at No. 8; Serena Rhinelander at No. 14; and William Rhinelander Stewart at No. 17. For their part, the Episcopalians of the Church of the Ascension refused to abandon their Richard Upjohn Gothic Revival building on Fifth Avenue at 10th Street. Ascension even attempted to bridge the divisions between its patrician parishioners (nearly 20 percent of whom were in the *Social Register*) and their multi-ethnic proletarian neighbors. For three years (1907–10), Ascension's social gospel minister, Percy Stickney Grant, ran an open discussion forum, which indeed drew enthusiastic working-class attendance. But the participants often expressed socialist views, which upset the vestrymen (who included several millionaires, notably August Belmont Jr.), and they put an end to it.

IT WAS TO THE SPACE SURROUNDED BY THESE TIGHT-KNIT COMMUNITIES—a middle-class residential district that lay between Washington and Sheridan Squares—that newcomers began trickling in from around the country during the 1910s. Most were young, white, and Protestant men and women of middle-class status and modest (or occasionally sizable) means, college grads disaffected from Victorian values and life in the provinces, people who saw themselves as a class apart, in need of a place apart. For them, all signs pointed to New York City.

Gotham seemed the preeminent site of modern possibilities, the perfect place from which to revolt against a century. It was the dynamic nucleus of the corporate revolution, pulsing with wealth and power. A cosmopolis, teeming with foreign cultures seemingly more vital than desiccated Anglophilia. A radical city, bustling with socialists, unionists, progressives, anarchists—and gender reformers like Emma Goldman. A literary and artistic marketplace and hub of the culture and head of the publishing industries, wherein they might find employment as writers, artists, and journalists—as "intellectuals," able to live by their wits and talents.

Within Gotham, Greenwich Village seemed the perfect greenhouse for would-be rebels. A small-town community in the skyscraper metropolis. Manageable, not alienating. Reportedly receptive to "bohemian" experiments with new ways of living. It was off the moral and physical grid. As Floyd Dell, one of the pioneers, recalled, "Where now the tide of traffic beats, / There was a maze of crooked streets; / The noisy waves of enterprise, / Swift-hurrying to their destinies, / Swept past this island paradise: / Here life went to a gentler pace, / And dreams and dreamers found a place."

The newcomers were also drawn by the light of Washington Square, the charm of secluded cul-de-sacs, the Jefferson Market Courthouse on Sixth Avenue, the dozens of bistros and bars, and above all the cheap rents as the neighborhood went down-market. Handsome town houses were converted to boardinghouses. Stables in MacDougal Alley and Washington Mews that had serviced north-side mansions became studios. Run-down row houses were partitioned into cold water flats.

What the newcomers would create here would be a space whose name would become—as were so many locales in New York—inextricably paired with a particular form of political, cultural, or commercial activity: Union Square with radicalism, Gramercy Square with progressive reform, Wall Street with moneymaking, Times Square with commercial culture, the Tenderloin with sin and ragtime, Fifth Avenue with millionaires and department stores. These names—trumpeted by Gotham's media megaphones—resonated far and wide beyond the city's borders. And now "Greenwich Village" would be added to the list as a locus of cultural and gender rebellion, and its fame would in turn attract other like-minded rebels to join the movement. Hutchins Hapgood, a participant observer in the process, suggested that "when the world began to change, the restlessness of women was the main cause of the development called Greenwich Village, which existed not only in New York but all over the country."

COUNTERCULTURE

The rebels arrived one by one.

One of the earliest was an exemplary New Woman, Mary Heaton Vorse. Born into a wealthy Amherst, Massachusetts, family, Vorse, after a sojourn at a Paris art school and a year at the Art Students League, sought work as a commercial illustrator, then turned to writing fiction about bachelor girls for *McClure's*, *Scribner's*, and *Harper's*. She lived first at 210 West 4th Street (across from Sheridan Square), and later on Waverly Place (one block from Washington Square). Both her publishing career and attraction to the Greenwich Village scene were boosted by her husband's connections to Lincoln Steffens's *Commercial Advertiser* network. Albert Vorse, whom Heaton married in 1898, was a close friend of Hutchins Hapgood, who was then living at the Benedick (an upscale bachelor hotel at 80 Washington Square East), and of Hapgood's wife-to-be, Neith Boyce, the only female reporter on the *Commercial Advertiser* staff. Boyce, who was publishing nonfiction magazine articles on the bachelor girl phenomenon, was then living in a tiny room at the Judson Hotel, on the south side of Washington Square. Vorse, who would later reside in the A Club for a time before returning to Sheridan Square, went on to become a labor reporter after she covered the Lawrence strike for *Harper's Weekly* in 1912. She considered herself part of the army of New Women who worked outside the home. "More and more and more of us are coming all the time," she believed, "and more of us will come until the sum of us will change the customs of the world."

Journalism was the mainstay of many of her successors. Djuna Barnes moved to Gotham from Cornwall-on-Hudson in 1912, and to Greenwich Village in 1915, having found work at the *Brooklyn Daily Eagle*, and then became a reporter-about-town, penning interviews, reviews, features, and short fiction for nearly every newspaper in New York.

Susan Glaspell, daughter of a Davenport, Iowa, hay farmer and public school teacher, worked for a hometown paper, and after college combined journalism with fiction writing for *Harper's*, *Munsey's*, and the *Ladies' Home Journal*. She moved to Chicago, composed her first novel in 1909, and in 1913 moved to Greenwich Village with her husband, George Cram Cook.

The radical press offered another support system. Dorothy Day, born in Brooklyn Heights in 1897, relocated with her family to San Francisco in 1904 and after the 1906 earthquake moved on to Chicago's South Side. In 1916 the family moved back to New York, where her father, a newspaperman, had gotten a job on the *Morning Telegraph*. She too wanted a job in journalism, and also—she was now 18—to get out of the family apartment. She wanted "to go on picket lines, to go to jail, to write, to influence others and so make my mark on the world," she later recalled. Day landed a spot on the Socialist Party's *New York Call* by proposing to live in Gotham as a single woman, on five dollars a week, and then write up her experience. The editor scoffed—though as Day pointed out, lots of waitresses and factory girls were doing just that—but said if she could pull it off for a month he'd hire her. She did, and he did, for twelve dollars a week.

JOURNALISM WAS ALSO A POINT OF ENTRY for many of the male migrants to New York's emerging Bohemia.

John Reed, born to a well-to-do Portland, Oregon, family, arrived in 1911 (aged 23), by way of Harvard and a brief Left Bank sojourn in Paris. He shared boardinghouse digs with four college chums at 42 Washington Square South. Lincoln Steffens, at the urging of Reed's father, an old friend, arranged a job for Jack at the *American Magazine*, reading manuscripts, writing poems and stories, and penning muckraking articles about "rich people who had too many motor cars and poor people who didn't have enough to eat." The city-savvy Steffens—who in 1912, recently widowed, took two rooms in Reed's boarding-house, thus becoming a senior citizen of the emerging Village neighborhood—guided young Reed's footsteps as he wandered the city in a state of constant wonderment. "New York was an enchanted city to me," Reed would recollect, in a piece that displayed more than a whiff of Whitman.[6] And in 1913 he wrote a long comic poem, *The Day in Bohemia; or, Life among the Artists*, celebrating the emergence of a separatist enclave, whose youthful creativity was a pointed challenge to a buttoned-up culture. ("Yet we are free who live in Washington Square," Reed rhymed. "We dare to think as Uptown wouldn't dare.") In a characteristic bit of hijinks, a small crew of rebels slipped to the top of the Washington Square Arch one January night in 1917, strung Chinese lanterns and balloons, uncorked wine, fired cap guns, and declared the birth of the Free and Independent Republic of Washington Square. (The Declaration consisted of the word "Whereas" repeated over and over.) Crusty critics who sought to dismiss the new radicals as bourgeois youths cavorting in what amounted to an overgrown college campus could point to Reed's observation: "There's no one to pry if we're tight, you and I, / Or demand how our evenings are spent." There *was* something larkish about this rebellion. It smacked at times of an adolescent blowout, prompted by pa-rental absence. But it quickly took on greater heft.

When Floyd Dell arrived in 1913, he moved in right next door to Reed, at 45 Washington Square South. Like Glaspell, Dell had grown up in Davenport, Iowa, though as the son of a failed butcher, he grew up much poorer. Being gifted and bookish, he was taken up by Davenport's intellectual set (descendants of German Forty-Eighters). He joined the Socialist Party at age 16 and moved into newspaper work, and in 1908 local backers aided his reloca-tion to Chicago, then undergoing a cultural flowering. Dell got a job editing an important literary supplement, came to know leading local writers, and as an editor encouraged Chicago's budding bohemian avant-garde. But like Glaspell and many other writers, he soon decided that given New York's incontestable command of the publishing industry, staying in Chicago would relegate him to regional rather than continental status, and he opted to join the Greenwich Village insurgency.

Max Eastman came down from an Elmira, New York, household—both parents were Congregational ministers, his mother one of the first women so ordained in America—and after graduating from Williams College in 1905 he had been reluctant to move to New York. But his sister, Crystal, then studying law at NYU, persuaded him to take the plunge, and in 1907 he moved south, sharing digs on 11th Street with her and other activists—until 1911, when he married Ida Rauh, a friend of Crystal's. Scion of a prosperous New York German

---

6. "I wandered about the streets, from the soaring imperial towers of downtown, along the East River docks, smelling of spices and the clipper ships of the past, through the swarming East Side, alien towns within alien towns, where the smoky glare of miles of clamorous pushcarts made a splendor of shabby streets. I knew Chinatown and Little Italy, Sharkey's and McSorley's saloons, the Bowery lodging houses and the places where the tramps gathered in winter, the Haymarket, the German village and the dives of the Tenderloin. The girls that walked the streets were friends of mine, and the drunken sailors off ships from the world's end."

Jewish family, Rauh was herself a lawyer and had been active in the Women's Trade Union League, especially during the 1909 strike.[7] In a small but telling break with convention, she kept her own name, and they displayed "Rauh" as well as "Eastman" on the bell of their sixth-floor walk-up on Charles Street. Eastman worked on a philosophy PhD with John Dewey up at Columbia, and though he completed the required work, he refused to take the degree, believing that an intellectual life was incompatible with an academic career.

ONCE IN "THE VILLAGE" (AS THEY CAME TO CALL IT), these and scores of other newcomers quickly discovered one another.

Cold-water flats being all that many could afford, the rebels met and mingled in warm restaurants and congenial bars. The Village abounded with ethnic eateries and drinkeries. There were Italian places like Mama Bertolotti's on West 3rd; its attractions included a fifteen-cent lunch, sawdust-covered floors, cod-oil lamps, and the cachet of being Poe's prior residence. There were Irish saloons like the Golden Swan at Sixth Avenue and 4th Street (the southeast corner), called "the Hell-Hole" by a roster of regulars that included gangsters (the Hudson Dusters), longshoremen, prostitutes, gamblers, and the usually inebriated Eugene O'Neill. There were bohemian-style bistros, too—intimate and artily decorated tea-rooms like the Mad Hatter, with wooden tables and candlelight. North of the Square at 8th Street and Fifth Avenue, the Brevoort Hotel's basement café afforded a Parisian flavor and was frequented by Emma Goldman and her cohort.

Polly's was something else again. In 1913 Paula Holladay, an anarchist from Evanston, opened a downstairs restaurant at 137 MacDougal (seventy years earlier the home of lithographer Nathaniel Currier). The idea had been suggested by her Czech anarchist lover, Hippolyte Havel, who wanted a nucleus around which scattered radicals could coalescence. Havel, who served as headwaiter, cook, and dishwasher, earned a cartoonish reputation for reviling uptowners as "bourgeois pigs" while taking their orders. But Havel was a serious guy. A committed militant—he'd been expelled from Austria-Hungary, Germany, and France—he was fluent in half a dozen languages, knew most anarchists in the international community, and, most important for Village circuitry, was a close associate (and former lover) of Emma Goldman. They had met in London in 1899 and traveled together to Paris, where they stayed ten months, and he returned with her to New York in 1900. Havel would become her right-hand man on *Mother Earth*, write the biographical introduction to her *Anarchism and Other Essays*, and found several journals of his own, including *Social War* and *Revolt*.

Polly's proved to be just the gravitational force Havel had envisioned, when the celebrated Liberal Club moved in one flight up. The club had begun life as a discussion society for progressive New Yorkers, and its meetings had been held in the Gramercy Park area. In 1913 a split developed when the majority refused opening membership to African Americans and declined to let Emma Goldman speak. A vigorous protest was mounted by Henrietta Rodman, who taught English at Wadleigh High School, and had been one of the unionized city school-teachers who had battled successfully with the city Board of Education over equal pay for female teachers. Rodman herself became an issue when she married a club member and then—shocking some—lived with him *and* his former wife. In the end Rodman led an exodus of members down to the Village, shifting from the progressive to the radical city. On the floor above Polly's they set up a "Meeting Place for Those Interested in New Ideas." After all,

---

7. Another Protestant-Jewish coupling, like Phelps Stokes and Pastor, or William Walling and Anna Strunsky.

Rodman argued, "Why shouldn't intelligent people to-day, have the same chance to know each other that the church and the tavern gave their grandparents." Here writers and artists—including John Reed, Susan Glaspell, Floyd Dell, Mary Heaton Vorse, and Hutchins Hapgood—drank wine, talked politics with Emma Goldman and Big Bill Haywood, listened to Horace Traubel reminisce about Walt Whitman (the Village's patron saint), and danced the tango and new ragtime steps.

THE COMPLEX EXPANDED YET AGAIN when Albert and Charles Boni, American-born sons of Russian Jewish immigrants, opened the Washington Square Bookshop at the adjacent 135 MacDougal. With the permission of the landlady, who owned both brownstones, the Bonis cut a doorway between their emporium and the Liberal Club. This not only allowed club members and writer visitors to circulate freely; it enhanced the flow of ideas about what kinds of books should be sold and, more important, published. In 1913, in conjunction with poet Alfred Kreymborg (a frequenter of the Liberal Club), the Bonis began publishing the *Glebe*, a little magazine (circulation 300) dedicated to "the best work of American and foreign authors"; the February 1914 issue included material by Ezra Pound, Amy Lowell, William Carlos Williams, and the as yet unknown James Joyce. The *Glebe* expired after ten issues, in part because of divided opinion over which to emphasize, foreign prose or American poetry. But in 1915, in another radical gambit, the Boni brothers founded the Little Leather Library. The tiny volumes (3" × 3.75") of classics and abridgements were sold through the mail at $2.98 for a set of thirty, and through Woolworth's five-and-ten-cent stores, reputedly at the rate of a million copies a year. In 1916 Albert (then 24) teamed up with bond salesman Horace Liveright (aged 29), to launch Boni & Liveright, which in 1917 began publishing reprints of European works in a series called the Modern Library; the earliest selections (Wilde, Dostoevsky, Strindberg, Wells, Ibsen) reflected the avant-garde tastes of Boni's Washington Square patrons and friends.

The arrival of Jewish Americans in the publishing industry opened a new era in the business, one daring in both content and marketing. The new houses provided an outlet for European authors—notably Russians, Italians, Spaniards, French, and Scandinavians—outside the traditional Anglo canon favored by conservative established houses, still under the influence of New England Brahman taste. The newcomers were also—not being tied in with established US authors—more responsive to the output of a new generation of Americans.

In addition to Boni & Liveright, Jewish American pioneers included Benjamin Huebsch, whose arrival in 1902 first cracked the solidly gentile facade of the often anti-Semitic publishing world, and Alfred A. Knopf. The latter entered Doubleday, Page & Co. in 1912 after graduating from Columbia and in 1914 switched to Mitchell Kennerley's eponymous firm. An immigrant from London, Kennerley was known for his openness to fresh talent; he published, for instance, Edna St. Vincent Millay's first book, *Renascence*, and Walter Lippmann's *Preface to Politics*. In 1915 Knopf and his wife, Blanche, went out on their own and began combing Europe for works to bring out under their Borzoi imprint. They focused particularly on Russian translations but also brought out local work by Floyd Dell, Max Eastman, and Konrad Bercovici, whose first book was a collection of short stories about the Lower East Side, with an introduction by John Reed. This new crop of publishers would secure New York's unquestioned leadership of the book trade in the United States.

THE BONIS' BOOKSTORE AT 135 MACDOUGAL PROVIDED THE VENUE for yet another cultural innovation, this one in drama. A group of Liberal Club members, dismayed with the state of the Broadway stage, decided to launch an experimental alternative that would rely on sub-scriptions rather than box-office sales. The amateur thespians included Rauh, Hutchins, Glaspell, Boyce, Eastman, Reed, and Vorse. Unable to afford to rent a theater space, they put on their first play in the Boni bookstore's back room. This inspired the formation of the Washington Square Players, who issued a manifesto, and moved uptown to challenge the Theatrical Syndicate on its home turf. But the Village amateurs did not abandon their project. In the summer of 1915, a group of them were vacationing on Cape Cod, where they wrote and staged several productions, first on the veranda of Hapgood and Boyce's rented ocean-view cottage, then in a makeshift theater on a wharf owned by Vorse. The following summer, word having spread, a much larger contingent of Villagers made their way to Provincetown— an escape from the broiling city that was far beyond the economic reach of their immigrant neighbors. The contingent included John Reed and his lover, writer Louise Bryant; painter Marsden Hartley; Max Eastman and Ida Rauh; Floyd Dell and Eugene O'Neill, who had been invited by Reed, the two having become close friends since O'Neill's dark and suicidal days at "Jimmy the Priest's" Fulton Street flophouse. The group staged his play *Bound East for Cardiff*, a great success, and on returning to New York formally organized as the Provincetown Players, committed to producing new American plays, and operating on a subscription basis. Mrs. Belardi (Jennie Ferreri), the ever-obliging landlady of 135 and 137 MacDougal, now rented them the parlor floor of 139, where they opened in November 1916, with three one-act plays (by O'Neill, Bryant, and Dell). By the end of their first season their subscription list had gone from 64 to 635, and the company needed a larger space. Just three doors down in the other direction, at 133, was an old stable, owned by the omnipresent Mrs. Belardi. It was rented and transformed into the Provincetown Playhouse.

MEANWHILE, BACK AT 137, POLLY'S HAD BECOME THE VENUE OF CHOICE for a luncheon club called Heterodoxy, "a little band of willful women," according to one member, a club for "women who did things and did them openly," according to another. It was founded in 1912 by Marie Jenny Howe, an ordained Unitarian minister who in 1910 had moved from Cleveland with her husband, urban reformer Frederick C. Howe, to West 12th Street in the Village. Its members included authors and journalists, doctors and lawyers, teachers and settlement workers, psychologists and anthropologists, playwrights and actresses, union-ists and radicals. Nearly all were economically independent; a few were well-off. At biweekly meetings they discussed issues of the day, their own work, and their personal affairs. Glaspell, Eastman, Milholland, Rauh, Rodman, Gurley Flynn, Pastor Stokes, Vorse, Anna Strunsky Walling, and Sara Josephine Baker were among the eventual sixty members. There were no restrictions as to race and religion, though Grace Nail Johnson, an activist married to James Weldon Johnson, was the only black member. While most were active in politics, labor, or social struggles, Heterodoxy itself did not take public stands. Indeed, the meetings were entirely off the record, and the injunction to secrecy was all but universally adhered to. Their luncheons were held in different places, usually somewhere in the Village, most often at Polly's.

VILLAGERS ALSO GATHERED IN SALONS. Most were low-key and low-budget—Rodman gave regular spaghetti dinners at her Bank Street place—but the rich and restless Mabel Dodge ran a grander version. Daughter of a wealthy Buffalo banker, she had married a Boston archi-tect of independent means and lived for several years in a villa above Florence, where she befriended Leo and Gertrude Stein, the art collector and literary innovator.

In 1912 Dodge (aged 32) moved to New York, took the second floor of a brick town house at 23 Fifth Avenue (and 9th Street), packed her estranged husband off to the Brevoort across the way, and threw herself into local affairs. "The city was teeming with potentialities," she recalled; "the old ways were about over and the new ways all to create." There was a problem, however, in "that there were a great many interesting men and women, all thinking and doing different things, but there didn't seem to be any *centralization*, any place where all *sorts* of people could meet under one roof and talk freely on all subjects." Encouraged by Lincoln Steffens and Hutchins Hapgood, she began in January 1913 to host weekly gatherings in her sumptuous apartment. Dodge selected a topic, perhaps a guest speaker, invited exciting people to her all-white abode, furnished plenty of food (also all white—usually turkey and Gorgonzola), and presided over an unstructured discussion. The gatherings attracted a luminous array of writers, artists, publishers, editors, society ladies, reformers, and radicals of every stripe. There were evenings devoted to sexual equality, free love, women's suffrage, good government, prison reform, unemployment, the labor movement, the Mexican question, the corrupting influence of money, and the modern movement in art. The more orderly-minded Walter Lippmann told Dodge: "Your categories aren't any good. They remind me of a Fourth Avenue antique shop." Leo Stein put it more succinctly: "Mabel Dodge / Hodge podge."[8]

But for Dodge, her chat room's catholicity of topics and participants was exactly what the moment needed. She liked mixing suffragists, birth controllers, clubwomen, and "Woman's-place-is-in-the-home Women." She particularly wanted to put "the Heads of things" in touch with one another, and on one evening arranged a confrontation between exponents of direct action (Wobbly chief Bill Haywood), anarchism (Goldman, Berkman, and Havel), and political socialism (represented by William English Walling), with 200 guests in attendance, half in evening dress, the other half in work clothes. It was not, Dodge thought, a success. Big Bill, mesmerizing before a crowd of thousands, "talked as though he were wading blindfolded in sand," and Goldman seemed a little schoolmarmish. Still, such encounters strengthened the link between political radicals and cultural rebels in the Village.

THE VILLAGE INTELLECTUALS CAME TOGETHER IN PRINT as well as conversation, most effectively in the *Masses*. In its first incarnation, begun in 1911, the magazine had been run by Piet Vlag, a Dutch immigrant socialist and a devout advocate of worker cooperatives. Essentially a party organ, it had been earnest, boring, and in short order defunct. Vlag departed, but the talented staff of writers and artists decided to resurrect it and remodel it after European satirical magazines. In August 1912 they informed Max Eastman: "You are elected editor of *The Masses*. No pay." Eastman, Dewey's former pupil, had been teaching up at Columbia, and had made it known he was looking for a job that would further the insurgent movement. "No pay" was not on his agenda, but he met with the staff, and was delighted to find they were talking "free-thought talk and not just socialism" and were motivated by "a sense of universal revolt and regeneration . . . in American art and literature and living-of-life as well as in politics." So he agreed to try on the editorship for one issue, and if it went well, he'd take the job—with pay.

Four months later the *Masses* was reborn. Its manifesto promised much. "We are going to make THE MASSES a *popular* Socialist magazine—a magazine of pictures and lively

---

8. Some critics, like Mary Heaton Vorse, thought she was just "a rich woman amusing herself in meeting celebrities of different kinds," but she would soon prove her radical bona fides, at least in the short term.

writing." No preachiness, no moral uplift, no sectarian squabbles. It would "have no further part in the factional disputes within the Socialist Party," a reference to the slugfest between Haywood and Hillquit, and would oppose "rigidity and dogma wherever it is found." The *Masses* would be "a magazine with a sense of humor and no respect for the respectable; frank, arrogant, searching for true causes." It would be "owned and published cooperatively by the editors. It has no dividends to pay and nobody is trying to make money out of it." It would be "a Revolutionary and not a Reform magazine," "a magazine whose final policy is to do as it pleases and conciliate nobody, not even its readers."[9]

They were as good as their words. The inaugural issue (December 1912) was sassy and slick. Artist John Sloan had come up with a lively design—elegant typography, bold heads, wide margins, large drawings—and artist Art Young contributed a two-page cartoon depicting the capitalist press as a whorehouse with the editor as madam, the advertisers as clients, the reporters as prostitutes.

Eastman stayed on. He wangled financial patronage from those Dell called the "Rebel Rich": Alva Belmont, Mabel Dodge, Samuel Untermyer (the counsel for Pujo), Adolph Lewisohn (copper king) and E. W. Scripps (publisher). Whenever expenses outran income, the *Masses* threw a fund-raising party at Webster Hall on East 11th Street. Those in costume were admitted at half price. Other Village groups did the same. The Liberal Club sponsored a Pagan Rout. Emma Goldman's *Mother Earth* staged a Red Revel. Soon costume spectaculars were the rage. Bacchanals patterned after those in the art-student quarter of Paris featured intellectual satyrs and nymphs romping in skimpy outfits and body paint.

In June 1913 Eastman moved the offices from 150 Nassau Street, on the edge of the jewelry district, to 91 Greenwich Avenue in the Village. This was convenient for editorial meetings, at which those assembled (including drop-in visitors like Haywood and Steffens) voted on articles and art. Things got a little chaotic, but they smoothed out when Eastman hired Dell as managing editor (he having learned the business in Chicago). Later Dell would hire Dorothy Day as his editorial assistant. (He also invited her to live with him and two others in a communal apartment on MacDougal Street, above the Provincetown Playhouse, where she met Eugene O'Neil and hung out with him at the Hell Hole, where she also drank the Hudson Dusters under the table.)

Its lively writing, witty cartoons, forceful artwork, spoofs of the rich and respectable, attacks on conventional religion (but support for "Comrade Jesus"), undogmatic socialism, and great good humor won the *Masses* a strong following (and 40,000 subscribers). Yet there was another aspect of its appeal to readers across the country—those Reed characterized as "a wide public, alert, alive, bored with the smug procession of magazine platitudes"—and that was its location in the Village. The editors made a point of dropping the lofty paternal voice of conventional magazine editors and adopting an accessible and equalitarian tone, in effect inviting readers out in the provinces to participate, at least imaginatively, in Gotham's bohemian free-speech world. Indeed, the Village was often described in its pages, in appealing terms; Eastman recalled "my then very great need to romanticize New York life." The *Masses* thus offered a politics, a temperament, and a home base.

IN APRIL 1913, A CONJUNCTION OF CULTURE AND POLITICS, art and revolution, was wrought during the Paterson silk workers strike, which had been going badly. At a dinner party in the

---

9. John Reed, who soon became a contributing editor, had submitted a draft manifesto to Eastman, suggesting the journal's broad purpose should be "to everlastingly attack old systems, old morals, old prejudices," but with "a rapier rather than a broad-axe."

Village, Bill Haywood was complaining that New York newspapers had imposed a virtual black-out on the events in New Jersey. No doubt he was remembering fondly how press coverage of the children's exodus from Lawrence had generated an outpouring of middle-class support, which totally transformed the strike's dynamics. Mabel Dodge suggested to Haywood that he consider bringing the workers to New York, hiring a big hall, and having them tell their own story by re-enacting the strike onstage. John Reed, also in attendance, jumped on the idea, and the next morning went to Paterson. He began talking with strikers at the mill gates and was promptly arrested and sentenced to twenty days in a jail already stuffed with incarcerated workers. There Reed approached Carlo Tresca, who was explaining the class struggle to a black prisoner, and asked him questions about the strike. Tresca, suspicious of the well-dressed young man, kept his distance, until later in the day, when Haywood arrived, having been arrested on arriving at the train station, and vouched for Reed's bona fides. Over the next days, Tresca and Haywood gave him a crash course in labor agitation, and IWW strikers told him their stories. After his release Reed immediately wrote a piece for the *Masses*. ("There is war in Paterson" was the lead.) His gripping report cracked the news boycott and encouraged an outpouring of support from fellow Villagers. Dodge drove out and transported picketers as needed. Sanger tried organizing runa-way shops in Hazleton, Pennsylvania. The Hapgoods and others opened their homes to Paterson children. Lippmann, Eastman, and Rodman trooped out on Sundays to hear Tresca, Flynn, and Haywood address mass meetings of Italians, Lithuanians, Poles, Greeks, and Jews.

But principally—putting a radical twist on a genteel form—they set about staging a co-lossal pageant, with the strikers as actors, to publicize the Jersey events in Manhattan. They raised the funds, partly from New York silk workers, partly from Dodge and other rebel rich. Steffens, Walling, Sinclair, Pastor Stokes, and Hapgood worked on publicity. Reed, assisted by scores of Villagers, rehearsed the nearly 1,500 participants and sorted out logistics. On June 7 the massed strikers marched from the Hoboken ferry landing to Madison Square Garden, where 10-foot-tall red electric letters blazed out "IWW" from all four sides of Stanford White's tower. Inside, spectators choked the cavernous arena. They roared their support as the enormous corps of unionists reenacted picket-line violence and strike meet-ings on a gigantic stage before a 200 foot painted backdrop of a silk mill by *Masses* artist John Sloan. The performance ended with more than 15,000 people singing "The Marseillaise."

The Paterson Strike Pageant was a smash hit with critics. Some hailed it as a new art form, the combined product of workers and intellectuals. Its impact on the strikers was more problematic. The massive publicity was welcome but proved unable to offset the mill owners' strategic advantages; Paterson wasn't Lawrence. Plus, the extravaganza failed to generate the hoped-for funds; indeed, it ran a deficit, as many of the midpriced tickets did not sell, and seats had been virtually given away to the huge crowds of workers wanting to get in. The strike itself crumbled a month later.

The pageant's organizers were the more lasting beneficiaries. Such connections pro-vided opportunities to reach and learn from working people. On the other hand, the class gulf was glaringly spotlit when Reed and Dodge (now lovers) sailed off for a vacation in Florence during the strike's dying days. They were understandably exhausted from their efforts, but there would be no R&R for the exhausted and defeated workers.

The pageant and his strike reporting were the making of Reed's career—Steffens suc-cessfully recommended him to *Metropolitan Magazine* as the ideal person to cover revolu-tionary events in Mexico—but it was the beginning of the end of Dodge's reign as a salonista. By the end of 1914, she recalled, she "had said good-by . . . to the Labor Movement, to Revolution, and to anarchy" and "turned more to Nature and Art." She gave up her evenings

Poster, Pageant of the Paterson Strike, Madison Square Garden, June 7, 1913. (Tamiment Library and Robert F. Wagner Labor Archives)

and rented a house in Croton, where she linked up with her neighbors—the very same afflu-ent owners of the Paterson mills "whom Reed and I had tried to defeat with our pageant!"—with whom she now "joined in sympathy, working together to help Beauty into the world."

Many other Villagers had more staying power and continued to support the labor move-ment. But the larger flow of influence and inspiration ran in the opposite direction. The working-class militancy evidenced in the era's great strikes (especially those by females) en-couraged a challenging of all existing power relations, those between sexes as well as classes. The Villagers' principal goal—"to everlastingly attack old systems, old morals, old prejudices," as Reed put it—seemed congruent with working-class struggles against capitalist exploitation. And opposition to the economic status quo seemed of a piece with assaults on the established gender order. Traditional socialists argued that winning women's equality was secondary to winning the class struggle, but the cultural radicals insisted that, to the contrary (as Eastman put it in the *Masses*), "the question of sex equality, the economic, social, political independence of woman, stands by itself parallel and equal in importance to any other question of the day."

FEMINISTS

Early in 1914 the conservative *Century Magazine* editorialized that "the time has come to define feminism; it is no longer possible to ignore it." For over a year the novel word had ricocheted around New York, with little agreement about its meaning beyond a sense of heightened female militancy. In February, Marie Howe and the Heterodoxy circle helped organize two "Feminist Mass Meetings" at Cooper Union to grapple with the issue. Various speakers—including Henrietta Rodman, Floyd Dell, Crystal and Max Eastman, Frances Perkins, Rose Schneiderman, and Charlotte Perkins Gilman—addressed the questions "What is Feminism?" and "What Feminism Means to Me."

Feminism, said Howe, meant "woman's struggle for freedom. Its political phase is woman's will to vote. Its economic phase is woman's effort to pay her own way. Its social phase is woman's revaluation of outgrown customs and standards." Taken together feminism meant "a changed psychology, the creation of a new consciousness in women."

There was widespread acceptance of this tripartite definition.

As to the first, there was universal agreement. For feminists, obtaining the suffrage was a bedrock issue.

The second, understood as women's right to work outside the home, in any job for which they were qualified, and on the basis of equal pay for equal work, was a position they shared with many non-feminist women but to which they brought a particular edge: women needed justly remunerated work to lessen their dependence on men.

As a concrete first step on the right-to-work front, Henrietta Rodman, shortly after the Cooper Union meetings, organized a Feminist Alliance to attack discriminatory practices in New York City. The alliance's manifesto demanded "the removal of all social, political, economic, and other discrimination which are based upon sex, and the award of all rights and duties in all fields on the basis of individual capacity alone." Among other campaigns, the group fought to further open up law schools, and went after the Board of Education's requirement that women teachers (though not men) who married must resign. They got that reversed, and when administrators then dismissed wives who became mothers (though not husbands who became fathers), the protestors got that overturned too.[10]

Female trade unionists and middle-class Women's Trade Union League allies were well represented at the Cooper Union conclaves, and they argued for making the right to organize a feminist demand. They saw young working-class women as exemplary shapers of their own destinies. As one wrote, "Working girls have a chance to be themselves because they earn their own wage and nobody owns them." Emma Goldman interjected a note of caution, asking, "How much independence is gained" for the great mass of working girls and women if "the narrowness and lack of freedom of the home is exchanged for the narrowness and lack of freedom of the factory, sweat-shop, department store or office?" It was, she thought, "no wonder that hundreds of girls are so willing to accept the first offer of marriage, sick and tired of their 'independence' behind the counter, at the sewing or typewriting machine. They are just as ready to marry as girls of the middle-class, who long to throw off the yoke of parental supremacy."

Some feminists argued for reframing the nature of work *inside* the home. Charlotte Perkins Gilman, a Manhattan-based theoretician of women's rights, was author of a utopian novel, *Herland*, that imagined an all-female society (it reproduced via parthenogenesis) in

---

10. The board's logic had been that married female teachers should resign so they could attend to their husbands' needs. Similarly they claimed they fired mothers in the interest of their infants—which protesters responded to by proposing and winning maternity leaves. But the *New York Times* made clear there were larger gender-order issues at stake when it complained in 1913 that "our public school system is a victim of that comparatively new and distressing malady called feminism. Time was when women married and took up the burdens of the conjugal relation expected thereafter to devote themselves to the care of their homes and the training of their children."

Henrietta Rodman, ca. 1910–15. (Library of Congress Prints and Photographs Division)

which women admirably filled all economic, political, and social roles. But in the there and then of twentieth-century New York, Gilman argued for rearranging the domestic sphere. Individual households, she suggested, were inefficient, outmoded, and particularly destructive to women. A smart and modern alternative was the cooperative home. Housekeeping should be delegated to central management and specialized workers, a strategy that dovetailed with New York's apartment-hotel boom, notably on Gilman's Upper West Side, where some buildings already included a centralized basement kitchen, centralized cleaning services, and centralized child care, with roof garden nurseries and kindergartens run by nurses and teachers. Such arrangements would allow women—with "professional" being the unstated and unexamined qualifier—to combine families and careers. Harriet Rodman, a disciple of Gilman, tried to have the Feminist Alliance actualize this project by constructing a Feminist Apartment House. She got it to the design stage—a twelve-story building near Greenwich Village—but the financing didn't materialize.

The most cultural of Howe's three components of "feminism" was her third, the movement's "revaluation of outgrown customs and standards," precisely those brassbound customs that Twain had thought unchallengeable a few years earlier.

Some of these customs and standards were at the level of everyday life, and within the ability of individuals to change, such as keeping one's "maiden" name, or throwing off the constraints of fashion. Many Village women, notably Rodman, bobbed their hair (cropped it short), discarded corsets, and adopted sandals, ethnic jewelry, and smock-like peasant dresses—handcrafted alternatives to mass-produced shirtwaists.

But most feminists had their eyes fixed on bigger-ticket items, like the consignment of women to the domestic sphere—what the *Times* called "taking up the burdens of the conjugal relation"—which required a self-effacing submersion in their roles as wives and mothers. Feminists talked less of sacrificial nurturance, more of expressing individuality; placed less emphasis on duties, more on rights.

Above all, feminists claimed the right to rethink sexuality. In general, they affirmed the inherent legitimacy, goodness, and healthfulness of sexual activity and relationships. In particular, they insisted that sexual instincts and passionate desires were as much a part of woman's nature as of man's, and that women, moreover, had an equal right to sexual fulfillment. Feminists invested sexuality with an importance that went beyond procreation; they saw it as an aspect of individual self-definition, a marker of identity. These gender radicals called for egalitarian sexual relationships that were not exclusively centered on marriage and reproduction. Specifically, sex before marriage should be taken off the forbidden list. As usual, Goldman was on the case before most others. Wasn't it outrageous, she asked in 1910, that a "healthy, grown woman, full of life and passion, must deny nature's demand, must subdue her most intense craving, undermine her health and break her spirit, must stunt her vision, abstain from the depth and glory of sex experience until a 'good' man comes along to take her unto himself as a wife?" Feminists advocated a single standard, not one that forced continence on males but rather one that granted equal sexual freedom to women. Then boys could be boys, girls could be girls, and geese and ganders could flock together.

Feminists were prepared to abandon claims to moral superiority based on their sexual purity. A feminist, said Gilman, was a woman who had jumped down from the pedestal and walked about on solid ground with "chains off, crown off, halo off," rejecting sentimental veneration. Members of older women's movements, who had staked a claim to public power based on their nurturing functions and superior virtue, were loath to give up such hard-won status.

Boldest of all was the reconsideration of marriage itself. Some feminists picked up on the anarchists' "free love" tradition, which declared that true love did not need the sanction of church or state, and if a marriage did not work out, the unsanctified or unlegalized union could and should be easily dissolved at the wish of either party. Most nineteenth-century "free lovers" had argued for monogamy, or at least serial monogamy, with the partners being sexually faithful for as long as a marriage lasted. Some twentieth-century feminists, however, females as well as males, believed couples need not be monogamous at all. Each party should be free to act on her or his attraction to others. Psychological or emotional fidelity was more significant than sexual fidelity, and so long as the basic union was solid, either or both parties should feel free to be with others as well.

Some Village radicals set out to put such theories into practice by living what Randolph Bourne called "the experimental life." Men and women sought to form relationships that blended passion and friendship while transcending sexual exclusiveness. "Emancipated" women explored their sexuality, having love affairs, discussing sex in mixed groups, writing up their thoughts and feelings on the subject.

The experimental life often proved painful. Women who rejected marriage and propriety lost the protections those institutions offered against the transience of love (much less lust). Unless economically independent, "free" women found themselves as powerless as their conventional sisters and vulnerable to manipulation by male bohemians. The men had their own problems. Some were simply cynical—justifying their old-fashioned tomcatting as new-fashioned feminist-approved liberation. But many male radicals honestly supported equal freedom for women—in theory—only to discover in practice that they were consumed by jealousy when women took the same liberties, and some decided they preferred a traditional wife to an emancipated partner.

Often, however, the women themselves did not take such liberties, not seeing sexual fulfillment as necessarily requiring multiple partners. This was the case for even the most militant. Emma Goldman argued that if love was genuine, an "outside attraction" would not destroy "mutual confidence and security," but her private letters reveal that she found her lover Ben Reitman's non-monogamy extremely hurtful. Elizabeth Gurley Flynn likewise suffered silently over the innumerable infidelities of Carlo Tresca.

WHAT ALL FEMINISTS AND RADICALS COULD AGREE UPON was condemning state intervention in private sexual activities, which they likened to the suppression of political speech in public. In 1902 libertarian radicals gathered at the Liberal Club and formed the Free Speech League (FSL). A Gotham-based organization, it was dedicated to protecting the rights of political dissidents—threatened by the new anti-anarchist laws—and the rights of those challenging the gender order, menaced by the Comstock Law's treating such speech as inherently obscene, hence subject to suppression. The Free Speech League was the latest manifestation of a long New York tradition of promoting civil liberties. The FSL's first president, Edward W. Chamberlain, was a New York lawyer who back in 1878 had led protests against Comstock's conviction of anarchist Ezra Heywood for mailing a pamphlet, *Cupid's Yokes*, that questioned traditional definitions of marriage. (Heywood was sentenced to two years at hard labor.) Chamberlain was succeeded in 1909 by E. B. Foote Jr., a wealthy physician and a second-generation defender of First Amendment rights for political and sexual radicals (his father having preceded him in this endeavor). The actual work of the Free Speech League was done by attorney Theodore Schroeder, who developed legal strategies for defending activists, notably IWW organizers, and most particularly Emma Goldman, whose lectures, whether on anarchism or marriage, were suppressed with great regularity.

Not content with defensive legal maneuvers, Villagers went on the offensive. Picking up on Goldman's critique of Comstock, radicals lampooned him endlessly, as in the *Masses* cartoon of a muttonchopped Comstockian figure hauling a mother before the bench and proclaiming: "Your Honor, this woman gave birth to a naked child!" They adopted, too, her pejorative label for the larger cultural complex for which Comstock served as enforcer. "To the modern young person," said Randolph Bourne, "there is no type so devastating and

Art Young, "Freedom of the Press," *The Masses* (December 1912). (Library of Congress Prints and Photographs Division)

harassing as the puritan." Soon condemnations of the "Puritanical policy of repression" became commonplace.

Some turned to the pre-Christian era for counter-models—casting themselves as the pagan antagonists of Puritan bigots. They particularly venerated the Greeks, for their athleticism and sensuality. Isadora Duncan was the embodiment of this trend. She studied Greek vases to ascertain steps of ancient dancers, dressed her dancers in simple tunics, and performed on an uncluttered stage akin to a Greek proscenium. She was adulated for her youth and beauty. She represented emancipation, sexual liberation, artistic freedom, and political protest.[11]

Sexual radicals in New York also called to their aid the latest thinking of European sexologists like Havelock Ellis, Edward Carpenter, and Ellen Key. Key insisted women were entitled to sexual satisfaction and should end marriages that didn't provide it. Carpenter argued that a just and equal society must promote the sexual and economic freedom of women. And Havelock Ellis, in his six-volume *Studies in the Psychology of Sex*, contested the Victorian sexual heritage in its entirety, advocating (among many other things) premarital sex, in the form of trial unions, to ensure sexual compatibility. But far and away the most potent of the European theorists was the one whom Villagers played an outsized role in introducing to the rest of the country.

ON SEPTEMBER 27, 1909, SIGMUND FREUD ARRIVED IN NEW YORK CITY. Invited to lecture at Clark University in Worcester, Massachusetts, he had budgeted an outing in the metropolis for the previous week. Dr. Abraham Arden Brill hosted Freud at his 88 Central Park West apartment (at 69th Street) and squired him around town. They took in Central Park,

11. Heterodoxy member Elsie Clews Parsons's anthropological writings further undermined the inherited gender order by setting it in a comparative sociological context in her feminist textbook *The Family* (1906).

"Your Honor, this woman gave birth to a naked child!"

Robert Minor, "Your Honor, This Woman Gave Birth to a Naked Child." *Masses*, September 1915.

Chinatown, the Lower East Side, and Coney Island. Freud saw his first movie, dined in Hammerstein's Roof Garden, and haunted the Metropolitan's collection of Grecian antiquities. Then he headed up to Worcester.[12]

For all New York's attractions, once back in Europe Freud wrote a follower urging that the American wing of his psychoanalytic movement be launched in New England: "I understand that all important intellectual movements in America have originated in Boston." Freud was off target here, both about past events and future prospects. Puritanical Boston shied away from his truculent emphasis on sexuality. It was New York that eagerly embraced his new theories.

There were several reasons for the city's affinity with psychoanalysis. One was the strong contingent of Jewish psychologists in the New York Psychoanalytic Society that Brill founded in February 1911. Their powerful commitment to advancing Freud's work drew sustenance both from their cultural connection to him and from their own outsider status vis-à-vis *Social Register* neurologists in the metropolis.

Brill's own career was emblematic. He had arrived from Austria-Hungary back in 1889—alone, aged 15, with three dollars in his pocket. He lived on the Lower East Side and worked his way through NYU sweeping out bars. He struggled through to a 1904 medical degree from Columbia's College of Physicians and Surgeons and then got a job in the state hospital system. (Many in the original group were associated not with private hospitals but

---

12. Freud was so taken with the Upper West Side that he told Brill: "Stay here, don't move from this spot; it is the nicest part of the city, so far as I can see."

with the public system—particularly the Psychiatric Institute of the New York State Hospitals on Ward's Island.) Brill discovered Freud when he studied psychiatry in Zurich in 1907. He returned to New York a dedicated disciple and set about translating the maestro's oeuvre into English. Within a decade of Freud's visit, Brill's dogged determination had helped make New York the center of the US movement.

But what really made psychoanalysis take off in Gotham was that it suited the needs of the Greenwich Village intellectuals then locked in combat with Comstock. In his 1908 essay "'Civilized' Sexual Morality and Modern Nervousness," Freud indicted the "code of sexual morality" then prevalent in Western society, arguing that an "undue suppression of the sexual life" led to neuroses and widespread social hypocrisy. In truth, he also defended some degree of repression as a social necessity; civilization was founded on the suppression of instinctual behavior, and the sublimation of sexual energy into higher cultural aims. In his 1909 Clark address, however, Freud repeated his concern that "the claims of our civilization make life too hard for the greater part of humanity," as the "excess of sexual repression" produced not "cultural gain" but rather "an aversion to reality" and a flight into mental illness.

Here was a high-powered antidote to the claims of the Social Hygiene movement that continence produced health. No, said the radicals—starting with Goldman—it produced crippling emotional illness, particularly in women. Goldman had been intrigued by Freud since she had attended a lecture of his in Vienna in 1885, and her admiration was confirmed by his presentations at Clark (where she had happened to be, as part of a New England lecture tour). Now Freud's mantle spread. Jung addressed the Liberal Club in 1912. Lippmann invited Brill to lecture at Dodge's salon in 1913, and she and Eastman entered analysis with him. Soon many Villagers were having themselves "done," and Freudian jargon flowed freely at parties. It got so, Susan Glaspell grumped, that "you could not go out to buy a bun without hearing of someone's complex."

The radicals did more than experience psychoanalysis; they popularized it. Dodge serialized her treatment in the Hearst press, and both Eastman and Dell wrote extended and accessible accounts. They presented Freud as an ally in their attack on outdated bourgeois morality, a simplified but not altogether wrong-headed reading, and one backed by Brill's defense of the tango and Turkey Trot as a welcome surfacing of repressed sexuality. In "The Psychopathology of the New Dances," a 1914 article in the *New York Medical Journal* that was summarized in the *New York Times*, Brill argued that the dancing mania sweeping Gotham was a "psychic epidemic," the "result of repressed emotions" finally breaking through. "Puritan prudery and Anglo-Saxon hypocrisy," Brill argued, "have for centuries acted the part of the ostrich and refused to acknowledge the existence of the sexual impulse." Noting prior dancing epidemics in the twelfth and thirteenth centuries, he rooted them in the "tyranny of the feudal system and the church," which had left no outlet for erotic emotions. Similarly, in New York, the phenomenon was due to prior repression. Happily, "the great majority, rich and poor, insist upon dancing the new dances, all objections to the contrary notwithstanding." And "thanks to the genius of Freud," it could now be seen that the phenomenon "must be considered as beneficial to our present social system," and indeed "should be encouraged."

Following Brill's psychoanalytic logic, it might be argued that the dance mania and the white slavery panic were opposite and opposing metropolitan responses to the erosion of the Victorian gender order, the one a fearful fantasy that fueled efforts to clamp down on female sexuality, the other a joyous shimmying off of half a century's repression.

FAIRIES

In October 1900, eight years after the Reverend Parkhurst had run gasping into the night from the Golden Rule Pleasure Club on West 3rd Street (just under the elevated where it curved north and headed up Sixth Avenue), Anthony Comstock led the vigilantes of his Society for the Suppression of Vice on a raid of another gay dive, the Black Rabbit, roughly a block south, at 183 Bleecker Street, steps away from MacDougal. "Never before" had he "raided a place so wicked," Comstock told the *Times*. "Sodom and Gommorah," he elaborated, "would blush for shame at hearing to what depths of vice its habitues had descended."

Loop-the-Loop. "Fairy" prostitute, Brooklyn, 1906. "Biography of a Passive Pederast," *American Journal of Urology and Sexology* 13 (October 1917).

But perhaps what's most remarkable is that despite nearly a decade of repeated closures, such "fairy places" continually managed to reopen. And for all Comstock's dismay, he and other vice patrollers paid far more attention to sites of heterosexual transgression than to places where same-sex encounters were the primary ones on offer. These were places straight men would to go watch the raucous entertainment, or arrange liaisons in back rooms with painted and powdered young men, attired in low-necked dresses and blond wigs, who adopted women's names as well as styles. (By the 1910s they were borrowing movie star monikers, with vamp Theda Bara's being particularly popular.)

In some degree, the young men of this and other working-class neighborhoods had sex with fairies—as these men performing "women" were called by themselves as well as others—out of sheer convenience. There was an immense number of young bachelors in the city; in 1900, two of every five men in Manhattan aged 15 or older were unmarried. Many were either highly transient—like sailors—or common laborers, irregularly and poorly paid; in either case, they were without the resources to support a family, even if they wanted to. Which many didn't. Working-class Irishmen married only in their early thirties, if at all, and their social life was largely organized around all-male groups. Many not only rejected domesticity but despised it, scorning the manners associated with the moralizing influence of women, as had their forebears, the B'hoys of yore. They weren't giving up on sex, to be sure, but given the numbers in their ranks, it was not easy to find willing sex partners, not even prostitutes. Fairies were an available substitute, and often a less expensive one.

And an *acceptable* one. Working-class Irish, Italians, and African Americans were fairly comfortable with same-sex encounters—more so than Jewish immigrants, whose community had a more balanced gender demographic—so long as their male partner acted the part of a woman, signaled either by costume, or putatively female mannerisms (limp wrists, tweezed eyebrows, swishy moves). Under the rules of their gender culture, using men, even regularly and repeatedly, implied nothing about their *own* gender. So long as they abided by masculine conventions—so long as it was they who did the penetrating—they retained their male status. No taint of abnormality was implied or accepted. "A man's a man for a' that," they might have said, redeploying Robbie Burns's formulation.

This was in tune with reigning scientific thought, and indeed probably preceded it. Fairies, or "inverts," to use the professional nomenclature, had the bodies of men but the souls of women. Their gender being had been turned upside down, inverted. An invert's sexual desire for men was not due to his "sexuality," considered as a distinct domain of personhood, but to his gender. The same-sex attraction was held to be a manifestation of the invert's woman-like character.

Accepting one's inner womanhood had pluses and minuses for male inverts. It exempted them from hewing to the codes of masculinity prescribed by the dominant culture. On the other hand, fairies, while tolerated in working-class neighborhoods, were not respected; they had forfeited their privileged status as men. Mockery and contempt came their way, and they were easy marks for gang bashings.

WHILE THE CITY'S MALE WORKING-CLASS SEX CULTURE remained the same, its middle-class male culture—gay and straight—was evolving in a new direction. Since at least the '90s, New York and other urban centers had been experiencing what some called a crisis of masculinity. The rise of the corporate economy had eroded or eliminated many traditional pathways to manhood status that had been afforded by the old artisanal order. The prospects of ascending from apprentice to journeyman to master craftsman—a position of substantial respect and responsibility in the city—were shrinking rapidly, as was the achievement of managerial status in the corporate office, clerical work having been largely feminized. And just as men were losing power at the workplace, they found it ebbing away at home. The New Woman phenomenon curtailed or sidestepped patriarchal authority in the household, and demands for the suffrage threatened to undermine the male prerogative of representing the family in the public sphere. Even leisure-time manly pursuits— bars, boxing, brothels—were under assault by largely female forces. Middle-class men, accordingly, fretted about their de-masculinization (not something that troubled most working-class males).

Teddy Roosevelt counseled middle-class men to toughen up. Rough sports, muscular Christianity, hunting, imperialism—all were prescribed as antidotes to over-civilization. Men were urged to define themselves in opposition to all that was soft and woman-like. Woman-like men challenged the supposed immutability of gender difference. Increasingly sexual connection with other men seemed a form of gender treason. The "fairy" thus became a pejorative identity against which male normality was measured. Denigration of "Miss Nancies" or "she-men" grew steadily more pronounced.

This dovetailed with advanced medical thinking on the subject. "Science" now began to insist that if a man had sex with another man, and found pleasure in doing so, then he was cut from the same cloth as his partner, even if he took the manly role. He was defined not by his male behavior but by his choice of sexual partner. His gender identity and his sexual identity parted company; he remained a male, but he was now also a "homosexual," as opposed to a "heterosexual." Male normality depended not on a man's masculine comportment but on his exclusive heterosexuality. A "real man" could only find sexual satisfaction with a female. Lines had been drawn, the ramparts of the great gender divide reinforced.

The Freudians had a hand in this. Brill, who in 1913 was chief of the Clinic of Psychiatry at Columbia, expressly classified "masculine" men who had sex with transvestite prostitutes as "homosexuals." The sex of the body with whom a man had sex was determinative.

This left middle-class gays in a pickle. For one thing, it ruled out adopting the persona of fairy. Faced with newly hardened gender trenches, they opted for the male side. Many were repelled by fairy behavior and the attendant loss of manly status. They also thought fairies were lower-class, which they usually were, and thus had little to lose by unconventional behavior, unlike themselves. They could live with the notion of being "homosexuals"—though "queer" was their (non-derogatory) term of choice. Queer men were not effeminate.[13] They agreed that their desire for men was a function of their sexual identity, not their gender style. This acceptance of "homosexuality" gave some pause, however, as psychiatrists were now labeling it as a pathological illness. Yet even this struck gays as an improvement over their being considered mortal sinners, deserving of death. And some European sexologists, notably Edward Carpenter, were arguing that homosexuality was a congenital condition, a normal part of the spectrum of human sexuality, and one that should be welcomed to the table. Havelock Ellis called for repeal of all laws criminalizing same-sex behavior. In the United States, however, that kind of social acceptance lay in the future, if there. Homosexual behavior was still subject to police arrests and vigilante raids.

One of the very few people in the country who publicly stood up for same-sex love was Emma Goldman, who began including in her speaking tours "The Intermediate Sex

---

13. Some queers argued that love for men was in fact *more* masculine than love for women and cited Whitman (and the ancient Greeks) as their authorities.

(A Discussion of Homosexuality)," a lecture whose title was borrowed from Edward Carpenter's 1908 work. The men and women who came up to her after this talk, she recalled, "confided to me their anguish and their isolation." "Most of them had reached an adequate understanding of their differentiation only after years of struggle to stifle what they had considered a disease and a shameful affliction. One young woman had never met anyone, she told me, who suffered from a similar affliction, nor had she ever read books dealing with the subject. My lecture had set her free; I had given her back her self-respect. Their pitiful stories made the social ostracism of the invert seem more dreadful than I had ever realized before."

SO IF OPEN EXPRESSION OF SAME-SEX LOVE would bring down the wrath of the heterosexual world and its defenders, and if fairy bars were not for them, but only for the young and poor and working-class, then where and how in the great city were they to meet and mingle with others of their sexual, gender, and class preference?

For men with money—businessmen, managers, professors, ministers, lawyers, clerks, to say nothing of the idle rich—there were quite a lot of possibilities.

Money bought circumspect housing in "bachelor" apartments and hotels, aimed at the single male market, which included (openly or not) men with homosexual preferences. Places like the Bachelor Apartments, at 15 East 48th, and the Hermitage Hotel, on Seventh Avenue just south of 42nd Street, were designed for the well-heeled single, and the St. George in Brooklyn was reputedly willing to accommodate avowedly gay men on a short- or long-term basis. Many lower-priced lodging houses readily rented to male couples, notably in neighborhoods near Union Square and Battery Park. The growing number of YMCA residential hotels emerged (quite unintentionally) as centers of gay sexual and social life. So did the contemporary Mills House No. 1, a single-room-occupancy venue at 156 Bleecker, though that had not at all been its progenitor's goal. Raines Law hotels provided additional options, thanks (if unwittingly) to vice reformers. In one instance, a hotel-saloon at 36 Myrtle Avenue, near the Brooklyn Navy Yard, was barred from admitting women, though it was soon discovered that "male perverts" were taking sailors to their rooms for "immoral purposes."

Bathhouses emerged as relatively safe havens—not the public ones, which were vigorously policed, but several private Russian and Turkish baths became amenable to a mixed or exclusively gay clientele. The Everard (all but inevitably a.k.a. "the Everhard") had been converted from a church to a bathhouse in 1888 and was located at 28 West 28th Street. In 1903 the Ariston Baths, in the basement of the twelve-story Ariston apartment hotel, at Broadway and 55th Street, were raided but subsequently ignored, probably as the managers paid for the privilege of uninterrupted operation. The Lafayette Baths, a gay haven at 403–405 Lafayette Street, just south of Cooper Union, were rendered in watercolors by Charles Demuth, a regular visitor in the 1910s.

Restaurants were another gathering spot. Like most young, single residents of rooming houses, gay men took meals at cheap cafeterias, like Child's or Horn and Hardart, and certain venues and tables within became known as gay gathering spots. So were public "comfort stations," especially those located near lodging houses for transients; the one in City Hall Park was widely known as a gay rendezvous, despite being subject to regular vice squad patrols.

Principally there were the streets and public places. The more commercial strips, where gay prostitutes worked alongside female counterparts, were in the vice districts, sites of assorted ribald entertainments—the Bowery, the Rialto (along East 14th Street between Third Avenue and Union Square), the Tenderloin (along Broadway and Sixth between 23rd and 40th), Times Square (at 42nd Street), and, seasonally, Coney Island. Gay men—their inclinations signaled perhaps by a red necktie—could also cruise for noncommercial companionship in public spaces, whose shifting locales were circulated on informal community networks. These notably included parks—Bryant, Prospect, and Central (in the 1900s Belvedere Castle near 63rd Street was the place to be; in the 1910s the hot spot was the southwest corner, at Columbus Circle, across from a Child's that was itself a major pickup site.)[14]

LESBIAN WOMEN HAD A HARDER TIME OF IT. It was much easier for men to live outside traditional families, as more of them worked and got paid better for doing so. Women wanting to survive in the city were more dependent on marriage, which all but precluded participation in a homosexual subculture. Men also had greater freedom to move about the city: many of the spaces in which they met, from streets to baths to public parks, were coded male.

On the other hand, there was a long-standing tradition of unmarried women openly living together in virtual marriages—"Boston marriages," they were called—which were accepted by respectable society. Dr. Sarah Josephine Baker, director of the city's Child Hygiene Bureau, lived in two successive Boston marriages. And Mary Dreier, head of the Women's Trade Union League, formed a close romantic bond with Frances Kellor, who in 1905 moved into Dreier's home in Brooklyn Heights. "Spinster" couples might or might not be sleeping together, but given reigning notions of female asexuality, the assumption was they weren't.[15] These connections in turn helped sustain a larger network of supportive friendship between single New Women, which collectively undergirded the settlement, feminist, and suffrage movements.

But the same altering of assumptions that led to the conviction that "real men" had to be exclusively heterosexual began, slowly, to lead to raised eyebrows about women who lived exclusively with other women. If women were indeed sexual beings, then "real women" should, it was ordained, form sexual attachments exclusively with men. Hitherto perfectly respectable ladies were increasingly defined as lesbians, and consequently as less respectable, indeed suspiciously abnormal, and this put a weapon in the hands of those opposed to their politics. Critics also began to discern homosexual elements in single-sex institutions like convents and boarding schools; doctors and psychologists scrutinized heretofore innocent schoolgirl "smashes" for signs of erotic content.

Ironically, such suspicions had a better chance of being borne out, precisely because young bachelor girls who were out of the domestic sphere, and acknowledging their sexuality while loosening its link with procreation, were opening up a space in which a lesbian subculture could be constructed. How the tension between a heightened demand for total heterosexuality, and the possibilities of creating a homosexual alternative, would play out remained to be seen.

14. Greenwich Village, despite its reputation for flouting bourgeois conventions, particularly those opposed to non-procreative sexuality, was not known as a rendezvous site. There were in fact a goodly number of gays in the bohemian world, but they were there as bohemians—artists, journalists, and feminists. (An estimated 20 percent of the Heterodoxy membership were lesbians.) Most mixed comfortably with their straight peers—though some bohemian men were troubled by the popular assumption that their unorthodox behavior and dress and long-haired style meant they were "queer" in a sexual sense—but resident queers had little interest in developing gay institutions.

15. Anne Morgan (J. P.'s daughter) established a ménage à trois with Elsie de Wolfe—a former actress who had recently opened an interior design business—and her lover, the theatrical agent Elisabeth Marbury. They had worked together in 1903 on founding the Colony Club, the first social club established in New York City by and for women. Morgan helped raise $500,000, and Stanford White designed the clubhouse, which went up at 120 Madison Avenue (East 30th/31st Streets) between 1904 and 1908.

In the meantime, it appeared, the overall balance between the tightening and lightening of repressive forces proved conducive to an ongoing flight of gays from the provinces to the metropolis, a migration not all that dissimilar to the arrival of bohemians from around the country. In 1913 Brill estimated that there were "many thousands of homosexuals in New York city among all classes of society."

BIRTH CONTROL

In the 1890s, when Emma Goldman practiced midwifery, she learned that poor women routinely jumped off tables, rolled on floors, or used blunt instruments to forestall yet another pregnancy. Deciding that contraceptive information was essential, she discovered it was unattainable. Comstock had banned it as "obscene," and doctors wouldn't buck him. Even physician-reformer William Josephus Robinson, who pleaded publicly for repeal of the Comstock Law, bowdlerized his popular advice books from fear of prosecution. In 1912 Robinson convinced Abraham Jacobi, newly elected president of the AMA, to denounce denying working people information to which respectable women had underground access. But Jacobi's colleagues refused to act.

Tackling Comstock would require direct and illegal action. In 1900 Goldman attended a secret contraceptive conference in Paris and smuggled devices back to New York. Her plan to make them available was halted by her temporary retirement after the McKinley assassination. A decade later, back on the lecture circuit, she talked occasionally (and cautiously) about contraception, as one topic of many. She avoided arrest on an issue with which she was not physically involved, due to her own infertility (from an inverted womb).

For Margaret Higgins, the Irish Catholic daughter of an upstate stonemason, the issue was intensely personal. Her father, a Henry George supporter, had his disagreements with the Church, but fertility control was not one of them. He impregnated his tubercular wife eighteen times. She birthed eleven children before dying at 49, of TB, complicated by cervical cancer, when Maggie was 16.

Higgins studied nursing but cut off her career with an impulsive marriage in 1902 to William Sanger, a McKim, Mead & White architect. After a dull decade of suburban motherhood in Hastings-on-Hudson, she engineered a move to Manhattan in 1910. There the couple plunged into the world of Greenwich Village radicalism. Bill Sanger had long been a member of the Socialist Party, and Margaret signed up, too. She went to the Liberal Club and Polly's, attended Dodge's salon and ran one of her own, enrolled her children in Goldman's Modern School, read the *Masses*, and befriended Flynn, Debs, Reed, Goldman, Rodman, and Haywood.

She also worked as a midwife with Lillian Wald's Visiting Nurses Association. Like Goldman before her, she heard women desperate at perpetual pregnancy plead for the "secret rich people have" of stopping babies. And she watched when they visited five-dollar abortionists or resorted to steel knitting needles, with periodically fatal results.

Margaret Sanger now began to write articles for the socialist *Call* on sex and reproduction. In November 1912 the Post Office declared her piece on physiology and venereal disease unmailable under the Comstock Law. The *Call* ran the heading—"What Every Girl Should Know"—above the words "NOTHING, by order of the Post-Office Department."

Sanger had problems with the Socialists. The party's men saw contraception as a trivial issue, a distraction from class struggle. Worse, they accepted the conventional definition of women's sphere and excoriated capitalism only for forcing women to work outside it, thus neglecting housework, motherhood, and husband care.

Margaret H. Sanger, ca. 1910–15. (Library of Congress Prints and Photographs Division, George Grantham Bain Collection)

She switched to the IWW, went to Lawrence in 1912, worked on the Paterson strike and pageant in 1913, and in March 1914, with IWW help, started publishing the *Woman Rebel*. In it, she advocated "birth control" (a term of her coinage) as a weapon of class struggle for workers, and as a way to win reproductive self-determination for all women. Rejecting sexual repression by "self-appointed and self-perpetuating masters," she declared: "It is none of Society's business what a woman shall do with her body." Goldman vigorously supported Sanger, and on her 1914 lecture tour recruited agents to distribute her publication.

The *Woman Rebel* acted as a red flag to a tired old bull. In recent years Anthony Comstock, jabbed repeatedly by *Masses* picadors, had also lost status with respectables. In 1913, he had made himself a laughingstock by ordering an art dealer to remove a decorous nude painting from his 46th Street display window. Judges were also tiring of his arrogant manner, and in September 1913 Judge Learned Hand critiqued a Comstock prosecution of publisher Mitchell Kennerley, in a decision that called into question (though it did not overturn) the entire legal substructure on which Comstock had been standing for forty years.[16]

---

16. In September 1913 Comstock made an unannounced raid on Kennerley's office, arresting him and seizing the plates and all copies of a novel, *Hagar Revelly*, about the sexual exploitation of a poor woman worker in New York. Kennerley petitioned to dismiss the indictment, challenging the "Hicklin test," spawned by a British decision, *Regina v. Hicklin* (1868), that had been repeatedly reaffirmed by American courts. Hicklin permitted juries to find a work obscene if it contained even a single passage that was judged "likely to deprave and corrupt" those "whose minds are open to such immoral influences," particularly children. (Comstock supplied a copy in which he had underlined some objectionable parts, though he hadn't read the whole novel, having

The *Woman Rebel* seemed the perfect vehicle for a comeback. Though Sanger had not yet dared offer specific contraceptive advice, Comstock got the June 1914 issue banned as "lewd, vile, filthy and indecent." She mailed it off anyway and now, desiring to be hanged for a sheep rather than a lamb, drafted *Family Limitation*, a sixteen-page pamphlet containing detailed and explicit information. She got William Shatoff, an IWW printer (and manager of Goldman's Ferrer Center), to secretly run off 100,000 copies. She then bundled them off to Wobbly and Socialist locals across the country, and in November 1914, facing forty-five years in jail, she jumped bail and sailed for Liverpool, cabling instructions to release the pamphlet once the vessel reached international waters. She would stay in Europe for nearly a year, studying the history, technology, and practice of birth control under the tutelage of Havelock Ellis.

Meanwhile, back in New York, in January 1915 Comstock entrapped Bill Sanger into selling a copy of *Family Limitation*, then offered to drop the charges if he'd divulge Margaret's whereabouts; Bill refused and was promptly arrested.

In March 1915 less radical women jumped in. Mary Ware Dennett, a suffrage organizer and Heterodoxy member, formed the National Birth Control League, the country's first such organization. Composed primarily of upper-middle-class liberal women, it set out to change the law, not defy it, by lobbying legislators, rather than practicing Goldman-style civil disobedience. It would proceed, Dennett said, in a "quiet business-like" way. Other leagues formed swiftly around the country.

Tried in September 1915, Bill Sanger got thirty days in the Tombs. It was Comstock's last triumph. The strain of the trial undid him. He contracted pneumonia and died, with Margaret still beyond his clutches.

Bill's conviction stirred a firestorm. Goldman now lectured on contraceptive use, in Yiddish and English. Wobblies, Socialists, and Village feminists took up the cause, distributing thousands of Sanger pamphlets, giving talks, and being hauled away. The *Masses* publicized Sanger's case, and requests for instruction in birth control techniques poured in from working-class readers.

When Margaret returned in October 1915 to face trial, she reached for respectable support. She apologized for scattershot militancy, committed to birth control as a single issue, distanced herself from Goldman, and organized a letter-writing campaign on her own behalf. Major magazines now treated her cause sympathetically, and she was escorted to the courthouse in January 1916 by fifty prominent men and women. On February 14, 1916, not wanting to buck this new trend, the US attorney dropped the charges.

Goldman continued in militant mode and was arrested in New York for distributing birth control information. Supporters arranged a mass protest meeting in Carnegie Hall on March 1, 1916 (John Reed and the Free Speech League's Theodore Schroeder were among

---

seen quite enough, he said.) Hand rejected Kennerley's petition, saying Hicklin could not simply be ignored, but then argued that in fact it should be discarded. For one thing, a literary work should be considered in its entirety; for another, "obscenity" should be considered as a historical phenomenon, not an eternal moral verity. An alternative definition might consider obscenity to be "the present critical point in the compromise between candor and shame at which the community may have arrived here and now." In this light, he found that "however consonant [the Hicklin ruling] may be with mid-Victorian morals," it "does not seem to me to answer to the understanding and morality of the present time." He particularly objected to restrictions that "reduce our treatment of sex to the standard of a child's library." More broadly he argued: "To put thought in leash to the average conscience of our time is perhaps tolerable, but to fetter it by the necessities of the lowest and least capable seems a fatal policy." At the subsequent trial, attended faithfully each day by a contingent of writers from the Village, on February 9, 1914, a jury found Kennerley innocent, despite the judge's having virtually directed a verdict of guilty.

The jury wasn't alone in getting tired of Comstock. At an arraignment hearing before Hand that May, Comstock kept popping up unbidden and interjecting comments, despite being admonished repeatedly by Hand. Finally the judge crashed his gavel down and said: "You might as well understand now that when I wish to hear from you, I will let you know." The put-down made headlines.

the speakers), and held an April 19 pre-trial banquet at the Hotel Brevoort, at which Rose Pastor Stokes handed out contraceptive information. At her April 20 trial Goldman defended birth control on radical grounds (workers with large broods would not dare go out on strike, join a revolutionary organization, or even express an opinion). She was sent to Queens County jail for fifteen days. On May 5 another Carnegie Hall event, chaired by Max Eastman, welcomed her on her release, and when Stokes again offered to hand out information slips, throngs of young working women rushed the stage in their eagerness to get hold of one.

Sanger was not quite through with civil disobedience. She rented two rooms on the first floor of a Brownsville tenement near Pitkin Avenue and opened a birth control clinic modeled on those she had seen in Holland. When no doctor would join her she enlisted her sister, Ethel Byrne, a trained nurse. They gave out handbills in English, Yiddish, and Italian and, for nine days after opening their doors on October 16, 1916, dispensed information to the Catholic and Jewish working women who poured in. Then the authorities shut down the clinic and arrested the sisters. Ethel got thirty days on Blackwell's Island. She went on a hunger strike. After seven days, authorities force-fed her via tubes shoved down her throat. (The story was reported by Dorothy Day in the *Call*.)

Sanger did her thirty days more cooperatively. When released she set up a sober new magazine, *Birth Control Review*, and her own organization, the Birth Control League of New York. She made a movie, *Birth Control*, shot on location in the city, with scenes comparing child-ridden slum streets to wealthy and virtually child-free precincts. The film, which depicted her clinic, trial, and incarceration, was suppressed by the New York City license commissioner as immoral and indecent.

Sanger's concessions and the pressure of larger events would redirect the birth control movement into more conservative channels. But the initial breakthroughs that had cracked the fifty-year ban on the provision of contraceptive information had been engineered by a linkage between New York's downtown socialists, anarchists, and feminists and its uptown professional and society women.

It was a similar alliance that gathered to abolish New York State's roughly 150-year ban on women being allowed to vote.

SUFFRAGISTS AND SUFFRAGETTES

The twenty-third of October, 1915, was a crisp fall day, splashed with sunshine, perfect for a parade. In midafternoon tens of thousands of women clad in white dresses and yellow sashes stepped out of Washington Square. They strode up Fifth Avenue arrayed in delegations of assorted age and station—letter carriers' wives from Queens, schoolgirls from Washington Irving High, ILGWU seamstresses, Henry Street settlement workers. Vendors hawked yellow pennants, yellow balloons, chrysanthemums of yellow paper. A quarter-million onlookers lined the sidewalks.

As the marchers passed Mayor Mitchel's reviewing stand at the public library, they hoisted high their banners.

REYKJAVIK VOTES; WHY NOT NEW YORK?

THE HOME IS THE BULWARK OF THE NATION. GIVE IT TWO VOTES INSTEAD OF ONE.

WE WANT OUR MOTHERS TO VOTE!

It took till moonrise for the last of the demonstrators to reach the finish line. The final contingent consisted of 2,000 men singing (to the tune of "John Brown's Body") "We will vote for Suffrage, / We will vote for Suffrage, / On next Election Day."

Flyer for 46 Amboy Street Birth Control Clinic in Three Languages, Brownsville, 1916. (Margaret Sanger Papers, Five College Archives & Manuscript Collections)

Whether a majority of the city's (and state's) men would join them in supporting female enfranchisement in the upcoming November 1915 referendum remained an open question. But win or lose, the city's suffrage movement—and hence the nation's—had been utterly transformed since its doldrum days twenty years earlier.

IN 1894 THE NATIONAL AMERICAN WOMAN SUFFRAGE ASSOCIATION (NAWSA), its roots dating back to 1869, was still under the control of its now-septuagenarian founders Elizabeth Cady Stanton and Susan B. Anthony, who set out to reenergize the stalled enterprise by tying it to New York's political reform movement. In particular, they urged the state constitutional convention of 1894 to pass a woman suffrage amendment, arguing in part that respectable elite ladies, once enfranchised, could help their husbands counter immigrant-backed bosses and bring domestic virtue to public life. Without the vote, the prominent proponent Dr. Mary Putnam Jacobi noted, women—"no matter how well born, how well educated, how intelligent, how rich, how serviceable to the State"—were the political inferiors of all men, "no matter how base-born, how poverty stricken, how ignorant, how vicious, how brutal."

Other women, however, of similar social standing and educational and professional attainment, opposed granting their sex the right to vote. They reaffirmed the traditional gender order—the respective domains of women (the home) and men (the state) were "divinely ordered"—and they denounced the call for the ballot as a selfish, individualistic demand, one incompatible with the selfless role of a true woman. Elite female "antis," as they were called, insisted that domesticity need not straitjacket women. They applauded and sought an extension of female higher education and access to the professions, goals for which the ballot was not deemed essential. And they argued that upper- and middle-class women had already emerged as a political force, by establishing reform organizations like the Woman's Municipal League, under whose banner—and clothed in domestic virtue and political nonpartisanship—females had been doing door-to-door canvassing in Tammany districts on behalf of reform campaigns. Elite women had in effect extended their sphere into the public arena, and antis believed that voting, and the consequent inevitable involvement in party politics, would only diminish their influence, not enhance it.

Antis also noted that women had been granted a variety of privileges and protections, which might be lost if they demanded political equality. They believed, too, that they already had the ear of power—their husbands—and were loath to dilute that influence. Crucially, they pounced on the fatal flaw in the suffragists' argument that voting would strengthen elite reformers. If the suffrage was granted, working-class women would vote, too, and the ranks of "the ignorant" would double. Dr. Jacobi assured the convention that elite women would be able to "so guide ignorant women voters that they could be made to counterbalance, when necessary, the votes of ignorant and interested men." But this was hardly a sure thing. Even less compelling was Stanton's politically preposterous proposal to restrict the ballot to educated or propertied women.

In the end, the all male delegates voted female suffrage down by 98–58, with the majority led by such paladins as Elihu Root, who argued that "in politics there is struggle, strife, contention, bitterness, heart-burning, excitement, agitation, everything which is adverse to the true character of woman." As a result, enfranchised women would become "hard, harsh, unlovable, repulsive; as far removed from that gentle creature to whom we all owe allegiance and to whom we confess submission, as the heaven is removed from earth." It was the convention's duty to spare them this awful fate.

With this setback, the movement seemed to have reached an impasse.

A SUGGESTED NEW DEPARTURE EMERGED FROM AN UNLIKELY QUARTER. Stanton's own daughter. Harriot Stanton Blatch publicly rejected NAWSA's unwillingness to include wage-earning women in either its vision or its strategy. Blatch wrote dismissively that the older group's effort "was being wasted on its supporters in private drawing rooms and in public halls where friends, drummed up and harried by the ardent, listlessly heard the same old arguments." She urged ladies of the "well-dressed movement" to make common cause with laboring women—maids, salesgirls, factory workers. Not that Blatch was disaffected from parlor society. She had married into a wealthy British family and had lived in England for many years. But she had also participated in the Fabian socialist and suffrage movements and gained a profound appreciation for the political and intellectual capabilities of working people.

When the elderly leadership recoiled from this approach, Blatch abandoned the suffrage movement. In 1905 she joined a more congenial group, the Women's Trade Union League. Blatch conducted investigations, organized mass meetings, and developed close relations with working-class leaders, especially Leonora O'Reilly and Rose Schneiderman. Their responsiveness to the suffrage issue strengthened Blatch's determination to wrest control of the stagnant movement from rich clubwomen.

In January 1907, with her mother and Anthony now in their graves, Blatch founded the Equality League of Self-Supporting Women (EL). It embraced college-educated professionals, doctors, lawyers, social workers, government employees, and reformers like Florence Kelley and Charlotte Perkins Gilman. Blatch considered these women the natural leaders of their sex. The EL also included milliners, shirt makers, and salesgirls—equally entitled to political voice, and, crucially, capable of affording access to working-class men (the majority, after all, of the electorate). Jewish working women on the Lower East Side were a prime target; the EL's first mass meeting, at Cooper Union on April 4, 1907, featured such speakers as Rose Schneiderman, Joseph Barondess, and Rabbi Stephen Wise.

With a changed constituency came a change in tactics. Blatch called for aggressive activism. Her model in part was the WTUL. Still greater inspiration came from the British suffrage movement led by Blatch's comrade from her Fabian days, Emmeline Pankhurst. In December 1907 the Equality League sponsored a talk by Anne Cobden-Sanderson, a visiting "suffragette." A packed house at Cooper Union thrilled to her report on the new tactics of civil disobedience practiced in London by the Women's Social and Political Union (formed in 1903), which were drawn from old working-class and Irish nationalist practice. Cobden-Sanderson had been one of the first to be arrested for the suffrage cause.

Cobden-Sanderson's visit catalyzed the New York movement. Days later, on December 31, 1907, an existing left-wing municipal reform group of actresses, artists, writers, teachers, and social welfare workers stole a march on Blatch. Led by librarian Maude Malone, president of the Harlem Equal Rights League (1905), and Bettina Borrman Wells, a visiting English suffragette, they organized a Progressive Woman Suffrage Union and started up a journal called the *American Suffragette*.[17] Using the continental term rather than the conventional "suffragist" designation signaled militant intentions on which they swiftly made good, holding an open-air meeting in Madison Square, a shocking departure for heretofore parlor-bound suffrage workers. Six weeks later they held New York's first all-woman parade, despite denial of a police permit. Though the tiny contingent of twenty-three women was dwarfed by the crowd of sympathetic workingmen looking on, it garnered enormous publicity. A follow-up march through Wall Street brought ruder treatment. Men jeered, hurled hard rolls and wet sponges. Undaunted, the group renounced "tea-table and drawing-room chat" forever, declaring: "The Suffragette is unwilling to wait for the ballot another sixty years. She wants it *now* and she wants it *quick*!"

---

17. In a remarkable example of intergenerational solidarity, they received financial aid from 75-year-old Tennessee Claflin (Victoria Woodhull's sister), now Lady Cook, the wife of a titled Englishman.

H. Riordan, "American Suffragette," January 27, 1910. (Library of Congress Prints and Photographs Division, George Grantham Bain Collection)

Blatch's group followed suit and slipped the constraints of respectable femininity. The EL held open-air meetings all around the city and organized the first sizable parade. In an interview with the *Times*, Blatch said it was imperative to reach men where they were, lauded the "value of publicity" as an aide to doing that, and argued that her "wide awake" methods had given a "brand new" sheen to the movement. In particular she pressed ahead with incorporating working women. She changed the EL's name to the Women's Political Union (WPU)—to be more welcoming to those who were not "self supporting," and also to underscore her affinity for the British suffragette organization (even adopting its colors—purple, green, and white—rather than the American jonquil yellow).

Both intentions were on evidence in Carnegie Hall on October 25, 1909, when Blatch arranged a talk by Sylvia Pankhurst, Emmeline's even more militant daughter. A capacity crowd of 3,000, with hundreds turned away, thrilled to her presentation. But they also marveled at the marshaled massing of Gotham womanhood. On stage sat 79 teachers, 6 dentists, 38 trained nurses, 120 trade unionists, 49 social workers, 8 actresses, 46 businesswomen, 10 musicians, 1 architect, 1 explorer, 16 authoresses, 2 sculptors, 4 journalists, 16 civil service workers, 25 lawyers, and an assortment of box makers, bookbinders, cigar makers, decorators, hat trimmers, librarians, potters, printers, stenographers, clerks, textile workers, telegraphers, and waitresses. In the boxes above sat leaders of reform organizations (NAWSA, the WTUL), and members of the suffragist rich, including Rose Pastor Stokes, Alice Lewisohn, Florence Jaffray Harriman (wife of banker J. Borden Harriman), Katherine Duer Mackay (wife of communications magnate Clarence Mackay), and, perhaps most formidable of all, Alva Smith Vanderbilt Belmont.

With the death of her second husband, O. H. P. Belmont, the flinty Alva (who long ago, as William Vanderbilt's wife, had crashed her way into Mrs. Astor's Four Hundred), now commanded two of the greatest fortunes in New York. In 1909 she threw her immense resources into the struggle. Entering the movement through NAWSA, she quickly determined that the national organization was too conservative and too inconspicuous. During a visit to England in April, as a NAWSA delegate to the International Woman Suffrage Alliance Convention, she was inspired by the militant tactics of the suffragettes and set out to remodel the mainstream US movement. In August she provided NAWSA, and its local affiliate the New York State Woman Suffrage Association, with luxurious office space, grounding the national movement in New York City. Occupying nearly an entire floor in 505 Fifth Avenue, a new tower at the corner of 42nd Street, the offices afforded room for a speakers bureau, a press bureau, and a printing establishment. It also housed Belmont's own suffrage group, the Political Equality Association, which consisted, principally, of Belmont herself. Untrammeled and resource rich, she now reached out to enroll the city's militant shirtwaist strikers in the suffrage movement.

On December 5, 1909, less than two weeks after Clara Lemlich had launched the ladies' garment walkout, Alva Belmont rented the mammoth Hippodrome for an event to promote and publicize the epochal rising of women. When somewhere between 6,000 and 8,000 strikers and allies jammed their way into the 5,300-seat venue, they found the cavernous venue festooned with banners hailing organized labor (WE DEMAND EQUAL PAY FOR EQUAL WORK) and organized women (GIVE WOMEN THE PROTECTION OF THE VOTE). Included along with labor and leftist speakers was the Reverend Dr. Anna Howard Shaw, president of NAWSA, who in the course of explaining the utility of the ballot found herself expanding her own movement's boundaries, despite the apprehensiveness of much of her membership at yoking the suffrage movement to the more radical labor movement. "Men keep telling us we should go back to the home and do the work our grandmothers did," she told the assembled throng. But "we can't; the men have taken that work out of the home, have put it in factories, and we must go out of the home to do it. . . . We don't go out to work because we like it. . . . We do those things because we have to."

Was the Hippodrome rally supporting "the cause of woman suffrage or the strikers?" the *New-York Tribune* asked, and answered: "It was hard to tell." Which was exactly the point. And it was why many strikers, who were suspicious about the motives of some Lady Bountiful allies, respected Belmont because she wanted something in return—their support for her suffrage cause, a cause that might well be of utility to them as well, hence the potential basis for a true alliance. The *Times* reported that many of the shirtwaist strikers had begun wearing suffrage buttons.

BY 1910, THE REENERGIZED AND EXPANDED SUFFRAGE MOVEMENT was fast becoming fashionable in metropolitan drawing rooms, college campuses, women's clubs, office buildings, and factory floors. And among (some) men as well as women.

The Men's League for Woman Suffrage, launched by Max Eastman in November 1909, was in part inspired by England's 1907 identically named association of left-wing intellectuals. Encouraged and aided by his mentor John Dewey (who hailed women's suffrage as an expansion of American democracy), Eastman pulled together roughly a hundred charter members, including Oswald Garrison Villard, Rabbi Wise, C. C. Burlingham (an admiralty lawyer), Charles Beard, William Dean Howells, Paul Kellogg, William Jay Schieffelin, Edward Devine, Ernest Poole, and Columbia professors Henry Seager and Joel Spingarn. In

1910, after the league's formal organization, it began providing contingents of male marchers to join in what became annual suffrage parades down Fifth Avenue.

FOR ALL THE GROWING VISIBILITY AFFORDED BY VIGOROUS PUBLIC ACTION TECHNIQUES, the
path to suffrage ran unavoidably through the formal political process, and the entity dedicated to winning legislative approbation was the New York City Woman Suffrage Party, the
creation of Carrie Chapman Catt. When Susan B. Anthony had retired from the presidency
of the National American Woman Suffrage Association in 1900, she had chosen Catt as her
successor, in large part because she'd shown a great flair for organizing. Catt had resigned the
presidency in 1904, to care for her ailing husband, and after his death in 1905 had confined
herself to the international suffrage movement, spending much of her time abroad. But in
1907 she turned her considerable talents to New York and set out to build a women's equivalent of Tammany Hall. First she took command of the Interurban Suffrage Council, a coalition of a few of the many small groups that had sprung up around the metropolis. Then she
pulled in many more, established a headquarters (at the Martha Washington Hotel), and set
up caucuses in every assembly district. These gatherings in turn chose 804 delegates to a
Convention of Disfranchised Women, which, on October 29, 1909, at a giant Carnegie Hall
meeting, founded the New York City Woman Suffrage Party (WSP). Though a subset of the
relatively conservative national and state organizations, the WSP also included virtually
every suffrage group in the city (including that of Blatch). While a substantial minority of the
new organization's leadership were *Social Register* ladies, the cadre also included numerous
union organizers and settlement house workers (Lillian Wald was honorary vice chairman)
and constituted a virtual Who's Who of Gotham's feminist political community.

Catt's strategy was to use Charlie Murphy's tactics—methods hitherto deemed degrading and undignified—to press for the ballot. In February 1910 the party set up headquarters
in the Metropolitan Life tower, started a journal (the *Woman Voter*), and hit the bricks—getting petitions signed on the street, canvassing door to door, organizing mass meetings, and
taking charge of the mounting of Fifth Avenue parades. Its first, on May 21, 1910, novelly
featured demonstrators riding in ninety automobiles, draped in yellow, followed by several
thousand marchers carrying banners like NEW YORK DENIES THE VOTE TO LUNATICS, IDIOTS,
CRIMINALS—AND WOMEN. The parade ended up at a rally in Union Square. With an estimated 10,000 participants, it was the largest women's suffrage demonstration ever mounted
in the United States.

Catt's Woman Suffrage Party welcomed socialists for their access to working women but
kept their leaders at arm's length, lest they alienate wealthy backers. The socialists were themselves divided on the issue. The party had been the only political organization to accept women
members and back women's rights. Debs (nationally) and Hillquit (locally) had championed
female suffrage. Yet many in the party were lackadaisical in support, considering it at best a
secondary issue. Some actively suspected a movement that for so long had denigrated immigrants. Even after the mainstream turned around in 1907, some socialists, pointing to
Belmont's participation, persisted in branding it an affair of rich faddists. (Wobbly syndicalists like Elizabeth Gurley Flynn were at first even less sympathetic, believing the vote largely
irrelevant to working-class women, who should concentrate on winning power at the workplace; Flynn also feared it might set working-class women at odds with working-class men.)

In 1908 the national Socialist Party backed suffrage, the only major party to do so. And
in 1909 US socialist women celebrated a "National Woman's Day"—with about women
turning out to hear speakers like Leonora O'Reilly, Charlotte Perkins Gilman, and Rose

Schneiderman. The Second International adopted the idea of such a celebration in 1910 and held its own in 1911. Meanwhile, socialist women forged an autonomous network of socialist suffrage clubs in all five boroughs and threw themselves into the struggle. The *New York Call* covered their activities extensively.

FROM 1910 ON, THE BROADER MOVEMENT EXPANDED ITS RANGE of advocacy techniques, from old-fashioned ward canvassing, to up-to-the-minute devices pioneered in the city's emerging mass-culture industry. Lavish society events drew the most press coverage: a suffrage card party and dance at the Hotel Astor; Louisine Havemeyer's benefit exhibit of her painting collection at the Knoedler gallery; exclusive balls; formal dress dinners at private homes and clubs. These aimed to establish the movement's respectability, influence wealthy men and politicians, and raise money. But the great bulk of work was done in middle- and working-class communities, where the votes lay. In 1913 Blatch held the annual WPU ball at an armory and invited striking shirt makers free. The "Shirtwaist Ball" was attended by 5,000, and press accounts goggled at the mingling of waltzers in shirtwaists with those in glittering gowns.

Campaigners sought out New Yorkers at play as well as work. The WSP sponsored Suffrage Days at baseball games. They draped banners across Polo Grounds boxes, sold suffrage candies, and held post-game open-air rallies. "Sandwich girls" walked the beach at Coney Island, advertising meetings. Suffragettes appeared as novelty attractions on the vaudeville stage and gave speeches between acts. At legitimate theaters they performed tableaux at matinees and sponsored suffrage plays. And they invaded the movie houses, not as protestors but as producers.

The new world of film had been notably hostile to suffragists. Studios ground out satires portraying them as man-hating anarchists bent on overturning the natural domestic order. A typical Pathé product, *A Day in the Life of a Suffragette* (1908), guffawed at harridans who ran amok, got thrown in jail, and ended by meekly following their husbands back to hearth and home. The movement fought film with film. In 1912 suffrage leaders produced *Votes for Women*. This melodrama depicted a haughty senator (and secret slum lord) won over to suffrage by his brave (and beautiful) fiancée. The film, which included newsreel footage shot at a Fifth Avenue suffrage parade, was exhibited at nickelodeons, fairs, and churches across the country. In 1913 *80 Million Women Want—?* opened at the Bryant Theatre. Starring Harriet Stanton Blatch and Emmeline Pankhurst, it featured a brave (and beautiful) female sleuth exposing a big-city boss.

The most striking events were the mass spectacles—demonstrations at the Statue of Liberty, bonfires on high hillsides, outdoor concerts, torchlit processions through ethnic communities, and, above all, the street parades—that bedrock form of urban entertainment and expression of strength and solidity. The Fifth Avenue parades grew larger with each passing year. By 1912 Macy's was selling marching gowns with matching bonnets and hatpins. Suffragettes set up their own suffrage shops, which sold message-bearing buttons, hats, fans, soap, rulers, matches, sewing kits, calendars, blotters, note paper, stickers, and greeting cards.

Above all, suffragettes sought to persuade through reasoned oratory. The WSP established schools to train organizers in public speaking. Hundreds of women took a ten-week course that included classes in suffrage history, the legal and social status of women, and organizing tactics. Graduates fanned out to address neighborhood groups, Protestant and Jewish congregations, and thousands of street meetings. Socialist women shared soapboxes with popular party leaders like London, Hillquit, and Debs.

"Book-Keepers and Stenographers, Women's Suffrage Parade, 1913." (Photo Researchers/Science Source)

The women allied with labor groups. In 1911 the WSP and WTUL teamed up to organize a New York Wage Earners' League for Suffrage and also created an Industrial Section within the WSP. Leonora O'Reilly presided over both. Rose Schneiderman, Mary Dreier, Rose Pastor Stokes, Florence Kelley, and ILGWU heroine Clara Lemlich (vice president of the WTUL) spoke at union meetings and factory gates. Margaret Hinchey, a rugged Irishwoman who worked in steam laundries, sought out workingmen in workshops, in subway excavations, and along the North River piers.

Speakers argued that votes for women were an "industrial necessity." Female workers could use the ballot to abolish the sweatshop, raise their wages, stop police harassment, win protective legislation, bring down food and housing costs, end child labor, and expand educational opportunities.

They made the same points in print. Suffrage groups ran off and distributed literature on a scale not seen since abolitionist days. Millions of small pamphlets, leaflets, and fliers were printed, in large type, on bright paper, in German, Italian, Yiddish, Scandinavian, and Bohemian, which were distributed with the help of settlement workers. The WSP also got suffrage news into the ethnic press. There were the occasional missteps. In March 1914 the WSP held a "cosmopolitan fete" aimed at ethnic groups, with booths representing nations. Unfortunately, the Italian booth featured an organ grinder with his monkey. This prompted the editor of *La Follia di New York* to acidly remind WSP leaders that "whilst their ancestors were still wandering, half naked, through the forests and plains," women professors were teaching philosophy, medicine, and literature at Bologna and Padua.

THE STEADY EXPANSION OF SUFFRAGE FORCES provoked a similar escalation by those who opposed extending the franchise. In 1895, in the wake of their successful campaign to beat back efforts at amending the state constitution, a coalition of women's groups came together at the home of Sarah Amelia Cooper Hewitt, the only surviving daughter of Peter Cooper, to form

"14-Yr. Old Striker, Fola La Follette, and Rose Livingston," 1913. (Library of Congress Prints and Photographs Division, George Grantham Bain Collection)

the New York State Association Opposed to Woman Suffrage. Its ranks grew slowly but steadily, from 12,000 in 1896 to 30,000 in 1914, much of the gain due to the leadership of Josephine Jewell Dodge, widow of wealthy businessman Arthur Murray Dodge and a leading philanthropist in her own right.

The New York organization became the vanguard of anti-suffragists throughout the United States, receiving a steady flow of requests for information, advice, or assistance from women in at least twenty different states. In 1911, galvanized by the surging local and national suffrage movement, notably its victory that year in California, the antis gathered in Dodge's Park Avenue home and founded the National Association Opposed to Woman Suffrage, of which Dodge took the helm. She also launched and edited the movement's official journal, the *Woman's Protest*.

The anti-suffrage leadership bore a marked resemblance to its suffrage counterpart. The women were wealthy, well educated, members of social clubs, and supporters of charities. Those who were professionals typically worked as authors or editors for genteel publications. Where the antis parted company with pro-vote social peers—apart from the fundamental disagreement on the desirability of enfranchising women—was in being uncomfortable with the contradiction between their professed abhorrence of stepping into the political arena and their ever-increasing involvement in politics. Slowly, reluctantly, always lagging behind their opponents, they graduated from ladylike parlor meetings to testifying at legislative hearings, giving speeches to mixed audiences, debating their suffrage opponents, erecting billboards and kiosks, and distributing fliers, buttons, and reams of anti-suffrage literature at public gatherings. They broke with the taboo against open-air meetings on April 15, 1912, with an event that drew about 800 people, perhaps a third of them men. Their outreach was limited, however, and despite pallid attempts to clone suffragette "wage-earner" organizations, they never put much energy into appealing for working-class or immigrant support, and they declined to "go out in carts or speak on street corners."

Anti-suffragists, as one wrote, were aware of the incongruity of "going into public life to say they can't go into it," but they pressed ahead because they believed that the suffrage movement had become increasingly associated with even more dangerous opponents: socialists and feminists. These evil twins, charged the National Association Opposed to Woman Suffrage, were out to destroy not just separate spheres but the patriarchal family itself. Their demands for "economic independence" would "depose man as the head of the home" and replace the "sacred marriage tie" with a "mere partnership contract"—an ideology "borrowed directly from socialism." Feminists, the antis argued, had "an aversion to motherhood," engaged in immoral behavior, practiced free love, and flaunted their "sex appeal" when parading through the streets. "Misdirected government is a bad thing," said Dodge, "but misdirected sex is a national tragedy, which, if not checked, will degenerate the race."

Anti-suffrage men were equally vehement and increasingly took a hand in the struggle. In May 1913 Everett P. Wheeler—a corporate lawyer, a founder of the New York Bar Association, a civil service reformer, and a founder of the Citizens' Union—launched and chaired the New York State Association Opposed to the Political Suffrage for Women. Wheeler soon changed the name to the more gender-specific Man-Suffrage Association Opposed to Woman Suffrage, though in private he whimsically referred to it as the Society for the Prevention of Cruelty to Women. Among those who flocked to his standard were some of the most powerful males of New York, including Charles S. Fairchild (corporate lawyer, railroad executive, bank president, and former secretary of the treasury), Francis Lynde Stetson (general counsel for United States Steel), Herbert L. Satterlee (J. P. Morgan's son-in-law), Cleveland Hoadley Dodge (of the Phelps, Dodge mining empire), and Elihu Root (former secretary of war, former secretary of state, and at that point one of New York's US senators). Within a year, the Man-Suffrage group claimed 309 members, many of whom hailed from old Knickerbocker families, had attended New England prep schools and Ivy League colleges, worked in Wall Street law firms, and were active in (all-male) clubs, national politics, philanthropy, charity, settlement houses, museums, and Society (two-thirds were in the *Social Register*). They also shared an extreme animosity to woman suffrage and a determination to fight it, even if it meant tackling all-female opponents. His members, Wheeler told a congressional committee, like all American males,

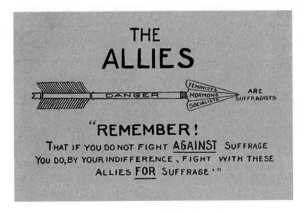

Anti-suffrage propaganda. "DANGER. The Allies Are Suffragists: Feminists, Mormons, Socialists." (New York State Library, Manuscripts and Special Collections)

"revere[d] womenhood," but if it came to a showdown, there would be "blows to give as well as blows to take."

THEN SHOWDOWN TIME ARRIVED.

The New York City Woman Suffrage Party had been pushing the state legislature, year after year, to authorize a referendum that would submit women's suffrage to a popular (if all-male) vote. In 1910 the measure died in the state senate. In 1911 it was shot down in both Albany houses. But in 1912 the constant battering forced politicians to give ground. Until that year, Democrats and Republicans at municipal, state, and federal levels had remained solidly anti-female-suffrage. New-model Tammany leaders like Al Smith and Robert Wagner feared women voters would back civic reform, prohibition, or third-party candidates. The consequences of inaction seemed increasingly dangerous. In 1912 Roosevelt's Progressive Party endorsed suffrage and garnered extensive female support. And the formidably well or-ganized suffrage movement bluntly warned politicos that once enfranchised they would take revenge on those who had blocked their way.

Both state parties decided to pass the issue on to the male electorate. In January 1913— the annus mirabilis of reform—Robert Wagner shepherded a referendum bill through the state senate, all the while declaring he was "just as much opposed to suffrage as he ever had been." Smith did the same in the assembly. Two years later, in February 1915, the next legis-lature ratified its predecessor's decision (as was required by the state constitution), and the issue was placed on the November 1915 ballot.

The *Times* responded immediately—editorially reminding readers that it was "totally opposed" to suffrage, which "would tend to disorganize society." With a referendum now unavoidable, "a grave issue faces the men," the paper said pugnaciously, "and they must meet it squarely." This the opposition men did, in the process largely taking control of the "anti" movement away from the women. They stressed, with increasing hysteria, that men were under attack from the "imitation-of-man" movement, which was thirsting for a "sex battle." Indeed, their "man hatred" had reached such a pitch that they wanted to "take him and kill him." And while women were the immediate oppressors in this gender fight, behind them lurked the left. One 1915 pamphlet listed the names of socialists enrolled in the suf-frage camp and concluded: "We are indeed threatened by a red peril in a yellow cloak."

CATT, TOO, REDOUBLED HER EFFORTS. She now generaled an Empire State Campaign Committee, leaving the City Woman Suffrage Party in the capable hands of her lieutenant Mary Garrett Hay.

Hay decided to canvass all of the 661,164 registered voters. Hundreds of women visited tenements, shops, factories, city and suburban homes, department stores, and office build-ings. It was estimated that 60 percent of the enrolled voters received personal appeals. The membership of the party was increased by 60,535 as women signed on to do canvassing.

The activists also embraced spectacular campaign activities that caught the public's at-tention. On the Night of the Interurban Council Fires, huge bonfires were lit on high bluffs in the different boroughs, and fireworks and balloons were sent up while music, speeches, and transparencies emphasized woman's evolution. There were torchlight rallies; street dances on the Lower East Side; Irish, Syrian, Italian, and Polish block parties; outdoor concerts, among them a big one in Madison Square, where a full orchestra played, opera singers sang, and eminent orators spoke; open-air religious services with the moral and religious aspects of suffrage discussed; a fête held in Dyckman Glen; flying squadrons of speakers whirling in autos from the Battery to the Bronx.

During the pre-referendum summer of 1915, they sponsored 5,225 outdoor meetings, organized suffrage hikes, ran telephone campaigns, and put on mime shows in department store windows. "Subway ladies" rode trains with posters on their laps. Various occupations were honored with their own "Suffrage Day," including firemen, lawyers, streetcar operators, longshoremen, and barbers. In June, Margaret Hinchey went down into a subway construction trench, carrying armfuls of green literature decorated with shamrocks, and asked in her thick brogue: "Brothers, are ye going to give us the vote in November?" "Sure we are," they cried back, and others down the way called out, "Send the big gurrl over here," and "Maggie Hinchey's all right."[18]

Optimism broke out. Observers noted that Tammany, while officially opposed, had begun to hedge its bets. In June, city Democrats agreed to let suffragettes use party clubrooms for meetings and offered assistance in canvassing. When Frances Perkins visited Murphy on another matter, the boss asked if she was one of "those woman suffragists." When Perkins allowed she was, Murphy responded: "Well, I am not, but if anybody ever gives them the vote, I hope that you will remember that you would make a good Democrat."

Perkins herself participated in an optimistic initiative, the founding in July 1915 of the New York Women's City Club. It was conceived at a meeting of about a hundred suffragists, so confident of winning the vote that they wanted an entity that could study and debate political initiatives, which women could promote with their newly won franchise. It set up shop in the fall, in a luxurious venue on the top floor of the Vanderbilt Hotel, and soon drew 440 charter members, forging a network of powerful women, prominent in their own right or through marriage to members of Gotham's political and intellectual elite.

The suffrage blitz climaxed with the magnificent parade on October 23—57 bands, 145 autos, 74 women on horseback—roughly two weeks before the referendum.

BUT THE REFERENDUM LOST. Big-time. New York's men defeated female suffrage 57–43 percent statewide and by a virtually identical margin in Gotham. Suffrage lost in all five boroughs. 238,098 voted in favor, 320,853 against, leaving an adverse majority of 82,755.

Suffragists raged. The WSP excoriated liquor dealers, politicians, and "arrogant young men flushed with the divine right of sex." Blatch, chagrined and furious, reverted to her mother's perspective and berated immigrants. It was humiliating, she fumed, that "men of twenty-six nationalities, not including the Indian," had "the power to pass upon me and upon the native born women of America, and a disgrace that the men of our country will force us to submit to it."

Lillian Wald rejected Blatch's blanket allegation of immigrant culpability and pointed to the election returns for decisive refutation.

It was true that German American men were antipathetic to suffrage, but that stance was anti-women only to the extent that they believed that once empowered, females would be more likely than males to support prohibition, another progressive reform then percolating, and indeed women had taken the lead in that movement for decades. Gotham's Germans were closely tied to the brewery industry—as owners, employees, and imbibers—and they viewed the suffrage campaign as an indirect assault on their livelihood and culture. Some

---

18. Socialists organized their own suffrage campaign, led by the Russian-born Theresa Malkiel, a pioneer agitator in the city's Jewish labor movement in the 1890s, an activist in the 1909 garment strike, a member of the Women's Trade Union League, and a Socialist Party militant. Socialist women took the suffrage case to women in immigrant communities, in conjunction with the party's language federations. Suffrage brigades distributed thousands of leaflets, held hundreds of street meetings on nearly every square block in the city, and arranged more convenient meetings in homes and public schools, proclaiming the link between suffrage and socialism, and covered the referendum drive in a "Votes for Women" column in the *Call*.

suffragists had in fact charged brewers with backing the anti campaign, despite Catt's injunctions not to do so, as there was no evidence to support the charge.

The Irish were less uniformly opposed, and Irish-dominated unions supported suffrage on paper. But the rank and file remained unenthusiastic. Longshoremen, building workers, firemen, policemen, and teamsters worked in all-male occupations. They shared neither workplace concerns nor political activism with Irish women, who worked overwhelmingly in nonunionized salesrooms and offices, or in isolated service jobs.[19] More troubling was the possible impact of suffrage on their metropolitan power bases—Tammany Hall and the Catholic Church. The local hierarchy had taken no official stand on suffrage, but there was little doubt where it stood. In 1909 the pope had declared: "Women can never be man's equal and cannot therefore enjoy equal rights." Priests and Catholic writers professed fear for the family (notably in Martha Moore Avery's denunciations of the "ungodly" sex rebellion, in contributions to Gotham-based journals like *America* or *Catholic Mind*). If women agreed with their husbands, they didn't need the vote. If they disagreed, empowering them would precipitate household schisms. Irish working-men had forced the Church hierarchy to a more progressive stance on labor issues. But Irish women lacked the clout to sway an utterly male and totally hierarchical institution, whereas Jewish and Protestant clergy were more exposed to pressure from the female laity.

Jewish gender relationships in general were dramatically different. Men and women shared workplace as well as family concerns. They had gone through the great garment strikes together (though in separate unions). In the voting, suffrage received extremely heavy support from predominantly Jewish assembly districts of the Lower East Side of Manhattan, the South Bronx, and parts of Brooklyn, and not a single Jewish-dominated district was opposed.

The Italians' response, to a degree, mirrored the Jews'. Few voted, so their numbers were not crucial to the outcome, and most uptown Italians voted no. But the Sicilian and Neapolitan precincts of Greenwich Village were solidly in favor. In many such families, female members had worked with their men in the garment trades and struggled alongside them (and their Jewish comrades) in the great general strikes. They were accessible to activists and open to arguments that voting would improve their family's lives. Priestly predictions of family fission no doubt seemed wildly improbable in their close-knit households.

TWO DAYS AFTER THE ELECTION, the WSP and NAWSA held a mass meeting at Cooper Union, where speeches were made and $100,000 pledged for a new campaign fund. The spirit of the members was shown in the words of a leader who wrote: "We know that we have gained over half a million voters in the State, that we have many new workers, have learned valuable lessons and with the knowledge obtained and undiminished courage we are again in the field of action."

The next referendum was slated for 1917.

THE PAST TWENTY YEARS HAD WITNESSED MULTIPLE CHALLENGES to the traditional gender order by the city's New Women. They would be marked as well by momentous (and overlapping) challenges to the city's long-standing racial order, launched by the city's black community, particularly its self-professed New Negroes.

---

19. One sample of registered voters found 53 percent of Irish men unmarried. Many of these bachelors lodged not with private families, but in all-male boardinghouses. And when they did marry—reluctantly and late—they spent little time with their wives, socializing instead with their "mates" in sex-segregated institutions.

21

Black Metropolis

RIOT

All day the twelfth of August 1900, the city roasted through a heat wave. Night brought no relief. In Hell's Kitchen, sleepless residents perched on stoops or fled to local watering holes. Arthur Harris, a 22-year-old, Virginia-born recent migrant, sought refuge at McBride's Saloon on the corner of Eighth Avenue and 41st Street, just down the block from the apartment in which he lived with his girlfriend, 20-year-old May Enoch. At 2:00 a.m., Enoch came by, asked him to "come on up home," then waited outside for him to join her. On departing, Harris found her struggling in a man's grip. He leapt to rescue her. The man produced a club and began battering him, shouting racist epithets. Harris pulled a knife and cut his assailant twice. Robert J. Thorpe, a plainclothes policeman who had been arresting Enoch for presumed soliciting, fell mortally wounded.

Harris was black. Thorpe was white. Three nights later the neighborhood exploded. Throngs of Irish residents howling "Lynch the niggers!" mobbed Eighth Avenue trolleys, dragged blacks off, beat them with lead pipes. Packs of young white men raced up and down the West 20s and 30s, screaming with rage at "black sons of bitches," hunting and stomping victims. Finally, the (overwhelmingly Irish) police force arrived—and promptly joined the rioters: smashing heads with nightsticks, shooting at apartment windows, dragging blacks to the 37th Street station house, where they were kicked, punched, and clubbed into insensibility. Before it was over, seventy blacks had been seriously injured, some crippled for life.

"Arthur Harris (from a photograph)." *Evening World*, August 16, 1900. (Chronicling America: Historic American Newspapers. Library of Congress)

The city's African American community demanded an investigation of police behavior. A grand jury held perfunctory hearings, then refused to indict anyone. The NYPD launched an internal review, a palpable sham that in the end would fully exonerate the accused officers, and indeed commend them for their "prompt and vigorous action."

Perceiving the whitewash in progress, the city's leading black ministers, organized by the Reverend Dr. William H. Brooks, pastor of St. Mark's Methodist Episcopal on West 53rd Street, formed a Citizens' Protective League (CPL) to undertake an independent investigation. On the night of September 12, a massive assemblage jammed into Carnegie Hall to ratify the CPL's founding, hurrah orators who protested the recent outrage, and denounce the failure of officials to punish those guilty. Brooks, angry but cautious, urged the throng to "fight for our rights," but "do nothing which will cost us the sympathy of the best people." Maritcha Lyons, a Brooklynite civil rights activist and the only female speaker, was more combative. "Let every negro get a permit to carry a revolver," she said. "You are not supposed to be a walking arsenal, but don't you get caught again."

With the support of good-government forces, the CPL hired prominent white lawyers—notably Frank Moss, head of the Society for the Prevention of Crime, and a longtime vigorous opponent of corruption and abuse in the Tammany-run police department. Securing affidavits from the victims and testimony from eyewitnesses, including white journalists on the

"The mob dragging Lavinie Johnson, a colored woman, from an Eighth Avenue car at Forty-third street." *Evening World*, August 16, 1900. (Chronicling America: Historic American Newspapers. Library of Congress)

scene, Moss and his associates sued the city for damages. But in the end, though overwhelming evidence of police brutality was presented, no black person received restitution for personal injuries or property losses. "The real offenders," concluded Police Commissioner Bernard York, "were the negroes who insisted in getting into the disorderly crowds that were pursuing them."

One unrepentant rioter rejoiced that New York was at last learning to deal with its "niggers" the way whites did "down south."

HEGIRA

Down south, where over 90 percent of the nation's African Americans lived, a vicious racial crackdown was under way. Southern states barred blacks from the polls and required Jim Crow segregation. Terrorists murdered thousands in grisly lynchings and pogrom-like riots. To some extent this campaign was an extension of the Ku Klux Klan's racial counterrevolution that had overthrown Reconstruction and imposed sharecropper servitude on African Americans. It had been spurred, more recently, by the biracial challenge of Populists to the Bourbon southern elite. And in part it was aimed at beating into submission the up-and-coming black generation, youngsters who were showing signs of voting with their feet. As one 15-year-old migrant explained, "The old people are used to their fare, and they never leave, but the children won' stand for the situation down there."

In addition to escaping the reach of a racist regime, these refugees were part of a larger tidal movement—white as well as black, western as well as southern—from the country to the city, an exodus spurred by ecological catastrophes like flooding and infestation. "Young people," explained a 19-year-old South Carolinian, "grow up now and say, 'I want to get 'ay from heah. No diggin' in de sile fo' me. Let other man do the diggin.'" Many headed for nearby cities. Between 1880 and 1910, the black population in the South's sixteen principal urban centers more than doubled. For many, however, these proved to be way stations as—increasingly encouraged by recruiting agents—thousands of young blacks fled north.

In the South Atlantic states—Virginia, the Carolinas, Georgia, and Florida—north mostly meant New York. The booming metropolis seemed a Promised City—job-laden, segregation-free, beyond the writ of Judge Lynch. Wildly misleading tales circulated about the high life awaiting them. "We hear 'out people in the North," said one would-be migrant, that "have automobile. Some have victrola." Poor blacks also heard that in Gotham "a man can earn ten dollars a week instead of the five he earns at him home." And that was true enough.

New York, moreover, was an easy boat ride from coastal cities. Steerage fare on Virginia's Old Dominion Steamship Company, with biweekly departures from Norfolk or Richmond, cost only six dollars, though it did mean traveling below decks with the household pets of white passengers.

So Arthur Harris and thousands like him commenced a hegira. Overwhelmingly single and young—for the most part between the ages of 15 and 26—they headed north, either directly from the field, or, for more than half, after first having sojourned in a southern city. And though the flow was a mere freshet compared to the torrent of Italians and Jews, it significantly boosted the size of New York's tiny black community. Between 1900 and 1910, migrants helped propel the African American population from 60,666 to 91,709, the majority of which was now southern-born.

CARIBBEAN CONNECTION

Alongside the coastal vessels steaming into New York's harbor, bearing black refugees from the South, came boats arriving from Port Antonio (Jamaica) and Bridgeport (Barbados), ferrying British West Indians to new lives in the metropolis. They had been set in motion by profound transformations under way in their home islands and throughout the Caribbean.

Back in the seventeenth and eighteenth centuries, when Jamaica, Barbados, and New York were co-colonies inside the British Empire, their interconnections were vital for both. Sugar and slaves flowed north; food and supplies traveled south. But those links were largely snapped by the Revolution. Gotham replaced them with ties to French sugar producers, until the uprising in Haiti, and then turned to the Spanish islands, preeminently Cuba, which in 1898 was transferred (at gunpoint) to the fledgling American Empire. New York capital underwrote a commercial revolution there, helping make Cuba the Caribbean's unrivaled leader in the production of sugar, accounting for just under 75 percent of the region's output. And after 1914 Cuba surged to new heights when, spurred by increased European demand, US investors expanded existing mills and built new ones. Within three years of being established in 1915, the New York–based Cuban Cane Corporation was the biggest sugar company in the world.

Jamaica's production, in sharp contrast, nose-dived in the nineties, and by the beginning of the new century its sugar industry had all but collapsed. Given its sugar-centric economy, this had a devastating impact, leading to widespread unemployment and impoverishment. It looked for a time as if the downturn might be reversed by a deft switch from sugar to bananas. The new agro-industry was the brainchild of an enterprising Cape Cod sea captain, one Lorenzo Dow Baker, who picked up some of the still-novel fruit in Jamaica and sold it to produce merchant Andrew Preston in Boston, who retailed the cargo for serious money. The duo now set up a base in Jamaica, bought and leased thousands of acres in the east of the island, and began growing for export. Incorporating in 1885 as the Boston Fruit Company, they rushed their perishable product to northeastern US cities, using the services of Britain's Atlas Steamship Line (which in New York docked at Pier 55, North River). In 1899 they joined forces with a similar operation, based in Central America, organized by Minor Cooper Keith. A Brooklyn-born railroad builder, Keith had established banana plantations in Costa Rica and Colombia, and was shipping product to New Orleans. Preston and Dow's Boston Fruit and Keith's Tropical Trading and Transport now consolidated into a New Jersey corporation, the United Fruit Company. Capitalized at $20 million, it soon acquired or crushed most competitors, and assembled an armada of steamships (the "Great White Fleet," whose initial vessels were navy surplus, left over from the Spanish-American War, fitted out with refrigeration capacity). Soon they added staterooms for tourists, and built pierheads on the East River that could handle both travelers and tropical fruit.

United Fruit quickly turned Jamaica into a world-class banana supplier, but it didn't do much for the island's depressed peasantry. Wielding a virtual monopoly of land and having a stranglehold over marketing, it drove independent producers out of business, then hired them on as agricultural workers, at miserable wages. With no manufacturing sector to provide employment, Jamaicans cast about for alternative sources of income. Barbadians found themselves in a similar but worse fix. The island's ruling plantocracy refused to abandon sugar, though the industry was in free fall, and instead made it pay by slashing wages to near-starvation levels.

The short-term solution for both populations was to leave their islands and find work elsewhere. Some labored on sugar plantations in Cuba, Puerto Rico, and the Dominican Republic, or on railroad construction projects in Central America, but most were drawn to the era's most colossal development project, the Panama Canal. During the peak period of construction, 1904–14, tens of thousands poured out of Jamaica and Barbados, to cut and blast a channel between the seas. Working conditions were atrocious and deadly. Horrible accidents devastated the workforce. And yellow fever, malaria, tuberculosis, and pneumonia scythed through the ranks, sending the death rate for black workers soaring (in 1905–6) to 49.01 per 1,000. To add social insult to physical injury, the American-controlled Isthmian Canal Commission imposed a US-style Jim-Crow racist regime. But all these impediments were trumped by wages substantially higher than those back home, money that could be remitted to families, and perhaps eventually used to buy land.

While the lower classes from Jamaica and Barbados found work in and around the Caribbean Sea, a different exodus was under way from these troubled islands—and others still under the British flag, including St. Kitts, Nevis, Antigua, Barbuda, St. Lucia, and Trinidad. This cohort headed north to the United States, preeminently to New York City. It was a much smaller one, in large part because the obstacles to relocation were substantial. Where many laborers were offered free passage to Panama, travel northward on banana boats (which now added migrants to their cargoes of tourists and fruit) was costly. Prospective emigrants were also required to post a thirty-dollar bond to demonstrate their financial solvency. And immigration law required that everyone seeking entry into the United States be met by a relative or guardian who agreed to assume financial responsibility for the newcomer. Resettlement costs thus screened out the most impoverished West Indians (though after 1914, when canal construction ended and thousands of unskilled laborers were evicted from the isthmus, there were some with enough "Panama money" in their pockets to make the leap to Gotham).

The occupational distribution of these New York–bound passengers was markedly different from that prevailing in their home islands. It was disproportionately drawn from professional, white-collar, and skilled artisanal ranks. Teachers and doctors, clerks and accountants, tradesmen and shopkeepers, tailors and carpenters, and dressmakers and seamstresses predominated. They were driven less by impoverishment than by ambition. They hoped to do better than they ever would under a colonial regime in which, though nowhere near as racially rigid as that in the United States, caste and custom reserved power and perquisites for the imperial elite and the whitest-skinned blacks. Though many had been beneficiaries of an excellent education at elite high schools like Harrison's College in Barbados, Kingston College in Jamaica, or Queen's Royal College in Trinidad, it was clear they would never be able to fulfill their potential.

BLACK NEWCOMERS FROM THE CARIBBEAN ARRIVED in far smaller numbers than did their southern counterparts. In 1900 foreign-born blacks were a mere 5,000—roughly 8 percent of the approximately 60,000 New Yorkers of African descent. By 1910 they'd grown to nearly 12,000 in number. As by then the overall black population had swelled to 90,000, the increase consisting mostly of southerners, the West Indians now constituted about 13 percent of the total. After another decade, a more vigorous migration stream had increased the foreign-born black total to nearly 37,000, out of a total of 152,467. This boosted them to just under a quarter of Gotham's blacks, making them the largest concentration of Caribbean-born blacks anywhere in the country, and making Gotham the only US city where Caribbeans were a significant presence.

Tension quickly developed between West Indians and US-born blacks, the antagonism rooted in real differences of condition and experience. The islanders arrived with higher literacy rates than African Americans (higher, indeed, than those of white Americans, whether foreign-born or native). That, plus their superior educational credentials, and greater white-collar work experience (compared to southerners, who'd been largely farmworkers or laborers), enabled them to attain a marginally greater presence in the black city's minuscule ranks of professionals, businessmen, and skilled workers. English-speaking West Indians, moreover, were reluctant to become US citizens, as they valued the modest degree of protection afforded by being subjects of the British crown. (They could and did call on the British consul in New York for support.) Their Anglican proclivities extended to the religious realm, in contrast to southerners' Baptist, Methodist, or Pentecostal preferences. Their cultural differences extended to patterns of speech (singsong lilt versus Carolina twang) and tastes in cuisine (rice, beans, and fried plantains vying with collard greens and ham hocks). More profoundly, West Indians hailed from countries that were virtually all black, giving residents a majoritarian consciousness, whereas southerners had been a minority hammered down by terrorist repression and racial segregation.

Each group accused the other of being "aggressive" and "clannish," and lobbed epithets featuring small mammals: southerners called West Indians "monkey chasers"; the latter called the former "possum eaters." (One ditty ran: "When a monkey-chaser dies / Don't need no undertaker / Just throw him in de Harlem River / He'll float back to Jamaica.") But what both sides soon enough discovered—as had generations of Irish and Italians who had initially been divided along county or village lines—was that distinctions that had loomed so large were barely discernible to the white New Yorkers who overwhelmed them demographically.

In 1910 nonblack people were 98.1 percent of the population. And just as most of these considered immigrants from County Clare and County Cork to be "micks," and those from Castellammarese and Corleone "wops," African descendants from Kingston or Mobile or Brooklyn were simply "niggers." "We were all strangers," one Panamanian immigrant recalled, speaking of the "black American" and "the black foreigner," and "we did not like one another, and the white foreigner liked us less and the white American hated all of us."

JIM CROW HOUSING

Disembarking migrants discovered that—in practice if not in law—New York was a Jim Crow town. In the early twentieth century, blacks lived predominantly in two neighborhoods in Manhattan, with a substantial minority arrayed in several concentrations in Brooklyn and smaller sprinklings in Queens. This was partly by preference—clustering being the default position for all arriving immigrants—and partly due to pressure imposed by rioting neighbors or club-wielding policemen.

The great bulk lived in the Tenderloin, that raucous strip of Manhattan's West Side famed for its licit and illicit entertainment venues. Black homes and churches were admixed with brothels and honky-tonks, as well as a dwindling number of Irish and German residents with whom they coexisted, albeit abrasively. The Tenderloin's boundaries, like most borders in Manhattan, were permeable, mutable, and on the move uptown. In the nineteenth century its perimeter had enclosed the territory between 23rd and 42nd Streets and Fifth and Seventh Avenues, with black residents densest in the lower 30s around Seventh. By 1900 the influx of African Americans moving up from Greenwich Village had expanded the Tenderloin northward to 53rd Street, a frontier to which they staked a spatial claim by planting along it major institutions, including St. Mark's Methodist Episcopal, Mount Olivet Baptist, St. Benedict the Moor (Catholic), the Colored Young Men's and Young Women's Christian Associations (YMCA, YWCA), and the Marshall and Maceo Hotels.[1] But when black renters began bulging west to Ninth Avenue, occupying crumbling tenements near the earsplitting elevated, they entered the solidly Irish terrain of Hell's Kitchen (which ran west down to the Hudson River), and there met with furious resistance. Clashes along the contested border involving black and Irish gangs—vanguards and sentinels of their respective communities—grew until in August 1898 they flared into four days of violence, which proved but a precursor to the full-blown Tenderloin race riot of 1900.

The second black domain was located just to the north of the Tenderloin and Hell's Kitchen, situated on a prominence called San Juan Hill. It was bisected vertically by Amsterdam and West End Avenues—as Tenth and Eleventh Avenues above 59th Street had been renamed in 1890, in an effort to attract genteel New Yorkers. Between 60th and 64th Streets, that effort failed. Instead, an upward tide of poor blacks had swept into those blocks, propelled by the migration from points south and by the dislocation generated by the building of Penn Station.

Beginning in 1901, the Pennsylvania Railroad had begun buying up (secretly, through agents) every building in the area bounded by West 31st and 33rd streets and Seventh and Ninth Avenues, an area described by one observer as "given up to the French and negro colonies." In February 1903, its ownership complete, the railroad began evictions from, and

---

1. The prestigious St. Philip's Protestant Episcopal remained for the moment on West 25th Street, to which it had relocated in 1886 from a Mulberry Street structure (which it had sold to Italians), as it had invested too heavily in bricks and mortar to follow the trend uptown during the 1890s.

demolition of, every brownstone, tenement, café, and saloon. Some 500 buildings covering 28 acres were demolished over the course of construction, squeezing black tenants northward.

Landlords welcomed newcomers by upping rents 30–50 percent and halting repairs. To make their payments, 40 percent of black families had to take in boarders. Congestion levels rivaled those on the Lower East Side. Overcrowding spurred deterioration and disease. So did the city's reluctance to pick up garbage or prosecute housing violations. Community organizations were thin on the ground, though in 1905 the Protestant Episcopal Mission Society did fund St. Cyprian's (at 169 West 63rd), which attracted Caribbean immigrants.

Among the new residents jamming into San Juan Hill's dilapidated buildings were some Buffalo Soldiers, black veterans of the Spanish-American War's key battle, for which the district was probably named, though perhaps it referred to the charges and countercharges up the hill's flanks as the Irish/African conflict had also migrated north. In July of 1905, after white and black street fighting broke out, the police joined the fracas, clubbing and (in an escalation from the 1900 affair) shooting black people, sometimes doing both: one Arthur Moody was first beaten then shot. Dozens of black men were arrested, taken to station houses, and forced to run a gauntlet of police armed with billy clubs. According to witnesses, each man was led "like an ox to the slaughter pen," and shoved into a long corridor where police officers "proceeded to beat them upon the head and bodies until they were nearly dead." Police Commissioner William McAdoo responded to protests by transferring out the precinct Captain, notorious in the black community as a "nigger hater," but also ordered the black population (though not the white) to "deposit their revolvers, blackjacks, and razors" with the police, as if they were the aggressors, not the victims. Then he left on summer vacation.

IN 1910 ROUGHLY 22,000 OF THE CITY'S 90,000 BLACKS LIVED IN BROOKLYN, which was, relatively speaking, a more peaceable kingdom for African Americans. In colonial times Brooklyn had had the biggest slave population, and in the decades between emancipation (1827) and the Civil War their descendants had settled into two quite different territories.

The first was in downtown Brooklyn, just east of Brooklyn City Hall, where their presence was evidenced by the principal black churches, clustered quite closely together. These included the Bridge Street African Wesleyan Methodist Episcopal (from 1854 at 309 Bridge), Concord Street Baptist (on Concord near Duffield Street), and Siloam Presbyterian (at 106 Prince Street between Myrtle and Willoughby). This population later extruded a few blocks eastward into the adjacent Fort Greene neighborhood, occupying better-quality housing above and below Fort Greene Park. (Siloam relocated to 404 Lafayette Avenue, not far from the Lafayette Avenue Presbyterian Church at South Oxford Street.) A few blocks farther north, backed up against the Navy Yard, was a poorer, rougher, vest pocket so-called Negro Quarter in Vinegar Hill, its tenants living in dilapidated frame houses along Hudson Avenue and adjacent streets. The combined downtown, Fort Greene, and Hudson Avenue neighborhoods hosted the great majority of Brooklyn's blacks, but they were largely immersed and interspersed in what were primarily white communities.[2]

---

2. These were not subjected to turf riots, as were the West Side communities in Manhattan, but there were occasional flash points that evoked southern-style crowd actions. In 1907 a *Brooklyn Daily Eagle* story reported that after one "Hudson avenue Negro," defending himself against another black resident, threw a stone that accidentally hit a 14-year-old white girl, a white crowd gathered and, believing a rape attack had been intended, rigged up a noosed rope and was preparing to lynch the man when the police arrived and rescued him.

The borough's other settlement, which also dated to the early nineteenth century, had long been a distinctly black territory. At its core were the communities of Weeksville and Carrsville, which lay roughly four miles to the east of downtown, remote enough from the then-independent city of Brooklyn to achieve a great degree of racial autonomy. When created in the 1830s as a refuge and real estate venture, these quasi-rural villages lay in the forested hills and hollows on the edge of the glacial moraine, high enough to afford a 360-degree view that took in Jamaica Bay, Long Island Sound, and far to the west the "roofs and spires" of Brooklyn. Its population was boosted in 1863 as refugees from the Draft Riots headed for the hills—the Bedford Hills, they were called, being just south of the crossroads town of Bedford. Here too, black churches—the African Methodist Episcopal (AME) and Berean Baptist—signified the predominant complexion.

Weeksville's seclusion came to a rapid end beginning in the 1870s when the impending arrival of the Brooklyn Bridge touched off a development boom. It was further spurred by the construction in the late 1880s of an elevated railway along Fulton Street, which, together with the Long Island Rail Road running along Atlantic Avenue, brought Bedford and the nearby farming area of Stuyvesant Heights within reasonable commuting distance of downtown Brooklyn and New York. Soon Bedford and Stuyvesant Heights were blanketed with row houses for middle- and upper-middle-class Germans, Irish, and Anglos. Then the development wave engulfed the Weeksville-Carrville communities. They were gridded and leveled, their hills dumped into hollows, and by the 1890s the African American villages were all but obliterated, apart from a few mid-nineteenth-century frame houses on Hunterfly Road.

In the early 1900s new black settlers arrived, some relocating east from downtown/Fort Greene, others floating in on the southern/Caribbean immigration stream. They did not move into the new upscale Bedford and Stuyvesant bedroom communities, wherein they were not welcome. Instead they were strewn along the miles-long commercial corridor formed by the Fulton and Atlantic arteries, which ran just below the all-white terrain, forming an axial aggregation rather than a distinctive community.

QUEENS HAD TWO PRINCIPAL COMMUNITIES, South Jamaica and Flushing, initially peopled by descendants of colonial slaves. Again, churches were the nuclei around which blacks settled. In South Jamaica, the Allen AME formally opened in 1844 at Washington Street (now 160th Street) and South Street (South Road). Like Weeksville, Jamaica, too, had lain amid fields and forests. As rapid transit arrived, the terrain north of the LIRR tracks was leveled, gridded, and developed for middle- and even upper-class whites, initially Germans and Irish moving out of Brooklyn. To the south, on the other side of the tracks, just below the business district, was the center of black population.

Black Flushing formed around another of Richard Allen's network of affiliated black Methodists—the Macedonia AME Church on Union Street. Established in the early 1800s by a black and Native American congregation, its first building went up in 1837, when about 25 percent of the population of Flushing was African American, attracted by the presence of a fiercely abolitionist Quaker community. At the turn of the century, its progressive environment attracted Lewis Latimer, the acclaimed black inventor and Edison associate, who purchased a house in 1903 in the predominantly white neighborhood. Latimer worked together with members of this community to establish a local chapter of the Unitarian Church, in part because of his belief in racial integration. Not all was peaches and cream, however. In 1905, when a colored Puerto Rican family built a house in Flushing, the structure was swiftly demolished. A sign staked up amid the ruins advised: "Do not try to build here anymore. No niggers wanted in this town."[3]

THERE WAS NOT MUCH NEW ABOUT ALL THIS. Gotham was no stranger to Jim Crow. White New Yorkers had had a hand in inventing de facto segregation back in the 1830s, hard on the heels of emancipation in 1827. Structural racism—backed by racial mini-pogroms—had deepened in the 1840s and '50s, as the city's economy grew ever more tightly intertwined with southern slavery. And blacks were lynched from lampposts on the sidewalks of New York during the draft riots of 1863, well before the practice became commonplace in the South. Still, there had been a moment, during Reconstruction, when, pursuant to the Fourteenth and Fifteenth Amendments, New York ended restrictions on black voting and passed civil rights legislation. But in the 1870s and '80s, when the former foes (Union and Confederate whites) built a rapprochement on the backs of former slaves, the state's commitment to charting a new course eroded as well.

In 1895, however, in a last gasp of racial reform, New York State passed the Malby Law. This legislation extended to all citizens "full and equal accommodations, advantages, facilities, and privileges of inns, restaurants, hotels, eating houses, bathhouses, barber shops, theaters, music halls, public conveyances on land and water, and all other places of public accommodation or amusement" without regard to color, race, or creed.

On paper, blacks had gained the protection of the law. But the law was widely flouted. Restaurants overcharged black patrons or served them spoiled food. Hotels claimed they were booked up. Broadway theaters and movie houses turned blacks away or restricted them to "nigger heaven," a balcony section. The courts dismissed suits challenging such practices. Or they issued exemptions: when white bootblacks refused to polish black men's shoes, jurists declared that shoe stands were not places of public accommodation. On paper, blacks had every right to use the city's parks, playgrounds, and public baths. In practice, menacing whites enforced an unofficial prohibition.

When Jim-Crowed Africans sued white proprietors, victories were not unknown. But as the *New York Times*, a caustic critic of the Malby Act, would point out, such triumphs could "not change the fact that white sentiment here is overwhelmingly against the close association of the two races in places of public entertainment." It was well, the paper observed, "not to go where one is not wanted, even when the lack of welcome is due to prejudice. To do it only makes the prejudice stronger—tends, if anything, to turn it into a reasonable dislike." And in a not-so-veiled warning of its own the *Times* added, "Everybody has rights that it is unwise to exercise."

While protests against denial of access to *private* venues were (on rare occasions) fought out in the courts, the denial of access to the city's streets, its most indisputably *public* spaces, was enforced at the "end of a policeman's nightstick," a practice for which there was in effect no legal remedy.[4]

---

3. There were smaller communities in Staten Island and the Bronx. In the former, a black neighborhood had existed in Castleton since at least 1801, when the Union American Methodist Episcopal Church was founded by manumitted slaves at 43 Tompkins Avenue. By 1900 black Staten Island numbered fewer than a thousand people.

In the Bronx, there were small enclaves in Wakefield-Williamsbridge, home to railroad workers and postal workers; in Mott Haven, near 144th Street and the Grand Concourse; in Morrisania, at 161st Street and Morris Avenue; and another nearby at 165th and Washington Avenue, whose residents worked on the railroads or local factories.

4. As per the NYPD's Inspector Clubber Williams's purported boast that "there is more law at the end of a nightstick then in all the statute books."

Black men seeking respite from crowded tenements frequently gathered on street corners (as did whites), especially if they were unemployed or worked nights, a practice that generated complaints to the municipal authorities. "Negroes congregate on the sidewalks and white people are compelled to take to the middle of the street," one Francis Legrange protested to Mayor Gaynor in 1912. Some black men were accused of "impudence" toward white women. "My wife came home from church on Sunday night," an aggrieved husband wrote, "and as she passed the place [where black men were standing], one of them niggers said some Bad word to her & she sat down and cried." Another begged the police to "do something with those Negroes" on 99th Street who made it "almost impossible for a white person to pass through on Sunday or any other day."[5]

The police were glad to oblige. Not long after the 1900 race riot, a fledgling patrolman, one Cornelius Willemse, encountered a group of black men "loitering" on a street corner, who (he said) had made offensive remarks to female passersby. He ordered them to "move on," threatening them (as he recounted in his autobiography) with "skull trouble, plenty of it." But "they shuffled off slowly, dragging their feet on the sidewalk, in a way which seemed to say, 'Feet, we'll be back as soon as this fool cop is gone.'" They did indeed return, and Willemse decided they were "ripe for a lesson." Without warning, he jumped into their midst and began beating any black man within reach, "work[ing] with the old nightstick as hard as I could," until within "two minutes, Negroes were lying all over the sidewalk, some of them half conscious, others bruised and bleeding." The point made, he didn't bother arresting them, instead leaving them "to scamper off to the best of their ability." But when he reported to his boss, Inspector "Smiling Dick" Walsh, Willemse learned that several had come in "with their heads swathed in bandages" to make a formal complaint. Walsh reassured Willemse that he had told them to get lost, indeed had commended the patrolman. Now he told him to go back "and show them all that you're boss on that corner." He did make one suggestion: "When you use your stick, always make a collar with it because, you understand"—here Walsh "smiled knowingly"—"you can always use force to overcome unlawful resistance," adding: "Don't forget that 'unlawful resistance' covers a multitude of sins."

ONCE "COLLARED," BLACKS ENTERED THE MAW of a racist criminal justice system. White juries, pre-convinced that Africans were natural-born criminals, returned guilty verdicts with alacrity. Unable to afford fines or hire good lawyers, convicted blacks—along with those guilty of other minor infractions like gambling or drunkenness—drew long jail terms. These were made longer still by judges who repeatedly tacked on fines, typically $500, to jail sentences. Failure to pay the fine meant remaining in custody even after the term had been served, an effective way of extending prison stays when the legal penalty was deemed insufficient. And incarceration proved an easy way to keep black people off the streets.[6]

JIM CROW JOBS

Like its housing market, Gotham's private-sector job market was informally but effectively segregated, from top to bottom.

---

5. Respectable middle-class blacks agreed. There had been, one wrote, "an alarming increase of the idlers who block up our street corners, hang about saloons and choke our concert halls."

6. This encompassed new arrivals, looking for a job or a bed, who were routinely arrested as vagrants.

The elite managerial and financial ranks of the new corporate economy were completely off limits to African Americans. A black person in one of Wall Street's dining clubs, in any capacity other than waiter, was an unthinkable thought.

Most professions also drew the color line. The American Bar Association barred black lawyers; hospitals refused staff privileges to black doctors. There was, however, a secondary sector of black lawyers and doctors (and teachers and clergymen) who had obtained credentials, but practiced exclusively within black communities. It was small: in 1900 twenty-six black lawyers and forty-two black physicians served 60,000 people.

White-collar jobs were reserved for white-skinned applicants. Department stores refused to hire black saleswomen; offices barred black clerks.

The skilled trades were largely inaccessible. One Caribbean immigrant, known as Panama, recalled a hiring boss who, though impressed by his qualifications, explained the facts of life: "I will tell you, if you wasn' a black fellow, if you was a white fellow, then you would have a job all your life here. But since you're a black fellow, I can' keep you here." Panama was forced to take work as a handyman. Skilled work, he angrily told an interviewer, was a white prerogative. "Do you think that you could go near an electrician's shop? Do you think that you could go near a bricklayer's job? They kill you. Those were white man's jobs."

The growing black community did, however, afford work for nonunion black carpenters, masons, painters, plumbers, tailors, printers, photographers, barbers, electricians, auto mechanics, and chauffeurs. Some of these men banded together in their own organizations, like the Negro Printers' Association (1907) and the Colored Chauffeurs' Association (1912), though that did not guarantee peaceful coexistence with white unions. As a black chauffeur explained, white drivers would "put mothballs in our gasoline tanks, short-circuit our ignition system and throw the carburetor out of adjustment. One man put emery into my gasoline tank."

New York had a huge industrial sector, from whose factories people of color were all but totally excluded. This included the ladies' garment industry. White women refused to work alongside black women, and factory owners imposed racial homogeneity in the city's female-dominated workplaces. The prejudice extended so far, explained one reformer, "as to prevent a colored woman from receiving home work when it entailed her waiting in the same sitting room with white women." This was particularly frustrating for the many Caribbean women who back home had worked as highly skilled seamstresses, and equally so for local black women who received training at New York trade schools in sewing, dressmaking, millinery, and artificial-flower making, only to discover they were barred from those industries.

Except when white workers went on strike. In the great walkout of 1909, when black female strikebreakers were much in evidence, the fledgling ILGWU invited them to join the union instead. The *New York Age* counseled rejecting this plea. "Negro girls were not asked to join the union" *before* the labor troubles began, the editor noted, so "why should Negro working girls pull white working girls' chestnuts out of the fire?" A few black women were enrolled, but in the strike's aftermath, they were again persona non grata.

The ranks of laborers, on the other hand, were packed with black men. They worked at the dirtiest and most dangerous jobs, in coal yards and subway construction sites. On the waterfront, there was room for African American longshoremen, given that the irregular and exhausting work turned off many whites. They toiled, too, as teamsters, draymen, and hackmen, and in the maritime trades as boatmen and sailors.[7] Almost completely un-unionized,

---

7. Many West Indian men detested manual labor, which they associated with slavery, and avoided becoming longshoremen, hostlers, furnace men, or street cleaners.

"A Quiet Spell 'Longshore," Manhattan, 1900. (The New York Public Library)

African American laborers were readily recruited into scab battalions and deployed against striking whites.

The great bulk of blacks worked in service trades, either commercial or domestic. The former, which included jobs like barbers, bootblacks, cooks, and waiters, were actually shrinking in availability, as new white immigrants crowded them out from traditional posts. Between 1900 and 1910, the number of black hostlers decreased 18 percent, black porters declined 36 percent, and black waiters found themselves virtually driven out of first-class hotels and restaurants (one reason they signed on as strikebreakers during the 1912 hotel workers walkout). Pullman porter jobs remained a black stronghold, though not a Caribbean one, as West Indians tended to react angrily when called "boy" or "George"—after George Pullman, the company's owner—and the firm avoided hiring them. Even in elite homes, where having black coachmen, footmen, or valets had been a mark of status (a legacy of slavery days), black servants had fallen out of fashion and were being supplanted by white (and Japanese) immigrants. This generated angry black nativist denunciations of the "scum of European society" who were displacing them.

What remained were bottom-barrel service jobs, like elevator operators, who were overwhelmingly men of color (half of them West Indians). Whites had good reasons for avoiding the job. Elevator men typically worked 168 hours every two weeks—70 hours one week and 98 the next—with no holidays or days off. They (and doormen) were hired as individuals and often worked in isolation, relating only to white people requiring their services. This left them unable to develop bonds of friendship or solidarity with coworkers, having none, and unable also to help kinfolk get jobs, the way Irish, Jewish, and Italian craftsmen or operatives might arrange a position for *landsmen* and *paisani*. Nor was the job deemed "manly," as it required subservience and docility.

The pay was poor, too, averaging $27.50 per month, less than $7.00 a week, or $2.00 a week less than the recommended minimum wage of $9.00 per week advocated for single women by the New York State Factory Investigating Committee. This wasn't unusual. According to a 1912 study, over 75 percent of black men working in twenty-four different domestic or personal service occupations received wages under $6.00 per week. A further 20 percent earned between $6.00 and $8.99.

"Elevator and Switchboard Operator," Manhattan, ca. 1910. (Landis Valley Museum, Landis Family Records)

BECAUSE HUSBANDS' WAGES WERE SO LOW, nearly a third of black wives had to work outside the home, whereas most white women retired on marriage. And those wives, along with their daughters, had to take the jobs white women disdained as demeaning. While a handful worked as nurses, midwives, beauticians, or boardinghouse keepers, overwhelmingly they entered service in white women's homes, or lugged washing back to scrub in their steaming apartments. Wages were low and working conditions difficult. Servants and laundresses earned between four and six dollars per week, a sum that even when combined with men's salaries left most black families impoverished. A live-in servant's time, moreover, was not her own. And her situation left her vulnerable to sexual assault. Prevailing stereotypes about black women's sexuality meant that if she brought charges of rape, New York's legal system would almost invariably throw them out of court. And black maids, like black elevator men, worked as individuals, cut off from community sources of support.[8]

---

8. Middle-class Caribbean women preferred live-in service to most alternative options. Though they hated doing for white people what others had done for them back home, it covered room and board, and helped accumulate the wherewithal to buy a house, their cherished ambition.

"Service at the Berkshire," Brooklyn, ca. 1910. (Landis Valley Museum, Landis Family Records)

WITH SO MUCH OF THE PRIVATE-SECTOR JOB MARKET OUT OF REACH, the public sector beckoned as a potentially more accessible source of employment. But here too there were roadblocks. Blacks lacked the political muscle required to land significant patronage positions, or to get jobs on public works or in public services. Partly this weakness was a matter of numbers; they were a tiny percentage of the population. Partly it was due to rampant racism, as pervasive in government as in business. And partly it was because the city's political parties had come up with an ingenious way of harvesting black votes without giving much in return.

Since the era of emancipation and reconstruction, Gotham's African American voters had all but unanimously backed Republicans, the party of Lincoln, which was arguably the wrong horse to pick in a Democratic town. But in addition to paying off a debt of gratitude, their solid support also reaped modest patronage rewards from Republican-run state and federal administrations. This pretty much exclusive affiliation continued until 1897, when a group of black Republican politicians, who had supported McKinley in the 1896 presidential race, failed to receive the government appointments they had been led to expect. Spurned, they passed word to Tammany Hall boss Richard Croker that they were prepared to defect.

Croker had a mayoral race coming up in 1897, which was looking uncomfortably close, and so was open to the overture. To demonstrate their capacity to deliver votes, the black politicos went all out to drum up support for Tammany's man, Robert Van Wyck, concentrating mainly on residents of San Juan Hill. When they produced over 600 votes, Croker decided to institutionalize this budding relationship with the black community. In January 1898 Croker appointed Edward "Chief" Lee, a Virginia-born African American who was head bellman at the Plaza Hotel, to lead a new party organization: the United Colored Democracy (UCD). Lee was to be in charge of delivering patronage to deserving black Democrats, starting with himself. (He was appointed deputy sheriff of New York County, a sinecure.)

This was a trap, into which the ex-Republicans scurried eagerly—not surprisingly, as they were some of its few beneficiaries, but shortsightedly, as it politically neutered the entire black community. The Tammany machine was highly centralized—with party leadership ultimately in the hands of the boss (at this point, Croker)—but also highly decentralized, with neighborhood leadership at the assembly district level in the hands of powerful district leaders (like Big Tim Sullivan), with whom the boss had to contend. Control of a district, in turn, gave the predominant ethnic group, usually clustered in political clubs, control of a significant chunk of political territory. Had Croker really wanted to recognize blacks as new players on the political scene, he could perhaps have carved out a Tenderloin/San Juan District, whose leader would have had an important say at party conclaves. But he didn't. Nor did the Democrats (or Republicans) allow blacks to join the territorially based district clubs where real power lay. Nor did either party support an African American for any elective office. Croker had set up a segregated but non-territorial entity, isolated from real influence. Lee was powerless, and so, by extension, was the scattered African American citizenry.

Gotham's Republicans did not establish a comparable organization, but they did anoint a liaison with the black community, Charles W. Anderson. A political broker who had risen through the party ranks, Anderson, chosen by the white establishment, was proclaimed a "leader" of the city's blacks (whom he often privately disparaged). He delivered votes to the Republicans in return for personal preferment and the right to dole out patronage from state and federal administrations. In 1898 Theodore Roosevelt, then the newly elected governor of New York, began to channel patronage for blacks through (and to) Anderson, a practice he continued when he ascended to the presidency. In 1904 TR made Anderson collector of internal revenue for the Wall Street district, a patronage plum. And Anderson funneled down less prestigious but respectable positions, mainly in the Post Office, which by the end of Roosevelt's term employed nearly 200 black men. The United Colored Democracy boasted that it generated far more jobs for the community, and between 1897 and 1913 it did deliver roughly 850 city positions—but over 600 of them were for doing heavy labor in the Street Cleaning Department.

IF NEW YORK CITY'S BLACK COMMUNITY FAILED TO GAIN significant job opportunities through the party system, it didn't fare much better when reform administrations were in power. Good-government types argued they would administer city affairs in a scientific, rational, efficient, and impartial way, selecting public employees based on merit only. But the bureaucrats proved anything but color-blind. Competitive examinations could be worked around. And the self-governing character of each autonomous agency facilitated their capture by one or another ethnic or professional group. Physicians in city hospitals, teachers in public schools, and officers in police and fire departments were drawn from specific constituencies, and none of them were black.

The boards governing city hospitals were dominated by medical societies, themselves controlled by white physicians who were strenuously opposed to the intrusion of nonwhite doctors. Even established black physicians could not gain a position at any of New York's public hospitals; nor could black medical students serve internships.

The educational bureaucrats who ran the public school system charted a more complex course. Manhattan's schools had been segregated since the eighteenth century. Until the mid-nineteenth century the black institutions had been run by white philanthropists. Then they were taken over by the Board of Education, under whose auspices they fared poorly, receiving far less funding per student than white schools. In 1873 white schools were opened to black pupils, and attendance at colored schools dwindled. In 1883 the board moved toward closing the remaining black institutions, but this met with a mixed reaction from black parents. Some favored integration, as it allowed their children access to better-funded schools.

Others favored maintaining some schools staffed and controlled by blacks, so long as attendance was voluntary, not mandatory. This latter group won a stay of execution for two black schools.

As some had feared, when colored schools were folded into the system, many black teachers were let go, and indeed found themselves virtually excluded from their profession. Occasionally a black student graduated from the city's Normal College—the gateway to jobs in the public system—but if there was no vacancy for her in one of the remaining colored schools, she received no appointment. This provoked an extensive legal battle. Black attorney T. McCants Stewart sued the Board of Education to allow black teachers to work in any school where there was a vacancy. Finally, in 1895, a Normal College black graduate, Susan Elizabeth Frazier, was appointed to an all-white faculty, and the heavens did not tremble.

Segregation persisted in Queens, which had entered Greater New York in 1898 with its own Board of Education. It maintained separate schools in Jamaica and Flushing into which all black children were funneled. Some black parents in South Jamaica refused to send their children to the colored school, claiming it was inferior to the white school, and the latter was closer to their home. They were convicted of violating the Compulsory Education Law. When they pressed the case, state courts ruled in 1900 (following the 1896 Supreme Court decision in *Plessy v. Ferguson*) that Queens County had the legal right to require black students to attend "separate but equal" schools. Immediately, pressure by pro-integrationists led Governor Theodore Roosevelt and the Republican-controlled legislature to pass a bill providing that no person should be refused admission or be excluded from any public school in the state on account of race or color. That put paid to official segregation. By 1913 there were at least a few black students in almost every school. But given restrictive residential patterns, 72 percent of the city's black students crowded into just nine schools. De facto segregation had replaced the de jure variant.

And while the door had been opened for hiring black teachers, resistance proved stiffer when it came to hiring black principals. First on the firing line was William Bulkley. Born in South Carolina, Bulkley was educated at Claflin University, Wesleyan College, and Syracuse University (where he received a PhD in ancient languages and literature) and did postdoctoral work at Strasburg University and the Sorbonne. He came to New York in 1899 and entered the New York City school system as a seventh-grade teacher in Canarsie. In 1901 he became principal of PS 80 on West 41st Street in the Tenderloin, whose students were virtually all black (this after the thirty people ahead of him on the civil service list had refused to go there). In 1909 he was transferred to PS 125 in lower Manhattan, a predominantly white school, the first African American to be placed in a position of authority. The teaching staff, appalled at the notion of having to answer to a black superior, almost unanimously requested transfers. The school board stood by Bulkley, but it would be in no hurry to repeat the experiment.

The city's uniformed services were even more adamantly opposed to black recruits. The overwhelmingly Irish firemen and policemen had long been able, with the support of Tammany Hall, to keep nonwhite entrants at bay, despite the institution of civil service reforms. The first African American to cross the color line was appointed to the Brooklyn Fire Department in 1898, just before the merger with Manhattan. The Virginia-born William H. Nicholson, who lived on Myrtle Avenue, was promptly detailed to the veterinary unit. Barred from fighting fires, he spent his entire career feeding horses and shoveling manure until he retired in 1912. A replacement was appointed in 1914, so the department could still say it was not exclusively white, but it was another five years before Wesley Williams, who would become a real challenger to the status quo, was appointed, thanks to Tammany connections of his own. Nevertheless, the day Williams reported for duty to Engine 55 in Manhattan, the captain retired on the spot rather than preside over a company that included a Negro, and every man requested a transfer (which was denied).

The city's first African American police officer also entered via the Brooklyn system, thanks to a concerted push by Timothy Thomas Fortune, editor of the *New York Age*; T. McCants Stewart, a black lawyer; Philip A. White, a black pharmacist; and Charles A. Dorsey, a black educator. They picked Wiley Grenada Overton, who had scored high on the civil service exam and, they believed, had the strength to overcome the sure hostility of white cops and citizens. In 1891 Overton was appointed a patrolman. Immediately there was a revolt. He was transferred from precinct to precinct because no white officer would sleep in the same dormitory with him, and superiors hounded him continuously, until he gave up and retired from the force. Nevertheless, others followed, and by the turn of the century a handful of African American officers were patrolling the Brooklyn streets, which put the borough way ahead of Manhattan. As were other cities: in Philadelphia there were fifty-six colored officers, and Boston, Chicago, Trenton, Camden, and Newark also had contingents.

Calls for hiring black cops came with increasing insistence from Manhattan's black community, whose determination gained force with each police riot against African Americans. In 1907 Reverdy C. Ransom, feisty pastor of the Tenderloin's Bethel AME church, said black officers would dampen unnecessary violence against black citizens, and also be better able to handle black lawbreakers. Given that an Italian Squad had been created, proponents called for equal treatment.

The pioneer proved to be Samuel Battle, who had been working at Grand Central Station as a "Red Cap," when he took the civil service examination in 1910 and passed, earning a rank in the top third. Normally that would have been sufficient for appointment, but Battle was repeatedly passed over. Finally he asked Fred Moore, then editor of the *New York Age*, for help. Moore assembled a pressure group, including Republican Anderson and Democrat Lee, and Battle finally became a member of the force in 1911. He was dispatched to the San Juan Hill district, where the white officers refused to speak to him or allow him to sleep in their quarters. (It didn't help that he refused to partake of graft opportunities in the local vice economy.) One day he found a note pinned over his bed "with a hole in it about the size of a bullet hole," and the message "Nigger, if you don't quit, this is what will happen to you." Battle was not deterred, but the department was, and by 1918 there were only five African American officers on the force.

GIVEN THAT THEY WERE BARRED FROM MOST DECENTLY PAID and respectable forms of labor, some black men spurned menial work and hustled their way into the underground economy alongside Jewish and Italian counterparts. Male entrepreneurs ran illicit brothels, gambling dens, poolrooms, policy shops, and faro banks. Others—lone hoodlums or organized gangsters—burgled, robbed, and preyed on their middle-class neighbors.

Similarly, some women chose prostitution over domestic work, though even in the sex trades blacks got the worst jobs. Working out of tenements or walking the streets, they catered to the poorest classes, in return for profits far below those garnered by white women in brothels that catered to a wealthy clientele. And as brothels cut immunity-for-cash deals with the cops, black sex workers were far more likely to be caught up in police street sweeps (as were any black women, no matter how respectable, as was the case with May Enoch, whose attempted arrest led to the race riot of 1900). African American women also had to deal with

African American pimps—essential protection for streetwalkers—who appropriated women's money and spent it on flashy clothing, in a bid to attain a modicum of respect, at least from their fellows on the street.

JIM CROW CULTURE

The culture of contempt that accompanied and undergirded racist repression was, like the stratification of jobs and housing, a vintage phenomenon in New York. It dated back at least to the birth of minstrel shows in 1832, when "Daddy" Rice first "jumped Jim Crow" at the Bowery Theatre. That racially charged entertainment form featured white actors in black-face, performing the stereotypical characters of Jim Crow, the slow-witted, irrepressibly comic "plantation darky," who represented the rural South, and Zip Coon, a fancied creature of the urban North, a foolish, foppish, self-satisfied dandy. In minstrelsy, which soon swept the nation, slavery was presented as right and natural; slaves as contented, lazy, and stupid; northern blacks as larcenous, immoral, and ludicrous. Threescore years later, the caricatures were still going strong but were about to turn uglier, as the character of Gotham's racism grew more vitriolic.

In considerable degree this was in response to global and national developments. When European imperialists—then swarming into Africa—proclaimed it their duty to lead or bludgeon "backward" peoples into "civilized" ways, the conviction steamed swiftly across the Atlantic, with New York its first port of call. Rudyard Kipling's "White Man's Burden" made its US debut in the February 1899 issue of *McClure's Magazine*. And metropolitan jingoes—then cheerleading America's charge into the Philippines and the Caribbean—swiftly scooped up and redeployed the argument. Teddy Roosevelt pronounced Filipinos "savages," patently unfit for self-government; others proclaimed Puerto Ricans equally in need of Anglo-Saxon tutelage.

Far more potent a driver was the poisonous miasma rolling up from the South, which added fear to the customary condescension. The master argument of the South's white ruling class at the century's turn, was that slavery had constrained Africans' "natural" tendencies to both indolence and savagery, and its abolition had loosed on the hapless white South all the furies of the Dark Continent. These were manifested in the nightmare of Reconstruction, when, goaded by northern Republicans who had given them the vote, blacks had run amok, until the Klan clamped down. Now, to ensure that this would never again happen, blacks had been stripped of the vote and subjected to firm but necessary measures (a.k.a. segregation and lynching). The North, southern spokesmen advised, should take heed and be aware that freed slaves and their progeny were "fast reverting" to the behavior that had "kept the African upon the lowest plane of humanity since the dawn of civilization." Phillip Bruce's *The Plantation Negro as a Freeman* (1889), the font of much of this, grew out of several articles he had written for the *New York Evening Post*, warning northern readers of the dangers presented by freed slaves. The notion that emancipation led to devolution mirrored the theory of degeneration popular with criminal anthropologists like the Italian Cesare Lombroso.

New Yorkers were not simply passive recipients of such ideologies, they made their own contributions to the era's recrudescent racism. In various domains wherein the city was expert—particularly the social and physical sciences (notably history, sociology, psychology, anthropology, and biology) and cultural production (notably journalism, book and magazine publishing, vaudeville, Tin Pan Alley, the theater, and the cinema)—New Yorkers amplified and broadcast white supremacist characterizations of black people.

GOTHAM-BASED HISTORIANS PROVIDED SUPPORT for the South's post–Civil War narrative. A group of scholars at Columbia University, led by Professor William Archibald Dunning, depicted Reconstruction as a dreadful inversion of the natural racial order but did so in the approved, "scientific," fact-based manner imported from German universities. Dunning was also influenced by John W. Burgess, another Columbia professor and a founder of the new discipline of political science, who denounced Reconstruction as "a monstrous thing." Dunning's work, beginning with his *Essays on the Civil War and Reconstruction* (1898), attracted students to New York, many of them southerners, who produced a series of monographs examining Reconstruction in a variety of southern states. Though their work differed from scholar to scholar, they all more or less rested their case on an essentialist characterization that depicted African Americans as either childlike ignorant dupes, manipulated by unscrupulous whites, or as savages, whose primal passions (particular black male lust for white women) had been unleashed by the end of slavery. Dunning's disciples captured many of the country's major history departments, particularly in the South, and their widely popularized work gave implicit or explicit sanction to Jim Crow regimes, north as well as south.

THOUGH THE DUNNING SCHOOL ATTRIBUTED a civilizing function to slavery, Dunning himself did not romanticize the old plantation order. That task was taken up by novelists and dramatists and filmmakers who, in the spirit of sectional reconciliation, began rehabilitating the Old South. Northerners who not long since had deprecated life on the plantation as languid, violent, and immoral now lamented its passing. Metropolitan belle-lettrists effused nostalgically over the Lost Cause in genteel magazines like *Harper's* and the *Century*, whose pages were festooned with engravings of rascally Sambos. Broadway plays praised the genteel manners, chivalry, and charm of white planters in the antebellum slave society and depicted the Civil War as a tragic mistake. David Belasco's first smash success was the spectacularly produced *The Heart of Maryland*, a Romeo and Juliet story in which a Confederate belle and a dashing Union officer transcend their country's division. First performed at the Herald Square Theatre in 1895, it ran for 240 performances, and was reincarnated in a film version in 1915.

The city's culture industry was even more forceful in its ratification of the southern white take on Reconstruction. In 1905 Doubleday published a novel by Thomas Dixon, forthrightly entitled *The Clansman: An Historical Romance of the Ku Klux Klan*, whose account of freed black slaves turning savage made it a best seller. Dixon, determined to eclipse the success of *Uncle Tom's Cabin* in all the media in which its anti-slavery forebear had triumphed, adapted *The Clansman* for the stage, retaining the original title. He sent the script to a theatrical agent in New York, who submitted it to a producer, who together with Dixon set up a new corporation, the Southern Amusement Corporation, to stage it. The New York crowd that attended its January 1906 premiere at the Liberty Theatre (recently opened on 42nd Street by Klaw and Erlanger's Theatrical Syndicate) applauded so vigorously that Dixon came onstage to declare that the drama's reception proved that "there is no longer a North and a South." *The Clansman*, too, was born again as a movie, in March 1915, when D. W. Griffith's *Birth of a Nation* opened at the same theater. American cinema's first authentic masterpiece embodied a vicious reading of history that featured hooded Klansmen rescuing blond heroines from black bucks. (Not *real* "bucks" but whites in blackface, as Griffith forbade actors with "black blood" to touch white actresses.) *Birth* ran for a spectacular eleven months, further polluting the already sulphurous air.

BUT THE LIVE-WIRE ISSUE WAS BLACK BEHAVIOR IN THE *NORTH*. Were the southerners right? Were black rapists and murderers breaching the Mason-Dixon Line and slouching toward the streets of New York? Again, newfound "scientific" evidence was wheeled out to support such anxieties. In 1890, for the first time, the US Census included prison statistics, which seemed to show that African Americans, though but 12 percent of the population, made up 30 percent of the nation's prison population. Did this indicate that a dangerous criminal population was swelling? Well, yes, according to white social scientists, who used the new crime data to make a supposedly objective, color-blind, and incontrovertible case.

With the new data in hand, German-born Frederick L. Hoffman, a statistician at the Prudential Life Insurance Company in Newark, produced a series of articles that were collected and published in May 1896 as *The Race Traits and Tendencies of the American Negro*. Hoffman found that "as regards the most serious of all crimes, the number of negro criminals is out of all proportion to the numerical importance of the race." According to Hoffman, the data proved that blacks, both male and female, were far more likely to steal or commit murder than any other race. The rape of white women by black men, he contended, was also on the increase. (This was "proved" by referencing the increasing number of southern lynchings.) Such outsized criminality could not be put down to individual immorality, in Hoffman's view, but rather constituted conclusive evidence that "the colored population is gradually parting with the virtues...developed under slavery" and that neither education, philanthropy, nor religion had been able "to develop a higher appreciation for the stern and uncompromising virtues of the Aryan race."

Commenting on Hoffman's work, Miles Menander Dawson, a New York actuary, drew the seemingly unarguable conclusion. If even in northern cities—"where abundant opportunities are given," where "legal processes are acknowledged to be fair," where "the Negro has the fullest educational opportunity," and where civil society was free of slavery's past and white supremacy's present—if even in exemplary New York blacks had higher arrest rates than their ignorant and oppressed brothers in the South, this was indisputable proof of black inferiority.[9]

THE ARGUMENT THAT NORTHERN BLACKS WERE INHERENTLY DANGEROUS was presented in less esoteric ways by Tin Pan Alley songsmiths (black ones included) and vaudeville writers, who negotiated the transition from the antebellum Zip Coon, a comic and ridiculous figure, to the menacing, razor-toting character who figured in hundreds of "coon songs" and vaudeville presentations. The earlier stance of bemused contempt was not, however, jettisoned altogether, as it was useful in explaining black men's supposed failure to gain entrée into the labor force (which bleeding hearts blamed on racist exclusionary practices). Coons might be murderous, but they were also lazy; they *chose* not to work, much preferring to rob or gamble or let women support them.

Black women were also cast in contradictory ways, as both sluts and mammies. Coon songs and vaudeville routines portrayed them as "mercenary wenches," libidinous and avaricious characters in hot pursuit of money and sex. They were thus innately predisposed

---

9. With premises like these, argumentation was superfluous, but the refusal to interrogate these assumptions, or to take into account the role of economic repression, or the criminal justice system's virtual vendetta against blacks, or even to properly evaluate their "data," would leave their conclusions vulnerable to critics who would soon shred their findings. But such treatises weren't readily falsifiable, because they were underscoring received wisdom.

to a life of prostitution. Where Caucasian sex workers were held to be helpless and innocent victims—the "captives" of "white slave" traders—black women were seen as aggressors who enticed unsuspecting white men into behaving immorally. Some went so far as to
argue that just as black women couldn't be "white slaves," they couldn't be raped either,
because of their inherent lack of virtue. On the other hand, beloved black mammies were
deemed perfectly suited to cooking and cleaning for white families, and to caring for their
children.

STATISTICAL ANALYSES AND COON-SONG CHARACTERIZATIONS OF BLACKS as essentially criminal still left wiggle room for those who pinned black lawlessness on environmental stresses
and strains (poverty, overcrowding, racism) and claimed it could be overcome (as criminologists believed was possible for whites, even Italian mobsters). What was lacking was definitive
evidence that black criminality, like black inferiority, was rooted in the nature of the race
itself. Here biologists and anthropologists stepped up to the plate for their turn at bat.

The rediscovery of Mendel's laws of heredity in 1900 handed a powerful analytical tool
to those who were seeking to root various forms of human behavior in biological soil. The
eugenics movement had been arguing that a vast array of social problems, such as alcoholism,
feeblemindedness, criminality, and perhaps poverty, were in fact inheritable phenomena. If
they were not environmental but congenital, then perhaps they could be addressed by refashioning the US population through "selective breeding."

New York became the national center for this enthusiasm. The gist of the approach had
already been advanced by Madison Grant, Henry Fairfield Osborn, and others of their circle,
and their project had found institutional havens at the Museum of Natural History and the
Bronx Zoo. But these men were amateurs, their approach lacked scientific rigor, and their
organizations were not devoted exclusively to eugenics. The early twentieth century would
see the emergence of serious professionals housed in purpose-built institutions.

The most important single figure in the emerging field of eugenics was Charles
Benedict Davenport, the Brooklyn Heights–born son of a New York real estate broker.
Educated as a civil engineer at Brooklyn Polytechnic, he then took a PhD in zoology at
Harvard. In 1899 he began teaching at the University of Chicago, where he got interested
in the emerging field of evolutionary biology. He set out to establish a biological farm—a
novel kind of experimental laboratory for studying heredity. In 1904 he prevailed on the
newly established Carnegie Institution of Washington to fund a Station for Experimental
Evolution (SEE). It was situated at Cold Spring Harbor, an old whaling village and resort
town on Long Island's North Shore, about forty miles from Manhattan, and Davenport
moved back east to direct it. At first the SEE focused on plants and nonhuman animals, but
the director grew increasingly intrigued by the possibility of exploring the laws of heredity
in *Homo sapiens*.

This urge was in the air. A cognate organization, the American Breeders' Association
(1903), had been partnering with Davenport on studying agricultural breeding, poultry genetics, and heredity in racehorses. But in 1906 the ABA established a Eugenics Committee
"to investigate and report on heredity in the human race" and "to emphasize the value of
superior blood and the menace to society of inferior blood." By 1908 Davenport had shifted
his attention mostly to eugenics and set out to hunt for funding. He urged philanthropists to
donate their funds to eugenics rather than social reform or charity, as neither addressed the
source of social problems, which lay not in the environment but in "bad genes." The goal
would be to increase the "aristogenic" gene pool while preventing propagation by the

"cacogenic"—those likely to have defective or undesirable offspring. This "scientific" approach would dry up the springs that "feed the torrent of defective and degenerate protoplasm."[10]

This struck a responsive chord in the millionairess Mary Harriman, who was readily converted to the eugenics cause, she said, as having been "brought up among well bred race horses helped her to appreciate the importance of a project to study heredity and good breeding in man." She gave half a million dollars to create the Eugenics Record Office (ERO), an 80-acre expansion of the SEE lab, to be overseen by Davenport and directed by his assistant Harry H. Laughlin. Another half million for operating expenses followed over the next eight years. The Rockefeller family made substantial contributions to Davenport's operation, as did Felix Adler, W. W. Astor, August Belmont, Cleveland Dodge, Daniel Guggenheim, J. P. Morgan, and Jacob Schiff. Foundations, including the Carnegie Institute of Washington, the New York Foundation, and the Russell Sage Foundation, provided support for laboratories, institutes, and journals that spread the gospel of genetic determinism, lending an air of respectability to racialist thinking.

Davenport and Madison Grant also established the Galton Society of New York (1918), whose membership was limited to "native Americans, who are anthropologically, socially, and politically sound," and whose purpose was to take back the anthropology profession from the "Jews" (notably Franz Boas) and promote instead "racial anthropology." The chosen people included Osborn, Laughlin, and Edward L. Thorndike, a Columbia University psychologist. Their major concern was the influx of Jews and Italians. Their major proposal for dealing with it was immigration restriction.

Blacks, too, were a matter of great concern. One young recruit, a recent Harvard history PhD named Lothrop Stoddard, had written a book called *The French Revolution in San Domingo* (1914), and he considered the Haitian Revolution a nightmarish template for a coming race war. Most Galtonians were less concerned about blacks rising up, however, than about the prospect of whites being dumbed down by admixing their superior blood with that of racial inferiors.[11] Roswell Hill Johnson, Davenport's assistant at the ERO, laid out the eugenicists' conventional wisdom on the consequences of miscegenation in a coauthored volume called *Applied Eugenics*. "Pure Negroes," the text announced, operated at but 60 percent of "white intellectual efficiency." The general population of blacks clocked in at 75 percent. Since most of them were mulattos, it meant that many 100 percent whites had been dragged down toward "pure Negro" level. The consequences were far more substantial than just diminished "intellectual efficiency," however, as blacks were also well known to have strong sexual impulses, low inhibitions, and a tendency to immoral conduct. They also lacked foresight, were content with immediate satisfactions, were less adept at organization, and were "lacking in that aggressive competitiveness which has been responsible for so much of the achievement of the Nordic race." That these were chiefly "germinal" characteristics, not merely the products of "social tradition," could be seen from a comparative study of Jamaicans, who manifested the same "fundamental, unchanged race traits."

---

10. One way to achieve this was through compulsory sterilization of the criminal and the insane. In 1912 New York State passed a sterilization law. But it never amounted to much. A total of forty-two procedures took place over a nine-year period, before New York courts declared the law unconstitutional.

11. Madison Grant thought blacks less dangerous than immigrants, as "negroes are never socialists and labor unionists." But eugenically they were a menace. Given that "the result of the mixture of two races, in the long run, gives us a race reverting to the more ancient, generalized and lower type," the fact was that "the cross between a white man and a negro is a negro," and "the cross between any of the three European races and a Jew is a Jew."

How to prevent the mongrelization of America? Some, like Earnest Sevier Cox, an earnest acolyte of Madison Grant, argued that as race mixing would result in the downfall of "White civilization," the removal of all blacks from the American continent was, in his own words, "a holy cause." Given that African Americans constituted roughly 10 percent of the US population, this was deemed impractical (though Grant would write an introduction to a book Cox produced on the subject). By and large, the authors of *Applied Eugenics* suggested, white society had already come to the almost-correct conclusion: the country should outlaw miscegenation. Already twenty-two states had passed statutes that forbade black-white intermarriage. (New York, unfortunately, was not among them, having tried in 1910 to win passage of an "Act to Amend the Domestic Relations Law, in Relation to Miscegenation," which would have not only banned interracial weddings but nullified already existing marriages *"contracted between a person of white or Caucasian race and a person of the negro or black race."* Subsequent campaigns had fallen similarly short). But even such laws were not enough, as most mulattos issued from extramarital relations. To preserve racial purity, therefore, it would be necessary to pass laws "to prohibit all sexual intercourse between the two races."

BLACK PROGRESSIVES

In the early twentieth century, Gotham's tiny elite black community struggled to keep its footing amid the influx of migrants. Their responses ranged from walling themselves off from the newcomers, to attempting to make them more presentable, to making common cause with white progressives in an effort to provide social services.

By metropolitan standards the black elite were not rich but upper-middle-class. Their fortunes had been made not in banking or commerce but in community-based professions like undertaking, teaching, or preaching. They tended to live in Brooklyn because housing options were somewhat better across the East River, and prejudice somewhat less marked. The most affluent owned their own brownstones, employed white servants, rode in private carriages, and sent their children to Howard and Oberlin. They joined black offshoots of the Masons, Elks, and Odd Fellows, borrowing their secret rituals, splendid regalia, and elaborate titles. The crème de la crème—the Negro Four Hundred—held their own exclusive balls, promenades, and concerts. They also formed genealogical organizations, like the Society of the Sons of New York (in Manhattan, on 53rd Street, alongside other leading African American institutions). Founded in 1884, roughly when Gotham's Anglo-Dutch descendants were establishing similar pedigree-based associations, the Sons traced their lineage to New York's "free people of color," whose escutcheon—unlike that of poor blacks and new immigrants—was unblotted by servitude. Its members, they boasted, had "the most delicate taste of gentlemen-like tone and behavior."

Despite some snobbery, the minuscule ranks of Knickerbocker blacks were open to talent. Successful professionals were welcome; so too were affluent West Indians and southern ministers. But they drew a class line between themselves and the mass of the city's black residents, on whom they gazed with much the same disdain as did the white elites they emulated, and whose approval they sought. "Respectable colored citizens" denounced those they called "riff-raff" as "ignorant and rough-mannered," "loud of mouth, flashy of clothes," "illiterate," "loafers," and "scum." Self-styled "Old Settlers" publicly blamed the "epidemic of negrophobia" on southern migrants. They "make it hard for us wherever they light," complained a black northerner. "The well meaning, industrious, progressive Negroes, as a rule, remain in the South to fight out the question there," whereas "the lazy, shiftless, worthless class come to northern cities to reduce our opportunities and privileges to a minimum."

In particular they laid the blame for black crime squarely on "the large and steady influx of Negroes from the Southern states." It was, said the *New York Age*, a migration that "has brought and will continue to bring a great many undesirable persons, criminally inclined, if not confirmed, before they leave the Southern states."

Initially the Knickerbockers pleaded with southerners and Caribbean islanders to remain where they were. It was "a sad mistake," the *Age* editor wrote, to think Gotham was "a paradise where employment of all kinds can be had for the asking." Shut out of jobs, immigrants might well find themselves living in abject poverty. "New York is a good place to shun," he summed up, "unless you have plenty of money or a position secured before coming here."

Such appeals proved futile. So one alternative was to forge ramparts around themselves, to establish enclaves of respectable gentility, ecclesiastical and secular, that would demonstrate to white opinion makers that they, at least, were not coons.

At the center of this initiative were the elite black churches, housed in grand structures, which allowed their parishioners to proudly display their aesthetic sensibilities and collective wealth. Inside these temples they jettisoned old-time styles of worship, replacing antebellum emotionalism with dignified and refined services, presided over by a trained ministry. The musical dimension shifted from participation to spectatorship—from clapping and shouting to listening and politely applauding concerts given by professional choirmasters and organists. Sunday services were the occasion to doff degrading uniforms and dress up in dark suits, bright dresses, elaborate hats, and white gloves—to look *fine*.

If these temples of respectability were also intended to set an example for the newcomers, they failed. Indeed, recent arrivals, used to southern-style ecstatic evangelism, were put off by the solemn services, deemed lacking in emotional sustenance, and instead reproduced their accustomed forms of worship in storefront churches that began to dot the ecclesiastical landscape. The Union Baptist Church, for example, first housed (1899) in a San Juan Hill brownstone on 63rd Street, was led by the Reverend Dr. George H. Sims of Virginia, who gathered together the "very recent residents of this new, disturbing city" and established a "shouting church" where Christianity came "alive Sunday morning." Pentecostal and Holiness churches sprang up, bringing their emphasis upon healing, gifts of prophecy, speaking in tongues, spirit possession, and religious dance. Musically, they drew on traditions of the slave past and reached out to embrace Gotham's secular black musical world, incorporating the sounds and rhythms of ragtime.

Elite black churches crusaded against illiteracy and fostered appreciation of art and literature, hoping to rebut the coonery image. Church societies provided libraries and classes, sponsored lectures and debates, hosted writing and speech contests. The premier example was the Brooklyn Literary Union, set up by the Siloam Presbyterian Church, which offered concerts, lectures on pertinent issues facing black Americans, and discussions of a "very high character." As the *Age* editorialized in 1908, "Those of the race who have had intellectual and mental training are to be the levers with which the masses are to be lifted."

While these programs were popular, there were many who did not care to be uplifted. Most young newcomers preferred New York's alluring nightlife to its religious and intellectual offerings. They spent more time at dances, theaters, clubs, and bars in tenement house basements that offered inexpensive alcohol, a pool table, and music. Back in the rural South, one migrant explained, "the only recreation we had was prayer meeting and little parties," but in New York City dances were held "every Saturday night." One woman even suggested, "That's why people move more than anything else." Migrants and immigrants both admitted that they attended church less frequently in the city than they had at home. Ministers took note and railed against dancing, gambling, drinking, and theatergoing. "The Negro race is dancing itself to death," thundered Adam Clayton Powell Sr.

INCREASINGLY, MEMBERS OF THE BLACK ELITE set out to improve the lot of the resident poor by offering social services that white charitable institutions had long refused to provide. Apart from the old Quaker-founded Colored Orphan Asylum (1836)—a response to the New York Orphan Asylum's (1809) having shut its doors against black children—virtually no white organization concerned itself exclusively with black welfare. White churches barred blacks from church-run orphanages and old-age homes. The YMCA, the Salvation Army, and Mills Hotels barred blacks from their facilities. New York Hospital refused to let black patients darken its wards. Even the settlement house movement at first concentrated its ameliorative efforts exclusively on white immigrants.

Then, in the 1890s and 1900s, black churches, led by female parishioners, began to increase their offerings. St. Mark's ran a day nursery, established a mutual aid society, and subsidized social work missions in upper Manhattan, Brooklyn, and the Bronx. The women at St. Cyprian, most of Caribbean ancestry, started up an employment agency for women domestics. The women of Abyssinian Baptist ran a home for the aged.

More and more, however, black women detached themselves from male-dominated ecclesiastical structures and, while maintaining their Christian affiliations, established female-run clubs and service organizations. The progenitors of these institutions often came from the ranks of Negro New Women, of whom a prime example was Victoria Earle Matthews.

Matthews's mother, born a slave in Georgia in 1861, had escaped to New York during the war but returned for her children in 1873. Educated in Gotham's public schools, Matthews worked as a domestic until her marriage in 1879, after which she became a well-known journalist, writing not only for the *New York Age* but for the white press as well, including the *New York Times*, the *New York Herald*, and the *Brooklyn Eagle*. She also lectured, most famously on "The Awakening of the Afro-American Woman."

In 1892 Matthews and others organized a highly successful fund-raising dinner in New York's Lyric Hall for Ida Bell Wells-Barnett, more commonly known as Ida B. Wells, a Memphis journalist who, driven out of her city for her exposés of lynching, had embarked on a crusade against racial terrorism. Matthews helped organize and became president of a secular organization, the Women's Loyal Union of New York and Brooklyn (WLU), which built a national reputation for New York's black activist women. In addition to supporting Wells's work, the WLU crusaded for expanding job opportunities for black women in the city, notably in sales, and providing relief for poor children during the mid-1890s depression. She was also active in fashioning the burgeoning black women's club movement. In 1896 Matthews helped arrange the merger of several such entities into the National Association of Colored Women (1896) and became its national organizer. The association was dedicated to aiding poor and working-class black women, promoting temperance, fighting for women's suffrage, and presenting "a positive image of the race to the world."

In 1897 Matthews founded the White Rose Association to aid black women migrants from the South. She began with a campaign to protect "fresh green country girls" from unscrupulous employment agents who lured them north with transport subsidies and promises of good jobs, only to place them as washerwomen or dispatch them to brothels. White Rose emissaries met boats departing Norfolk, and agents met trains and boats arriving in New York, to offer advice and assistance. She also opened a White Rose Mission on East 97th Street, which at first served as a base from which to make home visits to the substantial number of blacks who lived scattered about Manhattan's Upper East Side, from 59th to 127th between Park and First Avenues. She and a cadre of volunteers helped women with housework and child care and held mothers' meetings in various homes. In 1902 she was able to lease a brownstone on East 86th, in which she offered temporary lodging to homeless new arrivals and provided the kind of social services available at settlement houses—a kindergarten, a mothers' club, a library, classes in household skills (to prepare them for domestic jobs with churchgoing families), and programs about "race history" and black literature, including occasional lectures by the likes of poet Paul Lawrence Dunbar. In its first ten years of existence, the White Rose provided lodging to over 5,000 black working women. Though there were repeated efforts at raising money from members of the black community, given their straitened circumstances the great bulk of her funding came from wealthy white philanthropists like Grace Hoadley Dodge, Arabella (Mrs. Collis P.) Huntington, and Fanny Garrison (Mrs. Henry) Villard.

In part inspired by Matthews's example, black activists in Manhattan and Brooklyn pressured the all-white Young Men's Christian Association—and its equally white Young Women's Christian Association counterpart—into authorizing the founding of segregated but autonomous and self-governing facilities in black neighborhoods, and these, in turn, were able to attract support from wealthy whites.

In 1900 YMCA authorities agreed to establish a Colored Men's YMCA in the Tenderloin, at the urging of the Reverend Charles T. Walker. After assuming the pulpit at the prestigious Mount Olivet Baptist Church in 1899, Walker had quickly realized the need for an alternative to neighborhood dives, and for a place where young black men from the South could "come and find friends." He called a public meeting, won support from virtually every black pastor in the city, raised money (much of it garnered at church fairs sponsored by the United Tribes, an Olivet women's auxiliary), leased a brownstone for a year at 132 West 53rd (between Sixth and Seventh), and then, in December 1900, made application to the New York City YMCA Association for membership as a regular branch, which was accepted. It was so successful that it moved to larger quarters two blocks further west, at 252–254.

In Brooklyn the spark plug was Charles H. Bullock, black teacher and journalist, who in 1902 mobilized hundreds of members of the African American community in Brooklyn to pledge their support, and convinced financier George Foster Peabody to buy and equip a three-story building at 405 Carlton Avenue in Fort Greene. The "Colored Y" offered pleasant parlors, a reading room stocked with books, magazines, and newspapers, a game room, and a limited number of nicely furnished rooms. It also provided educational and Bible classes, and established a literary society, a glee club, an employment bureau, and a baseball team.

Black women activists pushed to establish Colored YWCAs. While resenting their exclusion from white branches, they appreciated the possibility of creating nondenominational institutions which they could control. In 1903 an African American branch was established in Brooklyn, on Lexington Avenue, which offered staples like training in cooking, serving, laundering, and seamstressing and, more unusually, a course in home nursing that provided a rudimentary grounding in anatomy and physiology. And in 1905 the United Tribes women from Mount Olivet founded a Manhattan branch, which eventually settled at 143 West 53rd (after first having rented space in San Juan Hill), just down the street from its male counterpart.

AT ROUGHLY THE SAME MOMENT, the white settlement movement turned its attention to Gotham's blacks. Lillian Wald's Henry Street had made no racial distinction in its programs, but she decided that a special effort should be made for residents of the black ghetto, and she dispatched black nurses up to San Juan Hill. In 1903 one of them reported back on the dreadful health conditions prevailing there and urged Wald to organize an uptown branch.

In 1905 a Negro nursing center was set up in a West 62nd Street tenement. A year later, Wald launched the Stillman Branch for Colored People, at 205 West 60th Street, supported by Mary Stillman Harkness and her sister, and named in memory of their father, a Wall Street lawyer who left them fortunes. It offered the full panoply of Henry Street settlement services, including a circulating library and a penny provident bank; classes in city history, folk dancing, carpentry, domestic science, and sewing; social clubs for all ages; a playground; and the Hope Day Nursery for Colored Children, which had been organized by African American mothers in 1902 and was then absorbed by the Stillman Branch. Demand for its offerings was so great that it moved to larger quarters at 203 West 63rd Street.

In 1908 Mary White Ovington opened a neighborhood center in a striking new philanthropic housing development at 233–247 West 63rd, virtually next door to Wald's operation. Ovington was born in the year of Lincoln's assassination into a well-to-do Brooklyn Heights family. Her father was an active anti-slavery man. Her grandmother, a friend of William Lloyd Garrison, raised her on stories about abolitionism. Ovington was educated at the Packer Collegiate Institute, from which she graduated in 1891, and Radcliffe College, from which she was forced to withdraw for financial reasons in 1893 (her father having been a depression casualty). She supported herself by working as a registrar at the Pratt Institute in Brooklyn. In 1895, under Pratt's auspices, she opened and for seven years headed a settlement house in Greenpoint, staffed by Pratt students and alumnae. Radicalized by her experiences in that white working-class community, she joined the Intercollegiate Socialist Society, then the Socialist Party itself (in 1905), and later wrote for the *Masses*.

Ovington developed an interest in doing settlement work in a black community after hearing a series of talks in 1903 at the Social Reform Club—a group of intellectuals and workers—that laid out the conditions of the Negro in New York. When she told Mary Simkhovitch of her desire, the Greenwich House head told her that she should undertake her own investigation of conditions among African Americans, as "you know nothing about the people you want to work with," and promptly arranged a Greenwich House fellowship to start it in 1904. Her ensuing seven-year analysis of black life in the city would culminate, in 1911, with publication of the little classic *Half a Man*, which was, as Franz Boas described it in his foreword, "a refutation of the claims that the Negro has equal opportunity with the whites, and that his failure to advance more rapidly than he has, is due to innate inability."

During this period Ovington looked about for possible financial support for her proposed settlement house. She knew of the philanthropic housing work being undertaken by former steel magnate Henry Phipps, including a complex in San Juan Hill, that would consist of four six-story buildings on West 63rd Street, to be called the Tuskegee Apartments. Ovington persuaded Phipps to allot her one of the apartments from which to do settlement work. When the project opened in 1908 she was the only white resident, and her rooms became a community gathering place. After eight months, however, Phipps discontinued the offer, but Ovington's stay there had given her an unparalleled vantage point for understanding racism in the city. And when she departed, she responded almost immediately to a proposal from Yerina Morton-Jones, a pioneering black woman doctor, that they open a settlement in downtown Brooklyn. The Lincoln Settlement, which they launched in 1908 at 105 Fleet Place, was located near the Hudson Avenue quarter, containing some of the worst poverty and slum dwellings in the borough. The settlement was supported principally by contributions from wealthy whites obtained by Ovington, who was in charge of fund-raising.

IN THE DECADE FOLLOWING THE RACE RIOT OF 1900, more and more powerful whites turned their attention to black life in New York. Their goals—a mix of moral, civic, business, and self-interested considerations—meshed neatly with those of middle-class black activists seeking to aid and uplift recent migrants. Out of this confluence came a relatively rapid crystallization of organizations.

In 1905 Frances Kellor, progressive activist and settlement researcher who had studied shady employment agencies, set out to scale up the work of Victoria Earle Matthews's White Rose Association. She organized the Association for the Protection of Colored Women, which fashioned an information network throughout the South. Using churches, schools, and newspapers, she aimed to alert young black women of the dangers that lay in wait for them in New York City and to direct them to a consortium of reputable black employment agencies. In 1906 a bevy of corporate executives, department store owners, investment bankers, and life insurance officials underwrote creation of the National League for the Protection of Colored Women, which brought together similar associations in Philadelphia, Baltimore, and other northern cities.

At the same time, William Bulkley, principal of the virtually all black PS 80, developed an evening school that offered classes in commercial and industrial skills, hoping to expand black employment. Bulkley approached William Jay Schieffelin, a trustee of the Hampton Institute in Virginia and other southern black industrial education projects, who agreed to prod fellow philanthropists into aiding northern blacks as well. This led in 1906 to the establishment of the Committee for Improving the Industrial Conditions of Negroes in New York to back Bulkley's approach; again it combined leading whites (Schieffelin and Ruth Baldwin, widow of philanthropist William Baldwin) and prominent blacks (Charles Anderson and Fred Moore).

A third organization, the Committee on Urban Conditions among Negroes, emerged in 1910, at the instigation of George Haynes. Born in Arkansas in 1880, Haynes got a BA from Fisk in 1903 and then a master's in sociology from Yale. After working for the YMCA, he enrolled in the graduate program jointly administered by Columbia and the New York School of Philanthropy and became the first African American to get a PhD in sociology. In 1910 he approached Frances Kellor and Ruth Baldwin and urged on them the importance of training black social workers to work in the black community, and particularly to serve newcomers from the South. Almost immediately the committee was established, and Haynes appointed its director.

In 1911 these three and other groups merged to form the National League on Urban Conditions among Negroes, soon known as the National Urban League (NUL). Its board mixed black notables—Dr. Bulkley, *Age* editor Moore, Abyssinian Baptist's Adam Clayton Powell—with white executives, philanthropists, lawyers, and bankers, including Schieffelin, Alfred T. White, and John D. Rockefeller Jr., the group's biggest contributor.

The NUL's overarching goal was to provide "Not Alms, but Opportunity," in the words of its motto, blazoned each month in its journal, *Opportunity*. This dovetailed with the self-help attitude appealing to many in the African American middle class. The organization believed the problems confronting blacks, particularly the newly arriving immigrants, were fixable, with a boost from supportive social workers and philanthropists.

The NUL set out to be a wide-spectrum social service operation. It sponsored vocational schools. It tried to convince white employers to hire blacks (without much luck: most of the few hundred men it placed each year worked as janitors). It trained black social workers and fostered uplift programs, hoping to instruct migrants about proper patterns of dress, cleanliness, speech, and behavior. It offered travelers' aid to new arrivals. It promoted housing bureaus, playgrounds, settlement houses, summer camps, clubs, community centers, and improved sanitation in black districts. It set up a "rescue home for unfortunate colored girls and women." It investigated Negro housing conditions and conducted health meetings at churches.

The Urban League's preferred tactics were those of businessmen, ministers, and teachers: negotiation, persuasion, education, investment. It eschewed protest, agitation, and the pursuit of reform legislation. It addressed symptoms, not causes. It did not go toe to toe with racism.

Mary White Ovington understood the limits of the efforts of groups like her Lincoln Settlement. It "does not hope to solve the race problem," she acknowledged, "but it trusts that the united efforts of white and colored to alleviate conditions in the eleventh ward may make their spot a better place to live." This was an honorable goal, no matter that it could be pursued for a wide variety of motives, not all of them altruistic.

But there were others in the city—including Ovington—who believed that what blacks were ultimately up against was deeply embedded structures of racism. They believed that while amelioration of misery was welcome, it would not get very far without directly confronting these deep structural barriers. At the same time the Urban League coalition of blacks and whites was deploying progressive measures, a different New York City coalition, also interracial, and with a certain degree of overlap, was mounting a more militant campaign.

CIVIL RIGHTS

Timothy Thomas Fortune, a Floridian born into slavery in 1856, grew up during Reconstruction, when his family was menaced repeatedly by the Ku Klux Klan, his father being an elected state representative. Fortune left the South in 1874, spent a year at Howard University, decided to become a journalist, and worked on various newspapers before moving to New York in 1879. In 1881 he founded a "race paper," the *New York Globe*, later changing its name twice, first to the *New York Freeman* in 1884, then to the *New York Age* in 1887. Fortune soon became the most prominent black journalist of the era, and the *Age* the most widely read black paper. In its pages he excoriated the southern regime for its lynch law, mob violence, segregation, disfranchisement, election fraud, debt peonage, chain gangs, and convict leasing. "Let us agitate! agitate! AGITATE! until the protest shall wake the nation from its indifference."

In 1887 Fortune organized the National Afro-American League, the first nationwide entity to challenge segregation and disenfranchisement. (Fortune promoted the term "Afro-American" as a more respectful alternative to "Negro.") A national association, based on local and state branches, it used the courts to protest infringements of civil and voting rights guaranteed by the Fourteenth and Fifteenth Amendments. But there were few successes. Nor was much support or funding forthcoming from either black leaders or the black masses. Except in New York, where the local branch leadership was in the hands of Fortune himself, the attorney T. McCants Stewart, and the Reverend Alexander Walters, a powerful new recruit.

Walters, born a slave in Kentucky, began preaching in 1877 at age 19, and served in various AME Zion pulpits before being assigned in 1888 to Gotham's Mother Zion Church; in 1892 he was made a bishop. But despite their joint efforts, and a few minor victories, the National Afro-American League fizzled out in 1893.

The black voice that *did* capture national attention was purveying a very different message.

Booker T. Washington, born a slave, had been educated at Hampton Institute in Virginia. In 1881 he became the principal of Tuskegee Normal and Industrial Institute in Alabama, an all-black school that trained teachers to provide vocational education. Assuming a larger role in southern affairs, Washington counseled his people to bend before the racist typhoon sweeping through the region, rather than engage, as did Fortune, in "mere political agitation." In 1895 Washington spelled out his vision in a speech in Atlanta addressed to both blacks and whites. He urged African Americans not to contest Jim Crow segregation, but rather to turn it to their advantage by building autonomous self-reliant communities. They should also accept their position at the bottom of the occupational hierarchy, and seek the practical education (the kind offered at Tuskegee) that would make them more efficient at such tasks. But they should also attempt to work their way up, by becoming black entrepreneurs and acquiring property and wealth: economic development, not political action, was the best route to racial uplift. All in all, his message was that by working hard, not making waves, embracing bourgeois virtues, and making money, blacks would eventually win acceptance and even respect from the white world. On the subjects of disenfranchisement and lynching he was all but mute.

Booker T. Washington (seated, right) and Theodore Roosevelt, speaking at the National Negro Business League, 1910. (Library of Congress Prints and Photographs Division, George Grantham Bain Collection)

To his white auditors, Washington insisted that blacks did not want and would not seek social equality. He also reminded them they had a good thing going for them—a "patient, faithful, law-abiding and unresentful" black workforce that would dig their mines, build their railroads, and pick their cotton, all "without strikes and labour wars" like those plaguing the North, where business relied on immigrants, with their "strange tongues and habits."

This speech was an instant smash hit with white folks, north as well as south, and garnered gobs of headlines in the white press. It appealed particularly to investors who wanted to develop the industrial resources of the South—its coal, its iron, its railroads—without getting sidetracked by the "Negro question." Leading capitalists fell all over one another in becoming ardent supporters of Booker T. Washington and his accommodationist message, and nowhere was he more popular than in New York City.

In December 1899, in Madison Square Garden's Concert Hall, corporate titans turned out en masse to hear Washington pitch for funds. August Belmont, Nicholas Murray Butler, Cleveland H. Dodge, William E. Dodge, Morris K. Jesup, Seth Low, J. Pierpont Morgan, George Foster Peabody, John D. Rockefeller Sr., J. G. Phelps Stokes, William Jay Schieffelin, and Jacob Schiff were among the crowd of capitalists motivated variously by missionary zeal, an abolitionist heritage, or the desire to cultivate a disciplined black labor force in an area where their investments lay. Tuskegee trustee William H. Baldwin Jr., president of the Long Island Rail Road and a former vice president of the Southern Railway system, had become convinced of the need for a trained black labor force in the South. As he told the Garden attendees: "The industrial education of the Negro—the education from the foundation up, as practiced at Tuskegee, is of vast business importance to all of us. The difference between 10 million ignorant Blacks and 10 million reasonably educated industrial workers, means more than sympathy, more than sentiment, more than our duty—it means wealth to the community." By "reasonably educated," Baldwin made clear, he meant they should be "taught the dignity of manual labor and how to perform it," period. He was, he explained, "bitterly opposed to the so-called higher education of Negroes," on the grounds that the black man should not be "educated out of his natural environment."[12]

New York philanthropists began to pump serious amounts of money southward. Some came from institutions. In 1902 Rockefeller Senior anted up a million in seed money to launch the General Education Board, chaired by Baldwin. The Southern Education Board, Phelps-Stokes Foundation, and John F. Slater Fund were also Gotham-based givers. Many made personal commitments. In addition to Baldwin, New Yorker trustees of Tuskegee included George Foster Peabody, Robert C. Ogden, J. G. Phelps Stokes, William Jay Schieffelin, George McAneny, and former mayor Seth Low. In 1903 Washington bagged the elephant. He had been trying to get the ear of Andrew Carnegie since 1899 but had been turned aside. Then his autobiography, *Up from Slavery*, came out in 1901. Carnegie, in admiration of another self-made man, now paid attention. He gave Tuskegee a library, then from 1902 a stipend of $10,000 a year; then, in April 1903, he gave $600,000, with the proviso that $150,000 be set aside, and the interest on it given directly to Washington and his wife, for life. (Washington prevailed on Carnegie to keep the size of the latter behest private.) "History is to tell of two Washingtons," Carnegie enthused, "one white, one black, both fathers of their people."

---

12. Baldwin assumed that the Negro would "willingly fill the more menial positions, and do the heavy work, at less wages," leaving to whites "the more expert labor." Baldwin's advice to the Negro was to "avoid social questions; leave politics alone; continue to be patient; live moral lives; live simply; learn to work…know that it is a crime for any teacher, white or black, to educate the negro for positions which are not open to him." In 1915 Washington was still sticking to this position: "We are trying to instil into the Negro mind that if education does not make the Negro humble, simple, and of service to the community, then it will not be encouraged."

Washington was also anointed as race spokesman by the nation's political leadership. Though President Roosevelt considered blacks stupid, shiftless, and prone to "vice and criminality," he thought qualified individual blacks were entitled to advancement, and, besides, the Republican Party was in need of black votes. So on October 16, 1901, Roosevelt invited Washington to dine in the White House (eliciting howls of protest from southern whites). Of greater consequence, TR made Washington his foremost confidant on race issues, and he became a key political adviser for many lesser Republican politicians as well.

Washington used his funds and patronage pull to develop a "Tuskegee machine" that rewarded supporters and punished enemies throughout the nation, but particularly in New York. At first, Washington's man in Manhattan was none other than Timothy Thomas Fortune. The militant *New York Age* editor and the accommodationst Alabamian struck up a friendship, despite their differing politics and temperaments, in part because Fortune believed that much of what Washington was promoting—thrift, hard work, economic development, self-sufficiency, and racial pride—was of value for blacks, and not inherently incompatible with demands for political and racial justice. He also knew all too well (and better than most northern blacks) how powerful were the racist currents Washington was trying to navigate. So in the early 1890s Fortune smiled on Washington's career and helped him win the mantle of top leader, even ghostwriting some of his books and speeches. The *New York Age* justified Washington's doings and defended him against a growing number of critics—and also came to depend on his (unacknowledged) patronage. But the more Fortune soft-pedaled his own views, the more he fell into drink and depression.

Occasionally, however, he would revert to full-fledged agitational mode. In June 1900, at a mass meeting in Brooklyn's Odd Fellows Hall commemorating the hundredth birthday of John Brown, the old Fortune flashed into view. It "has been said that we should make friends of the Southerners, but we must not make friends with any man who would deprive us of our rights as men and as citizens." On the contrary, Afro-Americans, now 10 million strong, were losing patience, and there would yet "come a time when they will get at the throats of the white men who have tried to wrong and outrage us as citizens." Indeed, he said, if the law doesn't protect us, "we should protect ourselves, and if need be die in the defense of our rights as citizens."

This was not the message Washington sought to convey, and, especially after Carnegie and Rockefeller and Roosevelt had climbed aboard the Tuskegee Express, he put an increasing amount of daylight between himself and his former mentor. He turned instead for advice and counsel to New York Republican politico Charles Anderson, who by 1904 had become his chief lieutenant. He also began grooming Frederick Moore, a devout accommodationist, as his journalistic spokesman. In 1905 he got Moore a position on the *Age*, and in 1907, with Washington's (unacknowledged) financing, Moore purchased the paper from Fortune when he was at a particularly low ebb, his health having collapsed. Washington also made friends and influenced people in the black business and church worlds, and among the black progressives. (He held fund-raising benefits for Victoria Earle Matthews's White Rose Mission and backed William Bulkley's vocational training approach.) When the National Urban League emerged, it was considered to be firmly in Booker T.'s camp. Gotham, it seemed, had become a Tuskegee town.

WASHINGTON'S RENUNCIATION OF RIGHTS, silence on abuses, and disparagement of higher education were beginning to pall. Not only had they patently failed to bring results, but in the decade after his Atlanta address, white supremacists had grown stronger, and lynchings had multiplied, as had Jim Crow segregation statutes. Many blacks were becoming frustrated and impatient, increasingly revisiting Fortune's advocacy of agitation.

In 1903 a powerful voice was added to the list of Washington's critics when W. E. B. Du Bois published *The Souls of Black Folk*, which contained an essay, "Of Mr. Booker T. Washington and Others," that attacked accommodationism. William Edward Burghardt Du Bois had been born in Great Barrington, Massachusetts, in 1868. In 1882, while still a high school student, he took on the task of distributing the *New York Globe*, Fortune being a man Du Bois admired, and between 1883 and 1885 the teenager himself became a contributor. In 1888 he got a degree from the all-black Fisk University; he got a second degree (in history) from Harvard in 1890, did graduate study at the University of Berlin in 1892, and in 1895 became the first African American to earn a doctorate from Harvard, in history. After a year teaching at Wilberforce University in Ohio, in 1896 he accepted a research position in sociology at the University of Pennsylvania, where he undertook a rigorous city survey of black Philadelphia. In 1897 he moved to Atlanta University to teach sociology and direct a series of empirical studies of the social, economic, cultural, and institutional lives of African Americans. In 1901 he published in the *New York Times* two articles on the history and sociology of blacks in New York City that were astonishingly insightful, deeply researched, and written in accessible prose and admirably brief compass.[13]

In his 1903 *Souls of Black Folk* Du Bois accused Washington of abandoning the fight for black political rights and accepting segregation in exchange for nonexistent economic gains. Du Bois in fact agreed with much of the Tuskegeean's counsel. He, too, advocated industrial training, supported black entrepreneurs, exhorted African Americans to develop purer morals, and hoped for eventual integration. But Du Bois indicted Washington for being fixated on vocational training at the expense of college education, whereas he wanted to develop a pool of university-trained black professionals (a "Talented Tenth") who might then uplift their "duller brethren."

A more pointed attack on Washington followed in 1904 when Du Bois declared blacks would only become free if they had "the courage and persistence to demand the rights and treatment of men and to cease to toady and apologize and belittle themselves." He called for a struggle to "gain every right and privilege open to a free American citizen." Du Bois also differed in developing a global perspective on the situation of US blacks, comparing them to overseas victims of imperialism. In *Souls* he asserted that "the problem of the twentieth century is the problem of the color-line,—the relation of the darker to the lighter races of men in Asia and Africa, in America and the islands of the sea."

In 1905 he gathered with supporters on the Canadian side of Niagara Falls, hotels on the US side being segregated, and formed an organization that came to be known as the Niagara Movement. Its basic demands were those Fortune had advanced twenty years before: full manhood suffrage; abolition of segregation; higher as well as vocational education; an end to discrimination in unions, the courts, and public accommodations; and real equality of economic opportunity. And, *pace* Washington's accommodationism, African Americans should "refuse to kiss the hand that smites us."

13. His two-part treatment—"The Black North, a Social Study: New York City," *New York Times*, November 17 and 24, 1901—was followed up in a fifth article (following on similarly deft pieces on Philadelphia and Boston), entitled "Some Conclusions," in the *Times* of December 15, 1901. Du Bois returned to the subject of black Gotham in *Some Notes on the Negroes in New York City* (1903), a five-page leaflet in the Atlanta University Studies series, which was really a sketchy rumination on census data.

That hand smote again in September of 1906, when supposedly progressive Atlanta experienced a vicious three-day riot, in which white crowds, reinforced by white police, raged through the city, killing scores, wounding hundreds, smashing black schools, businesses, and homes. Defections from Washington's camp were accelerated by outrage at his patron President Roosevelt's response to the riots—silence—and by his general capitulation to southern racism. Despite the postprandial hopes raised by his White House tête-à-tête with Booker T., TR had rapidly replaced African American officeholders with lily-white southerners, made no move to prevent the South from ejecting blacks from politics, and steadfastly failed to condemn mob violence. In New York, Bishop Walters (who since 1898 had headed the National Afro-American Council, a successor to the defunct Afro-American League) concluded that as "the President has abandoned us to our fate," the community must not stay silent. Walters proposed that Afro-Americans stage a march on Washington.

Worse, weeks after the Atlanta riot, in his Annual Message to Congress in December 1906, the president finally addressed the epidemic of lynching, but by saying that its "greatest existing cause" was the "perpetration, especially by black men, of the hideous crime of rape—the most abominable in all the category of crimes even worse than murder." True, he decried white mobs taking revenge for these "bestial" crimes, because it lowered them to the level of black criminals. The way to end lynching, he concluded, was to end black criminality, and the way to do that was to promote Booker T. Washington–style industrial education. This badly timed accolade was one the Tuskegee leader could have done without.

Then, in 1908, another shocking incidence of violence transformed the situation by winning Du Bois powerful white allies in New York City. A race riot broke out in the North, in Springfield, Illinois, near Lincoln's gravesite. In response, William English Walling, the wealthy Socialist and suffragist who had helped found the Women's Trade Union League back in 1903, penned an article—"The Race War in the North"—for the March 1908 *Independent*. Walling saw southern-style racial violence spreading northward. Halting it would require reviving "the spirit of the abolitionists." He proposed a national organization of "fair minded whites and intelligent blacks" to combat racial oppression.

Walling's challenge was taken up by settlement house organizer and Socialist activist Mary White Ovington, who arranged a meeting in January 1909 with Walling and prominent New York social worker Henry Moskowitz, then also associate leader of the New York Society for Ethical Culture. Years before, Ovington, who had known of Du Bois's scholarly work on Philadelphia and New York, had turned to the Atlanta University professor for help in her own analysis of Gotham's black community. Over the years, Ovington had become Du Bois's close friend and the city's leading white advocate of his ideas.

This trio—Du Bois, Ovington, and Moskowitz—quickly drew in other seasoned liberal reformers: William Henry Brooks (the black Methodist minister who had led the protest against New York's 1900 race riot), Lillian Wald, Florence Kelley, and Oswald Garrison Villard (publisher of the *New York Evening Post* and the *Nation*, grandson of the militant abolitionist, son of the wealthy railroad promoter, and a male mainstay of the women's suffrage movement). This inner circle put together a Call—issued on Lincoln's Birthday, 1909—signed by some sixty prominent whites and blacks. A National Negro Conference followed, held from May 30 to June 1, 1909, at Wald's Henry Street Settlement House. Du Bois played a key role in organizing the event and presided over the proceedings, out of which emerged an organization calling itself the National Negro Committee (NNC). Participants included, in addition to those already on board, Leonora O'Reilly, E. R. A. Seligman, Bishop Alexander Walters, Rabbi Stephen Wise, William Bulkley, John Dewey, Charles E. Russell,

Ida B. Wells, John Haynes Holmes, Dr. Verina Morton Jones, Lincoln Steffens, Ray Stannard Baker, and J. G. Phelps Stokes. At its second conference, on May 30, 1910, members renamed the NNC the National Association for the Advancement of Colored People (NAACP). Du Bois acknowledged the new organization's debt to T. Thomas Fortune and his Afro-American League forerunner.

The NAACP's initial platform demanded all civil and suffrage rights due under the Reconstruction amendments. Over the next few years it created a multi-layered protest strategy that used lobbying, boycotting, petitioning, voter education, calls for self-defense, and,

NATIONAL NEGRO COMMITTEE
500 FIFTH AVENUE
NEW YORK

Rev. W. H. Brooks, New York.
Prof. John Dewey, New York.
Paul Kennaday, New York.
Jacob W. Mack, New York.
Mrs. M. D. MacLean, New York.
Dr. Henry Moskowitz, New York.
John E. Milholland, New York.
Miss Leonora O'Reilly, New York.
Charles Edward Russell, New York.
Prof. Edwin R. A. Seligman, New York.
Rev. Joseph Silverman, New York.
Oswald G. Villard, New York.
Miss Lillian D. Wald, New York.

Wm. English Walling, New York.
Bishop Alexander Walters, New York.
Dr. Stephen S. Wise, New York.
Miss Mary W. Ovington, Brooklyn.
Dr. O. M. Waller, Brooklyn.
Rev. J. H. Holmes, Yonkers, N. Y.
Prof. W. L. Bulkley, Ridgefield Park, N. J.
Miss Maria Baldwin, Boston.
Archibald H. Grimke, Boston.
Albert E. Pillsbury, Boston.
Moorfield Storey, Boston.
Pres. Chas. P. Thwing, Cleveland, O.
Pres. W. S. Scarborough, Wilberforce, O.

Miss Jane Addams, Chicago.
Mrs. Ida Wells-Barnett, Chicago.
Dr. C. E. Bentley, Chicago.
Mrs. Celia Parker Woolley, Chicago.
Dr. William Sinclair, Philadelphia.
Miss Susan Wharton, Philadelphia.
R. R. Wright, Jr., Philadelphia.
L. M. Hershaw, Washington.
Judge Wendell P. Stafford, Washington.
Mrs. Mary Church Terrell, Washington.
Rev. J. Milton Waldron, Washington.
Prof. W. E. B. DuBois, Atlanta, Ga.
Leslie Pinckney Hill, Manassas, Va.

Platform Adopted by the National Negro Committee, 1909

We denounce the ever-growing oppression of our 10,000,000 colored fellow citizens as the greatest menace that threatens the country. Often plundered of their just share of the public funds, robbed of nearly all part in the government, segregated by common carriers, some murdered with impunity, and all treated with open contempt by officials, they are held in some States in practical slavery to the white community. The systematic persecution of law-abiding citizens and their disfranchisement on account of their race alone is a crime that will ultimately drag down to an infamous end any nation that allows it to be practiced, and it bears most heavily on those poor white farmers and laborers whose economic position is most similar to that of the persecuted race.

The nearest hope lies in the immediate and patiently continued enlightenment of the people who have been inveigled into a campaign of oppression. The spoils of persecution should not go to enrich any class or classes of the population. Indeed persecution of organized workers, peonage, enslavement of prisoners, and even disfranchisement already threaten large bodies of whites in many Southern States.

We agree fully with the prevailing opinion that the transformation of the unskilled colored laborers in industry and agriculture into skilled workers is of vital importance to that race and to the ration, but we demand for the Negroes, as for all others, a free and complete education, whether by city, State or nation, a grammar school and industrial training for all and technical, professional, and academic education for the most gifted.

But the public schools assigned to the Negro of whatever kind or grade will never receive a fair and equal treatment until he is given equal treatment in the Legislature and before the law. Nor will the practically educated Negro, no matter how valuable to the community he may prove, be given a fair return for his labor or encouraged to put forth his best efforts or given the chance to develop that efficiency that comes only outside the school until he is respected in his legal rights as a man and a citizen.

We regard with grave concern the attempt manifest South and North to deny black men the right to work and to enforce this demand by violence and bloodshed. Such a question is too fundamental and clear even to be submitted to arbitration. The late strike in Georgia is not simply a demand that Negroes be displaced, but that proven and efficient men be made to surrender their long-followed means of livelihood to white competitors.

As first and immediate steps toward remedying these national wrongs, so full of peril for the whites as well as the blacks of all sections, we demand of Congress and the Executive:

(1). That the Constitution be strictly enforced and the civil rights guaranteed under the Fourteenth Amendment be secured impartially to all.

(2). That there be equal educational opportunities for all and in all the States, and that public school expenditure be the same for the Negro and white child;

(3). That in accordance with the Fifteenth Amendment the right of the Negro to the ballot on the same terms as other citizens be recognized in every part of the country.

I herewith subscribe $_____ to the National Negro Committee, and desire to become a member of the permanent organization growing out of the present Conference.

(Make checks payable to Oswald G. Villard, Treasurer).

"Platform of the National Negro Committee," 1909. (Library of Congress, Manuscript Division, NAACP Records) centrally, a legal defense strategy, using persistent litigation to get the courts to uphold the Fourteenth and Fifteenth Amendments.

Though it called itself a "national" association, the fledgling organization's critical players were principally New Yorkers; indeed, half its thirty-member executive committee were required to live in Gotham. Du Bois himself moved from Atlanta to New York in the summer of 1910 and in November assumed his new duties as director of publicity and research, and editor, of the organization's journal, *The Crisis: A Record of the Darker Races*. Originally run out of Villard's Art Nouveau *Evening Post* building at 20 Vesey Street, it moved in 1914 to larger quarters in 70 Fifth Avenue (at 13th Street, one block from Union Square), after Villard and Du Bois had a falling-out.[14] The initial leadership was all white, apart from Du Bois, but the organization soon began incorporating African Americans into positions of authority—notably by selecting Bishop Walters as vice president in 1911, and in 1916 hiring as field secretary James Weldon Johnson, distinguished black journalist, diplomat and Broadway lyricist; over the next two years he spearheaded a phenomenally successful membership drive.

"W. E. B. (William Edward Burghardt) Du Bois," May 31, 1919. (Library of Congress Prints and Photographs Division)

---

14. Du Bois would attempt in 1912 to move his own household to Forest Hills Gardens, the model suburban community established by the Russell Sage Foundation, but the general manager of the RSF Homes Company wrote to say he regretted to inform Du Bois that, after much deliberation, it had been decided that "it would be a doubtful plan for you to settle in a community . . . of white people." The Du Bois family finally rented a small house in the Bronx at 3059 Villa Avenue.

The solid establishment of the NAACP instantly gave Gotham a claim to rival Tuskegee as the center of the country's organized black movement. And within the city it constituted an alternative to the Booker T. Washington–centric National Urban League, with its coalition of corporate elites and black progressives, an alternative consonant with its very different roots in the city's radical and reform movements.

The city's Protestant corporate elite failed to back the NAACP. The Carnegies and Rockefellers preferred Washington's emphasis on Negro obligations to Du Bois's demand for Negro rights. But if the NAACP's militancy cost its organizers one set of funders, it unexpectedly gained them another—some of the wealthiest members of New York's Jewish community.

Jewish reformers, to be sure, had been active from the beginning: Wald, Seligman, and Moskowitz had had a major role in planning the initial lift-off. Another Jewish intellectual, Columbia anthropologist Franz Boas, was invited to the second national conference in 1910 to give a presentation that shredded eugenicist arguments about the supposed inherent inferiority of African Americans; Du Bois immediately published Boas' lecture in the *Crisis*.[15] That same conclave passed resolutions protesting the recent expulsion of Jews from Kiev, and had Jacob Schiff address the meeting; Schiff became a major annual contributor, though he continued aiding Tuskegee as well. And in 1911 Joel Spingarn would sign on and play a critical part in the NAACP's development, becoming chairman of its board in 1913, replacing Villard.

Spingarn was born in New York City into a well-to-do family, his father an exile Austrian Jew who had prospered as a tobacco merchant. Spingarn attended New York public schools, got a doctorate in literature from Columbia, and stayed on to teach there, until his unorthodox approach to literary analysis—the "New Criticism"—and even more his opposition to Columbia president Nicholas Murray Butler's autocratic rule, led to his being fired in 1911. A liberal Republican and then a Progressive, Spingarn became active in promoting the NAACP's agenda in the public sphere. He was a terrific speaker, and he and Du Bois—who became close friends—drew large crowds on the lecture circuit, pounding away at Tuskegee-style accommodationism.

Still, many conservative and affluent Jews, averse to public agitation of racial issues, had only supported Booker T. Washington's approach—until 1915, when the Georgia lynching of Leo Frank, a Texas-born but Brooklyn-bred Jew, led several Jewish philanthropists to back the New York–based NAACP. Within a few years, second- and third-generation scions of the great German Jewish banking families were major NAACP players. Board chairman Joel Spingarn's brother, Arthur, became pro bono legal counsel, Herbert Lehman sat on its executive committee, and Herbert J. Seligman directed its public relations. Jews also joined the National Urban League, but white Protestants continued to dominate.

The establishment in New York of a civil rights coalition that combined blacks and Jews and liberal Protestants would prove to be of great significance for the city (and the country), but its immediate accomplishments were modest. Locally, in 1911 Joel Spingarn organized a New York Vigilance Committee to investigate and protest racial discrimination in the

---

15. Du Bois had invited Boas to give the 1906 commencement address at Atlanta University, and was astonished at the anthropologist's presentation, which described some of the major contributions to civilization that had come out of black sub-Saharan Africa. Boas also compared the position of Jews in Europe with Africans in the United States, noting the stubborn continuation of anti-Semitism, which, he told his audience, "illustrates the conditions that characterize your own position." The graduates should be aware that if they thought that programs of self-improvement would win "recognition or support" from their "white neighbor," as BTW argued, they were "destined to disappointment." And Boas's larger project—attacking the increasingly fashionable eugenicist version of evolutionary theory—was dismantling the presumed hierarchy of racial types that relegated both Jews and blacks to inferior status.

metropolis. In 1913, with strong black and Jewish support, the NAACP helped get the state legislature—then at progressive flood tide—to pass the Levy Act, which outlawed advertising intended to restrict access, on the basis of "race, color, or creed," to places of public accommodation (notably summer resorts) and amusement facilities.

At the federal level, the NAACP helped defeat an effort by southern congressmen to restrict immigration of West Indians. Southerners complained that Jamaicans who had been working on the now completed Panama Canal had gotten accustomed to relatively high wages, and were bringing such expectations with them to the United States, along with a racial culture that accepted social equality and permitted intermarriage across color lines. Given that the States had excluded the Chinese, who were "much superior to Negroes," why not forestall further "undesirable immigration"? The legislation passed the Senate in 1914 but was blocked in the House, thanks to a joint effort by the NAACP and Booker T. Washington's network.

THE NAACP'S MOST VISIBLE ACHIEVEMENT lay in providing W. E. B. Du Bois a platform. His harshly eloquent *Crisis* editorials raged at lynch mobs, crusaded against disfranchisement, and condemned "Anglo-Saxon civilization."[16]

Du Bois also cast about for possible political allies. The editor supported the principles of the Socialist Party (he was a member from 1910 to 1912), but was put off by its refusal to recognize racism as a priority. In 1912 he looked to the Progressive Party, even prepared a plank on black rights for the platform. But when Joel Spingarn, a Roosevelt supporter, passed it to TR, the former president rejected it—he was strenuously courting southern support—and told Spingarn he should be "careful of that man Du Bois," who was in Roosevelt's opinion a "dangerous person." The Republicans were running Taft again, a president who had gone on record in 1911 as saying the African American "ought to come and is coming more and more under the guardianship of the South." So NAACP militants endorsed Democrat Woodrow Wilson, in return for vague assurances of fair treatment. Big mistake. Once elected, the Virginia-born Wilson—when not telling "darky" stories at cabinet meetings—began segregating many government offices and firing or demoting scores of black federal employees. The NAACP's Oswald Garrison Villard met privately with Wilson to urge a change of policy, but got nowhere.

Du Bois's most successful outreach was to the women's suffrage movement, a movement divided on racial lines. Black women had been fighting for the vote on racial as well as gender grounds since at least the 1830s. First there'd been post-emancipation struggles to remove New York's property restrictions on black male voters. And after these were lifted by the Fifteenth Amendment, they sought the vote to strengthen the black community's ability to resist the various indignities and restrictions that were visited upon it. With the emergence of the black women's club movement, ever bigger suffragist battalions were mobilized.

White women suffragists were divided. Those aiming for a constitutional amendment worried about further alienating whites in the South, who were, after all, busily disenfranchising black men, and not likely to support opening the door to black women. And for many white women, working with black women as equal political partners was unthinkable.[17] In New York State, however, with the 1915 referendum looming, the more politically astute

---

16. Some of his editorials caused consternation in-house as well. In a September 1911 piece entitled "Social Equality," he declared, "Of course we want full social equality," which was "just as much a human right as political or economic equality." This led Florence Kelley to threaten resignation from the board unless the NAACP dissociated itself from that position.

17. In 1911 Mrs. John Dewey offered to host in her apartment a black and white suffrage meeting, but her white neighbors sought an injunction to block it, on the grounds that a "mixed" meeting violated the restrictive covenant laws that applied to the apartment building where the Deweys resided. The meeting was canceled.

white suffragists realized that black males would be voting on white women's future, and that black women might be able to sway them into supporting passage. Du Bois, meanwhile, was hammering away in the *Crisis*, telling black men it was in their own interest to expand the pool of black voters, and pointing out that the same arguments (about presumed female incapability) used to oppose suffrage for black women, were also used to oppose votes for black men. Slowly, white women suffragists began inviting African American clubwomen to form "colored" chapters. Alva Belmont funded a meeting room for black suffragists who joined her organization, the Political Equality Association. The Woman Suffrage Party opened a headquarters for black women on West 63rd Street.

DU BOIS ALSO, ON HIS OWN OR WITH OFFICIAL NAACP BACKING, took up the cudgels against New Yorkers whose intellectual or cultural interventions supported white supremacy.

He tackled head on the Dunning School's interpretation of Reconstruction. Invited by an unwary American Historical Association to address the 1909 annual convention—the first African American to be so honored—he astonished his listeners by presenting a paper, "Reconstruction and Its Benefits," which argued that the brief period of African American leadership in the South had accomplished three important goals: expansion of democracy, provision of free public schools, and adoption of new social welfare legislation.

He made another foray into counter-conventional history when on October 22, 1913, four months after the Paterson Pageant at Madison Square Garden, Du Bois staged a three-hour, 1,200-performer theatrical pageant in the 12th Regiment Armory in San Juan Hill. Called *The Star of Ethiopia*, it was his contribution to New York's commemoration of the

Promotional Poster, "'The Star of Ethiopia:' A History of the Negro Race," 1916. (National Endowment for the Humanities, Division of Preservation and Access)

fiftieth anniversary of the Emancipation Proclamation. It was not only an impressive spectacle and auditory treat, featuring music by black songwriters, but also presented a sweeping history of African peoples, from their glory days to the slave trade catastrophe to the accomplishments of diasporic African Americans.

Another intervention on the history front came in March 1915, when *Birth of a Nation* arrived at the Liberty Theatre, prefaced with an endorsement from Woodrow Wilson: "It is like writing history with lightning, and my only regret is that it is all so terribly true." The NAACP appealed to the National Board of Censorship of Motion Pictures to suppress the lie-laden film, and a 500-person-strong delegation led by Du Bois, Ovington, Villard, and Spingarn appealed to Mayor Mitchel. A few deletions were ordered—of a lynching and a forced marriage—but the film was soon released to theaters and drew huge lines. The NAACP picketed these theaters and distributed a pamphlet prepared by Mary White Ovington to inform the public of the film's fabrications. *Birth* nevertheless went on to a long and successful run.

During the brouhaha Griffith blasted the NAACP as a "pro-intermarriage" group bent on repealing miscegenation laws, which was half right. The organization did oppose them in states where they existed, but it did not advocate intermarriage. Instead it charged that such legislation would menace matrimony, by allowing lustful white men to seduce or coerce helpless colored girls, even set them up as concubines, with no possibility of forcing the seducer into marriage. Its protests helped block passage of such a law in New York.

AS DU BOIS'S PERSONAL RENOWN AND INFLUENCE GREW, that of Booker T. Washington declined, and after the latter died in 1915, his Tuskegee machine crumbled. In 1916, when membership in the NAACP had climbed above 10,000, and readership of the *Crisis* had passed the 45,000 mark, the NAACP called for a conference of black leaders that would unite Washington's supporters and NAACP activists behind a common program. Du Bois and Joel Spingarn held the conference on August 24–26, at Spingarn's estate near Amenia, New York. The roughly fifty conferees adopted a "Unity Platform" that pledged to forget old "hurts and enmities," and work together on behalf of both higher and vocational education for blacks, and toward recapturing political rights. The well-funded National Urban League, it was understood, would confine itself to research and socioeconomic issues.

The Amenia Conference marked the NAACP's ascendancy as the dominant force in the civil rights movement, with Gotham as its center. But dominant didn't mean triumphant. The limited success of the NAACP's legal and political campaigns didn't justify an optimistic assessment of its future. One of the reasons it had fallen short, it seemed, was that it was a Talented Tenth operation, very much a top-down affair, not rooted in a mass movement, not given to taking up popular methods of protest, or addressing the kinds of economic issues that concerned poor blacks. Another was its interracial leadership—numerically, at least, overwhelmingly white—also not calculated to appeal to the city's diasporic African working class.

In the two decades during which the NAACP gained its ascendancy, Gotham's black masses had been decidedly in motion—literally—pouring out of their respective slum quarters, heading uptown or cross-river, and collectively creating something totally unforeseen and utterly novel in New York, a densely populated, all-but-exclusively black district—Harlem—that would not only become a defensible metropolitan enclave but would begin to alter the racial balance of power in the city, and make Gotham the capital of black America.

HARLEM

African Americans had deep roots in Harlem. After roughly a century and a half of colonial rule, a 1790 census tally of the "Harlem division" found 115 slaves working upper Manhattan's farms and estates, roughly one-third the population. After emancipation in 1827, freedmen and -women, still working as farmers or servants on estates, crafted a community. From the 1830s it was centered around "Little Zion," an uptown mission established by downtown's "Mother Zion" (the AME church). Little Zion was housed from 1843 in a small brick building at 236 East 117th Street (between Second and Third). But as the farming economy waned, and Irish immigrant squatters moved into abandoned plots on which they tended pigs and grew vegetables, blacks began to diminish as a percentage of the total. Nothing happened fast, though, and sleepy Harlem remained disconnected from distant dynamic downtown; horsecar service arrived in 1853, but it still took an hour and a half to get to City Hall.

Harlem's insertion into the city, and its transformation into a white middle- and upper-class residential community, came in three great spurts of perfervid real estate development. Each was correlated closely to the larger boom-bust cycle of the macro-economy. The first ran from the post–Civil War boom of the late 1860s to the depression that began in 1873; the second, from recovery in the late 1870s to collapse in 1893; and the third spanned the years between the resurgence of 1898 and the puncturing of a real estate bubble in 1904, three years before the larger downturn of 1907.

In the postwar Gilded Age wave, key infrastructural and political foundations were set in place. Boss Tweed, an early promoter (and beneficiary) of rampant uptown development, got the state to lay out Seventh Avenue from West 110th Street to the Harlem River as a broad, tree-lined thoroughfare, and had elms planted along Sixth Avenue, soon to be renamed Lenox Avenue. Land speculators began furiously flipping uptown plots—purchasing and immediately reselling for a quick profit—until the frenzy fizzled out with the Panic of 1873, the year in which Harlem was officially annexed by New York.

The 1879–93 surge of speculative building was triggered by the arrival of transportation tendrils from downtown. In 1889 the Third Avenue Elevated linked South Ferry to 129th Street (with stops in the Harlem area at 106th, 116th, and 125th). The Second Avenue line arrived at 65th Street in 1880 (and subsequently at 99th, 105th, 111th, 117th, 121st, 125th, and 129th). And the Ninth Avenue El swooped around Suicide Curve at 110th and then swerved north, heading up Eighth Avenue, reaching 116th Street in 1892, and then rolling on to 125th, 130th, 135th, 140th, 145th, 151st, and 155th. These lines cut travel time to lower Manhattan roughly in half, making Harlem commutable.

Land values soared accordingly, sometimes doubling overnight, as speculators and developers outbid one another for tracts carved out of old estates and farms. West Harlem—the part closest to the Eighth Avenue El tracks—burst into elegant bloom, as apartment buildings and row houses flowered, in architectural varieties ranging from Italianate and Greek Revival, to Gothic or Second Empire, to Romanesque and neo-Renaissance. This was housing for white (English or Dutch or Irish or German Jewish) and wealthy (middle- and upper-class) commuters from downtown. Businessmen and professionals were drawn to streets like Doctor's Row, where 1880s brownstones filled the stretch of West 122nd between Mount Morris Park West and Lenox Avenue. Astor Row on West 130th Street near Lenox Avenue offered more reasonably priced single-family homes, within the reach of clerks. The King Model Houses, later known as Striver's Row, was a middle-income development, designed by Stanford White, of 146 row houses and three apartment buildings, on West 138th and West

139th Streets, between Eighth and Seventh Avenues, on which construction started in 1891. (This sustained burst of development was paralleled by the housing boom rolling from downtown Brooklyn east into Bedford, Stuyvesant Heights, and Crown Heights, and was aimed at buyers of similar class and racial makeup.)

The new Harlemites swiftly wove their terrain into the adjacent Manhattan tapestry.

They transplanted old houses of worship or built new branches—Episcopalian, Presbyterian, Methodist, Lutheran, Seventh-day Adventist, Congregationalist, Reform Jewish, and Unitarian. They shopped at fancy venues that now began to line 125th Street, like Blumstein's department store, which had been founded downtown in 1886 by the German Jewish immigrant Louis Blumstein but was relocated in 1888 to 230 West 125th Street (between Eighth and Seventh), its proprietor having recognized the emerging commercial opportunities. So did his competitor Henry C. F. Koch, who in 1891 opened Koch's, a six-story dry-goods emporium one block to the east, at 132 West 125th Street (between Seventh and Lenox), devoted to the latest ladies' fashions.

Harlemites erected familiar forms of entertainment, but more extravagantly sized. The Harlem Casino (1890) at Seventh Avenue and West 124th Street had its own outdoor amusement gardens that could hold 10,000 people. Oscar Hammerstein's Harlem Opera House at 207 West 125th Street (between Eighth and Seventh), the biggest in all New York, welcomed more than 1,000 people on opening night in 1889. But there were more intimate and exclusive venues, too, like the Harlem Club (1889) at the corner of Lenox and 123rd.

This world of West Harlem was a far cry from that of East Harlem, though it was only a few blocks away. Fifth Avenue was the generally accepted dividing line, but the more definitive border was on Fourth (a.k.a. Park, after 1888), along which ran the New York Central railroad tracks. Since 1874 they had been carried over a rocky brownstone viaduct between 98th and 111th, then continued along a shallow open cut through Harlem (until 1897, when at 111th the tracks would be lifted up onto a gigantic steel viaduct, an even more imposing boundary marker, which ran all the way to the Harlem River). To the east, on the other side of these tracks, lay tenement territory, the huge and rapidly expanding encampments of Eastern European Jews and southern Italians, who were pouring north from the Lower East Side via the Third and Second Avenue Els. There they shared space on the Harlem Flats, land that was among Manhattan's cheapest, given the proximity of noisome gas tanks, and the refuse from extensive industry and dozens of horse stables. The laboring classes of Little Italy and Little Russia—the latter as "lousy and congested as our East Side, with the same absence of light and air," according to the *Jewish Daily Forward*—would cover much of the area east of Third Avenue and south of 125th Street.

There was also an emerging concentration of blacks in the streets east of Third and south of 110th, down to roughly 94th Street, though the patch was not big enough to be called "Little" anything. It included people doing domestic labor for affluent whites to the west, and better-off blacks looking for an uptown alternative to the Tenderloin and San Juan Hill.

THE GOOD TIMES STOPPED ROLLING with the Wall Street crash of 1893, and the concomitant lurch downward of the housing market. Perhaps the most prominent casualties were the King Model Houses. Construction had commenced at the peak of the boom, in 1891, but was only completed in 1893, just as the economy fell off a cliff. Very few of the houses sold, the development failed, and in 1895 the Equitable Life Assurance Society, which had financed the project, foreclosed on almost all the units.

When the larger economy lifted off again in 1898, so did the housing market, spurred not only by the general prosperity but by the imminent arrival of the subway. Speculators had for years been trying to buy up properties adjacent to the proposed line's stations, but the process had dragged on for decades, and the project (and its route) remained dogged by uncertainty. No longer. Though there were still legal and technical obstacles to overcome, in 1900 the contracts were signed, and the ground was (literally) broken. The subway was coming, and it was heading straight for Harlem. The main line from City Hall would run up Broadway, while another line would peel off at 96th Street, dart under the corner of Central Park, and head uptown, smack through the middle of Harlem, stopping along Lenox Avenue at 110th, 116th, 125th, 135th, and 145th before ducking under the Harlem River to Mott Avenue in the Bronx.

Land values shot up stratospherically. Colossi of real estate capital like William Waldorf Astor and Henry Morgenthau, insurance companies like Equitable and Metropolitan Life, and investment syndicates like the Knickerbocker Real Estate Company (whose stockholders included Solomon Loeb of Kuhn, Loeb, and sugar king Henry O. Havemeyer) plunged into purchasing, selling, repurchasing, reselling, bidding prices and profits skyward. The speculative frenzy wasn't limited to the big boys; people up and down the class structure were collectively throwing vast amounts of money into real estate. And these were not all paper transactions; some also underwrote another physical transformation of Harlem. Investors filled in marshes, cleared out garbage dumps, and threw up New Law tenements, and gorgeous row houses, and luxurious apartment buildings along Lenox and Seventh Avenues in

Detail, Harlem. "Map Showing the Lines of the Interborough Rapid Transit Co." *The New York Subway: Its Construction and Equipment*, 1904.

the 130s and 140s.[18] Virtually all remaining vacant land vanished. The *Real Estate Record and Builders Guide*—which didn't impress easily—found the mammoth building boom in Central Harlem "astonishing."

Full-page ads advertised Harlem's charms, and affluent tenants and buyers stepped up to rent or purchase in the newly fashionable neighborhood. They were, however, *also* buying/renting elsewhere, as the subway line fertilized competing locations, like the entire Upper West Side. This might have given investors pause, but for the moment the boom roared heedlessly on.

AMONG THE ARRIVING RENTERS WAS A SMALL CONTINGENT of relatively well-off African Americans, who saw this as their opportunity to get out of the Tenderloin and San Juan Hill. Harlem looked like a Promised Land for blacks with money, since the informal racial barriers that kept them out of most downtown neighborhoods had not been set in place uptown. The *New York Age* carried advertisements of "Desirable Properties for Colored People"—apartments with closets, heated hallways, kitchen ranges, walnut mantelpieces, and marble fireplaces. Other landlords simply hung signs outside their buildings seeking "Colored Tenants." For all the general Negrophobia, many owners considered respectable blacks excellent tenants, not least because they could be hit up for higher rents than whites paid. Some builders even sought them out, like those who erected two apartment houses called the Summer and the Garrison, on Broadway between West 125th and West 126th Streets, blacks-only buildings named after white abolitionists. But some of the densest concentrations were along Lenox Avenue from 110th to 135th, and especially in the vicinity of the future station stop at Lenox and 135th.

An important agent of the black move uptown, and in particular the action around that strategic corner, was one Philip Payton, who had set up a real estate brokerage on 134th Street. Payton, born in 1876 in Massachusetts, had moved to New York in 1899 and despite having earned a college degree was unable to find anything but low end jobs. He worked as a barber and a handyman before getting a job as a porter in a real estate office. There he picked up the rudiments of the business and decided to enter the trade. His business plan was to approach white landlords in Harlem and offer to fill their buildings with Negroes who were able and willing to pay 10 percent above the market price. Payton would also manage the buildings, and collect rent from his black tenants. His first break came in late 1901 when two white landlords on West 134th Street had an ugly business dispute, and one decided to fill his buildings with black tenants, hopefully making his adversary's building unrentable to whites. Payton handled the transformation, and soon was moving black tenants into nearby blocks. By 1904 he was one of the city's most prominent black real estate men.

The impending arrival that year of the Lenox Avenue subway attracted bigger fish to the 135th Street corner. Entities like the Hudson Realty Company, whose directors included Joseph Bloomingdale of the department store family and Maximilian Morgenthau, brother of Henry Morgenthau (who'd been an initial director). Hudson's capital stock had been raised in 1902 from $100,000 (in $100 shares) to $1,000,000. The company wasn't satisfied with collecting relatively modest rents but wanted wealthier tenants, or perhaps to tear down

18. The largest and finest of the luxury buildings was Graham Court, the $500,000 eight-story apartment house commissioned by William Waldorf Astor in 1899. It opened in 1901 at Seventh Avenue and West 116th Street, one block from the elevated to the west, and the future subway to the east, and all its residents were rich and white.

small apartments and build taller, more profitable ones, especially at potential bonanza sites adjacent to subway stops.

In 1904 the Hudson syndicate bought up a tract of vacant land on the north side of 135th, near the corner of Lenox, intending to subdivide and sell to builders. To ensure the proper complexion, Hudson leased three tenements across the street and evicted their black tenants. Reading this as a first step toward racial cleansing, Payton made a remarkable move. With a group of partners he *bought* two five-story flats adjacent to Hudson's, valued at $50,000— heretofore he'd only *leased*—and promptly evicted the all-white tenants and moved in the recently evicted blacks. He thereby (as he later recounted) "stemmed the tide, which had it been successful in West 135th street, would surely have extended to West 134th street, which is almost entirely given over to our people." "Real Estate Race War Started in Harlem" was the way the *New York Times* would headline the story.[19] More skirmishes followed these initial moves, which left Payton in possession of the field.[20]

Not only the *Times* took notice. On May 3, 1904, Booker T. Washington wrote Payton: "I have read in yesterday's *World* how you turned the tables on those who desired to injure the race, and wish to congratulate you on this instance of business enterprise and race loyalty combined." Payton's next move was even more thrilling to the black capitalism crowd. Noting that "there is strength in financial combination"—a central mantra of the Morgan era—in July Payton incorporated the Afro American Realty Company (AARC), authorized to raise $500,000 (in $10 shares). For executive officers he cannily signed on such leading associates of Booker T. Washington as Fred Moore of the *New York Age*; Charles Anderson, the city's leading black Republican; Washington's New York attorney, Wilford H. Smith; and the Reverend William H. Brooks. The company then sold its stock to colored investors—real estate brokers, undertakers, lawyers, barbers—its prospectus offering buyers a chance to make a profit, and an opportunity to enable blacks to live wherever they could afford to. Funds in hand, Payton proceeded to buy buildings, evict white tenants, and replace them with blacks, preferably middle-class blacks. Moore's *Age* editorially encouraged the "better element of the race"—professionals, businessmen, the clergy—to move to Harlem. It didn't take much urging. The spacious homes on tree-lined streets were far and away the best available to blacks in the city, and rents, while high, were not extortionate.

By the time the 135th Street subway station opened, on November 23, 1904, Payton owned four tenements outright and was managing a dozen other buildings, collecting more than $100,000 in rent each year, and the AARC was worth more than $1 million.[21] In 1905 the *New York Herald* reported disconsolately that West 133rd to West 135th Streets between Lenox and Seventh Avenues had been "captured for occupancy by a Negro population."

Payton's success, and that of the score of black real estate men who jumped into the business, was rooted in more than mere acumen. Their timing was pitch-perfect because it was in 1904–5 that Harlem's overbuilt market collapsed. With so many other exciting neighborhoods having come on line, the supply of housing far outpaced demand. Landlords competed for tenants. Rents plummeted. Speculators fell behind in payments to financial institution lenders, who then threatened foreclosure. A wave of desperation sales followed. Owner losses

---

19. The *Times* piece was really tongue in cheek, not incendiary, for it stressed that whites had started the affair and more or less argued that turnabout was fair play, especially as the black tenants were "decent, hardworking negroes."

20. Partly because Hudson had much bigger fish to fry; it went on to purchase, for instance, the entire King Model Houses development from Equitable (in December 1904), flipped a piece of it, and set out to find buyers, refusing to rent to blacks.

21. Washington's *Negro in Business* (1907) devoted an entire chapter to lauding Payton's accomplishments.

"Philip A. Payton, Jr., Vice-President and Manager, Afro-American Realty Co., New York," 1907. (Schomburg Center for Research in Black Culture, Photographs and Prints Division)

ranged from one-third to two-thirds their original cost. Many of these buildings had never been inhabited. Facing ruin, some hitherto recalcitrant landlords decided to rent or sell to blacks.[22]

In 1906 the *Herald* predicted despondently that "the establishment of the Negroes in 135th Street is only the nucleus of a Negro settlement that will extend over a wide area of Harlem within the next few years." The *Herald* was right. Over the next decade, blacks from midtown, and immigrants from the South and Caribbean, poured through the beachhead Payton and others had established, especially after 1905, when the second major race riot rocked San Juan Hill, precipitating a mass breakout. Payton had solicited only the black bourgeoisie, but now lower-income blacks followed, though they had to double or triple up to meet the premium rents. By 1915, nearly two-thirds of Harlem's black apartment dwellers shared their rooms with lodgers.[23]

This migration was not only a one-by-one affair. Black churches, too, joined the acquisition frenzy, selling their valuable midtown properties and investing the profits in depreciated land uptown. In 1907 the rector of St. Philip's Protestant Episcopal Church, still down in the Tenderloin, began investing in Harlem real estate—in the 130s, west of Lenox. Rector Hutchens C. Bishop, the Maryland-born first black graduate of New York's General Theological Seminary, often passed for white in order to complete a transaction, then turned the property over to the church. He kept acquiring, culminating in a record-breaking $393,000 deal in 1911 involving ten buildings on West 135th Street, between Lenox and Seventh Avenues, whose white tenants were evicted and replaced with black ones. Bishop used the rental income, together with the proceeds from selling the church's midtown

---

22. Including Lillian Harris. Harris left her Mississippi Delta shanty in 1901. Arriving in New York with five dollars, she spent three on an old baby carriage and boiler, and two on pigs' feet, and opened a traveling restaurant. Soon known as "Pig Foot Mary," she hawked hog maws and chitterlings for sixteen years. Then she moved to Lenox Avenue, sank her profits in real estate, became a wealthy landlord—"Send it and send it damn quick," she wrote tardy tenants—and retired to California.

23. Payton kept buying, but he overextended AARC holdings, and was swept into bankruptcy by the Panic of 1907, though he bounced back, and maintained a modest but profitable real estate brokerage until his death in 1917.

property, to buy land at 210 West 134th Street, where New York's first black architect, Vertner Woodson Tandy, built a striking brick Gothic structure. It confirmed St. Philip's position as the most prestigious and wealthiest black church in the city, while simultaneously underscoring the African American presence in Harlem. Powell Senior's Abyssinian Baptist also invested heavily in uptown real estate. Soon the churches had become the largest black property owners in Harlem.

THIS PRESENCE DID NOT GO UNCONTESTED. In 1905 the *New York Indicator*, a journal devoted to (white) real estate interests, found the new black presence intolerable. "They should not only be disenfranchised," the paper said bluntly, invoking southern methodologies, "but also segregated in some colony in the outskirts of the city, where their transportation and other problems will not inflict injustice and disgust on worthy citizens." Eight years later, there were still people who thought blacks could be expunged from the landscape. As a white building owner demanded at a 1913 meeting of Harlem property owners: "Drive them out, and send them to the slums where they belong." But by then most whites were settling for a defensive game, rallying to stem further "invasion."

One popular method was to have all the white owners on a block agree to sign covenants committing them not to sell their property to black buyers. These agreements were legally binding—anyone who broke them could be sued by fellow signatories. Yet while these did create some "covenant blocks," which remained white even as blacks moved in and dominated nearby streets, such piecemeal efforts were soon deemed insufficient. More organized resistance outfits emerged. The most vociferous was the Harlem Property Owners Association.

It was spark-plugged by John G. Taylor, a retired police officer of Irish descent, who in 1903 had moved from Waverly Place (near the Greenwich Village black neighborhood) to West 136th Street, between Seventh and Eighth Avenues, a solidly white and middle-class block. In 1910 Taylor raised $20,000 for a campaign "to keep the negroes of 'Little Africa' just east of Lenox Avenue from further encroaching upon the street." Escalating, the association raised $100,000 to buy properties that were in danger of being sold to African Americans, started a "Harlem Redeemed" program offering discounts to white renters, opposed allowing blacks to use the New York Public Library branch at 103 West 135th Street, worked for resegregation of the Ninth Avenue El, and, most hysterically, advocated building a 24-foot-high wall along West 136th Street to keep blacks from moving north. Nothing worked, and in 1913 an almost despairing Taylor asked: "When will the people of Harlem wake up to the fact that they must organize and maintain a powerful anti-invasion movement if they want to check the progress of the black hordes that are gradually eating through the very heart of Harlem?" It was, he underscored, a "question of whether the white man will rule Harlem or the negro."[24]

By decade's end, the results were in. In 1911 an estimated 20,000 blacks had lived in the patch of land bordered by Fifth and Eighth Avenues and 132nd and 137th Streets. By 1920 73,000 had packed in, expanding the area of black predominance from 130th to 145th

---

24. Harlem's neighborhood associations did not, however, promote violence, and while there were street confrontations between black and white gangs, there were no instances of bombing new black homeowners, as happened in Chicago, or mob attacks on black homes in white neighborhoods, as in Detroit.

Some white churches were de facto allies of these white resistance groups, in that while their parishioners were declining in number as the catchment changed color, they refused to sell their buildings to black churches looking to move uptown. But in the end, they too joined the ranks of the departing, usually by selling to some third-party intermediary.

Streets.[25] In the process the center of black Gotham's gravity had shifted dramatically. In 1900 only 20 percent of Manhattan's African American population lived above 86th Street. By 1910 almost 50 percent did. By 1920 two-thirds did—and half the greater city's. Brooklyn's share of the city's total black population slid accordingly, from 30 percent in 1910 to 21 percent in 1920.

The transformation involved more than masses of individuals. Many of the city's black institutions flocked uptown as well. The black press—the *New York Age* and a newcomer, the *Amsterdam News*, founded with ten dollars in 1909 in San Juan Hill by James H. Anderson—relocated to Harlem. In 1912 Tammany's United Colored Democracy, following the mass of black voters, shifted uptown to West 136th Street. The leading churches, following St. Philip's lead, regrouped there, too—Mount Olivet to 120th Street, Bethel AME to 132nd, Mother Zion to 137th, Abyssinian Baptist to 138th. And the YMCA likewise shifted north, to 135th, as did the YWCA, to 137th. The NAACP opened a Harlem branch at 224 West 135th Street.

Black stores sprouted on 135th Street and along Lenox Avenue, though it proved hard for small, poorly capitalized shopkeepers to compete with the older, bigger, white establishments down on 125th Street. Many blacks preferred to patronize the Koch or Blumstein department stores: for all their rudeness and refusal to hire Afro-American salespeople, they offered larger stock and better credit.

The black business class succeeded in sectors where whites refused to serve blacks: hotels, restaurants, insurance, tailoring, undertaking, barbershops, and—most spectacularly—beauty parlors. The Louisiana-born Madame C. J. Walker discovered a hair-straightening process, parlayed it into a successful business in Indianapolis, moved to New York, opened a school that trained Harlem women to own and operate salons (using Walker products exclusively), and became New York's first black millionaire since Jeremiah G. Hamilton, antebellum Wall Street's "Prince of Darkness."[26] Walker became the center of a new social set of successful black professionals, clergy, businessmen, clubwomen, artists, and athletes. People vied for invitations to the receptions, balls, and dinner parties she held at her mansion on 136th Street, or her country estate, Villa Lewaro, up at Irvington-on-Hudson.

Other cultural institutions flourished. In the realm of polite letters, Arturo Schomburg helped form (in 1911) the Negro Society for Historical Research, and began amassing books and documents for its library. Schomburg's penchant for works on black history and culture was widely shared. Book clubs and stores like Young's Book Exchange on 135th Street did a brisk trade in volumes on African culture, the *Journal of Negro History* (1916), and the works of W. E. B. Du Bois.

Black theater, extinguished on Broadway, revived in Harlem. At first, the pre-migration playhouses down on 125th Street and along Seventh Avenue remained off-limits to blacks. But as white patronage dwindled, desperate proprietors at the Lafayette, the Alhambra, Proctor's, and Hurtig & Seamon's (later the Apollo) first opened segregated "nigger heavens," then actively encouraged black patronage. In 1915 the Anita Bush stock company moved into the Lafayette Theatre (132nd and Seventh), offering Shakespeare and black versions of Broadway melodramas; it was renamed the Lafayette Players in 1916. Black musical comedy,

---

25. In 1919 the area's last white bastion fell when the ninety-four town houses of the King Model Houses were sold to wealthy black purchasers.

26. Skin lighteners had been advertised in the *Age* since at least 1909, and hair straighteners from 1911. Harlem barbers sold Kink-No-More, called Conk for short.

"Madam C. J. Walker Portrait," ca. 1914. (Michael Ochs Archives/Stringer/Getty)

scarce since Williams and Walker's day, made a comeback. James Weldon Johnson noted that black performers "experienced for the first time release from the restraining fears of what a white audience would stand for." Remarkably, shows like the *Darktown Follies* (which scrapped minstrel formulas) drew whites uptown in droves.[27]

To the dismay of those in the Talented Tenth who sought to make Harlem an island of black gentility—a longing for respectability only too understandable in a city that routinely portrayed blacks as shiftless illiterates—less edifying cultural entrepreneurs also moved up from San Juan Hill. They opened poolrooms, saloons, liquor stores, gambling dens, brothels, cabarets, jook joints, and dance halls. They brought their own music, too.

James Reese Europe's Clef Club performed ragtime at the Manhattan Casino (at Eighth and 155th), an emergent center of Harlem's fashionable nightlife. By 1913, 4,000 dancers crowded its floor.[28] By 1914 the *New York Age* worried that Harlem was "infested" with saloons, and the next year the Urban League counted more than a hundred places in black Harlem to drink, dance, and listen to music. The first black nightclub was Leroy's Café, located

---

27. Cultural impresarios came, too: Ziegfeld bought the rights to about half the show for his own *Follies*, treading a fine line between admiration and expropriation.

28. Hotter stuff remained beyond the pale (as it were), even for some of the cultural radicals of Greenwich Village. When Carl Van Vechten got Mabel Dodge to invite two black entertainers to a session of her salon, it proved a disaster. Dodge recalled watching in horror while "an appalling Negress danced" and a man "sang an embarrassing song while she cavorted. They both leered and rolled their suggestive eyes and made me feel first hot and then cold, for I never had been so near this kind of thing before." The invitation was never repeated. The *Masses* crowd, made of sterner stuff, traveled en masse to black bars in Jersey to hear jazz.

in the basement of 2220 Fifth Avenue, at 135th Street. It had been opened in 1910 by Leroy Wilkins, who strictly opposed all forms of racial integration, admitting only blacks in black tie. His younger brother, Barron Wilkins, moved his West 35th Street Little Savoy nightclub to a basement space near Seventh Avenue and West 134th Street.

In truth, most of the saloons, clubs, and houses of prostitution were owned by white people, though they often hired black managers to run them. In 1914 only five of the saloons serving the black population of Harlem had black proprietors. Through whites' investments, Harlem became a "wide-open city" for all forms of "vice," notably prostitution, with the overwhelming bulk of sex-trade institutions owned and managed by whites. In this they were supported by the New York Police Department, which transferred its hands-off (and hands-out) policy from the Tenderloin, now transformed, with an assist from Committee of Fourteen zealots, into a respectable midtown business district, grown up around Penn Station.

NEW NEGROES

Harlem also spawned a new racial militancy. The unprecedented population density and novel sense of cultural control engendered security and self-confidence. Some Harlem new-comers—inspired by contemporary gender and class confrontations in the city—struggled to go beyond NAACP and NUL strategies for racial reform. Youthful agitators sought to create a new black politics, a new black culture, a new black socialism, a new black national-ism, a new black personality—indeed, in the parlance of the day, a New Negro.

WHEN A. PHILIP RANDOLPH ARRIVED IN NEW YORK by steamer in the spring of 1911, one month after the Triangle fire, he had no intention of becoming a radical activist but rather aspired to being a Shakespearean actor. Born in 1898 in Jacksonville, Florida, in moderate circumstances—his father was a tailor by profession and an AME minister by avocation—Randolph had worked as a railroad section hand. Inspired by Du Bois's *Souls of Black Folk*, he aspired to join the Talented Tenth, hoping to translate his resonant baritone, stylish manners, and cultivated English accent into a stage career. While waiting, he rented a room in Harlem and took a succession of menial jobs—elevator runner in a new downtown skyscraper, porter in an apartment building—from most of which he was fired for trying to organize fellow em-ployees. He took evening classes in public speaking, politics, and economics at CCNY, and joined other students in supporting IWW campaigns at Lawrence and Paterson.

Randolph met and married Lucille Campbell—a socialist, but also the owner of a beauty salon on 135th Street, a close friend of Madame Walker, and a member of black Society. Lucille introduced him (in 1915) to Chandler Owen, who had come up from North Carolina to attend the New York School of Philanthropy (on a social work fellowship from the National Urban League), and gone on to Columbia Law School. Owen shared Randolph's interest in radicalism. Together they read socialist literature at the New York Public Library, attended lectures at the Rand School, and befriended Hillquit and Debs. In 1916 they joined the Socialist Party, formed a branch in Harlem, and joined the soapbox orators on Lenox and 135th, a magnet for Harlemites.[29]

In 1917 the duo started the *Messenger*—financed from Lucille's hairdressing profits—calling it "the Only Radical Negro Magazine in America." In their journal, Randolph and Owen argued that Talented Tenth reformers, whether of NAACP or NUL persuasion, paid

---

29. It's interesting that Harlem's equivalent of Hyde Park Corner was at the very corner where Payton made his *coup de real estate*.

A. Philip Randolph and Chandler Owen, 1917. *Messenger* 1, no. 11 (November 1917).

insufficient attention to problems of the black masses—a lapse due either to their relatively privileged status or their financial dependence on whites. Randolph and Owen proposed instead to form a black workers' alliance—modeled on the IWW, the only labor organization that didn't draw the color line. It would mobilize railroad porters, elevator operators, longshoremen, and farm hands into one big, black union. In November 1917 Randolph made a start in this direction by organizing the United Brotherhood of Elevator and Switchboard Operators, enrolling 600 members within three weeks. Three years later he founded the Friends of Negro Freedom to unionize migrants, protect tenants, and "elevate the race" in New York City.

The pair faced insuperable obstacles. Harlem's clerics, businessmen, editors, and professionals insisted black labor's true interest lay with paternalistic white employers, not white workers. During the great garment strikes, the *Age* had urged black women to cross picket lines. Black workers, long excluded by racist trade unions, tended to agree, and for now those who advocated labor-based organizing were less successful than those—like Hubert H. Harrison—who promoted race-first radical politics.

Harrison—the "Father of Harlem Radicalism"—left his native St. Croix in 1900, aged 17, and arrived in New York a month after the West Side race riot. He lived at first on 62nd Street in San Juan Hill with his sister, a domestic. By day he worked, variously, as an elevator operator, bellhop, messenger, or stock clerk. By night he went to high school, became a superb student (winning second prize for oratory in the Board of Education finals), participated in lyceums at St. Benedict the Moor (which attracted black intellectuals of both Caribbean and US background), and tutored at the White Rose Mission and the 53rd Street YMCA.

In 1907 he moved to Harlem, settling on West 134th Street. He took and aced the Post Office exam and was appointed a clerk, first grade. Over the next four years Harrison was repeatedly promoted, attaining clerk, fourth grade status, accompanied by a salary of $1,000 a year, one of the highest-paid positions available to black males in the city. In 1910, however,

Hubert Harrison, n.d. (New York Public Library)

he wrote some powerful critiques of Booker T. Washington, which were published in the *New York Sun*. This led to his being fired from the Post Office in 1911, at the behest of Washington's hatchet man Charles Anderson.[30]

In 1911 he became a full-time organizer for the New York Socialist Party, which he had joined in 1909, attracted by its position on women and foreign-language federations. He worked at first for Piet Vlag's *Masses*, then wrote for the *Call*, promoting municipal Socialist candidates to black New Yorkers, and organized the Colored Socialist Club at 60 West 134th. Unlike Randolph, however, Harrison became disenchanted with the party's leadership, program, and practice. Many in its right wing were outright racists who supported segregation. The center believed the Negro Question (like the Woman Question) should be subordinated to class politics. And while left-wingers supported racial initiatives—in 1913, after a racial pogrom in Georgia, the *Masses* even urged blacks to armed resistance—they were bereft of power and had little to offer besides rhetoric.

So in 1914 Harrison became an independent radical, launching a full-time mission to Harlem. He gave mesmerizing outdoor lectures, becoming known as the "Black Socrates."

---

30. In September 1911 Anderson wrote Washington: "Do you remember Hubert H. Harrison? He is the man who wrote two nasty articles against you in the New York *Sun*. He is a clerk in the Post Office. The Postmaster is my personal friend, as you probably know. Harrison has had charges preferred against him and I think he is liable to be dismissed from the service. If not dismissed, he will get severe punishment." Three weeks later Anderson wrote again: "I am sure you will regret to learn that Mr. Hubert H. Harrison has been dismissed from his position as clerk in the New York Post Office. I am certain that you will also regret to hear that he is blaming me for his dismissal…He is now stumping for the Socialist party, and will probably have plenty of time in the future to learn that God is not good to those who do not behave themselves."

In addition to 135th and Lenox, Harrison gave street speeches at 125th/7th, 181st/St.Nicholas, 163rd/Prospect (in the Bronx), and even downtown, at 23rd/Madison and on Wall Street. In the summer of 1917 he began publication of the *Voice*, a newspaper whose circulation soon surged to within striking distance of the *Age*, and established the Liberty League, which met at the Bethel AME church on West 132nd Street.[31] In print and in person, Harrison urged a blend of socialism and black nationalism. Advocating the term "New Negro," he called on Harlemites to reject NAACP- and NUL-style cooperation with whites in favor of total self-reliance. He attacked racism in the country and in New York—running stories on police brutality under the Mitchel administration and demanding black police (and firemen) for Harlem. He also critiqued color discrimination *within* the black community—challenging the light-skinneds' presumption of leadership and denouncing the use of whiteners and straighteners.

Harrison was responding to Harlem's emergence as a potential base for political action. The route ahead for such politics was not obvious. Despite his nationalism (he admired Sinn Fein in Ireland) he was demanding not independence but equal rights. Despite his socialism, he was not foregrounding working-class issues (jobs, wages, rent, food prices) or using working-class tactics (boycotts, demonstrations, strikes). Harrison attracted the attention of Harlem's businessmen and professionals, though in the end they opted to pursue major-party politics.

As Harrison floundered, some of the artisans, small businessmen, intellectuals, journalists, and working people in his Liberty League began gravitating toward a Jamaican immigrant who had arrived in 1916, with no money or reputation, but possessed by a colossal ambition. In the next few years, Marcus Garvey would succeed in creating an immense, mass-based, all-black, internationally oriented political organization the likes of which the city (and country) had never seen.

GARVEY, BORN IN JAMAICA IN 1887, had been known among his café au lait schoolmates as "Ugly Mug" because of his coal-black color. Leaving school at 14, he learned the printer's trade and became a compositor. An active trade unionist, he helped lead a printers strike (1908–9), which failed. Branded a troublemaker, he was blacklisted by vengeful employers. In 1910 he joined a great exodus of Jamaicans who left their economically straitened island for the Central American banana plantations of the United Fruit Company. He worked first in Costa Rica as a timekeeper, a white-collar position obtained for him by an uncle there, and started a small paper chronicling the migrants' experience. Then he traveled and labored in Honduras, Ecuador, Colombia, Venezuela, and finally Panama, where, in Colón, he started another newspaper, which did poorly. Ill health forced his return to Kingston.

In 1912 he took to sea again, this time to London, where he was exposed to the germinating Pan-African movement. In 1911 the University of London had hosted the First Universal Races Congress, whose participants, contributors, and conveners from around the world (among them Du Bois, Ovington, Boas, and Felix Adler) had explored the science and politics of race, racism, and race relations. In 1912 a monthly magazine, the *African Times and Orient Review*, was established to continue the conversation. Its editor, Dusé Mohamed Ali, described it as a "Pan-Oriental Pan-African journal" that would lay out "the aims, desires, and intentions of the Black, Brown and Yellow races—within and without the Empire."

---

31. Reverdy Ransom, Bethel's minister, had his own history of militancy, having advised blacks, after an 1899 lynching, to learn the use of dynamite in order to protect their homes.

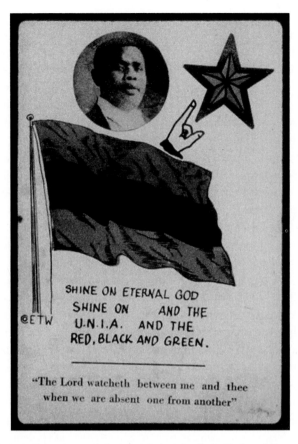

"Shine on Eternal God, Shine On, and the U.N.I.A. and the Red, Black and Green," 1918.
(Schomburg Center for Research in Black Culture, Photographs and Prints Division)

Garvey worked for a time as messenger, handyman, and then contributor (in 1913 Ali published his excoriating piece on European rapacity in the West Indies). In the British Museum's reading room Garvey immersed himself in the works of Edward Wilmot Blyden, the pioneering Liberian Pan-Africanist. In Hyde Park's Speakers' Corner he developed his vocal talents—he had taken elocution lessons in Jamaica—and became a regular in the verbal hurly-burly, talking about the West Indies, and discovering he could captivate an audience.

By 1914, having traveled widely in the Caribbean, Central America, England, and Europe, and having seen the common disabilities that Negroes suffered, Garvey became convinced that the race "must solidify itself through the medium of one great organization based on international principles." Rather than addressing varying national outrages separately, the racially oppressed should consider themselves a unit—Africa and its diaspora—and reformers should try to unite black people the world over in righting collective wrongs. On returning to Jamaica, accordingly, he immediately established the grandly monikered Universal Negro Improvement Association and African Communities (Imperial) League (UNIA). It didn't take off, however; the Jamaican middle classes dismissed it, and in March 1916 Garvey again set sail, this time for New York City.

On arriving he headed straight for Harlem, found lodgings with an expatriate Jamaican family, got intermittent printing jobs, and decided to establish himself as a lecturer. By April, a month after his arrival, he'd saved up enough to place a down payment on renting

St. Mark's Hall, 57 West 138th Street, to make his American debut. The 29-year-old Garvey, aware that he was unknown, needed a big name to back him, and he chose the biggest. Riding the subway downtown to the NAACP's office at 69 Fifth Avenue, he aimed to invite Du Bois, whom he had met briefly during a visit to the island, to chair his lecture. As a secretary politely informed him, the *Crisis* editor was out of town, which was just as well, as his May 9 evening proved a debacle. The replacement chair was half an hour late, Garvey was a bundle of nerves, the crowd (of thirty-six) heckled and whistled, and Garvey, from dizziness or on purpose, fell off the stage, curtailing the event.

Undaunted, or daunted only briefly, Garvey decided to take his show on the road. He traveled first to Boston, made his way to the Midwest (he visited Ida Wells in Chicago and learned about lynching), traveled extensively throughout the black-belt South (and learned firsthand about segregation) and, after a stop at Tuskegee, wound up his thirty-eight-state tour in March 1917 in Atlanta.

Back in New York he tried again to make his mark. He founded a New York branch of the UNIA in May and had a reentry event, again at St. Mark's, for which only a dozen disciples turned up. He turned to the soapboxes and stepladders at 135th and Lenox—black Gotham's Hyde Park—but his efforts didn't move the needle. (He'd actually experimented with public speaking before leaving on his tour, and had received a boost, literally, from A. Philip Randolph, when the black socialist, just finishing a speech, graciously stepped down from his ladder and offered it to the unknown Jamaican. Garvey "had a tremendous voice," Randolph recalled; "you could hear him from 135th to 125th Street," but the other auditors were not yet attracted by his message.)

Garvey was finally rescued by another master of the soapbox, Hubert Harrison. On June 12, 1917, the "Black Socrates" invited him to share the stage at the inaugural meeting of his Liberty League of Negro-Americans, in front of a huge crowd of Harlemites gathered at the Bethel AME church. Garvey's oration was well received. Harrison took him on as a regular warmup act, and he got more and more polished with every speech. He also evidenced an ability to draw West Indians and southerners, both finding attractive his plan to arrange an international alliance between components of the African diaspora. He received support, too, from Arturo Schomburg and his partner in the Negro Society for Historical Research, John Edward Bruce, a veteran journalist and contemporary of Blyden. Both men believed that collecting books, pamphlets, documents, and images from African American, African, and Caribbean sources would encourage the study of black history from an international perspective, and facilitate the forging of racial solidarity. Their burgeoning acquisitions, to which Garvey turned repeatedly, and New York's emergence as a nodal point on the Pan-Africanist grid, further encouraged him in his newfound belief that Gotham—not Kingston, not London or Liberia—was the place to pitch his organizational tent.

THE UNIA WOULD SOON DWARF, AND EVENTUALLY SUBSUME, THE LIBERTY LEAGUE. Before expiring, however, Harrison's movement helped Harlem crystallize its collective identity. In July 1917 a terrible racial pogrom swept East St. Louis in Illinois. Blacks were lynched, shot, and burned alive as entire neighborhoods were torched and their fleeing inhabitants thrown back into the flames. The NAACP, whose efforts to meet with President Wilson were turned aside, estimated perhaps 200 blacks dead, 6,000 rendered homeless. The Liberty League held a mass protest meeting—the largest ever held in Harlem. Over a thousand cheered speakers, among them Harrison, who called on the city's blacks to arm compatriots who were threatened by mob violence. Conservative blacks were appalled. Fred Moore of the *New York*

"Silent Protest Parade in New York against the East St. Louis Riots," July 18, 1917. (Library of Congress Prints and Photographs Division)

Age insisted the "representative Negro does not approve of radical socialistic outbursts, such as calling upon the Negroes to defend themselves against the whites." But a stunning variety of Harlemites, while not prepared for violence, were ready for dramatic protest. James Weldon Johnson of the NAACP proposed a giant parade. (Villard had suggested this, drawing on his participation in the women's suffrage marches.) An ad hoc group formed at St. Philip's drew together a cross-section of black leaders and organized the Negro Silent Protest Parade. On July 28, 1917, 10,000 to 15,000 blacks, dressed in their Sunday best, marched down Fifth Avenue from 56th Street to Madison Square, to the beat of muffled drums. Placards read MOTHER, DO LYNCHERS GO TO HEAVEN? and MR. PRESIDENT, WHY NOT MAKE AMERICA SAFE FOR DEMOCRACY? and YOUR HANDS ARE FULL OF BLOOD. Black Boy Scouts distributed NAACP circulars to thousands of white onlookers. It was the largest demonstration of African Americans in the history of New York City.

Blacks had established an African American enclave, comparable to those created by major ethnic groups, which proclaimed and would defend the black presence in the metropolis. It had also created the largest black urban center in the United States, and from now on, Harlem would be at the forefront of black America's resistance to white America's racism.

22

Insurgent Art

ART REBELS

Gotham's artists—both homegrown and newly arrived—sought to render and interpret the new city that was erupting before their eyes. But they found themselves hampered by inherited genteel protocols. Art—Victorian precepts had decreed—must foster Morality, by depicting the Beautiful. Which cities were not.

Patrons of the visual arts thought urban representations not worth seeing, certainly not worth buying. Morgan's Metropolitan, leading art dealers, and millionaire collectors stuck to Old Masters (though a minority embraced European impressionists). Most New York painters ignored the city scene. Mandarin juries at the National Academy of Design hung serene landscapes, historical tableaux, and cowboy art. The occasional glances they tossed at their host city consisted of sentimental paintings portraying street urchins; flattering close-ups of ladies of leisure, all satin and plumes; or shimmering Impressionist works depicting fashionable New Yorkers promenading through flower-laden parks and squares smoldering with color.

Writers, for their part, were disinterested in urban realism. In the depressed mid-1890s, William Dean Howells and Stephen Crane had pried open the limits of the permissible. But gentility frowned on further initiatives. The American Academy of Arts and Letters (1904), a newly fashioned citadel of Culture, defended the traditional canon against innovative departures in subject or style. Taking the Académie Française as its model, the academy set up shop as the "center and rallying point of the best literary and artistic opinions." The organization, said its chief organizer, Robert Underwood Johnson, should advocate "dignity, moderation and purity of expression" and oppose "vulgarity, sensationalism, meretriciousness, lubricity and other forms of degeneracy." The academy should also resist "the tyranny of novelty," said Johnson, and consider drawing up "well considered lists of words or meanings *taboo*." Academicians inveighed against "polyglot corrupters" of Anglo-Saxon English, and insisted that fiction uplift coarse and sordid people, not describe them. These convictions retained considerable currency in universities, publishing houses, and respectable magazines. And Comstockian vigilantes stood ready to pounce on renegades.

Younger artists were driven to generational revolt. Rejecting what some called the Art Trust, they opted for an artistic free market. They forged alternative institutions—little magazines, new exhibition spaces—in which to display their work. They reveled in "realist" or "modernist" approaches that drew upon European innovations or American popular culture. Above all, they scrapped taboos on subject matter, and set out to portray their own age, their own city.

Art rebels thus lined up alongside other mutinous New Yorkers: socialists and anarchists; labor, ethnic, and racial radicals; feminists and sexual revolutionaries. Many writers and painters drew inspiration from their insurgent counterparts. Often the circles of art and politics overlapped, especially (though not exclusively) in bohemian Greenwich Village, where cultural iconoclasts enlisted in the generalized assault on "Puritanism." Whatever their political affiliation, unconventional artists shared a common project: the fashioning of new ways of seeing, appropriate to new ways of being.

ASH CAN REALISTS

Some of the most daring interpreters of the new New York scene were commercial illustrators—transplants from the art departments of Philadelphia newspapers. These journeymen artists were dispatched to the sites of breaking stories—murders, fires, accidents—where they quickly sketched the scene and scrawled some notes, then dashed back to the office and rapidly worked up a drawing that was then prepared for the presses. In the 1890s, halftone technology made it possible to inexpensively replace such artwork with at-the-scene photographs, theoretically rendering the illustrators redundant. But editors often chose to stick with drawings, as the visible hand of the artist testified to the presence of a human witness, someone with whom readers could identify, thus giving the story a persuasive "you are there" quality.

Among the best of these Pennsylvanians were a small cohort of native-born middle-class artists, who combined illustrator chops with aspirations to fine art: John Sloan, William Glackens, George Luks, and Everett Shinn.

Sloan, born in 1871, grew up in Philadelphia. As a young man he worked in a bookstore that sold prints, and there began making etchings; later he designed greeting cards; in 1892 he began illustrating for the *Philadelphia Inquirer*. He also started taking evening classes at the Pennsylvania Academy of the Fine Arts, under the tutelage of Thomas Anshutz, himself a disciple of realist trailblazer Thomas Eakins, who believed art should reflect life, not hew to abstract aesthetic ideals. Glackens, another newspaper illustrator, was a classmate of Sloan's at the American Academy; Luks had studied there, too, then went on to European art schools before returning to a job at the *Philadelphia Press*, which was where Shinn, who also had taken classes at the academy, was likewise employed.

In 1892 Sloan and others formed the Charcoal Club, an art cooperative that hired models for an informal life drawing class. It developed into something more transformative when the journalists were joined by painter/art teacher Robert Henri (which he pronounced Henrye). Born in 1865, Henri was several years older than most of the group, and more advanced professionally. In 1888 he too had been admitted to the Pennsylvania Academy of the Fine Arts, where he'd studied anatomy and imbibed the Eakins credo. In 1888 he left for a stint of study in Paris, courtesy of a family allowance. Returning to Philadelphia in 1891, he began teaching at a design school for girls, and joined the Charcoal Club.

Henri hosted its weekly meetings in his studio, at which members socialized, drank, drew, and critiqued one another's work, with Henri assuming the role of mentor. He urged Sloan and the rest to shun genteel subjects in favor of vigorous depictions of everyday urban life, and to avoid academic polish when doing so—rejecting even Impressionism as a new variant of academicism, an art of mere surfaces. Such teachings fell on fertile soil, given the journalists' day jobs racing around the streets of Philadelphia, capturing the quotidian in quick-stroke style.

Increasingly, they eyed New York as an alternative place to work and make art. Photographers were horning in on their specialty, and the number of available venues in Philadelphia was limited, whereas Gotham was chockablock with illustrated monthlies and Sunday supplements of national newspapers. They were drawn to the thriving periodical center in the same way that songwriters were drawn to Manhattan's Tin Pan Alley, musicians to its recording industry, and novelists to its great publishing houses.

New York was also Art Central. It had been so for decades, and the boom years only strengthened its predominance. At the apex of a cluster of interlocking institutions sat a self-appointed body of tastemakers—the National Academy of Design (NAD, 1825)—whose elected artist members taught classes, and organized annual juried exhibitions. In the new century the NAD underwent a change in venue, and in the process helped remap the city's cultural geography. In 1899 it sold its Venetian Gothic Revival headquarters (1865), at Fourth Avenue and 23rd Street, to the Metropolitan Life Insurance Company. It moved its school way uptown, to Amsterdam Avenue and 109th, near the Morningside Heights acropolis. And its offices and exhibition space came to roost in the Fine Arts Building (1892) at 215 West 57th (between Broadway and Seventh Avenue, on the north side of the street).

Its arrival strengthened that structure's status as a leading locus of the city's artistic scene. The building had been erected by the American Fine Arts Society—an 1889 consolidation of the National Sculpture Society, the Architectural League, and the Society of American Artists (which in turn merged with the National Academy of Design in 1906). The Fine Arts Building also housed the Art Students League (1875)—a major feeder of new talent into the metropolitan art world. And a block farther east, 57 West 57th, sat another educational venue, the New York School of Art, founded in 1896 by William Merritt Chase. This potpourri of institutions helped establish 57th Street as the horizontal axis of Gotham's emerging art district.

The district's vertical axis ran north-south along Fifth Avenue, the favored location of galleries and dealers, who were selling to nearby millionaire collectors (Morgan, Altman, and Frick, et al.), who were then launching the boom era's art-buying binge. Well-established art-market figures, who had clustered near NAD's Madison Square location, moved steadily up-avenue, in pursuit of their clients, and were joined there by venturesome newcomers. Michael Knoedler, whose New York roots ran back to 1848, shifted in 1911 from Fifth at 22nd to a purpose-built Carrère and Hastings gallery at Fifth and 46th. Knoedler was joined in club territory by the Montross Gallery, which jumped in 1900 to 372 Fifth (at 35th), and then again in 1909 to 550 Fifth (at 46th). Gimpel & Wildenstein leapfrogged from 250 Fifth to 636 Fifth to 647 Fifth at 52nd (in 1918). The Bourgeois Gallery set up shop at 668 Fifth at 53rd in 1914. Jacques Seligmann opened a gallery at 55th Street. Joe Duveen opened a French Neoclassical palace at Fifth and 56th in 1912. And Durand-Ruel settled into 12 East 57th in 1913, thereby commanding the intersection of the district's horizontal (production) and vertical (consumption) axes.

Few of these dealers were devoted to American art, with the notable exception of the William Macbeth Galleries (1892) at Fifth and 40th. Most had long-standing ties to (or were branches of) the leading houses of Europe. They dealt chiefly in Old Masters or French Impressionists, and in effect oversaw the transfer of parts of Europe's art inheritance to American multi-millionaires, who were beginning to shift the major art marketplace from Europe to New York. In 1914, according to the trade press, Gotham boasted sixty-two art establishments, more than twice as many as London and Paris combined.

A significant lurch toward New York primacy came when the Anderson Auction Company scored a major coup. The death in 1909 of Robert Hoe, son of New Yorker Richard Hoe, inventor of the rotary press and a manufacturing magnate, opened the question of who would handle the estate sale of his fabulous collection. Hoe, co-founder and first president of the Grolier Club, had amassed the most valuable book trove ever put up for public sale; the Gutenberg Bible on vellum was only the most spectacular among his 14,500 volumes (not counting the hundreds of pornographic works handled in a private sale). London was still the accepted capital of the book auction trade. But with so many of the biggest buyers now being New Yorkers (Morgan, Huntington, et al.), the executors went with the Anderson. As a result, many distinguished European dealers were forced to travel to New York, repeatedly, as the books were sold off in seventy-nine separate sessions, spread over two years, all held in the Anderson's new home (1910), on 46th Street just off Fifth Avenue.

Finally—as the Philadelphians knew—New York was home to a critical establishment that routinely reviewed the exhibitions mounted by the National Academy, the galleries, and art-oriented gentlemen's clubs (particularly the Lotos, Salmagundi, National Arts, Century, and Union League). There were, as well, several specialized trade magazines, notably *American Art News* (1902) and *Art in America* (1913). In addition, at least eight metropolitan dailies had their own art critics, and dozens of Gotham-based national publications kept an eye on the local art scene. The Philadelphians understood that New York was the place where national and international reputations were made. Sloan observed in 1898 that "a good thing done in Philadelphia is well-done in Philadelphia," but "a good thing done in New York is heralded abroad." Besides, as Henri remarked after a trip to Gotham's galleries in 1897, "New York is so different from here—one feels alive there."

So one by one the Pennsylvanians relocated to the booming metropolis on the Hudson, and there regrouped. Luks landed a job at Pulitzer's *World* in 1896, where his assignments soon included drawing the pioneering Sunday comic *Hogan's Alley*, and penning *The Yellow Kid* after its creator defected to Hearst's *Journal*. Luks got a position on the *World* for Glackens, who later did sketching for the *Herald*, and was sent to Cuba by *McClure's* to cover the war. The two got a position for Shinn on his arrival in 1897; he also made drawings for guidebooks and magazine articles about New York. Sloan came in 1898 to work at the *Herald* but, feeling overwhelmed, retreated to Philadelphia. He and his wife, Dolly, only moved back permanently in 1904, when he began to "feel the necessity of New York as a residence." They found a place in Chelsea, at 165 West 23rd, and Sloan made the rounds with his portfolio, quickly winning illustrator assignments from *Collier's Weekly*, *Leslie's Monthly*, and the *Century*.

Henri arrived in 1900, after a two-year stay in Paris, and accepted teaching positions, first at a private girls' school, then, in 1902, at the prestigious New York School of Art. There the charismatic painter's classes soon rivaled in popularity those of the school's founder, William Merritt Chase. He attracted talented pupils such as Edward Hopper, Guy Pène du Bois, Rockwell Kent, and, in 1904, George Bellows, from Columbus, Ohio, who became his protégé and friend.

Henri enjoined his students to "go out into the streets and look at life"—rather as Pulitzer had once sent his staff walking down the Bowery. He had them study pictorial and literary realists like Daumier and Goya, Zola and Flaubert. And he, his students, and his Philadelphia colleagues deeply admired Whitman's way of seeing. Sloan often perused *Leaves of Grass* before setting out on urban expeditions.

Defying genteel injunctions, the newcomers rambled the city, searching for subjects, and finding them first and foremost on the sidewalks of New York. They perambulated the streets not as detached flaneurs, but as fellow participants in the flow of pedestrian traffic, comfortably curious about passing strangers whom they would never see again. They looked at people, who looked back, looked at each other, looked into shop windows; their paintings were full of eye contact.

They relished crowds. Where planners looked at the skyscraper-and-subway-spawned throngs and saw congestion, the painters saw fabulous energy and dynamic busyness. Their densely peopled canvases celebrated the crush of rush hour traffic; limned the throngs exiting ferryboats and elevateds, captured election-night revelers and last-minute Christmas shoppers and pushcart patrons. Swirling, darting paint strokes picked out distinct individuals while conveying the collective zest and buoyancy.

Like the Impressionists, urban realists flocked to the city's leisure zones. On occasion, they directed their feet to the city's fashionable precincts, painting elegant theaters and upscale restaurants. But usually they favored more plebeian venues. They painted the notorious Haymarket, McSorley's Bar, and Hammerstein's Roof Garden. Their canvases featured boxers at Sharkey's Athletic Club, patrons at five-cent movies and dance halls and vaudeville houses, and pleasure seekers at Coney Island, which they adored.

Unlike the Impressionists, they also chronicled workplaces. They painted men laboring in train yards and butcher shops, at the West Side docks and the Curb Exchange and the excavation site for Pennsylvania Station. They were far less interested in the new skyscrapers and bridges than in the men who built them. They observed women, too, working as nannies, laundresses, scrubwomen, shopgirls, office workers, and prostitutes (on the street or in Women's Night Court at the Jefferson Market).

They tramped through the tenement districts, convinced, like the Villagers, that "real life" was more likely found among working people, immigrants, and the derelict poor—people "undefiled by good taste." Slums teemed, vitally, in Luks's *Hester Street* (1905) and Bellows's *Cliff Dwellers* (1913). The artists tracked hoboes, probed breadlines, scanned dirt, dust, and slush. The ashcan would become their emblem.[1]

Yet theirs was a rose-tinted realism. They seldom weighed poverty's true burdens. They portrayed refuse and disorder with such delight, such smiling optimism, that it

---

1. Only occasionally did they glance at the rich, partly out of deliberate disinclination, partly because the wealthy were less accessible, unlike the poor, who spent so much time outdoors. They did capture some elite rituals of promenade and display, but didn't venture into the great hotels where the wealthy socialized in their quasi-public, quasi-domestic spaces. Nor, for that matter, did they care much about painting the monumental City Beautiful acropoli—the libraries, universities, museums, and train stations (once built). African Americans also figured rarely in their city scenography, partly as the artists seldom frequented black districts. And while they portrayed the rich and poor as occupying separate civic realms, they were seldom presented as being in conflict. Even Shinn's *Eviction (Lower East Side)* (1904) presented only the despairing victims.

George Bellows, *Men of the Docks*, 1912. (National Gallery, London)

George Bellows, *Cliff Dwellers*, 1913. (Los Angeles County Museum of Art)

turned to festive spectacle. Their mean streets were more erotic than squalid—pulsing (as Sloan put it) with the "warm blood and feeling of animal love." These artists rejoiced in shop windows bulging with brassieres, men cheerily urinating in gutters, tenement dwellers asleep on summer rooftops, bawdy beauties on the beach ("full of the real 'vulgar' human life," said Sloan).

THIS ROISTERING VISION IRKED THE CITY'S ART ESTABLISHMENT, which hewed to the notion that it was precisely the "everyday scrambling vulgarity of the street" that refined art should avoid. It was not as if they locked out the realists altogether. Henri, in particular, had been acceptable to National Academy of Design mandarins. He had studied in Paris. He held an important teaching post. His gallery shows, like a 1902 solo outing at William Macbeth's, had received good reviews. So he was elected to the Society of American Artists in 1903, and to the NAD itself in 1906, and invited to serve on juries. He in turn welcomed the opportunity to push for greater NAD accessibility from within.

But conservatives shoved back. In 1906, the year Comstock raided the Art Students League for having included student drawings of "unclothed human beings" in its annual catalog, the New York Watercolor Society refused to hang four of Sloan's etchings, declaring them "vulgar" and "indecent." Then, in 1907, the NAD jury evaluating submissions for the annual exhibition rejected pictures by Glackens, Luks, Shinn, and Sloan, and blackballed the application for membership of many Henri associates. A "mass veto," it was called.

Henri struck back. He not only withdrew his own work in protest; he took the realists' case to the press, denouncing the academy as a monopolistic Art Trust. This approach played well with journalists, partly because most of the Ash Can crowd had been fellow newsmen, partly because trustbusting was much in vogue, and partly because the ruckus sold copies. "The rebels are in arms," trumpeted the *World*, "their brushes bristling with fight and the conservatives stand in solid phalanx to resist the onslaught of radicalism."

Escalating, the media-savvy insurgents decided to mount their own independent exhibition, marketing it as an American Salon des Refusés. In February 1908 eight painters showcased their work at the Macbeth Galleries. The Eight, as critic James Huneker baptized them, included Henri, Sloan, Glackens, Luks, and Shinn—the Philadelphia Five—and three others, stylistically different but equally determined to crack open NAD's restrictive practices: symbolist Arthur B. Davies (who was well wired into wealthy New York collector circles), Impressionist/realist Ernest Lawson, and Postimpressionist Maurice Prendergast. (Davies and Lawson had been among the blackballed in 1907.)

The show was a great success. Charles FitzGerald, the influential art critic of the *Evening Sun*, heaped praise on the rebels. Opponents denounced the Eight as "Apostles of Ugliness," possessed of an "unhealthy nay even coarse and vulgar point of view," and chastised them, to boot, for their "poor drawing" and "weak technique." The curious packed in to see what the hoopla was about. By its close, over 7,000 visitors had flocked to 40th Street, and Gertrude Vanderbilt Whitney, one of the richest women in the world, had stepped up as the chief purchaser.[2]

---

2. Gertrude Vanderbilt, a great-granddaughter of the Commodore, was born in New York City in 1875, where she grew up in a 137-room French Renaissance château at 1 West 57th Street. When she married Harry Payne Whitney in 1896, they moved into a mansion across the street, at 2 East 57th, where they comingled their millions (which flowed from railroads, oil, tobacco, and stock market manipulation). Gertrude became a sculptor, studying at the Art Students League and in Paris, despite the disapproval of her family and her philandering playboy husband. Despite her immense wealth she met with establishment resistance to her work, one reason, perhaps, that she sympathized with the rebels. Nor was her support for the urban realists a one-off affair. In 1907 she

"New York's Art War and the Eight Rebels Who Have Dared to Paint Pictures of New York Life (Instead of Europe) and Who Are Holding Their Rebellious Exhibition All by Themselves." *Sunday World Magazine*, February 2, 1908.

Two years later the rebels raised the stakes. In 1910 Henri, Sloan, Davies, and Walt Kuhn (a Brooklyn-born cartoonist, graphic artist, and painter) mounted an unfiltered, no-jury, no-prize Exhibition of Independent Artists. With the Henri circle figuring prominently, 103 participants submitted more than 600 works, which were hung in alphabetical

set up an apartment and studio in Greenwich Village, remodeling a stable at 19 MacDougal Alley, just north of Washington Square, and made it available for informal exhibitions. In 1914 she bought the adjacent building (8 West 8th Street) and established therein a professional gallery, the Whitney Studio, which was managed by her lieutenant Juliana Force. She provided exhibition space to Bellows, Glackens, and Davies, and supported dozens of individual artists with stipends.

George Bellows, *Both Members of This Club,* 1909. (National Gallery of Art)

order. Crowds poured in—over 2,000 came to the opening. The *World*'s review of the exhibition was subtitled: "How the 'Art Rebels' of America Are Shocking the Older Schools by Actually Putting Prize Fights on Canvas [a reference to Bellows's *Stag at Sharkey's*] and Picturing Up-to-Date Life as It Really Is Here and Now." The *Globe* declared: "This is unmistakably the day of the Insurgent, the Revolutionist, the Independent, in art as in other directions."

AS THE ASH CAN PAINTERS DREW AWAY from the academy, they drew closer to radical politics. Henri and Bellows favored anarchism. At Emma Goldman's 1911 invitation, both taught at the Ferrer School. John and Dolly Sloan joined the Socialist Party in 1910. He contributed political cartoons to the *Call* (including a scathing 1911 memorial to the Triangle victims), and designed campaign posters (even ran himself for the New York State Assembly on the Socialist ticket, though unsuccessfully). The Sloans moved to the Village in 1912 (61 Perry Street), where Sloan became an art editor of the *Masses* (and brought George Bellows and Stuart Davis along with him). His March 1913 *Masses* cover depicted a wealthy couple in their opera box, captioned "The Unemployed." A rudely crayoned Davis image of two working girls parodied the glistening Gibsonesque cover girls favored by the slick commercial press; it was captioned "Gee, Mag, Think of Us Bein' on a Magazine Cover!"[3]

Sloan also painted the scenery for the June 1913 Paterson Pageant, the colossal art/political event held in Madison Square Garden, and was involved in planning for another 1913 event that would be the next step taken by the independent artists movement. In

---

3. In time, however, such captions irritated Sloan and company. They accused editors Eastman and Dell of transforming their humorous satire into didactic propaganda. Art Young countered that untitled "pictures of ash cans" were insufficiently theorized. Sloan and his friends resigned in 1916.

1912 the members of the Eight and others had organized what they intended to be a permanent alternative to the National Academy of Design, the American Association of Painters and Sculptors. Arthur B. Davies was chosen as president and Walt Kuhn as secretary. The organization began planning a blockbuster gathering for 1913 that would hopefully dwarf the 1908 and 1910 exhibitions. While it would predominantly feature American artists, it would also include a selection of European works, partly to set US artists in a transatlantic and historical context. It would be called the International Exhibition of Modern Art.

To gather information on the latest developments abroad, Davies sought to involve a friend of his, Alfred Stieglitz, a Fifth Avenue gallery owner who had been showing work by Parisian avant-garde figures and the handful of Americans who had been influenced by those French modernists. Stieglitz was something of an analog to Henri in being a vigorous advocate for a new—and, he claimed, revolutionary—approach to art. Stieglitz, like Henri, was himself an artist of repute, albeit in the field of photography. He was also someone who had dedicated himself to finding new ways of seeing New York City.

MODERNISTS' METROPOLIS

In 1890 Alfred Stieglitz, 26, returned to his native Gotham from a lengthy sojourn abroad, and fell into instant depression. In painful contrast to the great European capitals, his city seemed an unprepossessing subject for a man intent on proving photography a fine art, which had become his mission in life.

In 1871 Stieglitz's father, Edward, a German Jewish immigrant and successful wool merchant, had moved his family from Hoboken to a New York brownstone at 14 East 60th Street. Alfred was sent to the Charlier Institute, one of Gotham's best private schools for "Young Gentlemen," and in 1879 he entered City College. But his father decided its academic program was not up to snuff when measured against Germany's newly rigorous universities. So in 1881 Stieglitz père retired, sold his interest in the business for $400,000, and took the family for an extended stay in his homeland, where Alfred could get a proper education, and Edward could take up painting. Alfred studied mechanical engineering in Berlin, then segued into the developing field of photochemistry. In 1883 he bought his first camera. For the rest of the decade he immersed himself in the developing world of amateur photography. Traveling and shooting widely in France, Switzerland, and Italy, he entered competitions sponsored by gentlemen's camera clubs, won a number of prizes, and developed an international reputation.

When he returned in 1890 his father set him up in the photoengraving business—the family had sailed back in 1884—but what engaged Stieglitz was not transferring images to print, but making images himself. In late 1892 he bought his first handheld camera, and set out to reconnoiter the city. "From 1893 to 1895," he later recalled, "I often walked the streets of New York downtown, taking my hand camera with me. I wandered around the Tombs, the old Post Office, Five Points. I loathed the dirty streets, yet I was fascinated. I wanted to photograph everything I saw." He was particularly drawn to the immigrant poor. "Nothing charms me so much as walking among the lower classes, studying them carefully and making mental notes," he wrote in 1896. He was moved by "the derelicts, the secondhand clothing shops, the rag pickers, the tattered and torn"; he believed "there was a reality about them lacking in the artificial world in which I found myself."

In 1895, having married Emmeline Obermeyer, a wealthy brewery heiress, Stieglitz abandoned his business and plunged into full-time promotion of his vision of photography's future. His platform was the Camera Club of New York, which he helped form in 1896, and its journal, *Camera Notes*, of which he became editor. Stieglitz wanted to rescue photography from the condescension of "real" artists, who argued that there was no artistry in taking pictures, just mere mechanical reproduction. Stieglitz agreed. If photography was to take its place among the fine arts, it would have to go beyond point and shoot—the sort of work that produced postcards for tourists, all surface, no soul. Practitioners would have to use the camera as if it were a brush, a medium for expressing a unique artistic vision. The method Stieglitz and his colleagues propounded—"pictorialism"—required visible signs of intervention by the photographer, either through choice of subject matter, or darkroom manipulations of the image.

Stieglitz looked for "picturesque" subjects, though given his urban focus this was something of a stretch. The eighteenth-century aesthetic category referred to picture-worthy natural landscapes, but New York City was arguably the antithesis of nature. How to come up with a picturesque Manhattan?

As he roamed the streets with his hand camera, he figured out that the trick was to reinsert the city into nature. He shot New York in fog or snow, amid spring showers or winter blizzards, at dusk or night, until its dirt and angularity had been laundered, softened, rendered charming, atmospheric, picturesque. Some of his pictorialist colleagues achieved similar effects by chemical or mechanical means, using soft focus or greased lenses to effect the desired blur, but Stieglitz relied on weather and moonlight. His *Picturesque Bits of New York and Other Studies* (1898) gathered up a portfolio of twelve such photogravures, juxtaposing local scenes with ones from Venice and Paris, thus demonstrating that Gotham afforded equal opportunities for visual delectation.

In 1900 Stieglitz published in *Camera Notes* an essay by Sadakichi Hartmann, a poet and photography critic, which pushed this argument a step further. In "A Plea for Picturesqueness in New York," Hartmann said he was "astonished at the limited range of subjects which the artistic photographers attempt to portray." Such men believed there was little of pictorial interest in New York. Blinded by classical definitions of beauty, they were unable to see what was in front of their face. They seemed unaware that "the best art is that which is most clearly the outcome of the time of its production." They didn't understand that "the art signifying most in respect to the characteristics of its age is that which ultimately becomes classic." The photo-artist's goal should be "boldly to express the actual," to discover "all the various picturesque effects New York is capable of—effects which the eye has not yet got used to, nor discovered and applied in painting and literature." Hartmann rattled off examples: twilight seen from roof-garden restaurants when "all the distant windows began to glimmer like sparks, and the whole city seemed to be strewn with stars"; an elevated station at rush hour "when the populace goes to or returns from work" and "thousands and thousands climb up or down the stairs, reflecting in their varied appearances all the classes of society"; and, "for the lovers of proletarian socialism," pictures of "the hunger and the filth of the slums, the unfathomable and inexhaustible misery." All this awaited their cameras.[4] Hartmann also

---

4. In declaring the poor picturesque, Hartmann and Stieglitz (and numerous guidebook authors) were open to charges of tolerating the city's social inequities as "decorative enhancements," a charge that gains currency when compared to the chronologically contemporary but profoundly different work of photographer-activist Lewis Hine. Unlike Stieglitz, Hine packaged his work with numbers, words, and signed testimonies. His photographs appeared not in art galleries but in periodicals, reports, exhibitions, and slide show lectures. He aimed to publicize social evils by engendering empathetic responses to his subjects (resisting the

found prismatic poetry in "the gigantic parallelograms of office buildings and skyscrapers," and in the new century Stieglitz, too, turned his attention to the tall towers, deploying his picturesque landscaping techniques to integrate even these startlingly modern phenomena into nature. In his winter 1903 composition of the Flatiron Building, for example, he encompassed the looming structure in the snow-laden tree branches of Madison Square, rendering it lyrical, ethereal.

In 1901, impatient with foot-draggers in the Camera Club who resisted the pictorialist approach, Stieglitz and his supporters had "seceded" from the organization, founding the Photo-Secession group and establishing a new journal they called *Camera Work*. Its first issue, in December 1902, declared an "active protest" against the "conservatism and reactionary spirit" of those who "believe that the standards of yesterday must be the standards of all time to come." That the group and journal would become far more revolutionary than he had intended was thanks in considerable measure to his closest partner in the adventure, Edward Steichen. The two had met in 1900 when Steichen—a photographer and painter—was passing through New York from Milwaukee on his way to Paris, to further study painting. Stieglitz was impressed by the way Steichen blended the two media, and when the latter returned from Paris in 1902, and set up shop as a professional photographer, the two became inseparable.[5] They saw eye to eye on pictorialism; Steichen's Flatiron image of 1904 (colorized with gum bichromate) was a close cousin of Stieglitz's 1903 version. And together in 1905 they opened the Little Galleries of the Photo-Secession (at 291 Fifth, between 30th and 31st, which would come to be called "291"). Its initial exhibit of 100 prints by thirty-nine photographers was an instant success, and almost 15,000 visited during its first season.

But it was in painting that the partnership proved combustible. In Paris, Steichen had made the acquaintance of cutting-edge artists and sculptors, acquaintanceships renewed on repeated subsequent trips, which enabled him to send their work back to 291 for what were usually the artists' first US exhibitions. Between Steichen in Paris and Stieglitz in New York, a transatlantic transmission belt was established that reestablished Gotham's position as America's port of entry for overseas cultural innovations.

In January 1908 Steichen got Auguste Rodin (whom he had photographed extensively) to send a set of erotic nude drawings to 291; the *Times* review professed amazement that such a "challenge to the prurient prudery of our puritanism" had not been "raided by the blind folly that guards our morals." More startlingly, Steichen returned to New York in 1908 bearing a group of Matisse prints the artist had lent him, and the 291 Matisse exhibition mounted that April scored another first for the Photo-Secessionists. Yet it also marked a shift of focus away from photography to modern art. 1910 brought a Postimpressionist show, with works by Cézanne, Manet, Renoir, and Henri Rousseau. 291 began to buzz. Artists and enthusiasts frequented the small space to hear Stieglitz expound on the new styles, or to engage in

---

tendency of Jacob Riis, and some of his employers, to treat individuals as "cases"). And unlike the Ash Can artists, Hine was less interested in depicting "New York" than in surveying "urban society." But for all his focus on general "conditions," Hine brilliantly portrayed the city's very particular street traders, child laborers, Ellis immigrants, tenement home workers, and sweatshop and factory employees.

5. It was in this capacity that Steichen was hired in 1903 to assist a painter doing a portrait of J. P. Morgan, to minimize the banker's sitting time. After photographing Morgan in the pose requested, Steichen was permitted to make a second negative for himself, which proved far more revealing, as it caught Morgan in a flash of irritation at Steichen's posing instructions. When shown the two images, Morgan ordered a dozen copies of the first and ripped up the second. Steichen made a print for Stieglitz, who exhibited it, repeatedly; even Morgan came to like it.

debates among themselves. It became as much a salon as a gallery, less a place for silent looking than for stimulating conversation.

The year 1910 brought yet another transatlantic spark of connection, thanks to yet another Stieglitz talent scout, who had begun canvassing Parisian venues for 291 candidates. Marius de Zayas, a Mexican newspaper caricaturist, had arrived in Gotham in 1907, when his family was forced out of Mexico for opposing the dictatorship of Porfirio Díaz. De Zayas found work as a caricaturist at Pulitzer's *Evening World*, specializing now in depicting notable New Yorkers. Stieglitz exhibited them in 1909 and 1910, and the shows were wildly popular. On a trip to Paris in October 1910, de Zayas stumbled into Cubism, reporting back to Stieglitz that among practitioners of this bewildering approach it seemed "the real article is a Spaniard," whose name he did not recall. Within three months de Zayas had not only met Picasso but had done with him a pathbreaking in-depth interview, in their mutually native tongue. Stieglitz had it translated and published as a pamphlet accompanying Picasso's first US show, held at 291 in the spring of 1911. But this exhibition, consisting of eighty-three watercolors and drawings selected by de Zayas and Steichen, received mostly negative reviews. Only two of the works were sold, one for $12, and one (bought by Stieglitz) for $65. Stieglitz then offered the remaining eighty-one to the Met for $2,000, an average of $25 apiece. The curator who turned them down reportedly huffed that he "saw nothing in Picasso and vouched that such mad pictures would never mean anything in America."

Throughout 1911 and early 1912 Stieglitz continued organizing groundbreaking exhibits at 291 and promoting the new art in the pages of *Camera Work*. By the summer of 1912 he was so enthralled with painting that he published a special number of the magazine, devoted solely to Matisse and Picasso (with an essay by Gertrude Stein), which did not contain a single photograph.

Yet Stieglitz's own camera work underwent a marked transformation. In a burst of photo shoots around the city he abandoned pictorialism's blurred forms and picturesque effects, and adopted a "straight," crisply focused style. In *Old and New New York* (1910), taken from the corner of Fifth Avenue and 34th Street, he captured the way the unclad steel girders of the Vanderbilt Hotel, then under construction two blocks east on Park Avenue, loomed over a block of brownstones. The image, scrubbed free of fog, and all but stripped of people, was ambiguous. Did it suggest that a gigantic, abstract, and soulless new city was overmastering the old human-scaled one? Or did it pick up on Hartmann's decade-old call for a good picture of "an iron skeleton framework," suggesting there was "something wonderful in iron architecture, which as if guided by magic, weaves its networks with scientific precision over the rivers or straight into the air," creating "by the very absence of unnecessary ornamentation, new laws of beauty"? Or was he (as his title suggested) interested in rendering change, making visible the passage of time, no small challenge for a two-dimensional, fixed-time medium? And was he attempting, in marked contrast to the Ash Can School's focus on parts (streets, neighborhoods), to pull back the camera and grasp the city as a whole? *The City of Ambition* (1910) might be similarly read as a synoptic and change-capturing image, with its depiction of New York's sequentially developed but now coexistent macro-economic layers—maritime (the harborfront), industrial (West Side manufacturing belt), and corporate (the Singer-pinnacled skyscraper backdrop)—in an image bereft of people altogether.[6]

---

6. Stieglitz's submersion in European abstraction may have helped him discern new meaning in his own work. In 1907, aboard the fashionable *Kaiser Wilhelm II* on his way to Europe, Stieglitz (as he recalled much later) had spent the first few days at sea slouched in a steamer chair, his eyes closed, repelled by the sight of his nouveau-riche compatriots in First Class. To escape them

Alfred Stieglitz, *Old and New New York*, 1910. *Camera Work* 36 (October 1911).

IT WAS AT THIS TIME (1910–13) THAT STIEGLITZ BEGAN TO WORK with several youthful American artists who had imbibed Fauvist and Cubist approaches in Europe, and whom Stieglitz saw

he ventured far forward, discovered the steerage decks below, ran back to his stateroom, grabbed his Graflex, raced back, composed his shot, and exposed the plate—a spontaneous photo-slumming expedition that recapitulated his quest for the urban picturesque. But Stieglitz later claimed he had immediately recognized this image (*The Steerage*) as marking "another milestone in photography. . . . a step in my own evolution, a spontaneous discovery." He had not, he argued, seen people but rather "shapes related to one another"—the geometric pairings of round hat and round machinery, of crossed funnel/stairway and crossed white suspenders. In fact, he didn't make these comments at the time, but only after he'd been deeply influenced by European abstraction. Nor did he publish it until 1911, in an issue of *Camera Work*, pointedly pairing it with a Cubist drawing by Picasso (who had praised *The Steerage*'s forms and shifting depths).

Alfred Stieglitz, *City of Ambition*, 1910. (Everett Historical/Shutterstock)

as capable of transplanting modernism to Gotham. He offered them moral support, promotion of their work, and even shelter and financial aid. He was particularly taken with painters like John Marin and Max Weber who were inspired by the city itself, and who used abstraction to seize on some of its essential features (skyscrapers, crowds, lights) and qualities (speed, circulation, energy) to fashion a new metropolitan iconography.

As a youth, New Jersey–born John Marin had dabbled his way through architecture and the arts, finding no secure footing. In 1899, aged 29, he enrolled in the Pennsylvania Academy of the Fine Arts, and then at the Art Students League. In 1905 he left for Europe,

Alfred Stieglitz, *The Steerage*, 1907. *Camera Work* 36 (October 1911).

where he studied, traveled, and painted. In Paris in 1908 he met Steichen, who alerted Stieglitz to his promise; the latter confirmed this on a 1909 visit to Marin's Paris studio, and arranged Marin's first solo show at 291 in February 1910. But it was only that autumn, after Marin had returned to Gotham, that he began to reckon with his new subject, the new New York.

The city Marin saw was not picturesque or softly atmospheric. It was an ultra-modern city whose tremendous energy and power demanded a radically modern art. "I have just started some Downtown stuff," he wrote Stieglitz in 1911, "and to pile these great houses one upon each other with paint as they do pile themselves up there so beautiful, so fantastic—at times one is afraid to look at them." His etchings and watercolors of 1911–13 captured the exhilarating dynamics of city life, deploying both Cubist and Futurist techniques. "I try to express graphically what a great city is doing," he wrote in *Camera Work*. He did not, however, believe this required including its residents. "Shall we consider the life of a great city as confined simply to the people and animals on its streets and in its buildings?" Marin asked (in what was perhaps an indirect challenge to Ash Can ideology). "Are the buildings themselves dead?" No, was his resounding answer. When he examined the relation between the huge building masses contending for airspace in the skies over Manhattan he saw "great forces at work"—"warring, pushing, pulling forces." And to capture these he fractured the tall buildings into surging lines and fragmented planes, and sent them dancing along trafficked avenues. (Architect Cass Gilbert found Marin's Woolworth watercolors alarmingly "topsy turvy.") As one critic put it, rather than New Yorkers, "Marin sees New York itself, rearing monstrous pointed heads into a smiling sky; straining and growing and roaring."

Max Weber was similarly attentive to the city qua city. Born in 1881 in the Polish city of Bialystok, then part of the Russian Empire, Weber was brought to Williamsburg at the age of ten by his Orthodox Jewish parents. He left Boys' High without graduating to study at the Pratt Institute, from which he got a teaching degree in 1900. He also won a scholarship to study privately with Pratt's master teacher Arthur Wesley Dow, who had worked with Gauguin and helped introduce Postimpressionism and Japanese art to the United States. Weber, after teaching in public schools in Virginia and Minnesota (1901–5) to raise sufficient funds, then spent 1905–9 in Paris. There he studied at several academies, met Matisse, Picasso, and Rousseau, worked in the Cubist style, exhibited in the 1906 Salon, and in 1908 helped organize Matisse's art school, which he attended for a year. When he returned to New York in 1909, he was thoroughly fluent in Cubism. But as this remained an utterly alien tongue, he had great difficulty getting jobs or showing his work. At Steichen's suggestion Weber, at that point penniless, approached Stieglitz for help. Stieglitz took him on as an assistant, allowing him to live in 291 and to paint there before it opened to the public each morning.[7] He included Weber's work in a group exhibition in 1910 (along with Marin's) and then gave him a solo show in 1911 (which was thoroughly panned by uncomprehending critics).[8] Like Marin, Weber adopted the modern metropolis as a subject. And he, too, focused on the city's height, light, and speed. In *New York* (1913), huge blocks of angled skyscrapers crowded the canvas as abstract elevated lines snaked in and around them; in *Rush Hour, New York*, thrusting diagonals, cones, and semicircles conjured frenetic movement; in *New York at Night*, shafts of colored lights played among geometric shapes.

THE MODERNISTS' METROPOLIS WAS WONDROUS, EXHILARATING, dizzying, bewildering. And unpeopled. The citizens that crowded Ash Can canvases were ushered offstage from Stieglitz-circle photographs and paintings. The modernists also abandoned the pedestrian point of view. They saw the city from afar, or looked down from on high, or they synthesized many vantage points within a single canvas. But for all the real differences between the Henri and Stieglitz circles, they shared a disaffection from the domineering National Academy of Design, and it was in their capacity as "independent" artists that the American realists and modernists

---

7. It was probably in the capacity of assistant that Weber featured as the only prominent human in Stieglitz's *Old and New New York* photo—unless he was being deployed to some purpose, perhaps the role of the artist in the city.

8. Stieglitz and Weber fell out in 1911, and Weber transferred his allegiance from the 291 circle to the Ferrer Center anarchists, to whom he had been introduced by Henri, whom he had met at 291, where Henri was a frequent visitor.

undertook to conjointly produce a mammoth exhibition of their accumulated work, which they intended to be a knockout blow against the Art Trust, but which, given their incautious inclusion of European artists, would have colossally unanticipated consequences.

ARMORY SHOW

By January 1913 the promised International Exhibition of Modern Art was all but ready. During 1912 the organizers, led by Arthur B. Davies, a veteran of the Eight, and president of the new Association of American Painters and Sculptors (AAPS), had been busy. With pro bono help from John Quinn, a wealthy corporate lawyer and art collector (and Irish nationalist and supporter of Yeats), they had incorporated the AAPS, and leased the enormous 69th Regiment Armory at Lexington between 25th and 26th. They had assembled a group of wealthy backers, including Lillie P. Bliss (a faithful Davies patron), Gertrude Vanderbilt Whitney (despite having had her sculptures rejected), and Mabel Dodge (whose $500 check to Davies toward the $10,000 final cost was accompanied by a note declaring the exhibition "the most important thing [of its kind] that ever happened in America"). To ensure nationwide blockbuster status, the artists had hired a press agent, revved up a giant publicity machine, and designated the Pine Tree Flag of the American Revolution as official emblem. (Buttons bearing the logo would be distributed by the thousands.)

In September 1912, more importantly, Davies had dispatched Walt Kuhn to Europe to round up works for the European galleries. After travels in Germany and Holland, Kuhn arrived in Paris in late October. There he was plugged into the avant-garde scene by New Yorker (and former Henri student) Walter Pach, who had been coming to Europe repeatedly since 1903, as a student, and as agent for Henri's summer sessions abroad. Pach had lived in Paris for long stretches, and become close friends with, among many others, Matisse, Picasso, Albert Gleizes, Constantin Brancusi, and Marcel Duchamp. Pach also knew many of the prominent collectors in Paris, including the Stein families, and was on a first-name basis with the leading contemporary art dealers. Davies joined them in November, and together they began a whirlwind tour of galleries and studios and exhibitions. Doors swung open for the trio from Gotham, and loans were arranged for work by Pach's artists, and others, including Braque, Cézanne, Gauguin, Amedeo Modigliani, Francis Picabia, Renoir, Rodin, and Van Gogh. Gorged on Gallic art, they saw little need for Italian Futurists (none) or German Expressionists (virtually none, but one was Kandinsky). In the end, about a third of the estimated 1,368 works in the Armory Show (as it was quickly called) were European.[9]

THE SHOW OPENED FEBRUARY 17, 1913. New York Society turned out in force. Attendance rose steadily over its four-week run, eventually totaling 87,000, an unprecedented turnout. And, as intended, it provoked a media firestorm, though it was not the New Yorkers but the Parisians who garnered nearly all the attention. Many visitors rushed through the American galleries up front and stood on long lines at those in the rear—Gallery H, which housed

---

9. Quinn tried to eliminate a financial hurdle posed by the 1909 Payne-Aldrich tariff, which had slapped a duty of 15 percent on imported art less than twenty years old. Customs regulations even required works that were only *borrowed* from abroad, to post bond in advance for what they might owe if they were sold. (About a third of the Armory objects were required to front this deposit.) Quinn argued before the House Ways and Means Committee that the legislation was inequitable as it allowed the wealthiest to bring in their favored Old Masters duty free. "I prefer the art of my own time," Quinn declared, and he was successful, but the reversal of policy came only in October 1913, too late to affect the Armory event. It would, however, contribute to a post-show boom in sales of modern European art in America.

Matisse, and the adjacent Gallery I, next to the exit, wherein dwelt Duchamp and Picabia. (It was dubbed the Cubist Room or the Chamber of Horrors, depending on point of view.)

One camp of commentators, genially philistine, joked about the unintelligibility, and probable fraudulence, of works like Duchamp's *Nude Descending a Staircase.* Roosevelt's review good-humoredly hailed its value in educating "our people" about Eurodevelopments, lauded some nonrepresentational art (while preferring his Navajo rug), and jovially advised Americans to take much of the rest "no more seriously than we take P. T. Barnum's mermaids."

Other critics found the new art degenerate and dangerous. It was formless, immoral, a slap in the face to bourgeois taste. Duchamp's ironic, analytic figure—abstracted from time, space, sex, and physique—seemed deeply offensive, a mockery of the Female Form Divine. But the outrage and fearfulness in conservative quarters ran much deeper, because of the art's presumed relation to larger social, cultural, and political forces in play.

On March 16, the day the show closed, the *New York Times* ran a "straight from the shoulder" interview with Kenyon Cox, one of the National Academy of Design's most

"Seeing New York with a Cubist: The Rude Descending a Staircase (Rush Hour at the Subway)."
New York Evening Sun, March 20, 1913. (Granger)

prestigious painters and critics. Cox tipped his hat to TR's notion that the modernist project was essentially fraudulent, decrying the work of "charlatans" who "have seized upon the modern engine of publicity and are making insanity pay." But his deeper dismay was with the modernists' claim that art was and should be the "expression of the individual" artist, and their accompanying desire to "abandon all discipline, all respect for tradition." Those who make "art merely expressive of their personal whim," Cox warned, those who "make it speak in a special language only understood by themselves, are as truly anarchists as are those who would overthrow all social laws."

The *Times*'s editorial response to Cox picked up on his accusation of anarchism and ran with it. The Cubists and Futurists were "surely a part of the general movement, discernible all over the world, to disrupt and degrade, if not to destroy, not only art, but literature and society, too." The modernists were "cousins to the anarchists in politics, the poets who defy syntax and decency," the "cubists and futurists in religion who have made of faith a mockery," and to their counterparts in music, industrial movements, and philanthropy. They believed that "all that is old is bad, all that has been proved is false, all that has been cherished should be destroyed, all that is beautiful should be despised." Nor should anyone underestimate their appeal to "the disheartened, embittered, and discontented, as well as the mentally ill-balanced."

Some conservatives, like Royal Cortissoz, art critic of the *Tribune*, went beyond claiming ideological consanguinity to suggesting malevolent collusion. The radical canvases, he argued, were the work of "foolish terrorists" who wanted to "turn the world upside down." And in general there was much muttering about Wobblyesque paintings—the Armory Show itself having been bracketed by the Paterson strike, which had begun on February 1, days before the exhibition opened, and the IWW's Paterson Pageant, which took place three months after it closed, in Madison Square Garden, one block away from the armory.

In the case of the extraordinary abuse heaped upon Matisse in particular, perhaps the root of the loathing lay in his "primitivism," which touched on the era's deep anxieties about possible racial regression. Duncan Phillips, a Washington, DC, collector and critic who had been open to earlier and milder modernists, found Matisse's paintings "repellent because they turn humanity back to its brutish beginnings." Throwing off of centuries-old standards of art and beauty might threaten the very basis of Western civilization.[10]

To these charges, New York cultural radicals entered a cheery guilty plea. Hutchins Hapgood exulted that "beneficent agitation is as noticeable in art and in the woman's movement as it is in politics and industry." Whether in literature or the labor movement "we find an instinct to loosen up the old forms and traditions, to dynamite the baked and hardened earth so that fresh flowers can grow." The National Academy of Design had been thoroughly outflanked.

But so had—to their great chagrin—the Armory Show's Ash Can progenitors. The glare of French modernism illuminated the relative narrowness of the presumed gulf between Ash Canners and Academics. Both seemed suddenly old-fashioned, passé. Some thought the Pine Tree emblem a sour joke. "More than ever before," wrote AAPS cofounder and realist Jerome Myers, "our great country had become a colony; more than ever before, we had become provincials." Davies, Myers added dolefully, had "unlocked the door to foreign art and thrown the key away." And indeed, the Armory Show had provided a bitter and unanticipated lesson in the perils of cultural free trade.

---

10. Matisse, dismayed by the uproar, told an interviewer: "Oh, do tell the American people that I am a normal man; that I am a devoted husband and father, that I have three fine children, that I go to the theatre, ride horseback, have a comfortable home."

The vigorous and self-confident movement grew confused. Some jumped ship: Stuart Davis swung round to abstraction. Some tried to adapt: Sloan played with Van Gogh and Cézanne-like approaches to color. Many remained frankly hostile, denouncing abstraction as a betrayal of social and political responsibility, and a retreat from the city. The *Masses* mostly ignored the Armory Show, despite the fact that the magazine's editors and contributors were active participants, including Bellows, Sloan, Glackens, Henri, Art Young, and Davies himself. But they never included speeding cars or the Brooklyn Bridge in its pages, and the sole skyscraper to appear was a cartoon symbolizing big business. Their artwork stuck to the intimate city of old neighborhoods and alleyways, portraying not architecture but polyglot residents. Sloan did include a cartoon mildly spoofing the Cubists—"There was a cubic man and he walked a cubic mile…"—although when interviewed by *American Art News* about Matisse and the Cubists he said, "I think these a splendid symptom, a bomb under conventions." But that was a month before the show opened.

Stieglitz, however, was confirmed as a prophet; he had been way ahead of the curve. But the young American modernists he'd been nurturing—all but completely ignored during the media frenzy—now seemed tame, derivative, next to Matisse and the rest. As one of them wrote in *Camera Work* "the exhibition of the new art from Europe dropped like a bomb.... We are a generation behind Europe in the art." New galleries sprouted to showcase the new art, and exhibits of modernist works became commonplace, but the focus was on the Europeans. Even the Met trustees succumbed to the new craze (admittedly cautiously, and by a narrow majority) authorizing the purchase of a solitary Cézanne.[11]

Stieglitz shared the realists' worry that the flood of brilliant incoming work would overwhelm local efforts, and he continued to back his American modernist protégés. But he continued to showcase the "real article" as well. Two days after the Armory Show closed, Stieglitz opened at 291 an exhibit of the work of Picabia, including thirteen watercolors he had made since arriving in New York in January to attend the giant exhibition (the only European artist who did so). Picabia's new works were about Gotham, with titles like *New York as Seen from across a Body*, and—aware of the frenzied response to the modernists—he provided locals with an explanation of what he'd done, demonstrating how abstraction worked. "Did I paint the Flatiron Building, the Woolworth Building, when I painted my impression of these 'skyscrapers' of your great city? No! I gave you the rush of upward movement, the feeling of those who attempted to build the Tower of Babel—man's desire to reach the heavens, to achieve infinity." His works weren't representational, but they weren't meaningless, either. "They express the spirit of New York as I feel it, and the crowded streets of your city as I feel them, their surging, their unrest, their commercialism, and their atmospheric charm."

Picabia urged Gotham's artists to explore the "extreme modernity" of their own environment. As if in response, "fresh flowers" began to bloom almost immediately after the Armory exhibition and Picabia's exhortation. One of the most brilliantly colorful ones was Joseph Stella, whose personal trajectory had arced across the city's spectrum of artistic possibilities.

Stella, born in 1877 to a middle-class family in Italy, came to New York in 1896 intending to study medicine, but quickly turned instead to studying art. At the New York School of Art

---

11. Modernism swept as well into mass culture. An ad from Wanamaker's department store touted Cubist clothing, particularly hailing the vivid colors introduced by Matisse and others at the Armory. "*Color* is the vital thing," the text argued: "With the gown as pallete, the world has been painted over, intensified, vivified, made luminous, by putting it into dresses which express the color visions of the Modernists."

he worked with Henri, who introduced him to Whitman as well as realism. From 1905 to 1909 Stella prowled the streets of the immigrant enclaves, drawing Rembrandtesque depictions of slum life that were published in magazines. He veered in the direction of photographer Lewis Hine when his drawings of immigrant factory workers in *Survey* and *Outlook* led to a commission for a series on the miserable living and working conditions in industrial Pittsburgh—like the "infernal regions sung by Dante," Stella thought—work later published in the *Pittsburgh Survey*. Stella returned to Italy in 1909, encountered modernism, and relocated to Paris in 1911 (at the suggestion of Walter Pach) where, as he noted, "Fauvism, Cubism, and Futurism were in full swing." When he returned to New York in late 1912, he now saw the city with Futurist eyes, and thrilled to its "violent blaze of electricity" and its steel thrown to "hyperbolic altitudes." Moved by the Armory Show and inspired by Picabia, Stella created *Battle of Lights, Mardi Gras, Coney Island* (1913), conveying the surging crowd and revolving machines with a swooping and spinning tumult of glaring colors exploding in all directions.

Using a novel artistic form to capture a novel urban phenomenon—in this case a mass-culture carnival—seemed a supremely fitting match of eye and object, in the opinion of the European modernists, because, as Picabia put it: "New York is the cubist, the futurist city. It expresses in its architecture, its life, its spirit, the modern thought." The notorious Marcel Duchamp concurred. "I adore New York." He loved its engineering, its plumbing. It was *itself* "a complete work of art."

Joseph Stella, *Battle of Lights, Mardi Gras, Coney Island*, 1913–14. (Yale University Art Gallery)

IN THE LITERARY ARTS, New York also had its modernists and realists.

Among the former were experimental poets like Alfred Kreymborg. A New Yorker born and bred—his parents ran a cigar store, and he attended public schools—Kreymborg was active in the Greenwich Village scene. He frequented the Liberal Club, was the first literary figure to be included in Stieglitz's 291 circle, and was briefly associated with the Ferrer Center. He mocked the staid Poetry Society of America, whose members thought Yeats lacked "positive spirit," and whose offerings were "as smooth as one of Mr. Howells' editorials in *Harper's*." After his magazine the *Globe* expired in 1914, Kreymborg and others started up *Others: A Magazine of the New Verse* (1915–19), which featured work by Ezra Pound, T. S. Eliot, Amy Lowell, William Carlos Williams, Marianne Moore, and Wallace Stevens.

In 1917 Margaret Anderson and her new co-editor (and lover) Jane Heap moved their *Little Review* from Chicago to the basement of 24 West 16th Street, near Union Square. Founded in 1914, it had pioneered in publishing experimental fiction. Once in New York, Pound became foreign editor; Pound's backer John Quinn underwrote expenses, and the *Little Review* became a major conduit for modernist European work arriving from Yeats, Eliot, Wyndham Lewis, and Pound himself. The magazine's serialization of James Joyce's *Ulysses*, begun in March 1918, stung the culture police into action. Three issues with offending excerpts were burned by the Post Office, on grounds of being obscene, and finally the Society for the Suppression of Vice got Anderson and Heap arrested and convicted of violating the Comstock laws; the women were fined and forced to discontinue publication.

New York's realist camp were not as much in dialogue with European writers. Rather they drew nourishment from their deep roots in the city's literary and commercial culture, and took the city itself as their subject. Rebels could reach back to Whitman, take inspiration from Howells and Crane, and draw strength from the city's popular press and the probings of contemporary muckrakers. Some realist writers emphasized their disaffection from genteel conventions with roughened language and enlarged sympathies. But the best pursued wider, deeper agendas. They sought to capture the interplay of the new New York's enormous ensemble of social actors, to analyze its intersections of money, class, and power, to capture the nature of life in a modern capitalist city.

DREISER

In late November 1894, in the depths of the 1890s depression, Theodore Dreiser arrived in New York. He soon headed for City Hall Park, where he bulled his way into the *World* building, successfully evading the hired muscle who barred the doors of most Park Row newspapers, keeping desperate job seekers at bay. Once inside, he managed to land an unsalaried position as a space-rate reporter, paid by the column inch, on the strength of having served a lengthy journalistic apprenticeship in various midwestern cities.

Dreiser liked newsmen. He appreciated their cynical dissent from prevailing pieties. "One can always talk to a newspaper man," Dreiser would write, "with the full confidence that one is talking to a man who is at least free of moralistic mush."

His own life had rubbed him free of Victorian illusions. His family was grit-poor, his father a beaten man. The Dreisers were always on the move—being evicted or chasing cheaper rents—and ostracized as trash by "respectable" people. The slums of Terre Haute and Chicago taught him that life was hard, amoral, and indifferent to the individual—ideas reinforced by his readings of Spencer, Huxley, and Darwin.

Nevertheless, New York shocked him. "Nowhere before had I seen such a lavish show of wealth, or, such bitter poverty." On his "reporting rounds," Dreiser recalled, he was stunned by the numbers of "down-and-out men—in the parks, along the Bowery and in the lodging-houses that lined that pathetic street. They slept over gratings anywhere from which came a little warm air, or in doorways or cellar-ways," exhibiting a "dogged resignation to deprivation and misery."

He was astonished and "over-awed" by the "hugeness and force and heartlessness of the great city, its startling contrasts of wealth and poverty, the air of ruthlessness and indifference and disillusion that everywhere prevailed." Dreiser grew convinced that New York epitomized the Darwinian struggle for existence. In the "gross and cruel city" impersonal forces lifted up the arrogant rich; fire, disease, and winter storms carried off the shivering poor. He wondered why more New Yorkers didn't protest what Howells had called "the perpetual encounter of famine and of surfeit."

World work did not go well. He was given bottom-drawer assignments—covering suicides, Bellevue, the morgue—and not many of those, not enough to live on. "A crushing sense of incompetence and general inefficiency seemed to settle upon me, and I could not shake it off," he remembered. "Whenever I went out on an assignment—and I was always being sent upon those trivial, shoe-wearing affairs—I carried with me this sense of my unimportance." He began to worry he would wind up as yet another young man from the provinces who had been beaten down by the big city, like a character out of Balzac.

Theodore Dreiser, ca. 1907. (University of Pennsylvania, Rare Book & Manuscript Library Image Collections)

Around March 1895 he quit Pulitzer's paper. He tried writing fiction pieces and magazine articles but got nowhere. He rambled the streets with the throngs of depression-era itinerant poor, ate cheap at Child's, slept in flophouses. By May, nearly broke, he contemplated suicide. Then he was rescued by his brother Paul, a songwriter who composed for a start-up Tin Pan Alley firm that was then taking off, flush with profits from its hit ditty "The Sidewalks of New York." The Dreisers convinced the firm's principals to publish a monthly company magazine as a device for promoting its sheet music and to make Theodore the editor. *Ev'ry Month*—soon subtitled *The Woman's Magazine of Literature and Music*—was launched on October 1, 1895. Its mix of new sheet music—one could prop up the journal on the parlor piano's music rack—and poems, short stories, reviews of books (Crane, Cahan) and current New York plays was supplemented with editorial reflections from Dreiser.

These included ongoing observations about the city's rampant economic inequality. In an October 1896 piece he linked the fates of rich and poor, suggesting that wealth of the former was built on the labor of the latter. "Down in alleys and byways, in the shop and small dark chambers," he proposed, "are the roots of this luxurious high life," with the poor "starving and toiling the long year through, that carriages may roll and great palaces stand brilliant with ornaments." Dreiser did not attribute this state of affairs to the city's political economy; nor did he advance progressive or socialist proposals for the reformation or overthrow of capitalism. This was simply the way things were. Some were able to ruthlessly wield power and accumulate fortunes. Others either bore up under life's blows or went to the wall.

After nearly two years at the helm of *Ev'ry Month*, Dreiser moved on to full-time writing. He churned out pieces for the growing number of ten-cent magazines, concentrating on New York and New Yorkers, particularly successful ones. Indeed, of the almost 100 articles he published between the fall of 1897 and the fall of 1900, 30 appeared in a new magazine called *Success*, for which he interviewed Edison, Stieglitz, and his hero, Howells. His own fortunes rose as the city's economy revived. Making decent money, he got married at the end of 1898; the couple took an apartment on the Upper West Side at 6 West 102nd, and in the winter of 1899 he sat down to write a novel.

The plot of *Sister Carrie* drew heavily on the life of his sister Emma. She had had an affair with a married man, a cashier in a Chicago tavern. When his wife learned of the affair, he panicked, absconded with $3,500, and ran off with Emma to New York. In the book, it is George Hurstwood and Carrie Meeber who arrive at Grand Central Station.

It is soon clear to Hurstwood that, though a successful man in Chicago, "he would be an inconspicuous drop in an ocean like New York," a "common fish" in a sea "full of whales." His work schemes fall through. He indulges in Tenderloin dissipation, sinks into depression and impotence. He steps, as it were, on an escalator that glides slowly downward through layer below layer of metropolitan society, with Dreiser describing each meticulously.

The couple first move to a flat on 78th Street near Amsterdam Avenue, a bright new five-story building with steam heat, a call bell for the janitor, and a maid hired by the week. As circumstances straiten, they move to a cheaper, smaller flat on 13th Street, west of Sixth, a lesser but still respectable neighborhood. They scrimp, eat skimpier meals, wear shabbier clothes.

Hurstwood signs up as a scab during a Brooklyn trolley strike, is beaten by strikers, quits, subsides into immobility. Carrie leaves him. He moves to a third-rate Bleecker Street hotel with a moth-eaten lobby. He slips again, to a job in a hotel basement (and a bed in its attic). He notices a flaring announcement in the *World*—"80,000 people out of employment in New York this winter"—which "struck as a knife at his heart." He sinks farther down the island, to a Bowery lodging house. He begins begging. He joins the community of "pale, flabby, sunken-eyed, hollow-chested" bums—"a class which simply floats and drifts." He haunts the breadlines at the Sisters of Mercy and Fleischmann's bakery. Finally, during a lashing sleet storm, he takes a fifteen-cent flophouse room, stuffs its door cracks with his coat and vest, and turns on the gas without lighting it. His body is freighted off from the 26th Street pier to an unmarked grave in potter's field.

Long before Hurstwood hits the basement, Carrie has switched to the up escalator, having glimpsed high-life possibilities back on the Upper West Side, when a wealthy neighbor walked her around the Broadway shops and theaters and took her to Sherry's and the Plaza. She gets a job in the Casino chorus line (at $12 a week). She gets press attention and is promoted (salary $18). Her clothes improve. She leaves Hurstwood, moving up to a rented room on 17th Street. She's featured in magazines (salary $35). Her picture appears in a weekly. She transforms a bit part into a hit role. ($150 a week). Millionaires send mash notes. She moves to a showy new Seventh Avenue hotel, becomes a star, and finally settles into richly carpeted chambers in the newly erected Waldorf, snug against the storm that finishes off her former lover.

Carrie's success, perhaps even more than Hurstwood's nightmarish slide, contributed to the furor surrounding the novel's publication. Dreiser turned to the new firm of Doubleday, Page, which had published Frank Norris's daring *McTeague* the previous year, and indeed had hired him as a reader. Given Norris's enthusiasm, Walter Hines Page agreed to publish *Sister Carrie*. But when Frank Doubleday returned from Europe, he declared the book immoral and tried to kill the deal. Dreiser stood his legal ground, however, and the firm printed a grudging 1,000 copies in November 1900, of which only 456 sold. No surprise, given the majority of reviews. They condemned the book's dreary despair, its rejection of idealism, its condoning of unchastity, its crude characters, its use of colloquialisms. Given the prevailing taste for virtuous costume romances like *When Knighthood Was in Flower*, perhaps only Howells could have saved it. He demurred, unwilling to endorse a woman like Carrie Meeber.

DREISER CRUMBLED, TUMBLING INTO A DEPRESSION as deep as Hurstwood's. In an eerie recapitulation of his character's downward slide through the city, he and his wife moved in 1901 to a cheap apartment on East End Avenue and 82nd, overlooking gloomy Blackwell's Island, then to a 6' × 8' hall bedroom in a tattered rooming house at 113 Ross Street, near the Brooklyn Navy Yard. By 1903 he had lost twenty-nine pounds, his wife had left him, and he was hanging around the Wallabout Market, gleaning apples or potatoes that fell off wagons. Then he joined the lost souls in the Mills Hotel at 164 Bleecker, and was flirting with an East River suicide when his brother Paul again rescued him from the urban abyss, financing a five-week retreat at a sanitarium near White Plains. His wife rejoined him, and they moved to a modest apartment at 399 Mott Avenue in the Bronx.

In the decade following the *Carrie* catastrophe, Dreiser made a brilliant (if cynical) recovery by writing what the market would bear. He edited dime-novel cowboy thrillers for the Street & Smith publishing factory (whose unofficial motto was "The worse the swill, the more the public will buy"), and in 1905 was made editor of a new magazine called *Smith's*, which was aimed at "the every-day reader who seeks entertainment." In 1906 he jumpstarted the near-defunct *Broadway Magazine*, transforming that spicy rag into a respectable magazine featuring departments like "Beautiful Women of New York Society."

He and his wife moved again, to a larger apartment on Morningside Heights. In 1907, he took charge of the *Delineator*, a ladies' magazine put out by the Butterick Publishing

Company to boost sales of its fashion patterns. He rounded up genteel fiction (no slang, no coarseness) and corralled articles on homemaking, Santa Claus associations, pet animals, and the care and feeding of infants. (For the latter, he hired the childless H. L. Mencken, a Baltimore journalist who shared his contempt for bourgeois culture. Mencken began visiting New York regularly, dining with Dreiser at Luchow's when in town, and with Dreiser's help landed a spare-time job as book critic for the *Smart Set*.)

This idyll ended in 1910 when Dreiser was fired for ardent pursuit of the 17-year-old daughter of a coworker—not the sort of philandering that would have gone down well with the *Delineator*'s readership. Dreiser went back to full-time writing. The times seemed more propitious. He had gotten *Carrie* republished in 1907; this time it garnered respectful reviews and respectable sales. His *Jennie Gerhardt* (1911) and *Financier* (1912) did reasonably well. He discovered, moreover, a community of supporters among the rising generation who hailed him as a leader in the rebellion against literary conservatism.

He moved to West 10th Street and hovered on the fringe of the Greenwich Village scene. He went to the Anarchists Ball; cultivated Emma Goldman, Floyd Dell, and Hutchins Hapgood; joined the Liberal Club. When his flat was freezing he wrote in Polly's. He lauded the work of Henri and the Ash Can group and visited the studios of Everett Shinn and John Sloan to gather background for his next novel, *The "Genius"* (1915). This semi-autobiographical work tracked its realist painter protagonist from the Midwest to the bohemian Village, and dwelt at length on his sexual infidelities.

The "Genius" provoked a backlash. Genteel critics attacked its "Barbaric Naturalism." The thought police took note. Comstock's heir John S. Sumner toted up seventeen profane and seventy-five lewd passages, and in July 1916 his New York Society for the Suppression of Vice got the book banned as blasphemous and obscene. Dreiser's publisher, intimidated, recalled all copies.

Dreiser fought back, blasting "ignorant, impossible puritans." Mencken (who actually disliked the book) rallied 500 writers to defend the principle of literary liberty. Dreiser enlisted the radicals in the fight—Eastman, Dell, Rose Pastor Stokes—much to the annoyance of Mencken, who hated the "Washington Square mountebanks." Sumner was unmoved in his insistence that any book that might possibly corrupt a young girl should not be published. The book stayed banned, and Dreiser again stopped writing novels.[12] But if the legal superstructure supporting Victorian sensibilities still stood, it rested on badly weakened foundations.

WHARTON

Edith Wharton got a far different reception for a book that in some ways was remarkably similar to Dreiser's. It helped, of course, that she had started life at the opposite end of the social spectrum. Edith Newbold Jones was born into a family whose comfortable income from New York real estate holdings supported a Manhattan brownstone at 14 West 23rd street (just off Fifth Avenue and Madison Square Park), as well as summers in Newport, and extensive European travel. They moved in old New York's highest society, among a latticework of cousins that included Schermerhorns, Rhinelanders, and Gallatins.

But the Joneses failed to keep up with newer neighbors. The Vanderbilts and their ilk hopelessly inflated standards of wealth just as post–Civil War inflation was nibbling at the

---

12. Dreiser always felt himself to be a perilously perched visitor from the heartland. In 1913 he wrote: "I have lived in New York for years and years and yet I do not feel that it is My city. One always feels in New York, for some reason, as though he might be put out, or even thrown out."

Joneses' income. In 1866, to economize, the family leased their house and sailed for Europe, where they spent the next six years in cities like Rome, Paris, and Florence. They returned to New York in 1872, just before the economy tanked, and while their situation was anything but penurious, Edith's father was never completely free from money worries. When he died in 1880, Edith was bequeathed the income from $600,000 in property holdings, though the trust fund was controlled by her two brothers. Additional bequests would eventually bring her unearned income to $10,000 a year, enabling a handsomely affluent lifestyle.

To young Edith, old-monied New York—lower Fifth Avenue from Madison down to Washington Square—seemed confining and drab after the glories of European cities. Glancing backward she remembered "little low-studded rectangular New York, cursed with its universal chocolate-coloured coating of the most hideous stone ever quarried," as a "cramped horizontal gridiron of a town without towers, porticoes, fountains or perspectives, hidebound in its deadly uniformity of mean ugliness." Its "narrow houses so lacking in external dignity" were no better inside, with their interiors "crammed with smug and suffocating upholstery." As for the residents, they were distinguished more by their commitment to socializing than to social responsibilities; to birth and breeding rather than to ambition and accomplishment.

Edith wanted to be a writer, a socially dubious goal in her circles, but her parents indulged her, paying for discreet private printings of poetry and prose. In 1880 her brother sent some of her poems via an editor he knew to Henry Wadsworth Longfellow, who sent them to William Dean Howells, who published them in the highly respectable *Atlantic Monthly*. But she was now pushing up against the gender conventions of her conservative social strata. In 1882 she got betrothed to a young man due to inherit a vast fortune, though the engagement was broken off by his mother, a decision the elite gossip magazine *Town Topics* put down to "an alleged preponderance of intellectuality on the part of the intended bride."

Nor did she get respect from the man she did marry, three years later. Teddy Wharton was a jolly fellow—into shooting, fishing, wine, dogs, and horses—who lived off an allowance from his mother, and then off Edith's income. Teddy had no interest in ideas or writings, including those of his wife. Worse, her social circle ridiculed her career; some thought it disgraceful.[13] Wharton continued nevertheless to write small pieces, but most of her time was taken up in the ritual round of shopping, luncheons, teas, social calls, card-leaving, tedious dinners, balls, opera, theater, country weekends, and summers in Newport (where she was bored and unhappy). At her insistence the couple also spent several months in Europe every year between 1886 and 1897, principally Italy, and those were happier times, producing experiences from which she fashioned poems, stories, and articles that appeared in magazines like *Scribner's*. Still, in those first twelve years of her marriage, she was beset almost constantly by one or another recurrent illness—asthma, hay fever, bronchitis, exhaustion, nausea, depression—a sea of troubles she (and the era) labeled "neurasthenic."

She began to extract herself from her confining surroundings and to regain her health, partly by relocating. In 1891 the couple purchased a town house at Fourth Avenue and 78th Street (later 884 Park), on Lenox Hill, fifty-odd blocks north of Madison Square, which they redesigned, expanded, and occupied from 1897 as their winter home. She escaped from Newport by purchasing in 1901 113 acres near Lenox, in the Berkshire Hills of western Massachusetts, and thereon erecting a large house, The Mount, which they occupied in 1902. Edith would have lived there year-round, forgoing Gotham, but Teddy wanted to keep up his social life, which was centered in the city.

---

13. Whitman, for whose work she developed a great passion, was thought particularly shocking; *Leaves of Grass* was kept under lock and key in proper households and brought out, Wharton recalled, like tobacco, only in the absence of "the ladies."

More liberatory still were a string of literary accomplishments. In 1897 she published her first book, coauthored with architect Ogden Codman. *Decoration of Houses* was a critique of the interior arrangements of upper-class New York homes, like the one in which she'd been reared on West 23rd Street—cold formal homes of "exquisite discomfort." She loathed their Victorian stuffiness and clutter, advocating space and light instead. She also assaulted the new-monied's penchant for promiscuous eclecticism—Louis XV bedrooms, Queen Anne furniture, Renaissance ballrooms.

Even more life enhancing was her publication in 1899 of *The Greater Inclination*, her first book of stories, which "broke the chains which had held me so long in a kind of torpor." "For nearly twelve years," she related, "I had tried to adjust myself to the life I had led since my marriage; but now I was overmastered by the longing to meet people who shared my interests." She had decided that "the Land of Letters was henceforth to be my country, and I gloried in my new citizenship."

In 1902, accordingly, she sent Henry James a copy of *The Valley of Decision*, her recently published novel about the eighteenth-century Italian aristocracy. James praised it but encouraged her to focus on "the American subject." "Don't pass it by," he urged, "the immediate, the real, the one that's yours, the novelist it waits for. Take hold of it and keep hold, and let it pull you where it will." More exactly, he urged: "*Do New York!* The 1st-hand account is precious."

In 1905 Edith Wharton brought out *The House of Mirth*, a novel set almost entirely in Gotham. *Mirth* is a complex and capacious book in which a central concern is the clash of old

"Edith Wharton with Fur Collar and Muff," 1907. (University of Houston, Digital History)

and new New York. Wharton was interested less in physical than in social architecture, more concerned with the eruption of new wealth than the erection of new skyscrapers. In its own way *Mirth* is as much a work of exposure as the writings of her muckraker contemporaries— and perhaps even more incisive, for Wharton was poking behind the curtains of her own social world. Certainly few investigative journalists matched her caustic indictment of New York's rich, her excoriation of their mindless materialism and civic irresponsibility. And she was as ruthless as any investigating committee in laying bare hidden connections, revealing the interlocking directorates of Wall Street and Fifth Avenue. She was particularly attentive to interactions between the old-monied and the nouveaux riches. Analyzing their consumption patterns and mating rituals with an anthropological eye (she was taken with Thorstein Veblen's *The Theory of the Leisure Class* [1899]), she discerned both antagonism and accommodation.

Wharton's literary vehicles for exploring the changing topography of New York's elite were characters who, like Dreiser's, rode ascending and descending social escalators. (She admired *Sister Carrie.*) Here it is a woman on the downward course. Lily Bart, "a water-plant in the flux of the tides" is, like Hurstwood, a victim of implacable social forces. She was raised to be an exquisite ornament of genteel brownstone society. But her father goes bankrupt; her mother dies; her niggardly maiden aunt doles out funds and eventually disinherits her. Lily is left to circulate among her rich and fashionable friends and relations, serving as social secretary—a polite euphemism for tutoring ambitious arrivistes in how to spend their way into social acceptability. She also repeatedly makes halfhearted efforts to use her beauty and charm to snare a rich husband and thus become a social potentate in her own right. But just as repeatedly she balks, with varying degrees of self-awareness, in effect preferring to rent out her social skills and family connections, rather than sell herself as a commodity.

Her passed-up opportunities, coupled with betrayals by others—false accusations that blacken her reputation—send her spiraling downward through sequential social circles, with Wharton detailing each layer with great precision. In her heyday, Lily had been a favorite of European aristocrats: the Duchess of Beltshire had her to dine in Monte Carlo; Lady Skiddaw took her everywhere in Cannes; the Crown Princess of Macedonia had her stop for a week at Cimiez. She'd also been a fixture at the Fifth Avenue mansions, country houses, and private yachts of her Old Guard relations and connections the Tenors and Dorsets, descendants of the "well-fed and industrious stock of early New York," a class "who have always lived well, dressed expensively, and done little else." Then she drops to the more frankly pleasure-loving milieu of the Dormers, "a social outskirt which Lily had always fastidiously avoided" as being a "flamboyant copy of her own world, a caricature approximating the real thing as the 'society play' approaches the manners of the drawing-room." Nevertheless, it is a set of "rising consequence" and a source of income. She then slips down a notch to the milieu of Mrs. Hatch, whose circle live in the crudely opulent West Side apartment hotels—"a world over-heated, over-upholstered, and over-fitted with mechanical appliances for the gratification of fantastic requirements, while the comforts of a civilized life were as unattainable as in a desert."

She drops again, to the middle-class flat of Girty Fairish, a friend and social worker whose Girls Club offers shelter and support to poor women. This affords Lily her initial intimate contact with the working class. "She had always accepted with philosophic calm the fact that such existence as hers were pedestaled on foundations of obscure humanity," but this is the first time she "conceived of these victims of fate otherwise than in the mass." In an unusually philanthropic gesture, she pays for sending to a sanitarium a seduced and abandoned secretary who'd contracted tuberculosis.

Soon Lily herself falls to the "underworld of toilers," reduced to working in a fashionable millinery establishment, trimming hats destined for her former friends. She now lives in "a small private hotel" on the "edge of a fashionable neighborhood," with rooms that look out on "a sallow vista of brick walls and fire escapes," and a "dark restaurant" in which she takes her "lonely meals." This is in truth beyond her means, but it was "deemed of the utmost importance to keep up a show of prosperity." But then she is fired from her job—being hopelessly incompetent at any real-world occupation—and slides down yet farther (as had Dreiser) to the hall bedroom of a boardinghouse, with "blotched wallpaper and shabby paint," exposed to "the cries and rumblings" of a "New York street in the last stages of decline from fashion to commerce."

With her funds all but gone, Lily spends her days wandering the streets, and her nights drugging herself to sleep with chloral. One evening, exhausted and shivering, she rests on a bench in Bryant Park (Fifth Avenue and 41st Street), where she encounters Nettie Struthers, the girl whose treatment she had underwritten. Struthers takes her home to a tiny apartment, where she relates her return to health, her subsequent marriage to a solid workingman, and the birth of a daughter she has named in honor of Lily. Lily believes such a future is impossible for her—"I am a very useless person," she had explained to a friend earlier that day. "I was just a screw or a cog in the great machine I called life, and when I dropped out of it I found I was of no use anywhere else. What can one do when one finds that one only fits into one hole?" What Lily does is return to her solitary bed, and—carelessly? suicidally?—take a larger than usual dose and die.

LILY'S FALL IS COUNTERWEIGHTED BY SIMON ROSEDALE'S RISE. A Jewish financier, who "is mad to know the people who don't want to know him," Rosedale is at first shunned and treated with contempt. One socialite dismisses him as "the same little Jew who had been served up and rejected at the social board a dozen times." But he stages a masterly social ascent by "placing Wall Street under obligations which only Fifth Avenue could repay." A downward market lurch cuts into the income of the aristocrats, but Rosedale, who has presumably sold short, doubles his fortune. His seemingly magical touch (together with his affably offered market tips) sends his social stock soaring. All he needs now is "a wife whose affiliations would shorten the last tedious steps of his ascent."

Wharton herself shared the casual anti-Semitism of her characters, but she assigned Rosedale the attribute of honesty as well as vulgarity. He approaches Lily with an offer of marriage, presented bluntly as a business transaction. He would make her far richer than her enemies—"I'd put you where you could wipe your feet on 'em!"—in exchange for her helping him win social acceptance. "It takes just two things to do that, Miss Bart," Rosedale explains: "money, and the right woman to spend it." "I've got the money," he continued, "and what I want is the woman— and I mean to have her too." Lily is revulsed, but comes to appreciate his candor as her situation grows more desperate, yet by the time she decides to accept his offer, he withdraws it, as she is now damaged goods, and her sponsorship would impede his campaign, not advance it. Slowly, on his own hook, he begins to appear on municipal committees and charitable boards and gets invited to elite dinners, and "his candidacy at one of the fashionable clubs [is] discussed with diminishing opposition." In the end, among those "who rose to the surface with each recurring tide, and were either submerged beneath its rush or landed triumphantly beyond the reach of envious breakers," Rosedale is one of the winners.

THE HOUSE OF MIRTH WAS SERIALIZED in *Scribner's* over eleven months—its final installment in November was a national event—and coincident with the appearance of the book version. Scribner marketed it as an exposé, the book's wrapper declaring: "For the first time the veil has been lifted from New York society." Wharton protested vigorously; the publisher removed the offending text but kept feeding the press tidbits about the firsthand nature of her knowledge. The *New York Times Saturday Review of Books* ran a debate on whether or not *Mirth* had "Held New York Society up to Scorn," and though Wharton denied having done so, the book, with its myriad accounts of hypocrisy and heartlessness, cowardice and coarseness, pretentiousness and predatory sexuality, spoke for itself. Society was furious, though curious: Who was modeled on whom? Some genteel reviewers counterattacked, professing disgust at Wharton's having depicted such "vulgar, heartless, uninteresting, or immoral" characters. Others were taken aback by the author's gender politics. Wharton was no feminist, but her book was a patent indictment of constrictions on women.

Despite (or because of) such carping, *Mirth* was an instantaneous success. Most reviewers hailed it as an accomplished piece of fiction. It sold 30,000 copies in ten days. By year's end, there were 140,000 copies in print. It was the new century's first "serious book" blockbuster.

WHARTON REVISITED HER THEME in *Custom of the Country* (1913). Written during radicalism's high tide (though Wharton was no radical), her slashing attack on New York's elites was, in its own way, more telling than any *Masses* indictment or Village critique. There was nothing genteel about this ferocious work: "We move," said Henry James, "in an air purged at a stroke of the old sentimental and romantic values."

Custom's protagonist, the adventuress Undine Spragg, is a monstrous emblem of the prevailing pursuit of wealth and status. Undine (she's named for a hair-waver marketed by her father) is from Apex City, Kansas, the heartland of an America portrayed, with immense condescension, as provincial, vulgar, graceless, even grotesque. There Undine grows up dreaming of Fifth Avenue. "She knew all of New York's golden aristocracy by name, and the lineaments of its most distinguished scions had been made familiar by passionate poring over the daily press." Bereft of charm or cultivation—Wharton presents her as spoiled, ignorant, shallow, and amoral—she is well endowed with beauty and brass. Determined to infiltrate Gotham's "swell" society, she convinces her crude and complaisant parents to help mount an assault. They move to New York, establish a beachhead in the florid Hotel Stentorian on Central Park West, and spend two years plotting how to move across town: "Fifth Avenue is where she wanted to be!"

Her first conquest is Ralph Marvell, a Manhattan lawyer and occasional poet, who represents old and genteel New York. Marvell lives in Washington Square, which he calls a "Reservation" for "aboriginal" New Yorkers doomed to rapid extinction at the hands of the invading race of rich. Marvell is fond of prophesying that before long "its inhabitants would be exhibited at ethnological shows, pathetically engaged in the exercise of their primitive industries." Indeed, they have been complicit in turning over the keys to their city. "The daughters of his own race sold themselves to the Invaders; the daughters of the Invaders bought their husbands as they bought an opera-box. It ought all to have been transacted on the Stock Exchange."

Undine has not understood this. In distant Kansas she had bought into the myth of "old families" ruling Gotham "from a throne of Revolutionary tradition, with the new million-aires paying them feudal allegiance." She believes that in marrying Ralph she is lofting her-self to the apex of New York Society. But she comes to realize that the myth is "as obsolete as a mediaeval cosmogony." Washington Square, it transpires, has been superseded by "social systems far outside its ken, and as indifferent to its opinions as the constellations to the reck-onings of the astronomers; and all these systems joyously revolved about their central sun of gold." Undine had unwittingly "given herself to the exclusive and the dowdy when the future belonged to the showy and the promiscuous."

So she divorces Ralph and moves on; Marvell himself becomes extinct, committing sui-cide. After many adventures Undine pairs up with a leading Invader, Elmer Moffatt, who hails from her old hometown. One of the buccaneers boarding and seizing the city, Moffatt has advanced through bribery, blackmail, and corruption, up to stock speculation and corpo-rate reorganization. After pulling off the great "Apex consolidation," he has become a "bil-lionaire Railroad King." Among the wedding gifts he provides his new bride are "a necklace and tiara of pigeon-blood rubies belonging to Queen Marie Antoinette, a million dollar cheque," and a "new home, 5009 Fifth Avenue, which is an exact copy of the Pitti Palace, Florence." In the end, however, Undine remains restless. "She had everything she wanted, but she still felt, at times, that there were other things she might want if she knew about them."

DREAMS AND NIGHTMARES OF GREATER NEW YORK

Other writers joined Dreiser and Wharton in exploring the new New York by glissandoing fictional characters up and down the city's social keyboard.

In *The Rise of David Levinsky* (1917), the *Jewish Daily Forward* editor Abe Cahan tracks his immigrant hero's steady elevation. Levinsky arrives in 1885 with four cents to his name. He peddles baskets, remnants, and cheap hosiery. He sleeps in Bowery lodging houses or express-wagons on the streets. He becomes a machine operator in a cloak shop, then a petty garment manufacturer, then a grand factory owner with a magnificent establishment on Fifth Avenue near 23rd. As he grows rich he learns to eat in "high class restaurants" and "dress like a genteel American." He rises above people once "infinitely my superior," now "piteously beneath me."

In the end, however, though he's a millionaire tycoon—"one of the two or three leading men in the cloak-and-suit trade in the United States"—Levinsky is an unhappy man. His "sense of triumph," he admits, "is coupled with a brooding sense of emptiness and insignifi-cance, of my lack of anything like a great, deep interest." He envies "far more than I do a billionaire" those who've distinguished themselves in science, music, or art. "At the height of my business success I feel that if I had my life to live over again I should never think of a business career." He also feels cut off from his fellow immigrants: "I often long for a heart-to-heart talk with some of the people of my birthplace," he confesses. "I have tried to revive my old friendships with some of them, but they are mostly poor and my prosperity stands between us in many ways." Levinsky's commercial rise has been counterbalanced by a spirit-ual decline.

IN *THE SPORT OF THE GODS* (1902), Paul Laurence Dunbar—African American poet, novelist, and lyricist—charts the downward slide of three black southerners who seek refuge in the big city but are ruined by it instead. After emancipation, former slave Berry Hamilton works as a butler for a wealthy white man. He lives contentedly with his wife, Fannie, and two children, Joe and Kitty, on his employer's property, until he is falsely accused of stealing money. Convicted, he is sentenced to ten years hard labor. Fannie, Joe, and Kitty, evicted, and then ostracized by the small-town community, move far away, to New York's Tenderloin district. Dunbar's narrator observes that each is now at a fork in the road that every greenhorn confronts. After the first pangs of strangeness and homesickness, "the subtle, insidious wine of New York will begin to intoxicate him." At this point, "if he be wise, he will go away, any place,—yes, he will even go over to [New] Jersey." But "if he be a fool," he will stay on, "until the town becomes all in all to him; until the very streets are his chums and certain buildings and corners his best friends. Then he is hopeless, and to live elsewhere would be death."

Fannie suspects that there "could not be so many people together without a deal of wickedness," and she is soon proved right. Joe rapidly falls in with the wrong crowd, becoming a habitual gambler, a violent drunk, and eventually a murderer. He winds up jailed for life. Kitty becomes a successful singer and actress, but her character corrodes. Fannie, left alone, believing herself divorced, marries a wife-beater. Ultimately, Berry is exonerated and freed, travels to the big city, and is reunited with his wife (her new husband having been murdered at a racetrack), and they return, sans children, to their small-town existence in the South. Dunbar, speaking through a thinly disguised alter ego, summarizes the moral thusly: "Here is another example of the pernicious influence of the city on untrained negroes. Oh, is there no way to keep these people from rushing away from the small villages and country districts of the South up to the cities, where they cannot battle with the terrible force of a strange and unusual environment?" In a veiled nod to Jim Crow and mass lynchings, he admits "that the South has its faults—no one condones them—and its disadvantages, but that even what they suffered from these was better than what awaited them in the great alleys of New York. Down there, the bodies were restrained, and they chafed; but here the soul would fester, and they would be content."

A DECADE LATER, JAMES WELDON JOHNSON—Broadway lyricist, poet, diplomat, and future NAACP head—completed his novel *The Autobiography of an Ex-Colored Man* (1912), while finishing up his term as US consul in Nicaragua. He had the book published anonymously, by a small Boston firm, lest his diplomatic career be damaged by his story of a mulatto who passes as white.

At its beginning, Johnson's book seems like a replay of Dunbar's. On arriving in Gotham his unnamed narrator—born out of wedlock to a white Georgia gentleman and a light-skinned mulatto woman—is awed by the towers of Manhattan, shining "in a reflected light which gave the city an air of enchantment; and, truly, it is an enchanted spot." But this is not an endorsement. "New York City," he argues, "is the most fatally fascinating thing in America." It is a "great witch at the gate of the country, showing her alluring white face and hiding her crooked hands and feet under the folds of her wide garments—constantly enticing thousands from far within, and tempting those who come from across the seas to go no farther. And all these become the victims of her caprice." True, not all are immediately doomed: "Some she at once crushes beneath her cruel feet; others she condemns to a fate like that of galley slaves; a few she favors and fondles, riding them high on the bubbles of fortune; then with a sudden breath she blows the bubbles out and laughs mockingly as she watches them fall."

As had Dunbar's Joe, Johnson's narrator soon begins to "feel the dread power of the city; the crowds, the lights, the excitement, the gaiety." He, too, heads for the Tenderloin, becomes addicted to gambling, and begins to lead a dissolute life. But Johnson's narrator is saved from perdition by discovering an alternative to casinos. "The Club" (modeled on Ike Hines's West 27th Street establishment) is a "center of colored Bohemians and sports," and is suffused with a novel music. Having been trained as a classical pianist, the narrator is enthralled to discover ragtime, and over the next year his talent and determination spare him the need "to depend entirely upon the caprices of fortune at the gambling table": "I developed into a remarkable player of ragtime; indeed, I had the name at the time of being the best ragtime-player in New York." Whites as well as blacks flock to the club in large measure to hear him. Among them is an unnamed millionaire, who invites him to perform at a party for rich society figures. At first blasé, they are soon electrified, especially when he rags Mendelssohn's "Wedding March." The Tenderloin has arrived on Fifth Avenue.

Wealthy white women are also drawn to the club—for the music and to meet black lovers. One attractive and cultured woman, who has been seeing a man the narrator called "a surly black despot," begins to flirt with the narrator. Her black companion arrives, takes out a re-volver, and shoots the woman in the neck. The narrator flees the scene. Making his way west to Eighth Avenue, he heads down to 23rd Street, circumnavigating the Tenderloin, and then walks east across town until he reaches Fifth Avenue, where, by chance, his "millionaire friend" is passing in a cab. The narrator accepts his friend's offer to join him on an extended stay in Europe, where his ragtime virtuosity makes him a star in white society.

Eventually he decides he wants to return to the United States and compose music that is influenced by African American folk music. He travels throughout the rural South, "jotting down in my note-book themes and melodies, and trying to catch the spirit of the Negro in his relatively primitive state." Yet after he sees a black man doused with gasoline and burned alive by a white mob, a great wave of humiliation and shame sweeps over him: "Shame that I belonged to a race that could be so dealt with; and shame for my country, that it, the great example of democracy to the world, should be the only civilized, if not the only state on earth, where a human being would be burned alive." He gives up the idea of becoming a "colored composer"—and gives up being colored, too. He returns to Gotham as an "ex-colored man."

Becoming a real estate speculator, he makes pots of money and mixes with wealthy New Yorkers who have no idea he isn't white. He proposes marriage to a blond, blue-eyed woman, "as white as a lily," first confessing his genetic inheritance. She cringes initially ("the only time in my life that I ever felt absolute regret at being colored, that I cursed the drops of African blood in my veins and wished that I were really white"), but love triumphs. They have two children. She dies. He continues to pass, for his children's sake. ("There is nothing I would not suffer to keep the 'brand' from being placed on them.") But he is unhappy. Like Cahan's David Levinsky, he's given up his heritage (in this case racial, in Levinsky's ethno-religious) and deprived his children of theirs. His final words: "I cannot repress the thought, that, after all... I have sold my birthright for a mess of pottage."

COINCIDENTAL CONNECTION BETWEEN INDIVIDUALS normally at seriously separate social lo-cations also plays an important role in the work of William Sidney Porter, who arrived in New York in 1902, fresh from a three-year stretch in an Ohio pen for embezzlement. Fearing exposure as an ex-con, he lived anonymously, indeed pseudonymously—his most famous but by no means only pen name being O. Henry. Before dying of acute alcoholism in 1910, he churned out 272 adroit short stories, nearly 100 of them set in the city. Written for the *World's* Sunday supplement, and for popular magazines like *Everybody's* and *McClure's*, many were sheaved into volumes like *The Four Million* (1906)—its title an intended contrast with Mrs. Astor's "Four Hundred," the city's top 0.0001 percent.

Porter's fiction prowls the city's lower depths: the dance halls and dives of Hell's Kitchen, the Tenderloin, and the Bowery; the seedy rooming houses of the Lower West Side that housed the drifting and defeated. He wrote about New York's "little" people—hat pressers and soda jerkers, taxi drivers and bums. He paid particular and sympathetic attention to women locked into tedious jobs (waitresses, laundresses, typists, department store salesgirls), and preyed upon by employers. Porter's New York, like Dreiser's, is bleak, a "great cold city of stone and iron." It is also like "a monstrous quicksand, shifting its particles constantly, with no foundation, its upper granules of to-day buried to-morrow in ooze and slime."

But Porter was ultimately a romantic, a crafter of sentimental tales for a mass audience, and he rescues his sad and lonely isolates by connecting them with one another, or those higher up the social ladder, through the magic of coincidence. An adventurous piano salesman meets (and saves) a starving shopgirl through the fortuitous medium of an advertising card. A newspaper is blown hither and thither through the city streets, threading together a half-dozen individuals featured in its text. Tailor's apprentice Ikey Snigglefritz shakes the hand of Boss Billy McMahan, who shakes the hand of rich reformer Cortlandt Van Duyckink, who, on sudden impulse, while driving down Delancey, steps out and shakes the hand of Ikey Snigglefritz.

In some stories, O. Henry suggests it's possible to re-see the city through the eyes of another. In "Brickdust Row," a snotty young slumlord named Blinker hops the boat for Coney Island, out of boredom. On board he falls for Florence, a plucky hat trimmer (Lily Bart's job), who agrees to accompany him on his initial visit. At first Blinker is appalled. "Hoi polloi trampled, hustled and crowded him. Basket parties bumped him; sticky children tumbled, howling, under his feet, candying his clothes. Insolent youths strolling among the booths with hard-won canes under one arm and easily won girls on the other, blew defiant smoke from cheap cigars into his face." He is dismayed to see "the mob, the multitude, the proletariat shrieking, struggling, hurrying, panting, hurling itself in incontinent frenzy, with unabashed abandon, into the ridiculous sham palaces of trumpery and tinsel pleasures." The vulgarity of it, "its brutal overriding of all the tenets of repression and taste that were held by his caste, repelled him strongly."

Then, "by some miracle he suddenly saw Coney aright. . . . Counterfeit and false though the garish joys of these spangled temples were, he perceived that deep under the gilt surface they offered saving and apposite balm and satisfaction to the restless human heart." Blinkers removed, Coney was Romance, a "flight of Adventure," a "magic carpet that transports you to the realms of fairyland." He no longer saw a rabble but "his brothers seeking the ideal."

Then Blinker's new way of seeing smacks up against the windshield of reality. As he escorts Florence home, he discovers that she lives in one of his own tawdry and crumbling brick row houses, the very houses to which his attorney has been calling attention for five years. "There is something wrong; there is something wrong," he mutters on his way home, and the next day he washes his hands of further responsibility. "Do what you please with it," he tells the lawyer. "Remodel it, burn it, raze it to the ground. But, man, it's too late I tell you. It's too late. It's too late. It's too late." With this he leaves town (and, presumably, Florence as well). His sentimental holiday has come to an abrupt end. A momentary spark of empathy between distantly placed individuals can be all too rapidly extinguished.

A MORE SUSTAINABLE RE-SEEING IS ACHIEVED by Billy, protagonist of Ernest Poole's *The Harbor* (1915). This is in part because the object of his attention—New York's seaport—is itself undergoing a mammoth transformation, and in part because powerful personal and political forces spur his revaluation.

Poole—settlement worker, socialist, A Club member, and journalist of the Russian Revolution—introduces Billy as a child growing up in a Brooklyn Heights brownstone overlooking the harbor. Below lies the warehouse run by his father, a small businessman whose career had begun in the 1850s, when graceful clipper ships ruled the waves. Like his father, Billy finds only ugliness in the grimy new era of iron steamers, an antipathy exacerbated by his years in college, and then in Paris, pursuing Culture. Worse still, his father gets submerged in the wave of consolidations transforming the waterfront. Frozen out of business by a giant corporation that buys up two miles of docks and warehouses, including his, he becomes a hireling in his own former concern. Billy works there, too, but on the side begins writing magazine articles about the harbor.

At this point Billy comes under the spell of Mr. Dillon, father of a girl with whom he's fallen in love. Dillon is an engineer who's been hired by financiers to rationalize the port's facilities. He takes Billy on an aquatic tour of the harbor and lays out his plan to merge the welter of competing shipping firms, docks, and rail lines—currently "each for himself in a blind struggling chaos"—into a single planned, rational system. The goal is a unified New York Harbor, serving "a vast fleet of Yankee ships that should drive the surplus output of our teeming industries into all markets of the world."[14] As the boat rounds the Battery, they come upon "the skyscraper group, the homes of the Big Companies." Dillon explains that "in all you'll see while exploring the wharves, you'll find some string that leads back here. And you don't want to let that worry you. Let the muck-rakers worry and plan all they please," but the truth is that "there are men up there in Wall Street without whose brains no big thing can be done in this country. I'm working under their order and some day I hope you'll be doing the same. For they don't need less publicity, but more." Billy joins Dillon in worshipping "a new god, and its name was Efficiency." He begins writing puff pieces (as had Dreiser) profiling the rich and successful.

But Billy runs into his old college chum Joe Kramer, who has become one of those muckrakers Dillon alluded to. He's worked as a ship's stoker to ascertain conditions below decks, and is now helping organize a general strike in the Port of New York. He wants Billy to write a profile of Jim Marsh, the famous strike leader (modeled on Big Bill Haywood), who is, after all, also a "success," a "successful revolutionist." To provide background, Joe takes Billy on a harrowing tour of the hideous lower depths where men stoke the ship's engine with coal. This, together with the tremendous number of casualties among dockworkers, opens Billy's eyes to the effects of Dillon's system on the harbor's working class, and he becomes radicalized as a result.

Billy acts as publicity man for the walkout and helps organize a march of strikers along upper Fifth Avenue. (Here Poole drew on his own experience working on the Paterson strike and pageant.) "All around me as I marched," Billy recounts, "I heard an unending torrent of voices speaking many languages, uniting in strange cheers and songs brought from all over

---

14. New York, Billy says Dillon told him, "had developed its waterfront pell mell, each railroad and each ship line grabbing sites for its own use, until the port was now so clogged, so tangled and congested that it was able to grow no more. . . . Within a few years the Big Ditch would open across Panama, and the commerce of South America, together with that of the Orient, would pour into the harbor here to meet the westbound commerce of Europe. Ships of all nations would steam, through the Narrows, and we must be ready to welcome them all, with an ample generous harbor worthy of the world's first port. 'To get ready,' he said, 'what we've got to do is to organize this port as a whole, like the big industrial plant it is.'"

the ocean world." There was "no separation of races, all walked together in dense crowds, the whole strike family was here." The Harbor had come to Fifth Avenue.

The strike is broken by the men in the skyscrapers, but Billy's transformation is complete. "The last of my gods, Efficiency, whose feet had stood firm on mechanical laws and in whose head were all the brains of all the big men at the top, had now come tottering crashing down. And in its place a huge new god, whose feet stood deep in poverty and in whose head were all the dreams of all the toilers of the earth."

UPTON SINCLAIR, ANOTHER MUCKRAKER TURNED NOVELIST, had become a superstar after the tremendous reception accorded *The Jungle* (1906). Then he cast about for his next subject. "Do New York!" Arthur Brisbane told him—in essence Henry James's counsel to Wharton. Brisbane, managing editor of Hearst's flagship *New York Evening Journal*, had nearly gotten the naïve author to let the *Journal* run *The Jungle* excerpts free of charge. Sinclair's agent found out just in time to scuttle the deal and win a hefty payment for his client. But Brisbane took a liking to Sinclair and, whether out of generosity or mischievousness, suggested he write about the jungle that was Gotham's high society. He jump-started the project by inviting Sinclair to his country estate in Hempstead, Long Island, and introducing him to Alva Belmont. She proceeded, perhaps for her own amusement, to ply the notorious radical with racy stories about the haut monde, and introduced him to other grande dames with tales to tell. While the ladies briefed Sinclair about life on upper Fifth Avenue, other Brisbane contacts, including some of New York's leading corporate lawyers, were giving the charming revolutionary the lowdown on lower Manhattan. The stories thus gleaned became the basis for *The Metropolis* (1908), a scathing portrait of life among Gotham's rich and famous.

The plot of *Metropolis* is but a clothesline on which Sinclair hangs depictions and denunciations of elite customs and morals. His hero, Allan Montague, a 30-year-old lawyer from Mississippi, moves to New York to join his younger brother, Oliver, who had arrived several years earlier and wormed his way into the upper strata. Oliver introduces Allan (and the reader) to their members' world. Sinclair describes their homes, furniture, clothes, and objets d'art with the precision of an estate auctioneer pricing a decedent's possessions. He totes up the vast sums they lay out on sumptuous dinners, and costly toys (fancy cars, private trains) with which to relieve their ennui. He catalogs, too, their debauched lifestyle (alcoholism, affairs) and depraved characters (malicious, shallow).

The book was widely panned, more on literary than political grounds. The characters were "lifeless puppets"; the book was "more a travelogue than a novel." As a satirist of society Sinclair was declared "hopelessly out of it," especially (noted the *Times* critic) as the curious could more profitably turn to "Mrs. Wharton to picture social shortcomings," as well as to a host of lesser writers who had produced "fresh and entertaining studies of contemporary extravagance and vanity."

Sinclair's assessments had also been preceded by those of Veblen, who had underscored the functionality of conspicuous consumption, seeing "honorific waste" as an ancient and commonplace way that elites displayed power. But Sinclair, who had indeed studied Veblen, did not accept the archaic roots of rich New Yorkers' behavior. He argued instead that the fops of Fifth Avenue were quite specifically aping the ways of European aristocrats, and thus undermining American republicanism, which in 1776 had broken with the legatees of English feudalism. Fawning over French aristocrats was even more objectionable: Frenchiness stood for luxury and lust; French phrases used in conversation denoted affectation and effeminacy. The American rich were all the more dangerous as, in Sinclair's opinion, they had become what Jefferson had warned against: "an Aristocracy, founded on banking institutions and monied incorporations," with a predilection for parasitic stock market speculation or manipulation. Sinclair was actively involved in Socialist Party politics, though *The Metropolis* advocated not revolution but a revival of republican virtue.

A similar perspective marked Sinclair's sequel, *The Moneychangers* (also 1908), a fictionalized rendering of the just-concluded Panic of 1907. Here Sinclair portrays the panic as the fruit of a wicked conspiracy led by J. P. Morgan. Dan Waterman, Sinclair's stand-in for Morgan, is depicted as a villainous monster; all that's missing is a mustache to twirl. Waterman's plot to disrupt the American economy is driven not only by voracious greed but by sexual rapacity. He attempts to rape a young woman who refuses to be his mistress, but she is saved by Allan Montague, whom Sinclair ports over from the previous volume. Montague helps expose the conspiracy by aiding an investigative journalist (and former steeplejack) who rappels down a rope, dangled from their hotel window, to spy on the room below where Waterman, in secret conclave with fellow conspirators, is laying out his plan to throw the nation into turmoil.

Sinclair noted in his book prospectus that this melodramatic scene "will make a very effective story for [moving] picture purposes," but not only was there no movie, there was nearly no book. None of the major publishers in New York would bring it out; only a third-rate outfit took it on. Reviewers dismissed the novel as labored and incoherent; some thought it so turgid that they begged him to quit writing fiction; and many now wrote off the admired author of the *Jungle* as a crude propagandist.

Sinclair himself thought the book was weak, though its limitations were to some degree inherent in the genre within which he worked. Nineteenth-century popular fiction had often depicted financial panics as the deliberate work of a cabal of bankers, and in an era of buccaneer capitalism—Drew, Fisk, and Gould, et al.—this seemed a not implausible proposition. The transition from competitive to corporate capitalism, and the emergence of Wall Street bankers as organizers of the industrial economy, created new facts on the ground. On the one hand, the tremendous concentration of power gave even greater cause for worry about individual malfeasance. But on the other, the magnitude and complexity of the new economy seemed to transcend the ability of any set of actors to control it. By deploying melodrama (albeit heavy-handedly) Sinclair was implicitly insisting that financial crises were not systemic—inherent by-products of the capitalist accumulation process—but rather the consequence of machinations by Wall Street insiders. This assessment of causation affected what could be done about them. If panics were attributable to greedy financiers, their makers could be exposed and held morally accountable or criminally liable. If they were rooted in the larger economic order, citizens would have to undertake the more difficult and perhaps impossible task of either reversing the incorporation process (as populist writers desired), or putting the management or regulation of corporations in the hands of "the people" (as socialists or progressives urged). Sinclair favored the former approach—exposing the greedy, in effect the muckraker strategy—but argued that the willingness of many otherwise virtuous citizens to punish the guilty was undermined by their own complicity in the new order through the purchase of stocks. Sinclair's proposed solution was abstinence—the middle class should just get out of the market—a measure of dubious feasibility.

POPULAR WRITERS OVER THE PREVIOUS HALF CENTURY had imagined a more fantastic solution to the concentration of power in Wall Street, which was to fictionally blow it to kingdom come, and its host city with it. The apocalyptic tradition in American literature, the idea of purging the land with blood and building a better society on the ruins of the old, had produced scores of works depicting the destruction of New York City. The twentieth century brought a new crop of bloody-minded novels, often focusing on the new skyscrapers as lighting rods for disaster.

In January 1912 "The Last New Yorkers: A Weird Story of Love and Adventure in the Ruins of a Fallen Metropolis" began running in the *Cavalier*, one of Frank Munsey's pulp fiction magazines. Its eventual 103 episodes were also syndicated in the *New York Evening Mail*, and brought out as a trilogy of volumes (in 1912, 1913, and 1914) under the collective title of *Darkness and Dawn*. Its author was George Allan England, a staggeringly prolific and wildly popular writer. England, an army chaplain's son, had worked his way through Harvard and taken a job at a New York insurance company, but the onset of tuberculosis forced him to quit and retreat to his wife's childhood home in Maine. While recovering, he started producing magazine pieces (he sold his first story in 1903) and went on to churn out 300 short stories, twenty-five serials, eleven books, and innumerable newspaper and magazine articles, including works of science fiction, adventure, romance, travel—and socialism. England joined the Socialist Party, wrote pamphlets such as *Get Together!* (brought out by socialist publisher Gaylord Wilshire in 1908), and eventually received the party's nomination as candidate for governor of Maine in 1912. His novel *The Air Trust* (1915), about a capitalist's plot to corner the market in oxygen, was illustrated by John Sloan and dedicated to Eugene Debs.

Darkness and Dawn is a genre crossover, a mix of science fiction and socialist pamphlet. It begins with the hero and heroine—brainy engineer Allan Stern and his beauteous stenographer, Beatrice Kendrick—awakening from a millennium or so of suspended animation on the forty-eighth floor of the ruins of the Metropolitan Life Tower (in 1912 still the tallest building in the world). Climbing up to the observation platform, they see the forest-blanketed remains of Gotham: "Dead lay the city, between its rivers, whereon now no sail glinted in the sunlight, no tug puffed vehemently with plumy jets of steam, no liner idled at anchor or nosed its slow course out to sea." They surmise that they are the only survivors of some immense "world-ruin"; in episode 33 they discover it was an explosion that blew most of the Midwest (including Chicago) into orbit, and released poisonous gases into the atmosphere, gases that, happily, hadn't risen high enough to finish off the duo in their eyrie.

Allan, foraging for food and tools and, soon, weapons, explores the ruins while Beatrice sets about making "a real home out of the barren desolation of the fifth floor offices." But soon trouble arrives, Big Trouble, borne across the Hudson from New Jersey in thousands of canoes. It is the "Horde," the monstrous offspring of centuries of degeneration and miscegenation between the apes and nonwhite populations that also survived the catastrophe—and now, tom-toms beating, besiege them in their tower.

While they peer down at the newcomers in "Madison Forest," the couple speculate at length about their adversaries' color and nature. "Perhaps all the white and yellow peoples perished utterly in the cataclysm, leaving only a few scattered blacks," says Allan. "You know blacks are immune to several germ-infections that destroy other races," he adds. "Yes," says Beatrice. "And you mean—?" Indeed, says Allan, "it's quite possible these fellows are the far-distant and degenerate survivors of that other time." "So the whole world [says Beatrice] may have gone to pieces the way Liberia and Haiti and Santo Domingo once did, when white rule ceased?" Yes, Allan muses, probably the "degenerating people" left the city ruins, which they could not rebuild, all the while "going down, down, back toward the primeval state, down through barbarism, through savagery," and eventually to mating with animals, becoming "malformed human members, black and bestial," cannibal ape-men. Allan, the narrator

At any moment now, one of the gray devils might hurl itself at their throats. And once the taste of blood lay on those crimson tongues — good-bye!

See page 203

"At any moment now, one of the gray devils might hurl itself at their throats." George Allan England, *Darkness and Dawn: Illustrated*, 1914.

tells us, "realized now that he was in the presence of an unknown semi-human type, different in all probability from any that had ever yet existed. It was less their bestiality that disgusted him, than their utter, hopeless, age-long degeneration from the man-standard."[15]

Using the latest destructive technology—Pulverite bombs—Allan is able to destroy many of the Horde, yielding an "indistinguishable mass of ruin and of death." Still, masses remain, but then, amazingly, "thousands on thousands of the little monstrosities, fell prone and grovelling. Their hideous masklike faces hidden, there they lay on the moss and all among the undergrowth, the trampled, desecrated, befouled undergrowth of Madison Forest." Allan exults: "Gods! Gods we are now to them—to such of them as may still live. Gods we are; gods we shall be forever! The Great White Gods of Terror!"

Once the ape-men are annihilated or subdued, the new Adam and Eve set out to reconstitute civilization on the ruins of the past. They will build a cooperative commonwealth where "labor reaps its full reward": "The race of men, our race, must live again—shall live! . . . Once

---

15. This fleshed-out fantasy version of the nightmares of Madison Grant and Lothrop Stoddard was a commonplace in pulp magazines, which thrived on narratives of lost white races that had degenerated, sometimes by mating with apes. England was Munsey's second-biggest best seller, but pride of place went to Edgar Rice Burroughs, whose *Tarzan and the Apes* (with a different take on interspecies relationships) was running serially at virtually the same time.

more shall cities gleam and tower....A kinder and a saner world this time. No misery, no war, no poverty." (No people of color, no New Women.)

ANOTHER IMAGINED GLOBAL HOLOCAUST, STRIPPED OF HAPPY ENDING, flowed from the pen of H. G. Wells, who in *War of the Worlds* (serialized in 1897) had limned an invasion by Martians, and in 1908, in *The War in the Air*, conjured up an all-human conflagration, beginning with the destruction of New York City.

In Wells's book, the powerful nations of Europe, North America, and Asia have spent the first decades of the twentieth century secretly developing large forces of blimp-like "flying machines," and are preparing for war. The first move is made by Germany. Led by the bellicose Prince Karl Albert (who bears more than passing resemblance to Kaiser Wilhelm II), Germany sets out to force the United States, which has thwarted its imperial ambitions in South America, to abandon the Monroe Doctrine. The Prince takes direct command of the nation's air armada and, after sinking the American Atlantic Fleet—putting paid to the era of battleships—the great dirigibles, emblazoned with black iron crosses, carry on to New York. Flying in a flattened V at 12,000 feet, hence impervious to the ground fire coming from Staten Island, the airships come to rest over Jersey City. "There the monsters hung, large and wonderful in the evening light, serenely regardless of the occasional rocket explosions and flashing shell-bursts in the lower air." Millions watch from below, jammed onto river piers and Battery Park and Central Park and the cross-river bridges. From above, the occupants of the airships stare down at the tall buildings and mono-railways and crawling cars, "its collective effect so pacifically magnificent, that to make war upon it seemed incongruous beyond measure." But then three of the dark-hulled ships drop rapidly and noiselessly to hover over the Navy Yard, Brooklyn Bridge, and City Hall, while two more float over "the great business buildings of Wall Street and Lower Broadway." Then, all five off-load their bombs, with horrific effect. The main Post Office, adjacent to City Hall, which had housed a great multitude of workers, including many girls and women, is now a smoldering ruin, into which "volunteers with white badges entered behind the firemen, bringing out the often still living bodies, for the most part frightfully charred." Mayor O'Hagen, at the urging of "the terror-stricken property owners of lower New York," and with the consent of the White House, orders a white flag be flown from the Park Row skyscraper, then negotiates the terms of capitulation.

The surrender rouses the population's patriotic fury. " 'No!' cried New York, waking in the dawn. 'No! I am not defeated.' " Now "humming like a hive of bees—of very angry bees," an insurrectionary movement breaks out, manifested first by the "appearance in the morning sunlight of American flags at point after point above the architectural cliffs of the city." A party of young men hoist an artillery piece to the tenth floor of a building in Union Square. When the *Wetterhorn* drifts at quarter speed over Tiffany's pinnacles, the hidden one-gun battery fires two shells, and the "airship crumpled up like a can that had been kicked by a heavy boot, her forepart came down in the square, and the rest of her length, with a great snapping and twisting of shafts and stays, descended, collapsing athwart Tammany Hall."

The enraged Prince now orders a merciless bombardment of lower Manhattan, directing the air fleet to proceed in a column over Broadway, the *Vaterland* leading. There ensues "one of the most cold-blooded slaughters in the world's history, in which men who were neither excited nor, except for the remotest chance of a bullet, in any danger, poured death and destruction upon homes and crowds below." Sailing along, the airships "smashed up the city as a child will scatter its cities of brick and card." Below, "they left ruins and blazing conflagrations and heaped and scattered dead; men, women, and children mixed together as though they had been no more than Moors, or Zulus, or Chinese. Lower New York was soon a furnace of crimson flames, from which there was no escape. Cars, railways, ferries, all had ceased, and never a light lit the way of the distracted fugitives in that dusky confusion but the light of burning.... Dust and black smoke came pouring into the street, and were presently shot with red flame."

New York, Wells explains, "was the first of the great cities of the Scientific Age to suffer by the enormous powers and grotesque limitations of aerial warfare. She was wrecked as in the previous century endless barbaric cities had been bombarded, because she was at once too strong to be occupied and too undisciplined and proud to surrender in order to escape destruction."

And Gotham is just the beginning. The enraged Americans strike back at the Germans with their own secret weapons. France and England unveil huge fleets of deadly long-range airships. Berlin, London, and Paris all suffer the fate of New York. Then, while the Americans and their European allies are preoccupied with an attack on the "aerial Gibraltar" that the Germans have established at Niagara Falls, thousands of Japanese and Chinese airships suddenly darken the sky. The "Confederation of Eastern Asia" (China and Japan) has secretly been building a massive air force, and tensions between them and the United States, fueled by American denial of citizenship to Asian immigrants, lead to war. As one character exclaims, "The Yellow Peril was a peril after all!" The conflict escalates into a full-scale world war, accompanied by financial panic, famine, and pestilence. Modern civilization collapses; mankind slips into a new Dark Age.

Early in the novel, Wells's narrator muses on why New York had been targeted, apart from being the premiere city of the obstreperous USA, which had been standing in the way of Germany's manifest destiny. One suggestion is that in the head of Prince Karl Albert "were the vapours of romance: he was a conqueror, and this was the enemy's city. The greater the city, the greater the triumph." And Gotham was "the largest, richest, in many respects the most splendid, and in some the wickedest, city the world had ever seen. She had long

"As the airships sailed along they smashed up the city." H. G. Wells, *The War in the Air*, 1908.

ousted London from her pride of place as the modern Babylon, she was the centre of the world's finance, the world's trade, and the world's pleasure; and men likened her to the apocalyptic cities of the ancient prophets."

But New York was also a soft target. The city was utterly unprepared for the attack. "For many generations New York had taken no heed of war, save as a thing that happened far away, that affected prices and supplied the newspapers with exciting headlines and pictures." Its citizens "felt as secure as spectators at a bullfight." They "thought America was safe amidst all this piling up of explosives."

And then suddenly, "into a world peacefully busied for the most part upon armaments and the perfection of explosives, war came; came the shock of realising that the guns were going off, that the masses of inflammable material all over the world were at last ablaze."

PART FIVE

WARS

23

Over There?

PANIC AND PARALYSIS

The assassination of Archduke Franz Ferdinand of Austria by Serbian conspirators on June 28, 1914, had little immediate impact in New York. Virtually no one believed it would lead to a general European conflagration. But over the next month, state alliances clicked into place, like tumblers in a lock, and hell was loosed upon the earth.

On July 28 Austria-Hungary declared war on Serbia. On July 31 Russia, an ally of Serbia, mobilized its armed forces. The following day Germany declared war on Russia. On August 3 Germany declared war on France, a belligerency immediately reciprocated. On August 4 Germany invaded neutral Belgium, hoping to outflank the French army; in response, Britain entered the melee; and the United States declared its neutrality. On August 6 Austria-Hungary declared war on Russia, while Serbia followed suit against Germany. And on August 7 the first full blooded clash between French and German forces got under way.

In Gotham during these early days, great crowds thronged nightly in Herald and Times Squares to follow the breaking news posted on big red-lettered sheets hung in the windows of the great newspapers. An estimated 300,000-plus jammed Times Square on August 4 when a *Times* bulletin announced England had declared war on Germany. Many citizens of combatant countries who were resident in the United States were reservists in their respective armies and navies. Called to the colors, thousands besieged their consulates—most of which were clustered near Bowling Green—to sign up for a return to fight. Hundreds formed

"At German Consulate," enlisting, April–May 1914. (Library of Congress Prints and Photographs Division, George Grantham Bain Collection)

up in impromptu parades, singing anthems and waving national flags. On August 3 Germans trooped up Broadway singing "Die Wacht am Rhein," and French and Slavic reservists marched through downtown, belting out "The Marseillaise."

Though the gatherings were pacific, Mayor Mitchel, fearing disorder, issued a proclamation. "The population of this city," he declared on August 6, embraced "people of German, of French, of English, of Italian, of Austrian, and of Russian blood." Therefore, as "public demonstrations of sympathy by people of a particular race, while natural from their point of view, are calculated to breed ill feeling upon the part of their fellow-citizens of other blood and sympathies," such gatherings should "not take place in this cosmopolitan and entirely neutral city."

FOR ALL THIS TURMOIL IN THE STREETS, the first impact of the Great War had slammed into Gotham days before the serial declarations had been issued. The epicenter of upheaval lay a few blocks north of the Bowling Green consulates, at the corner of Wall and Broad, where sat the New York Stock Exchange and the Sub-Treasury building, on whose steps George Washington's statue stood sentinel. The dramatis personae were not would-be sailors and soldiers but civilian bankers and brokers. They had raced back to town from their summer verandas to deal with a crisis that threatened to topple the financial architecture of the United States.

Before their armies engaged, Europe's frantic combatants-to-be sought desperately to fill their vaults with gold, the wherewithal of war. But in pursuing this objective they brought on a panic that swamped their financial markets. To augment their stores of precious metal they began a pell-mell sell-off of the American stocks and bonds they had accumulated over decades. Paced by Britain, France, and Germany, Europeans had poured capital into industrializing the United States, underwriting its railroads and factories and mills and mines. By 1914 they held (very roughly) $4 billion worth of securities, which they now hurried to convert into cash.[1] But dumping vast quantities of stocks pummeled their prices down—instigating

1. As Europeans had invested far more in the United States ($7.1 billion) than Americans had in Europe ($3.5 billion), the United States in 1914 was a net debtor nation, to the tune of $3.6 billion ($3.8 billion when short-term debt is added to the mix).

more sales, and further falls. Then, on July 28, with combat breaking out, the race to the bottom accelerated, promising a crash of colossal proportions. To forestall this, one European exchange after another closed its doors, blocking further sales. By July 30 all but London's had been shuttered.

Much of the action now shifted across the Atlantic, where the NYSE remained open. Desperate sellers descended on the metropolis, with predictable consequences. In the immediate aftermath of Austria-Hungary's declaring war on Serbia, stock prices dropped 3.5 percent. Then, on Thursday, July 30, the enormous volume of new sales battered stocks down another 6 percent. As Friday dawned, judging by the mountain of sell orders that had accumulated overnight, it appeared that perhaps $100 million worth of US securities would be thrown on the market when the Exchange opened for business, a virtual guarantee of catastrophe.

Worse: stock sales were draining away the nation's supply of gold—the underpinning of US currency. Under gold standard rules, once a stock seller had a receipt in hand, he could take it to the nearest commercial bank and demand conversion of paper into metal. And if Wall Street banks ran out of gold, creditors could take their demand to the US Sub-Treasury. True, the public and private sectors held just over a billion dollars in gold or gold equivalents, which was trumpeted as a comforting figure. But if Europeans managed to unload just 25 percent of their holdings, demand would exceed supply, and the country would be forced off the gold standard, as it had been in 1907. This, in turn, might do serious damage to America's currency and international creditworthiness.

This was not a paranoid fantasy. In the last week of July alone, the North German Lloyd Line's enormous SS *Kronprinzessin Cecilie* had departed New York for Bremen laden with over $10 million worth of gold bars, while two London-bound vessels carried about $15 million more between them. Most of the specie had been subtracted from the coffers of institutions like Goldman Sachs, Lazard Frères, National City Bank, and Guaranty Trust. The first week of August saw another $30 million set sail.

To make matters still worse, there was another set of debts owed abroad, obligations incurred not by US corporations but by state and local governments. As it happened, far and away the biggest municipal debtor in the country was New York City, and a whopping chunk of its debt was about to come due.

To pay for its enormous development projects—water, streets, schools, docks, bridges, and subways—the City of New York had borrowed liberally. Its net debt had risen from $342 million in 1898 to $1.2 billion at the end of 1914 (an amount almost as large as the national debt). Most of this was owed to European creditors. Many loans were long term, running as high as fifty years. And the interest payments on those loans were considered a sustainable burden, given that the expanded infrastructure had helped boost the value of its real estate (from $2.5 billion to $8 billion), and taxes on property were the most significant source of municipal income.

Also seemingly safe were the city's substantial short-term borrowings. These were incurred not for capital projects but for day-to-day operating expenses, which came to $190 million per year (more than the gross annual earnings of the Pennsylvania Railroad). Since 1912 the city, seeking to avoid the high interest rates charged by local funders like J. P. Morgan and Kuhn, Loeb, had turned to English and French capital markets. The municipality had routinely issued short term "tax anticipation notes" (TANs), which were promptly repaid at tax collection time. Foreign lenders had insisted on the right to have their principal redeemed in gold, a clause that had seemed a harmless irrelevancy in peacetime. But in the summer of 1914, with war erupting, New York's government was looking at $80 million coming due between September 1914 and January 1915. Payable in gold. Which the city didn't have, partly because customary revenues had declined drastically due to the disruption of international commerce.

Worse yet: these debts were denominated in pounds sterling. Having borrowed pounds, the city had to repay with pounds. Normally, this was accomplished by converting dollars into gold (at a fixed rate), then shipping the metal across the Atlantic, where it was converted into sterling (also at a fixed rate). Importers and exporters didn't have to deal directly with this cumbersome procedure. It was handled by foreign exchange brokers, who would buy gold with dollars, add the costs of insuring and transporting the precious metal, tack on a profit kept moderate by competition, and, in London, complete its conversion into pounds. Normally, one could buy a pound for between $4.85 and $4.89. But there was nothing normal about the summer of 1914. As worries rose about America's ability to stay on the gold standard—to maintain its commitment and ability to keep the dollar at its fixed level—the currency's market value began to shrink. It required a steadily increasing number of dollars to purchase a single still-stable pound. In addition, with war under way, the rates for marine insurance skyrocketed, a cost that foreign exchange brokers passed along. The price of a pound rose rapidly, approaching $7.00. This meant that New York would have to pay its creditors not $80 million but somewhere between $95 million and $100 million.

Then paying even that inflated figure became simply impossible. On August 4, the gigantic four-funneled *Kronprinzessin Cecilie*, which in late July had steamed off into the Atlantic loaded with gold, arrived instead to the sleepy (and startled) port town of Bar Harbor, Maine. War having broken out while the ship was in mid-Atlantic, North German Lloyd, rather than risk having its liner captured by English or French cruisers, had ordered it to scurry back to neutral territory. The gold and the passengers were returned safely to New York. But insurance rates spiraled into the empyrean, then vanished altogether. No marine insurance was to be had at any price. Commerce jolted to a halt. The foreign exchange market shut up shop. Gotham would be unable to pay its debt. Bankruptcy loomed.

WHAT TO DO, AND WHO TO DO IT?

Wall Street—reflexively—looked to the House of Morgan, even though Morgan himself had passed from the scene. On January 7, 1913, shortly after his exhausting public joust with the Pujo Committee's Samuel Untermyer, Morgan had sailed for Egypt to view the progress of a Metropolitan Museum archaeological dig. He was 75, tired, and depressed, and as he traveled up the Nile, he suffered something akin to a nervous breakdown. His party turned back to Cairo, then went on to Rome, where he settled into a suite at the Grand Hotel. His health worsened; he fell into a coma, and died on March 31, 1913. His body was brought back to Manhattan, where it lay in state at the Morgan Library. Fifteen hundred pillars of Gotham's trinitarian class attended funeral services at St. George's on the morning of April 14, during which time trading on the Exchange was suspended, the only occasion on which the NYSE had been shuttered to honor a private citizen.[2]

Even had he lived, it was generally agreed that no one person could any longer muster the power Morgan had wielded during the 1907 crisis. The day after Morgan's death, the

---

2. Morgan's estate was estimated at $68 million, a much smaller sum than those that Frick, Harriman, Baker, and Rockefeller had amassed—to say nothing of Carnegie, who (reputedly) couldn't resist remarking: "And to think he was not a rich man." Senior's art collection, however, was valued at roughly $60 million. The Met had hoped he would donate it to the museum, but Junior— partly to cover his father's munificent bequests—sold off many of the finest pieces to Duveen and his rivals, who then resold them at hefty premiums to Frick and his rivals. Still, over 6,000 items remained, and were later given to the Met.

"Morgan and Posterity. The Financier. The Patron of Art." *Puck*, April 23, 1913. (Library of Congress Prints and Photographs Division)

Wall Street Journal had asserted that "now Wall Street is beyond the need or possibility of one-man leadership. There will be co-ordination of effort, union of resources, but Morgan will have no successor." Still, the financial district's response to the outbreak of war would be largely managed by Morgan's son, John Pierpont ("Jack") Morgan Jr. Young Morgan (aged 47) dropped "Junior" from his name, and began styling himself "Senior" (as had his father), but he was not as imperious as his pater. Jack was better at delegating authority to his capable partners Harry Davison, Thomas Lamont, and newcomer Dwight Morrow. This collegiality stood him in good stead when it came to coordinating the New York financial community's response to crisis.

Wall Street also recognized that Washington would have to play a critical role. But the Federal Reserve Bank, which had been set up in December 1913 in large part to deal with financial crises, was not yet operational during the war summer of 1914. (It would not become fully functional until November.) It was therefore unavailable to staunch the outflow of bullion by jacking up the interest rate, as the Bank of England had doubled its, from 4 percent to 8 percent. Instead, Morgan and his colleagues would deal directly with Secretary of the Treasury William Gibbs McAdoo, Gotham's tunnel entrepreneur, who had entered office with Woodrow Wilson. Together, Morgan and McAdoo, both as yet untested, now undertook a series of measures that alleviated the crisis.

FIRST ON THEIR AGENDA WAS RESCUING the imperiled New York Stock Exchange. On the morning of July 31, with an avalanche of sell orders waiting to be executed, Jack Morgan called an emergency session of the city's leading bankers; they got on the phone with McAdoo in DC and agreed to batten down the hatches. Less than fifteen minutes before the 10:00 a.m. opening bell, the exchange was shut down, a decision that generated a "wild outburst of cheering" from relieved brokers. The closure was the first since the Panic of 1873. That had lasted ten days; this would last four months.

Two days later, on Sunday August 2, McAdoo came up to New York's Hotel Vanderbilt to caucus with leading financiers (among them Morgan, Vanderlip of National City, and Hepburn of Chase National). The bankers feared runs on their institutions. The agreed-upon solution was to invoke the Aldrich-Vreeland Act, which, after the 1907 Panic, had authorized creation of emergency money. McAdoo announced that $500 million would be made available, and dramatized the decision by delivering next day a first shipment of $45 million worth of freshly printed banknotes, conveyed with fanfare by an armed convoy of twenty mail trucks to the back door of the Sub-Treasury building. The flood of paper currency did the trick. Runs were avoided.

The third initiative—dealing with New York City's debt—was more complicated but equally effective. Europeans, of course, wouldn't accept ersatz US money; they stuck to their demand for gold. So Morgan proposed organizing a mega-syndicate of every bank in Gotham. By pooling their gold resources, they could float a $100 million loan to the city, which would use the proceeds to pay off British and French creditors. Morgan would later say that he acted because a failure to "meet its obligations punctually" would "have dealt an almost irreparable blow to the credit of New York City, as well as cast discredit on the United States." But more than civic-mindedness was at work here. The bankers had played a major role in helping the city run up such a debt, by guaranteeing bond sales to ensure sufficient buyers; hence their own credibility was on the line. And the banking community's aspiration to play a bigger role in international finance might be mortally wounded if it let its host city go bankrupt. So, in an echo of Morgan Senior's strategy in 1907, Morgan and his partners Davison, Morrow, and Lamont muscled 126 banks into taking a piece of the gigantic loan, drawing on their gold supply to do so, from each according to its ability. Contributions ranged from the $3,005 anted up by the Tottenville National Bank to the $7,800,980 subscribed by the National City Bank.

The contract was signed on September 10, 1914. On September 15 the managers called for the first installment to be delivered to 23 Wall. Immediately bank messengers descended on the Corner bearing bags of gold certificates; these were redeemed for gold bars at the Sub-Treasury across the street; the gold was sealed in kegs and delivered by an express company to the railroad station, from which it was shipped to Ottawa—the Bank of England finessed the risks of sea transport by using a Canadian branch office—arriving twelve hours later.

The syndicate managers then resold the debt to wealthy individuals, insurance companies, and trusts. They made much of their refusal to charge the city their customary 0.5 percent commission, and their sharing with the city the resale profit of a little over $2 million. On the other hand, in return for the bailout, the bankers required New York City officials to adopt a "pay-as you go" policy. This forbade borrowing for any public works project that couldn't cover its own cost. Schools, parks, libraries, roads, and sewage treatment plants would have to be financed through general taxes (or not at all). The privilege of issuing bonds was reserved for the likes of rapid transit or new dockage. Mayor Mitchel was unhappy at the terms—and the 6 percent rate of interest (2 percent higher than the last city borrowing)—but he had no choice but to acquiesce.

The flow of gold to Canadian vaults—millions more followed in the next two months—and the clear determination of the federal government to remain on the gold standard when even Britain's commitment was faltering effectively calmed the troubled waters. By November, when the Federal Reserve arrived on the scene, the dollar had strengthened against the pound. And in December the NYSE reopened for business, albeit on a restricted basis.

As winter fell, it quickly became apparent that swift action by Washington and Wall Street had bailed out the banks and the city—but not its people.

RECESSION

Hard times had gotten harder since the previous winter (1913–14), when the IWW's Frank Tannenbaum had led the unemployed from church to church, seeking food, and shelter from the frigid weather. Not only was the city (like much of the country) suffering through a second winter (1914–15) of industrial unemployment; it was battered as well by a war-induced commercial crisis.

Immediately on their entry into the conflict on August 4, 1914, the British, brandishing their overwhelming sea power, announced a naval blockade of Germany, adopting a policy of economic strangulation. In short order—as per the hasty retreat beaten by the *Kronprinzessin Cecilie*—American trade with the Central Powers and neighboring neutral countries was essentially severed. So too was communication: on August 5, the British cut the transatlantic submarine cables connecting Germany's telecommunications service to Gotham.[3] At first the interdiction of commerce was relatively circumscribed. The British, not wanting to antagonize America, which insisted on minimal interference with its neutral shipping, forbade only conventionally defined contraband, and established their blockade perimeters close to German ports. After the First Battle of the Marne, in September 1914, halted Germany's invasion of France—at the cost of half a million dead or wounded—and the land conflict bogged down into trench-war stalemate, the British steadily expanded efforts to starve their enemies into submission. Soon their cruisers were stopping neutral vessels on the high seas, and in November the Royal Navy followed a (highly illegal under international law) policy of "distant blockade." Barring entrance to the English Channel and the North Sea, it forced merchant vessels to dock at British ports to be inspected, stripped of contraband (whose definition was dramatically widened to include foodstuffs), and then escorted through British-laid minefields to their destinations. German-American trade was effectively ended.

The war pummeled trade with Britain, too. Naval hostilities had made marine insurance prohibitively expensive. More to the point, there were few boats to be had. German vessels had hurried home or, like the *Kronprinzessin Cecilie*, been interned in neutral ports. Great Britain had diverted most of its huge tonnage to war-related activities in the European theater. And many of the foreign vessels that usually handled American commerce had dispersed to their countries of origin. (A US merchant marine had barely existed since Congress had scuttled the federal government's mail subsidy program in 1858; by 1914 less than 10 percent of the nation's commerce was carried in American bottoms.)

Commerce, accordingly, skidded to a virtual halt. Normally in the fall the United States shipped wheat and cotton abroad and got gold in return. But in 1914, though farmers had just brought in the biggest bumper crop in American history, there was no way to get the goods to Europe. Wheat was left to rot in grain elevators. Cotton, too, was going nowhere: where in August 1913 257,172 bales had been dispatched, in August 1914 a mere 21,210 left the country. The rest piled up on wharves, or was parked expensively in warehouses, along with similarly impeded manufactures. "Our foreign commerce is paralyzed," wailed the

---

3. The German government in Berlin was still able to communicate with the German consul in Gotham via the wireless transmitting station in Sayville, Long Island, 40 miles from New York, that had been built in 1912 by the German Telefunken Company. But England now had effective command over the flow of war news from the various fronts (to the great annoyance of the New York press). The disconnection would hamper as well the transatlantic passage of German capital.

National Foreign Trade Council. "Europe has placed an embargo on the commerce of the world," echoed the New York Chamber of Commerce.

As the principal port, Gotham was particularly hard hit. Not since the Embargo of 1807–9 had such a mass of ships ridden at anchor in New York harbor. "In this greatest port of this greatest neutral Nation," observed the *New York Press*, "lie strings of ships flying the flags of all the countries now grappling to the death in Europe." Here were to be found "British tramps and German liners, Russian emigrant ships and French freighters, Austrian hookers and many others, their ensigns all fluttering." Some of these, the paper speculated, "may grow weary of inaction, perhaps, and slip out past Sandy Hook, to brave the dangers of destruction or capture. How many will still be afloat a year from now?"

THE FINANCIAL AND COMMERCIAL CRISES DEEPENED the existing recession. Morgan partner Thomas Lamont noted that with ocean transportation "violently disarranged," the consequent "almost complete prostration of trade" had exacerbated the "general business depression that had existed for many months." By December 1914 an 8 percent reduction in the employment rate from the previous year—due in part to layoffs of export trade workers such as longshoremen and teamsters—drove Gotham's jobless tally to perhaps 325,000, in the estimate of the Association for Improving the Condition of the Poor (AICP). When the economy had lurched downward in 1913, suffering had reached levels not seen since the Panic of 1907; the winter of 1914–15 brought privation not seen since the terrible times of 1893–4.

Recession responses ran the usual gamut.

The *Wall Street Journal* called for a revival of religion to bring "employer and employed together on the common platform of love and fear of God." The paternalist and civic-minded rich opened their purses to the unemployment-battered poor. Newspapers like the *Evening Mail* raised relief funds for families facing eviction. Grumpy charity organizations chided the charitable rich and publicity-seeking papers for insufficiently scrutinizing claims to deservingness. And union leaders and social workers demanded the city government take action.

It did. In December 1914 the Mitchel administration appointed a Mayor's Council on Unemployment, chaired by Elbert H. Gary, the head of US Steel. (Gary had some expertise in the matter, USS having recently laid off 50,000 workers.) The council's eighty directors encompassed both big businessmen (Frank Vanderlip, Percy Straus) and civic reformers (Florence Kelley, Lillian Wald, Stephen Wise, and Rose Schneiderman). Being data-minded progressives, their first initiative was to measure the phenomenon carefully—for the first time in the city's history. Information provided by 602 business and industrial establishments was added to reports from tenement house inspectors and Metropolitan Life agents, then aggregated by the Bureau of Labor Statistics. The AICP, it turned out, had undershot the mark. Between 398,000 and 434,000 were out of work, the council concluded—between 16 and 18 percent of the city's wage-earning population, perhaps 50 percent more than had been jobless the previous winter.

The mayor and council responded with palliatives.

John Kingsbury, commissioner of charities, led some council members on a visit to the Municipal Lodging House at 438 East 25th Street, where on freezing nights—temperatures having plunged to four below zero, the coldest of the century to date—2,000 men, as well as dozens of women and a few children, queued up for shelter. This was nearly twice the number the facility could accommodate, and a minor percentage of the estimated 12,000 homeless in the city. Those turned away were taken to sleep in the City Morgue, or led to the Charities Department dock on East 26th Street, where three ferryboats were moored, on whose unheated decks they slept, under newspapers and overcoats, until awakened at 4:30 a.m. for breakfast. Stays were restricted to seven nights a month. Kingsbury told reporters that conditions were "absolutely inhumane, inadequate, and indecent," and declared "the city should meet the situation." By the night of January 14, the municipality had enclosed a recreation pier with a steel and glass shed and placed hundreds of cots therein, a humane but modest gesture. Kingsbury and Mitchel had debated a more ambitious plan—to transform Madison Square Garden into a massive dormitory—but it didn't pan out. Frederic C. Howe, the commissioner at Ellis Island, did offer federal sanctuary to 800 of the homeless.

Clothing needs were dealt with on "bundle days." The term had been coined that year to describe the practice of gathering castoffs and dispatching them to war sufferers in Europe. Now it was adapted for domestic consumption. The campaign to collect old clothes relied on volunteers, including society women mobilized by Frances Kellor of the National Progressive Service, Boy Scouts, firemen, police officers, and members of the Inter-Church Committee on Unemployment. The citizenry was exhorted—via newspaper ads, and slides projected in 600 movie theaters—to drop off secondhand apparel at collection centers established in 240 public schools, 99 parochial schools, 89 police stations, 7 railroad terminals, and numerous department stores. The donations were then sorted and repaired in workrooms where roughly 500 of the jobless were employed at a dollar a day.

Food provision was less successful. War disruption had caused prices to jump. The wholesale cost of beans in New York, per 100 pounds, rose from $3.85–$3.90 to $5.15–$5.25. A Mayor's Committee on Food Supply was initiated, led by George W. Perkins, who announced plans to organize several farmers' markets at which local producers could sell their crops direct to consumers. As Perkins admitted, however, these had little impact, especially in the winter months, and especially on the jobless. The Mayor's Committee had to content itself with issuing booklets like *How to Use Left-Overs*, which contained 125 recipes for "nourishing dishes" composed of things many housewives throw away. Their helpful hints— "left-over beef, lamb, mutton and veal are excellent for hash, scalloped dishes, croquettes, a loaf, and salads"—were of similarly marginal utility for the poor and unemployed.

Equally meager or nonexistent were municipal efforts to provide direct relief or public jobs. Plans to hand out emergency funds via churches and trade unions were vetoed by the organized charities, who rejected any evasion of the elaborate screening procedures with which they separated the deserving from the undeserving poor.

The Mayor's Committee did establish a temporary work program for the jobless, which paid men fifty cents a day to repair shoes and clothing and to roll bandages for hospitals and war supplies. Women were paid sixty cents to make clothing for themselves and their children. As of February 1915 the workshops were employing 1,072 men and 700 women, but the funds, largely contributed by committee members, had proved insufficient to deal with demand. The public, accordingly, was "urgently requested to help by sending checks to Henry P. Davison, Treasurer, J. P. Morgan & Co., 23 Wall Street." Proposals for more substantial public works projects were vetoed by the parsimonious Mitchel on fiscal and ideological grounds. While he acknowledged "an unusual condition of general unemployment," he saw no cause to entertain "various suggestions of an extreme nature."

Such suggestions were advanced by the city's socialists and more progressive progressives. Meyer London, in his November 1914 victory speech on the occasion of his election to the US Congress, declared that as a representative of the working class he would fight for legislation to mandate a minimum wage and a shorter working day, outlaw child labor, and institute a "national compulsory program of unemployment insurance." As London explained in a subsequent address, "We have learned that there is an obligation upon the community to protect the worker against loss by involuntary idleness, which is not an accident, but a feature of our industrial system." In February 1915 the Socialist Party, in conjunction with the United Hebrew Trades and other industrial unions, drew thousands to a Union Square rally against unemployment. (The American Federation of Labor [AFL] declined to participate.) London and other speakers urged the city to open public workshops that would employ workers at their own trade, hire people to build schools, extend loans to the jobless, and press the state legislature to pass unemployment insurance. They also lambasted Mayor Mitchel for "meeting a breakdown in industry with nothing better than a deluge of old clothes."

As so often, socialist prescriptions paralleled those of progressives who sought to reform but not transcend capitalism. John B. Andrews, secretary of the American Association for Labor Legislation, having been inspired by Britain's National Insurance Act (1911), which by 1913 was providing unemployment coverage to 2.3 million workers, had commissioned studies on its adaptability to US conditions. In December 1914 he summarized the findings in a twenty-page manifesto, *A Practical Program for the Prevention of Unemployment in America*. "The time is past when the problem of unemployment could be disposed of either by ignoring it," Andrews argued, "or by attributing it to mere laziness and inefficiency." It was, rather, "inherent in our present method of industrial organization." He called for public works, employment exchanges, regularizing seasonal industries (smoothing out their ups and downs), job sharing, and unemployment insurance. Andrews believed, however, that in the end, municipal resources would be insufficient to the task. He urged unemployment be tackled on a national scale, though regretfully understood that was beyond the bounds of present political possibility.

Wobblies called for immediate and direct action. At the IWW national convention in Chicago in September 1914, Big Bill Haywood said the One Big Union had to help the unemployed get through the upcoming winter. Workers shouldn't waste time appealing to municipal or state governments but rather, armed with pickaxes and crowbars, should head for the granaries and warehouses where food was locked up, and help themselves. Where houses were vacant, they should be occupied; where machinery was idle, it should be used. Some Wobblies counseled the hungry to go to restaurants, eat their fill, and charge the meals to the mayor. IWW members from the 4th Street headquarters did engage in "restaurant raids," ordering expensive dishes and billing Mitchel, and were arrested; at their trial they admitted to a policy of "taking instead of begging," and were consigned to the Workhouse. Joe Hill would write Elizabeth Gurley Flynn from the Salt Lake City jail cell where he was awaiting execution that she should organize a "Workers Moratorium League of New York," which would distribute certificates to give to unemployed workers to hand their landlords, entitling the bearer "to shelter without the paying of rent until able to secure a position." James Larkin, militant founder of the Irish Transport and General Workers' Union in Dublin, then in New York and working with the IWW, counseled more disciplined mass action, like a rent strike by the unemployed. It didn't pan out either.

Absent structural reforms or political upheaval, the recession might have been expected to drag on into a third year of privation, but instead, in the spring, as the snows and slush of winter melted away, hard times melted, too, and by the end of 1915 the city, and the country, were in the midst of an extravagant boom.[4]

---

4. To Mitchel's credit, he didn't drop the unemployment question, but in January 1916, with prosperity having broken out all around, he appointed a second Mayor's Committee on Unemployment, which included many of the players from the first one (Wald, Devine, Croly, Howe, Anne Morgan, Mary van Kleeck, and Henry Bruere, with William Delavan Baldwin, chairman of Otis Elevator, in the chair). Its mission was to get ahead of the game, as they were convinced recessions would recur, and responses

A PROSPEROUS NEUTRALITY

What turned things around was desperate cries from the charnel house of Europe for more implements of massive destruction. Rifles, bullets, gunpowder! Shells, grenades, machine guns, poison gas! Tanks, trucks, torpedo boats, fuel! Airplanes, locomotives, horses, mules! And barbed wire! Miles and miles of barbed wire to fence in the trenches along the Western Front, running from the English Channel, through Belgium and France, to the Swiss border. Chemical plants, steel mills, arms factories, the whole gamut of American industrial (and agricultural) production, leapt to life, galvanized by lucrative war contracts.[5]

The difficulties of getting goods to the killing fields were overcome by a series of public and private efforts. A Shipping Registry Act signed in mid-August 1914 allowed the government to transfer foreign-flag vessels to American registry, which expanded the merchant marine. Congress then offered the owners of these Americanized boats low-cost coverage from the War Risk Insurance Bureau, created in September. By the end of 1915 more than 1,200 vessels were criss-crossing the Atlantic, protected by government policies. But the shippers' true protector was the Royal Navy. Britannia ruled the waves, after all, and while it had, annoyingly, closed the sea lanes to America's German customers, it had opened a secure and profitable route to buyers in England and France.

Exports began to swell, surpassing imports by October 1914, then going into hyper-drive in 1915 when the war business got organized. With arms orders mounting chaotically and inefficiently, J. P. Morgan & Co. proposed to the British government that it act as the UK's purchasing agent in the United States, an idea accepted in January 1915, and in May the firm was signed up to represent France as well. Morgan purchasing chief Edward Stettinius dispatched 175 agents to scout out suppliers throughout the country, while also negotiating with the daily crush of agents hawking the wares of far-flung manufacturers. "The very atmosphere of Manhattan Island seems impregnated with 'war contractitis,'" noted a *Times* reporter.

By July 1915, as Morgan banker Lamont noted jubilantly, many manufacturers and merchants were "doing wonderful business in articles relating to the war." Among the most notable winners were Morgan-affiliated corporations like General Electric, United States Steel, DuPont, and Kennecott Copper (a firm Morgan helped the Guggenheims organize). Morgan itself did well: commissions on sales would net the firm $30 million.

By March 1915 the unprecedented boom in US exports had set a bull market to pawing the ground. And when remaining restrictions on stock trades were lifted that spring, the NYSE's brokers became a thundering herd.

Gold began trickling back across the Atlantic, then became a mighty current—$451 million sailed back in 1915, $686 million more in 1916—reversing, then dwarfing, the losses of 1914. Their vaults drained, the British and French recommenced their sell-off of US stocks, now that

should not be last minute catch-up affairs. They scrutinized the efforts that had been made in 1914–15 and proposed long-run solutions in a January 1917 report, *How to Meet Hard Times*. The committee admitted up front that it could not address "the fundamental economic, social and political maladjustments which are responsible for the recurrence of periodic trade crises and for thus depriving hundreds of thousands of workers of the opportunity to earn their daily bread." Its more delimited purview was how to avert or mitigate "the distressful effects of such crises," and at the municipal level. Moving closer to the Socialist/AALL position, it recommended compulsory unemployment insurance, pre-planned public works projects, vocational training programs, and reorganized public relief, though they hedged the proposals with caveats, arguing (under pressure from the organized charities) that "the doling out of bread, soup or money, even relief employment at a made job, come last, not first in a well worked-out program of preparedness."

5. Domestic demand was added to overseas orders when in March 1915 President Wilson signed a bill that provided for two battleships, six torpedo destroyers, and eighteen submarines.

the NYSE was again open for business. Vast quantities were effortlessly absorbed. From January 1915 to July 1916, roughly $1.3 billion in railroad securities alone was repurchased, and when industrials were added to the total, the total tally approached an astounding $2 billion.

And it still wasn't enough! More guns, more food! But by the summer of 1915 the Allies' money tanks were again running low. Now they began talking loans. Their initial requests to borrow funds had been vetoed by Secretary of State William Jennings Bryan, who considered loans a betrayal of "the true spirit of neutrality." In June 1915, however, Bryan had resigned, and his successor, Robert Lansing, had teamed up with Treasury Secretary McAdoo in urging President Wilson to reverse Bryan's policy. In August 1915 McAdoo reminded Wilson that the high prices foodstuffs were fetching had brought prosperity to farmers, just as munition sales had factories running at full capacity, benefiting industrialists and workers alike. And this could be only the beginning! "Great prosperity is coming," McAdoo argued, and it "will be tremendously increased if we can extend reasonable credits to our customers." The converse was true, too: "To maintain our prosperity we must finance it. Otherwise it may stop and that would be disastrous."

Two weeks later, Secretary Lansing vigorously underscored the downside of denying credit. "If European countries cannot find means to pay," he pointed out, "they will have to stop buying, and our present export trade will shrink proportionately." The consequence of that, he warned Wilson, "would be restriction of outputs, industrial depression, idle capital and idle labor, numerous failures, financial demoralization and general unrest and suffering among the laboring classes." The president should not let Bryan's "true spirit of neutrality" stand in the way of "our national interests, which seem to be seriously threatened."

Wilson agreed, and in October 1915 the House of Morgan, given the go-ahead, put together an American banking syndicate that lent $500 million (at 6 percent) to Britain and France. It was the biggest foreign loan in US history, and gave fresh evidence of New York's strength as a financial center.

But the $500 million—which promptly flowed back into the pockets of American corporations—was soon exhausted. England, France, Russia, Italy, and China lined up again, and again, at the tills of metropolitan banks. By April 1917 the House of Morgan alone had arranged over $1.5 billion in Allied credits, and loans by other private financiers brought the total to $2.6 billion, half the size of the US national debt.

In sharp contrast, between 1914 and 1917, loans issued in New York on behalf of the Central Powers amounted to only $35 million. This reflected the fact that the vast majority of bankers and financiers on Wall Street were pro-Allies. The Morgan partners, as Tom Lamont recalled, "wanted the Allies to win, from the outset of the War. We were pro-Ally by inheritance, by instinct, by opinion." The smaller contingent of German Jewish bankers, long the principal conduits for German capital, were themselves divided and under great pressure. As Jacob Schiff wrote a friend in 1914, "My sympathies are naturally altogether with Germany, as I would think as little to side against my own country as I would against my own parents." He also hated England's Russian ally, and when Jack Morgan organized the $500 million loan to the Allies, Schiff barred Kuhn, Loeb's participation, lest any of the funds find their way to the anti-Semitic czarist regime. His announced policy of bank neutrality aroused great ire among the Anglophiles, especially those, like Jack Morgan, who were already confirmed anti-Semites.[6] Schiff's partner Otto Kahn, on the other hand, was committed to the Allies. He not

6. Jack was even more an Anglophile than his father. He'd grown to love the haute-English lifestyle during his 1898–1905 exile. He seldom missed the August grouse shooting season in Scotland, where he mingled with merchant bankers and aristocrats, and often spent up to six months a year in England.

only subscribed personally to the big loan but turned his house in London's Regent Park into a home for blinded soldiers and sailors. Still, Schiff called the shots, and the firm's standing slipped. Goldman Sachs was even more deeply fractured. Henry Goldman was vigorously and publicly pro-German. He admired Prussianism (which Kahn deplored) and was fond of quoting Nietzsche. Walter Sachs, on the other hand, was staunchly pro-British and -French. Goldman blocked participation in the Allied loan, and though the chagrined Sachs personally subscribed, the bank became known as a "German firm" and was cut out of wartime finance. Goldman would eventually be forced to resign. The inability of the German Jewish banks to arrange equal German access to Gotham's capital markets would be a serious blow to the Kaiser's war effort.

WITH COMMERCE UNCORKED, THE PORT OF NEW YORK surged back to business. Grain flowed into the city and out across the Atlantic. In the first four months of 1915, the United States exported 98 million bushels of wheat, compared to 18 million during the same period a year earlier. Shipments through the city of cotton, steel, and munitions grew exponentially. By mid-1916 three-quarters of all American arms destined for Europe were being put aboard ships in Gotham's harbor. The biggest single transfer point was the Lehigh Valley Railroad's ten-pier freight yard on Black Tom, a peninsula jutting out into the harbor from the Jersey City shore, where thousands of boxcars delivered tons of foodstuffs, dry goods, and assorted explosives intended for the Western and Eastern Fronts. These were shifted into warehouses and storage pens, then transferred onto barges for delivery to freighters around the Upper Bay, poised for departure to Liverpool, Le Havre, and Archangel.

The soaring reemployment rates for warehousemen, truck drivers, longshoremen, and clerks were matched by vigorous hiring in the city's construction, finance, retail, and manufacturing sectors. By October 1915 a reporter was speculating that "every machine shop in New York and vicinity which can turn a few lathes must be engaged in making projectiles."

Unemployment evaporated. Indeed, wages rose as war orders swelled demand for labor, while a sharp drop in immigration reduced its supply. At the outbreak of conflict, the Hamburg-American and North German Lloyd lines, two of the steamship companies most widely used by immigrants, ceased operations. In 1914 878,052 immigrants passed through Ellis Island. In 1915 only 178,416 did. By 1918 a mere 28,867 trickled in.

CAT'S AWAY

Amidst the maelstrom of buying and selling, perspicacious observers discerned something at work more profound than simple profit taking. It seemed possible that a shifting of the axis of global economic power was under way, one that portended a profound transformation in the planetary position of New York City.

In an article in the July 1915 *Annals of the American Academy of Political and Social Science*, Thomas Lamont noted that "many people seem to believe that New York is to supersede London as the money center of the world." Lamont was not so sure. True, the first year of war had wrought a "tremendous reversal of conditions" in Gotham's relations with Europe. America's "wonderful business in articles relating to the war" had contributed to a "prodigious export trade balance." That in turn had provided the wherewithal to buy back immense quantities of securities held by foreign investors. And that had allowed the US to start lending to foreign nations and thus become a recipient, rather than a payer, of interest and dividends. If this state of affairs continued, Lamont believed, "then inevitably we shall become a creditor instead of a debtor nation, and such a development, sooner or later, would certainly tend to bring about the dollar, instead of the pound sterling, as the international basis of exchange."

All very encouraging, no doubt, but not sufficient. Replacing London as "the financial center of the world" would require that New York first become "the trade center of the world," and while that was "certainly a possibility," Lamont wasn't convinced it was a "probability." The problem was that up till then "our exports to regions other than Great Britain and Europe have been comparatively limited in amount." To achieve global supremacy, he believed, "we must cultivate and build up new markets for our manufacturers and merchants, and all that is a matter of time." It might take "many years."

Or perhaps not: "I think I am warranted," Lamont mused, "in saying that this question of trade and financial supremacy must be determined by several factors, a chief one of which is the duration of the war. If, as all humanity is bound to hope, the war should come to an end in the near future, our position would still be much different from, and more important than, what it was prior to the war." But Germany and England would swing back into "keen competition very promptly; and we should find that the building up of our foreign trade would be a much slower matter than if the war were to continue indefinitely, thus leaving those foreign fields of trade endeavor more open to us."

The thought had crossed other minds. As the *Wall Street Journal* noted: "War is a great evil but an evil wind may sometimes blow good to somebody." The "somebody" in this case was a New York–led business community itching to expand overseas, and aware (as another paper noted) that the war provided "a supreme opportunity for American manufacturers to gain world-wide markets." This was particularly true in Latin America—a territory long and gallingly contested by England and Germany. Now (as the *New York Commercial* exulted) it lay "invitingly open to the United States through the annihilation of Europe's foreign trade!"

It was also widely understood that exports of capital (not just commodities) could be expanded. In September 1915, on the eve of the big Allied loan, Edward Ewing Pratt, now chief of the Federal Bureau of Foreign and Domestic Commerce, stressed this in a speech to the Investment Bankers' Association of America. "We are getting accustomed nowadays to hearing New York spoken of as the financial center of the world," Pratt said, but "probably most of us would characterize this as somewhat too optimistic." London's goliath global status, after all, rested in considerable measure on Britain's investments abroad, from Japan to the Argentine, whereas most New York investors had never even heard of the securities (in rubber, rails, mines, governments) that were avidly sought after in Europe. Somewhat daringly, Pratt wondered aloud if the present focus on loaning money "to our best customers to enable them to destroy one another" was economically "sound." True, it was undoubtedly necessary, to keep foreign trade booming and to reap the attendant profits. But might it not be sensible to invest a portion of that money in "the undeveloped countries of South America, of Africa, of Australia, and of the Far East," who were, in fact, "ardently seeking capital with which not only to develop, but with which to keep the very wheels of commerce moving"? As the customary flow of billions in European capital had been violently disrupted and would probably not resume for years, "it remains to the United States to take up this work of development and expansion." (Lengthy applause followed.)

Certainly Frank Vanderlip at the National City Bank (NCB) thought so. The NCB, still known informally as the Rockefeller Bank, was a major participant in the Morgan-led Allied financing, though not with the same Anglophiliac gusto. Vanderlip thought the war less a high-minded defense of Civilization (as the British and French claimed), than a product of "greed and desire for trade expansion." He was also worried about placing so many eggs in the munitions basket. Yes, the economy was booming, but the business was patently, and dangerously, "ephemeral." Wars end. The NCB should therefore "disassociate ourselves from dependence upon war business and prepare the way for a continuing prosperity of a more rational and normal character." Indeed, he believed, "the sooner the war is over the better it will be for America in the long view," precisely the opposite of Lamont's not-so-hidden hope that the war would go on and on. Between the pursuit of immediate profit, and Anglo-American bonding, the House of Morgan (Vanderlip thought) had become virtually an adjunct of the Allies.

Vanderlip had his eyes on a larger prize. "We have an opportunity now to become the wellspring of capital for the world," he said, noting that "anxious hands are reaching toward us from every quarter." Seizing that opportunity, he put the full resources of Gotham's biggest commercial bank behind a super-ambitious plan to make National City "the most far-reaching world financial institution that there has ever been." It would have two components, a development consortium in New York, and a network of NCB branch banks throughout the world.

In November 1915 the NCB announced the formation of a mammoth holding company, the American International Corporation (AIC), to be headquartered at 25 Broad Street. Candidly admitting it was a response to "the withdrawal of capital that has been supplied by Great Britain, Germany, and France," the AIC announced its intention "to carry American capital into foreign fields," and "help make a world-wide market for our products." It was capitalized (for openers) at $50 million, and its directors included the brightest stars in the industrial/financial firmament, among them Percy Rockefeller of Standard Oil, Cyrus McCormick of International Harvester, J. J. Hill of the Great Northern Railroad, Robert S. Lovett of the Union Pacific, Charles A. Coffin of General Electric, John D. Ryan of Anaconda Copper, Joseph P. Grace of W. R. Grace, Theodore Vail of AT&T—and heavy hitters from the New York banking world such as Otto Kahn of Kuhn, Loeb, Albert H. Wiggin of Chase National, and, of course, the NCB's Vanderlip. The House of Morgan declined participation.[7]

The AIC's self-declared purview astonished Wall Street. According to its charter, the AIC was authorized to buy and sell domestic and foreign securities, contract with foreign governments for franchises and concessions, carry on a mercantile business in any part of the world, explore for and own mines, build and operate places of entertainment ("hotels, restaurants, shops, parks"), develop infrastructure projects ("gas, electric light and power works, water works, dams, flumes, water courses, aqueducts, sewage, drainage and sanitary works, wharves, piers, dry docks, basins, tugs, warehouses, oil tanks and other terminal facilities"), and more. Much more. Small-fry projects wouldn't interest them; $500,000 was the minimum loan application that would be accepted. Its goal, the AIC announced grandly, would be to have an "influence on American trade comparable with that which the East India Company exerted upon the development of England's Asiatic possessions."

Within a year the AIC had received 1,230 diverse proposals from all around the planet.

---

7. The AIC's vice president and intellectual spark plug was diplomat-banker Willard Dickerman Straight, who early in the new century, when he was US consul general in Manchuria, had been an advocate of a greater international role for the USA. Straight had become the agent in Peking of the American Group, a consortium of banks that had been encouraged to spearhead US economic penetration of China. When that venture ended in 1913, Straight signed on with J. P. Morgan & Co. But his belief that the war offered a golden opportunity for American businessmen to make commercial gains at Britain's expense was out of sync with what seemed to him the House of Morgan's virtual vassalage, and he jumped ship to work with the like-minded Vanderlip.

This development consortium was complemented by the establishment of a global network of National City Bank branches. Until 1913 overseas banking operations were forbidden by US law. This was a severe impediment to the expansion of trade. American companies wishing to access foreign markets were deprived of the kind of services and information commercial banks could provide, like accepting deposits, issuing letters of credit, handling commercial collections, providing credit information about foreign merchants, dealing in foreign exchange, collecting and evaluating information on local trade conditions, alerting US manufacturers to marketing opportunities, explaining customs protocols, and, more generally, facilitating interface with foreign cultures. Particularly onerous was the overseas unavailability of American banks that could issue and discount bankers' acceptances, the primary instrument of international trade.[8] For all these services, US exporters and importers were obliged to turn to local British banks, and for discounting facilities, they had to rely on London's Lombard Street financial institutions. The latter dependency was particularly annoying. The commissions US businesses were forced to pay London bankers, to finance US foreign trade, were considered a costly and unnecessary "tribute." And it wasn't unknown to find British bankers passing American commercial secrets to their British competitors.

The Federal Reserve Act swept away these prohibitions.

It authorized nationally chartered banks to establish branch offices abroad. Immediately the National City Bank began opening them, the first one in Buenos Aires, in November 1914. Over the next three years it established 17 more, 14 of them in Latin America, 2 in Russia, and 1 in Italy. In addition, the NCB took over an independent network, the International Banking Corporation, which had established offices in China, India, Japan, the Philippines, Latin America, and London, bringing the NCB's total to 40 branches (132, including sub-branches).

The Federal Reserve Act also allowed national banks to issue and discount acceptances. Even better, it allowed a national bank to turn around and "rediscount" discounted drafts, by reselling them to deep-pocketed institutions—no longer British banks, but rather the new-minted Federal Reserve Banks, principally the New York Fed. This ended the costly and humiliating dependence on London, and strengthened Gotham's financing capabilities.[9]

BE PREPARED!

Though there was general jubilation at the dramatic upswing and outreach of the economy, it was accompanied by two currents of unease. One was a moral concern: the awareness that

---

8. "Bankers Acceptance": When an importer wanted to order goods from a distant exporter, he could pay in advance with a draft payable to the exporter, at a specified time in the future, say, six months; it was akin to a postdated check. But if the parties didn't have an established relationship, and the exporter didn't know the importer's creditworthiness, the importer could ask his bank to guarantee payment of the draft by marking it "accepted." Once acknowledged as a bank liability, the draft was akin to a certified check, or a check drawn on an account with overdraft privileges. For this substitution of the bank's known credit standing for that of the unknown importer, the importer paid a fee.

"Discounting": A receiver of a banker's acceptance could wait until its date of maturation to cash it and receive the full face value. But he could also sell it immediately on receipt. He would not receive the face value—the payout would be "discounted"— but he'd have the cash in hand. Discounters were usually deep-pocketed banks.

9. Gotham had also begun strengthening inter-American trade relations by creating—with a boost from Senator Elihu Root—the Pan-American Society (1912). It drew hundreds of New York businessmen from banks, bond houses, industrial organizations, and steamship lines who were keen to cement the city's and country's standing in Latin America. They did so, among other ways, by entertaining distinguished Latin Americans when they came to town. The society's work fostered admiration for New York, particularly among modernizing elites. In the early 1900s when Buenos Aires urban planners envisioned their city's future, it looked like Gotham, not Paris.

American prosperity flowed from trenches filled with blood. The other was a worry that the United States might itself be dragged into combat by a Wall Street fearful of losing its multi-billion-dollar investment in an Allied victory, should the Kaiser win the war. As Georgia populist Tom Watson put it: "*Where Morgan's money went, your boy's blood must go,* ELSE MORGAN WILL LOSE HIS MONEY! That's all there is to it."[10]

Yet most Wall Streeters, whatever their personal predilections for one side or another, preferred *not* to get into the war, or any war. Indeed, since the turn of the century, leading New York financial and corporate executives had been investigating ways of expanding America's international role *without* getting sucked into Europe's clashes and arms races. As banker Frank Vanderlip observed, by avoiding a large military establishment, the United States had kept taxes down, freed manpower for industrial uses, and gained a competitive edge. But how to sustain this happy state of affairs given an increasingly armed and rivalrous Europe?

Lawyers, bankers, educators, and internationally minded businessmen (including representatives of leading import-export firms, steamship companies, and overseas mining interests) had been pondering the matter since at least 1895, when they had begun gathering annually at a posh hostelry in the Hudson Valley, 90 miles north of Gotham. Elihu Root was a regular at the Lake Mohonk Conference on International Arbitration, as were Perkins and Vanderlip and Nicholas Murray Butler. These gentlemen also figured prominently in the business-backed peace societies that flowered in the century's first decade, among them the New York Peace Society (1906), the fourth incarnation of the original, founded in Gotham in 1815 by Christian pacifists. This latest version was led by Root, Butler, Oscar Straus, and Andrew Carnegie (the last a bit improbably, given the millions he had made outfitting American battleships with steel plate armor). Carnegie had been helping finance sixteen of these societies, and was dismayed by their lack of coordination. Root, the preeminent corporate consolidator, counseled formation of what he called a "Peace Trust." Butler, who had long been fishing unsuccessfully for money from Carnegie, eagerly concurred. Carnegie agreed, and in December 1910 he created the Carnegie Endowment for International Peace (with Root as its first president), and seeded it with $10 million.

These businessmen advocated a variety of methods for preventing international disagreements from escalating into war. They promoted arbitration treaties. They sought a codification of international law. They urged creation of a World Court to settle disputes without messy and disruptive bloodshed. They argued for a Great Power league of nations with the ability to deploy economic sanctions and perhaps field its own police force. In 1912, in recognition of his having negotiated, as secretary of state, some forty reciprocal arbitration treaties, Root was awarded the Nobel Peace Prize.

On the other hand, the corporate class appreciated the usefulness of military power. Since the Spanish-Cuban-American War, Presidents Roosevelt and Taft (ably seconded by Root and Stimson, their respective secretaries of war) had often dispatched the navy southward to collect debts or defend commercial interests, and Wilson obligingly continued the tradition. In 1914 US Marines landed in Haiti, proceeded to the vaults of the National Bank, seized $500,000, carried it aboard the gunboat *Machias*, and transported it to New York, where it was deposited in the vault of the National City Bank. The subsequent Haitian-American

---

10. Watson focused too narrowly on "Morgan's money." True, there was the $30 million the House reaped by serving as the Allies' agent. And the House did want to secure the billions in loans it had helped arrange. But the smart money was after far bigger payoffs—the immense profits that would accrue from US and New York domination of the world's trade and financing. Judgments about the desirability of US intervention would not hinge merely on safeguarding "Morgan's money," but on how best to establish this new global position.

Treaty of 1915 gave the United States complete control over Haitian finances, and the right to intervene in the country whenever it was deemed necessary. The following year the Dominican Republic was also occupied at gunpoint.

The anti-war corporate elite didn't consider such actions betrayals of their pursuit of peace. It didn't count them as "wars" at all. That term was reserved for combat between equals. Their view of the islands' peoples was suffused with racist assumptions, particularly (and conveniently) concerning the natives' putative inability to govern themselves, lacking the Anglo-Saxon's natural talent in this regard. Like children, the Latins needed not only guidance but also protection, particularly from Germans. The Haitian incursion was spurred in part by a significant German cultural and economic presence on the island, one that US strategists feared might facilitate a German invasion aimed at securing a base from which to seize the Panama Canal, then approaching completion.

Which is why, despite their aversion to war, the New York elite continued to promote the naval buildup under way since the 1880s: their fledgling empire was on the line. In January 1915 Franklin Roosevelt, then assistant secretary of the navy, summarized the concern succinctly: "Without a strong navy," Roosevelt warned, "we should lose, in war time, Cuba, Samoa, Puerto Rico, the Panama Canal, Hawaii, and the Philippines." The Navy League agreed. Established in 1902 to promote naval expansion, it was by 1915 a powerhouse that included Wall Street bankers (seven directors from J. P. Morgan alone), corporate lawyers (like Root and Choate), and representatives of steel and shipbuilding companies (Bethlehem and United States Steel) that were recipients of multi-million-dollar contracts, and wanted more.[11]

The proponents of growing the army faced tougher resistance. Concerns about the dangers of a "standing army" retained potency, and the breadth of the surrounding oceans diminished its necessity. The principal calls for expanding land-based forces came from within the institution itself—its officer corps and civilian leadership—and what galvanized them was events in Mexico, a country with which the United States shared a 2,000-mile-long border.

In 1910 Major General Leonard Wood—co-creator of the Rough Riders, and former military governor, first of Cuba, then of the rebellious Moro province in the Philippines—was appointed army chief of staff. In 1911 he was joined by Henry Stimson, Taft's appointee as secretary of war. Both were alarmed at the outbreak of revolution in Mexico. The uprising against Porfirio Díaz that began in 1910 had many roots, but one of the thickest was widespread anger at the dictator's alliance with foreign (particularly American, particularly New York) capital. Powerful Mexican families were irked at seeing their interests subordinated or sacrificed to Guggenheims, Rockefellers, Hearsts, and Morgans, whose investments in rails, mines, agriculture, and oil had given them control of much of the economy. The armed insurrection launched by Francisco Madero (a scion of one of those families) alarmed President Taft. If Porfirio was toppled, Taft told Wood, 40,000 American lives and over a billion dollars' worth of investments might be put at risk.

In February 1911, accordingly, Taft and Wood decided to stage a show of strength along the border, but it proved a display of weakness. Many units were half strength, or filled with green or poorly trained recruits. And it took them three months to get to Texas, being scattered widely among fifty bases—most relics of the Indian wars, kept afloat by congressional

---

11. Navy League spokesmen also advanced collateral justifications. In October 1914 they argued that a stronger fleet would better ensure enforcement of restrictions on oriental immigration. And thus—given the "law of eugenics that the mixture of diverse races always results in a degenerative, mongrel race"—the maintenance of "race purity will also depend on the United States Navy."

pork. It became apparent that Root's earlier corporate-style centralization of the military command structure had been effected primarily on paper. Budgetary frugality, moreover, meant that funds were in short supply, so the embarrassingly inadequate border force was soon disaggregated and the units sent back to their many respective homes.[12]

Meanwhile, Mexico descended into full-scale civil war. In May 1911 Díaz relinquished power; in November 1911 Madero was elected president, but fighting continued between various rebel armies. In February 1913 Madero was betrayed, deposed, and murdered by his leading general, Victoriano Huerta, in collusion with US Ambassador Henry Lane Wilson, acting on his own (a loose cannon in a lame duck administration). In March 1913 newly in-augurated President Wilson, appalled at the assassination of Madero, refused to recognize Huerta's coup d'etat and imposed an arms embargo. Rebellions broke out against Huerta's regime—led by Zapata in the south, Venustiano Carranza and Pancho Villa in the north.[13]

In April 1914 Germany sent an arms-laden ship to bolster Huerta. To block delivery and pressure the dictator, Wilson had the US Navy seize and occupy Veracruz. For a time there was talk of war. On April 22 Wood's term in office expired, but he was given "supreme command" of a proposed US Army invasion force. Teddy Roosevelt was reportedly "burning with anxiety to get into the fray in Mexico," and ready to organize a brigade of cavalry. He would happily serve under Wood, his Rough Rider comrade-in-arms, but only if it was "a real war and not an exchange of bloodless talk between President Wilson and Gen. Huerta." Wilson, however, stuck to his policy of "watchful waiting," the crisis passed, the invasion was shelved, and the frustrated general, on July 10, 1914, assumed command of the Department of the East, with headquarters on Governors Island in New York's harbor.

Days later the Great War broke out. Wood, more than ever determined to expand the army, and prepare for possible US involvement, now launched a Gotham-based campaign to overcome his commander in chief's reluctance. That summer and fall Wood began ferrying across to Manhattan two or three times a week, then making his way up to the Harvard Club on West 44th Street. There he talked with powerful and influential civilians about the necessity of expanding the army to the massive levels Europeans had fielded, ideally by making military service an obligation of citizenship. "I am stirring up interest among the better class of men in New York," Wood told a friend, "and through them I shall hope to accomplish something. Through dinners, lunches, and meetings with men in law, business or finance, one has a chance to push things a little in a way of disseminating information about the army."

He was joined in this effort by another club member, Teddy Roosevelt, and the duo's partnership would prove a combustible collaboration. That fall of 1914, TR, too, began publicly insisting the United States was woefully underprepared to fight a major power like Germany. He was careful, however, to call only for preparedness, not active intervention, though both he and Wood believed war with Germany was inevitable, and desirable.[14] He also

12. America's land-based armed forces were only slightly larger than those of Mexico (or Belgium). The regular army had fewer than 100,000 men. And half these troops were stationed overseas, spread from Tientsin to the Canal Zone. According to one senior official, those remaining in the United States barely doubled the New York City Police Department.

13. In the autumn of 1913 John Reed was sent to Mexico by the *Metropolitan Magazine* to report on the Mexican Revolution. He traveled with Villa's army for four months and wrote a series of outstanding magazine articles (collected as *Insurgent Mexico*) that won him a national reputation as a war correspondent. Greenwich Village radicals were in general strongly supportive of the revolutionaries.

14. Wood believed that once the United States had acquired colonial possessions and status as a "great world power," it had inevitably and inextricably become involved in world affairs, particularly the imperial rivalry for markets. And if the country chose to remain weak (i.e., refused to build up its military), it would simply invite aggression by the strong, a clash that only the fittest would survive. Roosevelt agreed, and added his racialist spin: Anglo-Saxons were by nature driven to seek mastery and dominance,

took to denouncing Wilson as being spineless on Belgium, guilty of "supine inaction" in not coming to a fellow neutral's aid.[15] Wilson ignored the pressure, still assured of popular approbation for a pacific course.

On December 1, 1914, the proselytizing by Roosevelt and Wood helped precipitate organized action by the New York elite. Fifty prominent figures—industrialists, financiers, publishers, lawyers, and university presidents—gathered at the Hotel Belmont to found the National Security League (NSL). It had two key goals: a crash military buildup and compulsory universal military training. Within a month it was incorporated, with headquarters established at 31 Pine Street (one block north of Wall).

The propaganda agency's leading lights and top financial supporters included Roosevelt, Root, Stimson, Choate, Bacon, Morgan, Schiff, Baruch, Frick, the Guggenheim brothers, Cornelius Vanderbilt, and John D. Rockefeller Jr. It was overwhelmingly a New York City enterprise—in the next four years, 94.2 percent of substantial individual donations would come from Gothamites—but its target audience was national. Within a year, the NSL would set up seventy chapters in forty-two states, boasting 50,000 members, and would distribute a million pieces of "preparedness" literature.

In February 1915 a more action-oriented group of volunteers ferried over to Governors Island to get Wood's blessing for what they called the American Legion.[16] It would create a registry of men who had had military training, or possessed some skill that would be of military value. Those signing up pledged to serve in time of war. Wood gave the Legion not only his public support but an office in the Army Building on Governors Island. Within a week of its debut 20,000 had enrolled, including Roosevelt's four sons. (The ex-president himself chaired the Legion's executive committee, of which Stimson became a member.) This was altogether too much for Wilson, who ordered Wood to shut down the extralegal organization, and refrain from future involvements of this sort.

THEN CAME AN ABRUPT TURN OF EVENTS. In February 1915 the Kaiser had declared a submarine-enforced counter-blockade around Britain, whose interdiction of foodstuffs had been slowly starving the German population. On May 1, 1915, the Imperial German government placed a shipping notice in more than half a dozen New York newspapers. It warned that all English vessels were liable to destruction. It advised neutrals to avoid sailing on them.

That very morning the Cunard Line's *Lusitania* was taking on coal, cargo, and passengers at its 14th Street Chelsea Pier 54. Word of the notice spread rapidly. Voyagers could have

---

but their drive had been enervated by an excess of peace and profit seeking. Combat would toughen up their resolve. He had no truck with Root and Carnegie's penchant for international arbitration: only war could guarantee peace.

15. This required something of a pirouette on TR's part. At first, Roosevelt had actually *applauded* the German invasion, and as late as October 1914 he still spoke of it with a "thrill of admiration." He had seen it as proving yet again that Teutonic peoples—whom TR had long considered a root race of white America—were "a stern, virile, and masterful people." But once he decided that war with Germany might be imminent, his racial topography required revision. If the Germans were now to be reviled as moral monsters, the fault had to be laid at the door of their racial inheritance, which was, alas, disturbingly similar to his own. The Germans had to be assigned—posthaste and post hoc—a new pedigree, making them over into descendants not of freedom-loving Nordics, but of Asiatic hordes and "Huns." His racialist guru, Henry Fairfield Osborn, director of the American Museum of Natural History, proved equal to the task. After due reconsideration, the eugenicist capo discovered that while true Teutons were "long headed," the Kaiser and his crew had the round skull of Asiatic races. Diligent analysis traced "the Blood of the German Leaders" back to the "Wild Tartars" and the "Most Ancient Savages" of the steppes. Professor Osborn accordingly set his male museum employees to performing military drill in the parking lot two days a week, the better to defend the institution against "barbarous Teutonic hordes."

16. Not to be confused with the post-1918 Legion.

SUFFERING HUMANITY.

In the name of humanity, I want you to stop your submarine warfare. | In the name of humanity, I want you to stop the sale of ammunition.

Promotional Postcard, *The Fatherland*, 1915.

switched to the American Line's *New York*, sailing for Liverpool later that day. But the *New York* was a slow old tub. The *Lusitania* was the largest, fastest, most luxurious liner on the North Atlantic run, *and* it had reduced its fares. Besides, said a Cunard representative, passengers faced no "risk whatever" as the ship could outrun any sub. Only a few canceled. So when the great vessel steamed out of New York harbor shortly after noon, it was carrying 1,924 passengers and crew. It never reached Liverpool. On May 7, 1915, it was torpedoed off the Irish coast. Of the 1,198 lives lost, 124 were American.

Tremendous outrage ensued. Yet despite their furious indignation, Americans expressed little support for making the sinking a casus belli. Many observed that the United States bore some moral responsibility, having done nothing to discourage its citizens from sailing on a belligerent ship. But while the *Lusitania* didn't trigger a warlike response in the heartland, it heated to boiling the preparedness movement that had been percolating in New York City.

On Sunday, May 9, 1915, Grenville Clark and Elihu Root Jr., partners in the prestigious Manhattan law firm of Root, Clark, Buckner, and Howland, had scheduled a round of golf, but news of the sinking left them "too angry and horror stricken to play." The next day, May 10, Clark, heir to a banking and railroad fortune, and Root, the senator's son, gathered together fifteen other young lawyers in the Root, Clark office. They composed a petition asking Wilson to take action, which Theodore Roosevelt Jr. joined in signing, but that same day the president made his "too proud to fight" speech. The fifteen then telephoned fifty like-minded acquaintances and invited them to a luncheon the following afternoon at the Harvard Club "to talk over the Lusitania." A few days later a still larger meeting formed a Committee of 100, which consisted overwhelmingly of the sons and grandsons of New York's economic, social, and cultural elite.

By the end of May, Clark and his closest collaborator, DeLancey K. Jay, a direct descendant of John Jay on his father's side and of John Jacob Astor on his mother's, had come up with a way for their class's generation to demonstrate patriotism, manhood, and devotion to more than mere moneymaking. Their inspiration was a training program Wood had initiated in his last year as army chief of staff. Balked by Wilson in his goal of conscripting a citizen army, Wood decided to forge a corps of volunteers who could serve as officers of the mass army he was sure would eventually be required. To ensure a suitable social composition, he had hit on the idea of recruiting college students—almost by definition an elite constituency—to undertake a month-long summer training course that would provide a rudimentary introduction to military life, and, even more important, inculcate the idea that any vigorous foreign policy must be backed by force. In the summer of 1913, students flocked (at their own expense) to camps at Gettysburg, Pennsylvania, and Monterey, California. The college program had expanded in 1914, and was scheduled to be repeated in 1915. Clark and Jay proposed that one of those camps, at Plattsburgh, New York, a town on Lake Champlain near the Canadian border, recruit men of their class and age (in their late twenties and thirties). This Business Men's Camp, as it became known, would allow "our kind of people" to demonstrate they were willing to do something personally about military preparedness.

Wood, not surprisingly, loved the idea, and agreed to explain to a gathering of prospects what four weeks of training would entail. The organizers spread the word through professional and alumni associations, and on the evening of June 14 a thousand persons crammed their way into the Harvard Club. "Great crowd," the general noted in his diary. "Great interest in summer camps. Older type." Wood proceeded to secure authorization. A substantial donation from Bernard Baruch, the Wall Street financier and friend of President Wilson,

"Are You Trained to Defend Your Country? Plattsburg," 1917. (Library of Congress Prints and Photographs Division, Willard and Dorothy Straight Collection)

helped with initial expenses. Clark and his colleagues recruited candidates through gentlemen's clubs, college alumni organizations, and upper-class social networks. Soon Clark could boast to a friend that "the whole table at Delmonico's" had enrolled in the training course. "All the best families seem to have been drafted into a machine gun platoon," one New Yorker wrote. "Socially, it is already a tremendous success, as people like myself are already going around apologizing for not being there."

On August 15 twelve hundred volunteers began thirty-five days of rigorous drills and arduous marches. Wood—booted, spurred, and wielding a dog-headed riding crop—personally supervised the training. More important than mastering the arcana of artillery, the experience afforded the volunteers a brief immersion in the strenuous life preached by their idol Teddy Roosevelt. In an exercise in class and male bonding, the lawyers and brokers sat around campfires sharing feelings of brotherly exaltation, proving they were not mere deskbound and sissified money men. Though there was much talk, notably from Roosevelt and Wood, of the citizens' army being an agent of democratization, these gentlemen had little interest in sharing their pup tents with the lower orders. AFL chief Samuel Gompers complained to Wood that the cost of participation in time and money (participants had to pay their own way), along with the educational prerequisites (a high school diploma was mandatory), precluded participation by workingmen and had "a tendency to foster one of the evils of militarism, that is military castes."[17] And when TR urged Wood to accept a few qualified blacks, the general quashed the idea of accepting officer candidates "with whom our descendants cannot intermarry without producing a breed of mongrels; they must at least be white."

Plattsburgh proved to be a major media event, thanks to its elite participants, whose ranks included Mayor Mitchel and Police Commissioner Arthur Woods. (The latter brought along forty of New York's finest, the cops providing the only proletarian presence.)[18] The camp's press profile rose higher still after August 25 when, at Wood's invitation, TR showed up in his Rough Rider outfit to hail the volunteers, and accuse President Wilson of countenancing "the murder of American men, women, and children" on the high seas and of condoning continued upheaval in Mexico.

THE *LUSITANIA* SINKING SPURRED DEMANDS for a vast expansion of the navy and army. The Navy League called for a half-billion-dollar program to build ten battleships, six battle cruisers, ten scout cruisers, fifty destroyers, a hundred submarines, and eighty smaller vessels. Wilson approved, and the shipyards got busy. But when the National Security League called for an equivalent escalation—a volunteer army of a million men (Stimson laid out the case at a "Peace and Preparedness" mass meeting on June 14 in Carnegie Hall)—the proposal met with resistance from Wilson and much of the population. As one commentator remarked, "The big army sentiment is strong in the clubs and weak in the cheap restaurants."

To broaden support, preparedness backers hawked the idea that the country in general, and New York in particular, were in imminent jeopardy.

In early 1915 retired Major General Francis V. Greene, formerly governor general of the Philippines, and formerly New York City police commissioner, published *The Present Military*

---

17. Wood agreed that financing should be extended, but not until the government took over the camps were stipends made available, and a high school diploma remained a requirement.

18. Among those who passed through the first or subsequent iterations were Stimson himself, Robert P. Patterson, John J. McCloy, Robert Lovett, Ferdinand Eberstadt, and Alfred Loomis. Franklin Roosevelt missed the experience, due to an emergency appendectomy, but in 1916 he created a "Naval Plattsburgh," which provided a summer training cruise for civilian volunteers (notably yachtsmen) who were familiar with navigation, ships' engines, radios, and other maritime skills.

Theodore Roosevelt and General Wood, Plattsburg, August 25, 1915. (Everett Collection/Alamy)

Situation in the United States. Should the Kaiser declare war on the United States, Greene believed, German forces would "instantly strike at the vitals of our trade, commerce, industrial and financial system—that is, at New York." A fleet of transports carrying 240,000 infantry troops, escorted by battleships and scout cruisers, might anchor off Long Island, "probably quite near those beautiful houses where some of my dearest friends live at Southampton," and disgorge their quarter-million men. A four-day march would bring them to Long Island City. No doubt "our people" would blow up the East River bridges, but that would only delay, not stop, the overwhelming assault. On arriving in Manhattan, the Germans would hunt down and seize as hostages those who "occupy the commanding position in the world of affairs." Greene's list of the Germans' targets was quite precise: "John D. Rockefeller, Andrew Carnegie, J. P. Morgan, George F. Baker, Jacob H. Schiff, Frank A. Vanderlip, W. K. Vanderbilt, Henry C. Frick, Vincent Astor, and Harry Payne Whitney." Once captured, these worthies would be "placed in close confinement" until they collectively coughed up 5 billion war-sustaining dollars to the German invaders, "about twice the cost of our Civil War," Greene noted, "exclusive of pensions."

    J. Bernard Walker, a former *Scientific American* editor, brought out a book in 1915 entitled *America Fallen!*, in which he argued that the long-range guns in the six forts guarding New York harbor would not deter a German invasion. Under cover of night, enemy submarines could take Fort Hancock on Sandy Hook, Fort Hamilton at the Narrows, and the Brooklyn Navy Yard. Then the German surface fleet could bombard Manhattan skyscrapers—the

Woolworth Building, the Singer Building, the Municipal Building—and terrify New Yorkers into submission. Admiral Dewey endorsed the thesis.

Fallen New York was a favorite subject for filmmakers, too. Hudson Maxim, the inventor of smokeless gunpowder, wrote *Defenseless America* in 1915, which Vitagraph turned into a movie. As one reviewer reported: "You see the sky dotted with the oncoming air craft. You see bombs drop on the swaying crowd in Times Square, you see Long Island houses go up in flames." There was also a set piece in which a New York mother shoots her daughters to save them from being raped by licentious spike-helmeted soldiers, and promptly goes mad. The English-born producer consulted with Roosevelt and Wood; Wood, along with Dewey, offered on-screen endorsements.

Fall of a Nation, another of the genre, was directed by and based on a novel of Thomas Dixon Jr., whose *Clansman* had inspired Griffith's *Birth of a Nation*; some consider *Fall* the first-ever movie sequel. In Dixon's scenario a prominent New York businessman is revealed to be a foreign dignitary who takes advantage of New York's insufficient defenses to capture the city by unleashing a hidden army of foreign supporters posing as citizens, who then proceed to the (now formulaic) rape and slaughter of the populace.[19]

SUCH LURID FANTASIES WERE PREPOSTEROUS: the Atlantic, while shrinking, remained as yet a formidable barrier, and the Royal Navy and the US fleet were reliable shields against such hypothesized German invasions. But sabotage was possible, and indeed a fact of life, though it was never able to accomplish its objective of slowing, much less stopping, the flow of war materiel from New York to the Allies.

In January 1915 an explosion rocked a boat docked in the Erie Basin. Over the next three months, German agents, intent on disrupting deliveries to the Allies, collaborated with Irish longshoremen, eager to strike a blow against England, in placing incendiaries in the cargo holds of outbound ships. When they burst into flames, captains flooded their holds, ruining hundreds of tons of goods. Thirty-six ships were hit before Inspector Thomas Tunney of the New York Bomb Squad (formed in 1914 to combat anarchists) found and shuttered a bomb factory in the house of a Hoboken chemist.

On the morning of July 3, 1915, one Erich Muenter, a Cornell (and formerly Harvard) instructor of German, decided that a better way to interdict the flow of money and munitions would be to take Jack Morgan hostage. Armed with three sticks of dynamite and two loaded revolvers, Muenter forced his way into the banker's Glen Cove home. When Morgan resisted, Muenter shot him twice (inflicting only minor damage). Captured and arrested, Muenter told a justice of the peace he had not intended to harm Morgan—"I intended to stay there until something was done." He committed suicide three days later.

Some less violent proclivities on the German agenda were unveiled on the afternoon of July 23, 1915, when a Treasury Department agent aboard a Sixth Avenue El train snatched

---

19. In addition to these homegrown efforts, New York, being media capital of the United States, was target of a massive pro-British propaganda campaign, emanating from London's Wellington House. Sir Gilbert Parker, head of the American division of the newly formed War Propaganda Bureau, sent pamphlets and personal letters to thousands of "influential and eminent people of every profession," their names culled from *Who's Who*, to build "a backing for the British cause." The WPB published over 1,160 pamphlets during the war. Authors included Arthur Conan Doyle, Ford Madox Ford, John Galsworthy, Rudyard Kipling, and H. G. Wells. The bureau got commercial companies to print and publish the material so it wouldn't be seen as propaganda. Parker's men also fed their version of the war direct to New York papers and press services, most of whom used London as their base for covering European news, thereby guaranteeing that the British perspective would be read throughout the United States. Exaggerated reports of German atrocities against Belgian civilians, disseminated from Wellington House, filled the headlines of New York's dailies.

the briefcase of a dozing Heinrich F. Albert, a commercial attaché at the German embassy. In it were plans to encourage strikes in munitions factories, to corner the market in liquid chlorine (and thus hamper the manufacture of poison gas), and to subsidize, covertly but legally, pro-German propaganda efforts in New York. Wilson's chief adviser, Colonel Edward House, leaked the captured evidence to the pro-Wilson *New York World*, which began publishing the documents on August 15.

IN THE FALL OF 1915, fresh from his summer Plattsburgh experience, Mayor Mitchel, a passionate preparedness advocate, decided to bring the city government into the fray. Given that Congress was being "utterly supine," he deemed it the "duty of local Governments to stimulate public opinion within their own jurisdictions," and bring pressure to bear on representatives who were resisting Wood's and Roosevelt's clarion calls, "either through ignorant stupidity, or the venal service of special interests." On October 6 Mitchel established the Mayor's Committee on National Defense, whose executive committee got down to work the next day. The all-star membership included Willard Straight, Cornelius Vanderbilt, Cleveland H. Dodge, George Perkins, and Bernard Baruch. Its announced purpose was "to develop in this City an understanding of and a sentiment for an effective national defense."

On November 4, 1915, Wilson gave some ground. In a speech to New York's (Democrat oriented) Manhattan Club, the president backed creation of a volunteer force of 400,000. They would serve a three-year term but would not constitute "a standing army," as their service would be limited to undergoing "intensive training for a very brief period of each year." He would, moreover, continue to rely on the National Guard as the appropriate vehicle for expansion, rather than the regular army. He insisted he was preparing for defense, not for war, though of course this was TR's stance, too, at least publicly.[20]

In response, ten days later the mayor announced that he had selected a thousand New Yorkers who would push Congress (and the president) toward an "adequate state of military and naval preparedness." This Committee of 1,000—whose leadership included Cornelius Vanderbilt, Cleveland Dodge, George Perkins, Bernard Baruch, and Willard Straight—would also undertake an educational campaign for "promoting a popular understanding" of the issue's urgency, a cause that "every loyal" citizen should support.[21] That Wilson's initiative was deemed insufficient was made clear by a series of Stimson communiqués in early 1916, in which he promoted a further expansion of the army, and moved closer to urging intervention in the war itself. A German victory, he argued, would be "disastrous to our foreign trade, our time-honored Monroe doctrine in the Western hemisphere, our relation to Mexico and the Panama Canal, our republican institutions or our national solidarity as an English-speaking race." The key issue was no longer respecting the rights of neutrals, but rather the survival of democracy and civilization itself.

The city's preparedness proponents now took to the streets, staging a massive Preparedness Parade on May 13, 1916, to demonstrate that Gotham's populace was solidly behind their demands. Months of preparation went into fashioning the procession. (The grand marshal had organized the Sound Money Parade back in 1896.) The marchers would be arrayed

---

20. The speech brought a roar of outrage from pacifists and other opponents of militarism. Emma Goldman spoke of Wilson's betrayal, and concluded that there was no longer any difference between Theodore Roosevelt, "the born bully who uses a club," and Wilson, "the history professor who uses the smooth polished university mask."

21. In addition, to beef up metropolitan defenses, Police Commissioner Woods formed a Citizens Home Defense League to assist the police force in their duties should war break out. By April 1916 20,000 citizens had registered.

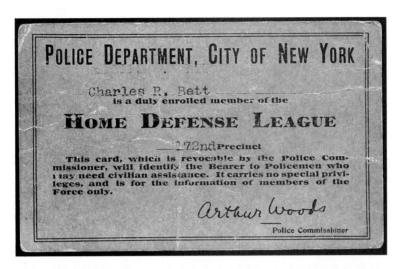

Membership Card, Home Defense League, Police Department, City of New York, 1917. (Image No. 42.5.10, Museum of the City of New York)

in ranks arranged by trades and professions, each preceded by a contingent of Plattsburg graduates. Biggest was the Financial Division, with 10,200 brokers, bankers, and employees. The Lighting (power companies) brigade mustered 9,000, the Wholesale Dry Goods 7,500, the Silk Trade 7,000, Insurance 7,000, Engineering 5,000, Paper Trades 2,500, Rubber Trade 2,100, Municipal Employees 2,000, plus lawyers, National Guardsmen, artists, actors, sculptors—115,000 in all, plus 20,000 women, largely office workers. Stepping off from City Hall Park, they marched twenty abreast past a reviewing stand at Madison Square (shared by Mayor Mitchel and General Wood), then onward up Fifth Avenue to 39th Street, where they passed another reviewing stand (from which Elihu Root waved) in front of the Union League Club. From there the ranks marched on to the Plaza at 59th Street, where they were mustered out.

It may have appeared that the entire metropolis had enlisted in the cause—"The anti-preparedness people are in a small minority," crowed the *Times*, "and their evil influence wanes daily"—but there were many citizens missing in action. As one worried observer reminded the paper, the preparedness mobilizers had "been successful in arousing a portion of the great so-called middle classes—largely the professional and business or mercantile elements," but "evidence of success is almost wholly lacking among industrial workers, especially the foreign contingent." Not only "were a large part of our people apathetic and indifferent in the face of national insult and danger," not only were workers "conspicuously absent" from the great Preparedness Parade, but the "banners of the great labor parade on May Day in New York," he noted indignantly, indicated outright opposition to preparedness. Given that the *Times* reported 100,000 had turned out to applaud Socialist Party speakers, who declared "To hell with preparedness," crying victory was indeed premature.

In fact, the ranks of dissenters extended well beyond the ranks of the city's socialists. Opponents included feminist/pacifist organizations like the Woman's Peace Party, which (the *Times* reported) had provided the only "disturbing incidents" to mar the official parade, when they attempted to break into the line of march with anti-preparedness banners and were arrested. There were also the progressive reformers who had created the American Union against Militarism, the pacifist clerics of the Fellowship for Reconciliation, and the labor dissenters of the Central Federated Union of New York City. Plus there were the vast numbers of "foreigners" who looked askance at the notion that the British were the standard-bearers of civilization and that real Americans (according to Anglophiles like Roosevelt and Root and Stimson, et al.). There were, after all, over 500,000 Germans, almost 68,500 Irish, and roughly 1,500,000 Jews in New York, and they had their own reasons for contesting a drift toward intervention on behalf of England, France, and czarist Russia.

PEACE NOW!

On August 29, 1914, a month after the outbreak of hostilities, 1,500 women staged a Woman's Peace Parade. They walked down Fifth Avenue, silent but for muffled drums. The women wore black dresses or black armbands and followed behind a yellow-fringed white banner depicting a dove and olive branch. Somber crowds lined the streets; men raised their hats as the peace flag went by.

The Peace Parade Committee embraced a broad spectrum of women activists, including suffragists Harriot Stanton Blatch and Carrie Chapman Catt; social workers Lillian Wald and Lavinia Dock; labor organizers Mary Dreier, Leonora O'Reilly, and Rose Schneiderman; and feminist intellectuals Mary Beard and Charlotte Perkins Gilman. Fanny Garrison Villard, a 70-year-old veteran of the peace movement, chaired. Most agreed (with Gilman) that in warfare "we find maleness in its absurdist extremes." Most concurred (with Catt) that "man's business of war and woman's business of conserving the race have clashed," and given the mass slaughter of women's husbands and sons, and the mass rapes to which women were subjected, it was time to make war the "undeniable business of women." Most had European friends and colleagues in the international women's movement, and believed/

Women's Peace Parade, Fifth Avenue, August 29, 1914. (Library of Congress Prints and Photographs Division, George Grantham Bain Collection)

hoped that ties of gender could overcome the hostilities of nationality. Most agreed that the male peace movement had been ineffective and there was need for an all-female organization, one that drew upon (and reinforced) the strength of the New York women's suffrage movement, then in full swing.

In November 1914 Crystal Eastman convened the first meeting of the Woman's Peace Party of New York City (WPPNY). The socialist-feminist attorney and journalist, who had authored New York State's first workman's compensation law, feared that entrance into war would end or even reverse the movement to improve industrial health and safety, and retard other social and labor reforms that women were championing. She and her fellow suffragists, socialists, and feminists—many of them members of Heterodoxy and participants in the Greenwich Village scene—also sought to address the causes of war, embedded in the economic structures of the United States. They adopted, for instance, an anti-imperialist stance, protesting the dispatch of troops to Haiti, the Dominican Republic, and Nicaragua.

In January 1915 Jane Addams of Chicago's Hull House led the way in establishing a nationwide Woman's Peace Party (WPP), seeking to mutually fortify the movements promoting international peace, domestic reform, and women's suffrage. It would be headquartered in Addams's hometown but would include a powerful contingent of New Yorkers, among them Crystal Eastman, Fanny Garrison Villard, Lillian Wald, Leonora O'Reilly, Florence Kelley, Mary Heaton Vorse, and Emily Balch.

In April 1915 the national Woman's Peace Party sent delegates to an International Congress of Women in The Hague. The delegates, from twelve countries—including Germany, Great Britain, Austria, and Hungary—appealed for US mediation to end the war, support for arbitration in settling disputes, democratic control of foreign policy, female suffrage so that women could have a say in such policies, general disarmament, and the voiding of secret treaties. The women were attacked in the press by Theodore Roosevelt, who described them as "hysterical pacifists" whose proposals were "both silly and base."[22]

THE WPPNY OVERLAPPED WITH A MORE NARROWLY FOCUSED Gotham-based organization, the American League to Limit Armaments (ALLA), whose formation in December 1914 came in direct response to the creation days earlier of the National Security League, which advocated an arms and army buildup. The ALLA was an awkward alliance of the conservative businessmen's peace movement and the newer, more militant one. Spearheaded by New York's Episcopal bishop David H. Greer, and Columbia University's Nicholas Murray Butler, the conservatives made clear they were only interested in pursuing arms restriction and arbitration *after* the current war had ended. But the radical wing wanted to contest the burgeoning preparedness drive, a clear and present danger. By March 1915 they had broken away and formed an Anti-Preparedness Committee, which they eventually renamed the American Union against Militarism (AUAM). Lillian Wald became the chairperson, and Crystal Eastman served as executive director. Prominent members included Oswald Garrison Villard (Fanny's son and the *Nation*'s publisher), philanthropist George Foster Peabody, Unitarian minister John Haynes Holmes, Morris Hillquit, Felix Adler, Rabbi Wise, Elsie Clews Parsons,

---

22. When Wilson refused to attempt mediation, Henry Ford proposed a private-sector intervention. Ford believed that "New York wants war," he said in June 1915, "but the United States doesn't. The peoples west of New York are too sensible for war." In November 1915 Ford traveled to Gotham, chartered a ship, and invited 115 well-known men and women to sail with him as peace commissioners and help set up a permanent peace conference in Europe. Bryan and Edison were among those who saw it off as a band played the most popular Tin Pan Alley song of 1915, "I Didn't Raise My Boy to Be a Soldier." The effort went nowhere, the belligerents being devoted to winning, not negotiating.

Carrie Chapman Catt, Adolph Lewisohn, and Jane Addams. By 1916 the New York–based organization had enrolled 15,000 members in twenty-two cities, distributed over half a million pieces of anti-war literature, and set up a national press bureau that delivered stories to 1,601 papers, including farmer and labor weeklies.

The Woman's Peace Party and American Union against Militarism went mano a mano with the National Security League. On June 15, 1915, the day after the NSL's mass "Peace and Preparedness" meeting at Carnegie Hall, the Woman's Peace Party staged a rebuttal gathering at Cooper Union. Crystal Eastman described the earlier meeting as one "at which certain learned gentlemen"—"well supported by gentlemen of great wealth"—had urged spending more of the people's money on national defense. The advocates, she argued, had used what seemed "to my poor feminine intellect like high school boy logic, fist logic." She reported that the WPP had sent the NSL chair a simple query—"Is Europe today your example of peace by preparedness?"—but had received no answer.

In another toe-to-toe gambit, on the very day of the NSL's Preparedness Parade, May 13, 1916, the WPP opened a "War against War" exhibition in 208 Fifth Avenue (at Madison Square). It offered anti-war displays and a daily program of noontime speakers (such as Wise, Villard, Holmes, and Hillquit), but its star attraction was Jingo, a papier-mâché dinosaur. The "military lizard" carried the following inscription: "This is Jingo, the armored dinosaur: All Armor Plate and No Brains. This animal believed in Huge Armaments—He is Now Extinct." Jingo, the exhibit noted, was of the species "Dinosaurus Theodorus Rooseveltus," and had been dug out of the mud at Oyster Bay. The exhibition attracted between 5,000 and 10,000 visitors a day, for months, to the intense annoyance of preparedness supporters. One such sputtered in a letter to the *Times* that he "viewed with much alarm the large attendance" at the "dastardly exhibit" whose "dangerous influence" was "insidious," its "purpose questionable if not treasonable"; it was something that "should be suppressed."

The WPP and AUAM also advanced concrete counterproposals. Given that (as Max Eastman observed) the "military excitement" seemed mainly "to have possessed our upper and leisure classes," those elites should pay for it, through income and inheritance taxes, "not by taxes which place the burden on the poor." More pointedly, they argued that the manufacture of munitions should be taken away from the war contractors in the Army and Navy Leagues—whose names and profits they exposed to public scrutiny—and turned over to the

"Jingo" the Dinosaur. "This animal believed in huge armaments; he is now extinct." *Survey,* April 1, 1916.

government, cutting costs dramatically by eliminating profits. They fought, too, against "the invasion of our public school system by military authorities and enthusiasts," but failed to block a New York State law that imposed military training on schoolboys aged 16 to 19—three hours of drill a week, two to four weeks at a camp during the summer; they did, however help forestall funding for such programs at the federal level.

WHERE ACTIVIST WOMEN HOPED THAT AFFINITIES OF GENDER might be able to transcend the enmities of nationalism, Christian pacifists felt similarly about the capability of their faith. A new generation of social gospelers—spiritual heirs of Walter Rauschenbusch—now came to the fore, among them Norman Thomas, of Marion, Ohio. His father was a Presbyterian minister, and the family was not well-off, but an affluent uncle paid Thomas's way through Princeton, where he studied with Woodrow Wilson. On graduating in 1905 Thomas was drawn to Gotham, where he did volunteer social work at the Spring Street Presbyterian Church and Neighborhood Center, helping the families of local laborers, many of them unemployed, in the run-down area between Varick Street and the Hudson River docks.

Though his father was of a conservative theological bent, Thomas in 1908 enrolled in Union Theological Seminary, a center of social gospel thought. Two of his teachers, Harry Emerson Fosdick and Henry Sloane Coffin, were great exponents of Rauschenbusch, whose work had a profound impact on the young man. While studying, he again did volunteer work, this time at Christ Presbyterian Church on West 36th Street, where he met Frances Violet Stewart, a visiting nurse from a wealthy, socially prominent family. When they married in 1910 she was summarily dropped from the *Social Register*. In 1911 Thomas graduated from the seminary and was ordained as a Presbyterian minister. Having been first in his class, he been sought out by, and could have stayed on at, the fashionable Brick Presbyterian Church on Fifth Avenue, at 37th, whose communicants were chauffeured to services in motorcars. But he and his wife opted for a ministry to the urban poor. He became pastor of the East Harlem Presbyterian Church, on 116th Street between Second and Third Avenues, where his congregants were Italians, Hungarians, Slovaks, and Swedes. In association with the Union Settlement on 104th Street (founded by Union Theological Seminary alumni), he sent coal to freezing communicants, provided nursing services, formed clubs, planted gardens, opened workshops, and in general sought funds from the rich to help the poor. But he came to believe that the conditions he was up against in East Harlem—"grotesque inequalities, conspicuous waste, gross exploitation, and unnecessary poverty"—were systemic in nature. And soon, he would later recall, he "came to the conclusion that it was extraordinarily difficult under the existing economic structure for many men and women of any class to carry out the ethics of Jesus."

When war broke out, Thomas was appalled by the "spectacle of men professing faith in the same Christ, using all possible means of destruction to kill one another." In 1916, therefore, he joined the fledgling Fellowship of Reconciliation (FOR), a Christian pacifist organization. In 1914 Henry Hodgkin, an English Quaker, and Friedrich Sigmund-Schultze, a German Lutheran, had pledged to find a way of working for peace even though their countries were at war. Out of this came a gathering of Christians in Cambridge, England, in December 1914, which founded the Fellowship. In 1915 Hodgkin came to the United States to meet with sixty-eight women and men at Garden City, New York, where the American FOR was founded on November 11; it opened offices at 125 East 27th Street. Among the prominent founders was John Haynes Holmes, Unitarian minister of the Church of the Messiah at Park Avenue and 34th Street. Placing the claims of religious faith above those of the nation-state, Holmes wrote: "No one is wise enough, no nation is important enough, no human interest is precious enough, to justify the wholesale destruction and murder which constitute the science of war." More emphatically still, he declared: "War is in open and utter violation of Christianity. If war is right, then Christianity is wrong, false, a lie."[23]

Thomas, too, became convinced that "war and Christianity are incompatible." He grew increasingly disturbed that clergymen, including those of his own denomination, supported preparedness, and even intervention, in the name of Jesus, rather than urging the United States to use its moral and economic strength to mediate a settlement between the warring parties. He began to work with the FOR, and the American Union against Militarism, speaking out on street corners and in local schools and colleges in opposition to compulsory military training. And, increasingly, he drew closer to the Socialist Party, which addressed both domestic and foreign ills in ways he found persuasive.

WHERE WOMEN COUNTED ON GENDER, and pacifist clerics counted on faith, socialists hoped that ties of class would outweigh those of nationality. New York socialists believed that workers of the world would unite in rejecting warfare. On August 8, 1914, within days of the outbreak of fighting, the party organized an anti-war protest in Union Square. Thousands attended the rally, where speakers railed—in English, German, French, Russian, Hungarian, and Swedish—against the spreading conflict. Behind them was a banner that read WAR IS

Irish socialist Cornelius "Con" Lehane, anti-war rally, Union Square, August 8, 1914. (Library of Congress Prints and Photographs Division, George Grantham Bain Collection)

---

23. Less well known than Holmes was a Thomas contemporary, Abraham Johannes (A. J.) Muste, a Dutch-born clergyman. From 1909 on Muste pastored at the Fort Washington Collegiate Church while studying at Union Theological, from which he earned a Bachelor of Divinity degree in 1913. He moved to Massachusetts in 1915, where, in 1916, he joined the local FOR.

Anti-war rally, Union Square, August 8, 1914. (Library of Congress Prints and Photographs Division, George Grantham Bain Collection)

HELL, SOCIALISM ALONE STANDS FOR BROTHERHOOD, WORKING MEN OF THE WORLD WILL WORK FOR SOCIALISM. To their shock and dismay, the world's workers did not unite. The spectacle of socialists killing socialists was all but unimaginable, given their premise that workers had no overweening national allegiance. But it seemed their comrades had been convinced that their respective countries faced invasion. Fear and hate had replaced solidarity, and all were "drawn into the maelstrom of confusion."

On August 12 the party declared that American workers would not be led to the slaughter. One of their contributions to forestalling such a fate was to offer an analysis of the forces that had led to war. Party theoretician Morris Hillquit penned an essay, published in early September, whose title got right to the point: "Murderous War in Europe Is the Inevitable Culmination of Murderous European Capitalism." Capitalists in European countries (like those in the United States), Hillquit argued, had confronted a structural overproduction/underconsumption crisis. Improved productivity via labor-saving devices had led to growing unemployment, which helped press down wages of those still employed, eroding their purchasing power. This left capitalists bereft of a home market large enough to absorb the commodities the workers had produced. Imperialism had seemed a potential solution, providing access to new markets. But then competition—constrained inside each country—had reared its head again on a global level. The collective capitalists of each nation vied for market share with their counterparts in other countries. Each saw salvation in robbing the others of colonies and markets. This led to military and naval rivalry—a necessary counterpart of commercial rivalry—and the competing nations, armed to the teeth, had stood threatening each other until finally "the cultured nations of Europe turned into one howling, savage mob, drunk with the lust of blood—shrieking for murder, murder, murder." European socialists had been powerless to prevent the appalling catastrophe because "the dark forces of capitalism" were simply too strong. Organized workers could not resist "the brutal logic of capitalist warfare," and "reluctantly but irresistibly they were drawn into the insane vortex of mutual slaughter."

Happily, US workers were less vulnerable to militarist blandishments, Hillquit suggested, "due principally to the fortunate position of geographical isolation of our country and partly also to the fact that as yet we have not been drawn very deeply into the economic rivalries of Europe, and have not had the opportunity to develop a pronounced imperialistic policy or a strong military regime." Yet Americans should "take warning from the horrible example of Europe. Already our capitalist classes are making a strong bid for the markets of the world. Already we are developing a 'colonial policy,' fortifying our army and building up a strong navy with steady and fatal consistency." That was why opposing preparedness was essential.

Congressman Meyer London agreed with Hillquit's focus on clashing economic interests—though he added some collateral cultural and political causes, like nationalist prejudice and race hatred, to Hillquit's narrow-gauge analysis—and he, too, thought expanding armies would exacerbate the situation. "When two men get into a fight," London observed, "if they have no revolvers they would not fight with revolvers, but if they have revolvers and ammunition and large stores of explosives at the very moment when their interests collide they will use the means they have at their disposal for destroying each other."

Hillquit, London, and the party leadership hammered out a peace program that included opposition to preparedness, proposals for mediation by the United States, and an embargo on financial assistance or shipment of food or munitions to all belligerents.

WHAT GAVE THESE DEMANDS POLITICAL MUSCLE was support from New York's labor movement, particularly the 300,000-strong Central Federated Union of New York City and Vicinity (CFU). On August 3, 1914, Ernest Bohm, secretary of the CFU, announced that his organization was inaugurating an anti-war campaign. During 1915, as the National Security League's preparedness campaign took off, the CFU remained staunchly opposed. In February the organization resolved that "whereas an attempt is being made by certain elements in our country to embroil it in the present European slaughter," the CFU "earnestly appeals to labor throughout this country to oppose in every way any and all attempts to inveigle the United States into the European conflict." On April 15, 1915, it invited Congressman London to address 3,000 unionists at Cooper Union. London argued that as the munition makers would never become conscience stricken—"business was business and they would supply hell with fire and brimstone if they could do so"—workers needed to paralyze "every industry that in any way helps to prolong the war." The assembled workers adopted a resolution (with great applause) that organized labor should "seriously consider at once the proposition of a general strike among those industries."[24] The torpedoing of the *Lusitania* did not deflect them. On June 19 the CFU and the Woman's Peace Party invited London and William Jennings Bryan to address a Carnegie Hall rally. London repeated his demands, and Bryan, arguing preparedness advocates "would provoke war instead of preventing it," observed of

---

24. The idea of a general strike proved to be too extreme for other socialists, and for the bulk of the CFU trade unions. It was too associated with syndicalists and Wobblies and anarchists. Which was exactly why it appealed to Emma Goldman: "Valuable as the work of the Women's Peace Party and other earnest pacifists may be," she would write in *Mother Earth*, "it is folly to petition the President for peace. The workers, they alone, can avert the impending war; in fact, all wars, if they will refuse to be a party to them. . . . The ordinary pacifist merely moralizes; the antimilitarist acts; he refuses to be ordered to kill his brothers. His slogan is: 'I will not kill, nor will I lend myself to be killed.' It is this slogan which we must spread among the workers and carry into the labor organizations."

Teddy Roosevelt that "he is so anxious to get into any contest that involves bloodletting that he cannot be trusted to deal with any phase of the subject."

The rally proved the last major pacifist endeavor sponsored by the CFU, as the organization slowly and reluctantly drifted toward the preparedness camp, following in the footsteps of Samuel Gompers, the AFL chieftain. Gompers had once promoted pacifism, believing war was bad for labor. By June 1915, however, he'd begun backing away from this stance—refusing to speak at the Carnegie Hall rally with London and Bryan—and by 1916 he had unreservedly endorsed Wilson's preparedness policy.

Why? Principally because Gompers believed it would be good for his skilled-worker constituency. If the preparedness movement succeeded, as he thought was increasingly likely in the aftermath of the *Lusitania* sinking, then becoming an early and eager convert would ingratiate labor with big business, with the Wilson administration (which had adopted pro-labor policies), and with the general public. Also, as supplying the Allies had uplifted a depressed economy and expanded employment opportunities, signing on to preparedness would extend this prosperity, and win the AFL a seat for workers at the wartime table. Gompers also thought preparedness would be good for Gompers. Joining that camp would, he believed, burnish his credentials as a "statesman of labor," a status he'd pursued at the National Civic Federation. And indeed, when Wilson appointed him to an Advisory Commission of the Council of National Defense, he was warmly embraced by the rich and powerful.

Still, through 1916, substantial forces in the AFL resisted Gompers's drift to martial militancy, particularly in New York. As late as February 1917, the CFU resolved by a near-unanimous vote to urge Wilson to resist those demanding intervention. Even stronger opposition came from outside the AFL/CFU network, among the Jewish and Italian needle workers in the International Ladies' Garment Workers Union and the Amalgamated Clothing Workers of America (ACWA), who believed the war was a brutal and inhuman conflict waged in the economic interests of the capitalist class (though, more pragmatically, the ACWA also demanded that labor get its fair share of preparedness profits).

THE NSL'S PREPAREDNESS PARADE OF MAY 13, 1916, observers had noted, was overwhelmingly composed of upper- and middle-class New Yorkers, and largely shorn of the industrial work-force, especially those of a socialist, pacifist, or feminist bent. The parade also came up short on "foreign" contingents—one reason, perhaps, that unlike in the Hudson-Fulton Parade of 1909, marchers were not arrayed by ethnicity. The parade, like the movement it promoted, could be seen as driven by economic elites and resisted primarily by sectors of the working class. Though it could also be seen, if viewed through a filter that highlighted countries of origin, as being chiefly promoted by New Yorkers of British and French descent, and opposed principally by citizens in German, Irish, and Jewish neighborhoods.

HYPHENS

German Americans, over 500,000 strong, were a prominent presence in Gotham, and had been since at least the 1840s. They commanded substantial swatches of territory—in Yorkville, Williamsburg, and Astoria, among other enclaves—wherein they had established a dense network of clubs, churches, and associations, from the German Society of the City of New York (1784) to the German Club (1847) to the German American Chamber of Commerce in New York (1914). The community boasted of its contributions to the city and country, and saw no contradiction in fervently supporting Germany's side in the war. From the minute hostilities broke out, many German Americans leapt to its aid. Young men lined up at the consulate to enlist, though most were balked by lack of boats.

Instead, the community sent money. The *Brooklyner Freie Presse* solicited funds "to help the widows and orphans of their suffering countrymen in Germany and Austria." Bazaars were held at which traditional German, Austrian, and Hungarian goods and foods were sold in order to raise cash. At a shop on Second Avenue, in a program organized by the German Historical Society, people donated precious objects—wedding bands, jewels, heirlooms—in return for an iron ring decorated with a Maltese cross and an inscription in German that read: "Loyalty to the Fatherland to evidence, gave I, in troublous time, gold for this iron." In October 1914 the *Times* estimated that over 10,000 of the iron rings were being worn across the city.

Others forthrightly backed the war effort itself—buying German war bonds, parading through the streets, attending large-scale events in the beer halls and parks in Manhattan, Brooklyn, and Queens, where both American and German anthems were sung and the flags of both nations flown. They saw no reason to mute their voices simply because other New Yorkers favored the Allies. The loudest voices came from the German American press, headed up by Herman Ridder's *New Yorker Staats-Zeitung* (founded in 1834), whose editorials weren't shy about supporting the Kaiser's imperial ambitions, praising him particularly for defending Civilization from Russian Barbarism. German newspapers argued for America's staying neutral, and criticized the preparedness movement as a step toward intervention on behalf of the British and French. (William Randolph Hearst's *Journal* was also vehemently pro-German, as was his German-language *Deutsches Journal*, Hearst being an Anglophobe of Scots-Irish descent.)

These voices were aided and amplified by the German state, which aimed to influence the New York press and populace. The German Information Service—a clandestine propaganda agency—published and distributed leaflets, pamphlets, and books arguing the German cause. In addition, the German ambassador, Count Johann von Bernstorff, established a multi-million-dollar slush fund to underwrite German- and English-language presses in the city. The most successful was the *Fatherland*, a pro-German weekly, written in English, established by George Sylvester Viereck in August 1914. Brought to New York in 1897, aged 12, Viereck graduated from City College in 1906 and went on to establish a national reputation as a poet. With the help of undisclosed subsidies from von Bernstorff's fund, Viereck set out to "break the power of England upon our government" through lively articles and editorials under the slogan "Fair Play for Germany and Austria-Hungary"; he soon claimed 75,000 subscribers.[25] The community's support for the Kaiser was not unanimous—German American socialists remained ardently opposed to the war—but they were bucking a strong tide, and their paper, the *Volkszeitung*, lost 5,000 subscribers in the first month of the conflict.

IRISH AMERICANS WERE NEVER GOING TO BE in England's corner, but the vehemence with which they opposed US intervention increased sharply, in response to shifting attitudes and dramatic events in Gotham and Ireland itself.

The New York Irish had been divided for many decades over how to deal with England's grip on Ireland. In the nineteenth century, New York's middle class and lace curtain elite had

---

25. Though there was much hullabaloo when its workings were exposed—thanks to Heinrich Albert's purloined papers—it was much less extensive, and far less successful, than its super-secret British counterpart directed from Wellington House.

tended to support movements for winning Home Rule—greater autonomy within the United Kingdom of Great Britain and Ireland—and they wanted to achieve it gradually and nonviolently, through constitutional electoral means. Working-class Irish Americans, however, tended to favor winning complete independence for Ireland and, if necessary, using physical force to attain it.

At the century's turn, there were two principal organizations promoting the contending positions—loosening versus eliminating British control—each linked with different Irish allies. The United Irish League of America (UILA,1901) aligned itself with the Irish Parliamentary Party (IPP) run by John Redmond, and aided his fight in Parliament to obtain Home Rule. The New York UILA leaders were conservative in their goals and tactics partly because they were men of wealth and social standing—bankers, contractors, and political leaders like John Purroy Mitchel, Tammany boss Charles Murphy, and famed Tammany orator/lawyer Bourke Cockran—those whom Redmond referred to as "the better class of Irish men of New York." Their local politics were cautious, too. They distanced themselves from James Connolly's Irish Socialist Federation (Connolly remained in New York exile from 1902 to 1910), while moving closer to the Catholic Church as a bulwark against social radicalism. Even the once pro-labor and anti-clerical Patrick Ford, UILA supporter and editor of the powerful *Irish World*, made peace with the hierarchy.[26]

The UILA was opposed by the Clan na Gael, founded in 1867, and led since the 1870s by the radical journalist John Devoy (whose own exile to New York had begun in 1871). Devoy reorganized the Clan in 1900. And three years later, at the age of 61, he started up the *Gaelic American* as a militant alternative to Ford's *Irish World*, and began lambasting parliamentarians. The Clan na Gael was linked with Ireland's paramilitary Irish Republican Brotherhood (IRB), a connection Devoy had himself established back in 1877. The IRB, a secretive organization, was composed of hard men prepared to use military means to establish an Irish Republic. The Clan na Gael leaders were also cultural nationalists, arguing that the Irish were a unique ethnicity, one decidedly distinct from English culture. They were strong supporters of the Gaelic Revival in Ireland and aided groups like the Gaelic League, the Gaelic Athletic Association, and Sinn Féin.

In the 1910s the UILA's conservative parliamentarians, not the Clan's revolutionary republicans, dominated Irish-American nationalism in New York—especially as it looked as if the former would succeed. UILA funding and political support helped Redmond win introduction of a Home Rule bill in Parliament in 1912. Roosevelt and Wilson both backed the measure. Membership in the UILA soared.

But the war changed everything. Home Rule finally passed in 1914, but Redmond—to demonstrate his loyalty—announced he was immediately postponing its execution, was supporting the British war effort, and was urging the paramilitary Irish Volunteers to enlist in the British Army. Redmond also claimed that "95 percent of the Irish Race in America" supported his position.

In fact, US support for the UILA, and Redmond, evaporated almost immediately, and the organization quickly collapsed. The Clan na Gael sprang into action. In its capacity as an underground revolutionary entity, it raised funds for an uprising in Ireland, and helped arrange German backing for the insurrection. On August 24, 1914, Devoy and other Clan

---

26. Some UILA backers, however, were fierce critics of the Church. John Quinn, the venturesome art patron and Armory Show supporter, saw the hierarchy as threatening artistic freedom, and he also believed, as he wrote William Butler Yeats, that it was essential to break the grip of the Catholic Church on education.

leaders met with Ambassador von Bernstorff and his military attaché Franz von Papen, at the luxurious German Club (112 Central Park South). They sought support for the planned uprising, requesting both arms and capable military officers; the Clan would supply the funding. Devoy also brought Sir Roger Casement into the discussion. Casement, who had arrived in the city on July 20, was an Anglo-Protestant Irish nationalist, who was working with the Irish Volunteers, and who proposed formation of an Irish Brigade to be recruited from among Germany's Irish prisoners of war. The Germans eventually agreed to send a boatload of arms.

While planning proceeded, and moneys were raised, the Clan worked aboveground to galvanize Irish-American support for the nationalist movement. This became the particular charge of Devoy's close confederate Daniel Florence Cohalan. Twenty-five years younger than Devoy, Cohalan was a second-generation Irish American, son of a building tradesman turned factory owner. By 1900 he'd become a successful lawyer and had started up the political ladder of Tammany Hall. By 1914 he'd been elected a grand sachem and appointed a state supreme court justice. In December of 1915 he and Devoy decided to sponsor a gathering that would "afford a rallying point for the union of the entire Irish Race at home and abroad." The Irish Race Convention was held March 4–5, 1916, in the Hotel Astor. It was striking for its size—more than 2,500 attended—and for its middle-class decorum, with Cohalan determined to shed any traces of rowdyism. But the tone of the speeches was uncompromisingly radical. Thus John W. Goff, an Irish-born Tammany judge, addressed the gathering, saying: "I want to see the power of England broken on land and sea. It is treason to our race to hope for or help in an English victory."

The convention also formed a new organization, the Friends of Irish Freedom, to broaden the movement's membership base, and allow the active participation of many previously excluded from Clan activities, notably women, who'd been strikingly subordinate or absent from the band of brothers-style Clan na Gael.

Meanwhile Devoy channeled $100,000 (from small donations) to the rebels in Dublin. On February 5, 1916, the Irish Republican Brotherhood sent him a coded message with the date of the rising: Easter Monday, April 24, 1916. It proved a disaster. First, on Good Friday, Casement had been captured after a German U-boat had set him ashore in County Kerry. The next day the boat, laden with arms from Germany, was stopped near the Irish coast and scuttled by its captain.[27] In Dublin, bands of IRB men and Volunteers forged ahead anyway, seizing sites around the city, taking the General Post Office as a headquarters, and declaring Ireland an independent republic. But thousands of British soldiers deploying heavy artillery suppressed the rebellion after six days of street fighting. Thirty-five hundred men and women involved or suspected of sympathy were arrested, nearly 2,000 were summarily shipped to prisons or internment camps, and fourteen of the leaders were executed in May in Kilmainham Jail. Casement was hanged for treason on August 3.

Both Dublin and New York were divided on the wisdom of the Rising. Some believed it irresponsible or poorly thought-through, while others believed it may have been a strategy to court martyrdom, with suppression of a foredoomed rebellion winning people to their cause.

---

27. Launched in New York, collaboration with the Germans may have been sunk there, too. On April 18, 1916, six days before the uprising, the US Secret Service raided the New York offices of Wolf von Igel, von Papen's successor as military attaché, and director of German intelligence operations in the United States. Confiscated papers included telegrams describing arms shipments and preparations for the rebellion. Devoy believed Casement's capture was due to information the Wilson administration furnished Great Britain. Secretary of State Lansing denied this, and it's possible that the British secret service on its own had deciphered intercepted German telegrams about the coming events in Ireland.

If so, it worked. In the aftermath of the Rising, independence gained the popular support in Ireland that resulted in the Sinn Fein electoral victories of 1918, which in turn brought on the War of Independence.

A wave of fury swept through Irish New York. On May 14, 1916, days after the executions, 3,500 crammed Carnegie Hall. (Four thousand more couldn't get in.) Devoy and Cohalan shared the stage with Bourke Cockran, who now repudiated his earlier moderate position. Father P. J. Duffy, chaplain of the "Fighting 69th" Regiment, declared that "British butchery" would unite the Irish as never before. And the meeting resolved that there should be no settlement of the European war that did not include a plan for the liberation of Ireland.

A month later, on June 10, the Friends of Irish Freedom held an "Irish Memorial Mass Meeting" in the more capacious Madison Square Garden (though again it seemed the crowd outside doubled the 20,000 within). Prior to the event 600 Irish Volunteers living in New York marched down Broadway from Columbus Circle to 23rd Street, carrying the flag of the Irish Republic that had floated over the Dublin Post Office during the uprising. In the rally, every mention of the United States, Ireland, and Germany touched off great demonstrations, while hisses and boos greeted every reference to the tyrannical British. Bourke Cockran declared that the executions had "forever doomed" any possible alliance between the US and the UK.

JEWISH AMERICAN REJECTION OF THE ANGLO–FRENCH–RUSSIAN ALLIANCE was coterminous with the outbreak of war, as terrible news flowed in from the Eastern Front, and was headlined in the Yiddish press. Czarist troops engaged in wholesale and sadistic savagery, along with massive expulsions of hundreds of thousands, often at twelve hours' notice. Conditions worsened in the winter months of 1914–15, as the Russians advanced into Galicia and Bukovina, spreading devastation and famine. By the spring of 1915, things were so bad in Russian Poland that, Jacob Schiff wrote in April, "Belgium's plight is a mere bagatelle in comparison." And it wasn't only the Russian regime, but Slavs in general, notably the Poles, who were responsible for atrocities. Jews had been "outraged in the most terrible manner," Schiff reported, "both by the Poles who denounced them to the Russians as enemies and spies and then by the Russians themselves, who treated them as such." It was only thanks to the Germans that the Jews ever received protection. "In saying this I do not want to be misjudged," Schiff insisted, "for it is well known that I am a German sympathizer. But the fact is that the Russians and the Poles alike have been inhumane to the Jewish population." When the German army in the summer of 1915 retook Austrian Gallicia, and the large Jewish centers of Warsaw, Bialystok, and Kovno, Gotham's Yiddish papers celebrated their liberation "from the rule of the Asiatic barbarian." Even radical Russian Jews like Chaim Zhitlovsky, steeped in Russian culture, admitted that if the war were only between Russia and Germany, "we would all be on Germany's side." Hungary, too, received plaudits in the city's Hungarian-Galician quarter, for Emperor Franz Joseph's protection of Jews from anti-Semitic Poles.

The city's Jews hastened to mobilize support for their badly mauled coreligionists, though at first in a segmented way. In October 1914 the American Jewish Relief Committee for Sufferers of the War was formed, with Felix Warburg (Jacob Schiff's son-in-law) and lawyer Louis Marshall at its head, in effect a creation of the American Jewish Committee, organ of the German Jewish establishment. At the same time, the city's Orthodox communities gathered together in a Central Relief Committee, and later, the People's Relief Committee was organized by the labor and socialist movements and chaired by Meyer London.[28] It was soon agreed that funds should be dispatched overseas through a single channel, and in November 1914 the Joint Distribution Committee was established. By 1917, operating out of Warburg's offices at 52 William Street, it had raised and transferred nearly $9 million.

GOTHAM'S COLLECTION OF CENTRAL AND SOUTHEASTERN EUROPEANS did support the Allies, not out of love for Britain, but in hopes that their victory might topple the Austro-Hungarian Empire that held their countries in thrall. There were perhaps a thousand Serbians in the city, who in July 1914 set up a Serbian National Defense League. Young men sought to return to their homeland to fight for national self-determination alongside their supporter, Czarist Russia. Gotham's Slovaks, numbering perhaps 10,000, were concentrated in Yorkville, in the East 70s and 80s between York and Third Avenues, as well as Long Island City, Sunnyside, Astoria, and Greenpoint. They, too, were aflame with nationalist sentiment, stoked by the newspapers *Slovak v Amerike* and *Newyorský Denník*. When the leading Croat-language paper, *Narodni List*, proved reluctant to push for statehood, the city's Croats turned to the more republican-minded *Hrvatski Svijet* or *Ilustrovani List*.

In addition to these initiatives, the communities quickly struck up informal collaborations to magnify their presence on the city scene. In July 1914 an array of ten Slavic-language newspapers issued a joint denunciation of the Austro-Hungarian Empire from Sokol Hall, located at 420 East 71st Street, a community center for Gotham's Slavic population. In August Serbians, Croats, Bohemians, Bosnians, Herzegovinians, Montenegrins, and Czechs met at the Central Opera House, on East 67th near Third, and pledged money and blood to the collective cause of liberation. The crowd sang the anthems of all the would-be nations, and many seemed to know the others' lyrics.

The Austro-Hungarian Empire itself had next to no support in New York, even from the German-language press, even from the Hungarians. The Dual Monarchy's biggest public splash came in July 1914 when Count Mihály Károlyi arrived in New York and drew over 10,000 Hungarian Americans to a rally in Washington Square. But Károlyi was a prominent member of the Hungarian opposition party, and his rally was to demand political reform of the empire.

WHEN ITALY JOINED THE ALLIES IN MAY 1915, having been offered territorial concessions should they win, the half-million inhabitants of East Harlem's Little Italy and other Italian neighborhoods in Brooklyn and the Bronx, hung flags and banners urging the Italian army to seize Trieste and Trento—which irredentists had long argued were predominantly Italian though under foreign rule. Thousands of recent emigrants—reservists in the Italian army and navy—lined up outside the Italian consulate on Spring Street, though in the end only about 15 percent of those eligible for military service boarded steamships for Genoa or Naples.

The community divided internally on the war. The great majority—driven by nationalist pride and spurred on by the *prominenti*, the clergy, and the consulate—turned out with gusto for rallies and parades. Most anarchists and socialists, from Galleani to Giovannitti,

---

28. The first initiative aided the approximately 59,000 Jews who were living in Palestine under Ottoman rule. The settlement—the Yishuv—was largely made up of Jews who had emigrated from Europe and were largely dependent on sources outside of Palestine for their income. The outbreak of war left the community destitute. The Yishuv's leaders appealed to Henry Morgenthau, then the US ambassador to Turkey. On August 31, 1914, Morgenthau cabled Schiff, requesting $50,000 in aid, which was swiftly forthcoming.

were fervently opposed to Italian participation. They urged workers not to fight and die for the imperialistic and dynastic ambitions of the House of Savoy. But many who had marched behind the red flag in Lawrence or Paterson now paraded behind the Italian tricolor. Even some of the syndicalists in the Italian Socialist Federation (ISF) underwent a drastic transformation. In June 1914 Giovannitti had been replaced as director of *Il Proletario* by a relative newcomer, Edmondo Rossoni, who at first attacked the war unrelentingly in the paper's pages and at meetings in Italian American communities. But Rossoni, shocked by American treatment of Italian workers, began to argue that proletarian internationalism would be possible only after Italy and Italians abroad were respected by outsiders. In August 1914 Rossoni declared his support for the Allies, and urged Italy to join the war effort in order to regain its past grandeur. Also, following the line advanced by Benito Mussolini, editor of *L'Avanti!*, the leading socialist daily in Italy, he argued that the passions aroused by the war would wake the working class from its stupor. He now attacked neutralists' masculinity, using violent and sexually laden imagery to charge they were lacking in courage. Not until June 1915 were IFS chapters able to force him out of the organization. Rossoni then founded *L'Italia Nostra*, a vehemently nationalist paper in Brooklyn, and in 1916 returned to Italy, where he eventually became head of Mussolini's Fascist labor organization. The ISF never regained its prominence in the Italian American community.

NEW YORK'S AFRICAN AMERICANS HAD NO EMPIRES to win or defend, no casualties of combat to succor, no cultural ties to the combatants. But as W. E. B. Du Bois argued from his NAACP editorial chair, and Hubert Harrison from his street-corner soapbox, Africa was in great measure what the war was all about.

In the November 1914 *Crisis*, Du Bois published "World War and the Color Line," in which he backed the socialist explanation of the conflict but added a crucial racial dimension. The war was not a "national" rivalry between Slavs, Teutons, and Latins, but rather a "wild quest for Imperial expansion" on the part of England, Germany, France, Belgium, Italy, Russia, and Austria-Hungary. The colonies they all coveted were "largely in tropical and semi-tropical lands and inhabited by black, brown and yellow peoples." There they confiscated land, worked the natives at low wages, made large profits, and opened markets for cheap European manufactures. And all this was justified by the purported inferiority of colored peoples. Desire for the untapped wealth of the "dark continent" had sparked a surge of "investment" in "color prejudice." In the process, "American color prejudice and race hatred" had "become all but universal in the greatest centers of modern culture."

In a follow-up piece in the May 1915 *Atlantic Monthly* called "The African Roots of War," Du Bois reiterated his charge that the "civilized nations are fighting like mad dogs over the right to own and exploit these darker peoples." Now he took the argument a step further by asking why supposedly progressive forces—parliamentary democrats, socialist parties, trade unions—had been unable to call off the dogs of war? Race was again crucial to the answer. White workingmen, he suggested, had been invited to "share the spoil of exploiting 'chinks and niggers.'" It was no longer just "merchants, bankers, and industrialists monopolizing the spoliation of the planet," but rather "a new democratic nation composed of united capital and labor." Nationalism was thus not simply sentimental patriotism; it was about winning power and pelf for all classes, including "the average citizen of England, France, and Germany."

Despite all this, African Americans should support the Allies. To be sure, England had been "primarily responsible for American slavery, for the starvation of India, and the Chinese opium traffic." But she had learned from her mistakes, Du Bois argued, and now "no white nation is fairer in its treatment of darker peoples than England." Not that England was fair, much less just, but that compared to Germany—with its genocidal campaigns in South-West Africa—Britain was "an angel of light." The "record of Germany as a colonizer toward weaker and darker people is the most barbarous of any civilized people and grows worse instead of better."

Some of this hyper-viciousness was due to Germany's being a latecomer to the colonial feast. It had looked toward South America, but the United States with its Monroe Doctrine had stood in the way. It had started for Africa but had secured only "one good colony, one desert and two swamps." So Germany decided to seize English or French colonies, and to this end feverishly expanded her navy and army. The country became a militaristic bully— the "Prussian strut had caught the nation's imagination"—and racist as well. Germany hadn't been anti-black at first, but now it was, and if it succeeded in world conquest it would become "one of the most contemptible of 'Nigger' hating nations." Given that England and France had begun to see the evils of racism—France, in particular, "draws no dead line of color"—and as colored Americans "fear race prejudice as the greatest of War-makers," the choice seemed clear.

IT DIDN'T TO HUBERT HARRISON. The orator's street-corner lectures shared much with Du Bois's narrative. He pointed out to his white audiences "that the racial aspect of the war in Europe was easily the most important, despite the fact that no American paper" presented "that side of the matter for consideration to its readers." The world, Harrison noted, "is made up of 17 hundred million people of which 12 hundred million are colored—black and brown and yellow." The "war in Europe is a war of the white race wherein the stakes of the conflict are the titles to possession of the lands and destinies of this colored majority in Asia, Africa, and the islands of the sea." Harrison didn't pick sides in this white "fratricidal strife," but remained militantly opposed to black participation in the war. He found some "consolation in the hope that when this white world shall have been washed clean by its baptism of blood, the white race will be less able to thrust the strong hand of its sovereign will down the throats of the other races."

ALL IN ALL, THEN, THE OUTBREAK OF WAR IN EUROPE had exacerbated tensions between European ethnic groups in New York. But one such group, the Anglo-Dutch Protestant elite, refused to accept such a characterization of the conflict. Rather than casting the debate as one between rival offshoots of contending European combatants, they posed it as a debate between *Americans* (themselves) and merely "*hyphenated* Americans." They presented, that is to say, a meta-critique of ethnicity—a status they claimed to have transcended—which awarded them a privileged position. From there it was but a short step to criticizing their opponents, not as backers of different European horses, but as *un*-Americans, whose stance could be defined as *disloyal*—despite the USA's continuing neutrality.

BE AMERICAN!

In Theodore Roosevelt's *New York: A Sketch of the City's Social, Political, and Commercial Progress from the First Dutch Settlement to Recent Times* (1891), he wrote that "the most important lesson taught by the history of New York City is the lesson of Americanism,—the lesson that he among us who wishes to win honour in our life, and to play his part honestly and manfully, must be indeed an American in spirit and purpose, in heart and thought and deed." More specifically, he enjoined citizens to "act as Americans; not as Americans with a prefix and qualification—not as Irish Americans, German Americans, Native Americans,—but as Americans pure and simple." This was particularly essential in the political sphere. It was, he declared, "an outrage for a man to drag foreign politics into our contests, and vote as an Irishman or German or other foreigner." Though it was "no less an outrage," Roosevelt insisted, "to discriminate against one who has become an American in good faith, merely because of his creed or birthplace."

Roosevelt elaborated on this thesis in an article called "True Americanism," which he contributed to the April 1894 issue of the *Forum Magazine*. "We welcome the German or the Irishman who becomes an American," he wrote, but "we do not wish German-Americans and Irish-Americans who figure as such in our social and political life." What exactly was the True Americanism to which these newcomers were expected to conform? In essence, it meant that foreigners should become more like "we"—the descendants of English and Dutch settlers. TR did not allude to the ethnic dimension of "we," opting for a general rather than a specific terminology when describing himself and his fellows, but it ran through his list of desiderata. "We believe that English, and no other language, is that in which all the school exercises should be conducted." Immigrants, or the children of immigrants, should not "cling to the speech, the customs, the ways of life, and the habits of thought of the Old World which they have left." The immigrant "must revere only our flag; not only must it come first, but no other flag should even come second. He must learn to celebrate Washington's birthday rather than that of the Queen or Kaiser, and the Fourth of July instead of St. Patrick's Day." Immigrants should adopt American "political ideas and principles," and the American "way of looking at the relations between Church and State."

How was this assimilation to be attained? Roosevelt was vague about the process. Mostly he believed it was almost inevitable that newcomers would shed old ways, as they were impossible to sustain in the American environment. "The immigrant cannot possibly remain what he was," his article asserted. "If he tries to retain his old language, in a few generations it becomes a barbarous jargon; if he tries to retain his old customs and ways of life, in a few generations he becomes an uncouth boor." Mainly, the United States could count on the foreigner's self-interest to accomplish the transformation, as "from his own standpoint, it is beyond all question the wise thing for the immigrant to become thoroughly Americanized." But in case of recalcitrance, TR made clear, "from our standpoint, we have a right to demand it."

Demanding proved more difficult than he'd imagined. The very next year, 1895, when as police commissioner he began raiding establishments that served liquor on Sundays, Roosevelt provoked a furious response from Gotham's Germans. Incensed at finding their "Continental Sunday" afternoons—spent in beer gardens listening to Strauss waltzes—banned as immoral, they mounted massive protest parades. Roosevelt delighted in facing down "the wrath of the asinine herd." But Mayor Strong, seeing his chances of reelection crumbling (Germans being an essential part of his political coalition), disavowed his commissioner.

Over the next decade, Roosevelt learned from Henry Fairfield Osborn and Madison Grant, his friends and advisers on matters racial, that eugenic "science" argued that not all peoples were *capable* of being Americanized—notably Asians, Africans, and Latin Americans. But TR remained sunnily optimistic about the possibility of an evolutionary absorption, at least of Europeans, which is why he was so ecstatic when, as president, he attended the opening night (October 5, 1908) of *The Melting Pot*, a play, dedicated to Roosevelt, by the noted

English author Israel Zangwill.[29] The drama centers on David Quixano, a Russian Jew who emigrates to New York after his family is slaughtered in a pogrom. His great ambition is to write a symphony that lauds America's ability to erase imported divisions. Quixano, addressing the immigrants at Ellis Island who "stand in your fifty groups, with your fifty languages and histories, and your fifty blood hatreds and rivalries," assures them they won't be like that long. America, he explains, "is God's Crucible, the great Melting-Pot where all the races of Europe are melting and re-forming!" So "a fig for your feuds and vendettas! Germans and Frenchmen, Irishmen and Englishmen, Jews and Russians—into the Crucible with you all! God is making the American."

In the play's climactic scene, David rhapsodizes before his bedazzled lover, Vera (an immigrant Russian Christian noblewoman), as they survey the city from the roof garden of a settlement house, on the evening of the Fourth of July. (The stage directions call for showing "a beautiful, far-stretching panorama of New York, with its irregular sky-buildings on the left, and the harbour with its Statue of Liberty on the right.") "Look!" says an exalted David. "There she lies, the great Melting Pot— listen! Can't you hear the roaring and the bubbling? There gapes her mouth (*He points east*)—the harbour where a thousand mammoth feeders come from the ends of the world to pour in their human freight. Ah, what a stirring and a seething! Celt and Latin, Slav and Teuton, Greek and Syrian,— black and yellow—. . . how the great Alchemist melts and fuses them with his purging flame! Here shall they all unite to build the Republic of Man and the Kingdom of God.... (*The sunset is swiftly fading, and the vast panorama is suffused with a more restful twilight, to which the many-gleaming lights of the town add the tender poetry of the night. Far back, like a lonely, guiding star, twinkles over the darkening water the torch of the Statue of Liberty. From below comes up the softened sound of voices and instruments joining in 'My Country, 'tis of Thee.' The curtain falls slowly.*)"

TR went wild. Sitting next to Mrs. Zangwill, he "positively raved" to her as the playwright took his bows, then leapt to his feet and bellowed across the theater: "That's a great play, Mr. Zangwill."

One can see where leaving the Americanization process in God's hands might finesse the knotty issue of precisely how such a melting would take place. Those who, like Roosevelt, believed that "we"—the Anglo-Dutch Protestant elite—were the mold into which melted immigrant ore should be poured, had long believed that relatively modest measures could be counted on to assist in doing the Lord's work. Measures like the 1909 Hudson-Fulton Parade, with its caboose of immigrant floats added to a train headed by Anglo-Dutch progenitors. Or the festooning of civic buildings with statues of Anglo-Dutch municipal patriots. Or the shepherding of immigrant children into Americanizing classrooms. But by the mid-1910s, the ongoing torrent of immigrants seemed vexingly determined to hold on to their old-world ways. They also stubbornly resisted Roosevelt's Anglophile preparedness movement, with its drift toward intervention on the side of the Allies. Increasingly more forceful measures seemed required. Two different approaches emerged, immigration restriction and coercive Americanization.

THE FIRST WAS A LONG-STANDING PROJECT, dating at least to the nativist movements of the 1840s, and institutionally represented in this era by the forthrighly named Immigration

---

29. Born to poor Russian immigrant parents, Zangwill was raised in London's Jewish East End. A popular novelist and spellbinding orator, he also became a Zionist, but one who believed Zion might lie not in Palestine but in Galveston, Texas. He convinced some of Gotham's German Jewish elite, notably Jacob Schiff and Henry Morgenthau, that it might be possible to divert to the West some of the East European Jews flooding into New York, but they had little success.

Mayor John Purroy Mitchel, City Hall, July 4, 1916. Reenactment of the First Congress meeting in Philadelphia. (Library of Congress Prints and Photographs Division, George Grantham Bain Collection)

Restriction League, of which Roosevelt was a strong supporter. In his 1894 "True Americanism" article, TR had declared it "urgently necessary to check and regulate our immigration, by much more drastic laws than now exist; and this should be done both to keep out laborers who tend to depress the labor market, and to keep out races which do not assimilate readily with our own, and unworthy individuals of all races—not only criminals, idiots, and paupers, but anarchists of the Most and O'Donovan Rossa type."

Twenty years further on, his concern about unassimilable races had been heightened by the eugenics movement. TR's close friend Madison Grant—they were both of similar standing in Gotham's social hierarchy—thought Roosevelt had got it all wrong in applauding Zangwill's play. "We Americans must realize," he insisted in his *Passing of the Great Race* (1916), that "the maudlin sentimentalism that has made America 'an asylum for the oppressed' " was sweeping the nation toward a racial abyss. "If the Melting Pot is allowed to boil without control," Grant warned, and we "deliberately blind ourselves to 'all distinctions of race, creed or color,' the type of native American of Colonial descent will become as extinct as the Athenian of the age of Pericles, and the Viking of the days of Rollo." For the dark truth was that, despite the undoubted superiority of those with Nordic blood in their veins, history taught they were not unconquerable. In the past, Nordics had been brought low by the corrupting influence and fecundity of Slavic Alpines, Mongoloid invaders, and the dark-skinned Mediterraneans of Southern Europe. Now, again, Nordics were facing disaster, on two fronts, and in both cases the catastrophes were largely of their own making.

First, the war itself. "From a race point of view," Grant noted, "the present European conflict is essentially a civil war and nearly all of the officers and a large proportion of the men on both sides are members" of the Nordic race, making the Great War another exercise in "race suicide."

Second, unrestricted immigration to the United States. The American's insistence on importing "serfs to do manual labor for him," Grant claimed, was "the prelude to his extinction." *Pace* Roosevelt, these immigrant laborers were *biologically* incapable of becoming true Americans and were all too capable of "breeding out their masters and killing by filth and by crowding as effectively as by the sword." Nowhere was this more self-evident than in Gotham, where the old-stock American "is to-day being literally driven off the streets of New York City by the swarms of Polish Jews." Immigrants "wear his clothes, they steal his name and they are beginning to take his women," which would no doubt "produce many amazing racial hybrids and some ethnic horrors that will be beyond the powers of future anthropologists to unravel." But it was clear to Grant that because "the result of the mixture of two races, in the long run, gives us a race reverting to the more ancient, generalized and lower type," it was the self-destructive Nordics that were melting away, in yet another instance of racial suicide.

Eugenicist Charles Benedict Davenport underscored this in a 1917 paper. A "hybridized people," Davenport concluded, were inevitably "badly put together…dissatisfied, reckless, ineffective," yet "this country is in for hybridization on the greatest scale that the world has ever seen." John Charles Van Dyke agreed: "With 750,000 Hebrews in New York City, and enough Sicilians to keep the police on the alert from dawn to dawn, there is little use of talking about absorption and assimilation. Indigestion and nausea are more appropriate because more truthful terms." And the Upper West Side developer and Davenport associate William Earl Dodge Stokes declared in his 1917 eugenics tract *The Right to Be Well Born* that "we cannot forever absorb this influx of the scum of the earth, this off-scouring, diseased, imported blood with its evil customs."

For the eugenics crowd, the only realistic solution was to halt the influx of non-Nordics. In 1916 Grant, a vice president of the Immigration Restriction League since its inception, helped win congressional approval of a bill that imposed a literacy test, expanded the list of undesirables to include "idiots, imbeciles, and feeble-minded persons," and added to the excluded Chinese all who resided in a forthrightly labeled "Asiatic Barred Zone," which encompassed India, Afghanistan, Persia (now Iran), Arabia, parts of the Ottoman Empire and Russia, Southeast Asia, and the Asian-Pacific islands. Wilson vetoed the legislation, but within a year, propelled by the growing xenophobia, his negative was overridden, and on February 5, 1917, the new barriers went into effect. Though restrictionists hailed the law, they deemed it insufficient, as it failed to filter out inferior Europeans, notably Italians and Jews. They adjusted their sights and soldiered on.

TO THIS SUPPLY-SIDE SOLUTION to the Americanization problem, was added a demand-side dimension, in the sense of Roosevelt's long-ago recognition that, in extremis, the core Americans ("we") were entitled to demand adherence to their cultural codes. TR himself took the lead in ratcheting up the rhetoric. In an October 1915 speech to the Knights of Columbus, he asserted that "there is no room in this country for hyphenated Americanism"; indeed, "a hyphenated American is not an American at all" but a menace to the Republic. In a 1916 follow-up address in St. Louis, he announced that "unless the immigrant becomes in good faith an American and nothing else, then he is out of place in this country, and the sooner he leaves it the better."[30]

On this issue, if little else, he found himself in agreement with Wilson. In May 1914 the new president dedicated a monument to an Irish American naval hero, John Barry, and took the occasion to contrast Barry, whose "heart crossed the Atlantic with him," with those Americans who "need hyphens in their names, because only part of them has come over." In May 1915 Wilson toughened his stance, declaring that "a man who thinks of himself as belonging to a particular national group in America has not yet become an American, and the man who goes among you to trade upon your nationality is no worthy son to live under the Stars and Stripes." In his November 1915 speech to New York's Manhattan Club urging expansion of the army and navy, he also declared it a matter of "grave concern" that some so-called Americans loved other countries better than they loved America.

By then, taking its cue from such national leaders, a movement had sprung up that rejected long-term assimilation in favor of "immediate Americanization." At its head was the former Progressive Party stalwart Frances Kellor, who by the end of 1914 had been eased out of her post running the Progressive Service. By spring 1915 Kellor had refocused her efforts from finding jobs and housing for immigrants to organizing the effort to accelerate their

Sheet music cover, "Let's All Be Americans Now," by Irving Berlin, Edgar Leslie, and George W. Meyer, 1917. (New York Public Library, Music Division)

---

30. In this Roosevelt (implicitly) dissented from the eugenicists' insistence that immigrants were biologically incapable of being melted, and instead sided (implicitly) with progressive anthropologists like Boas who believed immigrant customs were cultural, hence in theory malleable.

assimilation. In March she published an article entitled "Americanization" in the premiere issue of the *Immigrants in America Review* (published by the Committee for Immigrants in America, at 20 West 34th Street, with Kellor as editor). What the times demanded, she announced, was a "conscious effort to forge the people in this country into an American race that will stand together in time of peace or of war. Every effort should be bent toward an Americanization which will mean that there will be no 'German-Americans,' no 'Italian quarter,' no 'East Side Jew,' no 'Up-town Ghetto,' no 'Slav movement in America,' but that we are one people in ideals, rights and privileges and in making common cause for America." She made no mention of Anglo-Americans.

In May 1915 Kellor created the National Americanization Day Committee (NADC), with headquarters at 95 Madison Avenue. Aided by Helen Astor, Alice Vanderbilt, and Felix M. Warburg, she launched a crash program to make the upcoming Fourth of July an occasion for bringing the foreign-born—many of whom live "in colonies maintaining their foreign customs and standards and their own language"—together with the American-born, in a "common observance of the day and in a common understanding of America." The event, coordinated from New York, was celebrated in 107 cities throughout the country.

Other initiatives sought to push public schools to adopt compulsory English education, discourage cultural or political preferences considered un-American, encourage patriotism through celebratory courses in American history, and adopt a syllabus for immigrants that would "train" the foreign-born population to become "good, efficient and devoted" American citizens.[31] Kellor also struck up an alliance with the US Chamber of Commerce, adding to her Americanization curriculum a warning to immigrants that a proper American "is the natural foe of the I.W.W. and of the destructive forces that seek to direct unwisely the expression of the immigrant in the new country."

Kellor's National Americanization Committee (she dropped the "Day" when she expanded its purview) also struck up an informal alliance with the preparedness forces of the National Security League. Militarization and Americanization now marched hand in hand—notably on Fifth Avenue, where, two months after the NSL Preparedness Parade of May 1916, a flag-drenched Fourth of July parade was accompanied, reported the *Times*, by "Americanization and Preparedness" speeches in all five boroughs. (Childe Hassam paired the two events by naming his painting depicting the second one *The Fourth of July, 1916, the Greatest Display of the American Flag Ever Seen in New York, Climax of the Preparedness Parade in May*.)

President Wilson had paired Preparedness and Americanization more forcefully when he followed up his November 1915 speech, the one making his first concession to preparedness advocates, with his December 1915 State of the Union address, when he first asked Congress to authorize crackdown legislation. Speaking of citizens born under foreign flags, "who have poured the poison of disloyalty into the very arteries of our national life," he thundered that "such creatures of passion, disloyalty, and anarchy must be crushed out. They are not many, but they are infinitely malignant, and the hand of our power should close over them at once."

This sentiment was echoed in the May 1916 Preparedness Parade, when the marchers, on reaching the Union League Club, passed by a huge electric sign affixed to the building,

---

31. Roosevelt, as usual, put it more bluntly. On February 1, 1916, at a luncheon given by Helen Astor for the National Americanization Committee, the former president suggested: "Let us say to the immigrant not that we hope he will learn English, but that he has got to learn it. Let the immigrant who does not learn it go back."

"Absolute and Unqualified Loyalty to Our Country." *New York Times,* May 21, 1916. (Library of Congress Prints and Photographs Division)

whose bulbs, blinking on and off in the manner of Times Square commercials, spelled out the slogan: ABSOLUTE AND UNQUALIFIED LOYALTY TO OUR COUNTRY.

THE HYPHENATES WHOSE LOYALTY WAS BEING CALLED INTO QUESTION were perfectly aware of the sleight-of-hand embedded in one ethnic group's passing itself off as "American," substituting their part for the whole. In a piece entitled "The Hyphen in American History," which the *New Yorker Staats-Zeitung* ran in its September 4, 1916, issue, the author noted acerbically that Wilson and Roosevelt had discovered a "malignant malady," caused by a "mere mark of punctuation," that seemed to be "dangerous only in certain combinations. You may be an Anglo-Saxon, or a British-American, or Scotch-Irish, or a score of other things with hyphens, and the hyphen will be a mark of distinction and a badge of honor. But if you are a German-American—that is, during the past two years—the hyphen is as dreadful as the brand of Cain."

Such a specific critique could be dismissed as special pleading by suspect people. Yet a more powerful charge—also a meta-critique—had recently been leveled. It argued not only

Science Explains the Prussian Ferocity in War

A Comparison of the Round-Headed Savage Prussian Type of Skull (on the Right) and the Gentle Long-Headed Teuton Type (on the Left) Which Professor Osborn Says Represents Now Only Ten Per Cent of Germans.

Professor Osborn of the American Museum of Natural History, and Professor Gregory of the Chair of Evolution at Columbia University, Trace the Blood of the German Leaders Back Through the Wild Tartars to the Most Ancient Savages

"Science Explains the Prussian Ferocity in War." *Washington Times*, June 2, 1918. (Chronicling America: Historic American Newspapers. Library of Congress.)

that was the Americanization campaign a case of invidious special pleading but that its central propositions misunderstood the actually existing political and cultural order of the United States.

IN UNO PLURES

In February 1915 the *Nation* magazine had run a two-part essay, "Democracy versus the Melting Pot: A Study of American Nationality," by Horace Kallen, at that point a professor of philosophy at the University of Wisconsin in Madison. In a frontal challenge to the Americanization movement, Kallen argued that it promoted not a melding of many cultures but the predominance of one. "Jews, Slavs, Poles, Frenchmen, Germans, Hindus, Scandinavians and so on" were supposedly to be transmuted by the "'the miracle of assimilation' into beings similar in background, tradition, outlook, and spirit to the descendants of the British colonists, the Anglo-Saxon stock." The Anglo–Americans, in their guise as ur-Americans, presumed to rule by right of "cultural primogeniture." The first immigrants, through the accident of being first, had become an aristocracy, advocates "of the pride of blood." This was not only anti-democratic, but also authoritarian, as resistance by subordinated ethnics was met with coercive measures like the Anglo–supremacist public school system, which attempted to eradicate old-country ways by crushing the spirit of immigrant pupils.

Why did the Americanizers act this way? To some extent, it was a simple matter of self-interest; many advantages accrued to the firstborn son in a patriarchal culture. But Kallen believed the justification also rested on a confusion about the relationship between the state and civil society. The Anglo-Americans assumed that the survival of the nation hinged on cultural uniformity, as it did in European countries. A nation divided against itself could not stand. Dual loyalty was an impermissible contradiction in terms.

For Kallen this was a false dilemma. There was a fundamental difference, he argued, between a "nation of nations" and a "confederation of cultures." It was the latter term that summed up more precisely the peculiar status of the United States, a country constructed through an ingathering of peoples. The various "cultures" (a.k.a. "races" or "ethnicities" or "nationalities") were the building blocks of civil society. Each ethnic group expressed its emotional and voluntary life in its own language, using its own aesthetic and intellectual forms. Their enclaves were the sites of their most intimate social relations, the deepest sources of cultural identity, the domain of religion and kinship, and the terrain within which the citizen "lives and moves and has his being."

The state was an altogether different thing. It provided the framework for, and upheld the rules of, the democratic political system, and its proceedings were appropriately transacted in English, the lingua franca of the commonwealth. The role of the state, which should belong to no particular ethnicity, was to guarantee the independent existence of its component socio-cultural parts. The state's business was not to impose homogeneity but to protect difference. Its motto, Kallen might have said, should not be *E Pluribus Unum* (Out of Many, One), but *In Uno Plures* (In One, Many).

The Americanization process could also do with a better metaphor, Kallen thought— not the Zangwillian melting pot, but a symphony orchestra.[32] "As in an orchestra, every type of instrument has its specific timbre and tonality, founded in its substance and form; as every type has its appropriate theme and melody in the whole symphony, so in society each ethnic group is the natural instrument, its spirit and culture are its theme and melody, and the harmony and dissonances and discords of them all make the symphony of civilization." Kallen's focus, to be sure, was almost completely on the "harmony" piece, as was Zangwill's; he hoped that "'American civilization' may come to mean perfection of the cooperative harmonies of 'European civilization,' the waste, the squalor, and the distress of Europe being eliminated."

More broadly, Kallen thought the Anglo-conformist vision deeply misguided in scorning precisely what was most remarkable about the multi-cultural society that had emerged, unplanned, on the American strand. And in 1915, with Americanization advocates gaining strength, it seemed to Kallen that the country was approaching a crossroads. What do we want the United States to be, he asked, "a unison, singing the old Anglo-Saxon theme," or "a harmony, in which that theme shall be dominant, perhaps, among others, but one among many, not the only one?"[33]

---

32. In an afterword to the 1914 edition of his play, Zangwill said he'd been misunderstood: "The process of American amalgamation is not assimilation or simple surrender to the dominant type, as is popularly supposed, but an all-round give-and-take by which the final type may be enriched or impoverished." But Zangwill still envisioned a "final type."

33. Kallen had arrived at this position by two different routes, one sociological, one philosophical.

He had been born in Germany (his father an Orthodox rabbi), and brought to Boston as a 5-year-old, in 1887. Initially he rebelled against Judaism, wanting to be identified only as an American. He changed his mind while studying philosophy at Harvard. There he helped found the Harvard Menorah Society, dedicated to encouraging Jewish students to take pride in their cultural and religious heritage, and to feel comfortable with a dual identity, as both Jew and American. (In 1913 an Intercollegiate Menorah Association was formed, which in 1915 began publication of the *Menorah Journal* in New York, at 600 Madison Avenue.)

Philosophically, Kallen was greatly influenced by his teacher William James, who critiqued the absolute and monistic idealism then entrenched in philosophy. James argued that the universe was pluralistic, and that the craving to see it as a single unified system was deeply wrong-headed. He published the lectures in 1909 as *A Pluralistic Universe*. Kallen would call the social system he saw as having emerged in the United States an instance of "cultural pluralism."

KALLEN'S ESSAY ATTRACTED THE ATTENTION of another titan of pragmatism, John Dewey, whom he had met in Cambridge in 1905 or 1906. Kallen struck up a correspondence with the Columbia-based philosopher, and continued it when he accepted a teaching position at the University of Wisconsin. Kallen also visited Dewey in New York. During the summer of 1917, he taught at Columbia on Dewey's invitation, and was invited back in the spring of 1918 to give a course of lectures, after which he settled in Gotham permanently.

In responding to Kallen's essay, both in personal correspondence and public essays, Dewey agreed strongly with much of the analysis. "I never did care for the melting pot metaphor," he said. "To maintain that all the constituent elements, geographical, racial and cultural in the United States should be put in the same pot and turned into a uniform and unchanging product is distasteful." Indeed, "the concept of uniformity and unanimity in culture is rather repellent."

He agreed, too, that the "Americanization" campaign was a cover for Anglo-supremacists. "I want to see this country American," Dewey wrote Kallen, "and that means the English tradition reduced to a strain among others." In an essay of 1916 he underscored this, using Kallen's preferred metaphor, insisting that "Neither Englandism nor New-Englandism, . . . any more than Teuton or Slav, can do anything but furnish one note in a vast symphony."

Dewey also accepted that "our unity cannot be a homogeneous thing like that of the separate states of Europe." "Hyphenism" was to be welcomed. "Variety is the spice of life, and the richness and attractiveness of social institutions depend upon cultural diversity among separate units. In so far as people are all alike, there is no give and take among them. And it is better to give and take." The United States should extract "from each people its special good, so that it shall surrender into a common fund of wisdom and experience what it especially has to contribute. All of these surrenders and contributions taken together create the national spirit of America." Only in this sense was assimilation acceptable. Indeed, "genuine assimilation to one another—not to Anglo-Saxondom—seems to be essential to an American. That each cultural section should maintain its distinctive literary and artistic traditions seems to me most desirable, but in order that it might have the more to contribute to others."

Dewey did have some reservations about Kallen's argument. For one, it seemed to assume harmony was the default state of inter-ethnic relations. "I quite agree with your orchestra idea," Dewey explained, "but upon condition we really get a symphony and not a lot of different instruments playing simultaneously." Civic obligation was not sufficiently emphasized in Kallen's pluralism, focused as it was on the parts rather than the whole.

Provincialism was a second concern. "The dangerous thing is for each factor to isolate itself, to try to live off its past, and then to attempt to impose itself on other elements, or at least keep itself intact and thus refuse to accept what other cultures have to offer." This shoe best fit the Anglos, to be sure, but any ethnicity could fall prey to narrow loyalties and parochial prejudices.

Then there was Kallen's emphasis on ethnic continuity rather than change. Kallen implied that ethnics were virtually unmeltable, and suggested that Americanizers had been misled into thinking them readily remoldable because they concentrated on superficial externalities. It was true, Kallen argued, that greenhorns often embraced assimilation as an economic strategy, and adopted American speech, clothes, and manners. But once the immigrant attained a certain level of acceptance and stability, assimilation slowed, even stopped, and ideals of nationality resurged. The "wop changes into a proud Italian; the hunky into a proud nationalist Slav." At times Kallen seemed to suggest a biological basis to this stasis, with his talk about "ancestral endowments," though he never actually wandered into Madison Grant territory, and his focus on fixity could be put down to obdurate cultures.

A YEAR AFTER KALLEN'S *NATION* ESSAY, a more dynamic objection to the melting pot metaphor was advanced by Randolph Bourne, an acquaintance of Kallen and a disciple of Dewey. Bourne was not an academic, but a journalist and self-described member of New York's "younger intelligentsia," yet his relations with Columbia College had been transformative. He'd had a difficult childhood in suburban Bloomfield, New Jersey, where he'd suffered from the collapse of the family fortune in the Panic of 1893 and from multiple physical handicaps: his features had been badly mangled by a forceps at birth, and he'd developed a hunchback from a bout of spinal tuberculosis at the age of 4. In 1909 Columbia provided him with a full academic scholarship. There he was introduced to the writings of James and Boas, developed socialist politics in part through his classes with Beard, and became a student of Dewey, seeing in his pragmatism "an edge on it that would slash up the habits of thought, the customs and institutions in which our society has been living for centuries." After graduating in 1913, he spent a year in Europe, then moved to the Village and joined the radical scene. He got a staff job at the *New Republic* and published there in 1915 his series of articles applauding the Gary Plan. But feeling himself marginalized, he turned for outlets to other magazines, and in July 1916 he gave his "Trans-National America," a piece inspired by Kallen's work, to the *Atlantic Monthly*.

"No reverberatory effect of the great war," ran his opening sentence, "has caused American public opinion more solicitude than the failure of the 'melting-pot.'...We have had to watch hard-hearted old Brahmins virtuously indignant at the spectacle of the immigrant refusing to be melted...We have had to listen to publicists who express themselves as stunned by the evidence of vigorous traditionalistic and cultural movements in this country among Germans, Scandinavians, Bohemians and Poles, while in the same breath they insist that the alien shall be forcibly assimilated to that Anglo-Saxon tradition which they unquestioningly label 'American.'"

Far more vigorously than had Kallen—aided perhaps by himself being of ancient English stock—Bourne ripped into Anglo-American hypocrisy. The truth was "that no more tenacious cultural allegiance to the mother country has been shown by any alien nation" than by the Anglo-Saxon descendants in the United States. "English snobberies, English religion, English literary styles, English literary reverences and canons, English ethics, English superiorities, have been the cultural food that we have drunk in from our mothers' breasts." The war had exacerbated such sentiments, revealing the Anglos to be "still loving English things, owing allegiance to the English Kultur, moved by English shibboleths and prejudice. It is only because it has been the ruling class in this country...that we have not heard copiously and scornfully of 'hyphenated English-Americans.'" In truth, the Anglo-Saxon element "is guilty of just what every dominant race is guilty of in every European country: the imposition of its own culture upon the minority peoples." Fortunately, Americanization had failed. "The strong cultural movements represented by the foreign press, schools, and colonies" were positioned to save the United States from cultural stagnation, precisely because they "have not been melted down or run together, made into some homogeneous Americanism." Rather the country had become "a cosmopolitan federation of national colonies, of foreign cultures, from whom the sting of devastating competition has been removed. America is already the world federation in miniature, the continent where for the first time in history has been achieved that miracle of hope, the peaceful living side by side, with character substantially preserved, of the most heterogeneous peoples under the sun." America, Bourne asserted, "is a unique sociological fabric, and it bespeaks poverty of imagination not to be thrilled at the incalculable potentialities of so novel a union of men."

If "America is coming to be, not a nationality but a trans-nationality, a weaving back and forth, with the other lands, of many threads of all sizes and colors," then it follows, Bourne argued, that "any movement which attempts to thwart this weaving, or to dye the fabric any one color, or disentangle the threads of the strands, is false to this cosmopolitan vision." Trans-nationalism was the antidote to the "belligerent, exclusive, inbreeding" nationalism, "the poison of which we are witnessing now in Europe." Which was why he was "almost fanatically against the current programs of Americanism, with their preparedness, conscription, imperialism, integration issues, their slavish imitation of the European nationalisms which are slaying each other before our eyes."[34]

Bourne's cosmopolitanism, however, like Kallen's cultural pluralism, stopped at the color line. Both considered internationalism to embrace only white European cultures and migrants. They might profitably have considered the work of Du Bois, who had long preceded them in pondering duality. In "The Conservation of Races" (1897), Du Bois had suggested that many an African American must have asked himself: "Am I an American or am I a Negro? Can I be both? Or is it my duty to cease to be a Negro as soon as possible and be an American? If I strive as a Negro, am I not perpetuating the very cleft that threatens and separates black and white America? Is not my only possible practical aim the subduction of all that is Negro in me to the American? Does my black blood place upon me any more obligation to assert my nationality than German, or Irish or Italian blood would?" His answer, in *The Souls of Black Folk* (1903), was that the African American "ever feels his two-ness—an American, a Negro; two souls, two thoughts, two unreconciled strivings"—and longs to

---

34. In an even more drastic departure from parochial nationalism, Bourne hailed the "free and mobile passage of the immigrant between America and his native land again which now arouses so much prejudice among us." This was a planetary phenomenon, and a salutary one. In recent years "the demand for labor and colonists in all parts of the globe, the ease and cheapness of travel, have set in motion vast currents of immigration which render impossible the old tight geographical groupings of nationality. The political ideas of the future will have to be adjusted to a shifting world-population, to the mobility of labor, to all kinds of new temporary mixings of widely diverse peoples, as well as to their permanent mixings."

Bourne even suggested that "we may have to accept some form of that dual citizenship which meets with so much articulate horror among us [those who warred on hyphenization]." In a follow-up essay—"The Jew and Trans-National America" in the December 1916 issue of the *Menorah Journal*—Bourne suggested Jewish history and contemporary Zionism could serve as models for such duality: "Dispersion [analogous to the Jewish diaspora] is now the lot of every people. The Jewish ghetto in America is matched by the Italian, by the Slovac ghetto. The war will intensify this setting in motion of wandering peoples." Zionism (which he understood only in the abstract, without much sense of developments on the ground in Arab Palestine) seemed a pioneering instance of being able to be a political citizen of one country while maintaining cultural links to another. "I used to think," Bourne admitted, "that Zionism was incompatible with Americanism, that if your enthusiasm and energy went into creating a Jewish nation in the Orient, you could not give yourself to building up the State in which you lived." But it proved that "nothing could be falser than this idea." This dilemma of multiple allegiances would have to be solved in America, "and it is in the fertile implications of Zionism that I veritably believe the solution will be found."

Bourne did, however, add a caveat to his celebration of immigration: "I do not mean that we shall necessarily glut ourselves with the raw product of humanity. It would be folly to absorb the nations faster than we could weave them. We have no duty either to admit or reject. It is purely a question of expediency."

merge his double self into a better and truer self. But "in this merging he wishes neither of the older selves to be lost. He would not Africanize America, for America has too much to teach the world and Africa. He would not bleach his Negro soul in a flood of white Americanism, for he knows that Negro blood has a message for the world. He simply wishes to make it possible for a man to be both a Negro and an American, without being cursed and spit upon by his fellows, without having the doors of Opportunity closed roughly in his face."

IN FEW PLACES ON EARTH DID BOURNE'S VISION APPROACH FULFILLMENT more than in his own New York City, though reality proved more complicated than theory, especially when one added ingredients—notably class, race, and power—that were missing from or underdeveloped in the schemas of Messrs. Kallen, Dewey, and Bourne.

Vision and reality were most in accord on the fundamental precondition for a transnational or cultural pluralist city—the existence of immigrant enclaves large enough to sustain immigrant cultures. Gotham was replete with great encampments that were webbed together by a dense network of institutions: native-language newspapers and theaters, ethnic lodges and mutual benefit associations, houses of worship that were invitingly ethnic-oriented. (Even the universalistic Catholics offered national parishes.)

The borders of these ethnic quarters, moreover, were elastic, allowing districts to expand, checked only by counter-pressure from adjoining populations. Boundaries were constantly renegotiated, occasionally through clashes at the frontiers, more often via the market. If further expansion became impossible, nationality-neighborhoods could easily send out runners, given the superb and cheap mass transit system, and open up new "colonies" in the wide open outer-borough spaces. Not that living quarters were distributed equitably: nationality and race (like wealth and class) constrained a group's ability to command territory. Still, the city's cellularity allowed it to house, cheek by jowl, millions of people from wildly differing backgrounds—Czechs and Chinese, Germans and Greeks, Irish and Caribbean blacks, Poles and Puerto Ricans—while preserving a remarkable degree of domestic tranquility.

In part, this comparative stability could be attributed to New York's having had such extensive experience with immigration since the days of the Dutch. Over the course of its repeated remakings, Gotham had evolved into an urban organism superbly adapted for accommodating newcomers. These enclaves were more than colossal demographic facts on the ground; they were also points of entry—portals through which continuously passed the revitalizing demographic flows that kept the enclaves from petrifying, and allowed residents to keep in touch with their places of origin. These communities managed quite handily to handle duality, using such formulations as the homely Yorkville phrase "Germania our mother; Columbia our bride," or by pairing their home-country flag with the Stars and Stripes.

Multi-nationality, then, was a given in Gotham. New Yorkers carried in their heads mental maps of the city's ethnic geography. Newcomers quickly located the accessible portals and maneuvered their way inside. Master-race nativists might reject the patchwork status quo, but for most, pluralism was simply the way things were.

For outsiders, meanwhile, these ethnic neighborhoods became consumer goods. The enclaves afforded visitors a temporary immersion in other cultures—as witnessed by the new enthusiasm, fanned by the tourist industry, for sampling the city's varied sites and cuisines.

The Greenwich Village intellectuals, already engaged in diverse interactions in their particularly multi-cultural habitat, were delighted at the banquet of ethnicities available for tasting in the larger cosmopolis. "Within a block of my house," Jack Reed rhapsodized, "was all the adventure of the world; within a mile was every foreign country." The painter John Sloan saw the city as "a cosmopolitan palette in which all colors mingle and then appear sharply by turns." But for most of them, and particularly Randolph Bourne, perambulations around Gotham were intended to be transformative. They offered an opportunity to transcend the limitations of one's inherited culture, to develop a "new cosmopolitan outlook," to achieve a more complete human experience.

The city had been a consummate *practitioner* of multi-nationalism, but now it acquired an *ideology*, as some observers articulated and applauded actually existing pluralism. The Village radicals went further and depicted it as an oppositional culture. They hailed the everyday street-level internationalism as being the antithesis of—indeed, the antidote to— the simultaneously evolving alternative, advanced by New York's Americanizers and eugenicists, which recoiled from heterogeneity, and demanded the imposition of Anglo-conformity. For Bourne the city's trans-national ideology offered a basis for resistance. "Against the thinly disguised panic which calls itself 'patriotism' and the thinly disguised militarism which calls itself 'preparedness' the cosmopolitan ideal is set."[35]

THE ACADEMICS AND JOURNALISTS WHO CELEBRATED MULTIPLICITY paid less attention than they might have to the political-economic dimension of the pluralist city. The economy, after all, was also cellular—a pastiche of ethnic niches—with particular occupations being the all-but-wholly-owned possessions of specific nationalities. Official records might list job categories in nation-neutral terms—bankers, cops, construction workers, seamstresses—but New Yorkers knew these categories required additional adjectives: Anglo bankers, Irish cops, Italian construction workers, Jewish seamstresses. Even organized crime was sorted out along national lines.

The economy's structural segmentation provided multiple access points for immigrants and their offspring. Newcomers slotted themselves into long-established and closely held niches, passed down through generations, open only to compatriots. (One had an uncle in the garment biz, a paisan in the building trades.) And niches were as renegotiable as neighborhoods. A new group could muscle its way in (or up) by prying open an existing category, perhaps through political influence, perhaps through ethnic-based campaigns, perhaps through violence, perhaps through more or less peaceable succession. Again, the economic (like the spatial) order was neither equitable in its allocation of rewards, nor the product of intelligent design.

---

35. An early instance of extracting ideology from reality was an address called "The Genius of the Cosmopolitan City," given at the New-York Historical Society in 1903 by Hamilton Wright Mabie, a lawyer, journalist, and popular lecturer, who traced his ancestry to New Amsterdam. Mabie suggested that the city's demographic heterogeneity had, over the years, "given our friends, south and west, the opportunity of saying that New York is the least American of cities because it is the least homogeneous." Mabie argued the opposite. "It is fair to ask," Mabie countered, "which is the most distinctively American, the community in which the citizens are all of one blood, or that in which many races combine to create a new race?" Though starting from this proto-Zangwillian position, Mabie went on to anticipate Bourne's. "If America stands for a different order of society, a new kind of political and social unity...then New York is the most American of cities." Indeed, he asked, "this great city of ours with its diversities of race, of religion, of social, political and personal ideals—has it a unity which the country has as yet failed to recognize, a genius which belongs to the future rather than to the past, and which, because it is of the future, is slow to reveal itself?...Its very diversities are creating here a kind of city which men have not seen before; in which a unity of a more inclusive, if not a higher, order is slowly forming itself; a city the genius of which has the light of prophecy in it."

More to the point, not all niches were equal, either in recompense or power. Anglo bankers and Italian construction workers were not just different job classifications and incomes. The former were owners or commanders of capital; the latter were workers for wages. Corporate executives and investment bankers had a spectacularly greater impact on the city's economy, polity, and cultural institutions than did subway tunnelers.

Which is why the city's working class took up the cause of trans-nationalism. Not because they were entranced by the cultural possibilities of inter-ethnic interaction—though they lived such interactions every day (as evidenced by the common practice of intermarriage)—but because forging alliances with other ethnic groups was a practical necessity if they were to build a collective base of resistance to exploitation. *Pace* Kallen's harmonious orchestra metaphor, there had always been strenuous inter-ethnic competition over jobs, housing, and access to public resources, a jostling exacerbated by economic crisis, ethnoracial-religious tensions, and repercussions from overseas conflicts (as was currently the case). It did not escape Jewish and Italian seamstresses that such cultural divisions undermined the solidarity needed to win strikes, and they worked to overcome them, by learning each other's languages, celebrating together on birthdays, at baby showers, and at weddings, and organizing the labor movement side by side. Picket lines and Labor Day parades were routinely multi-ethnic affairs, marchers hoisting signs and banners in multiple languages. Industrial unionists were particularly determined to bridge ethnic fault lines: there were, as Big Bill Haywood put it, "no foreigners in the working class." Socialists were slower than syndicalists to embrace difference, partly because early Yiddish activists had adopted

"Garment Workers on Strike, New York City," 1913. (Glasshouse Images/Alamy Stock Photo)

a homogenizing vision of internationalism. They hoped a working-class melting pot might (in Abraham Cahan's words) "erase all boundaries between Jew and non-Jew in the labor world." But partly thanks to newly arrived critics like Zhitlovsky, who denounced the desire to amalgamate all nations into an undifferentiated mass class, the socialists reformulated internationalism as a cooperative alliance between different nationalities, exemplified in the establishment of Finnish, Italian, Bohemian, Polish, Scandinavian, and Hungarian ethnic/language federations.

The anarchists were equally receptive to working-class ethnic cross-connections. Most *circuli sovversivi* were composed of southern Italians, but many also opened their clubs to co-workers of Cuban, Spanish, Puerto Rican, Russian, French, and Bohemian descent, as well as native-born Americans. Emma Goldman thundered in *Mother Earth* that "the attempt to light the torch of the furies of war is the more monstrous when one bears in mind that the people of America are cosmopolitan. If anything, America should be the soil for international understanding, for the growth of friendship between all races. Here, all narrow, stifling national prejudices should be eradicated." But instead "the jingoes and war speculators are filling the air with the sentimental slogan of hypocritical nationalism, 'America for Americans,' 'America first, last, and all the time.'"

FOR MUCH OF 1916, IT LOOKED AS IF THE WAR PARTY—Anglophile and predominantly upper- and middle-class—would be held in check by widespread resistance throughout much of the

"Emma Goldman on a Street Car," 1917. (Library of Congress Prints and Photographs Division, George Grantham Bain Collection)

country, and, in Gotham, by a multi-ethnic and predominantly working-and-middle-class coalition. But then, in early 1917, a crescendo of external events shifted the balance of internal forces, and interventionists carried the day.

AND THE WAR CAME

On May 4, 1916, the German government, responding to Wilson's threat to sever diplomatic relations, had agreed to refrain from attacking all passenger ships, and to allow the crews of enemy merchant vessels to abandon their ships prior to any attack. This curtailed the German depredations that had been fueling the preparedness movement.

For a time, events in Mexico provided alternative grounds for promoting military expansion. On March 9, 1916, Pancho Villa's cavalry had swept across the border and shot up the frontier community of Columbus, New Mexico, killing eighteen Americans. Six days later, Wilson ordered General John J. Pershing to launch a "punitive expedition" with 10,000 regular army troops. Crossing the border, they dispersed Villa's forces, but failed to capture Villa himself, and their offensive revealed multiple shortcomings in military readiness. In addition, the expedition came up against a more formidable opponent, in the form of Venustiano Carranza's regular Mexican army, which raised the possibility of full-scale war. These developments helped win passage, on June 3, 1916, of the National Defense Act. It provided for an expanded army of 175,000 and an enlarged National Guard that could be called into federal service by the president. This Wilson did, on June 18, ordering about 110,000 guardsmen to patrol the border, including a New York division of 18,500. But by the end of July, when the bulk of the reinforcements finally arrived, the war crisis had abated, thanks to concessions by Carranza and patient diplomacy by Wilson.

PREPAREDNESS FORCES WERE ENERGIZED ALSO by an event in Gotham itself. On July 30, 1916, at two in the morning, German saboteurs snuck onto the Black Tom wharf, broke into the terminal, where over 2 million pounds of high explosives were awaiting transfer to Allied ships, and blew it up. A sequence of blasts shook skyscrapers, shattered thousands of windows in Jersey City, Brooklyn, and Manhattan, badly damaged buildings on Ellis Island, and pockmarked the Statue of Liberty. Sabotage was of course suspected, and galvanized anti-German sentiment, but no one *knew* that German agents had done it. (That was not proved until many years later.) Investigators eventually concluded it was probably an accident, though one made more likely by the Lehigh Valley Railroad's having crammed its facility with far more ammunition than it could safely store. Alternatives were bruited about, but, as the *New York Times* noted, any plan to remove "the thousands of tons of condensed destruction...would divert millions of dollars from New York."

DESPITE THE EVENTS IN MEXICO AND ON BLACK TOM, the major threat—involvement in the European war—receded in the summer and fall of 1916, thanks to Germany's continuing restrictions on its submarine warfare. But the issue would prove central in the upcoming presidential election, to which attention now shifted.

Woodrow Wilson was again the Democratic Party's standard-bearer, and his record of peace, prosperity, and progressivism was a formidable one. "He Kept Us out of War" was a potent slogan, given that the great majority of the country still opposed US entry. Business and workers and farmers were happy that arms and food sales had wiped out the recession. And progressives were pleased that Wilson had built up a substantial reform portfolio, by

John T. McCutcheon, "Uncle Sam's Reform School." *Chicago Daily Tribune,* March 13, 1916.

backing federal child labor legislation, supporting workers' compensation for federal employees, elevating the Department of Labor to cabinet rank, creating a Commission on Industrial Relations, and appointing lawyer-reformer Louis Brandeis to the Supreme Court. These accomplishments won him the support of many peace progressives, such as Stephen Wise and Lillian Wald, and even socialists like Congressman Meyer London and *Masses* editor Max Eastman.

Wilson also cautiously sought ethnic support, by modulating his anti-hyphen rhetoric, and stressing there were many "good" German Americans and Irish Americans, though he continued to equate dissent with disloyalty. Late in September the Irish American activist Jeremiah O'Leary cabled Wilson saying that his foreign policies—support for the British Empire, approval of war loans, and the traffic in munitions—were issues of concern in the Irish community. Wilson cabled back a widely republished reply: "Your telegram received. I would feel deeply mortified to have you or anybody like you vote for me. Since you have access to many disloyal Americans and I have not, I will ask you to convey this message to them."

Yet for all the strength of Wilson's position, he was confronting a changed political landscape. In 1912 he had won because Roosevelt had split the Republican vote with his third-party campaign. Now it looked like that breach would be healed, leaving Wilson to face a united Republican phalanx. But it was not clear who would emerge as the GOP's candidate. The choice lay between three candidates, all from New York City.

Representing the Republican Old Guard was Elihu Root, who in 1915 had returned to private life after fifteen years of public service, most recently a term in the US Senate. After the *Lusitania* sinking that May, Root had privately maintained that the United States should enter the conflict. In public he was a ferocious advocate of preparedness and Americanization. In January 1916, in an emotional address to the New York State Bar Association at the Hotel Astor, he vigorously counseled getting prepared to deal with "foreign foes" and the "more insidious foes within." The latter were drawn from the ranks of the "millions of immigrants who have come from the Continent of Europe," from "communities which have not the traditions of individual liberty, but the traditions of State control over liberty." As they still had these traditions in their blood, "it was the duty of the American people to see that the traditions of America were upheld."[36]

In February 1916 Root attacked Wilson's diplomacy before a Carnegie Hall audience as being "brave in words and irresolute in action." He also pushed against American neutrality, saying it was impossible to be "neutral between right and wrong, neutral between justice and injustice, neutral between humanity and cruelty, neutral between liberty and oppression." Root received the backing of Wall Street, and New York State's Republican machine, but he labored under multiple handicaps. If elected he'd be 72 at his inauguration. His domestic conservatism alienated progressive Republicans. His strident pro–British attitudes estranged German Americans. William Randolph Hearst damned him as "the attorney of privilege." And former president Taft considered him too close to the socially prominent "400 circles of New York City."

Theodore Roosevelt was another would-be candidate. He had refused the Progressive Party's nomination, effectively shutting down the organization, and returned to the regular Republican ranks. He received support from such conservative outlets as the *New York Tribune* and the *Bankers Magazine*. But in June 1916 he wrote Brigadier General Pershing: "I do not for one moment believe I shall be nominated. Just at present the American people are passing through a yellow streak, and their leaders have sedulously done everything in their power to broaden the yellow streak." He was right about being out of sync with majority opinion, and a tour of the Midwest during which he criticized German American opposition to neutrality effectively destroyed his chances.

Spurning both Root and Roosevelt, the Republicans nominated Charles Evans Hughes, associate justice of the Supreme Court, and previously a reform governor of New York State.[37] Hughes was thought the man most able to reconcile regulars and progressives. This proved a difficult tightrope to walk. On domestic issues, Hughes leaned too far toward conservative sentiment, and most former leaders of the Bull Moose Party endorsed Wilson instead. On the military front, he tried to reconcile the pro-war and pro-peace camps, endorsing "adequate" preparedness and "the firm and unflinching maintenance of all the rights of American citizens on land and sea" while backing proposals from more pacific quarters.

---

36. American lawyers had a particular obligation in this regard, he told his audience of attorneys. He found it disturbing that since he'd been away, the percentage of New York lawyers that were foreign-born had risen to 15 percent; 30 percent if one included the children of immigrants. These carried the virus of suspect legal traditions in their blood, and they would "hold those traditions until they are expelled by the spirit of American institutions." The distinguished Jewish American lawyer Louis Marshall penned a vigorous protest of Root's remarks in a letter to the *Times*.

37. A boomlet in favor of General Wood materialized, but fizzled.

On the Americanization front, Hughes sought to capitalize on hyphenate discontent with Wilson, and he won considerable German and Irish backing by supporting the right of citizens (like Jeremiah O'Leary) to differ with administration policies without having their patriotism besmirched. But here he was blind-sided by fellow Republican Roosevelt, whose pro-British and anti-hyphenate rhetoric grew increasingly violent. Hughes tried to tone him down. In mid-August he requested Roosevelt avoid the term "hyphenated American." In October his campaign asked TR to soft-pedal the preparedness rhetoric. No such luck, though requests to the defense societies and other interventionists to lie low proved more fruitful; Root obligingly gave just one speech. But Roosevelt was a Bull Moose loose in a china shop— it was as if *he* were running, and on a third-party ticket to boot. Democrats moved swiftly to capitalize on the "fear of TR" issue. Rumors circulated that were Hughes elected president, he would appoint the truculent Teddy as secretary of war or state. William Jennings Bryan's *Commoner* noted: "Mr. Roosevelt is still waging war on Mexico and Germany, but his shells are falling in the camp of one Charles Evans Hughes."

In the campaign finale, an affair of dueling speeches in New York, Wilson (on November 2) reaffirmed his commitment to neutrality before crowds at both Cooper Union and Madison Square Garden. Hughes (on November 4) called for preparedness but declared himself "a man of peace." And on November 3, at Cooper Union, Roosevelt really let fly, summoning against Wilson "the shadows of the men, women and children who have risen from the ooze of the ocean bottom and from graves in foreign lands; the shadows of the helpless whom Mr. Wilson did not dare protect lest he might have to face danger; the shadows of babies gasping pitifully as they sank under the waves; the shadows of women outraged and slain by bandits," etc., giving credence to Democratic accusations that Republicans sought war.

Wilson carried the country, by a whisker. He won New York City but lost New York State, his 40,000-vote majority in Gotham being insufficient to overcome Republican strength upstate. His anti-hyphenism had cost him some support among German and Irish voters, notably in Queens, where Republicans reversed a previous Democratic majority. Jews demonstrated continuing resistance to backing any alliance that included Czarist Russia by re-electing anti-war Socialist Meyer London, who was also endorsed by the Central Federated Union of Greater New York. Republican Fiorello La Guardia won a congressional seat in East Harlem, having campaigned in English, Yiddish, Italian, and Slovenian, mainly on domestic issues, notably Tammany corruption.

BY EARLY 1917 IT APPEARED AS IF NEUTRALITY had won the day. Then, on January 31, 1917, the first of several big shocks detonated when Ambassador von Bernstorff presented Secretary of State Lansing a note declaring that Germany would restart unrestricted submarine warfare the following day. U-boats would sink without warning belligerent and neutral ships found in a designated zone comprising waters around Great Britain, France, and Italy and in the eastern Mediterranean.

Britain's blockade of Germany had been effective. The country had suffered food shortages, leading to strikes and riots. Frustrated by failure to achieve a breakthrough on the Western Front, and facing a crisis in domestic morale, Germany placed its hopes on U-boat warfare. By sinking massive tonnage of merchant shipping and deterring neutrals from carrying goods to British ports, it could erode Britain's ability to prosecute the war. Yes, the United States might well intervene, but the high command reckoned that German submarines would win the conflict before the first US troopships arrived.

Foreign trade was immediately paralyzed. In New York, vessels lay in port; storage facilities overflowed. Standard Oil radioed its steamers to return home. Shipping companies postponed sailings indefinitely. The British ambassador reported a "stoppage of trade, a congestion in the ports, widespread discomfort and even misery on the coast and inland, even bread riots and a coal famine."

On February 3, 1917, Wilson went before Congress to announce that he had severed diplomatic relations with Germany. He added that he could not believe the Germans would actually destroy American ships and stressed that only "actual overt acts" would force him to seek a declaration of war.

The very next day, in New York City, the peace movement, alarmed that the president seemed to be moving toward intervention, stepped up its activities. On February 4 the half-dozen organizations housed in the Educational Building (70 Fifth Avenue at 13th Street, one block off Union Square)—including the Woman's Peace Party, the American Union against Militarism, the Church Peace Union, and the New York Peace Society—caucused with others in the peace camp, including the Socialist Party, the United Hebrew Trades, and the Amalgamated, and decided to establish an Emergency Peace Federation (EPF), also housed at 70 Fifth. They drew up an appeal to US citizens to join in demanding that a national referendum on whether or not to enter the war precede any congressional action; this was ratified the next evening at a mass meeting in Carnegie Hall. The EPF sent 1,500 telegrams to central labor bodies across the country, asking them to wire their congressional representatives, and telephoned all members of their respective organizations to do the same. By February 8 100,000 telegrams had rained down on Washington. Then they followed up by heading down to DC themselves, visiting congressmen, and staging a march on Lincoln's birthday behind a banner reading PEACE OR WAR? CONSULT THE PEOPLE! Some also urged keeping Americans out of the danger zone, thus removing the possibility of an "actual overt act" from occurring. Among the scores of New York activists involved in this organizing burst were Randolph Bourne, Crystal Eastman, Max Eastman, Morris Hillquit, John Haynes Holmes, Paul Kellogg, Benjamin C. Marsh, Leonora O'Reilly, Mary White Ovington, Harriet Rodman, Norman Thomas, and Fanny Garrison Villard.

THESE ANTI-WAR ACTIVISTS WERE OPPOSED by a newly emergent set of New York intellectuals who argued that, *pace* the pacifists' forebodings, war would have profoundly progressive consequences for the country's domestic arrangements. This group was gathered around the *New Republic* (*NR*), a journal founded in 1914 to advance the ideas its editor, Herbert Croly, had promulgated in his *Promise of American Life* (1909), and which had provided the ideological scaffolding for Roosevelt's Progressive Party platform (1912). With that party clearly on the ropes, Croly had wanted a vehicle—"radical without being socialistic"—to promote that same agenda: strong central government run scientifically by experts, regulation (but not dissolution) of corporations, support for (responsible) organized labor, and institution of social insurance programs.

Croly's project was taken up by social activist Dorothy Payne Whitney—a suffragist, Women's Trade Union League backer, settlement supporter, Junior League president, and, as the heiress of multiple fortunes, one of the richest women in the United States. Whitney had also drawn her husband, Morgan banker Willard Dickerman Straight, into the progressive movement, and now the formidable couple told Croly they would underwrite his proposed journal. They set him up in a four-story town house at 421 West 21st Street, between Ninth and Tenth Avenues, across from the General Theological Seminary, and fitted it out like a midtown men's club—replete with deep leather chairs, book-lined library, and French chef.

Croly recruited like-minded souls, most crucially Walter Lippmann. Scion of an affluent and assimilated German Jewish family, he had gone from Dr. Julius Sachs's School for Boys in Manhattan to Harvard where he discovered Fabian (top-down) socialism. He helped found a branch of the Intercollegiate Socialist Society and invited speakers like Lincoln Steffens, Florence Kelley, and Morris Hillquit up from New York. After graduating in 1910, Lippmann worked with Steffens investigating Wall Street, became part of the Village scene (a habitué of Mabel Dodge's salon), backed the Paterson strike, and did freelance journalism (writing for, among other venues, the *Masses* and the *New York Call*). Joining the *New Republic* meant repositioning himself in Manhattan's political landscape, from the radical Village to the progressive 20s (the same latitude as Gramercy Park and the Russell Sage Foundation folks). He broke with his former comrades, like Reed, now deemed impractically "romantic," and exchanged them for more "realistic" associates—or, the term increasingly preferred, "liberals." The *NR*, whose first issue arrived November 7, 1914, quickly attracted writers and advisers of the caliber of judge Learned Hand, attorney Felix Frankfurter, and Columbia professors Charles Beard and John Dewey. Within three months it was selling 2,500 copies a week.

Not surprisingly, the magazine promoted the fortunes of Teddy Roosevelt, hoping for a presidential comeback in 1916. But when the editors incautiously dared (in December 1914) to admonish TR—calling his denunciation of President Wilson's refusal to invade Mexico a "brutally unfair attack"—Roosevelt responded in full pit-bull mode, snarling that the editors, "three circumcised Jews and three anemic Christians," had been guilty of "personal disloyalty," for which he never forgave them. Lippmann then moved step by step into Woodrow Wilson's camp, encouraged by his embrace of progressive issues like child labor and the eight-hour day for railroad workers. In 1916, accordingly, the *New Republic* opted for Wilson. Lippmann wrote speeches for the president, went on the hustings himself, and blazed a trail for Bull Moosers to follow. On Election Day, virtually the entire contingent of Republican progressives supported the Democratic candidate, a backing that Wilson among others believed had been crucial, given the tightness of the race. Invitations to the White House followed, as did regular Lippmann and Croly meetings with Colonel House. The *New Republic* was soon perceived to be an administration organ. Its circulation shot up past 20,000.

Backing Wilson meant signing on to his neutrality policy. But Lippmann and his cohort began to argue that the president should change course and take the country into the war, not out of Rooseveltian belligerency, but rather from a liberal perspective. This stance— expressed forcefully in *NR* editorials—was based on Lippmann's observation of the measures to which European combatants had been driven over the past three years. In order to successfully prosecute the war, they had adopted long-resisted programs, like nationalizing railroads and shipping, that proved "that the old unorganized, competitive profiteering is unsound and wasteful." "Whatever else the war has done," he wrote in March 1917, "it has at least taught England and Germany and Canada and France that large-scale operations can be planned and executed," and "that the old scruples and dogmas of legalism and laissez-faire are old men's bogeys." If Europe's experience was any guide, then war would usher in long-sought but largely balked social and economic and political reforms. Military efficiency would dictate nationalizing railroads, strengthening labor's rights, abolishing child labor, providing vocational training (through the army), instituting social services, expanding and levying heavy taxes on incomes and excess profits, and strengthening the state's ability to direct the economy. Systematic, scientific, and expert national planning, characterized by cooperation between business and government, would facilitate the attainment of social and economic goals. "We stand at the threshold," Lippmann would say, "of a collectivism which is greater than any as yet planned by a socialist party." John Dewey argued similarly in the *NR*'s pages that the war had provided a "plastic juncture," a malleable moment in which the polity would be open to the guiding influence of reason, and the "use of science for communal purposes."

Pacifist Randolph Bourne, Dewey's former pupil, bitterly assailed the pro-war liberals as self-delusional and self-interested. The notion that only by being "on the craft, in the stream" would there be "any chance of controlling the current forces for liberal purposes" was a fantasy. Justifying the war in terms congenial to progressives would merely aid "the reactionaries" who in the end would "pull the strings of power." In their rush for a seat at the war table, the liberals would pave the way for the "riveting of a semi-military State-socialism on the country," and facilitate a "fatal backwash and backfire upon creative and democratic values at home."

ON MARCH 1 THE STAY-OUT-OF-WAR MOVEMENT was jolted by another German initiative that alienated great numbers of Americans. On that day the newspapers blazoned the news that back in mid-January, Germany's Foreign Minister Arthur Zimmerman had sent a telegram to the German ambassador in Mexico City, instructing him to notify the Mexican government (which he did on January 19) that Germany would be resuming unrestricted submarine warfare on February 1. Zimmerman hoped the United States would remain neutral, but if it did enter the war on the Allies' side, he proposed a deal. If Mexico declared war on the US, opening up a second front, Germany would help it recover territory lost in the Mexican-American War, including the states of Texas, Arizona, and New Mexico. The proposal was ridiculous. Germany was in no position to offer financial support, much less military assistance. President Carranza figured this out in short order and turned it down. That would have been that, but for the fact that British intelligence had intercepted and decrypted the telegram and, on February 24, forwarded it to President Wilson. Released four days later to the Associated Press, it was published nationwide on March 1.

The cable created an uproar. Most of the public thought that fighting for American "dignity" or the "rights of neutrals" was not worth the horrible cost, but promising entire states of the union to a foreign power was another matter altogether. In New York, the initial response within the German-language community was incredulity—perhaps it was the work of British forgers?—or embarrassment: the *New Yorker Staats-Zeitung* asserted, "No one could have expected such nonsense of a practical statesman."

Wilson chose to treat the telegram not as an act of war, but rather as a proposed policy that might become a hostile act if war actually broke out. He did, however, authorize a policy of "armed neutrality," giving merchant ships the right to shoot at any submarine acting in a threatening way. Then, on March 16, at 10:00 a.m., a U-boat attacked the *Vigilancia*, bound from New York to Le Havre with a cargo of iron, straw, asbestos, and dried fruits. It flew an American flag. Its name and home city—New York—were painted on the port and starboard bows in letters five feet high and could be read at a distance of three miles. The submarine commander made no effort to ascertain whether the craft was carrying contraband before he torpedoed the vessel. The steamer sank in seven minutes. Fifteen crewmen drowned, six of them Americans. The story reached the press March 19.

That same day, the highly troubled president met with Frank Cobb, the editor of the *New York World*. After noting that he had done everything possible to avoid war, Wilson expressed deep anxiety. Once the United States entered the conflict, "the spirit of ruthless brutality will enter into the very fiber of our national life, infecting Congress, the courts, the policeman on the beat, the man in the street." On the other hand, he was in receipt of a March 6 report from American ambassador Walter Hines Page who warned that Britain's gold resources were approaching exhaustion. If the country proved unable to pay its debts, its trade would crumble, paving the way to a German victory, and usher in a profound "world-wide panic for an indefinite period." "Perhaps," Page concluded, "our going to war is the only way in which our present preeminent trade position can be maintained and a panic averted."

On March 20 a cabinet meeting agreed that an "overt act" had been committed.

IF THE FUROR OVER EVENTS IN THE NORTH ATLANTIC hardened animosities toward Germany, a virtually simultaneous upheaval in Petrograd was removing one of the principal remaining roadblocks on the road to war, the refusal of Jews, particularly in New York, to ally with a despotic Russian regime. On March 15, 1917, Czar Nicholas II was forced to abdicate by a general strike in the recently renamed St. Petersburg, and by a mutiny of the troops sent to suppress it.

In Gotham, no one was more surprised than Leon Trotsky, a major figure in the 1905 Russian Revolution, who had been living in the Bronx (at 1522 Vyse Avenue and 172nd Street) since disembarking on January 13, a deportee from Spain. Though the day after his arrival he had written in the Russian-language *Novy Mir* (New World) that he had "profound faith in a coming revolution," privately he was prepared for a lengthy exile.

Trotsky was fascinated by the city. "Here I was in New York," he recalled in his autobiography, "city of prose and fantasy, of capitalist automatism, its streets a triumph of cubism, its moral philosophy that of the dollar. New York impressed me tremendously because, more than any other city in the world, it is the fullest expression of our modern age." It was also, he quickly discovered, the city whose capitalists were making a bid for global leadership. Virtually the first thing he did on disembarking was visit the New York Public Library. During his stay he would immerse himself in recent US economic history. He was "astounded" to discover the "figures showing the growth of exports during the war," and quickly understood what Wall Street was up to. As he told a Cooper Union meeting of welcome by local socialists, "It is a fact of supreme importance that the economic life of Europe is being blasted to its very foundations, whereas America is increasing in wealth. As I look enviously at New York—I who still think of myself as a European—I ask myself: 'Will Europe be able to stand it? Will it not sink into nothing but a cemetery? And will the economic and cultural centres of gravity not shift to America?'"

Most of Trotsky's attention, however, was focused on the local revolutionary scene, establishing a political presence, and earning a meager living from it. He joined the editorial board of *Novy Mir*, at 77 St. Mark's Place, which he co-edited with Nikolai Bukharin and Alexandra Kollontai (herself in constant touch with Lenin). He gave lectures to Russian, Finnish, Latvian, German, and Jewish socialists, at venues like Beethoven Hall on East 5th Street. He also frequented Café Monopole, a radical hangout at Second Avenue and 9th Street, and, being a vegetarian, patronized various Jewish dairy restaurants (where he became notorious for refusing to tip, on principle). The burden of his presentations was furious denunciations of the international socialist movement (especially the German SPD) for having caved in to nationalist war hysteria, and he raged, as well, at the American party, which hadn't. Partly he considered them culturally retrograde—he would tag Hillquit as "the ideal Socialist leader for successful dentists"—and partly he denounced them for insufficient militancy.

He quickly attracted American radical supporters —"a handful of revolutionary aster-oids revolving around a star of the first magnitude," as one observer recalled. On his second evening in the city Trotsky, Bukharin, and Kollontai were invited to a dinner party at the Brooklyn residence of Ludwig Lore, a left-wing editor of the *New York Volkszeitung*. Lore had assembled a small group of radicals who were disaffected with Hillquit's leadership—notably 25-year-old journalist Louis Fraina, and Louis Boudin, a lawyer and ofttimes Socialist candidate. After a debate over whether to secede and form a new party, the majority agreed with Trotsky's position—advanced with eloquence and passion though virtually no knowledge of local conditions—to stay in the Socialist Party but organize a Left-Wing fac-tion and launch a theoretical journal called the *Class Struggle*. In a major March 4 show-down at a Lenox Casino meeting of the New York local, Trotsky and Fraina, with backing from the Russian and Jewish national federations, proposed the party agree "to encourage strikes and resist recruiting in the event of war with Germany." Hillquit's supporters backed a more moderate resolution: party members should refuse to volunteer, but if conscription became lawful, they should not attempt to sabotage the draft. They successfully defeated Trotsky's formulation, which they branded as adventurist, suicidal, and out of touch with American realities. Four days later, however, the undeniably American Eugene Debs ad-dressed an overflow socialist and labor crowd at Cooper Union, urging (to roars of approval) that if the United States went to war, workers should declare a general strike, adding, "I'd rather be lined up against a wall and shot as a traitor to Wall Street than fight as a traitor to America."

Then came Petrograd. Already on March 13, before Nicholas stepped down, Trotsky wrote in *Novy Mir* that "we are the witnesses of the beginning of the second Russian revolu-tion." With abdication, he became the center of community and press attention, as inquiries and requests for lectures to explain events poured in. "The cosmopolitan working-class in New York was all excited," Trotsky recalled. "Meetings, extraordinary for their size and en-thusiasm, were held all over New York." On the evening of March 20, for example, various socialist groups held a jam-packed gathering at Madison Square Garden, Hillquit presiding, that hailed the removal of the Romanovs. Red flags hung from the balconies; a large band played "The Marseillaise" and "The Star-Spangled Banner," and congratulations were cabled to the new Russian government. Some of the more radical attendees saw the fall of the House of Romanov as presaging the fall of the Houses of Morgan and Rockefeller, as well as the overthrow of the Kaiser by German workers, followed swiftly by an end to the war.

Trotsky immediately applied at the Russian consulate for funds it had been instructed to provide refugees seeking to return. On March 26 his friends gave him a farewell party at the Harlem River Casino (127th Street and Second Avenue), at which he gave (said Emma Goldman) an electrifying parting address. He sailed the next morning, regretting (as he later recalled) that he had "only managed to catch the general life-rhythm of the monster known as New York. I was leaving for Europe, with the feeling of a man who has had only a peep into the foundry in which the fate of man is to be forged."

THE FOUNDRY ITSELF WAS ABLAZE with organizing and counterorganizing, charges and coun-tercharges. The Emergency Peace Federation was at the center of the vortex: holding Carnegie Hall rallies (at which mentions of Root and Roosevelt were met with boos and hisses); raising a peace fund to place ads in papers (Fanny Villard kicked off the campaign in her Park Avenue parlor where supporters anted up $10,000); organizing a March on Washington that sent thousands down to DC on April 2, the day Congress resumed business, despite Capitol police having revoked its permit.[38]

Meanwhile, a National Committee of Patriotic and Defense Societies asked its members to wire congressman asking them to pay no attention to the pacifist pilgrimage or the deluge of telegrams. The Women's Preparedness Committee of the National Civic Federation compared the Emergency Peace Federation to the Tories of the American Revolution and, borrowing a comparison earlier made by TR, the Copperheads of the Civil War. Charles A. Beard denounced pacifists for "terrorizing the President and paralyzing Congress," and headed a Columbia faculty committee that accused the EPF of being "inspired by German cunning and financed by German money." And counterdemonstrators headed down to Washington on April 2 to march in a Patriot Pilgrimage.

Tempers grew. At a Carnegie Hall rally of liberals and socialists to celebrate the Russian Revolution, the audience applauded Mayor Mitchel when he hailed the abdication as "the greatest triumph of democracy since the fall of the Bastille." But when he said that it was "inevitable" that the United States would soon join the war, rumblings of "No! No!" rolled down from the galleries, and when he declared Americans should be glad that "instead of fighting side by side with autocratic Russia, we shall be fighting side by side with democratic Russia," pandemonium ensued, fifteen minutes of solid noise that prevented further remarks. The mayor, "white with anger," shouted shrilly that the country was now "divided into only two classes—Americans and traitors!" He then stormed out. As he was leaving the hall, a reporter heard him mutter, "The time is coming when we will be standing up those kind of fellows against a stone wall."

ON APRIL 2, 1917, WITH CROWDS OF DEMONSTRATORS and counter-demonstrators milling in the streets, Wilson went before a joint session of Congress and requested a declaration of war against Germany. On April 4 the Senate voted yea. On April 6 the House concurred (with Congressman Meyer London among the few voting nay). The country was at war.

Also on April 6, Mayor Mitchel issued a proclamation. Noting that "millions of the people of this city were born in the countries engaged in this great war," he enjoined the citizenry to have "respect for each other" in "this time of stress and tension." Then he upped the stress and tension level. "There will be some exceptional cases of malign influence and malicious purpose among you," he continued, "and, as to them, I advise you all that full and timely preparation has been made adequate to the exigency which exists for the maintenance of order throughout the City of New York." To underscore his warning to "the ill-disposed," he cited a statute decreeing that whoever gave "aid and comfort" to the country's enemies was "guilty of treason," the punishment for which was death, or imprisonment for not less than five years. "All officers of the police," he added, "have been especially instructed to give their prompt and efficacious attention to the enforcement of this law." The notice, Mitchel concluded, was to be printed in English, Yiddish, Italian, and German, and distributed throughout the city by the police, to be displayed prominently "in public places, including store windows."

A more succinct formulation of the underlying message, promulgated that same day by the attorney general of the United States, said that "no German alien enemy . . . need have any fear of action by the Department of Justice so long as he observes the following warning: 'Obey the law. Keep your mouth shut.'"

---

38. The AUAM proposed to place ads in the subway but was turned down by the ad agency in charge.

24

Over Here

JOHNNY GET YOUR GUN

On the night of April 18, 1917, as Trinity's bells tolled twelve, Jean Earle Mohle, a young woman decked out in the uniform of a Continental soldier, mounted her horse in front of St. Bartholomew's at 44th and Madison, and set out to reenact the midnight ride of Paul Revere. After a trial trot to Times Square, she galloped flat-out down Broadway to 34th Street, flanked by two automobiles carrying blaring trumpeters. This was but the curtain raiser for a daylong Wake Up, America! event, dedicated to drumming up enlistments. After war had been declared two weeks earlier, on April 6, recruitment centers had popped up all over the city. But sign-ups had been anemic; hence the decision by the Mayor's Committee on National Defense to galvanize volunteering with a patriotic parade.

Ninety percent of the 60,000 marchers were women and children. Many of the former had been brought out by the Woman's Suffrage Party, much experienced in the art of parades; Mohle herself was a suffragist. Five hundred decorated autos filled with society women rolled downtown from 72nd Street, past the reviewing stand at the ever-ardent Union League Club, to Washington Square. The walkers and riders intermingled with giant floats designed by commercial artist James Montgomery Flagg ("One Flag One Country," "The Spirit of the Children of the Lusitania"). Overhead, from a squadron of planes out of Mineola Field, airborne Reveres dropped thousands of leaflets urging Gotham's men to take up arms as their forebears had back in 1776—a somewhat mixed historical metaphor, given that Britain, its new ally, had been the enemy against whom Revere had rallied his fellow colonists. At the Washington Square terminus, 300 chorus girls, who had ridden downtown on sightseeing-company open-air autos, disembarked and extended more personal invitations to young men who seemed likely candidates. A contingent of Camp Fire Girls carried a stretcher on which lay a dummy representing a dead pacifist. An explanatory banner read DEAD—HE CAN'T ENLIST, BUT YOU CAN.

The payoff was paltry. Over the next several days, only 107 signed up for the navy, and 117 joined the army. If hoped-for volunteers had been awakened by all the hoopla, they must have rolled over and gone back to sleep.

The disjuncture between effort and result was the more striking given the larger goal. If the US military was to field a force remotely comparable to the millions-strong English, French, and German armies, it had a long way to go. As late as 1914, the federal army had numbered under 100,000, while the National Guard (the state militias) had totaled around 115,000. The National Defense Act of 1916 had authorized increasing the army to 165,000 and boosting the National Guard to 450,000. But by 1917 the federal army had expanded only to 121,000, with the National Guard numbering just 181,000. When war was declared, Wilson asked for a million-man army. Six weeks later, only 73,000 had volunteered for service.

Still intent on coaxing, not coercing, Americans into a war so many had opposed, Wilson established, by executive order, a propaganda agency named the Committee on Public Information (CPI). George Creel was put in charge. Creel was a progressive western journalist who had co-authored an exposé of child labor, supported women's suffrage, and shaped publicity for Wilson's successful 1916 campaign. He promised to marshal public opinion to support the war. Not, he avowed, by negative means—"propaganda" and "censorship" were words to be avoided—but rather by clogging all channels of communication with officially approved information, leaving little leeway for rumor or "disloyal" reportage to reach the public. He intended to mold the American people into "one white-hot mass instinct of fraternity, devotion, courage, and deathless determination."

Officially headquartered in Washington, the CPI called perforce upon the resources clustered in Gotham, the country's media capital. Creel turned first to poster makers. Four days after Wilson handed him the job, Creel wired the country's preeminent illustrator, Charles Dana Gibson (of "Gibson Girl" fame). Gibson had been a zealous advocate for preparedness and was now "white-hot" for war. Indeed, Creel's telegram arrived just as Gibson was gaveling to order a meeting of the Society of Illustrators, assembled at the Hotel Majestic to discuss how to join the fray. Within days a Division of Pictorial Publicity had been set up (with Gibson in charge), headquarters established (at 200 Fifth Avenue, across from Madison Square Park), and a distinguished list of artists signed up. They included Joseph Pennell (best known for his lithographs and etchings, notably of the new New York), Ashcanners William Glackens and George Bellows, and Woolworth architect Cass Gilbert, who summarized the division's mission as being "to place upon every wall in America the call to patriotism and to service." The division proceeded to link Washington bureaucrats in need of images with one or more of the 279 artists and 33 cartoonists on call and have them arrange details over dinner at the nearby Keens Chop House.

Of the 1,438 division-produced designs for posters, cards, buttons, cartoons, and lantern pictures (to be used with speeches), the most spectacularly successful creation was a poster by James Montgomery Flagg. Using his own visage as model (though appending a white goatee), Flagg fashioned a portrait of Uncle Sam pointing his finger at the viewer, over text reading "I Want YOU for U.S. Army," below which was left a space in which to designate the "Nearest Recruiting Station." Over the eighteen-month duration of US participation in the war, over 4 million Uncle Sams were distributed. Even more visceral was another Flagg

James Montgomery Flagg, "Wake Up America Day—April 19, 1917." (Library of Congress Prints and Photographs Division)

"Destroy This Mad Brute: Enlist—U.S. Army," 1918. (World History Archive/Alamy Stock Photo)

poster depicting a red-headed young man, springing forward in pugnacious outrage, at whose feet was an open newspaper with the headline "HUNS KILL WOMEN AND CHILDREN!" Above him floated the text: "TELL THAT TO THE MARINES! At 24 East 23rd Street."

Other CPI initiatives rang changes on the pictorialists' public-private collaboration. The production of sheet music was never formally coordinated by Creel's agency, in part because Tin Pan Alley had been on the pro-war case before the CPI was even born. On the day after the April 6 declaration, a bellicose George M. Cohan dashed off score and lyrics for the rollicking "Over There."[1] When it was introduced to the public that fall, at a Red Cross benefit in New York, the song took off, and its original recording went on to sell over 1.5 million copies.

---

1. Johnny get your gun, get your gun, get your gun,
    Take it on the run, on the run, on the run;
    Hear them calling you and me,
    Every son of Liberty.
    Hurry right away, no delay, go today.
    Make your daddy glad,
    To have had such a lad,
    Tell your sweetheart not to pine,
    To be proud her boy's in line.

    Over there, over there,
    Send the word, send the word over there
    That the Yanks are coming, the Yanks are coming

"E-e-e-yah-yip! Go over with U.S. Marines. Apply at: 530 Willis Ave., Bronx, N.Y.," 1917. (Library of Congress Prints and Photographs Division, Willard and Dorothy Straight Collection)

The conjunction of patriotism and profit persuaded the pop music industry to do an abrupt musical turnabout, declaring war, as it were, on aural pacifism. "I Didn't Raise My Boy to be a Soldier," which had topped the charts in 1915, was still doing alarmingly well, so the industry fired off a volley of pro-war "mom songs," like "If I Had a Son for Each Star in Old Glory (Uncle Sam, I'd Give Them All to You)." Some lyrics went toe-to-toe, stanza-to-stanza with the pacifist anthem. The first verse of "Didn't Raise" began "Ten million soldiers to the war have gone who will never return again. / Ten million mothers' hearts must break for the ones who died in vain." The opener of "The Sentiment of Every American Mother: America, Here's My Boy" went "There's a million mothers waiting by the fireside bright / A million mothers waiting for the call tonight / And while within each heart there'll be a tear, / She'll watch her boy go marching with a cheer." And where the pacifist chorus commenced with "I didn't raise my boy to be a soldier," its challenger responded, "America, I raised a boy for you." The new material flooded into American parlors—in homes that *had* parlors—and where the poster makers sought wall space, the music men intended their colorful sheet music covers to occupy the nation's piano music stands.

The state-industry interface was a bit more complicated in the film world. New York and Hollywood producers leapt to the colors with the same alacrity as did Alleymen and artists—out

---

The drums rum-tumming everywhere.

So prepare, say a prayer,

Send the word, send the word to beware—

We'll be over, we're coming over,

And we won't come back till it's over, over there.

"The Navy needs you! Don't read American history—make it! U.S. Navy Recruiting Station, 34 East 23rd St., New York," 1917. (Library of Congress Prints and Photographs Division, Willard and Dorothy Straight Collection)

of patriotism, no doubt, but also with awareness that they could be shut down overnight as an unessential industry. Creel's agency appreciated cinema's propagandistic uses, but, being wary of the industry's largely Jewish (and German) makeup, it also established a Division of Films. The division collaborated with the movie men. It created treatments or scripts and passed them to producers, who generated the CPI-ordered movies and distributed them with their own. But it also bypassed the moguls by producing and distributing its own feature films.

The division also provided government-created film footage to be run as newsreels—"Roxy" Rothafel excelled at reweaving filmic threads into more compelling narratives—and made clear to the industry which themes it would and would not countenance. This was done most forthrightly in the case of films for export. Only productions that presented "the whole-some life of America, giving fair ideas of our people and our institutions," would receive the requisite license. Movies showing strikes and riots, hunger and poverty, or ghetto slum condi-tions were rejected on the grounds that they were a "bad testimonial to the value of democracy." By war's end Creel believed he had helped reverse the overseas image of the United States as "a land of cruel monopolists, our real rulers the corporations and our democracy a 'fake.'"[2]

---

2. Because of the large number of transatlantic cables making landfall in the city, and the presence in Gotham of the three cable company headquarters, New York City soon developed the largest censorship operation. Handling an average of 100,000 messages a week, the operation eventually swelled to a staff of 55 officers and 695 enlisted and clerical personnel (40 percent of whom were women).

Sheet music cover, "America Here's My Boy," 1917. (Library of Congress, World War I Sheet Music)

The CPI's Division of News drew on New York's deep bench of journalists, particularly its muckrakers. They were urged to turn their investigative sights on Germany, in the process making clear that Tammany corruption and Wall Street misdeeds were mere peccadillos when set alongside the monstrous doings of the country's arch foe. The CPI also paid close attention to adjusting overseas opinions of America—Creel appointed Ernest Poole to head up a Foreign Press Bureau—and the News Division established links, as well, with some 600 foreign-language papers published in the United States. A Division of Syndicate Features enlisted leading novelists, short story writers, and popular essayists to craft feature materials—for distribution via the nation's newspapers—that were more interesting and accessible than standard journalistic fare. It was not long before Creel realized the role Madison Avenue could play—"If ads could sell face cream and soap," he mused, "why not a war?"—and he "turned almost instinctively to the advertising profession for advice and assistance." A Division of Advertising was duly established, headquartered in Gotham's Metropolitan Tower.

Just a few blocks south from the CPI's advertising aerie in Madison Square, the city erected its most tangible piece of propaganda. Mayor Mitchel's Committee on National Defense hired the George A. Fuller Company to build a full-scale replica battleship in Union Square. "Launched" in May 1917 and christened the USS *Recruit*, it measured 200 feet in length and 40 in beam and was replete with gun turrets, torpedoes, and other wooden weapons. Inside the structure was a registration and examination room for potential recruits into the navy and marines. On its deck, bands performed Sousa marches, films were screened for large audiences, and war relief charities hosted fund-raising parties.

USS *Recruit*, Union Square, ca. 1917. (Library of Congress Prints and Photographs Division, George Grantham Bain Collection)

DESPITE THE MILLIONS OF POSTERS and copies of sheet music, news articles and speeches, films and pamphlets, the paucity of recruits nationwide all but foreordained congressional passage of the Selective Service Act. Signed into law by President Wilson on May 18, 1917, it required all men aged 21 to 30 to register for military service, after which local draft boards would interview them as to their health, occupation, and citizenship status, assess if they were exempt or eligible, and, if the latter, decide to which branch of the armed forces they would be assigned. (Volunteering for either the regular army or a state militia would forestall being drafted into the all-new, all-conscript National Army.) Unlike the Civil War draft act, the 1917 law explicitly forbade the hiring of substitutes.

Registration commenced on June 5, 1917. Memories of the Civil War draft riots cast a long shadow over the proceedings. New York police officers were on duty at all 2,123 locations. National Guard units were mobilized and placed on stand-by in their armories. Regular troops were dotted here and there throughout the city, with a machine-gun unit detailed to the largely Jewish sections of Brooklyn, where food riots had broken out earlier that year. But the day passed peacefully. Lines formed up outside neighborhood schools, barbershops, storefronts, and other familiar venues, yet apart from the unexpectedly large crowds threatening at moments to swamp the 8,000 officials, there were no problems. And though thousands failed to appear, 590,670 did, fairly close to the Census Bureau's estimate of 624,700 metropolitan males in that age bracket.

Deferments were granted for those with specified dependents, or for having an occupation deemed essential to home-front war work. The bulk of those declared eligible were unskilled and unorganized: office and sales clerks, laborers, and urban service workers—bartenders, waiters, bellboys, porters, elevator operators, and chauffeurs. Of those who appeared for pre-induction physicals, 70 percent displayed a marked lack of Cohan-like fervor by filing claims for exemption. Specific cases were adjudicated by the 189 draft boards sprinkled throughout the five boroughs of the city.[3]

RESISTANCE AND REPRESSION

THE METROPOLITAN PRESS REJOICED that "reds" and anarchists and pacifists had failed to disrupt registration day, hadn't even tried, perhaps because they were overawed by the overwhelming military presence. But that didn't signal acquiescence.

At an emergency national convention held in St. Louis, on April 7, 1917, the day after the declaration, the Socialist Party of America (SPA)—with Hillquit's New Yorkers in the forefront—denounced America's intervention. It had been instigated by "predatory capitalists." It was "a crime against the people of the United States." Unlike Europe's socialists, the SPA would refuse to back the war. It would demonstrate, it would petition, it would offer "continuous, active, and public opposition." If conscription (not yet enacted) were to be forced upon the people, the party would struggle to repeal it and support all mass movements that opposed it. If the government tried to pay for the war by taxing workers' necessities of life, or by issuing bonds that would burden future generations, the party would insist on handing the bill to the capitalist class that was responsible for the war ("Let those who kindled the fire furnish the fuel"). If the state adopted censorship of the press and mails, or restricted freedom of speech and assembly, or limited the right to strike, the socialists would offer vigorous resistance.

A few members dissented and defected—especially several high-profile, well-to-do intellectuals like William English Walling, J. G. Phelps Stokes, Robert Hunter, Charles Edward Russell, and Upton Sinclair. (Walling, who had been at odds with the party leadership, went so far as to assert that the SPA "under its present control is directed from Berlin.") These critics argued that the patriotic fervor whipped up by war might rally support for the socialist cause, but a party referendum demonstrated overwhelming support for the leadership's militant position.

The socialists, however, were well aware they would need allies in resisting the war. A few weeks later, accordingly, on May 2, 1917, they co-convened a planning session at the Hotel Astor. It included activists from the Emergency Peace Federation, the American Union against Militarism, and the Woman's Peace Party. There was general agreement that a new coalition of pacifists and radicals was needed to deal with the new situation. In search of a model, the organizers were drawn to developments in Russia, where the post-czarist Kerensky government, which had continued prosecuting the war against Germany, was facing growing opposition from an exhausted army and populace. Leading the charge for an immediate cease-fire were the workers and soldiers of the Petrograd "Soviet" (council), which in March 1917 had advanced a three-point peace plan—no forcible annexations, no punitive indemnities (reimbursements for loss), and self-determination of all peoples—that had attracted widespread international attention, especially in leftist German, French, and British circles. Borrowing the name and peace agenda of the Petrograd Soviet, the Astor organizers

---

3. Blacks, barred from skilled trades, were overdrafted and then sent to segregated units. The NAACP set aside its usual insistence on integration and concentrated on winning a (separate) training camp for black officers; Du Bois himself sought a commission in US Army Intelligence. Resident aliens (being citizens of other countries) were, of course, exempt. But as draft quotas were based on the total population, citizens found themselves penalized. In one Brooklyn district, a quarter of those registered were exempt Russians, and the first draft call carried off every eligible American. Furious protests forced a revision—quotas were refigured to be based only on eligible registrants— but vindictive draft boards drafted thousands of aliens anyway.

proposed creating a People's Council of America for Democracy and Peace (PCA). Such a body, they argued—particularly the socialists among them—would also address the unrepresentative nature of America's political institutions. Given their conviction that capitalists' domination of Congress had allowed them to maneuver the country into war, they suggested that a People's Council should struggle for greater democratization as well as peace.

WHILE THE PEOPLE'S COUNCIL readied its crusade, the city's anarchists embarked on direct action. Emma Goldman declared in *Mother Earth* her intent to resist conscription. She and Alexander Berkman organized the No-Conscription League of New York. Their manifesto proclaimed: "We oppose conscription because we are internationalists, anti-militarists, and opposed to all wars waged by capitalistic governments." Specifically, "we will resist conscription by every means in our power, and we will sustain those who, for similar reasons, refuse to be conscripted." The first important public activity of the No-Conscription League was a mass meeting on May 18, attended by 8,000 people, at the Harlem River Casino (126th Street and Second Avenue). Goldman, Louis Fraina, and Leonora O'Reilly, among others, denounced the draft, urged young men not to register, and called for a general strike to protest the war.

ON MAY 30, THE FLEDGLING PEOPLE'S COUNCIL packed Madison Square Garden for an organizational rally. Gaveled to order by the chairman, Rabbi Judah Magnes, the hall was filled with veterans of previous struggles: radicals and reformers, social workers and single taxers, Irish nationalists, feminists, and unionists. The organizers had signed up activists like Randolph Bourne, Roger Baldwin, Norman Thomas, Crystal and Max Eastman, Art Young, John Reed, Elizabeth Gurley Flynn, and Charles Beard. Powerful New York unions had come on board, including the Amalgamated, the teachers, and the typographers. The gathering proceeded to adopt the Petrograd Soviet's three-point peace program—no annexations, no indemnities, self-determination—which bore some similarity to Wilson's January 1917 proposal of a "peace without victory." They also called for universal disarmament, freedom of the seas, and arbitration of disputes by international tribunals. They condemned the conscription act, proclaimed themselves champions of organized labor, and called for reorganizing the economic order given that "Industrial plutocracy makes for war—Industrial democracy for peace." And to challenge the de facto capture of political power by economic oligarchs, they proposed building up a national network of Workmen's Councils—a nod to the All-Russian Congress of Soviets contesting Kerensky's Provisional Government—as a democratic supplement. They then ordered the printing up and distribution of 50,000 copies of a summary and manifesto by Magnes and agreed to hold an organizing convention for their proposed network in the fall.

THESE INITIATIVES IGNITED A FIERY BACKDRAFT. Earnest patriots appalled at seeming treason, and calculating men of power who had long craved an excuse to smash their enemies, now backed Wilson's insistence that "horses that kick over the traces" should be "put in the corral." The *Times* hailed the Selective Service Law as "a long and sorely needed means of disciplining a certain insolent foreign element in this nation." And Elihu Root told a cheering audience at the Union League Club: "There are men walking about the streets of this city tonight who ought to be taken out at sunrise tomorrow and shot for treason."

The war was swiftly sanctified by Billy Sunday, the country's leading revivalist, who arrived at Penn Station the day after hostilities were declared. He had come, the nondenominational evangelical announced, to storm the modern Babylon, the capital of Satan, the wickedest of wicked cities. But Sunday had powerful helpers inside the walls, including magnates, ministers, and leading pro-war activists.

Like the similar jumbo-scale revivals organized by Charles Grandison Finney in the 1830s and Dwight Moody in the 1870s, Sunday's operation was expensive and primarily supported by the rich. His chief backer, Rockefeller Jr., loaned opinion-shaping expert Ivy Lee to run public relations and helped underwrite the cost of hiring hundreds to work on the project. Carpenters constructed a sprawling wooden tabernacle at the corner of Broadway and 168th Street, the "largest structure for public meetings ever erected in New York." As the *Times* noted, Sunday and his helpers "were going after souls as a successful commercial corporation goes after sales."

For ten weeks Sunday bombarded full houses with colorful and vitriolic sermons. He lashed New York's iniquitous citizens, past as well as present, declaring that Walt Whitman was roasting in hell for his pernicious writings. He proposed a return to the morality of "our fathers" and a crackdown on sinners. Sinners included any who betrayed the "virtue of womanhood"—that "rampart of our civilization." White slavers should be "shot at sunrise."

Sinners most definitely included anti-war protestors. "In these days all are patriots or traitors to their country and the cause of Jesus Christ." Critics should be jailed—except for "that God-forsaken crew of I.W.W.'s," who "would have a firing squad at sunrise if I was running things." Sunday fed a war frenzy—and benefited from it. He drew a million and a half auditors, of whom 98,264 were converted. (Sunday was precise about such things.) Rockefeller Jr. was well pleased, except for Sunday's failure to "lay hold of the masses of the people." Industrial workers had stayed away in droves (as they had avoided his predecessors). Sunday's rhetoric—like the recruitment drives and preparedness marches—played best with the city's rapidly expanding middle class, among its ranks of office workers, salesmen, petty officials, and junior managers, and the members of its fraternal orders, businessmen's clubs, and civic welfare societies.[4]

"Cars and Pedestrian Traffic in front of Billy Sunday Tabernacle in New York City," 1917. (CriticalPast)

---

4. Sunday was not alone in the war pulpit. Liberals like Baptist Harry Emerson Fosdick also accepted the idea that the United States was engaged in a holy war.

"Billy Sunday Tabernacle in New York on Palm Sunday," 1917. (Library of Congress Prints and Photographs Division)

THE SECULAR ARM, TOO, PREPARED to battle "traitors." On June 15, 1917, Wilson signed the Espionage Law into being. It had little to do with spying, being mainly focused on outlawing criticism of, or resistance to, conscription. Willfully obstructing recruiting was declared punishable by a maximum fine of $10,000 or by imprisonment for not more than twenty years or both.

A host of municipal and federal forces were readied for enforcement action: the New York Police Department (particularly Inspector Tunney's Bomb Squad), the Citizens Home Defense League, the Special Committee on Loyalty of the Mayor's Committee on National Defense, the Department of Justice (especially its Bureau of Investigation), the Treasury Department's Secret Service, the army's Military Intelligence Division, the Office of Naval Intelligence, the Post Office Department, the United States Marshals Service, and, in a supporting role, the British Secret Service, run out of 44 Whitehall Street.

These official agencies were supplemented by an array of semiofficial vigilante groups. The National Security League (NSL), a child of the preparedness movement, acquired quasi-state-sanctioned status when its members were pressed into service on registration day in June 1917 and issued badges and identity cards. The American Defense Society (ADS) established a 100-man "Vigilante Patrol" whose mission it was to stop "seditious street oratory." The newcomer American Protective League (APL), formed in March 1917 by a wealthy Chicago advertising executive, was authorized by the Department of Justice to assist the Bureau of Investigation in "keeping an eye on disloyal individuals and making reports of disloyal utterances." Eventually the APL numbered 250,000 members in 600 cities. The New York branch, headed by the president of the Metropolitan Trust Company, industriously sniffed out "subversives," collected information on disloyal neighbors, and disrupted radical meetings, though for all its busyness, it never managed to catch a spy.

WITH THE NEW LAWS IN PLACE, these public and private agencies, jointly or severally, swung into action.

First on the target list were Emma Goldman and Alexander Berkman. On June 15, 1917, US Marshals and members of the NYPD Bomb Squad arrested them at their offices (20 East 125th Street), took them downtown to the Tombs, and charged them with violating the Selective Service Act. At their trial in the United States District Court, July 2–9, the defendants advanced a First Amendment defense, decrying the way American freedoms—one of the country's great contributions to world civilization—were being eroded. They lost. Each was sentenced to the maximum penalty of two years in jail for conspiring to "induce persons not to register."

In September federal agents raided IWW headquarters in Chicago, arresting 166 alleged conspirators, including Big Bill Haywood. There was no equivalent roundup in New York, the Wobblies by then having shifted most of their efforts to the West, efforts that did not in fact include interfering with conscription. But Elizabeth Gurley Flynn and Carlo Tresca were close at hand, and on September 29 Justice Department agents arrested Flynn at her Bronx apartment. They took her to the elevated station at 134th Street, and while they were awaiting a downtown train, Tresca arrived on an uptown train and spotted them across the tracks. "I tried to ignore him and to shoo him off," Flynn recalled, "but he rushed up to me and asked what was wrong." The agents arrested him on the spot and took them both to the Tombs. The *Times* applauded the local "I.W.W. Roundup," describing Tresca as "one of the most rabid of the I.W.W. troublemakers."

By federal lights, however, the bigger fish-in-the-making was the People's Council, planning to establish a "subversive" network in the fall. But over the summer the PCA faced defections from its constituent groups. Pacifist ranks shrank rapidly, as many believed it was not right to keep protesting when the country had committed to war. Other reformers, particularly those dependent on more conservative funders, or who had the ear of power and hoped they could steer it in more moderate directions, departed in droves. The American Union against Militarism melted away. The Woman's Peace Party lost half its membership. In August, Lillian Wald wrote Max Eastman that the proposed People's Council seemed like a case of "impulsive radicalism," particularly as it had hitched the organization to the Socialist Party and a group of revolutionary Russians. This was not shaping up to be a revitalization of the broad coalition of edgy radicals and respectable reformers that had helped forestall war for three long years. So, though she opposed conscription, Wald let the Henry Street Settlement be incorporated into the registration and drafting machinery. And she, along with other stalwart but moderate pacifists like Villard and Kellogg, declined to join the PCA.

More worrisome to PCA organizers, however, was that the administration now directly (and indirectly) entered the lists against them. Wilson shrewdly understood that what made the PCA potentially dangerous was its having brought into its fold a strong contingent of labor unions, and there was clearly considerable additional interest in resisting the "rich man's war," even among the more conservative Central Federated Union (CFU). Driving a wedge between activists and unionists would effectively neutralize the threat. So Wilson instructed propaganda-meister George Creel to enlist the support of Samuel Gompers, the American Federation of Labor chieftain. Gompers had firmly joined the pro-war ranks in 1915, in exchange for a seat at the power table and labor-friendly war policies. Now, with secret funding from Creel's Committee on Public Information, he set up a front group, the American Alliance for Labor and Democracy (AALD), whose avowed purpose was to shore up labor resistance to consorting with "subversives."

Gompers took two tacks. First, he denounced the Socialists as agents of the Kaiser; here he had the assistance of several SPA defectors, notably Walling and Russell, who saw in the AALD the possible kernel of a radical Labor Party. Second, he reminded CFU workers of the benefits they were enjoying—plentiful jobs, high wages—and those they would reap in the future, promising that out of war "will arise the golden days for the men who toil." This campaign effectively halted further labor support for the PCA. Then the Wilson administration offered extremely favorable war contracts to the Amalgamated Clothing Workers, and the union's support for the PCA accordingly cooled, until, at Hillman's insistence, it was officially withdrawn.

Thus weakened, the PCA was vulnerable to a knockout frontal assault. Government officials labeled the council a threat to national security. Publications coming out of its office (at 2 West 13th Street) were banned from the mails. Creel slammed the PCA as a haven for "traitors and fools" against whom "we are fighting…to the death." Having learned that the group planned to hold its fall "constituent assembly" in a hired hall in Minneapolis, Creel confidentially advised "patriotic societies" and civic organizations in that city to thwart the PCA as pro-German and disloyal. Their meeting arrangements were soon rescinded, and no other venue in the city would take them in. Efforts to shift to North Dakota or Wisconsin were similarly blocked. A hurried session in Chicago, before troops arrived to close it down, was the best they could manage. It wasn't good enough. Between official harassment and public distrust, the group would shrink to little more than its cadre in New York City.

AMONG THE PACIFISTS who did an abrupt volte-face that spring and summer was Nicholas Murray Butler, president of Columbia University. Butler had been a well-known participant in pacifism's corporate wing. He was also a longtime admirer of German *Kultur* and had had a personal audience with Kaiser Wilhelm in 1907. With the declaration of war, Butler decided he'd best put some daylight between himself and his former pacifism. He was particularly concerned to placate a conservative and activist board of trustees that contained the likes of Marcellus Hartley Dodge, head of the Remington Arms Company. To achieve maximum effect, the president devoted his commencement address of June 6, 1917, to banning dissident views—"what had been folly was now treason"—and warning that critics of US engagement would be promptly dismissed from Columbia. In short order he fired one professor for working with peace societies and another for petitioning Congress not to send conscripts to Europe. He also axed a young instructor who had worked (at Butler's urging) for the Association for International Conciliation but had failed to veer, as fast as had his mentor, from visions of world peace to sternly militant nationalism. Franz Boas wasn't fired, despite having written a letter to the *Times* protesting the anti-German hysteria being whipped up, but Butler was openly critical of the German-Jewish anthropologist, restricted his access to undergraduates, and curtailed his department's growth.

In response, historian and political scientist Charles Beard resigned, protesting the influence of trustees "who have no standing in the world of education, who are reactionary and visionless in politics, narrow and medieval in religion." Beard made clear he supported Wilson's intervention—a German victory, he believed, would plunge all into the "black night of military barbarism"—but those who didn't agree should be met with argument, not "curses and bludgeons."[5]

THE ESPIONAGE STATUTE THAT AFFORDED THE BASIS for arrests and imprisonment also authorized constraints on, or outright suppression of, printed matter. Censorship was accomplished by restricting or denying access to the mails. This methodology, which Anthony

---

5. In 1919, Beard would collaborate with James Harvey Robinson, Horace Kallen, Thorstein Veblen, Alvin Johnson, and Robert Bruere in founding the New School for Social Research, a sanctuary for threatened intellectuals and academics.

Comstock had pioneered and practiced successfully for decades, was now applied to political rather than sexual transgressions. In 1917 Postmaster General Albert Burleson—who among other achievements segregated the nation's postal service—promulgated rules about what would be allowed. The *New York Times* account, headlined "Burleson Tells Newspapers What They May Not Say," made clear he would monitor and prosecute any "seditious" utterances—as for instance allegations that "the Government is controlled by Wall Street or munitions manufacturers" or accounts "attacking improperly our allies." Such publications would be "dealt with severely." The arrows available in Burleson's quiver ranged from issuance of a warning, to barring of particular issues, to denial of second-class mailing privileges (first class being far more expensive), to complete banning from the mails, to outright suppression. In practice these were often accompanied by raids on offices and printing shops, seizures of files and mailing lists, and destruction of presses and back issues.

Burleson's first target was the *Masses*. In July 1917 he proscribed the socialist magazine for its furious opposition to "Woodrow Wilson's and Wall Street's war." Federal District Judge Learned Hand issued a temporary restraining order, arguing the journal's political agitation could not be equated with "direct incitement to violent resistance" and asserting that such censorship threatened "the tradition of English-speaking freedom." Hand was quickly reversed. Eastman, Young, Dell, and Reed were indicted for interfering with enlistments. After two hung juries, the indictments were dismissed, but though the editors survived, the *Masses* did not. Max and Crystal Eastman's successor magazine, the *Liberator*, while featuring many of its predecessor's writers, adopted a more cautious editorial stance.

Burleson went after other socialist magazines. He sent Abe Cahan's *Jewish Daily Forward* a letter saying that if the *Forward* continued to criticize the government's support for the Allies, it would lose its second-class postage rates. Cahan unrepentantly replied that though the paper would "not renounce its convictions," it "would desist from publishing them." Socialists, he declared, "obey the law even if they disagree with it." The Socialist Party's English-language paper, the *New York Call*, however, was denied second-class rates, on the startling ground that it was not, in Burleson's opinion, a newspaper at all (this despite its circulation of 35,000 copies). And his was the only opinion that counted.

The list went on and on. Emma Goldman's *Mother Earth* did not survive her incarceration: its last issue appeared in August 1917. The Italian socialist *Il Proletario* was denied mailing privileges. Tresca's *L'Avvenire* was not raided, though he was followed night and day by federal and local agents, and his office phone was tapped. But his paper struggled to pay for the "true translations" of all articles pertaining to the government and the war that the Espionage Act required foreign language newspapers to provide. African American papers were closely monitored. Du Bois was warned that the *Crisis* was edging close to the closure line. And when Randolph and Owen wrote that blacks shouldn't fight for the United States as it then existed, Department of Justice agents ransacked the *Messenger* offices, and Randolph was arrested, then released. Some of the ethnic presses came under assault too. Jeremiah A. O'Leary, already on Wilson's enemies list, was arrested, and his paper (*Bull*) was suppressed. Burleson also barred numerous issues of the *Gaelic American* and *Irish World* from the mails.[6]

---

6. Postal authorities went after book publishers, too. They informed the recently established firm of Boni & Liveright that a novel it brought out that called the war a "wholesale cripple-and-corpse factory" was banned from the mails. Its offices were placed under surveillance by military intelligence. National Security League pressure forced Putnam to withdraw Ellen Key's *War, Peace, and the Future*. And the allies of the Society for the Suppression of Vice head, John Sumner, beat back attempts to un-ban Dreiser's *Genius* by noting darkly how many of his supporters—Mencken, Huneker, Lewisohn, Untermyer, Knopf—had Central European names.

ULTIMATELY, HOWEVER, THE PREMIER TARGETS of official and vigilante zealotry were German Americans. The "Hun within our gates," said Theodore Roosevelt in September 1917, whether he is "the paid or the unpaid agent of Germany," whether he is "pro-German or poses as a pacifist," is "the enemy of the United States" and should not be allowed "to sow the seeds of treason and sedition in this country." German-language papers, he declared, "should be put out of existence for the period of this war." And every disloyal German-born citizen "should have his naturalization papers recalled and should be interned during the term of the war."

For his part, Wilson required all resident German citizens (a.k.a. "enemy aliens") to surrender any firearms, operate no wireless apparatus, and not reside within half a mile of a fort, camp, or arsenal, without a permit. He also sicced the American Protective League on German Americans, of whom more than 200,000 were eventually "investigated."

The National Security League began demanding that German American community groups in the city, such as the German Historical Society or Brooklyn's Germania Society, hold public meetings where their members could denounce the German government and declare their allegiance to the United States. Employers began requiring that applicants speak English.

Things German were increasingly proscribed. The German Theatre ceased production. The New York Philharmonic spurned music by living German composers. The Metropolitan Opera banned all German-language works, and leading German singers were summarily dismissed, the company explained, "lest Germany should make capital of their continued appearance to convince the German people that this nation was not heart and soul in the war." (London's Covent Garden, seemingly less worried about appearances, kept German operas in its repertory throughout the war.)

Then the zealots went after German itself. "We have room for but one language," Roosevelt decreed, and the patriotic societies set to work, particularly the American Defense Society (of which TR was honorary president and Madison Grant a trustee). Not settling for simply scrubbing away particular words or place names—"sauerkraut" gave way to "liberty cabbage," and in Brooklyn "Wilson Avenue" effaced "Hamburg Avenue"—it got New York City's schools to stop teaching German.[7] "The appalling and complete breakdown of German Kultur," said the ADS, "compels a sweeping revision of the attitude of civilized nations and individuals toward the German language, literature, and science." German was not a fit tongue "to teach clean and pure American boys and girls," according to an ADS publication, *Throw Out the German Language and All Disloyal Teachers.* Hopefully, "throughout every English-speaking country on the globe, the German language will be a dead language. Out with it forever!" Mayor Mitchel's Committee of Women on National Defense established an Americanization program intent on making New York City "one people with one language, instead of a group of foreign towns."

Finally, some went a step further and called for the eradication of the Germans themselves. The Reverend Dr. Newell Dwight Hillis of Brooklyn's Plymouth Congregational Church, believing that German blood stank of "putrefaction and decay," wrote approvingly of proposals for the mass sterilization of German men.[8] In the meantime, disloyal German Americans should be "arrested at dark, tried at midnight, and shot at daybreak."

---

7. In 1915, German was the first choice of 70 percent of the students who studied a second language; by war's end it had been superseded by Spanish.

8. "Statesmen, generals, diplomats, editors are now talking about the duty of simply exterminating the German people," Hillis reported, with surgeons suggesting that a "new painless method of sterilizing the men" might profitably be deployed in neutering Germany's ten million soldiers. When coupled with "the segregation of their women," it would make this generation of Germans the final one, and thus "civilized cities, states and races may be rid of this awful cancer that must be cut clean out of the body of society."

Under this barrage, many Germans opted for accelerated assimilation. Clubs ceased operation; the once powerful Turner gymnastic/political movement languished; singing societies sang only in English; boycotts of German-language newspapers were launched. The press and ethnic organizations exhorted German-Americans to display the flag, attend patriotic rallies, buy bonds, give blood. Institutions hauled down old names, hung out new shingles. The Germania Bank became the Commonwealth Bank; the German Savings Bank of Brooklyn morphed into the Lincoln Savings Bank of Brooklyn; the Germania Life Insurance Company quick-changed to the Guardian Life Insurance Company; and the German Hospital and Dispensary on Fourth Avenue between 76th and 77th, which had recently constructed the Kaiser Wilhelm Pavilion, reemerged as the Lenox Hill Hospital.

One hundred percent (Anglo) Americanism was hoving into sight in New York City. But there was one significant obstacle standing in the way.

ELECTORAL SHOWDOWNS

In November 1917, eight months after the United States entered the war, Gotham held a mayoral election. The contest proved to be the most fractious in the city's history, presenting an even starker choice of candidates and platforms than had the George-Hewitt-Roosevelt battle of 1886.

John Purroy Mitchel stood for reelection as the favorite son of the city's elite. He had lost the Republican endorsement when he was defeated in New York's first primary election (another reform mandated in 1913). So his nomination was bestowed by an independent Committee of 250, well stocked with bankers, lawyers, and corporate titans, who helped him assemble a war chest.

The mayor wisely decided not to run on his domestic accomplishments. His Bureau of Municipal Research and banker-backed drive for efficiency and cost-cutting commanded little popular support. He had infuriated Catholics by claiming their charities were corrupt, and had incensed parents who thought his Gary school plan would dilute their children's education.

Mitchel ran instead as the "embodiment of true Americanism," in supporter TR's words, and Elihu Root agreed: "All true Americans must vote for Mayor Mitchel." The candidate spent much of the campaign smearing German Americans (Robert Wagner was "the gentleman from Prussia") and denouncing "disloyal Irishmen," though he didn't hesitate to appeal to pro-war Italians in blatantly nationalist terms.

Morris Hillquit, the Socialist candidate, braved the Espionage Act and openly opposed the war. He condemned conscription, appealed for an immediate peace, denounced the suppression of civil liberties as the "transfer to American soil of Prussian militarism," and refused to buy war bonds, rejecting the "methods of moral terrorism" employed to sell them. These stands won him supporters among Irish nationalists (the newly established Irish Progressive League was in his corner) and pro-war liberals (like Harry Hopkins) who opposed government suppression of civil liberties. German American elites offered their backing, but Hillquit turned them down, saying that while he hated the war as a Socialist, his personal sympathies were with the Allies. In Harlem, Randolph and Owen's *Messenger* urged blacks to vote for the Socialists because they represented "the working people, and 99% of Negroes are working people," and because Hillquit dared to say (as did Du Bois) that the war was being fought "over the exploitation of darker peoples." Working-class Jews overwhelmingly backed the Socialists, to the dismay of the German Jewish elite, who feared an anti–Semitic backlash. Louis Marshall characterized Hillquit's pacifist pronouncements as "poison for the Jews" and, with Henry Morgenthau, Jacob Schiff, and Oscar Straus, issued a statement endorsing Mitchel. Rabbi Stephen S. Wise, for all his differences with Marshall et al., was with them on this one. "The eyes of the nation were turned on New York, fearful lest the metropolis should shame the nation by repudiating John Purroy Mitchel." Only the mayor's reelection, said Wise, would prevent the city's becoming "the American suburb of Berlin."

Hillquit devoted as much attention to municipal as to foreign affairs, issuing a "City for the People" platform. It called for municipal ownership of key industries (especially utilities), public provision of unemployment insurance, building affordable housing, improving schools and hiring more (and better-paid) teachers, and establishing municipal nurseries, tuberculosis centers, and a free beach at Coney Island. He devoted particular attention to the cost of food. Back in February, the diversion of foodstuffs to Europe and the manipulations of food brokers had spiraled prices upward. Poor families pawned possessions, depleted savings, ate spoiled goods. In February and March, Williamsburg women had begun a boycott of vegetables, chicken, and fish. It spread rapidly to other Jewish neighborhoods. Crowds of women engulfed shops, threatened butchers with cleavers, and poured kerosene over peddlers' pushcarts. More than 1,000 women marched from Rutgers Square to City Hall to demand Mayor Mitchel fix prices. A Madison Square demonstration of 5,000 women spilled over into a march on the Waldorf-Astoria, where Governor Whitman was rumored to be stopping. Protestors beat on its barricaded doors for two hours and dragged passengers from a passing car, shouting, "Yah! Yah! You ride in comfort while we walk and starve."

The Socialists called for lowering prices, adopting the slogan "Hillquit and 5 cents Bread." To achieve this, they urged the municipal government to buy and distribute food at cost, provide free school lunches, and set up publicly owned and managed terminal markets, bakeries, and ice plants. These proposals, which rallied support from 159 local organizations, remained a centerpiece of Hillquit's campaign. Labor issues were also high on his list. Addressing 2,500 East Side cloak makers in Cooper Union, Hillquit vowed that "if you elect me, police clubs will not be for the heads of honest working people trying to make a living and better their conditions, but for thugs and gangsters whom your employers hire to break your strikes."

Mitchel and his rattled supporters raised the invective level. The Business Men's League of New York called Hillquit's candidacy "a dangerous menace to New York City." The *World* said his victory would brand Gotham "a traitor town." The Chamber of Commerce denounced his "seditious and unpatriotic sentiments," deplored the fact that "many avenues of publicity are still permitted to disloyal persons," and urged the Department of Justice (DOJ) to arrest and prosecute Hillquit under the Espionage Act. Wilson had been paying close attention to the campaign—he'd sent his personal secretary Joseph Tumulty to assess the Socialists' strength—and he agreed that Hillquit deserved imprisonment. But the president decided that arresting him would only increase his support by making him a martyr. He settled for having DOJ stenographers transcribe all the candidate's speeches. As ever, Roosevelt shouted loudest. Hillquit—"the Hun inside our gates"—was "cowardly" as well as "treasonable." His entire campaign, TR bellowed, was a case of "yellow calls to yellow."[9]

The Democratic candidate, John F. Hylan, adopted a different strategy. Boss Murphy had chosen this obscure Brooklyn County Court judge in large part because Hylan's

---

9. Colonel House believed that Wilson "evidently feels he is in hostile territory" when in New York City. House noted in his diary that he had "tried to get [Wilson] to differentiate between the great mass of people" and the disloyal elements of the city, but to no avail.

advocacy of the municipal ownership of subway lines had won him the support of William Randolph Hearst. The publisher was widely reviled for his resistance to the war—the *Tribune* called him "Hears-s-s-t," and advertisers deserted in droves—but the city's Irish and German population sustained his papers' circulation, and he remained a powerful figure.

Hylan's biography also provided an appealing contrast with Mitchel's. Hylan's father was an Ulster Irish famine refugee. After fighting for the Union in the Civil War, he managed to get a mortgage on a 60-acre farm upstate in the Catskills, the income from which barely covered the interest payments. Young Hylan—raised a Catholic despite his mother's being a Methodist—worked on the farm, and each spring labored for a local railroad, clearing track. In 1887 he moved down to Brooklyn, got a job laying rails for the Brooklyn Union Elevated Railroad, and over the next nine years worked his way up to stoker, engine hostler, and eventually engineer, in the process joining the Brotherhood of Locomotive Engineers. His ambition was "a little engine that knew no rest" (as was said of Lincoln), and it drove him to become a lawyer. After crash studies to overcome his lack of elementary education, he entered New York Law School, where Woodrow Wilson, then teaching constitutional law, was among his professors. Then he practiced law for nine years, moved into Brooklyn Democratic politics, and rose through those ranks as well. His working-class background, professional accomplishments, and Irish Catholicism appealed to an offended hierarchy and enraged ethnics.

Hylan, Hearst, and Tammany boss Charlie Murphy tagged Mitchel as a flunky for the Rockefellers and a crony of the Vanderbilts. They pointed to the heavy involvement of the oil heir's associates in Mitchel's policy-making apparatus and claimed that "Rockefeller now controls the city." Mitchel was vulnerable on this score, partly because he had paid little attention to the populist issues he had promoted as a candidate—cheap transit fares, municipal ownership of utilities, improved housing, support for labor. He had cut waste but hadn't spent the money saved on expanding services. He gained the reputation of being a penny pincher, preoccupied with cost efficiency rather than people's needs.

The Hylan camp also poked fun at the mayor's upper-crust socializing. Mitchel was a regular guest at Society's dinner tables and charity balls, determined to prove that an Irish Catholic could hold his own with Union League Club types. He refused, moreover, to attend Passover balls or labor union functions—"I want to dance with my friends," he explained. Hearst lit into him as a social climber. The *Journal* pictured a night on which, "breathless and with a bright pink spot on each cheek," Mitchel "burst through his front door and cried, 'My dear, Mr. Vanderbilt called me Jack.'" Hearst delivery wagons promptly were emblazoned with "Call Me Jack" posters, displaying them all around the town.

Mitchel retaliated by assailing Hearst as "the spokesman of the Kaiser." The mayor declared he was running against "Hearst, Hylan and the Hohenzollerns." Mitchel's posters depicted him in a doughboy's uniform, bayonetting the Tammany Tiger. But Mitchel, running as an independent, had no vote-getting operation capable of matching the Democratic Party's machine, nor, for that matter, the Socialists'. The New York SP had developed an unprecedentedly sophisticated apparatus, capable of arranging from 125 to 150 meetings every night, at the campaign's height, and filling Madison Square Garden a half dozen times for rallies.

In fact, the Democrats worried more about Hillquit than about Mitchel. Murphy fought the Socialists first by Red-baiting them, then by adopting much of their program. Tammany Hall cried, "Vote for Hylan if you want to save the city from the socialists," and it sent wrecking crews to disrupt Hillquit street rallies. At the same time, its purloined planks offered

"'The City for the People': Socialist Party, for Mayor, Morris Hillquit." *Messenger* 1, no. 11 (November 1917).

heated denunciations of Rockefeller and the gas companies, and pledged "public ownership and operation of all traction systems, including marginal railways and docks, gas, electricity, and the telephone, as well as terminal markets, storehouses, and refrigerator plants."

The strategy worked. Hylan reeled in 313,956 votes, 46.3 percent of the vote, the greatest plurality in New York City's history. He pulled in the Gashouse and Hell's Kitchen Irish, the Yorkville Germans, and substantial numbers of Italians in lower Manhattan and South Brooklyn. He drew skilled and unskilled workers, Hearst supporters, and businessmen who feared Hillquit more than Hylan. He also rallied municipal employees: the 91,000 ballots cast for him by people on the city payroll represented nearly a third of his overall vote. (That the old patronage order was back in the saddle was made clear shortly after the election, when Hylan told the Civil Service Reform Association that "we have had all the reform that we want in this city for some time to come"—a more decorous version of Tammany's 1897 triumphal cry, "Well, well, well—Reform has Gone to Hell!") Hylan also denounced government by Bureau of Municipal Research "experts" as an attack on democracy and promised he would "fill the outgoing trains with 'experts,'" and in their place appoint "real New Yorkers" (i.e., machine Democrats), who understood the real-life problems faced by voters. Planners, too, would be shown the door, Hylan promised, and, indeed, after assuming office, his administration abolished the City Planning Committee and fired its staff.

All his flag-waving had garnered Mitchel only 155,497 votes—23.2 percent of the ballots, less than half his 1913 tally. His support came chiefly from the rich, the entrepreneurs, and the professionals in Manhattan (particularly on both sides of Central Park), as well as Flatbush,

Stuyvesant Heights, Crown Heights, and Flushing. The Irish and Germans opposed him—Hell's Kitchen and the Lower West Side gave him less than 5 percent, and Yorkville supplied only 11 percent. "Too much Fifth Avenue, too little First Avenue," was one analyst's verdict.

First Avenue went for Hillquit. His 145,332 votes (22.0 percent) placed him neck and neck with Mitchel—a spectacular fivefold gain over previous Socialist candidacies. To his backbone support from Eastern European Jews in Harlem and the Lower East Side was added that of German and Irish breakaways from Tammany. (Hillquit was most competitive in the Bronx, where he finished second, with more than 31 percent.) At the same time, ten Socialists won election to the state assembly; seven more were sent to the Board of Aldermen; and a Jewish Socialist, Jacob Panken, was elected a municipal judge.[10]

These results seemed to constitute a major defeat for Wilson. Two-thirds of New York City's voters were (in the *Globe*'s assessment) straight-out supporters of Kaiserism. But with the votes safely counted, Hylan proclaimed his support for the war, allowing a relieved press to argue his victory did not reflect peace sentiment.[11]

ON THE SAME DAY THAT HYLAN WON THE MAYORALTY, and Hillquit demonstrated impressive Socialist strength, New York State's women won the right to vote. The two outcomes were related in more ways than temporal proximity.

After its 1915 defeat, the suffrage movement had picked up its banners and begun again. The campaigners demanded and got a second referendum. Another blitz ensued, and this one ended in triumph. Where in 1915 the measure had lost by 89,000 votes, in 1917 it carried by more than 100,000, with New York City providing 92,696 of the ballots. Suffrage won in every borough, and in all but two of New York City's sixty-two assembly districts. How to explain this turnabout?

Much credit goes to the superb ground game organized and executed by Carrie Chapman Catt, president of the National American Woman Suffrage Association (NAWSA). Catt launched a yearlong, enormously ambitious grassroots campaign. NAWSA activists went root by root, house to house, woman to woman, asking each if she wanted the right to vote. Conservative groups, such as the National Association Opposed to Woman Suffrage (NAOWS), argued that most females didn't. Catt and her colleagues buried that claim by getting 1,030,000 women—a majority of the state's females—to sign a petition saying they did.

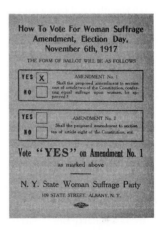

New York State Woman Suffrage Party, "How To Vote For Woman Suffrage Amendment, Election Day, November 6th, 1917." (Virginia Commonwealth University, Special Collections and Archives, James Branch Cabell Library)

---

10. The new aldermen promptly proposed startling bills: day nurseries for children of working parents; free school lunches; minimum wage legislation; a prohibition on using police as strikebreakers; and amnesty for political prisoners. All were indignantly rejected by regulars, who denounced the new members as traitors, especially after February 1918, when they refused to participate in a plan to sell war savings stamps, provoking a near-riot in the chamber.

11. When his term ended on December 31, 1917, Mitchel joined the Air Corps. On July 6, 1918, on a solo practice flight, without wearing a seat belt, he fell out during a dive and was killed. His funeral procession, from St. Patrick's Cathedral to City Hall, was accompanied by an airplane dropping flowers, and the War Department named a newly completed airfield on Long Island after him.

But not one of that million could vote. So the question remains: Why did the male electorate undergo such a tidal shift in sentiment? What had changed? America had entered the war, obviously, but how did that affect the suffrage movement? Basically, Catt and NAWSA took a pro-war stand, distancing themselves from radicals (thus making their own demands seem relatively moderate), from pacifists (making themselves acceptably patriotic), and from the conservative "antis" (making themselves partisans of democracy).

IN 1910, ALICE PAUL AND LUCY BURNS, NAWSA members who had been deeply involved in the British suffrage movement's civil disobedience campaigns, had urged Catt to push for a constitutional amendment guaranteeing the vote for women, rather than focusing only on a state-by-state strategy. In 1913, on the eve of Woodrow Wilson's inauguration, they organized a Woman Suffrage Procession on Pennsylvania Avenue, led by labor lawyer and Greenwich Village radical Inez Milholland astride a white horse; when half a million turned out to watch, or heckle, the event turned into a near-riot. Tensions over tactics developed within NAWSA. The Paul-Burns group broke away and created what became the National Woman's Party. Bankrolled in large part by Alva Belmont—at its founding convention in 1916 she pledged half a million dollars—it brought the militant tactics of British suffragettes to the nation's capital.

In January 1917 Woman's Party activists assembled outside the White House and began marching silently, carrying banners asking "How Long Must Women Wait for Liberty?" and describing the president as "Kaiser Wilson." Tolerated at first, once war was declared the picketers were attacked by enraged males, arrested by the police, and sentenced to the workhouse for up to seven months. There they insisted on being treated as political prisoners. When rebuffed, they went on hunger strikes. Force-fed, they won sympathy across the country.

Catt had been active in the peace movement before 1917 but viewed the war as an opportunity to show that women, if demonstrably patriotic, deserved full enfranchisement. Accordingly, on April 24, she herself accepted appointment as an administrator of the Women's Committee of the Council of National Defense. She also encouraged NAWSA members to march in Liberty Bond parades, roll bandages and knit socks for the men in the trenches, raise funds for the Red Cross and military hospitals overseas, gather food-conservation pledges from housewives, and register women for war service. Hence the support for the Wake Up, America! day. The *Times* headline, "Suffragists Aid Drive for Recruits," was precisely the publicity she was looking for. To drive the point home, she repudiated National Woman's Party tactics such as burning Wilson in effigy. NAWSA, she insisted, was a "bourgeois movement with nothing radical about it." It was, she said, "representative of the most coherent, tightest-welded, farthest reaching section of society—the middle." Perhaps "upper middle" would have been more accurate, as it was a board of wealthy women that had created the well-financed lobbying, advertising, and political organization, headquartered on two floors of a Manhattan skyscraper.[12] Such class credentials, and its stern dissociation from the Woman's Party's radical tactics, won over conservative males who, like Elihu Root, had opposed woman suffrage in the belief that women were natural-born pacifists, who if enfranchised would never let the country fight. The pro-war stance also appealed to soldiers and sailors, whose referendum votes, tabulated separately, showed them substantially more pro-suffrage than was the general population.

---

12. In 1914, Miriam Leslie, editor and powerful head of a publishing empire, died and left most of her $2 million estate to Carrie Chapman Catt for the cause of women's suffrage.

But the most important convert was President Wilson, who supported the more moderate NAWSA's referendum, casting it as a war measure.

The anti-suffragists complained that while they had patriotically immersed themselves totally in war relief work, the suffragists continued their campaign, diverting "Congress from the grave and solemn business before it," selfishly putting their interests above those of the country. But while this charge may have gained some traction for those castigating the Woman's Party suffragettes—who neither supported nor opposed the war—NAWSA suffragists were invulnerable to such assaults. They were patriots, and they had the socks to prove it.

The anti-suffragists also complained about the suffragists' affiliation with socialists and immigrants. Many observers did indeed credit the 1917 victory to a sharp increase in the number of registered Jewish voters—78 of the top 100 pro-suffrage electoral districts were Jewish, and Jews provided 24 percent of the overall pro vote. In part this was the consequence of a concerted Socialist Party registration drive in 1916; in part it was a function of the simultaneous mobilization under way by Hillquit's campaign. The Socialist candidate spoke out strongly on behalf of the referendum, arguing that "the suffrage is not a mere privilege, but lies at the most vital foundation of self-government or democracy," and it was "monstrous" that women were forced to rely for their rights on "the generosity of men." Given the synergy between the two campaigns, it's not surprising that a *Times* editorial labeled the referendum victory a "gift from Socialism," though it was not one that the "bourgeois" NAWSA cared to acknowledge; the group even excluded Socialist speakers from the victory celebrations.

Anti-suffragists convinced themselves that "pacifist, socialist, feminist, [and] suffragist" forces were "all parts of the same movement—a movement which weakens government, corrupts society and threatens the very existence of our great experiment in democracy." But on that score, given the war's rationale, the referendum's supporters clearly had the better argument. As Catt summarized the situation on the eve of Election Day: "Remember that our country is fighting for democracy, for the right of those who submit to authority to have a voice in their own government. Vote for woman suffrage, because it is part of the struggle toward democracy."

Given the next day's results, Catt was ecstatic. She believed this first suffrage victory in an eastern industrial state would be decisive in winning a national commitment to female voting, and she heralded the New York victory as "the Gettysburg of the woman suffrage movement." She was right. The principal convert was Wilson himself. He'd been waiting to see where the Democrats of the northern states would come down on the issue. The southern ones were opposed, hardly likely to enfranchise black women just as they were disenfranchising black men. Given Tammany's change of position, the president changed his own, and helped Catt push the proposed Nineteenth Amendment through the House. The Senate proved more obdurate. Despite Wilson's eloquent appeal—"We have made partners of the women in this war," he said. "Shall we admit them only to a partnership of suffering and sacrifice and toil and not to a partnership of privilege and right?"—and despite his repeated insistence that women's suffrage was "vitally essential to the successful prosecution of this great war," the Senate turned thumbs down. Not until mid-1919 did the upper house get on board. And it was only in the following year that it was ratified by the states, including New York, where Charlie Murphy, bowing to the inevitable, directed Tammany legislators to approve the amendment, and promptly began giving women positions within the machine. Anticipating this outcome, in May 1919, the New York Woman's Suffrage Party became the New York branch of the League of Women Voters.

"The Lady and the Tiger," November 7, 1917. (National Archives and Records Administration)

INTO THE TRENCHES

THE DAY AFTER HYLAN AND WOMEN'S SUFFRAGE WON, the Bolsheviks seized power in Petrograd. On November 7, 1917, with little opposition, their forces captured major military facilities, key communication installations, and the seat of Kerensky's government, the Winter Palace itself. At the forefront of the armed but remarkably bloodless insurrection was the chairman of the Petrograd Soviet, Leon Trotsky, late of 1522 Vyse Avenue in the Bronx.

Their takeover, and the subsequent withdrawal of Russia from the war, would have immense worldwide implications. In the United States, Wilson's responses were manifold and complicated, but the triumph of revolution in Russia seems to have strengthened his determination to stamp out internal dissent in the USA.

Crackdowns were more extensive in 1918 than they had been the previous year and reached higher up the political ladder, notably when Eugene Debs, a multiple past contender for the US presidency, was sentenced to jail for ten years. The legal underpinning for such governmental repression was cranked up considerably by a new piece of legislation. On May 16, 1918, Congress passed the Sedition Act—actually a set of amendments to the Espionage Act. It prohibited "any disloyal, profane, scurrilous, or abusive language about the form of government of the United States...or the flag of the United States, or the uniform of the Army or Navy." It banned, as well, the use of "contemptuous and slurring language about the President."

Wilson's greenlighting of suppression also facilitated measures to more vigorously enforce conscription. In September 1918 thousands of members of the American Protective League teamed up with federal agents from the DOJ's Bureau of Investigation, the New York Police Department, 1,000 sailors provided by the navy, and 2,000 soldiers rounded up from nearby army camps, and embarked on three harrowing days of combing the city for "slackers" (draft evaders). Another round of draft calls was coming up on September 12. All men aged between 18 and 45 would be required to register. To ensure compliance, the 20,000-strong posse would demonstrate what could happen to those who didn't have a draft card on their person in public.

On September 3, before the morning rush hour, the combined force of vigilantes and military men, the latter armed with rifles and fixed bayonets, blockaded the exits of every subway stop, ferry landing, and commuter train station in the city and refused to allow young men to pass through unless they could produce a valid draft card. By noon they had switched their attention to the midtown and downtown business districts, cordoning off whole blocks, barging into lunchrooms, cigar stores, office buildings, hotels, and streetcars. At night they muscled into cabarets, restaurants, saloons, billiard parlors, boardinghouses, and Times Square theaters. At each venue, young men were ordered to stand and present credentials. Those whose papers were missing or not in order, or who were too frightened to explain themselves, were hauled off in autos manned by APL wives to detention centers set up in armories, courthouses, or the Tombs. By the end of the first day, these impromptu camps were besieged by enraged relatives; at some armories, women with their men inside stormed the gates and had to be repulsed by the National Guard. Two more days of this followed. By the time incensed congressmen forced the Wilson administration to back off, between 300,000 and 500,000 New Yorkers had been interrogated, and more than 60,000 had been detained. Of these, 199 were eventually adjudged to be draft dodgers, and the number of "willful deserters" (who had deliberately ignored a call-up) was found to total 8. Wilson never apologized; indeed, he told his secretary of the navy (privately) that the raids had "put the fear of God in others just before the new draft."

THERE WAS A PROBLEM with this way of proceeding, quite apart from growing concerns about bands of vigilantes making unauthorized and illegal arrests, a phenomenon that many US senators of both parties criticized vociferously. Men might be dragooned into the military, but then what? How effective would a coerced army be, especially in a country whose citizenry highly prized their "American" rights and liberties?

There was a second problem, rooted in the closely associated efforts to impose 100 percent (Anglo) Americanism on the immense immigrant population. What to do with a conscript force that, notably in New York, was divided along ethnic lines? Some proposed using military discipline to compel the uniformity civilian authorities had failed to inculcate. But the War Department and army command, while sympathetic to the goal, feared the method might be counterproductive.

There was a third problem with using "the fear of God" as a method of mobilization. Given the limited size of the regular army, units of the National Guard would have to be deployed as well, and they depended on volunteers, who needed to be coaxed, not terrorized.

THERE WERE THREE DIFFERENT BRANCHES in the American Expeditionary Forces. Of the divisions that saw service in Europe, the regular army contributed eight, the state-based National Guard sixteen, and seventeen were provided by the brand-new National Army, whose ranks were composed entirely of draftees.[13] When the United States joined the war, General John

---

13. Divisions consisted of 28,000 men, divided into brigades, and further subdivided into regiments, battalions, companies, and platoons, commanded, respectively, by major generals, brigadier generals, colonels, lieutenant colonels, captains, and lieutenants.

J. Pershing rushed four divisions of regulars to the front, but helping their new allies stem German advances would require considerably more manpower, and quickly. With some reluctance—professionals were wary of National Guard volunteers' efficiency and readiness—Pershing turned first to existing units, who, though creatures of the states, could be and were now called up into federal service.

Of New York City's military entities, two of the most prominent were old established units, the 7th ("Silk Stocking") Regiment and the 69th ("Fighting 69th") Regiment; a third was the recently created 15th New York National Guard Regiment (eventually nicknamed the Harlem Hellfighters); and the fourth—far bigger—was the all-conscript 77th Infantry Division (known variously as the Melting Pot, Metropolitan, or Statue of Liberty Division).

As mobilization began, neither of the two veteran regiments—the 7th and the 69th—was at the minimum required strength of 2,002, so each embarked on a recruiting campaign. They appealed for volunteers on various grounds—patriotic fervor (as stoked by Creel's Committee on Public Information); anti-German feeling; the perception of war as an adventure, a rite of passage, a test of masculinity. If these weren't sufficient, there was the fact that given the Selective Service Act, young men were going to be drafted willy-nilly, and thrown together with who-knows-who. Wouldn't it be better to join up with people from a similar background, even friends and neighbors? Recruiters could also draw upon the conviction that membership in militias, which entailed the right and duty to participate in the common defense, was a hallmark of full citizenship. Moreover, joining a particular regiment meant affiliating with a particular collective identity, becoming part of a proud tradition, and connecting oneself to New York's history.

THE 7TH REGIMENT WAS THE OLDESt in the city, the oldest in the United States. It traced its roots back to 1806. It was famed for two other things as well. First, as proclaimed by its "Silk Stocking" label, it was, and always had been, composed of the city's patrician elite, or, more precisely, the elite's sons and grandsons—scions of Anglo-Dutch society like the Vanderbilts and Van Rensselaers, Roosevelts and Rhinelanders. The 7th did not enroll just anybody. Peacetime entry requirements had long been as rigorous as those for getting into an exclusive club, and indeed the 7th Regiment Armory (1880) on Park Avenue between 66th and 67th, resembled a lavishly appointed clubhouse.

The 7th also had a century-long tradition of serving as an unofficial municipal police force. Since before there *was* a police force, the unit's soldiers had been repeatedly called out to underwrite public order or, depending on one's perspective, intervene on behalf of their class. The regiment's roll call of campaigns fought consisted mainly of a lengthy list of strikes broken and riots suppressed.[14]

In August 1917 the 7th New York was called into federal service and set about recruiting. Immediately it ran into difficulties. One was a common problem that plagued all units with established pedigrees. Its time-honored number was retired and replaced with a bureaucratically assigned selection, and the regiment was bundled together with others and became a (small) part of a larger entity. In October, the 7th was merged with the plebeian 1st and 12th Regiments from upstate New York and retitled the 107th Infantry Regiment, 27th Division. Members were not happy about their shotgun wedding with the

---

14. The catalog included the Abolition Riot (1834), Stevedore Riot (1836), Flour Riot (1837), Anti-Rent War (1839), Croton Water Riot (1840), Astor Place Riot (1849), Police Riot (1857), Dead Rabbits Riot (1857), Draft Riots (1863), Orange Riot (1871), Railroad Strike (1877), Motormen's Strike (1895), and Croton Dam Strike (1900).

upstaters (a.k.a. "appleknockers"), and their distress was reciprocated by at least one north-country Guardsman, uncomfortable that the 7th was "made of college fellows, wealthy men and the like."

A more 7th-specific recruitment problem was that the sons and grandsons were not signing up en masse; indeed, some members were even jumping ship. It turned out that joining a class regiment was not as appealing as joining the officer class, the route to which ran through Plattsburgh. That was where one met one's fellows—the city's well-born, private-prep-school– and Ivy League–educated members of Gotham's highest business, political, and social circles. Graduates of the officer training camp would command the battalions, companies, and platoons of New York City's conscript 77th Division, thus porting their elite status from civilian into military life. They would not be limited to service in the 7th, which wasn't quite what it used to be, but would have the whole National Army as their oyster. The result, as a French military observer noted, was that "the officer corps is drawn almost entirely from the rich, cultured bourgeoisie."

THE 69TH WAS A MAJOR SOCIAL INSTITUTION for New York's Irish. It traced its roots to 1849 and had compiled a great Civil War record, at Fredericksburg and Gettysburg, as part of the famed Irish Brigade. Nevertheless, like other National Guard units, the 69th was under par in membership, so it launched into recruiting mode. Regimental representatives, including the military chaplain, Father Duffy, spoke on street corners, addressed audiences in theaters and movie houses, and tacked up posters invoking the lineage of the "famous Irish regiment." Cardinal John Murphy Farley called on every Catholic to enlist or register for the draft, warning that the "quality of our patriotism will be tested."[15]

Recruits arrived, including Duffy's Bronx parishioners, tough Irish teamsters and stevedores from Hell's Kitchen, residents of Manhattan's Gashouse District, and men from the Rockaways, Staten Island, Long Island City, and Coney Island. Many were drawn from Irish county societies or Catholic athletic clubs. By summer's end, though the roster included some German, French, Italian, and Polish names, they were totally outnumbered by the twenty-two Murphys, forty Kellys, and assorted O'Briens, O'Connells, O'Connors, and O'Reillys. Ninety-five percent of the regiment was reportedly Catholic.

But the 69th, like the 7th, feared looming dilution. The name went first, with the regiment now remonikered as the 3rd Battalion of the 165th Infantry, which with the 166th Ohio National Guard formed a brigade, which was in turn part of the 42nd Infantry (Rainbow) Division, itself a mixture of National Guard units gathered in from twenty-six states—an agglomeration suggested by Douglas MacArthur, an aide to Secretary of War Newton Baker. Worse, in August, just when the regiment had filled its ranks, the requisite minimum was upped from 2,002 to 3,600, leaving the 69th 1,600 short. Worse still, rather than renewing recruiting (time being of the essence), the brass assigned outsiders from other units to fatten up the 69th. One of the ransacked regiments, to its great dismay, was the 7th, a clear sign of

---

15. Francis P. Duffy had an unusual résumé for an army chaplain. Born in Ontario in 1871 to Irish Canadian parents, Duffy came to the United States as a young man and in 1896 was ordained a priest of the Archdiocese of New York. For fourteen years, Duffy was a professor at Dunwoodie, the major seminary of the archdiocese. There he played a key role in initiating and editing the controversial *New York Review: A Journal of Ancient Faith and Modern Thought*. An attempt to reconcile historical Christianity with modern science and philosophy, it was the leading American Catholic theological journal of its day. Its day passed in 1907 when Pius X condemned modernism. In 1909 Archbishop Farley fired the rector, and in 1912 the now Cardinal Farley dispatched Duffy to the Bronx, where he set about establishing Our Savior Parish and building a new church at Washington Avenue and 184th. In 1914 Farley appointed him chaplain of the 69th.

slipping status, but the 69th was equally discomfited by the dilution of its Irish and Catholic character. Nevertheless, the handoff was handled handsomely, with the 350 transferees (including the great-grandson of Cornelius Vanderbilt) escorted by the entire 7th on their grim march down to 26th Street, where the 69th's armory had been decorated with a huge (if perhaps not heartfelt) welcome sign.

IF THE 15TH NEW YORK NATIONAL GUARD REGIMENT had a historical tradition, it was one of aspiration. The city's African American community had been trying to win approval for a "colored" regiment since 1847. What finally made one possible was the rapid development of black Harlem, its population swelled by migrants from the South and the West Indies seeking employment in war industries. African American leaders, conscious of the enclave's growing size and strength, petitioned again for a regiment. In 1916, with the preparedness campaign in full swing, Governor Whitman appointed a prominent white Republican named William Hayward to be colonel of the new 15th New York.[16]

Recruiting began that July, but it was slow going, partly because the project was treated with such palpable contempt by the state, which provided none of the things normally supplied a National Guard regiment—no rifles, no helmets, no uniforms, no armory. The regiment's sponsors, accordingly, turned to sympathetic whites for financial contributions, and to the black community for other kinds of support. When James Reese Europe, the celebrated composer, bandleader, and Clef Club organizer, enlisted as a line officer, the sponsors appointed him regimental bandmaster and featured his musical performances at fund-raising affairs. Hayward also attracted Plattsburgh alums to serve as officers, like the amply pedigreed Hamilton Fish Jr., a descendant of Stuyvesants and Livingstons. Harlem theaters and dance halls and churches stepped up to serve as recruiting stations and drill halls.

The campaign drew in the neighborhood's elevator operators, shop owners, ballplayers, house painters, boxers, hustlers, porters, teachers, salesmen, and entertainers. But many Harlemites were skeptical. Watching a company of the 15th march by, a young man said, "They'll not take me out to make a target of me and bring me back to Jim Crow me." A man in a barbershop summed up his reservations thusly: "The Germans ain't done nothin' to me, and if they have, I forgive 'em." As was the case with the Anglo and Irish regiments, voluntary enlistments did not come in fast enough to allow the regiment to reach the minimum combat strength of 3,600 men, and the number was made up with draftees.

WHILE THE ANGLO, IRISH, AND AFRICAN AMERICAN REGIMENTS represented three strands of Gotham's population, the 77th Division embraced them all. It was indeed, as another of its several nicknames had it, "New York's Own Division." Its 27,000 draftees were dispatched for training to Camp Upton, a built-from-scratch facility on a 10,000-acre tract—a "wilderness of sand and scrub oak"—60 miles outside the city, near the hamlet of Yaphank, in the middle of Suffolk County, Long Island. An hour's train ride from Manhattan, Upton was in effect a satellite city. The eyes of all Gotham were upon it.

The city's English-language papers sent teams of correspondents out to report on the phenomenon but weren't quite sure what to make of this assemblage of troops from the tenements. For a generation the Anglo press had mockingly portrayed the city's Yids and Wops

---

16. Hayward was a member of the Union League Club of New York, which sponsored the 15th as it had the 20th US Colored Infantry in the Civil War.

and Chinks and Polacks as vaudeville-style caricatures, and stories from Upton tended to follow this convention, playing the immigrant soldier story for laughs.

Another trope represented the camp as a potpourri of peoples, truly representative of the city's cultural and social diversity, whose differences were happily being overcome as polyglot civilians were molded into a homogenous soldiery. Though off the mark as a description of reality, this assessment resonated with Americanizers and progressive reformers, who viewed this offshoot community of New York's working and middle classes as ripe for potential reformation. Secretary of War Baker established a Commission on Training Camp Activities (CTCA), headed by Raymond Fosdick, a former Henry Street resident, investigator of prostitution in the city, and associate of Rockefeller Jr.'s Bureau of Social Hygiene. Fosdick's CTCA campaign started with a program of sex education, alerting trainees to the dangers (and shame!) of venereal disease, and then expanded to inculcating conservative middle-class morals, the better to inoculate recruits against vice and depravity. With the aid of YMCA volunteers, the CTCA built facilities for wholesome recreations (sports, decorous dances, uplifting lectures). The CTCA also provided literacy classes and courses in US history and politics, and encouraged naturalization.

Moralizers were not only the ones watching. Nearly every Sunday, cars, trains, and buses brought thousands of friends and families to Yaphank. There they found it troubling that the special needs of minority populations were not being met. By early 1918 at least a quarter of the division was Jewish, and overwhelmingly Orthodox. Community leaders sought recognition and respect for such cultural differences. The Jewish Welfare Board (JWB) lobbied for the recruitment of Jewish military chaplains (there was not a single one in the entire US Army) and the provision of religious and social services for Jewish soldiers in the cantonment.

Secretary Baker agreed, and backed off from the 100 percent effort at Americanizing. Jewish services were authorized. So were Jewish military chaplains, and a Hebrew prayer book was prepared for their use. A kosher restaurant was set up off-base as an alternative to the mess hall. On Yom Kippur, the Mayor's Committee on National Defense arranged for special trains to take the draftees home, buying round-trip tickets for poor men who could not afford the expense. And it was agreed that if Jewish soldiers were killed in service, the army would bury them under the Star of David instead of the cross.

Other groups achieved similar recognition. The Knights of Columbus received permission to provide religious and social services for Catholic soldiers, particularly those of Italian origin. The Polish Falcons played a similar role, as did organizations representing the Armenian, Croat, Czech, Serb, Slovak, Slovene, and other Balkan groups.[17]

Concessions were made on the entertainment front as well. Broadway performers, overwhelmingly ethnic, insisted on their right to entertain the troops, some of whom were themselves professional comics and song-and-dance men. Draftee Irving Berlin pestered the camp commander into putting on an all-soldier review, in large part so he could minimize time spent on basic training. His grousing song "Oh! How I Hate to Get Up in the Morning" eschewed patriotic appeals in favor of comic fantasies of murdering the bugler; it became the war's *second*-most-popular song. (Berlin dropped his "God Bless America" from the show; it seemed a "little sticky," he thought.)

---

17. Such acknowledgment of ethnic requests was not matched by concessions to African Americans. Both the division and the camp were segregated.

In the end, however, the army turned Berlin's talents to inspirational ends. The show (*Yip, Yip, Yaphank*) was moved to Manhattan. After a smash-hit six-week run, it offered a closing night to remember. As usual, the company concluded its performance by marching offstage and down the aisles singing "We're on Our Way to France." Only this time they kept on marching, out into the street, where—followed by the crying, fainting, cheering audience—they tramped to their troop carrier and sailed away to France.

ON THE NIGHT OF JUNE 21, 1918, IN THE BACCARAT SECTOR of the Vosges Mountains of eastern France, men of the 308th Infantry Regiment, part of the Upton-trained 77th, were marching in single file up a road, when they encountered a column of men from the Fighting 69th (now the 165th Infantry) coming down. Father Duffy remembered the encounter as "Old Home Day," with the New Yorkers greeting one another—"Anybody here from Greenwich Village? . . . Any of you guys from Tremont?"—and at one point breaking into a rousing rendition of "East Side, West Side, All Around the Town."

The various New York forces served with distinction on a variety of fronts. The 107th Infantry of the 27th Division (the old 7th Regiment) fought in Belgium and France and took part in the ferocious attack against the famed Hindenburg Line, one of the strongest defensive systems ever devised; the assault was successful, but at a tremendous cost in lives.

The 77th Infantry Division arrived in France in April 1918, was sent to a quiet sector to learn trench warfare, and fought in the Battle of Château-Thierry in July and other engagements in August and September, before being assigned to participate in an assault on German positions in the heavily fortified Argonne Forest. On October 2 a detachment of more than 700 men broke through the German lines, only to be cut off and surrounded. For the next six days, though suffering tremendous losses (some inflicted by a friendly-fire bombardment), they repulsed repeated attacks by the Germans. Finally a "runner"—Private Abraham Krotoshinsky—"a little, stoop-shouldered Polish Jew," as he was described—got through to the division's headquarters and guided troops back to his beleaguered comrades. When the New Yorkers were finally relieved, fewer than 200 were able to leave the field on their own legs.

The story was recounted (and embroidered) by Damon Runyon, on the scene as a reporter for Hearst's *New York American*. The popular columnist was already renowned as a chronicler of the city's life, and his narrative made the men of the "Lost Battalion" into the "heroes of one of the Homeric fights of the war." Moreover, Runyon proclaimed, the hyphenates of the city slums had vindicated the Americanism of the immigrants in general, and of eastern European Jews in particular. The *New York Globe* agreed, identifying the 77th as a "Yiddish division" whose valor had underscored that "the East Side Jews are fighters, no mistake about it."

Perhaps the most successful record was compiled by the city's black regiment, which had to fight a two-front war, against the Germans and the US Army. It was the latter that heaped upon them one disrespect after another. It gave them a battered hulk of a troopship—it caught fire and sprung a leak—and refused to provide it with a naval escort. Furthermore, the army neglected to formally take the regiment into federal service, so it landed in France as the 15th New York, carrying state as well as national colors, the only regiment in the AEF to do so; it was belatedly renumbered as the 369th Infantry. When it arrived in France in January 1918, the regiment was sent to Saint-Nazaire to serve as a labor battalion, laying railroads and draining swamps.[18]

---

18. On February 12, in nearby Nantes, Lieutenant Europe conducted a performance of the regiment's sixty-piece marching band at the city's opera house. It included an up-tempo version of "The Marseillaise" that the French troops in attendance didn't recognize at first, then did and went wild. Hayward arranged for the band to go on tour, entertaining US troops as well as French

Then, on March 21, a German spring offensive opened with a massive assault against the British in Flanders, threatening a decisive breakthrough. In this crisis, Pershing offered the Allies the use of his few available units, one of them being the 369th Infantry. Before they could be deployed, the Germans ran out of steam. Pershing reclaimed his white divisions. But he made his black regiment a permanent gift to the French, who promptly deployed them as fighters, so often that they became more proficient than most white units of the AEF. In mid-May during one encounter, Private Henry Johnson held off a sneak attack and, despite having been shot, laid waste to an entire German platoon. Shortly after, Colonel Hayward arrived with three prominent journalists he had persuaded to visit his men. The *New York World* gave reporter Lincoln Eyre's account of "The Battle of Henry Johnson" a front-page spread, and it was reprinted throughout the country.

Between June and August, the 369th was heavily engaged as part of the French 4th Army opposing yet another German offensive and suffering grave losses. Its reward was pressure from American commanders in Pershing's headquarters to contain the tremendous admiration the French had developed for the African American troops. From their first arrival, the US military had warned the French that Negroes were prone to larceny, and might rape French women if allowed to fraternize. The French shrugged this off, but the US command continued to badger them to draw and respect a color line. On August 14, Colonel Linard, a French liaison officer at AEF headquarters, issued the document "Secret Information Concerning Black American Troops." The French should know, it explained, that American whites believed that displays of interracial friendship would encourage "intolerable pretensions to equality" and pose a threat when the troops came home. In particular, "Americans become greatly incensed at any public display of intimacy between white women and black men." Accordingly, French soldiers and civilians should not praise black troops too highly. "We must not eat with them, must not shake hands or seek to talk or meet with them outside the requirements of military service."

This cut no ice with the French high command, especially given the 369th's role in the Meuse-Argonne Offensive. On September 26, 1918, the Hellfighters (as by now they were known, for their prowess) began five days of continual assault against entrenched German positions, taking hundreds of prisoners, storming fortified Bellevue Ridge, and capturing the town of Sechault at a terrible cost in dead and wounded. Their casualties were so high that they had been destroyed as a fighting force. On October 1 the French withdrew them from the line and awarded the entire regiment the Croix de Guerre.

For all the differences in their wartime experience, New York's troops shared the hellish reality of "modern" combat, as did their British, French, and German counterparts. Little of the real horror made it past the respective censors. Slowly, however, the truth came out. In April 1919 the *Times* ran a story by Philip Gibbs, a celebrated English war correspondent, in which he apologized that he and his colleagues had been unable to "give the full picture of our men's agony." The untold sufferings—as summarized by the *Times* headline—included being "Shot to Pieces, Buried Alive, Seared Inside and Out by Poison Gas, Driven Insane by Shell Shock, Burned by Liquid Flames, and Drowned in the Bogs of Flanders." It was essential that the world be told, and the "beastliness and the terror of it all should be stripped

audiences. It wasn't the Europeans' first exposure to black music; Williams and Walker had performed at Buckingham Palace in 1903, Bob Cole and Rosamond Johnson had played in London and Paris in 1904, and Irving Berlin's "Alexander's Ragtime Band" sold over a million copies in Europe in 1914. But the 369th's music was perceived as a feature of American culture, not only that of African Americans.

of all their romantic 'camouflage' so that the truth should be etched deeply in the pages of history."

There were, however, some wartime horrors—also involving the deaths of thousands—about which New Yorkers did not have to wait to be apprised, as they transpired on the home front itself.

THE GERMS OF AUGUST

The virus arrived on August 11, 1918, aboard the Norwegian vessel *Bergensfjord*. The ship had wired ahead that ten passengers and eleven crew members had taken ill. The boat was met at the pier by ambulances and health officers, who whisked the sick to quarantine in Brooklyn's Norwegian Hospital. On August 16 the *Nieuw Amsterdam* out of Rotterdam made landfall bearing twenty-two stricken, and on September 4 the French liner *Rochambeau* brought in twenty-two more, along with the news that two others had died in passage. The city's Department of Health placed the afflicted in isolation at the Willard Parker Hospital on East 16th Street, and the French Hospital on West 34th.

On September 15 the first death from what was being called Spanish influenza was recorded. (There was nothing "Spanish" about the supremely contagious disease; it was rampant among all Europe's combatant armies and countries, but under-reported, due to military censorship, except in neutral Spain, where coverage was unchecked). On September 17, to gather information about the dimension of the onslaught, Dr. Royal S. Copeland, a homeopathic physician who in April had been appointed the city's health commissioner, required doctors to report instances of both flu and pneumonia. It quickly became clear that the number of cases was multiplying rapidly, as was the daily death toll. On September 30 physician reports showed that forty-eight people had died the previous day. And they were hard deaths, with patients gasping for breath as their lungs filled with bloody frothy fluid. As often as not, flu victims were finished off by pneumonia, a secondary infection that followed hard upon the flu virus's trail, constituting a lethal one-two punch.

In October the epidemic struck with full force. Morbidity soared. On October 4 physicians reported 999 new cases during the previous twenty-four hours. On October 9 that doubled to 2,000. On October 11 the count rose to 3,100. On October 12 there 4,300 new instances. And on October 19 4,875 new cases were tallied.

Mortality followed along. 126 died on October 6. 297 perished on October 13. Over 400 succumbed on October 16, and the daily death count fluctuated in the 400–500 range between October 16 and 26. On October 30 Mayor Hylan dispatched seventy-five men to the Calvary Cemetery to help inter bodies that had overflowed the facility's receiving vault.

Copeland's Department of Health opted for a two-part response to the epidemic: attempting to slow the spread of the disease; and treating the infected.

The containment strategy re-deployed public health measures worked out in New York over previous decades, in the course of dealing with various infectious diseases. The first line of defense was isolation of the ill. As Copeland explained to the *New York Times* on September 19, "When cases develop in private houses or apartments they will be kept in strict quarantine there. When they develop in boarding houses or tenements they will be promptly removed to city hospitals, and held under strict observation and treated there." In practice, home quarantine was voluntary, given the lack of sufficient physicians to oversee compliance. And hospital quarantine may have separated the sick from the general population, but couldn't isolate them from one another. The hyper-density of diseased patients was a function of the limited number of hospital beds, and the serious depletion of hospital staffs, as many doctors and nurses had answered US Army and Red Cross calls to set up and run military hospitals in France.[19] The New York hospitals were soon inundated, particularly the public ones, which hewed to their accept-all-comers policy, while private ones could and did limit admissions. (At one point Bellevue's grounds hosted ambulances from ten private hospitals waiting to discharge their refusés.) Bellevue patients were laid out on cots jammed together in every nook and cranny; children were packed three to a bed.

Other venues were pressed into service—armories, gymnasia, and the Municipal Lodging House, which was converted from homeless shelter to sick bay for the duration of the epidemic. Hard-hit military installations like Camp Mills, Camp Dix, and Camp Upton set up their own facilities. Upton hospitalized over a hundred new patients every day between September 15 and October 9—admissions peaked at 483 on October 4—in huge tent wards holding 900 infected; over 500 died at Upton alone.

On the slowing-the-spread front, Copeland tackled what he considered the biggest and least escapable dangers confronting still-healthy New Yorkers—the concentration and circulation of residents. Hallmarks of the post-Consolidation era, they also facilitated the spread of disease. Nothing packed bodies together as dangerously as the mass transit system. Subway and elevated cars almost certainly contained infected passengers who couldn't afford to skip work and stay home. The most menacing moments of the day and night came during morning and evening rush hours. To de-concentrate the crush, Copeland arranged with businesses to stagger work hours. White-collar offices would open at 8:40 and close at 4:30; wholesalers would start their days earlier, non-textile manufacturers would start later. Stores selling food and drugs were exempt.

Other obvious congestion points were schools and theaters, but where most US cities simply shut both down, Copeland went with a different strategy.

Schools, he reasoned, were often more sanitary than housing, particularly in the slums. New York City schools, moreover, boasted a well-established system of child health monitoring and care. Copeland, accordingly, kept the schools open. Under the direction of Dr. S. Josephine Baker, head of the Department of Health's Bureau of Child Hygiene, school physicians inspected children each morning and sent sick students home. It worked—few children caught the disease—and in addition the schools handed out printed material on how to avoid the flu, for passing along to parents.

Theaters seemed a more unequivocal danger, but Commissioner Copeland eschewed total closure. Many modern theaters were, after all, clean and well ventilated, and could be used to exhort audiences, urging them to adopt flu prevention measures. On October 11 Copeland announced that approved venues could stay open if they did not allow patrons to cough, sneeze, or smoke. Dirty and stuffy "hole-in-the-walls," as he called them, could be and were closed if they failed to meet sanitary standards.

Public health education campaigns, based on Gotham's experience with mitigating tuberculosis, were another way to slow the epidemic. By September 24 at least 10,000 posters had been placed around the city in railway stations, elevated train platforms, ferry landings, streetcars, store windows, police precincts, hotels, and other public places. These explained how the virus was transmitted, and instructed the citizenry to cover their coughs and sneezes,

---

19. Bellevue, quickest off the mark, established Base Hospital Unit #1, and was soon joined by personnel from New York Hospital, Presbyterian Hospital, and Mount Sinai, which set up Base Hospital #3 in a fifteenth-century monastery in Vauclaire, Dordogne, that at one point housed 2,800 patients.

and to refrain from spitting. A small army of Boy Scouts was detailed to hand printed cards to caught-in-the-act spitters, reading "You are in violation of the Sanitary Code." They were backed up by police, who rounded up New Yorkers caught spitting, and brought them before courts in large numbers. On October 4 134 men were fined one dollar each at the Jefferson Market Court.

When it came to treating the infected, the terrible truth was that no effective medical intervention existed; doctors were virtually helpless. But nurses were not. The best that could be done for the afflicted was to provide them with soups, baths, blankets, and fresh air, until the disease subsided or the patient died, which could happen within twenty-four hours of onset. This enormous task was taken on by a large army of women, generaled by the indefatigable Lillian Wald, who had pioneered the visiting nurse service that would now be writ large. Wald mobilized a multitude of nurses' organizations, church groups, municipal bureaucracies, civic entities, and social agencies into a Nurses' Emergency Council, which assembled volunteer nurses (a dangerous commitment, as in October roughly 20 percent came down with the disease), and enlisted women who could support them by answering phones, accompanying them on home visits, and arranging for and driving automobiles to carry linens, pneumonia jackets, and quarts of soup.[20]

The Department of Health provided additional backup. On October 7 Copeland established more than 150 emergency health centers in neighborhoods around the city, whose chief function was to coordinate the work of nurses making home visits in their district. On October 12 he created a special Emergency Advisory Committee to assist the department's initiatives, including representatives of private and public city hospitals, institutional and home nursing organizations, the Red Cross, the United States Public Health Service, the city's Department of Education, and the Mayor's Committee of Women on National Defense (which rounded up food and autos).

From October 26 onward, the number of deaths from both influenza and pneumonia first slackened, then swiftly declined. By early November, influenza and pneumonia mortality rates had returned to levels typical of the previous year's. The crisis was over. And so was the war. The Nurses' Emergency Council discontinued its central office on November 6, five days before the armistice was signed.

The plague months of September–November 1918, it turned out, had overlapped with the period of the American Expeditionary Force's maximum efforts, and while the military initiatives had been sanguinary for New Yorkers, the home front proved to have been more so. More Gothamites had died of disease in the city (roughly 20,000) than had died in the war (about 7,500). This civilian/military mortality ratio (2.6:1) actually understated the disparity, as the flu had sickened millions of soldiers, too. Of the 7,500 New York City soldier deaths, more than 2,000 were due to disease (for an adjusted ratio of 3.6:1). Similarly, while the trenches produced an ecological environment in which the flu virus could thrive and mutate into a lethal disease, the mobilization of Americans to fight abroad also created conditions that contributed to the death rate at home. Of the men assembled in highly vulnerable training camps, almost 30,000 were struck down before they got to France, while others died

---

20. According to a press release written by Wald, the council included the Bureau of Communicable Diseases, the Bureau of Child Welfare, the Red Cross, the Maternity Centers, the Association for the Aid of Crippled Children, the Milk Stations, the New York Diet Kitchen, the Social Service Department of Mt. Sinai, Presbyterian, and Beth Israel Hospitals, the Catholic Nursing sisterhoods, the Salvation Army, the Teachers College Department of Nursing, and virtually every social settlement and social agency in the city.

on the packed troopships, and some of the survivors carried viral reinforcement to the influenza attacking the front lines.[21]

New York's civilian fatalities, however, added relatively few to the colossal totals that ravaged the United States (675,000), to say nothing of the monstrous estimates of planetary mortality (at the very least 50 million), which reflected the very different social ecologies of India, China, and Russia, among others. "Global Flu" would have been a far more apposite name than "Spanish."

More pertinent, perhaps, is the comparison made at the time with other US cities, particularly Boston and Philadelphia. Gotham's death rate per 1,000 residents was reportedly 4.7, compared with 6.5 in Boston and 7.3 in Philadelphia. When asked in a *New York Times* postmortem interview to account for the difference, Health Commissioner Copeland attributed it to New York's long history of public health work, and particularly the alleviation of unhealthy conditions in streets, tenements, shops, and restaurants over the previous two decades.

THE POTOMAC AND THE HUDSON

Who was running New York during the war? Officially, it was the mayor, the Board of Estimate, and the Board of Aldermen. Unofficially, the Mayor's Committee on National Defense (MCND) served as a supplemental government. Set up in 1915 to lobby for preparedness, the committee had morphed into an activist organization, composed of subcommittees devoted to tackling war-related tasks. While the MCND was answerable to the mayor—first Mitchel, then Hylan—its considerable authority stemmed from its membership, drawn from the city's economic and social elite. During the war, the executive committee of the MCND included the likes of Elihu Root, Henry Stimson, Willard Straight, Cleveland H. Dodge, Nicholas F. Brady, Charles Schwab, and Al Smith. These were not mayoral flunkies.

Nor were the leaders of the subcommittees, of which there were dozens—among them Recruiting, Industry and Employment, Hospital and Medical Facilities, Shipping and Harbor Defense, Civic Finance, Transportation, Commerce, Labor, Aliens, Loyalty, and Investigation and Intelligence. Those in charge included eminent businessmen and civic leaders such as Robert de Forest, Henry Davison, George Baker, Mortimer Schiff, Thomas J. Ryan, Irving Bush, and George Perkins, along with leading professionals who specialized in a subcommittee's subject, like S. S. Goldwater (medicine) and Edward T. Devine (welfare). The subcommittees' rank and file were composed of businessmen, professionals, managers, and labor leaders. All in all, hundreds of prominent New Yorkers participated.

The Mayor's Committee on National Defense, clearly, was not answerable to Tammany Hall. Its members were not selected on partisan political grounds; nor were they vulnerable to being fired with a change of mayor.[22] Thanks to Hylan's win, Tammany had been able to purge "experts" from the official government, but the MCND—which included a small army of experts—was impervious to Boss Murphy's wishes. The goal of winning the war had

---

21. In 1922 Brigadier General J. Leslie Kincaid, then adjutant general of the State of New York, published a "Roll of Honor" that tabulated the types of fatalities suffered by citizens who died in the Great War. Of New York City residents in the US Army, he recorded the following: Killed in Action 2,993; Died of Wounds 1,037; Died of Disease 2,149; Accident 249; Drowned 72; Other Causes 128; for a total of New York City fatalities in the army of 6,630. The total of fatalities for the navy and Marine Corps was 816 (no data by cause was available). The total of NYC fatalities, in all branches and for all causes, was 7,446. Subtracting from this all non-disease fatalities (the army's 4,479, and an estimated 551 for the navy and Marine Corps) left a total of 5,030.

22. One of the more notable consequences of Hylan's ascendancy was the mayor's designation of his patron's wife, Millicent (Mrs. William Randolph) Hearst, as chair of the Mayor's Committee of Women on National Defense.

enabled an expansion of elite influence on municipal affairs that peacetime political reform movements had been unable to accomplish.

A similar transformation was under way at the federal level. Most of the critical decisions in wartime Washington were made by elected civilian officials (the president and Congress) or the military. But their work was supplemented by an extensive cadre of businessmen and professionals who came to DC to serve on wartime agencies tasked with homefront duties. Some of these boards and councils were without formal authority, like the National Defense Advisory Commission, but had considerable influence on Wilson's course of action. Others had decision-making powers of their own, and became pillars of an emerging administrative state. Many of their edicts would affect New York City more profoundly than any actions taken by Gotham's official or unofficial government, because they were addressing problems beyond solution at the municipal level.

IN THE WINTER OF 1917–18, the Port of New York was a mess. At the best of times, the harbor's complicated interlock of shore and marine operations, its crazy quilt of fragmented and competing rail lines, and its aged docks, antique equipment, and limited waterfront space, had made for levels of inefficiency and disorganization approaching chaos. When war sent wheat and weapons surging toward the port, it buckled under the strain. Piers were jammed, grain elevators crammed, waterfront arteries clotted with trucks and drays. It took days for teamsters to reach the piers. (At night they unhitched their horses and left their wagons in line.) Freight cars, unable to unload, were parked in yards and sidings—at one point, 65,000 of them were immobilized—and incoming trains were backed up as far as Pennsylvania. The massive snarl-up threatened to paralyze the war effort. In a winter of blizzards and subzero temperatures, lack of coal and food also threatened the life of the city itself.

Wilson took drastic action. On December 26, 1917, he put the railroads under control of a government-run United States Railroad Administration, directed by William Gibbs McAdoo, secretary of the treasury and builder of the Hudson and Manhattan Railroad. McAdoo initiated a government-overseen cartelization process, overcoming competition (in part by suspending antitrust laws). He also recapitalized the system, infusing half a billion dollars of federal funds, which went to making improvements and raising wages.[23] This kind of coerced coordination was something the European combatants had accomplished within days of the war's commencement. It was also seemingly akin to the nationalization that US radicals had long been urging, except for the critical fact that ownership and profits were left undisturbed. Still, once the companies were forced to act as interrelated units of a coordinated national system, without regard to ownership, the tracks and terminals were soon integrated into a network, and congestion dramatically reduced.

Wilson also created a War Board for the Port of New York, with Irving Bush as executive officer. This placed the port itself—for the first time in its history—under unified direction. Bush's own terminal was pressed into service as an army supply base while the military commissioned Cass Gilbert to design a new one. Within seventeen months, the Construction Division of the US Army (in consultation with Bush) had built in South Brooklyn (between 58th and 65th Streets) the best shipping terminal in the harbor. Its 6 million square feet of warehouses and 17 miles of track could handle 1,295 freight cars and load twelve 8,000-ton ships at the same time. Additional millions were poured into new piers, dry docks, and ship

---

23. To lure sufficient men back to the sea, the Seamen's Act of 1915 emancipated sailors from cruel punishments and abolished penalties for desertion; and the Shipping Board established an attractive wage scale.

repair facilities. Many of these were on the Jersey side of the harbor, calling for unprecedented levels of interstate cooperation. In 1917 the two governors appointed a joint Harbor Development Commission.

Across the Atlantic, William Wilgus (Grand Central's renovative engineer) was doing much the same in France. Based in Paris and reporting directly to Pershing, Wilgus set up the army's Transportation Service using methods he'd developed in working for the New York Central Railroad, and in designing freight delivery systems for Gotham. He successfully created a maritime-rail complex capable of receiving from New York and other seaboard ports the American Expeditionary Forces' men and equipment, and moving them smoothly to the front.

Wilson also set out to resurrect America's merchant marine, a goal he'd set himself even before the United States entered the war. Like many others in the Democratic Party, especially its southern cotton producers, he favored expanding foreign trade, for which shipping was essential. Private-sector efforts like Morgan's International Mercantile Marine Company had failed to develop a robust shipping sector. Government investment had been blocked by Republicans, who had little use for shipping, as they favored a tariff-protected industrial sector aimed at the domestic market. New York financiers, however, favored free trade and a merchant marine, as did more globally focused industrialists producing commodities (oil, sewing machines) that had worldwide sales.

Pressure for government intervention expanded with the outbreak of war in Europe, as demand for ships pulled further ahead of supply. With New York now the hub of world trade, ship brokers relocated there from European ports. The shipping district on lower Broadway rang with a babel of multilingual cries for "Bottoms at any price!" Prices shot up accordingly. In 1914 it cost 88¢ a ton to charter a transatlantic vessel for a month. By 1915 it cost $7.37; by 1917, $20.00.

In January 1916, Wilson set up a United States Shipping Board and gave it authority to buy, construct, or charter merchant ships suitable for use as naval auxiliaries. The following year, ten days after the declaration of war, on April 16, 1917, the Shipping Board created the Emergency Fleet Corporation (EFC) with a capital stock of $50 million. The EFC was given authority to acquire existing vessels and to construct new ones. Ships of enemy states interned in the United States were seized. Ninety-one German vessels were transferred into the US registry, adding nearly a million tons of shipping, including the *Kronprinzessin Cecilie*, which had been bottled up since its aborted bullion run, and the *Vaterland* (renamed the *Leviathan*), the second-largest boat afloat.

The EFC handed out war contracts to shipyards, a significant number of which were in the Greater New York area. The Standard Shipbuilding Company on Shooter's Island employed more than 4,000 workers in building cargo vessels for the transatlantic run. Old established boatyards in South Brooklyn (Morse, Tebo, Robins, and Shewan) were kept busy, as were Jersey-based yards in Elizabeth, Carteret, and Bayonne (where the Electric Launch Company [ELCO] built 448 110-foot submarine chasers and 284 boats of other types for the US Navy). The Brooklyn Navy Yard, after launching the battleship USS *Arizona* in October 1916, also turned its attention to sub chasers, given the clear and present U-boat danger, and turned out dozens of them, along with barges, scows, and service ships for the convoys to France.

As customary, the national government took responsibility for defending the port. Warships were dispatched to the harbor. A huge steel net was put in place to ward off U-boats. Obsolete guns in the harbor forts were replaced, electric mines laid, anti-aircraft batteries installed. These efforts proved strikingly successful. Though one German submarine (the *U-151*) did some damage to coastal shipping, the port itself remained unscathed.[24] A convoy system supported by minesweepers and seaplanes maintained an essentially uninterrupted flow of men and matériel to Europe, though the bulk of the credit belonged to the British navy.

THE FEDERAL GOVERNMENT ALSO INTERVENED in industrial production. Wilson appointed Bernard Baruch to head up a War Industries Board (WIB). The president had wanted someone who knew his way around Wall Street but was not too tied to the Republican establishment. Baruch (like McAdoo) fit the bill. A southerner, a Democrat, and a Jew, he was something of an outsider to the Street and its pieties. He believed, with Morgan, that combination and cooperation, not competition, were the keys to overcoming capitalist irrationality. But unlike Morgan (and like McAdoo), he believed that government—envisioned as a disinterested band of public servants—had to temper private enterprise with public authority.

Unlike McAdoo, who had been invested with managerial powers over at the Railroad Administration, Baruch lacked the authority to dictate terms to industrial titans. Instead, setting aside antitrust statutes, he set up a system of what amounted to government-sponsored cartels. Essentially, he allowed industry leaders to hammer out cooperative policies under the aegis of the state. The businessmen themselves, in consultation with military and home-front experts, mapped out production targets, allocated resources, allotted market share, and set prices of industrial products on a can't-lose cost-plus basis.

New York was soon awash in war contracts. Thirty-five hundred employees labored away in the Rosenwasser Brothers' shoe factory at Jackson Avenue and Orchard Street, just off Queens Plaza, in Long Island City. They produced not only army shoes but aviators' coats, gun covers, and, principally, gas masks, of which they turned out 17,000 a day. Long Island City also attracted aircraft manufacturers (like the Chance Vought Corporation), as did College Point (notably the LWF Engineering Company). The E. W. Bliss Company, a long-time armaments concern, handled big orders for shells and torpedoes in its plant on Adams and Plymouth Streets, at the Brooklyn end of the Manhattan Bridge. Nearby, on Manhattan Bridge Plaza at Flatbush Avenue, Elmer Sperry's Sperry Gyroscope Company (founded in 1910) had a small but vital research and development operation going on in several floors of the Carey Building, funded by the navy.

Washington agencies also inserted themselves into the combustible arena of labor relations. Given that the war effort depended on a steady flow of industrial output, Wilson deemed it essential to win the cooperation of most workers. The army of labor, like the army of draftees, could not be coerced into doing its utmost. The president had sought to win this cooperation by cutting a deal with Sam Gompers's AFL, which had been effective, but only up to a point, as there was a counterproductive dynamic built into the wartime economy that had to be addressed more creatively.

The war had wiped out unemployment, as millions of soldiers were subtracted from the workforce, and wartime immigration dropped sharply. This strengthened labor's bargaining position. Strikes increased in number, despite a no-strike pledge by Gompers, and wages went up accordingly. For a time, workers' standard of living rose and productivity remained

---

24. *U-151* was one of six subs dispatched in the late spring of 1918 to attack American shipping. It arrived off the East Coast, where, on May 28, the sub's crew "had our first sight of the bright lights of Broadway, the great glow that hangs over New York City after dark." It then laid mines off the Ambrose Channel and cut New York's cable links to Nova Scotia and Panama. On June 2, *U-151* sank six American ships and damaged two others off the coast of New Jersey, but as it either gave advance warning or picked up survivors, the only lives lost were caused by a capsized lifeboat.

Airplanes at the Lewis Vought Co. factory, Astoria, ca. 1918. (Cradle of Aviation Museum)

high. But inflation rose as well—an artifact of wartime financial arrangements—and ate up many of the gains, triggering a new round of strikes to restore the real wage level. Capital resisted but was in no position to hire strikebreakers or call in the police. Besides, when the government approved worker wage demands—which it did more often than not—it also approved an offsetting increase in prices and profits, as most contracts were awarded on the cost–plus basis. Government cash thus lubricated the machinery of war production.

Tensions over working conditions were tougher to deal with. Employers tried to use the war to justify a reduction of labor standards. The National Association of Manufacturers asked Congress to authorize suspension of the eight-hour day on government contracts. The Council of National Defense, dominated by business leaders, recommended that governors be allowed to modify protective restrictions in their labor laws, and tried to prevent the states from improving health and workplace conditions without its approval.

Labor and its allies resisted. Florence Kelley of the National Consumers' League fought attempts to dilute labor standards by arguing that poor working conditions hindered rather than helped production. To prove it, she pointed to the experience of British munitions makers, who had tried to increase output by lengthening the working day, only to discover that productivity declined. The British government then imposed an eight-hour workday, and improved work and living conditions, measures that led to more efficient production.

The US government on the whole accepted this rationale and tended to support workers' demands, especially when the government was itself the employer. The Railroad Administration formally recognized the rights of railroad workers to bargain collectively and granted higher wages and improved working conditions. The War and Navy Departments and the Emergency Fleet Corporation all prescribed labor standards in detail.

More broadly, a National War Labor Board (NWLB) was set up, which mandated labor-management negotiations. It even protected union organizers from employer interference, an unprecedented step for a federal agency. It set up arbitration machinery as well and recruited progressive reformers as labor relations experts, mediators, and welfare specialists. Much of the National Consumers League staff was drafted to oversee the treatment of wartime women workers. The Russell Sage Foundation's Mary van Kleeck became head of the Labor Department's Women in Industry Division.

The degree of federal intervention in New York's garment industry was extraordinary. When the quartermaster general's initial orders for uniforms went to nonunion concerns in Philadelphia, the Amalgamated's Sidney Hillman contacted Secretary of War Newton Baker. With help from Florence Kelley he convinced Baker to stop subsidizing sweatshop conditions. Baker went further and set up a Board of Control of Labor Standards for Army Clothing (with Kelley a key member). It awarded contracts only to firms that eliminated child labor, home-work, and unsanitary facilities, established an eight-hour day and a forty-eight-hour week, granted women equal pay, and recognized the Amalgamated (in exchange for its refraining from strikes). Manufacturers went along with this to get the lucrative contracts, especially as the government recompensed them for any wage increases the Board of Control demanded.

Two major consequences flowed from this federal intervention. First, Gotham turned out roughly 75 percent of all the military uniforms produced during the war. Second, as workers now had nothing to risk and much to gain, they poured into the Amalgamated, which became one of the nation's largest industrial unions. The same proved true for the American Federation of Labor, whose nationwide membership rose from 2 million in 1916 to over 3 million in 1919.

IN ADDITION TO WASHINGTON'S IMPACT on New York's labor relations, manufacturing, shipping, railroads, and port, the federal government altered its dealings with Wall Street.

The most immediate transformation concerned the New York financial community's relations with the country's new allies. The task of loaning England the money with which to buy US-produced war matériel was shifted from the consortiums of private investors assembled by the House of Morgan, to the federal treasury. These government-to-government loans would, over the course of the war, add another $9.5 billion to Europe's indebtedness. In August 1917, moreover, Allied purchasing of war goods was taken out of Morgan's hands and transferred to British-run war missions set up in the United States, though the Morgan firm continued to act as financial adviser.

The role of the New York Stock Exchange in providing corporations and municipalities with a marketplace where they could sell their stocks and bonds was modified as well. The Wilson administration wanted to regulate the financial markets so that capital would be channeled to industries central to the war effort and withheld, for the moment, from those deemed less vital. France, Germany, and England had already opted for such a managed marketplace. At the suggestion of the NYSE and the Investment Bankers of America, the United States now followed suit. A Capital Issues Committee (CIC) was established—another public/private entity—composed of federal officials and influential investment bankers. The CIC would prioritize proposed offerings of corporate and municipal issues, and the NYSE would refuse to list those deemed inessential.

The bigger question was how to finance the enormous and fast-mounting cost of the war itself. New York bankers advised the customary approach of issuing interest-bearing bonds that the wealthy would purchase, but they ran into strenuous opposition from progressives who proposed, instead, to tax the war boom's primary beneficiaries.

The ensuing battle was a continuation of one the country had recently fought, over whether or not to institute an income tax. Such a tax, having been deemed unconstitutional, required a constitutional amendment to make it legal. Populists and progressives argued in the 1900s and 1910s that the fruits of the corporate revolution were rising to the top. The rich had gotten richer and could afford to pay a bigger share.

Another argument for passing an income tax amendment came from those who believed that the federal government was excessively reliant on indirect taxes, like tariffs (the costs of which were passed along to consumers) and excise taxes on tobacco, liquor, wine, and beer (which fell more heavily on the masses as well). Such critics held that the government should levy a direct tax on the beneficiaries of the boom. This resonated with southern opponents of tariffs, and with members of the New York corporate elite, like Elihu Root, who also wanted to ditch tariffs but only if there was an alternative source for funding the state. The struggle led to ratification of the Sixteenth Amendment in 1913 and the enactment of a national income tax that same year. (A corporate income tax had been put in place four years earlier.)

At first the exactions placed on the wealthy and corporations were exceedingly modest. In 1914 income tax receipts provided less than 10 percent of federal revenues, while 90 percent were still harvested from the working and middle classes via the tariff and excise taxes.[25]

Then came the preparedness boom of 1915–16, the profits of which accrued overwhelmingly to the rich. The cry went up from progressives that those profits, particularly the income from selling munitions, should be taxed directly. Progressive senators like La Follette of Wisconsin charged that as the preparedness movement was a creature of the arms industry and Wall Street banks, they should be subject to higher taxation. These arguments proved to have broad appeal, and the 1916 Revenue Act provided for sharply increased income tax rates, as well as a tax on the profits of munitions manufacturers and a graduated federal inheritance tax.

Then the United States entered the war, with its skyrocketing costs. How were these to be paid? The progressives insisted on still steeper graduated income and inheritance taxes, and the imposition of a new "excess profits tax"—profits exceeding an amount determined by the rate of return on capital in a prewar base period, calculated at first to be 8 percent. Leading the campaign was a group of New York progressives, generaled by Amos Pinchot, a wealthy lawyer and a founder of the Bull Moose Party, who in 1916 had backed Wilson. Pinchot formed the American Committee on War Finance (ACWF), which in April and May of 1917 waged a vigorous lobbying effort. The ACWF argued that "the conscription of men and the conscription of wealth must go hand in hand." Taxing war profits would be more just, and it would improve public morale and help produce a united war effort. Pinchot's vision of its wartime benefits extended into peacetime. The ACWF, he admitted, wanted "to get an income tax started which, when once in operation, will be hard for the privileged interests to tear down after the war." He asserted that "if we ever get a big income tax on in war time, some of it—a lot of it—is going to stick. The men like Rockefeller and Morgan are doomed to moderate wealth in the future. . . . And the money boys know it."

Bankers and industrialists resisted. Jack Morgan said the government should avoid taxes that would fall "unjustly upon the investing class of the country," as that would curb enterprise and production. The *Commercial and Financial Chronicle* attacked the "Excessive Taxation of 'Excess' Profits" as "governmental confiscation of wealth." The *Wall Street*

---

25. In 1915, with a similar distribution, 40–45 percent of the income taxes collected came from New York. The city was clearly where the money was.

Journal similarly disparaged the excess-profits tax as "hasty and ill-advised legislation . . . rushed through Washington by politicians desiring political favor with the many by taxing the capital of the few."

By June "the many" had weighed in on the issue. More than 3 million people endorsed the ACWF plan. This show of strength played an important role in driving the War Revenue Act of 1917 through Congress. Treasury Secretary McAdoo had recommended a maximum total individual income tax of 42 percent on incomes over $2 million; the Ways and Means Committee increased this to 50 percent; the full House, to 62 percent; and the Senate, to 67 percent—the final figure incorporated in the record-breaking bill that became law on October 3, and generated $850 million. The law also enacted the levy on "excess profits," which brought in a billion more.

It wasn't enough.

So McAdoo turned to borrowing from the public. Four successful "Liberty Bond" campaigns—ballyhooed by Creel's Committee for Public Information—whooped up purchases through advertisements, posters, speeches, and all-star entertainment. One Century Theatre benefit featured Al Jolson, Sophie Tucker, George M. Cohan, and Enrico Caruso, who sang "Hover Dere" with rolled *r*'s but enormous gusto. Movie stars like Chaplin and Pickford drew immense crowds to public rallies in Times Square, on Wall Street, at the Plaza Hotel. Flag-drenched parades hurrahed down Fifth Avenue—inspiring Childe Hassam to two dozen canvases.

Poster, "HELLO! This Is Liberty Speaking—Billions of Dollars Are Needed and Needed NOW," 1918. (Library of Congress Prints and Photographs Division)

Joseph Pennell, "That Liberty Shall Not Perish from the Earth," 1918. (Library of Congress Prints and Photographs Division)

Not all inducements were so uplifting: families who resisted "flying squad" promotions might find their homes painted yellow. McAdoo himself warned: "If any man or woman with means to buy these bonds fails to buy them, America is no place for them." A large sign was erected in Times Square, made from several hundred light bulbs and claimed to be the largest electrical sign in the world, that advertised the bonds and later used electric dials to demonstrate the amount of loans bought by the public.

The four campaigns—not counting a postwar "Victory Bond" offering—brought in $17 billion ($9.5 billion of which was loaned to the Allies). As hoped, they had generated extremely widespread participation. But the majority of the money raised came from purchases of bonds in denominations of $1,000 or more, bought by corporations and wealthy individuals solicited by New York bank and trust companies. Gotham led the league in purchases. During the first Liberty Loan drive (May 14 to June 15, 1917), local subscription totals equaled one-third of the entire effort. *Life* magazine suggested that "this phenomenon is worth remembering when the next patriot mounts the stump and denounces New York as the enemy's country."[26]

26. Estimates of the sources of war financing suggest that 22 percent of the total came from taxes and 58 percent from borrowing, leaving 20 percent unaccounted for. Some economists suggest that this tranche was provided by McAdoo's expansion of the money supply—not by printing greenbacks, as had been done (disastrously) during the Civil War, but by selling certificates of indebtedness to banks, in part to cover the costs of their loaning money to those who wanted to buy Liberty Bonds. The banks in turn used these as reserves, which led to an explosive growth in the money supply, which from June 1916 to June 1919 expanded by

ALL THESE FEDERAL INTERVENTIONS IN MUNICIPAL AFFAIRS were highly visible, and each set some limits on metropolitan freedom of independent action. But there was another initiative that was deeply clandestine, and strengthened Gotham's ability to shape national and international affairs.

After the US entered the conflict in April 1917, its new allies brought to Wilson's attention that they had secretly signed agreements among themselves to divvy up what they hoped would be the spoils of war. This unseemly scramble for territory being a far cry from Wilson's noble war aims, he sent Colonel House to Paris in October 1917 to urge repudiation of the treaties. House was rebuffed. Then, in November, two weeks after the Bolshevik Revolution, People's Commissar for Foreign Affairs Leon Trotsky published the secret treaties (which the Kerensky government had left behind in its hasty exit), exposing the machinations of the prior czarist and Provisional Government regimes and their imperialist allies. The embarrassed Wilson administration tried to prevent the disclosures from being published in the US, but Oswald Garrison Villard, pacifist publisher of the *New York Evening Post*, blazoned their full texts in his pages.

This lent urgency to a super-secret project that Wilson had set in motion back in September, to develop American responses to these Allied demands, and generate war aims of its own. Laying out the desired boundaries of a post-imperial world would require a thorough assessment of the political, economic, demographic, and social state of affairs in Europe, the Middle East, and Asia. The president declined to give the assignment to the Department of State, considering it antiquated, inefficient, and (under Secretary Lansing) politically reactionary. Instead, the former Princeton professor turned to the academic community for the necessary expertise, and to New York City, rather than Washington, to host what would become the country's first foreign policy think tank.

In early September the president had set Colonel House to work on the project. House, in turn, gave the top job to Dr. Sidney E. Mezes, president of City College. A philosopher of religion and ethics, Mezes knew little of Europe's past or present, but he had one overriding qualification: he was House's brother-in-law and would be totally loyal to his relative. Professional supervision was turned over to Isaiah Bowman, one of the nation's top geographers, and since 1915 head of the American Geographical Society (AGS); and to James T. Shotwell, a Columbia University historian, who came up with a blandly generic name for the top secret operation, the "Inquiry." For someone to organize a small army of academics, and to write up their findings, House chose Walter Lippmann, with whom he'd worked during the president's reelection campaign, and made him general secretary.

When the war that Lippmann had advocated broke out, the *New Republic* editor, finding himself subject to the draft law, wangled his way out of service. His *NR* associate Felix Frankfurter had been recruited as a troubleshooter by Secretary of War Newton Baker (a prewar progressive). Lippmann asked if Frankfurter could "get me an exemption," so he could cogitate on approaches to peace. Rescued from the trenches, he worked on some smaller projects; then Baker seconded him to House's project.

At first the Inquiry directorate huddled in a cramped corner of the New York Public Library, but in November 1917, as scholars accumulated (roughly fifty by the beginning of 1918 and roughly three times that by year's end), the enterprise was transferred to the spacious quarters of the AGS building on Audubon Terrace (155th Street and Broadway), with

---

over $11 billion, helping drive consumer prices up nearly 66 percent, while the cost of living rose over 70 percent. This was a major source of the inflation that eroded wages and powered strikes.

access to its library and map collection (and that of Columbia, relatively nearby). Assembling information about nations and ethno-linguistic groups, and pairing that data with information on trading patterns and political movements, the Inquiry scholars would eventually produce nearly 2,000 separate reports and documents, and 1,200-plus maps, for use at a future peace conference.

On December 22 Lippmann gave House a summary memo of where things stood; Wilson returned it with instructions for clarification. On January 2 Lippmann gave House a revised version, organized into eight territory-based proposals, to which Wilson added six overarching diplomatic principles. And on January 8, 1918, the president presented his Fourteen Points to a joint session of Congress (including phrases that Lippmann was thrilled to see had been taken intact from his memo).

In a slap at his imperialist partners, Wilson not only called for "Open covenants of peace openly arrived at" but promised that in the future "there shall be no private international understandings of any kind, but diplomacy shall proceed always frankly and in the public view." He called, too, for freedom of the seas, removal of economic barriers between nations, reduction of armaments, the adjustment of colonial claims, with equal attention being paid to governments and populace, and a league of nations that would "guarantee political independence and territorial integrity to great and small states alike."

THE PUBLIC-SECTOR INQUIRY CONTINUED its work through the remainder of 1918, albeit out of public view. In June a comparable private-sector entity emerged, whose proceedings, though closed to the public, were covered in the press. It was proposed in a May 16, 1918, letter to the *New York Times* by Lindsay Russell, a Wall Street international customs lawyer with clients in Japan, who since 1910 had been president of the Japan Society. Russell suggested that as there were "less than one hundred men in the United States who think internationally," the country should make use of their experience and wisdom by creating "a council on foreign relations or a house of diplomats." His vision of it was a grand (if not grandiose) one; it should be modeled on the Federal Reserve Bank and be as independent as the Supreme Court. It would consist of former US ambassadors and "American citizens who have done constructive work internationally," and it would be charged with giving advice on foreign policy to the president and federal departments in Washington, though "its headquarters should be in New York."

Russell's entity never got off the ground, but on June 18, 1918, a more modest entity was established, a discreet club of (initially 108) Wall Street denizens, described as "high-ranking officers of banking, manufacturing, trading and finance companies, together with many lawyers." Following Russell's suggestion, the club adopted the name of Council on Foreign Relations, and adopted Russell himself as chairman—though the caliber of the body became clear when Elihu Root agreed to serve as honorary chair. The group got together regularly for dinner talks at the Metropolitan Club, with speakers who "were concerned primarily with the effect that the war and the treaty of peace might have on postwar business."

Between these two entities, the Inquiry and the Council—who would soon effect a merger that adopted the Council's name for the conjoint entity—the building blocks had been set in place for a Gotham-based foreign policy complex that would rival its social policy counterpart.

NEW YORK 1919

On November 7, 1918, a UPI correspondent mistook a momentary stand-down for a general cease-fire. He flashed a message to New York. It arrived by noon. By one o'clock, special editions were on the stands. Thousands abandoned desks, downed tools, and poured into the streets in frenzied celebration—only to discover they'd got it wrong. Which gave them a chance to do it all over again when, four days later, the real armistice arrived.

On December 18 Mayor Hylan appointed his patron William Randolph Hearst to take charge of welcoming the returning troops, but not a single dignitary would serve with the publisher. Instead, Henry Stimson and Charles Evans Hughes formed an independent committee and offered TR the chair. But Theodore Roosevelt had led his last charge: on January 6, 1919, he died in his sleep at Oyster Bay.

The celebrations went on without him. From February to May, at least once a month, returning regiments paraded along Fifth Avenue, passing through the Victory Arch—a full-sized replica of the Arc de Triomphe. The Anglo, Irish, black, and Melting Pot soldiers all had their day to be showered with affection and praise. In July the city gave a spectacular salute to Woodrow Wilson on his return from the Paris Peace Conference—replete with battleships, destroyers, seaplanes, and a blimp. In September, Gotham roared an exultant welcome to General Pershing as he rode on horseback from 110th Street to Washington Square, while crowds cast roses and laurel in his path.

More substantial rewards for the troops' service were, however, conspicuously absent. The only guaranteed benefit was a $60 demobilization "bonus," which wouldn't even buy a set of civvies. There was no system of veterans' benefits or pensions awaiting them, no plan for reintegrating them into the civilian economy. And the civilian economy itself was careening south. The papers were full of stories about rising unemployment, as war contracts were being rapidly terminated just as 4 million soldiers were reentering the job market. Peace would clearly end the Wilson administration's ability (and willingness) to cajole or coerce capital into keeping wages ahead of inflation.

This prognosis was all the more disconcerting when set alongside expectations that had emerged within the civilian workforce during the war. Labor had hoped its hard-won wage

Poster, "Forget it, Son, Come on with Me and Re-enlist," ca. 1918. (Pritzker Military Museum & Library)

level would be sustained, and that improvements in working conditions and social benefits would be made permanent parts of the postwar economy.

Since February 1918 workers and progressive allies (notably those in the *New Republic* circle) had been looking to England for a glimpse of a possible peacetime future. The British Labour Party had then issued a manifesto, *Labour and the New Social Order: A Report on Reconstruction*, that argued the war had put paid to the capitalist system. It proposed instead "a new social order, based not on fighting but on fraternity; not on the competitive struggle for the means of bare life, but on a deliberately planned co-operation." Specifically, it argued for a one-time massive "levy" on capital so that working people would not be stuck with the costs of the war, established a guaranteed minimum below which wages and working conditions would not be allowed to fall, and instituted a "democratic control of industry," starting with the nationalization of Britain's railways, mines, and electrical supply.

Labour and the New Social Order made a big splash in the United States. The *New Republic,* of course, ran it as a special supplement. The *Survey* was certain that "capitalism will not come back unchallenged and uncontrolled." In May 1918, six months before the armistice, the ILGWU and the Amalgamated endorsed the British blueprint. Not to be left behind, President Wilson in June of 1918 organized the Reconstruction Research Division, a brain trust of experts to develop a plan for the transition from a war to a peace economy. "The new social order is coming," philosopher Will Durant wrote in the *Dial* that same month, "and that is all there is to it."

With the armistice, progressive attorney and co-chair of the National War Labor Board Frank Walsh observed, the United States got caught up in "a perfect hurricane of reconstruction conferences and plans, projected by every group imaginable, highbrow, reactionary, labor and every other hand." Between November 1918 and mid-1919, the Federal Council of Churches, the US Chamber of Commerce, the National Catholic War Council, the American Federation of Labor, the Women's Trade Union League, and other organizations of social workers, farmers, and workers all came out with reconstruction programs. The Catholic bishops' "Social Reconstruction" plan advocated a minimum wage, an end to child labor, making labor's right to organize legally enforceable, and legislating programs to insure against unemployment, sickness, invalidity, and old age. The Central Conference of American Rabbis' program was much the same.

IN JANUARY 1919 RECONSTRUCTION GOT TAKEN UP by the newly elected governor of New York State, Al Smith, who had run as a progressive Tammany man—no longer a contradiction in terms. Though Smith was handed the nomination by Boss Murphy, his campaign received a critical boost from the progressive community, as mobilized by Abram I. Elkus, ambassador to Turkey, and former counsel to Smith and Wagner's Factory Investigating Commission. Elkus recruited other veterans of the industrial reform movement—social workers, lawyers, businessmen. A third of this cohort were women, now able to vote for the first time, including Mary Simkhovitch, Harriot Stanton Blatch, and, crucially, Belle Moskowitz (the former Belle Israels, who, after her first husband died in 1911, had in 1914 married settlement worker and multi-faceted reformer Henry Moskowitz). She introduced Smith to powerful and influential women in the Women's University Club, Colony Club, and Women's City Club, who would help overcome the resistance of patricians and professionals to supporting a Tammany man.

In November 1918 Smith swept by Governor Whitman, overcoming the Republican's upstate majority with a whopping Democratic margin in Manhattan and Brooklyn. He received strong support from Tammany's working-class base, as well as women, progressives, Jews, socialists—and soldiers and sailors, whose vote, polled separately, nearly tripled what they gave Whitman.

Immediately after taking office, Governor Smith, acting on a Moskowitz recommendation, set up a Reconstruction Commission to develop a comprehensive plan for transiting from war to peace. It proposed to address unemployment and poverty by establishing a minimum wage, expanding workmen's compensation benefits, instituting health insurance, protecting women and children in industry, improving education, fixing the tax system, and overhauling governmental operations. The commission, chaired by Elkus, included prestigious members like Bernard Baruch and Felix Adler, and was piloted by Mrs. M (as Smith liked to call Moskowitz) as executive secretary, with Robert Moses as chief of staff.

Immediately the commission ran into a brick Republican wall. Albany legislators flatly refused to fund it. Assembly Speaker (and manufacturer) Thaddeus Sweet called Smith's program "Bolshevik and socialistic." State Senator Clayton Lusk from Cortland County said the measures were "part of a German propaganda effort to break down the United States Government." The Republicans rejected inaugurating public works projects to relieve growing unemployment, saying it was not the state's duty to provide jobs for the jobless. Moskowitz raised funds privately for the commission's work and set up thirteen committees that between April 1919 and March 1920 issued reports that had little impact, given Republican intransigence.

Except in one arena.

The Reconstruction Commission's report on housing noted that a crisis existed, the product of a virtual cessation of construction during the war. Returning soldiers faced a severe shortage. The vacancy rate in Manhattan dropped to 3 percent in 1919 and to 0.6 percent the following year. Landlords jacked up rents, in part to keep ahead of rising costs, in part because of rampant speculation, in part because the shortage was there to be exploited. Tenants who didn't pay up were thrown out. By early 1919 thousands were being evicted each month. Warehouses throughout the city filled up with the furniture of the dispossessed. Desperate families turned back to the decrepit tenements they had fled (36,000 vacant apartments were reoccupied by 1920), and old slums gained a new lease on life.

Tenants began to resist. The Socialist Party and its allied labor unions helped Jewish and Italian workers to construct effective building and neighborhood organizations in the Bronx, in Washington Heights, in Williamsburg and Brownsville. Rent strikes forced hundreds of landlords to rescind increases and improve building conditions. Smaller groups came together in a Greater New York Tenants League, which called on the state legislature to limit rent increases.

Landlords called the tenant movement a Bolshevik plot but found the label harder to pin on the more conservative tenant groups that now emerged. These German and Irish associations, which had close ties to the Democratic Party and the municipal unions, were opposed to rent strikes but insistent that some action be taken. In April 1919 Mayor Hylan set up a Committee on Rent Profiteering. It held hearings and arranged temporary shelter in churches and armories for evicted families. But the cycle of increases, rent strikes, and evictions continued, clogging municipal courts with housing cases.

Smith's Reconstruction Commission proposed setting up a central housing agency and giving local housing boards authority to acquire land by condemnation and, if necessary, to undertake large-scale housing construction. The legislature refused. But finally, in September 1920, desperate to ward off "anarchy, riot and revolt" and forestall public housing, it passed

"A Rent Strike at 1294 Park Ave. in Harlem." *New York Times,* September 1919.

the Emergency Rent Laws, which gave municipal court judges the authority to block eviction of tenants for nonpayment of rent if the increase demanded was found to be "unjust, unreasonable and oppressive." The burden of justifying a rent hike was placed on the landlord, who was required to submit proof of gross income and expenses. Thus arrived the first, if still rudimentary, rent control program in the United States.

VISIONS OF SUSTAINING THE GOVERNMENT-IMPOSED wartime accords between capital and labor, much less expanding them into a new social and economic order, swiftly ran aground, as federal programs were rapidly dismantled. The Railroad Administration, the War Industries Board, the Emergency Fleet Corporation, the National War Labor Board, and the Capital Issues Committee were terminated, more or less abruptly. Wilson, exhausted from the fight over the League of Nations, declared that all readjustment programs would have to be handled by "spirited businessmen and self-reliant laborers."

With the federal government removed from the picture, capital and labor were once again directly face-to-face. This meant going toe-to-toe at the workplace.

The "spirited businessmen" who had chafed under what they considered impermissible infringements on their managerial authority and property rights, set out to rescind concessions granted under duress. Employers openly defied the last decisions of the War Labor Board and set out to roll back earlier ones. Corporations moved quickly to rid factories of unions and labor organizers, and to reestablish the open shop (now rebranded as the "American shop").

American laborers, well aware they could rely on no one but themselves, launched a nationwide offensive. In 1919, some 4 million employees went out on strike, roughly 20 percent of the workforce, far more than ever before in the country's history. Tremendous industrial battles were fought from Seattle to Boston, in coal, textiles, clothing, shipping, and steel—365,000 workers struck United States Steel—for pay raises and shorter hours, for locking in gains wartime administrators had awarded, and for making permanent the temporary right to organize conceded during the emergency.

Capital fought back by deploying its massive resources, often backed by the state, to smash resistance, justifying this by asserting that workers' real goal was to seize control of the economy and polity: "Unionism is nothing less than bolshevism," said the National Association of Manufacturers. "Heartiest congratulations on your stand for the open shop," Jack Morgan cabled US Steel president Elbert Gary, "with which I am, as you know, absolutely in accord. I believe American principles of liberty deeply involved and must win if we all stand firm."

The 1919 strike wave rocked New York City. Walkouts were called by tobacco workers and streetcar drivers, pressmen and painters, Chinese-restaurant waiters and power-plant stokers, garment-industry and building-trades workers, ferryboat crews and cigar makers, carpenters and drugstore clerks, jewelry workers and municipal employees. On one day in September a hundred strikes were in progress, overwhelmingly fought over wages, but also over the right to organize. One of the more dramatic was the strike that turned off the Great White Way.

During the war, the White Rats had again attempted to organize vaudeville performers, but their strike had been crushed by B. F. Keith and E. F. Albee's United Booking Office. Before expiring, the vaudevillians passed on their AFL charter to the broader-based Actors' Equity. In August 1919 the players struck, organized by a committee that included Ethel and Lionel Barrymore, Lillian Russell, Marie Dressler, Al Jolson, and Ed Wynn. Picket lines soon rang down the curtain on thirty-seven plays and prevented sixteen others from opening. The strikers gained public sympathy through adroit moves, such as presenting all-star variety shows, or sending a parade of 2,000 stars and chorus girls striding down Broadway from Columbus Circle to Madison Square.

Lee Shubert, head of the dominant theatrical empire, declared, "I am violently against a union of actors." Together with other members of the Producing Managers Association (PMA)—like Charles Dillingham, Lorenz Ziegfeld, and David Belasco—he set out to crush the insurgent actors. Shubert sued Equity officers and threatened to convert his playhouses to movie theaters. Ziegfeld tried a restraining order to keep his *Follies* going. George M. Cohan, by now as much producer as actor, was infuriated at the prospect of hewing to Equity regulations. Cohan brashly formed a company union—the Actors' Fidelity League—but its members, quickly dubbed Fidos, failed to undercut the strike. Then Gompers pledged support. Stagehands at the Hippodrome walked out, signaling that already organized theatrical workers would now weigh in. By early September, with managers losing millions, the PMA capitulated and recognized the union. Cohan, crushed and embittered, retired from the theater (albeit only temporarily).

The biggest strike of all did not go labor's way. In October 1919 the rank-and-file members of the International Longshoremen's Association (ILA)—defying union officials T. V. O'Connor and Joseph P. Ryan—went on strike, seeking a raise from seventy cents to a dollar an hour. As in 1907, the strike began in Brooklyn, sparked by Italians, and spread to the Irish-controlled Chelsea Piers. Soon the 60,000 longshoremen were joined by tens of thousands of other marine workers—teamsters, sailors, railroad and warehouse workers, and small armies of day laborers. Within a week 150,000 were out, not only Irish and Italians but blacks,

Hungarians, Swedes, and Russians. The port was all but paralyzed. Six hundred fifty ships were stranded, liners and freighters alike. ILA leaders ordered the men back to work. Massive rank-and-file meetings at Cooper Union and Brooklyn's Pilgrim Hall on Court Street repudiated them. O'Connor and Ryan tried turning the Irish against the Italians, then tried claiming the walkout was Wobbly-inspired, then at one meeting had armed bodyguards attack the strikers; all to no avail. Federal authorities sent troops to the harbor, though only to US Army docks. Shippers brought in strikebreakers (ex-servicemen from Oklahoma), and hired strong-arm men to protect them—leading to violent encounters in Greenpoint and elsewhere. After thirty days, the combination of the government, the US Shipping Board, the shipping companies, the ILA, and the AFL prevailed, as the strikers, some facing starvation, gave up.

AS 1919 WAS SUFFUSED WITH LABOR STRUGGLES, so too it was ablaze with racial conflict. Despite Du Bois's hopes, African American soldiers and civilians confronted not a grateful nation but whites panicked by black wartime advances and determined to restore the antebellum racial status quo. In the so-called Red Summer of 1919 there were full-blown racial pogroms in thirty cities, accompanied by seventy-seven lynchings—eleven by burning at the stake—including the murder of ten black veterans, some of whom were strung up in their uniforms. Armed groups of young black men and women, veterans among them, defended their neighborhoods but were generally overwhelmed.

New York's was a different story. There was no "race riot" in 1919—a term that almost invariably meant white crowds marauding through black neighborhoods—in good part because the black populace, badly mauled during the 1900 white invasion of San Juan Hill, had regrouped in Harlem. And Harlem had become impregnable. From 1917 to 1919 more than 70,000 blacks arrived in the city, and nearly all had headed straight uptown. By 1920 the territory bounded by 130th and 145th Streets and Fifth to Eighth Avenues was almost solidly African American and Caribbean, constituting two-thirds of Manhattan's black population. Harlem was now far from being the tempting target that smaller or scattered concentrations had been; plus, in 1919 it was home to hundreds of veteran Hellfighters, whose fearsome reputation gave even maddened racists pause. No longer would whites dream of invading Harlem.

The city's black leadership, moreover, was in a militant mood. In 1919 W. E. B. Du Bois abandoned his wartime accomodationism and urged militant action: "We return from fighting. We return fighting," he editorialized in the May issue of the *Crisis*. "Make way for Democracy! We saved it in France, and by the Great Jehovah, we will save it in the United States of America, or know the reason why."

James Weldon Johnson saw the wave of lynchings as an effort by upholders of "Anglo-Saxon superiority" to force blacks to cease aspiring to "the rights and privileges of freemen." But the "poor fools" didn't realize that "the mere thought of death" did not frighten a race whose "colored men died in France fighting for liberty."

Jamaican immigrant Claude McKay published a poem, "If We Must Die," in Max and Crystal Eastman's *Liberator* that called for "fighting back" against the "murderous, cowardly Pack."

Cyril Briggs, an immigrant from St. Kitts, responded to the racial pogroms by forming the African Blood Brotherhood, whose paper (the *Crusader*) proposed creating small militarized units for armed self-defense (inspired in part by the Irish Republican Brotherhood). Briggs merged black nationalism with Marxism—espousing workers' rights, black liberation, and anti-imperialism.

Members of the 369th Harlem Hellfighters, returning to New York after World War I, 1919.
(Schomburg Center for Research in Black Culture, Photographs and Prints Division)

A. Philip Randolph and Chandler Owen mixed denunciation of lynchings (in *Messenger* editorials like "The Hun in America," which called for defiance of white authority), with appeals for blacks to ally with white socialists, under the slogan "black and white workers unite." Calling the Soviet Revolution "the greatest achievement of the twentieth century," they became known as the "Lenin and Trotsky" of Harlem.

Looming over all these militants, in terms of popular appeal, was Marcus Garvey, whose Universal Negro Improvement Association (UNIA) had grown at a fantastic rate in 1918–19, exploding into an authentic mass movement. When his audiences outgrew Lafayette Hall he moved his meetings to the barnlike immensity of the Palace Casino at Fifth Avenue and 135th Street, and when the crowds burst the Casino's capacity, he bought the enormous Metropolitan Baptist Tabernacle (138th between Lenox and Seventh) and converted it into the UNIA Liberty Hall. He incorporated the organization, and started up a weekly, the *Negro World*, which was printed in multiple languages and distributed throughout the African diaspora. By 1919 UNIA dues-paying membership numbered roughly 7,500 in Harlem alone, with branches in twenty-five states of the Union, and divisions in the West Indies, Central America, and West Africa. While Garvey's claim in June 1919 of 2 million followers was wildly overblown, even such a critic as Du Bois credited him with 300,000. His militancy level had grown as well. He came out against the war—"Why go over to Europe and fight for the whites and lose an arm or leg when you can fight for a just cause?" And he developed an obviously popular analysis combining anti-racism and anti-imperialism—"White people are taking advantage of black men today because black men all over the world are disunited"— and an attendant strategy calling for global racial solidarity.

THE YEAR 1919 WAS ALSO AN ALARMING ONE for defenders of the traditional gender order. Wilson had delivered on his promise of support for the suffrage amendment. In June, Congress had officially proposed the Nineteenth Amendment and sent it to the states for ratification. Would this not, conservatives worried, turn the relations between men and women upside down?

The war itself had rattled old roles. Some women served in the AEF, as telephone operators or nurses. Many more went to France as volunteers with the YMCA or Red Cross. At home, several thousand women joined the city's workforce as telegraph messengers, elevator operators, letter carriers—jobs that paid substantially better wages than traditional "women's work." This was especially true on the transit lines, where female conductors could earn twenty-five dollars a week at a time when 92 percent of female workers made less than twenty. Piling out of domestic servanthood, women piled into war work, earning wages that enabled a new self-sufficiency. But now returning doughboys wanted their jobs back. The Central Federated Union said bluntly that "the same patriotism which induced women to enter industry during the war should induce them to vacate their positions after the war." Would they?

Women who had fought against suffrage also seized on what they believed might be the next stage, the kind of revolutionary change they were convinced radicals in Russia were engineering. Conservatives believed that Bolshevik commissars such as Aleksandra Kollontai had ordered the "nationalization of women," established a "bureau of free love," had forced educated ladies of property to do manual labor, and were, in general, intent on destroying the patriarchal family, which was the nation's primary bulwark against radicalism.

IN ALL THESE CONTESTS OVER THE RIGHTS of labor, blacks, and women, those opposed to locking in wartime improvements fervently (or cynically) accused their opponents of being subversive agents of alien forces—no longer Germans (until then the preferred term of abuse) but now Bolsheviks. In doing so they could point to upheavals not only in Russia but, in 1919, also in Europe; it seemed that westward the course of revolution might take its way. Certainly this was the goal of Russian leaders, who in March 1919 established the Communist International to fight "by all available means, including armed force, for the overthrow of the international bourgeoisie." Was there not evidence that such a goal had jumped the Atlantic and was now driving the American socialist movement?

During his brief stay in New York in 1917, Leon Trotsky had indeed urged disaffected local militants to organize an independent left wing inside the Socialist Party. Extrapolating from his experience with European social democrats, Trotsky regarded the US party as an obstacle to proletarian revolution. This position was attractive to those unhappy with the party's electoral focus.

Left-wing critics remained relatively quiescent until early 1919. Then the nationwide strike wave and ongoing repression appeared to render Hillquit's aims and methods inadequate to the moment. In February, left-wing socialists organized as a distinct section and adopted a manifesto declaring the Socialist Party a failure and calling for immediate revolution. Adopting European tactics wholesale, they called for a "proletarian dictatorship," workers councils, repudiation of national debts, and expropriation of all banks, railroads, and large aggregations of capital.

Branding Hillquit a barrier to revolution, they set out to take over, or bolt from, the Socialist Party. Backed by the large number of recent immigrants from Russia and Eastern Europe who had poured into the party's foreign-language federations, they made rapid gains. Hillquit's forces, which controlled the party's machinery, first denounced the prating about an American revolution as romantic, ill-informed, unhistorical claptrap. Then, in May, convinced it would be better to have two smaller ideologically coherent parties than one large one divided into squabbling factions, Hillquit began expelling and suspending about two-thirds of the membership. In June, the left wing gathered at the Manhattan Lyceum and agreed to try a takeover at the party's national convention in August. When that proved impossible, the left wing walked out and immediately split into two entities: the Communist Labor Party, with John Reed and other English-speakers in the lead, and the Communist Party of America, with Russian Federation members predominant, though their ideologies were all but identical.

The Socialists, numerically, were now a shadow of their former selves, having dropped from 109,000 members at their postwar peak to 36,000 by the end of 1919.

RATHER THAN HAILING THE SETBACK for the socialists, conservatives were petrified by the arrival of the communists. Observers found New York's elite "hag-ridden by the spectre of Bolshevism." Revolutionary rhetoric, amid a plethora of metropolitan protest, against a backdrop of national and international upheavals, had generated an agony of fear unseen in Gotham since the era of the Paris Commune. Many once reform-minded citizens lined up behind a campaign of official and unofficial repression.

Wartime patriotic societies like the National Security League, National Civic Federation, and American Defense Society howled for action. They were joined by the National Association of Manufacturers (eager to brand the labor movement as Bolshevik), by the new American Legion (launched under Theodore Roosevelt Jr. to commemorate the war and combat Reds), and by the reborn Ku Klux Klan (whose chapters, proliferating in Long Island and New Jersey, hated radicals, Jews, Catholics, foreigners, and blacks).

Metropolitan, state, and federal forces prepared for battle.

The city banned all displays of the red flag, barred the use of "alien tongues" in street demonstrations, dispatched Bomb Squad agents to all radical meetings, and trained thousands of police for riot duty.

The state established a Joint Legislative Committee against Seditious Activities, headed by Senator Lusk. The move came at the behest of Union League Club activists led by Archibald Stevenson, a New York lawyer who had scourged presumed Germanophiles as wartime chairman of the Committee on Aliens (a subsection of the Mayor's Committee on National Defense), and then smoothly segued to a crusade against Bolsheviks. Had Leninism not been spawned by Germany's Karl Marx? Whatever its origins, it was rampant among New York's workingmen and should be rooted out. The Lusk Committee agreed completely and assembled its own secret service of former American Protective League vigilantes.

At the national level, Attorney General A. Mitchell Palmer set to work, prompted by strikes, rising hysteria, and his own ambition and distrust of foreigners. Drawing on the $500,000 Congress appropriated to ferret out revolutionaries, he geared up the Justice Department's new General Intelligence Division. To head it up, he called on an eager, 24-year-old, middle-class crusader—fanatically loyal to Victorian culture, obsessed with the crimes and failings of the lower orders, and resentful of those in the upper classes who pampered them. Soon John Edgar Hoover's research operation had created an index file of more than 200,000 "radically inclined" individuals, and targeted particular organizations for attack.

The Military Intelligence Division of the US Army, in addition to its espionage and counterespionage operations, also conducted surveillance of domestic "subversives," particularly

Jews. Prejudice against Jews was traditional in the army, but in 1918 anti-Semitism had blossomed into a full-fledged conviction that an international conspiracy of radical Gotham Jews had been responsible for Russian Bolshevism—the revolution had been made in New York. (Some of the more capacious theories included Jacob Schiff, Felix Warburg, and American Jewish Committee head Louis Marshall as co-conspirators.) The MID men were bolstered in their conviction about Jewish conspiracies by their encounter in 1918 with the *Protocols of the Elders of Zion*, an anti-Semitic fabrication of the czarist police. The head of the MID's New York branch, Captain John B. Trevor, thought the *Protocols* were probably fraudulent, yet he was more than open to the emphasis on insidious Jewish conspiracies.

Trevor was a prosperous, nativist, Anglo-Saxon lawyer turned intelligence officer. Born to a prominent old New York family, he studied at the best prep schools and universities (BA Harvard, LLB Columbia) and traveled in the most prestigious social circles. A close friend of Madison Grant and other eugenicist ideologues, he served with Grant on the board of directors of the Museum of Natural History. Another of his close friends, Charles Stewart Davison, led the American Defense Society (ADS), a vigilante group with pronounced anti-immigrant and anti-Semitic sentiments.

In early 1919 Trevor directed MID investigators to research and design an "Ethnic Map of New York," to help guide army officers should there be need to suppress "an organized uprising" in the city. Trevor's men identified every "ethnic district" with colors and an explanatory alphabetical key: A = Russian Jews, B = Italians, C = Germans, D = Austro-Hungarians, E = Irish, and J = Negro. Superimposed on the map were designations of "radical meeting places," with the frequency of gatherings duly noted. Trevor distributed the map to the commander of the New York National Guard, the Adjutant General's Office, the New York Chamber of Commerce, and the New York City police commissioner (who found it intensely interesting "in view of the existing restlessness among the radical element of this city, and...throughout the world").

Trevor also drew up "Plans for the Protection of New York in Case of Local Disturbances." He suggested that 10,000 soldiers would be needed to defend Manhattan, with another 4,000 detailed to Brooklyn. He asked Washington to send pistols, rifles, pump shotguns, ammunition, and weapons for a special mobile Machine Gun Battalion, to be detailed "to the points where the emergency demands," which, "as indicated on our ethnic map," would likely be "the congested districts chiefly inhabited by Russian Jews." Washington dispatched 6,000 Springfield rifles but no machine guns.

INTO THIS TINDERBOX OF TENSION, on May Day 1919, radicals tossed some bombs, although they were not the Jewish communists with whom so many were obsessed, but Italian anarchists, almost certainly followers of Luigi Galleani, including members of East Harlem's Grupo Gaetano Bresci.

These bombings had a lengthy tit-for-tat backstory. Arguably, the triggering event that launched this latest round of retaliatory violence dated back to April 20, 1914, when a major act of violence was committed, not by anarchists but by capitalists, and not in Gotham but in Ludlow, Colorado. Miners there had been on strike since September 26, 1913, against the Colorado Fuel & Iron Company (CFI), notorious for its atrocious and dangerous working conditions, its miserable wages paid in scrip usable only in the company store, and its fanatical resistance to unionization. Faced with a strike, the CFI evicted its mostly southern and eastern European workers and their families from their company-owned shacks. The miners set up a tent colony off company property and hunkered down. Management hired armed

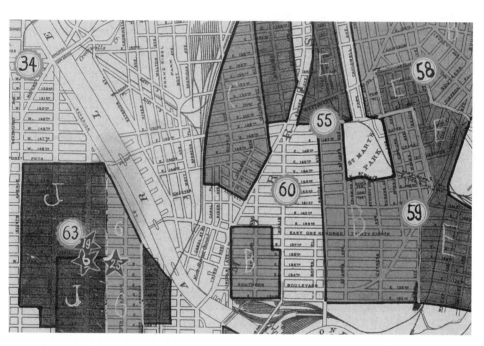

GERMANS .... **A** SCANDINAVIANS and FINNS .... **G**

RUSSIAN JEWS ..... **B** SYRIANS, TURKS, ARMENIANS, GREEKS ... **H**

ITALIANS .... **C** FRENCH .... **I**

AUSTRO-HUNGARIANS ... **D** NEGRO .... **J**

IRISH .... **E** MIXED .... *Uncolored*

CHINESE .... **F**

Detail, Harlem and the South Bronx. "Ethnic Map Prepared under the Direction of John B. Trevor, Special Deputy Attorney for the Joint Legislative Committee Investigating Seditious Activities," August 1919. Manhattan and the Bronx. (New York State Archives)

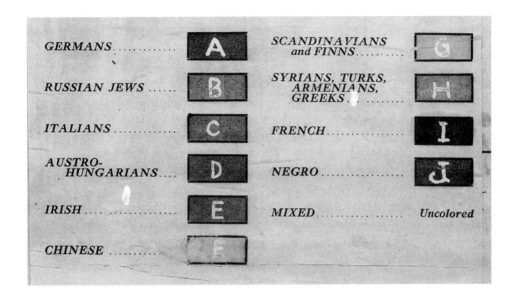

Detail, Lower East Side and west side. "Ethnic Map Prepared under the Direction of John B. Trevor, Special Deputy Attorney for the Joint Legislative Committee Investigating Seditious Activities," August 1919. Manhattan and the Bronx. (New York State Archives)

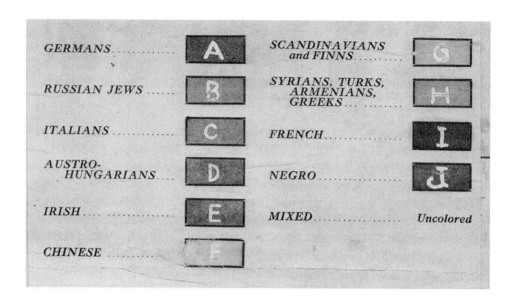

Detail, Williamsburg and north Brooklyn. "Ethnic Map Prepared under the Direction of John B. Trevor, Special Deputy Attorney for the Joint Legislative Committee Investigating Seditious Activities," August 1919. Brooklyn. (New York State Archives)

W. A. Rogers, *To Make America Safe for Democracy*, ca. 1919. (Library of Congress Prints and Photographs Division, Cabinet of American Illustration)

goons and private detectives, had them "deputized" by complaisant authorities, and engaged in sniper attacks. Workers dug under-tent pits for defense, and fired back.

This conflict received national attention because standing staunchly behind local management were the company's majority shareholders—the John D. Rockefellers, Senior and Junior both. Senior was already well known for his acerbic anti-unionism, but Junior's intransigence came as a surprise. In 1910, concerned that his virtuous Sunday school teacher image might be besmirched by the corruption seemingly endemic to the business world, he had resigned from the Standard Oil and other corporate boards (though not CFI's), intending to shift full-time into philanthropy. But when it came to labor unions, Junior hadn't fallen far from the paternal tree. He wrote to the Rockefellers' man in charge, "You are fighting a good fight, which is not only in the interest of your own company but of the . . . business interests of the entire country and of the laboring classes quite as much." On April 6, when summoned to testify before a congressional committee as to why the Rockefellers refused to negotiate, he explained that might lead to unionization, which they would resist at all cost. "And you will do that if it costs all your property and kills all your employees?" the chairman queried. To which Junior responded: "It is a great principle."

Two weeks later, the company went in for the kill. Armored cars mounted with machine guns raked the tents from an overlooking ridge; then the "militia" stormed the colony, smashing, looting, and murdering. (Three of the strike leaders were summarily executed; other strikers were shot in an exchange of gunfire). Then they set the tents ablaze, asphyxiating two mothers and eleven children who had taken shelter in the defense pits from which the oxygen was sucked by the firestorm above.

This "Ludlow Massacre" set off another firestorm—of nationwide opprobrium against the Rockefellers, and nowhere more so than in Gotham, their hometown. On April 27 3,500 socialists at a Carnegie Hall rally cheered Morris Hillquit's assertion that there was no difference between Charles Becker "who hired four gunmen to murder for pay, and John D. Rockefeller, Jr., who hired whole gangs of gunmen to murder for pay in Colorado." Protestors besieged 26 Broadway. Soon another contingent besieged his home. Junior kept a Smith & Wesson .38 pistol ready to hand, and posted watchmen on 54th Street. Then he took refuge at the family's Pocantico Hills estate near Tarrytown, some 30 miles north of New York. Demonstrators followed. During May and June, led by Alexander Berkman and Carlo Tresca, anarchists from the Ferrer Center repeatedly picketed the estate or assembled in Tarrytown's Fountain Square, only to be repeatedly attacked by local police and outraged villagers.

In late June Berkman and some Ferrer members apparently decided to escalate. They would avenge the Ludlow workers by blowing up the Tarrytown mansion, and perhaps the Rockefellers themselves. (Assassinations were much in the news with the June 28 murder in Sarajevo.) On the night of July 3, three of the group (not including Berkman) went to Tarrytown carrying a small package; hours later they returned, carrying the same package, their mission seemingly blocked or aborted. Next morning, July 4, shortly after 9:00 a.m., the apartment where they'd been storing dynamite was wracked by a tremendous explosion. The top three stories of the six-story brownstone at 1626 Lexington Avenue (between 103rd and 104th) were demolished. All three were killed.

Berkman staged a Union Square memorial service for the "martyrs" on July 11. He told the assembled 6,000 that "society has forced our friends to resist oppression with violence." One of the demonstrators, firebrand Becky Edelsohn, said, "When you train your machine guns on us, we will retaliate with dynamite." Emma Goldman, on the lecture circuit out west, was appalled on receiving the news—"I was aghast at the irresponsibility"—and further enraged when she received the July issue of *Mother Earth*, which Berkman had "filled with prattle about force and dynamite." ·

It was three weeks after the Union Square event that the NYPD established the Bomb Squad. But Inspector Tunney's men proved unable to prevent a subsequent rash of local bombings, all but certainly committed by anarchists. On October 13, the anniversary of the execution of Ferrer, bombs went off in St. Patrick's Cathedral, though doing only minor damage, and that same evening dynamite was found outside St. Alphonsus's Church, where Tannenbaum had been arrested. On November 11, the anniversary of the Haymarket executions, the Bronx County Courthouse was slightly damaged. On November 14 a bomb was disabled just before it exploded underneath a seat in the Tombs police court; the intended victim was the judge who had sentenced Tannenbaum to a year in prison. The Bomb Squad failed to track down those responsible, though they suspected it was the Bresci Group of Galleanistas (headquartered in the basement of 301 East 106th). And indeed Galleani himself, in a *Cronaca Sovversiva* assessment of the explosions, admitted they had been "*attentats*, more or less serious, more or less successful," and explicitly called on his disciples to "continue the good war," the war to exterminate "the vampires of capital."

In June 1917 Galleani was arrested, but released, then arrested again in May 1918, and again set free (though his paper was outlawed). In both cases the problem authorities faced was that they could not prove he had committed an illegal act. So in October 1918 Congress passed yet another immigration act. Its goal was to make it easier to detain and deport foreign-born anarchists—Galleani being target #1—along with anti-war protesters and members of radical labor unions, by removing the pesky due process obstacles embedded in existing law. Rather than having to prove that a suspected miscreant had actually acted on anarchist or revolutionary beliefs, simple membership in or affiliation with an organization that avowed such beliefs was deemed sufficient grounds for action. In January 1919, accordingly, Galleani was cleared for deportation. In February a circular appeared, signed by "the American Anarchists," that was unmistakably the work of Italians of the Galleani school. "Deportation will not stop the storm from reaching these shores," it said. "The storm is within and very soon will leap and crash and annihilate you in blood and fire." "You have shown no pity to us!" it concluded. "We will do likewise. And deport us! *We will dynamite you!*"

WHICH BRINGS US TO APRIL 28, 1919, shortly before May Day, when an aide in the office of Seattle's mayor opened a cardboard package that had come through the mail with the return address of "Gimbel Brothers, 32nd St. Broadway 33rd Street, New York City." It contained a bomb, which, luckily for him, failed to explode. Unluckily, when the next day Ethel Williams, a black domestic who worked for a Georgia senator, opened his box, it did blow up, and she lost both her hands. On reading the news, an alert New York Post Office clerk remembered that a cache of thirty-six identical packages had been held up—for insufficient postage—each addressed to a prominent man such as Morgan, Rockefeller, Palmer, and Hylan; each contained a bomb.

The discovery triggered May Day attacks on socialists and unionists. In New York police battled hundreds of ex-soldiers and sailors who tried to storm the gathering of moderate socialists at Madison Square Garden. Elsewhere in the city a crowd ransacked the offices of the *Call*, beating the workers and forcing them to sing the national anthem. Meetings in lower Manhattan were broken up, including a concert held by garment-trade unionists, and participants chased through the streets, beaten up, and clubbed.

On June 2, in a much better organized reprise of the failed May Day bombing, a network of radicals, the same Galleanistas responsible for the first event, planted pipe bombs in New York, Paterson, Philadelphia, Pittsburgh, Cleveland, Washington, Boston, and Newtown, Massachusetts, each set to explode around midnight. The one in New York, intended for a municipal court judge who had sent two Bresci members to jail, killed instead a 70-year-old night watchman, the only Gotham victim, and the one in Washington sheared off the front of Attorney General Palmer's house. At each bomb site they left a leaflet signed "The Anarchist Fighters."

Palmer now began the program of official denunciations, raids, arrests, and deportations that came to be known as the "Red Scare," using the first two bombing episodes as grounds for a wholesale roundup and deportation of radicals. The raids began on November 7, 1919, picked because it was the second anniversary of the Bolshevik Revolution. In New York, 700 city police, plainclothesmen, and Bomb Squad officers, together with agents of the Lusk Committee and the Justice Department, plus private vigilantes, swung into action. The Russian People's House on East 15th Street was attacked, home to the little-known Union of Russian Workers, an avowedly anarchist organization, though most of its members joined up for its courses in music, Russian literature, and auto mechanics. The contents were smashed and strewn about, its occupants beaten with makeshift clubs ripped from stair rails. The raiders also descended on the offices of the newly formed communist parties. Confiscating mailing lists, literature, and membership rosters, they forced those caught to run a gauntlet of clubs. The next day, directed by Lusk, raiders from the NYPD, Department of Justice, Immigration Service, and State Constabulary hit seventy-three radical centers, many connected to branches of the new communist parties. Lawyers examined 500 prisoners at police headquarters, held about 100 on charges of criminal anarchy, and confiscated "tons" of radical literature from fifty radical papers, which, with the aid of "wealthy parlor Bolsheviki of New York City," were "the backbone of the Red movement in this country." All told, about 1,000 were arrested. Some of the domestic communist leaders were tried and sent to Sing Sing. Aliens, about 650 of them, were interned on Ellis Island.

Two months later, in the predawn hours of December 21, 1919, 249 of the detainees were awakened and hurried through the freezing darkness onto barges and ferried to the SS *Buford*, a battered old army transport vessel. Most were poor immigrants, many with only the haziest knowledge of the political doctrines they were charged with spreading. But the boat of deportees (dubbed the "Soviet Ark" by a gleeful press), did, at the publicity-conscious Hoover's insistence, include one superstar—Emma Goldman, the Red Queen herself. Mayor Hylan hailed the expulsion of "alien fire-brands," saying they would "no longer have an opportunity to pollute the free breezes of America."

Despite protests from the National Civil Liberties Bureau, Palmer now promised to deport radicals by the thousands.[27] Hoover, Lusk, and New York vigilantes engineered another roundup in January 1920. Hundreds were dragooned—some dragged from bed—and the aliens among them dispatched to Ellis, joining others netted in simultaneous raids in thirty-three cities.

Also in January, the state legislature refused to seat five Socialist assemblymen from Manhattan, Brooklyn, and the Bronx. In the previous session Socialists had infuriated fellow legislators, hell-bent on rolling back reform, by introducing bills calling for a free state university, for old age, health, and unemployment insurance, and for extending factory legislation. Once unburdened of the Socialists, the legislature passed the quite different set of laws recommended by the Lusk Committee. These required loyalty checks for schoolteachers, established a secret service to counter subversives (a category that included the Amalgamated and ILGWU), and empowered an Albany court to strike undesirable political parties from the ballot.

Here the Red-hunters overreached. Governor Smith denounced the expulsions. He vetoed the Lusk bills, labeling them "hysterical" attempts to impose a police state. He was roundly supported by city notables like Charles Evans Hughes, Henry Stimson, and the New York Bar Association, all of whom condemned the ejections as official lawlessness. The metropolitan press, which had overwhelmingly backed the Red Raids, balked at peacetime sedition bills.

---

27. On July 1, 1917, before expiring, the American Union against Militarism had created a Civil Liberties Bureau (CLB). It was led by Crystal Eastman, the AUAM's executive secretary, and, just in from Missouri, Roger Nash Baldwin. Born into a prominent Boston family with strong liberal connections—Du Bois and Brandeis were family friends—Baldwin graduated from Harvard in 1905. At Brandeis's suggestion he became a settlement worker in St. Louis, from 1906 to 1917, and taught sociology at Washington University. He joined the AUAM and, after the draft was instituted, urged establishing a legal division to protect the rights of conscientious objectors. The CLB, which was the result, became a separate organization, the National Civil Liberties Bureau (NCLB), on October 1, 1917, headquartered in 70 Fifth Avenue, along with the NAACP and other activist organizations. Aided by lawyer Clarence Darrow, social gospel clergymen Harry F. Ward, John Haynes Holmes, and Norman Thomas, and labor activist Rose Schneiderman, the NCLB began providing legal advice and assistance for those being prosecuted under the Espionage Act of 1917 and later the Sedition Act of 1918. Beginning in early 1918, however, the NCLB itself came under attack. Its defense of the IWW led to investigations by Military Intelligence and the Bureau of Investigation. Baldwin tried to maintain good relations by cooperating with the government, even turning over confidential information on membership, but in August 1918 it too was raided by federal agents, and Union League Club vigilantes seized its files and turned them over to the Lusk Committee.

By the spring of 1920, the fever had broken. It was clear that no revolution was in the offing in the United States. Labor Department officials began canceling deportation for Ellis internees (though not before 591 were expelled). Palmer and Hoover tried to regain momentum. They predicted a communist-led uprising on May Day 1920. New York placed its entire 11,000-man police force on a twenty-four-hour alert. Nothing happened. Palmer was ridiculed. But there was to be one final act in this drama.

FIVE MINUTES BEFORE NOON ON SEPTEMBER 16, 1920, an old wagon rumbled to a stop directly across from the Wall Street offices of J. P. Morgan & Co. The driver disappeared. The wagon exploded. The dynamite blast drove holes in the pavement, punched out windows in a half-mile radius, and set awnings ablaze twelve stories above the street. It killed 38 people and injured over 300—most of them clerks, typists, and lunchtime passersby. One woman's head was blown off and plastered up against the bank's marble wall. Morgan himself was in Scotland, hunting; Thomas Lamont and Dwight Morrow were in a conference room at the other end of the building.

Palmer raced up from Washington and blamed a vast radical conspiracy. Hoover commenced an investigation but found nothing. Nevertheless, the New York Chamber of Commerce pronounced it an "act of war," and the police cracked down on radical meetings. But the nation as a whole, and soon the city as well, shrugged it off as the probable effort of a lone fanatic.[28]

LIKE MOST OTHER AMERICANS, NEW YORKERS—after five straight tension-filled years—felt wrung-out and strung-out, ready for the return to "normalcy" promised by the Republican campaign of 1920. GOP public relations experts, headquartered in New York City, churned out ads and movies, buttons and billboards, lithographs, photographs, and phonograph records—all purveying Warren G. Harding as a soothing alternative to the exalting but exhausting Wilson.

Gothamites didn't need much coaxing. The Republican tidal wave of 1920 drenched New York City. Harding carried sixty-one out of sixty-two assembly districts—including Boss Murphy's Gashouse stronghold. Governor Al Smith ran far ahead of the national ticket, but not far enough, and his departure from office allowed a gleeful legislature to repass the Lusk Laws. Tremors from the Red Scare would reverberate for the next few years. But by the end of 1920, the First World War in New York City was effectively over.

NEW WORLD ORDER

The ferocious battle over national reconstruction during 1919 overlapped with an equally contentious struggle over *international* reconstruction—an effort to fashion a new order for the postwar world, and reposition Gotham's place therein. The initiative got under way on December 4, 1918, when Woodrow Wilson and his party stepped off their direct-from-DC train at Hoboken's Pier 4 and boarded the *George Washington*, which then steamed off to the Narrows, past huge throngs lining the waterfronts waving Godspeed, and headed out into the North Atlantic, convoyed by the battleship *Pennsylvania* and a flotilla of destroyers. The

---

28. They were not far off the mark. The likely solitary terrorist was Mario Buda, another Galleanista, whose probable motive was revenge for the deportation of his comrades, and the September 11 indictments (for a murder they didn't commit) of his fellow revolutionary anarchists Nicola Sacco and Bartolomeo Vanzetti ("the best friends I had in America"), who had likely taken part with him in the June 2 bombings. In a Cedar Street mailbox, a few blocks from Broad and Wall, a postal worker found leaflets warning: "Free the Political Prisoners or it will be Sure Death for All of You!" They were signed, in by now familiar fashion: "American Anarchist Fighters."

president arrived in Brest on the French coast in Brittany, on the fourteenth; then he and the US delegation traveled on to Paris, where they settled into the Hotel Crillon and got to work with their victorious allies hammering out a peace treaty. Over the next month Wilson took time out to tour cities in France, England, and Italy, where his well-known and wildly popular Fourteen Points program brought millions into the streets to hail him as a Messiah who would bring lasting peace to the war-ravaged planet.

The president's program had vigorous support in New York as well, though different Points appealed to different parts of the populace. The distinction was particularly evident at the opposite ends of the demographic spectrum: Anglo-Protestant Wall Street and the great ethnic enclaves.

WALL STREET HOPED WILSON WOULD MAKE the world safe for investment. Although the city's financial and industrial magnates had made fortunes from the war, they believed that in the long run an orderly and sustainable peace would be more profitable. The chief obstacle to such stability was imperialism, the murderous competition between rivalrous nation-states to lock down markets, raw materials, and investment opportunities. In 1914 the combustible system had exploded into disruptive slaughter, and would again unless replaced by a better way of doing business.

Wilson's proposed solution was to expand the "open door" approach that US capital had embraced, eschewing conventional colonialism as costly and unnecessary. The other "great powers" should follow suit, forswearing construction of autonomous empires, and dismantling obstacles to the free flow of capital and commodities. Wilson's call for "freedom of navigation upon the seas, outside territorial waters, alike in peace and in war" (Point Two) and "removal, so far as possible, of all economic barriers and the establishment of an equality of trade conditions" (Point Three) spoke to the wishes of the Wall Street community.

Who would police this new post-imperialist world order? Wilson proposed creation (Point Fourteen) of a global community of nations whose members would collectively take action, military as well as economic, to guarantee "political independence and territorial integrity to great and small states alike." Wall Streeters could live with Wilson's League of Nations if, by whatever structural means necessary, effective authority was placed in the hands (and navies) of the United States and Great Britain. Where Wilson sought to transcend the traditional balance of great power politics, Wall Street preferred a Pax Anglo-Americana. Deeply Anglophilic before the war, the Street had become more so during the fighting. "For the long future," Thomas Lamont believed, "the safety and happiness of both America and Great Britain are dependent upon these two great nations working in accord," and "the peace of the whole world is dependent upon the same thing." Paul Cravath asserted in a July 1919 article for the *London Times* that "the best insurance of the peace of the world is a sound and lasting friendship between the English Speaking Nations." In particular, "the difficulties in negotiating the Treaty of Paris suggest the difficulties that will be encountered in enforcing it unless Great Britain and the United States co-operate in its enforcement."

But who would be the senior partner and who the junior? The US was far and away the stronger industrially, and financially the two countries had switched positions, with Britain now the debtor nation. Some Americans wanted the United States to seize the moment and supersede Britain as the military and economic guarantor of a liberal and capitalist world order, with New York replacing London as financial linchpin of the world economy. The "fortunes of war," declared National City Bank president Frank Vanderlip, "have given us a great opportunity to achieve a commanding position."

Yet the British were not inconsequential players, to be easily relegated to sidekick status. They had the Navy and the Empire. And London still had the edge on New York, or so Vanderlip believed. The massive credits built up during the war had left Wall Street awash in cash, and the ongoing inflow of interest and dividends "will undoubtedly give us the resources to conduct world operations." Yet "that alone will not of itself establish New York as the financial center of the world in the same sense that London has been in the past." The British capital had been "the place where the current trade of the world was financed," a centrality based on its geographical position, its great shipping interests, its superior communication systems, and a century's worth of accumulated commercial expertise. If America wanted to "create preeminence for New York," then "we must turn our eyes abroad and learn to be investors and traders the world around, and to correlate our industries on a fair exchange basis." Piling up credits (or gold bullion) was a problem, not a solution. "We cannot go over the world extracting honey and storing it in our hive, for the world's trade must be kept in balance." To achieve such stability, he concluded, we must make others "better able to trade with us."

This focus on attaining global equilibrium suggested, in turn, an approach to the issue of German reparations being hashed out in Paris—a debate that pitted Wilson and Wall Street against England and France. The latter powers wanted to demand an exorbitant amount from their defeated foe, a sum beyond Germany's ability to pay. The victors wanted this for vengeance, for rebuilding demolished infrastructure, for pensions for war widows, and for offsetting the $10 billion the Allies owed the US government. Lamont, a key player on the Reparations Committee, pushed for reducing the demand. American globalists, he explained, were anxious to restart the engine of commerce. Trading partners needed to be helped to buy US products, lest the US slip back into recession now that war orders had dried up.[29]

That meant reviving Europe, including Germany; and Germany couldn't be revived if all its resources were earmarked for payments to France and England. Wall Street not only pushed for lightening Germany's reparation burden; it proposed to write down or write off the $10 billion debt the Allies owed the US. Not only would clearing the decks speed their reintegration into the world economy; it would allow them to ease up on their demand for reparations. The bankers, moreover, believed wiping out past debt would clear a path for extending new credits, either by direct US government loans or by marshaling a massive government-backed bankers' consortium loan to restore Europe's shattered currencies. In effect, Wall Street was urging the US to step up and assume, either on its own or in co-operation with Great Britain, the position of arbiter and bankroller of a new world economic order.

IT DIDN'T HAPPEN. The United States did not join the League of Nations. It disavowed responsibility for European reconstruction. It failed to moderate the Allies' reparation demands on Germany or to write down the Allied debt. It rejected the notion of exercising the kind of global leadership Britain had assumed during the nineteenth century, and in the process slowed New York's march to the center of the world, which depended on federal backing.

---

29. America "cannot disentangle herself" from Europe, Lamont warned. Europe "is her greatest customer, her greatest purchaser of grains, cotton, copper, and all other raw materials. If our own industry and commerce are to be restored, if we are to get back to former prosperity, then, indeed, must we lend our own efforts to European restoration."

A lengthy list of reasons was advanced to explain the US pullback. Much of the blame fell on Wilson. He had made all kinds of tactical errors: freezing heavyweight Republicans like Root and Hughes out of the Paris deliberations, rejecting any compromise on key League provisions, refusing to discuss and defend his proposals in the public forum (perhaps a legacy of his crushing of conversation during the war—silencing critics by defining them as "seditious" might have gotten him out of the habit of listening).

Resistance to the project advanced by Wilson and the internationalists gathered in Gotham ran far deeper than reservations about the manner in which it was promoted. The initiative had raised the hackles of very powerful people in the US. Those players, labeled isolationist by some, were better understood as nationalists. They were either not interested in, or actively opposed to, the New York–based phalanx's desire to push out onto the planet. The continental United States was a gargantuan market and field for investment, and many domestic industrialists could satisfy their business goals without putting a foot offshore, rather as nineteenth-century imperialists had their hands full "winning" the West. Yes, Africa and Asia awaited, but their time would come.

New York's internationally minded complex, on the other hand, included industrial and agricultural sectors desiring to find extra-continental markets that could absorb surplus capital and commodities. The Great War had dramatically expanded this cohort, and by Treaty of Paris time it included mining and petroleum interests; producers of machinery and equipment (especially electrical appliances); makers of chemicals, rubber products, motor vehicles, and processed food; and providers of agricultural commodities, notably southern cotton. These business sectors accounted for well over half of all overseas investment in manufacturing.

No question, then, the internationalists were powerful, but they were not the only game in town. Indeed, they represented barely 20 percent of the country's manufacturing plant. Thus 80 percent of American industrialists were relatively uninvolved in producing for overseas markets. They remained indifferent to foreign economic affairs—not isolationist, just otherwise occupied.

Some nationalists, however, saw Wall Street's proposed initiatives as actively menacing. They were concerned that overseas investments and loans would indeed revive foreign competitors, especially in Germany, and such competition (especially if government subsidized) was not perceived as being in their interest. They were also worried that shipping capital abroad would deplete the pool of financing available to domestic producers. They were concerned, too, that loans to raw-materials producers might be used to organize producers' cartels that would raise prices charged to US industry.

Nowhere did nationalist and internationalist interests clash more directly than over tariff legislation. The New York crowd and their associates wanted to reduce or eliminate tariffs. This would allow overseas industrialists to sell their goods in the US market, and thus raise the foreign exchange they needed to pay the interest on Wall Street–underwritten debt. Opponents like the American Protective Tariff League warned (in 1918) that lowering tariff walls would leave "our domestic markets exposed to the competition of products made by low-paid labor of foreign lands," adding (in 1919) that free-traders were intent on stripping away adequate protection "for the industries and labor of the United States." The income from tariffs, moreover, provided a substantial percentage of the revenues needed to run the US government; if that income stream was clamped off, no doubt taxes would be raised on ordinary citizens to make up the deficit.

Wall Streeters responded that the nationalists were being short-sighted in not realizing that the international trading system depended on achieving equilibrium. Morgan banker

Harry Davison told a financial gathering on June 13, 1919: "The world has grown smaller. The man who thinks an economic Chinese wall can be built around America lacks knowledge."

Otto Kahn joined in the chiding. "Having become a creditor nation, we have got now to fit ourselves into the role of a creditor nation. We shall have to make up our minds to be more hospitable to imports. We shall have to outgrow gradually certain inherited and no longer applicable views and preconceptions and adapt our economic policies to the changed positions which have resulted from the late war." Some bankers did understand there would be losers as well as winners if their approach won the ear of power. Vanderlip allowed that "we shall have to be careful how we rapidly increase our importations of foreign goods or there may be injurious effects upon home production." In the end, he thought, the only way to keep things in balance without creating ill effects was to take the profits that now poured in from interest and dividends and immediately reinvest them abroad. "The logic of the situation seems to compel us to be in the future a great money-lending country," he said, but it was hard to see how this would comfort the nationalist manufacturers, as the profits (from fees) from arranging and servicing debt would accrue to financial rather than industrial capital. And domestic industrialists had political muscle. They constituted the historic core of the national Republican Party. When they insisted that Wall Street's proposed great leap outward was not in their (or the country's) best interest, politicians paid attention. The massive Republican victory of 1920 was about more than just "normalcy."

Wall Street's setback led the New York internationalists to better organize themselves as an ideological and political force. They did so by combining two of the institutions that had sprung up in Gotham in 1918–19 to ponder and promote greater involvement by the United States in world affairs. In Paris, on May 30, 1919, a group of American diplomats and scholars who had been members of the Inquiry gathered with their English counterparts at the Hotel Majestic, billet of the British delegation, and proposed to establish a cooperative Institute of International Affairs, with one branch in London, the other in New York, each to embrace mixed memberships. The British held up their end, as a Royal Institute of International Affairs was launched with great fanfare in London's Chatham House. The proposed American Institute of International Affairs, however, languished for lack of funding.

In the meantime, the New York dinner and discussion club known as the Council on Foreign Relations (1918), composed overwhelmingly of members of Gotham's leading law and banking firms, had slipped into desuetude. Roused by the setbacks in the political sphere, it was decided to revivify and merge the two entities, one well stocked with professional experts, the other including men of affairs and business who could tap fathomless resources. The honorary president of the new Council on Foreign Relations (CFR), as the conjoint community was named, was (all but inevitably) Elihu Root. Prominent early leaders included Lamont, Cravath, J. W. Davis, Polk, and Wickersham. Plans for mixed membership were scrapped—the CFR became wholly American, and Chatham House became wholly British—but the prevailing spirit in both was Anglo-American.

Wall Streeters did, however, have mixed feelings about the British Empire: annoyance at its violations of open door precepts (via a system of imperial preferences), yet admiration of it as a force for order, stability, and governance of peoples presumed incapable of self-rule. New York's ethnic enclaves, on the other hand, teemed with resolute anti-imperialists—among them Irish, African Americans, Jews, Poles, Syrians, and Indians—all of whom were hell-bent on liberating their country or community of origin from the overlordship of one empire or another. If Wall Streeters were drawn to a post-imperialist vision of global capitalism, many in the city's ethnic and racial communities dreamed of global decolonization.

NEW YORK ETHNICS, BY AND LARGE, HOPED that Wilson would make the world safe for ethno-nationalism. Initially this had not been his intention. None of his Fourteen Points contained the term "self-determination," and the notion that populations bound by a common language or shared history had a right to territorial independence was not originally part of his postwar program. Indeed, he had at first opposed the breakup of the multi-national Austro-Hungarian Empire, fearing consequent disorder, and called only for "autonomous development" within the existing imperial framework. Fearing the disaggregation of many (if not all) existing states, he cautiously proposed that "all well-defined national aspirations shall be accorded the utmost satisfaction that can be accorded them without introducing new or perpetuating old elements of discord and antagonism that would be likely in time to break the peace of Europe and consequently of the world."

Over time, however, self-determination loomed larger in his thinking. "National aspirations must be respected," he told Congress; "peoples may now be dominated and governed only by their own consent. 'Self-determination' is not a mere phrase. It is an imperative principle of actions which statesmen will henceforth ignore at their peril." Solving Europe's problems must be approached "with a view to the wishes, the natural connections, the racial aspirations, the security, and the peace of mind of the peoples involved."

New York liberationists proceeded to make the wishes and aspirations of their co-nationalists abundantly clear.

GOTHAM'S IRISH REPUBLICANS HAD HAD A TOUGH WAR. The Wilson administration had summarily barred issues of the *Gaelic American* and *Irish World* from the mails; police had arrested nationalist speakers; vigilantes had disrupted public meetings that promoted freeing Ireland from British tyranny. In addition, the vast majority of the New York Irish, while remaining steadfast supporters of self-determination, had been willing to wait till victory to press their case. Church, community, and political leaders all vigorously supported enlistment campaigns and bond drives.

The armistice unleashed the nationalists. Now *they* were supported by the vast majority, though with differences of opinion as to the form self-determination should take, ranging from dominion status to full independence. Mass organizations leapt into action. The Knights of Columbus, Ancient Order of Hibernians, Friendly Sons of St. Patrick, and Friends of Irish Freedom staged mammoth rallies, like one at Madison Square Garden on December 10, 1918, one month after the armistice, at which participants roared cheers for everything Irish. They cheered, too, for Woodrow Wilson, then sailing east on the *George Washington*, and they sent him a petition (by wireless) urging him "to demand at the Peace Congress self-determination for the people of Ireland." Four days later, the parliamentary election produced an overwhelming victory for Sinn Féin. The elected Sinn Féin members of Parliament then seceded from the House of Commons. They established instead an independent Irish parliament, the Dáil Éireann, which on January 21, 1919, declared independence and proclaimed an Irish Republic.

A month later, on February 22–23, the Friends of Irish Freedom (FOIF) held another Irish Race Convention, this time in Philadelphia. It drew 5,000 delegates, who hailed the success of Sinn Féin and huzzahed formation of the Republic, then set to work raising funds and mobilizing political support for the rebel government. The convention also appointed a three-man American Commission on Irish Independence to go to Paris and lobby for the Republic. To their dismay, the delegation was excluded. More shockingly, Woodrow Wilson refused his support. The United Kingdom, he declared (after the British had privately made clear to him that recognition of Irish independence would be a deal breaker), was not an empire but a democracy, and the Irish Question, being an internal affair, was beyond the purview of the peace convention. Irish Americans felt profoundly betrayed. Large numbers rushed to join the FOIF (275,000) and, in 1920, the American Association for Recognition of the Irish Republic (500,000), established by Éamon de Valera, the New York–born chairman of the Dáil Éireann, who arrived in Gotham on June 11, 1919, to urge US recognition. Over the next nineteen months, while a war for independence raged, de Valera spoke to massive crowds across the country, and raised substantial funding for the independence movement and its military arm, the Irish Republican Army.

FOUR DAYS BEFORE WILSON SET SAIL in the *George Washington*, W. E. B. Du Bois boarded the *Orizaba*, carrying the fifty-two-person press delegation. Once in Paris, the *Crisis* editor had no official role, Wilson having ignored his petition for status as an accredited observer. So he set out, virtually single-handedly, to create a black presence at Versailles by hastily organizing a Pan-African Congress that would seek to influence the discussion about the disposition of Germany's colonies in Africa.

First he needed to win French permission to hold such an event. For assistance he turned to Blaise Diagne, the Senegalese deputy to the French National Assembly and the highest-ranking African in French politics. Diagne, greatly regarded for his success in recruiting Africans for the French army (280,000 volunteers from Senegal alone), successfully lobbied Prime Minister Georges Clemenceau on Du Bois's behalf. (The American delegation suspected that Clemenceau had only granted permission in order to irritate Wilson, as the conference would certainly draw attention to the grievances of blacks in the US, though the French did stipulate that there was to be no publicity.)

Du Bois then assembled fifty-seven delegates representing fifteen countries and colonies, including Haiti, Liberia, the British West Indies, and the United States. (There would have been more had the British and American governments not refused passports and visas to citizens who wanted to come.) Nineteen were from Africa. The Pan-African Congress met discreetly in February 1919 at the Grand Hotel. Resolutions were passed, without publicity. The congress did not demand African self-determination. But it did ask the peace conference not to turn over Germany's colonial possessions to "mandates"—the fig leaf formula under which England and France were allowed to rule but not possess—but rather to the League of Nations directly. The congress also called for establishing a legal code of treatment "for the international protection of the natives of Africa." Though Du Bois got a polite hearing from House, Walter Lippmann, and other high Wilsonian advisors, he was not authorized to address the Peace Conference, and the congress's resolutions went nowhere.

Where Du Bois was the essentially solitary instigator of a black presence at Versailles, Marcus Garvey mobilized mass support for his campaign to influence the Peace Conference. On November 10, 1918, 3,000 to 5,000 answered his call in the *Negro World* to attend a meeting at the Palace Casino devoted to choosing delegates and advancing proposals. The assembly ratified the selection of Ida B. Wells and A. Philip Randolph as emissaries, and adopted a proposal that called for turning control of Germany's African colonies over not to the League of Nations, as the Pan-African Congress had suggested, but to a group "composed of the educated classes of

Negroes from America, the West Indies, Liberia, Hayti, Abyssinia, and the peoples of Japan and China and other enlightened sections of the African and European worlds."

On January 2, 1919, Garvey, Randolph, Chandler Owen, and the Reverend Adam Clayton Powell met with Madame C. J. Walker at her luxurious Villa Lewaro, and she agreed to help create an International League of Darker Peoples. This organization would in the short run coordinate the various black delegates heading for Paris. (She promised to pay their passage.) The founders also envisioned it becoming a permanent watchdog organization, "with a view of preventing the expropriation of the darker peoples of their national resources and labor."

Then racial reality intruded. The US refused to give visas to any of the would-be delegates. In the end the sole representative of the Universal Negro Improvement Association was Eliezier Cadet, a Haitian youth who had come to Garvey's attention when he wrote a letter to the *Negro World* denouncing the US military occupation of his country. Garvey had selected him to be the delegation's interpreter, but now, as he could travel on his Haitian passport, the UNIA chief charged him with presenting the organization's proposals to the Peace Conference. The utterly unknown Cadet got nowhere in Paris, though he haunted the offices of major Parisian newspapers, where his accounts of US lynching were listened to sympathetically but not set down in newsprint. Cadet covered up his (inevitable) failure by claiming Du Bois had sabotaged his mission, which widened an emerging split between Garvey and Du Bois.

IN DECEMBER 1914 LALA LAJPAT RAI, a Hindu lawyer from the Punjab and activist in the Indian National Congress, arrived in Gotham. For the next five years Rai would use the city as a base from which to mobilize US opinion behind the Indian nationalist cause. He focused particularly on winning support from New York intellectuals and activists, and built relationships with Du Bois, Oswald Garrison Villard, Norman Thomas, J. G. Phelps Stokes, Roger Baldwin, John Haynes Holmes, Felix Adler, Walter Lippmann, and George Kirchwey (former dean of the Columbia Law School). Once the US entered the war, favorable press coverage narrowed— the *Times* labeled his anti-British stance seditious—but his campaign was still supported by the *New York Evening Post*, the *Nation*, and the *New Republic*. In 1917 he founded the India Home Rule League, at 1400 Broadway. In 1918 he started up *Young India*, a monthly periodical, and an India Information Bureau, which provided US media outlets with antidotes to British propaganda.

THE CITY'S JEWISH COMMUNITIES had a dramatically different relationship with Great Britain and its empire than did Indian and Irish and African American nationalists, ever since the Balfour Declaration of November 2, 1917, in which His Majesty's Government was said to "view with favour the establishment in Palestine of a national home for the Jewish people, and will use their best endeavours to facilitate the achievement of this object."

The declaration had added a qualifier, however: "it being clearly understood that nothing shall be done which may prejudice the civil and religious rights of existing non-Jewish communities in Palestine." This reservation, as well as President Wilson's promotion of self-determination, helped galvanize resistance by New York's Syrian community. On November 8, 1917, one week after Balfour's declaration, 500 Syrians of the Palestine Antizionism Society gathered at Brooklyn's Hotel Bossert, convened by Fuad Shatara, a Christian Arab American of Palestinian descent who was a surgeon and instructor in the School of Medicine of Long Island College Hospital. The meeting resolved that "we protest against the formation of any Government or body politic based on religious principles, by a minority, contrary to the principles of the majority." It added: "We further protest against any scheme of artificial importation of Zionists flooding the country against its natural capacities and thus forcing an emigration of the rightful inhabitants."

A year later, on December 17, 1918, at the inaugural meeting of the American Jewish Congress (AJC) in Philadelphia, the organization issued a declaration supporting "the development of Palestine into a Jewish commonwealth" under the "trusteeship of Great Britain."

In early 1919 the Palestine Antizionism Society sent off resolutions to the Paris Peace Conference asking for self-determination for Greater Syria and urging that Zionist activities in Palestine be allowed only if they were undertaken by those willing to become "Syrian citizens" and act in accord with Syrian laws.

The issue was not immediately resolved.

The Jewish community had a related but more immediate issue on its postwar agenda. On the very day of the armistice, a wave of pogroms broke out in newly liberated Poland. From November 1918 through August 1919, hundreds of Jews were murdered in a hundred different Eastern European localities. Weeks later, in December 1918, the American Jewish Congress urged the Peace Conference to require that Poland and other new nations being carved out of old empires be required to adopt a comprehensive "Bill of Rights" to protect Jewish and other minority citizens, in effect establishing enclaves within nations (though not states within states).

Hundreds more murders in April triggered a major anti-pogrom campaign. On May 21, 1919, several hundred thousand Jews (factory workers, schoolchildren, shopkeepers, American Jewish veterans in uniform) took part in spontaneous Lower East Side street parades. That evening, before a giant throng in Madison Square Garden, Charles Evans Hughes accused Poland of "betray[ing] the cause for which we have fought," and Jacob Schiff asserted that "Poland cannot be free until it gives good guarantees that it will give protection for Jew and gentile alike."

Louis Marshall, who had played a significant role in drafting the AJC's Bill of Rights, worked during that spring and early summer on helping craft a specific version of it. What finally emerged was a Polish Minority Treaty, which the Polish government was obliged to sign, on the same day, June 28, 1919, that the Treaty of Versailles was passed. While it imposed some formal obligations to respect minority rights, it fell far short of establishing the quasi-autonomous regions Marshall had sought as a guard against internal imperialism—the oppression within a state of minorities by majorities. Wilson had played with a variant of this notion—giving the League of Nations blanket authority to intervene against internal discrimination—but it aroused a storm of opposition. As the British pointed out to the American president, such a provision would encourage "American negroes, Southern Irish, Flemings or Catalans" to appeal to the League over the heads of their own government. The Poles made exactly the same argument – furious that standards were hypocritically being imposed on the new states by old states that did not adhere to them.[30]

---

30. Dewey had suggested an alternate approach back in 1916. "If there is to be lasting peace, there must be a recognition of the cultural rights and privileges of each nationality, its right to its own language, its own literature, its own ideals, its own moral and spiritual outlook on the world, its complete religious freedom, and such political autonomy as may be consistent with the maintenance of general social unity." The model for this was the United States, which was itself home to many peoples and cultures. International by definition, the US had a vested interest in "promoting the efficacy of human intercourse irrespective of class, racial, geographical and national limits." The key to pulling this off was engineering "a complete separation of nationality from citizenship. Not only have we separated the church from the state, but we have separated language, cultural traditions, all that is called race, from the state—that is, from problems of political organization and power." He proposed to "make the accident of our internal composition into an idea, an idea upon which we may conduct our foreign as well as our domestic policy." Unity in diversity was the answer. "Let this idea fly abroad; it bears healing in its wings."

DESPITE THEIR VAST DIFFERENCES IN CULTURES AND HISTORIES, participants in the city's various national (or quasi-national) liberation movements often recognized a kinship of oppression, and a commonality of resistance. On September 28, 1919, Marcus Garvey inserted the black movement into a larger anti-colonial narrative. "Four millions of Irishmen and women are struggling for the independence of Ireland. Twelve millions of Jews are clamoring for the restoration of Palestine. The Egyptians are determined to get Egypt as an independent country. Three hundred millions of Indians are determined to have India. Four hundred million Negroes realize that the time has come to restore Africa to the Africans."[31]

Bilateral linkups were common. Between blacks and Jews: Garvey cultivated an image as "the Black Moses" and encouraged his followers to see his movement as a species of "black Zionism"; the Zionist press, in turn, offered favorable commentary on his movement. Between blacks and Irish: the Irish Progressive League invited Garveyite speakers to address its street meetings, and its *Bulletin* said the League sympathized with "people of whatever race, color, or creed who were struggling to live their lives as they themselves desired and not as alien exploiters would have them [live]." Between Irish and Indians: The *Gaelic American* extolled India's independence movement, and the St. Patrick's Day parade of 1920 featured Indian nationalists in its ranks.

There was even a League of Oppressed Peoples, founded by Dudley Field Malone. The son of a Tammany official, Malone studied law at Fordham, practiced law and politics, and backed Wilson in 1912 (for which he was awarded the city's most prestigious patronage plum, the Collector of the Port of New York). But he grew more radical, backed Hillquit in 1917 (though didn't join the Socialist Party), represented suffragettes, supported the NAACP, favored self-determination for Ireland, India, China, and Korea, and in 1919 formed the League, headquartered at 50 East 42nd Street. His board included Du Bois, Lala Lajpat Rai, Harriet Stanton Blatch, Abraham Cahan, Will Durant, the Reverend John Haynes Holmes, Frederic Howe, Rabbi Judah Magnes, Amos Pinchot, Rose Schneiderman, Norman Thomas, O. G. Villard, and Frank Walsh.

A touch grandiose in its ambitions and nomenclature, perhaps, but not only did the Military Intelligence Division suspect the worst—with the flocking to New York of radical agitators ("blacks and yellows from all parts of the world")—so did Madison Grant's disciple Lothrop Stoddard. His 1920 book *The Rising Tide of Color: The Threat against White World-Supremacy* foresaw an eventual awakening of peoples in Asia, Africa, and South America that would, he was sure, lead to colored domination, followed by the destruction of civilization through mongrelization.

ENDINGS AND BEGINNINGS

We've now come to the end of this volume, where two sets of conclusions await.

One offers a brief summary of Greater Gotham's tumultuous first decades—recounting its changing position on the planet, its shifting relations with the rest of the country, its altered macro economy, and its experience of the economy's ups and downs. This conclusion,

---

31. This catholicity was remarked upon by the federal intelligence community, which in mid-1919 fingered Garvey's Liberty Hall as "sort of a clearing house for all international radical agitators." Alarmingly, "blacks and yellows from all parts of the world" traipsed through its doors. One of them might have been Ho Chi Minh, who, according to him, had been living in Harlem, and had attended Garvey's talks. (This was before Ho himself went off to Paris, where he hoped to urge the Peace Conference to recommend that the Vietnamese be represented in France's colonial government. He, like Eliezer Cadet, proved unable to get a hearing, despite having rented a formal suit.)

however, is actually nestled back in the introduction ("Vantage Points"), as the brief summary offered there of the book's findings serves equally well as a big-picture review.

The second conclusion prepares readers for the eventual linkup with the next volume in the *Gotham* series, which will focus on the '20s, '30s, and early '40s.

The '20s, in popular imagination, boils down to a series of exclamation points: The economy boomed! Skyscrapers soared! So did the stock market! Organized crime flourished! Airplanes hopped the Atlantic! Radio arrived! Harlem had a renaissance! The overall takeaway casts the '20s as a dazzling decade that roared and partied its way up to a glittering Gatsbyesque apex atop a tall tower, from which it then jumped, plummeting to the grim '30s below.

This pack of flash cards does point to some key components of that era—though it leaves out others (like immigration restriction) that alter the overall picture—but the decade itself seems to come out of nowhere. Yet the Twenties evolved out of what preceded it. It was the resultant of innumerable choices made between competing potential pathways. Our second conclusion therefore doesn't say what happened next, but rather explores what contemporaries thought *might* happen next. It reviews some contending scenarios of the future that seemed plausible to New Yorkers in 1920, a year that was both an end and a beginning.

IT WAS PATENTLY OBVIOUS IN 1920 that the city's financial/corporate/commerce/real-estate complex had undergone a colossal expansion over the previous twenty years. Would it continue to swell? To some degree that would depend on how (or if) the nationalist-internationalist conflict got resolved. If the country opted for greater overseas involvement, and if New York surged past London, the resulting development of global trade and finance might accelerate Wall Street's growth exponentially. Even if the domestic economy remained the focus, the war-enhanced industrial sector would likely shift to peacetime production of consumer goods, and generate a ravenous appetite for financing. If so, the New York Stock Exchange, newly freed from federal constraints, might well expand its capacity to provide the necessary funds. Perhaps an economic boom would tempt the millions of wartime Liberty Bond buyers into making civilian stock purchases—leading to a democratization of capitalism, or perhaps only to a spreading of its risks.

Speaking of risk, might not bust rather than boom lie in the future? The city had just lived through a dizzying, two-decade-long roller-coaster ride: boom, panic, recession sputtering in-and-out, war boom, and postwar slump—the last triggered by the Fed's having doubled the interest rate to curb inflation. Indeed, as the decade began, unemployment and homelessness were again rife in Gotham. Were rent strikes, food riots, and a new round of labor and radical organizing in the offing?

If the economy did get its mojo back, what would be the physical ramifications for Wall Street? Would a boom summon up a new round of skyscrapers, fashioned by a new generation of architects who deployed new technologies and new materials to shape new styles (dictated in part by the new zoning laws)? If so, where would this new bumper crop of buildings arise—downtown? Or in midtown, the emerging rival business district mushrooming up around the new train stations? Would Wall Street remain on Wall Street?

"Permanence" being perhaps the least appropriate descriptor of New York City, observers in 1920 might have wondered if other sectors of the economy would be on the move. The garment and printing industries had swelled in size and jumped from downtown to midtown. The department stores had leapt from Sixth below 23rd to Fifth above 34th. Much heavy industry had remained (as did the great wholesale markets) on the Lower West Side and along the Brooklyn waterfront, but other large factories had continued to pull up stakes and regroup in Queens, the Bronx, and New Jersey. New York had also entrenched itself as the nation's media, communications, and entertainment capital, but the film industry's departure to Hollywood underscored the mutability of the economic landscape.

The port, too, was in flux. Under wartime federal administration, it had expanded its South Brooklyn and Jersey docking and warehousing operations, and preliminary steps had been taken toward better integrating the shared-but-separate New York–New Jersey harbor. Might the center of gravity of a more unified port not lurch decisively to the New Jersey side, situated as it was on continental terra firma? Also, as the strong governmental hand that curbed rampant railroad competition during the war had now been removed, might chaos return with the free market? And mightn't that allow more efficient cities to make inroads on the city's commercial supremacy?

And what of Gotham's geo-demographic profile? Where would people live and work in the future? The tea leaves were difficult to read. In the 1910s, spurred by housing legislation and transport extension, lower Manhattan's hyper-dense tenement district had begun to disaggregate. Better-off immigrants or their children departed Old Law slums for New Law apartment districts, reestablishing ethnic encampments, though in less huddled concentrations and more salubrious surroundings. But then history began running backward. Skyrocketing rents generated by inflation and the wartime construction freeze had forced recent escapees to return to denser but cheaper enclaves. Would dispersal continue to stall? Or would centripitalization resume?

That, in turn, would depend on the hydraulic pressure exerted by the inflow of new immigrants, a volume regulated by federal law, over which a congressional battle was brewing. The 1917 Asiatic Barred Zone Act had hugely expanded the most-unwanted list, forbidding immigration from India, Afghanistan, Central Asia, and the Arabian Peninsula. Now the Grants, Stoddards, Trevors, and Osborns—the Anglo-eugenics crowd that considered Jews and Italians and Caribbean blacks to be polluters of the city's gene pool—were prodding Congress to pass a "genuine 100 percent American immigration law." Would they be able to erect a legal wall high enough to block or filter out the "scum of the earth" (as W. E. D. Stokes so pithily put it)? Or would those who hailed the US as a multinational construct whose diversity was eminently worth preserving—like Kallen and Dewey and Boas but, alas, no longer Bourne, who had died in the flu epidemic—be able to keep the Golden Door open? The racial and ethnic composition of the metropolis would be influenced by the outcome.

Assuming that the restrictionists were beaten back, and that immigration (and domestic migration) ascended again to prewar levels, and that housing production expanded enough to keep pace, where would the populace go? The likeliest flow-ways would be along the subway lines that spiked deeply into the Bronx, Queens, and south Brooklyn. But a rival transport system had arrived. The automobile, no longer merely a plaything of the rich, was a workaday vehicle the middle class could afford. Would it challenge the primacy of New York's rail-based train and subway systems? Would bridges and tunnels henceforth be built for private cars rather than mass transit? Would highways (and garages) significantly expand the suburbs-within-the-city, increasing the percentage of homeowners and diminishing the ranks of renters?

And what political contests were on 1920's agenda?

Would the progressive movement recover? Would the prewar and wartime alliance of middle- and working-class reformers, badly weakened by the former's fear of aliens and Bolsheviks and labor unions, make a comeback? Would muckrakers again issue blistering critiques of the growing inequality of wealth, and corruption of the political process? Would the top 1 percent be condemned as plutocratic or hailed as Promethean? Would the great national debate over the new corporate order be resumed, or had the corporate condition become normalized?

Would advocates of social welfare initiatives again take up the cudgels on behalf of abolishing child labor, providing government insurance against ill health, unemployment, and old age, and establishing a minimum wage? Would Al Smith's Tammany Hall, beaten at the state level by conservative Republicans, be resuscitated as a vehicle for social democratic reconstruction? Or would John Hylan's Tammany Hall, in the municipal saddle since 1917, prefer patronage-driven politics?

Would radicalism revive from the heavy blows administered during the Red Scare? Would the quarreling Communists emerge from underground to become political factors? Would the numerically diminished Socialists remain a force to be reckoned with? Would the industrial union movement expand beyond the needle trades?

And what of racial politics? Would New Negro militancy and its cultural correlative make their mark on the broader New York scene? Which of the contending visions and plans of action would achieve predominance—that of Garvey, or Du Bois, or Randolph? Would Harlem continue to fill up with exiles from lynch-land? Would the revived Ku Klux Klan and other white supremacists gain a foothold in the metropolitan area?

And what of gender politics? Would ratification (in 1920) of the women's suffrage amendment turn the gender order upside down (as conservatives feared) or (as liberals hoped) give progressive legislation a boost? Would efforts by John Sumner's Society for the Suppression of Vice succeed in extending the sway of the Comstock Laws by arresting (in 1920) the publishers of *Ulysses*? Or would Margaret Sanger's revolt against repressive moralizing spill over into a wider rejection of censorship?

And what of religious politics? The Klan was as antagonistic to Catholicism as to people of color. Anti-Semitism was on the rise. And in 1920 an old fissure in metropolitan Protestantism widened as modernist theologians clashed with those who stressed certain fundamentals of belief. The modernists and fundamentalists also differed on the legitimacy of New York urban culture, the former applauding it, the latter devoting themselves to "*Fighting the Devil in Modern Babylon*."

Nowhere would these contending forces overlap more than in the looming struggle over prohibition. The Eighteenth Amendment would go into effect on January 16, 1920. How would prohibition play out in a city that had fought like a wildcat to block its passage? Would banning liquor usher in a new era of clean living, improved morals, and a saloon-free (and maybe even a Tammany-free) city, as "dry" proponents hoped? Or, as "wet" opponents worried, mightn't it lead to widespread evasion, massive corruption, and the development of a gigantic black market?

THIS ASSESSMENT OF HOW CONTEMPORARIES PONDERED THE FUTURE highlights the plasticity of their moment, and reminds us of paths not taken. It has other advantages. Attending more or less simultaneously to possible reconfigurations of the city's economy and culture, its polity and society, its demography and ecology, and its infrastructure and architecture stresses the sectors' interdependency, and enables a broad-spectrum analysis that avoids unduly privileging one factor over others. Tracking the conflicts between (and within) classes, ethnic groups, races, genders, and religions similarly ensures awareness of the tremendous complexity and dynamism of New York's civil society.

But all this focus on components and contentions has one serious drawback. It threatens to miss the whole for the parts, the forest for the trees, the city for its citizens.

John Dewey had worried about the perils of pluralism. He heartily endorsed maximizing autonomy for the nation's cultural subsets, but was concerned that excessive fragmentation might explode the polity, that diversity might overwhelm unity. The US, though exemplary in having assembled (if unintentionally) a substantial sampling of the world's peoples, had been factious from its foundation, and indeed had shattered into civil war. Yet since that rainy evening in 1898 that celebrated the concatenation of a huge number of wildly diverse peoples into a consolidated mega-city, there had been no signs of potential fracturing. While the new flag of Greater New York that was raised that night with such fanfare was hardly an object of veneration—probably few in the throng could have accurately described it the next morning—a metaphorical flag waved over the jumbled citizenry who, for all their divisions, showed no interest whatever in setting asunder what Andrew Haswell Green and associates had joined together. For all their varied backgrounds, New York's 5.6 million people were prepared to negotiate their differences within the domain represented by that common flag.

This is a remarkable fact—an instance of the dog not barking in the night. In 1920, peacemakers at Versailles were wrestling over redrawing national boundaries, arguing over minority rights in new states, and debating the interplay between ethnicity and citizenship. These were not academic discussions; they occurred in a context marked by civil wars, anti-colonial upheavals, revolutionary insurrections, bloody repressions, and threatened secessions. The stakes for the European order itself were super high.

Nothing remotely as apocalyptic was on the table in Greater New York, though it was itself a "new" political entity, being a scant twenty years old. Despite those two decades having witnessed nonstop battling between classes, races, ethnic groups, genders, and religions—verbally and at times violently—the center had held. It seems not to have occurred to anyone to break up or secede from the municipal union. It appears that the ties that bound—subways, bridges, schools, amusement parks, police, theaters, jobs, water, public health, Tammany, the excitement and pride of living in a great city—overmatched the innumerable antagonisms and kept them within bounds. If Greater Gotham's first score of years had been dedicated to testing whether a metropolis so conceived could long endure, a cautious observer in 1920 might well have been prepared to say: so far so good.

Acknowledgments

As decades go by, debts pile up.

My first thanks go to those who plowed through the whole manuscript, commenting on its conceptual underpinnings and pointing out infelicities (and felicities) of presentation. Ted Burrows, my longtime comrade, colleague, and co-author on volume 1, offered astute suggestions for additions and excisions. The distinguished urban historian, Columbia professor Elizabeth Blackmar, who twenty years ago scrutinized *Gotham*-in-progress, was again my most perceptive critic, rescuing me from errors large and small. NYU's Thomas Bender, celebrated historian of New York's intellectual life, advised an important structural shift, and Steve Fraser, eminent historian of labor and capital, posed questions I've hopefully answered adequately. Also much appreciated were the responses to successive drafts by students in my seminar on New York City in the twentieth century, given intermittently at the Graduate Center of the City University of New York (CUNY).

Thanks are due as well to Professors Blackmar, Joshua Freeman, and Peter Eisenstadt, for having read and critiqued hundreds of my pages on New York in the 1930s and '40s. These were originally slated for inclusion in this volume—the second in the *Gotham* series — conceived initially as spanning the first half of the twentieth century. When it became abundantly clear that such a book, twice the size of this one, would far exceed the capabilities of bindery technology (and reader patience!), the pages were detached from what became *Greater Gotham*, its bandwidth now narrowed to 1898–1919. The severed material will appear, in due time, in the series's third volume, which will tackle the boom-bust-war years of 1920–1945.

Thanks also to those who perused the galleys and jotted down some kind words of approbation for publication, including my old friend Eric Foner (who also offered salutary advice on publishing strategy) and the estimable Phillip Lopate, Ira Katznelson, Kathryn Kish Sklar, Louise Mirrer, and Kevin Baker.

Thanks, too, to friends and colleagues who responded graciously to requests for an evaluation of specific chapters, ones that fell within their area of interest or expertise. Among these commentators were Richard J. Bernstein, Daniel Bluestone, Hope Cooke, Daniel Czitrom, Victoria de Grazia, Elizabeth Fee, Joseph Horowitz, Richard Kahan, Peter Kwong, Harry Magdoff, Robert Padgug, Paolo Perulli, Marci Reaven, and Carol Willis.

My gratitude goes out as well to those who lent me their ears—who put up with my telling stories and trying out formulations, often around a dinner table. These listeners and verbal commentators included Marshall Berman, Paul Berman, Pablo Boullosa, Giuliana Bruno, Ric Burns, Cheryl Cipriani, Joan Davidson, Elisabeth Dyssegaard, Barbara Epstein, Andy Fierberg, Philip Hughes, Psiche Hughes, Kenneth Jackson, David Kallick, Enrique Krauze, Peter Kwong, Ana Luisa Liguori, Bill Lingle, Claudio Lomnitz, Phillip Lopate, Jeff Madrick, Andrea Martínez, James McCourt, Lucía Melgar, Dusanka Miscevic, Carlos Pereda, James Periconi, Julia Preston, Elisa Rios Simbeck, Sam Roberts, Anna Roth, Salman Rushdie, James Sanders, Andre Schiffrin, Leina Schiffrin, Arthur Schlesinger Jr., Michael Sorkin, Betsy Sussler, Bill Tabb, María Teresa Priego, Gustavo Velásquez, Vincent Virga, Anthony Viscusi, Margo Viscusi, Penny Wallace, Chris Wangro, and Naief Yehya.

Thanks, also, to those who answered specific and often arcane queries, including Emelise Aleandri, Peter Derrick, Eric Ferrara, Brian Horton, Michael Miscione, Martin Morand, Jennifer Roberts, and John Thorn.

*   *   *

Turning to the process of publication, Frances Goldin, my literary agent and dear friend for decades, battled as vigorously for this book and its predecessor as she fought for tenants, gay activists, and political prisoners. Now in her nineties, Frances has passed her agency into younger hands, including those of the capable Sam Stoloff, who now looks after my literary interests.

Plaudits, next, to the crack team at Oxford University Press that brought *Greater Gotham* from hard drive to hard copy. My editor, Tim Bent, was perspicacious and patient. Production editors Joellyn Ausanka (a veteran of volume 1) and Amy Whitmer were determined and efficient. Others who worked on building the book were Liza Grzan, Theresa Stockton, and production chief Deborah Shor. Farzana Razak updated the design. Lucas Heinrich did the excellent cover, helped by OUP's design chief, Brady McNamara. India Cooper, who had demonstrated her superb copyediting skill on *Gotham*, turned in a wonderful repeat performance. Drew Anderla and Alyssa O'Connell worked hard on obtaining images, assisted by Mariah White. Sarah Russo, Erin Meehan, and Angela Messina, the pros from publicity and marketing, are, as I write, shepherding the book into its commodity phase. And Niko Pfund, OUP USA's president, presided over a process somewhat akin to landing an aircraft carrier.[1]

*   *   *

In addition to these individuals and institutions, who've been supportive of the Book, there are many others who, in one way or another, have been supportive of its Author.

John Jay College of Criminal Justice (CUNY) has backed various projects of mine since I arrived there in 1971. During the writing of *Greater Gotham*, John Jay underwent a change of administration, with President Gerald Lynch and Provost Basil Wilson passing the torch to Jeremy Travis and Jane Bowers, respectively. Thanks to them for their institutional support, and to my History Department colleagues for their collegiality, especially my fellow members

---

1. In an era of rapid consolidation within the publishing industry, with the attendant subordination or extinction of venerable firms, it is appealing to have my book brought out by a house whose first big hit—in the seventeenth century— was the King James Bible, and whose first overseas branch (established in 1896) was planted in—where else?—New York City. It is also a source of satisfaction that so many of the books upon which I've drawn in constructing this synthesis appeared under the OUP imprimatur.

of the two-score-and-more-years club, Blanche Cook and Gerald Markowitz. Thanks also to my undergraduate students, on whom I tried out excerpts from this volume, testing its accessibility; to departmental secretary Melania Clavell; and to John Jay's Lloyd Sealy librarians Larry Sullivan, Bonnie Nelson, Kathleen Collins, Janice Dunham, Nancy Egan, Jane Davenport, Marvie Brooks, and Jeffrey Kroessler.

The New York Public Library's Frederick Lewis Allen reading room provided an ideal portal to the great repository's treasures, and herewith a thank you to Jay Barksdale.

At CUNY's Graduate Center, my thanks go to David Nasaw, one of the first to champion *Gotham* when others were (not unreasonably) dubious about its prospects. David, then chairperson of the History Department, brought me on board, and then, with Associate Provost Steve Brier, invited me to establish what became the Gotham Center for New York City History. I began by enlisting the aid of Suzanne Wasserman, a historian with whom I'd worked in the '80s when she was managing editor of the *Radical History Review*, a journal I and others had founded back in the late '60s, and which was then being run out of my John Jay office. The Gotham Center was launched in 2001, with the support of President Frances Horowitz, Provost William Kelly, and CUNY Vice Chancellor Louise Mirrer. Since then the Center has provided extensive public programming that brings the best new scholarship on New York history to the city's citizens and teachers. We also established a seminar on twentieth-century New York, co-directed by then department chair Joshua Freeman, at which I tried out segments of *Greater Gotham* in progress. In 2006, I turned over the directorship to Suzanne, who was ably assisted by education director Julie Maurer. A highly successful decade later she had to retire on health grounds (sadly, she died in June 2017), and oversight has been assumed by Peter-Christian Aigner, whose CUNY Ph.D.—a biography of Daniel Patrick Moynihan—will soon be published. Peter has added new features to our extensive website offerings (at gothamcenter.org), including a blog, and a bibliography of thousands of titles drawn from my database. Despite straitened budgets, Graduate Center President Chase Robinson, Interim Provost Louise Lennihan, and Provost Joy Connolly have kept the Center alive, and it continues to be an important contributor to New York City's cultural life.

* * *

Financial assistance for my work on the *Gotham* series was afforded by the New York Public Library's Dorothy and Lewis B. Cullman Center for Scholars and Writers, and by the John Simon Guggenheim Memorial Foundation. A belated thanks to the 1999 Pulitzer Prize jurors C. Vann Woodward, Henry F. Graff, and William H. Goetzmann; to the Municipal Arts Society of New York for its Brendan Gill Prize; and to the New York Society Library for its Book of the Year Award.

* * *

I have been fortunate indeed in being helped, serially, by a talented trio of assistants.

Stefan Fabien got the ball rolling during 2002, but was lured away by a prestigious British legal fellowship, and is now a sports attorney in Trinidad and Tobago.

In 2003 Michael Louis signed on. An undergraduate history major at St. Francis College, Mike set about organizing an artisanal workshop. He established and ran its computer operations, undertook research assignments, and as bibliographer compiled much of what eventually became a 30,000-item database; he also handled some of the work associated with my teaching duties. Over his stalwart nine-year tenure Mike finished college, went on to law school, and in 2012 departed—reluctantly, the book not having been completed—for a law practice in Dallas, where he now lives with his wife Nermeen and their children.

His place was taken by Joel Feingold, a student in my CUNY graduate seminar, whose impressive class papers and presentations led me to ask if he'd like to take over the workshop. Happily for me, he agreed. A knowledgeable and theoretically sophisticated historian, Joel served as an astute critic, offering invaluable commentary on the content and style of draft chapters as they emerged. He also undertook targeted and broad-spectrum research assignments, tracked down and corralled hundreds of images, constructed the chapter reference notes and bibliography, sorted out a variety of computer problems, and, for good measure, came up with the volume's title. I'm deeply appreciative of his manifold contributions.

* * *

In the *mens sana in corpore sano* department, grateful thanks to David Sumberg for helping me navigate some of life's rapids (while also offering sage advice on topics ranging from acquiring a mortgage to the secret of tying shoelaces). That my material (anatomical) base remains in reasonable working order is thanks in large part to the ministrations of Eric Kenworthy and Isaac Masri (also personal friends), as well as Caner Dinlenc, Leon Kavaler, Robert Klein, Gregory Lutz, Marion Skelly, and Philip Vasquez.

On the familial front, my sister Penny Wallace and her husband Bill Lingle, along with our cousins' club members Bob and Claudy, Julie and Elaine, David and Sandy, and Hedy and Henry, have been a perduring source of support and stability over the decades.

I met Carmen Boullosa on September 10, 2001, the first day of a yearlong residency at the Cullman Center for Scholars and Writers—me presumably a scholar, she indubitably a writer, indeed one of Mexico's foremost novelists, poets, and essayists. The next day the world was turned upside down, and it was some time before the seminar recommenced its operations. Over subsequent months, in the Center's congenial surroundings, Carmen and I got better acquainted, which led to love, and a few years farther on, to marriage. (Jean Strouse, who took over the Cullman directorship from Peter Gay, tells us that ours is so far the only wedding germinated at 42nd Street and Fifth Avenue, though less formal liaisons have been observed.)

Carmen hasn't been a direct influence on *Greater Gotham*—apart from inspiring me by her awesome productivity. But being half of a bi-national couple broadened my personal and historical horizons. At a moment when some propose building huge walls along the US-Mexico border, we've built some bridges.

Some of these followed naturally from living a split-screen existence between New York and Mexico City. There Carmen has provided me with a second family—her son Juan Aura and daughter María Aura, and their respective partners Aura Martínez and Alonso Barrera; a grandkiddy, León Barrera; and other members of her extended clan, including Pablo Boullosa and Lupina Becerra, and Pedro and Eliana Boullosa. She has also afforded me an entrée into Mexico's exhilarating world of writers and scholars, actors and directors, artists and activists.

More purposefully, she and I collaborated on some bi-national historical projects. We worked together on a museum exhibition and catalog called *Nueva York (1613–1945)*—itself a joint production of the New York Historical Society (presided over by Louise Mirrer) and El Museo del Barrio—that explored the centuries-long relationship between Gotham and the Spanish-speaking world. We also co-authored a book entitled *A Narco History: How the United States and Mexico Jointly Created the "Mexican Drug War."* The research that went into writing these histories directly informed parts of *Greater Gotham*.

Carmen also co-hosts *Nueva York*, an English-subtitled CUNY-TV show produced by Professor Jerry Carlson, in which capacity she interviews Spanish-speaking authors and journalists, artists and musicians, scientists and chefs, academics and architects, who live in the city, or who are passing through from Mexico, Latin America, or Spain. Constructing this portal between cultures has earned her five New York Emmies. And living in this bi-national flow has sensitized me to a major aspect of life in early twentieth-century New York, the epic clash over whether Gotham should hail or bewail its emergence as a cosmopolitan multi-national city.

*   *   *

Last, a tip of my scholarly mortarboard to the community of historians of New York City. I use the word "community" advisedly. Some think that writing is a solitary occupation, and it does require periods of isolation. But writing history also requires being in touch with a network of compatriots—keeping up with the fruits of their research, being aware of their battles over interpretation. Many who study New York's history are based in Gotham itself, where they congregate in organizations like the New York Academy of History, founded by Columbia University's Ken Jackson, the dean of New York City historians. But in scholarship, as in most arenas of life, the internet revolution has exploded geographical boundaries. Hunched over my keyboard I've been able to access a worldwide matrix of resources. My final and fathomless thanks are owed to those who have produced the books, articles, blogs, and dissertations without which this history would have been (literally) unthinkable.

References

INTRODUCTION TO SOURCES AND SUGGESTIONS FOR FURTHER READING

This book draws upon thousands of studies made by myriad specialists who in the last generation have rewritten the city's history. It is they who produced the strands of scholarship that I have woven into a narrative.

In the resource notes that follow, I have space to offer only the most truncated acknowledgment of the immense debt I owe those upon whose research and insights I have relied. The alphabetized author and date listings are intended only to suggest those works I found most valuable in sorting my way through the subject of each particular section. This approach does not allow me to differentiate between those interpretations I support and follow and those with which I disagree but nevertheless consider provocative or informative. Under these circumstances, it is more important than usual to insist that those I cite are to be held blameless for my infelicities of analysis and errors of fact.

PART ONE:
CONSOLIDATIONS AND
CONTRADICTIONS

CHAPTER 1:
MERGERS

Ali, 2010; Ayala, 1999;
Beard, 2003; Burrows et al.,
1999; Carosso, 1987;
Chandler, 1977; Chernow,
1990; Chernow, 1998;
Cohen, 1999; Dewing,

1913; Edwards, 1979; Ernst,
1940; Fraser, 2005; Garraty,
1960; Gibbs, 1984;
Goldman etal., 2003a;
Gordon et al., 1982;
Hammack, 1987; Hessen,
1990; Hoffmann, 1970;
Jessup, 1938; Klein, 1986;
Lamoreaux, 1985; Lasch,
1974; Leopold, 1954;
Livingston, 1986; Logan,
1981; Mitchell, 2007;

Morris, 2001; Nasaw, 2006;
Navin et al., 1955; Nelson,
1959; Painter, 1987; Porter,
1969; Reich, 1985; Sklar,
1988a; Skrabec, 2010;
Smiley, 1981; Smith et al.,
1993; Sobel, 1965; Sobel,
1968; Strouse, 1999;
Weitzenhoffer, 1986; White,
1982; Winkler, 1934;
Yablon, 2007;
Zimmermann, 2002

CHAPTER 2:
ACQUISITIONS

Allsep, 2008; Ameringer,
1963; Ayala, 1995; Ayala,
1999; Ayala et al., 2007;
Beisner, 1968; Benjamin,
1977; Bogart, 1999; Boyer,
1978; Brody, 2010; Burrows
et al., 1999; Cabranes, 1979;
Cantrell, 2004; Carosso,
1987; Chandler, 1977;
Clayton, 1985; Coates, 2010;

Conant, 1900a; Conant, 1900b; Davis, 1978; Dawley, 1991; Diaz Espino, 2003; Domosh, 2006; Eichner, 1969; Fabian, 1985; Foner, 1972a; Foner, 1972b; Frieden, 1987; Grauman, 1978; Harding, 1959; Harris, 2005; Hart, 1987; Hart, 2002; Healy, 1970; Healy, 1988; Hills, 2002; Hitchman, 1970; Hobsbawm, 1987; Hodgson, 1990; Hoffmann, 1970; Hofstadter, 1952; Hudson, 2007; Iglesias Utset, 2011; Irish, 1999; Jessup, 1938; Keller, 1963; Kiernan, 1978; Kinzer, 2006; LaFeber, 1998; Lasch, 1958; Lasch, 1974; Leopold, 1954; Livingston, 1986; Love, 2004; Magdoff, 1969; Malavet, 2008; Maldonado-Denis, 1972; May, 1959; McCallum, 2006; McPherson, 1995; Morris, 2001; Nasaw, 2006; O'Brien, 1989; O'Brien, 1996; O'Brien, 2007; Painter, 1987; Parrini, 1993; Pérez, 1999; Pletcher, 1998; Pratt, 1936; Pryor, 1987; Raustiala, 2009; E. Rosenberg, 1982; Rosenberg, 1999; Sanchez Korrol, 1983; Santamarina, 2000; Schmidt, 1987; Schmitz, 1986; Scrymser, 1915; Sinnette, 1989; Sklar, 1988a; Skolnik, 1964; Speck, 2009; Steel, 1980; Strouse, 1999; Swanberg, 1961; Thomas, 1998; Trachtenberg, 1982; Twomey, 2001; Veeser, 2002; Wallace, 2010; Welch, 1979; Wells, 2001; Wertz, 2008; White, 1982; Whittaker, 1969; Williams, 1959; Zerbe, 1969; Zimmermann, 2002

CHAPTER 3:
CONSOLIDATION

Allsep, 2008; Backus et al., 1890; Burrows et al., 1999; Ciucci, 1979; Cook, 1913; Flick, 1939; Foord, 1913; Graves, 1894; Green, 1893; Hall, 1898; Hammack, 1987; Hammack, 1994b; Hirsch, 1978; Jenkins, 1912; Jessup, 1938; Kaplan, 1975; Kaplan, 1979; Knerr, 1957; Kroessler, 2011; Kurland, 1969; Levine, 2002; Lui, 1993; MacCracken, 1905; Mazaraki, 1966; McElroy, 1975; McSeveney, 1972; Moehring, 1981; Morris,

2003; Nevins et al., 1948; Rosenwaike, 1972; Rosenzweig et al., 1994; Sayre et al., 1960; Schroth, 1974; Scobey, 1989; Scobey, 2002; Stiles, 1867; Stokes, 1928; Stone, 1969; Sullivan, 1995; Swanberg, 1961; Syrett, 1944; Teaford, 1984; Uggen, 2004; Waugh, 1992; Weidner, 1974; Wells et al., 1927; Wilder, 2000

CHAPTER 4:
WALL STREET

Ahamed, 2009; Alef, 2010; Allsep, 2008; Aronowitz, 1983; Barr, 1987; Beard, 2003; Berman, 1982; Bobinski, 1969; Bogart, 1989; Bonner, 1924; Cantrell, 2004; Carosso, 1970; Carosso, 1987; Cassis, 2010; Chapman, 2010; Chernow, 1990; Chernow, 1993; Chernow, 1998; Cleveland et al., 1985; Cohan, 2011; Cohen, 1999; Coit, 1957; Collins, 2002; Cremin, 1988; Ellis, 2008; Filler, 1976; Fraser, 2005; Frieden, 1987; Gambee, 1999; Garraty, 1960; Geisst, 2001; Geisst, 2004; Goodwyn, 1976; Gorelick, 1981; Grant, 1997; Hammack, 1987; Hobsbawm, 1987; Hobson, 1984; Hodgson, 1990; Hood, 2004; Hudson, 2007; Ingalls, 1975; Isaacson et al., 1986; Jessup, 1938; Keller, 1963; Klebaner, 1990; Kobler, 1988; Kouwenhoven, 1968; Kuhn, 1967; Landmarks Preservation Commission, 1997; Landmarks Preservation Commission, 1999; Leopold, 1954; Lisagor et al., 1988; Livesay, 1975; Livingston, 1986; Logan, 1981; Martin, 1970; Martin, 2005; Mitchell, 2007; Moody, 1919; Morison, 1960; Nasaw, 2006; National Park Service, 1977; Navin et al., 1955; Neal et al., 2007; Nevins et al., 1948; Norris, 1990; North, 1954; Ott, 2011; P. Lorillard Company, 1960; Painter, 1987; Powell, 1988; Pruessen, 1982; Roberts, 2007; Roth, 1983; Sarna, 2008; Scharff, 1986; Schmitz, 2001; Schwarz, 1981; Silber, 2007; Simpson, 1995; Sklar, 1988a; Skolnik, 1964; Smiley, 1981; Smith et al., 1993; Sobel, 1965;

Sobel, 1991; Starrett et al., 1938; Stern et al., 1983; Strouse, 1999; Stuart, 1901; Swaine, 2007; Swanberg, 1961; Tauranac et al., 1985; Weitzenhoffer, 1986; Wendt, 1982; Winkler, 1934; Zimmermann, 2002

CHAPTER 5:
CRITICS AND CRISIS

Muckrakers
Alexiou, 2010; Beard, 2003; Carosso, 1987; Chalmers, 1964; Cheape, 1980; Chernow, 1998; Devine, 1909a; Donnelly, 1982; Douglas, 1991; Edwards, 1979; Filler, 1939; Garraty, 1960; Goldman, 1978; Goodwyn, 1976; Gordon et al., 1982; Henretta, 2006; Hillstrom, 2010; Hofstadter, 1955; Huddleston, 1981; Keller, 1963; Lasch, 1965; Lawson, 1905; Lingenfelter, 2012; Malone, 2006; Marchand, 1998; May, 1959; McCormick, 1981; Miraldi, 2003; Mitgang, 1963; Morris, 2001; Munsey, 1907; Nasaw, 2000; North, 1954; Ohmann, 1996; Ott, 2011; Painter, 1987; Phillips, 1906; Schneirov, 1994; Smith et al., 1993; Trachtenberg, 1982; Wilson, 1983a; Zimmerman, 2006

Teddy
Aronson, 1975; Beard, 2003; Carosso, 1987; Chandler, 1977; Chernow, 1990; Chernow, 1998; Dorsey, 1995; Fraser, 2005; Hartshorn, 2011; Hofstadter et al., 1970; Jessup, 1938; Johnson, 1959; Keller, 1963; Kolko, 1963; Lasch, 1974; Leopold, 1954; May, 1959; McCullough, 1981; Mitchell, 2007; Morris, 2001; Painter, 1987; Sklar, 1988a; Smith et al., 1993; Strouse, 1999; Villard, 1939; Wesser, 1967; Zimmermann, 2002

Panic of 1907
Broesamle, 1990; Bruner et al., 2007; Carosso, 1987; Charles et al., 2011; Chernow, 1990; Chernow, 1998; Devine, 1909a; Devine, 1909b; Ellis, 2008; Feder, 1936; Fraser, 2005; Friedman et al., 1963; Garraty, 1960; Gibbs, 1984; Gordon et al., 1982; Hammack, 1987;

Hobsbawm, 1987; Hoffmann, 1970; Hooks, 1991; Huyssen, 2014; Jones, 2012; Kazin, 2006; Kolko, 1963; LaFeber, 1998; Lingenfelter, 2012; Livingston, 1986; Logan, 1981; Mitchell, 2007; Moody, 1919; Morris, 2001; Morris, 2010; Nasaw, 2006; Painter, 1987; Reinhart et al., 2009; Reinhart et al., 2012; Roth, 1983; Rothbard, 1984; Sautter, 1991; Seager, 1910; Silber, 2007; Sklar, 1988a; Sobel, 1968; Strouse, 1999; Tallman et al., 2010; Thelen, 1985; White, 1982; Wiebe, 1959; Winkler, 1934; Zinn, 1980

Other People's Money
Arnove, 1980; Broesamle, 1973; Bruner et al., 2007; Carosso, 1987; Cassis, 2010; Chernow, 1990; Fraser, 2005; Goodwyn, 1976; Greider, 1989; Gross, 2009; Hartshorn, 2011; Hofstadter, 1955; Josephson et al., 1969; Kennedy, 1980; Kolko, 1963; Livingston, 1986; Logan, 1981; Mitchell, 2007; Painter, 1987; Piketty, 2014; Rothbard, 1984; Seligman, 1911; Sklar, 1988a; Smith et al., 1993; Sobel, 1965; Steel, 1980; Strouse, 1999; Tomkins, 1970; Urofsky, 2009; Wells, 2004

CHAPTER 6:
WHO RULES NEW YORK?

Bosses and Businessmen
Allswang, 1977; Aronson, 1975; Bourgeois, 2004; Boyer, 1978; Bryk, 2006; Czitrom, 1991; Czitrom, 2016; Dash, 2007; Erie, 1988; Felt, 1973; Finegold, 1985; Freeman, 2001; Fronc, 2009; Hammack, 1987; Hartshorn, 2011; Johnson, 2002; Johnson, 2006; Kaplan, 1975; Kaplan, 1974; Landau et al., 1996; Lasch, 1965; Mackey, 2005; May, 1959; McClellan, 1956; McClymer, 1997; McCormick, 1981; Monoson, 1990; Murphy, 2008; New York Committee of Fifteen, 1902; O'Connor, 1963; Revell, 2003; Riordan, 1963; Sayre et al., 1960; Schiesl, 1977; Schneirov, 1994; Shanor, 1988; Sigerman, 1992; Skolnik, 1964; Steffens, 1903;

Steffens, 1904; Steffens, 1931; Steinberg, 2003; Steinberg, 2005; Stern et al., 1983; Swanberg, 1961; Taylor, 1966; Teaford, 1984; Thelen, 1975; Viteritti, 1989; Weiss, 1968; Welch, 2009; Williams et al., 1937

Radicals and Regulators
Aronson, 1975; Beard, 2003; Bone et al., 2006; Buhle, 1987a; Buhle, 1987b; Dubofsky, 1968b; Dubofsky, 1988; Erie, 1988; Fairfield, 1994; Fenton, 1957; Filler, 1976; Finegold, 1985; Finegold, 1995; Fogelson, 2001; Foner, 1982; Grout, 1897; Hammack, 1987; Hanford, 1909; Hanson, 2010; Henretta, 2006; Hillquit, 1903; Hillquit, 1909; Howe, 1976; Hulden, 2011; Kazin, 2006; Kipnis, 1972; Leinenweber, 1968; Levine, 2002; Malin, 2013; May, 1959; McCormick, 1981; McKivigan et al., 1996; Michels, 2005; Mitgang, 1963; Morris, 2001; Myatt, 1960; Nasaw, 2000; Pratt, 1979; Procter, 1998; Revell, 2003; Rodgers, 1998; Sanders, 1988; Shannon, 1955; Soll, 2009; Steel, 1980; Swanberg, 1961; Tax, 1980; Terwilliger, 1977; Weidner, 1974; Wesser, 1967; Yellowitz, 1965; Zipser et al., 1989

Experts
Allswang, 1977; Arnove, 1980; Aronson, 1975; Barrow, 2000; Barry, 2009; Bender, 1993; Blassingame, 1972; Braverman, 1975; Bureau of Municipal Research, 1907; Caro, 1974; Cerillo, 1973; Crocker, 2006; Dahlberg, 1966; Erie, 1988; Fairfield, 1994; Finegold, 1995; Fox, 1977; Freeman, 2001; Gilmartin, 1994; Goodnow, 1900; Gulick, 1976; Hammack, 1987; Hammack et al., 1994; Hofstadter, 1968; Jones, 2012; Kantor, 1971; Lewinson, 1965; Makielski, 1966; May, 1959; McClymer, 1997; McDonald, 2010; McFarland, 1975; Mitgang, 1963; Moses, 1914; Myatt, 1960; Nasaw, 2000; Recchiuti, 2006; Revell, 2003; Riordon, 1963;

Rodgers, 1952; Schiesl, 1977; Skolnik, 1964; Teaford, 1984; Thomas, 1969; Viteritti, 1989; Weiss, 1968

PART TWO:
CONSTRUCTION AND
CONNECTION

CHAPTER 7:
SKY BOOM

Skyline

Alexiou, 2010; Burchard et al., 1961; Ciucci, 1979; Domosh, 1985; Fenske, 2008; Fenske et al., 1992; Gibbs, 1984; Landau et al., 1996; Lowe, 1999; Rachlis et al., 1963; Shachtman, 1991; Shultz et al., 1959; Starrett et al., 1938; Stern et al., 1983; Yablon, 2004

Why Skies?

Ahamed, 2009; Bacon, 1986; Bender, 2002; Boyer, 1985; Cooke, 1995; Domosh, 1985; Fenske, 2008; Fenske et al., 1992; Fitch, 1977; Gibbs, 1984; Goldberger, 1981; Holleran, 1999; Keller, 1963; Kobler, 1988; Landau et al., 1996; Landmarks Preservation Commission, 2009c; Livingston, 1986; Mumford, 1925; Mumford, 1982; Nye, 1992; Shachtman, 1991; Shultz et al., 1959; Taylor, 1992b; Van Dyke et al., 1909; Van Leeuwen, 1988; Willis, 1995; Yablon, 2004

Builders, Engineers, Financiers

Alexiou, 2010; Blake, 2006; Fenske et al., 1992; Hendrickson, 1979; Holleran, 1999; Horowitz et al., 1937; Irish, 1998; Irish, 1999; Landau et al., 1996; Landmarks Preservation Commission, 1988b; Landmarks Preservation Commission, 1988c; Morgenthau, 1991; Morgenthau et al., 1922; New York Edison Company, 1913; Rachlis et al., 1963; Shachtman, 1991; Shultz et al., 1959; Starrett et al., 1938; Starrett, 1928; Thompson, 1912; Van Leeuwen, 1988; Weiss, 1992a; Weitzenhoffer, 1986; Zunz, 1990

Too Small?

Alexiou, 2010; Berman, 1982; Blackshaw, 1902;

Fenske, 2008; Fitch, 1977; Fogelson, 2001; Gilmartin, 1994; Landau et al., 1996; Rodgers, 1998; Shachtman, 1991; Steffens, 1897; Thompson, 1912; Van Leeuwen, 1988; Willis, 1995; Yablon, 2004; Yablon, 2010

City Beauticians

Alexiou, 2010; Bogart, 1989; Bogart, 1999; Boyer, 1978; Ciucci, 1979; Cooke, 1995; Croly, 1907; Fenske, 2008; Fenske et al., 1992; Fogelson, 2001; Foglesong, 1986; Gibbs, 1984; Gilmartin, 1994; Greenhalgh, 1988; Howe, 1915; James, 1907; Kantor, 1971; Landau et al., 1996; Levy, 1985; Peterson, 1983; Peterson, 2003; Revell, 2003; Revell, 2005; Rodgers, 1998; Shachtman, 1991; Shanor, 1988; Stern et al., 1983; Thompson, 1912; Trachtenberg, 1982; Trachtenberg, 1990; Wilson, 1989; Yablon, 2004

Too Tall!

Alexiou, 2010; Bacon, 1986; Bluestone, 1991; Bogart, 1989; Chappell, 1990; Ciucci, 1979; Croly, 1903; Fenske, 2008; Fenske et al., 1992; Fogelson, 2001; Gibbs, 1984; Gilmartin, 1994; Goldberger, 1981; James, 1907; H. James, 2005; Landau et al., 1996; Makielski, 1966; Mumford, 1925; Page, 1999; Revell, 1992; Rodgers, 1998; Schuyler, 1908; Shachtman, 1991; Shultz et al., 1959; Spengler, 1930; Starrett et al., 1938; Steffens, 1897; Stern et al., 1983; Thompson, 1912; Trachtenberg, 1990; Van Leeuwen, 1988; Weiss, 1991; Weiss, 1992a; Willis, 1995; Yablon, 2004

Zoning

Alexiou, 2010; Bacon, 1986; Boyer, 1983; Chappell, 1990; Ciucci, 1979; Fenske et al., 1992; Fitch, 1977; Fogelson, 2001; Gibbs, 1984; Gilmartin, 1994; Goldberger, 1981; Kantor, 1971; Kantor, 1983; Koolhaas, 1978; Landau et al., 1996; Lewinson, 1965; Lubove, 1963; Makielski, 1966; Revell, 1992; Revell, 2003;

Rodgers, 1998; Schuyler, 1913; Scott, 1969; Shachtman, 1991; Shultz et al., 1959; Spengler, 1930; Stern et al., 1983; Sutcliffe, 1981; Van Leeuwen, 1988; Weiss, 1992a; Weiss, 1992b; Willis, 1995

CHAPTER 8:
ARTERIES

Trains and Tunnels

Ammann, 1918; Anderson, 1981; Ballon et al., 2002; Broderick, 2010; Broesamle, 1973; Brooklyn League Committee on Industrial Advancement, 1914; T. Buckley, 1991; Burchard et al., 1961; Chamber of Commerce of the Borough of Queens et al., 1920; Collins, 2002; Condit, 1980a; Cudahy, 2002; Diehl, 1985; Fitzherbert, 1964; French, 1917; Gilmartin, 1994; Harlow, 1947; Hood, 2004; Jonnes, 2006; Konvitz, 1989; Miller, 2000; Mumford, 1925; Nevins et al., 1948; Revell, 2003; Roberts, 2013; Roth, 1983; Schlichting, 2012; Sherman, 1929; Stern et al., 1983; Strouse, 1999; Tauranac et al., 1985; Taylor, 1989; Tobier, 1988; Trager, 1990; Weiss, 1968; Wilson, 1983b; Wolf, 2010

Boats and Docks

Atlantic, 1916; Barnes, 1915; Betts, 1997; Bonner, 1924; Boyer, 1978; Brooklyn League Committee on Industrial Advancement, 1914; Brouwer, 1998; Bunker, 1979; Burgess, 2005; Buttenwieser, 1999; Carosso, 1987; Chamber of Commerce of the Borough of Queens et al., 1920; Chernow, 1990; Cresson, 1922; Cunningham, 2003; Gilmartin, 1994; Greenwich Village Society for Historic Preservation et al., 1986; Hammack, 1987; James, 1907; Kantor, 1971; Knerr, 1957; Konvitz, 1989; LaFeber, 1998; Lopate, 2004; Lord, 1976; Martin, 2005; Maxtone-Graham, 1972; Ment et al., 1980; Montgomery, 1987; New York City WPA Writers' Project, 1941; Poole, 1925; Port of New York Authority, 1941; Revell, 2003; Rischin, 1977; Rothbard et al., 1972;

Rush, 1920; Schoenebaum, 1977; Schoener, 1967; Simon, 2009; Skolnik, 1964; Stern et al., 1983; Tauranac et al., 1985; Uhl, 1985; Van Dyke et al., 1909; Waldman et al., 2002; Weiss, 1968; Zeisloft, 1899

Immigration Island
Cannato, 2009; Cunningham, 2003; Foner, 2000; Howe, 1976; Miller, 1985; Motomura, 2006; Pozzetta, 1971; Steiner, 1969; Unrau, 1984; Wells, 1906

Moving Freight
Black, 1981; Bogart, 1989; Bush, 1928; Chamber of Commerce of the Borough of Queens et al., 1920; Cresson, 1922; French, 1917; Hendrick, 2006; Irish, 1985; Konvitz, 1989; Miller, 2000; Revell, 2003; Riordan, 1963; Schlichting, 2012; Simon, 2009; Stern et al., 1983

Water
Bone, 2006; Bone et al., 1997; Church, 1913; Galusha, 2002; Henretta, 2006; Kroessler, 2011; Levine, 2002; Malin, 2013; Mitgang, 1963; Nasaw, 2000; Skolnik, 1964; Soll, 2009; Troesken et al., 2003; Weidner, 1974

Power
Bowker, 1901; Brooklyn League Committee on Industrial Advancement, 1914; Cheape, 1980; Chernow, 1998; Church, 1913; Collins, 1934; Committee on Coal and Power, 1928; ConEdison, 2001; Cook, 1913; Cunningham, 2012; Educational Service Bureau, 1960; Emmons, 1993; Green, 1989; Grout, 1897; Hammack, 1987; Hatheway, 2012; Henretta, 2006; Hirsch, 1948; Klein, 2008; Landmarks Preservation Commission, 2009a; Lurkis, 1982; Miller, 2000; Mitgang, 1963; Myers, 1974; Nasaw, 2000; New York Edison Company, 1907; New York Edison Company, 1913; Procter, 1998; Revell, 2003; Rodgers, 1998; Rose, 1995; Rudolph et al., 1986; Simon, 2012; Stotz et al., 1938;

Strouse, 1999; Teaford, 1984; Ware, 1951; Willensky et al., 1988

Food In
Bonner, 1924; Bulletin of the American Warehousemen's Association, 1916; Dolkart et al., 2009; Foner, 1982; Greenwich Village Society for Historic Preservation, 2002; Habstritt, 2009; Hauck-Lawson et al., 2008; Hyman, 1980; Landmarks Preservation Commission, 2003c; Mensch, 2007; Mayor's Market Commission et al., 1913; Sanders, 1969; Santlofer, 2017; Schoenebaum, 1977; Shulman, 2012; Slanetz, 1986; Tangires, 1997; Tangires, 2003; Wasserman, 2008; Willcox et al., 1920; Younger, 1978; Zeisloft, 1899

Garbage Out
Black, 1981; Corey, 1994; Hurley, 1994; Krogius, 1978; Kurlansky, 2006; Melosi, 1980; Miller, 2000; Mitchell, 2008; New York City Department of Environmental Protection, 2009; Rankin, 1939; Revell, 2003; Skolnik, 1964; Soll, 2009; Teaford, 1984; Waldman, 1999; Zeisloft, 1899

CHAPTER 9:
LIGAMENTS

Bridges
Ammann, 1918; T. Buckley, 1991; Chamber of Commerce of the Borough of Queens et al., 1920; Cohen, 2005; Dolkart et al., 2007; Greater Astoria Historical Society et al., 2008; Hammack, 1987; Hungerford, 1903; Johnson, 2002; Kroessler, 1991; Nevins et al., 1948; Reier, 2000; Revell, 2003; Rischin, 1977; Skolnik, 1964; Stern et al., 1983; Teaford, 1984; Wells, 1906

Els, Cables, Trolleys
Baker, 1905; Barth, 1980; Boyer, 1983; Carman, 1919; Carosso, 1987; Cheape, 1976; Cheape, 1980; Cudahy, 1995; Fischler, 1976; Goddard, 1996; Gompers et al., 1925; Hammack, 1987; Hirsch, 1948; Hurwitz, 1943; Katz, 1979; Kipnis, 1972; Levine,

2002; Moulton, 1964; Reed, 1978b; Revell, 2003; Rodgers, 1998; Skolnik, 1964; Walker, 1918

Planning the Subway
Baker, 1905; Bobrick, 1986; Carosso, 1987; Cheape, 1980; Collins, 2002; Cudahy, 1995; Derrick, 1979; Fairfield, 1985; Fischler, 1976; Fitch, 1985; Fogelson, 2001; Freeman, 1989; Hammack, 1987; Heller et al., 2004; Hirsch, 1948; Hood, 2004; Horan, 1985; Interborough Rapid Transit Company, 1904; Kantor, 1971; Katz, 1979; Levine, 2002; Revell, 2003; Rodgers, 1998; Skolnik, 1964; Stern et al., 1983; Strouse, 1999; Teaford, 1984; Thomas, 1969; Ultan et al., 1985; Walker, 1918; Weinstein, 1968; Yago, 1984

Building the System
Bobrick, 1986; Cheape, 1980; Cudahy, 1995; Daley, 1959; Derrick, 2001; Foner, 1964; Garn et al., 2004; Hood, 1979; Hood, 1986; Hood, 2004; Huyssen, 2014; Interborough Rapid Transit Company, 1904; Katz, 1979; Levine, 2002; Payne, 2002; Roth, 1983; Thomas, 1969; Weinstein, 1968

Expanding the System
Boyer, 1983; Broesamle, 1973; Cheape, 1980; Cudahy, 1995; Derrick, 1979; Derrick, 2001; Fischler, 1976; Foner, 1964; Hirsch, 1948; Hood, 1979; Hood, 1986; Horan, 1985; Huyssen, 2014; Katz, 1979; Lewinson, 1965; Mackay, 1987; Morgenthau et al., 1922; Nevins et al., 1948; Rodgers, 1998; Thomas, 1969; Walker, 1918

The Automobiling Class
Alexiou, 2010; Barth, 1980; Benardo et al., 2006; Black, 1981; Blanke, 2007; Bonner, 1924; Broesamle, 1973; Bronx Museum of the Arts, 1986; Carosso, 1987; Chandler, 1977; Chernow, 1990; Chernow, 1998; Chinitz, 1960; Clary, 1929; Corey, 1994; Dargan et al., 1990; De Leeuw, 1910; Finch, 1992; Flink, 1970; Flink, 1975; Fogelson, 2001; Foster, 1981; Fotsch, 2007; Goddard, 1996; Goodman,

1979; Grava, 1981; Green, 1920; Greene, 2008; Gurin, 1977; Hobsbawm, 1987; Hodges, 2007; Hood, 1986; Jackson, 1985; Kinney, 2004; Kirsch, 2000; Mallach, 1979; Martin, 2005; Mason, 1999; Mason, 2009; Mayer, 1958; McShane, 1979; McShane, 1994; McShane et al., 2007; Mom, 2004; Mom et al., 2001; Morris, 1996; Nevins et al., 1948; Ohmann, 1996; Powell, 1992; Rainone, 1985; Riess, 1989; Rosenblum, 2009; Rosenzweig et al., 1994; Salwen, 1989; Schrag, 2000; Schuster et al., 1966; Soll, 2009; Stern et al., 1983; Swaine, 2007; Swanberg, 1961; Volti, 2006; Weidner, 1974; Weiner, 2008; Wines, 1962

CHAPTER 10:
HOUSING

Old Law, New Law
Bacon, 1986; Bloom, 2008; Burrows et al., 1999; Fogelson, 2001; Gilmartin, 1994; Gurock, 1979; Hijiya, 1980; Howe, 1976; Jackson, 1976; Joselit, 1986; Knerr, 1957; Kosak, 2000; Lubove, 1961; Lubove, 1963; Mele, 2000; Montgomery, 2003; Nasaw, 1986; Orleck, 1995; Page, 1999; Plunz, 1990; Revell, 2003; Rodgers, 1998; Skolnik, 1964

Model Homes
Bacon, 1986; Carosso, 1987; Crocker, 2006; Lubove, 1963; Plunz, 1990; Rodgers, 1998; Stern et al., 1983

A Municipal Role?
Beard et al., 1987; Boyer, 1978; Giamo, 1989; Gilmartin, 1994; Hammack, 1987; Hopper, 2003; Howard, 2007; Veiller, 1910a

Fighting Congestion
Boyer, 1983; Foglesong, 1986; Gilmartin, 1994; Hartshorn, 2011; Jones, 2012; Kantor, 1983; Kraus, 1980; Lubove, 1963; Marsh, 1910; Morgenthau, 1991; Peterson, 2003; Revell, 2003; Rodgers, 1998; Schäfer, 2000; Schwartz, 1993; Scott, 1969; Stern et al., 1983; Weinberg et al., 1961; Wirka, 1996

Working-Class Neighborhoods: Manhattan, Brooklyn, Queens
Bayor, 1978; Benson et al., 2002; Brown, 1991; Cahan, 1917; Casey, 1996; Chamber of Commerce of the Borough of Queens et al., 1920; Chen, 1941; Derrick, 1979; Ekman, 1976; Fernandez, 2010; Flandro et al., 2008; Gualtieri, 2001; Gurock, 1979; Hammack, 1987; Henderson, 1976; Karatzas, 1990; Karvonides Nkosi, 1991; Kroessler, 1991; Landmarks Preservation Commission, 2009b; Levine, 2002; McCullough et al., 1983; Ment et al., 1980; Moore, 1981; Naff, 2000; O'Donnell, 2003; Pozzetta, 1971; Pritchett, 1997; Rainone, 1985; Revell, 1992; Revell, 2003; Rischin, 1977; Rosner, 1982; Sanchez Korrol, 1983; Sandis, 1982; Schoenebaum, 1977; Seyfried, 1984; Shelley, 2003; Simon, 2009; Snyder, 2015; Soyer, 2000; Stern et al., 1983; Thernstrom et al., 1980; Tobier, 1988; Totoricaguena et al., 2004; Varela-Lago, 2008; Varga, 2013; Vega, 1984; Vernon, 1960; Vouyouka Sereti, 1999; Wallace, 2010; Willensky, 1986; Zukin et al., 1985

The Bronx: Instant City
Ackerman, 2016; Bronx Museum of the Arts, 1986; Brown, 1991; Casey, 1996; Cheilik et al., 1977; Comfort, 1906; Condit, 1980b; Cook, 1913; Cudahy, 1995; Gonzalez, 2004; Hermalyn et al., 1997; Hermalyn et al., 1998; Hood, 1979; Jenkins, 1912; Jonnes, 2002; LaRuffa, 1988; Lubove, 1968; McNamara, 1985; Morgenthau, 1991; Morgenthau et al., 1922; Page, 1999; Rodgers, 1998; Rosenblum, 2009; Schick, 1982; Shachtman, 1991; Skolnik, 1964; Thatcher, 1996; Thomas, 1969; Trattner, 1968; Trotsky, 1930; Twomey et al., 2011; Ultan et al., 1985; Willensky et al., 1988

Housing the Middle Class: Brooklyn, Queens
Bluestone, 2011; Burchard et al., 1961; Chamber of Commerce of the Borough of Queens et al., 1920; Derrick, 1979; Foglesong, 1986; Hood, 2004; Kantor, 1971; Karatzas, 1990; Klaus, 2002; Kroessler, 1991; Landmarks Preservation Commission, 1979; Levine, 2002; Linder et al., 1999; Lubove, 1963; Mayer, 1979; Ment, 1979; Meyer, 1901; Meyer, 1930; Miller, 2000; Moore, 1981; O'Hanlon, 1982; Plunz, 1990; Rainone, 1985; Stern et al., 1983; Stern et al., 1987; Younger, 1978

Apartment Living in Manhattan
Alpern, 1975; Boyer, 1985; Cromley, 1990; Hawes, 1993; Landau et al., 1996; Montgomery, 2003; Norton et al., 1984; Osofsky, 1966; Stern et al., 1983; Tauranac et al., 1985; Trager, 1987

Housing Styles of the Rich and Famous
Alexiou, 2010; Bacon, 1986; Brooklyn Museum, 1979; Burchard et al., 1961; Chernow, 1990; Collins, 2002; Conrad, 1984; Cromley, 1990; Dearing, 1986; Gray, 1992; Gray et al., 2003; Kathrens, 2005; Katzman, 1978; Landau et al., 1996; Metcalf, 1988; Nasaw, 2000; Nasaw, 2006; Norton et al., 1984; Randall, 1987; Rosenzweig et al., 1994; Roth, 1983; Simon, 1978; Skrabec, 2010; Stern et al., 1983; Trager, 1987; Whibley, 1908

Summer Homes
Allsep, 2008; Birmingham, 1967; Black, 1981; Blackmar, 1979; Boyle, 2002; Brown, 2002; Casey, 1996; Chernow, 1990; Craven, 2009; Duffy, 1974; Epstein et al., 1985; Goddard, 2011; Goodman, 2004; Howe, 1976; Jackson et al., 1989; Kanfer, 1989; Kaplan et al., 2003; Kathrens, 2005; Kobler, 1988; Kraus, 1980; McCash, 1998; Mitgang, 1963; Montgomery, 2011; Paris, 2008; Randall, 1987; Richman, 1998; Rossano, 1984; Sloane, 1991; Stern et al., 1983; Swaine, 2007; Tauranac et al., 1985; Ward, 1989; Weitzenhoffer, 1986;

Wines, 1962; Winkleman, 1986; Zeisloft, 1899

CHAPTER 11:
INDUSTRIAL AND
COMMERCIAL CITY

Factory Town
Fraser, 1903; Hammack, 1987; Landmarks Preservation Commission, 1992; Nevins et al., 1948; *New York Times*, 1913; Pratt, 1968; Wells et al., 1927

Touring the Industrial City
Alexiou, 2010; Bao, 2001; Bender, 2004; Bender et al., 2003; Bobrow-Strain, 2012; Boyer, 1985; Bronx Museum of the Arts, 1986; Brooklyn League Committee on Industrial Advancement, 1914; Cahn, 1969; Chamber of Commerce of the Borough of Queens et al., 1920; Chandler, 1977; Clary, 1929; Cody, 2003; Comfort, 1906; Cook, 1913; Dolkart, n.d.; Dolkart et al., 2007; Dubofsky, 1968b; Fairfield, 1985; Fitch, 1977; Foner, 1982; Gill, 2011; Gonzalez, 2004; Gray, 2001; Green, 1992; Hammack, 1987; Hazelton, 1925; Howe, 1976; Hudson, 1987; Iardella, 1964; Keller, 1990; Killough, 1924; Kroessler, 1991; Landmarks Preservation Commission, 1992; Landmarks Preservation Commission, 2003a; Landmarks Preservation Commission, 2004; Landmarks Preservation Commission, 2005; Landmarks Preservation Commission, 2008; Landmarks Preservation Commission, 2011; Lieberman, 1995; Lubove, 1963; Magee, 1930; Makielski, 1966; Ment et al., 1980; Miller, 1990; Noble, 1977; Pope, 1983; Pope, 1983; Pratt, 1968; Quivik, 2004; Real Estate Record & Builders Guide, 1909; Reich, 1985; Sachs et al., 1988; Sanchez Korrol, 1983; Santlofer, 2017; Selekman et al., 1925; Seyfried, 1984; Simon, 2009; Snyder-Grenier, 1996; Stern et al., 1987; Tobier, 1988; Tobier, 1998; Twomey, 2007; Ultan

et al., 1985; Von Drehle, 2003; Waldinger, 1987; Wallace, 1986; Wells et al., 1927; Zeisloft, 1899

The City of Commerce
Alef, 2010; Carhart, 1911; Chandler, 1977; Cherington, 1913; Dolkart et al., 2007; Ellis, 2008; Federal Writers' Project, 1982; Fenske et al., 1992; Foner, 1972b; Gras, 1971; Hammack, 1987; Hendrickson, 1979; Hudson, 1987; Korom, 2008; Landmarks Preservation Commission, 1992; Landmarks Preservation Commission, 2008; Levinson, 2011; Livesay, 1975; Navin et al., 1955; Nevins et al., 1948; Ohmann, 1996; Pitrone, 2003; Plunkett-Powell, 1999; Pope, 1983; Scobey, 1989; Shultz et al., 1959; Smith, 2008; Smith, 2009; Taylor, 1989; Thompson, 1912; Wells, 2001; Winkler, 1970

Department Stores
Abelson, 1989; Banner, 1984; Beer, 1941; Benson, 1986; Boorstin, 1988; Boyer, 1983; Boyer, 1985; Bronx Museum of the Arts, 1986; Brooklyn Museum, 1979; Chase et al., 1954; Clary, 1929; Cook, 1913; Cooke, 1995; Devorkin, 1987; Hendrickson, 1979; Hower, 1943; Hungerford, 1922; Jasen, 1988; Kantor, 1971; Kramer, 1996; Kroessler, 1991; Leach, 1984; Leach, 1989; Leach, 1993; Lisicky, 2010; Lubove, 1963; Milbank, 1989; Musser, 1991; Nasaw, 1986; Nevins et al., 1948; Rantisi, 2004; Roth, 1983; Schoenebaum, 1977; Schorman, 2003; Schweitzer, 2008; Starrett et al., 1938; Stern et al., 1983; Trachtenberg, 1982

Commerce v. Industry
Benson, 1986; Blackmar, 1991; Boyer, 1983; Clary, 1929; Dolkart, 2011; Fairfield, 1985; Fitch, 1977; Fogelson, 2001; Gray, 1986; Hudson, 1987; Makielski, 1966; Page, 1999; Revell, 1992; Scott, 1969; Shachtman, 1991; Stern et al., 1983; Tobier, 1988; Weiss, 1992a

PART THREE:
CULTURES

CHAPTER 12:
ACROPOLI

Consolidating Culture
Boyer, 1978; Collins, 2002;
Croly, 1903; Fraser, 2005;
Jaher, 1982; Levine, 1988;
Livingston, 1986;
Sklar, 1988a

Art by the Cartload
Ardizzone, 2007; Behrman
et al., 2003; Beisel, 1997;
Bender, 2002; Bogart, 1989;
Briggs, 1969; Brooklyn
Museum, 1979; Browne,
2008; Carosso, 1987;
Chernow, 1990; Cohen, 2012;
Collins, 2002; Davis, 2005;
Fernandez, 2002; Gross,
2009; Harris, 1990;
Heckscher et al., 1995;
Higonnet, 2008; Horne,
1984; Jaher, 1982; Kagan,
2010; Levine, 2002; Mason,
1958; McCullough et al.,
1983; Ment et al., 1980;
Mumford, 1925; Nevins
et al., 1948; Norton, 1984;
Painter, 1987; Preston, 1986;
Reed, 1971; Remeseira, 2010;
Rosenzweig et al., 1994;
Roth, 1983; Saisselin, 1984;
Samuels et al., 1987; Secrest,
2004; Simon, 1978;
Simpson, 1986; Stern et al.,
1983; Strouse, 1999;
Swanberg, 1961; Tomkins,
1970; Varela-Lago, 2008;
Vidal, 1994; Wallace, 2010;
Watson, 1992; Weitzenhoffer,
1986

Fossil Philanthropy
Barkan, 1992; Cole, 1999;
Degler, 1991; Haraway, 1989;
Harper, 2000; Hegeman,
1998; Hellman, 1969;
Jacknis, 1985; Kennedy,
1968; Liss, 1990; Nevins
et al., 1948; Preston, 1986;
Quinn et al., 2006; Rainger,
1991; Regal, 2001; Spiro,
2000; Stocking, 1974

The Bronx Zoo
Bradford et al., 1992; Bridges,
1974; Horowitz, 1975; Jonnes,
2002; Mason, 1999; Mickulas,
2003; Newkirk, 2015; Spiro,
2000; Spiro, 2009

Wielding the Past
Bluestone, 2011; Bogart,
1989; Bogart, 2006; Boyer,
1978; Brouwer, 1998;
Browne, 2008; Burrows,

2008; Davies, 1955;
Gilmartin, 1994; Glassberg,
1990; Hall et al., 1910;
Harris, 1988; Hijiya, 1980;
Hood, 2002; Hosmer, 1965;
Jaher, 1982; Johnson, 2009;
Kammen, 1978; Kammen,
1979; Levine, 2002;
Livingston, 1986; Marling,
1988; Mason, 2009;
McNamara, 1997; Morrone,
1997; Norton, 1984; Page,
1999; Page et al., 2004;
Rhoads, 1985; Richards,
1984; Rosenzweig et al.,
1994; Salwen, 1989; Skolnik,
1964; Society of Iconophiles,
1930; Stern et al., 1983;
Stokes, 1915; Swanberg,
1961; Tauranac et al., 1985;
Trask, 2012; Vail, 1954;
Wallace, 1996a; Wallace,
1996b; Wells et al., 1927;
Yablon, 2004;
Zimmerman, 2012

Universities
Avrich, 1980; Barkan, 1992;
Barrow, 2000; Bender, 1987;
Brown, 1991; Brown et al.,
2002; Buhle et al., 1990;
Cohalan, 1983; Cremin,
1988; Dawley, 1969; Degler,
1991; Dolkart, 1998;
Fierstien, 1990; Frusciano et
al., 1997; Gannon, 1967;
Gettleman, 1970; Gleason,
1992; Gorelick, 1981;
Hammack, 1987; Handy,
1987; Hertzberg, 1997;
Jones, 2012; Jones, 1933;
Lasch, 1974; Liss, 1990;
Livingston, 1986;
McCaughey, 2003; Metzger,
1961; Miller, 1989;
Mumford, 1925; Nasaw,
2006; Nevins et al., 1948;
Newt Davidson Collective,
1974; Recchiuti, 1995;
Recchiuti, 2006; Rosenberg,
2004; Rosenthal, 2006; Roth,
1983; Rudy, 1949; Schroth,
2002; Shi, 1981; Spiro, 2000;
Spiro, 2009; Stern et al.,
1983; Ultan et al., 1985;
Wertheim, 1976

Libraries
Bender, 1987; Berrol, 1967;
Bobinski, 1969; Bogart,
1989; Cole, 1979; Cremin,
1988; Dain, 1972; Dain,
2000; Dierickx, 1996;
Garrison, 1979; Gorelick,
1981; Jaher, 1982; Lenin,
1977; Nasaw, 2006; Nevins
et al., 1948; Reed, 1986; Soll,
2009; Stern et al., 1983

Opera
Beard, 2003; Bloom, 2004;
Bloom, 2005; Collins, 2002;
Cone, 1966; Dizikes, 1993;
Eisler, 1984; Fiedler, 2001;
Horowitz, 1988; Horowitz,
2005; Jackson, 1972; Kobler,
1988; Kolodin, 1953; Levine,
1988; Lopate, 2011; Mayer,
1993; Phillips-Matz, 1984;
Phillips-Matz, 2002; Wagner,
2006

Symphony
Collins, 2002; Dizikes, 1993;
Horowitz, 1988; Jackson,
1972; Kobler, 1988; Kolodin,
1953; La Grange, 2008;
Levine, 1988; Levine, 2002;
Mayer, 1993; Ross, 2007;
Serafin, 2011; Shanet et al.,
1979;
Wagner, 2006

The New Theatre
Collins, 2002; Dale, 1910;
Dizikes, 1993; Hammack,
1996; Henderson, 1986;
Kolodin, 1953; Morehouse,
1971; Salwen, 1989; Stagg,
1968; Stern et al., 1983; The
New Theatre, 1909

CHAPTER 13:
SHOW BIZ

Times Square
Berman, 2006; Bianco, 2004;
Blackmar, 1991; Bloom,
1991; Boyer, 1988; Carroll,
1998; Cook, 1986; Erenberg,
1991; Gilfoyle, 1989; Grimes,
2009; Hammack, 1996;
Henderson, 1973;
Landmarks Preservation
Commission, 1987b;
Madsen, 2001; Real Estate
Record and Builders Guide,
1907; Starr et al., 1998; Stern
et al., 1983; Stokes, 1928;
Stone, 1982; Tell, 2007;
Traub, 2004; Wertheim, 2006

Broadway
Alexiou, 2010; Bernheim,
1964; Blackmar, 1991;
Bloom, 1991; Boyer, 1988;
Cahn, 1896; Carroll, 1998;
Carter, 1974; Davis, 1991;
Erenberg, 1991; Filippo,
1972; Hammack, 1996;
Henderson, 1973;
Henderson, 1986;
Henderson, 1989; Hirsch,
1998; Holmes, 2013;
Landmarks Preservation
Commission, 1987a;
Landmarks Preservation
Commission, 1987b;
McArthur, 1984;

McNamara, 1990; Mordden,
2008; Morrison, 1999; Pilat
et al., 1941; Poggi, 1968;
Register, 2001; Schweitzer,
2012; Snyder, 1989; Stagg,
1968; Stern et al., 1983;
Stone, 1982; Travis, 1958;
Wertheim, 2006

Vaudeville
Barth, 1980; P. Buckley,
1991; Cahn-Leighton Official
Theatrical Guide, 1912–13;
Carroll, 1998; Cullen, 2007;
Davis, 1991; Del Valle, 2010;
Erdman, 2004; Gilbert,
1940; Hamm, 1979;
Henderson, 1973; Herget,
2004; Hirsch, 1998; Holmes,
1994; Howe, 1976; Kasson,
1988; Kibler, 1999;
Landmarks Preservation
Commission, 1987b;
Leinenweber, 1977b; Nasaw,
1986; Segrave, 2008; Slide,
1994; Snyder, 1989; Snyder,
1991; Snyder, 1994; Stagg,
1968; Stone, 1982; Suisman,
2009; Weinstein, 1984;
Wertheim, 2006

Of Rats and Actors
Gilbert, 1940; Herget, 2004;
Holmes, 1994; Leinenweber,
1977b; McArthur, 1984;
Miller, 1987; Morehouse,
1971; Segrave, 2008; Snyder,
1994; Stagg, 1968

Tin Pan Alley
Barnouw, 1989; Bergreen,
1990; Brooks, 2002; Brooks
et al., 1999; Brooks et al.,
2004; Cohen, 1983; Conot,
1986; DeGraaf, 1995;
Erenberg, 1984; Furia, 1990;
Gelatt, 1977; Gronow, 1983;
Hamm, 1979; F. Hoffman,
2004; Jackson, 1972; Jasen,
1988; Kenney, 1999;
Marmorstein, 2007; Schicke,
1974; Stross, 2007; Suisman,
2009; Sutton, 2009a; Sutton,
2009b; Wallace, 2010;
Welch et al., 1994

Movies
Abel, 2005; Abel, 2006;
Alleman, 1988; Allen, 1980;
Barth, 1980; Bloom, 1991;
Bowser, 1990; Boyer, 1988;
Boyer, 1978; Brownlow, 1968;
Brownlow, 1990; Bruno,
1993; P. Buckley, 1991;
Carroll, 1998; Castonguay,
2006; Conot, 1986; Czitrom,
1991; Czitrom, 1992; Fisher,
1974; Friedman, 2000;
Gabler, 1988; Haenni, 2008;

Hansen, 1994; Jackson, 1972; Jacobs, 1939; Koszarski, 1990; Koszarski, 2004; Koszarski, 2008; Koszarski et al., 1983; MacKay et al., 1985; Manbeck et al., 2002; May, 1980; McArthur, 1984; Morehouse, 1971; Musser, 1984; Musser, 1990; Musser, 1991; Musser, 1995; Peiss, 1986; Pivar, 2002; Sanders, 2001; Sklar, 1975; Sklar, 1988b; Stagg, 1968; Stertz, 1992; Stokes, 1928; Tell, 2007; Thomas, 1969; Ultan et al., 1985; Vardac, 1987; Weinstein, 1984; Welch, 2009; Wertheim, 2006; Wu, 2011

Nightlife
Asbury, 1927; Baker, 1989; Banner, 1984; Batterberry et al., 1999; Bergreen, 1990; Berman, 2006; Bianco, 2004; Bloom, 1991; Bogart, 1995; Carter, 1974; Clement, 2006; Conrad, 1984; Cooke, 1995; DeArment, 2013; Erenberg, 1984; Erenberg, 1991; Garraty, 1960; Gilfoyle, 1989; Gilmartin, 1994; Gordon, 2010; Grimes, 2009; Moses King Inc. Publishers New York, 1914; Kobler, 1988; Lessard, 1996; Madsen, 2001; Nasaw, 1992; Nye, 1992; Roth, 1983; Salwen, 1989; Starr et al., 1998; Stern et al., 1983; Stone, 1982; Swanberg, 1961; Tell, 2007; Traub, 2004; Uruburu, 2008

Coney Island
Banner, 1984; Brown, 1994; Gillman, 1955; Hovey, 1998; Immerso, 2002; Kasson, 1978; Koolhaas, 1978; Lewinson, 1965; McCullough et al., 1983; Nasaw, 1993; Peiss, 1986; Pilat et al., 1941; Register, 2001; Roth, 1990; Rydell, 1984; Sally, 2006; Snyder-Grenier, 1996; Stanton, 1998; Stern et al., 1983; Swanberg, 1961; Weinstein, 1984; Younger, 1978

CHAPTER 14:
POPULAR CULTURES

Staging Ethnicity
Aleandri, 1999; American Heritage, 1968; Banner, 1984; Bencivenni, 2003; Bergreen, 1990; Bonner, 1997; P. Buckley, 1991;

Buhle, 2004; Carter, 1974; Cohen, 1983; Conolly-Smith, 1998; Distler, 1963; Dormon, 1991; Epstein, 2004; Erdman, 1997; Ferrara, 2011a; Goldman, 1992; Goldman, 1997; Grossman, 1991; Haenni, 2008; Hamm, 1979; Henderson, 1986; Howe, 1976; Huggins, 1971; Jasen, 1988; Kanellos, 1990; Kanfer, 2004; Kanfer, 2006; Kasson, 1988; Koegel, 2009; Lee, 1997; Levine, 1988; Lui, 2000; Maffi, 1995; May, 1959; Merwin, 2002; Moon, 2005; Mordden, 2008; Morehouse, 1971; Peiss, 1986; Rao, 2002; Romeyn, 1998; Romeyn, 2008; Seligman, 2016; Seller, 1983; Snyder, 1989; Snyder, 1994; Sotiropoulos, 2006; Stagg, 1968; Stone, 1982; Stone, 1985; Sturman, 1987; Swanberg, 1961; Thissen, 2002; Thissen, 2003; Thissen, 2008; Trager, 1987; Vega, 1984; Warnke, 2001; Warnke, 1996; Whitcomb, 1988

Ragtime
Alexander, 1999; Anderson, 1982; Badger, 1995; Banner, 1984; Benjamin et al., 2003; Bergreen, 1990; Berlin, 1994; Brooks et al., 2004; Carter, 2008; Chude-Sokei, 2006; Cohen, 1983; Cooke, 1995; Curtis, 1994; Daigle, 2009; Dizikes, 1993; Dormon, 1988; Erenberg, 1984; Forbes, 2008; Furia et al., 1998; Gilbert, 2011; Gilbert, 1940; Hamm, 1979; Hamm, 1997; Harrison-Kahan, 2010; Henderson, 1973; Henderson, 1986; Howe, 1976; Huggins, 1971; Jasen, 1988; Jasen et al., 1998; Johnson, 1930; Levy, 1973; Lewis, 1981; Magee, 2012; May, 1959; Moon et al., 2011; Morehouse, 1971; Morgan, 2004; Nasaw, 1986; Osofsky, 1966; Ovington, 1911; Peress, 2004; Scheiner, 1965; Schwartz, 2007; Slide, 1994; Snyder, 1989; Snyder, 1994; Sotiropoulos, 2006; Stagg, 1968; Stone, 1982; Suisman, 2009; Whitcomb, 1988; Woll, 1989; Wright, 2003

Chorus Line
Allen, 1991; Alpert, 1991; American Heritage, 1968;

Banner, 1984; Bergreen, 1990; Bianco, 2004; Boyer, 1988; Brooks et al., 2004; Carroll, 1998; Carter, 1974; Cohen, 1983; Dormon, 1988; Erenberg, 1991; Forbes, 2008; Golden, 2000; Grossman, 1991; Hammack, 1996; Henderson, 1973; Henderson, 1986; Hirsch, 1998; Kobler, 1988; Lessard, 1996; McArthur, 1984; Mizejewski, 1999; Mordden, 2008; Salwen, 1989; Schwartz, 2007; Seller, 1983; Shteir, 2004; Slide, 1994; Stagg, 1968; Stern et al., 1983; Stone, 1982; Stone, 1985; Swanberg, 1961; Tell, 2007; Trager, 1987; Traub, 2004; Uruburu, 2008; Waller, 2011; Woll, 1989

Everybody's Doin' It
Allen, 1991; Anderson, 1982; Antler, 1997; Badger, 1995; Banner, 1984; Batterberry et al., 1999; Berlin, 1994; Brooks et al., 2004; Brown, 1967; P. Buckley, 1991; Castle et al., 1958; Chude-Sokei, 2006; Clement, 2006; Daigle, 2009; Ecker et al., 2009; Erenberg, 1984; Erenberg, 1991; Fields, 2003; Fronc, 2009; Gilbert, 2011; Gilfoyle, 1992; Golden, 2007; Grimes, 2009; Harrison-Kahan, 2010; Lavitt, 1999; Leider, 2003; Lewis, 1981; Magee, 2012; May, 1980; Mordden, 2008; Peiss, 1986; Peiss, 1988; Perry, 1987; Sacks, 2006; Schriftgiesser, 1943; Sklar, 1975; Sotiropoulos, 2006; Street, 1913; Swanberg, 1961; Tell, 2007; Thomas, 1969; Walker, 1976; Whitcomb, 1988

CHAPTER 15:
SEEING NEW YORK

Adams, 1916; Auchincloss et al., 1998; Blake, 2006; Bramen, 2000a; Bramen, 2000b; Chambers, 1906; Childe, 1903; Cocks, 2001; Doyle, 1905; Engelhardt et al., 1902; Fenske, 2008; Fifth Avenue Bank of New York, 1915; Foster & Reynolds Co., 1917; *Gate to the Sea*, 1897; Gates, 1997; Haenni, 2008; Harris, 1988; Hughes et al., 1904; Hungerford, 1913; Huyssen, 2014; Jakle, 1985; Kaplan,

2006; Kasson, 1978; Landau et al., 1996; Landmarks Preservation Commission, 1988a; Landmarks Preservation Commission, 2012; Lankevich, 2003; Light, 1974; Lindner, 2015; Lui, 2000; Merchants Association of New York, 1906; Musser, 1990; Musser, 1991; "New York, the Unrivalled Business Centre," 1902; Petrulis, 2010; Rider et al., 1916; Romeyn, 2008; Ryan et al., 1982; Rydell, 1984; Sanders, 2001; Stern et al., 1983; "Strangers in New York," 1902; Street, 1913; Sutton, 1980; Tallack, 2005; Taylor, 1988; Tolman et al., 1904; Trachtenberg, 1990; Turkel, 2011; Van Dyke et al., 1909; Wigoder, 2002

PART FOUR:
CONFRONTATIONS

CHAPTER 16:
PROGRESSIVES

The Age of Reform
Boyer, 1983; Bremner, 1956; Chernow, 1998; Crocker, 2006; Croly, 1903; Fitzgerald, 2005; Fox et al., 1993; Fronc, 2009; Hammack, 1987; Hammack, 1994a; Henretta, 2006; Hijiya, 1992; Hofstadter, 1955; Huyssen, 2014; Kerr, 1980; Kraus, 1980; Leonard, 2005; Lubove, 1963; Mason, 2009; McGerr, 2003; McGuire, 2006; National Park Service, 1989; Rodgers, 1982; Rodgers, 1998; Rosenberg, 1969; Stokes, 1983; Stromquist, 2006

Settlements and Social Gospelers
Abell, 1980; Agnew, 2004; Arnove, 1980; Batlan, 2005; Bourgeois, 2004; Boyer, 1983; Boylan, 1998; Brown et al., 1997; Carson, 1984; Center for Migration Studies, 1975; Chen, 2013; Cook, 1979; Cook, 1992; Coss, 1989; Davis, 1964; Davis, 1984; Duke, 2003; Evans, 2004; Fastenau, 1982; Feld, 2008; Fitzgerald, 2005; Fox et al., 1993; Greeley, 1995; Hammack, 1987; Hammack, 1994a; Hijiya, 1992; Hulden, 2011; Huyssen, 2014; Jewish Social Service Association Inc., 1926; Kaufman, 1999;

Kehillah, 1919; King, 1981; Kraus, 1980; Lamb, 1909; Leonard, 2005; Livesay, 1978; Martin, 2005; Materese, 2006; McConnell, 1952; McGuinness, 2012; McGuire, 2006; Mervis, 1955; Morgenthau, 1991; Murphy, 2008; Polland et al., 2012; Raider, 2008; Robinson, 1981; Rodgers, 1998; Rosenberg, 2004; Rossinow, 2004; Rossinow, 2005; Sampson, 2012; Schmidt, 1978; Shapiro, 1984; Shelley, 1992; Simkhovitch, 1938; Singer, 1975; Skocpol, 1992; Soyer, 2000; Stromquist, 2006; Strong, 1997; Trolander, 1987; White et al., 1976; Winston, 1999; Yellowitz, 1965n

Child Labor
Abramovitz, 1988; Alchon, 1992; Bernhardt, 2000; Boylan, 1998; Bremner, 1956; Felt, 1965; Fitzpatrick, 1990; Foner, 1964; Hulden, 2011; Kantor et al., 1982; Katz, 1986; Kelley, 1995; Kraus, 1980; Leiby, 1978; Lubove, 1968; McClurken, 2011; McGuire, 2006; Nasaw, 1986; Recchiuti, 2006; Sklar, 1992; Sklar, 1995; Trachtenberg, 1990; Trattner, 1968; Van Kleeck, 1908; Yellowitz, 1965

Women's Work
Cook, 1992; Downey, 2009; Dubofsky, 1968b; Dubofsky et al., 1987; Dye, 1980; Fitzpatrick, 1990; Foner, 1982; Gordon, 1994; Hammack, 1994a; Henretta, 2006; Kantor et al., 1982; Kelley, 1995; Kraus, 1980; Lehrer, 1987; Leonard, 2005; McGuire, 2006; Recchiuti, 2006; Rodgers, 1998; Rosenberg, 2004; Schneider et al., 1941b; Sklar, 1995; Skocpol, 1992; Terwilliger, 1977; Urofsky, 2009; Van Kleeck, 1914; Varga, 2013

Poverty Wars
Arnove, 1980; Beckert, 2001; Bortz, 1970; Boylan, 1998; Bremner, 1956; Brown et al., 1997; Bruère et al., 1918; City Club of New York, 1903; Crenson, 1998; Ehrenreich, 1985; Fishback et al., 2000; Fitzgerald, 2005; Hammack, 1994a;

Henderson, 1909; Hijiya, 1992; Hopkins, 2011; Horowitz, 1985; Huyssen, 2014; Jewish Social Service Association Inc., 1926; Jones, 2012; Katz, 1986; Klips, 1980; Leff, 1973; Leonard, 2005; Lubove, 1968; McClymer, 1997; Morris, 1980; New York City Bureau of City Chamberlain et al., 1916; Piven et al., 1977; Rodgers, 1998; Schneider et al., 1941a; Skocpol, 1992; Trattner, 1968; Walkowitz, 1999; Waugh, 1992; Winston, 1999

Health
Abel, 2011; Aronson, 2009; Aufses et al., 2002; Bacon, 1986; Beito, 2000; Bonner, 1924; Bortz, 1970; Broderick, 2010; Brown, 1979; Brown et al., 2002; Burchard et al., 1961; Charity Organization Society of the City of New York, 1903; Cohalan, 1983; Condran, 1995; Corner, 1964; Daniels, 1979; Department of Health of the City of New York et al., 1908; Derickson, 2005; Dolkart, 1998; Dowling, 1982; Duffy, 1974; Epstein, 2013; Fee et al., 1995; Finegold, 1995; Fitch, 2006; Fitzgerald, 2005; Fox, 2006; Funigiello, 2005; Gardner, 1974; Gordon, 2003; Habstritt, 2009; Hanson, 2000; Hoffman, 2001; Hoyt, 1967; Huyssen, 2014; Jenkins, 1912; Jones et al., 2005; Katz, 1986; Kehillah, 1919; Kraus, 1980; Kreader, 1988; Larrabee, 1971; Lepore, 2009; Livesay, 1978; Lubove, 1963; Lubove, 1968; Markowitz et al., 1973; Materese, 2006; May, 1959; Mccauley, 1992; McGuire, 2013; Melosh, 1982; Morantz-Sanchez, 1985; Moss, 1996; Mottus, 1981; Musto, 1999; Nasaw, 2006; Nevins et al., 1948; New York City Bureau of City Chamberlain et al., 1916; New York Tuberculosis and Health Association et al., 1952; O'Grady, 1930; Opdycke, 1999; Quadagno, 2006; Race, 1918; Renner, 2008; Revell, 1992; Rodgers, 1998; Rosenberg, 1994; Rosenwaike, 1972; Rosner, 1982; Roth, 1983; Rothman, 1980; Sardell, 1988; Schiesl, 1977; Schlabach, 1968;

Schneider et al., 1941a; Skolnik, 1964; Stapleton, 2004; Starr, 1957; Starr, 1982; Starr, 1985; Stern et al., 1983; Stevens, 1989; Taylor, 1989; Teaford, 1984; Thomas, 1969; Trattner, 1968; Wells et al., 1927; Yee, 2012; Zeisloft, 1899

Schools
Aronson, 1975; Berrol, 1967; Bourne, 1916c; Brown, 1991; Brumberg, 1984; Cavallo, 1981; Cohen et al., 1979; Cohen, 1964; Cremin, 1961; Cremin, 1988; Dalton, 2002; Fass, 1989; Finegold, 1985; Finegold, 1995; Goodman, 1979; Gorelick, 1981; Greer, 1976; Hammack, 1994b; Hendrickson, 2001; Hofstadter, 1963; Huyssen, 2014; Kantor et al., 1982; Knerr, 1957; Kraus, 1980; Lacy, 2008; Landmarks Preservation Commission, 1983; Landmarks Preservation Commission, 1991; Landmarks Preservation Commission, 2003b; Larkins, 1905; Lasch, 1965; Levine, 2002; Lewinson, 1965; Martin, 2005; McCaughey, 2003; McClymer, 1997; McShane, 1994; Moore, 2006; Murphy, 1992; Nasaw, 1979; Nasaw, 1986; Newt Davidson Collective, 1974; Pozzetta, 1971; Ravitch, 1976; Riess, 1989; Rosenberg, 2004; Rosenthal, 2006; Rosenzweig et al., 1994; Salwen, 1989; Stern et al., 1983; Thayer-Bacon, 2012; Tyack, 1974; Tyack et al., 1982; Volk, 2005; Walkowitz, 2010; Westbrook, 1990

A Bully Moose
Abrahams, 1986; Berg, 2013; Bremner, 1956; Broesamle, 1990; Chace, 2004; Cooper, 1983; Davis, 1964; Dubofsky, 1968b; Ferguson, 1995; Fitzpatrick, 1990; Forcey, 1961; Furio, 1979; Gable, 1978; Garraty, 1960; Goodwin, 2013; Henretta, 2006; Hodgson, 2006; Hofstadter et al., 1970; Katz, 1986; Kazin, 2006; Keller, 1963; Kraus, 1980; Lasch, 1965; Leavell, 2015; Leinenweber, 1981; Levy, 1985; Link, 1947; May, 1959; Milkis, 2009; Morris, 2010; Mowry, 1946; Neu, 2015;

O'Toole, 2005; Orloff, 1988; Painter, 1987; Recchiuti, 2006; Rodgers, 1998; Rosenberg, 1969; Rosenthal, 2006; Sklar, 1981; Sklar, 1988a; Starr, 1982; Steel, 1980; Stromquist, 2006; Strong, 1997; Vanderlip et al., 1935; Weir et al., 1988; Yellowitz, 1965

CHAPTER 17:
REPRESSIVES

Gangs of New York
Asbury, 1927; Astor, 1971; Balsamo et al., 1988; Bonner, 1997; Campbell, 1977; Chen, 2014; Critchley, 2009; Dash, 2009; Downey, 2004; Ferrara, 2011b; Fox, 1993; Fried, 1980; Fronc, 2009; Gilfoyle, 1992; Hanson, 2010; Jones, 2012; Joselit, 1983; Katcher, 1958; Keefe, 2008; Kwong, 1979; Light, 1974; Lui, 2000; McIllwain, 1997a; McIllwain, 1997b; Monkkonen, 2001; Nelli, 1976; Nown, 1987; Orsi, 1985; Pozzetta, 1971; Rockaway, 2000; Seligman, 2016; Sims, 2006; Terwilliger, 1977; Tosches, 2005; Turner, 1909b; Welch, 2009

Cops and Robbers
Arons, 2008; Asbury, 1927; Astor, 1971; Bingham, 1908; Block, 1994; Critchley, 2009; Czitrom, 1991; Dash, 2007; Dash, 2009; Downey, 2004; Finegold, 1995; Fosdick, 1915; Fosdick, 1920; Fox, 1993; Hanson, 2010; Inciardi et al., 1977; Johnson, 2003; Johnson, 2002; Jones, 2012; Keefe, 2008; Kwong, 1979; Landmarks Preservation Commission, 1978; Lardner et al., 2000; Levine, 1971; McAdoo, 1906; Monkkonen, 2001; Moss, 1897; Nevins et al., 1948; *New Yorker*, 1960; Nown, 1987; O'Connor, 1993; Paddon, 1920; Schiesl, 1977; Sims, 2006; Steinberg, 2003; Steinberg, 2004; Stern et al., 1983; Thale, 1995; Thale, 2004; Thale, 2007; Thomas, 1969; Tosches, 2005; Turner, 1909b; Veiller, 1910b; Walsh, 1974

Vice and Vigilantes
Felt, 1973; Gilfoyle, 1986; Johnson, 2002; Mackey, 2005; Steinberg, 2003

Prostitution
Alexander, 1995; Anderson, 1982; Berman, 2006; Bianco, 2004; Bingham, 1911; Boyer, 1978; Bristow, 1982; Chernow, 1998; Cockburn, 2006; Committee of Fourteen, 1916; Connelly, 1980; Czitrom, 1991; Czitrom, 2016; D'Emilio et al., 1988; De Young, 1983; Donovan, 2006; Feldman, 1967; Felt, 1973; Fosdick, 1956; Fronc, 2009; Gardner, 1974; Gilfoyle, 1986; Gilfoyle, 1989; Gilfoyle, 1992; Goren, 1970; Grittner, 1990; Hobson, 1998; Howe, 1976; Johnson, 2002; Johnson, 2006; Jones, 2012; Joseph, 1986; Keefe, 2008; Keire, 1997; Keire, 2001; Kneeland, 1913; Kunzel, 1995; Lerner, 1999; Lubove, 1963; Lui, 2000; Mackey, 2005; May, 1980; Peters, 1918; Robertson, 2002; Robertson, 2005; Rockefeller, 1910; Roe, 1979; Rosen, 1982; Schenkel, 1990; Sealander, 1997; Sloat, 2002; Tell, 2007; Turner, 1909a; Turner, 1909b; Welch, 2009

Gambling
Alexander, 1999; Asbury, 1927; Asbury, 1938; Barth, 1980; Benson, 1989; Bruno, 2012; Cohen, 2006; Czitrom, 1991; Dargan et al., 1990; Dash, 2007; Flynt, 1907; Fried, 1980; Gilfoyle, 1989; Goodman, 1979; Gorn, 1986; Graham, 1952; Haller, 1990; Haller, 1991; Hammack, 1987; Henderson, 1976; Josephson et al., 1969; Katcher, 1958; Keefe, 2008; Logan, 1970; McIllwain, 1997a; McIllwain, 1997b; Nasaw, 1993; New-York Historical Society et al., 1980; O'Connor, 1963; Perry, 1987; Phillips, 1905; Pietrusza, 2003; Pilat et al., 1941; Reisler, 2002; Richardson, 1970; Riess, 1988a; Riess, 1988b; Riess, 1989; Riess, 1999; Riess, 2011; Sante, 1947; Steinberg, 2003; Steinberg, 2004; Stone, 1982; Sullivan, 1904; Thornley, 2000; Tosches, 2005; Trager, 1987; Valentine, 1947; Welch, 2009; Wesser, 1967

Drink
Asbury, 1927; Billings et al., 1905; Boyer, 1978; Critchley,

2009; Davis, 2006; Downey, 2004; Fronc, 2009; Gilfoyle, 1986; Hofstadter, 1955; Johnson, 2003; Katcher, 1958; Keefe, 2008; Kerr, 1985; Lerner, 1999; Levine, 1983; Levine, 1985; Light, 1974; McIllwain, 1997a; Okrent, 2010; Peiss, 1986; Rumbarger, 1989; Sante, 1947; Steinberg, 2003; Thomas, 1969; Timberlake, 1963; Tosches, 2005; Turner, 1909b

Drugs
Bonner, 1997; Boullosa et al., 2015; Campbell, 1977; Chen, 2014; Courtwright, 2001; Donati, 2010; Hanson, 2010; Jonnes, 1996; Keire, 1998; Light, 1974; Lui, 2000; McIllwain, 1997a; McIllwain, 1997b; Mensch, 1983; Musto, 1997; Musto, 1999; Schlieffelin & Co. New York, 1894; Schneider, 2008; Seligman, 2016; Spillane, 1999; Spillane, 2000; Young, 1961

CHAPTER 18:
UNION TOWN

Labor Day
Buhle, 1999; Dubofsky, 1968b; Finegold, 1985; Fitch, 2006; Foner, 1964; Gordon et al., 1982; Greene, 1998; Hammack, 1987; Hobsbawm, 1987; Hulden, 2011; Hurwitz, 1943; Irish, 1985; Lawbaugh et al., 1971–72; Leiter, 1957; Liazos, 1998; Livesay, 1978; Lorwin, 1924; McKivigan et al., 1996; Mendel, 1989; Mendel, 2003; Painter, 1987; Peiss, 1986; Rischin, 1977; Schlüter, 1910; Sklar, 1988a; Starrett et al., 1938; Yellowitz, 1965

Builders and Printers
Alexiou, 2010; Buhle, 1999; Butler, 2006; Clarkin, 1903; Commons, 1904; Delaney, 1983; Dubofsky, 1968b; Farley, 1903; Fine, 1995; Fitch, 2006; Foner, 1964; Galenson, 1983; Haber, 1930; Hulden, 2011; Hutchinson, 1970; Irish, 1985; Jacobs, 2006; Lawbaugh et al., 1971–72; Mendel, 2003; Morgan, 1930; Palladino, 2005; Powell, 1926; Rasenberger, 2004; Rischin, 1977; Robertson et al., 1996;

Seidman, 1938; Starrett et al., 1938; Starrett, 1928; Stevens, 1913; Winslow, 1913; Woodiwiss, 2001

Bang the Bell, Jack, I'm on Board
Arnesen, 2006; Barnett, 1916; Buhle, 1999; Cooper, 1987; Curran, 1978; Dubofsky, 1968b; Dubofsky et al., 1987; Dye, 1980; Erie, 1988; Fenton, 1957; Fitch, 2006; Foner, 1964; Gordon et al., 1982; Hammack, 1987; Higham, 1955; Hulden, 2011; Livesay, 1978; McKivigan et al., 1996; Mendel, 2003; Pozzetta, 1971; Ritterband, 2001; Terwilliger, 1977

Open-Shop Warriors
Alexiou, 2010; Buhle, 1999; Butler, 2006; Clarkin, 1903; Commons, 1904; Delaney, 1983; Dubofsky, 1968b; Farley, 1903; Fitch, 2006; Foner, 1964; Galenson, 1983; Haber, 1930; Hulden, 2011; Hutchinson, 1970; Irish, 1999; Jacobs, 2006; Lawbaugh et al., 1971–72; Livesay, 1978; Lorwin, 1924; Mendel, 2003; Morgan, 1930; Palladino, 2005; Powell, 1926; Rasenberger, 2004; Rischin, 1977; Robertson et al., 1996; Seidman, 1938; Starrett et al., 1938; Starrett, 1928; Stevens, 1913; Winslow, 1913; Woodiwiss, 2001

Let's Make a Deal
Chernow, 1998; Davies, 1982; Dubofsky, 1988; Feldberg, 1980; Fine, 1962; Foner, 1964; Gompers et al., 1925; Gordon et al., 1982; Hobsbawm, 1987; Hulden, 2011; Jessup, 1938; Kantor et al., 1982; Kolko, 1963; Kurland, 1971; Kwolek-Folland, 1994; Lasch, 1974; Levinson, 1935; Livesay, 1978; McGinley, 1949; Mitchell, 2007; Sandler, 1979; Strom, 1992; Weinstein, 1968

Hardball
Bernhardt, 2000; Brenner et al., 2009; Brody, 1998; Brouwer, 1989; Bunker, 1980-83; Fine, 1995; Fitch, 2006; Foner, 1964; Fredericks, 1905; Garraty, 1960; Gordon et al., 1982;

Hobsbawm, 1987; Huyssen, 2011; Kolko, 1963; Kurland, 1971; Lawbaugh et al., 1971–72; Levinson, 1935; Livesay, 1978; McGinley, 1949; Norwood, 1994; Norwood, 2002; Russell, 1966; Smith, 2003b; Terwilliger, 1977

Italians
Barnes, 1915; Bell, 1961; Boyer, 1947; Burnstein, 1993; Corey, 1994; Fenton, 1957; LaGumina et al., 2000; Levinson, 1935; Mondello, 2005; Montgomery, 1987; Nelli, 1976; Nelson, 1988; New York City WPA Writers' Project, 1941; Poole, 1925; Pozzetta, 1971; Smith, 2003b; Terwilliger, 1977; Winslow, 1998; Winslow, 2003

Jews
Asher, 1976; Bender, 2004; Buhle et al., 1990; Buhle, 1987a; Buhle, 1999; Cooper, 1987; DeVault, 2004; Dubofsky, 1968b; Dye, 1980; Fenton, 1957; Fitch, 2006; Foner, 1964; Green, 1992; Green, 1997; Gurock, 1998; Hammack, 1987; Hardy, 1935; Herberg, 1952; Howe, 1976; Hulden, 2011; Katz, 2011; Kipnis, 1972; Kosak, 1987; Kosak, 2000; Leinenweber, 1968; Livesay, 1978; Lorwin, 1924; Manor, 2009; Mendel, 1989; Mendel, 2003; Michels, 2000; Michels, 2005; Oneal, 1910; Orleck, 1995; Parmet, 2005; Pope, 1905; Pozzetta, 1971; Rand School of Social Science, 1916; Rischin, 1977; Sachar, 1992; Schappes, 1977; Schlüter, 1910; Schneider, 1994; Shuldiner, 1999; Sorin, 1985; Soyer, 2001; Stowell, 1918; Terwilliger, 1977; Waldinger, 1987; Yellowitz, 1965; Yellowitz, 1978

CHAPTER 19:
RADICALS

Jewish Radicals
Aronowitz, 1973; Ascher, 2004; Avrich, 1980; Avrich, 1988; Avrich et al., 2012; Bender, 1987; Boylan, 1998; Buhle, 1987a; Buhle, 1987b; Camp, 1995; Chalmers, 1914; Cohen, 1972; Davis, 1964; Donner, 1990; Dubofsky,

1968a; Dye, 1980; Fink, 1997; Foner, 1982; Frankel, 1981; Fraser, 1991; Glassgold, 2001; Goldberg, 2013; Goldman et al., 2003b; Gornick, 2011; Gray, 1979; Green, 1988; Hammack, 1987; Herberg, 1952; Hillquit, 1909; Hobsbawm, 1987; Howe, 1976; Jacobs, 1992; Jaffe, 1972; Johnson, 2003; Jones, 2012; Judge, 1992; Katz, 2011; Kazin, 2011; Kessner, 1977; Kipnis, 1972; Kotzin, 1998; Kraus, 1980; Lears, 1994; Lederhendler, 2008; Leinenweber, 1968; Leinenweber, 1974; Leinenweber, 1977a; Leinenweber, 1981; Lipsky, 2013; May, 1959; McSeveney, 1972; Mendes, 2014; Michels, 2005; Miller, 1990; Morgan, 1988; Orleck, 1995; Painter, 1987; Penkower, 2004; Poole, 1944; Pratt, 1979; Raffel, 2002; Recchiuti, 1995; Ribak, 2012a; Rischin, 1977; Rischin, 1986; Sanders, 1988; Shannon, 1955; Silver, 2008; Skolnik, 1964; Steel, 1980; Sumner, 1913; Tax, 1980; Terwilliger, 1977; Thompson, 1966; Vega, 1984; Von Drehle, 2003; Wertheim, 1976; Wexler, 1984; Yellowitz, 1965; Zipser et al., 1989

Italian Sovversivi
Baxandall, 1988; Bencivenni, 2011; Binder et al., 1995; Buhle et al., 1990; Buhle, 1987a; Buhle, 1999; Camp, 1995; Cannistraro et al., 2003; Donnelly, 1982; Dubofsky, 1968b; Dubofsky, 1988; Dubofsky et al., 1987; Durante et al., 2014; Fenton, 1957; Fitch, 2006; Foner, 1982; Furio, 1979; Gabaccia, 1986; Gabaccia, 1988; Gallagher, 1988; Guglielmo, 2010; Kazin, 2011; Kessner, 1977; Livesay, 1978; Lorwin, 1924; Morgan, 1988; Moses, 2015; Pernicone, 1999; Pernicone, 2005; Pozzetta, 1971; Salerno, 2003; Salerno, 2005; Tax, 1980; Terwilliger, 1977; Topp, 1996; Vecoli, 1976; Vecoli, 1983; Vecoli, 1988; Vellon, 2014; Zipser et al., 1989

Uprising in the Needle Trades
Asbury, 1927; Blumenson, 1949; Boylan, 1998;

Cannistraro et al., 2003; Chernow, 1990; Dubofsky, 1968b; Dubofsky et al., 1987; DuBois, 1987; Dye, 1980; Epstein, 1965; Fenton, 1957; Foner, 1982; Fraser, 1991; Frieburger, 1980; Fried, 1980; Furio, 1979; Gallagher, 1988; Goldberg, 2013; Goodman, 1979; Gorelick, 1981; Goren, 1970; Greenwald, 2005; Guglielmo, 2010; Hammack, 1987; Herberg, 1952; Howe, 1976; Huyssen, 2014; Jensen, 1996; Joselit, 1983; Katz, 2011; Kosak, 2000; Landmarks Preservation Commission, 2003a; Lehrer, 1987; Leinenweber, 1977a; Lerner, 1981; Lewinson, 1965; Lipsky, 2013; Lorwin, 1924; Orleck, 1995; Painter, 1987; Perry, 1987; Pratt, 1979; Sanders, 1988; Scheier, 1954; Seller, 1986; Shavelson et al., 1982; Tax, 1980; Terwilliger, 1977; Thomas, 1969; Von Drehle, 2003; Waldinger, 1987; Yellowitz, 1965; Zipser et al., 1989

Triangle and Tammany
Brownlow, 1990; Colburn, 1983; Cremin, 1988; Czitrom, 1991; Downey, 2009; Dubofsky et al., 1987; Dye, 1980; Erie, 1988; Finan, 2002; Foner, 1982; Furio, 1979; Goldberg, 2013; Greenwald, 2005; Handlin, 1958; Henderson, 1976; Hodgson, 1990; Howe, 1976; Huthmacher, 1968; Huyssen, 2014; Jensen, 1996; Josephson et al., 1969; Levy, 1985; Martin, 1976; Morison, 1960; Painter, 1987; Perry, 1987; Rodgers, 1998; Schmitz, 2001; Slayton, 2001; Stein, 1962; Tax, 1980; Von Drehle, 2003; Weiss, 1968; Yellowitz, 1965; Zinn, 1972

Wobblies and Socialists
Bencivenni, 2003; Best, 1914; Buhle et al., 1990; Buhle, 1987b; Buhle, 1999; Cannistraro et al., 2003; Chace, 2004; Clary, 1929; Draper, 1957; Dubofsky, 1968b; Dubofsky, 1987; Dubofsky, 1988; Durante et al., 2014; Fenton, 1957; Foner, 1950; Foner, 1965; Foner, 1982; Fraser, 1991; Furio, 1979; Gallagher, 1988; Goldberg, 2013; Golin, 1988;

Greenwald, 2005; Grimes, 2009; Guglielmo, 2010; Herberg, 1952; Huyssen, 2014; Kazin, 2011; Kessner, 1991; Kipnis, 1972; Leinenweber, 1968; Leinenweber, 1981; Levinson, 2013; Michels, 2005; Orleck, 1995; Pernicone, 2005; Rischin, 1977; Salvatore, 1982; Sione, 1992; Sumner, 1913; Terwilliger, 1977; Topp, 1996; Vecoli, 1976; Vecoli, 1983; Watson, 2005; Yellowitz, 1965; Zipser et al., 1989

The Army of the Unemployed
Avrich, 1980; Avrich et al., 2012; Feder, 1936; Foner, 1964; Foner, 1965; Gallagher, 1988; Hartshorn, 2011; Jones, 2012; Keyssar, 1986; McJimsey, 1987; Pernicone, 2005; Sautter, 1991; Sherwood, 1950; Wexler, 1984; Yeager, 2016

CHAPTER 20:
BENDING GENDER

Gorky
Garrison, 1989; Gorky, 1972; Holtzman, 1962; Levin, 1986; Poole, 1944; Pratt, 1979; Stansell, 2000; Thompson, 1966; Twain, 1962; Werner, 1949

New Women
Benson, 1986; Clement, 2006; Coble, 2006; D'Emilio et al., 1988; Davies, 1982; Dizikes, 1993; Dubbert, 1979; Epstein, 1984; Faderman, 1991; Fitzpatrick, 1990; Gordon, 1976; Grimes, 2009; Harrison-Kahan, 2010; Kantor et al., 1982; Katzman, 1978; Kennedy, 1970; Kwolek-Folland, 1994; Lasch, 1965; Lesy et al., 2013; Peiss, 1986; Peiss, 1989; R. Rosenberg, 1982; Sandler, 1979; Simmons, 1989; Simmons, 2009; Stansell, 2000; Strom, 1992; Werbel, 2014; Yablon, 2004; Zunz, 1990

Backlash
Boyer, 1978; Carter, 1985; Cattell, 1909; D'Emilio et al., 1988; Epstein, 1984; Gardner, 1974; Gilfoyle, 1992; Goldman, 1917a; Goldman, 1934; Goldman et al., 2003b; Gordon, 1976; Gurstein, 1996; Hovey, 1998;

Kennedy, 1970; Lasch, 1965; Rabban, 1997; Reed, 1978a; Simmons, 1989; Simmons, 2009; Stansell, 2000; Strouse, 1999; Wunsch, 1979

It Takes a Village
Beard et al., 1993; Bender, 1987; Boylan, 1998; Cain, 1988; Campbell, 2006; Dowling, 2001; Fishbein, 1982; Garrison, 1989; Green, 1988; Gurock, 1998; Hapgood, 1902; L. Harris, 2003; Hartshorn, 2011; Kanfer, 2004; Kanfer, 2006; Kaplan, 1974; Lipsky, 2013; May, 1959; McFarland, 2001; Miller, 1990; Parry, 1960; Rischin, 1986; Stansell, 2000; Steffens, 1931; Strausbaugh, 2013; Ware, 1965; Wasserman, 1990; Wertheim, 1976; Wetzsteon, 2001

Counterculture
Adickes, 1997; Antliff, 2001; Avrich et al., 2012; Ben-Zvi, 2005; Bender, 1987; Biel, 1992; Churchill, 1959; Colburn et al., 1983; Coles, 1987; Cook, 1993; Cook, 1978; Cott, 1987; Dowling, 2009; Fishbein, 1982; Gallagher, 1988; Gilmer, 1970; Golin, 1983; Golin, 1988; Gordon, 1976; Gosse, 1990; Gould, 1940; Green, 1988; Gurstein, 1996; Hale, 1971; Hartshorn, 2011; Hollinger, 1996; Hovey, 1998; Howe, 1976; Imholtz, 2005; Jones, 1981; Lane, 1990; Lasch, 1965; Lehman, 2002; Lehmann-Haupt, 1951; May, 1959; McArthur, 1984; Miller, 1990; Miller, 1982; Painter, 1987; Parry, 1960; Ramirez et al., 1990; Roazen, 1975; Roberts, 1982; Schwarz, 1986; Shi, 1981; Simmons, 2009; Stansell, 2000; Steel, 1980; Stone, 2004; Tebbel, 1975; Trimberger, 1984; Tripp, 1987; Ware, 1965; Wertheim, 1976; Wetzsteon, 2001; Wexler, 1984; Zipser et al., 1989; Zurier et al., 1988

Feminists
Abrahams, 1986; Adickes, 1997; Carter, 1985; Cott, 1987; D'Emilio et al., 1988; Goldman, 1917b; Goldman, 1917e; Goldman et al., 2003b; Gordon, 1976; Green, 1988; Guglielmo,

2010; Gurstein, 1996; Hale, 1971; Hayden, 1981; Jones, 1981; Lane, 1990; Lasch, 1965; Rabban, 1997; Roazen, 1975; Schwarz, 1986; Simmons, 2009; Stansell, 2000; Trimberger, 1984; Wertheim, 1976; Wexler, 1984; Wood, 2008; Zipser et al., 1989; Zurier et al., 1988

Fairies
Chauncey, 1989; Chauncey, 1994; Chernow, 1990; Chudacoff, 1999; Cox, 1984; D'Emilio, 1983; D'Emilio et al., 1988; Dubbert, 1974; Dubbert, 1979; Faderman, 1991; Fitzpatrick, 1990; Gilfoyle, 1992; Gordon, 1976; Katz, 1976; Katz, 1994; Kissack, 2008; Landmarks Preservation Commission, 2013c; Lynes, 1980; Miller, 1995; Schwarz, 1986; Simmons, 2009; Weeks, 1979

Birth Control
Biel, 1992; Brownlow, 1990; Chen, 1996; Clement, 2006; D'Emilio et al., 1988; Epstein, 1984; Fee et al., 1979; Fishbein, 1982; Goldman, 1917a; Gordon, 1976; Gray, 1979; Green, 1988; Gurstein, 1996; Hill, 1980; Hovey, 1998; Johnson, 1973; Kennedy, 1970; Reed, 1978a; Roberts, 2009a; Rosen, 2003; Wexler, 1984

Suffragists and Suffragettes
Benjamin, 1991; Bernikow, 2010; Brownlow, 1990; Buenker, 1973; Buhle, 1981; Dubbert, 1979; Dubofsky et al., 1987; DuBois, 1987; Ewen, 1985; Foner, 1982; Freeman, 2001; Gable, 1978; Goodier, 2013; Huyssen, 2014; Lerner, 1981; Lorwin, 1924; Lumsden, 1997; Marshall, 1997; McDonagh et al., 1985; Monoson, 1990; Painter, 1987; Perry, 1987; Perry, 1990; Schaffer, 1962; Sklar, 1999; Sloan, 1981; Sneider, 2008; Soffer, 2013; Vapnek, 2015; Weiss, 1968; Wetzsteon, 2001

CHAPTER 21:
BLACK METROPOLIS

Riot
Goldstein, 1977; Johnson, 2003; King, 2011; Citizens' Protective League et al., 1900; Osofsky, 1963; Osofsky,

1966; Richardson, 1970; Sacks, 2006; Salwen, 1989; Scheiner, 1965; Varga, 2013

Hegira
Connolly, 1977; Foner, 1988; Henri, 1975; Logan, 1965; Osofsky, 1966; Sacks, 2006; Woodward, 1951; Woodward, 1955; Woodward, 1991

Caribbean Connection
Brown, 2012; Domingo, 1925; Holder, 1987; Holder, 1998; Hudson, 2013; James, 1999; W. James, 2005; Kelley, 2009; Sacks, 2006; Striffler et al., 2003; Taylor, 1994; Taylor, 2002; Walter, 1981; Watkins-Owens, 1996; Watkins-Owens, 2001; Wilder, 2000

Jim Crow Housing
Ajarri, 1938; Connolly, 1977; Cromien, 1961; Eisenstadt, 2010; Greene, 2007; Greene, 1992; Jaher, 1985; Jonnes, 2006; Kelly, 2009; Landmarks Preservation Commission, 1971b; Landmarks Preservation Commission, 1991; Landmarks Preservation Commission, 2007; Landmarks Preservation Commission, 2013a; Landmarks Preservation Commission, 2013b; Maynard et al., 1988; Ogburn, 1909; Osofsky, 1966; Ottley et al., 1967; Ovington, 1911; Ovington, 1995; Peterson, 2011; Sacks, 2006; Scheiner, 1965; Taylor, 1994; Varga, 2013; Watkins-Owens, 1996; Wellman, 2014; Wilder, 2000; Willemse et al., 1931

Jim Crow Jobs
Browne, 2015; Faussette, 2002; Foner, 1982; Giddings, 1984; Goldstein, 1980; Gompers et al., 1925; Greer, 1976; Haynes, 1968; Holder, 1998; Johnson, 2003; Kantor et al., 1982; Katzman, 1978; Katznelson, 1973; Kraus, 1980; Lewis, 1981; McGruder, 2015; Osofsky, 1966; Otis, 2015; Ovington, 1911; Perry, 2009; Sacks, 2006; Scheiner, 1965; Seller, 1986; Sims, 2006; Skolnik, 1964; Terborg-Penn, 1985; Terborg-Penn, 1998; Terwilliger, 1977; Tyack, 1974

Jim Crow Culture
Alexander, 2012; Alleman, 1988; Anderson, 1982; Blight, 2002; Calavita, 1984; Cripps, 1963; Cruse, 1967; Floyd, 1902; Garland, 1986; Haller, 1984; Hellman, 1969; Lewis, 1994; Logan, 1965; May, 1959; May, 1980; Muhammad, 2010; Osofsky, 1966; Ottley et al., 1967; Painter, 1987; Popenoe et al., 1918; Reed, 1978a; Sacks, 2006; Sims, 2006; Slide, 2004; Smith et al., 2013; Snyder, 1994; Stoddard, 1914; Stokes, 2007; Sussman, 2014; Tucker, 2002; Welch, 1979; Woll, 1989; Woodward, 1955; Zipser et al., 1989

Black Progressives
Abramovitz, 1988; Adams et al., 2002; Alexander, 2012; Anderson, 1973; Boyd, 1998; Cash, 2001; Connolly, 1977; Dyckoff, 1914; Fortune, 2008; Fosdick, 1962; Gardner, 1990; Gardner, 1974; Gill, 2011; Gordon, 1991; Green et al., 1989; Hart, 2015; Haynes, 1968; Henri, 1975; Hicks, 2010; Johnson, 2003; Kantor et al., 1982; Katznelson, 1973; Kramer, 2006; Kraus, 1980; Lerner, 2005; Levine, 1977; Lincoln, 1973; McGruder, 2015; Ment, 1971; Moore, 1980; Morris, 2001; Osofsky, 1966; Ovington, 1911; Ovington, 1995; Painter, 1987; Peterson, 2011; Piott, 2014; Recchiuti, 2006; Rhodes-Pitts, 2011; Robertson, 2007; Sacks, 2006; Scheiner, 1965; Seraile, 2011; Sims, 2006; Skocpol et al., 2006; Skolnik, 1964; Stein, 1986; Taylor, 1994; Taylor, 2002; Terborg-Penn, 1998; Trager, 1987; Weisenfeld, 1997; Weiss, 1974; Wellman, 2014; Wilder, 2000; Wilder, 2001; Yellowitz, 1965

Civil Rights
Alexander, 2012; Anderson et al., 1999; Baker, 1998; Boylan, 1998; Brown, 2012; Coss, 2014; Cripps, 1963; Degler, 1991; Diner, 1995; Dowling, 2001; Du Bois, 1903; Fink, 1997; Fosdick, 1962; Gable, 1978; Genovese, 1971; Giles, 1976; Gill, 2011; Glassberg, 1990; Harlan, 1957; Herskovits, 1953;

Hyatt, 1990; Jonas, 2005; Kellogg, 1967; Lerner, 1981; Levy, 1973; Lewis, 1984; Lewis, 1994; Lewis, 2009; Logan, 1965; May, 1959; Osofsky, 1966; Ovington, 1911; Ovington, 1995; Painter, 1987; Popenoe et al., 1918; Ross, 1972; Rudwick, 1982; Scheiner, 1965; Sinnette, 1989; Stein, 1986; Stocking, 1974; Sullivan, 2009; Terborg-Penn, 1998; Washington, 1901; Washington, 1972a; Washington, 1972b; Weiss, 1974; Woodward, 1955; Zangrando, 1980

Harlem
Ackman, 1956; Adams et al., 2002; Anderson, 1982; Badger, 1995; Brooks et al., 2004; Browne, 2015; Bundles, 1992; Connolly, 1977; Cruse, 1967; Dunlap, 2004; Dyckoff, 1914; Gill, 2011; Gurock, 1979; Henri, 1975; Jones, 1998; Kahn et al., 1976; Katznelson, 1973; Krasner, 1997; Landmarks Preservation Commission, 1967; Landmarks Preservation Commission, 1971a; Landmarks Preservation Commission, 1981; Landmarks Preservation Commission, 1984; Lewis, 1994; Lincoln, 1973; McGruder, 2015; Morgenthau et al., 1922; Osofsky, 1966; Perry, 2009; Sacks, 2005; Sacks, 2006; Salwen, 1989; Scheiner, 1965; Schoener, 1995; Sinnette, 1989; Washington, 1907; White, 2015

New Negroes
Anderson, 1973; Anderson, 1982; Dubofsky et al., 1987; Fink, 1997; Fishbein, 1982; Foner, 1982; Grant, 2008; Harrison et al., 2001; James, 1999; Kersten, 2007; Kornweibel, 1975; Kornweibel, 2002; Levy, 1973; McGruder, 2015; Perry, 2009; Pfeffer, 1990; Rudwick, 1968; Rudwick, 1982; Taylor, 2002; Zangrando, 1980

CHAPTER 22:
INSURGENT ART

Ash Can Realists
Auchincloss et al., 1998; Barth, 1980; Beard et al., 1987; Belgrad, 2001; Berman, 1990; Bremner,

1956; Brown, 1955; Burchard et al., 1961; Colburn et al., 1983; Conrad, 1984; Coyle et al., 2007; Doezema, 1992; Gorn, 1986; Green, 1988; Homer et al., 1969; Kasson, 1978; Kleeblatt et al., 1991; Lindner, 2015; May, 1959; Mohl, 1971; Perlman, 1979; Perlman, 1988; Ramirez et al., 1990; Scott et al., 1999; St. John, 1965; Tallack, 2005; Tarbell, 1980; Taylor, 1992a; Trachtenberg, 1990; Trager, 1987; Watson, 1992; Watson, 1991; Wertheim, 1976; Zurier, 2006; Zurier et al., 1995

Modernists' Metropolis
Abrahams, 1986; Bender, 1987; Boelhower et al., 2004; Bramen, 2000a; Bramen, 2000b; Bremner, 1956; Brown, 1955; Burchard et al., 1961; Conrad, 1984; Corn, 1988; Cullen, 2009; Domosh, 1985; Fitzpatrick, 2009; Giamo, 1989; Green, 1988; Harris, 1998; K. Hoffman, 2004; Homer, 1977; Kasson, 1978; Kleeblatt et al., 1991; Kozloff et al., 2002; Levine, 1988; Lindner, 2015; Lukitsh, 2006; Mancini, 1998; May, 1959; Messenger, 2011; Norman, 1990; Scott et al., 1999; Sharpe et al., 1987; Stern et al., 1983; Stieglitz, 2000; Tallack, 2005; Taylor, 1992a; Trachtenberg, 1990; Wallace, 2005; Weinberg et al., 2004; Weinberg, 2001; Wertheim, 1976; Yochelson, 2010; Zayas et al., 1996

Armory Show
Agee, 2013; Antliff, 2001; Blake, 2013; Corn, 1999; Green, 1988; Haskell, 2013; Hegeman, 2013; Kasson, 1998; Kleeblatt et al., 1991; Kushner, 2013; Lobel, 2014; Lunday, 2013; Lynes, 1980; McCarthy, 2011; McCauley, 2013; Mecklenburg, 2013; Messenger, 2011; Orcutt, 2013a; Orcutt, 2013b; Orcutt, 2013c; Ottinger, 2013; Page, 2013; Ramirez et al., 1990; Reid, 1968; Scott et al., 1999; Stavitsky, 2013; Taylor, 2013; Tedeschi, 2013; Watson, 1991; Wertheim, 1976; White, 2013; Zilczer, 1974; Zilczer et al., 1978

Dreiser
Auchincloss et al., 1998; Berman, 2006; Conrad,

1984; Dickstein, 2005; Dreiser, 1907; Dreiser, 1923; Filler, 1993; Fishbein, 1982; Gelfant, 1970; Giamo, 1989; Green, 1988; Kazin, 1941; Lingeman, 1986; Loving, 2005; May, 1959; Miller, 2014; O'Connell, 1994; Swanberg, 1964; Wertheim, 1976; Zurier, 2006

Wharton
Auchincloss, 1971; Benert, 2007; Dickstein, 2005; Dwight, 1996; Franzen, 2012; Gates, 1987; Kazin, 1941; Lee, 2007; O'Connell, 1994; Walton, 1971; Wharton, 1905; Wharton, 1913

Dreams and Nightmares of Greater New York
Arthur, 2006; Blansfield, 1988; Bremner, 1956; Cahan, 1917; Daigle, 2009; Davis, 1998; Dickstein, 2005; Dowling, 2001; England, 1914; Howe, 1976; Lingeman, 1986; Lipsky, 2013; Miller, 2014; O'Connell, 1994; Henry, 1984; Page, 2008; Pittenger, 1994; Poole, 1925; Rideout, 1992; Sinclair, 1908a; Sinclair, 1908b; Swanberg, 1964; Taylor, 1992a; Varricchio, 2004; Wells, 1908; Yablon, 2004; Zimmerman, 2006; Zlotnick, 1971

PART FIVE:
WARS

CHAPTER 23:
OVER THERE?

Panic and Paralysis
Aitken, 1985; Bonner, 1924; Broesamle, 1973; Cassis, 2010; Chernow, 1990; Cleveland et al., 1985; Cohalan, 1983; Collins, 2002; Dawley, 1991; Eichengreen, 1989; Feder, 1936; Finegold, 1985; Finegold, 1995; Fitzpatrick, 1990; Furio, 1979; Gallagher, 1988; Goldberg, 2013; Hammack, 1994b; Harris, 2011; Henderson, 1976; Hobsbawm, 1987; Lamont, 1915; Lehman et al., 1928; Lewinson, 1965; Logan, 1981; Mitchell, 2007; Moody, 1919; Nevins et al., 1948; New York City WPA Writers' Project, 1941; Nicolson, 1935; Noyes, 1918;

Painter, 1987; Revell, 2003; Scheiber, 1969; Shachtman, 1991; Silber, 2007; Sobel, 1968; Wilkins, 1989; Wilkins, 2004; Williams, 1959; Wilson, 2014; Yellowitz, 1965

Recession
Avrich, 1980; Doenecke, 2011; Feder, 1936; Finegold, 1985; Foner, 1964; Foner, 1965; Fraser, 1991; Gallagher, 1988; Goldberg, 2013; Greenwald, 2005; Janicki, 2014; Jones, 2012; Kazin, 2011; Kellor, 1914; Kellor, 1915; Keyssar, 1986; Lamont, 1915; Mayor's Committee on Unemployment et al., 1917; Miller, 1990; New York City WPA Writers' Project, 1941; Pernicone, 2005; Ramirez et al., 1990; Revell, 2003; Sautter, 1991; Schneider et al., 1941a; Wertheim, 1976; Wexler, 1984; Wilson, 2014; Yellowitz, 1965

A Prosperous Neutrality
Bailey et al., 1975; Bonner, 1924; Broesamle, 1973; Carosso, 1987; Cassis, 2010; Chernow, 1990; Cohalan, 1983; Doenecke, 2011; Dye, 1980; Finegold, 1985; Frieden, 1987; Gardner, 1984; Hammack, 1994b; Hofstadter et al., 1970; Horn, 2000; Kennedy, 1980; LaFeber, 1998; Lamont, 1915; Lewinson, 1965; Logan, 1981; Magdoff, 1969; Mitchell, 2007; Moody, 1919; Myers, 1931; New York City WPA Writers' Project, 1941; Painter, 1987; Scheiber, 1969; Silber, 2007; Sobel, 1968; Unrau, 1984; Wilson, 2014

Cat's Away
Carosso, 1987; Cassis, 2010; Collins, 2002; Dawley, 1991; Doenecke, 2011; Frieden, 1987; Jessup, 1938; LaFeber, 1998; Lamont, 1915; Magdoff, 1969; May, 1959; Mayer, 1973; Parrini, 1969; Roberts, 1998; Roberts, 2002; Rosenthal, 2006; Russell, 2013; Scheiber, 1969; Silber, 2007; Strouse, 1999; Zimmermann, 2002

Be Prepared!
Bailey et al., 1975; Breen, 1984; Chernow, 1990; Clifford, 1972; Dawley, 1991;

Doenecke, 2011; Donner, 1990; Dyer, 1980; Finnegan, 1974; Frieden, 1987; Greene, 1915; Gutman et al., 1999; Healy, 1988; Hill, 2014; Kennedy, 1980; Kiernan, 1978; LaFeber, 1998; Lane, 2009; Lewinson, 1965; Marchand, 1972; Mayor's Committee on National Defense et al., 1917; Mayor's Committee on National Defense et al., 1918; McCallum, 2006; Nasaw, 2006; O'Brien, 1996; O'Brien, 2007; Page, 2008; Pearlman, 1984; Rosenthal, 2006; Safford, 1978; Schmitz, 2001; Shefter, 1993a; Shefter, 1993b; Shulman, 2000; Slotkin, 2005; Stimson, 1915; Tavenner, 1916; Walker, 1915; Ward, 1960; Wilson, 2014; Zimmermann, 2002

Peace Now!
Alonso, 1993; Bailey et al., 1975; Balanoff, 1985; Bencivenni, 2003; Bennett et al., 2014; Biel, 1992; Buckley, 1976; Buhle, 1999; Cannistraro et al., 2003; Clifford, 1972; Cook, 1973; Cook, 1978; Cook, 1979; Cottrell, 2000; Dawley, 1991; Deats, 2001; Dekar, 2005; Doenecke, 2011; Doyle, 1996; Dubofsky, 1961; Duke, 2003; Fabian, 1985; Goldberg, 2013; Goldman, 1915; Goldman, 1917d; Gregory, 2008; Hillquit, 1914; Holmes, 1917; Kazin, 2017; Kennedy, 1980; King, 1981; Kobler, 1988; Kornweibel, 1975; Lipsky, 2013; Livesay, 1978; Lusk et al., 1920; Marchand, 1972; May, 1959; McKivigan et al., 1996; McNickle, 1996; Milkis, 2009; Nasaw, 2006; Painter, 1987; Pernicone, 2005; Rosenthal, 2006; Rossinow, 2005; Scheiber, 1969; Swanberg, 1976; Terwilliger, 1977; Thomas, 2011; Thomas, 1917; Walker, 1990; Wilson, 2014; Wittner, 2015

Hyphens
Bencivenni, 2003; Brundage, 1996; Brundage, 2016; Buckley, 1976; Buhle et al., 1990; Chernow, 1990; Collins, 2002; Conolly-Smith, 2009; Cuddy, 1965;

Cuddy, 1969; Davidson, 1999; Du Bois, 1914; Ellis, 1992; Frankel, 1981; Guterl, 2001; Huggins, 1971; James, 1999; Johnson, 1968; Lewis, 1994; Morgenthau, 1991; Page, 1999; Painter, 1987; Pernicone, 1999; Pernicone, 2005; Raider, 2008; Ribak, 2012b; Schmuhl, 2016; Topp, 1996; Vecoli, 1983; Wilson, 2014

Be American!
Blake, 2006; Buhle, 1999; Chauncey, 1994; Cooney, 1986; Dowling, 2001; Dyer, 1980; Erdman, 1997; Fitzpatrick, 1990; Gates, 1997; Gerstle, 2001; Gleason, 1992; Guglielmo, 2010; Guterl, 2001; Hansen, 2003; Higham, 1984; Hobsbawm, 1987; Jacobson, 2000; Jaffe, 2012; Kazin, 2011; Lasch, 1965; Lederhendler, 2008; Leinenweber, 1968; Leinenweber, 1977a; Lewis, 1994; Liss, 1990; Lutzker, 1969; McFarland, 2001; Michels, 2005; Morgenthau, 1991; Morison, 1960; Morris, 2001; Romeyn, 1998; Roosevelt, 1891; Schneider, 2011; Sims, 2006; Spiro, 2000; Tucker, 2002; Van Dyke, 1908; Vecoli, 1996; Wald, 1987; Weiss, 1979; Wilson, 2014; Zangwill, 1909; Zimmermann, 2002; Zolberg, 2006

In Uno, Plures
Bencivenni, 2003; Bender, 1987; Bernstein, 2015; Biel, 1992; Bourne, 1916a; Bourne, 1916b; Bramen, 2000b; Cooney, 1986; Frankel, 1981; Fried, 2001; Gates, 1997; Gerstle, 2001; Gleason, 1992; Greene, 2011; Guglielmo, 2010; Guterl, 2001; Hansen, 2003; Higham, 1984; Hobsbawm, 1987; Hutchison, 2003; Huyssen, 2014; Hyatt, 1990; Jacobson, 2000; Jucan, 2010; Kallen, 1915a; Kallen, 1915b; Katz, 2011; Kazin, 2011; Kirshenblatt-Gimblett, 2001; Kraus, 1980; Kronish, 1982; Kushner, 2013; Lasch, 1965; Leinenweber, 1968; Leinenweber, 1977a; Lewis, 1994; Liss, 1990; Mabie et al., 1904; McFarland, 2001; Menand, 2001;

Michels, 2000; Mirel, 2002; Morgenthau, 1991; Morison, 1960; Morris, 2001; Romeyn, 1998; Salerno, 2003; Shumsky, 1975; Sims, 2006; Spiro, 2000; Stansell, 2000; Toll, 1997; Vecoli, 1996; Wald, 1987; Walzer, 1992; Weiss, 1979; Westbrook, 1990; Yee, 2012; Zangwill, 1909; Zimmermann, 2002; Zolberg, 2006

And the War Came
Alexiou, 2010; Bencivenni, 2003; Bird, 1992; Bourne, 1917; Buckley, 1976; Buhle et al., 1990; Carlisle, 2007; Clifford, 1972; Cook, 1978; Cooper, 1983; Cottrell, 2000; Cuff, 1989; Dawley, 1991; Deutscher, 1954; Doenecke, 2011; Draper, 1957; Frank, 1997; Giffin, 1968; Goldberg, 2013; Goldman, 1917c; Harris et al., 2015; Henderson, 1976; Henretta, 2006; Hofstadter, 1968; Jaffe, 2012; Kennedy, 1980; Lasch, 1965; Lears, 2012; McCaughey, 2003; Milkis, 2009; Miller, 2010; Millman, 2006; Mirel, 2002; Pernicone, 2005; Rauchway, 1999; Rosenthal, 2006; Ross, 2015; Scheiber, 1969; Stansell, 2000; Steel, 1980; Swanberg, 1976; Trotsky, 1930; Vought, 2004; Wilson, 2014; Wittner, 2015; Yellowitz, 1965; Zimmerman, 2002

CHAPTER 24:
OVER HERE

Johnny Get Your Gun
Axelrod, 2009; Capozzola, 2008; Clifford, 1972; Dawley, 2003; Griffeath, 2011; Jaffe, 2012; Kushner, 2013; Melnick, 2012; Merwood-Salisbury, 2009; Morehouse, 1971; Rawls, 1988; Schaffer, 1991; Tedlow, 1979; Wilson, 2014; Winkler, 2004

Resistance and Repression
American Defense Society, 1918; Anderson, 1973; Avrich, 1991; Bencivenni, 2011; Brundage, 1996; Buhle, 1999; Burgess et al., 2016; Capozzola, 2002; Capozzola, 2008; Clifford, 1972; Collins, 2002; Cook, 1973; Cook, 1978; Dawley, 1991; Dawley, 2003; Dizikes, 1993; Dubofsky, 1961; Ellis, 2001; Epstein, 2000; Fernandez, 2002; Frank,

1997; Gage, 2009; Garrison, 1989; Goldman, 1917c; Gregory, 2008; Grubbs, 1968; Hendrickson, 1970; Henri, 1975; Hillis, 1918; Jaffe, 2012; Jensen, 1969; Jensen, 1991; Johnson, 1999; Kennedy, 1980; Koegel, 2009; Lipsky, 2013; Luebke, 1974; Lusk et al., 1920; Marchand, 1972; McCormick, 2005; Metzger, 1961; Mills, 2013; Morgan, 1973; O'Neill, 1978; Pernicone, 2005; Preston, 1994; Recchiuti, 2006; Rischin, 1977; Rosenthal, 2006; Ross, 2015; Salerno, 2005; Slotkin, 2005; Stansell, 2000; Swanberg, 1976; Topp, 1996; Walker, 1990; Ward, 1960; Wexler, 1984; Wilson, 2014; Wittner, 2015; Young, 2005

Electoral Showdowns
Bernikow, 2010; Brown et al., 1997; Brundage, 1996; Buhle, 1981; Cooney, 2005; Erie, 1988; Finegold, 1995; Giffin, 1999; Goodier, 2013; Henderson, 1976; Hood, 2004; Kazin, 2011; Leinenweber, 1977a; Lewinson, 1965; Lewis, 2013; Lunardini, 1986; McClymer, 1997; McDonagh et al., 1985; Perry, 1987; Ravitch, 1976; Revell, 1992; Ross, 2015; Schaffer, 1962; Schaffer, 1991; Schiesl, 1977; Shannon, 1955; Skolnik, 1964; Soffer, 2013; Szajkowski, 1970; Weinstein, 1959; Weinstein, 1967

Into the Trenches
Badger, 1995; Bergreen, 1990; Capozzola, 2008; Chambers, 1987; Clifford, 1972; Coben, 1991; Dash, 2007; Eiler, 1997; Flick, 1935; Gilbert, 2011; Gill, 2011; Harris, 2001; S. Harris, 2003; Harris, 2006; Hogan, 1919; Huggins, 1971; Jacobson, 1920; Jaffe, 2012; Keene, 2001; Lukasik, 2008; Shelley, 1997; Slotkin, 2005; Sterba, 2003; Wilson, 2014

The Germs of August
Aimone, 2010; Aronson, 2009; Barry, 2005; Byerly, 2005; Chen, 2013; Crosby, 1989; Duffy, 1974; Iezzoni, 1999; Keeling, 2009; Opdycke, 1999; Pettit et al., 2008; Starr, 1957; University

of Michigan Center for the History of Medicine, 2016

The Potomac and the Hudson
Brouwer, 1990; Browning, 1994; Bunker, 1979; Cassis, 2010; Condit, 1980b; Cudahy, 1995; Cuff, 1989; Dawley, 1991; Dawley, 2003; Doenecke, 2011; Dubofsky, 1961; Fraser, 1991; Gage, 2009; Hammack, 1994a; Hillje, 1972; Hooks, 1991; Hudson, 2007; Hughes, 1971; Jaffe, 2012; Kennedy, 1980; Koistinen, 1967; Konvitz, 1989; Kuhlman, 2007; Mackey, 2005; Mayor's Committee on National Defense et al., 1917; Mehrotra, 2010; Miller, 2000; Mitchell, 2007; Nevins et al., 1948; New York City WPA Writers' Project, 1941; Painter, 1987; Perry, 1987; Pisano et al., 1992; Quivik, 2004; Revell, 2003; Rockoff, 2004; Rodgers, 1998; Rush, 1920; Safford, 1978; Schlichting, 2012; Schwarz, 1981; Schwarz, 1994; Simon, 2009; Steel, 1980; Sutch, 2015; Tell, 2007; Tucker, 1991; Vecoli, 1983; Waddell, 2001; Weinstein, 1968; Weisman, 2002; Wilson, 2014

New York 1919
Ackerman, 2016; Alonso, 1993; Avrich, 1991; Bendersky, 2000; Brenner et al., 2009; Buhle et al., 1990; Buhle, 1987a; Burner, 1967; Candeloro, 1979; Cannistraro et al., 2003; Castells, 1983; Chernow, 1990; Cohen, 1946; Colburn, 1973; Cottrell, 2000; Davis, 2007; Dawley, 1991; Dawley, 2003; Delegard, 2012; Draper, 1957; Dubofsky, 1961; Ellis, 2001; Fogelson, 2013; Fraser, 1991; Gage, 2009; Gill, 2011; Gleason et al., 2013; Grant, 2008; Guglielmo, 2010; Harris, 2001; Henderson, 1976; Henri, 1975; Herget, 2004; Hudson, 2007; Jackson, 1976; Jaffe, 1972; Jensen, 1991; Jobs, 2012; Kelley, 2002; Kornweibel, 2002; Leinenweber, 1977b; Levenstein, 1981; Lusk et al., 1920; McCormick, 2005; Miller, 1987; Montgomery, 1987; Morello, 2001; Morison, 1960; Murray,

1955; Nielsen, 2001; Orleck, 1995; Parascandola, 2006; Pernicone, 1999; Perry, 1987; Pfannestiel, 2003; Powers, 1987; Preston, 1994; Rand School of Social Science, 1920; Recchiuti, 1995; Rodgers, 1998; Ross, 2015; Schmitz, 2001; Scott, 1920; Segrave, 2008; Slotkin, 2005; Stansell, 2000; Stein, 1986; Vadney, 1968; Walker, 1990; Wexler, 1984; Wilder, 2000; Winslow, 2003

New World Order
Ahamed, 2009; Anderson, 2005; Bald, 2013; Brundage, 1996; Brundage, 2016; Buckley, 1976; Cantrell, 2004; Cassis, 2010; Chernow, 1990; Collins, 2002; Council on Foreign Relations, 1947; Davidson, 1999; Dawley, 1991; Dawley, 2003; Doyle, 1996; Ewing, 2014; Fink, 2008; Frieden, 1988; Frieden, 1987; Friedman, 1992; Garvey

et al., 1983a; Garvey et al., 1983b; Gill, 2011; Gould, 2006; Grant, 2008; Grose, 1996; Guterl, 1999; Haller, 1984; Hobsbawm, 1987; Hodgson, 2006; Jacobs, 2015; James, 1999; Kelley, 2002; Kornweibel, 1998; Lamont, 1994; Lamont, 1921; Lewis, 1994; Lewis, 2000; MacMillan, 2002; Manela, 2007; Morgenthau, 1991; Nelson, 2012; Pak, 2013; Parrini, 1969; Prins,

2014; Pruessen, 1982; Raider, 2008; Roberts, 1992; Roberts, 1994; Roberts, 1997; Roberts, 2002; Roberts, 2005; Roberts, 2007; Roberts, 2009b; Rosenberg, 2006; Schulzinger, 1984; Shoup, 1977; Silver, 2008; Simpson, 1995; Smith, 2003; Smith, 1993; Steel, 1980; Stein, 1986; Throntveit, 2011; Tooze, 2014; Westbrook, 1990

Bibliography

Abel, Emily. (2011) "Patient Dumping in New York City, 1877–1917." *American Journal of Public Health* 101: 789–95.

Abel, Richard. (2005) *Encyclopedia of Early Cinema*. New York.

———. (2006) *Americanizing the Movies and "Movie-Mad" Audiences, 1910–1914*. Berkeley, CA.

Abell, Aaron Ignatius. (1980) *American Catholicism and Social Action: A Search for Social Justice, 1865–1950*. Westport, CT.

Abelson, Elaine S. (1989) *When Ladies Go A-Thieving: Middle-Class Shoplifters in the Victorian Department Store*. New York.

Abrahams, Edward. (1986) *The Lyrical Left: Randolph Bourne, Alfred Stieglitz, and the Origins of Cultural Radicalism in America*. Charlottesville, VA.

Abramovitz, Mimi. (1988) *Regulating the Lives of Women: Social Welfare Policy from Colonial Times to the Present*. Boston, MA.

Ackerman, Kenneth D. (2016) *Trotsky in New York, 1917: A Radical on the Eve of Revolution*. Berkeley, CA.

Ackman, Lawrence D. (1956) *History of the Third Avenue Elevated Railroad, 1875–1956*. New York.

Adams, Franklin P. (1916) "It's a Fine Place to Visit, Yes—but I'd Hate to Live There." *Everybody's Magazine* 34: 181–89.

Adams, Michael Henry, and Paul Rocheleau. (2002) *Harlem, Lost and Found: An Architectural and Social History, 1765–1915*. New York.

Adickes, Sandra. (1997) *To Be Young Was Very Heaven: Women in New York before the First World War*. New York.

Agee, William C. (2013) "Henri Matisse at the Armory Show—and Beyond." In *The Armory Show at 100: Modernism and Revolution*, edited by Marilyn Satin Kushner and Kimberly Orcutt. New York.

Agnew, Elizabeth N. (2004) *From Charity to Social Work: Mary E. Richmond and the Creation of an American Profession*. Urbana, IL.

Ahamed, Liaquat. (2009) *Lords of Finance: The Bankers Who Broke the World*. New York.

Aimone, Francesco. (2010) "The 1918 Influenza Epidemic in New York City: A Review of the Public Health Response." *Public Health Reports* 125: 71–79.

Aitken, Hugh G. J. (1985) *The Continuous Wave: Technology and American Radio, 1900–1932*. Princeton, NJ.

Ajarri, James J. (1938) *A Black History of Jamaica: Emancipation Not Freedom, 1827–1900*. Jamaica, NY.

Alchon, Guy. (1992) "Mary Van Kleeck and Scientific Management." In *A Mental Revolution: Scientific Management since Taylor*, edited by Daniel Nelson. Columbus, OH.

Aleandri, Emelise. (1999) *The Italian-American Immigrant Theatre of New York City*. Charleston, SC.

Alef, Daniel. (2010) *Henry Goldman: Goldman Sachs and the Beginning of Investment Banking*. Santa Barbara, CA.

Alexander, Michael. (1999) "Jazz-Age Jews: Arnold Rothstein, Felix Frankfurter, Al Jolson, and the Jewish Imagination." Ph.D. diss., Yale University.

Alexander, Ruth M. (1995) *The Girl Problem: Female Sexual Delinquency in New York, 1900–1930*. Ithaca, NY.

Alexander, Shawn Leigh. (2012) *An Army of Lions: The Civil Rights Struggle before the NAACP*. Philadelphia, PA.

Alexiou, Alice Sparberg. (2010) *The Flatiron: The New York Landmark and the Incomparable City That Arose with It*. New York.

Ali, Omar H. (2010) *In the Lion's Mouth: Black Populism in the New South, 1886–1900*. Jackson, MS.

Alleman, Richard. (1988) *The Movie Lover's Guide to New York*. New York.

Allen, Robert Clyde. (1980) *Vaudeville and Film, 1895–1915: A Study in Media Interaction*. New York.

———. (1991) *Horrible Prettiness: Burlesque and*

American Culture. Chapel Hill, NC.

Allsep, L. Michael, Jr. (2008) "New Forms for Dominance: How a Corporate Lawyer Created the American Military Establishment." Ph.D. diss., University of North Carolina at Chapel Hill.

Allswang, John M. (1977) *Bosses, Machines, and Urban Voters: An American Symbiosis.* Port Washington, NY.

Alonso, Harriet Hyman. (1993) *Peace as a Women's Issue: A History of the U.S. Movement for World Peace and Women's Rights.* Syracuse, NY.

Alpern, Andrew. (1975) *Apartments for the Affluent: A Historical Survey of Buildings in New York.* New York.

Alpert, Hollis. (1991) *Broadway! 125 Years of Musical Theatre.* New York.

American Defense Society. (1918) *Hand Book of the American Defense Society.* New York.

American Heritage. (1968) *New York, N.Y.* New York.

Ameringer, Charles D. (1963) "The Panama Canal Lobby of Philippe Bunau-Varilla and William Nelson Cromwell." *American Historical Review* 68: 346–63.

Ammann, O. H. (1918) "The Hell Gate Arch Bridge and Approaches of the New York Connecting Railroad over the East River in New York City." *Transactions of the American Society of Civil Engineers* 82: 852–1039.

Anderson, Eric, and Alfred A. Moss Jr. (1999) *Dangerous Donations: Northern Philanthropy and Southern Black Education, 1902–1930.* Columbia, MO.

Anderson, Jervis. (1973) *A. Philip Randolph: A Biographical Portrait.* New York.

———. (1981) *This Was Harlem: A Cultural Portrait, 1900–1950.* New York.

———. (1982) *Harlem: The Great Black Way, 1900–1950.* New York.

Anderson, Lisa. (2005) "James T. Shotwell: A Life Devoted to Organizing Peace." In *Living Legacies at Columbia,* edited by William Theodore de Bary, Jerry Kisslinger, and Tom Mathewson. New York.

Antler, Joyce. (1997) *The Journey Home: Jewish Women and the American Century.* New York.

Antliff, Allan. (2001) *Anarchist Modernism: Art, Politics, and the First American Avant-Garde.* Chicago, IL.

Ardizzone, Heidi. (2007) *An Illuminated Life: Belle da Costa Greene's Journey from Prejudice to Privilege.* New York.

Arnesen, Eric. (2006) *Encyclopedia of U.S. Labor and Working-Class History.* New York.

Arnove, Robert F. (1980) *Philanthropy and Cultural Imperialism: The Foundations at Home and Abroad.* Boston, MA.

Aronowitz, Stanley. (1973) *False Promises: The Shaping of American Working Class Consciousness.* New York.

———. (1983) *Working Class Hero: A New Strategy for Labor.* New York.

Arons, Ron. (2008) *The Jews of Sing Sing: Gotham Gangsters and Gonuvim.* Fort Lee, NJ.

Aronson, David I. (1975) "The City Club of New York, 1892–1912." Ph.D. diss., New York University.

Aronson, Stanley M. (2009) *Perilous Encounters: Commentaries on the Evolution, Art and Science of Medicine from Ancient to Modern Times.* Bloomington, IN.

Arthur, Anthony. (2006) *Radical Innocent: Upton Sinclair.* New York.

Asbury, Herbert. (1927) *The Gangs of New York.* New York.

———. (1938) *Sucker's Progress: An Informal History of Gambling in America from the Colonies to Canfield.* New York.

Ascher, Abraham. (2004) *The Revolution of 1905: A*

Short History. Stanford, CA.

Asher, Robert. (1976) "Jewish Unions and the American Federation of Labor Power Structure 1903–1935." *American Jewish Historical Quarterly* 65: 215–27.

Astor, Gerald. (1971) *The New York Cops: An Informal History.* New York.

Atlantic, Gulf & Pacific Company. (1916) *Mill Basin: The New Industrial District on New York Harbor.* Brooklyn, NY.

Auchincloss, Louis. (1971) *Edith Wharton: A Woman in Her Time.* New York.

Auchincloss, Louis, and John Updike. (1998) *A Century of Arts and Letters: The History of the National Institute of Arts and Letters and the American Academy of Arts and Letters as Told, Decade by Decade, by Eleven Members.* New York.

Aufses, Arthur H., Jr., and Barbara Niss. (2002) *This House of Noble Deeds: The Mount Sinai Hospital, 1852–2002.* New York.

Avrich, Paul. (1980) *The Modern School Movement: Anarchism and Education in the United States.* Princeton, NJ.

———. (1988) *Anarchist Portraits.* Princeton, NJ.

———. (1991) *Sacco and Vanzetti: The Anarchist Background.* Princeton, NJ.

Avrich, Paul, and Karen Avrich. (2012) *Sasha and Emma: The Anarchist Odyssey of Alexander Berkman and Emma Goldman.* Cambridge, MA.

Axelrod, Alan. (2009) *Selling the Great War: The Making of American Propaganda.* New York.

Ayala, César J. (1995) "Social and Economic Aspects of Sugar Production in Cuba, 1880–1930." *Latin American Research Review* 30: 95–124.

———. (1999) *American Sugar Kingdom: The Plantation Economy of the Spanish Caribbean, 1898–1934.* Chapel Hill, NC.

Ayala, César J., and Rafael Bernabe. (2007) *Puerto Rico in the American Century: A History since 1898.* Chapel Hill, NC.

Backus, Truman Jay, and League of Loyal Citizens. (1890) *Against Consolidation: An Address.* Brooklyn, NY.

Bacon, Mardges. (1986) *Ernest Flagg: Beaux-Arts Architect and Urban Reformer.* Cambridge, MA.

Badger, Reid. (1995) *A Life in Ragtime: A Biography of James Reese Europe.* New York.

Bailey, Thomas A., and Paul B. Ryan. (1975) *The Lusitania Disaster: An Episode in Modern Warfare and Diplomacy.* New York.

Baker, Lee D. (1998) *From Savage to Negro: Anthropology and the Construction of Race, 1896–1954.* Berkeley, CA.

Baker, Paul R. (1989) *Stanny: The Gilded Life of Stanford White.* New York.

Baker, Ray Stannard. (1905) "The Subway Deal." *McClure's Magazine* 24: 451–69.

Balanoff, Elizabeth. (1985) "Norman Thomas: Socialism and the Social Gospel." *Christian Century,* January 30, 101–102.

Bald, Vivek. (2013) *Bengali Harlem and the Lost Histories of South Asian America.* Cambridge, MA.

Ballon, Hilary, and Norman McGrath. (2002) *New York's Pennsylvania Stations.* New York.

Balsamo, William, and George Carpozi Jr. (1988) *Under the Clock: The Inside Story of the Mafia's First Hundred Years.* Far Hills, NJ.

Banner, Lois W. (1984) *American Beauty.* Chicago, IL.

Bao, Xiaolan. (2001) *Holding Up More than Half the Sky: Chinese Women Garment Workers in New York City, 1948–92.* Urbana, IL.

Barkan, Elazar. (1992) *The Retreat of Scientific Racism: Changing Concepts of Race in Britain and the*

United States between the
World Wars. Cambridge,
UK.

Barnes, Charles B. (1915)
The Longshoremen. New
York.

Barnett, George E. (1916)
"The Stonecutters' Union
and the Stone-Planer."
*Journal of Political
Economy* 34: 417–44.

Barnouw, Erik. (1989)
*International Encyclopedia
of Communications*. New
York.

Barr, Brooke Jane. (1987)
"The Canyon of Heroes:
The History of New York
City's Ticker-Tape
Parades." M.A. thesis,
New York University.

Barrow, Clyde W. (2000)
*More than a Historian:
The Political and Economic
Thought of Charles A.
Beard*. New Brunswick, NJ.

Barry, Francis S. (2009) *The
Scandal of Reform: The
Grand Failures of New
York's Political Crusaders
and the Death of
Nonpartisanship*. New
Brunswick, NJ.

Barry, John M. (2005) *The
Great Influenza: The Epic
Story of the Deadliest
Plague in History*. New
York.

Barth, Gunther Paul. (1980)
*City People: The Rise of
Modern City Culture in
Nineteenth-Century
America*. New York.

Batlan, Felice. (2005)
"Gender in the Path of the
Law: Public Bodies, State
Power, and the Politics of
Reform in Late
Nineteenth-Century New
York City." Ph.D. diss.,
New York University.

Batterberry, Michael, and
Ariane Ruskin Batterberry.
(1999) *On the Town in New
York: The Landmark
History of Eating, Drinking,
and Entertainments from the
American Revolution to the
Food Revolution*. New
York.

Baxandall, Rosalyn F. (1988)
*Words on Fire: The Life and
Writing of Elizabeth Gurley
Flynn*. Piscataway, NJ.

Bayor, Ronald H. (1978)
*Neighbors in Conflict: The
Irish, Germans, Jews,
and Italians of New York

City, 1929–1941*.
Baltimore, MD.

Beard, Patricia. (2003) *After
the Ball: Gilded Age
Secrets, Boardroom
Betrayals, and the Party
That Ignited the Great Wall
Street Scandal of 1905*.
New York.

Beard, Rick, and Leslie
Berlowitz. (1993)
*Greenwich Village: Culture
and Counterculture*. New
Brunswick, NJ.

Beard, Rick, and Museum of
the City of New York.
(1987) *On Being Homeless:
Historical Perspectives*.
New York.

Beckert, Sven. (2001) *The
Monied Metropolis: New
York City and the
Consolidation of the
American Bourgeoisie,
1850–1896*. Cambridge,
MA.

Beer, Thomas. (1941) *Hanna,
Crane and the Mauve
Decade*. New York.

Behrman, S. N., and Saul
Steinberg. (2003) *Duveen*.
New York.

Beisel, Nicola Kay. (1997)
*Imperiled Innocents:
Anthony Comstock and
Family Reproduction in
Victorian America*.
Princeton, NJ.

Beisner, Robert L. (1968)
*Twelve against Empire: The
Anti-Imperialists,
1898–1900*. New York.

Beito, David T. (2000) *From
Mutual Aid to the Welfare
State: Fraternal Societies
and Social Services,
1890–1967*. Chapel Hill,
NC.

Belgrad, Daniel. (2001)
"Square Ring: American
Intellectual Life and the
Boxing Paintings of
Thomas Eakins and
George Bellows."
*Intellectual History
Newsletter* 23: 24–34.

Bell, Daniel. (1961) *The
End of Ideology*.
New York.

Ben-Zvi, Linda. (2005)
*Susan Glaspell: Her Life
and Times*. New York.

Benardo, Leonard, and
Jennifer Weiss. (2006)
*Brooklyn by Name: How
the Neighborhoods, Streets,
Parks, Bridges, and More
Got Their Names*. New York.

Bencivenni, Marcella. (2003)
"Italian American Radical
Culture in New York City:
The Politics and Arts of
the *Sovversivi*,
1890–1940." Ph.D. diss.,
City University of New
York.

———. (2011) *Italian
Immigrant Radical Culture:
The Idealism of the
Sovversivi in the United
States, 1890–1940*. New
York.

Bender, Daniel E. (2004)
*Sweated Work, Weak
Bodies: Anti-Sweatshop
Campaigns and Languages of
Labor*. New Brunswick, NJ.

Bender, Daniel E., and
Richard A. Greenwald.
(2003) *Sweatshop USA:
The American Sweatshop in
Historical and Global
Perspective*. New York.

Bender, Thomas. (1987) *New
York Intellect: A History of
Intellectual Life in New
York City, from 1750 to the
Beginnings of Our Own
Time*. New York.

———. (1993) "The
Historian and Public Life:
Charles A. Beard and the
City." In Bender, *Intellect
and Public Life: Essays in
the Social History of
Academic Intellectuals in the
United States*. Baltimore,
MD.

———. (2002) *The
Unfinished City: New York
and the Metropolitan Idea*.
New York.

Bendersky, Joseph W. (2000)
*The "Jewish Threat":
Anti-Semitic Politics of the
U.S. Army*. New York.

Benert, Annette. (2007) *The
Architectural Imagination
of Edith Wharton:
Gender, Class, and Power
in the Progressive Era*.
Madison, NJ.

Benjamin, Anne Myra
Goodman. (1991) *A
History of the Anti-Suffrage
Movement in the United
States from 1895 to 1920:
Women against Equality*.
Lewiston, NY.

Benjamin, Jules R. (1977)
*The United States and
Cuba: Hegemony and
Dependent Development,
1880–1934*. Pittsburgh, PA.

Benjamin, Rick, Paragon
Ragtime Orchestra, et al.

(2003) *Black Manhattan:
Theater and Dance Music of
James Reese Europe, Will
Marion Cook, and Members
of the Legendary Clef Club*.
Audio CD. New York.

Bennett, Scott H., and
Charles F. Howlett, eds.
(2014) *Antiwar Dissent and
Peace Activism in World
War I America: A
Documentary Reader*.
Lincoln, NE.

Benson, Kathleen, Philip M.
Kayal, et al. (2002) *A
Community of Many
Worlds: Arab Americans in
New York City*. New York.

Benson, Michael. (1989)
*Ballparks of North
America: A Comprehensive
Historical Reference to
Grounds, Yards, and
Stadiums, 1845 to Present*.
Jefferson, NC.

Benson, Susan Porter. (1986)
*Counter Cultures:
Saleswomen, Managers, and
Customers in American
Department Stores,
1890–1940*. Urbana, IL.

Berg, A. Scott. (2013)
Wilson. New York.

Bergreen, Laurence. (1990) *As
Thousands Cheer: The Life of
Irving Berlin*. New York.

Berlin, Edward A. (1994)
*King of Ragtime: Scott
Joplin and His Era*. New
York.

Berman, Avis. (1990) *Rebels
on Eighth Street: Juliana
Force and the Whitney
Museum of American Art*.
New York.

Berman, Marshall. (1982)
*All That Is Solid Melts into
Air: The Experience of
Modernity*. New York.

———. (2006) *On the Town:
One Hundred Years of
Spectacle in Times Square*.
New York.

Bernhardt, Debra. (2000)
*Ordinary People,
Extraordinary Lives: A
Pictorial History of
Working People in New
York City*. New York.

Bernheim, Alfred L. (1964)
The Business of the Theatre.
New York.

Bernikow, Louise. (2010)
"The 'Weaker Sex' Takes
Gotham: Fighting for
Women's Right to Vote."
Paper presented at
Gotham Center for New

York City History. New York.

Bernstein, Richard J. (2015) "Cultural Pluralism." *Philosophy and Social Criticism* 41: 347–56.

Berrol, Selma Cantor. (1967) "Immigrants at School: New York City, 1898–1914." Ph.D. diss., City University of New York.

Best, Harry. (1914) *The Men's Garment Industry of New York and the Strike of 1913*. New York.

Betts, Mary Beth. (1997) "Masterplanning: Municipal Support of Maritime Transport and Commerce, 1870–1930s." In *The New York Waterfront: Evolution and Building Culture of the Port and Harbor*, edited by Kevin Bone. New York.

Bianco, Anthony. (2004) *Ghosts of 42nd Street: A History of America's Most Infamous Block*. New York.

Biel, Steven. (1992) *Independent Intellectuals in the United States, 1910–1945*. New York.

Billings, John S., Francis Greenwood Peabody, et al. (1905) *The Liquor Problem: A Summary of Investigations Conducted by the Committee of Fifty, 1893–1903*. Boston, MA.

Binder, Frederick M., and David M. Reimers. (1995) *All the Nations under Heaven: An Ethnic and Racial History of New York City*. New York.

Bingham, Theodore A. (1908) "Foreign Criminals in New York." *North American Review* 188: 383–94.

———. (1911) *The Girl That Disappears*. Boston, MA.

Bird, Kai. (1992) *The Chairman: John J. Mccloy and the Making of the American Establishment*. New York.

Birmingham, Stephen. (1967) *"Our Crowd": The Great Jewish Families of New York*. New York.

Black, Frederick R. (1981) *Jamaica Bay: A History*. Washington, DC.

Blackmar, Elizabeth. (1979) "Going to the Mountains."

In *Resorts of the Catskills*, by John Margolies et al. New York.

———. (1991) "Uptown Real Estate and the Creation of Times Square." In *Inventing Times Square: Commerce and Culture at the Crossroads of the World*, edited by William R. Taylor. New York.

Blackshaw, Randall. (1902) "The New New York." *Century Magazine* 64: 493–513.

Blake, Angela M. (2006) *How New York Became American, 1890–1924*. Baltimore, MD.

Blake, Casey Nelson. (2013) "Greenwich Village Modernism: 'The Essence of It All Was Communication.'" In *The Armory Show at 100: Modernism and Revolution*, edited by Marilyn Satin Kushner and Kimberly Orcutt. New York.

Blanke, David. (2007) *Hell on Wheels: The Promise and Peril of America's Car Culture, 1900–1940*. Lawrence, KS.

Blansfield, Karen Charmaine. (1988) *Cheap Rooms and Restless Hearts: A Study of Formula in the Urban Tales of William Sydney Porter*. Bowling Green, OH.

Blassingame, Lurton W. (1972) "Frank J. Goodnow: Progressive Urban Reformer." *North Dakota Quarterly* 40: 22–30.

Blight, David W. (2002) "A Quarrel Forgotten or a Revolution Remembered? Reunion and Race in the Memory of the Civil War, 1875–1913." In Blight, *Beyond the Battlefield: Race, Memory, and the American Civil War*. Amherst, MA.

Block, Alan A. (1994) *Space, Time, and Organized Crime*. New Brunswick, NJ.

Bloom, Ken. (1991) *Broadway: An Encyclopedic Guide to the History, People and Places of Times Square*. New York.

———. (2004) *Broadway: Its History, People, and*

Places: An Encyclopedia. New York.

———. (2007) *The Routledge Guide to Broadway*. New York.

Bloom, Nicholas Dagen. (2008) *Public Housing That Worked: New York in the Twentieth Century*. Philadelphia, PA.

Bluestone, Daniel M. (1991) *Constructing Chicago*. New Haven, CT.

———. (2011) "Dutch Homesteads in Modern Brooklyn: The Unused Past." In Bluestone, *Buildings, Landscapes, and Memory: Case Studies in Historic Preservation*. New York.

Blumenson, S. L. (1949) "Revolt of the Reefer-Makers." *Commentary* 8: 62–70.

Bobinski, George S. (1969) *Carnegie Libraries: Their History and Impact on American Public Library Development*. Chicago, IL.

Bobrick, Benson. (1986) *Labyrinths of Iron: Subways in History, Myth, Art, Technology, and War*. New York.

Bobrow-Strain, Aaron. (2012) *White Bread: A Social History of the Store-Bought Loaf*. Boston, MA.

Boelhower, William Q., and Anna Scacchi, eds. (2004) *Public Space, Private Lives: Race, Gender, Class, and Citizenship in New York, 1890–1929*. Amsterdam.

Bogart, Michele. (1989) *Public Sculpture and the Civic Ideal in New York City, 1890–1930*. Chicago, IL.

———. (1995) *Artists, Advertising, and the Borders of Art*. Chicago, IL.

———. (1999) "Public Space and Public Memory in New York's City Hall Park." *Journal of Urban History* 25: 226–57.

———. (2006) *The Politics of Urban Beauty: New York and Its Art Commission*. Chicago, IL.

Bone, Kevin. (2006) "The Delaware System." In *Water-Works: The Architecture and Engineering of the New York City Water Supply*,

edited by Kevin Bone and Gina Pollara. New York.

Bone, Kevin, Mary Beth Betts, et al. (1997) *The New York Waterfront: Evolution and Building Culture of the Port and Harbor*. New York.

Bone, Kevin, and Gina Pollara, eds. (2006) *Water-Works: The Architecture and Engineering of the New York City Water Supply*. New York.

Bonner, Arthur. (1997) *Alas! What Brought Thee Hither? The Chinese in New York, 1800–1950*. Madison, NJ.

Bonner, William Thompson. (1924) *New York, the World's Metropolis, 1623–4–1923–4: A Presentation of the Greater City at the Beginning of Its Second Quarter Century of Amalgamated Government and the 300th Anniversary of Its Founding with Review of the Interim Accomplishments of Its Citizens*. New York.

Boorstin, Daniel J. (1988) *The Americans: The Democratic Experience*. London.

Bortz, Abe. (1970) "Historical Development of the Social Security Act." Paper presented at Social Security Administration. Baltimore, MD.

Boullosa, Carmen, and Mike Wallace. (2015) *A Narco History: How the United States and Mexico Jointly Created the "Mexican Drug War."* New York.

Bourgeois, Michael. (2004) *All Things Human: Henry Codman Potter and the Social Gospel in the Episcopal Church*. Urbana, IL.

Bourne, Randolph S. (1916a) "The Jew and Trans-National America." *Menorah Journal* 2: 277–84.

———. (1916b) "Trans-National America." *Atlantic Monthly* 118: 86–97.

———. (1916c) *The Gary Schools*. Boston, MA.

———. (1917) "The War and the Intellectuals." *Seven Arts* 2: 133–46.

Bowker, R. R. (1901) "The Piracy of Public Franchises." *Municipal Affairs* 5: 886–904.

Bowser, Eileen. (1990) *The Transformation of Cinema, 1907–1915*. Berkeley, CA.

Boyd, Robert L. (1998) "The Storefront Church Ministry in African American Communities of the Urban North during the Great Migration: The Making of an Ethnic Niche." *Social Science Journal* 35: 319–32.

Boyer, M. Christine. (1983) *Dreaming the Rational City: The Myth of American City Planning*. Cambridge, MA.

———. (1985) *Manhattan Manners: Architecture and Style, 1850–1900*. New York.

———. (1988) "Appearing on Broadway: Notes on Architectural Theatricalities, 1890–1930." Paper presented at Inventing Times Square Conference. New York.

Boyer, Paul. (1978) *Urban Masses and Moral Order in America, 1820–1920*. Cambridge, MA.

Boyer, Richard Owen. (1947) *The Dark Ship*. Boston, MA.

Boylan, James R. (1998) *Revolutionary Lives: Anna Strunsky and William English Walling*. Amherst, MA.

Boyle, Kevin. (2002) *Braving the Waves: Rockaway Rises—and Rises Again*. Scotts Valley, CA.

Bradford, Phillips Verner, and Harvey Blume. (1992) *Ota Benga: The Pygmy in the Zoo*. New York.

Bramen, Carrie Tirado. (2000a) "The Urban Picturesque and the Spectacle of Americanization." *American Quarterly* 52: 444–77.

———. (2000b) *The Uses of Variety: Modern Americanism and the Quest for National Distinctiveness*. Cambridge, MA.

Braverman, Harry. (1975) *Labor and Monopoly Capital: The Degradation*

of Work in the Twentieth Century. New York.

Breen, William J. (1984) *Uncle Sam at Home: Civilian Mobilization, Wartime Federalism, and the Council of National Defense, 1917–1919*. Westport, CT.

Bremner, Robert H. (1956) *From the Depths: The Discovery of Poverty in the United States*. New York.

Brenner, Aaron, Benjamin Day, and Immanuel Ness, eds. (2009) *The Encyclopedia of Strikes in American History*. Armonk, NY.

Bridges, William. (1974) *Gathering of Animals: An Unconventional History of the New York Zoological Society*. New York.

Briggs, John. (1969) *Requiem for a Yellow Brick Brewery: A History of the Metropolitan Opera*. Boston, MA.

Bristow, Edward J. (1982) *Prostitution and Prejudice: The Jewish Fight against White Slavery, 1870–1939*. New York.

Broderick, Mosette Glaser. (2010) *Triumvirate: McKim, Mead & White: Art, Architecture, Scandal, and Class in America's Gilded Age*. New York.

Brody, David. (1998) *Steelworkers in America: The Nonunion Era*. Urbana, IL.

———. (2010) *Visualizing American Empire: Orientalism and Imperialism in the Philippines*. Chicago, IL.

Broesamle, John J. (1973) *William Gibbs McAdoo: A Passion for Change, 1863–1917*. Port Washington, NY.

———. (1990) *Reform and Reaction in Twentieth Century American Politics*. New York.

Bronx Museum of the Arts. (1986) *Building a Borough: Architecture and Planning in the Bronx, 1890–1940*. The Bronx, NY.

Brooklyn League Committee on Industrial Advancement. (1914) *Brooklyn: A National Center of Commerce and Industry*. Brooklyn, NY.

Brooklyn Museum. (1979) *The American Renaissance, 1876–1917*. Brooklyn, NY.

Brooks, Tim. (2002) *High Drama in the Record Industry: Columbia Records, 1901–1934*. New York.

Brooks, Tim, and Brian Rust. (1999) *The Columbia Master Book Discography*. Westport, CT.

Brooks, Tim, and Richard K. Spottswood. (2004) *Lost Sounds: Blacks and the Birth of the Recording Industry, 1890–1919*. Urbana, IL.

Brouwer, Norman. (1989) "Improving Conditions for Seamen Ashore and Afloat." *Seaport* (Fall): 36–43.

———. (1990) "Fortress New York." *Seaport* (Summer): 36–41.

———. (1998) "The Port of New York: The Passenger Liner Era." *Seaport* (Fall): 36–41.

Brown, Dorothy M., and Elizabeth McKeown. (1997) *The Poor Belong to Us: Catholic Charities and American Welfare*. Cambridge, MA.

Brown, E. Richard. (1979) *Rockefeller Medicine Men: Medicine and Capitalism in America*. Berkeley, CA.

Brown, Eleanor Marie Lawrence. (2012) *The Blacks Who Got Their 'Forty Acres': A Theory of West Indian Migrant Asset Acquisition*. Los Angeles, CA.

Brown, Eve. (1967) *The Plaza: Its Life and Times*. New York.

Brown, Gary R. (1994) "The Coney Island Baby Laboratory." *American Heritage of Invention and Technology* 10: 24–33.

Brown, Mary Elizabeth. (1991) "'The Adoption of the Tactics of the Enemy': The Care of Italian Immigrant Youth in the Archdiocese of New York during the Progressive Era." In *Immigration to New York*, edited by William Pencak et al. New York.

Brown, Milton W. (1955) *American Painting from the*

Armory Show to the Depression. Princeton, NJ.

Brown, Phil, ed. (2002) *In the Catskills: A Century of Jewish Experience in "the Mountains."* New York.

Brown, Theodore M., and Elizabeth Fee. (2002) "Isaac Max Rubinow, Advocate for Social Insurance." *American Journal of Public Health* 92: 1224–25.

Browne, Arthur. (2015) *One Righteous Man: Samuel Battle and the Shattering of the Color Line in New York*. Boston, MA.

Browne, Dorothy M. (2008) "New York City Museums and Cultural Leadership, 1917–1940." Ph.D. diss., City University of New York.

Browning, Robert M., Jr. (1994) "The Coast Guard Captains of the Port." In *To Die Gallantly: The Battle of the Atlantic*, edited by Timothy J. Runyan and Jan M. Copes. Boulder, CO.

Brownlow, Kevin. (1968) *The Parade's Gone By*. New York.

———. (1990) *Behind the Mask of Innocence: Sex, Violence, Crime: Films of Social Conscience in the Silent Era*. New York.

Bruère, Henry Jaromir, Joseph Haag, et al. (1918) *Report on the Pension Funds of the City of New York*. New York.

Brumberg, Stephan F. (1984) "Going to America, Going to School: The Immigrant–Public School Encounter in Turn-of-the-Century New York City." *American Jewish Archives* 36: 86–135.

Brundage, David Thomas. (1996) "'In Time of Peace, Prepare for War': Key Themes in the Social Thought of New York's Irish Nationalists, 1890–1916." In *The New York Irish*, edited by Ronald H. Bayor and Timothy J. Meagher. Baltimore, MD.

———. (2016) *Irish Nationalists in America: The Politics of Exile, 1798–1998*. New York.

Bruner, Robert F., and Sean D. Carr. (2007) *The Panic of 1907: Lessons Learned from the Market's Perfect Storm*. Hoboken, NJ.

Bruno, Giuliana. (1993) *Streetwalking on a Ruined Map: Cultural Theory and the City Films of Elvira Notari*. Princeton, NJ.

Bruno, Joe. (2012) *The Wrong Man: Who Ordered the Murder of Gambler Herman Rosenthal and Why*. Sarasota, FL.

Bryk, William. (2006) "The Last Police Chief." Blog post, *Mr. Beller's Neighborhood: New York City Stories*, June 3.

Buckley, John Patrick. (1976) *The New York Irish: Their View of American Foreign Policy, 1914–1921*. New York.

Buckley, Peter. (1991) "Boundaries of Respectability: Introductory Essay." In *Inventing Times Square: Commerce and Culture at the Crossroads of the World*, edited by William R. Taylor. New York.

Buckley, Tom. (1991) "The Eighth Bridge." *New Yorker*, January 14, 37–59.

Buenker, John D. (1973) *Urban Liberalism and Progressive Reform*. New York.

Buhle, Mari Jo. (1981) *Women and American Socialism, 1870–1920*. Urbana, IL.

Buhle, Mari Jo, et al., eds. (1990) *Encyclopedia of the American Left*. New York.

Buhle, Paul. (1987a) *Marxism in the U.S.A.: From 1870 to the Present Day*. New York.

———. (1987b) "The Significance of Yiddish Socialism." In *Popular Culture in America*, edited by Paul Buhle. Minneapolis, MN.

———. (1999) *Taking Care of Business: Samuel Gompers, George Meany, Lane Kirkland, and the Tragedy of American Labor*. New York.

———. (2004) *From the Lower East Side to Hollywood: Jews in*

American Popular Culture. New York.

Bulletin of the American Warehousemen's Association. (1916) "About Washington Market (New York)." *Bulletin of the American Warehousemen's Association* 17: 25–28.

Bundles, A'Lelia P. (1992) "Carte De Visite: Madam C. J. Walker, 1867–1919." *Hayes Historical Journal* 12 (Fall–Winter): 65–67.

Bunker, John. (1979) *Harbor and Haven: An Illustrated History of the Port of New York*. Chicago, IL.

———. (1980–83) "A History of the SUI." 27 parts, *Seafarers Log*, June 1980–June 1983.

Burchard, John, and Albert Bush-Brown. (1961) *The Architecture of America: A Social and Cultural History*. Boston, MA.

Bureau of Municipal Research. (1907) *Purposes and Methods of the Bureau of Municipal Research*. New York.

Burgess, Douglas R. (2005) *Seize the Trident: The Race for Superliner Supremacy and How It Altered the Great War*. Camden, ME.

Burgess, Susan, and Kate Leeman. (2016) *CQ Press Guide to Radical Politics in the United States*. Los Angeles, CA.

Burner, David. (1967) *The Politics of Provincialism: The Democratic Party in Transition, 1918–1932*. New York.

Burnstein, Daniel Eli. (1993) "Clean Streets and the Pursuit of Progress: Urban Reform in New York City in the Progressive Era." Ph.D. diss., Rutgers University.

Burrows, Edwin G. (2008) *Forgotten Patriots: The Untold Story of American Prisoners during the Revolutionary War*. New York.

Burrows, Edwin G., and Mike Wallace. (1999) *Gotham: A History of New York City to 1898*. New York.

Bush, Irving T. (1928) *Working with the World*. Garden City, NY.

Butler, Gregory. (2006) *Disunited Brotherhoods: Race, Racketeering and the Fall of the New York Construction Unions*. Lincoln, NE.

Buttenwieser, Ann L. (1999) *Manhattan Water-Bound: Manhattan's Waterfront from the Seventeenth Century to the Present*. Syracuse, NY.

Byerly, Carol R. (2005) *Fever of War: The Influenza Epidemic in the U.S. Army during World War I*. New York.

Cabranes, José A. (1979) *Citizenship and the American Empire: Notes on the Legislative History of the United States Citizenship of Puerto Ricans*. New Haven, CT.

Cahan, Abraham. (1917) *The Rise of David Levinsky: A Novel*. New York.

Cahn, Julius. (1896) *Julius Cahn's Official Theatrical Guide*. New York.

Cahn-Leighton Official Theatrical Guide. (1912–13) *The Cahn-Leighton Official Theatrical Guide*. Vol. 16. New York.

Cahn, William. (1969) *Out of the Cracker Barrel: The Nabisco Story, from Animal Crackers to ZuZus*. New York.

Cain, William E. (1988) *F. O. Matthiessen and the Politics of Criticism*. Madison, WI.

Calavita, Kitty. (1984) *U.S. Immigration Law and the Control of Labor, 1820–1924*. New York.

Camp, Helen C. (1995) *Iron in Her Soul: Elizabeth Gurley Flynn and the American Left*. Pullman, WA.

Campbell, Rodney. (1977) *The Luciano Project: The Secret Wartime Collaboration of the Mafia and the U.S. Navy*. New York.

Campbell, W. Joseph. (2006) *The Year That Defined American Journalism: 1897 and the Clash of Paradigms*. New York.

Candeloro, Dominic. (1979) "Louis F. Post and the Red Scare of 1920." *Prologue* 11: 40–55.

Cannato, Vincent J. (2009) *American Passage: The*

History of Ellis Island. New York.

Cannistraro, Philip V., and Gerald Meyer, eds. (2003) *The Lost World of Italian-American Radicalism: Politics, Labor and Culture*. Westport, CT.

Cantrell, Phillip A., II. (2004) "A Talented and Energetic Young Man: John Foster Dulles and His Preparation for Statesmanship, 1888–1937." Ph.D. diss., West Virginia University.

Capozzola, Christopher. (2002) "The Only Badge Needed Is Your Patriotic Fervor: Vigilance, Coercion, and the Law in World War I America." *Journal of American History* 88: 1354–82.

———. (2008) *Uncle Sam Wants You: World War I and the Making of the Modern American Citizen*. New York.

Carhart, E. R. (1911) "The New York Produce Exchange." *Annals of the American Academy of Political and Social Science* 38: 206–21.

Carlisle, Rodney. (2007) "The Attacks on U.S. Shipping That Precipitated American Entry into World War I." *Northern Mariner/Le marin du nord* 17: 41–66.

Carman, Harry J. (1919) *The Street Surface Railway Franchises of New York City*. New York.

Caro, Robert. (1974) *The Power Broker: Robert Moses and the Fall of New York*. New York.

Carosso, Vincent P. (1970) *Investment Banking in America: A History*. Cambridge, MA.

———. (1987) *The Morgans: Private International Bankers, 1854–1913*. Cambridge, MA.

Carroll, John F. (1998) "Oscar Hammerstein I, 1895–1915: His Creation and Development of New York's Times Square Theatre District." Ph.D. diss., City University of New York.

Carson, Mina Julia. (1984) "'Settlement Folk':

Settlement Workers and the Settlement House Idea in the United States, 1885–1930." Ph.D. diss., Harvard University.

Carter, Marva Griffin. (2008) *Swing Along: The Musical Life of Will Marion Cook.* New York.

Carter, Patricia Anne. (1985) "A Coalition between Women Teachers and the Feminist Movement in New York City, 1900–1920." Ed.D. diss., University of Cincinnati.

Carter, Randolph. (1974) *The World of Flo Ziegfeld.* New York.

Casey, Marion R. (1996) "From the East Side to the Seaside: Irish Americans on the Move in New York City." In *The New York Irish*, edited by Ronald H. Bayor and Timothy J. Meagher. Baltimore, MD.

Cash, Floris Loretta Barnett. (2001) *African American Women and Social Action: The Clubwomen and Volunteerism from Jim Crow to the New Deal, 1896–1936.* Westport, CT.

Cassis, Youssef. (2010) *Capitals of Capital: The Rise and Fall of International Financial Centres, 1780–2009.* New York.

Castells, Manuel. (1983) *The City and the Grassroots: A Cross-Cultural Theory of Urban Social Movements.* London.

Castle, Irene, et al. (1958) *Castles in the Air.* Garden City, NY.

Castonguay, James. (2006) "The Spanish-American War in United States Media Culture." In *Hollywood and War: The Film Reader*, edited by J. David Slocum. New York.

Cattell, J. McKeen. (1909) "The School and the Family." *Popular Science Monthly* 74: 84–95.

Cavallo, Dominick. (1981) *Muscles and Morals: Organized Playgrounds and Urban Reform, 1880–1920.* Philadelphia, PA.

Center for Migration Studies. (1975) "American Catholicism Aids the Immigrant: Catholicism

and the Social Settlement." *Center for Migration Studies Special Issues* 1: 49–64.

Cerillo, Augustus, Jr. (1973) "The Reform of Municipal Government in New York City, from Seth Low to John Purroy Mitchel." *New-York Historical Society Quarterly* 57: 51–71.

Chace, James. (2004) *1912: Wilson, Roosevelt, Taft, and Debs—the Election That Changed the Country.* New York.

Chalmers, David Mark. (1964) *The Social and Political Ideas of the Muckrakers.* New York.

Chalmers, Henry. (1914) "The Number of Jews in New York City." *Publications of the American Statistical Association* 14: 68–75.

Chamber of Commerce of the Borough of Queens and Walter I. Willis. (1920) *Queens Borough, New York City, 1910–1920: The Borough of Homes and Industry.* New York.

Chambers, John Whiteclay II. (1987) *To Raise an Army: The Draft Comes to Modern America.* New York.

Chambers, Julius. (1906) *Seeing New York.* New York.

Chandler, Alfred, Jr. (1977) *The Visible Hand: The Managerial Revolution in American Business.* Cambridge, MA.

Chapman, Peter. (2010) *The Last of the Imperious Rich: Lehman Brothers, 1844–2008.* New York.

Chappell, Sally A. Kitt. (1990) "A Reconsideration of the Equitable Building in New York." *Journal of the Society of Architectural Historians* 49: 90–95.

Charity Organization Society of the City of New York. (1903) *A Handbook on the Prevention of Tuberculosis.* New York.

Charles, Amélie, et al. (2011) "A New Monthly Chronology of the US Industrial Cycles in the Prewar Economy." *Association Française de*

Cliométrie (AFC) Working Papers 2012 2: 1–19.

Chase, Edna Woolman, and Ilka Chase. (1954) *Always in Vogue.* Garden City, NY.

Chauncey, George, Jr. (1989) "From Sexual Inversion to Homosexuality: The Changing Medical Conceptualization of Female 'Deviance.'" In *Passion and Power: Sexuality in History*, edited by Kathy Peiss and Christina Simmons. Philadelphia, PA.

———. (1994) *Gay New York: Gender, Urban Culture, and the Making of the Gay Male World, 1890–1940.* New York.

Cheape, Charles W. (1976) "The Evolution of Urban Public Transit, 1880–1912: A Study of Boston, New York and Philadelphia." *Journal of Economic History* 36: 259–62.

———. (1980) *Moving the Masses: Urban Public Transit in New York, Boston, and Philadelphia, 1880–1912.* Cambridge, MA.

Cheilik, Michael, and David Gillison. (1977) *The Bronx Apartment House.* The Bronx, NY.

Chen, Constance M. (1996) *The Sex Side of Life: Mary Ware Dennett's Pioneering Battle for Birth Control and Sex Education.* New York.

Chen, Julia I. Hsuan. (1941) "The Chinese Community in New York: A Study in Their Cultural Adjustment, 1920–1940." Ph.D. diss., American University.

Chen, Michelle. (2013) "From Windows to Gateways on the Lower East Side: The Henry Street Settlement from the Progressive Era to the Great Society." *Historian* 75: 760–80.

———. (2014) "A Cultural Crossroads at the 'Bloody Angle': The Chinatown Tongs and the Development of New York City's Chinese American Community." *Journal of Urban History* 40: 357–79.

Cherington, Paul Terry. (1913) *Advertising as a*

Business Force. Garden City, NY.

Chernow, Ron. (1990) *The House of Morgan: An American Banking Dynasty and the Rise of Modern Finance.* New York.

———. (1993) *The Warburgs: The Twentieth-Century Odyssey of a Remarkable Jewish Family.* New York.

———. (1998) *Titan: The Life of John D. Rockefeller, Sr.* New York.

Childe, Cromwell. (1903) *New York: A Guide in Comprehensive Chapters.* Brooklyn, NY.

Chinitz, Benjamin. (1960) *Freight and the Metropolis: The Impact of America's Transport Revolutions on the New York Region.* Cambridge, MA.

Chudacoff, Howard P. (1999) *The Age of the Bachelor: Creating an American Subculture.* Princeton, NJ.

Chude-Sokei, Louis Onuorah. (2006) *The Last "Darky:" Bert Williams, Black-on-Black Minstrelsy, and the African Diaspora.* Durham, NC.

Church, Elihu Cunyngham. (1913) *The Bureau of Supplies of the Department of Water Supply, Gas and Electricity, New York City.* New York.

Churchill, Allen. (1959) *The Improper Bohemians: A Re-Creation of Greenwich Village in Its Heyday.* New York.

Citizens' Protective League and Frank Moss. (1900) *Story of the Riot.* New York.

City Club of New York. (1903) *The Department of Public Charities of the City of New York: A Statement of Facts.* New York.

Ciucci, Giorgio. (1979) *The American City: From the Civil War to the New Deal.* Cambridge, MA.

Clarkin, Franklin. (1903) "The Daily Walk of the Walking Delegate." *Century Magazine* 67: 298–304.

Clary, Martin. (1929) *Mid-Manhattan, That Section of the Greater City of New York between*

Washington Square and Central Park and the East and North Rivers in the Borough of Manhattan. New York.

Clayton, Lawrence A. (1985) *Grace: W. R. Grace & Co., the Formative Years, 1850–1930.* Ottawa, IL.

Clement, Elizabeth Alice. (2006) *Love for Sale: Courting, Treating, and Prostitution in New York City, 1900–1945.* Chapel Hill, NC.

Cleveland, Harold Van Buren, and Thomas Huertas. (1985) *The Bank for All: A History of Citibank, 1812–1970.* Cambridge, MA.

Clifford, John G. (1972) *The Citizen Soldiers: The Plattsburg Training Camp Movement, 1913–1920.* Lexington, KY.

Coates, Benjamin Allen. (2010) "Transatlantic Advocates: American International Law and U.S. Foreign Relations, 1898–1919." Ph.D. diss., Columbia University.

Coben, Stanley. (1991) *Rebellion against Victorianism: The Impetus for Cultural Change in 1920s America.* New York.

Coble, Alana Erickson. (2006) *Cleaning Up: The Transformation of Domestic Service in Twentieth Century New York City.* New York.

Cockburn, Alexander. (2006) "Nicholas Kristof's Brothel Problem." *CounterPunch Diary,* January 28, 2006: 1–3.

Cocks, Catherine. (2001) *Doing the Town: The Rise of Urban Tourism in the United States, 1850–1915.* Berkeley, CA.

Cody, Jeffrey W. (2003) *Exporting American Architecture, 1870–2000.* New York.

Cohalan, Rev. Msgr. Florence D. (1983) *A Popular History of the Archdiocese of New York.* Yonkers, NY.

Cohan, William D. (2011) *Money and Power: How Goldman Sachs Came to Rule the World.* New York.

Cohen, Gabriel. (2005) "For You, Half Price." *New York Times,* November 27.

Cohen, Julius Henry. (1946) "Rent Control after World War I—Recollections." *New York University Law Quarterly Review* 21: 267–81.

Cohen, Naomi Wiener. (1972) *Not Free to Desist: The American Jewish Committee, 1906–1966.* Philadelphia, PA.

———. (1999) *Jacob H. Schiff: A Study in American Jewish Leadership.* Hanover, NH.

Cohen, Rachel. (2012) "Priceless: How Art Became Commerce." *New Yorker,* October 8, 64–71.

Cohen, Ronald D., and Raymond A. Mohl. (1979) *The Paradox of Progressive Education: The Gary Plan and Urban Schooling.* Port Washington, NY.

Cohen, Sarah Blacher, ed. (1983) *From Hester Street to Hollywood: The Jewish-American Stage and Screen.* Bloomington, IN.

Cohen, Sol. (1964) *Progressives and Urban School Reform: The Public Education Association of New York City, 1895–1954.* New York.

Cohen, Stanley. (2006) *The Execution of Officer Becker: The Murder of a Gangster, the Trial of a Cop, and the Birth of Organized Crime.* New York.

Coit, Margaret L. (1957) *Mr. Baruch.* Boston, MA.

Colburn, David R. (1973) "Governor Alfred E. Smith and the Red Scare, 1919–1920." *Political Science Quarterly* 88: 423–44.

———. (1983) "Al Smith and the New York State Factory Investigating Commission, 1911–1915." In *Reform and Reformers in the Progressive Era,* edited by David R. Colburn and George E. Pozzetta. Westport, CT.

Colburn, David R. and George E. Pozzetta, eds. (1983) *Reform and Reformers in the Progressive Era.* Westport, CT.

Cole, Douglas. (1999) *Franz Boas: The Early Years, 1858–1906.* Seattle, WA.

Cole, John Y. (1979) "Storehouses and Workshops: American Libraries and the Uses of Knowledge." In *The Organization of Knowledge in Modern America, 1860–1920,* edited by Alexandra Oleson and John Voss. Baltimore, MD.

Coles, Robert. (1987) *Dorothy Day: A Radical Devotion.* Reading, MA.

Collins, Frederick L. (1934) *Consolidated Gas Company of New York: A History.* New York.

Collins, Theresa M. (2002) *Otto Kahn: Art, Money and Modern Time.* Chapel Hill, NC.

Comfort, Randall. (1906) *History of Bronx Borough.* The Bronx, NY.

Committee of Fourteen. (1916) *Annual Report, 1915–1916.* New York.

Committee on Coal and Power. (1928) *Power Development in New York State: The Secretary's Report to the Committee on Coal and Giant Power, with the Recommendations of the Committee, December, 1926.* New York.

Commons, John R. (1904) "The New York Building Trades." *Quarterly Journal of Economics* 18: 409–36.

Conant, Charles A. (1900a) "The Financial Future of the United States." *Bankers' and Trust Supplement to the Commercial & Financial Chronicle,* October 13, 42–44.

———. (1900b) *The United States in the Orient: The Nature of the Economic Problem.* New York.

Condit, Carl W. (1980a) *The Port of New York: A History of the Rail and Terminal System from the Beginnings to Pennsylvania Station.* Vol. 1. Chicago, IL.

———. (1980b) *The Port of New York: A History of the Rail and Terminal System from the Beginnings to Pennsylvania Station.* Vol. 2. Chicago, IL.

Condran, Gretchen A. (1995) "Changing Patterns of Epidemic Disease in New York City." In *Hives of Sickness: Public Health and Epidemics in New York City,* edited by David Rosner. New Brunswick, NJ.

Cone, John Frederick. (1966) *Oscar Hammerstein's Manhattan Opera Company.* Norman, OK.

Con Edison. (2001) *Waterside Station 1901–2001: One Hundred Years of Power at Waterside.* New York.

Connelly, Mark Thomas. (1980) *The Response to Prostitution in the Progressive Era.* Chapel Hill, NC.

Connolly, Harold X. (1977) *A Ghetto Grows in Brooklyn.* New York.

Conolly-Smith, Peter. (1998) "'*Ersatz*-Drama' and Ethnic (Self-) Parody: Adolf Philipp and the Decline of the New York's German-Language Stage, 1893–1918." In *Multilingual America: Transnationalism, Ethnicity, and the Languages of American Literature,* edited by Werner Sollors. New York.

———. (2009) "Transforming an Ethnic Readership through "Word and Image": William Randolph Hearst's *Deutsches Journal* and New York's German-Language Press, 1895–1918." *American Periodicals: A Journal of History and Criticism* 19: 66–84.

Conot, Robert E. (1986) *Thomas A. Edison: A Streak of Luck.* New York.

Conrad, Peter. (1984) *The Art of the City: Views and Versions of New York.* New York.

Cook, Blanche Wiesen. (1973) "Democracy in Wartime: Antimilitarism in England and the United States, 1914–1918." In *Peace Movements in America,* edited by Charles Chatfield. New York.

———. (1978) *Crystal Eastman on Women and Revolution.* New York.

———. (1979) "Female Support Networks and Political Activism: Lillian Wald, Crystal Eastman,

Emma Goldman." In *A Heritage of Her Own: Toward a New Social History of American Women*, edited by Nancy F. Cott and Elizabeth Hafkin Pleck. New York.

———. (1992) *Eleanor Roosevelt*, vol. 1, *The Early Years, 1884–1933*. New York.

———. (1993) "The Radical Women of Greenwich Village: From Crystal Eastman to Eleanor Roosevelt." In *Greenwich Village: Culture and Counterculture*, edited by Rick Beard and Leslie Berlowitz. New Brunswick, NJ.

Cook, Harry. (1913) *The Borough of the Bronx, 1639–1913: Its Marvelous Development and Historical Surroundings*. New York.

Cook, Karen. (1986) "Divine Signs: For a Half-Century, Artkraft Strauss Has Been Giving Times Square the Old Razzle-Dazzle." *Manhattan,inc.*, November.

Cooke, Hope. (1995) *Seeing New York: History Walks for Armchair and Footloose Travelers*. Philadelphia, PA.

Cooney, Robert. (2005) *Winning the Vote: The Triumph of the American Woman Suffrage Movement*. Santa Cruz, CA.

Cooney, Terry A. (1986) *The Rise of the New York Intellectuals: "Partisan Review" and Its Circle, 1934–1945*. Madison, WI.

Cooper, John M., Jr. (1983) *The Warrior and the Priest: Woodrow Wilson and Theodore Roosevelt*. Cambridge, MA.

Cooper, Patricia. (1987) *Once a Cigar Maker: Men, Women, and Work Culture in American Cigar Factories, 1900–1919*. Urbana, IL.

Corey, Steven Hunt. (1994) "King Garbage: A History of Solid Waste Management in New York City, 1881–1970." Ph.D. diss., New York University.

Corn, Wanda M. (1988) "The Artist's New York, 1900–1930." Paper presented at Conference

on the Comparative History of Metropolitan Transformation of Budapest and New York, 1870–1930. Budapest.

———. (1999) *The Great American Thing: Modern Art and National Identity, 1915–1935*. Berkeley, CA.

Corner, George Washington. (1964) *A History of the Rockefeller Institute, 1901–1953: Origins and Growth*. New York.

Coss, Clare. (1989) *Lillian D. Wald, Progressive Activist*. New York.

———. (2014) *Dr. Du Bois and Miss Covington*. New York.

Cott, Nancy F. (1987) *The Grounding of Modern Feminism*. New Haven, CT.

Cottrell, Robert C. (2000) *Roger Nash Baldwin and the American Civil Liberties Union*. New York.

Council on Foreign Relations. (1947) *The Council on Foreign Relations: A Record of Twenty-Five Years, 1921–1946*. New York.

Courtwright, David T. (2001) *Dark Paradise: A History of Opiate Addiction in America*. Cambridge, MA.

Cox, Anne F. (1984) *The History of the Colony Club, 1903–1984*. New York.

Coyle, Heather Campbell, Joyce K. Schiller, et al. (2007) *John Sloan's New York*. Wilmington, DE.

Craven, Wayne. (2009) *Gilded Mansions: Grand Architecture and High Society*. New York.

Cremin, Lawrence A. (1961) *The Transformation of the School: Progressivism in American Education, 1876–1957*. New York.

———. (1988) *American Education, the Metropolitan Experience, 1876–1980*. New York.

Crenson, Matthew A. (1998) *Building the Invisible Orphanage : A Prehistory of the American Welfare System*. Cambridge, MA.

Cresson, Benjamin Franklin, Jr. (1922) "Memoir of Calvin Tomkins." *Proceedings of the American*

Society of Civil Engineers 48: 140–42.

Cripps, Thomas R. (1963) "The Reaction of the Negro to the Motion Picture *Birth of a Nation*." *Historian* 25: 344–62.

Critchley, David. (2009) *The Origin of Organized Crime in America: The New York City Mafia, 1891–1931*. New York.

Crocker, Ruth. (2006) *Mrs. Russell Sage: Women's Activism and Philanthropy in Gilded Age and Progressive Era America*. Bloomington, IN.

Croly, Herbert. (1903) "New York as the American Metropolis." *Architectural Record* 13: 193–206.

———. (1907) " 'Civic Improvements': The Case of New York." *Architectural Record* 21: 347–52.

Cromien, Florence M. (1961) *Negroes in New York: From 1790 to 1960*. New York.

Cromley, Elizabeth C. (1990) *Alone Together: A History of New York's Early Apartments*. Ithaca, NY.

Crosby, Alfred W. (1989) *America's Forgotten Pandemic: The Influenza of 1918*. New York.

Cruse, Harold. (1967) *The Crisis of the Negro Intellectual*. New York.

Cudahy, Brian J. (1995) *Under the Sidewalks of New York: The Story of the Greatest Subway System in the World*. New York.

———. (2002) *Rails under the Mighty Hudson: The Story of the Hudson Tubes, the Pennsylvania Tunnels, and Manhattan Transfer*. New York.

Cuddy, Joseph Edward. (1965) "Irish-America and National Isolationism, 1914–1920." Ph.D. diss., State University of New York at Buffalo.

———. (1969) "Irish-Americans and the 1916 Election: An Episode in Immigrant Adjustment." *American Quarterly* 21: 228–43.

Cuff, Robert D. (1989) "United States Mobilization and Railroad

Transportation: Lessons in Coordination and Control, 1917–1945." *Journal of Military History* 53: 33–50.

Cullen, Deborah, ed. (2009) *Nexus New York: Latin/American Artists in the Modern Metropolis*. New York.

Cullen, Frank, et al. (2007) *Vaudeville, Old and New: An Encyclopedia of Variety Performers in America*. New York.

Cunningham, John T. (2003) *Ellis Island: Immigration's Shining Center*. Charleston, SC.

Cunningham, Joseph J. (2012) "Architect of Power: Thomas E. Murray and New York's Electrical System." *IEEE Power and Energy Magazine* 10: 80–94.

Curran, Robert Emmett. (1978) *Michael Augustine Corrigan and the Shaping of Conservative Catholicism in America, 1878–1902*. New York.

Curtis, Susan. (1994) *Dancing to a Black Man's Tune: A Life of Scott Joplin*. Columbia, MO.

Czitrom, Daniel J. (1991) "Underworlds and Underdogs: Big Tim Sullivan and Metropolitan Politics in New York, 1889–1913." *Journal of American History* 78: 536–58.

———. (1992) "The Politics of Performance: From Theater Licensing to Movie Censorship in Turn-of-the-Century New York." *American Quarterly* 44: 525–53.

———. (2016) *New York Exposed: The Gilded Age Police Scandal That Launched the Progressive Era*. New York.

D'Emilio, John. (1983) "Capitalism and Gay Identity." In *Powers of Desire: The Politics of Sexuality*, edited by Ann Snitow, Christine Stansell, and Sharon Thompson. New York.

D'Emilio, John, and Estelle B. Freedman. (1988) *Intimate Matters: A History of Sexuality in America*. New York.

Dahlberg, Jane S. (1966) *The New York Bureau of Municipal Research.* New York.

Daigle, Jonathan. (2009) "Paul Laurence Dunbar and the Marshall Circle: Racial Representation from Blackface to Black Naturalism." *African American Review* 43: 633–54.

Dain, Phyllis. (1972) *The New York Public Library: A History of Its Founding and Early Years.* New York.

———. (2000) *The New York Public Library: A Universe of Knowledge.* New York.

Dale, Alan. (1910) "The Shrine of Snobbery." *Cosmopolitan* 48: 475–80.

Daley, Robert. (1959) *The World beneath the City.* Philadelphia, PA.

Dalton, Thomas Carlyle. (2002) *Becoming John Dewey: Dilemmas of a Philosopher and Naturalist.* Bloomington, IN.

Daniels, Doris. (1979) "Building a Winning Coalition: The Suffrage Fight in New York State." *New York History* 60: 59–80.

Dargan, Amanda, and Steven J. Zeitlin. (1990) *City Play.* New Brunswick, NJ.

Dash, Mike. (2007) *Satan's Circus: Murder, Vice, Police Corruption, and New York's Trial of the Century.* New York.

———. (2009) *The First Family: Terror, Extortion, Revenge, Murder, and the Birth of the American Mafia.* New York.

Davidson, Lawrence. (1999) "Debating Palestine: Arab-American Challenges to Zionism, 1917–1932." In *Arabs in America: Building a New Future*, edited by Michael W. Suleiman. Philadelphia, PA.

Davies, Margery W. (1982) *Woman's Place Is at the Typewriter: Office Work and Office Workers, 1870–1930.* Philadelphia, PA.

Davies, Wallace Evan. (1955) *Patriotism on Parade: The Story of Veterans' and Hereditary Organizations in America, 1783–1900.* Cambridge, MA.

Davis, Allen F. (1964) "The Social Workers and the Progressive Party, 1912–1916." *American Historical Review* 69: 671–88.

———. (1984) *Spearheads for Reform: The Social Settlements and the Progressive Movement, 1890–1914.* New Brunswick, NJ.

Davis, John H. (1978) *The Guggenheims, 1848–1988: An American Epic.* New York.

Davis, Marni. (2006) "'On the Side of Liquor': American Jews and the Politics of Alcohol, 1870–1936." Ph.D. diss., Emory University.

Davis, Melvin Duane. (2005) "Collecting Hispania: Archer Huntington's Quest to Develop Hispanic Collections in the United States." Ph.D. diss., University of Alabama.

Davis, Mike. (1998) "Golden Ruins/Dark Raptures." In *Dark Raptures: Mike Davis' L.A.*, by Mike Davis et al. Berkeley, CA.

———. (2007) *Buda's Wagon: A Brief History of the Car Bomb.* London.

Davis, Peter A. (1991) "The Syndicate/Shubert War." In *Inventing Times Square: Commerce and Culture at the Crossroads of the World*, edited by William R. Taylor. New York.

Dawley, Alan. (1991) *Struggles for Justice: Social Responsibility and the Liberal State.* Cambridge, MA.

———. (2003) *Changing the World: American Progressives in War and Revolution.* Princeton, NJ.

Dawley, Powel Mills. (1969) *The Story of the General Theological Seminary: A Sesquicentennial History, 1817–1967.* New York.

De Leeuw, Rudolph M. (1910) *Both Sides of Broadway, from Bowling Green to Central Park, New York City.* New York.

De Young, Mary. (1983) "Help, I'm Being Held Captive! The White Slave Fairy Tale of the Progressive Era." *Journal of American Culture* 6: 96–99.

Dearing, Albin Pasteur. (1986) *The Elegant Inn: The Waldorf-Astoria Hotel, 1893–1929.* Secaucus, NJ.

DeArment, Robert K. (2013) *Gunfighter in Gotham: Bat Masterson's New York City Years.* Norman, OK.

Deats, Richard. (2001) "The Rebel Passion: Eighty-Five Years of the Fellowship of Reconciliation." *FOR's Blog*, March 29, 1–10.

Degler, Carl N. (1991) *In Search of Human Nature: The Decline and Revival of Darwinism in American Social Thought.* New York.

DeGraaf, Leonard. (1995) "Confronting the Mass Market: Thomas Edison and the Entertainment Phonograph." *Business and Economic History* 24: 88–96.

Dekar, Paul R. (2005) *Creating the Beloved Community: A Journey with the Fellowship of Reconciliation.* Telford, PA.

Del Valle, Cezar Joseph. (2010) *The Brooklyn Theatre Index.* Brooklyn, NY.

Delaney, Paul E. (1983) *Sandhogs: A History of the Tunnel Workers of New York.* New York.

Delegard, Kirsten Marie. (2012) *Battling Miss Bolsheviki: The Origins of Female Conservatism in the United States.* Philadelphia, PA.

Department of Health of the City of New York and Hermann Biggs. (1908) *Brief History of the Campaign against Tuberculosis in New York City: Catalogue of the Tuberculosis Exhibit of the Department of Health, City of New York.* New York.

Derickson, Alan. (2005) *Health Security for All: Dreams of Universal Health Care in America.* Baltimore, MD.

Derrick, Peter. (1979) "The Dual System of Rapid Transit." Ph.D. diss., New York University.

———. (2001) *Tunneling to the Future: The Story of the Great Subway Expansion That Saved New York.* New York.

Deutscher, Isaac. (1954) *The Prophet Armed: Trotsky, 1879–1921.* New York.

DeVault, Ileen A. (2004) *United Apart: Gender and the Rise of Craft Unionism.* Ithaca, NY.

Devine, Edward T. (1909a) *Report on the Desirability of Establishing an Employment Bureau in the City of New York.* New York.

———. (1909b) *Misery and Its Causes.* New York.

Devorkin, Joseph. (1987) *Great Merchants of Early New York: "The Ladies Mile."* New York.

Dewing, Arthur S. (1913) *A History of the National Cordage Company with a Supplement Containing Copies of Important Documents.* Cambridge, MA.

Diaz-Espino, Ovidio. (2003) *How Wall Street Created a Nation: J. P. Morgan, Teddy Roosevelt, and the Panama Canal.* New York.

Dickstein, Morris. (2005) *A Mirror in the Roadway: Literature and the Real World.* Princeton, NJ.

Diehl, Lorraine B. (1985) *The Late, Great Pennsylvania Station.* New York.

Dierickx, Mary B. (1996) *The Architecture of Literacy: The Carnegie Libraries of New York City.* New York.

Diner, Hasia R. (1995) *In the Almost Promised Land: American Jews and Blacks, 1915–1935.* Baltimore, MD.

Distler, Paul Antonie. (1963) "The Rise and Fall of the Racial Comics in American Vaudeville." Ph.D. diss., Tulane University.

Dizikes, John. (1993) *Opera in America: A Cultural History.* New Haven, CT.

Doenecke, Justus D. (2011) *Nothing Less than War: A New History of America's Entry into World War I.* Lexington, KY.

Doezema, Marianne. (1992) *George Bellows and Urban America.* New Haven, CT.

Dolkart, Andrew. (1998) *Morningside Heights: A History of Its Architecture and Development.* New York.

———. (2011) "The Fabric of New York City's Garment District: Architecture and Development in an Urban Cultural Landscape." *Buildings and Landscapes: Journal of the Vernacular Architecture Forum* 18: 14–42.

———. (n.d.) *American Manufacturing Company: A Brief History and Preliminary Analysis of Building Construction.* New York.

Dolkart, Andrew, and Landmarks Preservation Commission. (2007) *Dumbo Historic District Designation Report.* New York.

Dolkart, Andrew, and Matthew A. Postal. (2009) *Guide to New York City Landmarks.* Hoboken, NJ.

Domingo, W. A. (1925) "The Tropics in New York." *Survey* 53: 648–50.

Domosh, Mona. (1985) "Scrapers of the Sky: The Symbolic and Functional Structures of Lower Manhattan." Ph.D. diss., Clark University.

———. (2006) *American Commodities in an Age of Empire.* New York.

Donati, William. (2010) *Lucky Luciano: The Rise and Fall of a Mob Boss.* Jefferson, NC.

Donnelly, James Francis. (1982) "Catholic New Yorkers and New York Socialists, 1870–1920." Ph.D. diss., New York University.

Donner, Frank J. (1990) *Protectors of Privilege: Red Squads and Police Repression in Urban America.* Berkeley, CA.

Donovan, Brian. (2006) *White Slave Crusades: Race, Gender, and Anti-Vice Activism, 1887–1917.* Urbana, IL.

Dorman, James H. (1988) "Shaping the Popular Image of Post-Reconstruction American Blacks: The 'Coon Song'

Phenomenon of the Gilded Age." *American Quarterly* 40: 450–71.

———. (1991) "European Immigrant/Ethnic Theater in Gilded Age New York: Reflections and Projections of Mentalities." In *Immigration to New York*, edited by William Pencak, Selma Berrol, and Randall M. Miller. Philadephia, PA.

Dorsey, Leroy G. (1995) "Theodore Roosevelt and Corporate America, 1901–1909: A Reexamination." *Presidential Studies Quarterly* 25: 725–39.

Douglas, George H. (1991) *The Smart Magazines: 50 Years of Literary Revelry and High Jinks at "Vanity Fair," "The New Yorker," "Life," "Esquire," and "The Smart Set."* Hamden, CT.

Dowling, Harry Filmore. (1982) *City Hospitals: The Undercare of the Underprivileged.* Cambridge, MA.

Dowling, Robert M. (2009) *Critical Companion to Eugene O'Neill: A Literary Reference to His Life and Work.* New York.

———. (2001) "Slumming: Morality and Space in New York City from 'City Mysteries' to the Harlem Renaissance." Ph.D. diss., City University of New York.

Downey, Kirstin. (2009) *The Woman behind the New Deal: The Life of Frances Perkins, FDR's Secretary of Labor and His Moral Conscience.* New York.

Downey, Patrick. (2004) *Gangster City: A History of the New York Underworld, 1900–1940.* Fort Lee, NJ.

Doyle, H. J. (1905) *The Tourist's Hand-Book of New York: Landmarks, Historical Features, Chronology.* New York.

Doyle, Joe. (1996) "Striking for Ireland on the New York Docks." In *The New York Irish*, edited by Ronald H. Bayor and Timothy J. Meagher. Baltimore, MD.

Draper, Theodore. (1957) *The Roots of American Communism.* New York.

Dreiser, Theodore. (1907) *Sister Carrie.* New York.

———. (1923) *The Color of a Great City.* New York.

Du Bois, W. E. B. (1903) "Some Notes on the Negroes in New York City." In *Pamphlets and Leaflets*, edited by Herbert Aptheker. White Plains, NY.

———. (1914) "World War and the Color Line." *Crisis* 9: 28–30.

Dubbert, Joe L. (1974) "Progressivism and the Masculinity Crisis." *Psychoanalytic Review* 61: 443–55.

———. (1979) *A Man's Place: Masculinity in Transition.* Upper Saddle River, NJ.

Dubofsky, Melvyn. (1961) "Organized Labor in New York City and the First World War, 1914–1918." *New York History* 42: 380–400.

———. (1968a) "Success and Failure of Socialism in New York City, 1900–1918." *Labor History* 9: 361–75.

———. (1968b) *When Workers Organize: New York City in the Progressive Era.* Amherst, MA.

———. (1987) *"Big Bill" Haywood.* New York.

———. (1988) *We Shall Be All: A History of the Industrial Workers of the World.* Urbana, IL.

Dubofsky, Melvyn, and Warren R. Van Tine, eds. (1987) *Labor Leaders in America.* Urbana, IL.

DuBois, Ellen Carol. (1987) "Working Women, Class Relations, and Suffrage Militance: Harriet Stanton Blatch and the New York Woman Suffrage Movement, 1894–1909." *Journal of American History* 74: 34–58.

Duffy, John. (1974) *A History of Public Health in New York City, vol. 2, 1866–1966.* New York.

Duke, David Nelson. (2003) *In the Trenches with Jesus and Marx: Harry F. Ward

and the Struggle for Social Justice.* Tuscaloosa, AL.

Dunlap, David W. (2004) *From Abyssinian to Zion: A Guide to Manhattan's Houses of Worship.* New York.

Durante, Francesco, and Robert Viscusi. (2014) *Italoamericana: The Literature of the Great Migration, 1880–1943.* The Bronx, NY.

Dwight, Eleanor. (1996) *The Gilded Age: Edith Wharton and Her Contemporaries.* New York.

Dyckoff, E. F. (1914) "A Negro City in New York." *Outlook* 108: 949–54.

Dye, Nancy Schrom. (1980) *As Equals and as Sisters: Feminism, the Labor Movement, and the Women's Trade Union League of New York.* Columbia, MO.

Dyer, Thomas G. (1980) *Theodore Roosevelt and the Idea of Race.* Baton Rouge, LA.

Ecker, Susan, and Lloyd Ecker. (2009) *Sophie Tucker: Origins of the Red Hot Mama, 1910–1922.* Champaign, IL.

Educational Service Bureau, American Gas Association. (1960) *The History of Natural Gas.* Dallas, TX.

Edwards, Richard. (1979) *Contested Terrain: The Transformation of the Workplace in the Twentieth Century.* New York.

Ehrenreich, John H. (1985) *The Altruistic Imagination: A History of Social Work and Social Policy in the United States.* Ithaca, NY.

Eichengreen, Barry. (1989) "The U.S. Capital Market and Foreign Lending, 1920–1955." In *Developing Country Debt and the World Economy*, edited by Jeffrey Sachs. Chicago, IL.

Eichner, Alfred. (1969) *The Emergence of Oligopoly: Sugar Refining as a Case Study.* Baltimore, MD.

Eiler, Keith E. (1997) *Mobilizing America: Robert P. Patterson and the War Effort, 1940–1945.* Ithaca, NY.

Eisenstadt, Peter R. (2010) *Rochdale Village: Robert Moses, 6,000 Families, and

New York City's Great Experiment in Integrated Housing. Ithaca, NY.

Eisler, Paul E. (1984) *The Metropolitan Opera: The First Twenty-Five Years, 1883–1908*. Croton-on-Hudson, NY.

Ekman, Katri. (1976) "The Co-Operative Movement in Brooklyn, Manhattan, and the Bronx." In Ekman et al., *A History of Finnish American Organizations in Greater New York, 1891–1976: A Project of the Greater New York Finnish Bicentennial Planning Committee, Inc.* New York.

Ellis, Charles D. (2008) *The Partnership: The Making of Goldman Sachs*. New York.

Ellis, Mark. (1992) " 'Closing Ranks' and 'Seeking Honors': W. E. B. Du Bois in World War I." *Journal of American History* 79: 96–124.

———. (2001) *Race, War, and Surveillance: African Americans and the United States Government during World War I*. Bloomington, IN.

Emmons, William M., III. (1993) "Franklin D. Roosevelt, Electric Utilities, and the Power of Competition." *Journal of Economic History* 53: 880–907.

Engelhardt, George W., and Merchants' Association of New York. (1902) *New York, the Metropolis: The Book of Its Merchants' Association and of Co-operating Public Bodies*. New York.

England, George Allan. (1914) *Darkness and Dawn*. Boston, MA.

Epstein, Barbara. (1984) "Family, Sexual Morality, and Popular Movements in Turn-of-the-Century America." In *Powers of Desire: The Politics of Sexuality*, edited by Ann Snitow, Christine Stansell, and Sharon Thompson. London.

Epstein, Helen. (2013) "The Doctor Who Made a Revolution." *New York Review of Books*, September 26, 74.

Epstein, Jason, et al. (1985) *East Hampton: A History and Guide*. New York.

Epstein, Jonathan A. (2000) "German and English Propaganda in World War I." Paper presented at New York Military Affairs Symposium. New York.

Epstein, Lawrence J. (2004) *Mixed Nuts: America's Love Affair with Comedy Teams from Burns and Allen to Belushi and Aykroyd*. New York.

Epstein, Melech. (1965) *Profiles of Eleven: Profiles of Eleven Men Who Guided the Destiny of an Immigrant Society and Stimulated Social Consciousness among the American People*. Detroit, MI.

Erdman, Andrew L. (2004) *Blue Vaudeville: Sex, Morals and the Mass Marketing of Amusement, 1895–1915*. Jefferson, NC.

Erdman, Harley. (1997) *Staging the Jew: The Performance of an American Ethnicity, 1860–1920*. New Brunswick, NJ.

Erenberg, Lewis A. (1984) *Steppin' Out: New York Nightlife and the Transformation of American Culture, 1890–1930*. Chicago, IL.

———. (1991) "Impresarios of Broadway Nightlife." In *Inventing Times Square: Commerce and Culture at the Crossroads of the World*, edited by William R. Taylor. New York.

Erie, Steven P. (1988) *Rainbow's End: Irish-Americans and the Dilemmas of Urban Machine Politics, 1840–1985*. Berkeley, CA.

Ernst, Morris Leopold. (1940) *Too Big*. Boston, MA.

Evans, Christopher Hodge. (2004) *The Kingdom Is Always but Coming: A Life of Walter Rauschenbusch*. Grand Rapids, MI.

Ewen, Elizabeth. (1985) *Immigrant Women in the Land of Dollars: Life and Culture on the Lower East Side, 1890–1925*. New York.

Ewing, Adam. (2014) *The Age of Garvey: How a*

Jamaican Activist Created a Mass Movement and Changed Global Black Politics. Princeton, NJ.

Fabian, Larry L. (1985) *Andrew Carnegie's Peace Endowment: The Tycoon, the President, and Their Bargain of 1910*. New York.

Faderman, Lillian. (1991) *Odd Girls and Twilight Lovers: A History of Lesbian Life in Twentieth-Century America*. New York.

Fairfield, John D. (1985) "Neighborhood and Metropolis: The Origins of Modern Urban Planning, 1877–1935." Ph.D. diss., University of Rochester.

———. (1994) "The Scientific Management of Urban Space: Professional City Planning and the Legacy of Progressive Reform." *Journal of Urban History* 20: 179–204.

Farley, W. H. (1903) "Jurisdictional Arbitration in the New York United Board of Building Trades." *Official Journal of the Brotherhood of Painters, Decorators and Paperhangers of America* 17: 325–28.

Fass, Paula S. (1989) *Outside In: Minorities and the Transformation of American Education*. New York.

Fastenau, Maureen. (1982) "Maternal Government: The Social Settlement Houses and the Politicization of Women's Sphere, 1889–1920." Ph.D. diss., Duke University.

Faussette, Risa L. (2002) "Race, Migration, and Port City Radicalism: New York's Black Longshoremen and the Politics of Maritime Protest, 1900–1920." Ph.D. diss., State University of New York at Binghamton.

Feder, Leah Hannah. (1936) *Unemployment Relief in Periods of Depression: A Study of Measures Adopted in Certain American Cities, 1857–1922*. New York.

Federal Writers' Project. (1982) *The WPA Guide to*

New York City: The Federal Writers' Project Guide to 1930s New York. New York.

Fee, Elizabeth, and Evelynn M. Hammonds. (1995) "Science, Politics, and the Art of Persuasion: Promoting the New Scientific Medicine in New York City." In *Hives of Sickness: Public Health and Epidemics in New York City*, edited by David Rosner. New Brunswick, NJ.

Fee, Elizabeth, and Michael Wallace. (1979) "The History and Politics of Birth Control: A Review Essay." *Feminist Studies* 5: 201–15.

Feld, Marjorie N. (2008) *Lillian Wald: A Biography*. Chapel Hill, NC.

Feldberg, Roslyn L. (1980) " 'Union Fever': Organizing among Clerical Workers, 1900–1930." *Radical America* 14: 53–67.

Feldman, Egal. (1967) "Prostitution, the Alien Woman and the Progressive Imagination, 1900–1915." *American Quarterly* 19: 192–206.

Felt, Jeremy P. (1965) *Hostages of Fortune: Child Labor Reform in New York State*. Syracuse, NY.

———. (1973) "Vice Reform as a Political Technique: The Committee of Fifteen in New York, 1900–1901." *New York History* 54: 24–51.

Fenske, Gail. (2008) *The Skyscraper and the City: The Woolworth Building and the Making of Modern New York*. Chicago, IL.

Fenske, Gail, and Deryck Holdsworth. (1992) "Corporate Identity and the New York Office Building, 1895–1915." In *The Landscape of Modernity: Essays on New York City: 1900–1940*, edited by David Ward and Oliver Zunz. New York.

Fenton, Edwin. (1957) "Immigrants and Unions: A Case Study of Italians and American Labor, 1870–1920." Ph.D. diss., Harvard University.

Ferguson, Thomas. (1995) *Golden Rule: The Investment Theory of Party Competition and the Logic of Money-Driven Political Systems.* Chicago, IL.

Fernandez, James D. (2002) "'Longfellow's Law': The Place of Latin America and Spain in U.S. Hispanism, circa 1915." In *Spain in America: The Origins of Hispanism in the United States,* edited by Richard L. Kagan. Urbana, IL.

———. (2010) "The Discovery of Spain in New York, circa 1930." In *Nueva York, 1613–1945,* edited by Edward J. Sullivan. New York.

Ferrara, Eric. (2011a) *The Bowery: A History of Grit, Graft and Grandeur.* Charleston, SC.

———. (2011b) *Manhattan Mafia Guide: Hits, Homes and Headquarters.* Charleston, SC.

Fiedler, Johanna. (2001) *Molto Agitato: The Mayhem behind the Music at the Metropolitan Opera.* New York.

Fields, Armond. (2003) *Sophie Tucker: First Lady of Show Business.* Jefferson, NC.

Fierstien, Robert E. (1990) *A Different Spirit: The Jewish Theological Seminary of America, 1886–1902.* New York.

Fifth Avenue Bank of New York. (1915) *Fifth Avenue: Glances at the Vicissitudes and Romance of a World-Renowned Thoroughfare, Together with Many Rare Illustrations That Bring Back an Interesting Past.* Boston, MA.

Filippo, Ivan Joe. (1972) "Landmark Litigation in the American Theatre." Ph.D. diss., University of Florida.

Filler, Louis. (1939) *Crusaders for American Liberalism.* New York.

———. (1976) *The Muckrakers.* University Park, PA.

———. (1993) "Theodore Dreiser and the Anti-Progressive Drive." *Biography* 16: 249–57.

Finan, Christopher M. (2002) *Alfred E. Smith, the Happy Warrior.* New York.

Finch, Christopher. (1992) *Highways to Heaven: The Auto Biography of America.* New York.

Fine, Sidney. (1962) *Recent America: Conflicting Interpretations of the Great Issues.* New York.

———. (1995) *Without Blare of Trumpets: Walter Drew, the National Erectors' Association, and the Open Shop Movement, 1903–57.* Ann Arbor, MI.

Finegold, Kenneth. (1985) "Progressivism, Electoral Change and Public Policy: Reform Outcomes in New York, Cleveland and Chicago." Ph.D. diss., Harvard University.

———. (1995) *Experts and Politicians: Reform Challenges to Machine Politics in New York, Cleveland, and Chicago.* Princeton, NJ.

Fink, Carole. (2008) "Louis Marshall: An American Jewish Diplomat in Paris, 1919." *American Jewish History* 94: 21–40.

Fink, Leon. (1997) *Progressive Intellectuals and the Dilemmas of Democratic Commitment.* Cambridge, MA.

Finnegan, John Patrick. (1974) *Against the Specter of a Dragon: The Campaign for American Military Preparedness, 1914–1917.* Westport, CT.

Fischler, Stan. (1976) *Uptown, Downtown: A Trip through Time on New York's Subways.* New York.

Fishback, Price V., and Shawn Everett Kantor. (2000) *A Prelude to the Welfare State: The Origins of Workers' Compensation.* Chicago, IL.

Fishbein, Leslie. (1982) *Rebels in Bohemia: The Radicals of "The Masses," 1911–1917.* Chapel Hill, NC.

Fisher, Robert Bruce. (1974) "The People's Institute of New York City, 1897–1934: Culture, Progressive Democracy, and the People." Ph.D. diss., New York University.

Fitch, Robert. (1977) "Planning New York." In

The Fiscal Crisis of American Cities: Essays on the Political Economy of Urban America with Special Reference to New York, edited by Roger E. Alcaly and David Mermelstein. New York.

———. (1985) "The Family Subway: Space, Class, and Power in New York City, 1927–1940." *Research in Political Economy* 8: 163–200.

———. (2006) *Solidarity for Sale: How Corruption Destroyed the Labor Movement and Undermined America's Promise.* New York.

Fitzgerald, Maureen. (2005) *Habits of Compassion: Irish Catholic Nuns and the Origins of New York's Welfare System, 1830–1920.* Urbana, IL.

Fitzherbert, Anthony. (1964) "The Public Be Pleased": William G. McAdoo and the Hudson Tubes. New York.

Fitzpatrick, Ellen. (1990) *Endless Crusade: Women Social Scientists and Progressive Reform.* New York.

Fitzpatrick, Tracy. (2009) *Art and the Subway: New York Underground.* New Brunswick, NJ.

Flandro, Xsusha Carlyann, et al. (2008) *Progressive Housing in New York City: A Closer Look at Model Tenements and Finnish Cooperatives.* New York.

Flick, Alexander C. (1939) *Samuel Jones Tilden: A Study in Political Sagacity.* New York.

Flick, Ella. (1935) *Chaplain Duffy of the Sixty-Ninth Regiment, New York.* Philadelphia, PA.

Flink, James J. (1970) *America Adopts the Automobile, 1895–1910.* Cambridge, MA.

———. (1975) *The Car Culture.* Cambridge, MA.

Floyd, Silas Xavier. (1902) *Life of Charles T. Walker, D.D. ("the Black Spurgeon"): Pastor, Mt. Olivet Baptist Church, New York City.* Nashville, TN.

Flynt, Josiah. (1907) "The Telegraph and Telephone Companies as Allies of the

Criminal Pool-Rooms." *Cosmopolitan* 43: 50–57.

Fogelson, Robert M. (2001) *Downtown: Its Rise and Fall, 1880–1950.* New Haven, CT.

———. (2013) *The Great Rent Wars: New York, 1917–1929.* New Haven, CT.

Foglesong, Richard E. (1986) *Planning the Capitalist City: The Colonial Era to the 1920s.* Princeton, NJ.

Foner, Eric. (1988) *Reconstruction: America's Unfinished Revolution, 1863–1877.* New York.

Foner, Nancy. (2000) *From Ellis Island to JFK: New York's Two Great Waves of Immigration.* New Haven, CT.

Foner, Philip S. (1950) *The Fur and Leather Workers Union: A Story of Dramatic Struggles and Achievements.* Newark, NJ.

———. (1964) *History of the Labor Movement in the United States,* vol. 3, *The Policies and Practices of the American Federation of Labor.* New York.

———. (1965) *History of the Labor Movement in the United States,* vol. 4, *The Industrial Workers of the World, 1905–1917.* New York.

———. (1972a) *The Spanish-Cuban-American War and the Birth of American Imperialism,* vol. 1, *1895–1898.* New York.

———. (1972b) *The Spanish-Cuban-American War and the Birth of American Imperialism,* vol. 2, *1898–1902.* New York.

———. (1982) *Women and the American Labor Movement: From the First Trade Unions to the Present.* New York.

Foord, John. (1913) *The Life and Public Services of Andrew Haswell Green.* Garden City, NY.

Forbes, Camille F. (2008) *Introducing Bert Williams: Burnt Cork, Broadway, and the Story of America's First Black Star.* New York.

Forcey, Charles. (1961) *The Crossroads of Liberalism: Croly, Weyl, Lippman, and* the Progressive Era, 1900–1925. New York.

Fortune, Timothy Thomas. (2008) *T. Thomas Fortune, the Afro-American Agitator: A Collection of Writings, 1880–1928*, edited by Shawn Leigh Alexander. Gainesville, FL.

Fosdick, Raymond B. (1915) *European Police Systems.* New York.

———. (1920) *American Police Systems.* New York.

———. (1956) *John D. Rockefeller, Jr.: A Portrait.* New York.

———. (1962) *Adventure in Giving: The Story of the General Education Board, a Foundation Established by John D. Rockefeller.* New York.

Foster & Reynolds Co. (1917) *New York, the Metropolis of the Western World.* New York.

Foster, Mark S. (1981) *From Streetcar to Superhighway: American City Planners and Urban Transportation, 1900–1940.* Philadelphia, PA.

Fotsch, Paul Mason. (2007) *Watching the Traffic Go By: Transportation and Isolation in Urban America.* Austin, TX.

Fox, Daniel M. (2006) "The Significance of the Milbank Memorial Fund for Policy: An Assessment at Its Centennial." *Milbank Quarterly* 84: 5–36.

Fox, Kenneth. (1977) *Better City Government: Innovation in American Urban Politics, 1850–1937.* Philadelphia, PA.

Fox, Richard Wightman, and T. J. Jackson Lears, eds. (1993) *The Power of Culture: Critical Essays in American History.* Chicago, IL.

Fox, Stephen. (1993) *Blood and Power: Organized Crime in Twentieth-Century America.* New York.

Frank, Gelya. (1997) "Jews, Multiculturalism, and Boasian Anthropology." *American Anthropologist* 99: 731–45.

Frankel, Jonathan. (1981) *Prophecy and Politics:*

Socialism, Nationalism, and the Russian Jews, 1862–1917. Cambridge, UK.

Franzen, Jonathan. (2012) "A Rooting Interest: Edith Wharton and the Problem of Sympathy." *New Yorker*, February 13, 60–65.

Fraser, John Foster. (1903) *America at Work.* London.

Fraser, Steve. (1991) *Labor Will Rule: Sidney Hillman and the Rise of American Labor.* New York.

———. (2005) *Every Man a Speculator: A History of Wall Street in American Life.* New York.

Fredericks, B. T. (1905) "James Farley, Strike-Breaker." *Leslie's Monthly Magazine* 60: 106–10.

Freeman, Jo. (2001) "'One Man, One Vote; One Woman, One Throat': Women in New York City Politics, 1890–1910." *American Nineteenth Century History* 1: 101–23.

Freeman, Joshua B. (1989) *In Transit: The Transport Workers Union in New York City, 1933–1966.* New York.

French, James B. (1917) "The East New York Tunnel: A Part of the Bay Ridge Improvement of the Long Island Railroad." *Brooklyn Engineers' Club Proceedings* 20 (for 1916): 72–101.

Frieburger, William. (1980) "The Lone Socialist Vote: A Political Study of Meyer London." Ph.D. diss., University of Cincinnati.

Fried, Albert. (1980) *The Rise and Fall of the Jewish Gangster in America.* New York.

Fried, Lewis. (2001) "Creating Hebraism, Confronting Hellenism: The *Menorah Journal* and Its Struggle for the Jewish Imagination." *American Jewish Archives Journal* 43: 147–74.

Frieden, Jeffry A. (1988) "Sectoral Conflict and Foreign Economic Policy, 1914–1940." *International Organization* 42: 59–90.

———. (1987) *Banking on the World: The Politics of*

American International Finance. New York.

Friedman, Andrea. (2000) *Prurient Interests: Gender, Democracy, and Obscenity in New York City, 1909–1945.* New York.

Friedman, Isaiah. (1992) *The Question of Palestine: British-Jewish-Arab Relations, 1914–1918.* New Brunswick, NJ.

Friedman, Milton, and Anna J. Schwartz. (1963) *A Monetary History of the United States, 1867–1960.* Princeton, NJ.

Fronc, Jennifer. (2009) *New York Undercover: Private Surveillance in the Progressive Era.* Chicago, IL.

Frusciano, Thomas J., and Marilyn H. Pettit. (1997) *New York University and the City: An Illustrated History, 1831–1996.* New Brunswick, NJ.

Funigiello, Philip J. (2005) *Chronic Politics: Health Care Security from FDR to George W. Bush.* Lawrence, KS.

Furia, Philip. (1990) *The Poets of Tin Pan Alley: A History of America's Great Lyricists.* New York.

Furia, Philip, and Graham Wood. (1998) *Irving Berlin: A Life in Song.* New York.

Furio, Colomba Marie. (1979) "Immigrant Women and Industry: A Case Study—the Italian Immigrant Women and the Garment Industry, 1880–1950." Ph.D. diss., New York University.

Gabaccia, Donna R. (1986) "Neither Padrone Slaves nor Primitive Rebels: Sicilians on Two Continents." In *"Struggle a Hard Battle": Essays on Working-Class Immigrants*, edited by Dirk Hoerder. DeKalb, IL.

———. (1988) *Militants and Migrants: Rural Sicilians Become American Workers.* New Brunswick, NJ.

Gable, John A. (1978) *The Bull Moose Years: Theodore Roosevelt and the Progressive Party.* Port Washington, NY.

Gabler, Neal. (1988) *An Empire of Their Own: How*

the Jews Invented Hollywood. New York.

Gage, Beverly. (2009) *The Day Wall Street Exploded: A Story of America in Its First Age of Terror.* New York.

Galenson, Walter. (1983) *The United Brotherhood of Carpenters: The First Hundred Years.* Cambridge, MA.

Gallagher, Dorothy. (1988) *All the Right Enemies: The Life and Murder of Carlo Tresca.* New Brunswick, NJ.

Galusha, Diane. (2002) *Liquid Assets: A History of New York City's Water System.* Fleischmanns, NY.

Gambee, Robert. (1999) *Wall Street: Financial Capital.* New York.

Gannon, Robert I. (1967) *Up to the Present: The Story of Fordham.* Garden City, NY.

Gardner, Deborah S. (1990) "Practical Philanthropy: The Phelps-Stokes Fund and Housing." *Prospects* 15: 359–411.

Gardner, James F. (1974) "Microbes and Morality: The Social Hygiene Crusade in New York City, 1892–1917." Ph.D. diss., Indiana University.

Gardner, Lloyd C. (1984) *Safe for Democracy: The Anglo-American Response to Revolution, 1913–1923.* New York.

Garland, Allen E. (1986) "The Eugenics Record Office at Cold Spring Harbor, 1910–1940: An Essay in Institutional History." *Osiris* 2: 225–64.

Garn, Andrew, and New York Transit Museum. (2004) *Subway Style: 100 Years of Architecture and Design in the New York City Subway.* New York.

Garraty, John A. (1960) *Right-Hand Man: The Life of George W. Perkins.* New York.

Garrison, Dee. (1979) *Apostles of Culture: The Public Librarian and American Society, 1876–1920.* New York.

———. (1989) *Mary Heaton Vorse: The Life of an American Insurgent.* Philadelphia, PA.

Garvey, Marcus, et al. (1983a) *The Marcus Garvey and Universal Negro Improvement Association Papers*, vol. 1, *1826–August 1919*, edited by Robert Abraham Hill. Berkeley, CA.

———. (1983b) *The Marcus Garvey and Universal Negro Improvement Association Papers*, vol. 2, *August 1919–August 1920*, edited by Robert Abraham Hill. Berkeley, CA.

Gate to the Sea. (1897) Brooklyn, NY.

Gates, Jennifer. (1997) "Strangers in New York: Ethnic Tourism as Commodity, Spectacle, and Urban Leisure in Three Manhattan Neighborhoods." Ph.D. diss., New York University.

Gates, Robert A. (1987) "The Polarized City: Edith Wharton's *The House of Mirth* and Stephen Crane's *Maggie*." In Gates, *The New York Vision: Interpretations of New York City in the American Novel*. Lanham, MD.

Geisst, Charles R. (2001) *The Last Partnerships: Inside the Great Wall Street Money Dynasties*. New York.

———. (2004) *Wall Street: A History: From Its Beginnings to the Fall of Enron*. New York.

Gelatt, Roland. (1977) *The Fabulous Phonograph, 1877–1977*. London.

Gelfant, Blanche Housman. (1970) *The American City Novel*. Norman, OK.

Genovese, Eugene D. (1971) *In Red and Black: Marxian Explorations in Southern and Afro-American History*. New York.

Gerstle, Gary. (2001) *American Crucible: Race and Nation in the Twentieth Century*. Princeton, NJ.

Gettleman, Marvin E. (1970) "John H. Finley at CCNY—1903–1913." *History of Education Quarterly* 10: 423–39.

Giamo, Benedict. (1989) *On the Bowery: Confronting Homelessness in American Society*. Iowa City, IA.

Gibbs, Kenneth T. (1984) *Business Architectural Imagery in America, 1870–1930*. Ann Arbor, MI.

Giddings, Paula. (1984) *When and Where I Enter: The Impact of Black Women of Race and Sex in America*. New York.

Giffin, Frederick C. (1968) "Leon Trotsky in New York City." *New York History* 49: 391–403.

———. (1999) "Morris Hillquit and the War Issue in the New York Mayoralty Campaign of 1917." *International Social Science Review* 74: 115–28.

Gilbert, David. (2011) "The Product of Our Souls: Ragtime, Race, and the Marketplace in James Reese Europe's New York." Ph.D. diss., University of Wisconsin–Madison.

Gilbert, Douglas. (1940) *American Vaudeville: Its Life and Times*. New York.

Giles, James R. (1976) *Claude McKay*. Boston, MA.

Gilfoyle, Timothy J. (1986) "The Moral Origins of Political Surveillance: The Preventive Society in New York City, 1867–1918." *American Quarterly* 38: 637–52.

———. (1989) "From 'Tenderloin' to Times Square: The Policing of Sexuality in New York City, 1890–1930." Paper presented at Inventing Times Square Conference. New York.

———. (1992) *City of Eros: New York City, Prostitution, and the Commercialization of Sex, 1790–1920*. New York.

Gill, Jonathan. (2011) *Harlem: The Four Hundred Year History from Dutch Village to Capital of Black America*. New York.

Gillman, Lucy P. (1955) "Coney Island." *New York History* 36: 255–90.

Gilmartin, Gregory F. (1994) *Shaping the City: New York and the Municipal Art Society*. New York.

Gilmer, Walker. (1970) *Horace Liveright, Publisher of the Twenties*. New York.

Glassberg, David. (1990) *American Historical Pageantry: The Uses of Tradition in the Early Twentieth Century*. Chapel Hill, NC.

Glassgold, Peter. (2001) *Anarchy! An Anthology of Emma Goldman's "Mother Earth."* Washington, DC.

Gleason, Mildred Diane, and Hollis Micheal Tarver Denova. (2013) *Warren G. Harding: Harbinger of Normalcy*. New York.

Gleason, Philip. (1992) *Speaking of Diversity: Language and Ethnicity in Twentieth-Century America*. Baltimore, MD.

Goddard, David. (2011) *Colonizing Southampton: The Transformation of a Long Island Community, 1870–1900*. Albany, NY.

Goddard, Stephen B. (1996) *Getting There: The Epic Struggle between Road and Rail in the American Century*. Chicago, IL.

Goldberg, Gordon J. (2013) *Meyer London: A Biography of the Socialist New York Congressman, 1871–1926*. Jefferson, NC.

Goldberger, Paul. (1981) *The Skyscraper*. New York.

Golden, Eve. (2000) *Anna Held and the Birth of Ziegfeld's Broadway*. Lexington, KY.

———. (2007) *Vernon and Irene Castle's Ragtime Revolution*. Lexington, KY.

Goldman, Emma. (1915) *Preparedness, the Road to Universal Slaughter*. New York.

———. (1917a) "The Hypocrisy of Puritanism." In Goldman, *"Anarchism" and Other Essays*. New York.

———. (1917b) "Marriage and Love." In Goldman, *"Anarchism" and Other Essays*. New York.

———. (1917c) "The No-Conscription League." *Mother Earth* 12: 112–14.

———. (1917d) "The Promoters of the War Mania." *Mother Earth* 12: 17–19.

———. (1917e) "The Tragedy of Woman's Emancipation." In Goldman, *"Anarchism" and Other Essays*. New York.

———. (1934) *Living My Life*. New York.

Goldman, Emma, et al. (2003a) *Emma Goldman: A Documentary History of the American Years*, edited by Candace Falk et al. Vol. 1. Berkeley, CA.

———. (2003b) *Emma Goldman: A Documentary History of the American Years*, edited by Candace Falk et al. Vol. 2. Berkeley, CA.

Goldman, Eric F. (1978) "Public Relations and the Progressive Surge, 1898–1917." *Public Relations Review* 4: 52–62.

Goldman, Herbert G. (1992) *Fanny Brice: The Original Funny Girl*. New York.

———. (1997) *Banjo Eyes: Eddie Cantor and the Birth of Modern Stardom*. New York.

Goldstein, Michael. (1980) "Black Power and the Rise of Bureaucratic Autonomy in New York City Politics: The Case of Harlem Hospital, 1917–1931." *Phylon* 41: 187–201.

Goldstein, Michael L. (1977) "Preface to the Rise of Booker T. Washington: A View from New York City of the Demise of Independent Black Politics, 1889–1902." *Journal of Negro History* 62: 81–99.

Golin, Steve. (1983) "The Paterson Pageant: Success or Failure?" *Socialist Review* 69: 45–71.

———. (1988) *The Fragile Bridge: Paterson Silk Strike, 1913*. Philadelphia, PA.

Gompers, Samuel, and Florence Calvert Thorne. (1925) *Seventy Years of Life and Labor: An Autobiography*. New York.

Gonzalez, Evelyn Diaz. (2004) *The Bronx*. New York.

Goodier, Susan. (2013) *No Votes for Women: The New York State Anti-Suffrage Movement*. Urbana, IL.

Goodman, Cary. (1979) *Choosing Sides: Playground and Street Life on the Lower East Side*. New York.

Goodman, Fred. (2004) *The Secret City: Woodlawn Cemetery and the Buried History of New York*. New York.

Goodnow, Frank Johnson. (1900) *Politics and Administration: A Study in Government*. New York.

Goodwin, Doris Kearns. (2013) *The Bully Pulpit: Theodore Roosevelt, William Howard Taft, and the Golden Age of Journalism*. New York.

Goodwyn, Lawrence. (1976) *Democratic Promise: The Populist Moment in America*. New York.

Gordon, Colin. (2003) *Dead on Arrival: The Politics of Health Care in Twentieth-Century America*. Princeton, NJ.

Gordon, David M., Richard Edwards, and Michael Reich. (1982) *Segmented Work, Divided Workers: The Historical Transformation of Labor in the United States*. New York.

Gordon, Eric. (2010) *The Urban Spectator: American Concept Cities from Kodak to Google*. Hanover, NH.

Gordon, Linda. (1976) *Woman's Body, Woman's Right: A Social History of Birth Control in America*. New York.

———. (1991) "Black and White Visions of Warfare: Women's Welfare Activities, 1890–1945." *Journal of American History* 787: 559–90.

———. (1994) *Pitied but Not Entitled: Single Mothers and the History of Welfare, 1890–1935*. New York.

Gorelick, Sherry. (1981) *City College and the Jewish Poor: Education in New York, 1880–1924*. New Brunswick, NJ.

Goren, Arthur A. (1970) *New York Jews and the Quest for Community: The Kehillah Experiment, 1908–1922*. New York.

Gorky, Maksim. (1972) *The City of the Yellow Devil: Pamphlets, Articles and Letters about America*. Moscow.

Gorn, Elliott J. (1986) *The Manly Art: Bare-Knuckle Prize Fighting in America*. Ithaca, NY.

Gornick, Vivian. (2011) *Emma Goldman:*

Revolution as a Way of Life. New Haven, CT.

Gosse, Van. (1990) "Paterson 1913." *Radical History Review* 48: 169–76.

Gould, Harold A. (2006) *Sikhs, Swamis, Students, and Spies: The India Lobby in the United States, 1900–1946*. New Delhi.

Gould, Jack. (1940) "Mrs. Belardi Regrets." *New York Times*, January 2.

Graham, Frank. (1952) *The New York Giants: An Informal History*. New York.

Grant, Colin. (2008) *Negro with a Hat: The Rise and Fall of Marcus Garvey and His Dream of Mother Africa*. New York.

Grant, James. (1997) *Bernard M. Baruch: The Adventures of a Wall Street Legend*. New York.

Gras, Norman Scott Brien. (1971) *Business and Capitalism: An Introduction to Business History*. New York.

Grauman, Melody Webb. (1978) "Kennecott: Alaskan Origins of a Copper Empire, 1900–1938." *Western Historical Quarterly* 9: 197–211.

Grava, Sigurd. (1981) "The Bronx River Parkway: A Case Study in Innovation." *New York Affairs* 7: 15–23.

Graves, Edward C. (1894) *The Greater New York: Reasons Why*. Brooklyn, NY.

Gray, Christopher. (1986) "The Garment Center." *Avenue* 10: 95–103.

———. (1992) *Changing New York: The Architectural Scene*. New York.

———. (2001) "Streetscapes/Long Island City, Queens: After Hard Times, 1910 Auto Factory Gets New Life." *New York Times*, July 22.

Gray, Christopher, and Suzanne Braley. (2003) *New York Streetscapes: Tales of Manhattan's Significant Buildings and Landmarks*. New York.

Gray, Madeline. (1979) *Margaret Sanger: A Biography of the Champion of Birth Control*. New York.

Greater Astoria Historical Society and Roosevelt Island Historical Society. (2008) *The Queensboro Bridge*. Charleston, SC.

Greeley, Dawn. (1995) "Beyond Benevolence: Gender, Class and the Development of Scientific Charity in New York, 1882–1935." Ph.D. diss., State University of New York at Stony Brook.

Green, Andrew Haswell. (1893) *Municipal Consolidation Inquiry: Communication of Andrew H. Green to the Legislature of the State of New York*. New York.

Green, Charles, and Basil Wilson. (1989) *The Struggle for Black Empowerment in New York City: Beyond the Politics of Pigmentation*. New York.

Green, Fulton, Cunningham Company. (1920) *National Survey of the Economic Status of the Horse*. Detroit, MI.

Green, Laurie. (1989) "Lighting the City: Electric Streetlights and Urban Life in New York since 1880." In New York Department of Transportation et al., *Lights on New York! Streetlights and City Life in the Era of Electricity*. New York.

Green, Martin Burgess. (1988) *New York 1913: The Armory Show and the Paterson Strike Pageant*. New York.

Green, Nancy L. (1992) "Sweatshop Migrations: The Garment Industry between Home and Shop." In *The Landscape of Modernity: Essays on New York City, 1900–1940*, edited by David Ward and Oliver Zunz. New York.

———. (1997) *Ready-to-Wear and Ready-to-Work: A Century of Industry and Immigrants in Paris and New York*. Durham, NC.

Greene, Ann Norton. (2008) *Horses at Work: Harnessing Power in Industrial America*. Cambridge, MA.

Greene, Anthony C. (2007) "The Black Bronx: A Look at the Foundation of the

Bronx's Black Communities until 1900." *Bronx County Historical Society Journal* 44: 1–18.

Greene, Daniel. (2011) *The Jewish Origins of Cultural Pluralism: The Menorah Association and American Diversity*. Bloomington, IN.

Greene, Francis Vinton. (1915) *The Present Military Situation in the United States*. New York.

Greene, Julie. (1998) *Pure and Simple Politics: The American Federation of Labor and Political Activism, 1881–1917*. Cambridge, UK.

Greene, Veryl. (1992) "The Allen A.M.E. Church, Jamaica, NY, 1834–1900: The Role of the Black Church in a Developing 19th Century Community." *Afro-Americans in New York Life and History* 16: 31–39.

Greenhalgh, Paul. (1988) *Ephemeral Vistas: The Expositions Universelles, Great Exhibitions and World's Fairs, 1851–1939*. Manchester, UK.

Greenwald, Richard A. (2005) *The Triangle Fire, the Protocols of Peace, and Industrial Democracy in Progressive Era New York*. Philadelphia, PA.

Greenwich Village Society for Historic Preservation. (2002) "Gansevoort Market: A New York City Walking Tour." In *Save Gansevoort Market*, a project of the Greenwich Village Society for Historic Preservation.

Greenwich Village Society for Historic Preservation and Jeffrey P. Zaleski. (1986) *The Greenwich Village Waterfront: An Historical Study Prepared by the Greenwich Village Society for Historic Preservation*. New York.

Greer, Colin. (1976) *The Great School Legend: A Revisionist Interpretation of American Public Education*. New York.

Gregory, Raymond F. (2008) *Norman Thomas: The Great Dissenter*. New York.

Greider, William. (1989) *Secrets of the Temple: How the Federal Reserve Runs the Country.* New York.

Griffeath, Kristin. (2011) "War Sirens: How the Sheet Music Industry Sold World War I." M.M. thesis, University of Missouri–Kansas City.

Grimes, William. (2009) *Appetite City: A Culinary History of New York.* New York.

Grittner, Frederick K. (1990) *White Slavery: Myth, Ideology, and American Law.* New York.

Gronow, Pekka. (1983) "The Record Industry: The Growth of a Mass Medium." *Popular Music* 3: 53–75.

Grose, Peter. (1996) *Continuing the Inquiry: The Council on Foreign Relations from 1921 to 1996.* New York.

Gross, Michael. (2009) *Rogues' Gallery: The Secret History of the Moguls and the Money That Made the Metropolitan Museum.* New York.

Grossman, Barbara Wallace. (1991) *Funny Woman: The Life and Times of Fanny Brice.* Bloomington, IN.

Grout, Edward M. (1897) "New York City Should Own the Gas Supply." *Municipal Affairs* 1: 225–44.

Grubbs, Frank L., Jr. (1968) *The Struggle for Labor Loyalty: Gompers, the A.F. of L., and the Pacifists, 1917–1920.* Durham, NC.

Gualtieri, Sarah. (2001) "Becoming 'White': Race, Religion and the Foundations of Syrian/ Lebanese Ethnicity in the United States." *Journal of American Ethnic History* 20: 29–58.

Guglielmo, Jennifer. (2010) *Living the Revolution: Italian Women's Resistance and Radicalism in New York City, 1880–1945.* Chapel Hill, NC.

Gulick, Luther. (1976) "Beard and Municipal Reform." In *Charles A. Beard: An Appraisal,* edited by Howard K. Beale. New York.

Gurin, David. (1977) "Trolley Transit in New York." *National Railway Bulletin* 42: 4–14, 12–42.

Gurock, Jeffrey S. (1979) *When Harlem Was Jewish, 1870–1930.* New York.

———, ed. (1998) *East European Jews in America, 1880–1920: Immigration and Adaptation.* New York.

Gurstein, Rochelle. (1996) *The Repeal of Reticence: A History of America's Cultural and Legal Struggles over Free Speech, Obscenity, Sexual Liberation, and Modern Art.* New York.

Guterl, Matthew Pratt. (1999) "Investing in Color: A Cultural History of Race in Modern America, 1900–1940." Ph.D. diss., Rutgers University.

———. (2001) *The Color of Race in America, 1900–1940.* Cambridge, MA.

Gutman, Margarita, and Thomas Ford Reese. (1999) *Buenos Aires 1910: El imaginario para una gran capital.* Buenos Aires.

Haber, William. (1930) "Industrial Relations in the Building Industry." Ph.D. diss., University of Wisconsin.

Habstritt, Mary. (2009) "Manhattanville and New York City's Milk Supply." In *Archive of Industry,* edited by Mary Habstritt and Gerald Weinstein. New York.

Haenni, Sabine. (2008) *The Immigrant Scene: Ethnic Amusements in New York, 1880–1920.* Minneapolis, MN.

Hale, Nathan G., Jr. (1971) *Freud and the Americans: The Beginnings of Psychoanalysis in the United States, 1876–1917.* New York.

Hall, Edward Hagaman. (1898) *A Volume Commemorating the Creation of the Second City of the World.* New York.

Hall, Edward Hagaman, and Hudson-Fulton Celebration Commission. (1910) *The Hudson-Fulton Celebration, 1909: The Fourth Annual Report of the Hudson-Fulton Celebration Commission to the Legislature of the State of New York.* Albany, NY.

Haller, Mark H. (1984) *Eugenics: Hereditarian Attitudes in American Thought.* New Brunswick, NJ.

———. (1990) "Illegal Enterprise: A Theoretical and Historical Interpretation." *Criminology* 28: 207–36.

———. (1991) "Policy Gambling, Entertainment, and the Emergence of Black Politics: Chicago from 1900 to 1940." *Journal of Social History* 24: 719–39.

Hamm, Charles. (1979) *Yesterdays: Popular Song in America.* New York.

———. (1997) *Irving Berlin: Songs from the Melting Pot: The Formative Years, 1907–1914.* New York.

Hammack, David C. (1987) *Power and Society: Greater New York at the Turn of the Century.* New York.

———. (1994a) "A Center of Intelligence for the Charity Organization Movement: The Foundation's Early Years." In *Social Science in the Making: Essays on the Russell Sage Foundation, 1907–1972,* edited by David C. Hammack and Stanton Wheeler. New York.

———. (1994b) "Political Participation and Municipal Policy: New York City, 1870–1940." In *Budapest and New York: Studies in Metropolitan Transformation, 1870–1930,* edited by Thomas Bender and Carl E. Schorske. New York.

———. (1996) "Developing for Commercial Culture." In *Inventing Times Square: Commerce and Culture at the Crossroads of the World,* edited by William R. Taylor. New York.

Hammack, David C., and Stanton Wheeler, eds. (1994) *Social Science in the Making: Essays on the Russell Sage Foundation, 1907–1972.* New York.

Handlin, Oscar. (1958) *Al Smith and His America.* Boston, MA.

Handy, Robert T. (1987) *A History of Union Theological Seminary in New York.* New York.

Hanford, Benjamin. (1909) *Fight for Your Life! Recording Some Activities of a Labor Agitator.* New York.

Hansen, Jonathan M. (2003) *The Lost Promise of Patriotism: Debating American Identity, 1890–1920.* Chicago, IL.

Hansen, Miriam. (1994) *Babel and Babylon: Spectatorship in American Silent Film.* Cambridge, MA.

Hanson, Elizabeth. (2000) *The Rockefeller University: Achievements: A Century of Science for the Benefit of Humankind, 1901–2001.* New York.

Hanson, Neil. (2010) *Monk Eastman: The Gangster Who Became a War Hero.* New York.

Hapgood, Hutchins. (1902) *The Spirit of the Ghetto: Studies of the Jewish Quarter in New York.* New York.

Haraway, Donna. (1989) *Primate Visions: Gender, Race, and Nature in the World of Modern Science.* New York.

Harding, Earl. (1959) *The Untold Story of Panama.* New York.

Hardy, Jack. (1935) *The Clothing Workers: A Study of the Conditions and Struggles in the Needle Trades.* New York.

Harlan, Louis R. (1957) "The Southern Education Board and the Race Issue in Public Education." *Journal of Southern History* 23: 189–202.

Harlow, Alvin F. (1947) *The Road of the Century: The Story of the New York Central.* New York.

Harper, Kenn. (2000) *Give Me My Father's Body: The Life of Minik, the New York Eskimo.* South Royalton, VT.

Harris, Charles H., and Louis R. Sadler. (2015) *The Great Call-up: The*

Guard, the Border, and the Mexican Revolution. Norman, OK.

Harris, Christopher. (2005) "Edwin F. Atkins and the Evolution of American Cuba Policy, 1894–1902." *New England Quarterly* 78: 202–31.

Harris, Luther S. (2003) *Around Washington Square: An Illustrated History of Greenwich Village.* Baltimore, MD.

Harris, Max. (2011) "Full Faith and Credit: The United States' Response to the Panic of 1914." *Tempus* 12: 1–22.

Harris, Neil. (1988) "Urban Tourism and the Commercial City." Paper presented at Inventing Times Square Conference. New York.

———. (1990) "Collective Possession: J. Pierpont Morgan and the American Imagination." In Harris, *Cultural Excursions: Marketing Appetite and Cultural Tastes in Modern America.*

Harris, Peter B. (1998) "Some Teachable Ironies about the Alfred Stieglitz Photo *The Steerage* (1907), on the Cover of *The Heath Anthology of American Literature*, 3/E, Volume 2." Available online at http://college.cengage.com/english/heath/harris.htm.

Harris, Stephen L. (2001) *Duty, Honor, Privilege: New York's Silk Stocking Regiment and the Breaking of the Hindenburg Line.* Washington, DC.

———. (2003) *Harlem's Hell Fighters: The African-American 369th Infantry in World War I.* Washington, DC.

———. (2006) *Duffy's War: Fr. Francis Duffy, Wild Bill Donovan, and the Irish Fighting 69th in World War I.* Washington, DC.

Harrison-Kahan, Lori. (2010) *The White Negress: Literature, Minstrelsy, and the Black-Jewish Imaginary.* New Brunswick, NJ.

Harrison, Hubert H., and Jeffrey Babcock Perry.

(2001) *A Hubert Harrison Reader.* Middletown, CT.

Hart, John M. (1987) *Revolutionary Mexico: The Coming and Process of the Mexican Revolution.* Berkeley, CA.

———. (2002) *Empire and Revolution: The Americans in Mexico since the Civil War.* Berkeley, CA.

Hart, Tanya. (2015) *Health in the City: Race, Poverty, and the Negotiation of Women's Health in New York City, 1915–1930.* New York.

Hartshorn, Peter. (2011) *I Have Seen the Future: A Life of Lincoln Steffens.* Berkeley, CA.

Haskell, Barbara. (2013) "The Legacy of the Armory Show: Fiasco or Transformation?" In *The Armory Show at 100: Modernism and Revolution*, edited by Marilyn Satin Kushner and Kimberly Orcutt. New York.

Hatheway, Allen W. (2012) *Remediation of Former Manufactured Gas Plants and Other Coal-Tar Sites.* Boca Raton, FL.

Hauck-Lawson, Annie, and Jonathan Deutsch. (2008) *Gastropolis: Food and New York City.* New York.

Hawes, Elizabeth. (1993) *New York, New York: How the Apartment House Transformed the Life of the City.* New York.

Hayden, Dolores. (1981) *The Grand Domestic Revolution: A History of Feminist Designs for American Homes, Neighborhoods, and Cities.* Cambridge, MA.

Haynes, George Edmund. (1968) *The Negro at Work in New York City.* New York.

Hazelton, Henry Isham. (1925) *The Boroughs of Brooklyn, Queens, Counties of Nassau and Suffolk, L.I., N.Y., 1609–1924.* New York.

Healy, David. (1970) *United States Expansionism: The Imperialist Urge in the 1890s.* Madison, WI.

———. (1988) *Drive to Hegemony: The United States in the Caribbean, 1898–1917.* Madison, WI.

Heckscher, Morrison H., and Metropolitan Museum

of Art. (1995) *The Metropolitan Museum of Art: An Architectural History.* New York.

Hegeman, Susan. (1998) "Franz Boas and Professional Anthropology: On Mapping the Borders of the 'Modern.'" *Victorian Studies* 41: 455–83.

———. (2013) "A 'Wordminded People' Encounters the Armory Show." In *The Armory Show at 100: Modernism and Revolution*, edited by Marilyn Satin Kushner and Kimberly Orcutt. New York.

Heller, Vivian, and New York Transit Museum. (2004) *The City beneath Us: Building the New York Subways.* New York.

Hellman, Geoffrey. (1969) *Bankers, Bones and Beetles: The First Century of the American Museum of Natural History.* Garden City, NY.

Henderson, Charles Richmond. (1909) *Industrial Insurance in the United States.* Chicago, IL.

Henderson, Mary C. (1973) *The City and the Theatre: New York Playhouses from Bowling Green to Times Square.* Clifton, NJ.

———. (1986) *Theater in America: 200 Years of Plays, Players, and Productions.* New York.

———. (1989) "Broadway Bears and Bulls: The History of Play Producing in New York." Paper presented at Inventing Times Square Conference. New York.

Henderson, Thomas M. (1976) *Tammany Hall and the New Immigrants: The Progressive Years.* New York.

Hendrick, Daniel M. (2006) *Jamaica Bay.* Charleston, SC.

Hendrickson, Kenneth E., Jr. (1970) "The Pro-War Socialists, the Social Democratic League and the Ill-Fated Drive for Industrial Democracy in America, 1917–1920." *Labor History* 11: 304–22.

Hendrickson, Mary Ruth. (2001) "Role of the New York City Settlement Houses in the Education of Immigrant Women, 1890–1920." D.A. diss., St. John's University.

Hendrickson, Robert. (1979) *The Grand Emporiums: The Illustrated History of America's Great Department Stores.* New York.

Henretta, James A. (2006) "Charles Evans Hughes and the Strange Death of Liberal America." *Law and History Review* 24: 115–71.

Henri, Florette. (1975) *Black Migration: Movement North, 1900–1920.* Garden City, NY.

Henry, O. (1984) *41 Stories.* New York.

Herberg, Will. (1952) "The Jewish Labor Movement in the United States." *American Jewish Yearbook* 53: 3–74.

Herget, Danielle. (2004) "The Vaudeville Wars: William Morris, E. F. Albee, the White Rats and the Business of Entertainment, 1898–1932." Ph.D. diss., Tufts University.

Hermalyn, Gary, and Lloyd Ultan. (1998) "One Hundred Years of the Bronx." *Bronx County Historical Society Journal* 35: 63–68.

Hermalyn, Gary, and Peter Derrick. (1997) *The Great North Side: Centennial of the Bronx.* The Bronx, NY.

Herskovits, Melville J. (1953) *Franz Boas: The Science of Man in the Making.* New York.

Hertzberg, Arthur. (1997) *The Jews in America: Four Centuries of an Uneasy Encounter: A History.* New York.

Hessen, Robert. (1990) *Steel Titan: The Life of Charles M. Schwab.* Pittsburgh, PA.

Hicks, Cheryl D. (2010) *Talk with You like a Woman: African American Women, Justice, and Reform in New York, 1890–1935.* Chapel Hill, NC.

Higham, John. (1955) *Strangers in the Land:*

Patterns of American Nativism, 1860–1925. New Brunswick, NJ.

———. (1984) *Send These to Me: Immigrants in Urban America.* Baltimore, MD.

Higonnet, Anne. (2008) *A Museum of One's Own: Private Collecting, Public Gift.* Pittsburgh, PA.

Hijiya, James A. (1980) "Four Ways of Looking at a Philanthropist: A Study of Robert Weeks de Forest." *Proceedings of the American Philosophical Society* 124: 404–18.

———. (1992) *Lee de Forest and the Fatherhood of Radio.* Bethlehem, PA.

Hill, Mary Armfield. (1980) *Charlotte Perkins Gilman: The Making of a Radical Feminist, 1860–1896.* Philadelphia, PA.

Hill, Nancy Peterson. (2014) *A Very Private Public Citizen: The Life of Grenville Clark.* Columbia, MO.

Hillis, Newell Dwight. (1918) *The Blot on the Kaiser's 'Scutcheon.* New York.

Hillje, John W. (1972) "New York Progressives and War Revenue Act of 1917." *New York History* 53: 437–59.

Hillquit, Morris. (1903) *History of Socialism in the United States.* New York.

———. (1909) *Socialism in Theory and Practice.* New York.

———. (1914) "Murderous War in Europe Is the Inevitable Culmination of Murderous European Capitalism." *American Socialist* 1: 1–3.

Hills, Jill. (2002) *The Struggle for Control of Global Communication: The Formative Century.* Urbana, IL.

Hillstrom, Laurie Collier. (2010) *The Muckrakers and the Progressive Era.* Detroit, MI.

Hirsch, Foster. (1998) *The Boys from Syracuse: The Shuberts' Theatrical Empire.* Carbondale, IL.

Hirsch, Mark D. (1948) *William C. Whitney: Modern Warwick.* New York.

———. (1978) "Richard Croker." In *Essays in the History of New York City: A Memorial to Sidney Pomerantz,* edited by Irwin Yellowitz. Port Washington, NY.

Hitchman, James H. (1970) "U. S. Control over Cuban Sugar Production, 1898–1902." *Journal of Interamerican Studies and World Affairs* 12: 90–106.

Hobsbawm, Eric. (1987) *The Age of Empire, 1875–1914.* New York.

Hobson, Barbara Meil. (1998) *Uneasy Virtue: The Politics of Prostitution and the American Reform Tradition.* Chicago, IL.

Hobson, Wayne K. (1984) "Symbol of the New Profession: Emergence of the Large Law Firm, 1870–1915." In *The New High Priests: Lawyers in Post-Civil War America,* edited by Gerard W. Gawalt. Westport, CT.

Hodges, Graham Russell Gao. (2007) *Taxi! A Social History of the New York City Cabdriver.* Baltimore, MD.

Hodgson, Godfrey. (1990) *The Colonel: The Life and Wars of Henry Stimson, 1867–1950.* New York.

———. (2006) *Woodrow Wilson's Right Hand: The Life of Colonel Edward M. House.* New Haven, CT.

Hoffman, Beatrix Rebecca. (2001) *The Wages of Sickness: The Politics of Health Insurance in Progressive America.* Chapel Hill, NC.

Hoffman, Frank. (2004) *Encyclopedia of Recorded Sound.* Vol. 1. New York.

Hoffman, Katherine. (2004) *Stieglitz: A Beginning Light.* New Haven, CT.

Hoffmann, Charles. (1970) *The Depression of the Nineties: An Economic History.* Westport, CT.

Hofstadter, Richard. (1952) "Manifest Destiny and the Philippines." In *America in Crisis: Fourteen Crucial Episodes in American History,* edited by Daniel Aaron. New York.

———. (1955) *The Age of Reform: From Bryan to F. D. R.* New York.

———. (1963) *Anti-Intellectualism in American Life.* New York.

———. (1968) *The Progressive Historians: Turner, Beard, Parrington.* New York.

Hofstadter, Richard, and Michael Wallace. (1970) *American Violence: A Documentary History.* New York.

Hogan, Martin J. (1919) *The Shamrock Battalion of the Rainbow: A Story of the "Fighting Sixty-Ninth."* New York.

Holder, Calvin B. (1987) "The Causes and Composition of West Indian Immigration to New York City, 1900–1952." *Afro-Americans in New York Life and History* 11: 7–26.

———. (1998) "Making Ends Meet: West Indian Economic Adjustment in New York City, 1900–1952." *Wadabagei: A Journal of the Caribbean and Its Diaspora* 1: 31–84.

Holleran, Michael. (1999) "'The Machine That Makes the Land Pay': Recent Skyscraper Scholarship." *Journal of Urban History* 25: 860–67.

Hollinger, David A. (1996) *Science, Jews, and Secular Culture: Studies in Mid-Twentieth-Century American Intellectual History.* Princeton, NJ.

Holmes, John Haynes. (1917) *The Messiah Pulpit: A Statement to My People on the Eve of War.* New York.

Holmes, Sean Patrick. (1994) "Weavers of Dreams, Unite! Constructing an Occupational Identity in the Actors' Equity Association, 1913–1934." Ph.D. diss., New York University.

———. (2013) *Weavers of Dreams, Unite! Actor's Unionism in Early Twentieth-Century America.* Urbana, IL.

Holtzman, Filia. (1962) "A Mission That Failed: Gor'kij in America." *Slavic and East European Journal* 6: 227–34.

Homer, William Innes. (1977) *Alfred Stieglitz and the American Avant-garde.* London.

Homer, William Innes, and Violet Organ. (1969) *Robert Henri and His Circle.* Ithaca, NY.

Hood, Clifton. (1979) "The Impact of the IRT on New York City." Historic American Engineering Record, Survey Number HAER NY–122, 145–206.

———. (1986) "Underground Politics: A History of Mass Transit in New York City since 1904." Ph.D. diss., Columbia University.

———. (2002) "Journeying to 'Old New York': Elite New Yorkers and Their Invention of an Idealized City History in the Late Nineteenth and Early Twentieth Centuries." *Journal of Urban History* 28: 699–719.

———. (2004) *722 Miles: The Building of the Subways and How They Transformed New York.* Baltimore, MD.

Hooks, Gregory. (1991) *Forging the Military-Industrial Complex: World War II's Battle of the Potomac.* Urbana, IL.

Hopkins, June. (2011) "The Sacred and the Secular in Christodora Settlement House, 1897–1939." *Social Welfare History Project* website, VCU Libraries.

Hopper, Kim. (2003) *Reckoning with Homelessness.* Ithaca, NY.

Horan, Cynthia. (1985) "Agreeing with the Bankers: New York City's Depression Financial Crisis." *Research in Political Economy* 8: 201–32.

Horn, Martin. (2000) "A Private Bank at War: J. P. Morgan & Co. and France, 1914–1918." *Business History Review* 74: 85–112.

Horne, Donald. (1984) *The Great Museum: The Re-Presentation of History.* London.

Horowitz, Daniel. (1985) *The Morality of Spending: Attitudes toward the Consumer Society in America, 1875–1940.* Baltimore, MD.

Horowitz, Helen l. (1975) "Animal and Man in the New York Zoological Park." *New York History* 56: 426–55.

Horowitz, Joseph. (1988) *Understanding Toscanini: How He Became an American Culture-God and Helped Create a New Audience for Old Music.* Minneapolis, MN.

———. (2005) *Classical Music in America: A History of Its Rise and Fall.* New York.

Horowitz, Louis Jay, and Boyden Sparkes. (1937) *The Towers of New York: The Memoirs of a Master Builder.* New York.

Hosmer, Charles Bridgham. (1965) *Presence of the Past: A History of the Preservation Movement in the United States before Williamsburg.* New York.

Hovey, Elizabeth Bainum. (1998) "Stamping Out Smut: The Enforcement of Obscenity Laws, 1872–1915." Ph.D. diss., Columbia University.

Howard, Ella. (2007) "Skid Row: Homelessness on the Bowery in the Twentieth Century." Ph.D. diss., Boston University.

Howe, Frederic Clemson. (1915) *The Modern City and Its Problems.* New York.

Howe, Irving. (1976) *World of Our Fathers.* New York.

Hower, Ralph M. (1943) *History of Macy's of New York, 1858–1919: Chapters in the Evolution of the Department Store.* Cambridge, MA.

Hoyt, Edwin P. (1967) *The Guggenheims and the American Dream.* New York.

Huddleston, E. L. (1981) "The Generals up in Wall Street: Ray Stannard Baker and the Railroads." *Railroad History* 145: 69–86.

Hudson, James R. (1987) *The Unanticipated City: Loft Conversions in Lower Manhattan.* Amherst, MA.

Hudson, Peter James. (2007) "Dark Finance: An Unofficial History of Wall Street, American Empire

and the Caribbean, 1889–1925." Ph.D. diss., New York University.

———. (2013) "The National City Bank of New York and Haiti, 1909–1922." *Radical History Review* 115: 91–114.

Huggins, Nathan Irvin. (1971) *Harlem Renaissance.* New York.

Hughes, Rupert, and Henry Mayer. (1904) *The Real New York.* New York.

Hughes, Thomas Parke. (1971) *Elmer Sperry: Inventor and Engineer.* Baltimore, MD.

Hulden, Vilja. (2011) "Employers, Unite! Organized Employer Reactions to the Labor Union Challenge in the Progressive Era." Ph.D. diss., University of Arizona.

Hungerford, Edward. (1903) *The Williamsburg Bridge: An Account of the Ceremonies Attending the Formal Opening of the Structure.* Brooklyn, NY.

———. (1913) *The Personality of American Cities.* New York.

———. (1922) *The Romance of a Great Store.* New York.

Hurley, Andrew. (1994) "Creating Ecological Wastelands: Oil Pollution in New York City, 1870–1900." *Journal of Urban History* 20: 340–64.

Hurwitz, Howard Lawrence. (1943) *Theodore Roosevelt and Labor in New York State, 1880–1900.* New York.

Hutchinson, John. (1970) *The Imperfect Union: A History of Corruption in American Trade Unions.* New York.

Hutchison, William R. (2003) *Religious Pluralism in America: The Contentious History of a Founding Ideal.* New Haven, CT.

Huthmacher, J. Joseph. (1968) *Senator Robert F. Wagner and the Rise of Urban Liberalism.* New York.

Huyssen, David. (2011) "Class Collisions: Wealth

and Poverty in New York, 1890–1920." Ph.D. diss., Yale University.

———. (2014) *Progressive Inequality: Rich and Poor in New York, 1890–1920.* Cambridge, MA.

Hyatt, Marshall. (1990) *Franz Boas, Social Activist: The Dynamics of Ethnicity.* New York.

Hyman, Paula. (1980) "Immigrant Women and Consumer Protest: The New York City Kosher Meat Boycott of 1902." *American Jewish History* 70: 91–105.

Iardella, Albert B. (1964) *Western Electric and the Bell System: A Survey of Service.* New York.

Iezzoni, Lynette. (1999) *Influenza 1918: The Worst Epidemic in American History.* New York.

Iglesias Utset, Marial. (2011) *A Cultural History of Cuba during the U.S. Occupation, 1898–1902.* Chapel Hill, NC.

Imholtz, Arthur A., Jr. (2005) "Albert Boni: A Sketch of a Life in Micro-Opaque." *Proceedings of the American Antiquarian Society* 115 (2): 253–77.

Inciardi, James A., et al. (1977) *Historical Approaches to Crime: Research Strategies and Issues.* Beverly Hills, CA.

Ingalls, Robert P. (1975) *Herbert H. Lehman and New York's Little New Deal.* New York.

Interborough Rapid Transit Company. (1904) *The New York Subway: Its Construction and Equipment.* New York.

Immerso, Michael. (2002) *Coney Island: The People's Playground.* New Brunswick, NJ.

Irish, Sharon. (1985) "Cass Gilbert's Career in New York, 1899–1905." Ph.D. diss., Northwestern University.

———. (1998) "Paul Starrett." In *American National Biography*, edited by John A. Garraty and Mark C. Carnes. New York.

———. (1999) *Cass Gilbert, Architect: Modern Traditionalist.* New York.

Isaacson, Walter, and Evan Thomas. (1986) *The Wise Men: Six Friends and the World They Made.* London.

Jacknis, Ira. (1985) "Franz Boas and Exhibits: On the Limitations of the Museum Method of Anthropology." In *Objects and Others: Essays on Museums and Material Culture*, edited by George W. Stocking Jr. Madison, WI.

Jackson, Anthony. (1976) *A Place Called Home: A History of Low-Cost Housing in Manhattan.* Cambridge, MA.

Jackson, Kenneth T. (1985) *Crabgrass Frontier: The Suburbanization of the United States.* New York.

Jackson, Kenneth T., and Camilo J. Vergara. (1989) *Silent Cities: The Evolution of the American Cemetery.* New York.

Jackson, Stanley. (1972) *Caruso.* New York.

Jacobs, Jack Lester. (1992) *On Socialists and "the Jewish Question" after Marx.* New York.

Jacobs, James B. (2006) *Mobsters, Unions, and Feds: The Mafia and the American Labor Movement.* New York.

Jacobs, Lewis. (1939) *The Rise of the American Film: A Critical History.* New York.

Jacobs, Linda K. (2015) *Strangers in the West: The Syrian Colony of New York City, 1880–1900.* New York.

Jacobson, Gerald F. (1920) *History of the 107th Infantry U.S.A.* New York.

Jacobson, Matthew Frye. (2000) *Barbarian Virtues: The United States Encounters Foreign Peoples at Home and Abroad, 1876–1917.* New York.

Jaffe, Julian F. (1972) *Crusade against Radicalism: New York during the Red Scare, 1914–1924.* Port Washington, NY.

Jaffe, Steven H. (2012) *New York at War: Four Centuries of Combat, Fear, and Intrigue in Gotham.* New York.

Jaher, Frederick C. (1982) *The Urban Establishment: Upper Strata in Boston, New York, Charleston, Chicago, and Los Angeles.* Urbana, IL.

———. (1985) "White America Views Jack Johnson, Joe Louis and Muhammad Ali." In *Sport in America: New Historical Perspectives*, edited by Donald Spivey. Westport, CT.

Jakle, John A. (1985) *The Tourist: Travel in Twentieth-Century North America.* Lincoln, NE.

James, Henry. (1907) *The American Scene.* London.

———. (2005) *The New York Stories of Henry James*, selected and with an introduction by Colm Tóibín. New York.

James, Winston. (1999) *Holding Aloft the Banner of Ethiopia: Caribbean Radicalism in Early Twentieth-Century America.* London.

———. (2005) "The History of Afro-Caribbean Migration to the United States." In *In Motion: The African-American Migration Experience*, Schomburg Center for Research in Black Culture website.

Janicki, David A. (2014) "The British Blockade during World War I: The Weapon of Deprivation." *Student Pulse* 6: 1–5.

Jasen, David A. (1988) *Tin Pan Alley: The Composers, the Songs, the Performers, and Their Times: The Golden Age of American Popular Music from 1886 to 1956.* New York.

Jasen, David A., and Gene Jones. (1998) *Spreadin' Rhythm Around: Black Popular Songwriters, 1880–1930.* New York.

Jenkins, Stephen. (1912) *The Story of the Bronx, 1639–1912.* New York.

Jensen, Frances Brewer. (1996) "The Triangle Fire and the Limits of Progressivism." Ph.D. diss., University of Massachusetts Amherst.

Jensen, Joan M. (1969) *The Price of Vigilance.* Chicago, IL.

———. (1991) *Army Surveillance in America, 1775–1980.* New Haven, CT.

Jessup, Philip Caryl. (1938) *Elihu Root.* New York.

Jewish Social Service Association. (1926) *Fifty Years of Social Service: The History of the United Hebrew Charities of the City of New York, Now the Jewish Social Service Association, Inc.* New York.

Jobs, Sebastian. (2012) *Welcome Home, Boys! Military Victory Parades in New York City, 1899–1946.* Frankfurt, Germany.

Johnson, Arthur M. (1959) "Theodore Roosevelt and the Bureau of Corporations." *Mississippi Valley Historical Review* 45: 571–90.

Johnson, James Weldon. (1930) *Black Manhattan.* New York

Johnson, Kathleen Eagen. (2009) *The Hudson-Fulton Celebration: New York's River Festival of 1909 and the Making of a Metropolis.* New York.

Johnson, Marilynn S. (2003) *Street Justice: A History of Police Violence in New York City.* Boston, MA.

Johnson, Neil M. (1968) "George Sylvester Viereck: Poet and Propagandist." *Books at Iowa* 9: 22–36.

Johnson, Richard Christian. (1973) "Anthony Comstock: Reform, Vice, and the American Way." Ph.D. diss., University of Wisconsin–Madison.

Johnson, Val. (2002) "Defining 'Social Evil': Moral Citizenship and Governance in New York City, 1890–1920." Ph.D. diss., New School for Social Research.

———. (2006) "The Moral Aspects of Complex Problems: New York City Electoral Campaigns against Vice and the Incorporation of Immigrants, 1890–1901." *Journal of American Ethnic History* 25: 74–106.

Johnson, Wray R. (1999) "Black American Radicalism and the First World War: The Secret Files of the Military Intelligence Division." *Armed Forces and Society* 26: 27–54.

Jonas, Gilbert. (2005) *Freedom's Sword: The NAACP and the Struggle against Racism in America, 1909–1969.* New York.

Jones, Ernest. (1981) *The Life and Work of Sigmund Freud.* Vol. 2. New York.

Jones, Jacqueline. (1998) *American Work: Four Centuries of Black and White Labor.* New York.

Jones, Marian Moser, and New York City Department of Health and Mental Hygiene. (2005) *Protecting Public Health in New York City: 200 Years of Leadership, 1805–2005.* New York.

Jones, Thai. (2012) *More Powerful than Dynamite: Radicals, Plutocrats, Progressives, and New York's Year of Anarchy.* New York.

Jones, Theodore Francis. (1933) *New York University, 1832–1932.* New York.

Jonnes, Jill. (1996) *Hep-Cats, Narcs, and Pipe Dreams: A History of America's Romance with Illegal Drugs.* New York.

———. (2002) *South Bronx Rising: The Rise, Fall, and Resurrection of an American City.* New York.

———. (2006) *Conquering Gotham: A Gilded Age Epic: The Construction of Penn Station and Its Tunnels.* New York.

Joselit, Jenna Weissman. (1983) *Our Gang: Jewish Crime and the New York Jewish Community, 1900–1940.* Bloomington, IN.

———. (1986) "The Landlord as Czar: Pre–World War I Tenant Activity." In *The Tenant Movement in New York City, 1904–1984*, edited by Ronald Lawson and Mark Naison. New Brunswick, NJ.

Joseph, Judith Lee Vaupen. (1986) "The Nafkeh and the Lady: Jews, Prostitutes and Progressives in New York City, 1900–1930."

Ph.D. diss., State University of New York at Stony Brook.

Josephson, Matthew, Hannah Josephson, et al. (1969) *Al Smith, Hero of the Cities: A Political Portrait Drawing on the Papers of Frances Perkins.* Boston, MA.

Jucan, Marius. (2010) "Cultural Pluralism and the Issue of American Identity in Randolph Bourne's 'Trans-National America.' " *Journal for the Study of Religions and Ideologies* 9: 203–19.

Judge, Edward H. (1992) *Easter in Kishinev: Anatomy of a Pogrom.* New York.

Kagan, Richard L. (2010) "Blame It on Washington Irving: New York's Discovery of the Art and Architecture of Spain." In *Nueva York, 1613–1945*, edited by Edward J. Sullivan. New York.

Kahn, Alan Paul, and Jack May. (1976) *Manhattan and Bronx Elevated Railroads: 1920.* New York.

Kallen, Horace M. (1915a) "Democracy versus the Melting Pot: A Study of American Nationality: Part One." *Nation*, February 18, 190–94.

———. (1915b) "Democracy versus the Melting Pot: A Study of American Nationality: Part Two." *Nation*, February 25, 217–20.

Kammen, Michael. (1978) *A Season of Youth: The American Revolution and the Historical Imagination.* New York.

———. (1979) "The Rediscovery of New York's History, Phase One." *New York History* 60: 373–406.

Kanellos, Nicolás. (1990) *A History of Hispanic Theatre in the United States: Origins to 1940.* Austin, TX.

Kanfer, Stefan. (1989) *A Summer World: The Attempt to Build a Jewish Eden in the Catskills from the Days of the Ghetto to the Rise and Decline of the Borscht Belt.* New York.

————. (2004) "The Yiddish Theater's Triumph." *City Journal* 14: 102–21.

————. (2006) *Stardust Lost: The Triumph, Tragedy, and Mishugas of the Yiddish Theater in America*. New York.

Kantor, Harvey. (1971) "Modern Urban Planning in New York City, Origins and Evolution, 1890–1933." Ph.D. diss., New York University.

————. (1983) "Benjamin C. Marsh and the Fight over Population Congestion." In *The American Planner: Biographies and Recollections*, edited by Donald A. Krueckeberg. New York.

Kantor, Harvey, and David B. Tyack, eds. (1982) *Work, Youth, and Schooling: Historical Perspectives on Vocationalism in American Education*. Stanford, CA.

Kaplan, Barry J. (1975) "A Study in the Politics of Metropolitanization: The Greater New York City Charter of 1897." Ph.D. diss., State University of New York at Buffalo.

————. (1979) "Andrew H. Green and the Creation of a Planning Rationale: The Formation of Greater New York City, 1865–1890." *Urbanism Past and Present* 8: 32–39.

Kaplan, Justin. (1974) *Lincoln Steffens: A Biography*. New York.

————. (2006) *When the Astors Owned New York: Blue Bloods and Grand Hotels in a Gilded Age*. New York.

Kaplan, Lawrence, and Carol P. Kaplan. (2003) *Between Ocean and City: The Transformation of Rockaway, New York*. New York.

Karatzas, Daniel. (1990) *Jackson Heights: A Garden in the City*. New York.

Karvonides Nkosi, Joanna Electra. (1991) "Greek Immigrants in the Fur Manufacturing Industry in New York City, 1887–1943: Class and Ethnicity at the Workplace." Ph.D. diss., City University of New York.

Kasson, John F. (1978) *Amusing the Million: Coney Island at the Turn of the Century*. New York.

————. (1988) "The Performing Arts and the Disciplining of Spectatorship in New York City." Paper presented at Conference on the Comparative History of Metropolitan Transformation of Budapest and New York, 1870–1930. Budapest.

————. (1998) "Seeing Coney Island, Seeing Culture: Joseph Stella's Battle of Lights." *Yale Journal of Criticism* 11: 95–101.

Katcher, Leo. (1958) *The Big Bankroll: The Life and Times of Arnold Rothstein*. New Rochelle, NY.

Kathrens, Michael C. (2005) *Great Houses of New York, 1880–1930*. New York.

Katz, Daniel. (2011) *All Together Different: Yiddish Socialists, Garment Workers, and the Labor Roots of Multiculturalism*. New York.

Katz, Jonathan Ned. (1976) *Gay American History: Lesbians and Gay Men in the U.S.A.: A Documentary*. New York.

————. (1994) *Gay/Lesbian Almanac: A New Documentary*. New York.

Katz, Michael B. (1986) *In the Shadow of the Poorhouse: A Social History of Welfare in America*. New York.

Katz, Wallace B. (1979) "The New York Rapid Transit Decision of 1900: Economy, Society, Politics." Historic American Engineering Record, Survey Number HAER NY–122, 2–144.

Katzman, David M. (1978) *Seven Days a Week: Women and Domestic Service in Industrializing America*. New York.

Katznelson, Ira. (1973) *Black Men, White Cities: Race, Politics and Migration in the United States, 1900–30, and Britain, 1948–68*. New York.

Kaufman, David. (1999) *Shul with a Pool: The*

"Synagogue-Center" in *American Jewish History*. Hanover, NH.

Kazin, Alfred. (1941) "The Lady and the Tiger: Edith Wharton and Theodore Dreiser." *Virginia Quarterly Review* 17: 101–19.

Kazin, Michael. (2006) *A Godly Hero: The Life of William Jennings Bryan*. New York.

————. (2011) *American Dreamers: How the Left Changed a Nation*. New York.

————. (2017) *War against War: The American Fight for Peace, 1914–1918*. New York.

Keefe, Rose. (2008) *The Starker: Big Jack Zelig, the Becker-Rosenthal Case, and the Advent of the Jewish Gangster*. Nashville, TN.

Keeling, Arlene W. (2009) "'When the City Is a Great Field Hospital': The Influenza Pandemic of 1918 and the New York City Nursing Response." *Journal of Clinical Nursing* 18: 2732–38.

Keene, Jennifer D. (2001) *Doughboys, the Great War, and the Remaking of America*. Baltimore, MD.

Kehillah (Jewish Community) of New York City. (1919) *The Jewish Communal Register of New York City, 1917–1918*. New York.

Keire, Mara L. (1997) "The Committee of Fourteen and Saloon Reform in New York City, 1905–1920." *Business and Economic History* 26: 573–83.

————. (1998) "Dope Fiends and Degenerates: The Gendering of Addiction in the Early Twentieth Century." *Journal of Social History* 31: 809–22.

————. (2001) "The Vice Trust: A Reinterpretation of the White Slavery Scare in the United States, 1907–1917." *Journal of Social History* 35: 5–51.

Keller, Mollie. (1990) *How New York's Developers Reshaped the Metropolis*. Hilliard, OH.

Keller, Morton. (1963) *The Life Insurance Enterprise, 1865–1910: A Study in the Limits of Corporate Power*. Cambridge, MA.

Kelley, Florence. (1995) *The Selected Letters of Florence Kelley, 1869–1931*, edited by Kathryn Kish Sklar and Beverly Wilson Palmer. Urbana, IL.

Kelley, Robin D. G. (2002) *Freedom Dreams: The Black Radical Imagination*. Boston, MA.

————. (2009) *Thelonious Monk: The Life and Times of an American Original*. New York.

Kellogg, Charles Flint. (1967) *NAACP: A History of the National Association for the Advancement of Colored People*. Baltimore, MD.

Kellor, Frances A. (1914) "Is Unemployment a Municipal Problem?" *National Municipal Review* 3: 366–70.

————. (1915) "Unemployment in American Cities: The Record for 1914–15." *National Municipal Review* 4: 420–28.

Kelly, Wilhelmena Rhodes. (2009) *Crown Heights and Weeksville*. Charleston, SC.

Kennedy, David M. (1970) *Birth Control in America: The Career of Margaret Sanger*. New Haven, CT.

————. (1980) *Over Here: The First World War and American Society*. New York.

Kennedy, John Michael. (1968) "Philanthropy and Science in New York City: The American Museum of Natural History, 1868–1968." Ph.D. diss., Yale University.

Kenney, William Howland. (1999) *Recorded Music in American Life: The Phonograph and Popular Memory, 1890–1945*. New York.

Kerr, K. Austin. (1980) "Organizing for Reform: The Anti-Saloon League and Innovation in Politics." *American Quarterly* 32: 37–53.

————. (1985) *Organized for Prohibition: A New History*

of the Anti-Saloon League. New Haven, CT.

Kersten, Andrew Edmund. (2007) *A. Philip Randolph: A Life in the Vanguard.* Lanham, MD.

Kessner, Thomas. (1977) *The Golden Door: Italian and Jewish Immigrant Mobility in New York City, 1880–1915.* New York.

———. (1991) *Fiorello H. La Guardia and the Making of Modern New York.* . New York.

Keyssar, Alexander. (1986) *Out of Work: The First Century of Unemployment in Massachusetts.* Cambridge, UK.

Kibler, M. Alison. (1999) *Rank Ladies: Gender and Cultural Hierarchy in American Vaudeville.* Chapel Hill, NC.

Kiernan, V. G. (1978) *America, the New Imperialism: From White Settlement to World Hegemony.* London.

Killough, Lucy Winsor. (1924) *The Tobacco Products Industry in New York and Its Environs: Present Trends and Probable Future Developments.* New York.

King, Shannon. (2011) "'Ready to Shoot and Do Shoot': Black Working-Class Self-Defense and Community Politics in Harlem, New York, during the 1920s." *Journal of Urban History* 37: 757–74.

King, William McGuire. (1981) "The Emergence of Social Gospel Radicalism: The Methodist Case." *Church History* 50: 436–49.

Kinney, Thomas A. (2004) *The Carriage Trade: Making Horse-Drawn Vehicles in America.* Baltimore, MD.

Kinzer, Stephen. (2006) *Overthrow: America's Century of Regime Change from Hawaii to Iraq.* New York.

Kipnis, Ira. (1972) *The American Socialist Movement, 1897–1912.* New York.

Kirsch, David A. (2000) *The Electric Vehicle and the Burden of History.* New Brunswick, NJ.

Kirshenblatt-Gimblett, Barbara. (2001) "Imagining Europe: The Popular Arts of American Jewish Ethnography." In *Divergent Jewish Cultures: Israel and America,* edited by Deborah Dash Moore and S. Ilan Troen. New Haven, CT.

Kissack, Terence S. (2008) *Free Comrades: Anarchism and Homosexuality in the United States, 1895–1917.* Edinburgh.

Klaus, Susan L. (2002) *A Modern Arcadia: Frederick Law Olmsted Jr. and the Plan for Forest Hills Gardens.* Amherst, MA.

Klebaner, Benjamin Joseph. (1990) *American Commercial Banking: A History.* Boston, MA.

Kleeblatt, Norman L., and Susan Chevlowe. (1991) *Painting a Place in America: Jewish Artists in New York, 1900–1945.* New York.

Klein, Maury. (1986) *The Life and Legend of Jay Gould.* Baltimore, MD.

———. (2008) *The Power Makers: Steam, Electricity, and the Men Who Invented Modern America.* New York, NY.

Klips, Stephen. (1980) "Institutionalizing the Poor: The New York City Almshouse, 1825–1860." Ph.D. diss., City University of New York.

Kneeland, George Jackson. (1913) *Commercialized Prostitution in New York City.* New York.

Knerr, George F. (1957) "The Mayoral Administration of William L. Strong, New York City, 1895–1897." Ph.D. diss., New York University.

Kobler, John. (1988) *Otto the Magnificent: The Life of Otto Kahn.* New York.

Koegel, John. (2009) *Music in German Immigrant Theater: New York City, 1840–1940.* Rochester, NY.

Koistinen, Paul A. C. (1967) "The 'Industrial-Military Complex' in Historical Perspective: World War I." *Business History Review* 41: 378–403.

Kolko, Gabriel. (1963) *The Triumph of Conservatism: A Reinterpretation of American History, 1900–1916.* New York.

Kolodin, Irving. (1953) *The Story of the Metropolitan Opera, 1883–1950: A Candid History.* New York.

Konvitz, Josef W. (1989) "William J. Wilgus and Engineering Projects to Improve the Port of New York, 1900–1930." *Technology and Culture* 30: 398–425.

Koolhaas, Rem. (1978) *Delirious New York: A Retroactive Manifesto for Manhattan.* New York.

Kornweibel, Theodore. (1975) *No Crystal Stair: Black Life and the "Messenger," 1917–1928.* London.

———. (1998) *Seeing Red: Federal Campaigns against Black Militancy, 1919–1925.* Bloomington, IN.

———. (2002) *Investigate Everything: Federal Efforts to Compel Black Loyalty During World War I.* Bloomington, IN.

Korom, Joseph J. (2008) *The American Skyscraper, 1850–1940: A Celebration of Height.* Boston, MA.

Kosak, Hadassa. (1987) "The Rise of the Jewish Working Class, New York, 1881–1905." Ph.D. diss., City University of New York.

———. (2000) *Cultures of Opposition: Jewish Immigrant Workers, New York City, 1881–1905.* Albany, NY.

Koszarski, Richard. (1990) *An Evening's Entertainment: The Age of the Silent Feature Film Picture, 1915–1928.* New York.

———. (2004) *Fort Lee: The Film Town.* Bloomington, IN.

———. (2008) *Hollywood on the Hudson: Film and Television in New York from Griffith to Sarnoff.* New Brunswick, NJ.

Koszarski, Richard, and Astoria Motion Picture and Television Foundation. (1983) *The Astoria Studio*

and Its Fabulous Films: A Picture History with 227 Stills and Photographs. New York.

Kotzin, Daniel Phillip. (1998) "An American Jewish Radical: Judah L. Magnes, American Jewish Identity, and Jewish Nationalism in America and Mandatory Palestine." Ph.D. diss., New York University.

Kouwenhoven, John A. (1968) *Partners in Banking: An Historical Portrait of a Great Private Bank, Brown Brothers Harriman & Co., 1818–1968.* Garden City, NY.

Kozloff, Max, et al. (2002) *New York: Capital of Photography.* New Haven, CT.

Kramer, Rita. (1996) "Cathedrals of Commerce." *City Journal* 6: 78–104.

Kramer, Steve. (2006) "Uplifting Our 'Downtrodden Sisterhood': Victoria Earle Matthews and New York City's White Rose Mission, 1897–1907." *Journal of African American History* 91: 243–66.

Krasner, David. (1997) *Resistance, Parody, and Double Consciousness in African American Theatre, 1895–1910.* New York.

Kraus, Harry P. (1980) *The Settlement House Movement in New York City, 1886–1914.* New York.

Kreader, J. Lee. (1988) "America's Prophet for Social Security: A Biography of Isaac Max Rubinow." Ph.D. diss., University of Chicago.

Kroessler, Jeffrey A. (1991) "Building Queens: The Urbanization of New York's Largest Borough." Ph.D. diss., City University of New York.

———. (2011) "Brooklyn's Thirst, Long Island's Water: Consolidation, Local Control, and the Aquifer." *Long Island History Journal* 22: 1–17.

Krogius, Henrik. (1978) "The Collection on [*sic*]

Garbage." *Seaport* 12: 4–11.

Kronish, Ronald. (1982) "John Dewey and Horace M. Kallen on Cultural Pluralism: Their Impact on Jewish Education." *Jewish Social Studies* 44: 135–48.

Kuhlman, Erika (2007) "The 'Women's International League for Peace and Freedom' and Reconciliation after the Great War." In *The Women's Movement in Wartime: International Perspectives, 1914–19*, edited by Alison S. Fell and Ingrid Sharp. New York.

Kuhn, Loeb & Co. (1967) *A Century of Investment Banking*. New York.

Kunzel, Regina G. (1995) *Fallen Women, Problem Girls: Unmarried Mothers and the Professionalization of Social Work, 1890–1945*. New Haven, CT.

Kurland, Gerald. (1969) "The Amateur in Politics: The Citizens' Union and the Greater New York Mayoral Campaign of 1897." *New York Historical Society Quarterly* 43: 352–84.

———. (1971) *Seth Low: The Reformer in an Urban and Industrial Age*. New York.

Kurlansky, Mark. (2006) *The Big Oyster: History on the Half Shell*. New York.

Kushner, Marilyn Satin. (2013) "A Century of the Armory Show: Modernism and Myth." In *The Armory Show at 100: Modernism and Revolution*, edited by Marilyn Satin Kushner and Kimberly Orcutt. New York.

Kushner, Marilyn Satin, and Kimberly Orcutt, eds. (2013) *The Armory Show at 100: Modernism and Revolution*. New York.

Kwolek-Folland, Angel. (1994) *Engendering Business: Men and Women in the Corporate Office, 1870–1930*. Baltimore, MD.

Kwong, Peter. (1979) *Chinatown, New York:*

Labor and Politics, 1930–1950. New York.

La Grange, Henry-Louis de. (2008) *Gustav Mahler: A New Life Cut Short, 1907–1911*. Oxford, UK.

Lacy, Tim. (2008) "Fostering Unity amidst Diversity: The People's Institute and Great Books Idea, 1897–1930." Paper presented at Migration, Diaspora, Ethnicity, and Nationalism in History conference. Baltimore, MD.

LaFeber, Walter. (1998) *The New Empire: An Interpretation of American Expansion, 1860–1898*. Ithaca, NY.

LaGumina, Salvatore John, et al, eds. (2000) *The Italian American Experience: An Encyclopedia*. New York.

Lamb, Edwin Gifford. (1909) "The Social Work of the Salvation Army." Ph.D. diss., Columbia University.

Lamont, Edward M. (1994) *The Ambassador from Wall Street: The Story of Thomas W. Lamont, J. P. Morgan's Chief Executive*. New York.

Lamont, Thomas. (1921) "Reparations." In *What Really Happened at Paris: The Story of the Peace Conference, 1918–1919*, edited by Edward Mandell House and Charles Seymour. New York.

———. (1915) "The Effect of the War on America's Financial Position." *Annals of the American Academy of Political and Social Science* 60: 106–12.

Lamoreaux, Naomi R. (1985) *The Great Merger Movement in American Business, 1895–1904*. New York.

Landau, Sarah Bradford, and Carl W. Condit. (1996) *Rise of the New York Skyscraper, 1865–1913*. New Haven, CT.

Landmarks Preservation Commission. (1967) *St. Nicholas Historic District Designation Report*. New York.

———. (1971a) *Mount Morris Park Historic*

District Designation Report. New York.

———. (1971b) *Stuyvesant Heights Historic District Designation Report*. New York.

———. (1978) *Former Police Headquarters Building Designation Report*. New York.

———. (1979) *Prospect Lefferts Gardens Historic District Designation Report*. New York.

———. (1981) *10 West 130th Street House, (Part of Astor Row) Designation Report*. New York.

———. (1983) *Girls High School Designation Report*. New York.

———. (1984) *Graham Court Apartments Designation Report*. New York.

———. (1987a) *Belasco Theater Designation Report*. New York.

———. (1987b) *Palace Theater Designation Report*. New York.

———. (1988a) *St. Regis Hotel Designation Report*. New York.

———. (1988b) *Trinity Building Designation Report*. New York.

———. (1988c) *U.S. Realty Building Designation Report*. New York.

———. (1991) *Flushing High School Designation Report*. New York.

———. (1992) *Tribeca North Historic District Designation Report*. New York.

———. (1997) *14 Wall Street Building Designation Report*. New York.

———. (1999) *(Former) National City Bank Building Designation Report*. New York.

———. (2003a) *Brown Building (Originally Asch Building) Designation Report*. New York.

———. (2003b) *Erasmus Hall High School Designation Report*. New York.

———. (2003c) *Gansevoort Market Historic District Designation Report*. New York.

———. (2004) *Hecla Iron Works Individual Landmark*

Designation Report. New York.

———. (2005) *John De Groot House Designation Report*. New York.

———. (2007) *Crown Heights North Historic District Designation Report*. New York.

———. (2008) *West Chelsea Historic District Designation Report*. New York.

———. (2009a) *Consolidated Edison Building Designation Report*. New York.

———. (2009b) *Ridgewood North Historic District Designation Report*. New York.

———. (2009c) *S. Jarmulowsky Bank Building Designation Report*. New York.

———. (2011) *Bell Telephone Laboratories Complex Designation Report*. New York.

———. (2012) *Martha Washington Hotel Designation Report*. New York.

———. (2013a) *Bedford Stuyvesant/Expanded Stuyvesant Heights Historic District Designation Report*. New York.

———. (2013b) *Jamaica High School (Now Jamaica Learning Center) Designation Report*. New York.

———. (2013c) *South Village Historic District Designation Report*. New York.

Lane, Ann J. (1990) *To Herland and Beyond: The Life and Work of Charlotte Perkins Gilman*. New York.

Lane, Jack C. (2009) *Armed Progressive: General Leonard Wood*. Lincoln, NE.

Lankevich, George J. (2003) *Postcards from Manhattan*. Garden City Park, NY.

Lardner, James, and Thomas A. Reppetto. (2000) *NYPD: A City and Its Police*. New York.

Larkins, Charles D. (1905) "The Manual Training High School, Brooklyn, New York." *School Review* 13: 741–57.

Larrabee, Eric. (1971) *The Benevolent and Necessary Institution: The New York*

Hospital, 1771–1971. Garden City, NY.

LaRuffa, Anthony L. (1988) *Monte Carmelo: An Italian-American Community in the Bronx.* New York.

Lasch, Christopher. (1958) "The Anti-Imperialists, the Philippines, and the Inequality of Man." *Journal of Southern History* 24: 319–31.

———. (1965) *The New Radicalism in America, 1889–1963: The Intellectual as a Social Type.* New York.

———. (1974) "The Moral and Intellectual Rehabilitation of the Ruling Class." In Lasch, *The World of Nations: Reflections on American History, Politics, and Culture.* New York.

Lavitt, Pamela Brown. (1999) "First of the Red Hot Mamas: 'Coon Shouting' and the Jewish Ziegfeld Girl." *American Jewish History* 87: 253–90.

Lawbaugh, Bill, and Local 401. (1971–72) *An Informal History of the Iron Workers.* Philadelphia, PA.

Lawson, Thomas W. (1905) *Frenzied Finance.* New York.

Leach, William. (1984) "Transformations in a Culture of Consumption: Women and Department Stores, 1890–1925." *Journal of American History* 71: 319–42.

———. (1989) "Strategists of Display and the Production of Desire." In *Consuming Visions: Accumulation and the Display of Goods in America, 1880–1920,* edited by Simon J. Bronner. New York.

———. (1993) *Land of Desire: Merchants, Power, and the Rise of a New American Culture.* New York.

Lears, T. J. Jackson. (1994) *No Place of Grace: Antimodernism and the Transformation of American Culture, 1880–1920.* Chicago, IL.

———. (2012) "Pariahs' Progress: On

Isolationism." *Nation,* September 17, 27–31.

Leavell, Perry. (2015) "Finding a Man Who Will Take Advice: Woodrow Wilson and Edward House." *Proceedings of the American Philosophical Society* 159: 57–65.

Lederhendler, Eli. (2008) "Democracy and Assimilation: The Jews, America, and the Russian Crisis from Kishinev to the End of World War I." In *The Revolution of 1905 and Russia's Jews,* edited by Stefani Hoffman and Ezra Mendelsohn. Philadelphia, PA.

Lee, Hermione. (2007) *Edith Wharton.* New York.

Lee, Josephine D. (1997) *Performing Asian America: Race and Ethnicity on the Contemporary Stage.* Philadelphia, PA.

Leff, Mark. (1973) "Consensus for Reform: The Mothers' Pension Movement in the Progressive Era." *Social Service Review* 47: 397–417.

Lehman, Daniel W. (2002) *John Reed and the Writing of Revolution.* Athens, OH.

Lehman, Herbert H., and City Committee on Plan and Survey. (1928) *The Finances and Financial Administration of New York City: Recommendations and Report of the Sub-Committee on Budget, Finance, and Revenue, of the City Committee on Plan and Survey.* New York.

Lehmann-Haupt, Hellmut. (1951) *The Book in America.* New York.

Lehrer, Susan. (1987) *Origins of Protective Labor Legislation for Women, 1905–1925.* Albany, NY.

Leiby, James. (1978) *A History of Social Welfare and Social Work in the United States.* New York.

Leider, Emily Wortis. (2003) *Dark Lover: The Life and Death of Rudolph Valentino.* New York.

Leinenweber, Charles. (1968) "The American Socialist Party and 'New' Immigrants." *Science and Society* 32: 2–25.

———. (1974) "Socialism and Ethnicity." In *Failure of a Dream? Essays in the History of American Socialism,* edited by John H. M. Laslett and Seymour Martin Lipset. Garden City, NY.

———. (1977a) "Socialists in the Streets: The New York City Socialist Party in Working Class Neighborhoods, 1908–1918." *Science and Society* 41: 152–71.

———. (1977b) "Vaudeville in the Working Class Movement: The White Rats Actors Union." *Cultural Correspondence* 5: 20–27.

———. (1981) "The Class and Ethnic Bases of New York City Socialism, 1904–1915." *Labor History* 22: 31–56.

Leiter, Robert D. (1957) *The Teamsters Union: A Study of Its Economic Impact.* New York.

Lenin, V. I. (1977) "What Can Be Done for Public Education?" In *Lenin: Collected Works,* vol. 19, *March–December 1913.* Moscow.

Leonard, Thomas C. (2005) "Protecting Family and Race: The Progressive Case for Regulating Women's Work." *American Journal of Economics and Sociology* 64: 757–91.

Leopold, Richard W. (1954) *Elihu Root and the Conservative Tradition.* Boston, MA.

Lepore, Jill. (2009) "Preëxisting Condition." *New Yorker,* December 7, 29–30.

Lerner, Elinor. (1981) "Immigrant and Working Class Involvement in the New York City Woman Suffrage Movement, 1905–1917: A Study in Progressive Era Politics." Ph.D. diss., University of California, Berkeley.

Lerner, Gerda. (2005) *The Majority Finds Its Past: Placing Women in History.* Chapel Hill, NC.

Lerner, Michael Aloysius. (1999) "Dry Manhattan: Class, Culture, and Politics in Prohibition-Era New

York City, 1919–1933." Ph.D. diss., New York University.

Lessard, Suzannah. (1996) *The Architect of Desire: Beauty and Danger in the Stanford White Family.* New York.

Lesy, Michael, and Lisa Stoffer. (2013) *Repast: Dining out at the Dawn of the New American Century, 1900–1910.* New York.

Levenstein, Harvey A. (1981) *Communism, Anti-Communism, and the CIO.* Westport, CT.

Levin, Dan. (1986) *Stormy Petrel: The Life and Work of Maxim Gorky.* New York.

Levine, Harry G. (1983) "The Committee of Fifty and the Origin of Alcohol Control." *Journal of Drug Issues* 13: 95–116.

———. (1985) "The Birth of American Alcohol Control: Prohibition, the Power Elite, and the Problem of Lawlessness." *Contemporary Drug Problems* 12: 63–115.

Levine, Jerald Elliot. (1971) "Police, Parties, and Polity: The Bureaucratization, Unionization and Professionalization of the New York City Police, 1870–1917." Ph.D. diss., University of Wisconsin–Madison.

Levine, Lawrence W. (1977) *Black Culture and Black Consciousness: Afro-American Folk Thought from Slavery to Freedom.* New York.

———. (1988) *Highbrow/ Lowbrow: The Emergence of Cultural Hierarchy in America.* Cambridge, MA.

Levine, Steven A. (2002) "In Gotham's Shadow: Brooklyn and the Consolidation of Greater New York." Ph.D. diss., City University of New York.

Levinson, Edward. (1935) *I Break Strikes! The Technique of Pearl L. Bergoff.* New York.

Levinson, Marc. (2011) *The Great A&P and the Struggle for Small Business in America.* New York.

———. (2013) "Why 1913 Garment-Worker Strike Was among the Oddest Ever." *BloombergView*, January 15, 1–3.

Levy, David W. (1985) *Herbert Croly of the "New Republic": The Life and Thought of an American Progressive*. Princeton, NJ.

Levy, Eugene. (1973) *James Weldon Johnson: Black Leader, Black Voice*. Chicago, IL.

Lewinson, Edwin R. (1965) *John Purroy Mitchel: The Boy Mayor of New York*. New York.

Lewis, David Levering. (1981) *When Harlem Was in Vogue*. New York.

———. (1984) "Parallels and Divergences: Assimilationist Strategies of Afro-American and Jewish Elites, 1910 to the Early Thirties." *Journal of American History* 71: 543–64.

———. (1994) *W. E. B. Du Bois, 1868–1919: Biography of a Race*. New York.

———. (2000) *W. E. B. Du Bois, 1919–1963: The Fight for Equality and the American Century*. New York.

———. (2009) *W. E. B. Du Bois, 1868–1963*. New York.

Lewis, Susan Ingalls. (2013) "Women Win the Right to Vote in New York State." Blog post, *New York Rediscovered: Intriguing Stories from the History of New York State*, November 6.

Liazos, Theodore Christos. (1998) "Big Labor: George Meany and the Making of the Afl-CIO, 1894–1955." Ph.D. diss., Yale University.

Lieberman, Richard K. (1995) *Steinway & Sons*. New Haven, CT.

Light, Ivan. (1974) "From Vice District to Tourist Attraction: The Moral Career of American Chinatowns, 1880–1940." *Pacific Historical Review* 43: 367–94.

Lincoln, C. Eric. (1973) *The Black Muslims in America*. Boston, MA.

Linder, Marc, and Lawrence Zacharias. (1999) *Of Cabbages and Kings County: Agriculture and the Formation of Modern Brooklyn*. Iowa City, IA.

Lindner, Christoph. (2015) *Imagining New York City: Literature, Urbanism, and the Visual Arts, 1890–1940*. New York.

Lingeman, Richard. (1986) *Theodore Dreiser: At the Gates of the City, 1871–1907*. New York.

Lingenfelter, Richard E. (2012) *Bonanzas and Borrascas: Copper Kings and Stock Frenzies, 1885–1918*. Norman, OK.

Link, Arthur S. (1947) *Wilson: The Road to the White House*. Princeton, NJ.

Lipsky, Seth. (2013) *The Rise of Abraham Cahan*. New York.

Lisagor, Nancy, and Frank Lipsius. (1988) *A Law unto Itself: The Untold Story of the Law Firm of Sullivan & Cromwell*. New York.

Lisicky, Michael J. (2010) *Wanamaker's: Meet Me at the Eagle*. Charleston, SC.

Liss, Julia Elizabeth. (1990) "The Cosmopolitan Imagination: Franz Boas and the Development of American Anthropology." Ph.D. diss., University of California, Berkeley.

Livesay, Harold C. (1975) *Andrew Carnegie and the Rise of Big Business*. Boston, MA.

———. (1978) *Samuel Gompers and Organized Labor in America*. Boston, MA.

Livingston, James. (1986) *Origins of the Federal Reserve System: Money, Class, and Corporate Capitalism, 1890–1913*. Ithaca, NY.

Lobel, Michael. (2014) *John Sloan: Drawing on Illustration*. New Haven, CT.

Logan, Andy. (1970) *Against the Evidence: The Becker-Rosenthal Affair*. New York.

Logan, Rayford W. (1965) *The Betrayal of the Negro: From Rutherford B. Hayes to Woodrow Wilson*. New York.

Logan, Sheridan A. (1981) *George F. Baker and His Bank, 1840–1955: A Double Biography*. St. Joseph, MO.

Lopate, Phillip. (2004) *Waterfront: A Journey around Manhattan*. New York.

———. (2008) *Writing New York: A Literary Anthology*. New York.

———. (2011) "Here Brooklyn Gathers." In *BAM: The Complete Works*, edited by Steven Serafin. New York.

Lord, Walter. (1976) *A Night to Remember*. London.

Lorwin, Lewis L. (1924) *The Women's Garment Workers: A History of the International Ladies' Garment Worker's Union*. New York.

Love, Eric Tyrone Lowery. (2004) *Race over Empire: Racism and U.S. Imperialism, 1865–1900*. Chapel Hill, NC.

Loving, Jerome. (2005) *The Last Titan: A Life of Theodore Dreiser*. Berkeley, CA.

Lowe, David. (1999) *Stanford White's New York*. New York.

Lubove, Roy. (1961) "Lawrence Veiller and the New York State Tenement House Commission of 1900." *Mississippi Valley Historical Review* 47: 659–77.

———. (1963) *The Progressives and the Slums: Tenement House Reform in New York City, 1890–1917*. Pittsburgh, PA.

———. (1968) *The Struggle for Social Security, 1900–1935*. Cambridge, MA.

Luebke, Frederick C. (1974) *Bonds of Loyalty: German-Americans and World War I*. DeKalb, IL.

Lui, Adonica Yen-Mui. (1993) "Party Machines, State Structure, and Social Policies: The Abolition of Public Outdoor Relief in New York City, 1874–1898." Ph.D. diss., Harvard University.

Lui, Mary Ting Yi. (2000) "'The Chinatown Trunk Mystery': The Elsie Sigel Murder Case and the Policing of Interracial Sexual Relations in New York City's Chinatown, 1880–1915." Ph.D. diss., Cornell Univerisity.

———. (2007) *The Chinatown Trunk Mystery: Murder, Miscegenation, and Other Dangerous Encounters in Turn-of-the-Century New York City*. Princeton, NJ.

Lukasik, Sebastian Hubert. (2008) "Military Service, Combat, and American Identity in the Progressive Era." Ph.D. diss., Duke University.

Lukitsh, Joanne. (2006) "Alone on the Sidewalks of New York: Alfred Stieglitz's Photography, 1892–1913." In *Seeing High and Low: Representing Social Conflict in American Visual Culture*, edited by Patricia A. Johnston. Berkeley, CA.

Lumsden, Linda J. (1997) *Rampant Women: Suffragists and the Right of Assembly*. Knoxville, TN.

Lunardini, Christine A. (1986) *From Equal Suffrage to Equal Rights: Alice Paul and the National Woman's Party, 1910–1928*. New York.

Lunday, Elizabeth. (2013) *The Modern Art Invasion: Picasso, Duchamp, and the 1913 Armory Show That Scandalized America*. Guilford, CT.

Lurkis, Alexander. (1982) *The Power Brink: Con Edison, a Centennial of Electricity*. New York.

Lusk, Clayton R., and Joint Legislative Committee to Investigate Seditious Activities. (1920) *Revolutionary Radicalism: Its History, Purpose and Tactics with an Exposition and Discussion of the Steps Being Taken and Required to Curb It*. 2 vols. Albany, NY.

Lutzker, Michael Arnold. (1969) "The 'Practical' Peace Advocates: An Interpretation of the American Peace Movement, 1898–1917." Ph.D. diss., Rutgers University.

Lynes, Russell. (1980) *The Tastemakers: The Shaping of American Popular Taste*. New York.

Mabie, Hamilton Wright, and New-York Historical Society. (1904) *The Genius of the Cosmopolitan City: An Address Delivered before the New-York Historical Society on Its Ninety-Ninth Anniversary*. New York.

MacCracken, Henry Mitchell. (1905) *Andrew Haswell Green: A Memorial Address*. New York.

Mackay, Donald A. (1987) *The Building of Manhattan*. New York.

MacKay, Robert B., Geoffrey L. Rossano, and Carol A. Traynor, eds. (1985) *Between Ocean and Empire: An Illustrated History of Long Island*. Northridge, CA.

Mackey, Thomas C. (2005) *Pursuing Johns: Criminal Law Reform, Defending Character, and New York City's Committee of Fourteen, 1920–1930*. Columbus, OH.

MacMillan, Margaret. (2002) *Paris 1919: Six Months That Changed the World*. New York.

Madsen, Axel. (2001) *John Jacob Astor: America's First Multimillionaire*. New York.

Maffi, Mario. (1995) *Gateway to the Promised Land: Ethnic Cultures on New York's Lower East Side*. New York.

Magdoff, Harry. (1969) *The Age of Imperialism: The Economics of U.S. Foreign Policy*. New York.

Magee, Jeffrey. (2012) *Irving Berlin's American Musical Theater*. New York.

Magee, Mabel A. (1930) *Trends in Location of the Women's Clothing Industry*. Chicago, IL.

Makielski, S. J., Jr. (1966) *The Politics of Zoning: The New York Experience*. New York.

Malavet, Pedro A. (2008) "'The Constitution Follows the Flag . . . but Doesn't Quite Catch Up with It': The Story of *Downes v. Bidwell*." In *Race Law Stories*, edited by Rachel F. Moran and Devon W. Carbado. New York.

Maldonado-Denis, Manuel. (1972) *Puerto Rico: A Socio-Historic Interpretation*. New York.

Malin, Gwynneth C. (2013) "How Water Became Public in Progressive-Era New York, 1883–1917." Ph.D. diss., City University of New York.

Mallach, Stanley. (1979) "The Origins of the Decline of Urban Mass Transportation in the United States, 1890–1930." *Urbanism Past and Present* 8: 1–17.

Malone, Michael P. (2006) *The Battle for Butte: Mining and Politics on the Northern Frontier, 1864–1906*. Seattle, WA.

Manbeck, John B., and Robert Singer, eds. (2002) *The Brooklyn Film: Essays in the History of Filmmaking*. Jefferson, NC.

Mancini, J. M. (1998) "'The Safeness of Standing Alone': Alfred Stieglitz, *Camera Work*, and the Organizational Roots of the American Avant-Garde." *Canadian Review of American Studies* 28: 37–79.

Manela, Erez. (2007) *The Wilsonian Moment: Self-Determination and the International Origins of Anticolonial Nationalism*. New York.

Manor, Ehud. (2009) *Forward: The "Jewish Daily Forward" (Forverts) Newspaper: Immigrants, Socialism and Jewish Politics in New York, 1890–1917*. Portland, OR.

Marchand, C. Roland. (1972) *The American Peace Movement and Social Reform, 1898–1918*. Princeton, NJ.

———. (1998) *Creating the Corporate Soul: The Rise of Public Relations and Corporate Imagery in American Big Business*. Berkeley, CA.

Markowitz, Gerald E., and David Karl Rosner. (1973) "Doctors in Crisis: A Study of the Use of Medical Education Reform to Establish Modern Professional Elitism in Medicine." *American Quarterly* 25: 83–107.

Marling, Karal Ann. (1988) *George Washington Slept Here: Colonial Revivals and American Culture, 1876–1986*. Cambridge, MA.

Marmorstein, Gary. (2007) *The Label: The Story of Columbia Records*. New York.

Marsh, Benjamin C. (1910) "Economic Aspects of City Planning." *Municipal Engineers of the City of New York, Proceedings* 57: 73–87.

Marshall, Susan E. (1997) *Splintered Sisterhood: Gender and Class in the Campaign against Woman Suffrage*. Madison, WI.

Martin, George Whitney. (1970) *Causes and Conflicts: The Centennial History of the Association of the Bar of the City of New York, 1870–1970*. Boston, MA.

———. (1976) *Madam Secretary, Frances Perkins*. Boston, MA.

———. (2005) *CCB: The Life and Century of Charles C. Burlingham, New York's First Citizen, 1858–1959*. New York.

Mason, John Alden. (1958) *George G. Heye, 1874–1957*. New York.

Mason, Randall. (1999) "Memory Infrastructure: Preservation, 'Improvement,' and Landscape in New York City, 1898–1925." Ph.D. diss., Columbia University.

———. (2009) *The Once and Future New York: Historic Preservation and the Modern City*. Minneapolis, MN.

Materese, Michele M. (2006) "From Local to National: Lillian D. Wald, a Social Activist, 1893–1913." Ph.D. diss., State University of New York at Binghamton.

Maxtone-Graham, John. (1972) *The Only Way to Cross*. New York.

May, Henry Farnham. (1959) *The End of American Innocence: A Study of the First Years of Our Own Time, 1912–1917*. New York.

May, Lary. (1980) *Screening Out the Past: The Birth of Mass Culture and the Motion Picture Industry*. New York.

Mayer, Egon. (1979) *From Suburb to Shtetl: The Jews of Boro Park*. Philadelphia, PA.

Mayer, Grace M. (1958) *Once Upon a City: New York, 1890 to 1910*. New York.

Mayer, Martin. (1993) *The Met: One Hundred Years of Grand Opera*. New York.

Mayer, Robert. (1973) "The Origins of the American Banking Empire in Latin America: Frank A. Vanderlip and the National City Bank." *Journal of Interamerican Studies and World Affairs* 15: 60–76.

Maynard, Joan, and Gwen Cottman. (1988) *Weeksville Then and Now: The Search to Discover, the Effort to Preserve, Memories of Self in Brooklyn, New York*. Brooklyn, NY.

Mayor's Committee on National Defense and Thomas L. Chadbourne. (1917) *Report of the Executive Committee, Mayor's Committee on National Defense, New York City, November Twenty-First, 1917*. New York.

Mayor's Committee on National Defense and Henry MacDonald. (1918) *The Mayor's Committee on National Defense*. New York.

Mayor's Committee on Unemployment and William Delavan Baldwin. (1917) *How to Meet Hard Times: A Program for the Prevention and Relief of Abnormal Unemployment*. New York.

Mayor's Market Commission, Cyrus C. Miller, et al. (1913) *Report of the Mayor's Market Commission of New York City*. New York.

Mazaraki, George Alexander. (1966) "The Public Career of Andrew Haswell

Green." Ph.D. diss., New York University.

McAdoo, William. (1906) *Guarding a Great City.* New York.

McArthur, Benjamin. (1984) *Actors and American Culture, 1880–1920.* Philadelphia, PA.

McCallum, Jack Edward. (2006) *Leonard Wood: Rough Rider, Surgeon, Architect of American Imperialism.* New York.

McCarthy, Laurette E.. (2011) *Walter Pach (1883–1958): The Armory Show and the Untold Story of Modern Art in America.* University Park, PA.

McCash, June Hall. (1998) *The Jekyll Island Cottage Colony.* Athens, GA.

McCaughey, Robert A. (2003) *Stand, Columbia: A History of Columbia University in the City of New York, 1754–2004.* New York.

McCauley, Anne. (2013) "The 'Big Show' and the Little Galleries: Alfred Stieglitz and the Search for Modern Art Photography in 1913." In *The Armory Show at 100: Modernism and Revolution,* edited by Marilyn Satin Kushner and Kimberly Orcutt. New York.

McCauley, Bernadette. (1992) " 'Who Shall Take Care of Our Sick?' Roman Catholic Sisterhood and Their Hospitals, New York City, 1850–1930." Ph.D. diss., Columbia University.

McClellan, George B. (1956) *The Gentleman and the Tiger: The Autobiography of George B. McClellan, Jr.* Philadelphia, PA.

McClurken, Kara M. (2011) "Mary Abby van Kleeck (1883–1972): Settlement Worker, Researcher, Educator and Labor Reform Advocate on Behalf of Women and Children." *Social Welfare History Project* website, VCU Libraries.

McClymer, John F. (1997) "Of 'Mornin' Glories' and 'Fine Old Oaks': John Purroy Mitchel, Al Smith, and Reform as an Expression of Irish

American Aspiration." In *The New York Irish,* edited by Ronald H. Bayor and Timothy J. Meagher. Baltimore, MD.

McConnell, Francis John. (1952) *By the Way: An Autobiography.* New York.

McCormick, Charles H. (2005) *Hopeless Cases: The Hunt for the Red Scare Terrorist Bombers.* Lanham, MD.

McCormick, Richard L. (1981) "The Discovery That Business Corrupts Politics: A Reappraisal of the Origins of Progressivism." *American Historical Review* 86: 247–74.

McCullough, David G. (1981) *Mornings on Horseback: The Story of an Extraordinary Family, a Vanished Way of Life and the Unique Child Who Became Theodore Roosevelt.* New York.

McCullough, David W., and Jim Kalett. (1983) *Brooklyn—and How It Got That Way.* New York.

McDonagh, Eileen L., and H. Douglas Price. (1985) "Woman Suffrage in the Progressive Era: Patterns of Opposition and Support in Referenda Voting, 1910–1918." *American Political Science Review* 79: 415–35.

McDonald, Bruce D., III. (2010) "The Bureau of Municipal Research and the Development of a Professional Public Service." *Administration and Society* 42: 815–35.

McElroy, Robert McNutt. (1975) *Levi Parsons Morton: Banker, Diplomat, and Statesman.* New York.

McFarland, Gerald W. (1975) *Mugwumps, Morals and Politics, 1884–1920.* Amherst, MA.

———. (2001) *Inside Greenwich Village: A New York City Neighborhood, 1898–1918.* Amherst, MA.

McGerr, Michael E. (2003) *A Fierce Discontent: The Rise and Fall of the Progressive Movement in America, 1870–1920.* New York.

McGinley, James J. (1949) *Labor Relations in the New*

York Rapid Transit Systems, 1904–1944. New York.

McGruder, Kevin. (2015) *Race and Real Estate: Interracial Conflict and Co-Existence in Harlem, 1890–1920.* New York.

McGuinness, Margaret M. (2012) *Neighbors and Missionaries: A History of the Sisters of Our Lady of Christian Doctrine.* New York.

McGuire, John Thomas. (2006) "Making the Case for Night Work Legislation in Progressive Era New York, 1911–1915." *Journal of the Gilded Age and Progressive Era* 5: 47–70.

McGuire, Michael J. (2013) *The Chlorine Revolution: The History of Water Disinfection and the Fight to Save Lives.* Denver, CO.

McIllwain, Jeffrey Scott. (1997a) "From Tong War to Organized Crime: Revisiting the Historical Perception of Violence in Chinatown." *Justice Quarterly* 14: 25–52.

———. (1997b) "Organizing Crime in Chinatown: New York City's Chinatown and the Social System of Organized Crime in the United States of America during the Progressive Era." Ph.D. diss., Pennsylvania State University.

McJimsey, George. (1987) *Harry Hopkins: Ally of the Poor and Defender of Democracy.* Cambridge, MA.

McKivigan, John R., and Thomas J. Robertson. (1996) "The Irish American Worker in Transition, 1877–1914: New York City as a Test Case." In *The New York Irish,* edited by Ronald H. Bayor and Timothy J. Meagher. Baltimore, MD.

McNamara, Brooks. (1990) *The Shuberts of Broadway: A History Drawn from the Collections of the Shubert Archive.* New York.

———. (1997) *Day of Jubilee: The Great Age of Public Celebrations in New York, 1788–1909.* New Brunswick, NJ.

McNamara, John. (1985) "Irish in the Bronx." Paper presented at New York Celtic Medical Society. New York.

McNickle, Chris. (1996) "When New York Was Irish, and After." In *The New York Irish,* edited by Ronald H. Bayor and Timothy J. Meagher. Baltimore, MD.

McPherson, Alan. (1995) "Dollars Diplomacy and the Missing Link: A Socioeconomic Perspective on Cuban-American Relations, 1900–1934." *Ex Post Facto: Journal of the History Students at San Francisco State University* 4: 2–25.

McSeveney, Samuel T. (1972) *The Politics of Depression: Political Behavior in the Northeast, 1893–1896.* New York.

McShane, Clay. (1979) "Transforming the Use of Urban Space: A Look at the Revolution in Street Pavements, 1880–1924." *Journal of Urban History* 5: 279–307.

———. (1994) *Down the Asphalt Path: The Automobile and the American City.* New York.

McShane, Clay, and Joel A. Tarr. (2007) *The Horse in the City: Living Machines in the Nineteenth Century.* Baltimore, MD.

Mecklenburg, Virginia M. (2013) "Slouching toward Modernism: American Art at the Armory Show." In *The Armory Show at 100: Modernism and Revolution,* edited by Marilyn Satin Kushner and Kimberly Orcutt. New York.

Mehrotra, Ajay K. (2010) "Lawyers, Guns, and Public Moneys: The U.S. Treasury, World War I, and the Administration of the Modern Fiscal State." *Law and History Review* 28: 173–225.

Mele, Christopher. (2000) *Selling the Lower East Side: Culture, Real Estate, and Resistance in New York City.* Minneapolis, MN.

Melnick, Ross. (2012) *American Showman: Samuel "Roxy" Rothafel* and the Birth of the Entertainment Industry, 1908–1935. New York.

Melosh, Barbara. (1982) "The Physician's Hand": Work Culture and Conflict in American Nursing. Philadelphia, PA.

Melosi, Martin V. (1980) "Refuse Pollution and Municipal Reform: The Waste Problem in America, 1880–1917." In Pollution and Reform in American Cities, 1870–1930, edited by Marin V. Melosi. Austin, TX.

Menand, Louis. (2001) The Metaphysical Club. New York.

Mendel, Ronald. (1989) "Workers in Gilded Age New York and Brooklyn, 1886–1898." Ph.D. diss., City University of New York.

———. (2003) "A Broad and Ennobling Spirit": Workers and Their Unions in Late Gilded Age New York and Brooklyn, 1886–1898. Westport, CT.

Mendes, Philip. (2014) Jews and the Left: The Rise and Fall of a Political Alliance. New York.

Mensch, Barbara. (2007) South Street. New York.

Mensch, Jean Ulitz. (1983) "Social Pathology in Urban America: Desertion, Prostitution, Gambling, Drugs, and Crime among Eastern European Jews in New York City between 1881 and World War I." Ph.D. diss., Columbia University.

Ment, David. (1979) The Shaping of a City: A Brief History of Brooklyn. Brooklyn, NY.

Ment, David, and Mary S. Donovan. (1980) The People of Brooklyn: A History of Two Neighborhoods. Brooklyn, NY.

Ment, David Martin. (1971) "Racial Segregation in the Public Schools of New England and New York, 1840–1940." Ph.D. diss., Columbia University.

Merchants' Association of New York. (1906) Pocket Guide to New York. New York.

Mervis, Leonard J. (1955) "The Social Justice Movement and the American Reform Rabbi." American Jewish Archives 7: 171–230.

Merwin, Edward Paul. (2002) "In Their Own Image: New York Jews in Jazz Age American Popular Culture." Ph.D. diss., City University of New York.

Merwood-Salisbury, Joanna. (2009) "Patriotism and Protest: Union Square as Public Space, 1832–1932." Journal of the Society of Architectural Historians 68: 540–59.

Messinger, Lisa Mintz, ed. (2011) Stieglitz and His Artists: Matisse to O'Keeffe: The Alfred Stieglitz Collection in the Metropolitan Museum of Art. New York.

Metcalf, Pauline C. (1988) Ogden Codman and the Decoration of Houses. Boston, MA.

Metzger, Walter P. (1961) Academic Freedom in the Age of the University. New York.

Meyer, Henry A. (1901) Vanderveer Park: Reminiscences of Its Growth. Brooklyn, NY.

———. (1930) Looking through Life's Window: Personal Reminiscences. New York.

Michels, Tony. (2000) "'Speaking to Moyshe': The Early Socialist Yiddish Press and Its Readers." Jewish History 14: 51–82.

———. (2005) A Fire in Their Hearts: Yiddish Socialists in New York. Cambridge, MA.

Mickulas, Peter Philip. (2003) "Giving, Getting and Growing: Philanthropy, Science and the New York Botanical Garden, 1888–1929." Ph.D. diss., Rutgers University.

Milbank, Caroline Rennolds. (1989) New York Fashion: The Evolution of American Style. New York.

Milkis, Sidney M. (2009) Theodore Roosevelt, the Progressive Party, and the Transformation of American Democracy. Lawrence, KS.

Miller, Benjamin. (2000) Fat of the Land: Garbage of New York—the Last Two Hundred Years. New York.

Miller, Donald L. (1989) Lewis Mumford: A Life. New York.

Miller, Kenneth E. (2010) From Progressive to New Dealer: Frederic C. Howe and American Liberalism. University Park, PA.

Miller, Kerby. (1985) Emigrants and Exiles: Ireland and the Irish Exodus to North America. New York.

Miller, Kristin. (1987) "Work and Entertainment: The Radicalization of the Actors' Equity Association, 1913–1924." M.A. thesis, Columbia University.

Miller, Neil. (1995) Out of the Past: Gay and Lesbian History from 1869 to the Present. New York.

Miller, Stephen. (2014) Walking New York: Reflections of American Writers from Walt Whitman to Teju Cole. The Bronx, NY.

Miller, Terry. (1990) Greenwich Village and How It Got That Way. New York.

Miller, William D. (1982) Dorothy Day: A Biography. New York.

Millman, Chad. (2006) The Detonators: The Secret Plot to Destroy America and an Epic Hunt for Justice. New York.

Mills, Bill. (2013) The League: The True Story of Average Americans on the Hunt for WWI Spies. New York.

Miraldi, Robert. (2003) The Pen Is Mightier: The Muckraking Life of Charles Edward Russell. New York.

Mirel, Jeffrey. (2002) "Civic Education and Changing Definitions of American Identity, 1900–1950." Educational Review 54: 143–52.

Mitchell, Joseph. (2008) The Bottom of the Harbor. New York.

Mitchell, Lawrence E. (2007) The Speculation Economy: How Finance Triumphed over Industry. San Francisco, CA.

Mitgang, Herbert. (1963) The Man Who Rode the Tiger: The Life and Times of Judge Samuel Seabury. Philadelphia, PA.

Mizejewski, Linda. (1999) Ziegfeld Girl: Image and Icon in Culture and Cinema. Durham, NC.

Moehring, Eugene P. (1981) Public Works and the Patterns of Urban Real Estate Growth in Manhattan, 1835–1894. New York.

Mohl, Raymond A. (1971) Poverty in New York, 1783–1825. New York.

Mom, Gijs. (2004) The Electric Vehicle: Technology and Expectations in the Automobile Age. Baltimore, MD.

Mom, Gijs, and David A. Kirsch. (2001) "Technologies in Tension: Horses, Electric Trucks, and the Motorization of American Cities, 1900–1925." Technology and Culture 42: 489–518.

Mondello, Salvatore. (2005) A Sicilian in East Harlem. Youngstown, NY.

Monkkonen, Eric H. (2001) Murder in New York City. Berkeley, CA.

Monoson, S. Sara. (1990) "The Lady and the Tiger: Women's Electoral Activism in New York City before Suffrage." Journal of Women's History 2: 100–35.

Montgomery, David. (1987) The Fall of the House of Labor: The Workplace, the State, and American Labor Activism, 1865–1925. Cambridge, UK.

Montgomery, Gladys. (2011) An Elegant Wilderness: Great Camps and Grand Lodges of the Adirondacks, 1855–1935. New York.

Montgomery, Michael. (2003) "Keeping the Tenants Down: Height Restrictions and Manhattan's Tenement House System, 1885–1930." Cato Journal 22: 495–509.

Moody, John. (1919) The Masters of Capital: A Chronicle of Wall Street. New Haven, CT.

Moon, Krystyn R. (2005) Yellowface: Creating the

Chinese in American Popular Music and Performance, 1850s–1920s. New Brunswick, NJ.

Moon, Krystyn R., David Krasner, and Thomas L. Riis. (2011) "Forgotten Manuscripts: A Trip to Coontown." *African American Review* 44: 7–24.

Moore, Deborah Dash. (1981) *At Home in America: Second Generation New York Jews.* New York.

———. (2006) "At Home in America? Revisiting the Second Generation." *Journal of American Ethnic History* 25: 156–68.

Moore, Jesse T., Jr. (1980) "Resolving Urban Racial Problems: The New York Urban League, 1919–1959." *Afro-Americans in New York Life and History* 4: 27–43.

Morantz-Sanchez, Regina Markell. (1985) *Sympathy and Science: Women Physicians in American Medicine.* New York.

Mordden, Ethan. (2008) *Ziegfeld: The Man Who Invented Show Business.* New York.

Morehouse, Ward. (1971) *George M. Cohan: Prince of the American Theater.* Westport, CT.

Morello, John A. (2001) *Selling the President, 1920: Albert D. Lasker, Advertising, and the Election of Warren G. Harding.* Westport, CT.

Morgan, Austen. (1988) *James Connolly: A Political Biography.* Manchester, UK.

Morgan, Charlotte Elizabeth. (1930) *The Origin and History of the New York Employing Printers' Association: The Evolution of a Trade Association.* New York.

Morgan, David T. (1973) "The Revivalist as Patriot: Billy Sunday and World War I." *Journal of Presbyterian History* 51: 199–215.

Morgan, Thomas L. (2004) "The City as Refuge: Constructing Urban Blackness in Paul Laurence Dunbar's *The*

Sport of the Gods and James Weldon Johnson's *The Autobiography of an Ex-Colored Man.*" *African American Review* 38: 213–38.

Morgenthau, Henry, III. (1991) *Mostly Morgenthaus: A Family History.* Boston, MA.

Morgenthau, Henry, and French Strother. (1922) *All in a Life-Time.* Garden City, NY.

Morison, Elting Elmore. (1960) *Turmoil and Tradition: A Study of the Life and Times of Henry L. Stimson.* New York.

Morris, Charles R. (1980) *The Cost of Good Intentions: New York City and the Liberal Experiment, 1960–1975.* New York.

Morris, Edmund. (2001) *Theodore Rex.* New York.

———. (2010) *Colonel Roosevelt.* New York.

Morris, Lloyd R. (1996) *Incredible New York: High Life and Low Life from 1850 to 1950.* Syracuse, NY.

Morris, Roy. (2003) *Fraud of the Century: Rutherford B. Hayes, Samuel Tilden, and the Stolen Election of 1876.* New York.

Morrison, William. (1999) *Broadway Theatres: History and Architecture.* Mineola, NY.

Morrone, Francis. (1997) "The Ghost of Monsieur Stokes." *City Journal* 7: 98–111.

Moses, Paul. (2015) *An Unlikely Union: The Love-Hate Story of New York's Irish and Italians.* New York.

Moses, Robert. (1914) *The Civil Service of Great Britain.* New York.

Moss, David A. (1996) *Socializing Security: Progressive-Era Economists and the Origins of American Social Policy.* Cambridge, MA.

Moss, Frank. (1897) *The American Metropolis, from Knickerbocker Days to the Present Time.* Vol. 2. New York.

Motomura, Hiroshi. (2006) *Americans in Waiting: The Lost Story of Immigration*

and Citizenship in the United States. New York.

Mottus, Jane E. (1981) *New York Nightingales: The Emergence of the Nursing Profession at Bellevue and New York Hospital, 1850–1920.* Ann Arbor, MI.

Moses King Inc., Publishers. (1914) *King's How to See New York, a Complete Trustworthy Guide Book: 100 Illustrations, the Latest Map.* New York.

Moulton, Elizabeth. (1964) *St. George's Church, New York.* New York.

Mowry, George E. (1946) *Theodore Roosevelt and the Progressive Movement.* New York.

Muhammad, Khalil Gibran. (2010) *The Condemnation of Blackness: Race, Crime, and the Making of Modern Urban America.* Cambridge, MA.

Mumford, Lewis. (1925) *Sticks and Stones: A Study of American Architecture and Civilization.* New York.

———. (1982) *Sketches from Life: The Autobiography of Lewis Mumford: The Early Years.* New York.

Munsey, Frank Andrew. (1907) *The Founding of the Munsey Publishing-House, Quarter of a Century Old: The Story of the "Argosy," Our First Publication, and Incidentally the Story of "Munsey's Magazine."* New York.

Murphy, Kevin P. (2008) *Political Manhood: Red Bloods, Mollycoddles, and the Politics of Progressive Era Reform.* New York.

Murphy, Marjorie. (1992) *Blackboard Unions: The AFT and the NEA, 1900–1980.* Ithaca, NY.

Murray, Robert K. (1955) *Red Scare: A Study in National Hysteria, 1919–1920.* Minneapolis, MN.

Musser, Charles. (1984) "Another Look at the 'Chaser Theory.'" *Studies in Visual Communication* 10: 24–44.

———. (1990) *The Emergence of Cinema: The American Screen to 1907.* New York.

———. (1991) *Before the Nickelodeon: Edwin S. Porter and the Edison Manufacturing Company.* Berkeley, CA.

———. (1995) *Thomas A. Edison and His Kinetographic Motion Pictures.* New Brunswick, NJ.

Musto, David F. (1997) "History: The American Experience with Stimulants." Paper presented at the National Methamphetamine Drug Conference. Omaha, NE.

———. (1999) *The American Disease: Origins of Narcotic Control.* New York.

Myatt, James Allen. (1960) "William Randolph Hearst and the Progressive Era, 1900–1912." Ph.D. diss., University of Florida.

Myers, Gustavus. (1974) *History of Public Franchises in New York City.* New York.

Myers, Margaret G. (1931) *The New York Money Market,* vol. 1, *Origins and Development.* New York.

Naff, Alixa. (2000) "The Mother Colony in New York." Paper presented at A Community of Many Worlds: Arab Americans in New York City. New York.

Nasaw, David. (1979) *Schooled to Order: A Social History of Public Schooling in the United States.* New York.

———. (1986) *Children of the City: At Work and at Play.* New York.

———. (1992) "Cities of Light, Landscapes of Pleasure." In *The Landscape of Modernity: Essays on New York City, 1900–1940,* edited by David Ward and Oliver Zunz. New York.

———. (1993) *Going Out: The Rise and Fall of Public Amusements.* New York.

———. (2000) *The Chief: The Life of William Randolph Hearst.* Boston, MA.

———. (2006) *Andrew Carnegie.* New York.

National Park Service. (1977) *New York Life Building: National Register of Historic Places*

Inventory—Nomination Form. Washington, DC.

———. (1989) *National Register of Historic Places: United Charities Building Registration Form*. Washington, DC.

Navin, Thomas R., and Marian V. Sears. (1955) "The Rise of a Market for Industrial Securities, 1887–1902." *Business History Review* 29: 105–38.

Neal, Larry, and Lance E. Davis. (2007) "Why Did Finance Capitalism and the Second Industrial Revolution Arise in the 1890s?" In *Financing Innovation in the United States, 1870 to the Present*, edited by Naomi R. Lamoreaux and Kenneth Lee Sokoloff. Cambridge, MA.

Nelli, Humbert S. (1976) *The Business of Crime: Italians and Syndicate Crime in the United States*. New York.

Nelson, Bruce. (1988) *Workers on the Waterfront: Seamen, Longshoremen, and Unionism in the 1930s*. Urbana, IL.

———. (2012) *Irish Nationalists and the Making of the Irish Race*. Princeton, NJ.

Nelson, Ralph L. (1959) *Merger Movements in American Industry, 1895–1956*. Princeton, NJ.

Neu, Charles E. (2015) *Colonel House: A Biography of Woodrow Wilson's Silent Partner*. New York, NY.

Nevins, Allan, and John A. Krout. (1948) *The Greater City: New York, 1898–1948*. New York.

New Theatre. (1909) *The New Theatre, New York*. New York.

New-York Historical Society and Mary Black. (1980) *That Belmont Look: An Exhibition Celebrating the 75th Anniversary of Belmont Park*. New York.

New York City Bureau of City Chamberlain and Henry Jaromir Bruère. (1916) *New York City's Administrative Progress, 1914–1916: A Survey of Various Departments under the Jurisdiction of the Mayor*. New York.

New York City Department of Environmental Protection. (2009) *New York Harbor Survey Program: Celebrating 100 Years, 1909–2009*. New York.

New York City WPA Writers' Project. (1941) *A Maritime History of New York*. New York.

New York Committee of Fifteen. (1902) *The Social Evil, with Special Reference to Conditions Existing in the City of New York*. New York.

New York Edison Company. (1907) *Specifications for the New Waterside Power House of the New York Edison Company, New York, July 1907*. New York.

———. (1913) *Thirty Years of New York, 1882–1912: Being a History of Electrical Development in Manhattan and the Bronx*. New York.

New York Times. (1913) "First Industrial Survey of New York Is Now On: The Merchants' Association Is Directing a Remarkable Collection of Data Which Will Aid in Bringing Factories to New York City and in Bettering Facilities of Factories Now Here." *New York Times*, November 30.

New York Tuberculosis and Health Association, Godias J. Drolet, and Anthony M. Lowell. (1952) *A Half Century's Progress against Tuberculosis in New York City, 1900–1950*. New York.

"New York, the Unrivalled Business Centre." (1902) *Harper's Weekly* 46: 1673–87.

New Yorker. (1960) "The Talk of the Town: Infallible." *New Yorker*, February 6, 29–31.

Newkirk, Pamela. (2015) *Spectacle: The Astonishing Life of Ota Benga*. New York.

Newt Davidson Collective. (1974) *Crisis at CUNY*. CUNY Digital History Archive.

Nicolson, Harold. (1935) *Dwight Morrow*. New York.

Nielsen, Kim E. (2001) *Un-American Womanhood: Antiradicalism, Antifeminism, and the First Red Scare*. Columbus, OH.

Noble, David F. (1977) *America by Design: Science, Technology, and the Rise of Corporate Capitalism*. New York.

Norman, Dorothy. (1990) *Alfred Stieglitz: An American Seer*. New York.

Norris, James D. (1990) *Advertising and the Transformation of American Society, 1865–1920*. New York.

North, Douglass C. (1954) "Life Insurance and Investment Banking at the Time of the Armstrong Investigation of 1905–1906." *Journal of Economic History* 14: 209–28.

Norton, Thomas E. (1984) *100 Years of Collecting in America: The Story of Sotheby Parke Bernet*. New York.

Norton, Thomas E., and Jerry E. Patterson. (1984) *Living It Up: A Guide to the Named Apartment Houses of New York*. New York.

Norwood, Stephen H. (1994) "The Student as Strikebreaker: College Youth and the Crisis of Masculinity in the Early Twentieth Century." *Journal of Social History* 28: 331–49.

———. (2002) *Strikebreaking and Intimidation: Mercenaries and Masculinity in Twentieth-Century America*. Chapel Hill, NC.

Nown, Graham. (1987) *The English Godfather*. London.

Noyes, Alexander D. (1918) "Our International Banking in War Time." *Bankers Magazine* 97: 508–15.

Nye, David E. (1992) *Electrifying America: Social Meanings of a New Technology, 1880–1940*. Cambridge, MA.

O'Brien, Thomas F. (1989) "'Rich Beyond the Dreams of Avarice': The Guggenheims in Chile." *Business History Review* 63: 122–59.

———. (1996) *The Revolutionary Mission: American Enterprise in Latin America, 1900–1945*. New York.

———. (2007) *Making the Americas: The United States and Latin America from the Age of Revolutions to the Era of Globalization*. Albuquerque, NM.

O'Connell, Shaun. (1994) *Remarkable, Unspeakable New York: A Literary History*. Boston, MA.

O'Connor, Richard. (1963) *Courtroom Warrior: The Combative Career of William Travers Jerome*. Boston, MA.

———. (1993) *Hell's Kitchen*. New York.

O'Donnell, Edward T. (2003) *Ship Ablaze: The Tragedy of the Steamboat General Slocum*. New York.

O'Grady, John. (1930) *Catholic Charities in the United States: History and Problems*. Washington, DC.

O'Hanlon, Timothy James. (1982) "Neighborhood Change in New York City: A Case Study of Park Slope, 1850–1980." Ph.D. diss., City University of New York.

O'Neill, William L. (1978) *The Last Romantic: A Life of Max Eastman*. New York.

O'Toole, Patricia. (2005) *When Trumpets Call: Theodore Roosevelt after the White House*. New York.

Ogburn, William Fielding. (1909) "The Richmond Negro in New York City: His Social Mind as Seen in His Pleasures." M.A. thesis, Columbia University.

Ohmann, Richard. (1996) *Selling Culture: Magazines, Markets, and Class at the Turn of the Century*. New York.

Okrent, Daniel. (2010) *Last Call: The Rise and Fall of Prohibition, 1920–1933*. New York.

Oneal, James. (1910) *The Workers in American History*. Terre Haute, IN.

Opdycke, Sandra. (1999) *No One Was Turned Away: The Role of Public Hospitals in New York City since 1900.* New York.

Orcutt, Kimberly. (2013a) "Arthur B. Davies—Hero or Villain?" In *The Armory Show at 100: Modernism and Revolution,* edited by Marilyn Satin Kushner and Kimberly Orcutt. New York.

———. (2013b) "'Public Verdict': Debating Modernism at the Armory Show." In *The Armory Show at 100: Modernism and Revolution,* edited by Marilyn Satin Kushner and Kimberly Orcutt. New York.

———. (2013c) "Robert Henri's Manifesto." In *The Armory Show at 100: Modernism and Revolution,* edited by Marilyn Satin Kushner and Kimberly Orcutt. New York.

Orleck, Annelise. (1995) *Common Sense and a Little Fire: Women and Working-Class Politics in the United States, 1900–1965.* Chapel Hill, NC.

Orloff, Ann Shola. (1988) "The Political Origins of America's Belated Welfare State." In *The Politics of Social Policy in the United States,* edited by Margaret Weir, Ann Shola Orloff, and Theda Skocpol. Princeton, NJ.

Orsi, Robert A. (1985) *The Madonna of 115th Street: Faith and Community in Italian Harlem, 1880–1950.* New Haven, CT.

Osofsky, Gilbert. (1963) "Race Riot, 1900: A Study of Ethnic Violence." *Journal of Negro Education* 32: 16–24.

———. (1966) *Harlem: The Making of a Ghetto, Negro New York, 1890–1930.* New York.

Otis, Ginger Adams. (2015) *Firefight: The Century-Long Battle to Integrate New York's Bravest.* New York.

Ott, Julia C. (2011) *When Wall Street Met Main Street: The Quest for an Investors' Democracy.* Cambridge, MA.

Ottinger, Didier. (2013) "Off to the Armory Show!" In *The Armory Show at 100: Modernism and Revolution,* edited by Marilyn Satin Kushner and Kimberly Orcutt. New York.

Ottley, Roi, and William J. Weatherby. (1967) *The Negro in New York: An Informal Social History.* New York.

Ovington, Mary White. (1911) *Half a Man: The Status of the Negro in New York.* New York.

———. (1995) *Black and White Sat Down Together: The Reminiscences of an NAACP Founder,* edited by Ralph Luker. New York.

P. Lorillard Company. (1960) *Lorillard and Tobacco: 200th Anniversary, P. Lorillard Company, 1760–1960.* New York.

Paddon, Mary E. (1920) "Inferior Criminal Courts of New York City." *Journal of Criminal Law and Criminology* 11: 8–20.

Page, Max. (1999) *The Creative Destruction of Manhattan, 1900–1940.* Chicago, IL.

———. (2008) *The City's End: Two Centuries of Fantasies, Fears, and Premonitions of New York's Destruction.* New Haven, CT.

———. (2013) "The Armory Show in the Provisional City." In *The Armory Show at 100: Modernism and Revolution,* edited by Marilyn Satin Kushner and Kimberly Orcutt. New York.

Page, Max, and Randall Mason. (2004) *Giving Preservation a History: Histories of Historic Preservation in the United States.* New York.

Painter, Nell. (1987) *Standing at Armageddon: The United States, 1877–1929.* New York.

Pak, Susie. (2013) *Gentlemen Bankers: The World of J. P. Morgan.* Cambridge, MA.

Palladino, Grace. (2005) *Skilled Hands, Strong Spirits: A Century of Building Trades History.* Ithaca, NY.

Parascandola, Louis J. (2006) "Cyril Briggs and the African Blood Brotherhood: A Radical Counterpoint to Progressivism." *Afro-Americans in New York Life and History* 30: 7–18.

Paris, Leslie. (2008) *Children's Nature: The Rise of the American Summer Camp.* New York.

Parmet, Robert D. (2005) *The Master of Seventh Avenue: David Dubinsky and the American Labor Movement.* New York.

Parrini, Carl P. (1969) *Heir to Empire: United States Economic Diplomacy, 1916–1923.* Pittsburgh, PA.

———. (1993) "Charles A. Conant, Economic Crises and Foreign Policy, 1896–1903." In *Behind the Throne: Servants of Power to Imperial Presidents, 1898–1968,* edited by Thomas J. McCormick and Walter LaFeber. Madison, WI.

Parry, Albert. (1960) *Garrets and Pretenders: A History of Bohemianism in America.* New York.

Payne, Christopher. (2002) *New York's Forgotten Substations: The Power behind the Subway.* New York.

Pearlman, Michael D. (1984) *To Make Democracy Safe for America: Patricians and Preparedness in the Progressive Era.* Urbana, IL.

Peiss, Kathy. (1986) *Cheap Amusements: Working Women and Leisure in Turn-of-the-Century New York.* Philadelphia, PA.

———. (1988) "Gender, Race, Class and the Geography of Urban Leisure, 1900–1930." Paper presented at Conference on the Comparative History of Metropolitan Transformation of Budapest and New York, 1870–1930. Budapest.

———. (1989) "'Charity Girls' and City Pleasures: Historical Notes on Working-Class Sexuality, 1880–1920." In *Passion and Power: Sexuality in History,* edited by Kathy Peiss and Christina Simmons. Philadelphia, PA.

Penkower, Monty Noam. (2004) "The Kishinev Pogrom of 1903: A Turning Point in Jewish History." *Modern Judaism* 24: 187–225.

Peress, Maurice. (2004) *Dvořák to Duke Ellington: A Conductor Explores America's Music and Its African American Roots.* New York.

Pérez, Louis A., Jr. (1999) *On Becoming Cuban: Identity, Nationality, and Culture.* Chapel Hill, NC.

Perlman, Bennard B. (1979) *The Immortal Eight: American Painting from Eakins to the Armory Show, 1870–1913.* Westport, CT.

———. (1988) *Painters of the Ashcan School: The Immortal Eight.* Mineola, NY.

Pernicone, Nunzio. (1999) "Italian Immigrant Radicalism in New York." In *The Italians of New York: Five Centuries of Struggle and Achievement,* edited by Philip V. Cannistraro. New York.

———. (2005) *Carlo Tresca: Portrait of a Rebel.* New York.

Perry, Elisabeth Israels. (1987) *Belle Moskowitz: Feminine Politics and the Exercise of Power in the Age of Alfred E. Smith.* New York.

———. (1990) "Women's Political Choices after Suffrage: The Women's City Club of New York, 1915–1990." *New York History* 71: 417–34.

Perry, Jeffrey Babcock. (2009) *Hubert Harrison: The Voice of Harlem Radicalism, 1883–1918.* New York.

Peters, Rev. John P. (1918) "The Story of the Committee of Fourteen." *Journal of Social Hygiene* 4: 347–88.

Peterson, Carla L. (2011) *Black Gotham: A Family*

History of African Americans in Nineteenth-Century New York City. New Haven, CT.

Peterson, Jon A. (1983) "The City Beautiful Movement." In *Introduction to Planning History in the United States*, edited by Donald A. Krueckeberg. New Brunswick, NJ.

———. (2003) *The Birth of City Planning in the United States, 1840–1917*. Baltimore, MD.

Petrulis, Alan. (2010) "A Not So Concise History of the Evolution of Postcards in the United States." *Metropostcard.com*.

Pettit, Dorothy Ann, and Janice Bailie. (2008) *A Cruel Wind: Pandemic Flu in America, 1918–1920*. Murfreesboro, TN.

Pfannestiel, Todd J. (2003) *Rethinking the Red Scare: The Lusk Committee and New York's Crusade against Radicalism, 1919–1923*. New York.

Pfeffer, Paula F. (1990) *A. Philip Randolph: Pioneer of the Civil Rights Movement*. Baton Rouge, LA.

Phillips-Matz, Mary Jane. (1984) *The Many Lives of Otto Kahn*. New York.

———. (2002) *Puccini: A Biography*. Boston, MA.

Phillips, David Graham. (1905) "The Delusion of the Race-Track." *Cosmopolitan* 38: 251–62.

———. (1906) "The Treason of the Senate." *Cosmopolitan* 40: 487–502.

Pietrusza, David. (2003) *Rothstein: The Life, Times, and Murder of the Criminal Genius Who Fixed the 1919 World Series*. New York.

Piketty, Thomas. (2014) *Capital in the Twenty-First Century*, translated by Arthur Goldhammer. Cambridge, MA.

Pilat, Oliver Ramsay, and Jo Ranson. (1941) *Sodom by the Sea: An Affectionate History of Coney Island*. Garden City, NY.

Piott, Steven L. (2014) *Americans in Dissent: Thirteen Influential Social Critics of the Nineteenth Century*. Lanham, MD.

Pisano, Dominick, and National Air and Space Museum. (1992) *Legend, Memory, and the Great War in the Air*. Seattle, WA.

Pitrone, Jean Maddern. (2003) *F. W. Woolworth and the American Five and Dime: A Social History*. Jefferson, NC.

Pittenger, Mark. (1994) "Imagining Genocide in the Progressive Era: The Socialist Science Fiction of George Allan England." *American Studies* 35: 91–108.

Pivar, David J. (2002) *Purity and Hygiene: Women, Prostitution, and the "American Plan," 1900–1930*. Westport, CT.

Piven, Frances Fox, and Richard A. Cloward. (1977) *Poor People's Movements: Why They Succeed, How They Fail*. New York.

Pletcher, David M. (1998) *The Diplomacy of Trade and Investment: American Economic Expansion in the Hemisphere, 1865–1900*. Columbia, MO.

Plunkett-Powell, Karen. (1999) *Remembering Woolworth's: A Nostalgic History of the World's Most Famous Five-and-Dime*. New York.

Plunz, Richard. (1990) *A History of Housing in New York City: Dwelling Type and Social Change in the American Metropolis*. New York.

Poggi, Jack. (1968) *Theater in America: The Impact of Economic Forces, 1870–1967*. Ithaca, NY.

Polland, Annie, and Daniel Soyer. (2012) *Emerging Metropolis: New York Jews in the Age of Immigration, 1840–1920*. New York.

Poole, Ernest. (1925) *The Harbor*. New York.

———. (1944) "Maxim Gorki in New York." *Slavonic and East European Review* 3: 77–83.

Pope, Daniel. (1983) *The Making of Modern Advertising*. New York.

Pope, Jesse Eliphalet. (1905) *The Clothing Industry in New York*. Columbia, MO.

Popenoe, Paul Bowman, and Roswell Hill Johnson.

(1918) *Applied Eugenics*. New York.

Port of New York Authority. (1941) *The Port of New York*. New York.

Porter, Patrick G. (1969) "Origins of the American Tobacco Company." *Business History Review* 43: 59–76.

Powell, Leona Margaret. (1926) *The History of the United Typothetae of America*. Chicago, IL.

Powell, Michael J. (1988) *From Patrician to Professional Elite: The Transformation of the New York City Bar Association*. New York.

Powell, Richard E., Jr. (1992) "The Brewsters: Three Generations of American Carriage Builders." *Driving Digest Magazine* 73: 1992/5.

Powers, Richard Gid. (1987) *Secrecy and Power: The Life of J. Edgar Hoover*. New York.

Pozzetta, George Enrico. (1971) "The Italians of New York City, 1890–1914." Ph.D. diss., University of North Carolina at Chapel Hill.

Pratt, Edward Ewing. (1968) *Industrial Causes of Congestion of Population in New York City*. New York.

Pratt, Julius William. (1936) *Expansionists of 1898: The Acquisition of Hawaii and the Spanish Islands*. Baltimore, MD.

Pratt, Norma Fain. (1979) *Morris Hillquit: A Political History of an American Jewish Socialist*. Westport, CT.

Preston, Douglas J. (1986) *Dinosaurs in the Attic: An Excursion into the American Museum of Natural History*. New York.

Preston, William. (1994) *Aliens and Dissenters: Federal Suppression of Radicals, 1903–1933*. Urbana, IL.

Prins, Nomi. (2014) *All the Presidents' Bankers: The Hidden Alliances That Drive American Power*. New York.

Pritchett, Wendell Eric. (1997) "From One Ghetto to Another: Blacks, Jews

and Public Housing in Brownsville, Brooklyn , 1945–1970." Ph.D. diss., University of Pennsylvania.

Procter, Ben. (1998) *William Randolph Hearst: The Early Years, 1863–1910*. New York.

Pruessen, Ronald W. (1982) *John Foster Dulles: The Road to Power*. New York.

Pryor, Elizabeth Brown. (1987) *Clara Barton: Professional Angel*. Philadelphia, PA.

Quadagno, Jill S. (2006) *One Nation, Uninsured: Why the U.S. Has No National Health Insurance*. New York.

Quinn, Stephen C., and American Museum of Natural History. (2006) *Windows on Nature: The Great Habitat Dioramas of the American Museum of Natural History*. New York.

Quivik, Fredric L. (2004) *Kaiser's Richmond Shipyards with Special Emphasis on Richmond Shipyard No. 3*. Richmond, CA.

Rabban, David M. (1997) *Free Speech in Its Forgotten Years, 1870–1920*. New York.

Race, Joseph. (1918) *Chlorination of Water*. New York.

Rachlis, Eugene, and John E. Marqusee. (1963) *The Landlords*. New York.

Raffel, Martin J. (2002) "History of Israel Advocacy." In *Jewish Polity and American Civil Society: Communal Agencies and Religious Movements in the American Public Sphere*, edited by Alan Mittleman, Jonathan D. Sarna, and Robert Licht. Lanham, MD.

Raider, Mark A. (2008) "The Aristocrat and the Democrat: Louis Marshall, Stephen S. Wise and the Challenge of American Jewish Leadership." *American Jewish Journal* 94: 91–113.

Rainger, Ronald. (1991) *An Agenda for Antiquity: Henry Fairfield Osborn and Vertebrate Paleontology at*

the American Museum of
Natural History,
1890–1935. Tuscaloosa,
AL.

Rainone, Nanette, ed. (1985)
The Brooklyn Neighborhood
Book. Brooklyn, NY.

Ramirez, Jan Seidler, and
Museum of the City of
New York. (1990) Within
Bohemia's Borders:
Greenwich Village,
1830–1930: Interpretive
Script Accompanying an
Exhibition at the Museum of
City of New York. New
York.

Rand School of Social
Science. (1916) The
American Labor Year Book,
1916. New York.

———. (1920) The American
Labor Year Book,
1919–1920. New York.

Randall, Monica. (1987) The
Mansions of Long Island's
Gold Coast. New York.

Rankin, Rebecca B. (1939)
New York Advancing:
World's Fair Edition, the
Result of Five Years of
Progressive Administration
in the City of New York, F.
H. La Guardia, Mayor.
New York.

Rantisi, Norma M. (2004)
"The Ascendance of New
York Fashion."
International Journal of
Urban and Regional
Research 28: 86–106.

Rao, Nancy Yunhwa. (2002)
"Songs of the Exclusion
Era: New York
Chinatown's Opera
Theaters in the 1920s."
American Music 20:
399–444.

Rasenberger, Jim. (2004)
High Steel: The Daring
Men Who Built the World's
Greatest Skyline. New York.

Rauchway, Eric. (1999) "A
Gentlemen's Club in a
Woman's Sphere: How
Dorothy Whitney Straight
Created the New
Republic." Journal of
Women's History 11: 60–85.

Raustiala, Kal. (2009) Does
the Constitution Follow the
Flag? The Evolution of
Territoriality in American
Law. New York.

Ravitch, Diane. (1976) The
Great School Wars: New
York City, 1805–1973.
New York.

Rawls, Walton H. (1988)
Wake Up, America! World
War I and the American
Poster. New York.

Real Estate Record and
Builders Guide. (1907)
"Changes in Long Acre
Square." November 16,
1907: 799.

———. (1909) "A New City
in the Bronx." April 17,
1909: 753–54.

Recchiuti, John Louis.
(1995) "The Rand School
of Social Science during
the Progressive Era: Will
to Power of a Stratum of
the American Intellectual
Class." Journal of the
History of the Behavioral
Sciences 31: 149–61.

———. (2006) Civic
Engagement: Social Science
and Progressive-Era Reform
in New York City.
Philadelphia, PA.

Reed, Henry Hope. (1971)
"The Vision Spurned:
Classical New York—the
Story of City Planning in
New York." Classical
America 1: 31–41.

———. (1986) The New
York Public Library: Its
Architecture and
Decoration. New York.

Reed, James. (1978a) From
Private Vice to Public Virtue:
The Birth Control Movement
and American Society since
1830. New York.

Reed, Robert Carroll.
(1978b) The New York
Elevated. South
Brunswick, NJ.

Regal, Brian. (2001)
"Terrible Monkeys: Henry
Fairfield Osborn, Race,
and the Search for Origins
of Man." Ph.D. diss.,
Drew University.

Register, Woody. (2001) The
Kid of Coney Island: Fred
Thompson and the Rise of
American Amusements.
New York.

Reich, Leonard S. (1985) The
Making of American
Industrial Research: Science
and Business at GE and Bell,
1876–1926. New York.

Reid, B. L. (1968) The Man
from New York: John
Quinn and His Friends.
New York.

Reier, Sharon. (2000) The
Bridges of New York.
Mineola, NY.

Reinhart, Carmen M., and
Kenneth S. Rogoff. (2009)
This Time Is Different:
Eight Centuries of Financial
Folly. Princeton, NJ.

———. (2012) "Sorry, U.S.
Recoveries Really Aren't
Different." Bloomberg,
October 26, 1–4.

Reisler, Jim. (2002) Before
They Were the Bombers:
The New York Yankees'
Early Years, 1903–1915.
Jefferson, NC.

Remeseira, Claudio Iván.
(2010) "A Splendid
Outsider: Archer Milton
Huntington and the
Hispanic Heritage in the
United States." In
Hispanic New York: A
Sourcebook, edited by
Claudio Iván Remeseira.
New York.

Renner, Andrea. (2008) "A
Nation That Bathes
Together: New York City's
Progressive Era Baths."
Baths." Journal of the
Society of Architectural
Historians 67: 504–31.

Revell, Keith D. (1992)
"Regulating the
Landscape: Real Estate
Values, City Planning, and
the 1916 Zoning
Ordinance." In The
Landscape of Modernity:
Essays on New York City:
1900–1940, edited by
David Ward and Oliver
Zunz. New York.

———. (2003) Building
Gotham: Civic Culture and
Public Policy in New York
City, 1898–1938.
Baltimore, MD.

———. (2005) "Law Makes
Order: The Search for
Ensemble in the
Skyscraper City,
1890–1930." In The
American Skyscraper:
Cultural Histories, edited
by Roberta Moudry. New
York.

Rhoads, William. (1985)
"The Colonial Revival and
the Americanization of
Immigrants." In The
Colonial Revival in
America, edited by Alan
Axelrod. New York.

Rhodes-Pitts, Sharifa.
(2011) Harlem Is
Nowhere: A Journey to the
Mecca of Black America.
New York.

Ribak, Gil. (2012a) Gentile
New York: The Images of
Non-Jews among Jewish
Immigrants. New
Brunswick, NJ.

———. (2012b) "'A Victory
of the Slavs Means a
Deathblow to Democracy':
The Onset of World War I
and the Images of the
Warring Sides among
Jewish Immigrants in New
York, 1914–16." In War
and Peace in Jewish
Tradition: From the Biblical
World to the Present, edited
by Yigal Levin and Amnon
Shapira. London.

Richards, Pamela Spence.
(1984) Scholars and
Gentlemen: The Library of
the New-York Historical
Society, 1804–1982.
Hamden, CT.

Richardson, James F. (1970)
The New York Police,
Colonial Times to 1901.
New York.

Richman, Jeffrey I. (1998)
Brooklyn's Green-Wood
Cemetery: New York's
Buried Treasure. Brooklyn,
NY.

Rideout, Walter B. (1992)
The Radical Novel in the
United States, 1900–1954:
Some Interrelations of
Literature and Society.
New York.

Rider, Fremont, et al. (1916)
Rider's New York City and
Vicinity, Including Newark,
Yonkers and Jersey City: A
Guide-Book for Travelers,
with 16 Maps and 18 Plans.
New York.

Riess, Steven A. (1988a)
"Only the Ring Was
Square: Frankie Carbo
and the Underworld
Control of American
Boxing." International
Journal of the History of
Sport 5: 29–52.

———. (1988b) "Sports and
Machine Politics in New
York City, 1870–1920." In
The Making of Urban
America, edited by
Raymond A. Mohl.
Wilmington, DE.

———. (1989) City Games:
The Evolution of American
Urban Society and the Rise
of Sports. Urbana, IL.

———. (1999) Touching
Base: Professional Baseball
and American Culture in the

Progressive Era. Urbana, IL.

———. (2011) *The Sport of Kings and the Kings of Crime: Horse Racing, Politics, and Organized Crime in New York, 1865–1913*. Syracuse, NY.

Riordon, William L. (1963) *Plunkitt of Tammany Hall: A Series of Very Plain Talks on Very Practical Politics*. New York.

Rischin, Moses. (1977) *The Promised City: New York's Jews, 1870–1914*. Cambridge, MA.

———, ed.. (1986) *Grandma Never Lived in America: The New Journalism of Abraham Cahan*. Bloomington, IN.

Ritterband, Paul. (2001) "Counting the Jews in New York, 1900–1991: An Essay in Substance and Method." In *Papers in Jewish Demography 1997: Selected Proceedings of the Demographic Sessions Held at the 12th World Congress of Jewish Studies, Jerusalem, 1997*, edited by Sergio DellaPergola and Judith Even. Jerusalem.

Roazen, Paul. (1975) *Freud and His Followers*. New York.

Roberts, Dorothy. (2009a) "Margaret Sanger and the Racial Origins of the Birth Control Movement." In *Racially Writing the Republic: Racists, Race Rebels, and Transformations of American Identity*, edited by Bruce Baum and Duchess Harris. Durham, NC.

Roberts, Nancy Lee. (1982) "Dorothy Day and the *Catholic Worker*, 1933–1982." Ph.D. diss., University of Minnesota.

Roberts, Priscilla. (1992) "'All the Right People': The Historiography of the American Foreign Policy Establishment." *Journal of American Studies* 26: 409–34.

———. (1994) "The First World War and the Emergence of American Atlanticism, 1914–1920." *Diplomacy and Statecraft* 5: 569–619.

———. (1997) "The Anglo-American Theme: American Visions of an Atlantic Alliance, 1914–1933." *Diplomatic History* 21: 333–64.

———. (1998) "Willard Straight, the First World War, and 'Internationalism of All Sorts': The Inconsistencies of an American Liberal Interventionist." *Australian Journal of Politics and History* 44: 493–511.

———. (2002) "Frank A. Vanderlip and the National City Bank during the First World War." *Essays in Economic and Business History* 20: 145–66.

———. (2005) "Paul D. Cravath, the First World War, and the Anglophile Internationalist Tradition." *Australian Journal of Politics and History* 51: 194–215.

———. (2007) "The First World War as Catalyst and Epiphany: The Case of Henry P. Davison." *Diplomacy and Statecraft* 18: 315–50.

———. (2009b) "The Transatlantic American Foreign Policy Elite: Its Evolution in Generational Perspective." *Journal of Transatlantic Studies* 7: 163–83.

Roberts, Sam. (2013) *Grand Central: How a Train Station Transformed America*. New York.

Robertson, Nancy Marie. (2007) *Christian Sisterhood, Race Relations, and the YWCA, 1906–46*. Urbana, IL.

Robertson, Raymond J., and International Association of Bridge, Structural, and Ornamental Iron Workers. (1996) *Ironworkers 100th Anniversary, 1896–1996: A History of the Iron Workers Union*. New York.

Robertson, Stephen. (2002) "Age of Consent Law and the Making of Modern Childhood in New York City, 1886–1921." *Journal of Social History* 35: 781–98.

———. (2005) *Crimes against Children: Sexual Violence and Legal Culture in New York City, 1880–1960*. Chapel Hill, NC.

Robinson, Jo Ann. (1981) *Abraham Went Out: A Biography of A. J. Muste*. Philadelphia, PA.

Rockaway, Robert A. (2000) *But He Was Good to His Mother: The Lives and Crimes of Jewish Gangsters*. New York.

Rockefeller, John D., Jr. (1910) "Grand Jury Presentment: White Slave Traffic." Appended to *The House of Bondage*, by Reginald Wright Kauffman. New York.

Rockoff, Hugh. (2004) "Until It's Over, Over There: The U.S. Economy in World War I." *NBER Working Paper* 10580: 3–44.

Rodgers, Cleveland. (1952) *Robert Moses, Builder for Democracy*. New York.

Rodgers, Daniel T. (1982) "In Search of Progressivism." *Reviews in American History* 10: 113–32.

———. (1998) *Atlantic Crossings: Social Politics in a Progressive Age*. Cambridge, MA.

Roe, Clifford Griffith. (1979) *The Great War on White Slavery*. New York.

Romeyn, Esther. (1998) "My Other/My Self: Impersonation, Masquerade, and the Theatre of Identity in Turn-of-the-Century New York City." Ph.D. diss., University of Minnesota, Twin Cities.

———. (2008) *Street Scenes: Staging the Self in Immigrant New York, 1880–1924*. Minneapolis, MN.

Roosevelt, Theodore. (1891) *New York*. London.

Rose, Mark H. (1995) *Cities of Light and Heat: Domesticating Gas and Electricity in Urban America*. University Park, PA.

Rosen, Robyn L. (2003) *Reproductive Health, Reproductive Rights: Reformers and the Politics of Maternal Welfare,* 1917–1940. Columbus, OH.

Rosen, Ruth. (1982) *The Lost Sisterhood: Prostitution in America, 1900–1918*. Baltimore, MD.

Rosenberg, Arnold S. (1969) "The New York Reformers of 1914: A Profile." *New York History* 50: 198–206.

Rosenberg, Charles E. (1994) *The Care of Strangers: The Rise of America's Hospital System*. Baltimore, MD.

Rosenberg, Emily. (1982) *Spreading the American Dream: American Economic and Cultural Expansion, 1890–1945*. New York.

———. (1999) *Financial Missionaries to the World: The Politics and Culture of Dollar Diplomacy, 1900–1930*. Cambridge, MA.

Rosenberg, Jonathan. (2006) *How Far the Promised Land? World Affairs and the American Civil Rights Movement from the First World War to Vietnam*. Princeton, NJ.

Rosenberg, Rosalind. (1982) *Beyond Separate Spheres: Intellectual Roots of Modern Feminism*. New Haven, CT.

———. (2004) *Changing the Subject: How the Women of Columbia Shaped the Way We Think about Sex and Politics*. New York.

Rosenblum, Constance. (2009) *Boulevard of Dreams: Heady Times, Heartbreak, and Hope along the Grand Concourse in the Bronx*. New York.

Rosenthal, Michael. (2006) *Nicholas Miraculous: The Amazing Career of the Redoubtable Dr. Nicholas Murray Butler*. New York.

Rosenwaike, Ira. (1972) *The Population History of New York City*. Syracuse, NY.

Rosenzweig, Roy, and Elizabeth Blackmar. (1994) *The Park and the People: A History of Central Park*. New York.

Rosner, David. (1982) *A Once Charitable Enterprise: Hospitals and Health Care in Brooklyn and New York, 1885–1915*. New York.

Ross, Alex. (2007) *The Rest Is Noise: Listening to the*

Twentieth Century. New York.

Ross, Barbara Joyce. (1972) *J. E. Spingarn and the Rise of the NAACP, 1911–1939.* New York.

Ross, Jack. (2015) *The Socialist Party of America: A Complete History.* Lincoln, NE.

Rossano, Geoffrey. (1984) "Suburbia Armed: Nassau County Development and the Rise of the Aerospace Industry, 1909–1960." In *The Martial Metropolis: U.S. Cities in War and Peace,* edited by Roger W. Lotchin. New York.

Rossinow, Doug. (2004) "'The Model of a Model Fellow Traveler': Harry F. Ward, the American League for Peace and Democracy, and the 'Russian Question' in American Politics, 1933–1956." *Peace and Change* 29: 177–220.

———. (2005) "The Radicalization of the Social Gospel: Harry F. Ward and the Search for a New Social Order, 1898–1936." *Religion and American Culture* 15: 63–106.

Roth, Leland. (1983) *McKim, Mead & White, Architects.* New York.

Roth, Ronald O. (1990) "New York 1918: Bronx International Exposition." In *Historical Dictionary of World's Fairs and Expositions, 1851–1988,* edited by John E. Findling and Kimberly D. Pelle. Westport, CT.

Rothbard, Murray N. (1984) "The Federal Reserve as a Cartelization Device: The Early Years, 1913–1930." In *Money in Crisis: The Federal Reserve, the Economy, and Monetary Reform,* edited by Barry N. Siegel. San Francisco, CA.

Rothbard, Murray N., and Ronald Radosh, eds. (1972) *A New History of Leviathan: Essays on the Rise of the American Corporate State.* New York.

Rothman, David J. (1980) *Conscience and Convenience: The Asylum and Its Alternatives in*

Progressive America. Boston, MA.

Rudolph, Richard, and Scott Ridley. (1986) *Power Struggle: The Hundred-Year War over Electricity.* New York.

Rudwick, Elliott. (1968) *W. E. B. Du Bois: Propagandist of the Negro Protest.* Philadelphia, PA.

———. (1982) *W. E. B. Du Bois: Voice of the Black Protest Movement.* Urbana, IL.

Rudy, S. Willis. (1949) *The College of the City of New York: A History, 1847–1947.* New York.

Rumbarger, John J. (1989) *Profits, Power, and Prohibition: Alcohol Reform and the Industrializing of America, 1800–1930.* Albany, NY.

Rush, Thomas E. (1920) *The Port of New York.* New York.

Russell, Daniel E. (2013) "The Day Morgan Was Shot." *Glen Cove Heritage* 2013: 1–26.

Russell, Maud. (1966) *Men along the Shore.* New York.

Ryan, Dorothy B., and George Miller. (1982) *Picture Postcards in the United States, 1893–1918.* New York.

Rydell, Robert W. (1984) *All the World's a Fair: Visions of Empire at American International Expositions, 1876–1916.* Chicago, IL.

Sachar, Howard M. (1992) *A History of the Jews in America.* New York.

Sachs, Charles L., and Nancy H. Waters. (1988) *Made on Staten Island: Agriculture, Industry, and Suburban Living in the City.* Staten Island, NY.

Sacks, Marcy S. (2005) "'To Show Who Was in Charge': Police Repression of New York City's Black Population at the Turn of the Twentieth Century." *Journal of Urban History* 31: 799–819.

———. (2006) *Before Harlem: The Black Experience in New York City before World War I.* Philadelphia, PA.

Safford, Jeffrey J. (1978) *Wilsonian Maritime*

Diplomacy, 1913–1921. New Brunswick, NJ.

Saisselin, Rémy G. (1984) *The Bourgeois and the Bibelot.* New Brunswick, NJ.

Salerno, Salvatore. (2003) "No God, No Master: Italian Anarchists and the Industrial Workers of the World." In *The Lost World of Italian American Radicalism: Politics, Labor, and Culture,* edited by Philip V. Cannistraro and Gerald Meyer. Westport, CT.

———. (2005) "Paterson's Italian Anarchist Silk Workers and the Politics of Race." *WorkingUSA: The Journal of Labor and Society* 8: 611–25.

Sally, Lynn. (2006) *Fighting the Flames: The Spectacular Performance of Fire at Coney Island.* New York.

Salvatore, Nick. (1982) *Eugene V. Debs: Citizen and Socialist.* Urbana, IL.

Salwen, Peter. (1989) *Upper West Side Story: A History and Guide.* New York.

Sampson, E. J. (2012) "Educational Alliance: A History of a Lower East Side Settlement House." *Social Welfare History Project* website, VCU Libraries.

Samuels, Ernest, and Jayne Samuels. (1987) *Bernard Berenson: The Making of a Legend.* Cambridge, MA.

Sánchez Korrol, Virginia E. (1983) *From Colonia to Community: The History of Puerto Ricans in New York City, 1917–1948.* Westport, CT.

Sanders, James. (2001) *Celluloid Skyline: New York and the Movies.* New York.

Sanders, Ronald. (1969) *The Downtown Jews: Portraits of an Immigrant Generation.* New York.

———. (1988) *Shores of Refuge: A Hundred Years of Jewish Emigration.* New York.

Sandis, Eva E. (1982) "The Greek Population of New York City." In *The Greek American Community in Transition,* edited by Harry

J. Psomiades and Alice Scourby. New York.

Sandler, Mark Stuart. (1979) "Clerical Proletarianization in Capitalist Development." Ph.D. diss., Michigan State University.

Santamarina, Juan C. (2000) "The Cuba Company and the Expansion of American Business in Cuba, 1898–1915." *Business History Review* 74: 41–48.

Sante, Luc. (1947) *Low Life: Lures and Snares of Old New York.* New York.

Santlofer, Joy. (2017) *Food City: Four Centuries of Food-Making in New York.* New York.

Sardell, Alice. (1988) *The U.S. Experiment in Social Medicine: The Community Health Center Program, 1965–1986.* Pittsburgh, PA.

Sarna, Jonathan D. (2008) "Two Jewish Lawyers Named Louis." *American Jewish Journal* 94: 1–19.

Sautter, Udo. (1991) *Three Cheers for the Unemployed: Government and Unemployment before the New Deal.* New York.

Sayre, Wallace S., and Herbert Kaufman. (1960) *Governing New York City: Politics in the Metropolis.* New York.

Schäfer, Axel R. (2000) *American Progressives and German Social Reform, 1875–1920: Social Ethics, Moral Control, and the Regulatory State in a Transatlantic Context.* Stuttgart.

Schaffer, Ronald. (1962) "The New York City Woman Suffrage Party, 1909–1919." *Quarterly Journal of the New York State Historical Association* 43: 269–87.

———. (1991) *America in the Great War: The Rise of the War Welfare State.* New York.

Schappes, Morris U. (1977) "The Political Origins of the United Hebrew Trades, 1888." *Journal of Ethnic Studies* 5: 13–45.

Scharff, Edward E. (1986) *Worldly Power: The*

Making of the "Wall Street Journal." New York.

Scheiber, Harry N. (1969) "World War I as Entrepreneurial Opportunity: Willard Straight and the American International Corporation." *Political Science Quarterly* 84: 486–511.

Scheier, Paula. (1954) "Clara Lemlich Shavelson: 50 Years in Labor's Front Line." *Jewish Life* 9: 7–11.

Scheiner, Seth M. (1965) *Negro Mecca: A History of the Negro in New York City, 1865–1920*. New York.

Schenkel, Albert Frederick. (1990) "The Rich Man and the Kingdom: John D. Rockefeller, Jr., and the Protestant Establishment, 1900–1960." Ph.D. diss., Harvard University.

Schick, Sandor Evan. (1982) "Neighborhood Change in the Bronx, 1905–1960." Ph.D. diss., Harvard University.

Schicke, C. A. (1974) *Revolution in Sound: A Biography of the Recording Industry*. Boston, MA.

Schiesl, Martin J. (1977) *The Politics of Efficiency: Municipal Administration and Reform in America, 1800–1920*. Berkeley, CA.

Schlabach, Theron. (1968) "Labor Unions: Organization without Rationalization." In *Rationality and Welfare: Public Discussion of Poverty and Social Insurance in the United States, 1875–1935*, prepared for the Social Security Administration. Washington, DC.

Schlichting, Kurt C. (2012) *Grand Central's Engineer: William J. Wilgus and the Planning of Modern Manhattan*. Baltimore, MD.

Schieffelin & Co. (1894) *One Hundred Years of Business Life, 1794–1894*. New York.

Schlüter, Hermann. (1910) *The Brewing Industry and the Brewery Workers' Movement in America*. Cincinnati, OH.

Schmidt, Hans. (1987) *Maverick Marine: General*

Smedley D. Butler and the Contradictions of American Military History. Lexington, KY.

Schmidt, William J. (1978) *Architect of Unity: A Biography of Samuel McCrea Cavert*. New York.

Schmitz, Christopher. (1986) "The Rise of Big Business in the World Copper Industry, 1870–1930." *Economic History Review* 39: 392–410.

Schmitz, David F. (2001) *Henry L. Stimson: The First Wise Man*. Wilmington, DE.

Schmuhl, Robert. (2016) *Ireland's Exiled Children: America and the Easter Rising*. New York.

Schneider, David M., and Albert Deutsch. (1941a) *The History of Public Welfare in New York State, 1867–1940*. Vol. 1. Chicago, IL.

———. (1941b) *The History of Public Welfare in New York State, 1867–1940*. Vol. 2. Chicago, IL.

Schneider, Dorothee. (1994) *Trade Unions and Community: The German Working Class in New York City, 1870–1900*. Urbana, IL.

———. (2011) *Crossing Borders: Migration and Citizenship in the Twentieth-Century United States*. Cambridge, MA.

Schneider, Eric C. (2008) *Smack: Heroin and the American City*. Philadelphia, PA.

Schneirov, Matthew. (1994) *The Dream of a New Social Order: Popular Magazines in America, 1893–1914*. New York.

Schoenebaum, Eleanora. (1977) "Emerging Neighborhoods: The Development of Brooklyn's Fringe Areas, 1850–1930." Ph.D. diss., Columbia University.

Schoener, Allon. (1967) *Portal to America: The Lower East Side, 1870–1925*. New York.

———. (1995) *Harlem on My Mind: Cultural Capital of Black America, 1900–1968*. New York.

Schorman, Rob. (2003) *Selling Style: Clothing and Social Change at the Turn of the Century*. Philadelphia, PA.

Schrag, Zachary M. (2000) "'The Bus Is Young and Honest': Transportation Politics, Technical Choice, and the Motorization of Manhattan Surface Transit, 1919–1936." *Technology and Culture* 41: 51–79.

Schriftgiesser, Karl. (1943) *Oscar of the Waldorf*. New York.

Schroth, Raymond A. (1974) *The "Eagle" and Brooklyn: A Community Newspaper, 1841–1955*. Westport, CT.

———. (2002) *Fordham: A History and Memoir*. Chicago, IL.

Schulzinger, Robert D. (1984) *The Wise Men of Foreign Affairs: The History of the Council on Foreign Relations*. New York.

Schuster, George N., and Tom Mahoney. (1966) *The Longest Auto Race*. New York.

Schuyler, Montgomery. (1908) "To Curb the Skyscraper." *Architectural Record* 24: 300–302.

———. (1913) *The Woolworth Building*. New York.

Schwartz, Joel. (1993) *The New York Approach: Robert Moses, Urban Liberals, and Redevelopment of the Inner City*. Columbus, OH.

Schwartz, Michael. (2007) "A Matter for Experts: Broadway 1900–1920 and the Rise of the Professional Managerial Class." Ph.D. diss., University of Pittsburgh.

Schwarz, Jordan A. (1981) *The Speculator: Bernard M. Baruch in Washington, 1917–1965*. Chapel Hill, NC.

———. (1994) *The New Dealers: Power Politics in the Age of Roosevelt*. New York.

Schwarz, Judith. (1986) *Radical Feminists of Heterodoxy: Greenwich Village, 1912–1940*. Norwich, VT.

Schweitzer, Marlis. (2008) "American Fashions for

American Women: The Rise and Fall of Fashion Nationalism." In *Producing Fashion: Commerce, Culture, and Consumers*, edited by Regina Lee Blaszczyk. Philadelphia, PA.

———. (2012) "A Failed Attempt at World Domination: 'Advanced Vaudeville,' Financial Panic, and the Dream of a World Trust." *Theatre History Studies* 32: 53–79.

Scobey, David M. (1989) "Empire City: Politics, Culture, and Urbanism in Gilded-Age New York." Ph.D. diss., Yale University.

———. (2002) *Empire City: The Making and Meaning of the New York City Landscape*. Philadelphia, PA.

Scott, Emmett J. (1920) *Negro Migration during the War*. New York.

Scott, Mel. (1969) *American City Planning since 1890*. Berkeley, CA.

Scott, William B., and Peter M. Rutkoff. (1999) *New York Modern: The Arts and the City*. Baltimore, MD.

Scrymser, James Alexander. (1915) *Personal Reminiscences of James A. Scrymser in Times of Peace and War*. Easton, PA.

Seager, Henry R. (1910) *Social Insurance, a Program of Social Reform*. New York.

Sealander, Judith. (1997) *Private Wealth and Public Life: Foundation Philanthropy and the Reshaping of American Social Policy from the Progressive Era to the New Deal*. Baltimore, MD.

Secrest, Meryle. (2004) *Duveen: A Life in Art*. New York.

Segrave, Kerry. (2008) *Actors Organize: A History of Union Formation Efforts in America, 1880–1919*. Jefferson, NC.

Seidman, Harold. (1938) *Labor Czars: A History of Labor Racketeering*. New York.

Selekman, Benjamin Morris, Henriette Rose Walter, and W. J. Couper. (1925) *The*

Clothing and Textile Industries in New York and Its Environs. New York.

Seligman, Edwin R. A. (1911) *The Income Tax: A Study of the History, Theory and Practice of Income Taxation at Home and Abroad.* New York.

Seligman, Scott D. (2016) *Tong Wars: The Untold Story of Vice, Money, and Murder in New York's Chinatown.* New York.

Seller, Maxine Schwartz, ed. (1983) *Ethnic Theatre in the United States.* Westport, CT.

———. (1986) "The Uprising of the Twenty Thousand: Sex, Class, and Ethnicity in the Shirtwaist Makers' Strike of 1909." In *"Struggle a Hard Battle": Essays on Working-Class Immigrants,* edited by Dirk Hoerder. DeKalb, IL.

Serafin, Steven, ed. (2011) *BAM: The Complete Works.* New York.

Seraile, William. (2011) *Angels of Mercy: White Women and the History of New York's Colored Orphan Asylum.* The Bronx, NY.

Seyfried, Vincent F. (1984) *300 Years of Long Island City, 1630–1930.* Queens, NY.

Shachtman, Tom. (1991) *Skyscraper Dreams: The Great Real Estate Dynasties of New York.* Boston, MA.

Shanet, Howard, et al. (1979) *Early Histories of the New York Philharmonic.* New York.

Shannon, David A. (1955) *The Socialist Party of America: A History.* New York.

Shanor, Rebecca Read. (1988) *The City That Never Was: Two Hundred Years of Fantastic and Fascinating Plans That Might Have Changed the Face of New York City.* New York.

Shapiro, Robert Donald. (1984) "A Reform Rabbi in the Progressive Era: The Early Career of Stephen S. Wise." Ph.D. diss., Harvard University.

Sharpe, William, and Leonard Wallock, eds. (1987) *Visions of the*

Modern City: Essays in History, Art, and Literature. Baltimore, MD.

Shavelson, Clara Lemlich, and Morris U. Schappes. (1982) "Remembering the Waistmakers General Strike, 1909." *Jewish Currents* 36: 300–303.

Shefter, Martin. (1993a) "New York's National and International Influence." In *Capital of the American Century: The National and International Influence of New York City,* edited by Martin Shefter. New York.

———. (1993b) "New York City and American National Politics." In *Capital of the American Century: National and International Influence of New York City,* edited by Martin Shefter. New York.

Shelley, Thomas J. (1992) "John Cardinal Farley and Modernism in New York." *Church History* 61: 350–61.

———. (1997) "What the Hell Is an Encyclical? Governor Alfred E. Smith, Charles C. Marshall, Esq., and Father Francis P. Duffy." *U.S. Catholic Historian* 15 (Spring): 87–107.

———. (2003) *Greenwich Village Catholics: St. Joseph's Church and the Evolution of an Urban Faith Community, 1829–2002.* Washington, DC.

Sherman, Franklin J. (1929) *Building Up Greater Queens Borough: An Estimate of Its Development and the Outlook.* Brooklyn, NY.

Sherwood, Robert Emmet. (1950) *Roosevelt and Hopkins: An Intimate History.* New York.

Shi, David E. (1981) *Matthew Josephson, Bourgeois Bohemian.* New Haven, CT.

Shoup, Laurence H. (1977) *Imperial Brain Trust: The Council on Foreign Relations and United States Foreign Policy.* Lincoln, NE.

Shteir, Rachel. (2004) *Striptease: The Untold History of the Girlie Show.* New York.

Shuldiner, David Philip. (1999) *Of Moses and Marx:*

Folk Ideology and Folk History in the Jewish Labor Movement. Westport, CT.

Shulman, Mark R. (2000) "The Progressive Era Origins of the National Security Act." *Dickinson Law Review* 104: 289–330.

Shulman, Robin. (2012) *Eat the City: A Tale of the Fishers, Trappers, Hunters, Foragers, Slaughterers, Butchers, Farmers, Poultry Minders, Sugar Refiners, Cane Cutters, Beekeepers, Winemakers, and Brewers Who Built New York.* New York.

Shultz, Earle, and Walter Simmons. (1959) *Offices in the Sky.* Indianapolis, IN.

Shumsky, Neil Larry. (1975) "Zangwill's *The Melting Pot*: Ethnic Tensions on Stage." *American Quarterly* 28: 29–41.

Sigerman, Harriet Marla. (1992) "Daughters of the Book: A Study of Gender and Ethnicity in the Lives of Three American Jewish Women." Ph.D. diss., University of Massachusetts Amherst.

Silber, William L. (2007) *When Washington Shut Down Wall Street: The Great Financial Crisis of 1914 and the Origins of America's Monetary Supremacy.* Princeton, NJ.

Silver, Matthew. (2008) "Louis Marshall and the Democratization of Jewish Identity." *American Jewish History* 94: 41–69.

Simkhovitch, Mary Kingsbury. (1938) *Neighborhood: My Story of Greenwich House.* New York.

Simmons, Christina. (1989) "Modern Sexuality and the Myth of Victorian Repression." In *Passion and Power: Sexuality in History,* edited by Kathy Peiss and Christina Simmons. Philadelphia, PA.

———. (2009) *Making Marriage Modern: Women's Sexuality from the Progressive Era to World War II.* New York.

Simon, James F. (2012) *FDR and Chief Justice Hughes: The President, the Supreme*

Court, and the Epic Battle over the New Deal. New York.

Simon, Kate. (1978) *Fifth Avenue: A Very Social History.* New York.

Simon, Malka. (2009) "The Space of Production: Brooklyn and the Creation of an Urban Industrial Landscape." Ph.D. diss., New York University.

Simpson, Christopher. (1995) *The Splendid Blond Beast: Money, Law, and Genocide in the Twentieth Century.* Monroe, ME.

Simpson, Colin. (1986) *Artful Partners: Bernard Berenson and Joseph Duveen.* New York.

Sims, Kimberly Joyce. (2006) "Blacks, Italians, and the Progressive Interest in New York City Crime, 1900–1930." Ph.D. diss., Harvard University.

Sinclair, Upton. (1908a) *The Metropolis.* New York.

———. (1908b) *The Moneychangers.* New York.

Singer, C. Gregg. (1975) *The Unholy Alliance.* New Rochelle, NY.

Sinnette, Elinor Des Verney. (1989) *Arthur Alfonso Schomburg, Black Bibliophile and Collector: A Biography.* New York.

Sione, Patrizia. (1992) "Industrial Work, Militancy, and Migrations of Northern Italian Workers in Europe and in Paterson, New Jersey, 1880–1913." Ph.D. diss., State University of New York at Binghamton.

Sklar, Kathryn Kish. (1992) "Explaining the Power of Women's Political Culture in the Creation of the American Welfare State, 1890–1930." In *Gender and the Origins of Welfare States in Western Europe and North America,* edited by Seth Koven and Sonya Michel. Boston, MA.

———. (1995) *Florence Kelley and the Nation's Work.* New Haven, CT.

———. (1999) "Reinventing Woman Suffrage." *Reviews in American History* 27: 243–49.

Sklar, Martin J. (1981) "The Corporate Ascendancy and

the Socialist Acquiescence: An Inquiry into Strange Times." *Maryland Historian* 12: 49–59.

———. (1988a) *The Corporate Reconstruction of American Capitalism, 1890–1916: The Market, the Law, and Politics.* New York.

Sklar, Robert. (1975) *Movie-Made America: A Cultural History of American Movies.* New York.

———. (1988b) "Oh! Althusser! Historiography and the Rise of Cinema Studies." *Radical History Review* 41: 10–35.

Skocpol, Theda. (1992) *Protecting Soldiers and Mothers: The Political Origins of Social Policy in the United States.* Cambridge, MA.

Skocpol, Theda, Ariane Liazos, and Marshall Ganz. (2006) *What a Mighty Power We Can Be: African American Fraternal Groups and the Struggle for Racial Equality.* Princeton, NJ.

Skolnik, Richard. (1964) "The Crystallization of Reform in New York City, 1890–1917." Ph.D. diss., Yale University.

Skrabec, Quentin R. (2010) *Henry Clay Frick: The Life of the Perfect Capitalist.* Jefferson, NC.

Slanetz, Priscilla Jennings. (1986) "A History of the Fulton Fish Market." *Log of Mystic Seaport* 38: 14–25.

Slayton, Robert A. (2001) *Empire Statesman: The Rise and Redemption of Al Smith.* New York.

Slide, Anthony. (1994) *The Encyclopedia of Vaudeville.* Westport, CT.

———. (2004) *American Racist: The Life and Films of Thomas Dixon.* Lexington, KY.

Sloan, Kay. (1981) "Sexual Warfare in the Silent Cinema: Comedies and Melodramas of Woman Suffragism." *American Quarterly* 33: 412–36.

Sloane, David Charles. (1991) *The Last Great Necessity: Cemeteries in*

American History. Baltimore, MD.

Sloat, Warren. (2002) *A Battle for the Soul of New York: Tammany Hall, Police Corruption, Vice, and Reverend Charles Parkhurst's Crusade against Them, 1892–1895.* New York.

Slotkin, Richard. (2005) *Lost Battalions: The Great War and the Crisis of American Nationality.* New York.

Smiley, Gene. (1981) "The Expansion of the New York Securities Market at the Turn of the Century." *Business History Review* 55: 75–85.

Smith, Andrew F. (2008) "The Food and Drink of New York from 1624 to 1898." In *Gastropolis: Food and New York City,* edited by Annie Hauck-Lawson and Jonathan Deutsch. New York.

———. (2009) *Eating History: 30 Turning Points in the Making of American Cuisine.* New York.

Smith, George David, and Richard Sylla. (1993) "The Transformation of Financial Capitalism: An Essay on the History of American Capital Markets." *Financial Markets, Institutions and Instruments* 2: 1–62.

Smith, John David, and J. Vincent Lowery, eds. (2013) *The Dunning School: Historians, Race, and the Meaning of Reconstruction.* Lexington, KY.

Smith, Neil. (2003) *American Empire: Roosevelt's Geographer and the Prelude to Globalization.* Berkeley, CA.

Smith, Robert Freeman. (1993) "Thomas W. Lamont." In *Behind the Throne: Servants of Power to Imperial Presidents, 1898–1968,* edited by Thomas J. McCormick and Walter LaFeber. Madison, WI.

Smith, Robert Michael. (2003b) *From Blackjacks to Briefcases: A History of Commercialized Strikebreaking and Unionbusting in the United States.* Athens, OH.

Sneider, Allison L. (2008) *Suffragists in an Imperial Age: U.S. Expansion and the Woman Question, 1870–1929.* New York.

Snyder-Grenier, Ellen M. (1996) *Brooklyn! An Illustrated History.* Philadelphia, PA.

Snyder, Robert W. (1989) *The Voice of the City: Vaudeville and Popular Culture in New York.* New York.

———. (1991) "Vaudeville and the Transformation of Popular Culture." In *Inventing Times Square: Commerce and Culture at the Crossroads of the World,* edited by William R. Taylor. New York.

———. (1994) "Immigrants, Ethnicity, and Mass Culture: The Vaudeville Stage in New York City: 1880–1930." In *Budapest and New York: Studies in Metropolitan Transformation, 1870–1930,* edited by Thomas Bender and Carl E. Schorske. New York.

———. (2015) *Crossing Broadway: Washington Heights and the Promise of New York City.* Ithaca, NY.

Sobel, Robert. (1965) *The Big Board: A History of the New York Stock Market.* New York.

———. (1968) *Panic on Wall Street.* New York.

———. (1991) *The Life and Times of Dillon Read.* New York.

Society of Iconophiles. (1930) *History of the Society of Iconophiles of the City of New York,* compiled by Richard Hoe Lawrence et al. New York.

Soffer, Jonathan. (2013) "Modern Women Persuading Modern Men: The Nineteenth Amendment and the Movement for Woman Suffrage, 1916–1920." Gilder Lehrman Institute of American History *History by Era* website.

Soll, David. (2009) "Watershed Moments: An Environmental History of the New York City Water Supply." Ph.D. diss., Brandeis University.

Sorin, Gerald. (1985) *The Prophetic Minority: American Jewish Immigrant Radicals, 1880–1920.* Bloomington, IN.

Sotiropoulos, Karen. (2006) *Staging Race: Black Performers in Turn of the Century America.* Cambridge, MA.

Soyer, Daniel. (2000) "Brownstones and Brownsville: Elite Philanthropists and Immigrant Constituents at the Hebrew Educational Society of Brooklyn, 1899–1929." *American Jewish History* 88: 181–207.

———. (2001) "Class Conscious Workers as Immigrant Entrepreneurs: The Ambiguity of Class among Eastern European Jewish Immigrants to the United States at the Turn of the Twentieth Century." *Labor History* 42: 45–59.

Speck, Mary Elizabeth. (2009) "Let There Be Candy for Everyone: The Politics of Sugar in Cuba, 1902–1952." Ph.D. diss., Stanford University.

Spengler, Edwin H. (1930) *Land Values in New York in Relation to Transit Facilities.* New York.

Spillane, Joseph F. (1999) "Making a Modern Drug: The Manufacture, Sale, and Control of Cocaine in the United States, 1880–1920." In *Cocaine: Global Histories,* edited by Paul Gootenberg. New York.

———. (2000) *Cocaine: From Medical Marvel to Modern Menace in the United States, 1884–1920.* Baltimore, MD.

Spiro, Jonathan Peter. (2000) "Patrician Racist: The Evolution of Madison Grant." Ph.D. diss., University of California, Berkeley.

———. (2009) *Defending the Master Race: Conservation, Eugenics, and the Legacy of Madison Grant.* Burlington, VT.

St. John, Bruce, ed. (1965) *John Sloan's New York Scene.* New York.

Stagg, Jerry. (1968) *The Brothers Shubert*. New York.

Stansell, Christine. (2000) *American Moderns: Bohemian New York and the Creation of a New Century*. New York.

Stanton, Jeffrey W. (1998) "Coney Island—Lunda Park." *Westland.net*.

Stapleton, Darwin H., ed. (2004) *Creating a Tradition of Biomedical Research: Contributions to the History of the Rockefeller University*. New York.

Starr, John. (1957) *Hospital City*. New York.

Starr, Paul. (1982) *The Social Transformation of American Medicine*. New York.

Starr, Roger. (1985) *The Rise and Fall of New York City*. New York.

Starr, Tama, and Ed Hayman. (1998) *Signs and Wonders: The Spectacular Marketing of America*. New York.

Starrett, Paul, and Webb Waldron. (1938) *Changing the Skyline: An Autobiography*. New York.

Starrett, William Aiken. (1928) *Skyscrapers and the Men Who Build Them*. New York.

Stavitsky, Gail. (2013) "Walt Kuhn: Armory Showman." In *The Armory Show at 100: Modernism and Revolution*, edited by Marilyn Satin Kushner and Kimberly Orcutt. New York.

Steel, Ronald. (1980) *Walter Lippmann and the American Century*. Boston, MA.

Steffens, Lincoln. (1897) "The Modern Business Building." *Scribner's Magazine* 22: 37–61.

———. (1903) "New York: Good Government in Danger." *McClure's Magazine* 22: 84–92.

———. (1904) *The Shame of the Cities*. New York.

———. (1931) *The Autobiography of Lincoln Steffens*. New York.

Stein, Judith. (1986) *The World of Marcus Garvey: Race and Class in Modern Society*. Baton Rouge, LA.

Stein, Leon. (1962) *The Triangle Fire*. Philadelphia, PA.

Steinberg, Allen. (2003) "The 'Lawman' in New York: William Travers Jerome and the Origins of the Modern District Attorney in Turn-of-the-Century New York." *University of Toledo Law Review* 34: 753–79.

———. (2004) "The Becker-Rosenthal Murder Case: The Cop and the Gambler." In *Famous American Crimes and Trials*, edited by Frankie Y. Bailey and Steven M. Chermak. Westport, CT.

———. (2005) "Narratives of Crime, Historical Interpretation and the Course of Human Events: The Becker Case and American Progressivism." In *Crime and Culture: An Historical Perspective*, edited by Amy Gilman Srebnick and René Lévy. Burlington, VT.

Steiner, Edward Alfred. (1969) *On the Trail of the Immigrant*. New York.

Sterba, Christopher M. (2003) *Good Americans: Italian and Jewish Immigrants during the First World War*. New York.

Stern, Robert A. M., Gregory Gilmartin, and John Massengale. (1983) *New York 1900: Metropolitan Architecture and Urbanism, 1890–1915*. New York.

Stern, Robert A. M., Gregory Gilmartin, and Thomas Mellins. (1987) *New York 1930: Architecture and Urbanism between the Two World Wars*. New York.

Stertz, Stephen A. (1992) "The Edison Studio in the Bronx." *Bronx County Historical Society Journal* 29: 1–12.

Stevens, George A. (1913) *New York Typographical Union No. 6: Study of a Modern Trade Union and Its Predecessors*. Albany, NY.

Stevens, Rosemary. (1989) *In Sickness and in Wealth: American Hospitals in the Twentieth Century*. New York.

Stieglitz, Alfred. (2000) *Stieglitz on Photography: His Selected Essays and Notes*, edited by Sarah Greenough, with an essay by Richard Whelan. New York.

Stiles, Henry Reed. (1867) *A History of the City of Brooklyn*. 3 vols. Brooklyn, NY.

Stimson, Henry L. (1915) *The Duty of Preparedness Today: Address of Henry L. Stimson before the National Security League at Carnegie Hall, June 14, 1915*. New York.

Stocking, George W., Jr, ed. (1974) *The Shaping of American Anthropology, 1883–1911: A Franz Boas Reader*. New York.

Stoddard, T. Lothrop. (1914) *The French Revolution in San Domingo*. Boston, MA.

Stokes, I. N. Phelps. (1915) *The Iconography of Manhattan Island, 1498–1909*. Vol. 1. New York.

———. (1928) *The Iconography of Manhattan Island, 1498–1909*. Vol. 5. New York.

Stokes, Melvyn. (1983) "American Progressives and the European Left." *Journal of American Studies* 17: 5–28.

———. (2007) *D. W. Griffith's "The Birth of a Nation": A History of "the Most Controversial Motion Picture of All Time."* New York.

Stone, Elaine Murray. (2004) *Dorothy Day: Champion of the Poor*. New York.

Stone, Jill. (1982) *Times Square: A Pictorial History*. New York.

Stone, Richard. (1969) "The Annexation of the Bronx, 1874." *Bronx County Historical Society Journal* 6: 1–24.

Stone, Rosaline Biason. (1985) "The Ziegfeld Follies: A Study of Theatrical Opulence from 1907 to 1931." Ph.D. diss., University of Denver.

Stotz, Louis, and Alexander Jamison. (1938) *History of the Gas Industry*. New York.

Stowell, Charles Jacob. (1918) *The Journeymen Tailors' Union of America: A Study in Trade Union Policy*. Urbana, IL.

"Strangers in New York." (1902) *Harper's Weekly* 46: 266–67.

Strausbaugh, John. (2013) *The Village: 400 Years of Beats and Bohemians, Radicals and Rogues: A History of Greenwich Village*. New York.

Street, Julian. (1913) *Welcome to Our City*. New York.

Striffler, Steve, and Mark Moberg, eds. (2003) *Banana Wars: Power, Production, and History in the Americas*. Durham, NC.

Strom, Sharon Hartman. (1992) *Beyond the Typewriter: Gender, Class, and the Origins of Modern American Office Work, 1900–1930*. Urbana, IL.

Stromquist, Shelton. (2006) *Reinventing "the People:" The Progressive Movement, the Class Problem, and the Origins of Modern Liberalism*. Urbana, IL.

Strong, Douglas M. (1997) *They Walked in the Spirit: Personal Faith and Social Action in America*. Louisville, KY.

Stross, Randall E. (2007) *The Wizard of Menlo Park: How Thomas Alva Edison Invented the Modern World*. New York.

Strouse, Jean. (1999) *Morgan: American Financier*. New York.

Stuart, Percy C. (1901) "The New York Stock Exchange." *Architectural Record* 11: 525–52.

Sturman, Janet Lynn. (1987) "Zarzuela in New York: Contributions of Lyric Theatre to Hispanic Identity." Ph.D. diss., Columbia University.

Suisman, David. (2009) *Selling Sounds: The Commercial Revolution in American Music*. Cambridge, MA.

Sullivan, Joseph Patrick. (1995) "From Municipal Ownership to Regulation: Municipal Utility Reform in New York City, 1880–1907." Ph.D. diss., Rutgers University.

Sullivan, Mark. (1904) "The Pool-Room Evil." *Outlook* 77: 212–16.

Sullivan, Patricia. (2009) *Lift Every Voice: The NAACP and the Making of the Civil Rights Movement*. New York.

Sumner, Mary Brown. (1913) "The Parting of the Ways in American Socialism." *Survey* 29: 623–30.

Sussman, Robert W. (2014) *The Myth of Race: The Troubling Persistence of an Unscientific Idea*. Cambridge, MA.

Sutch, Richard. (2015) "Financing the Great War: A Class Tax for the Wealthy, Liberty Bonds for All." Berkeley Economic History Laboratory Working Paper 2015–09.

Sutcliffe, Anthony. (1981) *Towards the Planned City: Germany, Britain, the United States and France, 1780–1914*. Oxford, UK.

Sutton, Allan. (2009a) *A Camden Chronology: The Evolution of the Victor Talking Machine Company Complex (1899–1929)*. Denver, CO.

———. (2009b) "Camden, Philadelphia, or New York? The Victor Studio Conundrum (1900–20)." *Vintage Jazz Mart*, Autumn.

Sutton, Horace. (1980) *Travelers: The American Tourist from Stagecoach to Space Shuttle*. New York.

Swaine, Robert T. (2007) *The Cravath Firm and Its Predecessors*, vol. 1, *1809–1906*, and vol. 2, *The Cravath Firm since 1906*. Originally published 1946, 1948. Clark, NJ.

Swanberg, W. A. (1961) *Citizen Hearst: A Biography of William Randolph Hearst*. New York.

———. (1964) *Dreiser*. New York.

———. (1976) *Norman Thomas, the Last Idealist*. New York.

Syrett, Harold. (1944) *The City of Brooklyn, 1865–1898: A Political History*. New York.

Szajkowski, Zosa. (1970) "The Jews and New York

City's Mayoralty Election of 1917." *Jewish Social Studies* 32: 286–306.

Tallack, Douglas. (2005) *New York Sights: Visualizing Old and New New York*. Oxford, UK.

Tallman, Ellis W., and Elmus R. Wicker. (2010) "Banking and Financial Crisis in United States History: What Guidance Can History Offer Policymakers?" Federal Reserve Bank of Cleveland Working Paper 10–09.

Tangires, Helen. (1997) "Feeding the Cities: Public Markets and Municipal Reform in the Progressive Era." *Prologue: Quarterly of the National Archives* 29: 16–26.

———. (2003) *Public Markets and Civic Culture in Nineteenth-Century America*. Baltimore, MD.

Tarbell, Roberta K. (1980) "Gertrude Vanderbilt Whitney as Patron." In *The Figurative Tradition and the Whitney Museum of American Art: Paintings and Sculpture from the Permanent Collection*, by Patricia Hills, Roberta K. Tarbell, and Whitney Museum of American Art. Newark, DE.

Tauranac, John, and Christopher Little. (1985) *Elegant New York: The Builders and the Buildings, 1885–1915*. New York.

Tavenner, Clyde Howard. (1916) *The Navy League Unmasked*. Washington, DC.

Tax, Meredith. (1980) *The Rising of the Women: Feminist Solidarity and Class Conflict, 1880–1917*. New York.

Taylor, Clarence. (1994) *The Black Churches of Brooklyn*. New York.

———. (2002) *Black Religious Intellectuals: The Fight for Equality from Jim Crow to the 21st Century*. New York.

Taylor, Michael R. (2013) " 'The Cuban Who Outcubed the Cubists': Francis Picabia and the 1913 Armory Show." In *The Armory Show at 100: Modernism and Revolution*,

edited by Marilyn Satin Kushner and Kimberly Orcutt. New York.

Taylor, Robert Lewis. (1966) *Vessel of Wrath: The Life and Times of Carry Nation*. New York.

Taylor, William R. (1988) "The Launching of a Commercial Culture: New York City, 1860–1930." In *Power, Culture, and Place*, edited by John H. Mollenkopf.

———. (1989) "The Evolution of Public Space in New York City: The Commercial Showcase of America." In *Consuming Visions: Accumulation and the Display of Goods in America, 1880–1920*, edited by Simon J. Bronner. New York.

———. (1992a) *In Pursuit of Gotham: Culture and Commerce of New York*.

———. (1992b) "A Place That Words Built: Broadway, Damon Runyon, and the Slanguage of Lobster Alley." In Taylor, *In Pursuit of Gotham: Culture and Commerce of New York*.

Teaford, Jon C. (1984) *The Unheralded Triumph: City Government in America, 1870–1900*. Baltimore, MD.

Tebbel, John. (1975) *A History of Book Publishing in the United States*. Vol. 2. New York.

Tedeschi, Martha. (2013) "A Pre-Emptive Strike: John Marin and the Armory Show." In *The Armory Show at 100: Modernism and Revolution*, edited by Marilyn Satin Kushner and Kimberly Orcutt. New York.

Tedlow, Richard S. (1979) *Keeping the Corporate Image: Public Relations and Business, 1900–1950*. Greenwich, CT.

Tell, Darcy. (2007) *Times Square Spectacular: Lighting Up Broadway*. New York.

Terborg-Penn, Rosalyn. (1985) "Survival Strategies among African-American Women Workers: A Continuing Process." In *Women, Work and Protest*,

edited by Ruth Milkman. New York.

———. (1998) *African American Women in the Struggle for the Vote, 1850–1920*. Bloomington, IN.

Terwilliger, Marlene P. (1977) "Jews and Italians and the Socialist Party, New York City, 1901–1917: A Study of Class, Ethnicity and Class Consciousness." Ph.D. diss., Union Graduate School.

Thale, Christopher. (1995) "Civilizing New York City: Police Patrol, 1880–1935." Ph.D. diss., University of Chicago.

———. (2004) "Assigned to Patrol: Neighborhoods, Police, and Changing Deployment Practices in New York City before 1930." *Journal of Social History* 37: 1037–64.

———. (2007) "The Informal World of Police Patrol: New York City in the Early Twentieth Century." *Journal of Urban History* 33: 183–216.

Thatcher, Ian D. (1996) "Leon Trotsky in New York City." *Historical Research* 69: 166–80.

Thayer-Bacon, Barbara J. (2012) "Maria Montessori, John Dewey, and William H. Kilpatrick." *Education and Culture* 28: 3–20.

Thelen, David P. (1975) "Lincoln Steffens and the Muckrakers: A Review Essay." *Wisconsin Magazine of History* 58: 313–17.

———. (1985) *Robert M. La Follette and the Insurgent Spirit*, edited by Oscar Handlin. Madison, WI.

Thernstrom, Stephan, et al. (1980) *Harvard Encyclopedia of American Ethnic Groups*. Cambridge, MA.

Thissen, Judith. (2002) "Charlie Steiner's Houston Hippodrome: Moviegoing on New York's Lower East Side, 1909–1913." In *American Silent Film: Discovering Marginalized Voices*, edited by Gregg Bachman and

Thomas J. Slater. Carbondale, IL.

———. (2003) "Reconsidering the Decline of the New York Yiddish Theatre in the Early 1900s." *Theatre Survey* 44: 173–97.

———. (2008) "Film and Vaudeville on New York's Lower East Side." In *The Art of Being Jewish in Modern Times*, edited by Barbara Kirshenblatt-Gimblett and Jonathan Karp. Philadelphia, PA.

Thomas, Hugh. (1998) *Cuba; or, The Pursuit of Freedom*. New York.

Thomas, Lately. (1969) *The Mayor Who Mastered New York: The Life and Opinions of William J. Gaynor*. New York.

Thomas, Louisa. (2011) *Conscience: Two Soldiers, Two Pacifists, One Family: A Test of Will and Faith in World War I*. New York.

Thomas, Norman M. (1917) *War's Heretics: A Plea for the Conscientious Objector*. New York.

Thompson, Arthur W. (1966) "The Reception of Russian Revolutionary Leaders in America, 1904–1906." *American Quarterly* 18: 452–76.

Thompson, Hugh. (1912) "The Remaking of New York." *Munsey's Magazine* 47: 893–906.

Thornley, Stew. (2000) *Land of the Giants: New York's Polo Grounds*. Philadelphia, PA.

Throntveit, Trygve. (2011) "The Fable of the Fourteen Points: Woodrow Wilson and National Self-Determination." *Diplomatic History* 35: 445–81.

Timberlake, James H. (1963) *Prohibition and the Progressive Movement, 1900–1920*. Cambridge, MA.

Tobier, Emanuel. (1988) "Manhattan's Business District in the Industrial Age." In *Power, Culture, and Place: Essays on New York City*, edited by John H. Mollenkopf. New York.

———. (1998) "The Bronx in the Twentieth Century:

Dynamics of Population and Economic Change." *Bronx County Historical Society Journal* 35: 69–103.

Toll, William. (1997) "Horace M. Kallen: Pluralism and American Jewish Identity." *American Jewish History* 85: 57–74.

Tolman, William Howe, and Charles Hemstreet. (1904) *The Better New York*. New York.

Tomkins, Calvin. (1970) *Merchants and Masterpieces: The Story of the Metropolitan Museum of Art*. New York.

Tooze, J. Adam. (2014) *The Deluge: The Great War, America and the Remaking of the Global Order, 1916–1931*. New York.

Topp, Michael Miller. (1996) "The Italian-American Left: Transnationalism and the Quest for Unity." In *The Immigrant Left in the United States*, edited by Paul Buhle and Dan Georgakas. Albany, NY.

Tosches, Nick. (2005) *King of the Jews*. New York.

Totoricaguena, Gloria P., Emilia Sarriugarte Doyaga, and Anna M. Renteria Aguirre. (2004) *The Basques of New York: A Cosmopolitan Experience*. Reno, NV.

Trachtenberg, Alan. (1982) *The Incorporation of America: Culture and Society in the Gilded Age*. New York.

———. (1990) *Reading American Photographs: Images as History, Mathew Brady to Walker Evans*. New York.

Trager, James. (1987) *West of Fifth: The Rise and Fall and Rise of Manhattan's West Side*. New York.

———. (1990) *Park Avenue: Street of Dreams*. New York.

Trask, Jeffrey. (2012) *Things American: Art Museums and Civic Culture in the Progressive Era*. Philadelphia, PA.

Trattner, Walter I. (1968) *Homer Folks, Pioneer in Social Welfare*. New York.

Traub, James. (2004) *The Devil's Playground: A Century of Pleasure and*

Profit in Times Square. New York.

Travis, Steve. (1958) "The Rise and Fall of the Theatrical Syndicate." *Educational Theatre Journal* 10: 35–40.

Trimberger, Ellen Kay. (1984) "Feminism, Men, and Modern Love: Greenwich Village, 1900–1925." In *Powers of Desire: The Politics of Sexuality*, edited by Ann Snitow, Christine Stansell, and Sharon Thompson. London.

Tripp, Anne Huber. (1987) *The I.W.W. and the Paterson Silk Strike of 1913*. Urbana, IL.

Troesken, Werner, and Rick Geddes. (2003) "Municipalizing American Waterworks, 1897–1915." *Journal of Law, Economics, and Organization* 19: 373–400.

Trolander, Judith Ann. (1987) *Professionalism and Social Change: From the Settlement House Movement to Neighborhood Centers, 1886 to the Present*. New York.

Trotsky, Leon. (1930) *My Life: An Attempt at an Autobiography*. New York.

Tucker, David M. (1991) *The Decline of Thrift in America: Our Cultural Shift from Saving to Spending*. New York.

Tucker, William H. (2002) *The Funding of Scientific Racism: Wickliffe Draper and the Pioneer Fund*. Urbana, IL.

Turkel, Stanley. (2011) *Built to Last: 100+ Year-Old Hotels in New York*. Bloomington, IN.

Turner, George Kibbe. (1909a) "The Daughters of the Poor: A Plain Story of the Development of New York City as a Leading Centre of the White Slave Trade of the World, under Tammany Hall." *McClure's Magazine* 34: 45–61.

———. (1909b) "Tammany's Control of New York by Professional Criminals." *McClure's Magazine* 33: 117–34.

Twain, Mark. (1962) "The Gorky Incident." In

Letters from the Earth, edited by Bernard DeVoto. New York.

Twomey, Bill. (2007) *The Bronx: In Bits and Pieces*. Bloomington, IN.

Twomey, Bill, and Thomas X. Casey. (2011) *Northwest Bronx*. Charleston, SC.

Twomey, Michael J. (2001) "A Century of Foreign Investment in Mexico." University of Michigan–Dearborn Economics Working Paper 98.

Tyack, David B. (1974) *The One Best System: A History of American Urban Education*. Cambridge, MA.

Tyack, David B., and Elisabeth Hansot. (1982) *Managers of Virtue: Public School Leadership in America, 1820–1980*. New York.

Uggen, John F. (2004) "Archer Harman y la construcción del Ferrocarril del Sur." *Procesos: Revista Ecuatoriana de Historia* 20: 37–54.

Uhl, Robert. (1985) "Art, Trade, and Mystery: The Pilots of Sandy Hook." *Seaport* 19: 11–17.

Ultan, Lloyd, and Gary Hermalyn. (1985) *The Bronx in the Innocent Years, 1890–1925*. The Bronx, NY.

University of Michigan Center for the History of Medicine. (2016) "New York, New York." In *The American Influenza Epidemic of 1918–1919: A Digital Encyclopedia*, website.

Unrau, Harlan. (1984) *Ellis Island: Statue of Liberty National Monument Historic Resource Study*. Washington, DC.

Urofsky, Melvin I. (2009) *Louis D. Brandeis: A Life*. New York.

Uruburu, Paula. (2008) *American Eve: Evelyn Nesbit, Stanford White, the Birth of the "It" Girl, and the Crime of the Century*. New York.

Vadney, Thomas E. (1968) "The Politics of Repression: A Case Study of the Red Scare in New

York." *New York History* 49: 56–75.

Vail, R. W. G. (1954) *Knickerbocker Birthday: A Sesqui-Centennial History of the New-York Historical Society, 1804–1954.* New York.

Valentine, Lewis Joseph. (1947) *Night Stick: The Autobiography of Lewis J. Valentine.* New York.

Van Dyke, John Charles. (1908) *The Money God: Chapters of Heresy and Dissent concerning Business Methods and Mercenary Ideals in American Life.* New York.

Van Dyke, John Charles, and Joseph Pennell. (1909) *The New New York: A Commentary on the Place and the People.* New York.

Van Kleeck, Mary. (1908) "Child Labor in New York City Tenements." *Charities and the Commons* 19: 1405–20.

———. (1914) *Working Girls in Evening Schools.* New York.

Van Leeuwen, Thomas A. P. (1988) *The Skyward Trend of Thought: The Metaphysics of the American Skyscraper.* Cambridge, MA.

Vanderlip, Frank A., and Boyden Sparkes. (1935) *From Farm Boy to Financier.* New York.

Vapnek, Lara. (2015) *Elizabeth Gurley Flynn: Modern American Revolutionary.* Boulder, CO.

Vardac, A. Nicholas. (1987) *Stage to Screen: Theatrical Origins of Early Film: David Garrick to D. W. Griffith.* New York.

Varela-Lago, Ana María. (2008) "Conquerors, Immigrants, Exiles: The Spanish Diaspora in the United States (1848–1948)." Ph.D. diss., University of California, San Diego.

Varga, Joseph J. (2013) *Hell's Kitchen and the Battle for Urban Space: Class Struggle and Progressive Reform in New York City, 1894–1914.* New York.

Varricchio, Mario. (2004) "The Wasteful Few:

Upton Sinclair's Portrait of New York's High Society." In *Public Space, Private Lives: Race, Gender, Class, and Citizenship in New York, 1890–1929,* edited by William Boelhower and Anna Scacchi. Amsterdam.

Vecoli, Rudolph J. (1976) "Pane e Giustizia." *La Parola del Popolo* 26: 55–61.

———. (1983) "The Italian Immigrants in the United States Labor Movement from 1880 to 1929." In *Gli italiani fuori d'Italia: Gli emigrati italiani nei movimenti operai dei paesi d'adozione 1880–1940,* edited by Bruno Bezza. Milan.

———. (1988) " 'Primo Maggio' in the United States: An Invented Tradition of the Italian Anarchists." In *May Day Celebration,* edited by Andrea Panaccione. Quaderni della Fondazione G. Brodolini. Venice.

———. (1996) "Primo Maggio: May Day Observances among Italian Immigrant Workers, 1890–1920." *Labor's Heritage: The Quarterly of the George Meany Memorial Archives* 7: 28–41.

Veeser, Cyrus. (2002) *A World Safe for Capitalism: Dollar Diplomacy and America's Rise to Global Power.* New York.

Vega, Bernardo. (1984) *Memoirs of Bernardo Vega: A Contribution to the History of the Puerto Rican Community in New York,* edited by César Andreu Iglesias. New York.

Veiller, Lawrence. (1910a) *The National Housing Association.* New York.

———. (1910b) "A New Aid to Justice: The Committee on Criminal Courts." *Survey,* October 29, 3–7.

Vellon, Peter G. (2014) *A Great Conspiracy against Our Race: Italian Immigrant Newspapers and the Construction of Whiteness in the Early 20th Century.* New York.

Vernon, Raymond. (1960) *Metropolis 1985: An*

Interpretation of the Findings of the New York Metropolitan Region Study. Cambridge, MA.

Vidal, Jaime R. (1994) "The Rejection of the Ethnic Parish Model." In *Puerto Rican and Cuban Catholics in the U.S., 1900–1965,* edited by Jay P. Dolan and Jaime R. Vidal. Notre Dame, IN.

Villard, Oswald Garrison. (1939) *Fighting Years: Memoirs of a Liberal Editor.* New York.

Viteritti, Joseph P. (1989) "The Tradition of Municipal Reform: Charter Revision in Historical Context." *Proceedings of the Academy of Political Science* 37: 16–30.

Volk, Kenneth S. (2005) "The Gary Plan and Technology Education: What Might Have Been?" *Journal of Technology Studies* 31: 39–48.

Volti, Rudi. (2006) *Cars and Culture: The Life Story of a Technology.* Baltimore, MD.

Von Drehle, David. (2003) *Triangle: The Fire That Changed America.* New York.

Vought, Hans P. (2004) *The Bully Pulpit and the Melting Pot: American Presidents and the Immigrant, 1897–1933.* Macon, GA.

Vouyouka Sereti, Maria. (1999) "Entrepreneurship and Ethnicization: The Greek Community of Astoria in Transition." Ph.D. diss., State University of New York at Stony Brook.

Waddell, Brian. (2001) *The War against the New Deal: World War II and American Democracy.* DeKalb, IL.

Wagner, Mary H. (2006) *Gustav Mahler and the New York Philharmonic Orchestra Tour America.* Lanham, MD.

Wald, Alan M. (1987) *The New York Intellectuals: The Rise and Decline of the Anti-Stalinist Left from the 1930s to the 1980s.* Chapel Hill, NC.

Waldinger, Roger. (1987) "Another Look at the

International Ladies' Garment Workers' Union." In *Women, Work, and Protest: A Century of US Women's Labor History,* edited by Ruth Milkman. New York.

Waldman, John R. (1999) *Heartbeats in the Muck: The History, Sea Life, and Environment of New York Harbor.* New York.

Waldman, Stuart, and Zack Winestine. (2002) *Maritime Mile.* New York.

Walker, Alexander. (1976) *Rudolph Valentino.* New York.

Walker, James Blaine. (1918) *Fifty Years of Rapid Transit, 1864–1917.* New York.

Walker, John Bernard. (1915) *America Fallen!* New York.

Walker, Samuel. (1990) *In Defense of American Liberties: A History of the ACLU.* New York.

Walkowitz, Daniel J. (1999) *Working with Class: Social Workers and the Politics of Middle-Class Identity.* Chapel Hill, NC.

———. (2010) *City Folk: English Country Dance and the Politics of the Folk in Modern America.* New York.

Wallace, Christina Lee. (1986) "The Evolution of Reinforced Concrete Technology, 1848–1918." M.A. thesis, Columbia University.

Wallace, Mike. (1996a) "Razor Ribbons, History Museums, and Civic Salvation." In Wallace, *Mickey Mouse History and Other Essays on American Memory,.* Philadelphia, PA.

———. (1996b) "Visiting the Past: History Museums in the United States." In Wallace, *Mickey Mouse History and Other Essays on American Memory,.* Philadelphia, PA.

———. (2005) "Stieglitz in Steerage." In *Foto Grafia,* edited by Fundación Televisa/DGE Tightrope. Madrid.

———. (2010) "Nueva York, the Back Story: New York City and the Spanish-

Speaking World from Dutch Days to the Second World War." In *Nueva York, 1613–1945*, edited by Edward J. Sullivan. New York.

Waller, David. (2011) *The Perfect Man: The Muscular Life and Times of Eugen Sandow, Victorian Strongman*. Brighton, UK.

Walsh, George. (1974) *Gentleman Jimmy Walker, Mayor of the Jazz Age*. New York.

Walter, John C. (1981) "The Caribbean Immigrant Impulse in American Life, 1900–1930." *Revista/Review Interamericana* 11: 522–44.

Walton, Geoffrey. (1971) *Edith Wharton: A Critical Interpretation*. Teaneck, NJ.

Walzer, Michael. (1992) *What It Means to Be an American*. New York.

Ward, David. (1989) *Poverty, Ethnicity, and the American City, 1840–1925: Changing Conceptions of the Slum and the Ghetto*. New York.

Ward, Robert D. (1960) "The Origin and Activities of the National Security League, 1914–1919." *Mississippi Valley Historical Review* 47: 51–65.

Ware, Caroline Farrar. (1965) *Greenwich Village, 1920–1930: A Comment on American Civilization in the Post-War Years*. New York.

Ware, Louise. (1951) *George Foster Peabody: Banker, Philanthropist, Publicist*. Athens, GA.

Warnke, Bettina. (2001) "Reforming the New York Yiddish Theater: The Cultural Politics of Immigrant Intellectuals and the Yiddish Press, 1887–1910." Ph.D. diss., Columbia University.

Warnke, Nina. (1996) "Immigrant Popular Culture as Contested Sphere: Yiddish Music Halls, the Yiddish Press, and the Processes of Americanization, 1900–1910." *Theatre Journal* 48: 321–35.

Washington, Booker T. (1901) *An Autobiography: The Story of My Life and Work*. Toronto, Canada.

———. (1907) *The Negro in Business*. Boston, MA.

———. (1972a) *The Booker T. Washington Papers*, edited by Louis R. Harlan. Vol. 1. Urbana, IL.

———. (1972b) *The Booker T. Washington Papers*, edited by Louis R. Harlan. Vol. 2. Urbana, IL.

Wasserman, Suzanne. (1990) "The Good Old Days of Poverty: The Battle over the Fate of New York City's Lower East Side during the Depression." Ph.D. diss., New York University.

———. (2008) "Hawkers and Gawkers: Peddling and Markets in New York City." In *Gastropolis: Food and New York City*, edited by Annie Hauck-Lawson and Jonathan Deutsch. New York.

Watkins-Owens, Irma. (1996) *Blood Relations: Caribbean Immigrants and the Harlem Community, 1900–1930*. Bloomington, IN.

———. (2001) "Early-Twentieth-Century Caribbean Women: Migration and Social Networks in New York City." In *Islands in the City: West Indian Migration to New York*, edited by Nancy Foner. Berkeley, CA.

Watson, Bruce. (2005) *Bread and Roses: Mills, Migrants, and the Struggle for the American Dream*. New York.

Watson, Peter. (1992) *From Manet to Manhattan: The Rise of the Modern Art Market*. New York.

Watson, Steven. (1991) *Strange Bedfellows: The First American Avant-Garde*. New York.

Waugh, Joan. (1992) "Unsentimental Reformer: The Life of Josephine Shaw Lowell." Ph.D. diss., University of California, Los Angeles.

Weeks, Jeffrey. (1979) "Movements of Affirmation: Sexual Meanings and Homosexual Identities." *Radical History Review* 20: 164–79.

Weidner, Charles H. (1974) *Water for a City: A History of New York City's Problem from the Beginning to the Delaware River System*. New Brunswick, NJ.

Weinberg, Arthur, and Lila Shaffer Weinberg, eds. (1961) *The Muckrakers*. New York.

Weinberg, H. Barbara, and Elizabeth E. Barker. (2004) *Childe Hassam, American Impressionist*. New Haven, CT.

Weinberg, Jonathan. (2001) "The Family of Stieglitz and Steichen." *Art in America* 89: 50–57.

Weiner, Edward. (2008) *Urban Transportation Planning in the United States: History, Policy, and Practice*. New York.

Weinstein, James. (1959) "Anti-War Sentiment and the Socialist Party, 1917–1918." *Political Science Quarterly* 74: 215–39.

———. (1967) *The Decline of Socialism in America, 1912–1925*. New York.

———. (1968) *The Corporate Ideal in the Liberal State, 1900–1918*. Boston, MA.

Weinstein, Stephen Frederick. (1984) "The Nickel Empire: Coney Island and the Creation of Urban Seaside Resorts in the United States." Ph.D. diss., Columbia University.

Weir, Margaret, Ann Shola Orloff, and Theda Skocpol, eds. (1988) *The Politics of Social Policy in the United States*. Princeton, NJ.

Weisenfeld, Judith. (1997) *African American Women and Christian Activism: New York's Black YWCA, 1905–1945*. Cambridge, MA.

Weisman, Steven R. (2002) *The Great Tax Wars: Lincoln to Wilson—the Fierce Battles over Money and Power That Transformed the Nation*. New York.

Weiss, Marc. (1991) "The Politics of Real Estate Cycles." *Business and Economic History* 20: 1–8.

———. (1992a) "Density and Intervention: New York's Planning

Traditions." In *The Landscape of Modernity: Essays on New York City: 1900–1940*, edited by David Ward and Oliver Zunz. New York.

———. (1992b) "Skyscraper Zoning: New York's Pioneering Role." *Journal of the American Planning Association* 58: 201–11.

Weiss, Nancy J. (1974) *The National Urban League, 1910–1940*. New York.

———. (1968) *Charles Francis Murphy, 1858–1924: Respectability and Responsibility in Tammany Politics*. Northampton, MA.

Weiss, Richard. (1979) "Ethnicity and Reform: Minorities and the Ambience of the Depression Years." *Journal of American History* 66: 566–85.

Weitzenhoffer, Frances. (1986) *The Havemeyers: Impressionism Comes to America*. New York.

Welch, Richard E., Jr. (1979) *Response to Imperialism: The United States and the Philippine-American War, 1899–1902*. Chapel Hill, NC.

Welch, Richard F. (2009) *King of the Bowery: Big Tim Sullivan, Tammany Hall, and New York City from the Gilded Age to the Progressive Era*. Albany, NY.

Welch, Walter L., and Leah Brodbeck Stenzel Burt. (1994) *From Tinfoil to Stereo: The Acoustic Years of the Recording Industry, 1877–1929*. Gainesville, FL.

Wellman, Judith. (2014) *Brooklyn's Promised Land: The Free Black Community of Weeksville, New York*. New York.

Wells, Allen. (2001) "Did 1898 Mark a Fundamental Transformation for the Cuban Sugar Industry?" Paper presented at Latin America and Global Trade Conference. Stanford, CA.

Wells, Donald R. (2004) *The Federal Reserve System: A History*. Jefferson, NC.

Wells, H.G. (1906) *The Future in America: A*

Search after Realities. New York.

———. (1908) *The War in the Air, and Particularly How Mr. Bert Smallways Fared While It Lasted.* New York.

Wells, James L., et al. (1927) *The Bronx and Its People: A History, 1609–1927.* 4 vols. New York.

Wendt, Lloyd. (1982) *The "Wall Street Journal": The Story of Dow Jones and the Nation's Business Newspaper.* Chicago, IL.

Werbel, Amy. (2014) "The Crime of the Nude: Anthony Comstock, the Art Students League of New York, and the Origins of Modern American Obscenity." *Winterthur Portfolio* 48: 249–82.

Werner, M. R. (1949) "L'affaire Gorky." *New Yorker,* April 30, 62.

Wertheim, Arthur Frank. (1976) *The New York Little Renaissance: Iconoclasm, Modernism, and Nationalism in American Culture, 1908–1917.* New York.

———. (2006) *Vaudeville Wars: How the Keith-Albee and Orpheum Circuits Controlled the Big-Time and Its Performers.* New York.

Wertz, Daniel. (2008) "American Imperialism and the Philippine War." B.A. thesis, Wesleyan University.

Wesser, Robert F. (1967) *Charles Evans Hughes: Politics and Reform in New York, 1905–1910.* Ithaca, NY.

Westbrook, Robert. (1990) "Lewis Mumford, John Dewey, and the 'Pragmatic Acquiescence.'" In *Lewis Mumford: Public Intellectual,* edited by Thomas P. Hughes and Agatha Hughes.

Wetzsteon, Ross. (2001) *Republic of Dreams: Greenwich Village, the American Bohemia, 1910–1960.* New York.

Wexler, Alice. (1984) *Emma Goldman: An Intimate Life.* New York.

Wharton, Edith. (1905) *The House of Mirth.* New York.

———. (1913) *The Custom of the Country.* New York.

Whibley, Charles. (1908) *American Sketches.* London.

Whitcomb, Ian. (1988) *Irving Berlin and Ragtime America.* New York.

White, Eric B. (2013) *Transatlantic Avant-Gardes: Little Magazines and Localist Modernism.* Edinburgh.

White, Gerald Taylor. (1982) *The United States and the Problem of Recovery after 1893.* Tuscaloosa, AL.

White, Ronald C., Jr., and Charles Howard Hopkins. (1976) *The Social Gospel: Religion and Reform in Changing America.* Philadelphia, PA.

White, Shane. (2015) *Prince of Darkness: The Untold Story of Jeremiah G. Hamilton, Wall Street's First Black Millionaire.* New York.

Whittaker, William George. (1969) "Samuel Gompers, Anti-Imperialist." *Pacific Historical Review* 38: 429–45.

Wiebe, Robert H. (1959) "The House of Morgan and the Executive, 1905–1913." *American Historical Review* 65: 240–47.

Wigoder, Meir. (2002) "The 'Solar Eye' of Vision: Emergence of the Skyscraper-Viewer in the Discourse on Heights in New York City, 1890–1920." *Journal of the Society of Architectural Historians* 61: 152–69.

Wilder, Craig Steven. (2000) *A Covenant with Color: Race and Social Power in Brooklyn.* New York.

———. (2001) *In the Company of Black Men: The African Influence on African American Culture in New York City.* New York.

Wilkins, Mira. (1989) *The History of Foreign Investment in the United States to 1914.* Cambridge, MA.

———. (2004) *The History of Foreign Investment in the United States, 1914–1945.* Cambridge, MA.

Willcox, William Russell, and New York, New Jersey Port and Harbor Development Commission. (1920) *Joint Report with Comprehensive Plan and Recommendations.* Albany, NY.

Willemse, Cornelius W., George James Lemmer, and Jack Kofoed. (1931) *Behind the Green Lights.* New York.

Willensky, Elliot. (1986) *When Brooklyn Was the World, 1920–1957.* New York.

Willensky, Elliot, Norval White, and Fran Leadon. (1988) *AIA Guide to New York City.* San Diego, CA.

Williams, C. Dickerman, and Peter R. Nehemkis, Jr. (1937) "Municipal Improvements as Affected by Constitutional Debt Limitations." *Columbia Law Review* 37: 177–211.

Williams, William Appleman. (1959) *The Tragedy of American Diplomacy.* New York.

Willis, Carol. (1995) *Form Follows Finance: Skyscrapers and Skylines in New York and Chicago.* New York.

Wilson, Christopher P. (1983a) "The Rhetoric of Consumption: Mass-Market Magazines and the Demise of the Gentle Reader, 1880–1920." In *The Culture of Consumption: Critical Essays in American History, 1880–1980,* edited by Richard Wightman Fox and T. J. Jackson Lears. New York.

Wilson, Richard Guy. (1983b) *McKim, Mead & White: Architects.* New York.

Wilson, Ross J. (2014) *New York and the First World War: Shaping an American City.* Burlington, VT.

Wilson, William H. (1989) *The City Beautiful Movement.* Baltimore, MD.

Wines, Roger. (1962) "Vanderbilt's Motor Parkway: America's First Auto Road." *Journal of Long Island History* 2: 14–28.

Winkleman, Michael. (1986) *The Fragility of Turf: The Neighborhoods of New York City.* New York.

Winkler, John K. (1934) *The First Billion.* New York.

———. (1970) *Five and Ten: The Fabulous Life of F. W. Woolworth.* Freeport, NY.

Winkler, Jonathan Reed. (2004) "Wiring the World: U.S. Foreign Policy and Global Strategic Communications, 1914–1921." Ph.D. diss., Yale University.

Winslow, Calvin, ed. (1998) *Waterfront Workers: New Perspectives on Race and Class.* Urbana, IL.

———. (2003) "Italian Workers on the Waterfront: The New York Harbor Strikes of 1907 and 1919." In *The Lost World of Italian American Radicalism: Politics, Labor, and Culture,* edited by Philip V. Cannistraro and Gerald Meyer. Westport, CT.

Winslow, Charles Henry. (1913) *Conciliation and Arbitration in the Building Trades of Greater New York.* Washington, DC.

Winston, Diane H. (1999) *Red-Hot and Righteous: The Urban Religion of the Salvation Army.* Cambridge, MA.

Wirka, Susan Marie. (1996) "The City Social Movement: Progressive Women Reformers and Early Social Planning." In *Planning the Twentieth-Century American City,* edited by Mary Corbin Sies and Christopher Silver. Baltimore, MD.

Wittner, Lawrence. (2015) "New York's 200-Year Conspiracy for Peace." *CounterPunch,* March 9, 1–18.

Wolf, Donald E. (2010) *Crossing the Hudson: Historic Bridges and Tunnels of the River.* New Brunswick, NJ.

Woll, Allen L. (1989) *Black Musical Theatre: From 'Coontown' to 'Dreamgirls.'* Baton Rouge, LA.

Wood, Janice Ruth. (2008) *The Struggle for Free Speech in the United States, 1872–1915: Edward Bliss Foote, Edward Bond Foote,* and *Anti-Comstock Operations*. New York.

Woodiwiss, Michael. (2001) *Organized Crime and American Power: A History*. Toronto, Canada.

Woodward, C. Vann. (1951) *Origins of the New South, 1877–1913*. Baton Rouge, LA.

———. (1955) *The Strange Career of Jim Crow*. New York.

———. (1991) *Reunion and Reaction: The Compromise of 1877 and the End of Reconstruction*. New York.

Wright, Jill Yvonne Gold. (2003) "Creating America on Stage: How Jewish Composers and Lyricists Pioneered American Musical Theater." Ph.D. diss., Claremont Graduate University.

Wu, Tim. (2011) *The Master Switch: The Rise and Fall of Information Empires*. New York.

Wunsch, James Lemuel. (1979) "Prostitution and Public Policy: From Regulation to Suppression, 1858–1920." Ph.D. diss., University of Chicago.

Yablon, Charles M. (2007) "The Historical Race: Competition for Corporate Charters and the Rise and Decline of New Jersey: 1880–1910." *Journal of Corporation Law* 32: 323–81.

Yablon, Nick. (2004) "The Metropolitan Life in Ruins: Architectural and Fictional Speculations in New York, 1909–1919." *American Quarterly* 56: 308–47.

———. (2010) *Untimely Ruins: An Archaeology of American Urban*

Modernity, 1819–1919. Chicago, IL.

Yago, Glenn. (1984) *The Decline of Transit: Urban Transportation in German and U.S. Cities, 1900–1970*. Cambridge, MA.

Yeager, Matthew G. (2016) *Frank Tannenbaum: The Making of a Convict Criminologist*. New York.

Yee, Shirley J. (2012) *An Immigrant Neighborhood: Interethnic and Interracial Encounters in New York before 1930*. Philadelphia, PA.

Yellowitz, Irwin. (1965) *Labor and the Progressive Movement in New York State, 1897–1916*. Ithaca, NY.

———, ed. (1978) *Essays in the History of New York City: A Memorial to Sidney Pomerantz*. Port Washington, NY.

Yochelson, Bonnie. (2010) *Alfred Stieglitz: New York*. New York.

Young, James Harvey. (1961) *The Toadstool Millionaires: A Social History of Patent Medicines in America before Federal Regulation*. Princeton, NJ.

Young, Virginia Heyer. (2005) *Ruth Benedict: Beyond Relativity, beyond Pattern*. Lincoln, NE.

Younger, William Lee. (1978) *Old Brooklyn in Early Photographs, 1865–1929: 157 Prints from the Collection of the Long Island Historical Society*. New York.

Zangrando, Robert L. (1980) *The NAACP Crusade against Lynching, 1909–1950*. Philadelphia, PA.

Zangwill, Israel. (1909) *The Melting-Pot: Drama in Four Acts*. New York.

Zayas, Marius de, and Francis M. Naumann. (1996) *How, When, and Why Modern Art Came to New York*. Cambridge, MA.

Zeisloft, E. Idell. (1899) *The New Metropolis: Memorable Events of Three Centuries, 1600–1900; from the Island of Mana-Hat-Ta to Greater New York at the Close of the Nineteenth Century*. New York.

Zerbe, Richard. (1969) "The American Sugar Refinery Company, 1887–1914: The Story of a Monopoly." *Journal of Law and Economics* 12: 339–75.

Zilcer, Judith K. (1974) "'The World's New Art Center': Modern Art Exhibitions in New York City, 1913–1918." *Archives of American Art Journal* 14: 2–7.

Zilcer, Judith K., and Hirshhorn Museum and Sculpture Garden. (1978) *"The Noble Buyer": John Quinn, Patron of the Avant-Garde*. Washington, DC.

Zimmerman, David A. (2006) *Panic! Markets, Crises, and Crowds in American Fiction*. Chapel Hill, NC.

Zimmerman, Jean. (2012) *Love, Fiercely: A Gilded Age Romance*. Boston, MA.

Zimmerman, Jonathan. (2002) "Ethnics against Ethnicity: European Immigrants and Foreign-Language Instruction, 1890–1940." *Journal of American History* 88: 1383–1404.

Zimmermann, Warren. (2002) *First Great Triumph: How Five Americans Made Their Country a World Power*. New York.

Zinn, Howard. (1972) *LaGuardia in Congress*. Westport, CT.

———. (1980) *A People's History of the United States*. New York.

Zipser, Arthur, and Pearl Zipser. (1989) *Fire and Grace: The Life of Rose Pastor Stokes*. Athens, GA.

Zlotnick, Joan. (1971) "Abraham Cahan, a Neglected Realist." *American Jewish Archives* 23: 33–46.

Zolberg, Aristide R. (2006) *A Nation by Design: Immigration Policy in the Fashioning of America*. New York.

Zukin, Sharon, and Gilda Zwerman. (1985) "Housing for the Working Poor: A Historical View of Jews and Blacks in Brownsville." *New York Affairs* 9: 3–18.

Zunz, Olivier. (1990) *Making America Corporate, 1870–1920*. Chicago, IL.

Zurier, Rebecca. (2006) *Picturing the City: Urban Vision and the Ashcan School*. Berkeley, CA.

Zurier, Rebecca, et al. (1988) *Art for the Masses: A Radical Magazine and Its Graphics, 1911–1917*. Philadelphia, PA.

Zurier, Rebecca, Robert W. Snyder, and Virginia M. Mecklenburg. (1995) *Metropolitan Lives: The Ashcan Artists and Their New York*. Washington, DC.

Index of Names

Page numbers in bold indicate figures.

Index of Subjects

Page numbers in bold indicate figures.